DEEP LEARNING IN QUANTITATIVE FINANCE

DEEP LEARNING IN QUANTITATIVE FINANCE

ANDREW GREEN

WILEY

Published by John Wiley & Sons, Inc., Hoboken, New Jersey.

For general information on our other products and services please contact our Customer Care Department with the U.S. at 877-762-2974, outside the U.S. at 317-572-3993 or fax 317-572-4002.

Wiley also publishes its books in a variety of electronic formats. Some content that appears in print, however, may not be available in electronic format.

Library of Congress Cataloging-in-Publication Data has been applied for:

Hardback: 9781119685241
ePDF: 9781119685258
epub: 9781119685227
oBook: 9781119685289

Cover Design: Wiley
Cover Image: © Dmitry Vikarchuk/iStock/Getty Images Plus/Getty Images
Printed and bound by CPI Group (UK) Ltd, Croydon, CR0 4YY
C9781119685241_030226
The manufacturer's authorized representative according to the EU General Product Safety Regulation is Wiley-VCH GmbH, Boschstr. 12, 69469 Weinheim, Germany, e-mail: Product_Safety@wiley.com.

For Simone

Contents

Acknowledgements

I would like to express my sincere gratitude to Chris Dennis and Ryan Ferguson for their thoughtful reviews of various sections of the text and for the insightful discussions on deep learning throughout the creation of this book. Special thanks go to my Scotiabank colleagues Shuqing Ma, Karin Bergeron and Gabriel Buteler, who provided their support from the project's conception through to its final production.

Needless to say, completing this book took far longer than initially anticipated, evolving dramatically as the entire field of AI research advanced at an incredible pace. Therefore, my deepest appreciation goes to Simone for her exceptional patience and unwavering support throughout the lengthy writing journey.

Finally, I must acknowledge the contributions of Milou, Nounours, Chouchou and Loulou, the enthusiastic team of Pomeranians, and Pelotte, my discerning feline editor, whose collective wisdom and insistence on regular breaks undoubtedly enhanced the quality (and duration!) of this endeavour.

PART

One

Introducing Deep Neural Networks

CHAPTER 1

Introduction

furor est profecto, furor egredi ex eo et, tamquam interna eius cuncta plane iam nota sint, ita scrutari extera, quasi vero mensuram ullius rei possit agere qui sui nesciat, aut mens hominis videre quae mundus ipse non capiat.

It is madness, perfect madness, to go out of this world and to search for what is beyond it, as if one who is ignorant of his own dimensions could ascertain the measure of anything else, or as if the human mind could see what the world itself cannot contain.

Pliny the Elder, Natural History 2.1

1.1 WHAT THIS BOOK IS ABOUT

This book is about deep learning or, as it is more popularly known, *artificial intelligence (AI)*, and its application to problems in traditional quantitative finance. It grew from a desire on my own part to learn as much as possible about the subject. Before 2017, I had extensive experience in quantitative finance and in the numerical algorithms typically employed in pricing models, particularly in the context of XVA, the subject of my first book *XVA: Credit, Funding and Capital Valuation Adjustments* (Green, 2015). XVA typically involves high-performance computing (HPC) and, in my particular case, experience with GPUs. I also had exposure to algorithmic differentiation. While I had limited previous experience in machine learning beyond simple regression models, deep learning, using GPUs and gradient-based learning, seemed like a natural fit for quantitative finance.

The first concrete application of deep learning in quantitative finance I explored was replicating a basket option as described in Ferguson and Green (2018). This basket option was chosen because it was of moderate dimension and, simultaneously, challenging because the replicated underlying model used a Monte Carlo simulation. The work aimed to demonstrate that an accurate replicating model could be trained to handle noisy input and that the performance during inference would exceed the original model once trained. It also allowed the impact of hyperparameter tuning to be presented. The experiment was successful; however, simple replication of a pricing function has proved to be a small subset of the capabilities of deep learning in quantitative finance.

What category of method is deep learning? Quantitative analysts have historically used numerical methods to construct models, such as partial differential equation (PDE) solvers and Monte Carlo simulations. Deep learning and, more broadly, machine learning are no different. Deep neural networks are approximation models with weights that are *learned*. A better description would be that the weights are optimised using gradient-based optimisers that are variants of stochastic gradient descent. Neural networks should be seen as another numerical method in the arsenal of such methods available to quantitative analysts and the broader community of scientists. Neural networks have strengths and weaknesses like any other method.

Deep Learning in Quantitative Finance, First Edition. Andrew Green.

However, deep learning is not without controversy in quantitative finance as elsewhere. Like any new approach, it has its sceptics and supporters. The accompanying AI revolution and media hype have not been conducive to the wider adoption of deep learning in quantitative finance. Deep learning is connected with the search for *artificial general intelligence (AGI)* and the timeless quest for humans to create an intelligence like themselves. Media hype there has been, but the last decade has genuinely seen a revolution with the advent of tools like *large language models (LLM)* that are clearly transformative in many fields.

Deep learning is an *empirical* and practical discipline. While mathematical, it is usually limited to linear algebra and hence is relatively straightforward. Training a neural network model, however, is not always straightforward, and making advances requires practical experience. Neural networks are often criticised as 'black boxes' and this opacity can be extended to both the training stage and inference time. It is not always clear why results from a particular network configuration perform poorly or well. Hence, this book contains many examples coded in Python and presented in Jupyter Notebooks. The examples are presented 'warts and all'; many work well, but some do not. Working with deep neural networks means developing experience and intuition to make things work.

The book has two main blocks of chapters. The first block explores deep learning techniques in their original content. This means covering many topics that are not related to quantitative finance at all, such as image classification and image generation. This is justified as it is how I have personally explored the deep learning discipline and provides a firm foundation for using neural network models in any context. The second block of chapters explores deep learning in quantitative finance, building on the foundation of the earlier general chapters. Hence, the book aims to serve two purposes: firstly, to provide a practical introduction to a wide variety of neural network models and, secondly, to explore the application of those techniques in traditional quantitative finance. The selection of topics is personal, reflecting the areas I am interested in. I have made it reasonably comprehensive, but there are inevitably omissions. This is in no small part due to the explosive growth of AI research in the last decade and during the writing of this text.

1.2 THE RISE OF AI

Figure 1.1 presents a timeline of the main developments in AI since 1900. What is notable in this image is the fact that half the entries are from developments in the last 25 years, reflecting the rise of AI in this period. Quantitative finance has explored the use of neural networks since the 1980s. However, practical applications have only arisen since the re-emergence of deep learning in recent years, with a significant increase in interest after 2016. The key challenge this has presented in writing a book has been the pace of change. This has inevitably meant the contents of the book's conclusion are different than they were at the project's inception. For example, when starting to write about generative models, generative adversarial networks (GANs) were the pre-eminent models, but around 2022, diffusion-based models became the leaders and GANs were quickly left behind. This has necessitated an almost constant updating of the text at specific points to reflect ongoing developments.

1.2.1 LLMs

One development that happened part way through this project was the arrival of highly capable LLMs like GPT-4 from OpenAI and Claude 3 from Anthropic. Writing assistants like Grammarly now embed generative AI tools within their workflow. I have used LLMs and Grammarly as writing assistants and as a coding copilot to accelerate the preparation of examples since the release of these tools in 2023. LLMs are helpful as productivity tools, a subject I will return to later in Chapter 20.

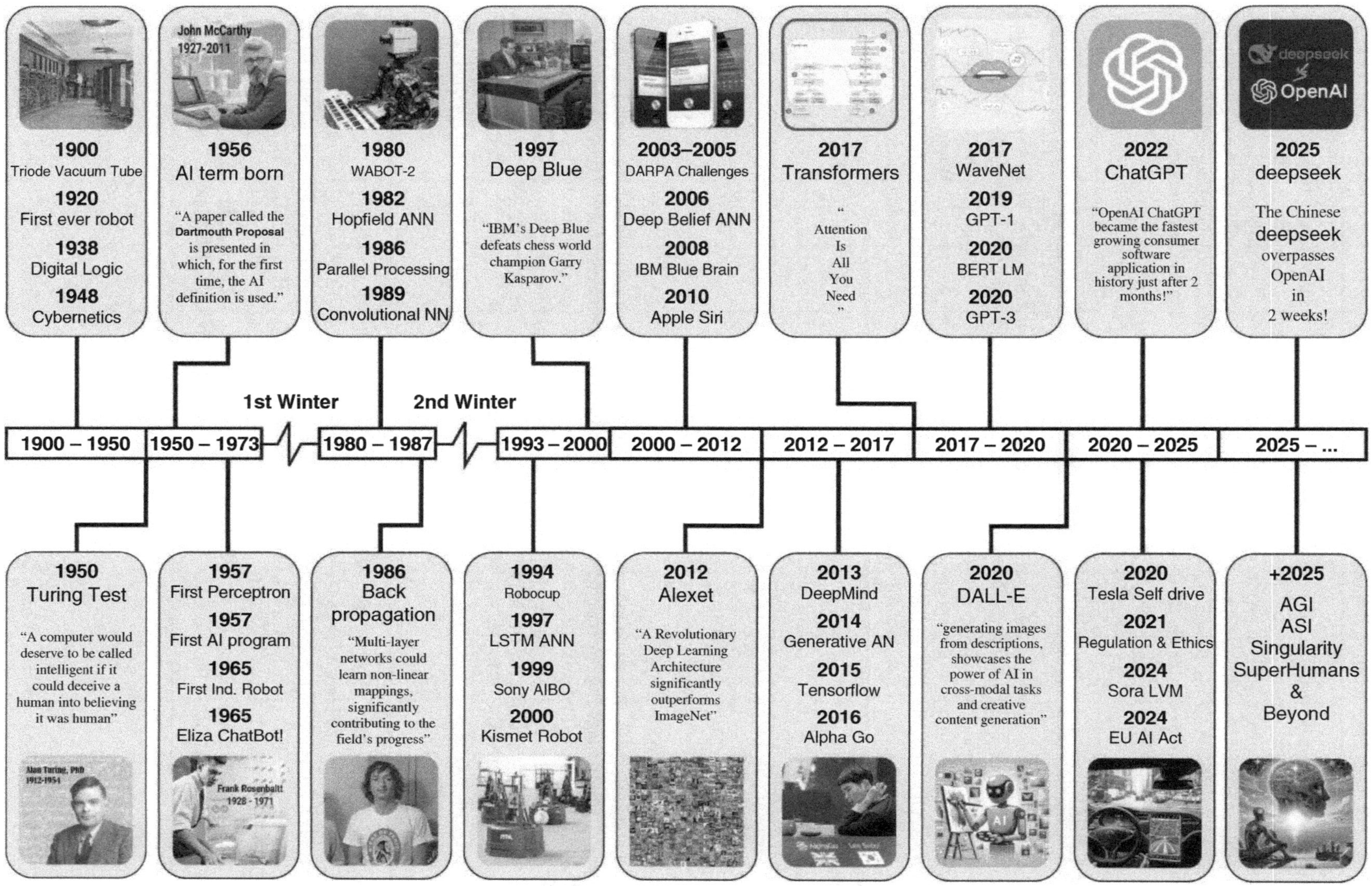

FIGURE 1.1 A timeline of the history of AI. *Source*: Tarjomyar on Wikimedia Commons. Licensed under CC BY-SA 4.0 https://creativecommons.org/licenses/by-sa/4.0/deed.en. Printed versions have been converted to greyscale.

1.3 THE PROMISE OF AI IN QUANTITATIVE FINANCE

One driver for this book is the *promise* of neural networks in traditional quantitative finance. While many and varied examples of deep learning are covered in the later chapters, that promise is not yet fulfilled. There is limited evidence of many deep learning models in production applications at the time of writing in 2025. This reflects partly on the inertia of financial market participants, where more traditional techniques still hold sway. However, quants are steadily finding new ways to use neural networks, and initial scepticism is slowly being replaced by practical steps forward. There is more to do; hence, this work also advocates using deep learning models. Deep learning will never replace traditional methods, but it does *complement* them well.

1.4 PRACTICALITIES

As noted earlier, deep neural networks are often seen as 'black boxes' that cannot be understood. In reality, they are, at best, 'grey boxes' that can sometimes be characterised through exploring the features they learn, as can be seen from the various methods to visualise features in computer vision applications as described in Chapter 6. This is only possible with small models; it is impossible for LLMs with trillions of parameters. While there are essential theoretical results such as the *universal function approximation theorem* (Hornik et al., 1989, 1990; Cybenko, 1989; Hornik, 1991), they are limited in number. Advances in deep learning have typically come through experiment and data science. Experience gained through practice is invaluable in guiding research.

1.4.1 The Examples

The examples are available on the GitHub repo:

```
https://github.com/greandrew/DeepLearningBookExamples
```

Each chapter with examples has its subdirectory, and the Python packages are grouped by chapter. Using Python virtual environments to manage the dependencies is possible, but I recommend using Docker containers. All examples are presented in Jupyter Notebooks or through Jupyter Lab. A small number of Python files are sometimes used to manage utilities. Some examples are computationally demanding, and a reasonably powerful consumer GPU card with NVIDIA® CUDA™ capability is strongly recommended (NVIDIA Corporation, 2007).[1] Most models have been trained using an NVIDIA RTX™3060 or NVIDIA RTX™4090.[2]

Note that all code examples either presented in the book or the accompanying code repository are subject to the following disclaimer:

> THERE IS NO WARRANTY FOR THE PROGRAM, TO THE EXTENT PERMITTED BY APPLICABLE LAW. EXCEPT WHEN OTHERWISE STATED IN WRITING THE COPYRIGHT HOLDERS AND/OR OTHER PARTIES PROVIDE THE PROGRAM 'AS IS' WITHOUT WARRANTY OF ANY KIND, EITHER EXPRESSED OR IMPLIED, INCLUDING, BUT NOT LIMITED TO, THE IMPLIED WARRANTIES OF MERCHANTABILITY AND FITNESS FOR A PARTICULAR PURPOSE. THE ENTIRE RISK AS TO THE QUALITY AND PERFORMANCE OF THE PROGRAM IS WITH YOU. SHOULD THE PROGRAM PROVE DEFECTIVE, YOU ASSUME THE COST OF ALL NECESSARY SERVICING, REPAIR OR CORRECTION.

[1] NVIDIA® CUDA™ is a trademark of the NVIDIA Corporation in the United States and/or other countries.
[2] NVIDIA RTX™ is a trademark of the NVIDIA Corporation in the United States and/or other countries.

1.4.2 Python and PyTorch

Python is the language of choice for AI model development and training, which has been true for the last decade. For deep learning model development, I have adopted PyTorch

```
https://pytorch.org/
```

exclusively. Python is a powerful and succinct language which facilitates rapid development. It is normally interpreted and hence is not as fast as compiled languages like C++. However, given that most of the operations used in deep learning happen inside dedicated AI frameworks like PyTorch, this is not generally a problem. Python is among the best-supported languages, with many libraries and tools available.

All languages have weaknesses of one type or another, and Python is no exception. Python's Achilles heel is compatibility, and while there are many tools available, not all of these are compatible with each other and often depend on specific versions of Python or dependent packages. Resolving these dependencies can be complex, and while installation tools like `pip` do an excellent job of finding compatible packages, they can be slow and sometimes fail. Managing a self-consistent base version of Python and all the required packages is impossible; hence, virtual environments are essential. However, even virtual environments can prove problematic if different versions of CUDA and the associated packages are also needed. This has led me to switch to containers for Python development and Docker.

1.4.3 Docker

Docker provides *containerisation*, that is, it provides a service that allows applications to be isolated from each other but use fewer resources than a full virtual machine:

```
https://www.docker.com/
```

Docker containers make managing software environments straightforward. In particular, it allows different versions of libraries, like those that form part of CUDA, to coexist on the same physical workstation or server without conflict. They can run applications without human intervention, but they can also be run interactively and support an external web browser. The ability to run a container with a browser output means it can be used interactively with Jupyter Notebook and Jupyter Lab, as with these examples.

Each chapter with examples provides two or three files:

- `docker-compose.yml` – A YAML configuration file.
- `Dockerfile` – A command file that tells Docker how to build the container.
- `requirements.txt` – Some chapters have a separate requirements file that is used to install Python packages with `pip`.

The `docker-compose.yml` file should be modified to specify the location of the chapter example directly on the host machine. The `volumes` parameter tells Docker where to map the internal container directory. So, for example:

```
version: '3'
services:
jupyter:
runtime: nvidia
build:
context: .
dockerfile: Dockerfile
working_dir: /home/notebooks
```

```
shm_size: 32gb
ports:
- "8888:8888"
deploy:
resources:
reservations:
devices:
- capabilities: [gpu]
volumes:
- PUT_YOUR_PATH_HERE:/home/notebooks
- .:/app
```

In this example, the default size is 32 GB, which may need to be modified if you have less RAM.

To build the docker container:

```
$ docker-compose build
```

To start the docker container:

```
$ docker-compose up
```

Shutting down the Jupyter Notebook or Lab will shut down the container.

1.5 READING THIS BOOK

The book is organised into four parts: Introducing Deep Neural Networks, Foundations, Applications and The Future.

The first part contains this introduction. Part II comprehensively reviews deep learning methodology. Chapter 2 introduces *feedforward neural networks* or *multilayer perceptrons*, the most basic type of deep network. Training neural networks by stochastic gradient descent is the subject of Chapter 3, while Chapter 4 introduces various regularisation techniques. Choosing good values for hyperparameters is essential for successful deep learning and is discussed in depth in Chapter 5, including several different methodologies for hyperparameter search. Computer vision tasks have been dominated by *convolutional neural networks (CNNs)*, and this is explored in Chapter 6 in their original context of images. However, CNNs are also a pre-requisite for *generative* models and find application elsewhere, such as in time-series generation and market prediction. Sequence models are another primary type of neural network model, discussed in Chapter 7. Sequence models include recurrent neural networks but now include *attention* mechanisms and *transformers*. Like CNNs and images, sequence models are most naturally introduced in the context of *natural language processing (NLP)*. Autoencoders, neural networks that reproduce their input, are introduced in Chapter 8; the *variational* type of autoencoder is applied in generative modelling. The block of chapters from 2 through 8 provides the foundation upon which all subsequent chapters rely.

The last two chapters in Part II discuss generative models (Chapter 9) and deep reinforcement learning (Chapter 10), respectively. Generative models are introduced in their original context of image generation. However, this chapter provides the key background for the later application of generative models to market data generation in Chapter 18. Reinforcement learning (RL) is a subdiscipline of machine learning in its own right, and deep RL is the subset that uses neural networks for function approximation. Chapter 10 provides a basic introduction to RL and deep RL and is essential background for Chapter 19 on *deep hedging*.

Part III presents a series of chapters, each focused on a key application of deep neural networks to traditional quantitative finance. Chapter 11 trains deep neural networks to replicate derivative valuation functions. PDEs and backward stochastic differential equations can be solved by deep learning, which is the subject of Chapter 12, while Monte Carlo methods can also be accelerated by neural networks, which are discussed in Chapter 13.

Chapter 13 also includes *deep optimal stopping* and the application of neural networks to the pricing of Bermudan and American-style options. *Static replication* models have a long history in quantitative finance, and the neural network variant of these models is explored in Chapter 14. Chapters 15 and 16 discuss the closely related applications of volatility surface modelling and model calibration. Chapter 17 reviews the applications of neural networks to XVA that are not discussed elsewhere in the book. Derivative valuation and deep optimal stopping are directly applicable to XVA as well. Generating realistic synthetic market data is the key application of generative models in quantitative finance and is reviewed alongside classical techniques in Chapter 18. Similarly, deep hedging is the critical application of deep RL in quantitative finance and is explored in detail in Chapter 19.

The book concludes with Part IV and the last chapter, Chapter 20. Here, the future of quantitative finance is discussed, and the expanding influence of AI is considered.

PART Two

Foundations

CHAPTER 2

Feedforward Neural Networks

'Externally', Jase said in its usual, calm, measured tones, 'it is an ellipsoid. Fields up, it looks like a very small ship. It's about ten metres long and two and a half in diameter. Internally it's made up of millions of components, but the most important ones are the thinking and memory parts of the mind proper; those are what make it so heavy because they're so dense. It weights nearly fifteen thousand tonnes. It is fitted with its own power, of course, and several field generators, any of which could be pressed into service as emergency motors, and indeed are designed with this in mind. Only the outer envelope is constantly in real space, the rest – all the thinking parts, anyway – stay in hyperspace'.

Iain M. Banks, Consider Phlebas (1987)

2.1 INTRODUCING NEURAL NETWORKS

(Deep) feedforward networks, also known as multilayer perceptrons, are the simplest type of deep neural network. They consist of a series of layers of artificial neurons, fed by an input layer, proceeding through a series of *hidden* layers and ending in an output layer. Figure 2.1 illustrates an example of the architecture. The layers of a deep neural network form a *directed acyclic graph (DAG)*. DAGs are finite graphs in which no loops return to the start of the graph. DAGs are an essential part of neural network software packages and are used to control calculation flow, and indeed, this is explicit in Tensorflow. In the older style of Tensorflow programming, a static graph was defined

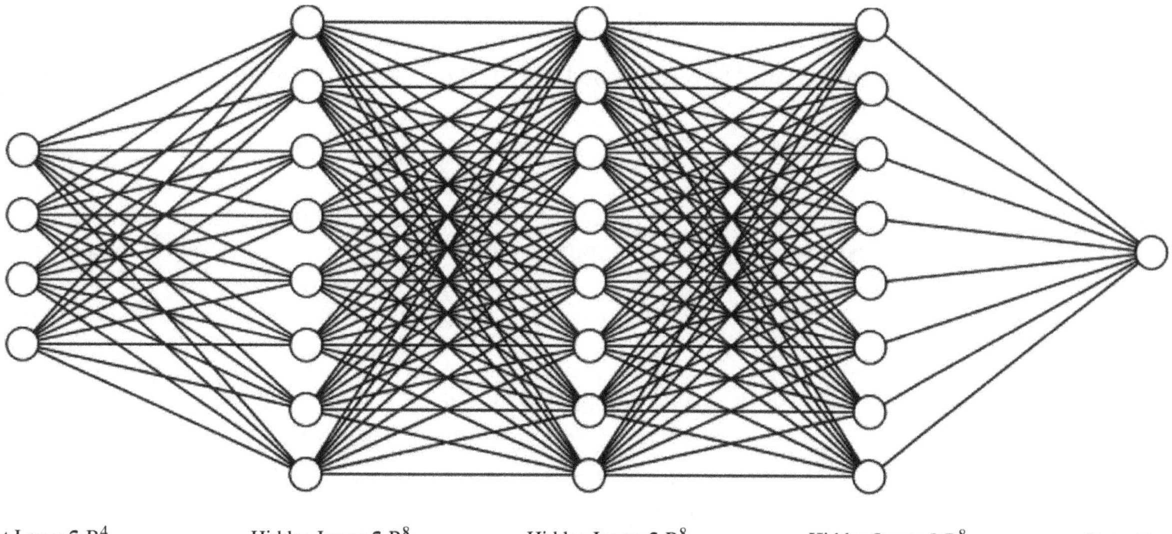

FIGURE 2.1 A feedforward network with four inputs, three hidden layers of eight neurons and a single output.

Deep Learning in Quantitative Finance, First Edition. Andrew Green.

and compiled prior to execution. A *feedforward* network has one of the simplest DAGs as data is propagated only from the input, through successive hidden layers, to the output. For general deep neural networks, the layers can take many forms, but for feedforward networks, they are *dense* layers of neurons; that is, all the neurons of one layer connect to the neurons of the next layer.

The size of the input layer decides the number of input data points or *features*, while the nature of the problem determines the output layer. For example, a single-class classifier model will have a single output, as will a univariate regression model. A multi-class and multi-label classifier will have as many outputs as classes in the problem. The main parameters of a feedforward network are the number of hidden layers and the width of each layer. *Shallow* networks contain only a single hidden layer, while *deep* networks contain more than one layer. Modern neural networks can contain hundreds of layers and many millions of parameters. For example, the award-winning *AlexNet* from 2012, then top ranked in the *ImageNet Large Scale Visual Recognition Challenge*, used around 63 million parameters, while the LLM GPT-4 from OpenAI is believed to use over 1 trillion parameters.

The output of each neuron feeds through an *activation function* that is usually a non-linear operation. Each layer will use the same activation function; typically, all the activation functions in all hidden layers will be the same. The output layer activation function is determined by the type of problem, so, for example, a regression problem will likely have a linear output. At the same time, a single-class classifier will use the sigmoid function. Section 2.3 describes activation functions.

The choice of neural network properties, that is, the number of hidden layers, the width of those layers and the activation functions, form the *architecture* of the network. The topology of a neural network is defined by the connections between its neurons and the weights that govern their operation (Miikkulainen, 2010). The *hypothesis space* is the set of all hypotheses that can be returned by a machine learning model (Blockeel, 2010). In the context of neural networks, this corresponds to the set of all possible weight vectors. Hence, the hypothesis space is determined by the topology of the network, and the choice of topology constrains what the network can learn (Chollet, 2018, p. 59).

The network operation is explained mathematically and summarised in Table 2.1. Each neuron takes a vector of inputs from the previous layer, $a_j^{[l-1]}$, and applies a weight vector, $W_j^{[l]}$ and a bias, $b_j^{[l]}$, so that

$$Z_j^{[l]} = W_j^{[l]} a^{[l-1]} + b_j^{[l]} \tag{2.1}$$

or in matrix notation

$$Z^{[l]} = W^{[l]} a^{[l-1]} + b^{[l]}, \tag{2.2}$$

which is, of course, a purely linear operation. The result from layer l is then given by applying a non-linear *activation function* $g(Z)$,

$$a^{[l]} = g(Z^{[l]}). \tag{2.3}$$

Many different choices of activation functions are available (see §2.3). In this way the input vector $x = a^{[0]}$ is propagated forward through the network to give the output $y = a^{[L]}$. The operation is, therefore, a sequence of linear algebra operations coupled with the application of a function to all elements of the matrix $Z^{[l]}$. GPUs and other parallel-processor architectures are ideal for neural networks as they allow for efficient parallel computation during training and inference.

TABLE 2.1 Neural Network Notation Used in This Book

Notation	Description
x; x_j	Input layer, jth element of input layer
$\hat{y}$	Output (vector or scalar depending on problem context)
$\hat{y}^{(i)}$	Output value from the neural network for training example i

$(x^{(i)}, y^{(i)})$	ith training example
(X, Y)	Matrices of all training examples
$W^{[l]}; W_j^{[l]}$	Weight matrix for the lth layer and jth component vector
$b^{[l]}; b_j^{[l]}$	Bias vector for the lth layer and jth element
L	Number of layers in the neural network
$g(z)$	Non-linear activation function
$Z^{[l]} = W^{[l]}X + b^{[l]}$	Result of matrix operations on layer l
$a^{[l]} = g(Z^{[l]})$	Results of activation function on layer l
$a^{[0]} = x; a^{[L]} = y$	Input and output layers
$J(W^{[l]}, b^{[l]})$	Loss function
$\odot$	Element-wise multiplication
α	Learning rate
θ	Set of all trainable parameters in a neural network

2.1.1 Why Activation Must Be Non-Linear

Why, in general, should activation functions be non-linear? This need for non-linearity is straightforward to understand; consider two layers, l and $l + 1$, with both layers having linear activation functions, $g(z) = z$. The output of layer l is given by

$$\begin{aligned} a^{[l]} &= g(Z^{[l]}) \\ &= Z^{[l]} \\ &= W^{[l]}X + b^{[l]}. \end{aligned} \tag{2.4}$$

Input this into the second layer to give

$$\begin{aligned} Z^{[l+1]} &= W^{[l+1]}a^{[l]} + b^{[l+1]} \\ &= W^{[l+1]}(W^{[l]}X + b^{[l]}) + b^{[l+1]}, \end{aligned} \tag{2.5}$$

$$\begin{aligned} a^{[l+1]} &= g(Z^{[l+1]}) \\ &= Z^{[l+1]} \\ &= W^{[l+1]}(W^{[l]}X + b^{[l]}) + b^{[l+1]}. \end{aligned} \tag{2.6}$$

The second layer's output is completely linear and can be expressed with just one linear layer. Therefore, if all the activation functions within the network are linear, there is no advantage to having extra layers. The neural network would reduce to basic linear regression.

2.1.2 Learning Representations

What do the layers in a deep neural network do? The key to deep learning and why it works well is that layers learn *representations* of the input data; that is, they learn to extract meaningful features for the task at hand. As noted by Bengio et al. (2013), feature engineering is an essential element of most machine learning algorithms. However, it reflects their weakness in that they rely on human knowledge of the problem domain to devise a suitable input representation of the data. The majority of machine learning algorithms are incapable of learning the representation directly.

Deep learning is different in that the layers of a neural network can learn useful representations of the data directly, and this became clear with the introduction of the *deep belief network* (Hinton and Salakhutdinov, 2006) and the series of papers that followed it. The critical element of these early papers on deep learning was the use of *greedy layer-wise unsupervised pre-training* (Bengio et al., 2013), in which a series of *restricted Boltzmann machines (RBMs)* were trained successively using the features learned in the previous layer as input. Neural network classifiers and other models, including the deep Boltzmann machine (Salakhutdinov and Hinton, 2009), were created by stacking the layers. Modern deep learning shows the same behaviour, with the layers learning a hierarchy of representations, with layers closest to the input learning basic features and layers closer to the output learning aggregate features that combine the essential elements. As shown in Chapter 6, this is visible in the layers of a convolutional neural network where the learned features can be visualised directly at successive layers.

Hence, deep learning has a distinct advantage over other machine learning techniques because extensive feature engineering is generally not required. The only exception is when only limited data is available for training.

2.2 REGRESSION AND CLASSIFICATION

Feedforward networks are used in supervised learning tasks, that is, they support regression and classification tasks through function approximation. Here, two examples are provided: multi-class classification using MNIST, the dataset discussed above, and regression approximation of the Black–Scholes function.

EXAMPLE 2.1: MULTI-CLASS CLASSIFICATION USING MNIST

The MNIST dataset of handwritten digits consists of 60,000 training examples and 10,000 test examples (LeCun et al., 2012) and each example is a 28×28 greyscale image (this example is included in the Jupyter Notebook collection that accompanies this chapter and can be found in `MNIST basic.ipynb`). The dataset is available online from http://yann.lecun.com/exdb/mnist/ and is supplied as standard in Tensorflow, Keras and PyTorch.

Here, PyTorch is used. To load MNIST, we must import the `datasets` class that allows the loading of built-in datasets and then load the data

```
from torchvision import datasets, transforms
transform = transforms.Compose([transforms.ToTensor()])
train_set = datasets.MNIST('~/.pytorch/MNIST_data/',
                           download=True, train=True, transform=transform)
test_set = datasets.MNIST('~/.pytorch/MNIST_data/',
                          download=True, train=False, transform=transform)
```

Input must be a floating-point vector for a standard feedforward network. As discussed in detail in Chapter 3, we also prefer the magnitude of the input values to be close to 1.0. Hence, the images must first be flattened from the 2D image into a 1D vector, then converted to floating-point numbers and divided by 255, the number of discrete intensity levels in each image pixel. The labels are converted from integer values into categorical variables, that is, into a vector with a binary indicator to determine which class (number) the image represents. There are 10 digits; hence, the labels become binary vectors of length 10. The PyTorch function `one_hot`, which is part of `torch.nn.functional`, provides this transformation, commonly known as *one-hot encoding*.

```
import torch.nn.functional as F
train_x = train_set.data.reshape((60000, 28*28))
train_x = train_x.float() / 255
test_x = test_set.data.reshape((10000, 28 * 28))
test_x = test_x.float() / 255
num_classes = train_set.targets.max() + 1
```

```
train_y = F.one_hot(train_set.targets, num_classes=num_classes).float()
test_y = F.one_hot(test_set.targets, num_classes=num_classes).float()
```

The next step is to build the neural network, which will be done by building a neural network class that derives from `torch.nn.module`. Here, two layers, with 200 neurons in each, are used, with the ReLU activation function. The input is the flattened image vector at length 28×28. The last layer is a linear layer passed through the special softmax function used to represent the probability that the input image represents the integers from 0 to 9. The softmax is embedded within the cross-entropy loss function in PyTorch. Given this probability, the sum of the final-layer output values will be 1.0. When using the model for inference and evaluation, the entry with the highest probability will be used to determine the classification.

```
import torch.nn as nn
class NeuralNetwork(nn.Module):
def __init__(self):
    super(NeuralNetwork, self).__init__()
    self.fc1 = nn.Linear(28 * 28, 200)
    self.fc2 = nn.Linear(200, 200)
    self.fc3 = nn.Linear(200, 10)

def forward(self, x):
    x = x.view(-1, 28 * 28)
    x = F.relu(self.fc1(x))
    x = F.relu(self.fc2(x))
    x = self.fc3(x)
    return x
```

For optimal performance, a GPU is used if available, and the `device` is selected appropriately.

```
if torch.cuda.is_available():
    device = torch.device("cuda:0")
else:
    device = torch.device("cpu")
print("Device:", device)
```

The model and then later other tensors are transferred to the device.

```
model = NeuralNetwork().to(device)
```

To train the model, an optimiser and loss function must be chosen. Here, the `rmsprop` optimiser and `crossentropy` loss function are used.

```
import torch.optim as optim
optimizer = optim.RMSprop(model.parameters(), lr=0.001)
loss_fn = nn.CrossEntropyLoss()
```

PyTorch data loaders are used to manage the batches of data and these are imported and constructed after the data is moved to the GPU.

(*Continued*)

(*Continued*)

```
train_x = train_x.to(device)
train_y = train_y.to(device)
train_dataset = TensorDataset(train_x, train_y)
train_loader = torch.utils.data.DataLoader(train_dataset, batch_size=128,
                                           shuffle=True, drop_last=True)

test_x = test_x.to(device)
test_y = test_y.to(device)
test_dataset = TensorDataset(test_x, test_y)
test_loader = torch.utils.data.DataLoader(test_dataset, batch_size=128,
                                          shuffle=False, drop_last=True)
```

A training function and the loops over the epochs performing the training loop are defined. The function loops over all batches from the data loader for each epoch. The loss is calculated for each, then the gradient is calculated, and one step of stochastic gradient descent is applied. The training loss and training accuracy are then calculated and stored. After all the batches for the current epoch have been completed, the model is switched to evaluation mode. Then, with no gradient calculation, the model is evaluated using the test set, and test loss and test accuracy are calculated. The `tqdm` package is used to monitor the training progress, as this shows a progress bar in the Jupyter Notebook and allows the metrics to be reported at each epoch end in the status bar. Once training is complete, the losses and accuracy figures are stored in a dictionary and returned.

```
def train_model(model, train_loader, test_loader, loss_fn, optimizer,
                epochs):
    train_errors = []
    test_errors = []
    train_accuracies = []
    test_accuracies = []

    tqdm_epoch = trange(epochs)
    for epoch in tqdm_epoch:
        model.train()
        train_loss = 0.0
        correct_train = 0.0

        # Train
        for batch_X, batch_y in train_loader:
            outputs = model(batch_X)
            loss = loss_fn(outputs.squeeze(), batch_y)
            optimizer.zero_grad()
            loss.backward()
            optimizer.step()

            train_loss += loss.item() * batch_X.size(0)
            predicted = torch.argmax(outputs.squeeze(), dim=1)
            targets = torch.argmax(batch_y, dim=1)
            correct_train += (predicted == targets).sum().item()

        train_loss /= len(train_loader.dataset)
        train_accuracy = 100 * correct_train / len(train_loader.dataset)
        train_errors.append(train_loss)
        train_accuracies.append(train_accuracy)
```

```
        # Evaluation on test set
        model.eval()
        test_loss = 0.0
        correct_test = 0.0
        with torch.no_grad():
            for batch_X, batch_y in test_loader:
                outputs = model(batch_X)
                loss = loss_fn(outputs.squeeze(), batch_y)
                test_loss += loss.item() * batch_X.size(0)
                predicted = torch.argmax(outputs.squeeze(), dim=1)
                targets = torch.argmax(batch_y, dim=1)
                correct_test += (predicted == targets).sum().item()

        test_loss /= len(test_loader.dataset)
        test_accuracy = 100 * correct_test / len(test_loader.dataset)
        test_errors.append(test_loss)
        test_accuracies.append(test_accuracy)

        tqdm_epoch.set_description(f"Epoch {epoch+1}/{epochs} \
            - Train loss: {train_loss:.4f}, Test loss: {test_loss:.4f}, \
            Train Acc: {train_accuracy:.2f}%, \
            Test Acc: {test_accuracy:.2f}%")

    history = dict()
    history['train_loss'] = train_errors
    history['test_loss'] = test_errors
    history['train_acc'] = train_accuracies
    history['test_acc'] = test_accuracies

    return history
```

The model is trained through 20 epochs with a batch size of 128.

```
epochs = 20
history_dict = train_model(model, train_loader, test_loader,
                           loss_fn, optimizer, epochs)
```

The training accuracy and loss for the model are illustrated in Figure 2.2. A final test accuracy of 98.07% was obtained in the trained model but will vary slightly between training runs because of differences in random initialisation of weights and biases.

(*Continued*)

(*Continued*)

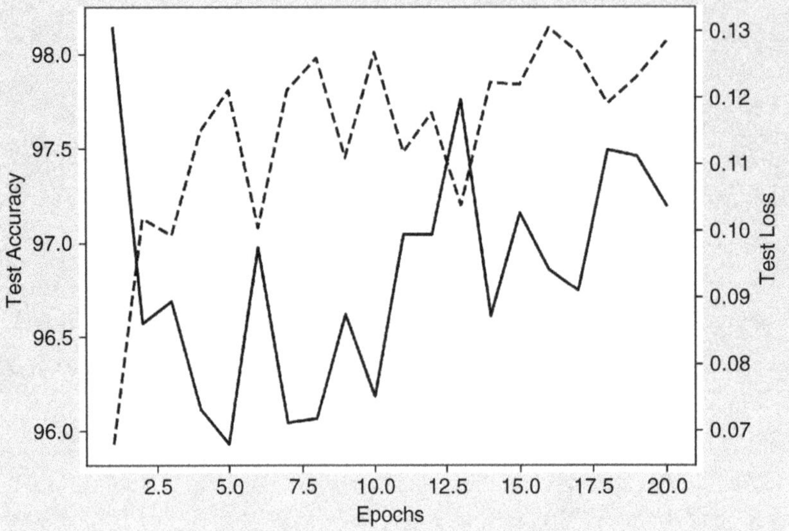

FIGURE 2.2 Training accuracy and loss from training a two-layer neural network with MNIST.

EXAMPLE 2.2: REGRESSION APPROXIMATION OF BLACK–SCHOLES

As an example of a regression problem, a feedforward network is fitted to the Black–Scholes model (Black and Scholes, 1973; Black, 1976) (the Black–Scholes model is included in the Jupyter Notebook collection that accompanies this chapter and can be found in `Black-Scholes Basic.ipynb`).

$$V_C(F, K, T, \sigma, r) = e^{-rT}\left(FN(d_1) - KN(d_2)\right)$$
$$V_P(F, K, T, \sigma, r) = e^{-rT}\left(KN(-d_2) - FN(-d_1)\right)$$

where

$$d_1 = \frac{1}{\sigma\sqrt{T}}\left[\log\left(\frac{F}{K}\right) + \frac{1}{2}\sigma^2 T\right]$$
$$d_2 = d_1 - \sigma\sqrt{T}$$

and F is the forward price of the asset, T is the maturity, K is the strike, r is the interest rate and σ is the volatility of the asset returns. Black–Scholes is a low-dimensional problem; it serves as a useful test case. We simplify the problem by setting the interest rate $r = 0$ or equivalently fitting the undiscounted model. If we divide $V_C(F, K, T, \sigma, r)$ and $V_P(F, K, T, \sigma, r)$ throughout with the strike, we see that only the ratio F/K appears. Hence, we only need to use the strike or the forward as an input to the neural network, reducing the dimensionality (this is known as the 'homogeneity hint' and is discussed again in Chapter 11). Here, we will assume the strike $K = 100$ and use the forward as an input. We fit both call and put prices, introducing a categorical variable to indicate put or call. Finally, we have four inputs that we will fit: forward F, volatility σ, maturity T and put/call indicator function, which equals 1 for a call and 0 for a put.

A dataset for neural network training is being generated using Monte Carlo simulation and the QuantLib library to obtain option values corresponding to random input parameter sets, following the approach outlined in Ferguson and Green (2018). No stochastic dynamics are imposed on the inputs, and each one is generated independently using separate marginal distributions selected for each input parameter. The exception to this process is the put/call indicator; when generating the training set, both put and call values are generated from each set of three random inputs (forward, maturity and volatility). Hence, the training set always contains both. When the dataset is used for training, the put and call values are separated into individual training examples, and the put/call indicator is set appropriately. The distributions used to generate the three inputs are given in the equations below and illustrated in Figure 2.3. One million sets of example inputs were generated, giving two million option values split between calls and puts (a Jupyter Notebook with code to generate the training set is included in the examples for this chapter, `Generate Option Training Data.ipynb`).

$$\sigma \sim U(0.0, 1.0)$$

$$F = 100\exp(z) \quad \text{where} \quad z \sim N(0.5, 0.25)$$

$$T = \frac{z^2}{365.0} \quad \text{where} \quad z \sim U(1.0, 43.0).$$

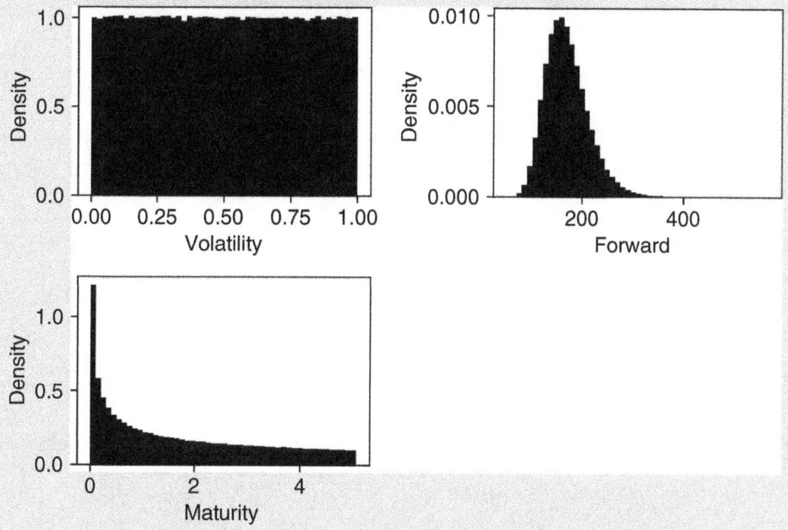

FIGURE 2.3 Distribution of training-set examples for the Black–Scholes model.

Before commencing the network's construction and training, we must undertake data loading and preprocessing, and this entails generating an input pandas data frame containing the three real-valued inputs and the put/call categorical variable, as well as a corresponding output value array. Notably, the initial three real-valued inputs necessitate scaling to ensure a mean of zero and a variance of one. We accomplish this by utilising the `StandardScaler` function from *scikit-learn*.

```
from sklearn.preprocessing import StandardScaler
scalar = StandardScaler()
X[['Vol','Spot','T']] = sscalar.fit_transform(X[['Vol','Spot','T']])
```

Next, the data is split into training and testing sets using `train_test_split`, again from *scikit-learn*.

```
from sklearn.model_selection import train_test_split
X_ta, X_te, y_ta, y_te = train_test_split(X, y, test_size=0.04,
                                          random_state=42)
```

(*Continued*)

(*Continued*)

The network uses PyTorch and has two hidden layers, each with 50 neurons. Both hidden layers use ReLU activation, and the output layer, given this is a regression model, uses linear activation. (Note that in this case, given that we know the option price is always positive, we could also use ReLU activation in the output layer. In general, however, regression models use a linear output layer.) The choice of network architecture is based on *hyperparameter tuning* across several different possible architectures (I will discuss hyperparameter tuning later in Chapter 5). Again, the *rmsprop* optimiser is used with its default settings, but the loss function is now changed to *mean square error (MSE)*, which is an appropriate choice for regression problems.

```
class NeuralNetwork(nn.Module):
    def __init__(self):
        super(NeuralNetwork, self).__init__()
        self.fc1 = nn.Linear(4, 50)
        self.fc2 = nn.Linear(50, 50)
        self.fc3 = nn.Linear(50, 1)

    def forward(self, x):
        x = F.relu(self.fc1(x))
        x = F.relu(self.fc2(x))
        x = self.fc3(x)
        return x

model = NeuralNetwork().to(device)
```

The training loop is modified slightly from the previous example as the accuracy is not relevant.

```
optimizer = optim.RMSprop(model.parameters(), lr=0.001)
loss_fn = nn.MSELoss()

def train_model(model, train_loader, test_loader,
                loss_fn, optimizer, epochs):
    train_errors = []
    test_errors = []

    tqdm_epoch = trange(epochs)
        for epoch in tqdm_epoch:
            model.train()
            train_loss = 0.0
            correct_train = 0

            # Training
            for batch_X, batch_y in train_loader:
                outputs = model(batch_X)
                loss = loss_fn(outputs.squeeze(), batch_y)
                optimizer.zero_grad()
                 loss.backward()
                optimizer.step()
                train_loss += loss.item() * batch_X.size(0)

             train_loss /= len(train_loader.dataset)
            train_errors.append(train_loss)

        # Test
```

```
        model.eval()
        test_loss = 0.0
        correct_test = 0
        with torch.no_grad():
            for batch_X, batch_y in test_loader:
                outputs = model(batch_X)
                loss = loss_fn(outputs.squeeze(), batch_y)
                test_loss += loss.item() * batch_X.size(0)

        test_loss /= len(test_loader.dataset)
        test_errors.append(test_loss)

        tqdm_epoch.set_description(f"Epoch {epoch+1}/{epochs} \
            - Train loss: {train_loss:.4f}, Test loss: {test_loss:.4f}")

    history = dict()
    history['train_loss'] = train_errors
    history['test_loss'] = test_errors
    return history
```

Training runs for 50 epochs with a batch size of 10,000. GPU training accelerates this small model, making it quick despite the large training set and batch size. The training loss as a function of epoch is illustrated in Figure 2.4.

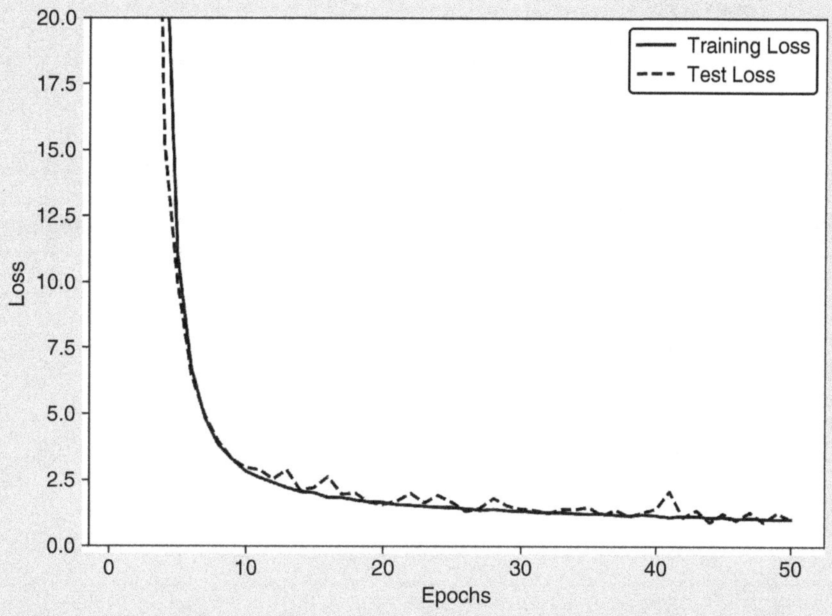

FIGURE 2.4 Training and test loss as a function of epoch for the Black–Scholes model.

The final training loss was 1.0291, while the test loss was similar at 0.9992.

2.3 ACTIVATION FUNCTIONS

There are, in fact, a large number of different activation functions available for use in neural networks. This section describes the more essential functions in active use today and those of historical interest. As noted above, we can identify two types of activation functions, those used in hidden layers and those used in output layers, with a small number of functions applicable in both contexts. The possible uses of each type of activation function described here are given in Table 2.2.

2.3.1 Linear

The linear activation function is the simplest possible as the output is the same as the input. Linear activation functions are only used as the output layer for regression problems where the range of output values lies on the entire real line. The properties are given in Table 2.3.

2.3.2 Sigmoid (Logistic)

The sigmoid or logistic activation function is the output function for single-class classifier problems. Such problems generate a probability value, which must lie between 0 and 1, and sigmoid satisfies this. Before the widespread adoption of ReLU around 2010, sigmoid and the similar hyperbolic tangent were much more widely used in hidden layers, not just the output (see discussion below in Sections 2.3.5 and 2.3.4, respectively). The properties of the function are given in Table 2.3.

TABLE 2.2 Activation Function Uses

Activation Function	Uses
Linear	Output
Sigmoid (logistic)	Both
Heaviside (binary)	Both
Hyperbolic tangent (tanh)	Both
Rectified linear unit (ReLU)	Hidden
Leaky ReLU	Hidden
Parametric rectified linear unit (PReLU)	Hidden
Gaussian error linear unit (GELU)	Hidden
Exponential linear unit (ELU)	Hidden
Scaled exponential linear unit (SELU)	Hidden
Swish	Hidden
Scaled exponentially regularised linear units (SERLU)	Hidden
Softmax	Output

2.3.3 Heaviside (Binary)

The Heaviside or binary function was frequently used in early neural networks such as the McCulloch–Pitts neuron 1943, the Mark I Perceptron (Rosenblatt, 1957) and Adaline (Widrow and Huff, 1960). The activation function has fallen out of use as it has zero gradients for its entire range, making it unsuited to gradient-based training. The properties of the Heaviside function are given in Table 2.4.

TABLE 2.3 Linear and Sigmoid Activation Functions

Linear		Sigmoid (Logistic)	
Prop	**Description**	**Prop**	**Description**
Func	$g(z) = z$	Func	$g(z) = \sigma(z) = \frac{1}{1+e^{-z}}$
Deriv	$g'(z) = 1$	Deriv	$g'(z) = \sigma(z)(1 - \sigma(z))$
Cont	C^{∞}	Cont	C^{∞}
Output	$[-\infty, \infty]$	Output	$[0, 1]$
Plot	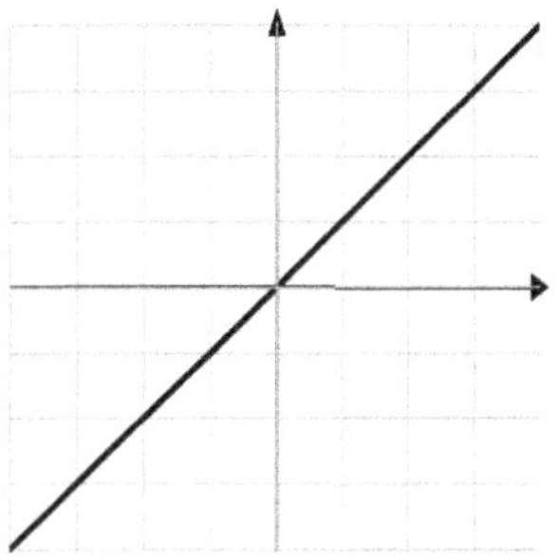	Plot	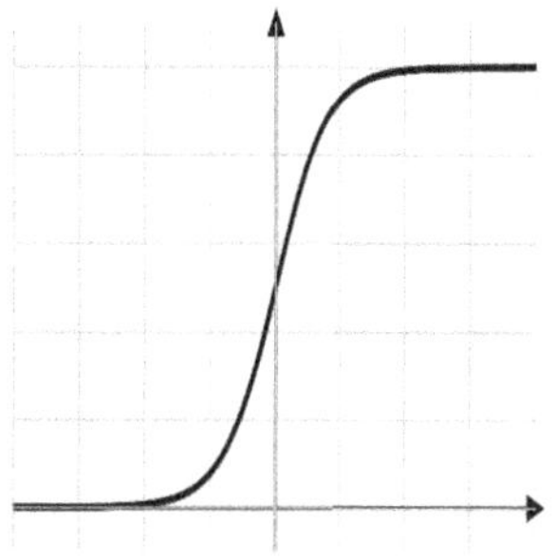

TABLE 2.4 Heaviside and Hyperbolic Tangent Activation Functions

Heaviside (Binary)		Hyperbolic Tangent (tanh)	
Prop	**Description**	**Prop**	**Description**
Func	$g(z) = \begin{cases} 0 & \text{for } z < 0 \\ 1 & \text{for } z \geq 0 \end{cases}$	Func	$g(z) = \frac{(e^{z}-e^{-z})}{(e^{z}+e^{-z})}$
Deriv	$g'(z) = \begin{cases} 0 & \text{for } z \neq 0 \\ \text{undef} & \text{for } z = 0 \end{cases}$	Deriv	$g'(z) = 1 - g(z)^2$
Cont	C^0	Cont	C^{∞}
Output	$[0, 1]$	Output	$[-1, 1]$

(Continued)

TABLE 2.4 Heaviside and Hyperbolic Tangent Activation Functions (*Continued*)

Plot	Plot
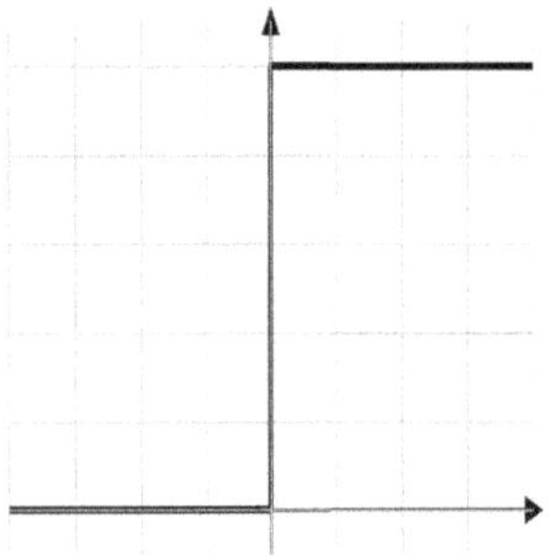	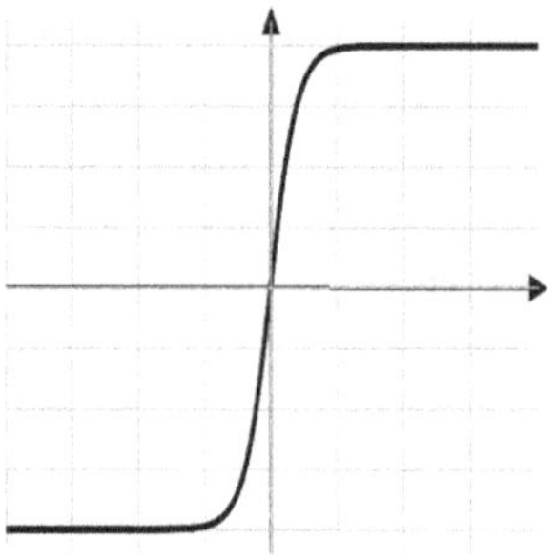

2.3.4 Hyperbolic Tangent (tanh)

The hyperbolic tangent function is closely related to the sigmoid function,

$$\begin{aligned}\tanh(z) &= \frac{e^z - e^{-z}}{e^z + e^{-z}} \\ &= \frac{1 - e^{-2z}}{1 + e^{-2z}} \\ &= \frac{2 - (1 + e^{-2z})}{1 + e^{-2z}} \\ &= 2\frac{1}{1 + e^{-2z}} - 1 \\ &= 2\sigma(2z) - 1.\end{aligned} \tag{2.7}$$

As noted above, before ReLU was introduced, the sigmoid and hyperbolic tangent functions were used as activation functions in hidden layers. Both functions saturate at high and low values of z and, indeed, saturate for low positive and negative values of z, making the gradient close to 0 for much of the range, which can slow the learning process significantly. Contrast this with ReLU, which has a non-zero gradient from half of the real line. Of course, both sigmoid and hyperbolic tangent are infinitely differentiable, which can be necessary in some applications. Goodfellow et al. (2016) suggest that of the two, the hyperbolic tangent performs better given that $\tanh(0) = 0$ and, therefore, is close to the identify function at the origin. The properties of hyperbolic tangent can be found in Table 2.4. Note that tanh should be used with the *hinge* and *squared hinge* loss functions described in Sections 3.4.2.2 and 3.4.2.3, respectively.

$$\begin{aligned}&\lim_{z\to-\infty} \tanh(z) = -1 \quad \lim_{z\to-\infty} \sigma(z) = 0 \\ &\lim_{z\to\infty} \tanh(z) = 1 \quad \lim_{z\to\infty} \sigma(z) = 1.\end{aligned}$$

2.3.5 Rectified Linear Unit (ReLU)

The rectified linear unit (ReLU) was first introduced by Hahnloser et al. (2000), motivated on biological grounds. It was later applied in the context of RBMs by Nair and Hinton (2010) and in computer vision and sentiment analysis by Glorot et al. (2011). The gradient is consistent and large for positive values of z, making it easier to train than sigmoid or hyperbolic tangent. Nevertheless, the lack of gradient over half of the input range has prompted a series of generalisations, including *leaky ReLU* and *PReLU* described below. The second derivative is zero across the full range of input values, which may cause problems in some applications.

TABLE 2.5 Rectified Linear Unit (ReLU) and Leaky Rectified Linear Unit (Leaky ReLU)

Rectified Linear Unit (ReLU)		Leaky Rectified Linear Unit (Leaky ReLU)	
Prop	**Description**	**Prop**	**Description**
Func	$g(z) = \max(z, 0)$	Func	$g(z) = \begin{cases} 0.01z & \text{for } z < 0 \\ z & \text{for } z \geq 0 \end{cases}$
Deriv	$g'(z) = \begin{cases} 0 & \text{for } z \leq 0 \\ 1 & \text{for } z > 0 \end{cases}$	Deriv	$g'(z) = \begin{cases} 0.01 & \text{for } z < 0 \\ 1 & \text{for } z \geq 0 \end{cases}$
Cont	C^0	Cont	C^0
Output	$[0, \infty]$	Output	$[-\infty, \infty]$
Plot	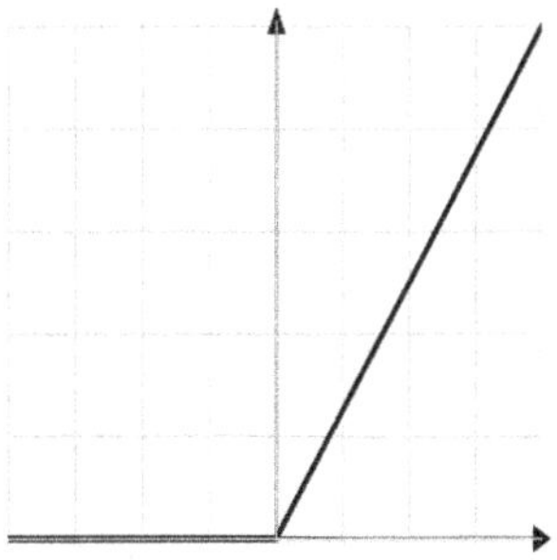	Plot	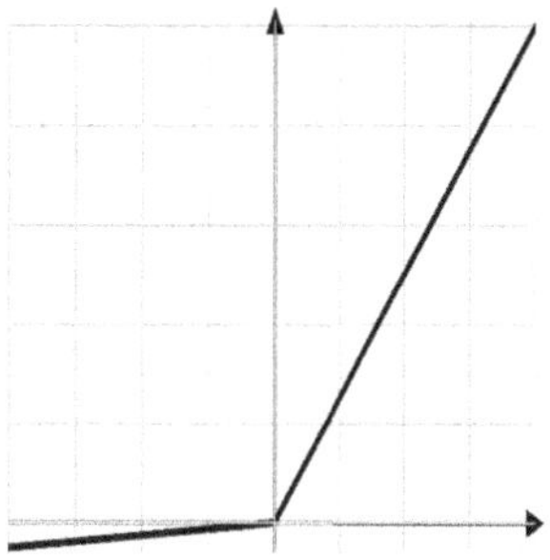

Given that ReLU is a simple *max* function, the computational performance is much better than more complex functions. ReLU is universally acknowledged as the most popular activation function for hidden units today. The properties are given in Table 2.5.

2.3.6 Leaky ReLU

Leaky rectified linear unit was introduced by Maas et al. (2013). It provided a non-zero output and non-zero gradient for $z < 0$, designed to ensure easier training as the gradient is non-zero everywhere while remaining non-linear. The second derivative remains zero, however. The properties of leaky ReLU are given in Table 2.5.

2.3.7 Parametric Rectified Linear Unit (PReLU)

The parametric rectified linear unit is a generalisation of leaky ReLU with the output for $z < 0$ equal to $\alpha_i z$. PReLU treats this parameter as learnable, with each layer learning a parameter value, while leaky ReLU fixes it at 0.01. PReLU was introduced by He et al. (2015), using it to surpass human-level performance on ImageNet classification.

2.3.8 Gaussian Error Linear Unit (GELU)

Hendrycks and Gimpel (2016) introduced the Gaussian error linear unit, which is based on the Gaussian cumulative distribution function. GELU has a similar shape to ReLU but is infinitely differentiable. For faster performance the function can be approximated (Hendrycks and Gimpel, 2016),

$$g(z) = z\Phi(z) \approx 0.5z\left(1 + \tanh\left[\sqrt{2/\pi}\left(z + 0.044715z^3\right)\right]\right). \tag{2.8}$$

The authors provide evidence of better performance than ReLU across computer vision, natural language processing and speech tasks. Table 2.6 provides more details.

TABLE 2.6 Parametric Rectified Linear Unit (PReLU) and Gaussian Error Linear Unit (GELU)

Parametric Rectified Linear Unit (PReLU)		Gaussian Error Linear Unit (GELU)	
Prop	Description	Prop	Description
Func	$g(z) = \begin{cases} \alpha z & \text{for } z < 0 \\ z & \text{for } z \geq 0 \end{cases}$	Func	$g(z) = z\Phi(z)$
Deriv	$g'(z) = \begin{cases} \alpha & \text{for } z \leq 0 \\ 1 & \text{for } z > 0 \end{cases}$	Deriv	$g'(z) = \Phi(z) + z\phi(z)$
Cont	C^0	Cont	C^∞
Output	$[-\infty, \infty]$	Output	$[-0.17, \infty]$
Plot	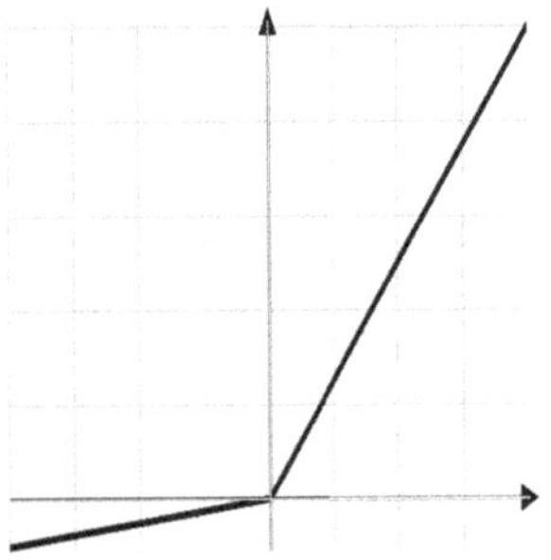	Plot	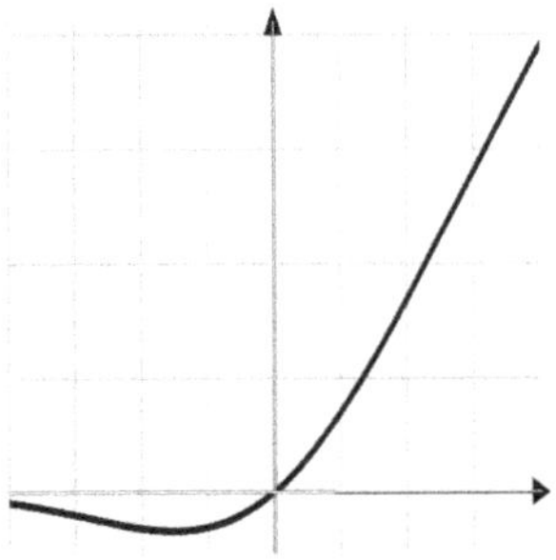

2.3.9 Exponential Linear Unit (ELU)

The exponential linear unit is another ReLU-like function, which can be made once differentiable if the parameter $\alpha = 1$. Clevert et al. (2016) introduced ELU and claimed better performance than ReLU or its derivatives because it allows negative values and tends to a fixed activation as $z \to -\infty$. Negative values push mean activations towards zero, benefiting learning. Table 2.7 provides details.

2.3.10 Scaled Exponential Linear Unit (SELU)

The scaled exponential linear unit was introduced as part of *self-normalising networks* (Klambauer et al., 2017). SELU is a variant of ELU with different parameter values selected based on the Banach fixed-point theorem to satisfy the self-normalising property; activations must have mean zero and variance one. Klambauer et al. (2017) tested 121 different tasks from the UCI Machine Learning repository, showing SELU outperforming ReLU-based feedforward networks. More details are in Table 2.7.

2.3.11 Swish

Swish is an activation function that is simply $z \times \sigma(z)$ and as such is a C^∞ function that is ReLU-like. Ramachandran et al. (2017) suggest that it performs better than ReLU in deep networks and improves performance on ImageNet and Inception-ResNet-v2. Table 2.8 presents more details.

TABLE 2.7 Exponential Linear Unit (ELU) and Scaled Exponential Linear Unit (SELU)

Exponential Linear Unit (ELU)		**Scaled Exponential Linear Unit (SELU)**	
Prop	**Description**	**Prop**	**Description**
Func	$g(\alpha, z) = \begin{cases} \alpha\,(e^z - 1) & \text{for } z \leq 0 \\ z & \text{for } z > 0 \end{cases}$	Func	$g(\alpha, z) = \begin{cases} \lambda\alpha\,(e^z - 1) & \text{for } z \leq 0 \\ \lambda z & \text{for } z > 0 \end{cases}$
Deriv	$g'(\alpha, z) = \begin{cases} \alpha\,(e^z) & \text{for } z < 0 \\ 1 & \text{for } z \geq 0 \end{cases}$	Deriv	$g'(\alpha, z) = \begin{cases} \lambda\alpha\,(e^z) & \text{for } z < 0 \\ \lambda & \text{for } z \geq 0 \end{cases}$
Cont	C^0(unless $\alpha = 1$ then C^1)	Cont	C^0
Output	$[-\alpha, \infty]$	Output	$[-\lambda\alpha, \infty]$
Plot	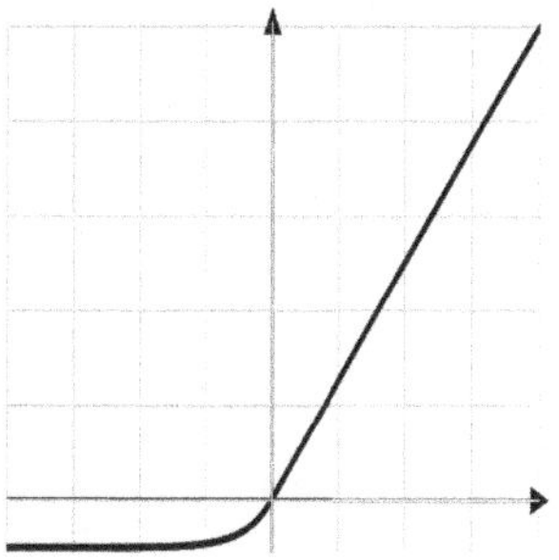	Plot	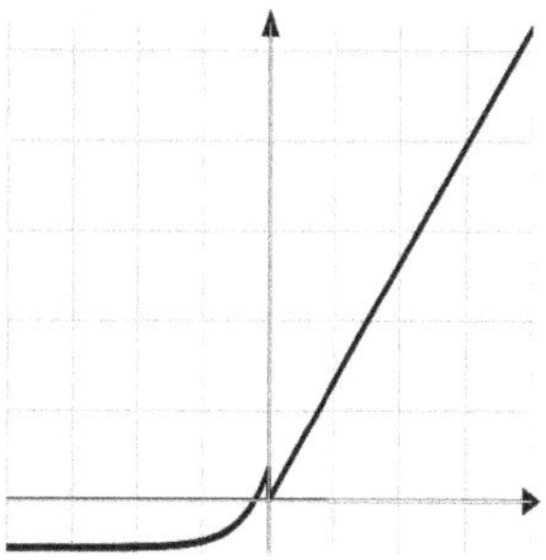

TABLE 2.8 Swish and Scaled Exponentially Regularised Linear Units (SERLU)

Swish		**Scaled Exponentially Regularised Linear Units (SERLU)**	
Prop	**Description**	**Prop**	**Description**
Func	$g(z) = z\sigma(z)$	Func	$g(z) = \lambda_{serlu} \begin{cases} z & z \geq 0 \\ \alpha_{serlu} z e^z & \text{otherwise} \end{cases}$
Deriv	$g'(z) = \sigma(z) + z\sigma(z)(1 - \sigma(z))$	Deriv	$g'(z) = \lambda_{serlu} \begin{cases} 1 & z \geq 0 \\ \alpha_{serlu}(1 + z)e^z & \text{otherwise} \end{cases}$
Cont	C^∞	Cont	C^0(unless $\alpha = 1$ then C^1)
Output	$[-0.278, \infty]$	Output	$[-1.15242, \infty]$
Plot	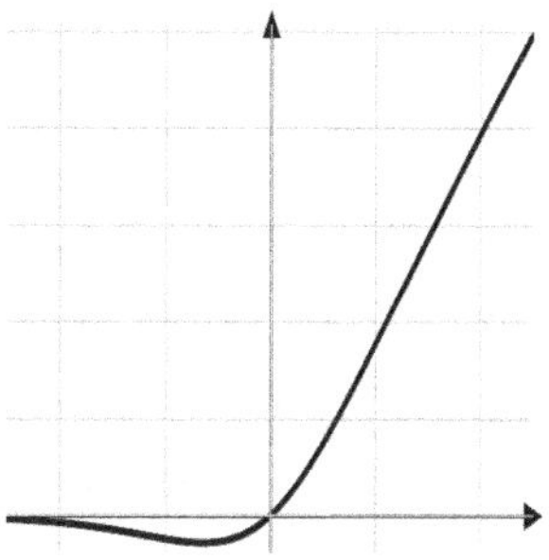	Plot	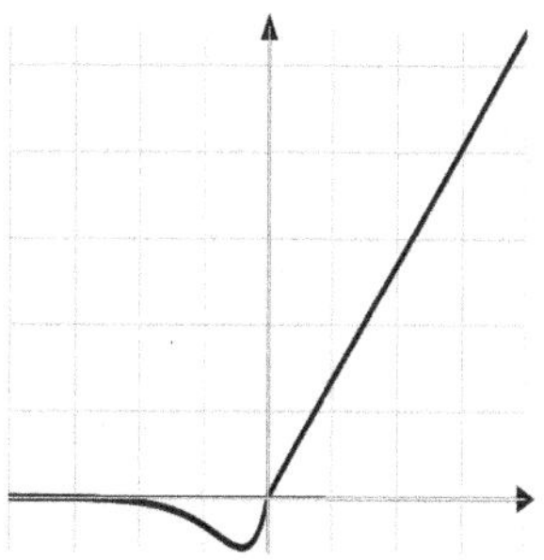

2.3.12 Scaled Exponentially Regularised Linear Unit (SERLU)

Scaled exponentially regularised linear units are also associated with self-normalising networks. Zhang and Li (2018) propose SERLU as an alternative to SELU that is not monotonic. The optimal choice of parameters is given in Equation (2.9), and Table 2.8 provides full details of the function.

$$\begin{aligned} \lambda_{\text{serlu}} &= 1.07862 \\ \alpha_{\text{serlu}} &= 2.90427 \end{aligned} \tag{2.9}$$

2.3.13 Softmax

Softmax is a specialised output activation function for multi-class classification problems, although rarely, it can also be used inside the model (see Goodfellow et al., 2016, p. 179). Unlike other activation functions, softmax applies over the output layer as it represents the probability distribution across all n output classes. That is, the output layer represents a vector of probabilities,

$$y_i = P(z_i = 1|\boldsymbol{x}), \tag{2.10}$$

and hence we require

$$\sum_i y_i = 1. \tag{2.11}$$

The softmax function satisfies this constraint through normalisation, and we define it as follows:

$$\text{softmax}(z) = \frac{\exp(z)}{\sum_i \exp(z_i)}. \tag{2.12}$$

The function as written is numerically unstable because of the use of the exponential, which could overflow. To solve this, note that the function is invariant to the addition of a constant,

$$\begin{aligned} \text{softmax}(z + c) &= \frac{\exp(z + c)}{\sum_i \exp(z_i + c)} \\ &= \frac{\exp(c)\exp(z)}{\exp(c)\sum_i \exp z_i} \\ &= \text{softmax}(z). \end{aligned} \tag{2.13}$$

Hence, to implement softmax, use a constant equal to the largest value of z_i, and this ensures that the arguments of the exponential functions all remain negative and relative to the largest value.

EXAMPLE 2.3: TESTING ACTIVATION FUNCTIONS WITH MNIST

In order to evaluate the effectiveness of various activation functions in the hidden layers, a test was conducted using the same MNIST network as described in Section 2.1. The results were generated using a Jupyter Notebook named *MNIST_Activation.ipynb*.

In PyTorch, most activation functions are available as built-in layers in version 1.13, which is being used here. Swish and SERLU, however, are not and must be defined, so this must be done first.

```
class Swish(nn.Module):
    def __init__(self):
        super(Swish, self).__init__()
```

```
    def forward(self, x):
        return x * torch.sigmoid(x)

def serlu(x):
    return 1.10786 * F.relu(x) + 3.1326 * torch.min(x, torch.tensor(0.0)) *
        torch.exp(torch.min(x, torch.tensor(0.0)))

class SERLU(nn.Module):
    def __init__(self):
        super(SERLU, self).__init__()

    def forward(self, x):
        return serlu(x)
```

Then, a dictionary of activation names is created and passed to the neural network class as a string name.

```
activation_functions = {
'relu': nn.ReLU(),
'sigmoid': nn.Sigmoid(),
'tanh': nn.Tanh(),
'leaky_relu': nn.LeakyReLU(),
'elu': nn.ELU(),
'prelu' : nn.PReLU(),
'selu' : nn.SELU(),
'gelu' : nn.GELU(),
'swish' : Swish(),
'serlu' : SERLU()
}
```

The neural network is essentially the same as the earlier MNIST example with an additional argument and activation function lookup.

```
class NeuralNetwork(nn.Module):
    def __init__(self, activation_name):
        super(NeuralNetwork, self).__init__()
        self.activation = activation_functions[activation_name]
        self.fc1 = nn.Linear(28 * 28, 200)
        self.fc2 = nn.Linear(200, 200)
        self.fc3 = nn.Linear(200, 10)

    def forward(self, x):
        x = x.view(-1, 28 * 28)
        x = self.activation(self.fc1(x))
        x = self.activation(self.fc2(x))
        x = self.fc3(x)
        return x
```

The model was trained for five epochs with a batch size of 128 to compare the impact of different activation functions on training accuracy and performance. Table 2.9 shows the results for all 10 activation functions. The accuracy variation between activation functions is slight, with the more complex ones showing slightly worse performance.

(*Continued*)

(*Continued*)

TABLE 2.9 Accuracy and Time for Different Activation Functions Using MNIST

Activation Function	Accuracy	Time
ReLU	97.67%	5.54s
Sigmoid	96.32%	5.30s
tanh	97.59%	5.57s
ELU	97.39%	5.57s
Leaky ReLU	97.76%	4.77s
Swish	97.77%	6.95s
PReLU	97.59%	7.42s
SELU	97.01%	5.96s
GELU	97.63%	5.64s
SERLU	97.68%	8.88s

EXAMPLE 2.4: ACTIVATION FUNCTIONS AND GRADIENTS

It is helpful to return to the Black–Scholes problem discussed in Section 2.2 to evaluate the performance of the different activation functions in the context of a regression problem. This example aims to assess accuracy in valuation and gradients and can be found in the Jupyter Notebook `Black-Scholes Activation Function and First Order Gradients.ipynb`. With that aim, the underlying dataset captured from QuantLib also contains the analytic delta, vega and theta for both puts and calls. The first-order gradients from the trained neural network will be compared with these analytic results using the test set.

The input CSV file contains the training inputs (volatility, forward and time to maturity), the target put and call values, and several sensitivities. The data must be prepared similarly to that described in Section 2.2 with the input values split from the target values and Greeks. Unlike in the previous example, we need to retain the Greeks for each example, so we no longer use `test_train_split` to separate test and training sets. Given that each line in the input is generated randomly, there is no need to use a random split between test and training datasets. Hence, we split the raw input file, containing both put and call data, into two once loaded into the pandas data frame, with the last 20,000 rows of the one million examples separated to form the test set. Both training and test datasets can then be processed to generate input data, with the real-valued input being split away from the data frame and then duplicated for call-and-put inputs. The top half of the now doubled dataset is appended with an additional categorical variable representing the 'put/call' flag. The target vector is initially arranged to have all call and put values, so the categorical variable must be set consistently. The test set can be left in this form, but the training set should be shuffled so that each minibatch contains both put and call values.

```
from sklearn.utils import shuffle
X, y = shuffle(X, y, random_state=42)
```

The input real values must be scaled appropriately, and `StandardScaler` is again used for this purpose. Fitting is done on the training set, with the transform applied separately to the test set.

```
from sklearn.preprocessing import StandardScaler
scalar = StandardScaler()
X[['Vol','Spot','T']] = sscalar.fit_transform(X[['Vol','Spot','T']])
X_test[['Vol', 'Spot', 'T']] = sscalar.transform(X_test[['Vol', 'Spot', 'T']])
```

A neural network class similar to the one used in the MNIST example was developed to rebuild the network with different activation functions. The training loop function is identical to the one used in the previous Black–Scholes example.

The model is trained through 500 epochs with a batch size of 10,000 to ensure good convergence. The test loss is evaluated using the test set once the training is complete. PyTorch autograd functionality was used to calculate the first-order gradients. The code block obtains the sensitivities of the model output with respect to the inputs.

```
X_input = torch.tensor(X_test.to_numpy(), dtype=torch.float32).to(device)
X_input.requires_grad_(True)
y_output = model(X_input)
y_output.backward(torch.ones_like(y_output))
dy_dx = X_input.grad
dy_dx = dy_dx[:,:3].detach().cpu().numpy()
```

Once the gradients for each test set input have been obtained, the mean square error versus the sensitivities obtained from the analytic derivatives of the Black–Scholes equation was calculated. Given the scaling process, the sensitivities need to be divided by the fitted scaling values.

```
scaled_grads = dy_dx / standard_scalar.scale_
```

The test set loss and the mean squared error for each activation function are given in Table 2.10. In each case, the model was trained through 500 epochs with a batch size of 10,000 samples. The lowest test loss values are given by tanh, leaky ReLU, Swish and GELU, while Swish and GELU give the lowest errors in sensitivities. Overall, Swish and GELU should be preferred based on this test case. The error distribution plots for value with ReLU and Swish are given in Figures 2.5 and 2.7, respectively, while sensitivities can be found in Figures 2.6 and 2.8.

TABLE 2.10 Mean Square Errors for Put and Call Value, Delta, Vega and Theta

	ReLU	Sigmoid	tanh	ELU	Leaky ReLU	Swish	PReLU	SELU	GELU	SERLU
Call Delta MSE	0.002527	0.000509	0.001116	0.000571	0.001445	0.000477	0.000742	0.000987	0.000397	0.003741
Put Delta MSE	0.003887	0.000342	0.000831	0.001222	0.002748	0.000584	0.000755	0.001655	0.001589	0.003822
Call Vega MSE	0.003291	0.000984	0.000966	0.000870	0.003490	0.000698	0.001970	0.001963	0.000964	0.004450
Put Vega MSE	0.003345	0.000628	0.000622	0.001457	0.003294	0.000536	0.000936	0.003675	0.000736	0.005052
Call Theta MSE	0.000159	0.000146	0.000154	0.000156	0.000131	0.000135	0.000091	0.000143	0.000172	0.000196
Put Theta MSE	0.000150	0.000087	0.000093	0.000169	0.000118	0.000113	0.000075	0.000158	0.000126	0.000156
Loss	0.000397	0.000157	0.000781	0.000306	0.000353	0.000249	0.000136	0.000838	0.000282	0.000462

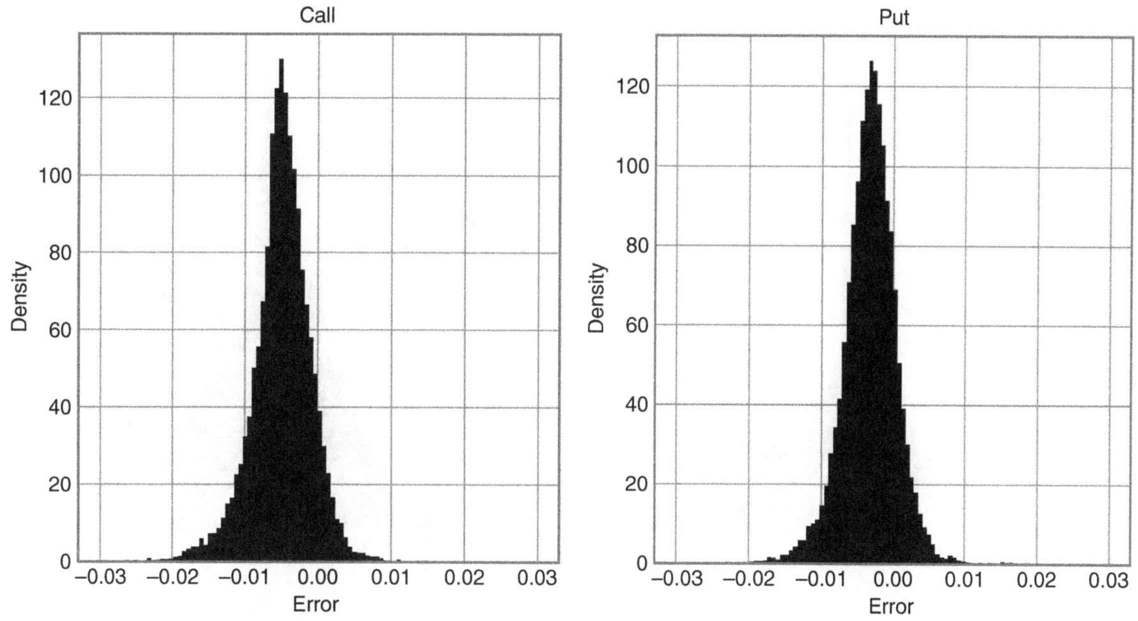

FIGURE 2.5 Value error distribution for the Black–Scholes neural network model with ReLU activation.

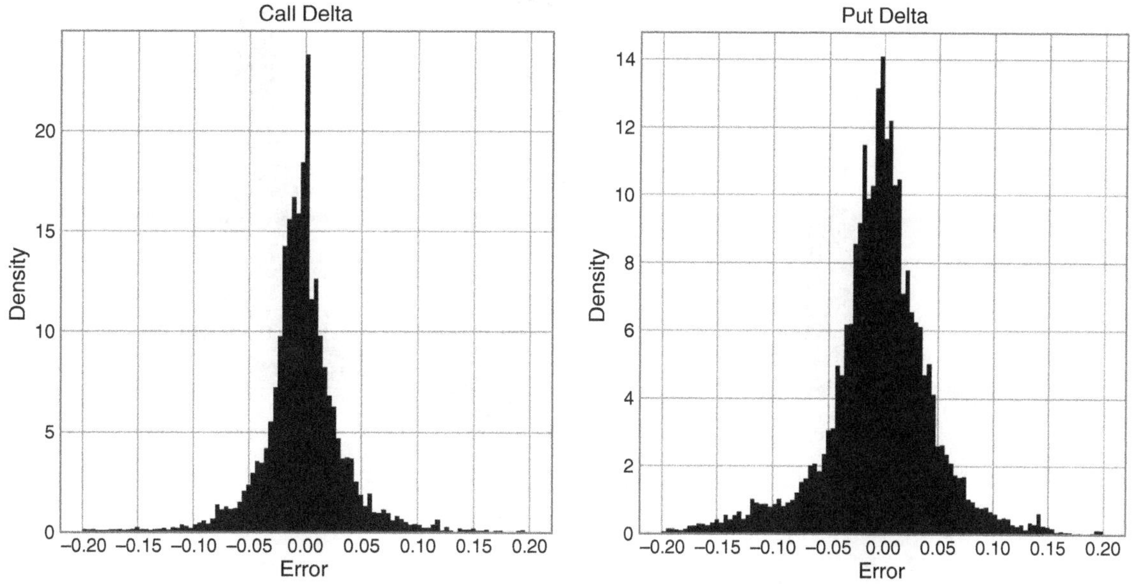

FIGURE 2.6 *Continued*

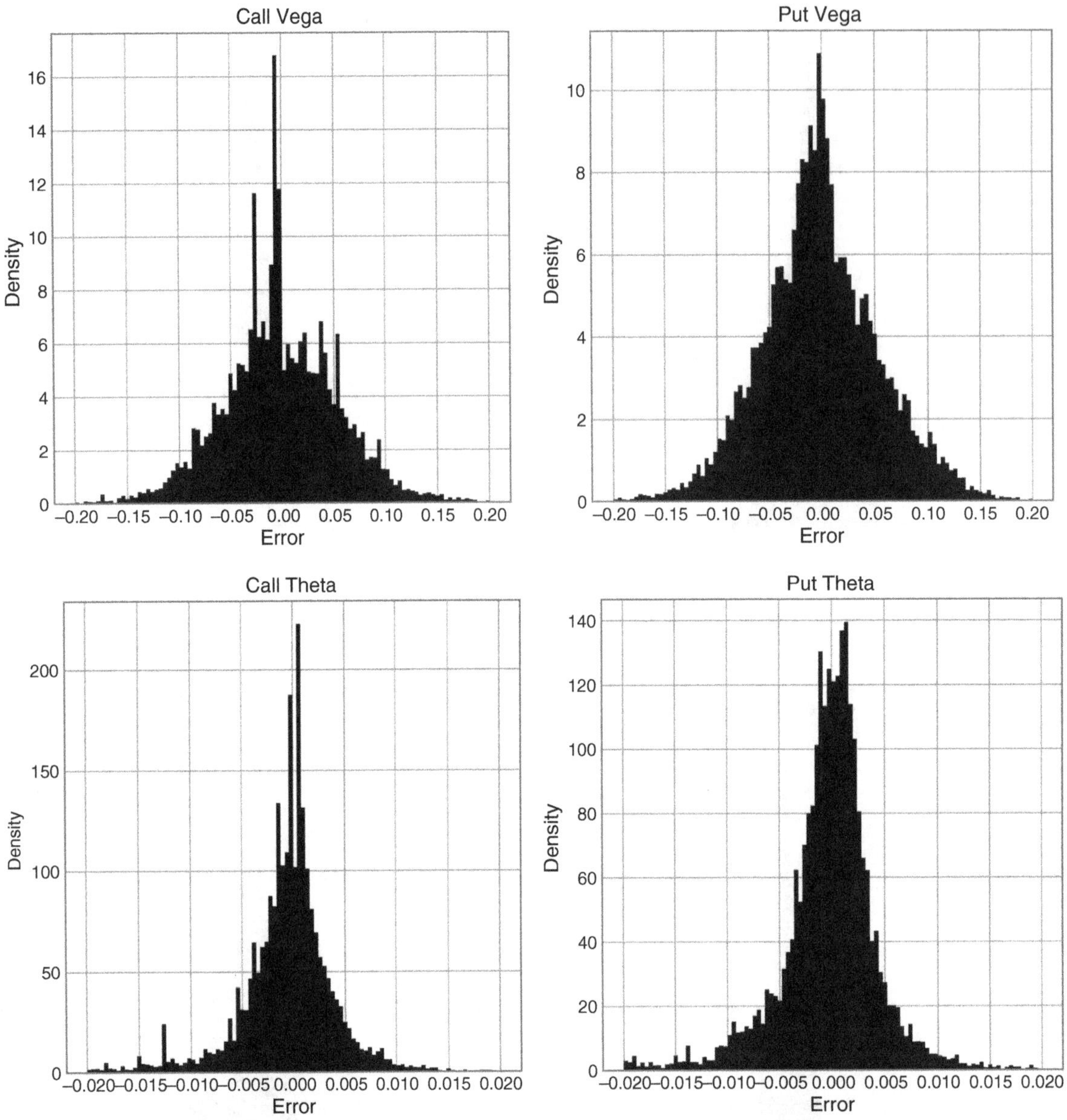

FIGURE 2.6 Sensitivity error distribution for the Black–Scholes neural network model with ReLU activation.

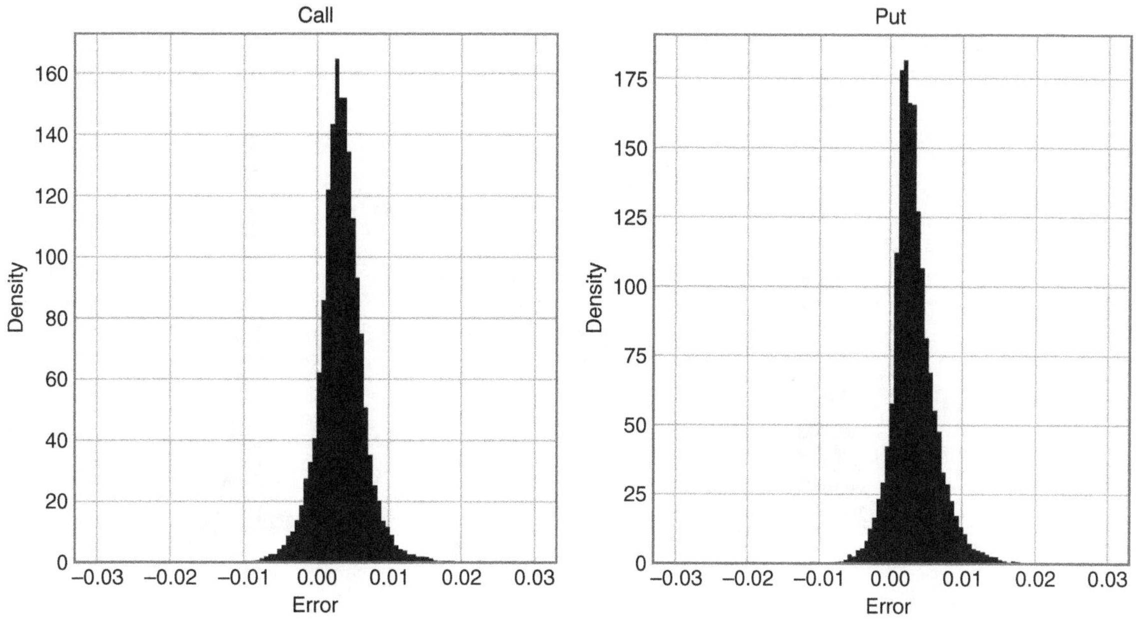

FIGURE 2.7 Value error distribution for the Black–Scholes neural network model with Swish activation.

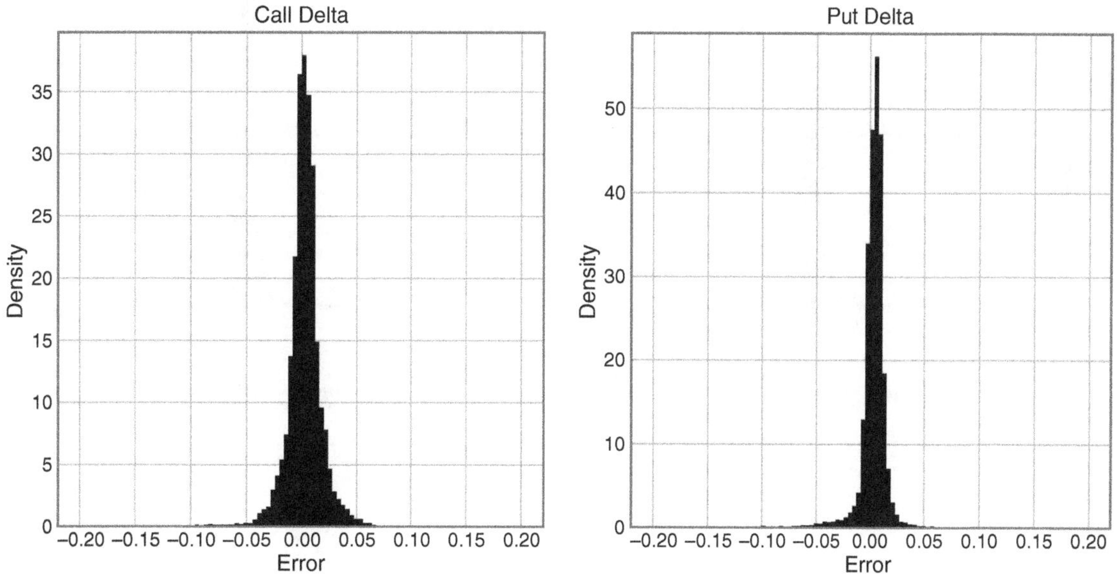

FIGURE 2.8 *Continued*

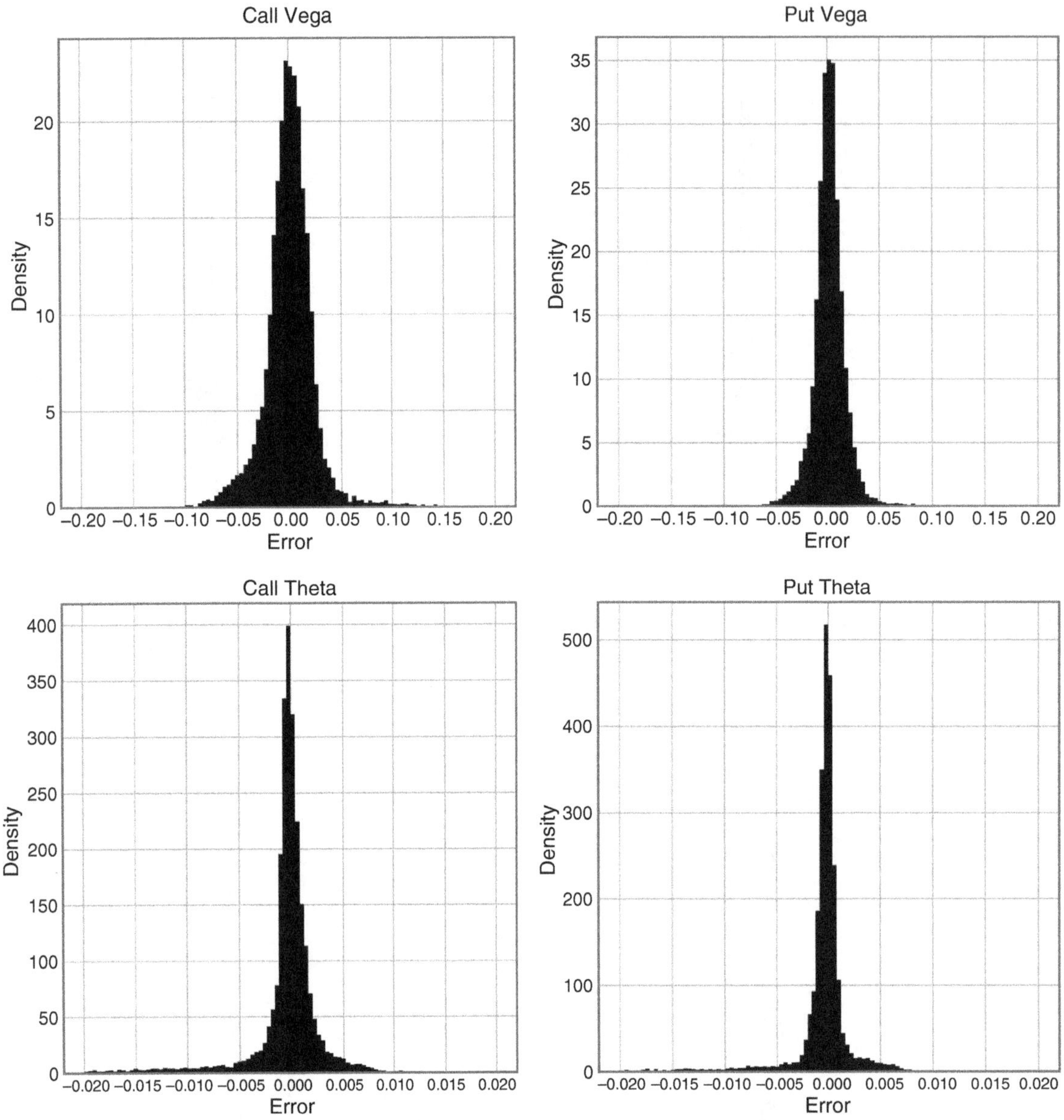

FIGURE 2.8 Sensitivity error distribution for the Black–Scholes neural network model with Swish activation.

2.4 THE UNIVERSAL FUNCTION APPROXIMATION THEOREM

Deep neural networks are function approximators, whether the function being approximated is real-valued or a probability in a classifier problem. We know this works in practice, but can we establish mathematical results demonstrating what functions can be approximated and what choices of activation function, layer width and network depth are required?

The *universal function approximation theorem* was developed independently by Cybenko (1989), Hornik et al. (1989, 1990) and Hornik (1991).

Theorem 2.1 ***(Universal Function Approximation Theorem)*:** *Multilayer feedforward networks with as few as one hidden layer using arbitrary squashing functions*[1] *are capable of approximating any Borel measurable function*[2] *from one finite-dimensional space to another to any desired level of accuracy, provided sufficiently many hidden units are available.*

Hornik et al. (1990) further extend this theorem to include the function's derivatives, including the case where the function possesses only a generalised derivative such as a piecewise differentiable function.

The critical observation is that it is *always* possible to find a feedforward network that can represent a function and its derivatives to arbitrary precision. Of course, the theorem says nothing about whether this is achievable in practice, nor does it say how big the neural network should be. Furthermore, the theorem says nothing at all about network depth. It does imply that should the neural network fail to approximate a function, then it must be either because it was too small or because the training process failed.

The issue of the network size required was first tackled by Barron (1993). The key result is that in a feedforward network with a single layer and sigmoid activation functions, the integrated squared error is of order $O(1/n)$, where n is the number of neurons. Of course, the results place a theoretical bound; they do not say anything about how to achieve this in real-world applications.

The initial function approximation theorem was only proved for squashing functions like the sigmoid function. The result was later generalised to a broader class of functions, including piecewise continuous activation functions like ReLU by Leshno et al. (1993).

Montufar et al. (2014) studied function approximation by deep feedforward networks with piecewise linear activation functions like ReLU. Empirically, it is clear that deep networks are favoured over shallow ones, and intuitively, this can be understood by the function composition behaviour of deep networks. Montufar et al. (2014) analysed deep networks and obtained the following key result.

Theorem 2.2 ***(Montufar et al.)*:** *A rectifier neural network with n_0 input units and L hidden layers with $n \geq n_0$ can compute functions that have $O((n/n_0)^{(L-1)n_0} n^{n_0})$ linear regions.*

Theorem 2.2 shows that the number of linear regions a network has grows exponentially in the number of layers and polynomially in layer width. Hence, we see immediately why deep networks perform better than shallow ones. The deeper layers can often exponentially reuse the functions computed by lower network levels. The results from Montufar et al. (2014) also apply to other network architectures, such as convolutional neural networks.

Theorem 2.1 shows that networks with one hidden layer and arbitrary width are universal function approximators. Can a bound be placed on the width of hidden layers if the depth is not bounded? Lu et al. (2017) proved the following theorem for such width-bound networks.

---

[1] A function $\Psi : \mathbb{R} \to (0,1)$ is a *squashing function* if it is non-decreasing, $\lim_{\lambda\to\infty} \Psi(\lambda) = 1$ and $\lim_{\lambda\to-\infty} \Psi(\lambda) = 0$ (Hornik et al., 1989, Definition 2.3, p. 300).

[2] A function $f : X \to Y$ between two topological spaces is called Borel measurable if $f^{-1}(A)$ is a Borel set for any open set A (Skvortsov, 2012). Note that any continuous function on a closed and bounded subset of $\mathbb{R}^n$ is Borel measurable (Goodfellow et al., 2016, p. 192).

Theorem 2.3 *(**Universal Function Approximation Theorem for Width-Bound Networks**)*: *For any Lebesgue-integrable function* $f : \mathbb{R}^n \rightarrow \mathbb{R}$ *and any* $\epsilon > 0$*, there exists a fully connected ReLU network* $\mathcal{A}$ *of width* $d_m \leq n + 4$ *such that the function* $F_{\mathcal{A}}$ *represented by this network satisfies*

$$\int_{\mathbb{R}^n} \left| f(x) - F_{\mathcal{A}}(x) \right| < \epsilon.$$

In other words, an n-dimensional function can be approximated by a neural network with ReLU activation of width $n + 4$ and arbitrary depth. Hanin (2019) demonstrates that for continuous functions, the hidden layer width $n + 3$ is sufficient and for continuous convex functions, width $n + 1$ is sufficient. Kidger and Lyons (2020) prove similar results for arbitrary activation functions.

2.5 CONCLUSIONS

This chapter introduced feedforward neural networks and their two modes of operation as regression approximators and classifiers. It covered the architecture of feedforward networks and their various non-linear activation functions, which play a critical role in their performance. Additionally, the chapter discussed the 'universal function approximation theorems' that support the notion that neural networks are excellent function approximators and that deep networks outperform shallow ones.

The chapter presented two case studies to showcase the use of neural networks. The first was a classifier using the famous MNIST dataset and the second was a regression example using the Black–Scholes equation. The accuracy of first-order sensitivities was evaluated in the Black–Scholes equation case study and different activation functions were tested in both case studies.

The next chapter will provide a comprehensive guide on training, covering the process in detail.

CHAPTER 3
Training Neural Networks

Good morning, Dr. Chandra. This is Hal. I am ready for my first lesson.

Arthur C. Clarke, 2010: Odyssey Two (1982)

This chapter discusses the training of neural networks in all its aspects. The critical algorithm that made deep neural networks feasible is *backpropagation*. This is discussed first, alongside *adjoint algorithmic differentiation*, an example of the latter being familiar to many quantitative analysts. The chapter then proceeds stepwise through the training process, beginning with data preparation and scaling – the initialisation of weights and biases is discussed next, and several different approaches are presented. The choice of loss or objective function is partially determined by the problem at hand, with different classes of loss function appropriate to regression, binary classification and multi-class classification.

Nonetheless, several options are available for each class of problem, which are presented in the chapter. Optimisation algorithms for neural networks are based on gradient descent methods, and the primary method is described along with the concept of *momentum*. The most popular algorithms are then reviewed in detail, along with numerical case studies. The chapter explores the evaluation and validation of neural networks during and after training, an issue critical to successfully optimising network parameters. Batch normalisation is a common addition to neural networks that enhances training performance, described in Section 3.7. Section 3.8 discusses techniques for appropriately evaluating and validating models to complete the training successfully. Finally, the chapter discusses using function gradients during training in the process known as *Sobolev training*.

3.1 BACKPROPAGATION AND ADJOINT ALGORITHMIC DIFFERENTIATION

The famous backpropagation algorithm has made deep learning possible because it facilitates gradient-based training. During the training phase, the weights and bias parameters of the model are systematically updated to minimise the error between the training data labels and estimates generated by the model. A set of m_{train} training examples are used, and the error is given by a loss function J, given in Equation (3.1):

$$J(\mathbf{W}^{[l]}, b^{[l]}) = \sum_{i}^{m_{\text{train}}} \mathcal{L}(\hat{y}^{(i)}, y^{(i)}) = \mathcal{L}(\hat{y}, y), \tag{3.1}$$

where the function $\mathcal{L}$ depends on the choice of loss measure with the available choices described in Section 3.4 below.[1]

The minimum is found using an optimisation procedure, and the standard approach uses batch gradient descent or a variant of it (see 3.5). Such optimisation procedures require the gradients of the loss function,

$$d\mathbf{W}^{[l]} = \frac{\partial J}{\partial \mathbf{W}^{[l]}}, \tag{3.2}$$

[1]Note that the notation used in this chapter is defined in Table 2.1.

Deep Learning in Quantitative Finance, First Edition. Andrew Green.

$$db^{[l]} = \frac{\partial J}{\partial b^{[l]}}, \tag{3.3}$$

which are used to update the weights,

$$W^{[l]} = W^{[l]} - \alpha dW^{[l]}, \tag{3.4}$$

$$b^{[l]} = b^{[l]} - \alpha db^{[l]}. \tag{3.5}$$

Backpropagation recursively applies the chain rule to propagate derivatives back through the computational graph of the neural network model. Beginning with the output layer, the derivative $da^{[L]}$ is defined by

$$da^{[L]} = \nabla_{a^{[L]}=\hat{y}} \mathcal{L}(\hat{y}, y). \tag{3.6}$$

The derivative $dZ^{[L]}$ is then given by

$$dZ^{[L]} = da^{[L]} \odot g'(Z^{[L]}). \tag{3.7}$$

Hence, the derivatives of the weights for layer L are given by

$$dW^{[L]} = \frac{1}{m} dZ^{[L]}.a^{[L-1]}, \tag{3.8}$$

$$db^{[L]} = \frac{1}{m} dZ^{[L]}. \tag{3.9}$$

The derivative $da^{[L-1]}$ for the next layer is then given by

$$da^{[L-1]} = (W^{[L]})^T.dZ^{[L]}, \tag{3.10}$$

and hence, the derivatives can be propagated backwards through the network to obtain all the $dW^{[l]}$ and $db^{[l]}$. Figure 3.1 illustrates forward and backward propagation.

3.1.1 Adjoint Algorithmic Differentiation

Adjoint algorithmic differentiation (AAD) was introduced to quantitative finance through the seminal paper by Giles and Glasserman (2006).[2] Many quants have adopted AAD in model libraries to obtain fast, stable risk from computationally intensive models. This is particularly beneficial for derivative valuation adjustments or XVAs as these models rely on Monte Carlo simulation and involve many stochastic factors as they span many different assets. Not only does this imply computationally intensive models, but it also means that many sensitivities must be generated. AAD can provide a considerable performance gain over traditional finite difference techniques, at least two to three orders of magnitude (Malakian, 2019).

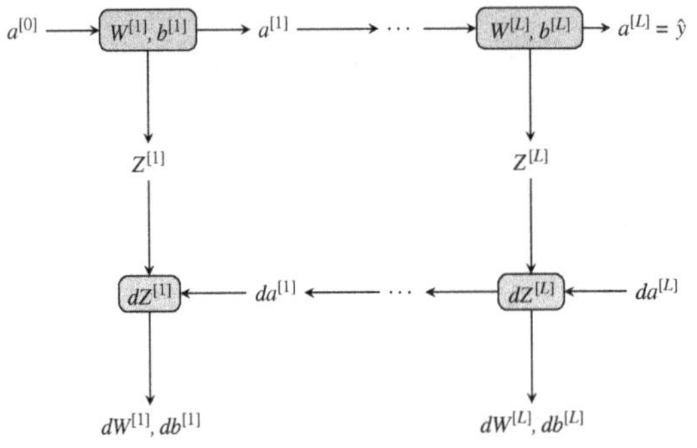

FIGURE 3.1 Forward and backward propagation algorithms for a neural network with L layers.

[2]For a comprehensive treatment of algorithmic differentiation, including higher-order sensitivity calculation, the reader is referred to Griewank and Walther (2008), Naumann (2012) or Savine (2019).

Consider a function that maps from $\mathbb{R}^n$ to $\mathbb{R}^m$,

$$Y = f(X), \tag{3.11}$$

where Y is an m-dimensional vector and X is an n-dimensional vector. The function f is then implemented as a computer program, with steps and intermediate values U and V. The steps can be considered lines of code within a program in a high-level language or as individual instructions on the processor. The program proceeds from input to output through the intermediate steps,

$$X \to \cdots \to U \to V \to \cdots \to Y.$$

We seek to calculate the Jacobian matrix of output sensitivities to inputs, that is,

$$\begin{aligned} J &= \frac{\partial Y}{\partial X}, \\ J_{ij} &= \frac{\partial Y_i}{\partial X_j}. \end{aligned} \tag{3.12}$$

To generate the elements of the Jacobian using AAD, we form the adjoint of X,

$$\bar{X}_i = \sum_{j=1}^{m} \bar{Y}_j \frac{\partial Y_j}{\partial X_i}. \tag{3.13}$$

So to obtain the elements of the Jacobian, J_{ij}, we seed the elements of the adjoint vector, $\bar{Y}_j$, equal to 1 in turn while keeping the remaining elements of the vector 0 (in the language of machine learning, $\bar{Y}$ is set equal to a sequence of *one-hot* vectors). Given that the computer program goes through a series of intermediate steps, we apply the chain rule,

$$\begin{aligned} \bar{X}_i &= \sum_{j=1}^{m} \bar{Y}_j \frac{\partial Y_j}{\partial X_i} \\ &= \sum_{j=1}^{m} \bar{Y}_j \sum_k \frac{\partial Y_j}{\partial U_k}\frac{\partial U_k}{\partial X_i} \\ &= \sum_{j=1}^{m} \bar{Y}_j \sum_k \sum_l \frac{\partial Y_j}{\partial V_l}\frac{\partial V_l}{\partial U_k}\frac{\partial U_k}{\partial X_i}. \end{aligned} \tag{3.14}$$

The adjoints of the intermediate variables can be formed in a similar way to Equation (3.13),

$$\bar{V}_l = \sum_{j=1}^{m} \bar{Y}_j \frac{\partial Y_j}{\partial V_l}, \tag{3.15}$$

$$\bar{U}_k = \sum_l \bar{V}_l \frac{\partial V_l}{\partial U_i}, \tag{3.16}$$

and this means that it is possible to proceed by forming the adjoint of each intermediate step and work backwards from the end with $\bar{Y}$ seeded with a one-hot vector, calculating the intermediate adjoints and propagating them through to obtain the adjoint vector $\bar{X}$. This vector will then contain one complete Jacobian column,

$$\bar{X} \leftarrow \cdots \leftarrow \bar{U} \leftarrow \bar{V} \leftarrow \cdots \leftarrow \bar{Y}.$$

The benefit of doing this in the context of derivative models becomes evident in the case that $m < n$ and for XVA models $m \ll n$, given that there are typically thousands of inputs and one output, the valuation adjustment.

It should also be clear that this process is identical to the backpropagation algorithm, which is AAD applied to a neural network. When applied to general code, algorithmic differentiation usually relies on software tools to support the generation of the adjoints and backpropagation. For the neural network case, the adjoints are calculated explicitly, which is straightforward given that the forward propagation algorithm consists of linear algebra operations coupled with an activation function that is at least differentiable over most of the real line. Gradient descent optimisation involves using these gradients to update the weights of each layer. The backpropagation algorithm is employed to compute the gradient of the loss function with respect to these weights during the neural network training process. However, it is also possible to use backpropagation to obtain the sensitivity of the output of a trained network to its inputs. In this case, the procedure is identical to that described here, with the adjoint of the output layer seeded with one-hot vectors and backpropagated through the network layer to the input, where the sensitivities can be read off.

3.2 DATA PREPARATION AND SCALING

As with other machine learning techniques, the data must be prepared appropriately for use with neural networks before commencing training.

3.2.1 Vectorisation

In general, inputs to the neural network must be tensors of floating-point numbers (Chollet, 2018, p. 101). For the Black–Scholes example in Chapter 2, this was already true of three of the four inputs (volatility, time and spot), but the indicator of whether the option was a put or a call had to be represented as a number, with call set equal to 1.0 and put set equal to 0.0. In general, such categorical data needs to be *one-hot* encoded, and *scikit-learn*, *TensorFlow* and *PyTorch* provide tools to do this. Other types of transform may also be required; for example, with the MNIST dataset example explored in Chapter 2, the input data takes the form of greyscale images and the data needs to be flattened to be fed into a feedforward network.[3]

The output labels must be scaled appropriately to match the activation function in the output layer (Brownlee, 2019a). This is the case for classifier problems, where the output uses sigmoid (binary and multi-class, multi-label) or softmax (multi-class), and then the training labels will be one-hot encoded. No scaling may be necessary for regression problems that can take any value on the real line, but if, for example, the output uses a ReLU unit, then the labels must always be positive.

3.2.2 Input Normalisation

In general, all the floating-point values should have similar magnitudes and take small values of absolute magnitude in the range 0 to 1 (Chollet, 2018, p. 101). Suppose this is not true, and there is a significant variation in parameter scales. In that case, the problem becomes ill-conditioned, with the loss function becoming over-sensitive to some parameters and under-sensitive to others, and this affects the performance of gradient descent methods (Aggarwal, 2018, p. 127).[4] The need to normalise inputs for neural networks was recognised by at least the mid-1990s (LeCun et al., 1998b). There are two main types of input normalisation: *standard (z-scale) normalisation* and *min–max normalisation*.

---

[3]Note that images are generally used with convolutional neural networks and with such networks the flattening process occurs after the convolutional layers and hence does not form part of data preparation. However, sometimes image inputs will need to be resized. Convolutional neural networks are discussed in Chapter 6.

[4]A related phenomenon is *covariate shift*, which occurs when the training and test set are not drawn from the same distribution, which can occur in real-world problems (Dharani et al., 2019). The related term *internal covariate shift* is discussed in Section 3.7 below.

3.2.2.1 Standard (z-scale) Normalisation Standard scaling shifts the mean of a given input feature to 0.0 and its variance to 1.0,

$$\hat{x}^{(i)} = \frac{x^{(i)} - \bar{x}}{\sigma}, \tag{3.17}$$

where

$$\bar{x} = \frac{1}{n}\sum_{i}^{n} x^{(i)}, \tag{3.18}$$

$$\sigma = \mathrm{Var}(x^{(i)}). \tag{3.19}$$

This transformation can easily be done using several Python packages but is also readily performed by the `StandardScalar` from scikit-learn, and this was used in the Black–Scholes examples.

```
from sklearn.preprocessing import StandardScaler
sscalar = StandardScaler()
X[['Vol', 'Spot', 'T']] = sscalar.fit_transform(X[['Vol', 'Spot', 'T']])
```

Scikit-learn scalers have three essential functions: `fit` that fits the scaler object to the data, `transform` that transforms the data, given a fitted scaler object, and `fit_transform` that both fits and transforms.

3.2.2.2 Min–Max Normalisation Min–max normalisation scales all values to lie in the range (0, 1),

$$\hat{x}^{(i)} = \frac{x^{(i)} - \min(x)}{\max(x) - \min(x)}, \tag{3.20}$$

where the minimum and maximum are taken across each dimension of the input vector x separately. Scikit-learn provides a scaler object implementation, `MinMaxScalar`. We saw min–max scaling in the context of the MNIST example in Chapter 2. The pixel values were integer greyscale intensity values between 0 and 255, and these were converted to floating-point numbers by dividing throughout by 255.

EXAMPLE 3.1: IMPACT OF SCALING

How much impact does scaling have on training performance? The Black–Scholes regression example will be used again to explore the concept. A Jupyter Notebook containing this test case is included in the associated chapter folder, named `Test Scaling Methodology.ipynb`. A network was trained with the same basic architecture as before, with two hidden layers of 50 neurons using ReLU activation. Three networks were trained through 100 epochs using mean squared error as the loss function and *RMSProp* as the optimiser. The three networks were trained with unscaled data, standard scaled data and min–max scaled data, and the training loss as a function of the epoch is plotted in Figure 3.2. It is immediately apparent that even with this simple example, the learning performance of the unscaled case is significantly worse than either of the two scaling types. Standard scaling performs slightly better than min–max for this example.

(*Continued*)

(*Continued*)

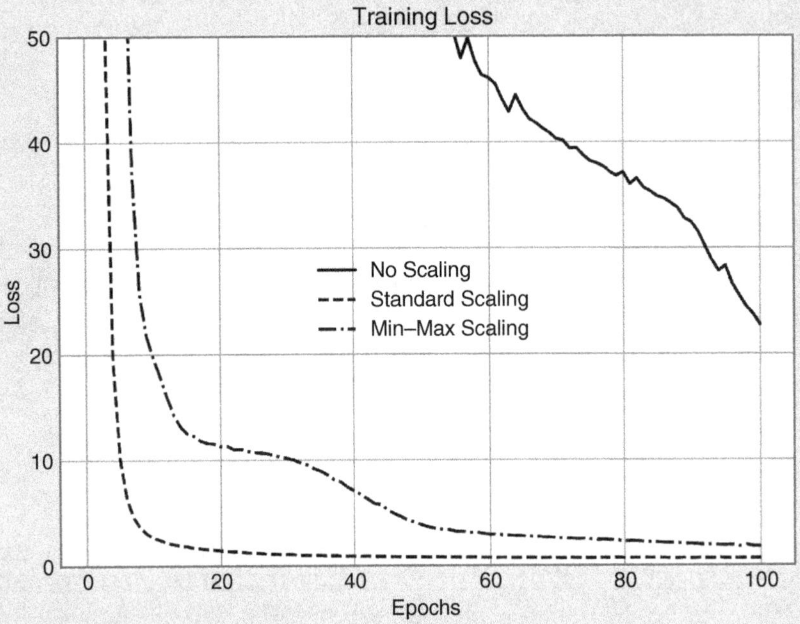

FIGURE 3.2 The training loss for the Black–Scholes model example with no scaling, standard scaling and min–max scaling of the three floating-point input values.

3.2.3 Handling Test and Validation Data

The training data as a whole needs to be scaled, and indeed, any data used later for inference in the trained model will also need to be scaled, and this means that the scaling parameters will need to be saved and distributed with the model. Test and validation data also needs to be scaled, but should the scaling parameters be calculated across the training before or after it is split into test, train and validation sets? As Section 3.8 will make clear, test and validation data should be independent of the training data. Hence, the best practice is to fit the scaler only to the training dataset, which with scikit-learn corresponds to either the `fit` or `fit_transform` methods (Brownlee, 2019a). The test and validation datasets should then be scaled using the fitted scaling parameters using the `transform` function.

3.2.4 Feature Engineering?

Feature engineering (also known as *feature extraction*), that is, the careful handcrafting of input features, is common practice in machine learning (Bishop, 2006; Murphy, 2012). As noted in Section 2.1.2, feature engineering is less common with neural networks, as one of the key features they exhibit is the ability to learn representations, that is, to learn their features and then compose these features in successive layers. The one exception is in situations with limited data, and here, neural networks can benefit from feature engineering (Chollet, 2018, pp. 102–103).

3.3 WEIGHT INITIALISATION

Deep neural networks rely on iterative optimisation techniques, which means a starting set of weights $W^{[l]}$ and $b^{[l]}$ must be supplied. The optimisation algorithms are sensitive to the starting point, and it will determine if the algorithm converges and, if it does, how quickly it converges (Goodfellow et al., 2016, p. 292). Hence, weight initialisation is an integral part of the learning process, and in this section, the available methods are reviewed. Most initialisation methods have limited theoretical justification, primarily based on empirical testing of what works and what does not. Weight initialisation is considered first, followed by bias initialisation.

3.3.1 Initialising Weights

Could all the weights be initialised to zero? While this might be attractive, it will not work, and as Aggarwal (2018) points out, it will lead to nodes working in 'lock-step' as each node in a layer will calculate the same function, and training will fail. Hence, it is essential to *break symmetry* of the initial weight matrices, which has prompted approaches that use random numbers. Given the need to ensure that all neurons calculate different functions, Goodfellow et al. (2016) propose an optimal solution to identify an orthogonal basis via Gram–Schmidt orthogonalisation. However, such a process would be expensive computationally, and a random initialisation is likely to similarly ensure that all neurons are initialised appropriately at a lower cost.

The magnitude of the initialised weights is subject to considerable debate. There is also a tension between the requirements of optimisation and the requirements of generalisation (Goodfellow et al., 2016, p. 294). Larger weights give stronger symmetry breaking, which helps propagate information and the optimisation process but, at the same time, can cause problems for recurrent neural networks and, more generally, could cause activations to saturate. Generalisation demands small weights, and as Goodfellow et al. (2016) suggest, the initial weights act like a Bayesian prior, suggesting it is better to have the initial weights close to zero. In general, the approaches that have been proposed are based on heuristics and primarily focus on controlling the variance of each layer. These techniques aim to avoid numerical problems, particularly vanishing and exploding gradients discussed in Section 3.6.5 below.

3.3.1.1 Gaussian The simplest of all initialisation strategies is to use a simple Gaussian distribution for the weights with zero mean and a small variance, say 10^{-2} (Aggarwal, 2018, p. 129). The problem here is that this is not sensitive to the number of inputs to the layer, so the variance of the whole later will scale linearly with the number of inputs, n. Hence a more common approach is to initialise using (LeCun et al., 1998b)

$$W_0 \sim N\left(0, \frac{1}{n}\right), \tag{3.21}$$

which is sometimes known as *LeCun normal initialisation*. Of course, a normal distribution can still yield high and low values as the distributions run to positive and negative infinity. Hence, some packages provide a truncated normal distribution for initialisation. Keras, for example, provides a truncated normal that redraws any values above and below two standard deviations from the mean (Chollet et al., 2015).

3.3.1.2 Uniform An alternative to a normal distribution is to use a symmetric uniform distribution (Goodfellow et al., 2016, p. 295),

$$W_0 \sim U\left(-\frac{1}{\sqrt{n}}, \frac{1}{\sqrt{n}}\right). \tag{3.22}$$

This is also known as *LeCun uniform initialisation*.

3.3.1.3 Xavier or Glorot Glorot and Bengio (2010) introduced a new scheme they called *normalised initialisation*,

$$W_0 \sim U\left(-\frac{\sqrt{6}}{\sqrt{n^{[l]} + n^{[l+1]}}}, \frac{\sqrt{6}}{\sqrt{n^{[l]} + n^{[l+1]}}}\right), \tag{3.23}$$

where $n^{[l]}$ is the number of nodes in layer l. Note that the variance of a uniform distribution, $U(a, b)$, is $\frac{1}{12}(b-a)^2$ and hence this corresponds to a layer variance of

$$\text{Var}\left(W_0^{[l]}\right) = \frac{2}{n^{[l]} + n^{[l+1]}}. \tag{3.24}$$

This approach balances the desire to maintain activation variances during forward propagation and gradient variances during backpropagation. By including the number of nodes in the current and next layers, they include the impact of multiplication through layers. There is also a Gaussian version of this initialisation scheme,

$$W_0 \sim N\left(0, \frac{2}{n^{[l]} + n^{[l+1]}}\right). \tag{3.25}$$

3.3.1.4 Kaiming or He He et al. (2015) performed similar variance-based analysis to that of Glorot and Bengio (2010), but adding in consideration of rectified activation functions.[5] For ReLU, they obtained a desired layer variance of

$$\mathrm{Var}(W_0^{[l]}) = \frac{2}{n^{[l]}} \tag{3.26}$$

and for PReLU,

$$\mathrm{Var}(W_0^{[l]}) = \frac{2}{(1 + a^2)n^{[l]}}, \tag{3.27}$$

where a is the value of the coefficient. There are normal and uniform versions:

$$W_0 \sim U\left(-\frac{\sqrt{6}}{\sqrt{(1 + a^2)n^{[l]}}}, \frac{\sqrt{6}}{\sqrt{(1 + a^2)n^{[l]}}}\right), \tag{3.28}$$

$$W_0 \sim N\left(0, \frac{2}{(1 + a^2)n^{[l]}}\right), \tag{3.29}$$

with $a = 0$ for ReLU.

3.3.1.5 Sparse Sparse initialisation was introduced by Martens (2010). The idea is to fix the number of non-zero weights in each layer, which means this number is independent of layer size. As Goodfellow et al. (2016) note, this provides a strong differentiation between units at initialisation but also provides a strong prior on the non-zero weights and can cause problems for some units, such as the max out.

3.3.1.6 Orthogonal Saxe et al. (2013) proposed an orthogonal initialisation procedure in which the weight tensor in each layer is initialised with the QR decomposition of a matrix of random numbers. The output matrix will have orthogonal rows if there are fewer rows than columns; otherwise, the columns will be orthogonal.

3.3.2 Initialising Biases

The most common bias initialisation is setting them all to zero, which is compatible with most weight-initialisation schemes (Goodfellow et al., 2016; Aggarwal, 2018). Some practitioners argue that for ReLU, it is better to initialise the bias parameters with a small value, say 0.1 or 0.01, to ensure all the ReLU units fire at the start of training. However, there is no universal agreement that this performs better (Li et al., 2020). Some network structures can either benefit from non-zero bias initialisation, including autoencoders and Boltzmann machines, or should not have zero bias, such as long short-term memory units. With classifiers, it can be beneficial to initialise the bias to give the correct marginal distribution at the output layer (Goodfellow et al., 2016, p. 297).

---

[5] This initialisation scheme is sometimes known as *Kaiming initialisation* and sometimes as *He initialisation* after the first author's given name and family name, respectively.

EXAMPLE 3.2: INITIALISATION IMPACT

Two examples are considered to explore the empirical impact of initialisation schemes. The first example involves a regression model using a deep neural network to approximate a basket option model. In contrast, the second example is a classifier training on the MNIST fashion dataset (Xiao et al., 2017). The basket option was selected as an example of a deep feedforward network with more layers than the Black–Scholes example considered earlier. The MNIST fashion dataset was used to train a CNN, and the driver behind this choice is that for CNNs, the number of neurons per layer varies quite significantly. Most training problems manifest in deeper networks, so these test cases are based on deeper networks than the earlier Black–Scholes and MNIST examples.

Basket Option

The basket option example uses the same approach adopted by Ferguson and Green (2018), which is explored in detail in Chapter 11 (this example is available in the workbook `Basket Option Weight Initialisation.ipynb` in the folder for this chapter). For this example, a dataset of one million barrier options was generated with the input parameters randomly generated using Monte Carlo simulation. The basket option is a worst-of-call option on a basket of six underlying stocks with the payoff

$$V = \max(0, \min(S_1, S_2, S_3, S_4, S_5, S_6) - K).$$

Most input parameters can be generated using the same approach used in the Black–Scholes example except for the correlations, which require special handling using the C-vine method of Lewandowski et al. (2009). The value for each example is generated by the *QuantLib* basket option pricer.

The network architecture was fixed for all initialisation, with an input layer of width 28 followed by six layers of width 200, ReLU activation and a linear output for the final value.

The network was initialised using all the methods described above, apart from *Sparse,* for which no initialisation was available. A model with configurable weight initialisation was created using PyTorch, which provides a series of initialisation routines in `torch.nn.init`. Note that LeCun initialisation is approximated using the similar Kaiming initialisation scheme.

```
class FeedForwardNN(nn.Module):
    def __init__(self):
        super(FeedForwardNN, self).__init__()
        self.hidden_layers = nn.ModuleList([nn.Linear(28, 200)] +
            [nn.Linear(200, 200) for _ in range(4)])
        self.output_layer = nn.Linear(200, 1)

    def forward(self, x):
        for layer in self.hidden_layers:
            x = torch.relu(layer(x))
            x = self.output_layer(x)
        return x

    def initialize_weights(self, init_type):
        if init_type == "normal":
            for layer in self.hidden_layers:
                init.normal_(layer.weight, mean=0.0, std=0.01)
        elif init_type == "uniform":
            for layer in self.hidden_layers:
                init.uniform_(layer.weight, a=-0.03, b=0.03)
        elif init_type == "lecun_normal":
```

(*Continued*)

(*Continued*)

```
        for layer in self.hidden_layers:
            init.kaiming_normal_(layer.weight, mode='fan_in',
                                 nonlinearity='linear')
    elif init_type == "lecun_uniform":
        for layer in self.hidden_layers:
            init.kaiming_uniform_(layer.weight, mode='fan_in',
                                  nonlinearity='linear')
    elif init_type == "truncated_normal":
        for layer in self.hidden_layers:
            init.trunc_normal_(layer.weight, mean=0.0,
                               std=0.01)
    elif init_type == "glorot_normal":
        for layer in self.hidden_layers:
            init.xavier_normal_(layer.weight)
    elif init_type == "glorot_uniform":
        for layer in self.hidden_layers:
            init.xavier_uniform_(layer.weight)
    elif init_type == "he_normal":
        for layer in self.hidden_layers:
            init.kaiming_normal_(layer.weight, mode='fan_in',
                                 nonlinearity='relu')
    elif init_type == "he_uniform":
        for layer in self.hidden_layers:
            init.kaiming_uniform_(layer.weight, mode='fan_in',
                                  nonlinearity='relu')
    elif init_type == "orthogonal":
        for layer in self.hidden_layers:
            init.orthogonal_(layer.weight)
    else:
        raise ValueError("Unknown initialization type")
```

The network was trained through 100 epochs with a batch size of 10,000 in each case, and the training and validation loss was captured. Figure 3.3 shows the training loss for each initialisation method as a function of epoch, while Figure 3.4 shows the smoothed validation loss. The results show that in this case, the three best initialisation schemes are *LeCun uniform*, *LeCun normal* and *Glorot uniform*. However, in practice, the benefit is limited, with the best-performing scheme achieving a given validation loss around 15 epochs earlier than the worst-performing one.

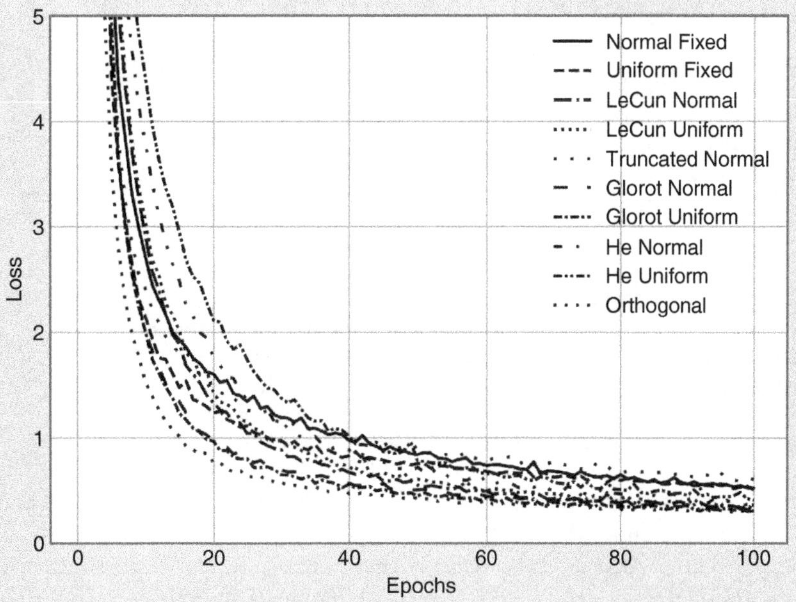

FIGURE 3.3 Training loss as a function of epoch for the basket option model with different weight-initialisation schemes.

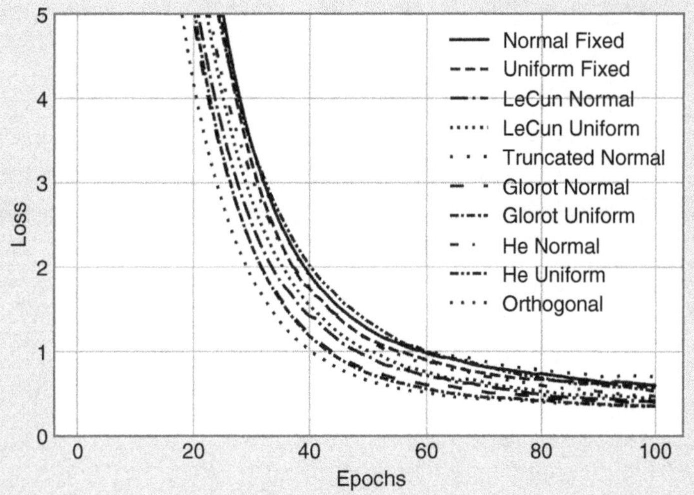

FIGURE 3.4 Smoothed validation loss as a function of epoch for the basket option model with different weight-initialisation schemes.

Fashion MNIST

The MNIST fashion dataset is a collection of 28 × 28 greyscale images of fashion items in 10 classes (Xiao et al., 2017) that was designed as an alternative to MNIST digits (this example can be found in the Jupyter Notebook `MNIST Fashion Weight Initialization.ipynb`). The dataset contains 60,000 training images and 10,000 test images. It is part of torchvision datasets and hence can easily be accessed. Preparing the data differs from that used with MNIST earlier, as a CNN will be used. As previously, the image pixels must be converted from integer values to floating-point numbers between 0 and 1. However, the images must not be flattened and should remain three-dimensional tensors.

(*Continued*)

(*Continued*)

```
from torchvision import datasets, transforms

transform = transforms.Compose([
    transforms.ToTensor(),
    transforms.Normalize((0.5,), (0.5,))
])

trainset = datasets.FashionMNIST('~/.pytorch/F_MNIST_data/', download=True,
                                 train=True, transform=transform)
train_loader = DataLoader(trainset, batch_size=64, shuffle=True)
testset = datasets.FashionMNIST('~/.pytorch/F_MNIST_data/', download=True,
                                train=False, transform=transform)
test_loader = DataLoader(testset, batch_size=64, shuffle=False)
```

The network structure consists of three, two-dimensional convolutional layers and two *max pooling* layers before the structure is flattened, and a standard dense layer leads into an output layer. The output layer implicitly has a softmax output with multi-class classification built into the PyTorch cross-entropy loss function. The operation of the convolutional layers will be discussed in Chapter 6, but for now, it suffices to say that these provide significant advantages for image data. The model is built using the following class.

```
class FashionMNISTCNN(nn.Module):
    def __init__(self):
        super(FashionMNISTCNN, self).__init__()
        self.conv1 = nn.Conv2d(1, 32, kernel_size=3)
        self.conv2 = nn.Conv2d(32, 64, kernel_size=3)
        self.conv3 = nn.Conv2d(64, 64, kernel_size=3)
        self.fc1 = nn.Linear(64 * 3 * 3, 64)
        self.fc2 = nn.Linear(64, 10)

    def forward(self, x):
        x = torch.relu(self.conv1(x))
        x = nn.MaxPool2d(2, 2)(x)
        x = torch.relu(self.conv2(x))
        x = nn.MaxPool2d(2, 2)(x)
        x = torch.relu(self.conv3(x))
        x = torch.flatten(x, 1)
        x = torch.relu(self.fc1(x))
        x = self.fc2(x)
        return x

    def initialize_weights(self, init_type):
        for m in self.modules():
            if isinstance(m, nn.Conv2d) or isinstance(m, nn.Linear):
                if init_type == 'normal':
                    init.normal_(m.weight, mean=0.0, std=0.01)
                elif init_type == 'uniform':
                    init.uniform_(m.weight, a=-0.03, b=0.03)
                elif init_type == 'lecun_normal':
                    init.kaiming_normal_(m.weight, mode='fan_in',
                                         nonlinearity='linear')
                elif init_type == 'lecun_uniform':
                    init.kaiming_uniform_(m.weight, mode='fan_in',
                                          nonlinearity='linear')
```

```
            elif init_type == 'truncated_normal':
                init.trunc_normal_(m.weight, mean=0.0, std=0.01)
            elif init_type == 'glorot_normal':
                init.xavier_normal_(m.weight)
            elif init_type == 'glorot_uniform':
                init.xavier_uniform_(m.weight)
            elif init_type == 'he_normal':
                init.kaiming_normal_(m.weight, mode='fan_out',
                                     nonlinearity='relu')
            elif init_type == 'he_uniform':
                init.kaiming_uniform_(m.weight, mode='fan_out',
                                      nonlinearity='relu')
            elif init_type == 'orthogonal':
                init.orthogonal_(m.weight)

        if m.bias is not None:
            init.constant_(m.bias, 0)
```

The critical point for the initialisation schemes is that the number of trainable parameters in each layer varies significantly. Hence, the number of ingoing and outgoing connections differs per layer, and the numbers of connections are used by the *Glorot* initialisation schemes.

The network was trained through 20 epochs with a batch size of 64 for each initialisation scheme. Since this is a classifier problem, training and validation accuracy were monitored during training. Figure 3.5 shows the training accuracy as a function of epoch, while Figure 3.6 shows the validation accuracy. In the training accuracy chart, three schemes underperform the others, *truncated normal*, *uniform* and *normal*, while the remaining schemes all show training accuracy levels that are similar. The smoothed validation accuracy flattens off at around 90% for all schemes, suggesting that the network is overfitting and that the initialisation schemes do not play a significant role.

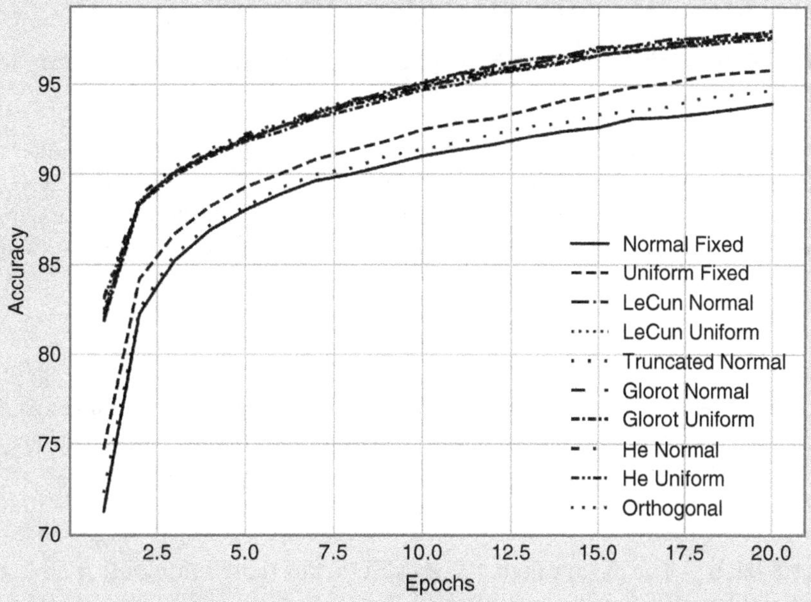

FIGURE 3.5 Training accuracy as a function of epoch for the MNIST fashion CNN model with different weight-initialisation schemes.

(*Continued*)

(*Continued*)

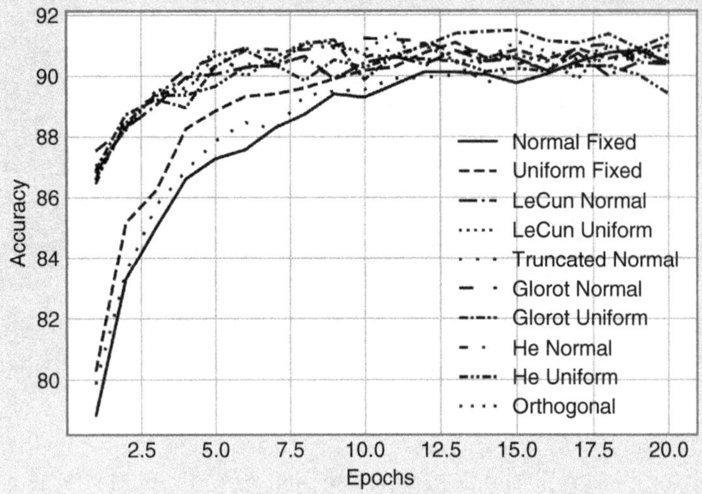

FIGURE 3.6 Validation accuracy as a function of epoch for the MNIST fashion CNN model with different weight-initialisation schemes.

3.4 THE CHOICE OF LOSS FUNCTION

The loss function, also known as the cost, error or objective function, measures the distance between the true output value and that predicted by the neural network. We defined the loss function by

$$J(\mathbf{W}, \mathbf{b}) = \frac{1}{m} \sum_{i=1}^{m} \mathcal{L}(\hat{y}^{(i)}, y^{(i)}), \tag{3.30}$$

where $\mathcal{L}$ is the loss from example i. The task of the optimiser is to minimise this function over the training set using gradient descent methods. There are many different measures of loss appropriate to different problem types and with different treatments of individual differences, particularly how larger differences are penalised. We can break down the types of loss functions according to the categories of supervised learning problem, regression, binary classification and multi-class classification.

3.4.1 Regression

Regression problems output real values; hence, for this problem class, we seek measures of distance that operate well across the real line. In this section, four different loss functions are discussed: *mean square error*, *mean absolute error*, *Huber* and *log-cosh*. The form of each loss function as a function of the difference between predicted and true values, $\hat{y} - y$, is given in Figure 3.7. Example 3.7 gives a test example using each loss function.

3.4.1.1 Mean Square Error (MSE) The mean square error (MSE) is the most commonly used loss function for regression problems. It is defined by

$$J_{MSE} = \frac{1}{m} \sum_{i=1}^{m} (y^{(i)} - \hat{y}^{(i)})^2, \tag{3.31}$$

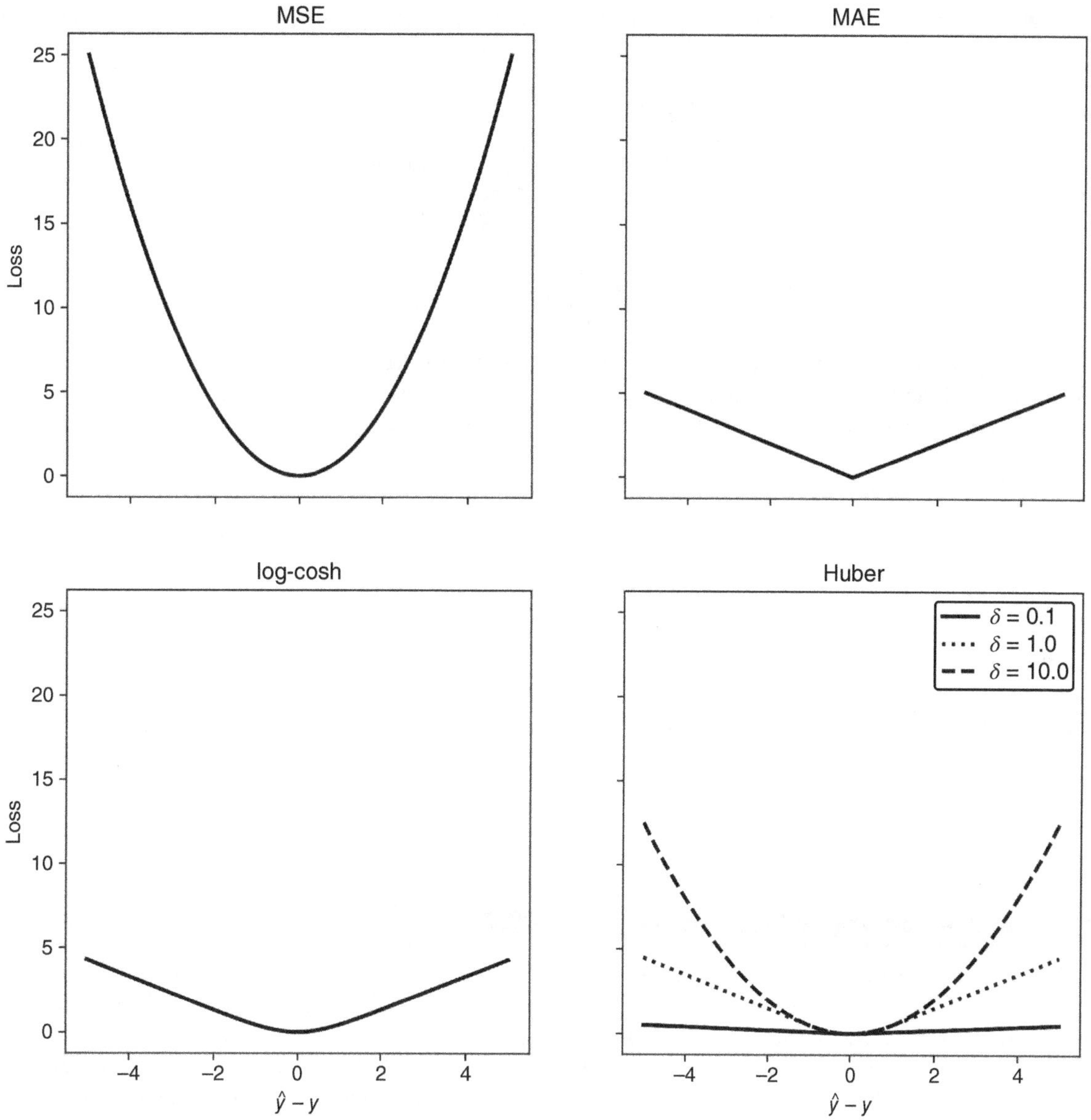

FIGURE 3.7 Four types of loss function suitable for use with regression problems.

that is, the sum of the square of the differences between the true value and the predicted value or the square of the L_2 norm. Given that the measure is the square of the difference, large differences are penalised heavily compared to smaller ones.

3.4.1.2 Mean Absolute Error (MAE) The mean absolute error (MAE) or L_1 loss is the sum of the absolute difference between actual and predicted values; it is the L_1 norm of the vector of actual and predicted values,

$$J_{MAE} = \frac{1}{m}\sum_{i=1}^{m} ||y^{(i)} - \hat{y}^{(i)}||. \tag{3.32}$$

Unlike MSE, MAE does not penalise outliers, which makes it robust to them because if the dataset is corrupted with large negative or positive values, then it will be less affected by them than MSE (Grover, 2018). However, the gradient of the MAE loss function is constant for all loss values, unlike MSE, which has a decreasing gradient as the loss decreases. For gradient descent algorithms, this is problematic and could lead to overshooting the minimum.

3.4.1.3 Huber The Huber loss function is a parameterised hybrid of MSE and MAE, behaving like MAE for large errors and MSE for small,

$$L_{\text{Huber}}(\delta, i) = \begin{cases} \frac{1}{2}(y^{(i)} - \hat{y}^{(i)})^2 & \text{for } |y^{(i)} - \hat{y}^{(i)}| \leq \delta \\ \delta |y^{(i)} - \hat{y}^{(i)}| - \frac{1}{2}\delta^2 & \text{otherwise} \end{cases} \tag{3.33}$$

and

$$J_{\text{Huber}} = \sum_{i=1}^{n} L_{\text{Huber}}(\delta, i). \tag{3.34}$$

The value of the parameter δ determines the transition point between MSE and MAE-style loss. Huber effectively solves the issue of outliers while still retaining a decreasing gradient close to the minimum point. The cost of this is to add a hyperparameter, δ, which will need to be tuned appropriately (Grover, 2018).

3.4.1.4 Log-Cosh Log-cosh is another function with a decreasing gradient close to the minimum point and a constant gradient for significant losses,

$$J_{\text{log-cosh}} = \sum_{i=1}^{n} \log\left(\cosh\left(y^{(i)} - \hat{y}^{(i)}\right)\right), \tag{3.35}$$

and

$$\lim_{\Delta y \to 0} \log(\cosh(\Delta y)) = \frac{\Delta y^2}{2},$$

$$\lim_{||\Delta y|| \to \infty} \log(\cosh(\Delta y)) = ||\Delta y|| - \log(2).$$

EXAMPLE 3.3: LOSS FUNCTION IN THE BASKET OPTION NETWORK

Several models were trained with the basket option dataset as an example of using different loss functions to train a regression model (this example can be found in the Jupyter Notebook `Basket Option Loss Functions.ipynb`). As with the previous example using different weight-initialisation schemes, the network architecture was fixed with six hidden layers, each with 200 neurons. ReLU activation was used in the hidden layers with orthogonal initialisation and the Adam optimiser. Six examples were trained, each with a different loss function used: mean square error, mean absolute error, Huber ($\delta = 0.1$), Huber ($\delta = 1.0$), Huber ($\delta = 10.0$) and log-cosh. At each epoch, the training and validation root mean square error was calculated to measure the performance of the models during and after training, using a common measurement of error.

PyTorch provides a series of loss functions as part of the neural network component of the library, nn. All of the above are built-in, except log-cosh, which must be implemented by hand.

```
class LogCoshLoss(nn.Module):
    def __init__(self):
        super(LogCoshLoss, self).__init__()

    def forward(self, y_pred, y_true):
        loss = torch.log(torch.cosh(y_pred - y_true))
        return loss.mean()
```

The results of training the basket option regression model with different loss functions are shown in Figures 3.8 and 3.9. The RMSE shows little difference on the training set, with the Huber loss with $\delta = 10.0$ performing marginally better than the other types of loss function. Evaluated on the validation set, mean absolute error and log-cosh perform slightly worse than the other functions between epochs 30 and 50, but there is little difference at 100 epochs.

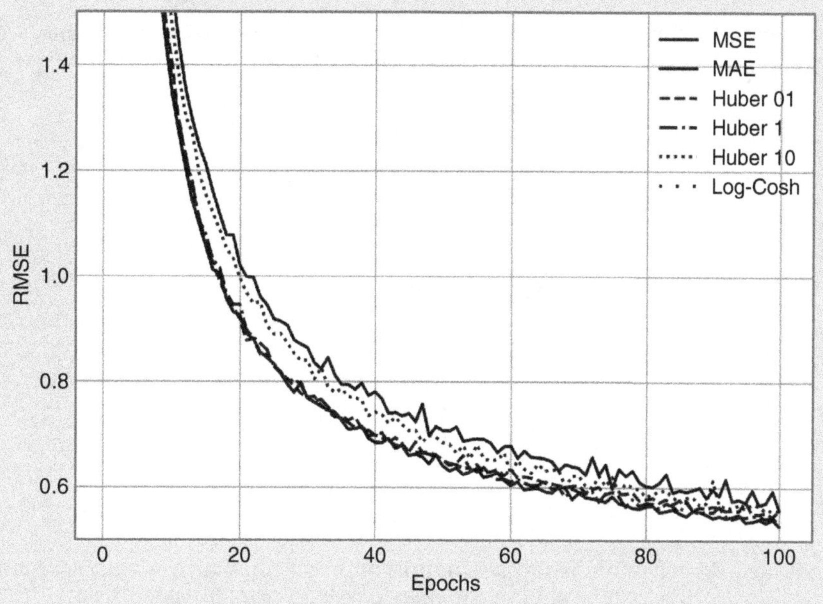

FIGURE 3.8 Training RMSE as a function of epoch for the basket option model with different loss functions.

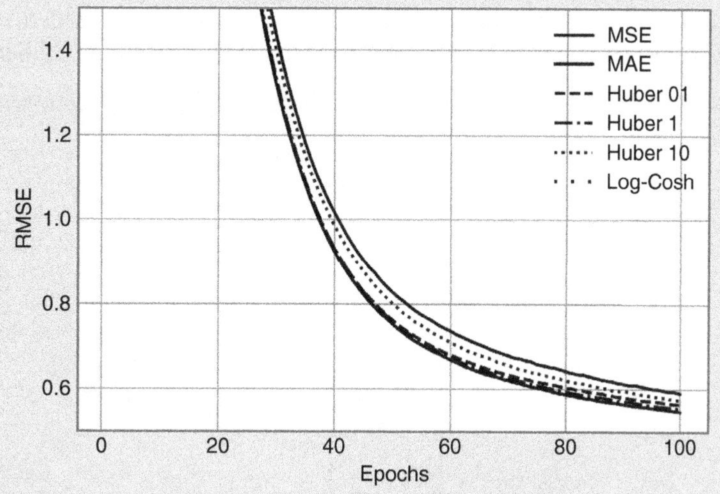

FIGURE 3.9 Validation RMSE as a function of epoch for the basket option model with different loss functions.

3.4.2 Binary Classification

Binary classification problems determine whether the input should be classified as class 'A' or class 'B'. However, the neural network's output is a probability that the input falls into class 'A', and as such, the output is constrained to lie between 0 and 1. We, therefore, seek loss functions that perform well in determining the error in a probability distribution.

3.4.2.1 Binary Cross-Entropy The binary cross-entropy loss function is given by

$$J_{BCE} = -\frac{1}{m}\sum_{i=1}^{m}\left[y^{(i)}\log\hat{y}^{(i)} + (1-y^{(i)})\log(1-\hat{y}^{(i)})\right], \tag{3.36}$$

which is identical to the loss function applied in simple logistic regression. To interpret this, we identify the output value with the conditional probability distribution $P(y|\boldsymbol{x})$ (Ng, 2018a),

$$\text{if} \quad y = 1 \quad P(y|\boldsymbol{x}) = \hat{y},$$

$$\text{if} \quad y = 0 \quad P(y|\boldsymbol{x}) = 1 - \hat{y},$$

hence

$$P(y|\boldsymbol{x}) = \hat{y}^{y}(1-\hat{y})^{(1-y)}. \tag{3.37}$$

Finally, we can recognise the loss function as

$$\begin{aligned} J_{BCE} &= -\frac{1}{m}\sum_{i=1}^{m}\log P(y|\boldsymbol{x}) \\ &= \mathbb{E}\left[\log\left(\frac{1}{P(y|\boldsymbol{x})}\right)\right]. \end{aligned} \tag{3.38}$$

So when we train the model, we are minimising the quantity in brackets, which is the *cross-entropy*.

We define the entropy $H(X)$ of a discrete random variable X using (Gylberth, 2019)

$$H(X) = -\sum_{x} p(x)\log p(x). \tag{3.39}$$

If we have a true distribution $p(x)$ and an approximation to it $q(x)$, then we can define the relative entropy or Kullback–Leibler distance between the distribution using (Goodfellow et al., 2016; Gylberth, 2019)

$$\begin{aligned} D_{KL}(p||q) &= \mathbb{E}_{X\sim p(x)}\left[\log p(x) - \log q(x)\right] \\ &= \mathbb{E}_{X\sim p(x)}\left[\log\frac{p(x)}{q(x)}\right]. \end{aligned} \tag{3.40}$$

We define the cross-entropy as

$$\begin{aligned} H(p,g) &= H(p) + D_{KL}(p||q) \\ &= \mathbb{E}_{X\sim p(x)}\left[\log\frac{1}{p(x)}\right] + \mathbb{E}_{X\sim p(x)}\left[\log\frac{p(x)}{q(x)}\right] \\ &= \mathbb{E}_{X\sim p(x)}\left[\log\frac{1}{q(x)}\right]. \end{aligned} \tag{3.41}$$

So, by minimising the cross-entropy, we minimise the difference between the two distributions, true and approximate, given by the neural network model.

Consider the probability distribution of the model $q(x;\theta)$ as a function of the set of weights and biases that we call generically θ. The maximum-likelihood estimator of parameter vector θ, given a set of independent examples $x^{(i)}$, is given by

$$\theta_{ML} = \underset{\theta}{\operatorname{argmax}}\prod_{i=1}^{m} q(x^{(i)};\theta). \tag{3.42}$$

Taking the log on the right-hand side does not change the maximisation, but it replaces the product with a sum,

$$\theta_{ML} = \underset{\theta}{\text{argmax}} \sum_{i=1}^{m} \log q(x^{(i)}; \theta). \tag{3.43}$$

We can further write that

$$\begin{aligned} \theta_{ML} &= \underset{\theta}{\text{argmax}} \sum_{i=1}^{m} \frac{1}{m} \log q(x^{(i)}; \theta) \\ &= \underset{\theta}{\text{argmax}}\ \mathbb{E}_{X\sim p(x)} \left[\log q(x^{(i)}; \theta)\right] \\ &= \underset{\theta}{\text{argmin}} - \left(\mathbb{E}_{X\sim p(x)} \left[\log q(x^{(i)}; \theta)\right]\right) \\ &= \underset{\theta}{\text{argmin}}\ \mathbb{E}_{X\sim p(x)} \left[\log \frac{1}{q(x^{(i)}; \theta)}\right]. \end{aligned} \tag{3.44}$$

Thus, we conclude that minimising the cross-entropy is equivalent to constructing the maximum-likelihood parameter vector for the neural network model.

3.4.2.2 Hinge Hinge loss is an alternative to binary cross-entropy that was originally associated with *support vector machines (SVMs)* (Murphy, 2012, p. 214). It is intended for use with labels ± 1; hence, applications with labels 0 and 1 must be converted. The output layer will also need to be consistent with the label range, and hence *tanh* should be used as the activation function rather than *sigmoid*. The loss function is given by

$$J_{\text{Hinge}} = \frac{1}{m} \sum_{i=1}^{m} \max(0, 1 - \hat{y}^{(i)} \cdot y^{(i)}). \tag{3.45}$$

Note that the loss function is not differentiable at $\hat{y}^{(i)} \cdot y^{(i)} = 1$, and to avoid this, smoothed versions could be used instead (Zhang, 2004; Rennie, 2005).

3.4.2.3 Squared Hinge Squared hinge loss is simply the square of the hinge loss, which is smoother and easier to handle numerically. The loss is given by

$$J_{\text{SqrdHinge}} = \frac{1}{m} \sum_{i=1}^{m} [\max(0, 1 - \hat{y}^{(i)} \cdot y^{(i)})]^2. \tag{3.46}$$

As with the hinge loss, labels should be ± 1 and a tanh output layer should be used.

EXAMPLE 3.4: TAIWANESE CREDIT CARD DEFAULTS

An example was used to demonstrate the influence of the loss function on a binary classifier. The example is based on the default of credit card clients in Taiwan and can be found in the Jupyter Notebook named `Taiwan Credit Classifier Loss.ipynb` (Yeh and Lien, 2009). The dataset is available in the CSV file `default of credit card clients.csv`. The raw input data parameters are given in Table 3.1, while the output was a binary value with 1 indicating default has occurred. Given the parameter values, the task is to predict which clients will default. The categorical input variables were one-hot encoded, while the remainder were treated as floating-point values, including the integer values for the number of months in arrears (PAY_1 to PAY_6). The input dataset consists of 30,000 customers, and this was divided into training, test and validation data with an 18,000; 6000; 6000 split. Real-valued inputs were scaled using the standard scaler from scikit-learn.

(*Continued*)

(*Continued*)

TABLE 3.1 Input Parameters for the Taiwanese Credit Card Default Example

Parameter	Type	Description
LIMIT_BAL	Real	Credit limit
SEX	Categorical	Gender
EDUCATION	Categorical	Educational level
MARRIAGE	Categorical	Marital status
AGE	Integer	Age in years
PAY_1 to PAY_6	Integer	Months in arrears
BILL_AMT1 to BILL_AMT6	Real	Bill amount last 6 months
PAY_AMT1 to PAY_AMT2	Real	Payment last 6 months

A neural network with two hidden layers, each with 50 neurons, was constructed, with the single output value using sigmoid activation with the binary cross-entropy loss and tanh with hinge and squared hinge losses. In PyTorch, binary cross-entropy loss is implemented using the built-in loss function `nn.BCELoss()`. However, both hinge and squared hinge must be implemented as follows, noting the adjustment for the binary labels to match the use of the tanh activation function that these loss functions expect.

```
class HingeLoss(nn.Module):
    def __init__(self):
        super(HingeLoss, self).__init__()

    def forward(self, outputs, labels):
        # Ensure the labels are -1 or 1
        labels = 2 * labels - 1
        loss = torch.mean(torch.clamp(1 - labels * outputs, min=0))
        return loss

class SquaredHingeLoss(nn.Module):
    def __init__(self):
        super(SquaredHingeLoss, self).__init__()

    def forward(self, outputs, labels):
        # Ensure the labels are -1 or 1
        labels = 2 * labels - 1
        loss = torch.mean(torch.clamp(1 - labels * outputs, min=0)**2)
        return loss
```

The models were each trained through 100 epochs with a batch size of 1000. To compare the results of the three cases, test and validation accuracy were plotted as a function of epoch and the charts are shown in Figures 3.10 and 3.11. In both cases, the squared hinge loss function performs slightly worse than BCE and hinge, achieving a validation accuracy of just under 82%.

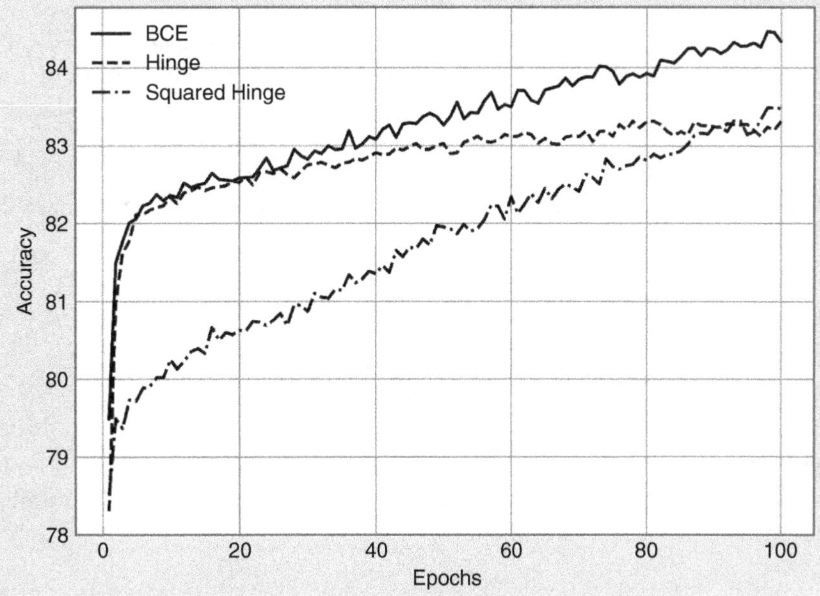

FIGURE 3.10 Training accuracy as a function of epoch for the Taiwanese credit card default classifier.

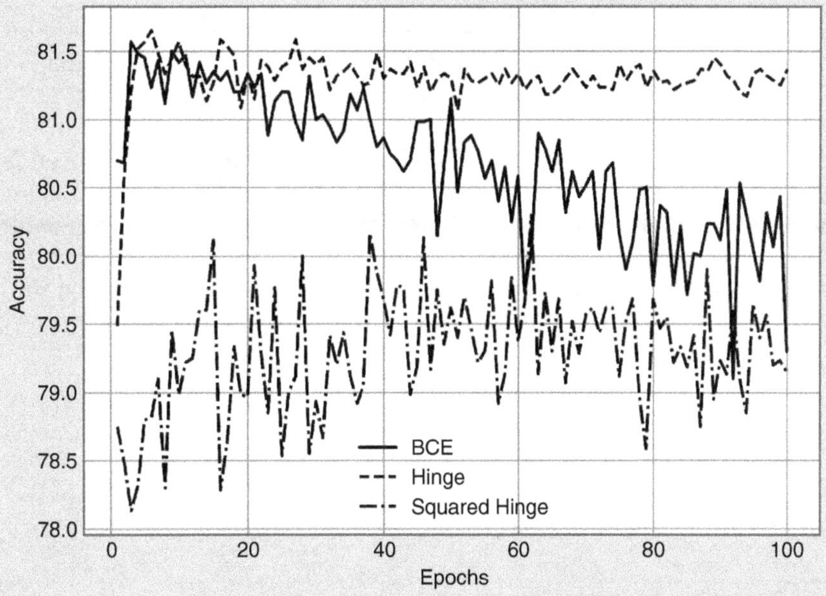

FIGURE 3.11 Validation accuracy as a function of epoch for the Taiwanese credit card default classifier.

3.4.3 Multi-Class Classification

Multi-class classification involves assigning input examples to one of N exclusive categories. Two examples of this have already been presented: MNIST digits and MNIST fashion. The output layer for these problems is a softmax layer in which the probabilities of each category sum to 1.0, and the example is classified according to the highest probability.

3.4.3.1 Categorical Cross-Entropy Categorical cross-entropy is the generalisation of binary cross-entropy to the multi-class case. The loss function is given by

$$J_{CCE} = -\frac{1}{m}\sum_{i=1}^{m}\sum_{j=1}^{N} y^{(i)} \log \hat{y}^{(i)}, \tag{3.47}$$

which is identical with Equation (3.36) if $N = 2$.

3.4.3.2 Kullback–Leibler Divergence Kullback–Leibler divergence was defined in Equation (3.40) in the discussion relating cross-entry to maximum likelihood and is a measure of the difference between two probability distributions. It can also be used directly as a loss function in the form

$$J_{KL} = \frac{1}{m}\sum_{i=1}^{m} y^{(i)} \log\left(\frac{y^{(i)}}{\hat{y}^{(i)}}\right). \tag{3.48}$$

EXAMPLE 3.5: MNIST FASHION AND LOSS FUNCTIONS

As an example of multi-class classification with different loss functions, the MNIST fashion example described is used again (this example can be found in the Jupyter Notebook `MNIST Fashion Loss Functions.ipynb`). Here, the two multi-class loss functions described above, categorical cross-entropy and Kullback–Leibler (KL) divergence, were used. In PyTorch, categorical cross-entropy loss is implemented using the built-in loss function `nn.CategoricalCrossEntropy`. Recall that this loss function has the softmax function built in, and the ground truth labels can be integers. The KL divergence loss is implemented using the following custom class. The KL divergence implementation in the functional library component of PyTorch requires the labels to be one-hot encoded and the log-softmax function to be applied to the model output. Hence, these are implemented in the custom class and have the same input requirements as the categorical cross-entropy loss implementation.

```
class KLDivergenceLoss(nn.Module):
    def __init__(self, num_classes):
        super(KLDivergenceLoss, self).__init__()
        self.num_classes = num_classes

    def forward(self, y_pred, y_true):
        y_true_one_hot = F.one_hot(y_true,
            num_classes=self.num_classes).to(torch.float)
        y_pred_log_softmax = F.log_softmax(y_pred, dim=1)
        return F.kl_div(y_pred_log_softmax, y_true_one_hot,
                        reduction='batchmean')
```

The model's training and validation accuracy was measured during training across 20 epochs as in the previous example, and the results are plotted in Figure 3.12. In this case, there is little to choose between the two loss functions regarding performance, although, as discussed above, they are closely related measures.

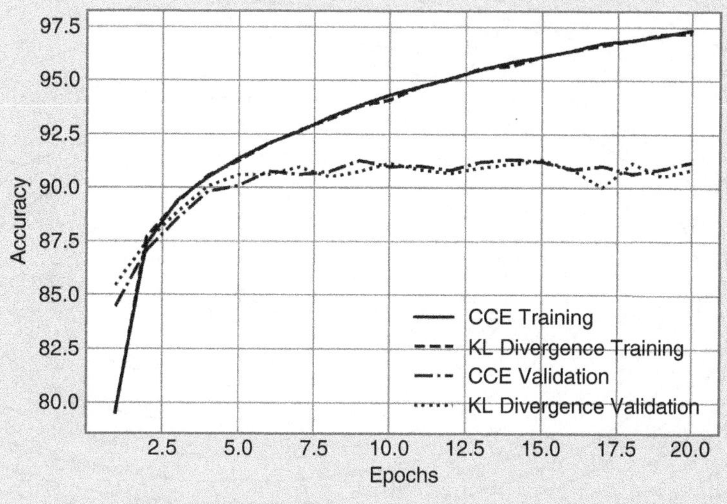

FIGURE 3.12 Training and validation accuracy as a function of epoch for the MNIST fashion classifier.

3.4.4 Multi-Label Classification

Multi-label classification problems involve datasets where the classifier selects several output categories for the example. In multi-class classification, the output categories are mutually exclusive, while in the multi-label classification, they are not. The output layer will have as many outputs as categories. However, the outputs now represent the probability that the example falls into each category, and the output values no longer sum to 1. Typically, the sigmoid activation function is used in this output layer, and the loss function will be a sum of losses for each category. So, for example, binary cross-entropy could be used for each class, and the overall loss function is the sum across all classes.

3.5 OPTIMISATION ALGORITHMS

The heart of training a neural network is an optimisation algorithm that, in almost all cases, is based on *gradient descent*. The origin of gradient descent methods lies with Cauchy (1847), although its convergence properties and widespread use followed from the 1940s onwards. The section begins by describing gradient descent methods and using *momentum* as a refinement. Modern optimisers for deep learning typically use adaptive learning rates, and three methods and their variants are considered: AdaGrad, RMSProp and Adam.

3.5.1 Basic Techniques

3.5.1.1 Gradient Descent Methods The basic equations of gradient descent are presented above in Equations (3.2) through (3.5) with learning rate α. The weights and biases in each layer are successively updated in the direction that will reduce the loss value. The learning rate governs how large a step is taken in each iteration. Figure 3.13 illustrates the process in a simple two-dimensional case, with the arrows each representing one step. We can define three basic types of stochastic gradient descent, differentiated by the fraction of the training set used in each update (Ruder, 2016; Ng, 2018b).

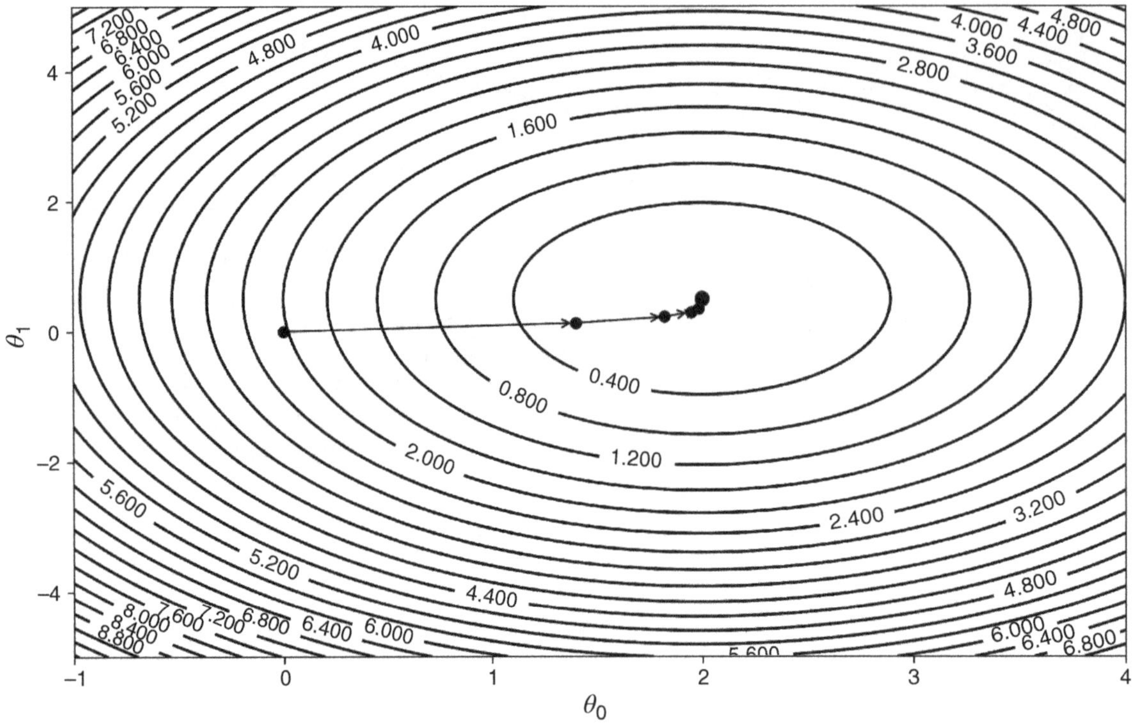

FIGURE 3.13 A visualisation of gradient descent. The contour plot represents the loss surface while the sequence of arrows represents successive steps of gradient descent approaching the minimum point.

Batch Gradient Descent (BGD) In batch gradient descent, the whole training set is processed through the cost function and its gradient before the weights are updated. Define θ as the collection of all trainable parameters in the network, that is,

$$\theta \equiv [W^{[1]}, W^{[2]}, \dots, W^{[L]}; b^{[1]}, b^{[2]}, \dots, b^{[L]}]. \tag{3.49}$$

Then, the weight update is calculated over all training examples i,

$$\theta_{t+1} = \theta_t - \alpha \nabla_\theta J(\theta_t). \tag{3.50}$$

As Ruder (2016) notes, there are several problems with batch gradient descent. Firstly, it can be slow, mainly if the training set is large, as all examples must be processed before any update is made. Indeed, it can be intractable if the dataset cannot fit into the computer's memory and must be loaded partially from external storage during each iteration. This is also a problem with single GPU cards, which typically have lower amounts of memory available. Deep learning frameworks using GPU acceleration will typically reserve a block of GPU memory to hold all examples in the batch. Even with modest training sets like MNIST, this may not be possible. Secondly, the method does not allow any online updating with new examples.

Stochastic Gradient Descent (SGD) Stochastic gradient descent represents the other extreme to batch gradient descent in that it updates the weights after every single training example, that is,

$$\theta_{t+1} = \theta_t - \alpha \nabla_\theta J(\theta_t; x^{(i)}, y^{(i)}). \tag{3.51}$$

Training is much faster than batch gradient descent and proceeds directly through the epoch rather than at the end. Training samples are shuffled prior to the start of each epoch, so they are applied in random order. The variance of the updates is very high, so the loss function can be very noisy. The high variance is a double-edged sword in that it can be beneficial as a jump may lead to the optimiser finding a new, better local minimum. However, it can also lead to overshooting the minimum and 'bouncing' around the solution. A small learning rate may be required to ensure stable updates. Note that while the impact of training with a single sample is immediate, it may not take the best advantage of multi-core hardware such as GPUs (Goodfellow et al., 2016, p. 272). SGD can be shown to have the same convergence behaviour as BGD if the learning rate is slowly decreased as training proceeds (Ruder, 2016, p. 2).

Mini-Batch Gradient Descent Mini-batch gradient descent lies between batch and stochastic gradient descent extremes. It uses small batches of samples to perform the gradient descent update as defined in Equation (3.52):

$$\theta_{t+1} = \theta_t - \alpha \nabla_\theta J(\theta_t; x^{(i):(i+n)}, y^{(i):(i+n)}), \tag{3.52}$$

where n is the number of samples in the mini-batch. The ordering of the samples is shuffled at the start of each epoch to ensure that each mini-batch is independent, and this ensures that the gradient estimate from each mini-batch is independent or bias could be the result (Goodfellow et al., 2016, p. 273).

Using more than one sample reduces the variance of parameter updates compared to SGD but is faster than BGD (Ruder, 2016). The use of mini-batches can better utilise multi-core hardware, and indeed, for some hardware, mainly GPUs, there is a minimum batch size below which there is no reduction in execution time (Goodfellow et al., 2016, p. 272). Similarly, there can be an upper limit to batch size, and again, with GPU hardware, the memory size on the card limits the number of samples that can be processed in a single batch. For the most efficient use of GPU hardware, the use of batch sizes that are a power of 2 is favoured as GPUs typically use blocks of 32 threads[6] and hence batch sizes in the range 32–256 are most common. Wilson and Martinez (2003) found that models with small batches show improved generalisation and that for any given learning rate, batch training underperforms mini-batch and stochastic gradient descent. Mini-batch gradient descent and its variants are the most common optimisation algorithms for deep learning.

EXAMPLE 3.6: MNIST MINI-BATCH GRADIENT DESCENT AS A FUNCTION OF BATCH SIZE

An experiment was conducted using the MNIST fashion dataset to investigate the impact of batch size on learning rate and execution time. A convolutional network structure was trained, as described in Example 3.2, with various batch sizes over 50 epochs. This example can be found in the Jupyter Notebook titled `MNIST Gradient Descent.ipynb`. All batch sizes were powers of 2 and range from 2^4 to 2^{14}. The executing time was monitored and stored in the training loop.

The results are shown in Figure 3.14, where the validation accuracy is plotted against time. The smaller batch sizes show higher accuracy in line with the findings of Wilson and Martinez (2003), while the largest batch sizes learn slowly or not at all. The smaller sizes also take longer to execute overall, while the examples with batch sizes 4096, 8192 and 16,384 take the same time to complete 50 epochs at around 40 seconds, and this shows that the maximum level of parallelism for the GPU used here, an NVidia RTX 4090, has already been achieved. Overall, getting the best performance per unit training time requires a compromise between a small batch size, which will benefit training speed per epoch, and a batch size chosen to make as much use of the available cores on the hardware as possible.

(*Continued*)

[6] Known as a *warp* in CUDA development.

(Continued)

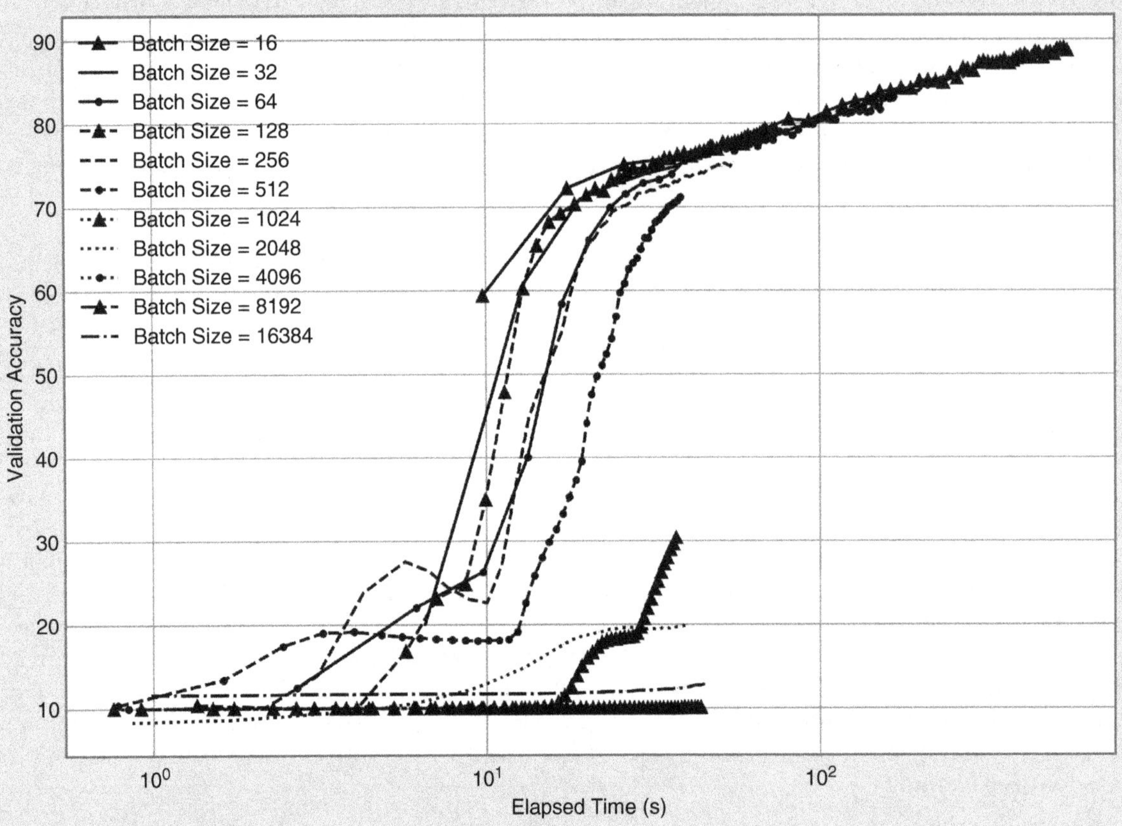

FIGURE 3.14 The validation accuracy of the MNIST fashion CNN trained with 11 different batch sizes and plotted as a function of elapsed training time.

The Learning Rate The learning rate, α, is a hyperparameter that needs to be selected. In the examples presented, this has typically been left at its default value, which for SGD in PyTorch is $\alpha = 0.001$. However, this need not be the optimal choice. We must first choose the appropriate scale for the learning rate, which would be, say, [0.0001, 1.0], and then use a log-scale to choose a series of learning rates and then observe the training performance for each value (Ng, 2018c). Hence, a sequence like the following might be used:

$$0.0001, 0.001, 0.01, 0.1, 1.0$$

or

$$0.0001, 0.0003, 0.001, 0.003, 0.01, 0.03, 0.1, 0.3, 1.0$$

with two steps per order of magnitude.

In practice, reducing the learning rate as training proceeds in a process known as *learning rate decay* or *learning rate annealing* is common, and this makes sense as the model descends deeper into the loss function. A lower learning rate can be used to avoid chaotically jumping around the minimum and instead descend smoothly towards it (Li et al., 2020).

Step and Linear Decay Step decay reduces the learning rate by some factor after a set number of epochs, say reducing it by half every five epochs (Li et al., 2020). The exact decay schedule will depend on the problem; the decay rate is another hyperparameter to select. Goodfellow et al. (2016) recommend linear decay in learning rate until a pre-determined iteration τ_i is reached,

$$\alpha = \left(1 - \frac{\tau}{\tau_i}\right)\alpha_0 + \frac{\tau}{\tau_i}\alpha_\tau, \tag{3.53}$$

and thereafter the learning rate remains at α_τ.

$1/\tau$ ***Decay*** The learning rate is specified as a function of iteration τ (or equivalently epoch number),

$$\alpha = \frac{1}{1 + k\tau}\alpha_0, \tag{3.54}$$

where k is the decay rate and α_0 is the initial learning rate (Ng, 2018b; Li et al., 2020).

Exponential Decay The learning rate follows an exponential decay profile,

$$\alpha = \alpha_0 b^{\tau/\tau_d}, \tag{3.55}$$

where b is the base and τ_d is the decay steps (Ng, 2018b; Li et al., 2020) with $b = 1/e$ if desired.

Manual Decay In manual decay, the learning rate is adjusted manually and reduced when the validation error stops reducing.

All the above methods apply the same learning rate to all parameters, but this approach is rather crude. Hence, the methods discussed below in Section 3.5.2 adapt the learning rate to each parameter.

EXAMPLE 3.7: MNIST MINI-BATCH GRADIENT DESCENT AS A FUNCTION OF LEARNING RATE

The impact of the choice of learning rate on training was explored with the MNIST fashion dataset and a CNN in the Jupyter Notebook `MNIST Learning Rates.ipynb`. The same network described in Example 3.2 was trained using nine different learning rates: 0.0001, 0.0003, 0.001, 0.003, 0.01, 0.03, 0.1, 0.3 and 1.0. These were used with the PyTorch stochastic gradient descent optimiser over 20 epochs, with a batch size of 64. As a measure of the effectiveness of training with different learning rates, the validation accuracy was plotted as a function of epoch for all nine learning rates, and this can be seen in Figure 3.15. In this case, the optimal learning rate was quite large at 0.1, with smaller learning rate values like 0.0001 being too small to progress rapidly, while a learning rate of 1.0 was too large, and the network did not learn at all.

(*Continued*)

(*Continued*)

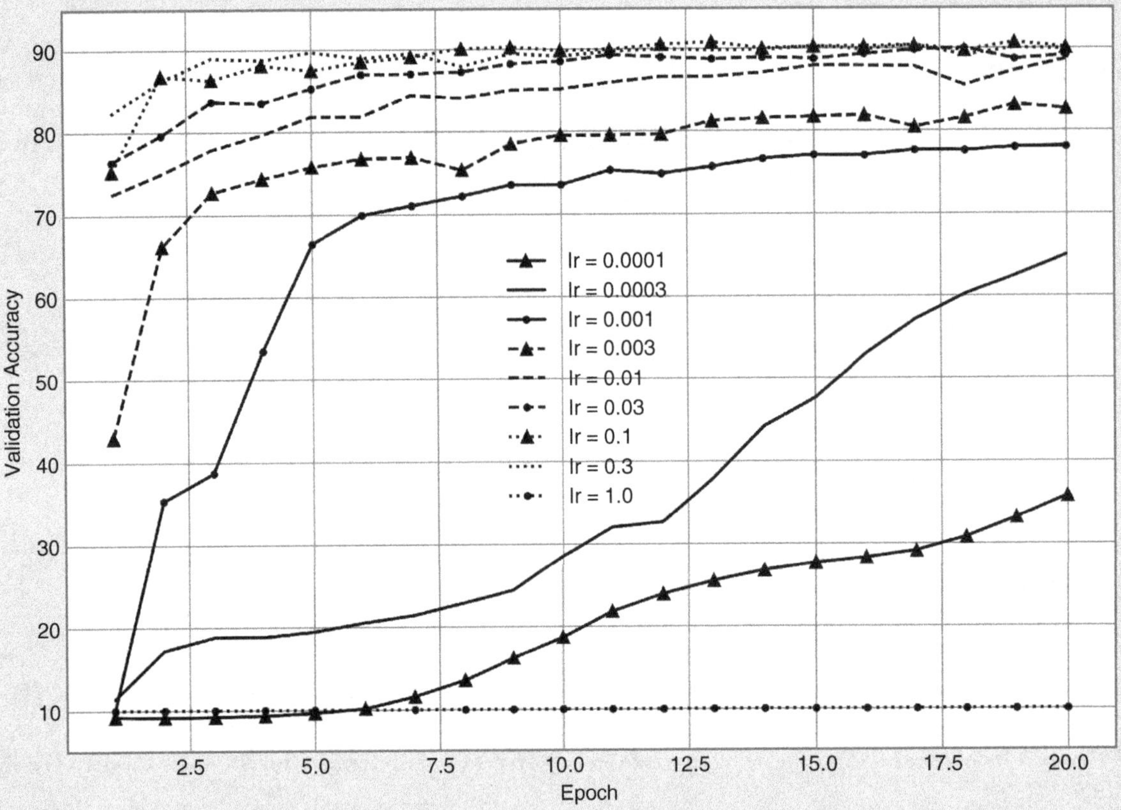

FIGURE 3.15 The validation accuracy of the MNIST fashion CNN trained with nine different learning rates.

3.5.1.2 Momentum Sutton (1986) identified that SGD has particular problems with *ravines* in the loss function, regions where the gradient is much steeper in some directions than others. Using the memory of the previous update step to accelerate SGD in the right direction can help prevent oscillations (Ruder, 2016). Figure 3.16 shows the impact of aligned and misaligned gradient and momentum step vectors, illustrating the acceleration and damping behaviour. Polyak (1964) introduced the momentum algorithm, which defines a velocity v_t that is formed of the exponentially decaying moving average of past gradients as defined in Equation (3.56),

$$v_t = \gamma v_{t-1} + \alpha \nabla_\theta J(\theta), \tag{3.56}$$

$$\theta_{t+1} = \theta_t - v_t. \tag{3.57}$$

The typical choice for the parameter is $\gamma = 0.9$, although it can be increased as iterations proceed, with the learning rate now less important (Goodfellow et al., 2016).

3.5.1.3 Nesterov Momentum Nesterov momentum is a variant of the momentum algorithm with a *predictor* type step. Rather than calculate the gradient at the current position, it uses the current momentum to shift the position at which the gradient is calculated. Hence, the update rule becomes

$$v_t = \gamma v_{t-1} + \alpha \nabla_\theta J(\theta_t - \gamma v_{t-1}), \tag{3.58}$$

$$\theta_{t+1} = \theta_t - v_t. \tag{3.59}$$

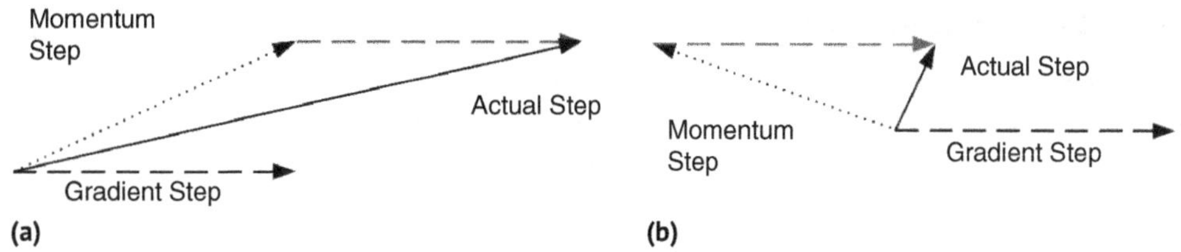

FIGURE 3.16 The momentum update step, when the gradient and momentum steps are aligned (a) and when they are misaligned (b).

Nesterov momentum was introduced into the training of deep neural networks by Sutskever et al. (2013) and is based on work by Nesterov (1983).

EXAMPLE 3.8: BASKET OPTION WITH MOMENTUM

Three basket option models were trained using standard SGD, SGD with momentum and SGD with Nesterov momentum (this example can be found in the Jupyter Notebook `Basket Option Momentum.ipynb`). A learning rate of 0.001 was used, as higher rates were found to cause numerical issues when momentum was selected, and the momentum parameter, γ, was set to the usual default value of 0.9. The neural network architecture was identical to that used in the previous basket examples, with six hidden ReLU layers, each with 200 nodes. The results are shown in Figure 3.17, and it is immediately apparent that training is significantly faster with momentum but that, in this case, Nesterov momentum does not offer an additional advantage.

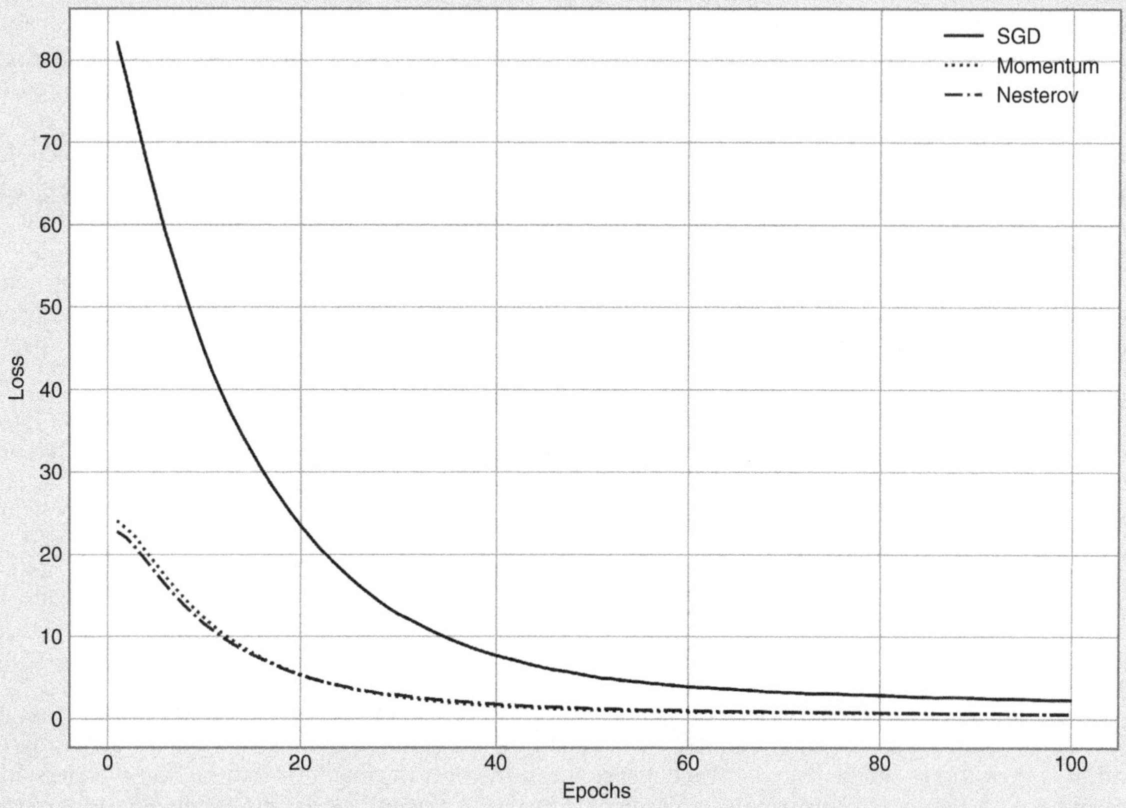

FIGURE 3.17 The validation loss for basket option models trained with standard SGD, momentum and Nesterov momentum.

3.5.2 Optimisers with Adaptive Learning Rates

3.5.2.1 AdaGrad and Variants The AdaGrad optimiser, introduced by Duchi et al. (2011), differs from standard SGD in that it adapts the learning rate individually to each parameter. The inverse squared accumulated gradient for each parameter scales the effective learning rate. Consider the gradient with each parameter, i, given by

$$\begin{aligned} g_{t,i} &= \nabla_{\theta_i} J(\theta_{t,i}), \\ g_t &= \nabla_{\theta} J(\theta_t). \end{aligned} \tag{3.60}$$

We can accumulate this gradient,

$$\begin{aligned} r_{t,i} &= \sum_{\tau=1}^{t-1} g_{\tau,i}^2, \\ r_t &= \sum_{\tau=1}^{t-1} g_\tau \odot g_\tau. \end{aligned} \tag{3.61}$$

The parameter update becomes

$$\begin{aligned} \theta_{t+1,i} &= \theta_{t,i} - \frac{\alpha}{\sqrt{r_{t,i} + \epsilon}} g_{t,i}, \\ \theta_{t+1} &= \theta_t - \frac{\alpha}{\sqrt{r_t + \epsilon}} \odot g_t, \end{aligned} \tag{3.62}$$

where ϵ is a small constant to ensure numerical stability. The advantage of this approach is that the learning rate is adapted to each parameter individually according to its gradient history and hence the learning rate, α, can be left untuned at a default value of, say, 0.01 (Ruder, 2016). However, as the gradient accumulates, the effective learning rate falls and can do so too early, effectively choking off learning (Goodfellow et al., 2016, p. 299).

AdaDelta Zeiler (2012) introduced AdaDelta to improve on the known problem with AdaGrad's accumulating gradients leading to the learning rate declining too aggressively. There are two key changes: firstly, the gradient is only accumulated over a fixed-size window instead of across steps and secondly, to correct the units of the update equation with a Hessian approximation.

To accumulate over a fixed window directly would require storing the w previous updates, which would be inefficient. Hence, AdaGrad replaces the accumulation of the gradient with an exponentially decaying average of the squared gradient. At time t the average is given by

$$\mathbb{E}[g^2] = \rho \mathbb{E}[g^2]_{t-1} + (1-\rho) g_t^2. \tag{3.63}$$

We need the square root of Equation (3.63) in the denominator of the update, that is, the root mean squared gradient

$$RMS[g]_t = \sqrt{\mathbb{E}[g^2]_t + \epsilon}. \tag{3.64}$$

Making these changes to the AdaGrad update in Equation (3.62) gives

$$\theta_{t+1} = \theta_t - \frac{\alpha}{RMS[g]_t} \odot g_t. \tag{3.65}$$

Looking at the update equations for SGD, momentum and AdaGrad, we can see that the update term does not have units of the parameter. Rather, in the case of SGD and momentum, it is in the units of the gradient, and for AdaGrad, it is the ratio of gradients, which is dimensionless. In contrast, methods that rely on the Hessian or an approximation to it do use the correct units, and for such methods, the update has the following proportionality:

$$\Delta\theta \propto \frac{g}{H}, \tag{3.66}$$

where H is the Hessian matrix. So, to correct this, AdaDelta replaces the learning rate by $RMS[\Delta\theta]_t$, which is defined by

$$RMS[\Delta\theta]_t = \sqrt{\mathbb{E}[\Delta\theta^2]_t + \epsilon}, \tag{3.67}$$

$$\mathbb{E}[\Delta\theta^2]_t = \eta\mathbb{E}[\Delta\theta^2]_{t-1} + (1-\eta)\Delta\theta_t^2. \tag{3.68}$$

Given that $RMS[\Delta\theta]_t$ is unknown, it is approximated by its value at the previous step. Hence, the update is given by

$$\theta_{t+1} = \theta_t - \frac{RMS[\Delta\theta]_{t-1}}{RMS[g]_t} \odot g_t. \tag{3.69}$$

Moreover, the input learning rate has been removed.

RMSProp Hinton et al. (2014) developed RMSProp but only published it in University of Toronto undergraduate lecture notes. RMSProp is an adaptive learning rate variant of AdaGrad that is identical to the first step of AdaDelta described above, with the update

$$\theta_{t+1} = \theta_t - \frac{\alpha}{RMS[g]_t} \odot g_t. \tag{3.70}$$

The recommended default parameter values are $\rho = 0.9$ in Equation (3.63) and $\alpha = 0.001$.

3.5.2.2 Adam and Variants Adaptive moment estimation (Adam) is an adaptive learning rate optimisation scheme introduced by Kingma and Ba (2015). Adam uses biased corrected estimates of the first and second moments of the gradients to adapt the learning rate to individual parameters. The method first calculates exponentially decaying moving averages of the mean and variance of the gradients

$$m_t = \beta_1 m_{t-1} + (1-\beta_1)g_t, \tag{3.71}$$

$$v_t = \beta_2 v_{t-1} + (1-\beta_2)g_t^2. \tag{3.72}$$

Initialising the running averages to zero causes them to be biased, and so Kingma and Ba (2015) derive a correction, which is given below:

$$\hat{m}_t = \frac{m_t}{1-\beta_1^t}, \tag{3.73}$$

$$\hat{v}_t = \frac{v_t}{1-\beta_2^t}. \tag{3.74}$$

The update rule is then given by

$$\theta_{t+1} = \theta_t - \frac{\alpha\hat{m}_t}{\sqrt{\hat{v}_t} + \epsilon}, \tag{3.75}$$

with recommended default values of $\beta_1 = 0.9$, $\beta_2 = 0.999$ and $\epsilon = 10^{-8}$. Adam is one of the most popular optimisers for training neural networks.

AdaMax Kingma and Ba (2015) also introduce a variant of Adam based on the infinity norm, AdaMax. The L_2 norm in Equation (3.72) is replaced by the stable L_∞ norm

$$\begin{aligned} u_t &= \beta_2^\infty v_{t-1} + (1-\beta_2^\infty)|g_t|^\infty \\ &= \max(\beta_2 v_{t-1}, |g_t|). \end{aligned} \tag{3.76}$$

Hence, the AdaMax update is given by

$$\theta_{t+1} = \theta_t - \frac{\alpha\hat{m}_t}{u_t}. \tag{3.77}$$

Nadam Given that Adam is based on classic momentum, the Nadam optimiser combined Adam with Nesterov momentum. To do this, we must rewrite Nesterov momentum in a slightly different form (Ruder, 2016, p. 9). Firstly, write Nesterov momentum in the notation used for Adam,

$$\begin{aligned} g_t &= \nabla_{\theta_t} J(\theta_t - \gamma \boldsymbol{m}_{t-1}), \\ \boldsymbol{m}_t &= \gamma \boldsymbol{m}_{t-1} + \alpha g_t, \\ \theta_{t+1} &= \theta_t - \boldsymbol{m}_t. \end{aligned} \tag{3.78}$$

Next, the update is modified to use the look-ahead vector directly, thus eliminating the need to apply it before calculating the gradients,

$$\begin{aligned} g_t &= \nabla_{\theta_t} J(\theta_t), \\ \boldsymbol{m}_t &= \gamma \boldsymbol{m}_{t-1} + \alpha g_t, \\ \theta_{t+1} &= \theta_t - (\gamma \boldsymbol{m}_t + \alpha g_t). \end{aligned} \tag{3.79}$$

The Adam update is then expanded to be written in terms of $\boldsymbol{m}_{t-1}$ and g_t,

$$\theta_{t+1} = \theta_t - \frac{\alpha}{\sqrt{\hat{v}_t} + \epsilon} \left(\frac{\beta_1 \boldsymbol{m}_{t-1}}{1 - \beta_1^t} + \frac{(1 - \beta) g_t}{1 - \beta_1^t} \right). \tag{3.80}$$

Then, noting that $\hat{\boldsymbol{m}}_{t-1} \approx \boldsymbol{m}_{t-1}/(1 - \beta_1^t)$ gives

$$\theta_{t+1} = \theta_t - \frac{\alpha}{\sqrt{\hat{v}_t} + \epsilon} \left(\beta_1 \hat{\boldsymbol{m}}_{t-1} + \frac{(1 - \beta) g_t}{1 - \beta_1^t} \right). \tag{3.81}$$

Replacing $\hat{\boldsymbol{m}}_{t-1}$ by its current value $\hat{\boldsymbol{m}}_t$ gives the Nadam update rule,

$$\theta_{t+1} = \theta_t - \frac{\alpha}{\sqrt{\hat{v}_t} + \epsilon} \left(\beta_1 \hat{\boldsymbol{m}}_t + \frac{(1 - \beta) g_t}{1 - \beta_1^t} \right). \tag{3.82}$$

EXAMPLE 3.9: MNIST WITH ADAPTIVE LEARNING ALGORITHMS

The Jupyter Notebook titled `MNIST Adaptive Learning Rate Optimizers.ipynb` contains an example that revisits the classic MNIST handwritten digits classification problem to evaluate various optimiser algorithms. The convolutional network architecture used in the earlier MNIST fashion examples was trained through 20 epochs using seven optimisers: SGD, AdaGrad, AdaDelta, RMSProp, Adam, AdaMax and Nadam. All optimisation algorithms were trained using their default parameter values in PyTorch. In PyTorch, all optimisers can be found in `torch.nn.optim`.

The results of the example are given in Figures 3.18 and 3.19, which show the training accuracy as a function of epoch. In this case, SGD performs worst, followed by RMSProp. All the *Ada*-type optimisers show similar training and validation performance.

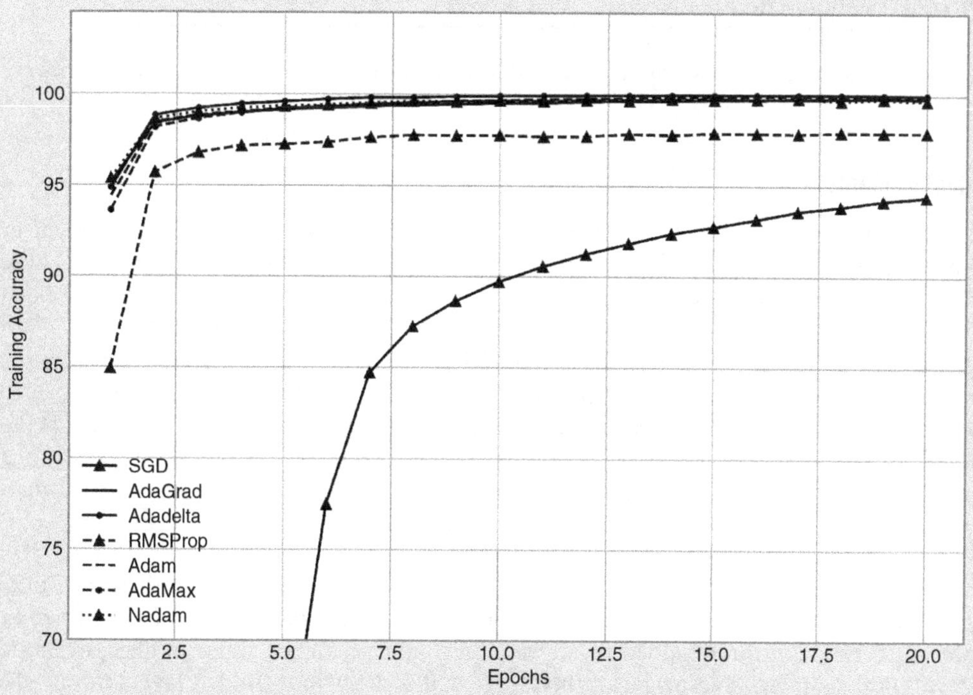

FIGURE 3.18 Training accuracy for different optimisation algorithms with the MNIST dataset over 20 epochs.

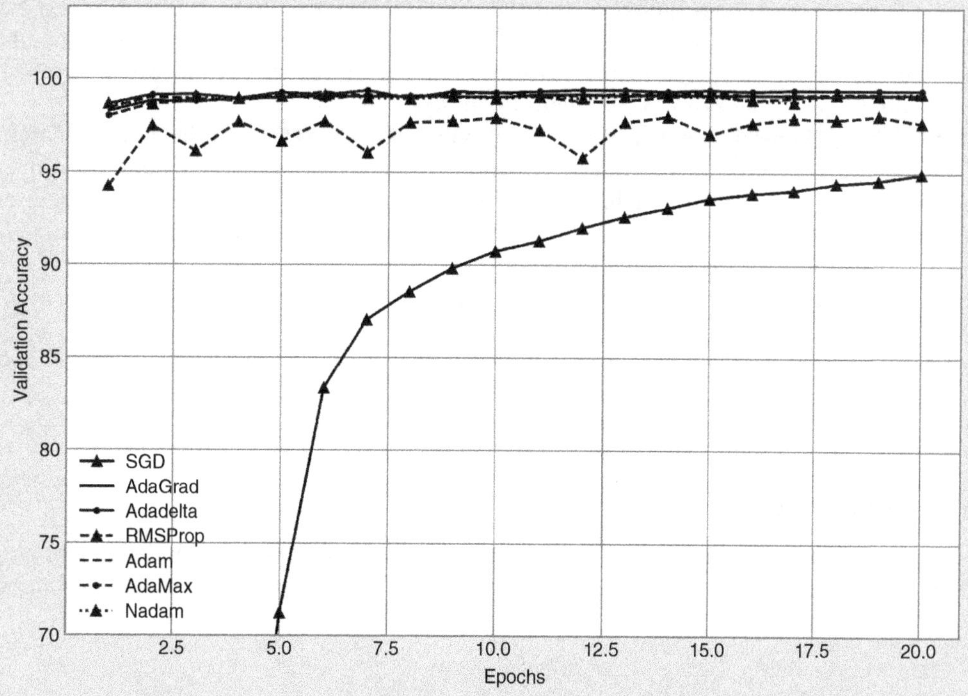

FIGURE 3.19 Validation accuracy for different optimisation algorithms with the MNIST dataset over 20 epochs.

3.6 COMMON TRAINING PROBLEMS

This section describes the most common actual and perceived problems encountered during the training of deep neural networks.

3.6.1 Overfitting/Underfitting

A central issue in deep neural networks is the quality of the model that fits the data. We want to ensure an excellent fit to the training data that generalises well to the test and validation sets unseen by the model. The two conditions we must avoid are *overfitting* and *underfitting*.

3.6.1.1 Underfitting Underfitting, also known as *high bias* (Ng, 2018e), occurs when the training and validation loss plateau at a high level, and this means that the model does not have sufficient *learning capacity* to represent the desired function; the function is too complex to be able to be represented by the architecture of the neural network. Adding additional training data will not affect the network's performance, nor will the addition of regularisation. While training the model for longer or using a better optimisation algorithm might improve matters, typically, underfitting will require changes to the neural network architecture, such as increasing the depth of the network or increasing the size of layers.

As an example of underfitting, consider Figure 3.20, which shows a series of models with different numbers of dense layers.[7] Each model had 200 neurons in each layer but had between two and six hidden layers. The loss for the examples with two and three hidden layers remains higher than the other models, even after 20 epochs, training across 960,000 samples. It seems clear, therefore, that at least four hidden layers are needed to represent the function. On the other hand, there is no additional benefit from using five or six hidden layers.

3.6.1.2 Overfitting Overfitting, also known as high variance (Ng, 2018e), occurs when the model becomes too closely attuned to the specifics of the training set and fails to generalise well to previously unseen data such as the test and validation sets or when the network is deployed in an actual application, and this manifests itself as a gap between training and validation performance, with training performance continuing to improve but validation performance plateauing or, in some cases, peaking and then declining.

An example of this behaviour is shown in Figure 3.21, which illustrates the training and validation accuracy for three different models trained on the MNIST fashion dataset.[8] The three models were dense feedforward networks with 2, 6 and 10 layers of 200 neurons each, rather than using convolutional layers. For all three models, the validation accuracy plateaus at around 89%, while the training accuracy continues to increase, with all three models achieving over 97.5% accuracy on the training set after 100 epochs.

To correct overfitting there are a number of options (Ng, 2018c):

1. Use more data, or if more data is not available, use data augmentation (see Sections 4.5, 6.4 and Chapter 9).
2. Apply one or more regularisation techniques (see Chapter 4).
3. Change the network architecture, specifically reduce the network size.

3.6.2 Defining Bias and Variance Mathematically

We can define bias and variance mathematically by considering the errors that arise under function approximation (Aggarwal, 2018). Consider the function f applied to an input example $x^{(i)}$ and its approximation by a neural network $\hat{f}$ giving

$$y^{(i)} = f(x^{(i)}), \tag{3.83}$$

$$\hat{y}^{(i)} = \hat{f}(x^{(i)}). \tag{3.84}$$

[7] See the Jupyter Notebook `Basket Option Underfitting %26 Overfitting.ipynb`.

[8] The Jupyter Notebook `MNIST Under and Overfitting.ipynb` contains this example.

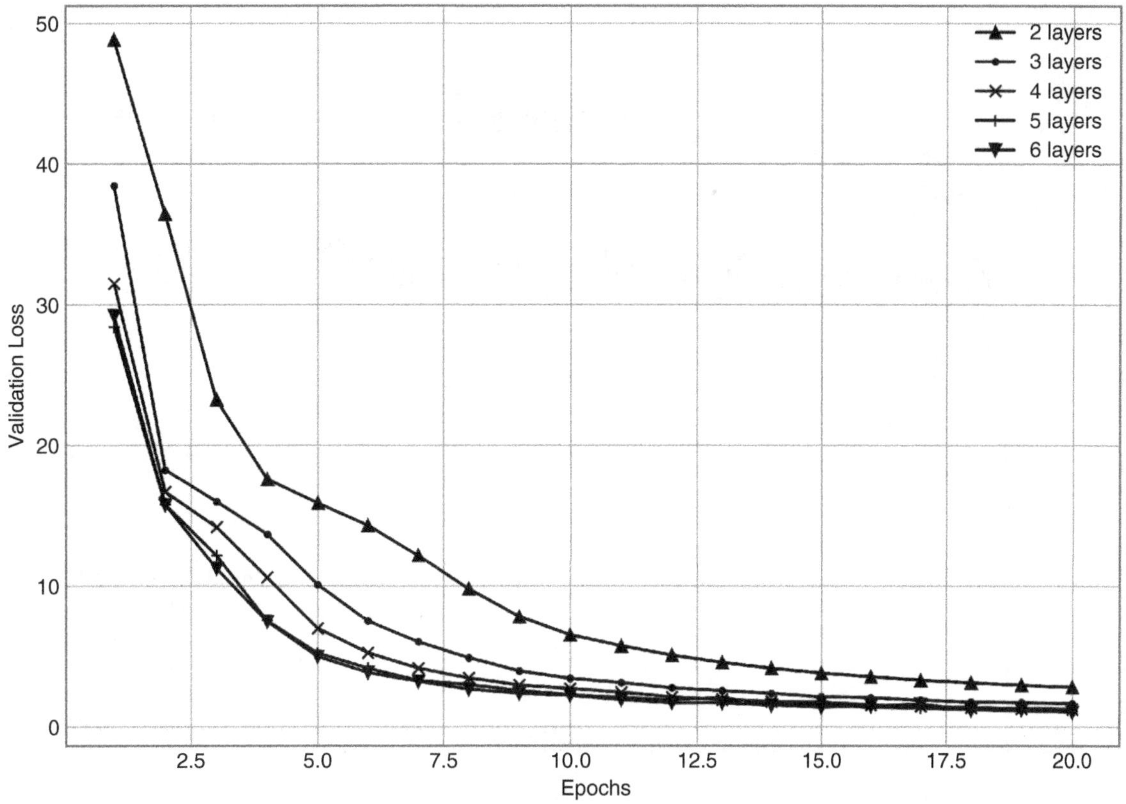

FIGURE 3.20 Validation loss for feedforward networks with two to six hidden layers, each with 200 neurons, trained on the basket option dataset.

Next, consider the average expected mean square approximation error across some test set with t elements, which gives

$$\mathbb{E}[MSE] = \frac{1}{t}\sum_{i=1}^{t}\mathbb{E}\left[(\hat{f}(x^{(i)}) - f(x^{(i)}))^2\right]. \tag{3.85}$$

We can add and subtract $\mathbb{E}[\hat{f}(x^{(i)})]$ within the squared bracket,

$$\mathbb{E}[MSE] = \frac{1}{t}\sum_{i=1}^{t}\mathbb{E}\left[(\hat{f}(x^{(i)}) - f(x^{(i)}) + \mathbb{E}[\hat{f}(x^{(i)})] - \mathbb{E}[\hat{f}(x^{(i)})])^2\right] \tag{3.86}$$

$$= \frac{1}{t}\sum_{i=1}^{t}\mathbb{E}\left[\left\{(f(x^{(i)}) - \mathbb{E}[\hat{f}(x^{(i)})]) + (\mathbb{E}[\hat{f}(x^{(i)})] - \hat{f}(x^{(i)}))\right\}^2\right]. \tag{3.87}$$

The square of the sum can be expanded into three separate terms, but the cross term is equal to zero because $\mathbb{E}[\mathbb{E}(\hat{f}(x^{(i)})) - \hat{f}(x^{(i)})] = \mathbb{E}(\hat{f}(x^{(i)})) - \mathbb{E}(\hat{f}(x^{(i)})) = 0$. Hence, the final expression contains two terms,

$$\mathbb{E}[MSE] = \frac{1}{t}\sum_{i=1}^{t}\left\{f(x^{(i)}) - \mathbb{E}[\hat{f}(x^{(i)})]\right\}^2 + \frac{1}{t}\sum_{i=1}^{t}\mathbb{E}\left[\left\{\mathbb{E}[\hat{f}(x^{(i)})] - \hat{f}(x^{(i)})\right\}^2\right], \tag{3.88}$$

where the first term is the *bias* and the second term is the *variance*. The bias measures the error in the approximation versus the ground-truth function, and the variance measures the uncertainty in the approximation.

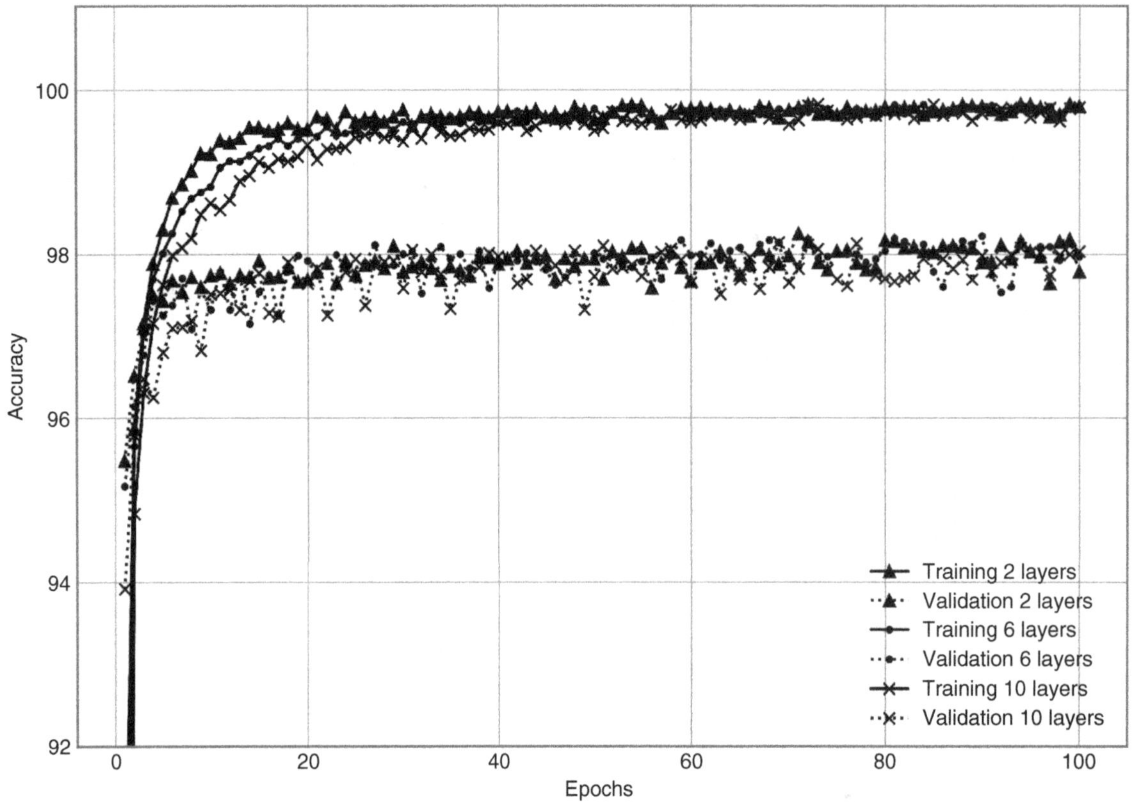

FIGURE 3.21 Training and validation accuracy for feedforward networks with 2, 6 and 10 hidden layers, each with 200 neurons, trained on the MNIST fashion dataset.

3.6.3 Local Minima

Many machine learning techniques have been carefully designed to have a convex objective function, leading to a relatively straightforward convex optimisation to find the solution (Goodfellow et al., 2016, p. 276). For convex problems, there is only one minimum; the global minimum and distinct local minima are not observed. Unfortunately, deep neural network loss functions are not convex and have many local minima. As Goodfellow et al. (2016) point out, this is partly due to the *model identifiability problem*. Neural networks have weights that can be exchanged in location, and a feedforward network with m layers and n nodes per layer has $n!^m$ different ways of arranging the weights, leading to a large number of equivalent local minima. Goodfellow et al. (2016) further note that there are potentially other sources of model non-identifiability in deep neural networks.

Local minima are a potential problem in any optimisation problem if the loss associated with the local minimum significantly differs from the global minimum and the optimisation algorithm is susceptible to becoming stuck in the local minimum. For many years, it was believed that local minima were a severe problem in training deep neural networks, but opinion has now changed (Ng, 2018b). It is now understood that in the high-dimensional space of neural network optimisation, the most common type of stationary point is a saddle point rather than a local minimum.

3.6.4 Saddle Points and Second-Order Methods

Saddle points such as the example shown in Figure 3.22 are common in the high-dimensional non-convex loss functions applied in deep neural networks (Dauphin et al., 2014, p. 9), while local minima are comparatively rare. Saddle points are stationary points where the Hessian has some positive components while others are negative. While the lack of local minima is encouraging, saddle points present some problems. Gradients may become small,

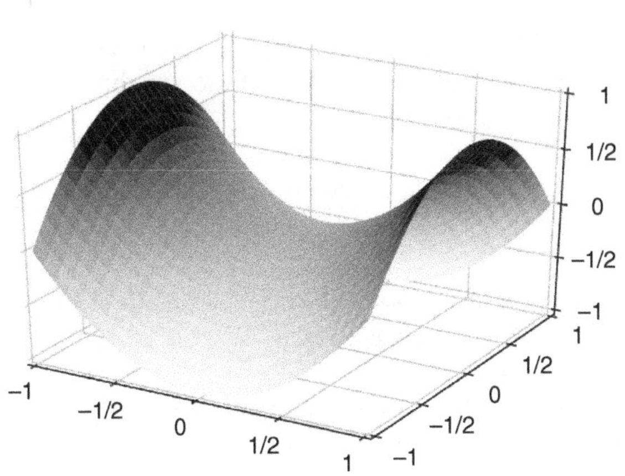

FIGURE 3.22 A saddle point.

close to saddle points, which would slow learning, although, in practice, gradient descent methods seem to be able to navigate them (Goodfellow et al., 2016, p. 279).

Second-order optimisation methods have yet to be widely adopted in deep learning. The best-known second-order method is that of Newton, but given that it solves for stationary points, it is not suitable when there are a large number of saddle points (Goodfellow et al., 2016, pp. 279–280). Furthermore, the method requires computation of the inverse Hessian, which is computationally expensive, and also needs to store a sizeable Hessian matrix to perform updates, which is memory intensive (Tan and Lim, 2019). A *saddle-free* Newton method has been developed by Dauphin et al. (2014) but is challenging to scale up to handle large neural networks (Goodfellow et al., 2016, p. 280). There are several other second-order methods, including *conjugate gradient, quasi-Newton, Gauss–Newton, Levenberg–Marquardt, Hessian-free* and *approximate greatest descent* (see Tan and Lim, 2019, for a review). However, all have computational and memory overheads associated with them. Gradient descent methods, therefore, remain the only mainstream method of training neural networks.

3.6.5 Vanishing and Exploding Gradients

Recall the backpropagation equations for the derivatives of $Z^{[L]}$ and $a^{[L]}$ given by Equations (3.7) and (3.10), respectively. Consider the expression for the gradient dZ^1, which drives the weights update at layer 1. We can write this as a recursion back through the layers,

$$\begin{aligned} dZ^{[1]} &= da^{[1]} \odot g'(Z^{[1]}) \\ &= (W^{[2]})^T.dZ^{[2]} \odot g'(Z^{[1]}) \\ &= (W^{[2]})^T.W^{[3]})^T.dZ^{[3]} \odot g'(Z^{[2]}) \odot g'(Z^{[1]}) \\ &= (W^{[2]})^T \dots (W^{[L]})^T da^{[L]} \odot g'(Z^{[L]}) \dots g'(Z^{[1]}). \end{aligned} \tag{3.89}$$

Assume that all the weight matrices are identical and diagonal with the same value for all diagonal elements, λ. If $\lambda < 1$, then with a deep network, the gradient signal from the loss function will rapidly decrease through the layers and potentially *vanish*. If, however, $\lambda > 1$, the gradient will grow rapidly during backpropagation and possibly *explode*. Furthermore, Equation (3.89) is also a function of the derivative of the activation function. Hence, the choice of activation function and the possibility of its saturating also significantly impact the propagation of the gradient signal. ReLU and its variants, such as leaky ReLU, will behave better than saturating functions like sigmoid and tanh. This saturation behaviour leads to the vanishing and exploding gradient problem; small gradients slow learning, while large ones lead to instability (Goodfellow et al., 2016, p. 282). While it can be an issue with deep feedforward networks and deep convolutional networks, the use of ReLU and related activation functions has alleviated the problem, and indeed, vanishing gradients due to saturation is the significant driver away from the use of sigmoid and tanh activation functions in hidden layers. In recurrent networks, the same weights matrix is repeatedly multiplied, making the problem more challenging to avoid (Bengio et al., 1994; Sussillo and Abbott, 2014). The *long short-term memory* unit was developed as a solution to this problem (Hochreiter and Schmidhuber, 1997) and will be discussed in detail in Chapter 7.

3.6.5.1 Gradient Clipping Gradient clipping is a heuristic approach to dealing with exploding gradients. There are two basic approaches.

Element-Wise Clipping This approach was introduced by Mikolov (2012) in his PhD thesis. The threshold value replaces any element of the gradient vector that exceeds it.

Norm-Based Clipping Pascanu et al. (2012) introduced norm-based clipping, where the gradient vector is scaled if the gradient norm exceeds a threshold,

$$\begin{aligned} &\text{if} \quad ||\mathbf{g}|| > h \\ &\mathbf{g}' = \frac{h\mathbf{g}}{||\mathbf{g}||}, \end{aligned} \tag{3.90}$$

where h is the threshold, $\mathbf{g}$ is the gradient vector and $\mathbf{g}'$ is the clipped gradient vector.

Norm-based clipping has the advantage that the direction of the gradient vector remains unchanged. However, in practice, both methods show similar results, and indeed, taking a random step if the gradient exceeds a threshold also works (Goodfellow et al., 2016, p. 403). It should be noted that gradient clipping does introduce bias in the gradient descent scheme. Gradient clipping can be viewed as a similar approach to learning rate decay optimisers but one that can respond instantaneously to large gradients (Pascanu et al., 2012).

3.7 BATCH NORMALISATION

Batch normalisation was introduced by Ioffe and Szegedy (2015) and is an essential component in many neural networks and can be considered essential in some applications such as *generative adversarial networks* (see, for example, Radford et al., 2016; Zhou et al., 2020a). Section 3.2.2 already discussed the need to normalise inputs to the neural network. Batch normalisation extends this to each layer of the network. Indeed, as Ioffe and Szegedy (2015) show, we can view the inputs to a deeper layer of a neural network in precisely the same way as the inputs to the first layer of the network and hence should expect to see similar issues if these inputs are not normalised.

Definition 3.1 ***(Internal Covariance Shift)***: *Internal covariance shift* is defined as the change in the distribution of network activations due to changes in network parameters during training (Ioffe and Szegedy, 2015, p. 2).

Consider the impact on activation functions to see the problem that internal covariance shift can lead to. As the input distribution shifts, the activation functions can become saturated, leading to vanishing gradients and slow learning, as noted earlier. Intuitively, a network layer will behave better during training when the input values are normalised to have mean zero and a variance–covariance matrix equal to the identity matrix.

The ideal way to proceed would be to construct a normalising transformation that created a transformed input $\hat{a}^{(i)}$ based on all inputs to the layer l across the training set, $a^{(i)\ldots(m)}$, that is,

$$\hat{a}^{(i)} = \text{Norm}(a^{(i)}, a^{(i)\ldots(m)}). \tag{3.91}$$

The problem with this approach is that it would be costly to use, as backpropagation would require the Jacobians for this transformation and the transformation would require the calculation of the variance–covariance matrix of $\mathbf{a}$.

To avoid such computationally intensive calculations, Ioffe and Szegedy (2015) proposed a simpler approach that normalised each input dimension individually, so for input dimension (k), the transformation is given by

$$\hat{a}^{(k)} = \frac{a^{(k)} - \mathbb{E}[a^{(k)}]}{\sqrt{\text{Var}[a^{(k)}]}}, \tag{3.92}$$

with the expectation and variance calculated across the whole training set. This approach avoids decorrelating the inputs but still speeds up convergence. Making this transformation can affect the behaviour of the neural network and, in particular, could lead to problems with sigmoid activation as all inputs would lie in the linear region of the function. To deal with this, Ioffe and Szegedy (2015) introduced two learned parameters for each (k) and so performed a linear transformation of the normalised value,

$$y^{(k)} = \gamma^{(k)}\hat{a}^k + \beta^{(k)} \equiv BN_{\beta,\gamma}(a^{(k)}). \tag{3.93}$$

Hence, the full batch normalisation calculation is given by

$$\mu_B = \frac{1}{m}\sum_{i=1}^{m} a^{(i)}, \tag{3.94}$$

$$\sigma_B^2 = \frac{1}{m}\sum_{i=1}^{m} (a^i - \mu_B)^2, \tag{3.95}$$

$$\hat{a}^{(i)} = \frac{a^{(k)} - \mu_B}{\sigma_B + \epsilon}, \tag{3.96}$$

$$y^{(i)} = \gamma\hat{a}^i + \beta. \tag{3.97}$$

To backpropagate through the batch normalisation requires the analytic derivatives of the loss function with respect to $\hat{a}^{(i)}$, $a^{(i)}$, σ_B, μ_B, γ and β, which can be obtained by simple application of the chain rule.

Once the network is trained, normalisation will still be required during inference but must depend only on the input and be deterministic. Hence, the normalisation is frozen with the mini-batch mean, μ_B, and variance, σ_B^2, replaced by the mean and variance across the whole training set in Equations (3.96) and (3.97).

Batch normalisation can be applied to both dense and convolutional layers. PyTorch provides distinct `BatchNorm1d` and `BatchNorm2d` layers.

The key benefit of batch normalisation is that it avoids training slowdown due to saturation of the activation function, and this translates to allowing the user to increase the learning rate and reduce or remove regularisation such as *dropout* layers.

EXAMPLE 3.10: BASKET OPTION WITH BATCH NORMALISATION

The impact of batch normalisation on feedforward networks was investigated by comparing the training and validation performance of networks trained using the basket option dataset. The study focused on observing the effects of batch normalisation on network performance. An example of this can be found in the Jupyter Notebook titled `Basket Option Batch Normalisation.ipynb`. The basic network architecture remained, with six hidden layers containing 200 nodes. In the case of batch normalisation, the PyTorch layer was added immediately after each dense layer. The code to create the network becomes

```
class FeedForwardNN(nn.Module):
    def __init__(self, no_layers, use_batch_norm=False):
        super(FeedForwardNN, self).__init__()
        self.use_batch_norm = use_batch_norm

        layers = [nn.Linear(28, 200)]
        if self.use_batch_norm:
            layers.append(nn.BatchNorm1d(200))

        for _ in range(no_layers):
            layers.append(nn.Linear(200, 200))
            if self.use_batch_norm:
                layers.append(nn.BatchNorm1d(200))
```

(*Continued*)

(*Continued*)

```
        self.hidden_layers = nn.ModuleList(layers)
        self.output_layer = nn.Linear(200, 1)

    def forward(self, x):
        for layer in self.hidden_layers:
        if isinstance(layer, nn.Linear):
            x = layer(x)
            x = torch.relu(x)
        elif isinstance(layer, nn.BatchNorm1d) and self.use_batch_norm:
            x = layer(x)
        x = self.output_layer(x)
        return x
```

The Adam optimiser was used to train both networks with five different learning rates: 0.00001, 0.0001, 0.001, 0.01 and 0.1. The networks were trained through 50 epochs with a batch size of 2048.

Figure 3.23 shows the validation loss for all the examples. The case with Adam and a learning rate of 0.1 does not appear as their performance was poor. The case with batch normalisation and a learning rate of 0.1 shows the loss exploding after just over 20 epochs. The figure shows that the best-performing model uses Adam with batch normalisation and a learning rate of 0.01. Batch normalisation appears to allow higher learning rates. There is additional computational cost as the training time per epoch with batch normalisation averaged around 9.38 seconds per epoch, slightly slower than the model without it at 9.12 seconds per epoch.

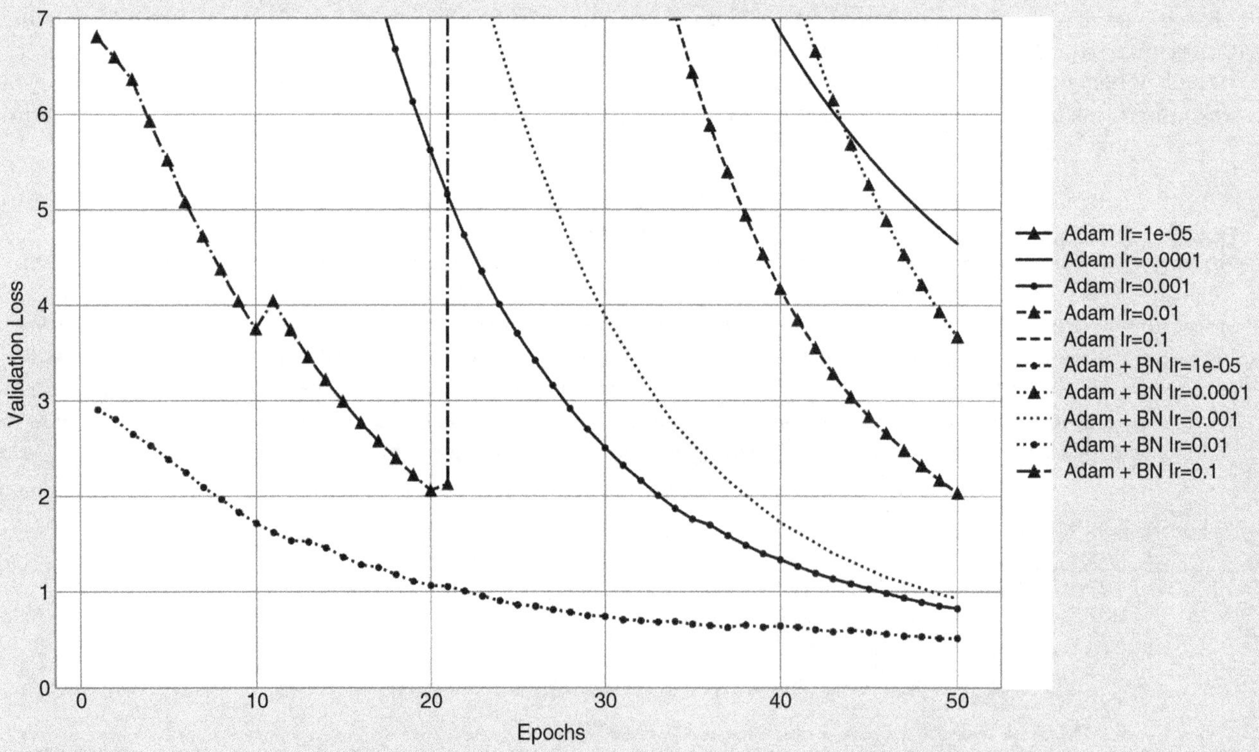

FIGURE 3.23 The validation loss for basket option models trained with Adam with and without batch normalisation and five different learning rates.

EXAMPLE 3.11: MNIST WITH BATCH NORMALISATION

As an example of batch normalisation in a convolutional network, it was applied to the MNIST fashion task. As with the basket option, models were trained with and without the batch normalisation layer and the same five learning rates, 0.00001 to 0.1, were used with the Adam optimiser. The models were trained through 20 epochs with a batch size of 64.

The training and validation accuracy are shown in Figures 3.24 and 3.25. In this case, the best training results are given by batch normalisation with a learning rate of 0.001, while the best-performing case with no batch normalisation has a learning rate of 0.001 and lies a few per cent below it. The validation accuracy is less clear-cut as the results with and without batch normalisation and a learning rate of 0.001 are similar. In general, the batch normalisation cases perform better than those without and allow higher learning rates to be used. However, the computational cost is higher, with batch normalisation taking 5.3 seconds per epoch, compared to 3.8 seconds without it.

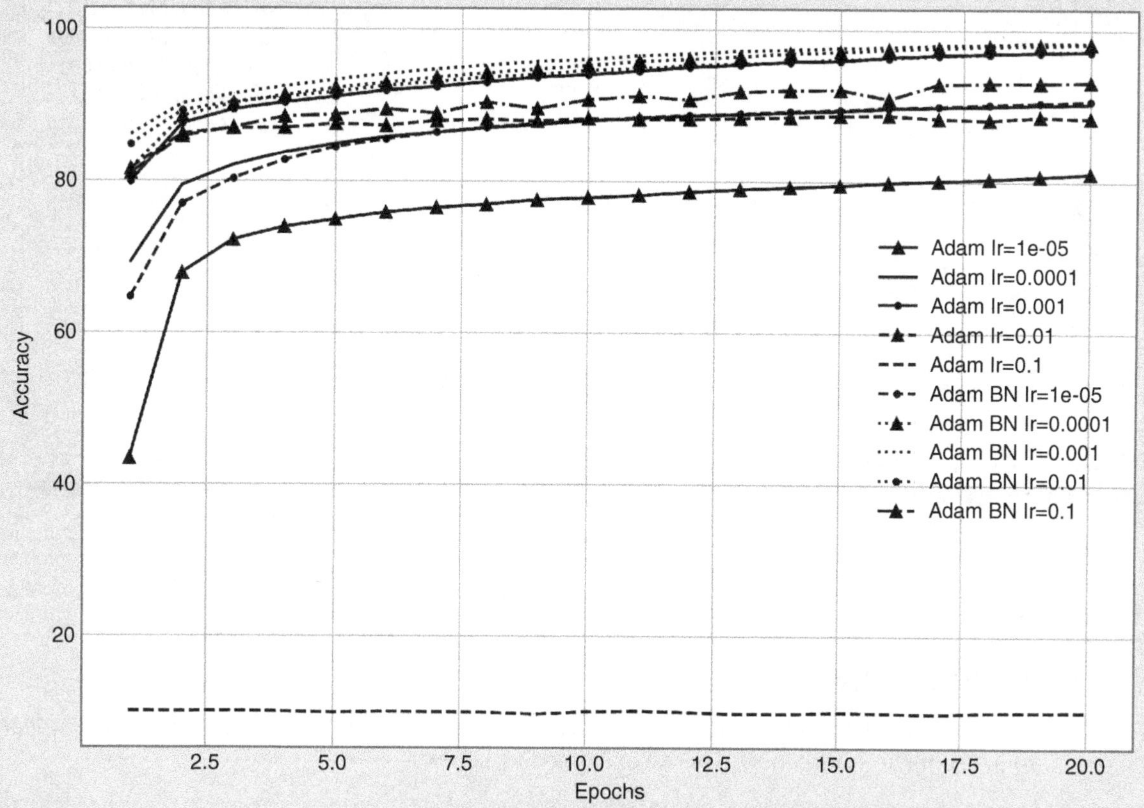

FIGURE 3.24 MNIST fashion test accuracy with and without batch normalisation and five different learning rates.

(Continued)

(*Continued*)

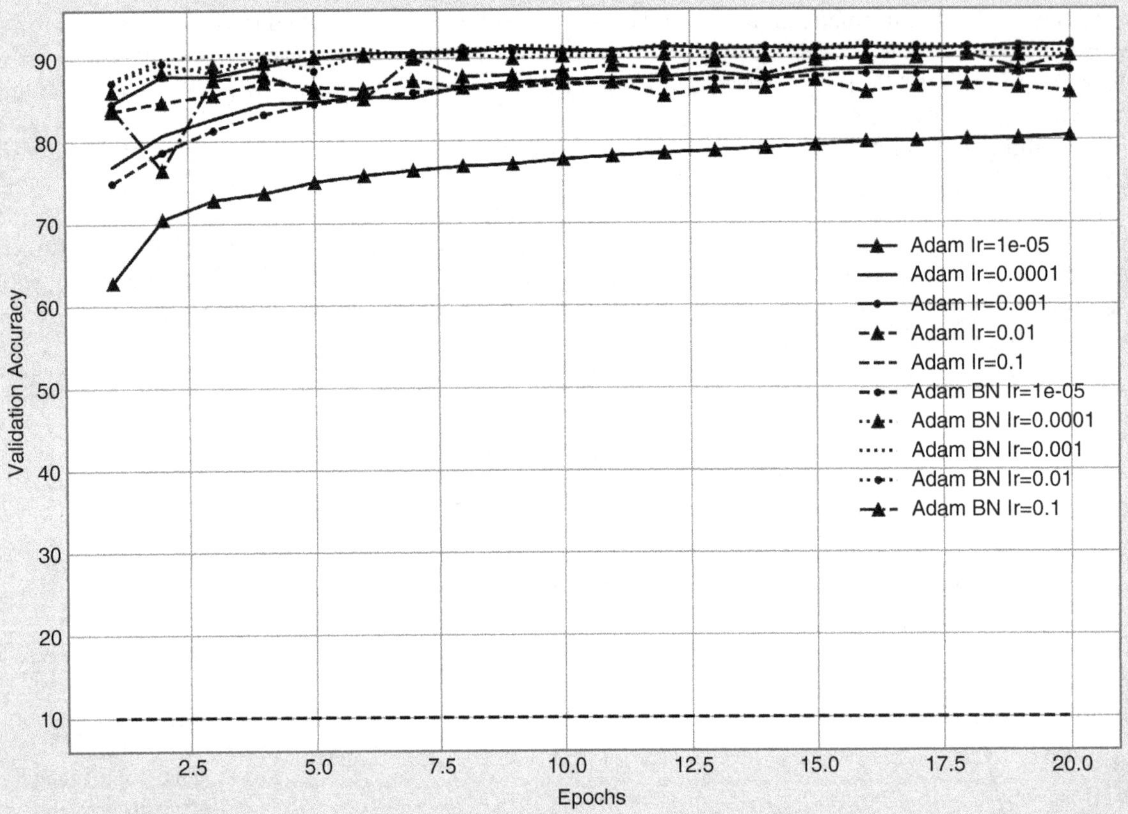

FIGURE 3.25 MNIST fashion validation accuracy with and without batch normalisation and five different learning rates.

3.8 EVALUATION AND VALIDATION

3.8.1 The Train/Test/Validation Split

When discussing data preparation in Section 3.2.3, I noted the need to split the input data into three independent subsets for *training*, *testing* and *validation*. These are defined as follows.

Definition 3.2 ***(Training Set)*:** The training set is the data upon which the model parameters are trained.

Definition 3.3 ***(Test Set)*:** The test set is an independent dataset from the training set used to perform a final test of the trained model on previously unseen data, and this will determine how well the model is generalising from the training set and hence indicate if the model has *overfitted* the training data. As discussed earlier, the test data should be drawn from the same distribution as the training data or *covariate shift* can occur.

Definition 3.4 ***(Validation Set)*:** The validation set is a second hold-out dataset independent of training and test sets. It is used to monitor model performance during training on an independent dataset. The primary purpose of the validation set is for *hyperparameter* tuning to identify which model hyperparameters give the best-performing model. As Chollet (2018) points out, hyperparameter tuning is also a form of learning, although indirect, which means that information about the validation data can 'leak' into the model. Furthermore, the model can overfit

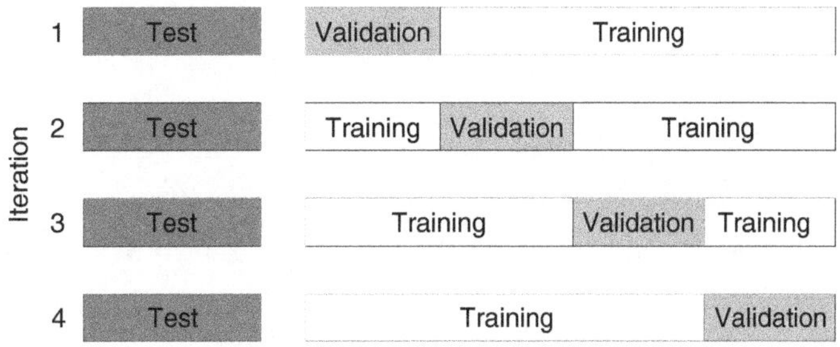

FIGURE 3.26 k-Fold cross-validation with $k = 4$. The dataset is split into the test and training/validation sets. The training/validation set is then subdivided into k blocks, with each block playing the role of the validation set for one iteration. A total of k iterations are then performed with the validation scores averaged over all iterations.

validation data, as it can overfit training data. Hence, the validation dataset must be distinct from and independent of the test set.

How should the data be split? The split between data subsets depends on the total data available for training. Ng (2018b) recommends that for small datasets with up to 10,000 samples, the training/test/validation split should be 60%/20%/20%, while for datasets with one million examples or more, the division should be 98%/1%/1%, and for intermediately sized datasets the split should be approximately interpolated between these two endpoints.

The division between training, test and validation sets should be random, so the dataset should be shuffled before the division is made. In some cases, however, the data is already randomised, such as with the basket option examples, and no further shuffling is needed.

3.8.1.1 *k*-Fold Cross-Validation and Small Datasets If the dataset is small, a further technique is available to assist, *k-fold cross-validation*. This method divides the input dataset into k equal parts. The method then performs k iterations, reserving one part for validation purposes and training on the remaining data. The validation metrics are calculated for each iteration and then averaged to obtain an overall metric. An independent test set should be reserved before the k-fold split is made. The process is illustrated in Figure 3.26.

EXAMPLE 3.12: TAIWANESE CREDIT CARD DEFAULT USING *k*-FOLD CROSS-VALIDATION

The Taiwanese credit card default example is a relatively small dataset at 30,000 examples. Hence, it can be used with k-fold cross-validation (see the Jupyter Notebook `Taiwan Credit Classifier Using K-Fold.ipynb`). The algorithm can be implemented manually but is available as an object in scikit-learn, alongside a series of related algorithms.

```
from sklearn.model_selection import KFold

no_splits = 5
kf = KFold(n_splits=no_splits)
```

Then, the iterations are looped over, training a model each time and recording the validation accuracy for each fold.

```
X_train = X_train.to_numpy()
all_histories = []
current_split = 0
for train_index, val_index in kf.split(X_train, y_train):
 iX_train, iX_val = X_train[train_index], X_train[val_index]
 iy_train, iy_val = y_train[train_index], y_train[val_index]
```

(Continued)

(*Continued*)

```
 train_loader = createDataLoader(iX_train, iy_train, True)
   val_loader = createDataLoader(iX_val, iy_val, False)

 print("Processing fold: {0}".format(current_split))
 current_split = current_split + 1

 model = BinaryClassifier(input_cols, 50).to(device)
 loss_fn = nn.BCELoss()
 optimizer = optim.Adam(model.parameters(), lr=0.001)
 history_dict = train_model(model, train_loader, val_loader,
 loss_fn, optimizer, no_epochs)
 val_history = history_dict['test_acc']
 all_histories.append(val_history)
```

The validation accuracy history is then averaged to get a final average validation accuracy, which can be plotted and examined.

```
average_history = [np.mean([x[i] for x in all_histories])
                   for i in range(no_epochs)]
```

3.8.2 Evaluation Metrics

During and after training, various statistical metrics are available to evaluate model performance. The loss function is one metric used to monitor training, but as has already been presented, monitoring additional metrics during training is frequently beneficial. For classifiers, this typically involves monitoring *accuracy*. However, essentially, any loss function can also be used for evaluation, and this was used in Example 3.3. The loss function already encountered in the context of regression problems is best suited to model evaluation. However, several additional metrics are helpful in classification, as defined in this section. Before defining individual metrics, the *confusion matrix* is presented. Note that some model types, such as GANs, have specific evaluation metrics, which will be discussed in the relevant chapters.

3.8.2.1 Binary Confusion Matrix Consider first a binary classifier with two classes *positive* and *negative*; each sample has a true and a predicted class. The confusion matrix illustrated in Figure 3.27 best illustrates the four possible classification outcomes. A series of binary classification metrics can now be defined.

		Predicted Class	
		Positive	Negative
Actual Class	Positive	True Positive (TP)	False Negative (FN)
	Negative	False Positive (FP)	True Negative (TN)

FIGURE 3.27 The binary confusion matrix illustrates the four possible binary classification outcomes.

Accuracy For classifiers, accuracy is the default metric, and in the binary or multi-class case, it can be defined by

$$\text{Accuracy} = \frac{\text{No. Correct Predictions}}{\text{Total Predictions}}. \tag{3.98}$$

Accuracy can also be written in terms of the confusion matrix variables,

$$\text{Accuracy} = \frac{TP + TN}{TP + TN + FP + FN}. \tag{3.99}$$

What is clear is that accuracy does not separate false positives and negatives.

Consider the following example:

$$\begin{vmatrix} TP = 450 & FN = 50 \\ FP = 150 & TN = 350 \end{vmatrix}. \tag{3.100}$$

In this case, the model's accuracy is $(450 + 350)/1000 = 80\%$, which is reasonably high and similar to the performance achieved on the Taiwan classifier. However, it is not clear that the model performs better in identifying true positives than true negatives; that is, the fraction of true positives identified amongst all positive cases is 90%, while the model only identifies 70% of true negatives amongst actual negatives and of the positives identified by the model, 25% are false positives.

Next, consider the case where the classes are imbalanced, and the positives vastly outnumber the negatives. In this case, the accuracy will remain high even if the classifier only poorly distinguishes true from false negatives. Consider the following example confusion matrix:

$$\begin{vmatrix} TP = 925 & FN = 25 \\ FP = 25 & TN = 25 \end{vmatrix}. \tag{3.101}$$

The accuracy for this example is $(925 + 25)/1000 = 95\%$, but the classifier only accurately predicts half of the cases that fall into the negative class. While accuracy is helpful as a single-number performance measure, it can hide significant errors in identification.

Precision and Recall Precision and recall are two metrics that attempt to rectify the issues identified in the accuracy metric. Precision measures how well the model predicts positives (Grandini et al., 2020) and is defined as

$$\mathcal{P} = \frac{TP}{TP + FP}. \tag{3.102}$$

Recall measures how accurately the model identifies positives and is defined as

$$\mathcal{R} = \frac{TP}{TP + FN}. \tag{3.103}$$

Precision and recall, therefore, do separate the impact of false positives and false negatives. In the example defined by Equation (3.100), we obtain a precision of $450/(450 + 150) = 0.75$ and a recall of $450/(450 + 50) = 0.9$, showing that precision does pick up the generation of a significant number of false positives. For the second example defined by Equation (3.101), we obtain a precision of $925/(925 + 25) = 0.97$ and similarly a recall of $925/(925 + 25) = 0.97$, showing that precision and recall do not perform that well in the unbalanced case.

Balanced Accuracy Balanced accuracy in the binary case is defined by (Pedregosa et al., 2011)

$$\text{Balanced Accuracy} = \frac{1}{2}\left(\frac{TP}{TP + FN} + \frac{TN}{TN + FP}\right). \tag{3.104}$$

This metric is defined to deal with unbalanced datasets. Consider the first example defined by Equation (3.100): balanced accuracy equals 81.25%, close to the standard accuracy measure. In a second unbalanced example, the balanced accuracy is equal to 48.6%, showing that the balanced accuracy can distinguish poor performance in negative cases.

F_β-Score The disadvantage presented by precision and recall is that two numbers are required rather than one, and a single metric is more desirable as an evaluation target. The F_β-score is a harmonic mean of the precision and recall and thus combines them into a single metric,

$$F_\beta = (1 + \beta^2)\left(\frac{\mathcal{P} \cdot \mathcal{R}}{\beta^2 \mathcal{P} + \mathcal{R}}\right). \tag{3.105}$$

Typically, $\beta = 1$ balances precision and recall in the F_1-score. $\beta < 1$ favours recall while $\beta > 1$ favours precision. The F_1-score, for example one is 0.818 and for example two is 0.974.

AUC The *area under a ROC curve (AUC)* is another metric used to analyse the output of classifiers. It is the integrated area under a *receiver operating characteristic (ROC)* curve.

The ROC metric is a plot of the percentage of the true positive rate against the false positive rate on a 2D chart, which normally has the true positive rate on the y-axis and the false positive rate on the x-axis (see, e.g., Fawcett, 2006). The plot on a ROC chart gives a single point for a discrete classifier. However, most classification algorithms and neural networks give a probability measure. For binary classifiers, we apply this probability to a discrete prediction using a threshold value, normally set at 0.5, so that any sample with an output greater than 0.5 is positive. Otherwise, it is negative. We could use a different threshold value to separate positive and negative. The ROC is generated by plotting the true positive and false positive values obtained by varying the threshold probability from 0.0 to 1.0. An example ROC curve from the Taiwanese credit card default example is shown in Figure 3.28.[9]

The AUC value always lies between 0.0 and 1.0, given that the ROC curve is plotted on the unit square. Fawcett (2006) suggests that no classifier should have an AUC value less than 0.5, and a higher score than this is desirable.

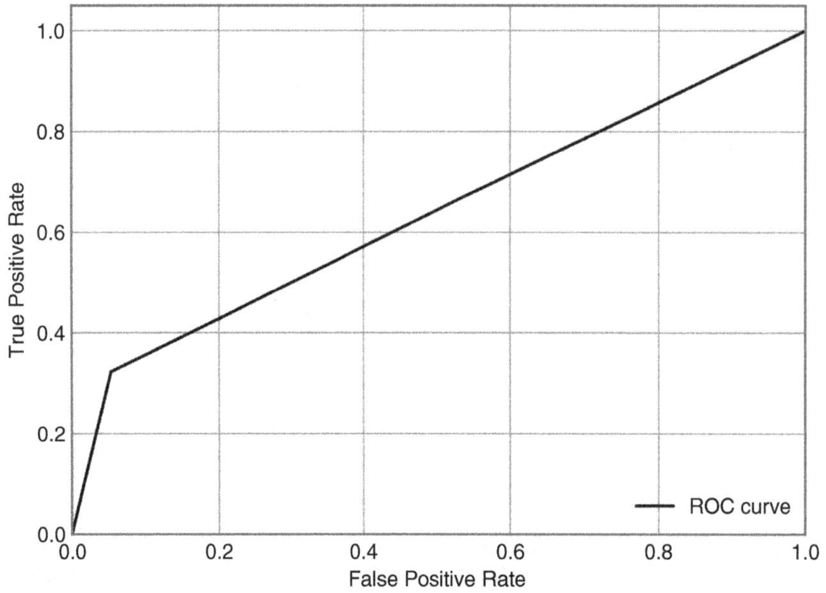

FIGURE 3.28 The ROC curve for the Taiwanese credit card default classifier.

[9]The code to generate this curve can also be found in the Jupyter Notebook `Taiwan Credit Classifier Using K-Fold.ipynb`.

EXAMPLE 3.13: TAIWANESE CREDIT CARD DEFAULT EVALUATION METRICS

The Taiwanese credit card default model trained also provides a suitable basis, for example, evaluation metrics for a binary classifier. These examples can be found in the same Jupyter Notebook as the *k*-fold example, `Taiwan Credit Classifier Using K-Fold.ipynb`. The metrics are all available in scikit-learn (Pedregosa et al., 2011). We need actual predictions from the model for all metrics apart from AUC. Hence, the first step is to apply a probability threshold of 0.5 and identify the predicted defaults on the test set.

```
y_predict = model.predict(X_test)
y_pred = np.array([1 if i > 0.5 else 0 for i in y_predict])
```

Next, the metrics are calculated, importing the required metric from `sklearn.metrics`.

```
# Accuracy
from sklearn.metrics import accuracy_score
accuracy = accuracy_score(y_test, y_pred)
print("Accuracy = {}".format(accuracy))

# Balanced Accuracy
from sklearn.metrics import balanced_accuracy_score
balanced_accuracy = balanced_accuracy_score(y_test, y_pred)
print("Balanced Accuracy = {}".format(balanced_accuracy))

# Precision
from sklearn.metrics import precision_score
precision = precision_score(y_test, y_pred)
print("Precision = {}".format(precision))

# Recall
from sklearn.metrics import recall_score
recall = recall_score(y_test, y_pred)
print("Recall = {}".format(recall))

# F1-Score
from sklearn.metrics import f1_score
f1 = f1_score(y_test, y_pred)
print("F1-Score = {}".format(f1))

# AUC
from sklearn.metrics import roc_auc_score
# Note the use of raw probabilities
auc = roc_auc_score(y_test, y_predict)
print("AUC = {}".format(auc))
```

The results are given in Table 3.2. The accuracy of the model is 81.3%. However, it is clear from the other metrics that the performance of the model is ‘middling’, and the low recall shows that the model is producing a lot of false negatives. This may be due to the relatively small dataset at 30,000 samples or the lack of explanatory power of the input variables.

(*Continued*)

(Continued)

TABLE 3.2 Results from Evaluating the Taiwanese Credit Card Default Classifier Model

Metric	Value
Accuracy	0.8098
Balanced accuracy	0.6346
Precision	0.6272
Recall	0.3229
F_1-score	0.4263
AUC	0.6346

3.8.2.2 Multi-Class Confusion Matrix The confusion matrix can be extended to the multi-class context by adding columns and rows per class. We can then score the classifier's output and place the results in each cell in the matrix. We can label as before, but now the four category labels, true positive, false positive, true negative and false negative, can only be applied to each class individually, as illustrated in Figure 3.29.

3.8.2.3 Multi-Class and Multi-Label Metrics Metrics are generalised from the binary case in the multi-class and multi-label classification context. Some metrics do this by treating the problem as a collection of binary classification tasks and then applying some form of averaging; other metrics generalise more naturally to higher dimensions. Scikit-learn (Pedregosa et al., 2011) defines four types of average operation:

- *macro* calculates the mean of the collection of binary metrics with equal weight given to each class;
- *micro* calculates the sum of the numerators and denominators of the binary metrics together before dividing them to give an overall metric;
- *weighted* calculates a weighted average of the binary metric where the weight is the class weight in the true label distribution;
- *samples* applies only to multi-label problems and constructs a sample weighted average of the metric for each label.

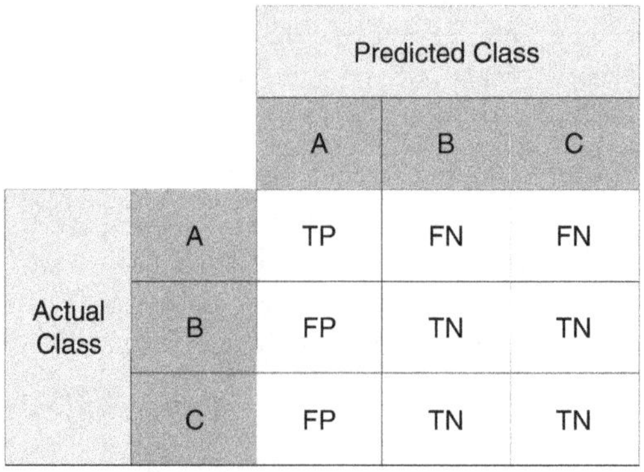

FIGURE 3.29 A multi-class confusion matrix for three classes A, B and C. The labels represent outcomes from the perspective of class A.

Precision, Recall and F_1-Score The basic precision and recall values are now calculated on a per-class basis,

$$\mathcal{P}_k = \frac{TP_k}{TP_k + FP_k}, \tag{3.106}$$

$$\mathcal{R}_k = \frac{TP_k}{TP_k + FN_k}. \tag{3.107}$$

The macro, micro, weighted and samples versions of precision, recall and F_1-score are all in Table 3.3. Here, w_k is the true population weight for class k, and s_k is the sample population weight for class k.

Balanced Accuracy In the multi-class and multi-label context, balanced accuracy becomes (Dei, 2019)

$$\text{Balanced Accuracy} = \frac{1}{K}\sum_{k=1}^{K} w_k TP_k. \tag{3.108}$$

AUC and ROC Curves In the multi-class context, the ROC chart will contain one ROC curve per class, each presenting a 'one-vs-rest' classification. AUC can also be extended using averaging, and two broad types are available in scikit-learn. The *one-vs-one algorithm* (Hand and Till, 2001) uses a weighted average over pairwise AUC computations, with two weighting schemes, uniform and by class prevalence. The class prevalence weighted version is defined by

$$AUC_{ovo}\frac{2}{K(K-1)}\sum_{j=1}^{K}\sum_{k=1}^{K} w_{jk}(AUC(j|k) + AUC(k|j)), \tag{3.109}$$

where w_{jk} is the prevalence of the pair. The second algorithm constructs a weighted average of one-vs-rest ROC curves (Provost and Domingos, 2000; Fawcett, 2006), where again the weight can be uniform or by class prevalence,

$$AUC_{ovr}\sum_{k=1}^{K} w_k AUC_k. \tag{3.110}$$

TABLE 3.3 Macro, Micro, Weighted and Samples Versions of Precision and Recall for Multi-Class/Multi-Label Classifier Models

Average	Precision	Recall	F_β-Score
Macro	$\frac{\sum_{k=1}^{K}\mathcal{P}_k}{K}$	$\frac{\sum_{k=1}^{K}\mathcal{R}_k}{K}$	$(1+\beta^2)\left(\frac{Ma_{\mathcal{P}}\cdot Ma_{\mathcal{R}}}{\beta^2 Ma_{\mathcal{P}}+Ma_{\mathcal{R}}}\right)$
Micro	$\frac{\sum_{k=1}^{K}TP_k}{\sum_{k=1}^{K}TP_k+\sum_{k=1}^{K}FP_k}$	$\frac{\sum_{k=1}^{K}TP_k}{\sum_{k=1}^{K}TP_k+\sum_{k=1}^{K}FN_k}$	$(1+\beta^2)\left(\frac{Mi_{\mathcal{P}}\cdot Mi_{\mathcal{R}}}{\beta^2 Mi_{\mathcal{P}}+Mi_{\mathcal{R}}}\right)$
Weighted	$\frac{1}{\sum_{k=1}^{K}w_k}\sum_{k=1}^{K}w_k\mathcal{P}_k$	$\frac{1}{\sum_{k=1}^{K}w_k}\sum_{k=1}^{K}w_k\mathcal{R}_k$	$\frac{(1+\beta^2)}{\sum_{k=1}^{K}w_k}\sum_{k=1}^{K}w_k\left(\frac{\mathcal{P}_k\cdot\mathcal{R}_k}{\beta^2\mathcal{P}_k+\mathcal{R}_k}\right)$
Samples	$\frac{1}{\sum_{k=1}^{K}s_k}\sum_{k=1}^{K}s_k\mathcal{P}_k$	$\frac{1}{\sum_{k=1}^{K}s_k}\sum_{k=1}^{K}s_k\mathcal{R}_k$	$\frac{(1+\beta^2)}{\sum_{k=1}^{K}s_k}\sum_{k=1}^{K}s_k\left(\frac{\mathcal{P}_k\cdot\mathcal{R}_k}{\beta^2\mathcal{P}_k+\mathcal{R}_k}\right)$

Other Metrics Other metrics not discussed in this section can also be considered. These include *Matthews correlation*, *Cohen's kappa*, *Jaccard similarity* and the *Hamming loss*. For more details, see the scikit-learn documentation and Grandini et al. (2020).

EXAMPLE 3.14: MULTI-CLASS METRICS AND THE MNIST FASHION CLASSIFIER

The MNIST fashion dataset with the CNN classifier used in previous examples was used to explore multi-class metrics. This example can be found in the Jupyter Notebook `MNIST Evaluation Metrics.ipynb`. After training the classifier, the predicted classes for the test set were generated. The model output of the matrix of probability values must be turned into class predictions using argmax.

```
y_predict = model.predict(test_norm)
y_pred = tf.one_hot(tf.argmax(y_predict, axis=1), y_predict.shape[1]).numpy()
```

Some of the multi-class evaluation metrics in scikit-learn can accept a one-hot representation of multi-class data, but others cannot, so both test labels and predicted labels were re-encoded back into categorical indices, giving a one-dimensional representation.

```
enc_test_labels =np.argmax(test_labels,axis=-1)
enc_y_pred = np.argmax(y_pred, axis=-1)
```

Numerical metrics can then be calculated using the same function as in the binary case but with the averaging method specified. So, for example, the weighted precision can be calculated using

```
# Weighted Precision
from sklearn.metrics import precision_score
wprecision = precision_score(enc_test_labels, enc_y_pred, average='weighted')
print("Weighted Precision = {}".format(wprecision))
```

In this case, the numerical metrics only give a sense of the overall performance, not the performance of individual categories. Hence, two ROC curves and the confusion matrix charts are generated, as shown in Figures 3.30 and 3.31, respectively. The scikit-learn `roc_curve` function was used to generate the ROC curves. The confusion matrix was generated using the scikit-learn `confusion_matrix` function, which gives a matrix of counts, and this was then plotted using the `heatmap` function in the `seaborn` Python graphics library, which itself builds on `matplotlib` functionality. The ROC curves plot shows that the classifier generally performs well but with some dispersion across the different classes, and in particular, the 'shirt' class is the worst performing. The confusion matrix shows the same behaviour, and the classifier sometimes confuses shirts and T-shirts, which is unsurprising given the similar shapes.

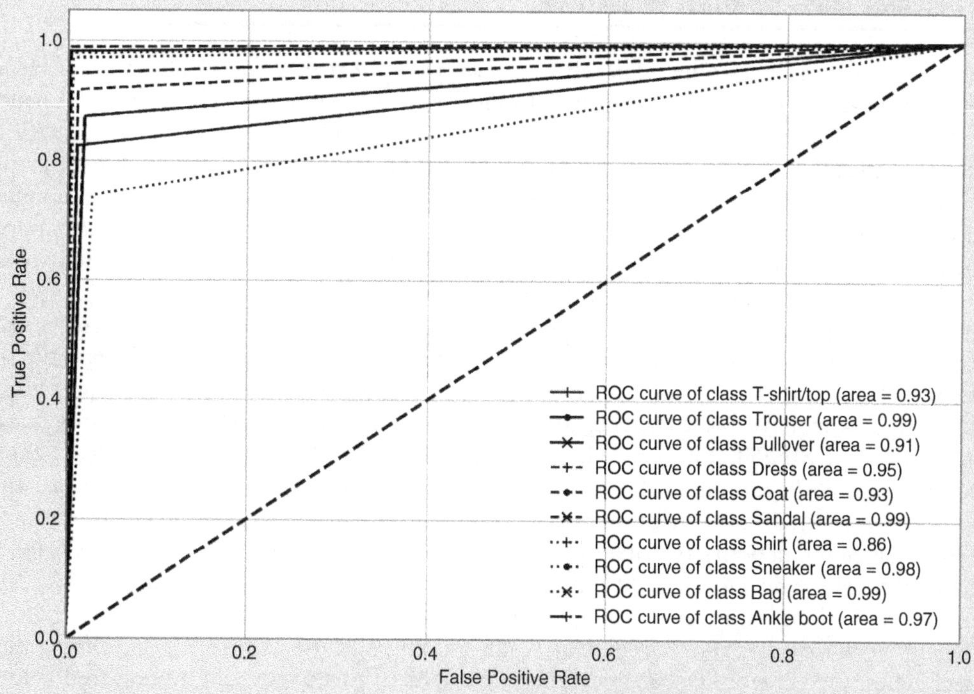

FIGURE 3.30 The ROC curves for each class in the MNIST fashion dataset. Only the top left corner of the full chart is shown, so the curves can be easily distinguished.

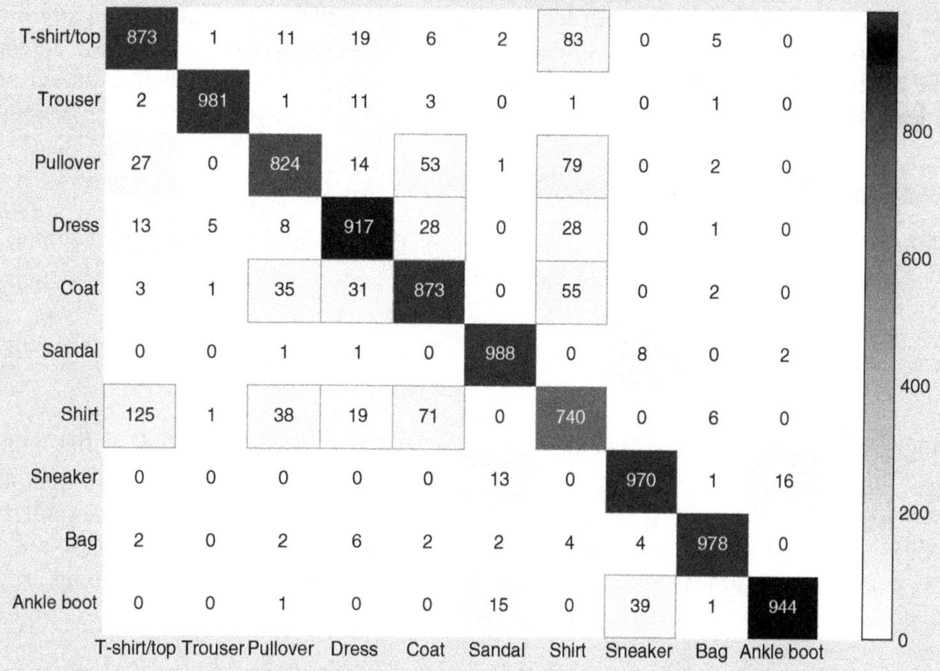

FIGURE 3.31 The confusion matrix for the MNIST fashion dataset.

3.9 SOBOLEV TRAINING: USING FUNCTION DERIVATIVES

In all the examples of supervised learning explored so far, only the *label* or *value* has been used. Hence, we might call this type of training *value training*. In many, if not most, use cases for supervised training of neural networks, there is no other information available, and in particular, we often do not know what the sensitivities of the value are to the function inputs. However, in some contexts, the derivatives of the function we seek to approximate with a neural network are available. In particular, if we wanted to train a neural network to replicate a financial derivative valuation function, the derivatives may be available analytically via AAD, using finite difference approximation or some other scheme. Hence, the question 'Can we use function derivatives to improve neural network training?' is valid and of specific interest in quantitative finance applications.

Several authors have approached the problem of using function derivatives in neural network training, either in the general case or in the context of tackling a specific problem. Many of these authors have independently rediscovered the use of function derivatives, apparently unaware of previous attempts. The first published attempt to use derivatives appears to have been Drucker and Le Cun (1992), who developed a *double backpropagation* algorithm in the context of MNIST numbers. Mitchell and Thrun (1992) and Masuoka (1993) explored the use of gradients in neural network training in the context of reinforcement learning applications. Lee and Oh (1997) developed a Jacobian learning rule for general neural networks, demonstrating accelerated learning speed and better generalisation. Fitting a neural network to potential-energy surfaces and corresponding force fields led to derivative-based training by Witkoskie and Doren (2005) and Pukrittayakamee et al. (2009). Rifai et al. (2011) used the Jacobian of encoder activations with respect to inputs when training autoencoders.

The most recent work on using function derivatives in training and the name *Sobolev training* derive from the work of Czarnecki et al. (2017) from DeepMind. The key results of this paper will be explored below. The name, *Sobolev*, derives from *Sobolev spaces*, which are the metric spaces associated with functions and their derivatives. Hornik (1991) used Sobolev spaces to prove his universal function approximation theorems. Kissel and Diepold (2020) tested the performance of Sobolev training with approximated derivatives using a linear least-squares derivative approximation and finite difference, while Hartmann et al. (2019) considered using higher-order derivatives. Avrutskiy (2021) similarly considered higher-order derivatives up to fifth order but specifically in the context of neural networks used to solve differential equations.[10] Finally, Huge and Savine (2020) used derivatives obtained using AAD in the context of derivative valuation using Monte Carlo regression, where a neural network is used instead of linear least squares.[11]

3.9.1 Incorporating Derivatives

All the papers discussed above adopt a similar approach to incorporating derivatives into training and extending the loss function. Hence, they replace Equation (3.30) with

$$J(\mathbf{W}, b) = \frac{1}{m}\sum_{i=1}^{m}\left[\mathcal{L}(\hat{y}^{(i)}, y^{(i)}) + \sum_{j=1}^{K}\lambda_j\mathcal{L}_j(D^j_{\mathbf{X}}\hat{y}^{(i)}, D^j_{\mathbf{X}}y^{(i)})\right], \tag{3.111}$$

where K is the highest order of derivative included, λ_j is a weight applied to order j, $\mathcal{L}_j$ is the loss for derivatives of order k on example i and $D^j_{\mathbf{X}}$ is the differential operator of order j with respect to input vector $\mathbf{X}$. Given that these are mostly regression problems, $\mathcal{L}$ is typically the L_2 norm. For large K and where the underlying function f is multivariate, Czarnecki et al. (2017) note that the Jacobian could be expensive to calculate and hence propose using a technique from Rifai et al. (2011) in which the Jacobian is projected onto a random variable v, sampled from the unit sphere, and this gives a revised loss function,

$$J(\mathbf{W}, b) = \frac{1}{m}\sum_{i=1}^{m}\left[\mathcal{L}(\hat{y}^{(i)}, y^{(i)}) + \sum_{j=1}^{K}\mathbb{E}_{v^j}\left[\lambda_j\mathcal{L}_j(\langle D^j_{\mathbf{X}}\hat{y}^{(i)}, v^j\rangle, \langle D^j_{\mathbf{X}}y^{(i)}, v^j\rangle)\right]\right]. \tag{3.112}$$

[10] See Chapter 12.

[11] This paper will be discussed in more detail in Chapter 11.

Several authors advocate using a weight λ_j with the derivative loss term. As will be seen when regularisation is discussed in Chapter 4, this makes the term and this method look remarkably like a regularisation technique. However, there is a difference in that regularisation terms generally reduce variance at the cost of some bias. Here, the derivative term is unbiased, and the aim is to match the input derivatives exactly (Czarnecki et al., 2017; Huge and Savine, 2020). The choice of weight varies between authors, with Kissel and Diepold (2020) advocating decreasing the weight after each epoch of training and Hartmann et al. (2019) suggesting it should be set adaptively with reference to the quotient of the derivative error for a given order.

3.9.2 Key Theorems

Czarnecki et al. (2017) proved two key theorems underlying Sobolev training.

Theorem 3.1: *Given any two functions $f : S \to \mathbb{R}$ and $g : S \to \mathbb{R}^d$ on $S \subseteq \mathbb{R}^d$ and a finite set $\Sigma \subset S$, there exists a neural network h with a ReLU (or leaky ReLU) activation such that $\forall x \in \Sigma$, $f(x) = h(x)$ and $g(x) = \frac{\partial h}{\partial x}$.*

Define $K_{reg}(\mathcal{F})$ as a measure of the amount of data required to learn some target function and $\mathcal{F}$ as a parametrised family of functions. Similarly, K_{sob} is the data required to learn the target function using Sobolev training.

Theorem 3.2: *For any $\mathcal{F}$, there holds $K_{sob}(\mathcal{F}) \leq K_{reg}(\mathcal{F})$.*

Hence, Czarnecki et al. (2017) demonstrated that for ReLU-based neural networks, Sobolev training would not require more training than regular value training. They further demonstrated that if $\mathcal{F}$ is drawn from the family of Gaussian PDFs or linear element-wise functions, then the amount of data required for Sobolev training is strictly less than value training. So, we have reasonable theoretical grounds for expecting Sobolev training to perform better than value training.

3.9.3 Empirical Results

The common observation from all authors and virtually all test cases is that Sobolev training outperforms value training for a given dataset size. One example from Czarnecki et al. (2017) where Sobolev training performs worse was on the rapidly oscillating Ackley function with 100 data points or less. Intuitively, the low sampling of the gradients in this case could lead to worse performance, but with a larger dataset of 10,000 points, Sobolev outperformed value training. The benefit gained does change with the function and size of the training set and lies in the range of a small multiplier up to around three orders of magnitude for a bowl-shaped function with a small dataset and fourth-order derivatives used (Hartmann et al., 2019). A typical figure for the benefit in the test cases found in Czarnecki et al. (2017), Hartmann et al. (2019) and Kissel and Diepold (2020) is one order of magnitude. The benefit declines with increasingly complex function shapes and training set sizes. Kissel and Diepold (2020) demonstrated that Sobolev with approximate derivatives provides benefit over value training, although exact derivatives provide more benefit than approximate.

EXAMPLE 3.15: SOBOLEV TRAINING WITH BLACK–SCHOLES

Can the benefits of Sobolev training be observed in the simple case of a feedforward network trained to replicate the Black–Scholes function (see the Jupyter Notebook `Sobolev Training Black-Scholes.ipynb` for this example)? In the example, the neural network estimate of the delta, vega and theta was used with the analytic delta, vega and theta for each example generated by QuantLib to construct the adjusted Sobolev loss function.

In PyTorch, implementing Sobolev training requires modifying the training loop presented earlier. The new training loop calculates the gradients of the outputs with respect to the inputs. It compares these with the supplied derivative values to calculate the gradient loss, weighted by the supplied value of λ to give the overall loss.

(Continued)

(*Continued*)

```
def train_model(model, train_loader, test_loader, loss_fn,
                optimizer, lambda_1, epochs):
    train_errors = []
    test_errors = []
    grad_errors = []

    tqdm_epoch = trange(epochs)
    for epoch in tqdm_epoch:
        model.train()
        train_loss = 0.0
        grad_loss_accum = 0.0

        for batch_X, batch_ydy in train_loader:
            batch_X.requires_grad_(True)

            # Split the input labels into value and gradients
            batch_y = batch_ydy[:, 0]
            dy_dx = batch_ydy[:, 1:]

            # Forward pass
            outputs = model(batch_X)
            value_loss = loss_fn(outputs.squeeze(), batch_y)

            # Compute gradients of outputs with respect to inputs
            outputs_grad = grad(outputs.sum(), batch_X,
                                create_graph=True)[0]
            grad_loss = loss_fn(outputs_grad[:,0:3], dy_dx)

                # Combine losses
            loss = value_loss + lambda_1 * grad_loss

            # Backward pass and optimization
            optimizer.zero_grad()
            loss.backward()
            optimizer.step()

            train_loss += value_loss.item() * batch_X.size(0)
            grad_loss_accum += grad_loss.item() * batch_X.size(0)

        train_loss /= len(train_loader.dataset)
        grad_loss_accum /= len(train_loader.dataset)
        train_errors.append(train_loss)
        grad_errors.append(grad_loss)

        # Evaluation on the test set
        model.eval()
        test_loss = 0.0
        with torch.no_grad():
            for batch_X, batch_ydy in test_loader:
                batch_y = batch_ydy[:, 0]
                outputs = model(batch_X)
                loss = loss_fn(outputs.squeeze(), batch_y)
                test_loss += loss.item() * batch_X.size(0)
```

```
        test_loss /= len(test_loader.dataset)
        test_errors.append(test_loss)

        tqdm_epoch.set_description(f"Epoch {epoch+1}/{epochs} - \
                                     Train loss: {train_loss:.4f}, \
                                     Grad loss: {grad_loss_accum:.4f}, \
                                     Test loss: {test_loss:.4f}")

    history = dict()
    history['train_loss'] = train_errors
    history['grad_loss'] = grad_errors
    history['test_loss'] = test_errors
    return history
```

The model used was the same two-hidden-layer network described in Chapter 2 with 200 nodes per layer. The activation function used was Swish rather than ReLU, ensuring that the activation function is differentiable everywhere.

Models were trained for 50 epochs for three different sample sizes, 10,240, 102,400 and 512,000, with a batch size of 1024. Three different lambda values were used, $\lambda = 0.0$ to switch off the gradient term entirely, $\lambda = 0.1$ and $\lambda = 1.0$.

The validation loss as a function of the epoch is shown in Figure 3.32. The number of samples per epoch differs for each sample size, but the chart allows an assessment of performance in each of the four groups of models and an overall assessment of performance. For the cases with a sample size of 10,240, there is little difference between the results for different values of λ. For the cases with 102,400 and 512,000 samples, the $\lambda = 1.0$ case does show better performance than $\lambda = 0.0$ and $\lambda = 0.1$, showing that there is benefit from using Sobolev training. However, the benefit is relatively small and dwarfed by the benefit of a more extensive training set. It should also be noted that the gradient loss is lower with Sobolev training than without, suggesting that the models trained with Sobolev will have more accurate gradients than those trained on values, which could be significant in some contexts.

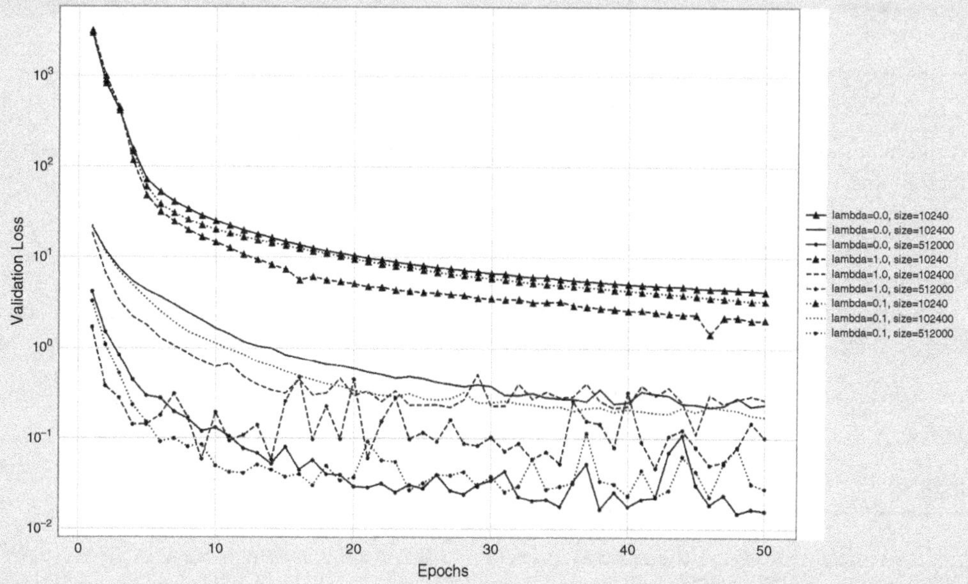

FIGURE 3.32 Validation loss for neural networks trained to replicate the Black–Scholes function with loss plotted as a function of epoch.

(Continued)

(*Continued*)

Each sample case can also be run for the same number of iterations and run more epochs for the cases with smaller sample sizes (see `Sobolev Training Black-Scholes - Train equal sample iterations.ipynb`). The validation loss plotted as a function of iteration is shown in Figure 3.33 and shows the same pattern. The smaller number of samples at 1024 and 10,240 do not generalise well, irrespective of the addition of Sobolev training. The cases with 102,400 and 512,000 samples generalise much better and benefit from Sobolev training.

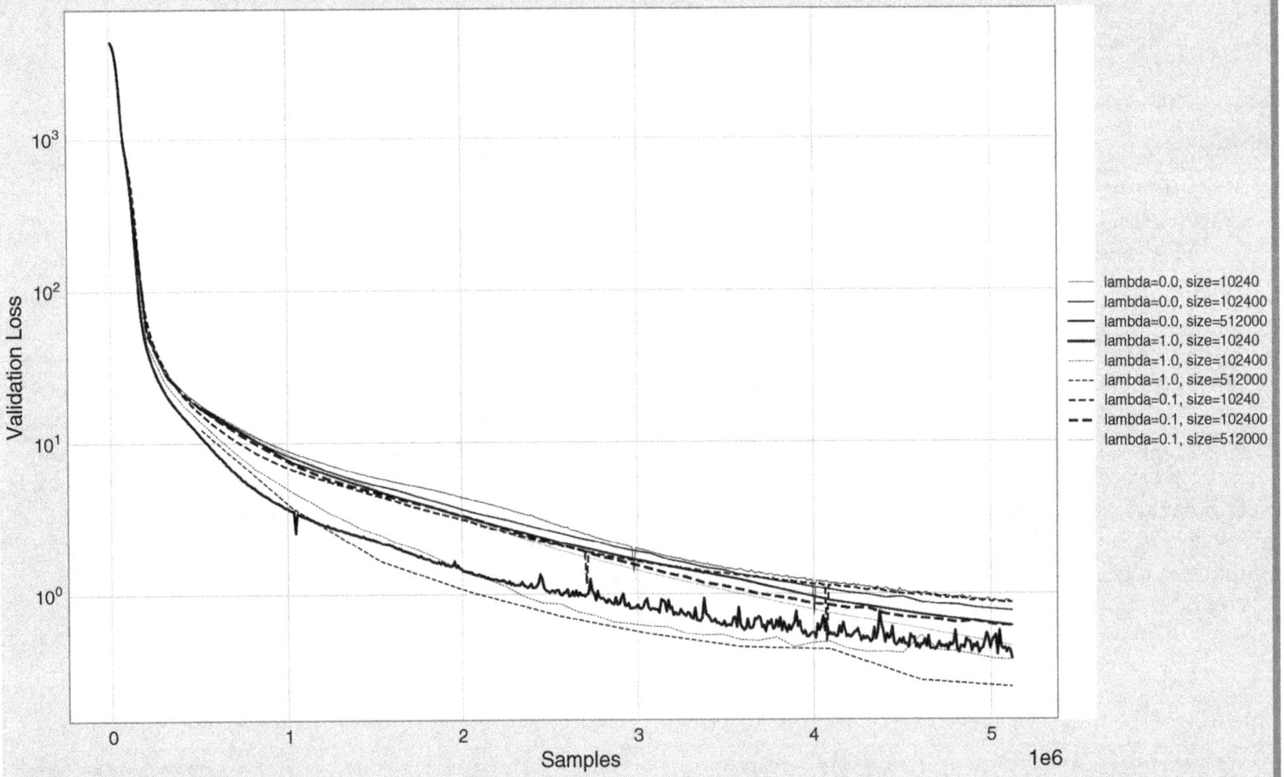

FIGURE 3.33 Validation loss for neural networks trained to replicate the Black–Scholes function with loss plotted as a function of iteration.

In conclusion, if sufficient samples are used for good generalisation behaviour, then a fixed dataset size using Sobolev training will further improve the model and the gradients. However, just increasing the number of samples will give a similar boost in performance. Hence, the decision to use Sobolev will be a trade-off between the cost of obtaining extra data with derivatives and the slower runtime that Sobolev training involves.

3.10 CONCLUSIONS

This chapter has thoroughly explored the critical aspects of training neural networks, beginning with the foundational algorithm: backpropagation. The importance of data preparation was emphasised, including scaling techniques and input normalisation, as well as the careful handling of test and validation data. Neural network weights need to be randomly initialised, and discussion on weight initialisation underscored strategies for setting initial weights and biases to facilitate efficient learning. The choice of the loss function must be tailored carefully to the task that was reviewed, as were optimisation algorithms, highlighting both basic methods and those with adaptive learning rates. Common training challenges like overfitting, underfitting, local minima, saddle points and vanishing or exploding gradients were examined, along with solutions such as batch normalisation. The chapter also covered evaluation and validation practices, stressing the significance of proper data splitting and appropriate metrics. Sobolev training was introduced, showcasing how incorporating function derivatives can enhance learning. Together, these topics provide a comprehensive understanding of the techniques for effectively training neural networks.

CHAPTER 4

Regularisation

Interviewer: David, what makes you sad?

David: War, poverty, cruelty, unnecessary violence. I understand human emotions, although I do not feel them myself. This allows me to be more efficient and capable and makes it easier for my human counterparts to interact with me.

Prometheus (directed by Ridley Scott, 2012)

4.1 INTRODUCTION: REGULARISATION AND GENERALISATION

Recall from Section 3.6 that the two critical issues in training neural networks are bias and variance or, equivalently, underfitting and overfitting. Models that are overfitted to the training data do not generalise well to unseen examples, and given that generalisation is precisely the goal of machine learning, this is a severe issue (Aggarwal, 2018, p. 169). As we have already seen, neural networks tend to overfit, and the complexity of the model architecture determines this. Furthermore, the only solutions seen so far are to increase the training data or reduce the model complexity. Fortunately, there is a third solution, *regularisation*.

How might we define regularisation formally? Goodfellow et al. (2016) adopt the following definition.

Definition 4.1 ***(Regularisation)*:** Regularisation is any modification to a machine learning algorithm intended to reduce its generalisation error but not its training error.

Kukačka et al. (2017) adopt a similar definition in their review of regularisation techniques for deep learning.

Definition 4.2 ***(Regularisation)*:** Regularisation is any supplementary technique for improving the model's generalisation (i.e., producing better results on the test set).

These broad definitions reflect that various regularisation techniques have been applied to deep learning models.

Kukačka et al. (2017) identified five categories of regularisation motivated by the form of the loss function. Write the deep learning optimisation problem in the following form (see Equation (3.30)),

$$\underset{\theta}{\operatorname{argmin}} \frac{1}{m} \sum_{i=1}^{m} \mathcal{L}(\hat{f}(x^{(i)}, \theta), y^{(i)}) + R, \tag{4.1}$$

where R has been added to represent a regularisation term. The five classes of regularisation technique can be directly related to Equation (4.1).

1. m: Data/training set
2. $\hat{f}$: Model family
3. $\mathcal{L}$: Error function

Deep Learning in Quantitative Finance, First Edition. Andrew Green.

4. R: Regularisation term
5. argmin_{θ}: Optimisation procedure

In practice, these categories are not mutually exclusive, and some regularisation techniques can belong to multiple classes.

This chapter reviews the main regularisation techniques in widespread use with deep learning, *weight decay*, *early stopping*, *dropout* and *data augmentation*. Data augmentation is often used in computer vision; hence, the details of that specific application will be discussed in Chapter 6. The chapter will review other techniques that provide regularisation as a byproduct in Section 4.6.

4.2 WEIGHT DECAY

The most popular form of regularisation for neural networks is *weight decay*, so called because it adds a regularisation term to the loss function that penalises large weight values. Hence, the loss function takes the form

$$\begin{aligned} J(\theta) &= \frac{1}{m} \sum_{i=1}^{m} \mathcal{L}(\hat{y}^{(i)}, y^{(i)}) + R \\ &= \frac{1}{m} \sum_{i=1}^{m} \mathcal{L}(\hat{y}^{(i)}, y^{(i)}) + \lambda\Omega(\theta). \end{aligned} \tag{4.2}$$

Machine learning practitioners widely apply this type of regularisation. In the context of linear regression models, it is known as *ridge* or *Tikhonov* regression when using the L_2 norm (Tikhonov, 1943; Phillips, 1962), and as *lasso* regression when applying the L_1 norm (Santosa and Symes, 1986; Tibshirani, 1996).

Generally, practitioners apply this form of regularisation only to network weights and not to bias parameters (Goodfellow et al., 2016, p. 222), although deep learning frameworks enable regularisation of the bias vector if desired. The bias directly contributes to only a single layer, whereas weights multiply the results of previous layers. Thus, weights have a more pervasive impact than bias and benefit significantly more from regularisation. Often, practitioners use the same multiplier, λ, for all layers, but programming frameworks can specify this on a per-layer basis if necessary. The practice of weight decay in neural networks, with benefits recognised in the 1980s and early 1990s, has a long history (Hinton, 1987; Krogh and Hertz, 1992; Moody, 1992).

4.2.1 L_2 Regularisation

For L_2 regularisation the weight penalty, Ω, is the L_2 norm of the weights,

$$\Omega(\theta) = ||\mathbf{W}||_2 = \sum_i W_i^2. \tag{4.3}$$

The regularisation term can be motivated by considering the case of a linear network, which is linear regression. Recall the definition of learning variance from Equation (3.88). Writing the function $\hat{f}(x^{(i)})$ as a linear function and setting the bias vector to zero gives

$$\hat{f}(x^{(i)}) = \mathbf{W} \cdot x^{(i)}. \tag{4.4}$$

Substituting this into the expression for the variance gives

$$\begin{aligned} \mathbb{E}\left[\left\{\mathbb{E}[\hat{f}(x^{(i)})] - \hat{f}(x^{(i)})\right\}^2\right] &= \frac{1}{t}\sum_{i=1}^{t}\left[\left\{\frac{1}{t}\sum_{j=1}^{t}\mathbf{W}\cdot x^{(j)} - \mathbf{W}\cdot x^{(i)}\right\}^2\right] \\ &= \frac{1}{t}\sum_{i=1}^{t}\left\{\mathbf{W}\cdot\tilde{x}^{(i)}\right\}^2, \end{aligned} \tag{4.5}$$

where

$$\tilde{x}^{(i)} = \frac{1}{t}\sum_{j=1}^{t} x^{(j)} - x^{(i)}. \tag{4.6}$$

We can place an upper bound on the L_2 norm on the right-hand side of Equation (4.5) since

$$||\mathbf{W} \cdot \boldsymbol{x}||_2 \leq ||\mathbf{W}||_2 ||\boldsymbol{x}||_2 \tag{4.7}$$

and hence

$$\mathbb{E}\left[\left\{\mathbb{E}[\hat{f}(\boldsymbol{x}^{(i)})] - \hat{f}(\boldsymbol{x}^{(i)})\right\}^2\right] \leq \frac{1}{t}\sum_{i=1}^{t} ||\mathbf{W}||_2 ||\widetilde{\boldsymbol{x}}^{(i)}||_2. \tag{4.8}$$

So, targeting the L_2 norm of the weights directly through the regularisation term will reduce the variance in the linear case.

L_2 regularisation is the most popular type of weight decay, penalising larger weights more heavily than L_1 regularisation and often outperforming it. The equivalence of L_2 regularisation to other methods can be demonstrated in specific instances. For example, the addition of Gaussian noise to each input demonstrates equivalence to L_2 regularisation (see Aggarwal, 2018, pp. 182–183), as does the technique of *early stopping* (see Section 4.3).

4.2.2 L_1 Regularisation

As might be expected, L_1 regularisation uses the L_1 norm as the regularisation term, and so

$$\Omega(\theta) = ||\mathbf{W}||_1 = \sum_i |W_i|. \tag{4.9}$$

The SGD weight update equation is then given by

$$W_{i,t+1} = W_{i,t} - \alpha \nabla_{W_i} J_{W_i} - \alpha\lambda \cdot sgn(W_i), \tag{4.10}$$

where *sgn* is the signum function. Of course, this is not well defined when $W_i = 0$ but in general, that is not a problem as the weights are initialised to non-zero values, and floating-point operations will then likely guarantee that the weights are never exactly zero (Aggarwal, 2018, p. 184).

L_1 regularisation exhibits different behaviour from L_2 regularisation because the penalty's gradient is not linear in W_i but a constant instead. With weights initialised to small random values, weight decay regularisation acts to confine them within a specific region of the origin, $||\mathbf{W}||_p \leq B$, where the shape of this region depends on the applied regularisation type (Murphy, 2012, pp. 432–433). In two dimensions, this region forms a diamond for L_1 regularisation, intersecting the axes at $(0, B)$, $(B, 0)$, $(0, -B)$ and $(-B, 0)$, while for L_2 regularisation it shapes into a circle with radius B. The optimal solution, constrained by the region, aligns with the loss function J's minimum value intersecting the region's edge. Unlike L_2, L_1 regularisation often finds the minimum near the axes, where the diamond-shaped region's points are furthest from the origin, as illustrated in Figure 4.1. Therefore, L_1 regularisation tends to push one or more weights close to zero, preferring sparse solutions. This characteristic is beneficial in linear regression for feature selection.

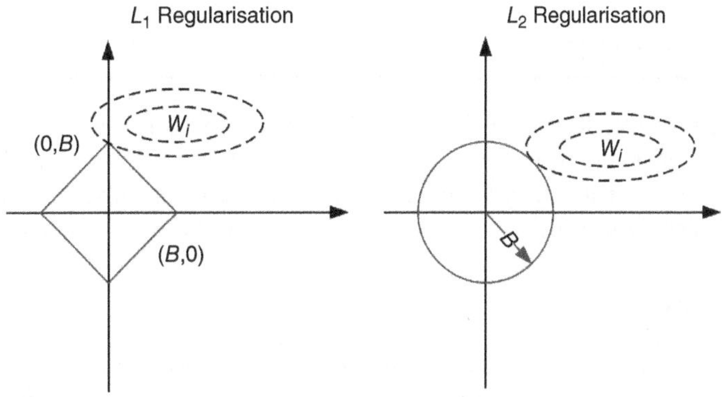

FIGURE 4.1 The action of L_1 and L_2 regularisation on parameter values is to constrain them to a region near the origin with the region's shape dictated by the form of the norm that is applied.

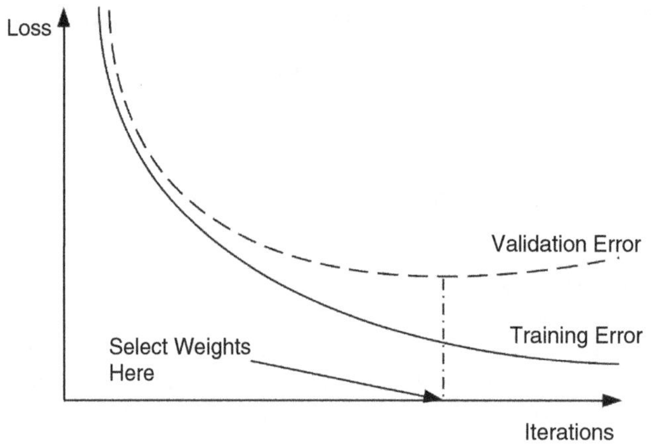

FIGURE 4.2 Early stopping: select the model at the point of lowest validation error.

4.3 EARLY STOPPING

Early stopping is the most straightforward available regularisation technique as it simply stops training when the selected validation metric is at its lowest, as illustrated in Figure 4.2. The parameters for the current lowest point would be stored until enough iterations proceeded to guarantee that this was the lowest error by training past it to obtain the true point of the lowest validation error. However, in practice, one could also monitor for the point at which the validation error began to increase and use the parameters associated with that point instead. The method could be viewed as a very efficient hyperparameter selection method, with the hyperparameter being the optimal number of training iterations (Goodfellow et al., 2016, p. 240).

To see the action of early stopping, consider the behaviour of SGD from the initial weight values W_0 until early stopping at time τ,

$$W_\tau = W_0 - \alpha \sum_{t=1}^{\tau-1} \nabla J(W_t). \tag{4.11}$$

Denoting the maximum gradient by $\nabla J_{\max}$, the maximum change in the weights is given by

$$|W_t - W_0| \leq \alpha(\tau - 1)\nabla J_{\max}, \tag{4.12}$$

and so the weights are constrained to stay within a limited distance of the origin, like *weight decay* (Bishop, 2006; Khapra, 2019). It can further be shown that with a quadratic approximation of the loss function in the vicinity of the optimal weight vector, early stopping behaves like L_2 regularisation (Goodfellow et al., 2016, pp. 242–245).

4.4 ENSEMBLE METHODS AND DROPOUT

Ensemble methods combine multiple learned models to increase the performance of machine learning algorithms and reduce generalisation errors. There are several such algorithms, many situated in a Bayesian framework. In the context of neural networks, one method stands out, *dropout*, and this can be seen as a development of *bootstrap aggregation (bagging)*. In this section, I present an overview before moving on to discuss dropout.

4.4.1 Bootstrap Aggregating (Bagging)

It is possible to train n different models to solve the same problem. If there is a regression problem, then the output of the models could be averaged to give a final result, and for classifier problems, the models could be polled to give a majority verdict. Formally, suppose we have n regression models $y_i = f(x)$, then the final predicted value can be obtained by averaging (Bishop, 2006; Goodfellow et al., 2016),

$$\bar{y} = \frac{1}{n}\sum_{i=1}^{n} y_i. \tag{4.13}$$

Assume that each model can be written in terms of the true value $h(x)$ and an error ϵ_i,

$$y_i = h(x) + \epsilon_i. \tag{4.14}$$

Further assume that the errors are drawn from the multivariate normal distribution with zero mean, $\mathbb{E}[\epsilon_i] = 0$, and covariance $\mathbb{E}[\epsilon_i\epsilon_j] = \sigma_i j$. The mean squared error is then given by

$$\begin{aligned} MSE &= \mathbb{E}\left[\left(\frac{1}{n}\sum_{i=1}^{n}\epsilon_i\right)^2\right] \\ &= \frac{1}{n^2}\mathbb{E}\left[\sum_{i=1}^{n}\sum_{j=1}^{n}\epsilon_i\epsilon_j\right] \\ &= \frac{1}{n^2}\sum_{i=1}^{n}\sum_{j=1}^{n}\sigma_{ij}. \end{aligned} \tag{4.15}$$

Assume that all the errors have the same variance v and all covariances are given by $\sigma = v^2\rho$, then we have

$$MSE = \frac{v^2}{n} + \frac{(n-1)v^2\rho}{n}. \tag{4.16}$$

So

$$\rho = 1 \quad MSE = v^2, \tag{4.17}$$

$$\rho = 0 \quad MSE = \frac{v^2}{n}. \tag{4.18}$$

The error of the ensemble is no worse than that of the individual models and will be significantly better if the errors are uncorrelated.

How should the n models be trained? The models will need to be trained using different datasets, and given that there is typically only one finite-sized dataset available, the n individual training sets will need to be obtained by sampling. There are two possibilities: sampling with replacement and sampling without replacement (Aggarwal, 2018, pp. 186–187). Sampling with replacement, yielding true *bagging*, involves taking a sample of size s from the original m training examples, drawing on the complete set of m examples each time. Sample size s must be less than or equal to m, but often m samples are used. These samples will include some duplicates, and some examples will be missing from each sampled training set. Sampling without replacement gives *subsampling* and essentially divides the original training set into n parts and then uses the subtraining sets to train each model. The variance of either approach will be lower than that of a single model trained using the entire dataset. However, this comes at the cost of training multiple models, although each of the n models can be trained in parallel.

4.4.2 Dropout

Dropout (Hinton et al., 2012; Srivastava et al., 2014), recognised as a potent regularisation technique, acts as a form of bagging while being computationally efficient and convenient (Goodfellow et al., 2016, pp. 251–252). During training with dropout, models temporarily eliminate nodes from the network for a single mini-batch. Each input and hidden unit in a given mini-batch has a defined probability of exclusion from the network. When a node gets dropped out, its output switches to zero, severing all its outgoing connections. Figure 4.3 depicts a fully connected network showcasing three dropout configurations. This procedure generates a collection of 'thinned' networks that share weights, where a network with n nodes presents 2^n potential thinned configurations. Out of these numerous possible networks, only a minuscule fraction undergo training, and even then, for only a single

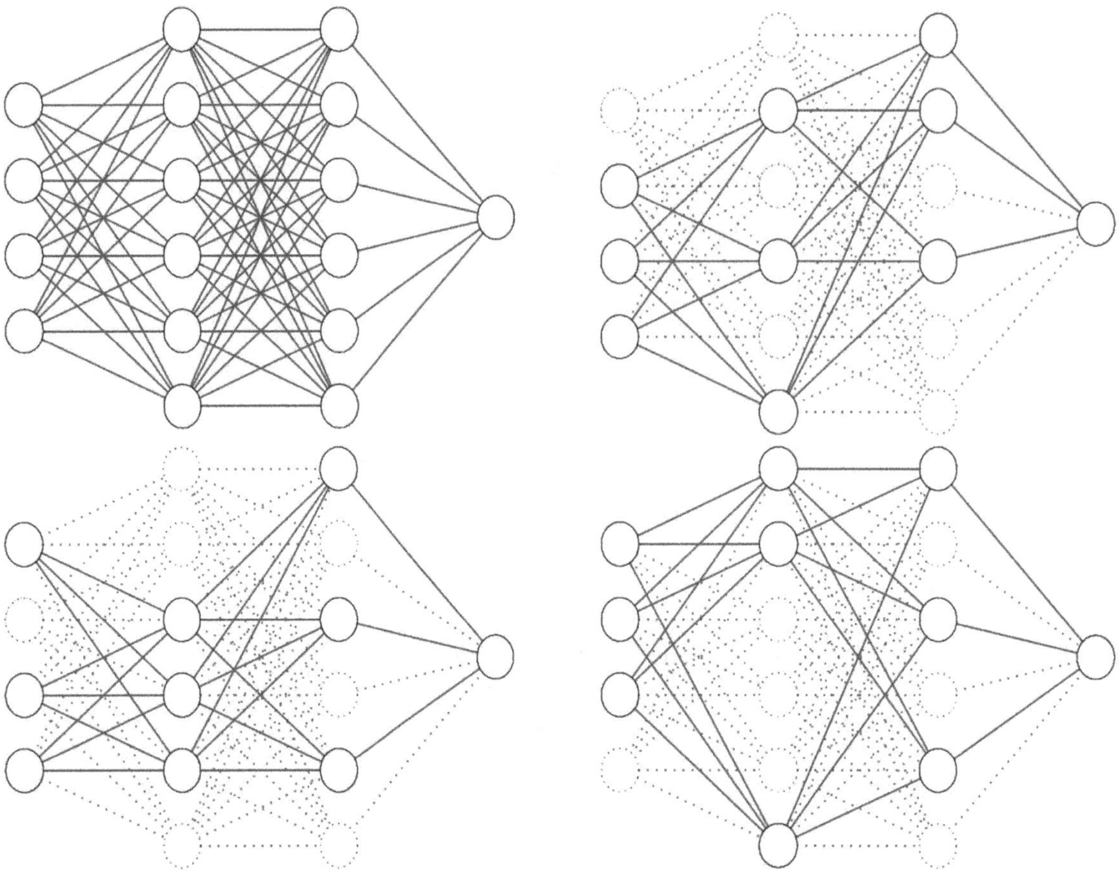

FIGURE 4.3 Dropout on a neural network with two hidden layers of six nodes. The full network is illustrated in the top left, and the three remaining networks show the impact of different dropout configurations in which one input node is dropped out along with three each from the two hidden layers.

mini-batch. While it is impractical to formally enumerate and average each subnetwork during the inference and testing phase, a straightforward weighting strategy is applied. The network's output weights are multiplied by the dropout probability to achieve the averaging effect.

Formally, the equations of a simple feedforward network are replaced by the following:

$$r^{[l]} \sim \text{Bernoulli}(p), \tag{4.19}$$

$$\tilde{a}^{[l]} = r^{[l]} \odot a^{[l]}, \tag{4.20}$$

$$Z^{[l+1]} = W^{[l]}\tilde{a}^{[l]} + b^{[l]}, \tag{4.21}$$

$$a^{[l]} = g(Z^{[l+1]}). \tag{4.22}$$

The vector r is drawn from the Bernoulli distribution, which generates 1 with probability p and is a random binary vector. This vector then masks off the previous layer's output, and the remaining equations are unchanged. Backpropagation is also unchanged, although the binary vector will mask off the gradient contributions to the previous layer.

Dropout can be applied to nearly all network types, including CNNs, RNNs, restricted Boltzmann and deep Boltzmann machines. Notwithstanding the explanation of dropout as generating exponentially many bagged subnetworks, it can also be understood through its effect on neural network nodes. Srivastava et al. (2014) suggest that dropout prevents *co-adaptation* by groups of nodes within the network; in standard networks, errors in some nodes are compensated for by other neighbouring nodes. These co-adaptations are specific to the training set and do not generalise. With dropout, there is no guarantee that a specific node will be present in any given mini-batch; hence, co-adaptations are challenging to form.

The effect on features was further explored by Srivastava et al. (2014) by examining the intermediate feature maps generated when training a CNN with MNIST.[1] Hidden layers trained using dropout showed significantly clearer feature detection than layers trained without, suggesting that co-adaptation was not present with dropout.

Analysis of networks trained with dropout reveals significantly higher sparsity than those without, echoing the behaviour seen with L_1 regularisation. Like observations in Sobolev training from Section 3.9, dropout does not benefit small training sets, indicating potential model overfitting to the training data even with dropout applied. Conversely, intermediate and larger datasets exhibit advantages from dropout, though, for MNIST, the benefits decrease as the fraction of the full dataset used increases (Srivastava et al., 2014). Srivastava et al. (2014) identified the optimal dropout probabilities as $p = 0.2$ for input nodes and $p = 0.5$ for hidden nodes. While dropout on the input layer is less common, a default probability of 0.5 for hidden layers has become standard. Treating p as a hyperparameter allows for its optimisation through hyperparameter tuning.

There is a computational cost associated with dropout, although it is relatively small. Dropout networks do take longer to train than networks without dropout layers but with the benefit of lower generalisation errors. Hence, as with most neural network training techniques, there is a trade-off between computational cost and error.

4.4.2.1 Gaussian Dropout Dropout strongly resembles the additional stochastic noise noted above in the context of L_2 regularisation, and this can be made explicit by swapping the Bernoulli distribution for the multivariate Gaussian distribution. The equations describing a feedforward network become

$$r^{[l]} \sim \mathcal{N}(1, \sigma^2), \tag{4.23}$$

$$\widetilde{a}^{[l]} = r^{[l]} \odot a^{[l]}, \tag{4.24}$$

$$Z^{[l+1]} = W^{[l]}\widetilde{a}^{[l]} + b^{[l]}, \tag{4.25}$$

$$a^{[l]} = g(Z^{[l+1]}). \tag{4.26}$$

Given that the expected value does not change in this case, no further scaling of values is required during the inference and testing phase. Srivastava et al. (2014) showed that Bernoulli dropout and *Gaussian dropout* performed equally well on MNIST and CIFAR-10 datasets.

Note that while this approach is still called *dropout*, neurons are no longer dropping out of use entirely. Instead, their output is scaled by a random variable drawn from a Gaussian distribution centred on 1.0, and this is just adding random noise to the layers of the network.

EXAMPLE 4.1: TAIWANESE CREDIT CARD DEFAULT WITH REGULARISATION

As an example of applying different regularisation techniques, consider the Taiwanese credit card default dataset that has been used for examples in Chapter 3 (see the Jupyter Notebook `Taiwan Credit Classifier Regularization.ipynb`). This dataset is relatively small, so overfitting is a risk. This case study uses a model that will overfit to illustrate different regularisation techniques and show the impact. So, the base model is a neural network with five layers of 100 nodes, much larger than the small network with two layers of 50 nodes used previously in Example 3.4. The behaviour of this base case can be seen alongside the regularisation cases in Figure 4.4. The model peaks at a validation accuracy of around 69% after about 20 epochs before falling back to around 64% after 200 epochs. The base model starts to overfit, and generalisation starts to worsen.

(Continued)

[1]Note that it is possible to visualise the features that the hidden layers of CNNs detect, and this will be covered in Chapter 6.

(*Continued*)

In PyTorch, L_2 regularisation is added as an option in the optimiser as seen here, with the `weight decay` set to a non-zero value.

```
l2_optimizer = optim.Adam(l2_model.parameters(), lr=0.001,
                          weight_decay=0.01)
```

L_1 regularisation has to be implemented inside the training loop by summing the absolute value of the model weights only, with bias parameters excluded. Here, the L_1 term is weighted with 0.001, smaller than the 0.01 used with L_2 regularisation.

```
def l1_regularizer(model):
    lossl1 = 0
    for model_param_name, model_param_value in \
        model.named_parameters():
        if model_param_name.endswith('weight'):
            lossl1 +=  torch.norm(model_param_value, 1)
            return lossl1
```

When using PyTorch, the appropriate dropout function must be used after each dense layer. For standard dropout, this is `F.dropout`; for Gaussian dropout, it is `F.dropout2d`, and both take the probability as an argument. Hence, the dropout network is constructed using the following class:

```
class BinaryClassifier(nn.Module):
    def __init__(self, input_size, dropout_type=None,
                 dropout_rate=0.5):
        super(BinaryClassifier, self).__init__()
        self.fc1 = nn.Linear(input_size, 100)
        self.fc2 = nn.Linear(100, 100)
        self.fc3 = nn.Linear(100, 100)
        self.fc4 = nn.Linear(100, 100)
        self.fc5 = nn.Linear(100, 100)
        self.output_layer = nn.Linear(100, 1)
        self.relu = nn.ReLU()
         self.dropout_type = dropout_type
        self.dropout_rate = dropout_rate
        self.output_activation = nn.Sigmoid()

    def forward(self, x):
        x = self.fc1(x)
        x = self.relu(x)
        x = self._apply_dropout(x)
        x = self.fc2(x)
        x = self.relu(x)
        x = self._apply_dropout(x)
        x = self.fc3(x)
        x = self.relu(x)
        x = self._apply_dropout(x)
        x = self.fc4(x)
```

```
        x = self.relu(x)
        x = self._apply_dropout(x)
        x = self.fc5(x)
        x = self.relu(x)
        x = self._apply_dropout(x)
        x = self.output_layer(x)
        x = self.output_activation(x)
        return x

    def _apply_dropout(self, x):
        if self.dropout_type == 'standard':
            return F.dropout(x, self.dropout_rate,
                             training=self.training)
        elif self.dropout_type == 'gaussian':
            return F.dropout2d(x, self.dropout_rate,
              training=self.training) if self.training else x
        return x
```

In PyTorch, early stopping can be implemented in the training loop, as illustrated in this code fragment. Training is stopped if the `early_stopping_patience` is supplied and there is no improvement during the patience period.

```
# Early Stopping
if early_stopping_patience is not None:
    if test_loss < best_test_loss:
        best_test_loss = test_loss
        epochs_no_improve = 0
    else:
        epochs_no_improve += 1
        if epochs_no_improve == early_stopping_patience:
            print(f"Early stopping triggered after {epoch + 1} epochs.")
            break
```

Returning to Figure 4.4, all of the regularisation methods performed equally well, reaching 69.5% accuracy and remaining stable, with the dropout methods performing marginally better than L_1 and L_2. Early stopping stops after 13 epochs with an accuracy of 69%, achieving a similar accuracy to the other methods but for less computational cost. The small model from earlier examples is also included in the figure and shows very similar results to the regularised cases, and this raises the question of whether it is better to use a smaller unregularised model or a larger regularised one. This will be discussed further in Section 4.7.

(*Continued*)

(*Continued*)

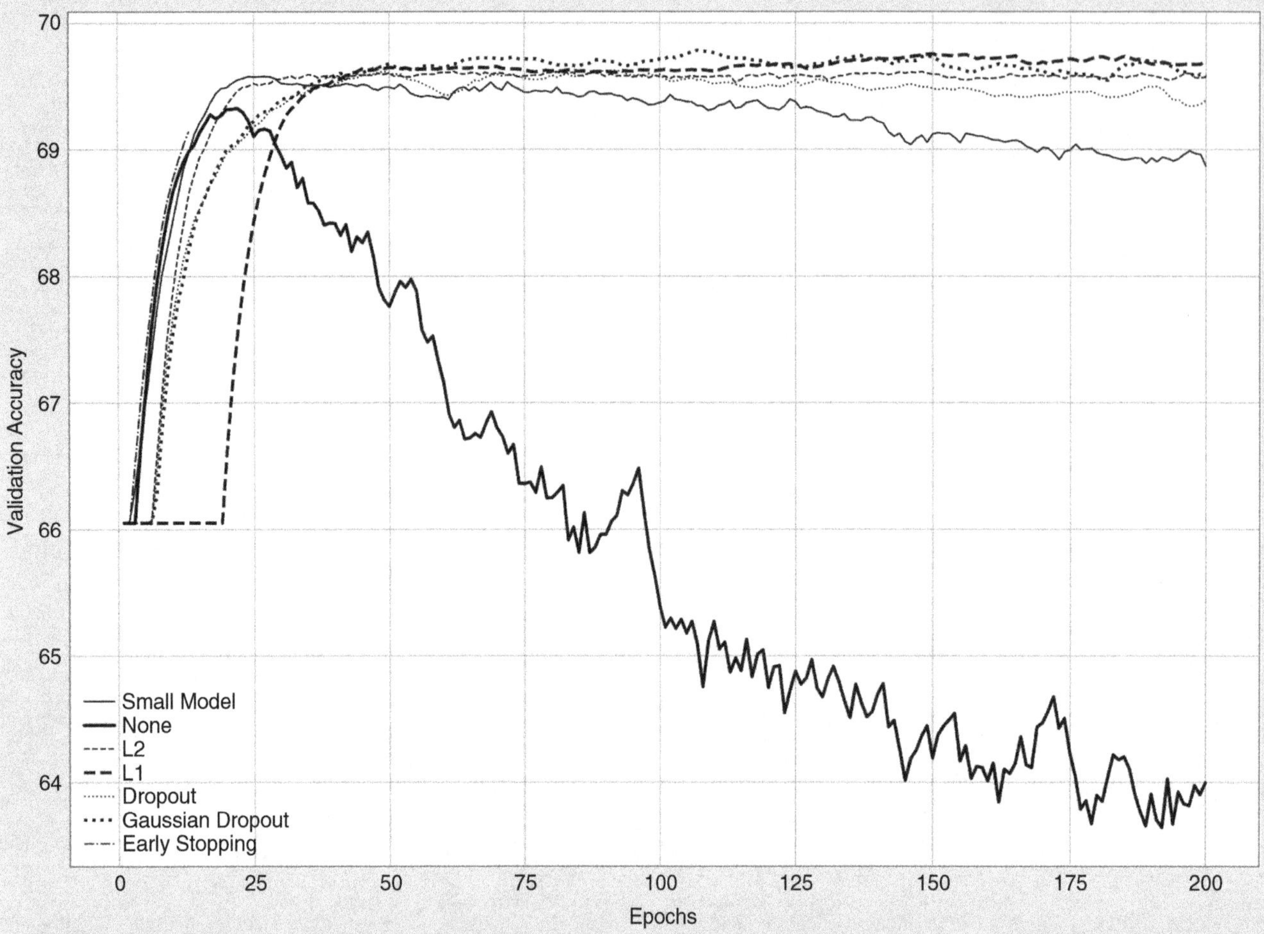

FIGURE 4.4 Smoothed validation accuracy for the Taiwanese credit card default classifier models trained with no regularisation, L_1, L_2, dropout, Gaussian dropout and early stopping. The results from the original model with 2×50 neurons are also shown. All five regularisation techniques perform equally well in this call, although early stopping is much more computationally efficient. The small model from earlier experiments is also included on the chart and shows results similar to those of regularised cases.

4.5 DATA AUGMENTATION

Data augmentation enhances regularisation by enriching the training dataset and adding extra examples derived from the current ones. Although theoretically general, data augmentation is domain-specific, finding substantial success, particularly in image-related machine learning problems. The technique involves modifying training examples through standard transformations like rotation, shear and zoom for images. Considering the predominant application of data augmentation is in imaging, and standard tools cater specifically to this, further elaboration will occur in Chapter 6. It is also worth noting that generative models, such as GANs, can create additional training data, a topic that Chapter 9 will explore.

4.6 OTHER REGULARISATION METHODS

4.6.1 Batch Normalisation as Regularisation

Batch normalisation was introduced in Section 3.7, and its regularisation properties have already been noted. Several authors have either conjectured that batch normalisation acts as a regulariser or noted empirical evidence. Ioffe and Szegedy (2015) suggested that batch normalisation acts as an implicit regulariser. At the same time, Szegedy et al. (2016), in work on the Inception CNN, suggested that the better performance observed with either dropout or batch normalisation suggests that the latter also acts as a regularisation technique. Empirical evidence for regularisation behaviour from batch normalisation has been provided by Zhang et al. (2016), Gitman and Ginsburg (2017) and others.

Luo et al. (2018) explored the regularisation behaviour of batch normalisation theoretically. Their key result was to decompose batch normalisation into two effects: population normalisation and a regularising effect they call 'gamma decay'. They note that the batch mean discourages reliance on a single node and that the batch standard deviation reduces the kurtosis of the input distribution and the correlation between nodes. Luo et al. (2018) further demonstrated that gamma decay allows the network to converge with a significant maximum learning rate compared to a network trained without batch normalisation. The authors further demonstrated that batch normalisation gives better generalisation than vanilla SGD or weight normalisation.

In summary, batch normalisation is a regulariser, behaving similarly to dropout and adding random noise to weights.

4.6.2 Multitask Learning

Multitask learning (Caruana, 1997) is another way to improve model generalisation. The idea here is that a network that is constructed to output multiple related values from the same input data will perform better than multiple networks trained on the same data but with a single output, and this makes sense as the multitask model will be forced to learn more general representations that suit multiple tasks. Baxter (1995) proves that a model with n tasks requires $O(a + b/n)$ examples per task to ensure good generalisation, where a and b are constants. Hence, multitask models require fewer examples to generalise well. Of course, this can only hold if there is a meaningful statistical relationship between the tasks (Goodfellow et al., 2016, p. 239).

We can also relate multitask learning to Sobolev training, as discussed in Section 3.9. As noted there, Sobolev training appears to be a regularisation term, albeit unbiased. We can argue that Sobolev training is a regulariser because it forces the network to perform multitask learning.

EXAMPLE 4.2: MULTITASK LEARNING WITH BLACK–SCHOLES

Multitask learning is straightforward to demonstrate with Black–Scholes (see the Jupyter Notebook `Black Scholes Multi-output.ipynb`). In this example, the performance of two networks trained to produce put and call option values individually is compared with that of a network trained to produce put and call values simultaneously for a given set of inputs. The network architecture for the three models is essentially the same, with two hidden layers of 200 nodes, with the call and put networks having a single linear output and the multitask network having two linear outputs for both call and put values. In this case, all models have three inputs: volatility, spot value and maturity. All models were trained through 50 epochs with a mini-batch size of 1024. After training the three models, the performance was evaluated against the test set, and the results are given in Table 4.1. In this case, multitask learning has not provided a benefit.

(*Continued*)

(*Continued*)

TABLE 4.1 Test MSE for Neural Networks That Learn to Put and Call Values Separately and Together Through Multitask Learning

Model	Test MSE
Call	0.0252
Put	0.0109
Multi: Call	0.0278
Multi: Put	0.0312

4.7 CONCLUSIONS: REGULARISATION STRATEGY

The critical question is: What is the best strategy for regularisation? In the Taiwanese credit card example (Example 4.1), the result of the large regularised networks was very similar to a much smaller network without regularisation. Is regularisation worth the extra computational cost of the larger network? Theoretically, a larger network with regularisation can better generalise as the neurons in the network will be less individually specialised. The best strategy, in general, is to use larger networks with regularisation. However, there are cases where the larger network may require too much storage for the desired application or where only limited training time is available. A more pragmatic approach with a smaller network or early stopping might be better. Ultimately, the choice of regularisation strategy is best guided by empirical results and the nature of the model being trained.

CHAPTER 5

Hyperparameter Optimisation

The concept of waiting bewilders me. There are always deadlines. There are always ticking clocks. That is why you must manage your time.

Mr. Robot, Mr. Robot created by Sam Esmail (2018)

5.1 INTRODUCTION

Hyperparameter optimisation (HPO) or tuning is critical to building machine learning models. However, unlike the weights and biases of a neural network, hyperparameters cannot be learned using gradient-based algorithms. Hyperparameters are usually specified exogenously to the machine learning algorithm, as discussed in Chapters 2 and 3. Many hyperparameters are associated with deep learning, and subsequent chapters will introduce many more. They can take many forms; for example, discrete parameters define the architecture of a neural network, the number of layers and the number of nodes per layer; the learning rate is real-valued and categorical variables define the choice of activation functions or the selection of regularisation techniques. Some choices lead to additional hyperparameters, such as momentum.

HPO as a formal element within machine learning dates back to at least the early 1990s (Feurer and Hutter, 2019; Yu and Zhu, 2020). Generally, HPO is the first stage of model design and training, which operates before finalising the model. What is the purpose of HPO? Feurer and Hutter (2019) suggest three key use cases:

1. Reduce the human effort, particularly of AI/ML experts.
2. Improve the performance of ML algorithms.
3. Improve the reproducibility of scientific studies using ML.

As the complexity of neural network models increases, and with the availability of many architecture and training algorithm choices, there is an increasing need for HPO. State-of-the-art computer vision and natural language processing models are now vast and expensive to train. Hence, it is crucial to identify the optimal choice of hyperparameters, but the large number of them makes HPO a computationally expensive problem. Not all models are large; however, with neural networks also targeted at consumer devices such as smartphones or embedded systems, size and computational cost constraints play a role. HPO is also needed to ensure that the model is suited to the final environment to which it is targeted.

Automated machine learning is a technology designed to apply machine learning in a way that is automated, objective and driven by data (Hutter et al., 2019, p. 8). The aim is to make machine learning accessible to other scientific disciplines without expert knowledge. As such, HPO is a critical component of auto ML.

Deep Learning in Quantitative Finance, First Edition. Andrew Green.

Feurer and Hutter (2019) identify four reasons why HPO is a difficult problem to solve in practice:

1. Evaluating the 'objective' function can be computationally expensive if the model and dataset are large or if the machine learning pipeline is complex.
2. The space of hyperparameter configurations is complex and high dimensional, containing continuous, categorical and conditional parameters.
3. Normally, HPO cannot be performed using gradient-based optimisation techniques as the gradient is either unavailable or undefined.
4. Optimisation for generalisation performance is impossible due to the limited size of training sets.

The HPO problem can be defined as follows (Feurer and Hutter, 2019, p. 16). Given a machine learning algorithm $\mathcal{A}$ with N hyperparameters, each parameter n has a domain Λ_n. The *hyperparameter configuration space* is then defined by

$$\Lambda = \Lambda_1 \times \Lambda_2 \times \cdots \times \Lambda_n. \tag{5.1}$$

A particular selection of hyperparameters is denoted by $\lambda \in \Lambda$. Let D_t be the training set and D_v be the validation set. The HPO problem is defined by

$$\lambda^* = \underset{\lambda \in \Lambda}{\text{argmin}}\, \mathbb{E}_{D_t, D_v} J(\mathcal{A}_\lambda, D_t, D_v), \tag{5.2}$$

where J is the loss function for the model with the given set of hyperparameters. This can be written in terms of the *hyperparameter response function* $\Psi(\lambda)$ (Bergstra and Bengio, 2012),

$$\lambda^* \equiv \underset{\lambda \in \Lambda}{\text{argmin}}\, \Psi(\lambda). \tag{5.3}$$

In general, little is known about the form of $\Psi(\lambda)$ and the most appropriate approach to the optimisation problem is to find the minimum over a set of trial points S,

$$\lambda^* \approx \underset{\lambda \in \{\lambda^{(1)}, \ldots, \lambda^{(S)}\}}{\text{argmin}}\, \Psi(\lambda). \tag{5.4}$$

Hence, the HPO problem is reduced to choosing the most efficient sample points given a particular computational budget.

One key empirical observation about the hyperparameter response function is its low effective dimension. Bergstra and Bengio (2012) tested a problem with seven hyperparameters and concluded that the effective dimensionality was in the range of one to four. One difficulty is that different datasets and problems respond differently to the same set of hyperparameters, so one problem may be susceptible to a particular parameter while another may not. In general, it is impossible to determine which are the most important hyperparameters a priori. Hence, taking advantage of the low effective dimension through deliberate experimental design is challenging.

5.1.1 Types of Hyperparameter

We can categorise hyperparameters into two broad types: training hyperparameters that control the learning process and model design hyperparameters that govern the structure of the neural network.

5.1.1.1 Training Hyperparameters Training hyperparameters concern the training of neural networks and, fundamentally, the speed at which training occurs. The learning rate is the most critical training parameter of central concern to all stochastic gradient descent methods. Choosing an appropriate learning rate is essential to efficient training; training will proceed too slowly if it is too small, and if it is too large, the model may fail to converge. Of course, in many situations the learning rate will not be a single number but rather involve one of the types of learning rate decay described in Section 3.5.1.1.

Moving beyond stochastic gradient descent brings additional hyperparameters into play, and these are examples of conditional hyperparameters. Momentum and Nesterov momentum require *gamma* to be specified, while optimisers based on adaptive learning rates require a variety of optimiser-specific parameters to be specified.

Other training hyperparameters include the size of the mini-batch, the choice of weight initialisation scheme (§3.3), the choice of loss function (§3.4) and the use of techniques like batch normalisation (§3.7).

5.1.1.2 Model Design Hyperparameters

Model design hyperparameters govern the structure of the neural network and, hence, its fundamental learning capacity. Regularisation techniques come in two forms: adjustments to the loss function, which appear to be training-related, and changes to the network structure, such as dropout layers, which relate to the network's architecture. Regularisation affects how well a neural network model can generalise, so regularisation-related parameters belong to model design hyperparameters.

For a feedforward network, the number of layers and the size of those layers are key hyperparameters. Heaton (2017) provides some 'rules of thumb' on the number of neurons, w, per layer:

1. $w_{\text{input}} < w < w_{\text{output}}$.
2. $w = \frac{2}{3}w_{\text{input}} + w_{\text{output}}$.
3. $w < 2w_{\text{input}}$.

In general, however, the choice of network structure is much more complex. In CNNs, convolutional and pooling layers are used with additional parameters such as the stride and filter size, while RNNs use specialised units such as LTSM and GRU. Many advanced network structures use blocks constructed from simpler units. Hence, determining the optimal architecture may involve more than simply determining the number and size of layers.

The choice of the activation function (§2.3) is also a significant element in network design, but in recent years the default choice for hidden layers has been ReLU, with the output layer determined by the type of problem. However, as discussed earlier, other choices are available and may be required if there is a need for second-order sensitivities.

In Chapter 4, regularisation techniques were discussed at length. The choice of regularisation techniques forms one hyperparameter choice, and then different techniques have their conditional hyperparameters. Data augmentation for images, for example, has multiple parameters that govern the range of transformations applied to the existing dataset to generate new examples.

5.1.2 Types of HPO

Two broad types of HPO technique can be identified: *(parallel) search* algorithms and *sequential* optimisation (Jaderberg et al., 2017). Parallel search algorithms run many sets of hyperparameters and train networks associated with them in parallel. They find the best set of hyperparameters from the examples sampled from the distribution. They do not learn during this process, and no information gained from earlier examples is used to inform later choices of hyperparameters. Examples of parallel search include *grid search*, *random search*, *successive halving*, *hyperband* and *asynchronous successive halving*. The archetypal sequential optimisation algorithm is *Bayesian optimisation*, which uses all the results of all prior training runs to guide the selection of future ones via a probabilistic model. The problem with such methods is that they are inherently sequential and cannot take advantage of compute clusters. A final class of HPO techniques use a hybrid between parallel search and sequential optimisation, and examples of this type of algorithm include *BOHB* and *population-based training*.

5.2 MANUAL

The simplest form of HPO is manual search. Goodfellow et al. (2016) suggest that the goal of manual hyperparameter tuning is to find the lowest generalisation error subject to a runtime and memory budget and that to do this requires the model developer to understand the relationship between hyperparameters, training error, generalisation error and computational resources. Hence, manual search depends heavily on the knowledge and experience of the model developer, and this might be a viable strategy when working on problems similar to those with existing solutions. However, suppose there is limited access to deep learning expertise. Some automated search is appropriate, although expert knowledge can influence the search domain. Of course, manual search does afford insight into the problem to the researcher (Bergstra and Bengio, 2012).

5.3 GRID SEARCH

Grid search represents the most straightforward method for automated HPO. The method involves selecting a set of evaluation points for each hyperparameter. Then, for a fixed number of epochs, the model undergoes training at each point within the hypercube defined by the hyperparameter configuration space. This technique can handle binary and categorical variables as discrete points along an axis. Although real-valued parameters can be searched on a linear scale, a log scale often proves more effective. Earlier, in Section 3.5.1.1 and the associated Example 3.6, selecting the best learning rate demonstrated this approach. However, setting the bounds for the search range and determining the appropriate step size still require expert knowledge.

Additionally, one can employ adaptive grid refinement starting with a coarse grid to pinpoint the most promising search areas, which can then be refined using a denser grid of search points. Grid search suffers from the *curse of dimensionality* like all grid methods, meaning the computational cost escalates exponentially with the number of hyperparameters and remains practical only for configurations involving three or fewer parameters (Goodfellow et al., 2016, pp. 420–422). Nevertheless, the independence of all search points allows for the parallelisation of the grid search, which helps mitigate the computational cost.

Bergstra and Bengio (2012) found that grid search performed poorly compared to random and manually guided searches. They concluded that the low effective dimensionality coupled with the difficulty in determining which dimensions were important were the primary explanations for this. In grid search, many trials are wasted on dimensions that are not sensitive to the problem.

EXAMPLE 5.1: BASKET OPTION GRID SEARCH

Consider running a grid search for the hyperparameters of the basket option neural network model considered in earlier chapters (this example can be found in the Jupyter Notebook `Hyperparameter Optimization - Grid Search.ipynb`). The `Optuna` Python package (Akiba et al., 2019) provides several HPO algorithms, including the grid search used here.

The basket option data is loaded and prepared as in previous examples. A class is defined to build the feedforward network, where the number of layers and the number of neurons per layer can be specified.

```
class FeedForward(nn.Module):
    def __init__(self, no_layers=1, no_neurons=1, input_shape=28):
        super(FeedForward, self).__init__()
        self.layers = nn.ModuleList()
        prev_size = input_shape
        size = no_neurons
        for _ in range(no_layers):
            self.layers.append(nn.Linear(prev_size, size))
            prev_size = size
        self.output_layer = nn.Linear(prev_size, 1)

    def forward(self, x):
        for layer in self.layers:
            x = F.relu(layer(x))
            x = self.output_layer(x)
        return x
```

The model is created and trained for trial using the following function:

```
def create_optimizer(name, learning_rate, parameters):
    if name == 'Adam':
        opt = Adam(parameters, lr=learning_rate)
```

```
    elif name == 'RMSprop':
        opt = RMSprop(parameters, lr=learning_rate)
    else:
        opt = Adagrad(parameters, lr=learning_rate)
    return opt

def objective(trial):
    no_layers = trial.suggest_int('no_layers', 1, 6)
    layer_width = trial.suggest_int('hidden_size', 32, 512, step=32)
    optimizer_name = trial.suggest_categorical('optimizer',
                         ['Adam', 'RMSprop', 'AdaGrad'])
    lr = trial.suggest_float('lr', 1e-4, 1e-2, log=True)
    print(f"no_layers: {no_layers}, layer_width: {layer_width},  \
           optimizer_name: {optimizer_name}, lr: {lr}")
    model = FeedForward(no_layers, layer_width).to(device)
    optimizer = create_optimizer(optimizer_name, lr, model.parameters())
    loss_fn = nn.MSELoss()
    history = train_model(model, train_loader, val_loader, loss_fn,
                          optimiser, no_epochs)
    return history['test_loss'][-1]
```

where the `train_model` function is the same as in previous examples.

The hyperparameters are entered as lists in a dictionary with names equal to those used in the `trial.suggest_` functions in the objective function.

```
param_grid = {
'lr': [1e-4, 1e-3, 1e-2],
'optimiser': ['Adam', 'RMSprop', 'AdaGrad'],
'no_layers': [1, 3, 5],
'hidden_size': [16, 64, 256]
}
```

The *Optuna* study is configured and run as follows:

```
study = optuna.create_study(sampler=optuna.samplers.GridSampler(param_grid))
study.optimize(objective, n_trials=3*3*3*3)
```

The lowest loss after 30 epochs was obtained from a network with five layers, each with 256 neurons per layer and the Adam optimiser with a learning rate of 0.001.

5.4 RANDOM SEARCH

Bergstra and Bengio (2012) introduced random search, which converges to a suitable set of hyperparameters much quicker than grid search. First, each hyperparameter has a marginal distribution assigned. So, for continuous variables, this might be a uniform distribution; for discrete variables, this could be a multinoulli distribution (or Bernoulli if a binary parameter). To generate each sample point, $\lambda^{(i)}$, using the marginal distributions, means drawing either random or pseudo-random numbers for each hyperparameter dimension. Quasi-random number sequences such as Sobol (Sobol, 1967) did not offer a significant advantage over pseudo-random numbers in the study performed by Bergstra and Bengio (2012). However, they perform well in Monte Carlo applications in moderate dimensions.

Quasi-random sequences also have the disadvantage that the generated points are not independent and that if a point is missing because the model training failed, the overall parameter search will suffer.

Bergstra and Bengio (2012) list four advantages of random search:

1. Researchers can stop an experiment at any time.
2. If additional computational resources become available, researchers can schedule additional trials without adjusting a grid.
3. Trials are independent and may run asynchronously and, hence, in parallel.
4. If a trial fails, researchers can abandon it without impacting other trials.

Random search offers significant performance and operational advantages over grid search with minimal added complexity. However, more sophisticated algorithms have superseded it today. These algorithms are supported by hyperparameter frameworks that simplify operations.

EXAMPLE 5.2: BASKET OPTION RANDOM SEARCH

As an example of a random search, the earlier HPO for a basket option can be repeated using the `Optuna` package, and the code can be found in the Jupyter Notebook `Hyperparameter Optimization - Random Search.ipynb`. This is almost identical to the grid search, and the only differences are in the structure of the objective function and the study.

```
def objective(trial):
    no_layers = trial.suggest_int('no_layers', 1, 6)
    layer_width = trial.suggest_int('hidden_size', 32, 512, step=32)
    optimizer_name = trial.suggest_categorical('optimizer',
                          ['Adam', 'RMSprop', 'AdaGrad'])
    lr = trial.suggest_float('lr', 1e-4, 1e-2, log=True)
    model = FeedForward(no_layers, layer_width).to(device)
    optimizer = create_optimizer(optimizer_name, lr, model.parameters())
    loss_fn = nn.MSELoss()
    history = train_model(model, train_loader, val_loader, loss_fn,
    optimizer, no_epochs, trial)
    return history['test_loss'][-1]

study = optuna.create_study(sampler=optuna.samplers.RandomSampler())
```

Three layers with 512 neurons and the Adam optimiser, with a learning rate of 0.008851, gave the lowest loss after 30 epochs.

5.5 BAYESIAN OPTIMISATION

HPO is a type of black-box optimisation problem in which only values are available, and function evaluation is expensive and needs to be minimised (Grosse, 2017). Here, the objective function $f(\theta)$ is the error on the validation set, and θ is a vector of hyperparameters. In such situations, *Bayesian optimisation* can be used to find the set of hyperparameters that minimises the validation error.

Bayesian optimisation constructs a probabilistic model for the objective $f(\theta)$ and then uses this model to decide where next to evaluate the objective (Snoek et al., 2012). Each value obtained then updates the model. Hence, unlike gradient-based techniques or second-order methods that rely on local gradients and Hessians to perform the update, Bayesian optimisation uses all the previous function evaluations. Two main choices are required: the prior distribution of the surrogate model, which in most cases is a Gaussian process, and the *acquisition function*, which is a function of the model posterior and determines where to evaluate the function next.

Bayesian optimisation efficiently finds the minimum of a complex non-convex function, such as the one in HPO problems, with relatively few function evaluations. However, in its basic form, it performs only one function evaluation at a time serially and cannot exploit any parallelism beyond what the evaluation of $f(\theta)$ provides. Snoek et al. (2012) suggest using *Monte Carlo acquisition*, a method for parallelising Bayesian optimisation, which we discuss below. A more effective form of parallelism results from integrating Bayesian optimisation with Bandit-based techniques to create BOHB, as described in Section 5.6.

The steps in the Bayesian HPO process are as follows (Yu and Zhu, 2020, p. 19):

1. Build the prior distribution of the surrogate model.
2. Obtain the hyperparameter vector that performs best on the model.
3. Compute the acquisition function with the current surrogate model.
4. Evaluate the hyperparameter set by calculating the objective function $f(\theta)$.
5. Update the surrogate model.
6. Repeat steps 2–5 until a satisfactory set of hyperparameters is identified.

5.5.1 The Gaussian Process Surrogate Model

Gaussian processes (GPs) are the most common prior distribution for Bayesian optimisation because of their convenience as marginals, and conditionals can be computed in the closed form (Snoek et al., 2012). The Gaussian process can be defined as follows (Rasmussen and Williams, 2006).

Definition 5.1 ***(Gaussian Process)*****:** A GP is a collection of random variables, any finite number with a joint Gaussian distribution.

A GP is specified by a mean function and a covariance function. Given some process $f(x)$, the mean function and covariance function are defined by

$$m(x) = \mathbb{E}[f(x)], \tag{5.5}$$

$$k(x, x') = \mathbb{E}[(f(x) - m(x))(f(x') - m(x'))]. \tag{5.6}$$

The mean function is commonly set to zero, $m(x) = 0$, while the covariance function drives the ability of the GP to express the distribution on functions (Snoek et al., 2012, p. 3). Define the quantity r^2 by the expression

$$r^2(x, x') = \sum_{d=1}^{D} \frac{(x_d - x'_d)^2}{\psi_d^2}, \tag{5.7}$$

where ψ_d are D length-scale hyperparameters of the GP. The default choice of *kernel* for the GP is the *automatic relevance determination (ARD) squared exponential kernel*, which is defined by

$$k_{SE}(x, x') = \psi_0 \exp\left\{-\frac{1}{2} r^2(x, x')\right\}. \tag{5.8}$$

However, the *ARD Matérn 5/2 kernel* is preferred for HPO problems as it is twice differentiable but not unrealistically smooth (Snoek et al., 2012, pp. 3–4), and this is defined by

$$k_{M52}(x, x') = \psi_0 \left(1 + \sqrt{5r^2(x, x')} + \frac{5}{3} r^2(x, x')\right) \exp\left\{-\sqrt{5r^2(x, x')}\right\}. \tag{5.9}$$

In both these expressions, ψ_0 is the covariance amplitude and another hyperparameter of the GP.

The objective function, $f(\theta)$, is assumed to be drawn from a GP prior. The observations of the objective function take the form

$$\{\theta_n, y_n\}_{n=1}^{N}, \tag{5.10}$$

where

$$y_n \sim \mathcal{N}(f(\theta_n), \nu), \tag{5.11}$$

and ν is the observation noise variance and is another GP hyperparameter.

5.5.2 The Acquisition Function

The acquisition function, a, determines the next point to be evaluated via

$$\theta_{N+1} = \underset{\theta}{\operatorname{argmax}}\, a(\theta). \tag{5.12}$$

The most common choice of acquisition function is expected improvement (Snoek et al., 2012; Grosse, 2017), which is defined by

$$a_{EI}(\theta; \{\theta_n, y_n\}, \psi) = \sigma(\theta; \{\theta_n, y_n\}, \psi)(\gamma(\theta)\Phi(\gamma(\theta)) + \mathcal{N}(\gamma(\theta); 0, 1)) \tag{5.13}$$

$$\gamma(\theta) = \frac{f(\theta_{\text{best}}) - \mu(\theta; \{\theta_n, y_n\}, \psi)}{\sigma(\theta; \{\theta_n, y_n\}, \psi)}, \tag{5.14}$$

where ψ is the vector of GP hyperparameters, μ is the predictive mean function and σ^2 is the predictive variance function. A second alternative is the *upper confidence bound* acquisition function, which is given by

$$a_{UCB}(\theta; \{\theta_n, y_n\}, \psi) = \mu(\theta; \{\theta_n, y_n\}, \psi) - \kappa\sigma(\theta; \{\theta_n, y_n\}, \psi), \tag{5.15}$$

where κ is another hyperparameter used to tune the amount of exploitation and exploration.

The GP has its own set of hyperparameters, ψ, that must be set. Bishop (2006) suggests that the simplest approach is to use a point estimate of the parameters obtained by maximising the log-likelihood. However, Snoek et al. (2012) propose marginalising over all the hyperparameters and using an *integrated acquisition function* given by

$$\hat{a}(\theta; \{\theta_n, y_n\}) = \int a(\theta; \{\theta_n, y_n\}, \psi) p\left(\psi | \{\theta_n, y_n\}_{n=1}^{N}\right) d\psi. \tag{5.16}$$

5.5.3 Enhancements for Bayesian Hyperparameter Optimisation

Snoek et al. (2012) suggest two enhancements specifically for Bayesian optimisation of machine learning hyperparameters: modelling cost and Monte Carlo acquisition.

In particular, machine learning models and deep learning can vary enormously in execution time. For example, a deep neural network with 10 layers of 1000 units will run considerably slower than one with 5 layers of 100 units. When performing HPO, different hyperparameter selections can lead to significant differences in the time taken to evaluate the objective function. As Snoek et al. (2012) point out, in such circumstances, the number of function evaluations is less significant than the actual runtime. Hence, they propose optimising *expected improvement per second*. To do this, they model an additional *duration function* $c(\theta)$ alongside $f(\theta)$, again with a GP.

Assuming a budget of $N + J$ evaluations, with N already completed, the Monte Carlo acquisition works by performing the remaining J evaluations. Ideally, the next point should be selected using the expected acquisition function over all remaining points J, which is given by

$$\hat{a}(\theta; \{\theta_n, y_n\}, \psi, \{\theta_j\}) = \int_{\mathbb{R}^J} a\left(\theta; \{\theta_n, y_n\}, \psi, \{\theta_j, y_j\}\right) p(\{y_j\}_{j=1}^{J} | \{\theta_j\} j = 1^J, \{\theta_n, y_n\}_{n=1}^{N}\right) dy_1 \ldots dy_J. \tag{5.17}$$

This expression is the expectation of the acquisition function under a J-dimensional Gaussian distribution, which can be sampled through Monte Carlo. Parallelisation of Monte Carlo sampling is possible.

EXAMPLE 5.3: BASKET OPTION BAYESIAN HYPERPARAMETER OPTIMISATION

As an example of Bayesian HPO, the basket option model will be used again as a testbed (the example is contained in the Jupyter Notebook `Hyperparameter Optimization - Bayesian.ipynb`). *Optuna* provides a GP sampler for Bayesian HPO.

```
study = optuna.create_study(sampler=optuna.samplers.GPSampler())
```

Here, the GP sampler has been used as the sampler type. The hyperparameter configuration search is then performed by

```
study.optimize(objective, n_trials=20)
```

Detailed output of the trials can be obtained as a dataframe by calling

```
df = study.trials_dataframe(attrs=("number", "value", "params", "state"))
```

giving the results in Table 5.1 for the basket option.

TABLE 5.1 Bayesian Hyperparameter Optimisation Results for the Basket Option Example

No.	Value	Hidden Size	lr	No. layers	Optimiser	State
0	20.355416	320	0.000133	5	AdaGrad	COMPLETE
1	3.754281	224	0.002298	5	AdaGrad	COMPLETE
2	1.364038	160	0.001512	6	RMSProp	COMPLETE
3	18.566416	160	0.000368	4	AdaGrad	COMPLETE
4	1.043743	192	0.000198	6	RMSProp	COMPLETE
5	4.961308	416	0.000649	1	Adam	COMPLETE
6	0.403963	288	0.003238	3	Adam	COMPLETE
7	2.517597	384	0.004808	2	AdaGrad	COMPLETE
8	0.944607	512	0.003871	2	RMSProp	COMPLETE
9	1.702074	416	0.004324	5	AdaGrad	COMPLETE
10	1.242773	32	0.010000	6	Adam	COMPLETE
11	3.317538	512	0.010000	1	Adam	COMPLETE
12	4.670111	32	0.010000	6	AdaGrad	COMPLETE
13	1.144660	32	0.003128	6	Adam	COMPLETE
14	4.997100	512	0.000597	1	RMSProp	COMPLETE
15	2.071150	32	0.010000	6	RMSProp	COMPLETE
16	1.670309	512	0.003563	6	Adam	COMPLETE
17	5.243203	32	0.000100	6	RMSProp	COMPLETE
18	16.943757	32	0.004160	1	Adam	COMPLETE
19	**0.360194**	**384**	**0.005002**	**4**	**Adam**	**COMPLETE**

5.6 BANDIT-BASED

Bandit-based HPO algorithms are based on *multi-armed bandits*. Consider a row of slot machines or one-armed bandits, with each machine offering a different probability distribution of reward. A player with a fixed budget of arm-pulls seeks to obtain the maximum reward possible but does not know the properties of each slot machine. The player must decide which machines to play and must balance *exploration* in which he or she tries different machines to sample the rewards offered and *exploitation* where rewards are gained by, say, repeatedly playing the machine that is perceived to give the best reward. This is known as the multi-armed bandit problem and is a classic in *reinforcement learning* (Sutton and Barto, 2018, pp. 25–27).

The first bandit-based algorithm, *successive halving* or *SHA*, is the basis for the three subsequent algorithms, *hyperband*, *BOHB* and *asynchronous successive halving* or *ASHA*. Hence, it is helpful to define some standard notation, and this is given in Table 5.2.

Note that *resources* can be measured in several different ways:

- *Epochs*. The number of training epochs is an obvious measure but leads to significant differences in wall-clock training time for different hyperparameter configurations.
- *Time*. Wall-clock time is a good measure if there is a focus on overall computational cost.
- *Dataset subsampling*. R could be the full training dataset, and then r could be some fraction of it.

5.6.1 Successive Halving (SHA)

The successive halving algorithm (Jamieson and Talwalkar, 2016; Li et al., 2018a) is an adaptive approach that uses intermediate results from multiple hyperparameter configurations to select the best-performing examples and successively refine them until the best is identified. The steps of the algorithm are as follows:

1. Select n different configurations of hyperparameters, typically selected randomly.
2. Allocate a small budget to all configurations and train each model.
3. Evaluate the performance of each configuration by, for example, calculating the validation loss.
4. Keep the top $1/\eta$ configurations and discard the rest.
5. Increase the budget for the remaining configurations by a factor of η.
6. Repeat steps 3–5 until the maximum R budget is reached.
7. Return the best-performing configuration.

TABLE 5.2 Notation Used for Bandit-Based Hyperparameter Optimisation Algorithms

Parameter	Description
n	Number of configurations
R	Maximum resource that can be allocated to a single configuration
r	Minimum resource that can be allocated to a single configuration
time(R)	Execution time for training with resource R
B	Resource budget – algorithm budget could be a multiple
η	Reduction factor – each *rung* of SHA promotes $1/\eta$ configurations
$s \in \{s_{\max}, \dots, 0\}$	Bracket index
$s_{\max} = \lfloor \log_\eta(R) \rfloor$	Maximum bracket index
$s_{\min}$	Minimum bracket index
T	Collection of hyperparameter configurations

SHA is formally defined in Algorithm 5.1 (Li et al., 2018a), with three key functions that will also appear in later algorithms:

- `get_hyperparameter_configuration`(n). This function returns n different hyperparameter configurations sampled randomly from the search space.
- `run_then_return_val_loss`(θ, r). This function trains a model with the given hyperparameters, then calculates and returns the validation loss.
- `top_k`($T, L, n_i/\eta$). This function calculates the top k performing configurations from the index i and returns them.

Algorithm 5.1: Successive Halving (SHA)

Input: Number of configurations n, minimum resource r, maximum resource R, reduction factor η, minimum bracket $s_{\min}$

$s_{\max} \leftarrow \lfloor \log_\eta(R) \rfloor$;

require $n \geq \eta^{s_{\max} - s_{\min}}$;

$T \leftarrow$ `get_hyperparameter_configuration` (n);

for $i \leftarrow 0$ **to** $s_{\max} - s_{\min}$ **do**

  $n_i \leftarrow \lfloor n\eta^{-i} \rfloor$;

  $r_i \leftarrow r\eta^{i+s_{\min}}$;

  $L \leftarrow$ `run_then_return_val_loss` (θ, r_i) : $\theta \in T$;

  $T \leftarrow$ `top_k` ($T, L, \lfloor n_i/\eta \rfloor$);

Output: best configuration in T

SHA can be described as a series of *rungs*, as illustrated in Figure 5.1. Rung 0 corresponds to the initial evaluation of all n hyperparameter configurations. After that initial evaluation, the top $1/\eta$ performing configurations are promoted to rung 1 and then re-evaluated. The evaluation process, reduction to the top $1/\eta$ cases and promotion to the next rung, continues until only one configuration remains.

Li et al. (2018a) describe two possible ways of parallelising SHA. The first method proposes dividing the initial hyperparameter configurations across multiple workers and running SHA on each. The difficulty with this approach is that the runtime for each instance of SHA is at a minimum no. rungs × time(R), where R is the computational resource allocated to each rung. The second approach to parallelisation of SHA is to distribute the training of surviving configurations of each rung, which Li et al. (2018a) label *synchronous SHA*, and start new groups of

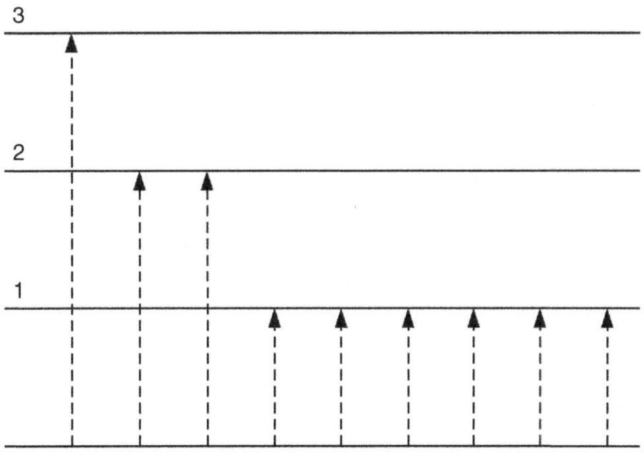

FIGURE 5.1 Successive halving can be described in terms of *rungs*. This experiment evaluates nine different hyperparameter configurations in the first round. The best-performing configurations are evaluated further in the second round, after which the best configuration is selected and promoted to the third round.

hyperparameter configurations (*brackets*) if no jobs are available in current groups. They suggest this approach suffers from two problems: firstly, that it is sensitive to cases that train slowly or fail as all configurations must be completed before moving to the next rung, and secondly, that the estimate of top configurations does not improve with more brackets as the promotion process is independent for each bracket. Li et al. (2018a) propose *asynchronous SHA*, described below in Section 5.6.4, as an alternative.

5.6.2 Hyperband

Hyperband (Li et al., 2018b) extends successive halving and calls it a subroutine in the inner loop of the algorithm. One of the shortcomings of SHA is that it requires the user to specify the number of configurations, n, and SHA then allocates B/n resources on average to each configuration. However, Li et al. (2018b) point out that for any given problem, it is unclear whether it is better to consider many configurations for a short period or fewer configurations for a longer time. The critical factor in this observation is that for any given HPO problem, the observed validation loss of some configuration v_i(*resources*) is surrounded by an *envelope* of uncertainty. To resolve whether or not the loss from the best configuration v_1 can be distinguished from the second best, v_2, requires the envelopes of both results to be non-overlapping. However, in practice, the distribution of terminal loss is unknown, and we do not know how quickly the width of each envelope reduces with resources.

To address the uncertainty in the appropriate choice of n, hyperband considers a range of values for a given budget B and performs a grid search over n. For each choice of n, n_i, a minimum resource r_i is allocated to all configurations on the base rung of SHA. The algorithm has two components:

1. An outer loop over different values of n and r.
2. An inner loop that invokes SHA for the given values of n and r.

Each *bracket* of SHA is configured to use approximately the same budget B. Hence, the total cost of a single run of hyperband is $(s_{\max} + 1)B$, as $s_{\max} + 1$ different values of n are evaluated beginning with the maximum exploration case with $n = s_{\max}$. Subsequent brackets reduce n by approximately η until the final bracket with $s = 0$ corresponds to a classical random search. Hyperband is formally defined in Algorithm 5.2 and uses the same three functions as SHA, `get_hyperparameter_configuration`, `run_then_return_val_loss` and `top_k`.

As an example of the algorithm, consider the case where $R = 64$ and $\eta = 4$, as presented in Table 5.3. Here, $s_{\max} = \log_4(64) = 3$ and hence $B = 4R = 256$. Given these parameters, the base rung of each bracket can be determined. Subsequent rungs divide the configurations by 4, rounding down and multiplying the resources used by 4.

Algorithm 5.2: Hyperband

Input: Maximum resource R, reduction factor η
$s_{\max} \leftarrow \lfloor \log_\eta(R) \rfloor$;
$B \leftarrow (s_{\max} + 1)R$;
for $s \in \{s_{\max}, s_{\max} - 1, \ldots, 0\}$ **do**
  $n \leftarrow \left\lceil \frac{B}{R} \frac{\eta^s}{(s+1)} \right\rceil$;
  $r \leftarrow R\eta^{-s}$;
  `// begin SUCCESSIVEHALVING with` (n, r) `inner loop`
  $T \leftarrow$ `get_hyperparameter_configuration` (n);
  for $i \leftarrow 0$ **to** s **do**
    $n_i \leftarrow \lfloor n\eta^{-i} \rfloor$;
    $r_i \leftarrow r\eta^{i+s_{\min}}$;
    $L \leftarrow$`run_then_return_val_loss` $(\theta, r_i) : \theta \in T$;
    $T \leftarrow$`top_k` $(T, L, \lfloor n_i/\eta \rfloor)$;

Output: Configuration with smallest intermediate loss

TABLE 5.3 Hyperband Configuration for an Example with $R = 64$ and $\eta = 4$

	$s = 3$		$s = 2$		$s = 1$		$s = 0$	
i	n_i	r_i	n_i	r_i	n_i	r_i	n_i	r_i
0	64	1	21	4	8	16	4	64
1	16	4	4	16	2	64		
2	4	16	1	64				
3	1	64						

The two parameters of hyperband, R and η, must still be selected by the user, and Li et al. (2018b) provide some guidance. R is the maximum amount of resources that can be allocated to any configuration and is also the number of configurations in the bracket that does the most exploration (i.e., $s = s_{\text{max}}$). In many problems, there is a natural scale for R, such as the size of the training set. If R is unknown, then an *infinite-horizon* version of hyperband is possible in which the budget B is doubled over time and for each B tries all possible values of $n \in \{2^k : k \in \{1, \ldots, \log_2(B)\}\}$. There may also be a desire to limit the number of configurations, and then $R = n_{\text{max}}$ and $s_{\text{max}} = \lfloor \log_\eta(n_{\text{max}}) \rfloor$.

η controls how aggressive elimination is during the inner SHA loop. Increasing η will reduce the budget per bracket by reducing the number of rungs. Li et al. (2018b) suggest that the result is not very sensitive to the value of η and that on theoretical grounds, the optimal choice is $\eta = e = 2.718$. Selecting η to be 3 or 4 works best.

Hyperband can easily be parallelised along two axes. Firstly, the outer loop over brackets can be run in parallel as these are strictly independent of each other. Secondly, the inner SHA loop can be parallelised by running each configuration at a given rung.

EXAMPLE 5.4: HYPERBAND FOR THE BASKET OPTION

Optuna incorporates the concept of *samplers* and *pruners*. *Samplers* sample the hyperparameter space using the specified algorithm, which includes techniques such as random and grid search, as well as Bayesian algorithms like the earlier-used Gaussian process sampler and the tree-structured Parzen estimator discussed below. *Pruners* terminate training when continuing is not cost-effective. In the previous Bayesian example with Optuna, the system ran all trials to completion. However, the *hyperband* pruner is used, which implements the hyperband algorithm described above. To accommodate the pruning process, slight modifications in the code are necessary, as shown in the Jupyter Notebook `Hyperparameter Optimization - Hyperband.ipynb`. The `train_model` function now accepts a `trial` object as an argument. Additionally, after calculating the validation error, the training loop includes a new check to consult the pruning algorithm and decide if the trial should be pruned.

```
trial.report(test_loss, epoch)
if trial.should_prune():
    raise optuna.TrialPruned()
```

The `study` now takes the pruner as an argument.

```
study = optuna.create_study(sampler=optuna.samplers.RandomSampler(),
            pruner=optuna.pruners.HyperbandPruner(
            min_resource=1, max_resource=no_epochs,
            reduction_factor=3
        ),)
```

The minimum and maximum resources must be specified as the R or resource parameter, and η is the reduction factor. Table 5.4 shows the complete results.

(*Continued*)

(Continued)

TABLE 5.4 Hyperband Optimisation Results for the Basket Option Example

No.	Value	Hidden Size	lr	No. Layers	Optimiser	State
0	20.269392	384	0.000139	4	AdaGrad	COMPLETE
1	22.728516	288	0.000997	2	AdaGrad	PRUNED
2	**0.349539**	**352**	**0.004267**	**5**	**Adam**	**COMPLETE**
3	0.865670	320	0.000302	2	Adam	COMPLETE
4	8.181525	352	0.002985	5	RMSProp	PRUNED
5	1.454640	128	0.001437	5	RMSProp	COMPLETE
6	3.377052	128	0.004040	6	AdaGrad	PRUNED
7	56.761163	384	0.000396	2	AdaGrad	PRUNED
8	1.274808	480	0.002447	4	Adam	PRUNED
9	12.380232	224	0.004910	3	AdaGrad	PRUNED
10	38.233740	480	0.000321	3	AdaGrad	PRUNED
11	0.419570	192	0.000509	6	Adam	COMPLETE
12	53.662291	64	0.001683	2	AdaGrad	PRUNED
13	8.088780	320	0.008747	5	AdaGrad	PRUNED
14	2.656605	256	0.005020	2	RMSProp	PRUNED
15	64.096948	480	0.000752	1	AdaGrad	PRUNED
16	3.207479	320	0.002702	4	AdaGrad	PRUNED
17	0.565391	96	0.004514	5	Adam	PRUNED
18	12.693985	192	0.000203	4	Adam	PRUNED
19	15.230120	32	0.000741	6	RMSProp	PRUNED

5.6.3 BOHB

BOHB or *Bayesian optimisation hyperband* is a hyperparameter tuning algorithm that combines hyperband with Bayesian optimisation (Falkner et al., 2018). The technique is designed to address shortcomings in both Bayesian optimisation and hyperband. Firstly, Bayesian optimisation in its basic form gives robust hyperparameter tuning, but it is a sequential method. Secondly, in its most common form, Bayesian optimisation uses GPs to construct its probability model, which does not scale well to large dimensions with cubic complexity in the number of points. Hyperband is highly parallel and gives results with an overall budget similar to fully training a model. It is flexible and scalable to high dimensions, but it is based on a purely random search and does not learn from previous results. In combining Bayesian optimisation and hyperband, Falkner et al. (2018) seek to use the best of both approaches.

BOHB uses a surrogate model based on *tree of Parzen estimators (TPEs)* (Bergstra et al., 2011). TPE uses non-parametric kernel density estimators (KDEs) to model the distribution of good and bad configurations x, using a reference value α that is defined as a percentile of the loss values y over observations with a given budget,

$$l(x) = p(y < \alpha | x, D), \tag{5.18}$$
$$g(x) = p(y > \alpha | x, D). \tag{5.19}$$

Given this form for the surrogate model, the expected improvement (EI) acquisition function is straightforward. It can be shown (Bergstra et al., 2011, p. 4) that

$$EI_\alpha(x) = \frac{q\alpha l(x) - l(x) \int_{-\infty}^{\alpha} p(y)dy}{ql(x) + (1-q)g(x)}, \tag{5.20}$$
$$\propto \left(q + \frac{g(x)}{l(x)}(1-q) \right)^{-1}. \tag{5.21}$$

Hence, to optimise EI, the ratio $\frac{l(x)}{g(x)}$ can be used instead and $l(x)$ sampled. TPE scales linearly in the number of observations and in the number of hyperparameters, which compares favourably to GPs. For more details of the TPE probability fitting process, see Falkner et al. (2018) and Bergstra et al. (2011) and references therein.

The BOHB algorithm uses hyperband to set the budget and continues to use the SHA inner loop. The random sample is, however, replaced by the Bayesian optimisation sampling procedure given in Algorithm 5.3.

Algorithm 5.3: Sampling in BOHB

Input: Observations D, fraction of random runs ρ, percentile q, number of samples N_s, minimum number of points in a model $N_{\min}$
Output: Next configuration to evaluate
if `rand()` $< \rho$ **then**
  return *random configuration*
$b = \text{argmax}\{D_b : |D_b| > N_{\min} + 1\}$;
if $b = 0$ **then**
  return *random configuration*
$\alpha = q$-percentile of all $y \in D_b$;
fit KDE probabilities $l(x) = p(y < \alpha | x)$, $g(x) = p(y > \alpha | x)$;
draw N_s samples $\sim l(x)$;
return *sample with highest ratio* $l(x)/g(x)$

Parallelism in BOHB comes from two sources: TPE and hyperband. Section 5.6.2 discussed how hyperband can be parallelised. Falkner et al. (2018) suggest that TPE samples used to optimise EI can be evaluated in parallel, limiting the number of samples to obtain diversity. The parallelisation procedure described by Falkner et al. (2018) is as follows:

- Start with the first SHA run from hyperband: the most aggressive bracket.
- Follow Algorithm 5.3 until (1) all workers are busy or (2) enough configurations have been sampled for SHA.
- When a new worker is available:
  1. Sample a new configuration.
  2. Start the next SHA run in parallel using Algorithm 5.3.

BOHB was found by Falkner et al. (2018) to outperform hyperband and Bayesian optimisation in several numerical test cases, including feedforward networks.

EXAMPLE 5.5: BOHB AND THE BASKET OPTION

To implement the BOHB algorithm, Optuna can again be used, this time with a Bayesian tree-structured Parzen estimator sampler coupled with the hyperband pruner, as seen in the Jupyter Notebook `Hyperparameter Optimization - BOHB.ipynb`. The only change from the hyperband case is the code to set up the study object

```
study = optuna.create_study(sampler=optuna.samplers.TPESampler(),
          pruner=optuna.pruners.HyperbandPruner(
          min_resource=5, max_resource=no_epochs,
          reduction_factor=3
      ),)
```

The results of the trials are given in Table 5.5.

TABLE 5.5 BOHB Optimisation Results for the Basket Option Example

No.	Value	Hidden Size	lr	No. Layers	Optimiser	State
0	1.109032	192	0.008374	5	AdaGrad	COMPLETE
1	3.469169	384	0.007211	1	Adam	COMPLETE
2	67.999121	32	0.000362	6	AdaGrad	PRUNED
3	0.840804	96	0.000338	6	Adam	COMPLETE
4	3.300582	480	0.000420	2	RMSProp	PRUNED
5	15.945552	224	0.001313	3	AdaGrad	PRUNED
6	**0.283885**	**224**	**0.001376**	**4**	**Adam**	**COMPLETE**
7	2.090543	480	0.002923	6	AdaGrad	PRUNED
8	3.348642	160	0.000257	6	Adam	PRUNED
9	0.594277	416	0.009978	2	Adam	COMPLETE
10	1.482933	320	0.001135	4	RMSProp	PRUNED
11	6.247121	320	0.000120	3	Adam	PRUNED
12	7.147333	384	0.002445	1	Adam	PRUNED
13	0.358115	288	0.003683	4	Adam	COMPLETE
14	0.392367	256	0.003702	4	Adam	COMPLETE
15	0.391610	128	0.001692	5	Adam	COMPLETE
16	5.770144	288	0.000669	4	RMSProp	PRUNED
17	0.503251	224	0.004299	5	Adam	PRUNED
18	1.266917	96	0.000840	3	Adam	PRUNED
19	3.506367	320	0.005160	4	RMSProp	PRUNED

5.6.4 Asynchronous Successive Halving (ASHA)

Asynchronous successive halving (ASHA) is a HPO algorithm introduced by Li et al. (2018a) to improve upon SHA and address the observed shortcomings of naive parallel implementation. The key aim of ASHA is to address the issues observed in SHA by making the algorithm asynchronous, that is, problems with 'stragglers', or slow-running hyperparameter sets and hyperparameter choices that lead to training failure.

The SHA algorithm is modified as follows, assuming there are several workers available that operate in parallel:

1. For each free worker, get a job.
   (a) Check if there is a *promotable* configuration available.
      - That is, for the rungs $k, \dots, 0$, is there a candidate in the top $1/\eta$ configurations?
   (b) Return the configuration if available.
   (c) Otherwise, draw a random configuration from the base rung.
   (d) Launch asynchronous training/evaluation of the configuration.
2. Repeat until *desired*.
3. Return the best-performing configuration.

The algorithm promotes configurations whenever possible; however, if less than the full set of configurations has been completed for a given rung, there is a risk that the promoted configuration will not be in the final top $1/\eta$ configurations, and the promotion was incorrect. In general, this does not cause any problems, and the probability of an incorrect promotion decreases with the number of tested hyperparameter configurations. For free workers with no promotions available, extend the base rung with more randomly generated hyperparameter sets. The algorithm does not require the user to specify the number of initial base configurations; the stopping criterion is essentially open. However, Li et al. (2018a) does make a recommendation (see below).

Algorithm 5.4: Asynchronous Successive Halving (ASHA)

```
Input: minimum resource r, maximum resource R, reduction factor η, minimum bracket s_min
repeat
    for each free worker do
        (θ, k) ← get_job ();
        run_then_return_val_loss (θ, rη^(s_min+k));
    for completed job(θ, k) with loss l do
        Update configuration θ in rung k with loss l;
until desired;
Output: best configuration in T

function get_job()
    for k ← ⌊log_η(R/r)⌋ − s_min − 1, ..., 1, 0 do
        candidates ←top_k (T_k, |T_k|/η);
        promotable ← {t ∈ candidates : t not promoted};
        if |promotable | > 0 then
            return promotable [0], k + 1;
        Draw random configuration θ;
        return θ, 0
```

The ASHA algorithm is formally defined by Algorithm 5.4 (Li et al., 2018a), where the two functions `run_then_return_val_loss` and `top_k` were defined in Section 5.6.1 and a third function, `get_job` is defined in the algorithmic block.

Li et al. (2018a) demonstrate that ASHA can return a completely trained model in a time

$$\left(\sum_{i=s}^{\log_\eta(R)} \eta^{i-\log_\eta(R)} \right) \times \text{time}(R) \leq 2\ \text{time}(R), \tag{5.22}$$

where s is the minimum early stopping rate. The authors note that when training is iterative, ASHA can return an answer in just time(R) as incremental training means that configurations can be stopped and resumed. Comparing this with the SHA algorithm for the case with nine initial configurations that could be completed in 3 time(R) shows that AHSA performs significantly better. In practical tests with *neural architecture benchmarks (NAS)*, AHSA outperformed SHA and BOHB by nearly a factor of 2.

To make ASHA usable in practice, Li et al. (2018a) propose the following default settings:

- Set the reduction factor $\eta = 4$ so that each rung promotes 25% of hyperparameter sets.
- Set the maximum early stopping rate to allow for a maximum of five rungs, implying a minimum resource of $r = \frac{1}{4^4}R = \frac{R}{256}$.
- Run the three most aggressive early stopping brackets with $s = 0, 1, 2$.
- Use n, the number of configurations evaluated as the stopping criterion.

ASHA is designed for large-scale parallel implementation and is available in several HPO frameworks.

EXAMPLE 5.6: ASHA AND THE BASKET OPTION

The ASHA algorithm is utilised in the Sherpa Python library, which is demonstrated in the Jupyter Notebook named `Hyperparameter Optimization - AHSA.ipynb`. The data preparation step in this example is the same as in previous examples, which involves creating a training and validation set. The model build function retrieves the necessary hyperparameters from a trials object provided by the Sherpa library.

```
def buildModel(trial):
    lr = trial.parameters['learning_rate']
    no_layers = trial.parameters['no_layers']
    layer_width = trial.parameters['hidden_size']
    optimizer_name = trial.parameters['optimizer']
    model = FeedForward(layer_width, no_layers).to(device)
    optimizer = create_optimizer(optimizer_name, lr, model.parameters())
    loss_fn = nn.MSELoss()
    return model, optimiser, loss_fn
```

The Sherpa `study` object configures the optimisation run. A list of Sherpa parameter objects, which describe the distribution of each hyperparameter under evaluation, is collected. This list and the algorithm object are passed to the study object creator function.

```
parameters = [sherpa.Continuous('learning_rate', [1e-4, 1e-2], 'log'),
sherpa.Discrete('hidden_size', [32, 64, 128, 256, 512]),
sherpa.Discrete('no_layers', [1, 2, 3, 4, 5]),
sherpa.Choice('optimiser', ['Adam', 'RMSprop', 'Adagrad'])]
algorithm = alg = sherpa.algorithms.SuccessiveHalving(r=1, R=9, eta=3, s=0,
max_finished_configs=1)
study = sherpa.Study(parameters=parameters,
algorithm=algorithm,
optimiser          lower_is_better=True,
dashboard_port=8995)
```

The user must supply a port number and choose whether the objective is minimised or maximised using the boolean `lower_is_better` parameter, and this is `True` here, as the objective is the validation loss. A temporary directory is needed to store intermediate model files and this is done using the `tempfile` package

```
model_dir = tempfile.mkdtemp()
```

The study object is an iterable container of trials, and to run the optimisation, these are looped over.

```
for trial in the study:
    print(trial.parameters['resource'])
    initial_epoch = {1: 0, 3: 1, 9: 4, 27: 13,
                     81: 40 }[trial.parameters['resource']]
    epochs = trial.optimisationresource'] + initial_epoch

    print("-"*100)
    print(f"Trial:\t{trial.id}\nEpochs:\t{initial_epoch} to \
        {epochs}\nParameters:{trial.parameters}\n")

    if trial.parameters['load_from'] == "":
        print(f"Creating new model for trial {trial.id}...\n")
        model, optimizer, loss_fn = buildModel(trial)
    else:
        print(f"Loading model from: ", \
        os.path.join(model_dir, trial.parameters['load_from']),
          "...\n")
          model, optimizer, loss_fn = buildModel(trial)
        model_state_dict = torch.load(os.path.join(model_dir,
        trial.parameters['load_from']))
        model.load_state_dict(model_state_dict)

    # Train model
    train_model(model, train_loader, val_loader, loss_fn, optimizer,
            initial_epoch, epochs, study)

    study.finalize(trial=trial)
    print(f"Saving model at: ", \
        os.path.join(model_dir, trial.parameters['save_to']))
    torch.save(model.state_dict(),
           os.path.join(model_dir, trial.parameters['save_to']))
    study.save(model_dir)
```

The core of the loop is a decision as to whether to build a new model or load and continue to train a model that was trained earlier and saved down. After the optimisation process has finished, the best results can be obtained from the study object

```
study.get_best_result()
```

giving

```
{'Trial-ID': 74,
'Iteration': 115,
'hidden_size': 385,
'learning_rate': 0.000456optimisation8,
```

(Continued)

(*Continued*)

```
'load_from': '61',
'no_layers': 4,
'optimiser': 'Adam',
'resource': 81,
'rung': 4,
'save_to': '74',
'Objective': 0.17233774719238282,
'loss': 0.17233774719238282}
```

Note that the total number of layers is one larger than the output indicates, as seen from the implementation above.

5.7 POPULATION-BASED TRAINING (PBT)

Population-based training (PBT) was introduced by Jaderberg et al. (2017) from DeepMind. PBT is designed to bridge the two broad classes of hyperparameter tuning discussed in this chapter: parallel search and sequential optimisation. Hence, the motivation for the approach is similar to that of BOHB, and like that algorithm, PBT is also designed for asynchronous operation on a cluster. However, the inspiration for PBT is quite different, and it is closer to a genetic algorithm in the way it operates.

The process starts with a population $\mathcal{P}$ containing N models with parameters $\{\theta^i\}_{i=1}^N$, each optimised with different hyperparameters $\{\lambda^i\}_{i=1}^N$. PBT aims to find the best model across a population not simply by selecting a set of hyperparameters but rather by updating both λ and θ according to the performance of the population. Hence, PBT produces a schedule of hyperparameters rather than simply selecting the best hyperparameter vector. PBT uses two key methods: *exploit*, which determines whether or not a worker process should continue or switch focus to a better parameter set, and *explore*, which generates a new set of hyperparameters to explore the solution space given a current solution and hyperparameters.

PBT is presented in Algorithm 5.5. There are five key functions:

- `step`$(\theta|\lambda)$ takes a training set and updates parameters θ given the current set of hyperparameters λ. For a deep neural network, this is a step in gradient descent.
- `eval`(θ) evaluates the model with parameters θ, and this could involve evaluating the validation loss or accuracy, or some other metric.
- `ready`$(p, t, \mathcal{P})$ determines whether the model is ready for exploitation/exploration, and this could mean a predetermined number of training steps has been performed or a specific level of performance has been reached.
- `exploit`$(\lambda, \theta, p, \mathcal{P})$ determines whether the worker should continue with the current set of parameters and hyperparameters or whether these should be replaced with a better set. The form of the exploit function depends on the nature of the machine learning task. For example, in the context of a reinforcement learning task, Jaderberg et al. (2017) propose two types of exploitation: *T-test selection* and *truncation selection*. T-test selection uniformly samples another agent in the population and compares the last 10 episodic rewards with the current agent using Welch's *t*-test (Welch, 1947). Truncation selection ranks all agents according to the episodic reward. If the current agent is in the bottom 20%, then the weights and hyperparameters are replaced with those taken from an agent sampled from the top 20%. Jaderberg et al. (2017) also apply T-test selection to machine translation and truncation selection to GANs.
- `explore`$(\lambda', \theta', \mathcal{P})$ generates a new set of hyperparameters using the current solution and hyperparameters. The form of the function is also dependent on the type of machine learning problem. Jaderberg et al. (2017) propose two strategies in the context of reinforcement learning: *perturb* and *resample*. Perturb randomly shifts each hyperparameter by a factor of 1.2 or 0.8 and resamples each hyperparameter from the prior distribution. The perturb strategy is also used by Jaderberg et al. (2017) in the context of machine translation and GANs.

Algorithm 5.5: Population-Based Training (PBT)

Input: Initial population $\mathcal{P}$
for $(\theta, \lambda, p, t) \in \mathcal{P}$*(asynchronously in parallel)* **do**
    while *not end of training* **do**
        `// Optimise using hyperparameters h`
        $\theta \leftarrow$`step` $(\theta|\lambda)$;
        $p \leftarrow$`eval` (θ);
        if `ready` $(p, t, \mathcal{P})$ **then**
            `// Use remaining population to find better solution`
            $\lambda', \theta' \leftarrow$ `exploit` $(\lambda, \theta, p, \mathcal{P})$;
            if $\theta \neq \theta'$ **then**
                `// generate new hyperparameters h`
                $\lambda, \theta \leftarrow$`explore` $(\lambda', \theta', \mathcal{P})$;
                $p \leftarrow$`eval` (θ);
        update $\mathcal{P}$ with new $(\theta, \lambda, p, t+1)$
Output: θ with highest p in $\mathcal{P}$

Jaderberg et al. (2017) apply PBT to three challenging problems in machine learning involving deep learning: *deep reinforcement learning*, *machine translation* using a *transformer* network and *GANs*. They report consistent improvements in model accuracy, training time and stability. Li et al. (2018a) report that ASHA outperformed PBT in their test cases.

EXAMPLE 5.7: PBT AND THE BASKET OPTION

Population-based training is also one of the featured algorithms in *Sherpa*, and this example is in the Jupyter Notebook `Hyperparameter Optimization - PBT.ipynb`. The setup is almost identical to that of the ASHA algorithm described above, with the exception that the algorithm creator function changes.

```
algorithm = sherpa.algorithms.PopulationBasedTraining(
population_size=80,
num_generations=8,
perturbation_factors=(0.8, 1.2))
```

The population size is the number of initial models in the population $\mathcal{P}$ sampled from the hyperparameter space, and the number of generations is the number of generations for evolving the models through. The perturbation factors shift the real-valued parameters, the learning rate in this example.

The training loop itself is slightly different from the ASHA case.

```
for trial in study:
     generation = trial.parameters['generation']
     load_from = trial.parameters['load_from']
     training_lr = trial.parameters['learning_rate']

     print("-"*100)
     print("Generation {}".format(generation))
     print(f"Trial:\t{trial.id}\nParameters:{trial.parameters}\n")

     if load_from == "":
         print(f"Creating new model for trial {trial.id}...\n")
         model, optimizer, loss_fn = buildModel(trial)
```

(Continued)

(*Continued*)

```
    else:
        model, optimizer, loss_fn = loadModel(trial)

    # Train model for 10 epochs
    train_model(model, train_loader, val_loader, loss_fn, optimizer, 10,
                study)

    study.finalize(trial=trial)
    print(f"Saving model at: ", os.path.join(model_dir,
        trial.parameters['save_to']))

    torch.save(model, os.path.join(model_dir, trial.parameters['save_to']))
    study.save(model_dir)
```

The main difference from the ASHA algorithm is the learning rate perturbation step when a model from a previous generation is loaded. The final results of the search are as follows:

```
{'Trial-ID': 57,
'Iteration': 6,
'generation': 3,
'hidden_size': 422,
'learning_rate': 0.005017846595624772,
'lineage': '2,21,',
'load_from': '21',
'no_layers': 1,
'optimiser': 'Adam',
'save_to': '57',
'Objective': 0.5319786865234375,
'loss': 0.5319786865234375}
```

Note that the total number of layers is one larger than the output indicates, as seen from the implementation above.

5.8 CONCLUSION

This chapter explored several HPO schemes, from simple manual search to complex asynchronous processes such as ASHA and PBT. As deep neural networks become increasingly complex and computationally expensive to train, HPO is becoming increasingly important. The idea of fully automated machine learning is still some way off, and all of the methods discussed in this chapter require some degree of user input, particularly in specifying sensible ranges and distributions for individual hyperparameters. Nevertheless, relatively few parameters are associated with any HPO schemes, and their use is relatively straightforward.

Table 5.6 lists the optimal hyperparameter set identified by each of the examples in the chapter. The same dataset was used for all examples, including the basket option, and in all cases, the same four hyperparameters were selected for tuning. The maximum budget for all optimisation schemes was approximately 30 epochs, so that the final results could be compared. Notably, the Adam optimiser was selected by all but one of the seven approaches, but the remaining parameters show a fair amount of variation. The number of layers varies between one and five. However, the preference is for four or five, the optimal layer width varies from 224 to 512, and the learning rate ranges from $4e^{-4}$ to $8e^{-3}$. This suggests that a range of models show comparable performance in this case.

TABLE 5.6 Optimal Choice of Hyperparameters for the Basket Option Example from Each HPO Method

HPO	No. Layers	Layer Width	Optimiser	Learning Rate
Grid	5	256	Adam	0.001
Random	3	512	Adam	0.008851
Bayesian	4	384	Adam	0.005002
Hyperband	5	352	RMSProp	0.004267
BOHB	4	224	Adam	0.001376
ASHA	4	385	Adam	0.000456
PBT	1	422	Adam	0.005018

Of course, the wall-clock time needed to obtain the optimal choice depends heavily on the HPO method. The grid approach took a long time, while the *pruning* methods of hyperband and BOHB achieved their results at significantly lower computational cost.

CHAPTER 6

Convolutional Neural Networks

I've seen things you people wouldn't believe: attack ships on fire off the shoulder of Orion. I've watched C-beams glitter in the dark near the Tannhäuser Gate. All those ... moments ... will be lost in time, like ... tears ... in rain.

Roy Batty, Blade Runner (directed Ridley Scott, 1982)

6.1 INTRODUCTION

Convolutional neural networks (CNNs) are neural networks that contain one or more *convolutional layers* (Goodfellow et al., 2016, p. 321). Convolutional layers utilise the mathematical convolution operation described in Section 6.2.1. Unlike dense layers that learn global patterns from the input space, convolutional layers learn local patterns from their input (Chollet, 2018, p. 122). Convolutions are specialised for grid-structured data in one or two dimensions. Given the application of convolution operations in signal and image processing (see, e.g., Appel, 2007, pp. 217–219), the application of convolutional layers to time series in one dimension and images in two dimensions is unsurprising.

CNNs are primarily applied to computer vision, including image classification and object detection. CNNs have also been utilised in reinforcement learning, processing the video feed from Atari 2600 games (Mnih et al., 2015). Convolutional layers are also critical in image applications of *generative adversarial networks*, which will be discussed in Chapter 9.

This chapter describes CNNs, and given that their main application is to computer vision, this will also be the focus of both the text and the examples. Computer vision is an odd digression in the context of a book on quantitative finance. However, it is justified as developing intuition about convolution through images is much easier. There are financial applications of convolutions, one-dimensional for time series discussed in Chapter 7 and two-dimensional for volatility surfaces discussed in Chapter 15.

The chapter organises itself as follows: Section 6.2 defines the convolution operation, describing the mathematics of the continuous and discrete cases and then discussing the neural network implementation. This section also discusses two vital elements: handling edge effects through padding and managing multiple channels, which are essential for dealing with colour images. Section 6.3 discusses operations that reduce the sizes of the inputs through downsampling, strided convolutions and pooling layers. Section 6.4 describes data augmentation to enhance the effective size of the training set, a method commonly used with images but applicable in other contexts. Section 6.5 discusses transfer learning, which is widely used with computer vision applications. Section 6.6 addresses several methods of visualising the features that convolutional layers detect. Finally, Section 6.7 discusses the architecture of several prominent CNNs.

Deep Learning in Quantitative Finance, First Edition. Andrew Green.

6.2 CONVOLUTIONS

6.2.1 Mathematics of Convolutions

The convolution of two functions f and g is defined by (Appel, 2007, p. 211)

$$h(x) \equiv \int f(t)g(x-t)dt, \tag{6.1}$$

and is denoted by

$$h = f * g. \tag{6.2}$$

In this function, f is the input and g is the kernel. Of course, in a deep neural network context, the convolution is discrete, and x can only take a fixed set of values on the real line. The discrete convolution is given by (Goodfellow et al., 2014, p. 323)

$$h(x) = \sum_{x=-\infty}^{\infty} f(t)g(x-t). \tag{6.3}$$

In deep learning, the input function and the kernel are defined on a discrete set of points forming the tensor. The usual assumption is that the function is zero everywhere except at those points. Given that the tensors are finite, the sum becomes finite. Assuming two-dimensional tensors, the convolution becomes (Goodfellow et al., 2016, p. 323),

$$h(i,j) = \sum_m \sum_n F(m,n)G(i-m, j-n) \tag{6.4}$$

$$= \sum_m \sum_n F(i-m, j-n)G(m,n), \tag{6.5}$$

where the second line relies on the commutative property of convolutions. In practice, many software packages implement the closely related cross-correlation function

$$h(i,j) = \sum_m \sum_n F(i+m, j+n)G(m,n). \tag{6.6}$$

In a deep learning application, the input tensor F is convolved with a smaller kernel G, which learns weights. The convolution operation can be viewed as matrix multiplication with constraints (Goodfellow et al., 2016, p. 324).

As an example, consider convolving the following tensor:

$$F = \begin{bmatrix} 8 & 0 & 0 & 4 & 8 & 1 \\ 6 & 1 & 6 & 5 & 5 & 1 \\ 8 & 9 & 2 & 7 & 5 & 1 \\ 9 & 9 & 2 & 3 & 1 & 5 \\ 7 & 8 & 0 & 4 & 5 & 5 \\ 3 & 0 & 2 & 9 & 9 & 7 \end{bmatrix}, \tag{6.7}$$

with the Scharr filter

$$G = \begin{bmatrix} 3 & 0 & -3 \\ 10 & 0 & -10 \\ 3 & 0 & -3 \end{bmatrix}. \tag{6.8}$$

This is equivalent to performing element-wise multiplication and summation of each sub-block of F by G (that is 'sum-product'), giving

$$F * G = \begin{bmatrix} 42 & -46 & -23 & 67 \\ 81 & 26 & -24 & 66 \\ 109 & 78 & -14 & -5 \\ 94 & 31 & -68 & -10 \end{bmatrix}. \quad (6.9)$$

The resulting tensor is 4×4 because the 3×3 G tensor will only 'fit' four times horizontally and vertically over the F tensor.

EXAMPLE 6.1: MNIST EDGE DETECTION

Convolution with a filter detects features in an image (see the Jupyter Notebook `MNIST Edge Detection.ipynb`). CNNs learn the filter weights, but some known filters can illustrate feature detection, with the Scharr filter as one example. Figure 6.1 shows eight handwritten numbers drawn from the MNIST training set as a basic example.

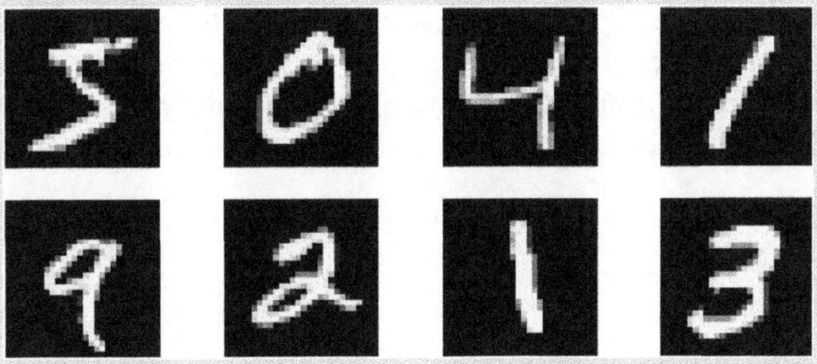

FIGURE 6.1 Eight images from the MNIST training set.

These images can be convolved with the Scharr filter using the `convolve2d` function from the package `scipy.signal`.

```
scharr = np.array([[ -3-3j, 0-10j,  +3 -3j],
                   [-10+0j, 0+ 0j, +10 +0j],
                   [ -3+3j, 0+10j,  +3 +3j]])

grad = signal.convolve2d(train_images[image_index], scharr, boundary='symm',
                         mode='same')
```

Note that the Scharr filter is defined as an array of complex numbers here and that, in general, CNNs work purely in the real domain. The resulting images illustrated in Figure 6.2 clearly show the edges of the numbers.

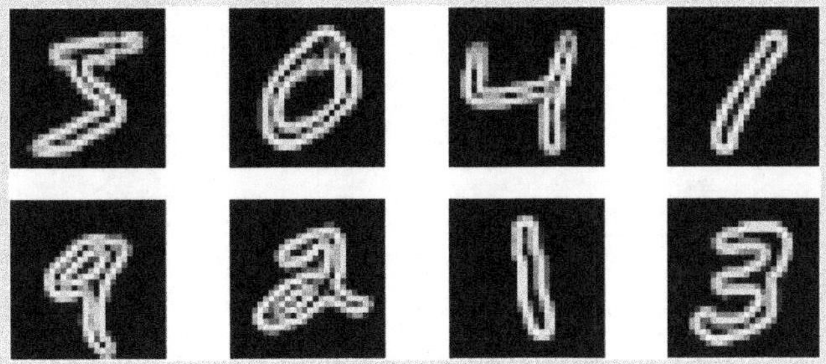

FIGURE 6.2 The eight images from the MNIST training set convolved with a Scharr filter.

6.2.2 Convolutional Layers

Goodfellow et al. (2016) note three key motivations for using convolutional layers: sparse interactions, parameter sharing and equivariant representations.

In a convolutional layer, the filter (kernel) size is usually significantly smaller than the input size, say 3×3 or 5×5. The model will typically use a block of such filters in each layer. The number of filters per layer will typically increase with depth in the network.[1] The number of parameters in such a layer is significantly less than would be used for a corresponding dense layer.

In Example 6.2, a feedforward network is compared to a CNN with the MNIST dataset. The first layer of the dense network has an input dimension of $28 \times 28 = 784$ and an output dimension of 200, giving 157, 000 trainable weights. The CNN, in contrast, has the exact input dimension, but this does not impact the number of weights, which is provided by the number of filters multiplied by the size of the filter with a single bias parameter per filter, giving $32 \times 3 \times 3 + 32 = 320$ trainable parameters. Using fewer parameters will significantly reduce memory requirements and the number of computational operations.

Sparse connectivity also means that the receptive field is narrow between two layers. For a fully connected layer, the concept of receptive field is meaningless as all units in one layer are connected to all units in the next layer. For a CNN, however, the size of the receptive field is dictated by the filter size, so if the filter is 3×3, then this is also the size of the receptive field for input to the next layer. Of course, the effective receptive field grows deeper into the network, with later layers seeing more and more of the original image, as illustrated in Figure 6.3.

For a feedforward network, each weight is used precisely once, and there is no sharing (Goodfellow et al., 2016, p. 328). For a CNN, however, the weights of each filter are used at every position of the input, with the possible exception of points on the edge of the image. The sparsity of parameters does not reduce the computational cost but does reduce the memory footprint considerably.

The convolution operation is translation equivariant, and this property arises from the use of parameter sharing (Goodfellow et al., 2016, p. 329). A function f is equivariant to another function g if

$$f(g(x)) = g(f(x)). \tag{6.10}$$

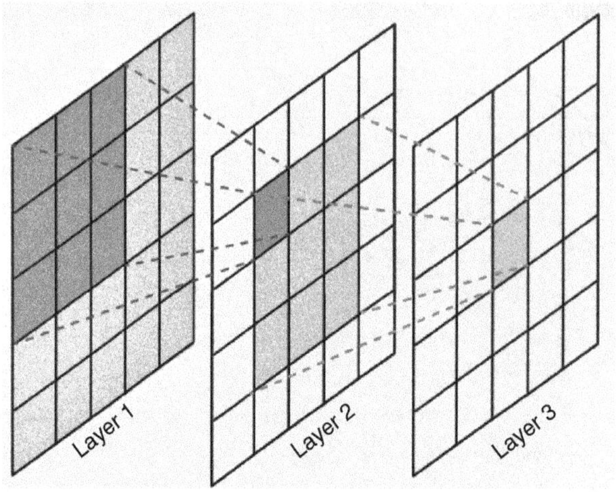

FIGURE 6.3 The receptive field of a CNN for a 3×3 filter through three layers. *Source*: Lin et al. (2017). Modified to greyscale from the original colour. Available via license: Creative Commons Attribution 4.0 International https://creativecommons.org/licenses/by/4.0/.

[1]For a discussion on the size of filters, see Section 6.2.5, while Section 6.2.6 explores how to select the number of filters optimally.

The parameter sharing ensures that the convolutional layer is translation equivariant so that if g is a translation operation, then convolution f is equivariant to it (Trivedi and Kondor, 2017). In the context of images, this means that if the input is shifted, the output is also shifted, or applying the convolution after the shift gives the same result as performing the convolution and then using the shift (Mishra, 2020). Translation equivariance is useful, for example, in computer vision applications where multiple occurrences of an object are in object detection applications. Translation invariance, discussed below in Section 6.3, should be distinct from translation equivariance.

EXAMPLE 6.2: COMPARING FEEDFORWARD AND CONVOLUTIONAL NETWORKS WITH MNIST

Earlier chapters trained feedforward and CNN models against the MNIST and MNIST fashion datasets without directly comparing the models. This example uses the previously trained network architectures and can be found in `Comparing Feed Forward Networks and CNNs with MNIST.ipynb`. The MNIST dataset undergoes the usual scaling. The data requires flattening into vectors of length 28^2 for the feedforward network but remains two-dimensional for input to the CNN. Training the models occurred through 200 epochs with a batch size of 2048, and both utilised the Adam optimiser.

The feedforward network architecture is described by print on the model.

```
NeuralNetwork(
(fc1): Linear(in_features=784, out_features=200, bias=True)
(fc2): Linear(in_features=200, out_features=200, bias=True)
(fc3): Linear(in_features=200, out_features=10, bias=True)
(relu): ReLU()
(softmax): Softmax(dim=1)
)
```

Similarly, the CNN architecture is as follows:

```
CNNModel(
(conv1): Conv2d(1, 32, kernel_size=(3, 3), stride=(1, 1))
(conv2): Conv2d(32, 64, kernel_size=(3, 3), stride=(1, 1))
(conv3): Conv2d(64, 64, kernel_size=(3, 3), stride=(1, 1))
(pool): MaxPool2d(kernel_size=2, stride=2, padding=0, dilation=1,
          ceil_mode=False)
(fc1): Linear(in_features=576, out_features=64, bias=True)
(fc2): Linear(in_features=64, out_features=10, bias=True)
)
```

Comparing the two, it is clear that the CNN has less than half the trainable parameters of the feedforward network. When training them, however, the feedforward network processes each epoch faster than the CNN (in 1.18s compared to 2.27s). The validation accuracy of both models is plotted as a function of epoch in Figure 6.4. CNN is slightly more accurate than the feedforward network.

(*Continued*)

(*Continued*)

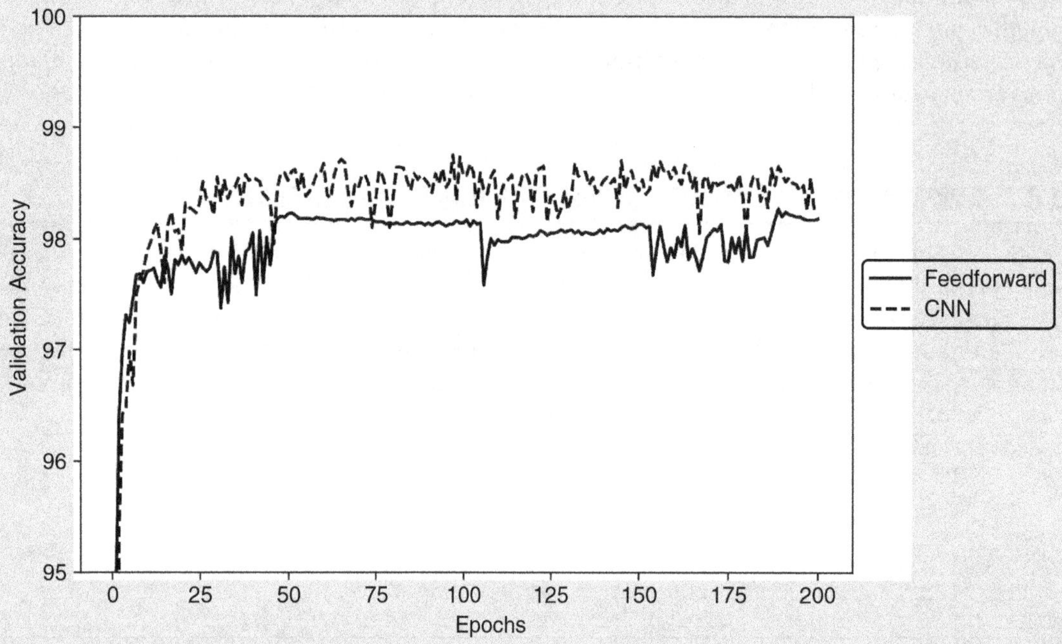

FIGURE 6.4 Validation accuracy for a feedforward network and CNN trained for 200 epochs using the MNIST dataset.

6.2.3 Edge Effects: Padding

Recall Figure 6.3, which illustrates the receptive field for a CNN with a 3×3 filter; it should be clear that without any special consideration of the edge pixels, the size of the output will be two units less than the input for the spatial dimensions. This effect is also evident in the CNN used in Example 6.2, which also uses a 3×3 filter size; the input to the first layer is 28×28 while the first two dimensions of the output are 26×26. We may want more control over this behaviour by using *padding*, and three common types are illustrated in Figure 6.5.

The default behaviour with no changes is known as *valid padding*. In this case, the filter is applied directly to the input, and the output is reduced in size as determined by the size of the filter. If the input is of width m and the kernel is of width k, then the output is of width $m - k + 1$. While it is common practice to use square input images and square filters, rectangular inputs and filters can also be used so that the output size can vary by dimension.

Same padding ensures that the output has the same dimension as the input. This method adds a border with zero value to the edge of the input wide enough to ensure that the output size matches the input once the filter has been applied. A 3×3 filter requires a border width of 1 pixel, while a 5×5 filter needs a width of 2 pixels.

Full padding adds border zeros so that each pixel in the input has the filter applied the same number of times in each direction. This approach pads the input with enough zeros so that the first application of the filter will touch the corner pixel. For a 3×3 filter, two border rows are added and filled with zeros, resulting in an output one element larger in width and height than the input. Goodfellow et al. (2016) note that full padding can lead to difficulty learning a kernel that performs well across the input. In practice, valid and same padding is more common than full padding.

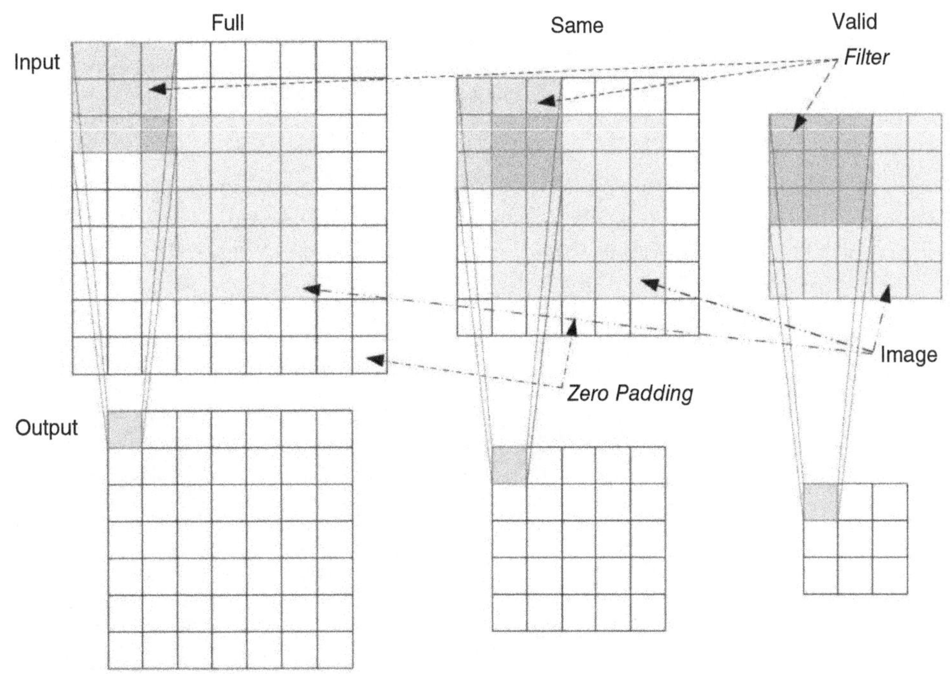

FIGURE 6.5 The three different types of padding are full, same and valid (see text for explanation).

6.2.4 Multi-Channel Convolutions

The MNIST dataset is a set of greyscale images that consists of a single channel containing intensity values. However, there are many data instances with multiple channels, such as RGB images. The input is expanded to three channels in the context of colour images, and the filters in the input layer now must have a matching depth (Aggarwal, 2018, p. 320). Note that, given that the depth of the filter is governed entirely by the number of channels in a layer, it is not specified separately and only the user determines the width and height. Hence, the weight matrix associated with each filter is a three-dimensional tensor $\mathbf{W}$ containing width × height × depth weights, and there is one additional bias parameter per filter.

EXAMPLE 6.3: THE CIFAR-10 DATASET

The CIFAR-10 dataset (Krizhevsky, 2009) from the *Canadian Institute for Advanced Research* consists of 60,000 32 × 32 colour images in 10 classes: aeroplane, automobile, bird, cat, deer, dog, frog, horse, ship and truck (see Figure 6.6). A model using CIFAR-10 is trained in the Jupyter Notebook `Colour CNN Example.ipynb`. The dataset is built into PyTorch and so can be loaded similarly to MNIST.

```
transform = transforms.Compose([
    transforms.ToTensor(),
    transforms.Normalize((0.5, 0.5, 0.5), (0.5, 0.5, 0.5))
])

trainset = torchvision.datasets.CIFAR10(root='./data', train=True,
                                        download=True, transform=transform)
trainloader = torch.utils.data.DataLoader(trainset, batch_size=2048,
                                          shuffle=True)

testset = torchvision.datasets.CIFAR10(root='./data', train=False,
                                       download=True, transform=transform)
```

(*Continued*)

(*Continued*)

```
testloader = torch.utils.data.DataLoader(testset, batch_size=2048,
                                         shuffle=False)
```

The data preparation follows the same pattern as that of MNIST. Conversion of the image data to floating point and division by 255 reduces the intensity values to the range [−1.0, 1.0]. The labels remain as integers in the [0, 9] range. The CNN construction mirrors the earlier MNIST example, with the input shape changed to (:, 3, 32, 32), where the second entry represents the colour channels.

FIGURE 6.6 Ten images from the CIFAR-10 dataset. Note that the images are pixelated as the underlying images are 32 × 32 pixels.

The output of the model summary is as follows.

```
CNNModel(
    (conv1): Conv2d(3, 32, kernel_size=(3, 3), stride=(1, 1))
    (conv2): Conv2d(32, 64, kernel_size=(3, 3), stride=(1, 1))
    (conv3): Conv2d(64, 64, kernel_size=(3, 3), stride=(1, 1))
    (pool): MaxPool2d(kernel_size=2, stride=2, padding=0,
                      dilation=1, ceil_mode=False)
    (fc1): Linear(in_features=256, out_features=64, bias=True)
    (fc2): Linear(in_features=64, out_features=10, bias=True)
)
```

The following formula gives the number of parameters in the first layer:

$$
\begin{aligned}
\text{no.param} &= \text{no.filters} \times (\text{height} \times \text{width} \times \text{channels} + 1) \\
&= 32 \times (3 \times 3 \times 3 + 1) \\
&= 896.
\end{aligned}
$$

The same formula works for the deeper convolutional layers, too. After training for 200 epochs, the model had a validation accuracy of 70%.

6.2.5 Selecting Filter Sizes

How should the size of a filter be chosen? For example, in Example 6.3, 3×3 filters were used, which is the most common choice today but is not the only possible one. The first thing to note is that, in general, odd filter sizes are preferred because odd sizes lead to a symmetric division of the previous layer pixels. In contrast, even sizes can lead to distortions (Pandey, 2020). A 1×1 filter will act to reduce the number of channels and not act spatially across the plane of the image, and so can be considered a particular case. In early CNNs such as AlexNet (see Section 6.7.2), filter sizes were larger, with AlexNet using 5×5 and 11×11 (Krizhevsky et al., 2012). However, the computational cost of large filters has proved to be prohibitive and hence, today, 3×3 is more common (Pandey, 2020). Inception version 3 (Szegedy et al., 2016) (see Section 6.7.4) uses factorised convolutions where a $1 \times n$ convolution is followed by an $n \times 1$ convolution, where n is odd.

EXAMPLE 6.4: DIFFERENT FILTER SIZES WITH THE CIFAR-10 DATASET

Classifier models were trained using the CIFAR-10 dataset to see the impact of filter size on accuracy and training time, and this example can be found in the Jupyter Notebook `Changing Filter Size.ipynb`. Square filters were used with odd sizes ranging between 3 and 7, with one additional case using factorised filters with a layer using 1×3 followed by one using 3×1. To compare these models, it makes sense to use the 'same' padding so that the convolution does not reduce the size of each output layer and then rely on max pooling to downsample. The model construction function for the square filter case becomes

```
class CNNModel(nn.Module):
    def __init__(self, filter_size=3):
        super(CNNModel, self).__init__()
        self.conv1 = nn.Conv2d(3, 32, kernel_size=filter_size,
                               padding='same')
        self.pool = nn.MaxPool2d(kernel_size=2, stride=2)
        self.conv2 = nn.Conv2d(32, 64, kernel_size=filter_size,
                               padding='same')
        self.conv3 = nn.Conv2d(64, 64, kernel_size=filter_size,
                               padding='same')
        self.flatten = nn.Flatten()
        self.fc1 = nn.Linear(64 * 8 * 8, 64)
        self.fc2 = nn.Linear(64, 10)
        self.relu = nn.ReLU()

    def forward(self, x):
        x = self.relu(self.conv1(x))
        x = self.pool(x)
        x = self.relu(self.conv2(x))
        x = self.pool(x)
        x = self.relu(self.conv3(x))
        x = self.flatten(x)
        x = self.relu(self.fc1(x))
        x = self.fc2(x)
        return x
```

A pair of layers replaces each convolutional layer to handle the factorised filters.

```
class CNNFactorizedModel(nn.Module):
    def __init__(self, filter_size=3):
        super(CNNFactorizedModel, self).__init__()
```

(*Continued*)

(*Continued*)

```
        self.conv1_1 = nn.Conv2d(3, 32, kernel_size=(1, filter_size),
                                 padding='same')
        self.conv1_2 = nn.Conv2d(32, 32, kernel_size=(filter_size, 1),
                                 padding='same')
        self.pool = nn.MaxPool2d(kernel_size=2, stride=2)
        self.conv2_1 = nn.Conv2d(32, 64, kernel_size=(1, filter_size),
                                 padding='same')
        self.conv2_2 = nn.Conv2d(64, 64, kernel_size=(filter_size, 1),
                                 padding='same')
        self.conv3_1 = nn.Conv2d(64, 64, kernel_size=(1, filter_size),
                                 padding='same')
        self.conv3_2 = nn.Conv2d(64, 64, kernel_size=(filter_size, 1),
                                 padding='same')
        self.flatten = nn.Flatten()
        self.fc1 = nn.Linear(64 * 8 * 8, 64)
        self.fc2 = nn.Linear(64, 10)
        self.relu = nn.ReLU()

    def forward(self, x):
        x = self.relu(self.conv1_1(x))
        x = self.relu(self.conv1_2(x))
        x = self.pool(x)
        x = self.relu(self.conv2_1(x))
        x = self.relu(self.conv2_2(x))
        x = self.pool(x)
        x = self.relu(self.conv3_1(x))
        x = self.relu(self.conv3_2(x))
        x = self.flatten(x)
        x = self.relu(self.fc1(x))
        x = self.fc2(x)
        return x
```

Figure 6.7 shows the validation accuracy of the six models with different filter sizes trained using the CIFAR-10 dataset. It is immediately apparent that the models with smaller filters perform better. Given the relatively small image size of 32×32, larger filters may smear out features too much and reduce the level of accuracy that can be obtained. Training time is also a consideration, with smaller filters expected to be more computationally efficient. This is illustrated in Table 6.1, which shows the time taken to train each model through 200 epochs. The 3×3 case gives the best computational performance.

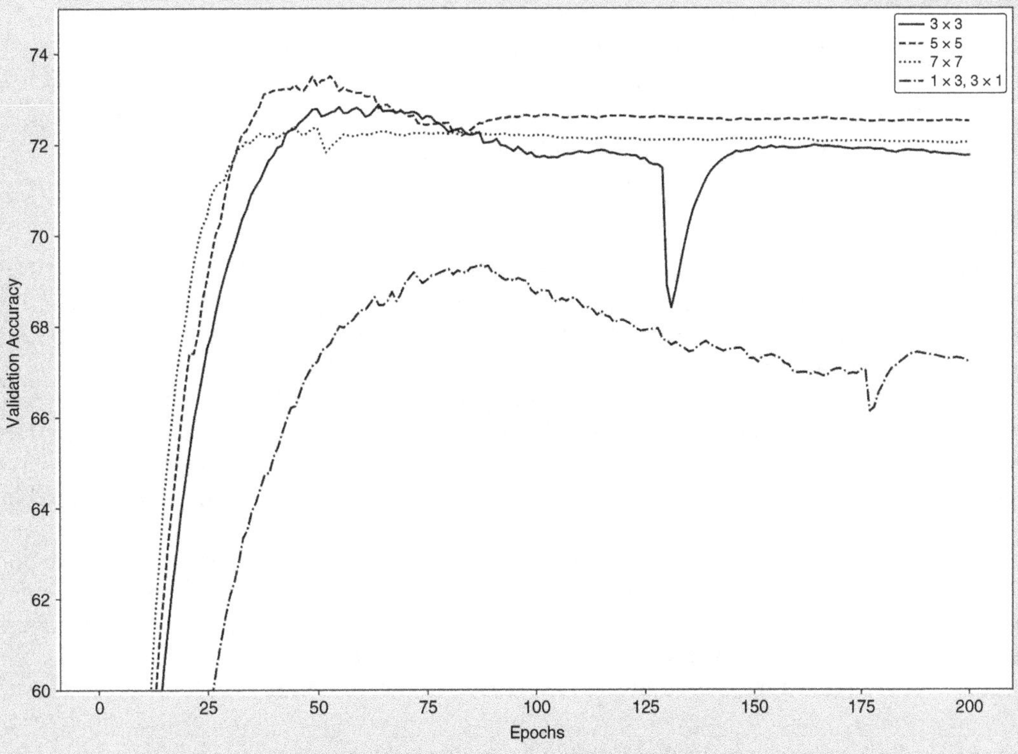

FIGURE 6.7 Smoothed validation accuracy for CIFAR-10 with different filter sizes.

TABLE 6.1 Time to Train a Model Using the CIFAR-10 Dataset as a Function of Filter Size. All Models Were Trained Through 200 Epochs

Filter Size	Training Time (s)
3 × 3	146.328155
5 × 5	159.312209
7 × 7	182.096126
1 × 3, 3 × 1	216.462546

6.2.6 Choosing the Number of Filters

Each filter represents a learned feature, and the number of filters in each convolutional layer represents another hyperparameter that can be tuned. Typically, the number of filters is chosen to be a power of two and ranges from 16 to 512. It is relatively common for the number of filters to double for each successive convolutional layer.

6.3 DOWNSAMPLING

In general, in CNNs, the image size must be compressed deeper into the network as the number of filters gradually increases. This *downsampling* can be accomplished in several different ways. Firstly, we have seen that in the absence of padding, the image plane is naturally reduced in size by the convolution operation because of image effects. In practice, however, two methods are used to downsample: *strided convolutions* and *pooling* layers.

6.3.1 Strided Convolutions

Strided convolution achieves downsampling straightforwardly. Instead of applying a filter to every pixel in the input plane, the filter applies to pixel locations separated by *stride* pixels in the x and y directions. A stride of 2 leads to downsampling by a factor of 2 (Chollet, 2018, p. 127). Generally, strided convolutions are rarely used, with pooling operations serving as the preferred mechanism for downsampling.

6.3.2 Pooling

Pooling functions replace their input with an array of summary statistics (Goodfellow et al., 2016, p. 330). The pooling operator acts on a range of inputs of size (p, q) and provides a single output from each operator. Unlike the convolution operator, pooling layers act on each filter or channel separately, so the output of a pooling layer has the same number of channels as the input.

We want the neural network to have shift-invariance properties for applications like image recognition. For example, if we train a CNN to recognise cats, we would like it to detect cats wherever they occur in the input image (Goodfellow et al., 2016, p. 331). Pooling operations provide this translation-invariance property in CNNs. Pooling, by downsampling, also increases the receptive fields of later layers and, therefore, helps build learned hierarchies of features.

Max pooling, the most common form of pooling operation, is illustrated in Figure 6.8. Max pooling selects a square region of size (p, q) from the input and chooses the highest numerical value to pass to the output. The operator typically applies to the input with a stride larger than 1. A standard configuration uses max pooling with size 2×2 and a stride of 2, resulting in an output half the input size.

Other types of pooling have been used in the past. *LeNet-5* (LeCun et al., 1998a) (see Section 6.7.1 below) employed *average pooling*, which averages the values inside the operator. Additional pooling types are possible, such as those based on the L_2 norm or using weighted averages (Goodfellow et al., 2016, p. 330). However, these alternative methods are rarely used in practice.

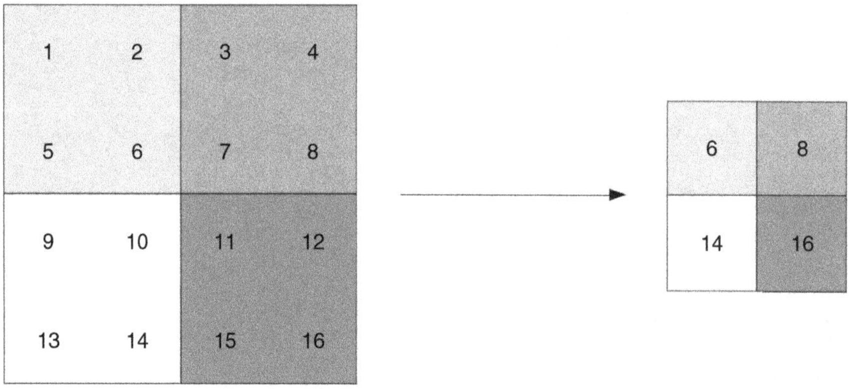

FIGURE 6.8 Max pooling using a 2×2 pooling size and a stride of 2 in each direction.

EXAMPLE 6.5: DOWNSAMPLING

Three models were trained using the CIFAR-10 dataset using *max pooling*, *average pooling* and *strided convolutions* to explore the impact of different types of downsampling (see the Jupyter Notebook `Pooling Operations.ipynb`). All the earlier CNN examples have used max pooling, which adds a `MaxPooling2D` layer after a convolutional layer. In PyTorch, this is done using

```
nn.MaxPool2d(2, 2)
```

Average pooling is similarly specified in PyTorch using

```
nn.AvgPool2d(2, 2)
```

For the strided convolution case, the pooling layers are dropped entirely, and the convolutional layers are then specified with a (2, 2) stride. The first convolutional layer is then specified as follows:

```
def calculate_same_padding(kernel_size, stride):
    return (kernel_size - 1) // 2 if stride == 1 \
        else ((stride - 1) + kernel_size - 1) // 2

nn.Conv2d(32, 64, kernel_size=3, stride=2,
          padding=calculate_same_padding(3, 2))
```

The validation accuracy for the three models is shown in Figure 6.9 with training over 200 epochs, with max pooling giving the best performance.

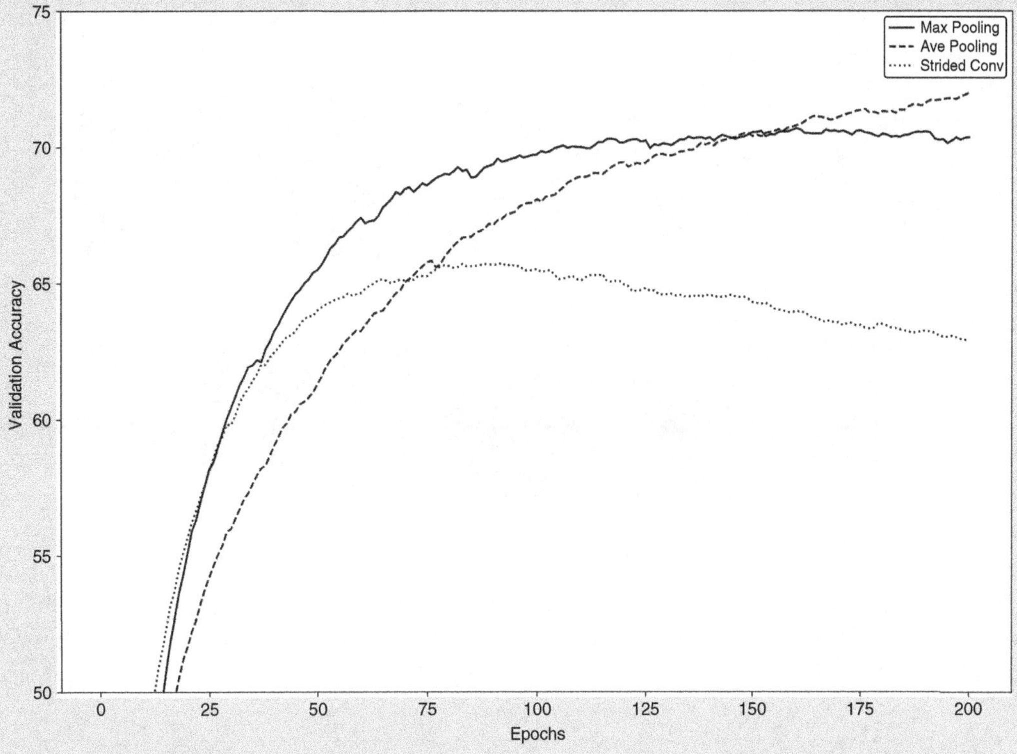

FIGURE 6.9 Validation accuracy from models with three different types of downsampling: max pooling, average pooling and strided convolutions.

6.4 DATA AUGMENTATION

Section 4.5 briefly described data augmentation in the context of regularisation, noting its common use in computer vision applications. The general idea involves creating fake data by transforming the training data. Transformations applied to images can include translations, rotations and scaling. However, care is required. Consider the MNIST dataset of handwritten images: inverting the images of sixes would result in what appeared to be nines (Goodfellow et al., 2016, p. 234). Hence, the range of admissible transformations depends on the context. An example best illustrates data augmentation.

EXAMPLE 6.6: USING DATA AUGMENTATION WITH THE Galaxy10 DECals DATASET

The Galaxy10 DECals dataset (Leung and Bovy, 2017) consists of 17,736 256 × 256 images of galaxies classified into 10 categories. The underlying images were initially sourced from the *Sloan Digital Sky Survey (SDSS)* via the Galaxy Zoo project (Lintott et al., 2008). Figure 6.10 illustrates 10 examples from the dataset. Here, we use the dataset to train a galaxy-type classifier and demonstrate the impact of data augmentation. The example is in the Jupyter Notebook `Data Augmentation with Galaxy10 DECals Dataset.ipynb`.

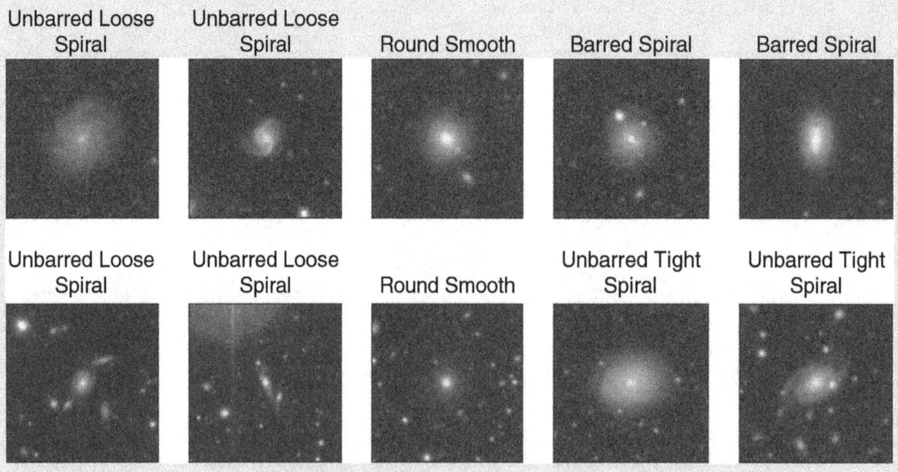

FIGURE 6.10 Ten examples of galaxies from the Galaxy10 DECals dataset.

The data must first be downloaded from the *astroNN* website, https://astro.utoronto.ca/~hleung/shared/Galaxy10/Galaxy10_DECals.h5, and this is a large file at 2.54 GB and will take some time to download. The file then needs to be loaded in Python and split into an array of images and labels.

```
import h5py
import numpy as np

with h5py.File('Galaxy10_DECals.h5', 'r') as gF:
images = np.array(gF['images'])
labels = np.array(gF['ans'])
```

The images and labels must then be shuffled randomly using `sklearn.utils.shuffle` and split into training and test sets using `train_test_split`. Finally, the labels need to be converted to categorical variables, and the images converted to `float32` and scaled by dividing by 255.

The model trained is a simple CNN with three convolutional layers, with 32, 64 and 64 features and using 3×3 filters. There are two, 2×2, max-pooling layers with stride 2 to reduce dimensions. Finally, there is a dense layer followed by a softmax output.

To use data augmentation in PyTorch, `transforms` are used. The following class defines a series of random data augmentations.

```
class CustomAugmentations:
    def __init__(self, rotation_range, width_shift_range, height_shift_range,
                 shear_range, zoom_range, horizontal_flip):
        self.rotation_range = rotation_range
        self.width_shift_range = width_shift_range
        self.height_shift_range = height_shift_range
        self.shear_range = shear_range
        self.zoom_range = zoom_range
        self.horizontal_flip = horizontal_flip

    def __call__(self, img):
        # Random rotation
        angle = torch.empty(1).uniform_(-self.rotation_range,
                                        self.rotation_range).item()
        img = TF.rotate(img, angle,
                        interpolation=TF.InterpolationMode.NEAREST)

        # Random width shift
        width_shift = torch.empty(1).uniform_(-self.width_shift_range,
                                              self.width_shift_range).item()
        img = TF.affine(img, angle=0,
                        translate=(width_shift * img.shape[2], 0), scale=1,
                        shear=0, interpolation=TF.InterpolationMode.NEAREST)

        # Random height shift
        height_shift = torch.empty(1).uniform_(-self.height_shift_range,
                                               self.height_shift_range).item()
        img = TF.affine(img, angle=0,
                        translate=(0, height_shift * img.shape[1]), scale=1,
                                   shear=0,
                                  interpolation=TF.InterpolationMode.NEAREST)

        # Random shear
        shear = torch.empty(1).uniform_(-self.shear_range,
                                        self.shear_range).item()
        img = TF.affine(img, angle=0, translate=(0, 0), scale=1, shear=shear,
                        interpolation=TF.InterpolationMode.NEAREST)

        # Random zoom
        zoom = torch.empty(1).uniform_(1 - self.zoom_range,
                                       1 + self.zoom_range).item()
        img = TF.affine(img, angle=0, translate=(0, 0), scale=zoom, shear=0,
                        interpolation=TF.InterpolationMode.NEAREST)

        # Random horizontal flip
        if self.horizontal_flip and torch.rand(1).item() > 0.5:
            img = TF.hflip(img)

        return img
```

(*Continued*)

(*Continued*)

The image transform is constructed using the following code:

```
custom_transforms = transforms.Compose([
    CustomAugmentations(rotation_range=40,
                        width_shift_range=0.2,
                        height_shift_range=0.2,
                        shear_range=0.2,
                        zoom_range=0.2,
                        horizontal_flip=True)
])
```

The parameters above are defined as follows.

- **rotation_range:** an integer specifies the range in degrees [0–180] to randomly rotate the image.
- **width_shift_range:** float [0–1] that specifies a range of random horizontal translation.
- **height_shift_range:** float [0–1] that specifies a range of random vertical translation.
- **shear_range:** float shear intensity.
- **zoom_range:** float or (upper, lower) tuple that specifies the range for random zooms.
- **horizontal_flip:** randomly flip images horizontally.
- **fill_mode:** set the mode to fill new pixels generated when transformation occurs.

A bespoke dataset class is constructed to apply the transforms to the fly.

```
class AugmentedDataset(torch.utils.data.Dataset):
 def __init__(self, dataset, transform=None):
     self.dataset = dataset
     self.transform = transform

 def __len__(self):
     return len(self.dataset)

 def __getitem__(self, idx):
     x, y = self.dataset[idx]
     if self.transform:
        x = self.transform(x)
     return x, y
```

The dataset and data loader were then constructed as follows, with the test data loader remaining unchanged.

```
aug_train_dataset = AugmentedDataset(train_dataset,
                                     transform=custom_transforms)

train_loader = DataLoader(aug_train_dataset, batch_size=128, shuffle=True)
```

The model with and without data augmentation was trained through 200 epochs with a batch size of 128. The training and validation accuracy for both cases is illustrated in Figure 6.11. In the case without data augmentation, the model overfits drastically to the small training test and then fails to generalise. The model with data augmentation performs significantly better with no overfitting and has a similar training and validation accuracy that slowly improves as a function of epoch.

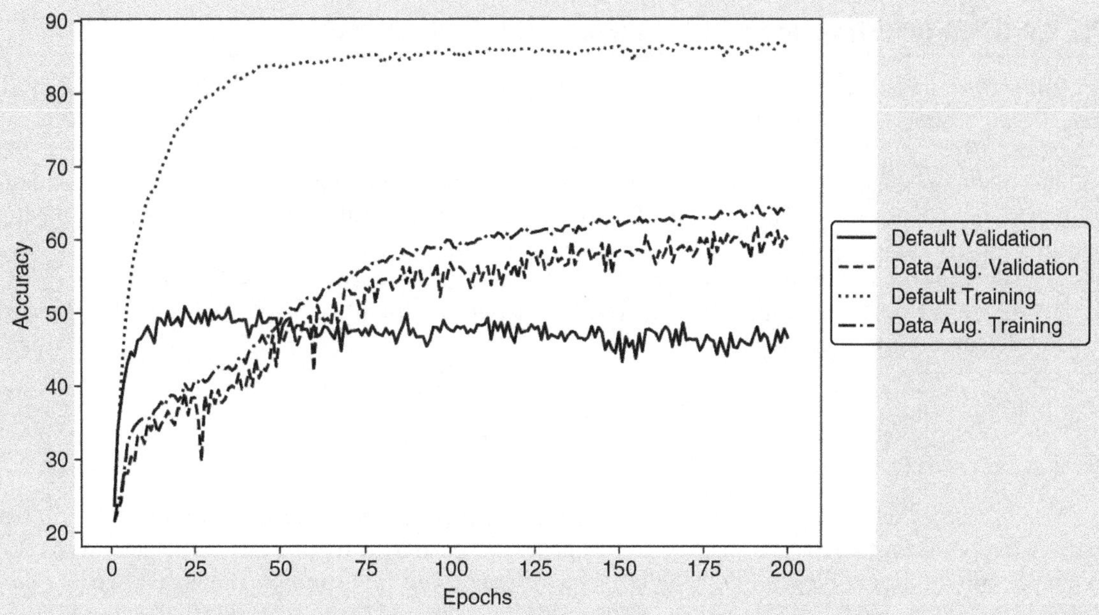

FIGURE 6.11 Training and validation accuracy for a CNN trained against the Galaxy10 DECals dataset both with and without data augmentation.

6.5 TRANSFER LEARNING: USING PRE-TRAINED NETWORKS

Transfer learning involves reusing a trained network for another application, which is relatively common in computer vision and natural language processing applications. Transfer learning relies on the learned representation or features being meaningful more generally than in the original application. Images share many low-level elements such as edges and shapes (Goodfellow et al., 2016, p. 527). So, a CNN would learn these low-level features in the early layers of a network and then compose them into complex and domain-specific features in later layers. This behaviour can be visualised as illustrated in Section 6.6. The GPT-3 natural language model shows similar behaviour. Once trained, the basic model can be applied to several tasks when fine-tuned using a small number of examples (Brown et al., 2020; Metz, 2020).

There are several drivers behind the use of transfer learning. One is simply the cost of training. The CNNs described in Section 6.7 are all modest by current standards but still take many hours to train from scratch using a recent GPU card. The state-of-the-art natural language model GPT-3 has 175 billion parameters and requires several thousand petaflop/s-days of computing to train (Brown et al., 2020, p. 39). A *second issue* is the available labelled data, which may not be sufficient to support training from scratch. Transfer learning, however, can often be done with a minimal amount of data.

Many trained models are available in standard packages such as Keras, Tensorflow and PyTorch. First, download the weights of the trained models, then use them to instantiate the neural network structure; for transfer learning, some retraining element is required. In some cases, this could involve replacing the dense layers at the end of a CNN and freezing all the weights of the downloaded model. However, the later features in the model may not be appropriate to the new task, and hence, some of the later layers of the trained model are subject to fine-tuning with the new dataset.

EXAMPLE 6.7: USING TRANSFER LEARNING WITH THE Galaxy10 DECals DATASET

As an example of transfer learning, consider using a model trained on ImageNet as the basis of a galaxy classifier using the Galaxy10 DECals dataset (see the Jupyter Notebook `Transfer Learning with Galaxy10 DECals Dataset.ipynb`), and this might not seem an obvious thing to do, given that ImageNet does not contain any images of galaxies. However, the same general features and shapes in terrestrial images are also present in galaxies, so reusing the early layers of a pre-trained network still makes sense. However, the higher-level features are probably undesirable, so these will be retrained.

The Galaxy10 dataset is prepared in Example 6.6, and data augmentation is also used here. The base model to be reused is *ResNet50* from PyTorch, a residual network with 50 layers described in detail in Section 6.7.5 below. To load this model, we call

```
import torchvision.models as models

resnet50 = models.resnet50(pretrained=True)
```

The next step specifies which layers undergo fine-tuning using the galaxy dataset and which remain frozen. Each parameter block contains a `.required_grad` property settable to true or false. The network is divided into five large convolutional blocks, with the last block undergoing fine-tuning. The layers are looped over with the required grad set to false. Adaptation of the last fully connected layer is necessary due to the 10 classes rather than the 1000 of ImageNet. A dense layer with 256 nodes and a softmax layer output replaces this layer.

```
freeze_layers = ['conv1', 'bn1', 'relu', 'maxpool', 'layer1', 'layer2',
                 'layer3']
for name, param in resnet50.named_parameters():
    if any(freeze_layer in name for freeze_layer in freeze_layers):
        param.requires_grad = False

num_features = resnet50.fc.in_features
resnet50.fc = nn.Sequential(
    nn.Linear(num_features, 256),
    nn.ReLU(),
    nn.Linear(256, 10),
    nn.Softmax(dim=1)
)
for param in resnet50.fc.parameters():
    param.requires_grad = True
```

The results are shown in Figure 6.12, and the final validation accuracy was 62.6% after 50 epochs. The experiment succeeded even though the underlying model was trained using completely different training data without overlapping with galaxy images.

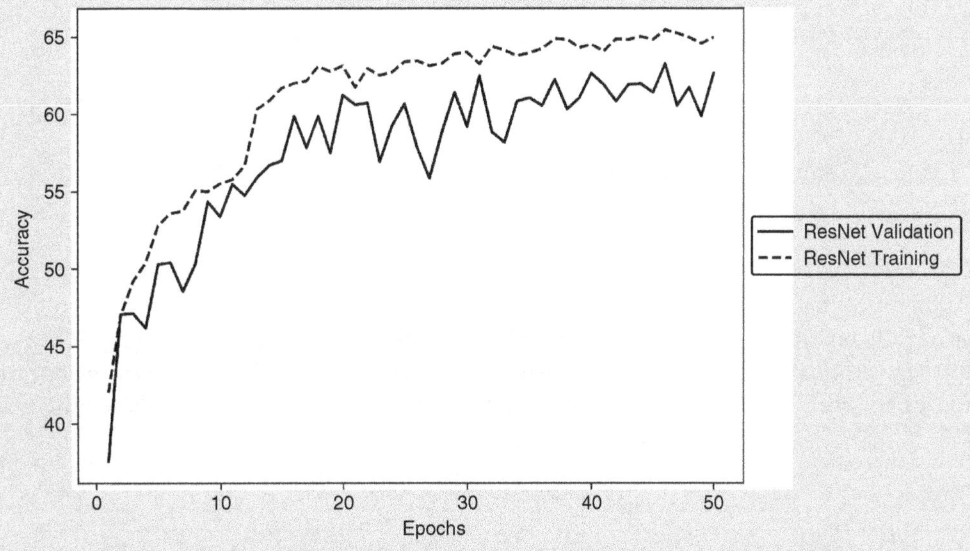

FIGURE 6.12 Training and validation accuracy for a ResNet retrained as a galaxy classifier.

6.6 VISUALISING FEATURES

One major criticism of neural network models is the need for more transparency and explainability in obtaining their output values, particularly with classifiers. In the case of computer vision applications, this is not true, and there has been a sustained effort since Zeiler and Fergus (2013) to explore how CNNs 'see' the world. This section will discuss and implement numerous methods to explore computer vision in Example 6.8.

6.6.1 Visualising Filters and Feature Activations

This most straightforward possible approach to visualising CNNs is to look at the trained two-dimensional filters (Aggarwal, 2018, p. 352). Once training is complete, the weights for each filter in a convolutional layer can be extracted and plotted as an intensity map. Furthermore, this gives a visual representation of the filters and allows a basic understanding of what role each filter plays, and this is very meaningful for the first convolutional layer as the channels correspond directly to the three RGB pixel intensities. Beyond that, however, the filters operate on the output of the filters of the previous layer, and it becomes difficult to interpret meaningfully. Some of the first layer filters for a galaxy classifier model are shown in Figure 6.13.

Another simple approach to visualisation is to examine the feature activations given a specific image (Chollet, 2018, pp. 160–166), and this is done by using an input image for model inference, while retaining the intermediate activations in the convolutional layers and plotting them. With a trained model, the expected pattern is to see a progression in the behaviour of each layer (Chollet, 2018, p. 166). The first layer is expected to provide simple features such as edge detection. Later layers become more challenging to interpret and are expected to contain information about the features in the image rather than the image itself. Features in later layers may become blank, indicating that the particular element encoded in that feature is not present in the input image. The feature activations for three convolutional layers given an input barred spiral galaxy are illustrated in Figure 6.15.

6.6.2 Gradient-Based Visualisation

Perhaps the most obvious way to try to understand the relationship between the inputs and outputs of a model is to use gradients, and several authors have adopted this approach (see, e.g., Szegedy et al., 2013; Zeiler and

Fergus, 2013; Springenberg et al., 2014; Simonyan and Zisserman, 2015; Selvaraju et al., 2017). The first choice is to examine the sensitivity of a given output o with respect to an input pixel x_{ij},

$$\frac{\partial o}{\partial x_{ij}}, \tag{6.11}$$

which gives the *saliency map* (Simonyan and Zisserman, 2015), and this can be extended to any intermediate activation h,

$$\frac{\partial h}{\partial x_{ij}}. \tag{6.12}$$

Calculating these gradients uses backpropagation as usual, which is now extended to the input layer. The standard backpropagation algorithm applies, but two alternatives exist: *deconvnet* and *guided backpropagation*. In deconvnet, application of the ReLU activation function to the backpropagated gradient modifies the gradient g_i from (Aggarwal, 2018, p. 355)

$$g_i = g_{i+1} \odot \max(z_i, 0) \tag{6.13}$$

to

$$g_i = g_{i+1} \odot \max(g_{i+1}, 0). \tag{6.14}$$

Guided backpropagation further modifies this by adding back the original max function to give

$$g_i = g_{i+1} \odot \max(g_{i+1}, 0) \odot \max(z_i, 0). \tag{6.15}$$

The gradient visualisation depends on the input image, necessitating a second choice of what input image to use. Using an actual image allows the gradient to highlight pixels contributing to a particular activation, such as an output class. Figure 6.16 shows a saliency map of this type.

Grad-CAM (Selvaraju et al., 2017) provides a heat map of activation response for a given category of output and the input image. This approach calculates the gradient of a score for a given class, y^c, with respect to the features of a convolutional layer h^k,

$$\frac{\partial y^c}{\partial h^k}. \tag{6.16}$$

These gradients are then averaged/pooled to give *neuron importance weights*,

$$a_k^c = \frac{1}{Z}\sum_i \sum_j \frac{\partial y^c}{\partial h_{ij}^k}. \tag{6.17}$$

These weights are then used to give a weighted average of forward activation maps,

$$L_{\text{Grad-CAM}}^c = \max\left(\sum_k a_k^c h^k, 0\right). \tag{6.18}$$

This can be used as a heat map and overlain on the image to show the areas in the image that are important to class c. Figure 6.17 shows an example of the classified galaxy.

EXAMPLE 6.8: VISUALISING A GALAXY CLASSIFIER

This example will apply several visualisation techniques to a galaxy classifier model trained on the Galaxy10 DECals dataset. The same simple model with three convolutional layers trained with data augmentation in Example 6.6 will be used here. The examples are in the Jupyter Notebook `Visualising Features with Galaxy10 DECals Dataset.ipynb`.

The first way to visualise what the model has learned is to look at the filters physically. The filters can be extracted from each convolutional layer and then plotted (Brownlee, 2019b), and this can be done quickly with PyTorch by extracting the first layer from the model and then getting the weights from the layer. The weights can then be normalised and scaled to sit in the range [0, 255] to present a series of intensity values that can be plotted.

```
layer = cnn_model.conv1

weights = layer.weight.data.cpu().numpy()
max_val = weights.max()
min_val = weights.min()
abs_max = max(abs(min_val), abs(max_val))
weights = (weights / abs_max) * 255
weights = weights.astype(np.uint8)

plt.figure(figsize=(15, 5))
n_filters, ix = 16, 1
for i in range(n_filters):
    f = weights[i]
    # Loop over the RGB channels
    for j in range(3):
        ax = plt.subplot(3, n_filters, ix)
        ax.set_xticks([])
        ax.set_yticks([])
        # Plot filter channel in grayscale
        plt.imshow(f[j], cmap='gray')
        ix += 1
```

The plots for the first 16 filters, out of 32 for the first layer of the galaxy classifier, are shown in Figure 6.13. The three lines of filters represent red, green and blue channels, respectively. The filters are all 3×3 in size, matching the architecture of the first convolutional layer and showing various simple patterns that correspond to features such as edge detectors.

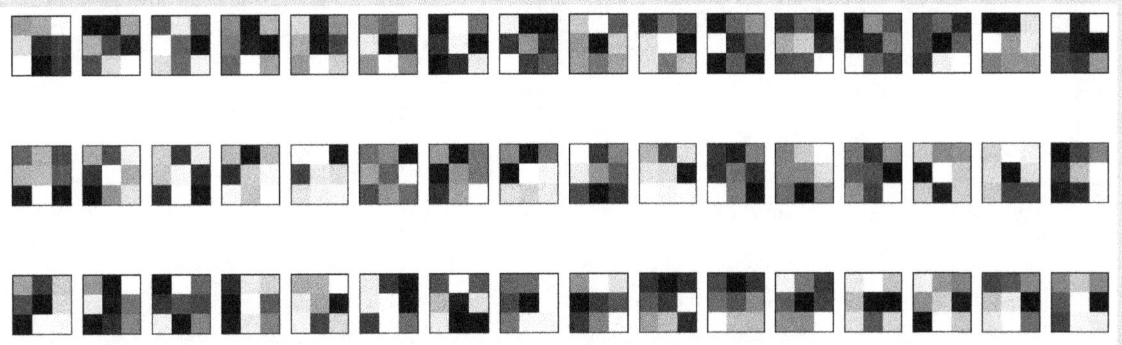

FIGURE 6.13 The first 16 filters from the three red, green and blue channels for the first convolutional layer in the example network trained on the Galaxy10 DECals dataset.

The second approach to visualisation is to examine the intermediate activation responses in the convolutional layers of a given image. A new image, not in the training or test set, is used for this purpose, and in this case, a Hubble Space Telescope image of NGC 4680 is used and is illustrated in Figure 6.14. This high-resolution image is reduced to 256×256 for use with the classifier.

(*Continued*)

(*Continued*)

FIGURE 6.14 The spiral galaxy NGC 4680 taken with the Hubble Space Telescope. *Image Source:* ESA/Hubble & NASA, A. Riess et al.

The first step is to use the image with the classifier, and the model classifies NGC 4680 as a barred spiral. The following code is used to extract the intermediate activations.

```
# Extract the activations
act = {}
def get_activation(name):
    def hook(model, input, output):
        act[name] = output.detach()
    return hook

for name, layer in cnn_model.named_modules():
    if isinstance(layer, torch.nn.Conv2d):
        layer.register_forward_hook(get_activation(name))

# Perform a forward pass to get the activations
with torch.no_grad():
    _ = cnn_model(img_tensor)
```

The next step is to define a function that will display the intermediate activations for each layer, and this needs to increase the contrast in the activations.

```
def plotActivations(layer_act, img_per_row, filename=None, cmap='gist_gray'):
```

```
layer_act = layer_act.squeeze().cpu().numpy()
features = layer_act.shape[0]
size = layer_act.shape[1]
cols = features // img_per_row
display_grid = np.zeros((size * cols, img_per_row * size))

for col in range(cols):
    for row in range(img_per_row):
        ch_img = layer_act[col * img_per_row + row]

        # Enhance the contrast
        ch_img_min = ch_img.min()
        ch_img_max = ch_img.max()
        diff = (ch_img_max - ch_img_min + 1e-5)
        ch_img = ch_img * 255 / diff
        display_grid[col * size : (col + 1) * size,
                     row * size : (row + 1) * size] = ch_img

scale = 1.0 / size
plt.figure(figsize=(scale * display_grid.shape[1],
scale * display_grid.shape[0]))
plt.grid(False)

fig = plt.imshow(display_grid, aspect='auto', cmap=cmap, vmin=0,
                 vmax=255)
fig.axes.get_xaxis().set_visible(False)
fig.axes.get_yaxis().set_visible(False)
if filename is not None:
    plt.savefig(filename, dpi=300, bbox_inches='tight')
```

Figure 6.15 shows one of the intermediate activations for the NGC 4680 image.

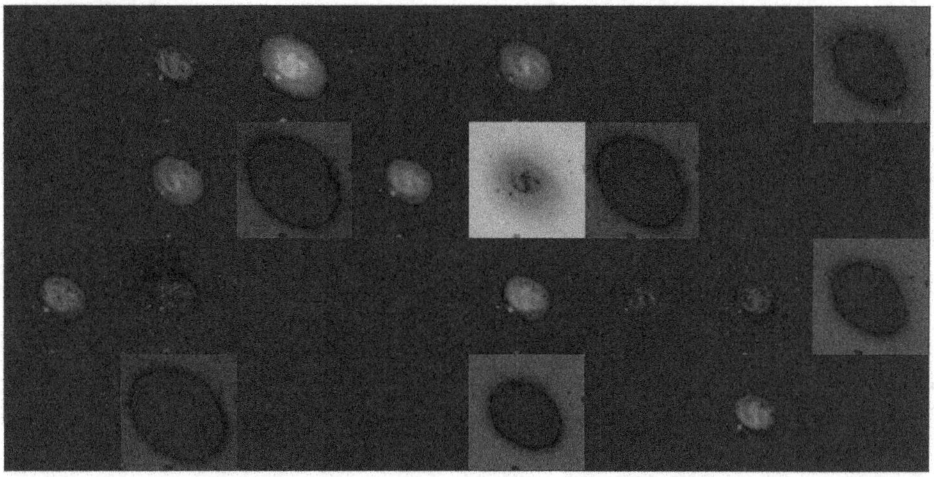

FIGURE 6.15 Activations from the first convolutional layer.

(Continued)

(*Continued*)

Creating the saliency map for a given image is straightforward using the built-in classes in the package `Captum`, which works with PyTorch models. The input image is the galaxy NGC 4680, and the output map can be displayed directly using `matplotlib.pyplot.imshow`, giving the result in Figure 6.16.

```
cnn_model.eval()

# Replace the model's last activation function to a linear one
class ReplaceToLinear(nn.Module):
    def __init__(self, model):
        super().__init__()
        self.model = model
        self.replace_last_layer()

    def replace_last_layer(self):
        self.model.fc2 = nn.Linear(self.model.fc2.in_features,
                                   self.model.fc2.out_features)

    def forward(self, x):
        return self.model(x)

cnn_model_da = ReplaceToLinear(cnn_model)
cnn_model_da = cnn_model_da.to(device)

# Define the score function
class CategoricalScore:
    def __init__(self, target_class):
        self.target_class = target_class

    def __call__(self, model_output):
        return model_output[:, self.target_class]

# Get the predicted class
score = CategoricalScore(ipred)

# Create a Saliency object
saliency = Saliency(cnn_model_da)

# Compute saliency map
saliency_map = saliency.attribute(img_tensor, target=ipred)

# Convert the saliency map to a NumPy array and visualize it
saliency_map = saliency_map.squeeze().permute(1, 2, 0).cpu().numpy()

sa_max = saliency_map.max()
sa_min = saliency_map.min()
saliency_map = (saliency_map - sa_min) * 255 / (sa_max - sa_min)

saliency_map = saliency_map.astype(np.uint8)[:,:,0]

fig = plt.imshow(saliency_map, cmap='binary', norm=norm)
fig.axes.get_xaxis().set_visible(False)
fig.axes.get_yaxis().set_visible(False)
plt.savefig('SaliencyMap.png', dpi=300, bbox_inches='tight')
```

FIGURE 6.16 A saliency map for the barred spiral image.

The final visualisation type in this example is Grad-CAM. The implementation is similar to the saliency map using the `LayerGradCAM` class from PyTorch. The resulting image is given in Figure 6.17.

```
layer_gradcam = LayerGradCam(cnn_model_da, cnn_model_da.model.conv3)

# Generate heatmap with GradCAM
attributions = layer_gradcam.attribute(img_tensor, target=ipred)

# Upsample the attributions to the input image size
upsampled_attributions = LayerGradCam.interpolate(attributions,
                                                   img_tensor.shape[-2:])

# Convert the attributions to a NumPy array and visualize it
heatmap = upsampled_attributions.squeeze().cpu().detach().numpy()
heatmap = np.uint8(cm.jet(heatmap)[..., :3] * 255)

# Overlay the heatmap on the input image
img_array_np = img_tensor.squeeze().permute(1, 2, 0).cpu().detach().numpy()
img_array_np = np.uint8((img_array_np - img_array_np.min()) / \
               (img_array_np.max() - img_array_np.min()) * 255)

fig, ax = plt.subplots()
ax.imshow(img_array_np)
ax.imshow(heatmap, cmap='jet', alpha=0.5)  # overlay
ax.axis('off')
plt.savefig('GradCAM.png', dpi=300, bbox_inches='tight')
```

(Continued)

(*Continued*)

FIGURE 6.17 GradCAM output.

6.7 FAMOUS CNNs

CNNs have played a significant role in the development of deep learning in the early twenty-first century. In this section, a selection of the most important networks is presented.

6.7.1 LeNet

LeCun et al. (1998a) introduced the first true convolutional neural network, applying it to the MNIST handwritten number dataset (LeCun et al., 1989). LeCun named his networks *LeNet*, with *LeNet-5* proving the most successful of a series of designs. Figure 6.18 illustrates the network's architecture.

As an early convolutional network, LeNet-5's architecture contains elements no longer used in modern CNNs. Table 6.2 provides a detailed layer description. The input size was larger than the actual image size at 32×32 compared to the dataset's 28×28 images. Convolutional layers used 5×5 filters with a 1×1 stride and hyperbolic tangent activation functions. Subsampling layers averaged over a 2×2 window with a 2×2 stride, resembling *average pooling*. Unlike modern pooling layers, these also had a trainable coefficient and bias, with the output passing through a sigmoid activation function. Sparse connections linked S2 and C3, with each of the six features in S2 connecting to 10 of the 16 features in C3. The last convolutional layer, C5, was dense with 120 neurons. The final layer had 10 outputs, one for each class, and used a Gaussian activation, contrasting with modern networks' use of a softmax layer.

LeCun et al. (1998a) broadly compared LeNet-5 with several alternative techniques, including standard deep neural networks, SVMs and K-NN methods. LeNet-5 achieved a test error of 0.95% in its native form after 20 epochs of training and outperformed all other techniques apart from those trained with a dataset augmented with artificially distorted examples.

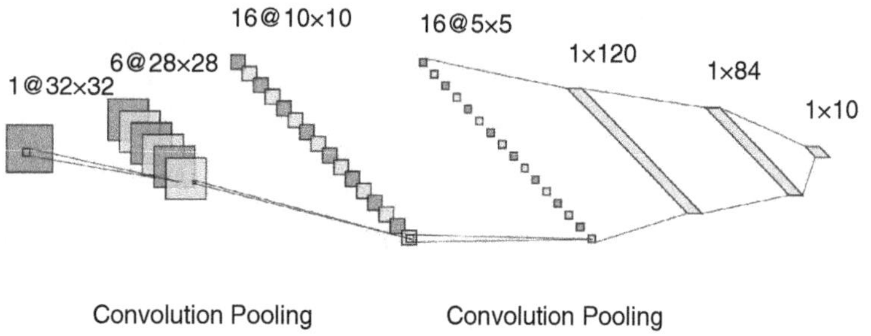

FIGURE 6.18 The architecture of the LeNet-5 neural network (LeCun et al., 1998a).

TABLE 6.2 Detailed Description of the Layers in LeNet-5

Layer	Type	Features	Filter/Pool Size	Input Size	Strides	Activation
Input	Image (padded)			32 × 32		
C1	Convolution	6	5 × 5	28 × 28	1 × 1	tanh
S2	Subsampling	6	2 × 2	14 × 14	2 × 2	sigmoid
C3	Convolution	16	5 × 5	10 × 10	1 × 1	tanh
S4	Subsampling	16	2 × 2	5 × 5	2 × 2	sigmoid
C5	Convolution	120	5 × 5	1 × 1	1 × 1	tanh
F6	Dense	84				tanh
Output	Dense	10				Gaussian

EXAMPLE 6.9: BUILDING LeNet-5 IN PyTorch

Building a modern version of *LeNet-5* using PyTorch is straightforward, although some changes are necessary (see the Jupyter Notebook `LeNet-5.ipynb`). The input layer can directly accept MNIST images at 28 × 28 without padding to 32 × 32. Replication of the convolutional layers uses the PyTorch `Conv2D` layer with padding set to `'same'`, a `(5, 5)` filter size and the activation function set to `'tanh'`. `AveragePooling2D` with a pool size of `(2,2)` and the default stride of 2 × 2 best replaces subsampling. A simple dense layer with 120 neurons replaces the last convolutional layer, and a softmax layer replaces the Gaussian output in the output layer. The function to create the network is given by

```
class LeNet5(nn.Module):
 def __init__(self):
     super(LeNet5, self).__init__()
     self.conv1 = nn.Conv2d(1, 6, kernel_size=5, padding=2)
     self.pool1 = nn.AvgPool2d(kernel_size=2, stride=2)
     self.conv2 = nn.Conv2d(6, 16, kernel_size=5)
     self.pool2 = nn.AvgPool2d(kernel_size=2, stride=2)
     self.fc1 = nn.Linear(16 * 5 * 5, 120)
     self.fc2 = nn.Linear(120, 84)
     self.fc3 = nn.Linear(84, 10)

 def forward(self, x):
     x = torch.tanh(self.conv1(x))
```

(*Continued*)

(Continued)

```
        x = self.pool1(x)
        x = torch.tanh(self.conv2(x))
        x = self.pool2(x)
        x = x.view(-1, 16 * 5 * 5) # Flatten the tensor
        x = torch.tanh(self.fc1(x))
        x = torch.tanh(self.fc2(x))
        x = F.softmax(self.fc3(x), dim=1)
        return x
```

After training for 50 epochs, the LeNet-5 reached a validation accuracy of 98.49%.

6.7.2 AlexNet

AlexNet (Krizhevsky et al., 2012) won the ILSVRC-2012 image classification contest with a top-5 error of 15.3%, which was a significant advance on previous winners that had scored a top-5 error of 25% or more (Aggarwal, 2018, p. 341). The *ImageNet Large Scale Visual Recognition Challenge (ILSVRC)* (Russakovsky et al., 2015) was an image recognition challenge that ran annually from 2010 until 2017 using various editions of ImageNet, an extensive database of images. At the time of the 2012 contest, the dataset contained around 1.2 million training images categorised into 1000 different classes, and today contains over 14 million labelled images.

Figure 6.19 illustrates the architecture of AlexNet. The model comprises five convolutional layers and three fully connected layers, with details of these layers provided in Table 6.3. Training of the network utilised two GPU cards, each with 3 GB of memory, splitting the model layers between the two cards, as represented in Figure 6.19. Convolutional layers 2, 4 and 5 lacked interconnection with the other half of the network located in the memory of the other GPU card. The first convolutional layer and the output softmax layer remained unsplit across GPUs, while the third convolutional layer and hidden fully connected layers connected to the kernel maps on both GPUs. AlexNet employed *response normalisation*, described below after the first two convolutional layers and max pooling after each response normalisation and the fifth convolutional layer. The max pooling used a pool size of 3 × 3 and a stride of 2 × 2, ensuring overlap of the pooling areas. Unlike many previous networks, AlexNet utilised the ReLU activation function.

AlexNet used three critical forms of regularisation: data augmentation and dropout. The data augmentation used a series of image transformations described in Section 6.4. A second type of augmentation involved applying random changes to the principal components of intensities in each RGB channel. Dropout (see Section 4.4.2) was applied to the two hidden fully connected layers with a probability of 0.5. Finally, AlexNet used L_2 regularisation with a weight decay multiplier of 0.0005 in the weight update equation.

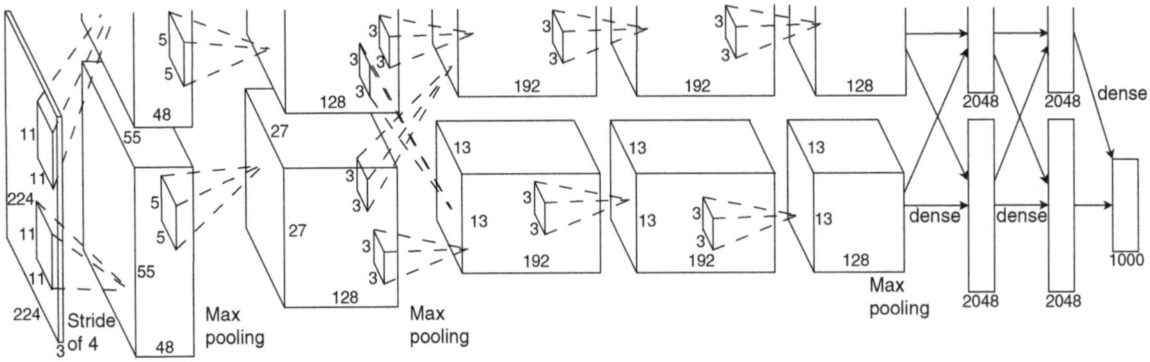

FIGURE 6.19 The architecture of AlexNet (Krizhevsky et al., 2012).

TABLE 6.3 Detailed Description of the Layers in AlexNet

Layer	Type	Features	Filter/Pool Size	Output Size	Strides	Activation
Input	Image			227 × 227		
C1	Convolution	96	11 × 11	55 × 55	4 × 4	ReLU
N1	Response norm			55 × 55		
P1	Max pooling	96	3 × 3	27 × 27	2 × 2	
C2	Convolution	256	5 × 5	27 × 27	1 × 1	ReLU
N2	Response norm			27 × 27		
P2	Max pooling	256	3 × 3	13 × 13	2 × 2	
C3	Convolution	384	3 × 3	13 × 13	1 × 1	ReLU
C4	Convolution	384	3 × 3	13 × 13	1 × 1	ReLU
C5	Convolution	256	3 × 3	13 × 13	1 × 1	ReLU
P5	Max pooling	256	3 × 3	6 × 6	2 × 2	
FC6	Dense	4096				ReLU
FC7	Dense	4096				ReLU
Output	Dense	1000				Softmax

The model was trained using SGD with a batch size of 128. The momentum update was used with the parameter set to the default of 0.9. During training, the learning rate was reduced by an order of magnitude three times.

AlexNet holds significant historical importance as the first CNN to win the ILSVRC contest, dramatically improving performance over previous winners (Aggarwal, 2018). Convolutional layers followed by max pooling have become standard for CNNs, although overlapping pooling windows have fallen out of use. AlexNet marked a turning point in the use of ReLU as an activation function; while ReLU had seen previous use, its application in AlexNet greatly popularised it. Dropout and data augmentation using image transformation have also become standard methods for regularising CNNs. Distribution of training across multiple GPUs is now essential for large deep models. However, *data parallelism* has become a more common distribution strategy than the *model parallelism* used by AlexNet.

EXAMPLE 6.10: TRAINING AlexNet ON Galaxy10 DECals

Training of the original AlexNet used the vast ImageNet database, which is impractical for examples. This implementation trains AlexNet on the much smaller Galaxy10 DECals dataset, coupled with data augmentation (see the Jupyter Notebook `AlexNet with Galaxy10 DECals Dataset.ipynb`).

Example 6.6 prepares the data. The construction of AlexNet follows the code given below. The output softmax is replaced with 10 units rather than the original 1000 to match the 10 categories in this problem. Batch normalisation replaces the original local response normalisation, and Adam replaces the original optimiser.

```
class AlexNet(nn.Module):
    def __init__(self):
        super(AlexNet, self).__init__()
        self.conv1 = nn.Conv2d(3, 96, kernel_size=11, stride=4, padding=2)
        self.bn1 = nn.BatchNorm2d(96)
        self.pool1 = nn.MaxPool2d(kernel_size=2, stride=2)
```

(*Continued*)

(Continued)

```
        self.conv2 = nn.Conv2d(96, 256, kernel_size=5, padding=2)
        self.bn2 = nn.BatchNorm2d(256)
        self.pool2 = nn.MaxPool2d(kernel_size=2, stride=2)

        self.conv3 = nn.Conv2d(256, 384, kernel_size=3, padding=1)
        self.bn3 = nn.BatchNorm2d(384)

        self.conv4 = nn.Conv2d(384, 384, kernel_size=3, padding=1)
        self.bn4 = nn.BatchNorm2d(384)

        self.conv5 = nn.Conv2d(384, 256, kernel_size=3, padding=1)
        self.bn5 = nn.BatchNorm2d(256)
        self.pool3 = nn.MaxPool2d(kernel_size=2, stride=2)

        self.fc1 = nn.Linear(256 * 7 * 7, 4096)
        self.bn6 = nn.BatchNorm1d(4096)
        self.dropout1 = nn.Dropout(0.4)

        self.fc2 = nn.Linear(4096, 4096)
        self.bn7 = nn.BatchNorm1d(4096)
        self.dropout2 = nn.Dropout(0.4)

        self.fc3 = nn.Linear(4096, 1000)
        self.bn8 = nn.BatchNorm1d(1000)
        self.dropout3 = nn.Dropout(0.4)

        self.fc4 = nn.Linear(1000, 10)
        self.bn9 = nn.BatchNorm1d(10)

    def forward(self, x):
        x = F.relu(self.bn1(self.conv1(x)))
        x = self.pool1(x)

        x = F.relu(self.bn2(self.conv2(x)))
        x = self.pool2(x)

        x = F.relu(self.bn3(self.conv3(x)))

        x = F.relu(self.bn4(self.conv4(x)))

        x = F.relu(self.bn5(self.conv5(x)))
        x = self.pool3(x)

        x = x.view(-1,  256 * 7 * 7)  # Flatten the tensor
        x = F.relu(self.bn6(self.fc1(x)))
        x = self.dropout1(x)

        x = F.relu(self.bn7(self.fc2(x)))
        x = self.dropout2(x)

        x = F.relu(self.bn8(self.fc3(x)))
        x = self.dropout3(x)
```

```
        x = F.softmax(self.bn9(self.fc4(x)), dim=1)

        return x
```

The training and validation error as a function of the epoch is illustrated in Figure 6.20. The final validation error after 50 epochs is 62.34%, slightly higher than the simple model used earlier. However, the training process was much noisier, with the validation error showing considerable volatility. The training accuracy was higher than the validation error, indicating that the model overtrained, even with data augmentation. Of course, this model is considerably larger than the three-layer convolutional architecture used earlier.

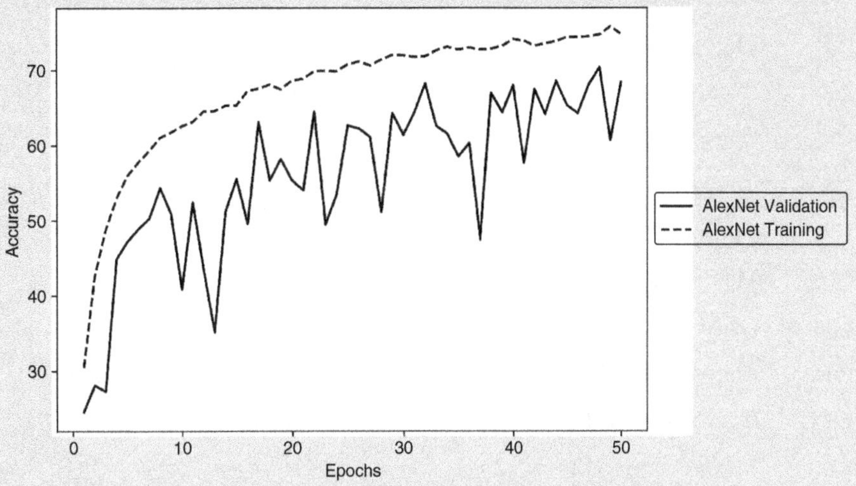

FIGURE 6.20 The training and validation error as a function of epoch for AlexNet trained on the Galaxy10 DECals dataset with data augmentation.

6.7.3 VGG

Simonyan and Zisserman (2015) introduced two models: VGG-16 with 16 trainable layers and VGG-19 with 19 trainable layers, named after the *Visual Geometry Group* at the University of Oxford where the research was completed. An ensemble of seven VGG models came second to *GoogLeNet* in 2014 but contained several features that later became standard (Aggarwal, 2018, p. 342).

The structure of the 16-layer variant is shown in Table 6.4 and Figure 6.21. The 19-layer variant adds an extra convolutional layer in each of the last three blocks of convolutional layers with max pooling. Unlike AlexNet, VGG uses small filter sizes of 3×3 throughout but is significantly deeper. Simonyan and Zisserman (2015) compare a block of three convolutional layers using 3×3 filters with a single layer using a 7×7 filter. Both give the same receptive field of 7×7, but the block of three layers has fewer weights at $3(3^2 C^2) = 27C^2$ compared to $7^2 C^2 = 49C^2$, where C is the number of channels. The max pooling layers all use a 2×2 window with a 2×2 stride and do not overlap, unlike AlexNet. The first two dense layers use dropout regularisation and are identical to the last layers of AlexNet.

Initialisation used pre-training with a shallower architecture to initialise the first four convolutional and dense layers. Subsequently, the authors report that they were able to successfully initialise and train using Glorot initialisation (see Section 3.3.1.3).

TABLE 6.4 Detailed Description of the Layers in VGG-16

Layer	Type	Features	Filter/Pool Size	Output Size	Strides	Activation
Input	Image			224×224		
C1	Convolution	64	3×3	224×224	1×1	ReLU
C2	Convolution	64	3×3	224×224	1×1	ReLU
P3	Max pooling	64	2×2	112×112	2×2	
C4	Convolution	128	3×3	112×112	1×1	ReLU
C5	Convolution	128	3×3	112×112	1×1	ReLU
P6	Max pooling	128	2×2	56×56	2×2	
C7	Convolution	256	3×3	56×56	1×1	ReLU
C8	Convolution	256	3×3	56×56	1×1	ReLU
C9	Convolution	256	3×3	56×56	1×1	ReLU
P10	Max pooling	256	2×2	56×56	2×2	
C11	Convolution	512	3×3	28×28	1×1	ReLU
C12	Convolution	512	3×3	28×28	1×1	ReLU
C13	Convolution	512	3×3	28×28	1×1	ReLU
P14	Max pooling	512	2×2	14×14	2×2	
C15	Convolution	512	3×3	14×14	1×1	ReLU
C16	Convolution	512	3×3	14×14	1×1	ReLU
C17	Convolution	512	3×3	14×14	1×1	ReLU
P18	Max pooling	512	2×2	7×7	2×2	
FC6	Dense	4096				ReLU
FC7	Dense	4096				ReLU
Output	Dense	1000				Softmax

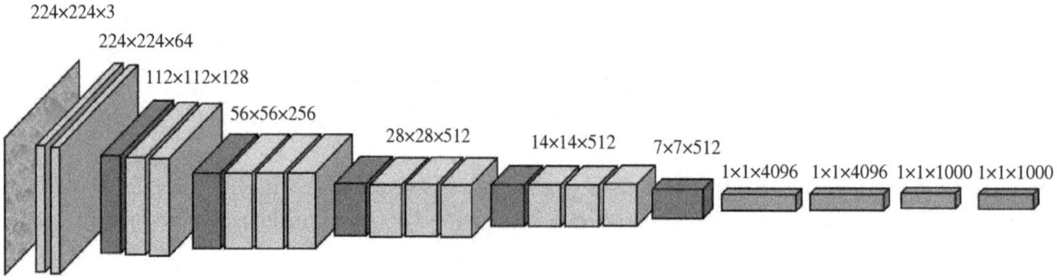

FIGURE 6.21 The architecture of VGG-16 (Simonyan and Zisserman, 2015). *Source:* Nshafiei, Wikimedia Commons licenced under the Creative Commons Attribution-Share Alike 4.0 International licence https://creativecommons.org/licenses/by-sa/4.0/deed.en. The image has been converted from colour to greyscale.

The training utilised SGD with a momentum parameter of 0.9 and a batch size of 256. L_2 weight decay provided regularisation. The initial learning rate of 10^{-2} underwent reduction by an order of magnitude three times during training whenever validation accuracy ceased improving. The ImageNet dataset for the 2012–2014 ISLVRC contests served to train the models. Data augmentation applied three techniques: random image cropping, random horizontal flips and random RGB colour shifts.

The VGG models mark a significant step because of the use of smaller filter sizes and greater depth than previous convolutional networks, and this has now become a standard part of CNNs. Non-overlapping max pooling layers have also become standard. The use of greater depth networks revealed a greater sensitivity to initialisation (Aggarwal, 2018, p. 343).

EXAMPLE 6.11: VGG WITH THE Galaxy10 DECals DATASET

For this example, a cut-down VGG network was trained with the Galaxy10 DECals dataset, and it is located in the Jupyter Notebook `Small VGG with Galaxy10 DECals Dataset.ipynb`. A shallower network was used than the best-known VGG-16, as the deeper network proved difficult to train. The code to build the network is given by

```
class CNNModel(nn.Module):
    def __init__(self):
        super(CNNModel, self).__init__()
        self.conv1 = nn.Conv2d(3, 32, kernel_size=3, padding=1)
        self.pool = nn.MaxPool2d(kernel_size=2, stride=2)
        self.conv2 = nn.Conv2d(32, 64, kernel_size=3, padding=1)
        self.conv3 = nn.Conv2d(64, 128, kernel_size=3, padding=1)
        self.conv4 = nn.Conv2d(128, 256, kernel_size=3, padding=1)
        self.conv5 = nn.Conv2d(256, 256, kernel_size=3, padding=1)
        self.flatten = nn.Flatten()
        self.fc1 = nn.Linear(256 * 8 * 8, 256)
        self.fc2 = nn.Linear(256, 256)
        self.fc3 = nn.Linear(256, 10)

    def forward(self, x):
        x = F.relu(self.conv1(x))
        x = self.pool(x)

        x = F.relu(self.conv2(x))
        x = self.pool(x)

        x = F.relu(self.conv3(x))
        x = self.pool(x)

        x = F.relu(self.conv4(x))
        x = self.pool(x)

        x = F.relu(self.conv5(x))
        x = self.pool(x)

        x = self.flatten(x)
        x = F.relu(self.fc1(x))
        x = F.relu(self.fc2(x))
        x = F.log_softmax(self.fc3(x), dim=1)
        return x
```

(Continued)

(*Continued*)

Figure 6.22 shows the training and validation accuracy. The final accuracy of this model is around 72% after 50 epochs, although there is some evidence of overtraining.

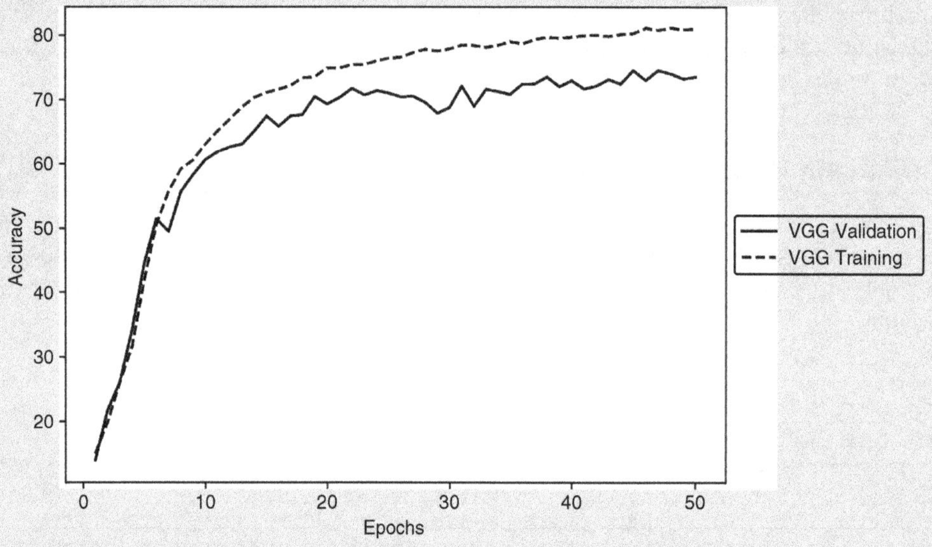

FIGURE 6.22 Training and validation accuracy for a cut-down VGG-style network.

6.7.4 Inception

6.7.4.1 GoogLeNet *GoogLeNet* was the winner of ILSVRC-2014, beating VGG by a small margin, the name being a homage to LeNet. The model introduced the *inception module*, which is a network within a network (Szegedy et al., 2014, p. 2) using an idea from Lin et al. (2013). Inception networks are significantly more computationally efficient than traditional forms like VGG but at the cost of considerable architectural complexity.

The two primary motivations behind the inception module are computational efficiency and critical information in images available at different levels of detail (Szegedy et al., 2014; Aggarwal, 2018). The standard way to increase performance from a CNN is to increase the number of layers and the width of each layer. The difficulty with this is the significant increase in computational cost, even for convolutional layers, which use significantly fewer parameters than dense layers, and this led Szegedy et al. (2014) to look for a sparse structure that could be created using readily available components. To give the network the ability to extract information from the image on different length scales, the inception module uses three convolutional layers with different filter sizes in parallel: 1×1, 3×3 and 5×5. Using a 5×5 filter on top of a convolutional layer with many filters is computationally expensive. So, the inception module uses dimensional reduction in the form of 1×1 convolutions before the 3×3 and 5×5 convolutions. Each parallel path's outputs are then concatenated before the next layer. The inception module used in GoogLeNet is illustrated in Figure 6.23.

The entire network architecture of GoogLeNet is illustrated in Figure 6.24 and described in Table 6.5. The inception *modules* can be considered specialised convolutional layers in the centre of a more conventional CNN structure that begins with standard convolutional and max pooling layers and ends with a softmax layer. Note that average pooling reduces the final grid output from the last inception layer to a dense layer. Dropout regularisation is used before a linear layer, allowing the network to adapt to a different layer set. GoogLeNet uses two auxiliary classifiers after the first and second blocks of inception layers, and this is to encourage discrimination in the lower sections of the network and increase the gradient backpropagation signal (Szegedy et al., 2014, p. 6). The loss from the two auxiliary classifiers is weighted by 0.3 in the loss function and discarded after the training is complete. The auxiliary classifiers have five layers, described in Table 6.6.

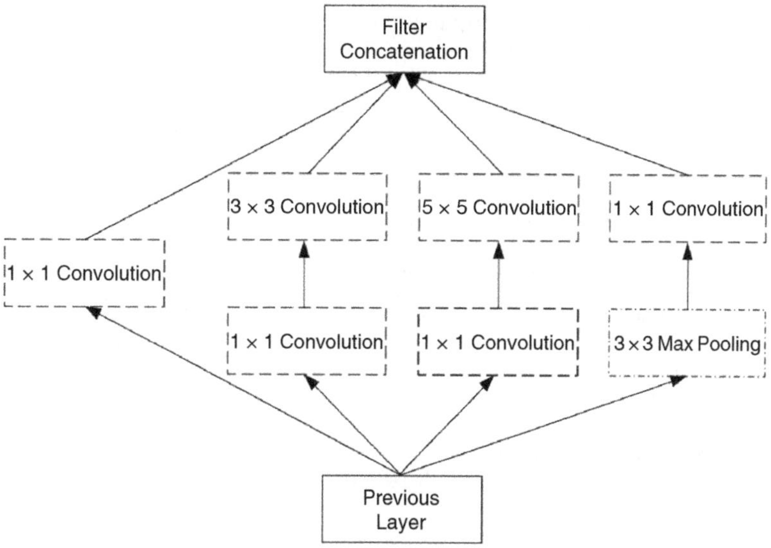

FIGURE 6.23 The inception module as used in GoogLeNet (Szegedy et al., 2014).

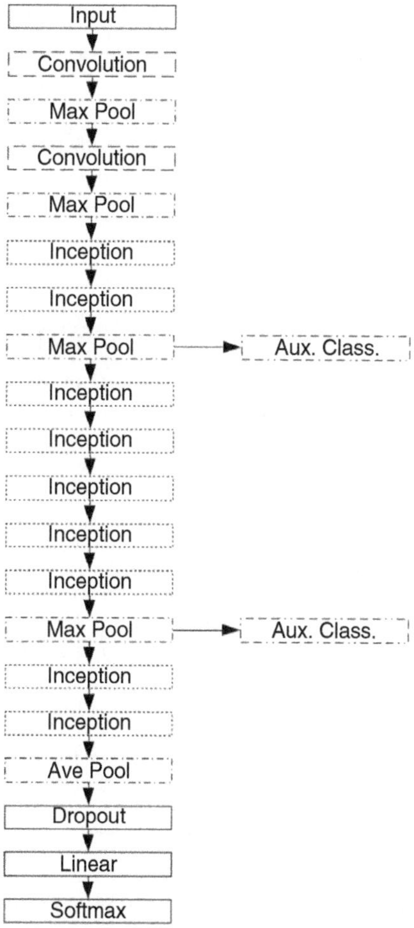

FIGURE 6.24 The full structure of GoogLeNet (Szegedy et al., 2014).

TABLE 6.5 Detailed Description of the Layers in GoogLeNet

Type	Features	Filter/Pool Size	Output Size	Strides
Input	3		224 × 224	
Convolution	64	7 × 7	112 × 112	2
Max pooling	64	3 × 3	56 × 56	2
Convolution	192	3 × 3	56 × 56	1
Max pooling	192	3 × 3	28 × 28	2
Inception	256		28 × 28	
Inception	480		28 × 28	
Max pooling	480	3 × 3	14 × 14	2
Inception	512		14 × 14	
Inception	512		14 × 14	
Inception	512		14 × 14	
Inception	528		14 × 14	
Inception	832		14 × 14	
Max pooling	832	3 × 3	7 × 7	2
Inception	832		7 × 7	
Inception	1024		7 × 7	
Average pooling	1024	3 × 3	1 × 1	1
Dropout (40%)	1024		1 × 1	
Linear	1024		1 × 1	
Softmax	1000		1 × 1	

TABLE 6.6 Detailed Description of the Auxiliary Classifiers in GoogLeNet

Type	Features	Filter/Pool Size	Output Size	Strides
Average pooling	512/528	5 × 5	4 × 4	3
Convolution	128	1 × 1		
Dense (ReLU)	1024			
Dropout (70%)	1024		1 × 1	
Softmax	1000		1 × 1	

Training employed asynchronous SGD with momentum, using the default parameter value of 0.9. The learning rate decreased on a fixed schedule by 4% every eight epochs. Distribution of training used both model and data parallelism. Data augmentation utilised four techniques: sampling patches of the original images in the range 8% to 100% original size, aspect ratio shifts between 3/4 and 4/3, photometric distortions and random interpolation (Szegedy et al., 2014, p. 8).

GoogLeNet introduced the innovative inception architecture, which saw improvement in several further versions. Many techniques introduced in GoogLeNet, such as separate paths with filters of different granularity and the use of auxiliary classifiers during training, have now fallen out of use in favour of *ResNets* (see Section 6.7.5 below). The critical step involved recognising that networks could not indefinitely grow deeper and wider and that computational efficiency constituted a vital design consideration.

EXAMPLE 6.12: GoogLeNet WITH THE Galaxy10 DECals DATASET

For this example, GoogLeNet is trained with the Galaxy10 DECals dataset, and the example is in the Jupyter Notebook `GoogLeNet with Galaxy10 DECals Dataset.ipynb`. The inception architecture is significantly more complex than any of the model architectures explored until now. Two helper functions are defined to create an inception block and an auxiliary classifier. The inception block constructs the four separate branches and then combines these using the PyTorch `concatenate` function.

```
class InceptionBlock(nn.Module):
    def __init__(self, in_channels, c1, c2_1, c2_2, c3_1, c3_2, c4):
        super(InceptionBlock, self).__init__()
        self.branch1 = nn.Conv2d(in_channels, c1, kernel_size=1, padding=0)


        self.branch2_1 = nn.Conv2d(in_channels, c2_1, kernel_size=1,
                                   padding=0)
        self.branch2_2 = nn.Conv2d(c2_1, c2_2, kernel_size=3, padding=1)

        self.branch3_1 = nn.Conv2d(in_channels, c3_1, kernel_size=1,
                                   padding=0)
        self.branch3_2 = nn.Conv2d(c3_1, c3_2, kernel_size=5, padding=2)

        self.branch4_pool = nn.MaxPool2d(kernel_size=3, stride=1, padding=1)
        self.branch4_1 = nn.Conv2d(in_channels, c4, kernel_size=1, padding=0)

    def forward(self, x):
        branch1 = F.relu(self.branch1(x))

        branch2 = F.relu(self.branch2_1(x))
        branch2 = F.relu(self.branch2_2(branch2))

        branch3 = F.relu(self.branch3_1(x))
        branch3 = F.relu(self.branch3_2(branch3))

        branch4 = self.branch4_pool(x)
        branch4 = F.relu(self.branch4_1(branch4))

        outputs = [branch1, branch2, branch3, branch4]
        return torch.cat(outputs, 1)
```

The auxiliary and main classifiers are reduced to 10 units to reflect the 10 classes in this dataset. The auxiliary classifier helper is defined by

```
class AuxiliaryClassifier(nn.Module):
    def __init__(self, in_channels, num_classes=10):
        super(AuxiliaryClassifier, self).__init__()
        self.pool = nn.AvgPool2d(kernel_size=5, stride=3)
        self.conv = nn.Conv2d(in_channels, 128, kernel_size=1, padding=0)
        self.fc1 = nn.Linear(128 * 4 * 4, 1024)
```

(*Continued*)

(Continued)

```
        self.dropout = nn.Dropout(0.7)
        self.fc2 = nn.Linear(1024, num_classes)

    def forward(self, x):
        x = self.pool(x)
        x = F.relu(self.conv(x))
        x = torch.flatten(x, 1)
        x = F.relu(self.fc1(x))
        x = self.dropout(x)
        x = self.fc2(x)
        return x
```

The model is now constructed using the helper functions and here, the optimiser used is Adam.

```
class GoogLeNet(nn.Module):
    def __init__(self, num_classes=10):
        super(GoogLeNet, self).__init__()
        self.conv1 = nn.Conv2d(3, 64, kernel_size=7, stride=2, padding=3)
        self.maxpool1 = nn.MaxPool2d(kernel_size=3, stride=2, padding=1)
        self.bn1 = nn.BatchNorm2d(64)

        self.conv2_1 = nn.Conv2d(64, 64, kernel_size=1, padding=0)
        self.conv2_2 = nn.Conv2d(64, 192, kernel_size=3, padding=1)
        self.maxpool2 = nn.MaxPool2d(kernel_size=3, stride=2, padding=1)
        self.bn2 = nn.BatchNorm2d(192)

        self.inception3a = InceptionBlock(192, 64, 96, 128, 16, 32, 32)
        self.inception3b = InceptionBlock(256, 128, 128, 192, 32, 96, 64)
        self.maxpool3 = nn.MaxPool2d(kernel_size=3, stride=2, padding=1)

        self.inception4a = InceptionBlock(480, 192, 96, 208, 16, 48, 64)
        self.aux1 = AuxiliaryClassifier(512, num_classes)

        self.inception4b = InceptionBlock(512, 160, 112, 224, 24, 64, 64)
        self.inception4c = InceptionBlock(512, 128, 128, 256, 24, 64, 64)
        self.inception4d = InceptionBlock(512, 112, 144, 288, 32, 64, 64)
        self.aux2 = AuxiliaryClassifier(528, num_classes)

        self.inception4e = InceptionBlock(528, 256, 160, 320, 32, 128, 128)
        self.maxpool4 = nn.MaxPool2d(kernel_size=3, stride=2, padding=1)

        self.inception5a = InceptionBlock(832, 256, 160, 320, 32, 128, 128)
        self.inception5b = InceptionBlock(832, 384, 192, 384, 48, 128, 128)

        self.avgpool = nn.AdaptiveAvgPool2d((1, 1))
        self.dropout = nn.Dropout(0.4)
        self.fc = nn.Linear(1024, num_classes)

    def forward(self, x):
        x = F.relu(self.conv1(x))
        x = self.maxpool1(x)
        x = self.bn1(x)
```

```
        x = F.relu(self.conv2_1(x))
        x = F.relu(self.conv2_2(x))
        x = self.maxpool2(x)
        x = self.bn2(x)

        x = self.inception3a(x)
        x = self.inception3b(x)
        x = self.maxpool3(x)

        x = self.inception4a(x)
        aux1 = self.aux1(x) if self.training else None

        x = self.inception4b(x)
        x = self.inception4c(x)
        x = self.inception4d(x)
        aux2 = self.aux2(x) if self.training else None

        x = self.inception4e(x)
        x = self.maxpool4(x)

        x = self.inception5a(x)
        x = self.inception5b(x)

        x = self.avgpool(x)
        x = torch.flatten(x, 1)
        x = self.dropout(x)
        x = self.fc(x)

        if self.training:
            return x, aux1, aux2
        else:
            return x
```

The results from training are shown in Figure 6.25. The final validation error was 75.4%, noisier than that of the VGG network but less than that seen with AlexNet. The model is overtrained, as seen in the divergence between training and validation errors.

(*Continued*)

(*Continued*)

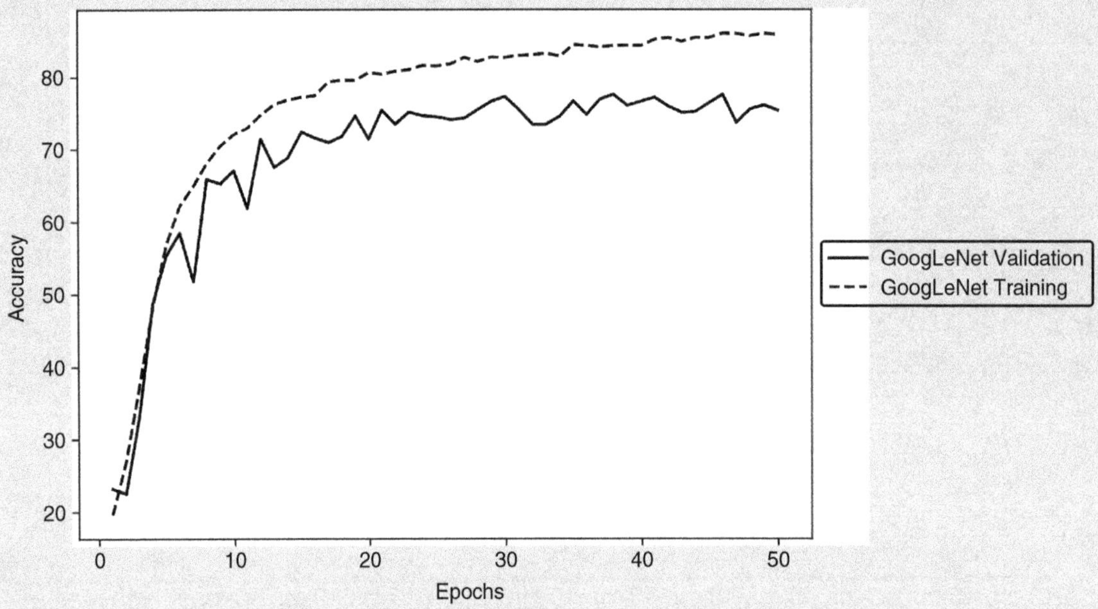

FIGURE 6.25 Training and validation accuracy for GoogLeNet.

6.7.4.2 Inception v2 and v3 Szegedy et al. (2016) introduced further enhancements to the inception architecture and versions 2 and 3 of the network. The revised network structure is given in Table 6.7 with version 3 distinguished by batch normalisation with the fully connected layer. In contrast, version 2 uses batch normalisation just with the convolutional layers. Three different types of inception modules are used in the network, labelled 2a, 2b and 2c in the table and illustrated in Figures 6.26, 6.27 and 6.28.

TABLE 6.7 Detailed Description of the Layers in Inception v2 and v3

Type	Features	Filter/Pool Size	Input Size	Strides
Convolution	32	3×3	299×299	2
Convolution	32	3×3	149×149	1
Convolution (padded)	64	3×3	147×147	1
Pooling	64	3×3	147×147	2
Convolution	80	3×3	73×73	1
Convolution	192	3×3	71×71	2
Convolution	288	3×3	35×35	1
$3 \times$ Inception 2a	768		35×35	
$5 \times$ Inception 2b	1280		17×17	
$2 \times$ Inception 2c	2048		8×8	
Pooling	2024		8×8	1
Softmax	1000		1×1	

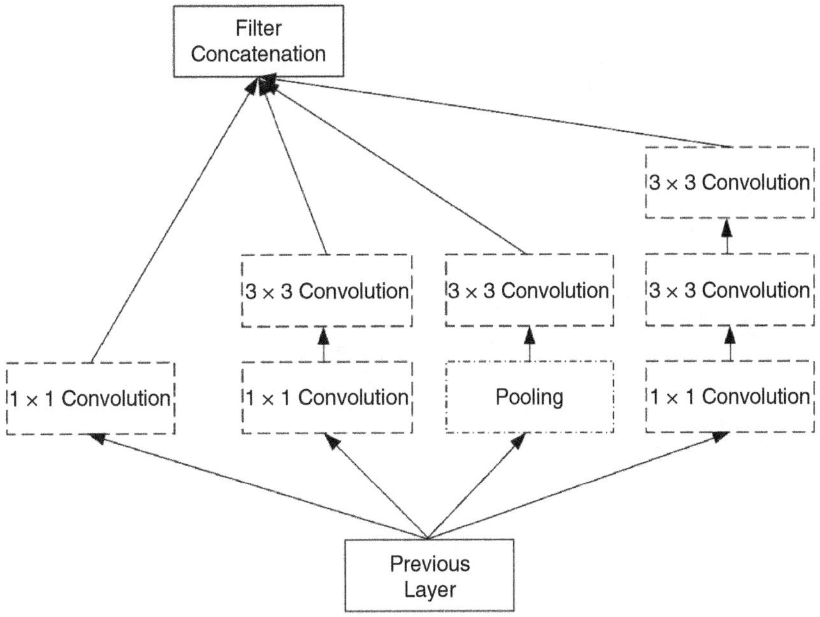

FIGURE 6.26 The inception module 2a as used in inception v2 and v3 (Szegedy et al., 2016).

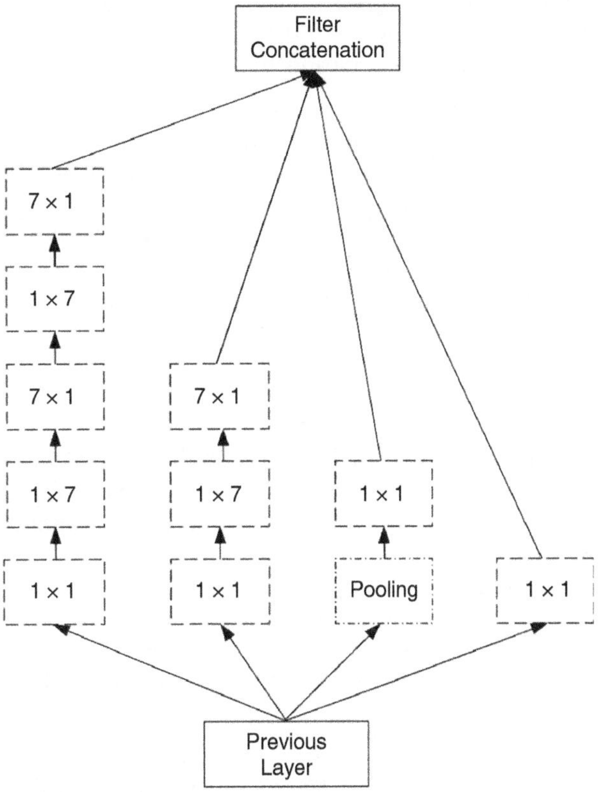

FIGURE 6.27 The inception module 2b as used in inception v2 and v3 (Szegedy et al., 2016).

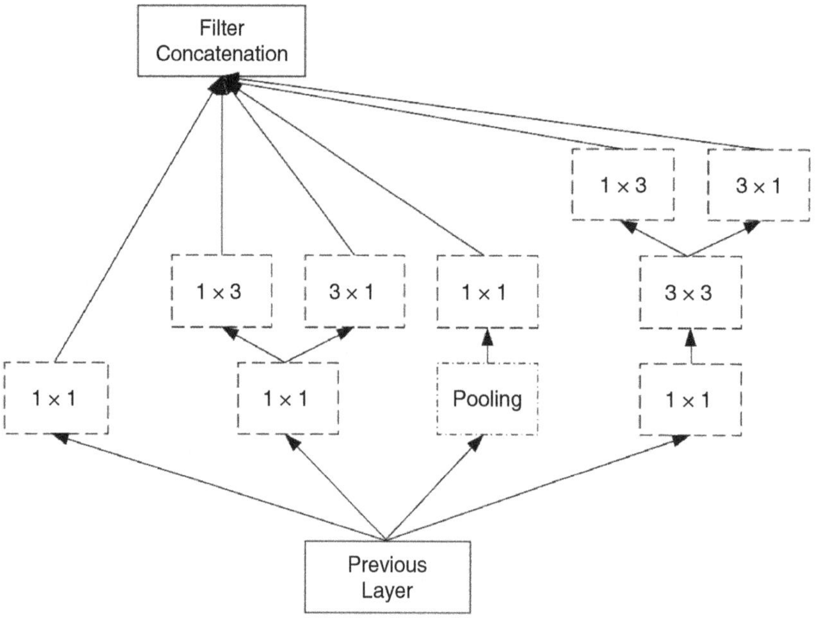

FIGURE 6.28 The inception module 2c as used in inception v2 and v3 (Szegedy et al., 2016).

Module 2a in Figure 6.26 is a minor modification of the original inception module in which the 5×5 convolutional layer has been replaced by two successive 3×3 convolutional layers. This factorisation retains the same receptive field as a 5×5 convolution but has fewer parameters and a net reduction of computation by a factor of $\frac{2 \times 9}{25}$ (Szegedy et al., 2016, p. 3).

Inception module 2b effectively has a 7×7 receptive field but reduces the computation cost by factorising each 7×7 convolution into a pair of 1×7 and 7×1 convolutions, as discussed in Section 6.2.5, and this, again, results in a significant reduction in computational costs.

The last type of inception module, 2c, is a minor modification of type 2a, in which the final 3×3 convolution in each branch is factorised into a pair of 1×3 and 3×1 convolutions. This layer is used on the coarse 8×8 grids of the lower part of the network and is designed to promote high-dimensional representations (Szegedy et al., 2016, p. 5).

6.7.5 ResNet

Residual networks, or *ResNets,* were introduced by He et al. (2016) to address the *degradation* problem. This problem is observed during the training of very deep networks. For a given problem, as deeper and deeper networks are trained initially, training and test errors decrease as a function of depth until, eventually, accuracy becomes saturated. Deeper networks then have higher training errors. This effect is not caused by overfitting but instead reflects optimisers' difficulty in training deeper networks.

To combat this problem, He et al. (2016) introduce *residual mappings* or *skip connections.* Each block in the ResNet consists of several layers, each with a ReLU activation function, combined with an identity mapping from the input to the output. So if the input is x, and the layer calculates $f(x)$, then the output is given by

$$y = f(x) + x, \tag{6.19}$$

as illustrated in Figure 6.29. If we wish the network to learn the mapping $\mathcal{H}(x)$, then the layer block is tasked with learning the residual function $f(x) = \mathcal{H}(x) - x$.

He et al. (2016) cite several motivations for ResNets from earlier neural network architectures and other sources. One such motivating method is *multigrid* (Brandt, 1977; Green, 2000; Trottenberg et al., 2001), which is a PDE solver that uses a hierarchical decomposition of residuals on different scales. Multigrid approaches do converge faster than direct solvers. Several other types of network use shortcut connections, and He et al. (2016) note the

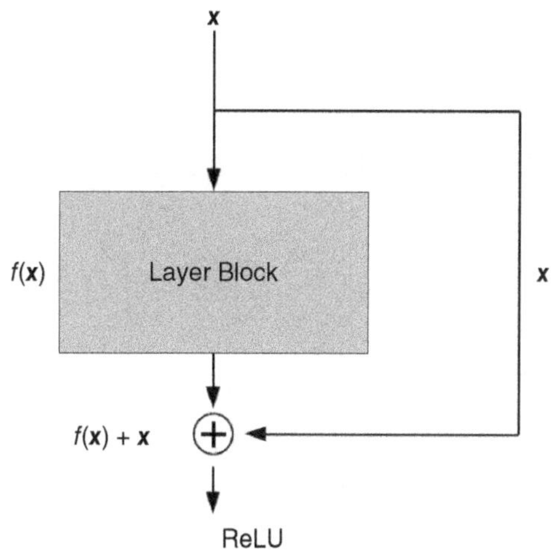

FIGURE 6.29 A *residual network* block. A shortcut or *skip connection* is provided around the block of layers.

(a) Block A	(b) Block B	(c) Block C	(d) Block D
$3 \times 3, 64$	$3 \times 3, 128$	$3 \times 3, 256$	$3 \times 3, 512$
$3 \times 3, 64$	$3 \times 3, 128$	$3 \times 3, 256$	$3 \times 3, 512$

FIGURE 6.30 Two-layer residual network block definitions.

highway networks proposed by Srivastava et al. (2015a,b) as using gated and parameterised shortcut connections. Recurrent neural network units like LTSM and GRU are based on similar principles (Aggarwal, 2018, p. 348).

How may we interpret the use of skip connections in ResNets? We can use the residual interpretation proposed by He et al. (2016), but there are other possibilities. We can similarly interpret them as inception networks: networks that allow the network to learn the appropriate length of the path for different features (Aggarwal, 2018). ResNets have more flexibility than inception networks, as the shortcuts directly enable the choice of several layer blocks to include for each feature. The skip connections also allow backpropagation of the full gradient signal to all layer blocks, alleviating the vanishing gradient problem even if He et al. (2016) suggest this is not the source of the degradation problem. We have seen the use of auxiliary classifiers in GoogLeNet, which is intended to solve this same problem, although again, the ResNet solution appears both more straightforward and more flexible.

The critical part of the residual network is implementing the skip connection itself. When the input and output have the same dimensions, it is straightforward to implement using element-wise addition. If the dimensions of input and output are not the same, then a linear projection is used with a square matrix W_S,

$$y = f(x) + W_S x. \tag{6.20}$$

Residual networks are constructed from blocks of two or three convolutional layers alongside the skip connection. The shallower networks with 18 and 34 layers tested by He et al. (2016) contain blocks with two convolutional layers, each with 3×3 filters, as defined in Figure 6.30. The deeper networks with 50, 101 and 152 layers all use blocks of three layers, starting and ending with 1×1 convolutions with a 3×3 convolution in between (Figure 6.31). The configuration described in terms of the block structure is given in Table 6.8.

He et al. (2016) demonstrated that ResNets solve the degeneration problem and compared the performance of 18- and 34-layer plain networks to 18- and 34-layer ResNets. In the plain networks, the 18-layer training and validation performance was better than that of the 34-layer network, while the reverse is true for the ResNets. In 2015, a single 152-layer ResNet outperformed all previous winners of ILSVRC using ensembles of models. An ensemble of ResNets, including two 152-layer models, significantly outperformed the 2014 winners of ILSVRC and won in 2015.

(a) Block E	(b) Block F	(c) Block G	(d) Block H
$1 \times 1, \mathbf{64}$	$1 \times 1, \mathbf{128}$	$1 \times 1, \mathbf{256}$	$1 \times 1, \mathbf{512}$
$3 \times 3, \mathbf{64}$	$3 \times 3, \mathbf{128}$	$3 \times 3, \mathbf{256}$	$3 \times 3, \mathbf{512}$
$1 \times 1, \mathbf{256}$	$1 \times 1, \mathbf{512}$	$1 \times 1, \mathbf{1024}$	$1 \times 1, \mathbf{2048}$

FIGURE 6.31 Three-layer residual network block definitions.

TABLE 6.8 Block Structure of ResNets of Different Depths. The Number of Filters Is in **Bold**, and Stride Is *Italic* If Not 1. The Block Definitions Are Given in Figures 6.30 and 6.31

Layer	Output Size	18-Layer	34-Layer	50-Layer	101-Layer	152-Layer
1	112×112	7×7, **64**, *2*				
2	56×56	3×3, Max pooling, *2*				
		$A \times 2$	$A \times 3$	$E \times 3$	$E \times 3$	$E \times 3$
3	28×28	$B \times 2$	$B \times 4$	$F \times 4$	$F \times 4$	$F \times 8$
4	14×14	$C \times 2$	$C \times 6$	$G \times 6$	$G \times 23$	$G \times 36$
5	7×7	$D \times 2$	$D \times 3$	$H \times 3$	$H \times 3$	$H \times 3$
6	1×1	Average pooling, 1000 dense layer, Softmax				

EXAMPLE 6.13: ResNet 34 WITH THE Galaxy10 DECals DATASET

ResNet 34 is trained with the now familiar Galaxy10 DECals dataset and can be found in the Jupyter Notebook `ResNet with Galaxy10 DECals Dataset.ipynb`. ResNet has a much simpler architecture than inception but is very deep. Two helper classes are defined to construct standard blocks that have the same input and output sizes and reduction blocks that reduce the output by a factor of two.

```
class ResNetStandardBlock(nn.Module):
    def __init__(self, in_channels, out_channels):
        super(ResNetStandardBlock, self).__init__()
        self.conv1 = nn.Conv2d(in_channels, out_channels, kernel_size=3,
                               stride=1, padding=1)
        self.bn1 = nn.BatchNorm2d(out_channels)
        self.conv2 = nn.Conv2d(out_channels, out_channels, kernel_size=3,
                               stride=1, padding=1)
        self.bn2 = nn.BatchNorm2d(out_channels)

    def forward(self, x):
        x_shortcut = x
        x = F.relu(self.bn1(self.conv1(x)))
        x = self.bn2(self.conv2(x))
        x += x_shortcut
        x = F.relu(x)
        return x
```

```
class ResNetReductionBlock(nn.Module):
    def __init__(self, in_channels, out_channels, stride):
        super(ResNetReductionBlock, self).__init__()
        self.conv1 = nn.Conv2d(in_channels, out_channels, kernel_size=3,
                               stride=stride, padding=1)
        self.bn1 = nn.BatchNorm2d(out_channels)
        self.conv2 = nn.Conv2d(out_channels, out_channels, kernel_size=3,
                               stride=1, padding=1)
        self.bn2 = nn.BatchNorm2d(out_channels)
        self.conv_shortcut = nn.Conv2d(in_channels, out_channels,
                                       kernel_size=1, stride=stride,
                                       padding=0)
        self.bn_shortcut = nn.BatchNorm2d(out_channels)

    def forward(self, x):
        x_shortcut = self.bn_shortcut(self.conv_shortcut(x))
        x = F.relu(self.bn1(self.conv1(x)))
        x = self.bn2(self.conv2(x))
        x += x_shortcut
        x = F.relu(x)
        return x
```

The final network can then be constructed.

```
class ResNet34(nn.Module):
    def __init__(self, num_classes=10):
        super(ResNet34, self).__init__()
        self.conv1 = nn.Conv2d(3, 64, kernel_size=7, stride=2, padding=3)
        self.bn1 = nn.BatchNorm2d(64)
        self.maxpool = nn.MaxPool2d(kernel_size=3, stride=2, padding=1)

        # conv2_x
        self.layer1 = nn.Sequential(
            ResNetReductionBlock(64, 64, 2),
            ResNetStandardBlock(64, 64),
            ResNetStandardBlock(64, 64)
        )

        # conv3_x
        self.layer2 = nn.Sequential(
            ResNetReductionBlock(64, 128, 2),
            ResNetStandardBlock(128, 128),
            ResNetStandardBlock(128, 128),
            ResNetStandardBlock(128, 128)
        )

        # conv4_x
        self.layer3 = nn.Sequential(
            ResNetReductionBlock(128, 256, 2),
            ResNetStandardBlock(256, 256),
            ResNetStandardBlock(256, 256),
            ResNetStandardBlock(256, 256),
            ResNetStandardBlock(256, 256),
            ResNetStandardBlock(256, 256)
        )
```

(*Continued*)

(*Continued*)

```
        # conv5_x
        self.layer4 = nn.Sequential(
            ResNetReductionBlock(256, 512, 2),
            ResNetStandardBlock(512, 512),
            ResNetStandardBlock(512, 512)
        )

        self.avgpool = nn.AdaptiveAvgPool2d((1, 1))
        self.fc = nn.Linear(512, num_classes)

    def forward(self, x):
        x = F.relu(self.bn1(self.conv1(x)))
        x = self.maxpool(x)

        x = self.layer1(x)
        x = self.layer2(x)
        x = self.layer3(x)
        x = self.layer4(x)

        x = self.avgpool(x)
        x = torch.flatten(x, 1)
        x = self.fc(x)

        return x
```

The training and validation accuracy for ResNet34 is shown in Figure 6.32. The model has overtrained in common with several architectures discussed in this section. The final validation accuracy was 74.6%, but the training process was very noisy, with periods where the validation accuracy fell sharply. This model is significantly deeper than any other model discussed so far, and the presence of skip connections allows gradients to propagate properly.

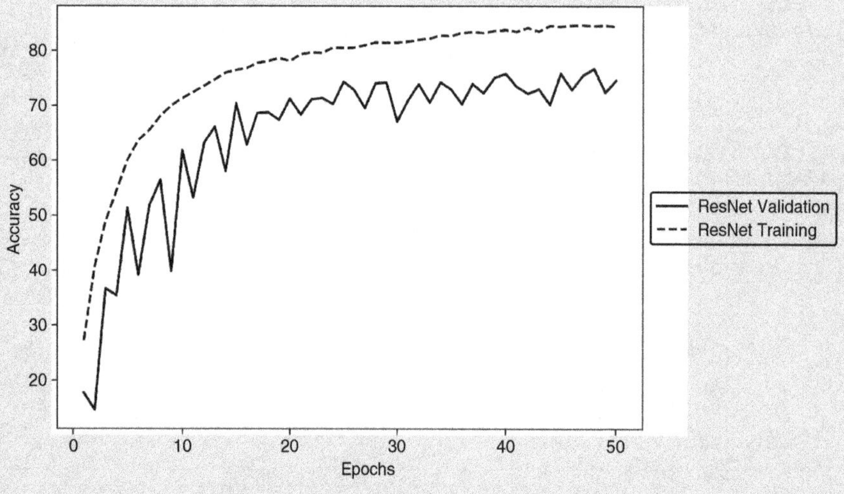

FIGURE 6.32 Training and validation accuracy for ResNet34.

6.8 CONCLUSIONS ON CNNs

This chapter explored the essential components of convolutional neural networks, a pivotal architecture in deep learning, particularly in the context of computer vision, but applicable more widely. The chapter began with a review of the mathematics of convolutions and their implementation in convolutional layers. Design considerations such as selecting appropriate filter sizes and determining the number of filters were discussed to optimise model performance. Downsampling is essential to transform the image into semantic space, and strided convolutions and pooling approaches were explored. The significance of data augmentation was highlighted as a strategy to enhance model generalisation. Transfer learning, leveraging pre-trained networks to expedite model development for new tasks, was reviewed. Feature visualisation techniques were presented to provide deeper insights into the model's inner workings. Lastly, CNN architectures that have significantly influenced the evolution of deep learning were presented: LeNet, AlexNet, VGG, inception and ResNet.

CHAPTER 7

Sequence Models

'The first ten million years were the worst', said Marvin, 'and the second ten million years, they were the worst too. The third ten million years I didn't enjoy at all. After that, I went into a bit of a decline'.

Douglas Adams, The Restaurant at the End of the Universe (1980)

7.1 INTRODUCING SEQUENCE MODELS

Sequence models are a fundamental type of deep learning model designed to process data sequences with contextual relationships. The most common sequence type is text, but they also embody time-series data, which is fundamental to financial data and its analysis. Hence, this chapter presents the necessary background to models of financial time series as a foundation to generative models of time series in Chapter 18. It also presents the application of sequence models to NLP, from its foundation to the development of *transformers* and *large language models*.

Sequence data, in its formal definition, refers to a collection of elements arranged in a specific, meaningful order where the position of each element is significant. Temporal order is the most common, but sequences can follow a different logical order. Each element in this sequence is related to its immediate predecessor or successor and contextualised within the overall structure. Time-series data in finance exemplifies temporal sequence data, as it records market prices chronologically. DNA sequences consist of ordered chains of nucleotides and are an example of biological sequence data. In music, notes form sequences that create melodies and harmonies. Sequence data can be found in various economic, scientific and cultural domains.

Sequence models have various applications across domains due to their unique ability to interpret and predict ordered data (Ng, 2018d; Drori, 2022). Machine translation and speech recognition are two tasks in NLP that rely heavily on these tools. Time series of financial data can be used to predict market trends for economic purposes of price prediction for algorithmic trading. Sequence models in healthcare can be used to analyse patient data and predict disease progression or aid in treatment. Generative sequence models can be used to create new music compositions. Self-driving vehicles need to process sequence data to predict the trajectories of other objects in their environment.

Sequence models can be broadly categorised into three types based on their input–output relationships: one-to-many, many-to-one and many-to-many (Drori, 2022). One-to-many models take a single input, generate a sequence of outputs and are used in applications such as image captioning. Conversely, many-to-one models process sequences of inputs to produce a single output, as seen in sentiment analysis, where a sequence of words, like a sentence or document, undergoes analysis to determine a single sentiment rating. Lastly, many-to-many models work with sequences as inputs and outputs, and this is a typical scenario in machine translation, where a sequence of words in one language gets translated into a sequence of words in another language. Table 7.1 provides illustrations of these examples.

There are two fundamental approaches to handling sequences for deep learning: recurrence and fixed-size input window. Recurrence leads to RNNs, where the model processes sequences by maintaining a memory of previous inputs. The memory or hidden state is updated as the network processes the sequence of inputs, allowing it to capture temporal dependencies. Models with fixed input windows, such as CNNs or transformers, process sequences by

Deep Learning in Quantitative Finance, First Edition. Andrew Green.

TABLE 7.1 Types of Sequence Models and Their Applications

Model Type	Examples of Application
One-to-many	Image captioning (single image to a sequence of words)
	Music generation (single emotion cue to a sequence of notes)
Many-to-one	Sentiment analysis (sequence of words to a single output sentiment)
	Time-series forecasting (sequence of historical data to a single future value)
Many-to-many	Machine translation (sequence in one language to another language)
	Video captioning (sequence of video frames to a sequence of words)

considering a pre-determined data segment at a time. This approach prevents the model from processing arbitrary length sequences but allows considerable gains in computational efficiency.

The remainder of this chapter explores sequence models in deep learning, addressing a range of model architectures and methods that have found success. Section 7.2 analyses the architecture of the critical types of RNNs, including gated units such as GRUs and LSTMs. This section also addresses challenges like the vanishing gradient problem and extends into discussions on bidirectional and deep RNNs, supplemented by practical case studies.

Natural language processing is a central focus of sequence models and is discussed beginning with Section 7.3.1, which outlines the basics of NLP and their importance. The chapter then explores NLP preprocessing techniques in Section 7.3.2. The discussion progresses to *n*-grams in Section 7.3.3, a crucial element in the computational processing of language structure. Section 7.3.4 reviews the various evaluation metrics used in NLP. Section 7.3.5 explores the *neural probabilistic language model* of Bengio et al. (2003), covering the early application of neural networks to NLP. *Word embeddings* are central to how neural networks process text sequences and described in Section 7.3.6, highlighting significant contributions from *Word2Vec* and *GloVe*. The text explores the application of RNNs to NLP in Section 7.3.7. The chapter then moves to a comprehensive discussion on *sequence-to-sequence models* in Section 7.3.8, followed by an in-depth examination of *attention mechanisms* in Section 7.3.9. Finally, Section 7.3.10 covers transformers and their application in *large language models*. This section offers an overview of the transformer model, its unique encoder–decoder structure, self-attention and positional encoding, and insights into landmark models like BERT and GPT.

7.2 RECURRENT NEURAL NETWORKS

Introduced by Rumelhart et al. (1986), RNNs represent a neural network architecture capable of processing input sequences of indeterminate length (Goodfellow et al., 2016). RNNs can handle sequences ranging from scalar values to tensors of any dimension. RNNs share parameters across time, akin to CNNs sharing parameters across spatial dimensions. This shared parameter approach enables RNNs to manage information at various positions within a sequence and to process sequences of varying lengths.

The aim is for the network to recognise a word as the same, regardless of its position in a sentence. A recurrent network can overcome this limitation, unlike a feedforward network, which cannot naturally do this and needs to build separate word detectors for each position in a fixed-length input. The network can apply recurrence in a forward direction to model time-explicit sequences, such as financial time series. Additionally, it can employ bidirectional recurrence for series where modelling long-range dependencies in both directions is crucial. In a sentence, for instance, words appearing later can be as important to the context of the current word as those preceding it. Section 7.2.2 discusses bidirectional RNNs in detail.

RNNs can operate in any of the three input–output modes described earlier with variable input and output lengths. Recurrence does introduce a significant problem in that it deepens the computational graph, potentially leading to vanishing and exploding gradients, and this issue is explored in more detail in Section 7.2.4.

7.2.1 Shallow RNNs

The RNN is a dynamical system with the form (Goodfellow et al., 2016):

$$h^{(t)} = f(h^{(t-1)}, x^{(t)}; \theta), \tag{7.1}$$

where $h^{(t)}$ is the state of the system at time t, $x^{(t)}$ is the input at time t and θ are the model parameters. Unrolling the recurrence relation gives,

$$\begin{aligned} h^{(t)} &= f(h^{(t-1)}, x^{(t)}; \theta), \\ h^{(t-1)} &= f(h^{(t-2)}, x^{(t-1)}; \theta), \\ &\vdots \\ h^{(1)} &= f(h^{(0)}, x^{(1)}; \theta), \\ h^{(0)} &= \text{initial state.} \end{aligned}$$

The recurrence relation can be illustrated in graphical form in both the rolled and unrolled state as illustrated in Figure 7.1.

The RNN can be formally defined by the equations (Goodfellow et al., 2016; Ng, 2018d)

$$z^{(i)} = Wh^{(t-1)} + Ux^{(t)} + b, \tag{7.2}$$

$$h^{(t)} = g_1(z^{(i)}), \tag{7.3}$$

$$o^{(t)} = Vh^{(t)} + c, \tag{7.4}$$

$$\hat{y} = g_2(o^{(t)}), \tag{7.5}$$

where $h^{(t)}$ is the hidden state at t, $x^{(t)}$ is the input at t, W, U and V are weight matrices, b and c are bias vectors and g_1 and g_2 are activation functions. The computational graph is illustrated in Figure 7.2. Concatenating the hidden state and input gives $\bar{x}^{(t)} = [h^{(t-1)}; x^{(t)}]^T$, with the weight matrices W and U similarly concatenated to $\bar{W} = [W; U]$ (Drori, 2022), allowing Equation (7.3) to be written as

$$h^{(t)} = g_1(\bar{W}\bar{x}^{(t)} + b). \tag{7.6}$$

The loss functions used for RNNs are identical to those used in standard feedforward networks as described in Section 3.4. Recurrence adds another level of summation: the loss for an element in the sequence is $J_{elem}(y^{(i)}, \hat{y}^{(i)})$ and the loss for an individual sequence is therefore

$$J_{seq}(y, \hat{y}) = \sum_{i=1}^{t} J_{elem}(y^{(i)}, \hat{y}^{(i)}), \tag{7.7}$$

and the total overall m sequences in a mini-batch are given by

$$J_{total}(y, \hat{y}) = \sum_{j=1}^{m} \sum_{i=1}^{t} J_{elem}(y^{(i)}, \hat{y}^{(i)}). \tag{7.8}$$

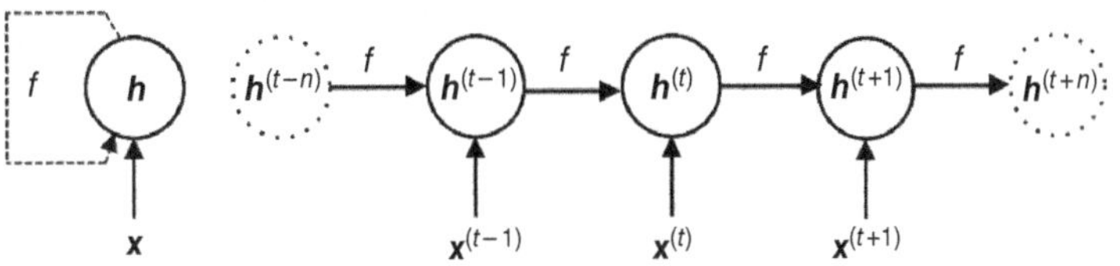

FIGURE 7.1 The computational graph for the recurrence relation in Equation (7.1) shown in rolled and unrolled form.

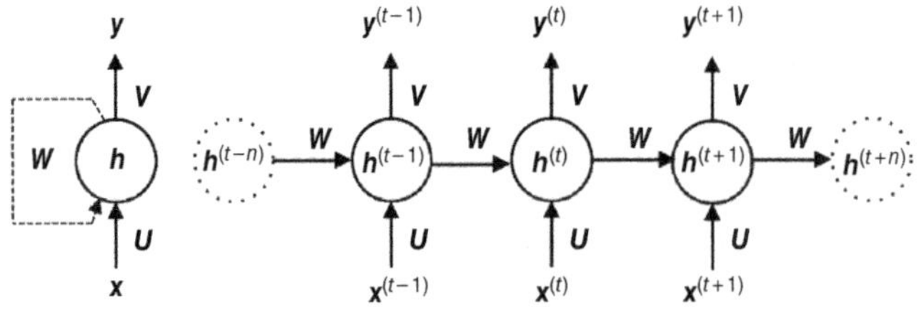

FIGURE 7.2 The computational graph for the (shallow) RNN is shown in rolled and unrolled form.

The gradient of the loss with respect to parameters θ is given by

$$\begin{aligned}\frac{\partial J_{total}}{\partial \theta} &= \sum_{j=1}^{m}\sum_{i=1}^{t}\frac{\partial J_{elem}(y^{(i)}, \hat{y}^{(i)})}{\partial \theta} \\ &= \sum_{j=1}^{m}\sum_{i=1}^{t}\frac{\partial J_{elem}(y^{(i)}, \hat{y}^{(i)})}{\partial \hat{y}^{(i)}}\frac{\partial \hat{y}^{(i)}}{\partial \theta}.\end{aligned} \tag{7.9}$$

Replacing θ by the weight matrices and bias vectors gives the following expressions:

$$\begin{aligned}\frac{\partial \hat{y}^{(i)}}{\partial c} &= \frac{\partial \hat{y}^{(i)}}{\partial o^{(i)}}\frac{\partial o^{(i)}}{\partial c} \\ &= \frac{\partial \hat{y}^{(i)}}{\partial o^{(i)}};\end{aligned} \tag{7.10}$$

$$\begin{aligned}\frac{\partial \hat{y}^{(i)}}{\partial V} &= \frac{\partial \hat{y}^{(i)}}{\partial o^{(i)}}\frac{\partial o^{(i)}}{\partial V} \\ &= \frac{\partial \hat{y}^{(i)}}{\partial o^{(i)}}h^{(i)};\end{aligned} \tag{7.11}$$

$$\begin{aligned}\frac{\partial \hat{y}^{(i)}}{\partial b} &= \frac{\partial \hat{y}^{(i)}}{\partial o^{(i)}}\frac{\partial o^{(i)}}{\partial b} \\ &= \frac{\partial \hat{y}^{(i)}}{\partial o^{(i)}}\frac{\partial o^{(i)}}{\partial h^{(i)}}\frac{\partial h^{(i)}}{\partial b} \\ &= \frac{\partial \hat{y}^{(i)}}{\partial o^{(i)}}\frac{\partial o^{(i)}}{\partial h^{(i)}}\frac{\partial h^{(i)}}{\partial z^{(i)}}\frac{\partial z^{(i)}}{\partial b} \\ &= \frac{\partial \hat{y}^{(i)}}{\partial o^{(i)}}\frac{\partial o^{(i)}}{\partial h^{(i)}}\frac{\partial h^{(i)}}{\partial z^{(i)}};\end{aligned} \tag{7.12}$$

$$\begin{aligned}\frac{\partial \hat{y}^{(i)}}{\partial U} &= \frac{\partial \hat{y}^{(i)}}{\partial o^{(i)}}\frac{\partial o^{(i)}}{\partial U} \\ &= \frac{\partial \hat{y}^{(i)}}{\partial o^{(i)}}\frac{\partial o^{(i)}}{\partial h^{(i)}}\frac{\partial h^{(i)}}{\partial U} \\ &= \frac{\partial \hat{y}^{(i)}}{\partial o^{(i)}}\frac{\partial o^{(i)}}{\partial h^{(i)}}\frac{\partial h^{(i)}}{\partial z^{(i)}}\frac{\partial z^{(i)}}{\partial U} \\ &= \frac{\partial \hat{y}^{(i)}}{\partial o^{(i)}}\frac{\partial o^{(i)}}{\partial h^{(i)}}\frac{\partial h^{(i)}}{\partial z^{(i)}}x^{(i)};\end{aligned} \tag{7.13}$$

$$\begin{aligned}\frac{\partial \hat{y}^{(i)}}{\partial U} &= \frac{\partial \hat{y}^{(i)}}{\partial o^{(i)}} \frac{\partial o^{(i)}}{\partial W} \\ &= \frac{\partial \hat{y}^{(i)}}{\partial o^{(i)}} \frac{\partial o^{(i)}}{\partial h^{(i)}} \frac{\partial h^{(i)}}{\partial W} \\ &= \frac{\partial \hat{y}^{(i)}}{\partial o^{(i)}} \frac{\partial o^{(i)}}{\partial h^{(i)}} \frac{\partial h^{(i)}}{\partial z^{(i)}} \frac{\partial z^{(i)}}{\partial W} \\ &= \frac{\partial \hat{y}^{(i)}}{\partial o^{(i)}} \frac{\partial o^{(i)}}{\partial h^{(i)}} \frac{\partial h^{(i)}}{\partial z^{(i)}} \left(h^{(i-1)} + W \frac{\partial h^{(i-1)}}{\partial W} \right),\end{aligned} \tag{7.14}$$

where the last term must be iterated backwards to the initial state h_0. This is a potential issue and will be returned to in Section 7.2.4 below.

EXAMPLE 7.1: RNN REGRESSION FOR SUNSPOT ACTIVITY

The first example demonstrates a simple shallow RNN in a regression problem precisely to predict the next value in a sequence. It employs a time series of sunspot data and is presented in the Jupyter Notebook titled `RegressionRNNSunspots.ipynb`. Various example models using this dataset are available on Kaggle, as is the dataset https://www.kaggle.com/datasets/robervalt/sunspots, downloadable as a CSV file. This file comprises three columns: an index, a date marking each month's end and the monthly mean total sunspot number. The data series spans the period from January 1749 to August 2017. The number of sunspots visible on the solar surface correlates with the approximately 11-year solar cycle. However, the magnitude of a solar maximum and the number of sunspots vary from one cycle to another.

The dataset undergoes preparation once downloaded and read into a Pandas data frame. In this process, the RNN learns to predict the next value through supervised training, where the network receives a sequence of a pre-determined length and then predicts the next value, addressing a many-to-one problem. This approach involves sourcing data and targets from the time series using a sliding-window technique. Initially, the dataset gets split chronologically into training and test segments, dedicating the last 20% of the data for testing and the remainder for training. This split occurs using `train_test_split` with the shuffle argument set to false. The training and test datasets were then created using the following Python function:

```
def create_sequences(data, train_win, tar_win):
    sequences = []
    targets = []
    for i in range(len(data) - train_win - tar_win + 1):
        sequences.append(data[i:(i + train_win)])
        targets.append(data[(i + train_win):(i + train_win + tar_win)])
    return np.array(sequences), np.array(targets)
```

The creation of PyTorch data loaders follows from the resulting numpy arrays. Maintaining the dataset's chronological structure is crucial; hence, setting the data loaders to keep the data unshuffled is necessary.

A PyTorch class constructs the RNN model featuring a single RNN layer. This layer necessitates input data with dimension ordering: batch size, sequence length and input size. The model includes a linear layer for output. The design specifies 64 units for the hidden layer and 12 for the input, reflecting 12 months, while the output is a scalar.

```
class SimpleRNN(nn.Module):
    def __init__(self, input_size, hidden_size, output_size):
        super(SimpleRNN, self).__init__()
        self.rnn = nn.RNN(input_size, hidden_size, batch_first=True)
```

(Continued)

(*Continued*)

```
        self.linear = nn.Linear(hidden_size, output_size)

    def forward(self, x):
        out, _ = self.rnn(x)
        out = out[:, -1, :]
        out = self.linear(out)
        return out
```

As illustrated in previous examples, the training was performed using a standard PyTorch training loop function. The batch size was 32, and optimisation was done using Adam with a learning rate of 10^{-4} over 100 epochs. The training and test losses during training are shown in Figure 7.3.

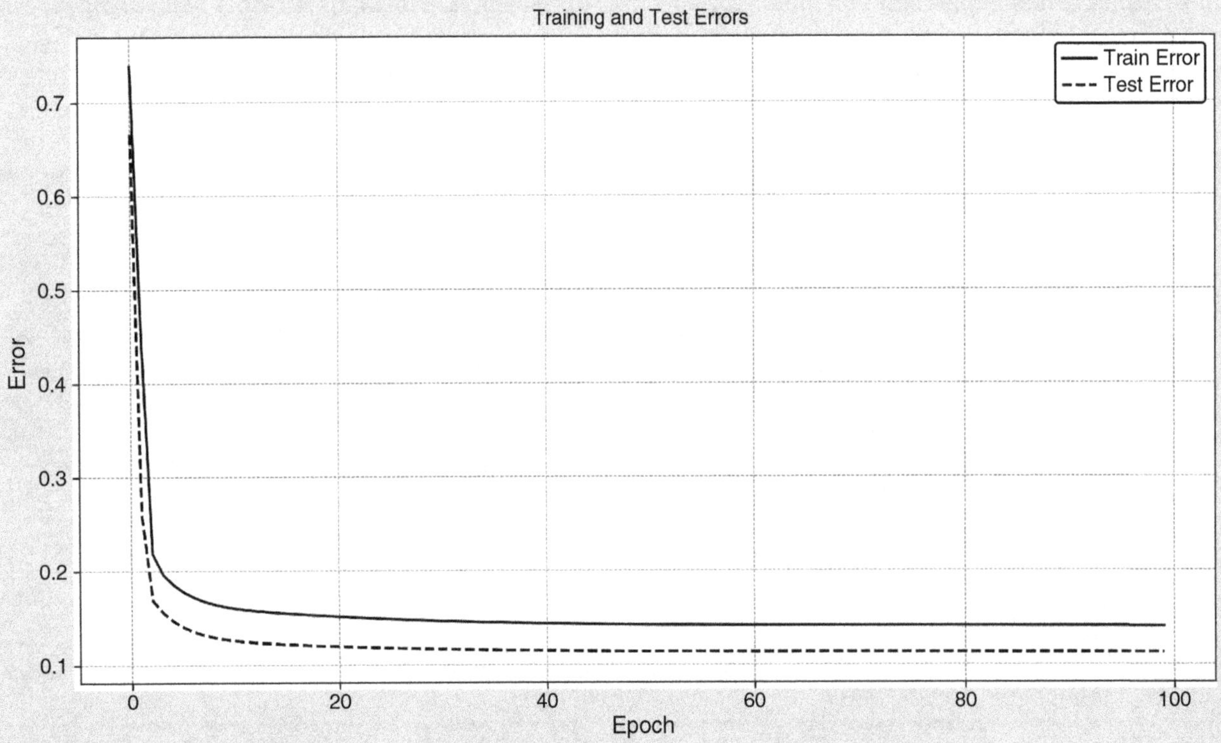

FIGURE 7.3 Training and test losses for the sunspot regression RNN as a function of epoch.

A plot was created to compare the predicted values with the actual values for all data points in the training and test sets in order to demonstrate the model's performance. The resulting chart is shown in Figure 7.4. As can be seen, the predicted values are generally very close to actual values in both the in-sample and out-of-sample regions. The model also reproduces the *Dalton minimum* with low solar and sunspot activity in the first half of the nineteenth century and the recent weaker solar cycle. However, the model fails to reproduce the intense peaks of some solar cycles.

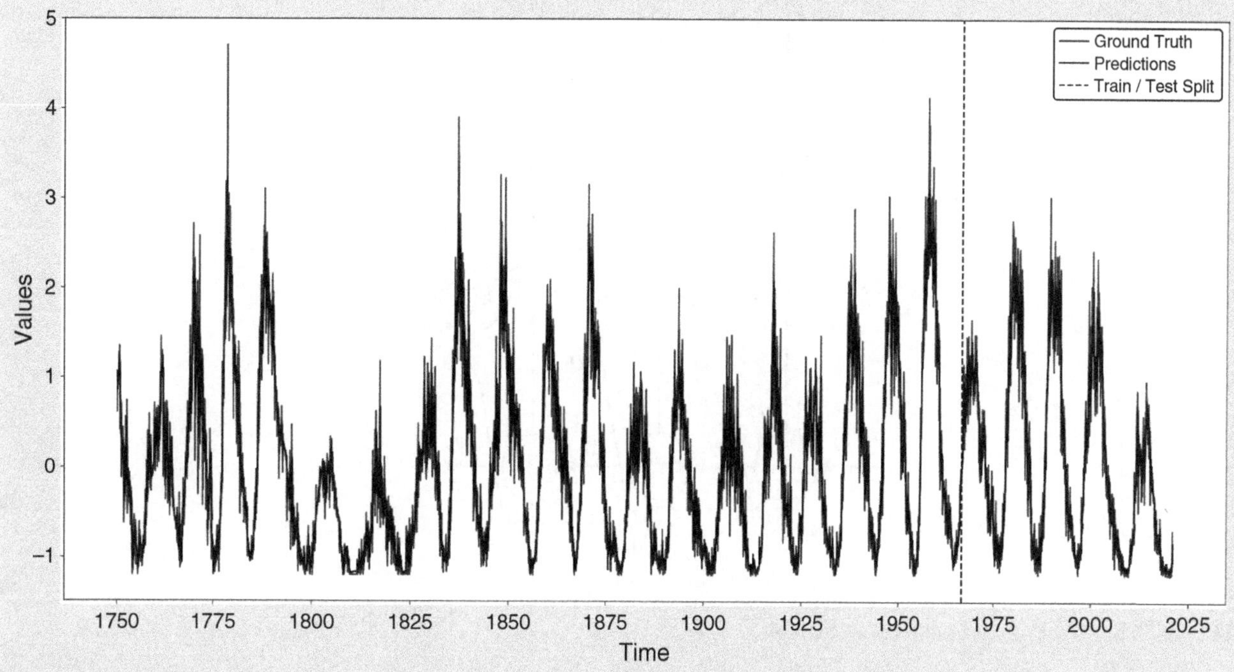

FIGURE 7.4 Ground truth and predicted values from the RNN for the sunspot time series. The dashed vertical line gives the split between the dates used for training to the left and those used for testing to the right.

7.2.2 Bidirectional RNNs

A bidirectional RNN has connections in both directions, with forward propagation of information in 'time' as with the standard RNN and backward propagation in addition, and this means that there are now two sets of weight matrices. Equations (7.2) through (7.5) are then replaced by

$$z^{(i)} = Wh^{(t-1)} + Ux^{(t)} + b, \tag{7.15}$$

$$\widehat{z}^{(i)} = \widehat{W}\widehat{h}^{(t+1)} + \widehat{U}x^{(t)} + \widehat{b}, \tag{7.16}$$

$$h^{(t)} = g_1(z^{(i)}), \tag{7.17}$$

$$\widehat{h}^{(t)} = g_1(\widehat{z}^{(i)}), \tag{7.18}$$

$$o^{(t)} = V[h^{(t)}; \widehat{h}^{(t)}] + c, \tag{7.19}$$

$$\widehat{y} = g_2(o^{(t)}). \tag{7.20}$$

The network output is formed from the concatenated outputs of the forward and backward recurrent networks. The structure of the bidirectional RNN is illustrated in Figure 7.5.

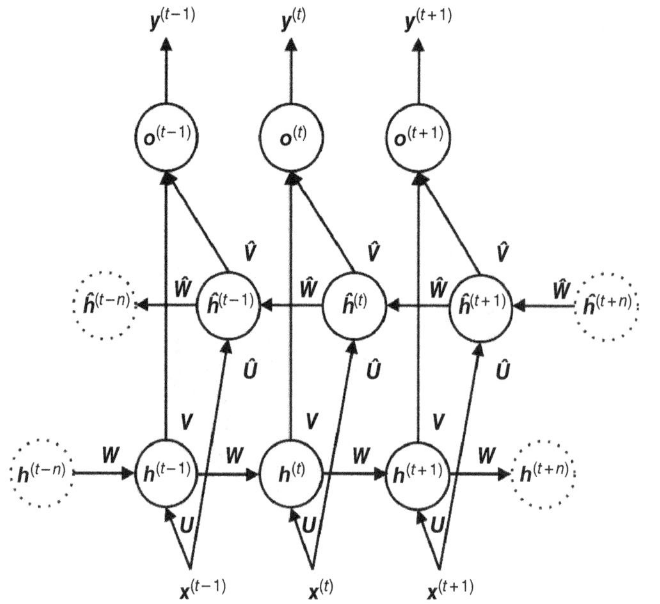

FIGURE 7.5 The structure of a bidirectional RNN.

EXAMPLE 7.2: GENOMIC SEQUENCE CLASSIFICATION USING A BIDIRECTIONAL RNN

This example demonstrates the classification of genomic sequences using a shallow bidirectional RNN model, detailed in the Jupyter Notebook `ClassificationBiRNNGenomics.ipynb`. The model utilises genomic sequences from the Python package `genomic-benchmarks` (Grešová et al., 2023). This package offers a variety of datasets suitable for genomic machine learning tasks. Specifically, the example employs the *human or worm* dataset, comprising 100,000 sequences with 200 base pairs each, evenly split between human and worm sequences. The dataset reserves 25% for testing purposes, and an example sequence appears below.

GAAAATAAAACAGATTTACGTGTAAAAATAGATCATACCAAACTTTAGAAAT

ACCGTATAGTTGTTATTAGTTGTGAACCCATACATTTTTTAGAAAGATGTGA

TGAATGTAAAATTTAAATAATTAAAATAAAGCAGAACCAATGAGTACAGCAT

CTTTTGTTGCCTTAAACGATGGGTTTTCCAAGCTCTTTTCAGAC

The sequences are the first letter of the four bases: adenine, guanine, cytosine and thymine, and this gives a vocabulary of four characters, but four additional characters can be found in the data – 'N', '<eos>', '<bos>' and '<unk>' – giving a total vocabulary of eight.

The sequences must be tokenised, and the genomics benchmark package utilities provide the vocabulary, which is then used to convert the sequences to integers.

```
from genomic_benchmarks.data_check import list_datasets, info
from genomic_benchmarks.dataset_getters.utils import LetterTokenizer, build_vocab
from genomic_benchmarks.dataset_getters.pytorch_datasets import DemoHumanOrWorm

train_dset = DemoHumanOrWorm(split='train', version=0)
test_dset = DemoHumanOrWorm(split='test', version=0)
```

The sequences must be tokenised, and the genomics benchmark package utilities must provide the vocabulary and then convert the sequences to integers.

```
tokenizer = get_tokenizer(LetterTokenizer())
vocabulary = build_vocab(train_dset, tokenizer, use_padding=False)
vocab_dict = vocabulary.get_stoi()

def char_to_int_sequence(data, char_to_int):
    int_data = []
    label_data = []
    for string, label in data:
        int_data.append([char_to_int[char] for char in string])
        label_data.append(label)
    return int_data, label_data

train_int_data, train_lbl = char_to_int_sequence(train_dset, vocab_dict)
test_int_data, test_lbl = char_to_int_sequence(test_dset, vocab_dict)
```

To prepare the input sequences, they must convert to PyTorch tensors and one-hot encoding, achievable using PyTorch functions. Contrary to the previous example, these data loaders should shuffle the data, as the downloaded sequences initially appear in two blocks for 'human' and 'worm'.

The RNN class in this example mirrors the previous one, with one notable adjustment: modifying the RNN layer to operate bidirectionally. Additionally, the inputs to the linear output layer double in size.

```
self.rnn = nn.RNN(input_size, hidden_size, batch_first=True,
                  bidirectional=True)
self.linear = nn.Linear(hidden_size*2, output_size)
```

Here, the input size is eight; given the vocabulary size and one-hot encoding size, the number of hidden units is 64, and a single linear value gives the output. Note that the loss function is `torch.nn.BCEWithLogitsLoss()`, which embeds the sigmoid. The model was trained through 100 epochs using the Adam optimiser with a learning rate of 10^{-5} using a standard classifier training loop similar to those described earlier. During training, the loss and accuracy on training and test sets were monitored and are shown in Figure 7.6. Table 7.2 shows a series of evaluation metrics as described in Chapter 3. The final accuracy of 62.5% is not that high, reflecting the use of a small shallow RNN.

(*Continued*)

(*Continued*)

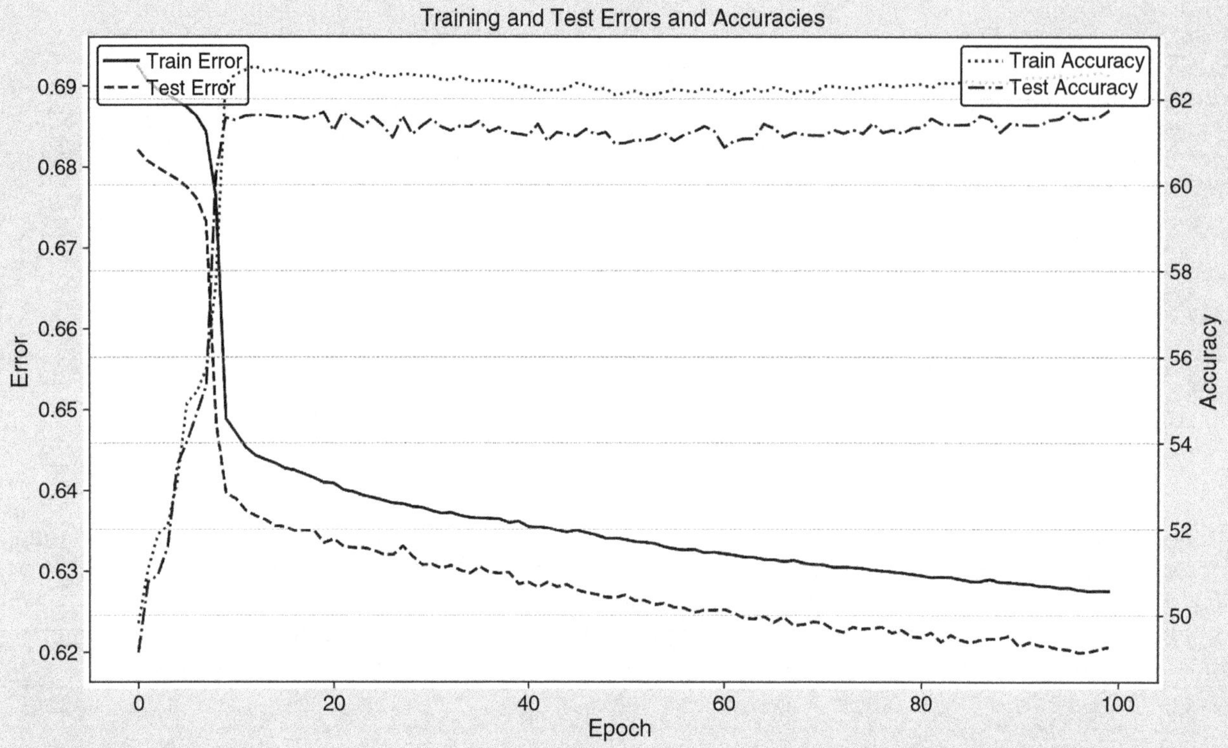

FIGURE 7.6 Training and test loss, and accuracy for the genomics binary classifier using a bidirectional RNN.

TABLE 7.2 Performance Metrics for the Genomics Binary Classifier Using a Bidirectional RNN

Metric	Value
Accuracy	0.62497
Balanced accuracy	0.62476
Precision	0.70452
Recall	0.42908
F_1-score	0.53334
AUC	0.62476

7.2.3 Deep RNNs

Both standard and bidirectional RNNs can be deep and consist of L layers. Additional layers can also be used in between the RNN layers, such as dropout. The equations for a standard deep RNN can be written as follows:

$$z_0^{(t)} = W_0 h_0^{(t-1)} + U_0 x^{(t)} + b_0, \tag{7.21}$$

$$h_0^{(t)} = g_1(z_0^{(t)}), \tag{7.22}$$

$$\vdots$$

$$z_L^{(t)} = W_L h_L^{(t-1)} + U_L h_{L-1}^{(t)} + b_L, \tag{7.23}$$

$$h_L^{(t)} = g_1(z_L^{(t)}), \tag{7.24}$$

$$o^{(t)} = V h_L^{(t)} + c, \tag{7.25}$$

$$\hat{y} = g_2(o^{(t)}). \tag{7.26}$$

EXAMPLE 7.3: GENOMIC SEQUENCE CLASSIFICATION USING A DEEP BIDIRECTIONAL RNN

This example repeats the previous one but uses a deep bidirectional RNN instead. The preprocessing and training steps are identical, but the network has been changed to reflect the use of a deep RNN with dropout, and this can be achieved with the same PyTorch RNN unit with additional settings. The RNN class now becomes

```
class DeepRNN(nn.Module):
    def __init__(self, input_size, hidden_size, output_size, num_layers=3,
                 dropout=0.5):
        super(DeepRNN, self).__init__()
        self.rnn = nn.RNN(input_size, hidden_size, num_layers=num_layers,
                          batch_first=True, bidirectional=True,
                          dropout=dropout)
        self.linear = nn.Linear(hidden_size * 2, output_size)

    def forward(self, x):
        out, _ = self.rnn(x)
        out = out[:, -1, :]
          out = self.linear(out)
        return out
```

The accuracy and loss for training and test sets during training are illustrated in Figure 7.7, which still shows improvement after 100 epochs, suggesting better results could be obtained from training longer. The performance metrics after 100 epochs are given in Table 7.3 and are significantly better than those obtained with the shallow bidirectional RNN.

(*Continued*)

(*Continued*)

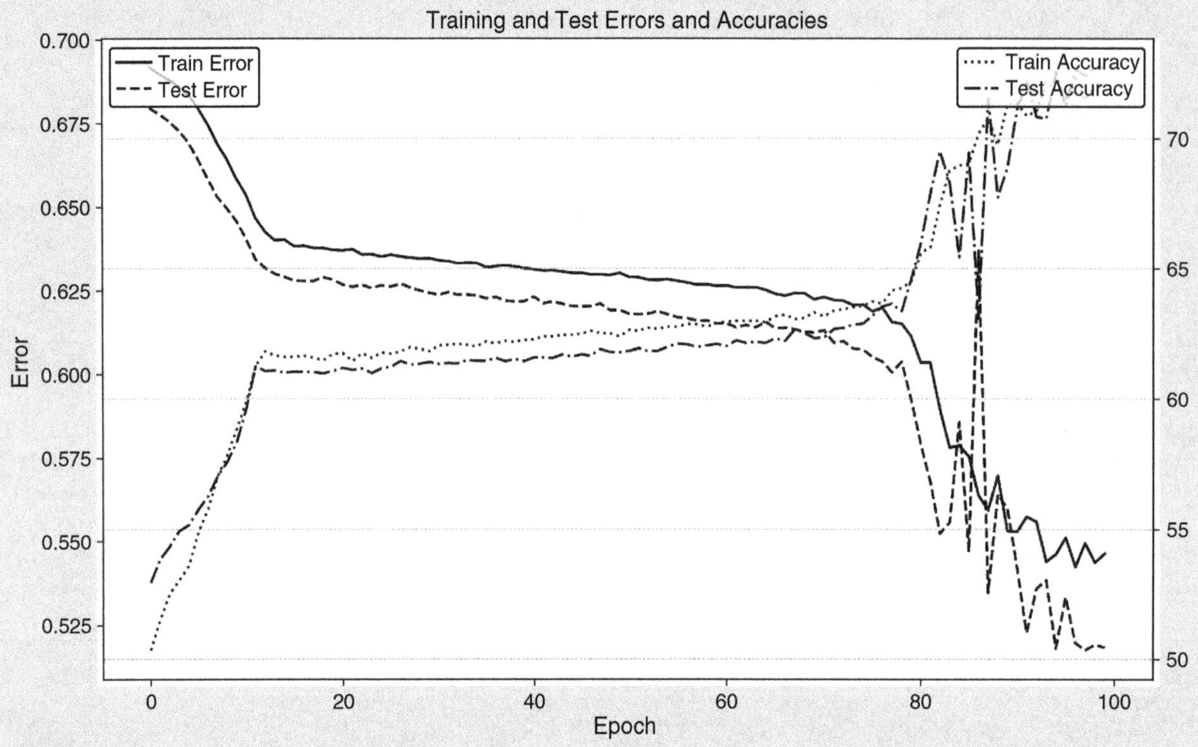

FIGURE 7.7 Training and test loss and accuracy for the genomics binary classifier using a deep bidirectional RNN.

TABLE 7.3 Performance Metrics for the Genomics Binary Classifier Using a Deep Bidirectional RNN

Metric	Value
Accuracy	0.73943
Balanced accuracy	0.73941
Precision	0.72364
Recall	0.77519
F_1-score	0.74853
AUC	0.73941

7.2.4 Vanishing and Exploding Gradients

Recall Equation (7.14), which describes how to backpropagate gradients for weights W. Considering the second term and iterating backwards in time gives

$$\frac{\partial \hat{y}^{(i)}}{\partial U} = \frac{\partial \hat{y}^{(i)}}{\partial o^{(i)}} \frac{\partial o^{(i)}}{\partial h^{(i)}} \frac{\partial h^{(i)}}{\partial z^{(i)}} \left(W \frac{\partial h^{(i-1)}}{\partial W} \right) \tag{7.27}$$

$$= \frac{\partial \hat{y}^{(i)}}{\partial o^{(i)}} \frac{\partial o^{(i)}}{\partial h^{(i)}} \frac{\partial h^{(i)}}{\partial z^{(i)}} \frac{\partial h^{(i-1)}}{\partial z^{(i-1)}} W^2 \frac{\partial h^{(i-2)}}{\partial W} + \cdots \tag{7.28}$$

If the sequence length is N, then the weight matrix W multiplies at each step, resulting in W^N during backpropagation. Therefore, if the weight matrix's eigenvalues are less than 1, gradients will vanish, while eigenvalues greater than 1 lead to exploding gradients (Drori, 2022). This characteristic makes training standard RNNs notoriously challenging.

While gradient clipping can address exploding gradients, vanishing gradients are more complex. Consequently, RNNs struggle to learn long-range dependencies (Mourri et al., 2021). The remedy involves breaking the multiplication chain using gated units like LSTM and GRU. Additionally, LSTM units incorporate a memory *cell* to handle long-term dependencies.

7.2.5 Long Short-Term Memory (LSTM)

Hochreiter and Schmidhuber (1997) introduced the LSTM unit to tackle the vanishing gradient problem in standard RNNs and enable the learning of long-range dependencies. Figure 7.8 illustrates the LSTM architecture.

The LSTM's core advance is the *cell memory* state, a second hidden state flowing through the unit (Mourri et al., 2021). Unlike an RNN's hidden state, the cell memory in an LSTM traverses the unit with the pointwise addition of a candidate memory, akin to a skip connection. This mechanism facilitates the easy backpropagation of information and gradients. Three gates control information flow, all utilising sigmoid activation to produce a value between 0 and 1.

7.2.5.1 Forget Gate The forget gate determines what information will be 'forgotten' from the cell memory. It uses information from the current value of the hidden state, $h^{(t-1)}$, and the input $x^{(t)}$ to make this choice (Mourri et al., 2021; Drori, 2022),

$$f^{(t)} = \sigma(W_f h^{(t-1)} + U_f x^{(t)} + b_f). \tag{7.29}$$

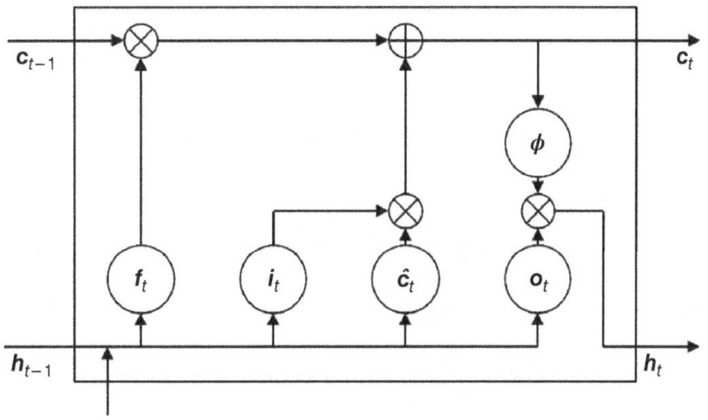

FIGURE 7.8 The LSTM cell structure. f_t is the forget gate, i_t is the input gate, $\hat{c}_t$ is the candidate memory and o_t is the output gate.

7.2.5.2 Candidate Cell Memory A candidate for storing information in the cell memory is formed using the current value of the hidden state and the input,

$$\hat{c}^{(t)} = \phi(Wh^{(t-1)} + Ux^{(t)} + b), \tag{7.30}$$

where ϕ is the activation function, normally tanh.

7.2.5.3 Input Gate The third stage of the processing selects what information to store in the cell state. The input gate controls how much candidate memory is passed to the new cell memory state,

$$i^{(t)} = \sigma(W_i h^{(t-1)} + U_i x^{(t)} + b_i), \tag{7.31}$$
$$c^{(t)} = f^{(t)} c^{(t-1)} + i^{(t)} \hat{c}^{(t)}, \tag{7.32}$$

7.2.5.4 Output Gate The final step is the output, controlled by the output gate, which determines how much of the cell memory state is passed to the hidden state. Again, this uses the current value of the hidden state and the input,

$$o^{(t)} = \sigma(W_o h^{(t-1)} + U_o x^{(t)} + b_o), \tag{7.33}$$
$$h^{(t)} = o^{(t)} \phi(c^{(t)}). \tag{7.34}$$

7.2.5.5 Stacked LSTMs LSTMs can be made deep by stacking like RNNs and bidirectional RNNs.

7.2.5.6 Peephole LSTM Gers and Schmidhuber (2000) introduced additional *peephole* connections into the LSTM to overcome the limitation that all gates can only observe the previous hidden state and input. In the standard LSTM, the gates have no direct access to the cell memory state. The peephole connections add access to the previous cell state for the input and forget gates and the current cell state for the output gate, and this modifies the expressions for the gates as follows:

$$f^{(t)} = \sigma(W_f h^{(t-1)} + P_f c^{(t-1)} + U_f x^{(t)} + b_f), \tag{7.35}$$
$$i^{(t)} = \sigma(W_i h^{(t-1)} + P_i c^{(t-1)} + U_i x^{(t)} + b_i), \tag{7.36}$$
$$o^{(t)} = \sigma(W_o h^{(t-1)} + P_o c^{(t)} + U_o x^{(t)} + b_o). \tag{7.37}$$

7.2.6 Gated Recurrence Unit (GRU)

Cho et al. (2014) introduced the *gated recurrence unit (GRU)* as a simplified form of the LSTM unit that was faster to compute. The forget and input gates of the LSTM are combined in the GRU as the reset gate, and there is only one hidden state $h^{(t)}$. The reset gate and the update gate use sigmoid activation and are functions of the previous hidden state and the input (Drori, 2022),

$$r^{(t)} = \sigma(W_r h^{(t-1)} + U_r x^{(t)} + b_r), \tag{7.38}$$
$$z^{(t)} = \sigma(W_z h^{(t-1)} + U_z x^{(t)} + b_z). \tag{7.39}$$

The reset gate controls the candidate update,

$$\hat{h}^{(t)} = \phi(W(r^{(t)} \odot h^{(t-1)}) + Ux^{(t)} + b), \tag{7.40}$$

while the update gate controls the new memory state,

$$h^{(t)} = z^{(t)} \odot h^{(t-1)} + (1 - z^{(t)}) \odot \hat{h}^{(t)}. \tag{7.41}$$

The GRU structure is illustrated in Figure 7.9.

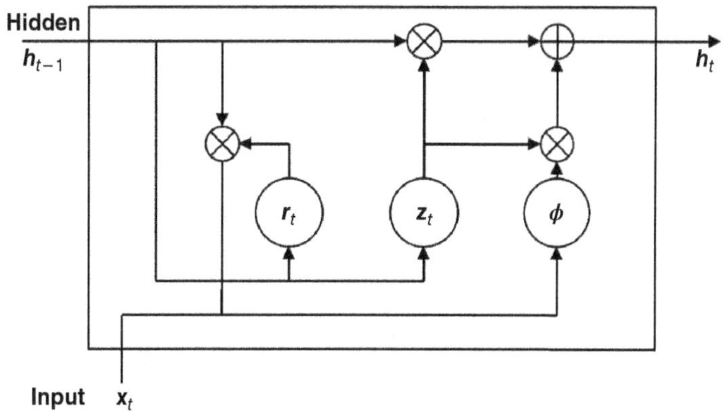

FIGURE 7.9 The structure of a GRU. r_t is the reset gate and z_t is the update gate.

EXAMPLE 7.4: GENOMIC SEQUENCE CLASSIFICATION USING DEEP BIDIRECTIONAL LSTMs AND GRUs

The genomic sequence classification example above was repeated for LSTM and GRU units, and the code can be found in the Jupyter Notebooks `ClassificationLSTMGenomics.ipynb` and `ClassificationGRUGenomics.ipynb`. In both cases, the model was three layers deep and bidirectional, as the earlier model with the hidden dimension was also the same at 64 units. The one parameter difference was using a higher learning rate at 10^{-4}.

The code to build the LSTM and GRU models differs slightly from that for the bidirectional RNN. The LSTM class is given by

```
class DeepLSTM(nn.Module):
    def __init__(self, input_size, hidden_size, output_size, num_layers=3,
                 dropout=0.5):
        super(DeepLSTM, self).__init__()
        self.lstm = nn.LSTM(input_size, hidden_size, num_layers=num_layers,
        batch_first=True, bidirectional=True, dropout=dropout)
        self.linear = nn.Linear(hidden_size * 2, output_size)

    def forward(self, x):
        out, (h_n, c_n) = self.lstm(x)
        out = out[:, -1, :]
        out = self.linear(out)
        return out
```

The LSTM unit initialisation drops in with the same arguments as the bidirectional RNN. However, the unit's outputs differ, as the hidden state and the cell memory are outputs. The following code gives the GRU class; the output is the same as the bidirectional RNN.

```
class DeepGRU(nn.Module):
    def __init__(self, input_size, hidden_size, output_size, num_layers=3,
                 dropout=0.5):
        super(DeepGRU, self).__init__()
        self.gru = nn.GRU(input_size, hidden_size, num_layers=num_layers,
        batch_first=True, bidirectional=True, dropout=dropout)
        self.linear = nn.Linear(hidden_size * 2, output_size)
```

(*Continued*)

(*Continued*)

```
    def forward(self, x):
        out, h_n = self.gru(x)
        out = out[:, -1, :]
        out = self.linear(out)
        return out
```

Figure 7.10 shows the loss and accuracy for the LSTM model during training, while Figure 7.11 shows the same for the GRU model. Table 7.4 shows the final performance metrics for both models. LSTM and GRU networks demonstrate significantly higher accuracy than any RNN-based models across all metrics, with the GRU slightly outperforming LSTM. The training loss and accuracy profiles vary between LSTM and GRU, with the GRU exhibiting a faster and smoother progression towards the final result.

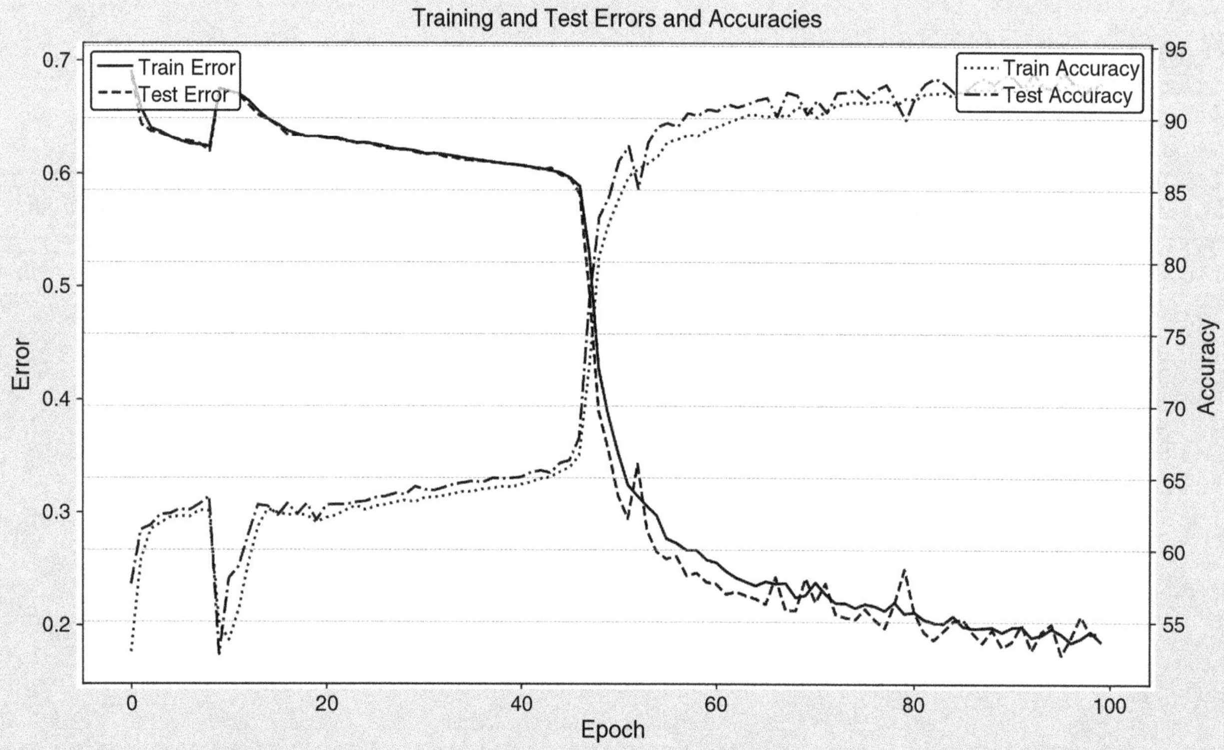

FIGURE 7.10 Training and test loss and accuracy for the genomics binary classifier using a deep bidirectional LSTM.

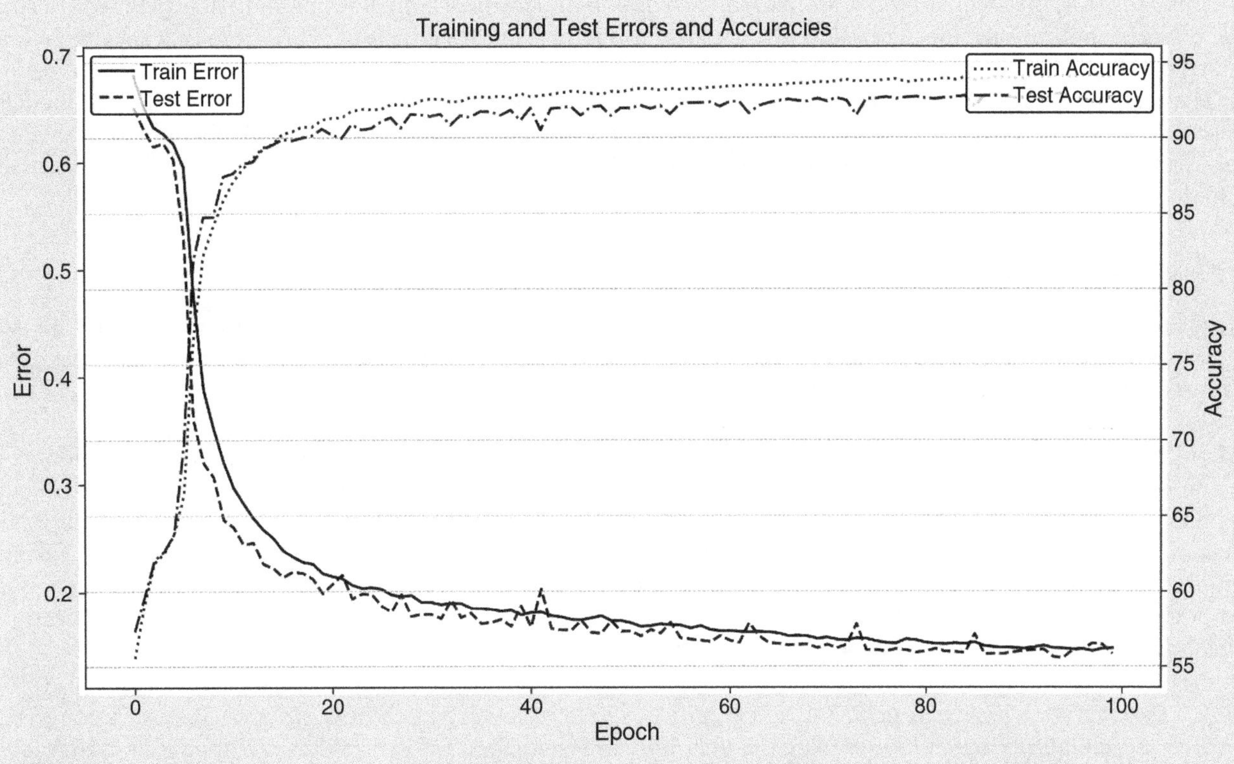

FIGURE 7.11 Training and test loss and accuracy for the genomics binary classifier using a deep bidirectional GRU.

TABLE 7.4 Performance Metrics Comparison Between LSTM and GRU Models

Metric	LSTM	GRU
Accuracy	0.92284	0.94384
Balanced accuracy	0.92284	0.94384
Precision	0.95226	0.92474
Recall	0.89033	0.96632
F_1-score	0.92025	0.94507
AUC	0.92284	0.94384

7.3 NEURAL NATURAL LANGUAGE PROCESSING

7.3.1 Introducing NLP

This section introduces neural NLP, a field that has developed alongside advancements in sequence modelling. Neural NLP uses neural networks to process, understand and generate human language. Critical applications include machine translation and automated text generation. This section applies sequence models to tackle complex NLP tasks with broader applications to general sequence data. Although NLP has direct financial applications, such as sentiment analysis, the techniques discussed here, such as one-dimensional convolutions and attention mechanisms, have broader applications. It is natural to discuss these techniques in the context of NLP, given that they were first applied there.

The remainder of this section outlines the development of neural NLP models. Before discussing the models, however, it is important to briefly describe the techniques explicitly developed for text handling and model evaluation. Hence, Section 7.3.2 describes preprocessing steps, Section 7.3.3 explains *n*-grams and Section 7.3.4 discusses evaluation methods for NLP tasks.

7.3.2 NLP Preprocessing

Before processing sequences of text, several essential steps are required to convert that text data into a form suitable to be processed by a model. This section provides a brief overview, but for a more detailed perspective, please see a dedicated text on NLP such as Eisenstein (2019).

7.3.2.1 Tokenisation Tokenisation breaks down a piece of text into smaller units known as tokens. Depending on the context, these tokens can be individual words, symbols or other relevant elements. The primary goal of tokenisation is to transform unstructured data into a structured format. For example, take the sentence 'Tokenisation is essential for NLP'. In tokenisation, this sentence would be broken down into individual tokens, such as ['Tokenisation', 'is', 'essential', 'for', 'NLP']. This breakdown makes it easier to perform word-by-word sentence analysis and prepares the text for other NLP tasks such as part-of-speech tagging, parsing and model input preparation. Tokenisation is the first step in almost all NLP workflows.

7.3.2.2 Lowercasing Lowercasing in NLP is a preprocessing step in which all the text in a given dataset is converted to lowercase, standardising and simplifying the text. In many languages, the same word can appear in varied cases (e.g., 'House', 'house' and 'HOUSE' all refer to the same concept), and treating these variations as distinct can unnecessarily increase the vocabulary size and computational complexity. NLP systems can match and analyse words more easily by converting everything to lowercase, regardless of their original casing. This process is helpful for tasks such as counting word frequency, looking up words in a dictionary and training machine learning models, as it ensures that words are consistently represented, which improves performance. However, converting words to lowercase can eliminate particular semantic distinctions, such as the difference between proper and common nouns, or alter the meaning when capitalisation is essential.

7.3.2.3 Removing Punctuation, Numbers and Special Characters A common preprocessing step in NLP is to remove punctuation, numbers, special characters and emojis. Punctuation marks can introduce unnecessary complexity in NLP tasks by increasing the variability of tokens. Similarly, numbers and special characters, unless specifically relevant to the task (e.g., in financial text analysis), are typically removed to reduce the size of the text. Emojis may have considerable expressive power, but they are challenging to interpret in a standardised way. These text elements are commonly removed from the text to make processing easier for algorithms. However, for some NLP applications, it is essential to retain these items as they carry meaning and significance for the task.

7.3.2.4 Stop Words Removal Stop words removal is a preprocessing step in many NLP tasks and involves eliminating frequently occurring words with minimal semantic importance from the text. Stop words typically include articles, conjunctions and prepositions such as 'the', 'and', 'but', 'or', 'is' and 'in'. Such words contribute little to the overall meaning of a text. By removing stop words, NLP models can focus on more meaningful words, leading to more efficient processing and potentially more accurate results. However, in some tasks like sentiment analysis or language translation, the context provided by these words can be crucial. Therefore, the decision to remove stop words should be made based on the application.

7.3.2.5 Removing Handles and URLs Removing handles (commonly used in social media usernames) and URLs can be vital with certain types of text, such as data from social media platforms like X (Twitter) or Facebook. Handles and URLs often appear in tweets and posts but do not contribute meaningful content for NLP tasks such as sentiment analysis, topic modelling or text classification. However, these elements should be retained and analysed in contexts where a handle or URL is significant.

7.3.2.6 Stemming Stemming in NLP refers to reducing words to their base or root form, consolidating different word forms into a common representation (Manning et al., 2008). In text processing, the meaning is often more important than the exact form of a word. Stemming algorithms operate by cutting off the ends of words using a heuristic approach. For example, stemming transforms words like ‘running’ and ‘runs’ into their root word ‘run’. This method is quick and straightforward but can be inaccurate. While stemming helps reduce the complexity of textual data and improves the performance of various NLP tasks like search and information retrieval, it must be used carefully.

7.3.2.7 Lemmatisation Lemmatisation reduces words to their base or dictionary form, known as the lemma (Manning et al., 2008). The aim of lemmatisation is, like stemming, to reduce a word to its base form, but unlike stemming, it is to do so using the words’ context and morphological analysis. Hence, lemmatisation relies on detailed knowledge of the language and its vocabulary. Lemmatisation is especially useful in tasks that require precise semantic understanding and consistency in word forms. However, it is computationally more intensive than stemming and may only be necessary for some NLP applications.

EXAMPLE 7.5: NLP PREPROCESSING

The Jupyter Notebook `NLPPreprocessing.ipynb` demonstrates the essential NLP preprocessing steps discussed earlier. All of the steps can be accomplished either by using the Python standard libraries or using the *Natural Language Toolkit*, `nltk` (https://www.nltk.org/).

Tokenisation. Tokenisation can be done using the `nltk` word tokenisation tool. The appropriate library must be downloaded before the word tokeniser can be used.

```
from nltk.tokenize import word_tokenize
nltk.download('punkt')
sentence = "Natural Language Processing with Python is fun!"
tokens = word_tokenize(sentence)
```

Lowercasing. The `lower` command performs lowercasing in Python.

```
sentence = "Natural Language Processing with Python is Exciting!"
lowercased_sentence = sentence.lower()
```

Removing Punctuation, Numbers and Special Characters. Remove punctuation, numbers and special characters, including emoji, using the `string` library and the `re` regex library. For emojis, a regex pattern needs to be defined.

```
import string
import re

text = "Hello, World! This is a test text with numbers 123, \
        special characters @#$ and emoji  ."

# Define a regex pattern for matching emojis
emoji_pattern = re.compile("["
                        u"\U0001F600-\U0001F64F"  # emoticons
```

(Continued)

(*Continued*)

```
                        u"\U0001F300-\U0001F5FF"  # symbols & pictographs
                        u"\U0001F680-\U0001F6FF"  # transport & map symbols
                        u"\U0001F1E0-\U0001F1FF"  # flags (iOS)
                        "]+", flags=re.UNICODE)

# Remove punctuation
text = text.translate(str.maketrans('', '', string.punctuation))

# Remove numbers
text = re.sub(r'\d+', '', text)

# Remove special characters and emojis
text = re.sub(r'[^A-Za-z0-9 ]+', '', text)
```

Stop Words Removal. Stop words can be removed using the `nltk` stopword functionality. The text needs to be tokenised first, and then stopwords must be removed using the data provided by `nltk`.

```
from nltk.corpus import stopwords

nltk.download('stopwords')
text = "This is a sample sentence, demonstrating the removal of stop words."
tokens = word_tokenize(text)

stop_words = set(stopwords.words('english'))
filtered_sentence = [word for word in tokens if not word in stop_words]
```

Removing Handles and URLs. Handles and URLs can be removed using the regex library.

```
text = "This is a tweet by @user, and it contains a URL https://example.com"

# Remove handles - anything that starts with @
# followed by any number of characters
text_without_handles = re.sub(r'@\S+', '', text)

# Remove URLs - a simple regex for common URL patterns
text_without_handles_urls = re.sub(r'http\S+|www.\S+', '',
                                   text_without_handles)
```

Stemming. `nltk` provides a stemmer class, `PorterStemmer`, that can be used for stemming.

```
from nltk.stem import PorterStemmer

porter = PorterStemmer()
words = ["running", "runs", "run", "runner", "easily", "fairly"]
stemmed_words = [porter.stem(word) for word in words]
```

Lemmatisation. Lemmatisation is also provided by `nltk` as the `WordNetLemmatizer`.

```
nltk.download('wordnet')

from nltk.stem import WordNetLemmatizer
lemmatizer = WordNetLemmatizer()

sentence = "The leaves are falling and the cats are running around."
tokens = word_tokenize(sentence)
lemmatized_words = [lemmatizer.lemmatize(word) for word in tokens]
```

7.3.3 *n*-Grams

In NLP, an *n-gram* is defined as a contiguous sequence of n items extracted from a sample of text or speech (Shannon, 1951). These items could be as small as phonemes or as large as words, varying with the specific application. n-Grams are used to evaluate the pattern of occurrence of word sequences. The analytical capability of n-grams makes them indispensable for several NLP tasks, including text prediction, where they forecast the subsequent sequence of words; spelling correction by identifying and suggesting the most likely alternatives; and language identification, where they help determine the language of a given text. A unigram is a single word; a bigram is two consecutive words; a trigram is three. Higher-order n-grams capture longer sequences but are less used because of data sparsity and heightened computational demand.

7.3.3.1 Probability and *n*-Grams To define the probability of a sentence using the chain rule, consider a sentence composed of words $w_1, w_2, \dots, w_n$. The probability of the sentence is the joint probability of these words occurring in sequence. Using the chain rule of probability, this can be expressed as (Mourri et al., 2021; Jurafsky and Martin, 2023)

$$\begin{aligned} P(w_1, w_2, \dots, w_n) &= P(w_1) \times P(w_2|w_1) \times P(w_3|w_1, w_2) \times \cdots \times P(w_n|w_1, w_2, \dots, w_{n-1}) \\ &= \prod_{i=1}^{n} P(w_i|w_1, w_2, \dots, w_{i-1}). \end{aligned} \tag{7.42}$$

The Markov assumption for n-grams, particularly in the context of language modelling, simplifies the computation of word probabilities by assuming that the probability of a word depends only on a fixed number of immediately preceding words. For an n-gram model, the probability of a word w_i given all its preceding words $w_1, w_2, \dots, w_{i-1}$ is approximated by considering only the $n-1$ most recent words, and is written as

$$P(w_i|w_1, w_2, \dots, w_{i-1}) \approx P(w_i|w_{i-(n-1)}, \dots, w_{i-1}), \tag{7.43}$$

where n is the order of the n-gram model.

- For a bigram model ($n = 2$), it assumes $P(w_i|w_1, \dots, w_{i-1}) \approx P(w_i|w_{i-1})$.
- For a trigram model ($n = 3$), it assumes $P(w_i|w_1, \dots, w_{i-1}) \approx P(w_i|w_{i-2}, w_{i-1})$.
- And so on for higher-order n-gram models.

In practice, the probability of an n-gram is computed based on the occurrences of that sequence in a corpus. For a bigram model (2-grams), for example, the probability of a word w_i following a word w_{i-1} is given by

$$P(w_i|w_{i-1}) = \frac{\text{Count}(w_{i-1}, w_i)}{\text{Count}(w_{i-1})}, \tag{7.44}$$

where $\text{Count}(w_{i-1}, w_i)$ is the count of the bigram (the two words appearing consecutively) in the corpus, and $\text{Count}(w_{i-1})$ is the count of the first word appearing in the corpus. This concept extends to n-grams (where $n > 2$):

$$P(w_i|w_{i-(n-1)}, \dots, w_{i-1}) = \frac{\text{Count}(w_{i-(n-1)}, \dots, w_{i-1}, w_i)}{\text{Count}(w_{i-(n-1)}, \dots, w_{i-1})}. \tag{7.45}$$

A common issue in n-gram models is zero probability for unseen n-grams in the training data. To handle this, techniques like Laplace smoothing (add-one smoothing) are used:

$$P_{\text{smoothed}}(w_i|w_{i-1}) = \frac{\text{Count}(w_{i-1}, w_i) + 1}{\text{Count}(w_{i-1}) + V}, \tag{7.46}$$

where V is the vocabulary size, and 1 is added to each count to ensure no zero probabilities.

7.3.3.2 Advantages and Disadvantages n-Gram models present advantages and disadvantages. They are simple, easy to understand and implement and very suited to tasks with limited computational resources. They often perform well on small datasets where more complex models may struggle because of insufficient data. n-Grams are versatile and suited to text prediction and language detection applications. However, n-grams provide only limited context of a short text section, which may be insufficient to discern the meaning of a whole sentence. The available context increases as the size of the n-gram but requires exponentially more data as n increases. n-Grams are also not well suited to handling rare or new words and word combinations that enter the language. Perhaps the biggest issue is that the size of n limits their ability to capture long-range dependencies in text.

7.3.4 Evaluation Metrics for NLP

7.3.4.1 Classification Metrics Evaluation metrics for classification tasks received a detailed discussion in Section 3.8.2. The same metrics apply to classification tasks in NLP, such as supervised learning approaches to sentiment analysis and fake news detection. Therefore, *accuracy*, *precision*, *recall*, *F-scores* and *AUC* remain equally valid in this context.

7.3.4.2 Machine Translation and Text Generation Metrics

BLEU (Bilingual Evaluation Understudy) The BLEU metric, an acronym for Bilingual Evaluation Understudy, is a widely used method for evaluating the quality of text which has been machine-translated from one natural language to another. Developed by Papineni et al. (2002), BLEU assesses the correspondence of a machine-generated translation to one or more reference translations. The core idea of BLEU is to compare the n-grams of the machine-generated translation's n-grams with the reference text and count the number of matches. These matches are then divided by the number of n-grams in the machine-generated text. The final BLEU score is calculated as the weighted average of individual BLEU scores for n-grams of different lengths, usually up to 4-grams. BLEU is language-independent and correlates with human judgement, making it a reliable measure of translation quality. However, it is mechanical and based on short n-grams, and so it is criticised for lacking sensitivity to fluency and grammatical correctness. Nevertheless, it is a standard benchmark for machine translation.

$$\text{BLEU} = \min\left(1, \frac{\text{Output Length}}{\text{Reference Length}}\right)\left(\prod_{i=1}^{N} \frac{\text{Number of Matching } n\text{-Grams}}{\text{Number of Total } n\text{-Grams in Output}}\right)^{\frac{1}{N}}. \tag{7.47}$$

The BLEU score ranges from 0 to 1, where 1 perfectly matches the reference translation. In practice, scores are often presented as a percentage.

ROUGE (Recall-Oriented Understudy for Gisting Evaluation) ROUGE, which stands for Recall-Oriented Understudy for Gisting Evaluation, is an evaluation metric primarily employed in automatic summarisation and machine translation. Lin and Hovy (2003) developed this metric to estimate the quality of a summary by comparing it to reference summaries written by humans. This measurement quantifies the overlap in terms of n-grams, word sequences and word pairs. Several variants of ROUGE exist, with the most commonly used ones being the following.

- ROUGE-N: Measures the overlap of n-grams between the generated summary and the reference summaries. Commonly, ROUGE-1 (unigrams) and ROUGE-2 (bigrams) are used (Lin and Hovy, 2003; Lin, 2004).
- ROUGE-L: Considers the longest common subsequence between the generated and reference summaries. It is particularly sensitive to sentence-level structure similarity (Lin and Och, 2004).

- **ROUGE-S**: Focuses on skip-bigrams, measuring the pair of words in their sentence order, allowing for arbitrary gaps (Lin and Och, 2004).

The ROUGE scores are calculated in recall, precision and F1 variants, so, for example, ROUGE-N recall is calculated as

$$\text{ROUGE-N} = \frac{\sum_{s \in \{\text{Reference Summaries}\}} \sum_{n\text{-gram} \in s} \text{Count}_{\text{match}}(n\text{-gram})}{\sum_{s \in \{\text{Reference Summaries}\}} \sum_{n\text{-gram} \in s} \text{Count}\,(n\text{-gram})}. \tag{7.48}$$

7.3.4.3 Language Modelling Metrics

Perplexity Perplexity is a widely used metric in NLP, particularly in language modelling. The metric was initially introduced in the context of speech recognition by Jelinek et al. (2005). It is a measure of how well a probability model predicts a sample. In language models, perplexity quantifies how well a model predicts a sequence of words.

The perplexity of a language model on a given text is defined as the inverse probability of the test set, normalised by the number of words. For a model M and a test set $W = w_1, w_2, \dots, w_N$, the perplexity is given by

$$\text{Perplexity}(W) = \sqrt[N]{\frac{1}{P(w_1, w_2, \dots, w_N)}}. \tag{7.49}$$

Lower values of perplexity indicate better predictive performance of the model. A lower perplexity score means the probability distribution estimated by the model is closer to the true distribution of the words in the test data.

7.3.4.4 Text Similarity and Correlation Metrics

Levenshtein Distance The Levenshtein distance (Levenshtein, 1965), or edit distance, measures the similarity between two strings. The minimum number of single-character edits (insertions, deletions or substitutions) is required to change one word into the other. This metric is handy in spell checking, DNA sequencing and NLP tasks like text correction and similarity checking.

Given two strings, a and b, with lengths $|a|$ and $|b|$, respectively, the Levenshtein distance $d(a, b)$ can be computed using dynamic programming. The algorithm constructs a matrix D where $D[i][j]$ represents the Levenshtein distance between the first i characters of a and the first j characters of b. The value of $d(a, b)$ is then found at $D[|a|][|b|]$.

The recursive formula to compute the entries of matrix D is as follows:

$$D[i][j] = \begin{cases} 0 & \text{if } i = 0 \text{ and } j = 0 \\ i & \text{if } j = 0 \text{ and } i > 0 \\ j & \text{if } i = 0 \text{ and } j > 0, \\ \min \begin{cases} D[i-1][j] + 1 \\ D[i][j-1] + 1 \\ D[i-1][j-1] + \mathbf{1}(a_i \neq b_j) \end{cases} & \text{otherwise} \end{cases} \tag{7.50}$$

where $\mathbf{1}(a_i \neq b_j)$ is an indicator function, 1 if a_i and b_j are different and 0 if they are the same. The Levenshtein distance is valuable in providing a quantitative measure of the difference between two strings, enabling algorithms to make informed decisions in tasks involving textual data.

Jaccard Index The Jaccard index, or Jaccard similarity coefficient (Jaccard, 1908), measures the similarity of sample sets. It is commonly used in various fields, including NLP, ecology and data mining, to compare the similarities between the two sets.

The Jaccard index, J, is defined as the intersection of the two sets divided by their union. Hence, for two sets A and B,

$$J(A, B) = \frac{|A \cap B|}{|A \cup B|}. \tag{7.51}$$

In NLP, the Jaccard index can measure the similarity between two text documents. Here, the documents are converted into sets of tokens (such as words), and the Jaccard index is computed based on these sets. The Jaccard index ranges from 0 to 1, where 0 indicates no similarity (i.e., the sets do not share any elements) and 1 indicates that the sets are identical. This metric is beneficial in text analysis for tasks such as document clustering, plagiarism detection and measuring the similarity in textual content.

7.3.5 A Neural Probabilistic Language Model

The first neural network model applied to NLP was Bengio et al. (2003). When the paper was published, the prevailing models in NLP were n-gram models, using the probabilistic approach highlighted above in Section 7.3.3.

One problem for language modelling is the curse of dimensionality, which results from the vast vocabulary size of natural languages. The Bengio et al. (2003) model addresses this issue by representing words as continuous feature vectors, thereby reducing the dimensionality of the input space. The model learns distributed representations for words, which means that a dense vector represents each word in a continuous vector space. Bengio et al. (2003) used a feedforward neural network with one hidden layer. The network was trained to predict the next word in a sentence given the previous words, with backpropagation used to update the weights with SGD.

The paper demonstrated that the neural probabilistic language model outperformed traditional n-gram models on two text databases. The neural network model capitalised on broader contexts and grasped more intricate word associations, enhancing generalisation and superior accuracy in predicting the next word in a sequence. Overall, the results demonstrated the effectiveness of the proposed approach in addressing the curse of dimensionality in statistical language modelling and improving the performance of language models in NLP applications, and this paved the way for standardised word embeddings, as discussed below in Section 7.3.6.

EXAMPLE 7.6: A NEURAL PROBABILISTIC LANGUAGE MODEL

This example provides an implementation of the *Neural Probabilistic Language Model* as developed by Bengio et al. (2003), and the code can be found in the Jupyter Notebook `Neural ProbabiliticLanguageModel.ipynb`.

The example has two models: a simple n-gram model and a neural network model with a single hidden layer. These are essentially the models that Bengio et al. (2003) used, but here, the n-gram model is a simple implementation rather than the more sophisticated *modified Kneser–Ney* algorithm.

Both n-gram and neural network models are trained using the *Brown* text corpus as used by Bengio et al. (2003), and this is available from the `nltk` library and must be downloaded and accessed via the API.

```
import nltk
nltk.download('brown')
from nltk.corpus import brown

corpus_sentences = brown.sents()
```

The downloaded data comes as a tokenised sentence list but is otherwise unprocessed. The data must be split into training and test sets, which is done by generating a split index and dividing the list into two parts: `train_corpus_sentences` and `test_corpus_sentences`, with a 0.8 : 0.2 split used.

n-Gram Model

For the *n*-gram model, the training data is further processed to change the tokenised text to lowercase and to flatten the structure to a single list of tokens. A sliding-window approach employs a flat list of tokens to generate a list of *n*-grams. Finally, the *n*-gram model is 'trained' by walking through the list of *n*-grams and counting the occurrences of the next word in the text, and this generates a `defaultdict` structure, which has the *n*-gram as the key and values a second dictionary containing all of the words that follow that *n*-gram in the text as keys and with values of the corresponding conditional probability.

```
def preprocess_corpus(corpus):
    # Convert to lowercase and flatten the list of sentences
    return [word.lower() for sentence in corpus for word in sentence]

def create_ngrams(words, n=2):
    ngrams = list(zip(*[words[i:] for i in range(n)]))
    return ngrams

def train_ngram_model(corpus, n=2):
    # Preprocess and create ngrams
    words = preprocess_corpus(corpus)
    ngrams = create_ngrams(words, n)

    # Calculate frequencies
    ngram_freqs = Counter(ngrams)
    context_freqs = Counter([ngram[:-1] for ngram in ngrams])

    # Calculate probabilities
    model = defaultdict(lambda: defaultdict(float))
    for ngram, freq in ngram_freqs.items():
        context = ngram[:-1]
        word = ngram[-1]
        model[context][word] = freq / context_freqs[context]

    return model

context_size = 3
n = context_size + 1
ngram_model = train_ngram_model(train_corpus_sentences, n)
```

Now that the model is prepared, it can be used to predict the next work, given an *n*-gram context. Of course, in this simplistic *n*-gram model, if the context does not exist in the training set, it will not be able to generate a word. The following code is used to predict the next word, given a context as a string: the code tokenises the input string and performs quick checks before finding all the possible words associated with that context. The word with the highest probability is then selected. Alternatively, the model could be used generatively by sampling these probabilities and selecting the word based on a random draw.

```
def preprocess_sentence(sentence):
    sentence = word_tokenize(sentence)
    return [word.lower() for word in sentence]

def predict_next_word(model, context, n=2):
    processed_context = preprocess_sentence(context)
```

(*Continued*)

(*Continued*)

```
    if len(processed_context) < n - 1:
        raise ValueError(f"Context must be at least {n - 1}
                          words for an {n}-gram model.")

    # Use the last (n-1) words as the context for prediction
    ngram_context = tuple(processed_context[-(n - 1):])

    if ngram_context not in model:
        return None

    # Find the word with the highest probability
    possible_words = model[ngram_context]
    next_word = max(possible_words, key=possible_words.get)
    return next_word
```

With the context 'that the city', the predicted next word is 'executive'. The perplexity can be calculated from the probabilities by walking through a text using a sliding window.

```
def calculate_perplexity_ngram(model, test_data, n):
    total_log_prob = 0
    total_word_count = 0
    for i in range(n - 1, len(test_data)):
        context = tuple(test_data[i - n + 1:i])
        word = test_data[i]
        word_probability = model[context].get(word, 0)
        total_log_prob += math.log(word_probability + 1e-12)
        total_word_count += 1

    avg_log_prob = total_log_prob / total_word_count
    perplexity = math.exp(-avg_log_prob)
    return perplexity
```

If this is calculated on the training set, the perplexity is very low at 1.52. However, if calculated on the test set, the result is terrible with a perplexity of 152×10^9. The model is not generalising at all, which is not surprising, given that there is no smoothing in the *n*-gram model.

Neural Network Model

The neural network model has a single hidden layer. However, a trainable embedding layer is included to convert the input contexts, which will be vectors of indices, to real-valued vectors in the embedding space. The model has a linear output as the `CrossEntropyLoss` in PyTorch embeds the softmax function.

```
class BengioLanguageModel(nn.Module):
    def __init__(self, vocab_size, embedding_dim, hidden_dim, context_size):
        super(BengioLanguageModel, self).__init__()
        self.embeddings = nn.Embedding(vocab_size, embedding_dim)
        self.linear1 = nn.Linear(context_size * embedding_dim, hidden_dim)
        self.linear2 = nn.Linear(hidden_dim, vocab_size)
```

```
    def forward(self, inputs):
        embeds = self.embeddings(inputs)
        embeds = embeds.view(embeds.size(0), -1)
        out = torch.relu(self.linear1(embeds))
        return self.linear2(out)
```

The process determines the vocabulary size by constructing a vocabulary dictionary during preprocessing. The embedding and hidden dimensions are set to 64. The neural network model uses a processing step that converts input contexts to vector indices. A word-to-index dictionary is created to perform this conversion, and a reverse index-to-word dictionary is used during inference. The system replaces low-frequency words with an 'unknown' token, `<UNK>`.

```
def build_vocab_and_index(data, min_freq, unk_token="<UNK>"):
    # Count the frequency of each token in the data
    counter = Counter(data)

    # Create vocabulary: map each frequent word to a unique index and
    # infrequent words to the 'unknown' token index
    unk_index = 0  # Typically, the unknown token is indexed at 0
    vocab = {unk_token: unk_index}
    idx_to_word = {unk_index: unk_token}
    idx = 1

    for word, freq in counter.items():
       if freq >= min_freq:
           vocab[word] = idx
           idx_to_word[idx] = word
           idx += 1
       else:
           vocab[word] = unk_index

    return vocab, idx_to_word

min_freq = 4
vocab, idx_to_word = build_vocab_and_index(tokenized_text, min_freq)
```

Further preprocessing is required to create PyTorch datasets and data loaders. A bespoke `Dataset` is used, which can then be combined with the standard `DataLoader`.

```
def create_context_target_pairs(data, context_size, vocab):
    for i in range(context_size, len(data)):
        context = [vocab.get(data[j], vocab['<UNK>']) for j in \
                   range(i - context_size, i)]
        target = vocab.get(data[i], vocab['<UNK>'])
        yield context, target

class BengioDataset(Dataset):
    def __init__(self, corpus, context_size, vocab, device):
        self.data = [(torch.tensor(context, dtype=torch.long, device=device),
                      torch.tensor(target, dtype=torch.long, device=device))
                      for context,
```

(*Continued*)

(*Continued*)

```
                        target in create_context_target_pairs(corpus,
                        context_size, vocab)]

    def __len__(self):
        return len(self.data)

    def __getitem__(self, idx):
        return self.data[idx]
```

Training and test data loaders can then be constructed, and here, a batch size of 512 was used, reflecting the availability of a GPU for training. The model was then trained through 20 epochs with the Adam optimiser and a learning rate of 0.001. The training loop was similar to those used for classification problems earlier, although this is a multi-class classification task. The model can predict the next word, given a context. The code to do this is more complex than for the *n*-gram as the input string needs to be encoded to indices and the output decoded back to words. As with the *n*-gram model, the most likely word is selected using softmax and argmax to find the most probable word. Unlike the *n*-gram model, this spans the entire vocabulary, not just the words found in the training set associated with the *n*-gram. Hence, in theory, the neural network is more generalisable than the simplistic *n*-gram model.

```
def predict_next_word_nn(model, context, vocab, idx_to_word,
                        context_size, device):
    model.eval()

    # Convert context words to indices, handling unknown words
    context_indices = [vocab.get(word, vocab['<UNK>']) for word in context]

    # Ensure the context is of the right size for the model
    if len(context_indices) != context_size:
        raise ValueError(f"Context should be exactly \
                         {model.context_size} words.")

    # Convert to tensor and add batch dimension
    context_tensor = torch.tensor([context_indices],
                                  dtype=torch.long).to(device)

    # Get model output and convert to probability distribution
    with torch.no_grad():
        output = model(context_tensor)
        probabilities = torch.softmax(output, dim=1)

    # Get the most likely next word index
    predicted_index = torch.argmax(probabilities, dim=1).item()

    # Convert index to word
    predicted_word = idx_to_word[predicted_index]
    return predicted_word
```

For the same context used earlier, the neural network selects 'was' as the most likely word. The perplexity can be calculated, this time using PyTorch cross-entropy functions.

```
def calculate_perplexity(model, data_loader, device):
    model.eval()
    total_loss = 0.0
    total_words = 0

    with torch.no_grad():
        for batch_X, batch_y in data_loader:
            batch_X, batch_y = batch_X.to(device), batch_y.to(device)
            outputs = model(batch_X)
            loss = F.cross_entropy(outputs, batch_y, reduction='sum')
            total_loss += loss.item()

            # Count the total number of words in the target
            total_words += batch_y.numel()

    average_loss = total_loss / total_words
    perplexity = math.exp(average_loss)
    return perplexity
```

On the training set, the perplexity was 153, but on the test set, it was 627, which is much lower than for the *n*-gram model, showing that the neural network is much more generalisable. Bengio et al. (2003) obtained better results than this and compared their neural network models with the KN *n*-gram model. They obtained a 24% improvement over the best *n*-gram model.

7.3.6 Word Embeddings

The two prominent word embedding approaches are *Word2Vec* and *GloVe*. The Python library `gensim` (https://radimrehurek.com/gensim/) provides open-source downloadable word embeddings based on Word2Vec and GloVe. Word embeddings based on transformer models like BERT can be obtained using the `transformers` Python library maintained by *HuggingFace* (https://huggingface.co/docs/transformers/index).

EXAMPLE 7.7: USING WORD EMBEDDINGS

This example downloads the relevant word embeddings or language model and then explores the vector relationship between words. The code can be found in the Jupyter Notebook `WordEmbeddings.ipynb`.

Word2Vec and GloVe are both available in several versions from the `gensim` library, which provides an `info()` method on the API to give details of the available models. For the Word2Vec case, `word2vec-google-news-300` was used, while for GloVe, the model variant was `glove-wiki-gigaword-300`. The API to load the model is straightforward.

```
glove_model = api.load('glove-wiki-gigaword-300')
```

The model provides a dictionary-style interface and the vector for a given word is given by

```
word2vec_model['computer']
```

Table 7.5 lists a series of related word pairs chosen to present the word embeddings in vector form. The process extracts the word vectors for all the words and uses PCA to reduce them to a three-dimensional representation. The PCA implementation comes from `sklearn.decomposition`.

(*Continued*)

(*Continued*)

```
word_vectors = [model[word] for word in words]
pca = PCA(n_components=3)
word_vectors_3d = pca.fit_transform(word_vectors)
```

The points for each word were then plotted in three dimensions, and the pairs of related words connected with a line to show the relationships. Figure 7.12 shows the plot for Word2Vec, while Figure 7.13 shows the same for GloVe.

TABLE 7.5 Word Pairs to Illustrate Word Embeddings

Word 1	Word 2
man	king
woman	queen
paris	france
london	england
apple	orange
car	bicycle

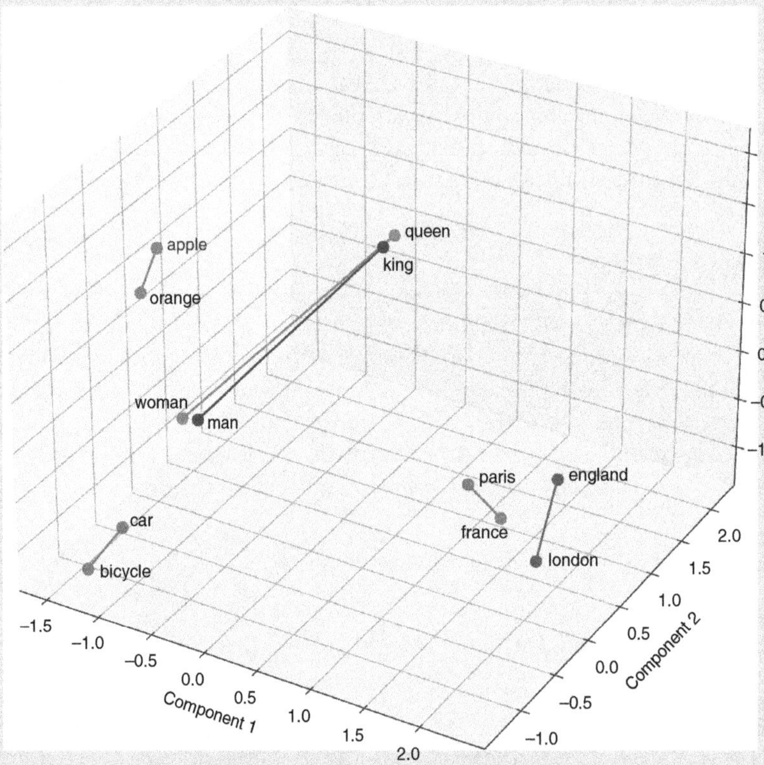

FIGURE 7.12 Test word vectors generated from Word2Vec and reduced to three dimensions using PCA. Lines join related words.

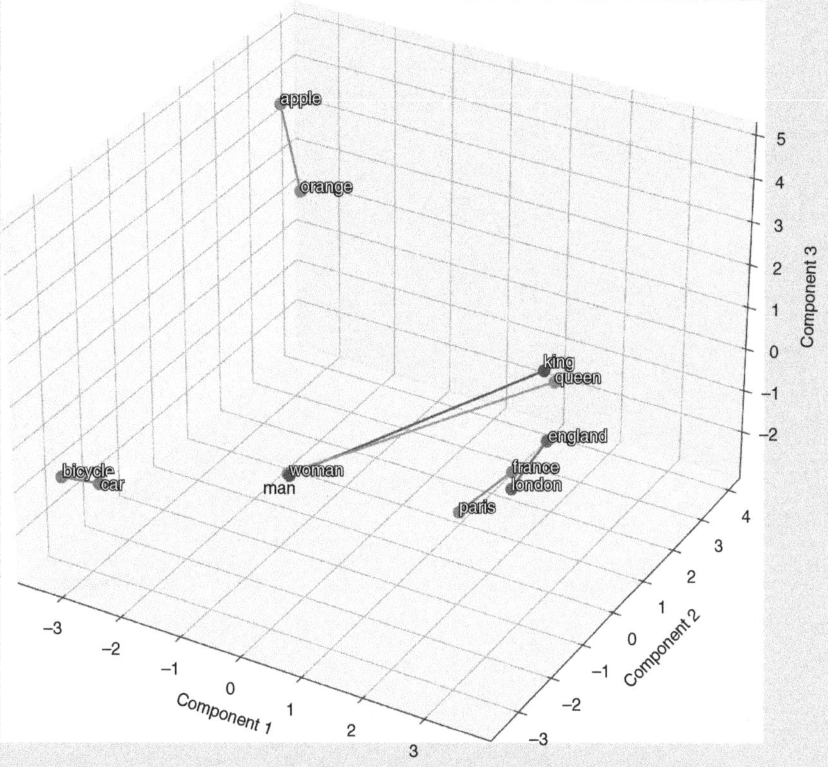

FIGURE 7.13 Test word vectors generated from GloVe and reduced to three dimensions using PCA. Lines join related words.

Accessing word embeddings from the BERT transformer model is slightly more involved. `BertTokenizer` and `BertModel` from the transformers library are used to generate a dictionary of word-to-word vectors. Figure 7.14 illustrates the word embeddings for the BERT model.

```
from transformers import BertTokenizer, BertModel
import torch

def get_bert_embeddings(word_list):
    # Load pre-trained model tokenizer (vocabulary)
    tokenizer = BertTokenizer.from_pretrained('bert-base-uncased')

    # Load pre-trained model
    model = BertModel.from_pretrained('bert-base-uncased')

    word_embeddings = {}
    for word in word_list:
        # Encode text
        encoded_input = tokenizer(word, return_tensors='pt')

        # Forward pass, get hidden states
        with torch.no_grad():
            outputs = model(**encoded_input)

        # Get the embeddings of the first token ([CLS] token)
```

(*Continued*)

(*Continued*)

```
        embeddings = outputs.last_hidden_state[:, 0, :]
        word_embeddings[word] = embeddings.detach().numpy().tolist()[0]

    return word_embeddings
```

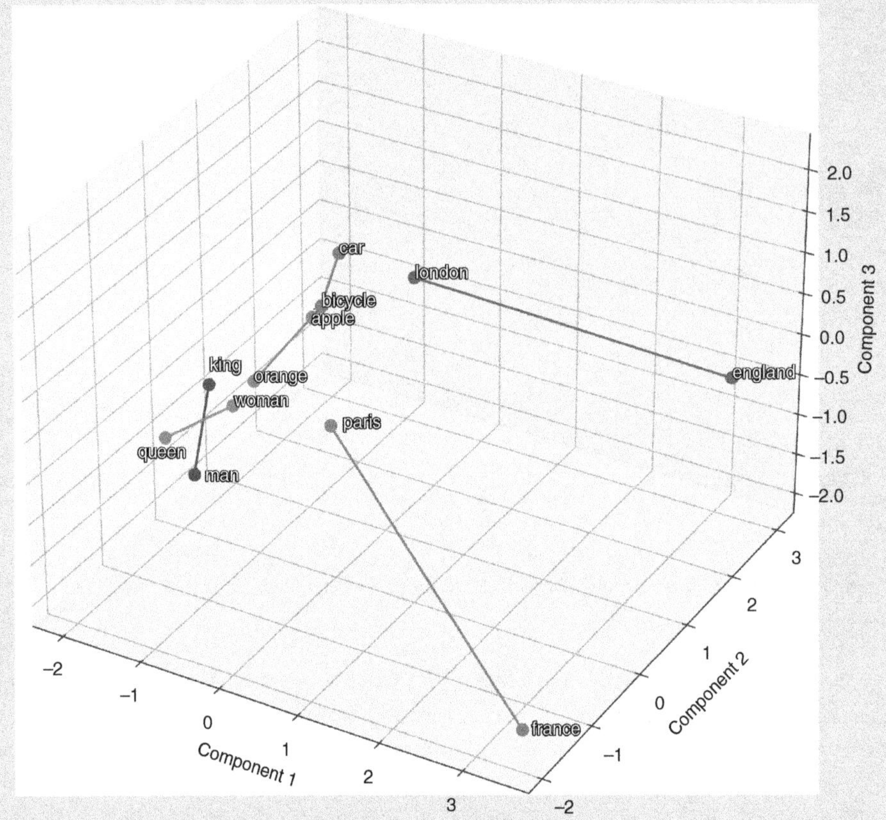

FIGURE 7.14 Test word vectors generated from BERT and reduced to three dimensions using PCA. Lines join related words.

Exploring the figures, we see that for both Word2Vec and GloVe, there is a clear vector relationship for the pairs (man, woman) and (king, queen). The lines connecting man–king and woman–queen are parallel, which is not true for BERT. However, BERT embeddings establish a similar vector relation between the pairs (London, Paris) and (France, England).

7.3.7 RNNs and NLP

Mikolov et al. (2010) represents the first application of RNNs to language modelling. They applied several model configurations to the problem of language modelling in a similar way to Bengio et al. (2003), but using an RNN as the core model. Also, like Bengio et al. (2003), the authors compared the results with Kneser–Ney n-gram models and tested configurations that combined RNN and n-gram. By current standards, the hidden layer's size in the shallow RNN was small, at 30–500 hidden units in a single layer. The dataset used in the experiments was drawn from the *New York Times* section of English Gigaword, which had 37 million words, of which the authors used 6.4 million. Training took several weeks for the most complex models. Mikolov et al. (2010) outperformed a Kneser–Ney 5-gram model with the larger RNN and combined models, showing lower perplexity and word error rates on the test set.

EXAMPLE 7.8: LANGUAGE MODEL WITH GRUs

Mikolov et al. (2010) used a single-layer RNN for their language model. This example uses a multi-layer GRU to build a language model. The code for the example can be found in the Jupyter Notebook `GRULanguageModel.ipynb`. The model will be trained using the smaller of two datasets based on Wikipedia entries from Huggingface, `wikitext-2-raw-v1`, and this can be downloaded using the `load_dataset` function from the `datasets` library provided by Huggingface.

```
from datasets import load_dataset
dataset = load_dataset("wikitext", "wikitext-2-raw-v1")
```

The dataset comprises 36,718 strings in the training set, 4358 in the test set and 3760 in the validation set, totalling around 1.8 million words in the training set. The `torchtext` library, part of PyTorch (Wisam, 2022), can tokenise the dataset. The first step involves building the vocabulary from the training set, requiring a minimum frequency threshold of three. After building the vocabulary, it includes additional tokens for *end of string* `<eos>` and *unknown* `<unk>`, with the latter set as the default value returned for tokens not in the dictionary.

```
from torchtext.data.utils import get_tokenizer
from torchtext.vocab import build_vocab_from_iterator

tokenizer = get_tokenizer('basic_english')
tokenize_data = lambda example, \
                tokenizer: {'tokens': tokenizer(example['text'])}
tokenized_dataset = dataset.map(tokenize_data, remove_columns=['text'],
                                fn_kwargs={'tokenizer': tokenizer})
vocab = build_vocab_from_iterator(tokenized_dataset['train']['tokens'],
                                  min_freq=3)
vocab.insert_token('<unk>', 0)
vocab.insert_token('<eos>', 1)
vocab.set_default_index(vocab['<unk>'])
```

The actual conversion to numeric index values is performed using the following function:

```
def prepare_tokenized(dataset, vocab):
    data = []
    for item in dataset:
        if item['tokens']:
            tokens = item['tokens'].append('<eos>')
            tokens = [vocab[token] for token in item['tokens']]
            data.append(tokens)
    return data

train_data = prepare_tokenized(tokenized_dataset['train'], vocab)
test_data = prepare_tokenized(tokenized_dataset['test'], vocab)
```

Note that the `<eos>` token is added to the end of every string in the list, yielding lists of integer tokens of varying lengths.

(*Continued*)

(*Continued*)

The next question is how to organise the model's architecture and how the training data should be presented to the model for training. The purpose of the model is to predict the next token given a prompt. The adopted approach is similar to the previous example inspired by *n*-grams and Bengio et al. (2003). The whole corpus is concatenated into a single list of tokens. Then, a sequence of length `window_size` is presented to the model, with the next token being the target, which is achieved using a sliding window across the whole corpus.

The data is batched by dividing the entire sequence into parts of equal length, each consisting of `batch_size` units. These parts are then presented to the model as a batch, sliding the window from left to right over the text blocks. An epoch is complete when the window reaches the end of the block of sequences. It is important to note that this is not the only possible arrangement. For example, the sequences could be presented without concatenation, with them all padded up to the length of the longest sequence. This is a user choice and depends on what empirically gives the best results.

A custom PyTorch dataset class is implemented to generate a list of inputs and targets, which are then returned to the data loader. Note that the tensors are generated on the fly and passed to the device during the training loop, and this is to limit the amount of data used on the device. Once constructed, the training and test datasets were used to initialise data loaders with a window size of 5 and a batch size of 128. Note that these are not set to shuffle, as the sliding window should be retained during training to be consistent with the hidden state usage.

```
class FlattenedSequenceDataset(Dataset):
    def __init__(self, sequences, window_size=5, num_batches=128):
        self.window_size = window_size
        self.num_batches = num_batches

        # Step 1: Flatten the sequences
        flat_sequence = [token for seq in sequences for token in seq]

        # Step 2: Determine the length of each subsequence
        total_length = len(flat_sequence) - window_size
        self.subseq_length = math.ceil(total_length / num_batches)

        # Create the input-target pairs
        self.data = []
        for i in range(0, total_length, self.subseq_length):
            subseq = flat_sequence[i:i+self.subseq_length + window_size]
                for j in range(len(subseq) - window_size):
                    self.data.append((subseq[j:j+window_size],
                                      subseq[j+window_size]))

    def __len__(self):
        return len(self.data)

    def __getitem__(self, idx):
        input_seq, target = self.data[idx]
        return torch.tensor(input_seq), torch.tensor(target)
```

The GRU-based model class is similar to previous RNN models with an embedding layer mapping the input index sequences to vectors in the embedding space. The model only returns the last output from the RNN layer, a single-word vector. The final layer is fully connected because the output is also mapped back to index vectors. It performs the inverse transformation to the input, as the hidden layer is the same size as the embedding dimension, and this allows the weights to be tied between the embedding and output layers. The model class also provides initialisation for the hidden state.

```
class RNNLanguageModel(nn.Module):
    def __init__(self, vocab_size, embedding_dim, hidden_dim, n_layers,
                 device, dropout=0.5):
        super(RNNLanguageModel, self).__init__()
        self.embedding = nn.Embedding(vocab_size, embedding_dim)
        self.rnn = nn.GRU(embedding_dim, hidden_dim, n_layers,
                          dropout=dropout, batch_first=True)
        self.fc = nn.Linear(hidden_dim, vocab_size)
        self.device = device
        self.vocab_size = vocab_size
        self.embedding.weight = self.fc.weight

    def forward(self, x, hidden):
        embedded = self.embedding(x)
        output, hidden = self.rnn(embedded)
        last_output = output[:, -1, :]
        return self.fc(last_output), hidden

    def init_hidden(self, batch_size):
        return torch.zeros(self.rnn.num_layers, batch_size,
                           self.rnn.hidden_size).to(self.device)
```

Here, the embedding and hidden dimensions were set to 1024, two layers were used and dropout was set to 50%.

The training loop was similar to those used earlier for multi-class classification. Note that the hidden state does need to be handled during training. The hidden state is initialised before each epoch and then passed back to the model at each step.

Cross-entropy loss was used with the Adam optimiser with the learning rate set at 10^{-3}. Given the focus on the text, the perplexity, the loss was scaled up by the batch size and used to calculate the perplexity, which is simply the exponential of the cross-entropy loss. The model was trained through 20 epochs, yielding a final training set perplexity of 167 and a test set perplexity of 331. The following function was used to predict the next word, given a prompt, and this tokenises the prompt, initialises the hidden state and passes the prompt to the model. The function then obtains the output, applies a softmax to obtain the probabilities and finds the maximum to give the most probable word. The token is then converted to a word using the vocabulary object.

```
def predict_nextword(prompt, model, tokenizer, vocab, device):
    model.eval()
    tokens = tokenizer(prompt)
    indices = [vocab[t] for t in tokens]
    batch_size = 1
    hidden = model.init_hidden(batch_size)
    with torch.no_grad():
        src = torch.LongTensor([indices]).to(device)
        prediction, hidden = model(src, hidden)

        probs = torch.softmax(prediction, dim=-1)
        predicted_index = torch.argmax(probs, dim=1).item()

    itos = vocab.get_itos()
    token = itos[predicted_index]
    return token
```

7.3.8 Sequence-to-Sequence Models

Sutskever et al. (2014) was a pivotal paper for NLP and machine translation. The paper introduced *sequence-to-sequence* models built on neural networks and demonstrated their capability through a machine translation task. Sutskever et al. (2014) could show BLEU scores comparable to those obtained from state-of-the-art machine translation models when translating sentences from French to English.

The model presented by Sutskever et al. (2014) features an encoder–decoder structure, paralleling the autoencoders in Chapter 8. This design integrates two recurrent neural networks: one encodes the input sequence into a fixed-length vector, while the other decodes this vector back into the output sequence. The encoder and decoder are built using deep LSTM networks comprising four layers of LSTMs with 1000 cells each. Additionally, an embedding layer with 1000 dimensions is incorporated.

Twelve million sentences from the WMT 2014 English–French dataset were used to train the model. The vocabulary was limited to the *N* most frequent words in each language, with 160,000 words for the French source and 80,000 for the English target. Reversing the order of words in the source sentence enhanced the performance. The model was trained through 7.5 epochs in 128-sentence batches, organised to have approximately equal sentence lengths. Gradient clipping was employed to prevent LSTM gradient explosion. Parallel training was executed on an 8-GPU server.

Sutskever et al. (2014) were able to achieve a BLEU score of 34.81 for their best ensemble model, which compared favourably with the BLEU score of 37.0, which was achieved by the then best-in-class model, which was a phrase-based system (Durrani et al., 2014). The authors also showed that their LSTM model showed no degradation with less than 35 words in a sentence and mild degradation in performance for longer sentences.

7.3.8.1 Aside: Teacher Forcing *Teacher forcing* is a training technique for recurrent neural network models, including LSTM and GRU. During the training phase, the model is fed the correct output (the 'ground truth') from the previous time step as the current input rather than its prediction from the previous time step. This approach is analogous to a teacher providing the correct answer while a student is still learning, hence the term 'teacher forcing'. RNNs predict a sequence of tokens one at a time for sequence generation tasks. During standard training, the model bases each prediction on the preceding one. However, this approach may cause compounding errors if the initial prediction is incorrect, as the upcoming predictions rely on that incorrect output.

Teacher forcing in neural NLP models accelerates training convergence by aligning model predictions with correct sequences, thereby minimising error propagation that could derail the learning process. However, it can create a discrepancy known as exposure bias, where the model performs well in training with correct previous outputs but struggles during real-world inference. The model can become overly reliant on these teacher signals, inhibiting its ability to self-correct mistakes. Teacher forcing, therefore, involves a trade-off between accelerating training and potential problems with the trained model.

EXAMPLE 7.9: SEQUENCE-TO-SEQUENCE NEURAL MACHINE TRANSLATION

This example, found in the Jupyter Notebook `Seq2Seq.ipynb`, trains a sequence-to-sequence neural translation model to perform German–English translation of simple sentences.

The dataset available at https://www.manythings.org/anki/ provides tab-delimited sentence pairs in multiple languages, sourced from the *Tatoeba* project at https://tatoeba.org/en. Its moderate size and straightforward sentences offer an advantage and facilitate quick learning by a sequence-to-sequence model. Alternatively, the extensive WMT 2014 dataset could be used and is accessible via Huggingface. It includes about 40 million English–French sentence pairs featuring complex language. However, due to its size and complexity, WMT 2014 proves impractical for training simple examples, requiring significant time and computing resources.

The dataset presents data in a tab-delimited format: *English + TAB + Other Language + TAB + Attribution*. The initial step involves using the `csv` library with a tab delimiter to read the file and extract sentences into a list of lists, with German as the first element and English as the second. After processing the file, sentences exceeding 10 words in either language are discarded to maintain brevity. The next stage includes preprocessing to eliminate punctuation, numbers and non-standard characters and converting all text to lowercase. Given that the text is in Unicode format, the first preprocessing step converts it to ASCII using the `unicodedata` library. Subsequent functions are responsible for performing this normalisation.

```
import unicodedate
import string
import re

def unicode_to_ascii(s):
    return unicodedata.normalize('NFKD', s).encode('ascii',
            'ignore').decode('ascii')

def normalize(s):
    s = unicode_to_ascii(s)
    s = s.translate(str.maketrans('', '', string.punctuation))
    s = s.lower().strip()
    s = re.sub(r'\d+', '', s)
    s = re.sub(r'[^A-Za-z0-9 ]+', '', s)
    return s.strip()

def process_pairs(pairs):
    return [[normalize(pair[0]), normalize(pair[1])] for pair in tqdm(pairs)]
```

After processing, there are just under 250,000 pairs. The data is split into training and test sets, with 5% of the data reserved for testing.

The `torchtext` library is utilised to tokenise the data and build vocabularies for German and English. Underlying this, however, is a tokeniser library, and here `spacy` is used (https://spacy.io/api/tokenizer). The `spacy` library and language modules must be separately installed, for German `de_core_news_sm` is used as the language module and for English `en_core_web_sm`. The first step is to build the vocabulary, including four special tokens for unknown (<unk>), padding (<pad>), the beginning of a sentence (<bos>) and the end of a sentence (<eos>). The minimum count for inclusion here is 20, which limits the vocabulary size.

```
import torchtext
from torchtext.data.utils import get_tokenizer
from torchtext.vocab import build_vocab_from_iterator

def yield_tokens(data, idx, token_lang):
    tokenizer =  This ('spacy', language=token_lang)
    for item in tqdm(data):
        text = item[idx]
        tokenized_text = tokenizer(text)
        yield tokenized_text

german_vocab = build_vocab_from_iterator(
    yield_tokens(ftrain_pairs, 0, 'de_core_news_sm'),
    specials=['<unk>', '<pad>', '<bos>', '<eos>'],
    min_freq=20)
german_vocab.set_default_index(german_vocab['<unk>'])
```

Once constructed, the vocabulary objects enable the tokenisation of sentence pairs into lists of integers. This process yields two lists of sentences representing each language. The same tokenisation method applies to the test data.

(*Continued*)

(*Continued*)

The implementation employs PyTorch datasets and data loaders, necessitating creating a custom `Dataset` class to manage the data effectively. This class incorporates `<bos>` and `<eos>` tokens into the sentences and provides a collation function for the data loader. Additionally, it utilises the PyTorch utility `pad_sequence` to ensure all sequences in a batch achieve uniform length.

```
from torch.nn.utils.rnn import pad_sequence
from torch.utils.data import Dataset, DataLoader

class TokenizedPairsDataset(Dataset):
    def __init__(self, source_sequences, target_sequences,
                 src_vocab, trg_vocab):
    assert len(source_sequences) == len(target_sequences), \
        "Source and target sequences must have the same length."
    self.src_seq = [torch.tensor([src_vocab['<bos>']] + seq +
                    [src_vocab['<eos>']]) for seq in source_sequences]
    self.trg_seq = [torch.tensor([trg_vocab['<bos>']] + seq +
                    [trg_vocab['<eos>']]) for seq in target_sequences]
    self.src_pad_idx = src_vocab['<pad>']
    self.trg_pad_idx = trg_vocab['<pad>']

def __len__(self):
    return len(self.src_seq)

def __getitem__(self, idx):
    return self.src_seq[idx], self.trg_seq[idx]

def collate_fn(self, batch):
    src_batch, trg_batch = zip(*batch)
    src_padded = pad_sequence(src_batch,
                     padding_value=self.src_pad_idx, batch_first=True)
    trg_padded = pad_sequence(trg_batch,
                     padding_value=self.trg_pad_idx, batch_first=True)
    return src_padded, trg_padded
```

The dataset can be used with a data loader, but passing the collate function as an argument is important.

```
train_dataloader = DataLoader(train_dataset, batch_size=batch_size,
                              shuffle=True,
                              collate_fn=train_dataset.collate_fn,
                              drop_last=True)
```

The encoder–decoder model can now be defined. For both the encoder and decoder, LSTM units are used, coupled with embedding layers. The encoder model is defined as follows:

```
class Encoder(nn.Module):
    def __init__(self, input_dim, emb_dim, hidden_size, num_layers=1,
                 dropout=0.0):
        super(Encoder, self).__init__()
        self.hidden_size = hidden_size
```

```
        self.num_layers = num_layers
        self.embedding = nn.Embedding(input_dim, emb_dim)
        self.lstm = nn.LSTM(emb_dim, hidden_size, num_layers,
                            dropout=dropout, batch_first=True)

    def forward(self, src):
        embedded = self.embedding(src)  # [batch_size, sequence_len, emb_dim]
        outputs, hidden = self.lstm(embedded)
        return outputs, hidden
```

The encoder `input_size` equals the vocabulary length for the input language, and this forms the input to the embedding layer, which projects the input token indices into the embedding space with dimension `emb_dim`, here selected to be 128 in size. The embedding layer performs a linear transformation, so there is no activation function after it. The LSTM layers come next with the hidden size specified to be 128, two layers used and dropout set to 0.5. The output is a fixed length vector 128 units in size.

The decoder has a similar structure with an embedding layer followed by LSTM. The output is a linear layer that projects from the hidden size to the output size, equal to the vocabulary length for the output language. There is no softmax as this is embedded in the enclosing sequence-to-sequence class.

```
class Decoder(nn.Module):
    def __init__(self, input_dim, emb_dim, hidden_size, output_size,
                 num_layers=1, dropout=0.0):
        super(Decoder, self).__init__()
        self.hidden_size = hidden_size
        self.num_layers = num_layers
        self.embedding = nn.Embedding(output_size, emb_dim)
        self.lstm = nn.LSTM(emb_dim, hidden_size, num_layers,
                            dropout=dropout, batch_first=True)
        self.out = nn.Linear(hidden_size, output_size)

    def forward(self, input, hidden):
        input = self.embedding(input)
        output, hidden = self.lstm(input, hidden)
        output = self.out(output)
        return output, hidden
```

The decoder's hidden and embedding dimensions are 128; the LSTM used two layers with dropout. The `Seq2Seq` class combines the encoder and decoder models and implements a combined `forward` method. The encoder's hidden state is passed to the input of the decoder. The decoder input at the first step is a vector containing the beginning-of-sequence token. For subsequent steps, the input depends on whether `teacher_force_ratio` is non-zero. There is no teacher forcing during inference, so the input to the next step is the output of the previous step. If the teacher forcing ratio is non-zero, then sampling is used to determine if teacher forcing, that is, using the ground truth, is used for the current step. After completing the steps, the results are collated and passed through a softmax to create the probabilities of each word in the output vocabulary object.

(*Continued*)

(*Continued*)

```
class Seq2Seq(nn.Module):
    def __init__(self, encoder, decoder, device, bos_token):
        super(Seq2Seq, self).__init__()
        self.encoder = encoder
        self.decoder = decoder
        self.device = device
        self.bos_token = bos_token

    def forward(self, src, trg, teacher_forcing_ratio=0.5):
        batch_size = src.size(0)
        trg_len = trg.size(1)
        trg_vocab_size = self.decoder.out.out_features
        encoder_output, encoder_hidden = self.encoder(src)
        decoder_input = torch.empty(batch_size, 1, dtype=torch.long,
                                    device=device).fill_(self.bos_token)
        decoder_hidden = encoder_hidden
        decoder_outputs = []

        for i in range(trg_len):
            decoder_output, decoder_hidden = self.decoder(decoder_input,
                                                          decoder_hidden)
            decoder_outputs.append(decoder_output)
            teacher_force = random.random() < teacher_forcing_ratio

            if teacher_force:
                # Teacher forcing: Feed the target as the next input
                decoder_input = trg[:, i].unsqueeze(1) # Teacher forcing
            else:
                # Without teacher forcing:
                # use its own predictions as the next input
                _, topi = decoder_output.topk(1)
                decoder_input = topi.squeeze(-1).detach()
        decoder_outputs = torch.cat(decoder_outputs, dim=1)
        decoder_outputs = F.log_softmax(decoder_outputs, dim=-1)
        return decoder_outputs
```

The training loop for the model closely resembles those of previous classification models but includes two key additions. First, the teacher forcing ratio undergoes annealing to zero with a half-life of 10 steps. Second, to prevent gradient explosion, gradients are clipped to stay below 0.25, using the PyTorch utility function `torch.nn.utils.clip_grad_norm_`. LSTMs remain prone to exploding gradients, which justifies the application of gradient clipping. The model's training, conducted over 10 epochs, employs the Adam optimiser with a 10^{-3} learning rate. `NLLLoss` serves as the loss function, given the inclusion of the softmax function in the model.

A function was written to support translation with the trained model:

- take a German source sentence
- tokenise it
- input sequence to the model
- receive back word probabilities
- identify the most likely word for each word in the output

- decode the tokens into English

```
def translate(model, src_sentence, src_vocab, trg_vocab, src_tokenizer,
              device, max_length=10):
    model.eval()
    s = normalize(src_sentence)
    tokens = [src_vocab['<bos>']] + \
        [src_vocab[token] for token in src_tokenizer(s)] + \
        [src_vocab['<eos>']]
    src_tensor = torch.LongTensor(tokens).unsqueeze(0).to(device)

    with torch.no_grad():
        _, encoder_hidden = model.encoder(src_tensor)
        decoder_input = torch.empty(1, 1, dtype=torch.long,
                                    device=device).fill_(trg_vocab['<bos>'])
        decoder_hidden = encoder_hidden
        decoder_outputs = []

        for i in range(max_length):
            decoder_output, decoder_hidden = model.decoder(decoder_input,
                                                           decoder_hidden)
            decoder_outputs.append(decoder_output)
            _, topi = decoder_output.topk(1)
            decoder_input = topi.squeeze(-1).detach()
        decoder_outputs = torch.cat(decoder_outputs, dim=1)
        decoder_ids = torch.argmax(decoder_outputs, dim=-1).squeeze()
        decoded_words = []
        for idx in decoder_ids:
            if idx.item() == trg_vocab['<eos>']:
                decoded_words.append('<eos>')
                break
            decoded_words.append(trg_vocab.get_itos()[idx.item()])
    return decoded_words
```

As a test, the trained model was asked to translate the German *Ich mag Eis* and the model response was `['<bos>', 'i', 'like', 'the', 'ice', 'cream', '<eos>']`, which is a good translation. The final step was to calculate the BLEU score, which can be done by averaging the score obtained by translating sentences from the test set and comparing with the ground truth using the `sentence_bleu` function from `nltk.translate.bleu_score`. The trained model gave modest results of 0.08 on the test set.

7.3.9 Attention Mechanisms

Human attention is the process whereby humans selectively focus on specific stimuli and ignore others. Humans distribute attention across multiple tasks over time, shifting their attention to tackle specific goals. Attention is finite and must be electively allocated according to perceived importance and cognitive load.

Attention, with its selective focus, translates well to neural networks. Selective focus allows for more efficient information processing, particularly in tasks involving large inputs or sequences of natural language or images for classification and segmentation. Attention mechanisms have significantly improved the performance of neural networks, and they are now a standard technique when designing network architectures.

This section provides an introduction to four key types of attention mechanisms that have proved influential, namely *Bahdanau attention* (Bahdanau et al., 2015), *dot-product* or *Luong attention* (Luong et al., 2015), *self-attention* and *multi-head attention* (Vaswani et al., 2017). Many more attention variants are in use today, and their impact on deep learning has been pivotal.

7.3.9.1 Bahdanau Attention The early neural translation models were encoder–decoder models with a fixed-length vector state in between, as described in Section 7.3.8 above. Bahdanau et al. (2015) argue that this state compression can be limiting, especially for long sequences, as the model might lose important information.

In an encoder–decoder model the encoder processes the input sequence $(x_1, x_2, \dots, x_T)$ and produces a series of hidden states $(h_1, h_2, \dots, h_T)$, where T is the length of the input sequence. Similarly, at each time step t in the decoding phase, the decoder has a hidden state s_t, which is computed as

$$s_i = f(s_{i-1}, y_{i-1}, c_i), \tag{7.52}$$

where y_{i-1} is the previous output and c_i is the context vector. In the attention model, this context vector is not fixed but dynamic and depends on a weighted sum of the encoder states. The *attention* weights, $\beta_{t,i}$, determine how much emphasis is put on different parts of the input sequence,

$$c_t = \sum_{i=1}^{T} \beta_{t,i} h_i. \tag{7.53}$$

The alignment scores between the decoder's current hidden state s_t and each of the encoder's hidden states h_i is parametrised using a feedforward neural network with trainable weights $\boldsymbol{W}_a$, U_a and bias $\boldsymbol{b}_a$, and applying an activation function, g, like tanh. The alignment score $\alpha_{t,i}$ is computed as follows:

$$\alpha_{t,i} = \boldsymbol{V}_a^{\mathrm{T}} g(\boldsymbol{W}_a s_t + U_a h_i + \boldsymbol{b}_a), \tag{7.54}$$

where $\boldsymbol{V}_a$ is another weight vector. The alignment scores for each encoder hidden state are then normalised using the softmax function to produce the attention weights, and this ensures that the weights sum up to 1, forming a probability distribution:

$$\beta_{t,i} = \frac{\exp(\alpha_{t,i})}{\sum_{j=1}^{T} \exp(\alpha_{t,j})}. \tag{7.55}$$

Bahdanau et al. (2015) used a bidirectional RNN as the encoder model and a standard RNN as the decoder, both with 1000 hidden units. They trained models with sentences up to 30 words and with sentences up to 50 words. The models were trained using the Adadelta optimiser using the WMT 2014 French–English dataset. Bahdanau et al. (2015) obtained significantly higher BLEU scores than those obtained for benchmark encoder–decoder models.

EXAMPLE 7.10: SEQUENCE-TO-SEQUENCE NMT WITH BAHDANAU ATTENTION

This example is in the Jupyter Notebook `Seq2Seq-Bahdanau.ipynb`. It repeats the previous German–English translation but adds Bahdanau attention to the decoder while reducing the number of LSTM layers to one. Bahdanau attention is represented as a class implementing Equations (7.54) and (7.55).

```
class BahdanauAttention(nn.Module):
    def __init__(self, hidden_size):
        super(BahdanauAttention, self).__init__()
        self.W = nn.Linear(hidden_size, hidden_size)
        self.U = nn.Linear(hidden_size, hidden_size)
        self.V = nn.Linear(hidden_size, 1)

    def forward(self, query, keys):
        query = query.permute(1, 0, 2)
```

```
        scores = self.V(torch.tanh(self.W(query) + self.U(keys)))
        scores = scores.squeeze(2).unsqueeze(1)
        weights = F.softmax(scores, dim=-1)
        context = torch.bmm(weights, keys)
        return context, weights
```

The decoder needs to be modified to add the attention layer and feed it the query, which is the decoder's hidden state, and the keys, which are the encoder output. The input to the LSTM unit is the concatenated output from the attention layer and the decoder input. The forward function also returns the attention weights used for visualisation below.

```
class Decoder(nn.Module):
    def __init__(self, input_dim, emb_dim, hidden_size, output_size,
                 num_layers=1, dropout=0.0):
        super(Decoder, self).__init__()
        self.hidden_size = hidden_size
        self.num_layers = num_layers
        self.attention = BahdanauAttention(hidden_size)
        self.embedding = nn.Embedding(output_size, emb_dim)
        self.lstm = nn.LSTM(emb_dim + hidden_size, hidden_size, num_layers,
                            dropout=dropout, batch_first=True)
        self.out = nn.Linear(hidden_size, output_size)

    def forward(self, input, hidden, encoder_outputs):
        input = self.embedding(input)  # [batch_size, 1, emb_dim]
        context, attn_weights = self.attention(hidden[0], encoder_outputs)
        lstm_input = torch.cat((input, context), dim=2)
        output, hidden = self.lstm(lstm_input, hidden)
        output = self.out(output)
        return output, hidden, attn_weights
```

Minor changes are also needed to the `Seq2Seq` class to pass the encoder outputs to the decoder and capture and concatenate the attention values to the output.

The model was trained identically to the previous example. After 10 epochs, the training and test loss was lower than in the model without attention. The BLEU score was also higher, at 0.128.

(*Continued*)

(*Continued*)

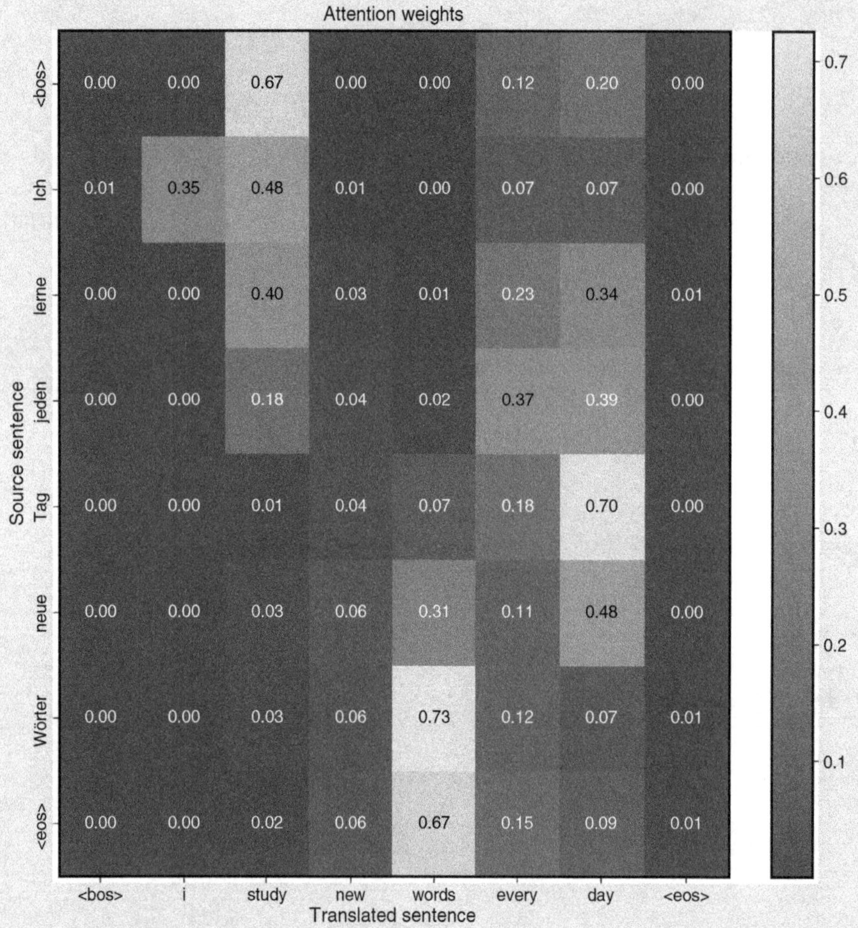

FIGURE 7.15 Visualisation of Bahdanau attention from the trained sequence-to-sequence model between the input German and output English sentences.

The attention weights between an input and output sentence can be visualised as a heat map. Figure 7.15 illustrates the attention weights between the input sentence 'Ich lerne jeden Tag neue Wörter' and the output 'I study new words every day'.

7.3.9.2 Dot-Product Attention Luong et al. (2015) introduced dot-product attention in the same encoder–decoder model context, which is a simpler attention model than that of Bahdanau et al. (2015) but effective.

The softmax function still gives attention weights over the alignment scores, as per Equation (7.55), but the scores are calculated differently. Luong et al. (2015) proposed three *global* attention variants in which the score function α_t is calculated as follows:

$$\alpha_t(h_t, s_t) = \begin{cases} h_t^{\top} s_t & \text{dot} \\ h_t^{\top} W_a s_t & \text{general} \\ W_a [h_t; h_s] & \text{concat} \end{cases}. \tag{7.56}$$

Of these three, the simplest *dot* was the most effective. The authors also proposed two local attention mechanisms: *monotonic alignment* and *predictive alignment*. Unlike global attention, which considers all encoder states, local attention focuses on a window of encoder states around a certain aligned position p_t. In monotonic alignment, $p_t = t$, while in predictive alignment, p_t is given by a feedforward network,

$$p_t = S \cdot \text{sigmoid}\,(v_p^\top \tanh(W_p s_t)), \tag{7.57}$$

where S is the sentence length. The window is defined by a range of positions around p_t, say $[p_t - D, p_t + D]$, where D is the window size. For each position i within this window, the attention weight $\alpha_{t,i}$ is calculated using a score function.

Luong et al. (2015) trained a series of models using the WMT 2014 German–English dataset. They concluded that the dot attention mechanism works best with global attention, while the general score function performs best for local attention. Overall, local attention and the general score gave the best BLEU score.

7.3.9.3 Self-Attention and Multi-Head Attention The paper by Vaswani et al. (2017) stands as one of the most influential contributions in deep learning history. It introduces three significant architectural advancements: self-attention or scaled dot-product attention, multi-head attention (both discussed here) and the transformer model (elaborated in Section 7.3.10).

The self-attention mechanism takes as input the matrix $X = [x_1, \dots, x_n]$, composed of d-dimensional word vectors x_i. These vectors originate from input sentence words processed through a pre-calculated word embedding layer (Drori, 2022). It then generates three matrices: queries (Q), keys (K) and values (V), each being linear projections of the input sentence matrix:

$$Q = XW^Q, \tag{7.58}$$
$$K = XW^K, \tag{7.59}$$
$$V = XW^V, \tag{7.60}$$

where W^i are square matrices of learned parameters. The alignment score emerges from the dot-product of the query and key matrices, scaled by the square root of the dimension. The final attention matrix applies the softmax function to the alignment score, also scaled by the square root of the dimension,

$$\beta(Q, K, V) = \text{softmax}\left(\frac{QK^T}{\sqrt{d}}\right) V. \tag{7.61}$$

Multi-head attention is illustrated in Figure 7.16. Instead of just projecting the queries, keys and values once, in multi-head attention, this is done h times through different learnable transformations, giving the matrices

$$Q_h = XW_h^Q, \tag{7.62}$$
$$K_h = XW_h^K, \tag{7.63}$$
$$V_h = XW_h^V. \tag{7.64}$$

Each head has its self-attention mechanism as given by Equation (7.61). The output of all the heads is concatenated together,

$$\text{Concat}(\text{head}_1, \dots, \text{head}_h) = \text{Concat}(\text{Attention}(Q_1, K_1, V_1), \dots, \text{Attention}(Q_h, K_h, V_h)). \tag{7.65}$$

Finally, this concatenated result is again linearly transformed using another learnable weight matrix W^O,

$$\text{Multi-Head}(Q, K, V) = \text{Concat}(\text{head}_1, \dots, \text{head}_h) W^O. \tag{7.66}$$

In summary, multi-head attention allows the model to process the same input information differently simultaneously (each head potentially capturing different types of information). Then, it combines the different 'perspectives' provided by the multiple heads to produce a comprehensive output.

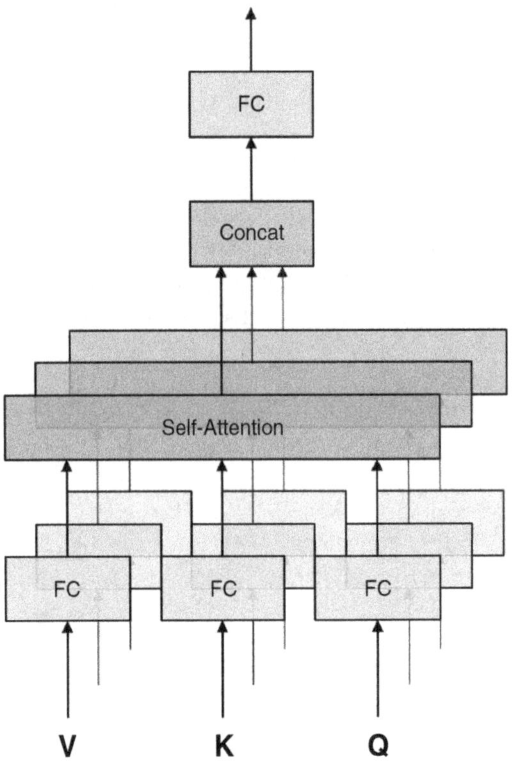

FIGURE 7.16 Multi-head attention.

7.3.10 Transformers and Large Language Models

RNNs, including their more advanced variants like LSTMs and GRUs, have significantly advanced NLP. However, their sequential processing makes them computationally inefficient for long sequences, leading to challenges in capturing long-range dependencies within a text. The vanishing and exploding gradient problems are partially addressed by LSTM and GRU units, but problems with long-range dependencies remain. Fundamentally, the sequential nature of RNNs makes them less parallelisable, which limits their scalability and training speed, a significant drawback in an era when data size and model complexity are ever-increasing.

Vaswani et al. (2017) introduced the transformer architecture. The transformer architecture revolutionises the handling of sequence data, effectively addressing the limitations of recurrent NLP models. Transformers process full sequences simultaneously, not sequentially, and leverage self-attention mechanisms. This parallel processing vastly improves computational efficiency and scalability, particularly for longer sequences. Self-attention allows the model to learn relationships between distant elements in a sequence.

Transformers do not suffer from the vanishing gradient problem, as their computational graphs are much shallower than those found in RNNs, which facilitates training.

Transformers have been found to excel at a wide range of NLP tasks, including machine translation and text generation, outperforming earlier RNN models in both speed and accuracy. The inherent parallelism has also allowed transformer models to scale up to vast sizes, as seen in models like GPT-4, and this would not have been possible with recurrent architectures.

7.3.10.1 Attention and Positional Encoding The critical component of the transformer is multi-head attention layers, as introduced above in Section 7.3.9.3. As model sizes have increased, the number of heads in the multi-head attention layers has also increased.

Transformer models do not operate sequentially and require a supply of positional encoding information. Mathematically, positional encodings are added to the input embeddings, ensuring that the model retains awareness of the position of each word in the sequence. For a given position i and dimension j in the input sequence, the positional encoding is calculated using sinusoidal functions (Vaswani et al., 2017):

$$PE(i, 2j) = \sin(i/10{,}000^{2j/d_{\text{model}}}), \tag{7.67}$$

$$PE(i, 2j+1) = \cos(i/10{,}000^{2j/d_{\text{model}}}), \tag{7.68}$$

where d_{model} represents the dimension of the input embedding. This formula generates a unique encoding for each position, and the wave-like pattern of the sinusoids facilitates the model's learning of relative positions and distances between words.

7.3.10.2 Architecture of the Transformer Three transformer models are used in NLP applications: autoencoding, autoregressive and sequence-to-sequence, each targetted at different tasks (Drori, 2022).

- Autoencoding Transformers
  - *Description*: Autoencoding transformers are designed to reconstruct or predict parts of the input from masked versions of that input. They process the entire input sequence at once and are trained to predict the original unmasked input, excelling in understanding and representing context.
  - *Examples*
    - **BERT (Bidirectional Encoder Representations from Transformers):** Trained on a masked language model task, BERT predicts original words from masked sentences, used in sentiment analysis, named entity recognition and question answering (Devlin et al., 2018).
    - **RoBERTa (A Robustly Optimised BERT Pre-training Approach):** An optimised version of BERT with improved pre-training and better performance on various NLP benchmarks (Liu et al., 2019c).
- Autoregressive Transformers
  - *Description*: Autoregressive transformers generate sequences in a left-to-right fashion, predicting the next element based on previously generated elements, ideal for generative tasks like language modelling and text generation.
  - *Examples*
    - **GPT (Generative Pre-trained Transformer):** Models like GPT-2 and GPT-3 generate contextually relevant text by predicting the next word in a sequence (Radford et al., 2018, 2019; Brown et al., 2020; OpenAI, 2023).
    - **XLNet:** Captures bidirectional context by permuting the input sequence during autoregressive training (Yang et al., 2019).
- Sequence-to-Sequence Transformers
  - *Description*: Seq2Seq transformers, with an encoder for processing input and a decoder for generating output, are suited for converting one sequence into another, like in translation or summarisation.
  - *Examples*
    - **T5 (Text-to-Text Transfer Transformer):** Frames all NLP tasks as text-to-text problems, handling tasks like translation and summarisation in a unified format (Raffel et al., 2019).
    - **BART (Bidirectional and Auto-Regressive Transformers):** Combines bidirectional encoding and autoregressive decoding, effective for tasks requiring input understanding and coherent output generation (Lewis et al., 2020).

All types of NLP transformer models are built from encoder blocks and decoder blocks, and the structure of those used by Vaswani et al. (2017) is described below.

Encoder Block The encoder block used by Vaswani et al. (2017) has the following structure, with the embedding and positional encoding forming the input to a stack of encoder blocks formed by the remaining layers. Vaswani et al. (2017) used six blocks in total.

- **Input Embedding Layer**
  - Converts input tokens into vectors of fixed dimensionality.
  - Embeddings capture the semantic meaning of the tokens.

- **Positional Encoding**
  - Adds position information to the input embeddings.
  - Helps the model to understand the order of tokens in the sequence.
- **Multi-Head Attention Mechanism**
  - Each token attends to all other tokens in the input sequence.
  - Computes a weighted sum of all input embeddings, where the relevance of other tokens determines weights.
  - Helps the model to capture contextual information from the entire sequence.
- **Add & Norm (Residual Connection and Layer Normalisation)**
  - Applies a residual connection that adds the output of the self-attention layer to its input.
  - Followed by layer normalisation to stabilise the learning process.
- **Feedforward Neural Network**
  - This is a standard feedforward network with a ReLU activation function applied between the two layers.
  - Each position in the encoder goes through the same feedforward network independently.
- **Add & Norm (Residual Connection and Layer Normalisation)**
  - Another residual connection followed by layer normalisation.
  - Adds the output of the feedforward network to its input and then normalises.

Decoder Block Vaswani et al. (2017) used a decoder block with the following structure, with all but the input embedding and positional encoding repeated in each block. The authors used six decoder blocks, followed by a linear layer and softmax, to generate output probabilities.

- **Input Embedding Layer**
  - Converts target tokens into vectors of fixed dimensionality.
  - Embeddings are used to represent the output sequence tokens.
- **Positional Encoding**
  - Adds position information to the output embeddings.
  - Essential for the model to understand the sequence order of the output tokens.
- **Masked Multi-Head Attention Mechanism**
  - Similar to the self-attention mechanism in the encoder.
  - Masking prevents each token from attending to subsequent tokens in the sequence, ensuring causality in generation.
  - Focuses on the appropriate parts of the output sequence for accurate prediction.
- **Add & Norm (Residual Connection and Layer Normalisation)**
  - Applies a residual connection around the masked self-attention layer.
  - Followed by layer normalisation.
- **Encoder–Decoder Attention Mechanism**
  - The decoder attends to the output of the encoder.
  - Helps in aligning and translating the input sequence to the output.
- **Add & Norm (Residual Connection and Layer Normalisation)**
  - Another residual connection and layer normalisation is applied after encoder–decoder attention.
- **Feedforward Neural Network**
  - Consists of a two-layer neural network with an activation function between them.
  - Processes each position in the decoder output independently.
- **Add & Norm (Residual Connection and Layer Normalisation)**
  - Final residual connection and layer normalisation step in the decoder block.
  - Stabilises the output before passing it to the next decoder block or the output layer.

7.3.10.3 Training Transformers The training of transformer models in NLP is a two-step process with pre-training and fine-tuning.

Pre-Training In this stage, the model is exposed to a vast and diverse corpus of text, ranging from the entirety of Wikipedia to a collection of books and websites. Pre-training provides the model with an internal representation of the language, encompassing grammar, context, semantics and standard language patterns. The learning process here is typically self-supervised. For instance, models like BERT (Devlin et al., 2018) involve the masked language model (MLM) task, where random words in a sentence are masked and the model learns to predict them based on their context. In contrast, models like GPT (Radford et al., 2018, 2019; Brown et al., 2020; OpenAI, 2023) use a different approach where the model predicts the next word in a sequence given all previous words, thus learning a probabilistic understanding of language sequences.

Fine-Tuning Fine-tuning adapts the base model for specific tasks. The model is trained using a small task-specific training set. Fine-tuning is supervised and requires an appropriately labelled dataset, allowing the model to improve its performance on tasks such as question answering, summarisation and translation.

The integration of pre-training and fine-tuning gives transformer models their power and versatility. Pre-training equips the model with a comprehensive internal language representation while fine-tuning moulds this broad knowledge into a task-specific tool. Transformer models can be fine-tuned for multiple tasks, making them adaptable tools for NLP.

EXAMPLE 7.11: LLM FOR SENTIMENT

Large language model training is highly computationally demanding and requires vast hardware. In practice, the only viable solution for modest projects is to use a pre-trained model and apply it as is or perform a small fine-tuning. Many models have been released open-source, and sites like Huggingface are excellent accessible resources. This example, found in the Jupyter Notebook `LLMSentiment.ipynb`, uses a pre-trained model from Huggingface that has also been fine-tuned for sentiment analysis on financial text.

The Huggingface `transformers` and `datasets` libraries provide easy access to trained model pipelines and datasets. Here, a fine-tuned version of *FinancialBERT* is used, a version of BERT trained on a corpus of financial text.

```
from transformers import pipeline
from datasets import load_dataset

sentiment_analysis = pipeline("sentiment-analysis",
                              model="Sigma/financial-sentiment-analysis")
dataset = load_dataset("financial_phrasebank", "sentences_allagree")
dataset2 = load_dataset("FinanceInc/auditor_sentiment", "sentences_allagree")
```

The exercise here is to classify the financial text as negative, neutral or positive, and both datasets have the same labels, 0, 1 and 2, respectively. The pipeline can be used directly for this and automatically tokenises the input. The output classification comes as a string in the form `'LABEL_'` *label*. The following code runs through the dataset, collecting the predicted labels.

```
def pipeline_label_to_number(label):
    if label == "LABEL_0":
        return 0
    elif label == "LABEL_1":
        return 1
    elif label == "LABEL_2":
        return 2

predictions = []
ground_truths = []
for example in dataset["train"]:
    result = sentiment_analysis(example["sentence"])[0]
    predicted_label = pipeline_label_to_number(result["label"])
    predictions.append(predicted_label)
    ground_truth_label = example["label"]
      ground_truths.append(ground_truth_label)
```

(*Continued*)

(*Continued*)

The code is run for both datasets, and the confusion matrix defined in Section 3.8.2 is plotted as shown in Figure 7.17. The financial phrasebank results are outstanding because this is the dataset on which the model was fine-tuned. The second dataset, auditor sentiment, is unseen, but the results remain excellent.

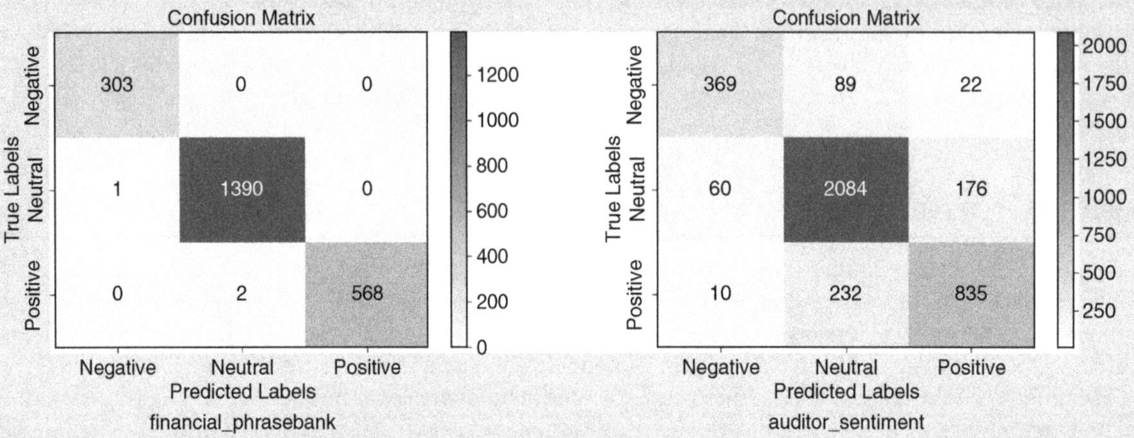

FIGURE 7.17 Confusion matrices from financial sentiment analysis using the pre-trained `Sigma/financial-sentiment-analysis` model from Huggingface.

7.3.10.4 Transformers Outside NLP The transformer architecture has evolved to have various applications across various fields. Here are some key applications:

- **Computer Vision.** Transformers have been successfully applied to image recognition, showing excellent results on benchmarks like ImageNet and CIFAR-100. They can be used without convolutional networks, as seen in vision transformer (ViT) models (Dosovitskiy et al., 2021).
- **Time-Series Analysis.** Transformers have been used to perform time-series analysis (Ahmed et al., 2023).
- **Medical Image Analysis.** In medical imaging, transformers have proven their capability in classification, segmentation and detection, offering advantages over conventional CNNs (Azad et al., 2024).
- **Graph Machine Learning.** Transformers have been adapted for graph-based tasks, like molecule property prediction and graph neural networks, leveraging their ability to represent complex interactions (Choukroun and Wolf, 2022).
- **3D Vision.** Transformers are being used in 3D vision for tasks like segmentation, detection and pose estimation, addressing the unique challenges of three-dimensional data representation (Lahoud et al., 2022).
- **Multimodal Learning.** Transformers are being integrated to handle text and tabular data for various applications (Gu and Budhkar, 2021).

The transformer architecture is now ubiquitous and is widely used across deep learning applications.

7.4 CONCLUSIONS ON SEQUENCE MODELS

This chapter has explored sequence models and NLP. It has reviewed the early applications of RNNs, including the significant advances provided by LSTMs. The chapter presented the transformer architecture and the key forms of attention mechanisms, including Bahdanau, dot-product attention, self-attention and multi-head attention. The transformer *revolution* culminated in LLMs like BERT and GPT but has also found application across deep learning.

CHAPTER 8

Autoencoders

Yoda: Blind we are, of creation of this clone army we could not see.
Mace Windu: I think it is time we inform the senate that our ability to use the force has diminished.
Yoda: Only a Dark Lord of the Sith knows of our weakness. If informed the senate is, multiply our adversaries will.

George Lucas, Star Wars: Episode II – Attack of the Clones (2002)

8.1 INTRODUCTION

Autoencoders are neural networks that copy their input to the output, resulting in an output layer the same size as the input. The structure typically exhibits symmetry around the central hidden layer, as Figure 8.1 illustrates. A neural network that learns the identity function perfectly, replicating the input, offers little interest. Therefore, autoencoders usually approximate the input rather than replicating it perfectly. This approximation occurs in several ways, the simplest being a restriction on the size of the hidden layer or layers. Fewer neurons in the hidden layers than in the input and output layers create an *undercomplete autoencoder*, discussed in Section 8.3. Regularisation methods achieve the same behaviour, particularly those inducing sparseness on the hidden layer, and Section 8.4 reviews these methods. The hidden layer can still exceed the size of the input and output layers, resulting in an *overcomplete autoencoder*.

Autoencoders perform dimension reduction, closely relating to classical dimension reduction techniques like *singular value decomposition (SVD)* and *principal component analysis (PCA)*, and Section 8.2 explores this relationship. *Denoising autoencoders* remove noise, typically from images. Training involves adding noise to the input data while presenting the true data as output. Section 8.5 presents denoising autoencoders. Finally, Section 8.6 explores the relationship between autoencoders and generative models, with the *variational autoencoder (VAE)* being a specific derivative of the basic autoencoder.

8.1.1 Encoders and Decoders

The critical observation about autoencoders is that they are a subset of deep neural networks, and this means that all of the theoretical and practical development of deep neural networks, as described in Chapters 2 through 5, applies here too. Early work on autoencoders can be found in LeCun (1987) and Bourlard and Kamp (1988).

The central hidden layer in an autoencoder is known as the *code*, and hence the first part of the network is the *encoder* and the second part is the *decoder*. The two parts can often be used separately, so the encoder is used for dimension reduction. Defining the hidden state vector as $\boldsymbol{h}$, we have (Goodfellow et al., 2016, p. 493),

$$\text{encoder} \quad \boldsymbol{h} = f(\boldsymbol{x}), \tag{8.1}$$
$$\text{decoder} \quad \bar{\boldsymbol{x}} = g(\boldsymbol{h}), \tag{8.2}$$

with the training process seeking to find parameters such that

$$g(f(\boldsymbol{x})) = \boldsymbol{x}. \tag{8.3}$$

Deep Learning in Quantitative Finance, First Edition. Andrew Green.

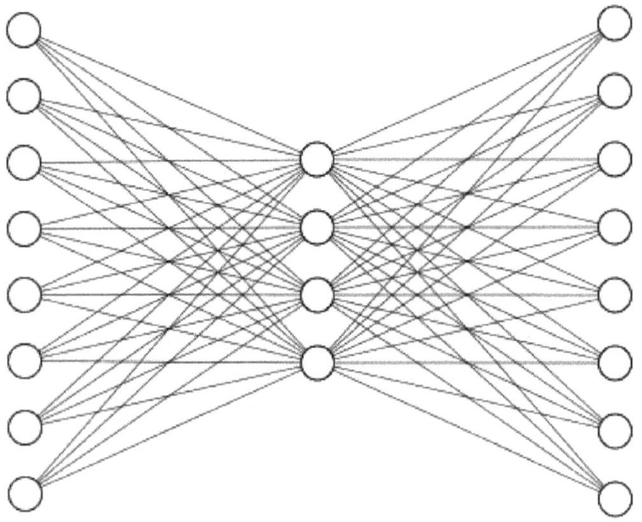

FIGURE 8.1 The structure of an autoencoder neural network.

8.2 AUTOENCODERS AND SINGULAR-VALUED DECOMPOSITION

8.2.1 PCA and SVD

Principal component analysis (PCA) is a numerical technique that linearly transforms a dataset to a new space defined by a set of orthogonal principal components. The transforms are such that the greatest variance in the data is associated with the first principal component, the second greatest variance with the second principal component and so on (Jolliffe, 2002, p. 1). This is also known as the Karhunen–Loève transformation (Murphy, 2012, p. 389). PCA can be useful for identifying the key sources of variance in a dataset. However, its main application is a dimension reduction technique. Dimension reduction can be used directly for visualisation, with another modelling technique, or a machine learning method such as naïve Bayes or random forests.

PCA is performed as follows:

1. Given a data matrix with N examples in rows, each with D features, the data $\boldsymbol{X}$ is first centred by subtracting the mean,

$$\bar{\boldsymbol{X}} = \boldsymbol{X} - \mu_X. \tag{8.4}$$

2. The covariance matrix is formed using

$$\Sigma_X = \bar{\boldsymbol{X}}^T \bar{\boldsymbol{X}}. \tag{8.5}$$

3. The principal components consist of an orthogonal set of basis vectors $\boldsymbol{v}_i$ for $i = 1, \dots, D$. It can be shown (see, e.g., Murphy, 2012, p. 389ff) that these basis vectors are, in fact, the eigenvectors of the covariance matrix Σ_X, ordered such that the eigenvector associated with the largest eigenvalue is the first principal component and so on to the smallest, that is we have

$$\Sigma_X \boldsymbol{v}_i = \lambda_i \boldsymbol{v}_i, \tag{8.6}$$

where $\lambda_1 > \cdots > \lambda_D$. If we form the matrix $\boldsymbol{V}$ with columns that are the eigenvectors and a matrix Λ with the ordered eigenvalues on the diagonal and zero elsewhere, then we obtain

$$\Sigma_X \boldsymbol{V} = \boldsymbol{V}\Lambda. \tag{8.7}$$

4. We can project the original data into the principal directions using V,

$$Z = VX. \tag{8.8}$$

5. To perform the dimensional reduction, we need to find a low-dimensional approximation such that the *reconstruction error*,

$$J = \|X - \widehat{X}\|_F^2, \tag{8.9}$$

is minimised.
6. Assume L eigenvectors are used with $L \leq D$, then we form a matrix V_L of the first L eigenvectors. We can project the data into this L-dimensional space using

$$Z_L = V_L X. \tag{8.10}$$

7. The data can be reconstructed using the transpose of V_L so we have

$$\begin{aligned}\widehat{X} &= V_L^T Z_L \\ &= V_L^T V_L X.\end{aligned} \tag{8.11}$$

Clearly, if $L = D$, then $V_L = V_L$ and $V^T V$ is the identity matrix.

Singular value decomposition (SVD) is closely related to PCA and the eigenvalue decomposition. Any real or complex matrix X can be decomposed into a product of three matrices,

$$X = USV^T. \tag{8.12}$$

If the matrix X has dimension $m \times n$, then the three decomposition matrices have the properties:

- U is a complex unitary[1] matrix of dimension $m \times m$.
- S is a diagonal matrix of dimension $m \times n$ with $r = \min(m, n)$ non-negative real values on the diagonal.
- V is a complex unitary matrix of dimension $n \times n$.

If X is real, then U and V are also guaranteed to be real. To obtain the relationship between SVD and the eigenvector decomposition, pre-multiply X by its transpose,

$$\begin{aligned}X^T X &= VS^T U^T USV^T \\ &= VS^T SV^T \\ &= V\Lambda^V V^T,\end{aligned} \tag{8.13}$$

where $\Lambda_V = S^T S$ is a diagonal matrix. Post-multiplying both sides by V gives

$$X^T XV = V\Lambda_V, \tag{8.14}$$

showing that V is a matrix containing the eigenvectors of $X^T X$ with Λ_V being a diagonal matrix with the corresponding eigenvalues. Similarly, it can be shown that

$$XX^T U = U\Lambda_U, \tag{8.15}$$

and hence the matrix U consists of the eigenvectors of XX^T, with eigenvalues on the diagonal of Λ_U.

SVD generates a low-rank approximation of X via the theorem of Eckart and Young (1936). The best approximation of X with rank $L < D$ follows:

$$\hat{X} = U\hat{S}V^T, \tag{8.16}$$

[1] A unitary matrix has the property that $U^T U = UU^T = I$, the identity matrix.

where $\widehat{S}$ contains the largest L singular values and zeros elsewhere. In practice, $\widehat{S}$ reduces to an $L \times L$ matrix, and both U and V truncate to L columns, and this allows the direct performance of PCA using SVD. Furthermore, the reconstruction expresses, in terms of the original dataset $\boldsymbol{X}$, using Equations (8.12) and (8.16):

$$\begin{aligned}\widehat{X} &= U\widehat{S}V^T \\ &= U\widehat{S}S^T U^T X \\ &= U\widehat{S}\widehat{S}^T U^T X \\ &= W^T W X.\end{aligned} \tag{8.17}$$

This uses $\widehat{S}S^T = \widehat{S}\,\widehat{S}^T$, given that the last $N - L$ entries on the diagonal of $\widehat{S}$ are zero, and defines $W^T = U\widehat{S}$. Noting that this minimises the reconstruction error:

$$J = |X - W^T W X|_F^2, \tag{8.18}$$

which indicates that the matrix W represents a set of weights that minimises the mean square error when multiplied by its transpose.

8.2.2 Linear Autoencoders Replicate SVD

Consider a shallow autoencoder with one hidden layer containing L units and an input/output layer with D units where $L \leq D$. Assume there are N training examples arranged into an input matrix $\boldsymbol{X}$ of dimension $D \times N$. The hidden layer has a linear activation function and so calculates

$$Z = WX + b, \tag{8.19}$$

where the weight matrix W has dimension $L \times D$ and $\boldsymbol{b}$ is a bias vector of dimension L. The output layer with a weight matrix $\widehat{W}$ of dimension $D \times L$ is also linear and calculates

$$\begin{aligned}\widehat{X} &= \widehat{W}Z + \widehat{b} \\ &= \widehat{W}Z(WX + b) + \widehat{b}.\end{aligned} \tag{8.20}$$

Setting the two bias vectors to zero and assuming that the weights of input and output are shared so that $\widehat{W} = W^T$ gives

$$\widehat{X} = W^T W X, \tag{8.21}$$

which is the same as Equation (8.17). The weights are trained using gradient descent with the mean squared error as the loss function. Hence, linear autoencoders learn the same weights as would be generated by SVD (Bourlard and Kamp, 1988).

EXAMPLE 8.1: PCA, SVD AND AUTOENCODERS

This example compares dimension reduction and data reconstruction using classic PCA, SVD and a linear autoencoder (and can be found in the Jupyter Notebook `PCA, SVD and Autoencoders.ipynb`). The dataset is *overnight index swap (OIS)* rates for GBP, known as SONIA, for 60 different maturities out to 5 years in maturity. The curves are provided for every business date from 2009 until now and are split between two files. The data can be found at https://www.bankofengland.co.uk/-/media/boe/files/statistics/yield-curves/oisddata.zip.

After downloading the data, `StandardScaler` from *scikit-learn* scales it. This process subtracts the mean and scales the values by the standard deviation of the data. The scaling step is not strictly necessary for PCA.

PCA can be performed using routines from the *numpy* library first to calculate the correlation matrix of the data and then to calculate the eigenvectors and eigenvalues. Given the scaled data in the numpy array `X_bar` arranged as a row per business date with the yield curve rates as columns, this is done using

```
rho = np.corrcoef(X_bar.T)
eigenvalues, eigenvectors = np.linalg.eig(rho)
```

The first four eigenvalues explain 99.98% of the variance, so the data is reduced to four dimensions by ignoring the remaining eigenvectors and values. The data is then reconstructed from the four eigenvectors using

```
ZL = np.dot(X_bar, np.real(eigenvectors[:,:4]))
X_hat_bar = np.dot(ZL, np.real(eigenvectors[:,:4].T))
X_hat = scaler.inverse_transform(X_hat_bar)
```

Note that `np.real` removes any small residual complex part of the eigenvectors, which can result from numerical noise in the eigenvalue routine. Calculating the reconstruction error as a fraction of the norm of the input data array shows a relative error of 0.5743%.

SVD can be applied directly to the scaled data matrix `X_bar`.

```
U, S, Vh = np.linalg.svd(X_bar, full_matrices=False)
```

The diagonal matrix of singular values is returned as a vector, so some manipulation is required to return it to a diagonal matrix. Furthermore, only the first four singular values are taken to perform the same dimension reduction as done with PCA above.

```
S_hatd = copy.deepcopy(S)
S_hatd[4:] = 0.0
S_hat = np.zeros((len(S_hatd), len(S_hatd)))
np.fill_diagonal(S_hat, S_hatd)
```

The data is then reconstructed by multiplying the matrices using $X^T XV = V\Lambda_V$.

```
X_hatsvd_bar = np.dot(U, np.dot(S_hat, Vh))
X_hatsvd = scaler.inverse_transform(X_hatsvd_bar)
```

The final relative reconstruction error is almost identical to that of PCA and is highly numerically accurate.

The final comparison is with a linear autoencoder. The autoencoder is shallow, with a single hidden layer with four nodes and linear activation. The input and output weights are shared, and the output weight matrix is the transpose of the input weight matrix. It is helpful to create a specialised layer for this purpose when using *tied* weights in PyTorch.

```
class DenseTied(nn.Module):
    def __init__(self, dense, activation=None, use_bias=True):
        super(DenseTied, self).__init__()
        self.dense = dense
```

(*Continued*)

(*Continued*)

```
        if activation is not None:
            self.activation = activation
        else:
            nn.Identity()
        self.use_bias = use_bias
        if self.use_bias:
            self.biases = nn.Parameter(torch.zeros(dense.in_features))

    def forward(self, inputs):
        z = torch.matmul(inputs, self.dense.weight)
        if self.use_bias:
            outputs = self.activation(z + self.biases)
        else:
            outputs = self.activation(z)
        return outputs
```

The class constructor uses a dense layer as an argument, so the tied layer reuses its weights. The class also allows the activation function to be specified and a boolean parameter to determine whether biases are used or not. Here, the activation is linear, and no bias is used. The autoencoder can now be built using the class.

```
class LinearAutoencoder(nn.Module):
    def __init__(self, input_dim, hidden_width, activation=None,
                 use_bias=True):
        super(LinearAutoencoder, self).__init__()
        self.dense = nn.Linear(input_dim, hidden_width, bias=False)
        self.tied_dense = DenseTied(self.dense, activation=activation,
                                    use_bias=use_bias)

    def forward(self, x):
        encoded = self.dense(x)
        decoded = self.tied_dense(encoded)
        return decoded

    def build_linear_autoencoder(input_dim, hidden_width):
        model = LinearAutoencoder(input_dim, hidden_width,
                                  activation=nn.Identity(), use_bias=False)
        return model
```

Training of the model occurred through 10,000 epochs with a batch size of 512. Upon completion, the entire dataset passed through the network to generate the reconstructed data, followed by the calculation of the reconstruction error. This process yielded a value of 0.5762%, very close to that obtained using both PCA and SVD. The reconstruction of a yield curve directly demonstrates this similarity. Figure 8.2 displays the reconstruction error of the OIS curve on 2 January 2009 as a function of maturity. All three methods exhibit very similar errors as a function of maturity, demonstrating that the linear autoencoder replicates the other methods almost exactly.

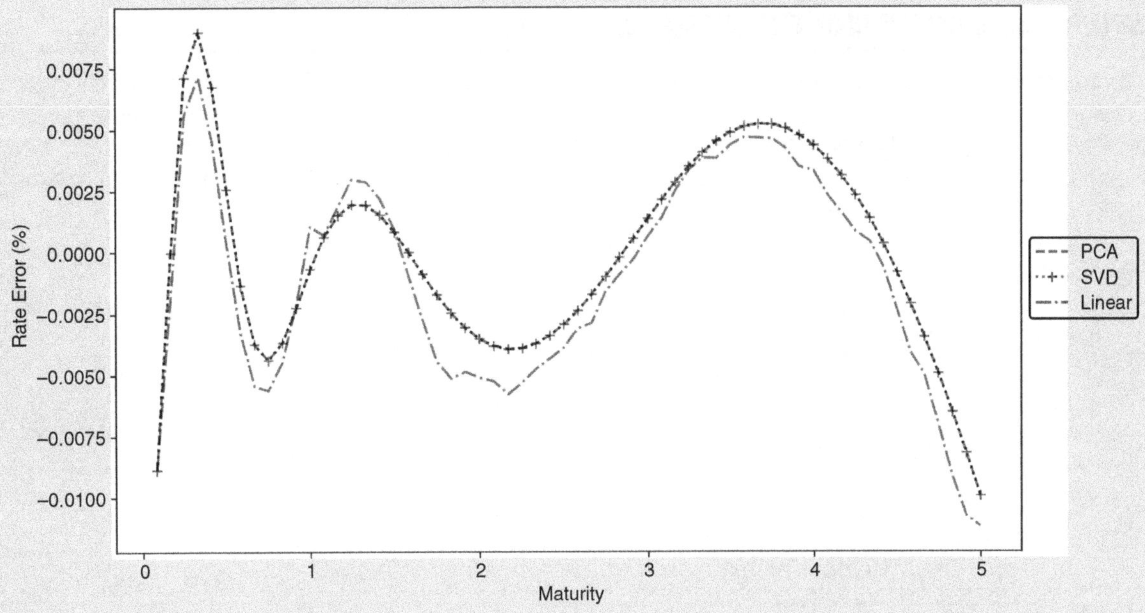

FIGURE 8.2 Reconstruction errors from PCA and SVD using four dimensions and a linear autoencoder with four hidden units for the SONIA curve on 2 January 2009.

8.2.3 Autoencoders as Non-Linear PCA

As we have already demonstrated in Section 2.1.1, activation functions need to be non-linear to gain any benefit from using multiple layers. It is also evident from the above section that a shallow linear autoencoder network replaces SVD. Given that training a linear autoencoder will take significantly longer than applying an SVD routine, there is no practical benefit to this. Hence, it is clear that autoencoders only offer an advantage over traditional dimension reduction techniques if non-linear activation functions are used. The non-linear activations must be used only on hidden layers, as the output layer has to mirror the input and cover the same domain.

A non-linear autoencoder can, therefore, be used to perform non-linear PCA, although typically, this does require a deep network (Aggarwal, 2018, p. 78). Non-linear PCA is more effective than standard PCA, mapping data into much lower-dimensional spaces (Aggarwal, 2018, p. 78) and outperforming PCA significantly (Kramer, 1991, p. 242)

8.3 SHALLOW AND DEEP AUTOENCODERS

A basic shallow autoencoder consists of an input layer and an identically sized output layer with a single hidden layer in the middle. As in the above example, the hidden layer is usually restricted to have fewer nodes than the input and output. As noted earlier, this is an *undercomplete* autoencoder. A deep autoencoder has multiple hidden layers, usually arranged symmetrically around a central hidden layer. However, there is no absolute requirement for such symmetry, and indeed, any encoder can be coupled with any decoder structure as long as the input and output have the same shape.

Given that autoencoders are feedforward networks, deep autoencoders should be expected to outperform shallow ones (Aggarwal, 2018, p. 79). Like standard deep neural networks, deep autoencoders form a hierarchical representation of the training data. Deep networks can approximate any mapping from input to code layer to arbitrary precision with sufficient hidden nodes, can reduce the computational cost of computing certain functions and can reduce the required amount of training data (see Goodfellow et al., 2016, p. 500 and Section 2.4). Hinton and Salakhutdinov (2006) show that deep autoencoders work much better than PCA to produce dimension reduction.

EXAMPLE 8.2: SHALLOW AND DEEP AUTOENCODERS WITH MNIST

This example trains shallow and deep undercomplete autoencoders to encode and decode the MNIST dataset (see the Jupyter Notebook `Shallow and Deep Autoencoders.ipynb`). Here, simple dense layers are used, although it is perfectly possible to use two-dimensional convolutional layers in an autoencoder. The data is prepared in the usual way and flattened to a vector of length 784 for a dense layer input. Unlike the earlier example, the encoder and decoder sections do not share weights for simplicity.

The shallow autoencoder uses a single hidden layer with 32 nodes and a ReLU activation function and is constructed using

```
class ShallowAutoencoder(nn.Module):
    def __init__(self, hidden_width=32):
        super(ShallowAutoencoder, self).__init__()
        self.encoder = nn.Sequential(
            nn.Linear(28*28, hidden_width),
            nn.ReLU()
        )
        self.decoder = nn.Sequential(
            nn.Linear(hidden_width, 28*28),
            nn.Linear(28*28, 28*28)
        )

    def forward(self, x):
        x = self.encoder(x)
        x = self.decoder(x)
        return x
```

The deep autoencoder is constructed with five hidden layers of dimension 128, 64, 32, 64 and 128, all with ReLU activation.

```
class DeepAutoencoder(nn.Module):
    def __init__(self):
        super(DeepAutoencoder, self).__init__()
        self.encoder = nn.Sequential(
            nn.Linear(28*28, 128),
            nn.ReLU(),
            nn.Linear(128, 64),
            nn.ReLU(),
            nn.Linear(64, 32),
            nn.ReLU()
        )
        self.decoder = nn.Sequential(
            nn.Linear(32, 64),
            nn.ReLU(),
            nn.Linear(64, 128),
            nn.ReLU(),
            nn.Linear(128, 28*28),
            nn.Linear(28*28, 28*28)
        )

    def forward(self, x):
        x = self.encoder(x)
        x = self.decoder(x)
        return x
```

Training does not use labels; input and output are the training images. Both networks were trained through 50 epochs with a batch size of 256. The validation loss for both shallow and deep networks is shown in Figure 8.3, and it is clear that the shallow network quickly runs out of representational capacity, while with the deep network, the loss continues to reduce throughout training.

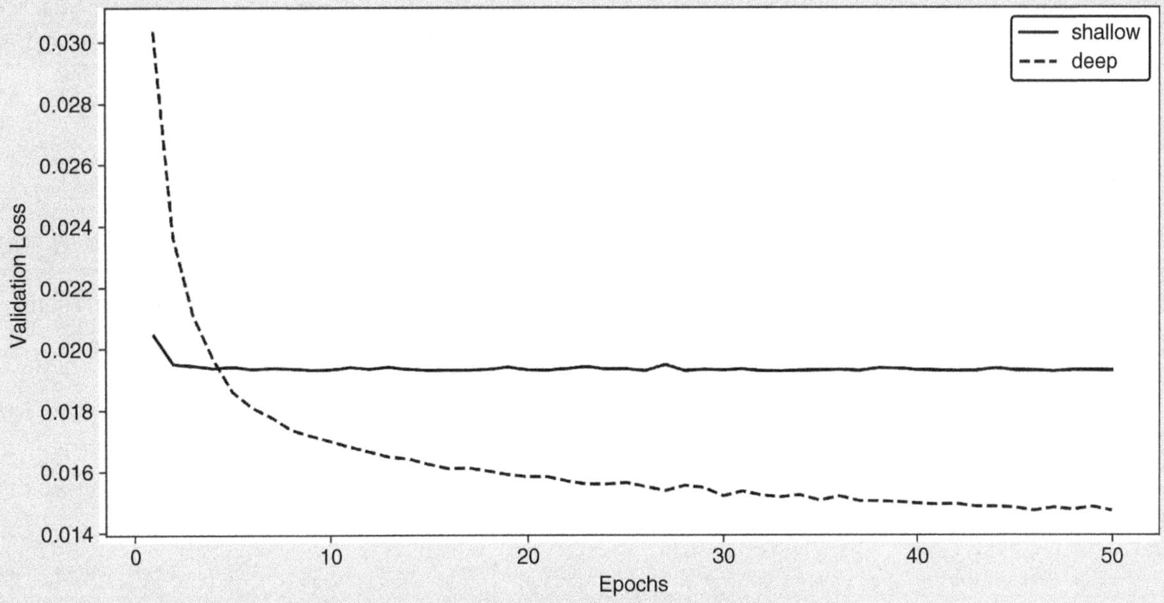

FIGURE 8.3 Validation loss for shallow and deep autoencoders trained with MNIST.

To further assess the networks, it is helpful to visually compare the reconstructed outputs of the networks with the original input, and this can be seen in Figure 8.4, which shows that the reconstructions from the deep network in the third row contain fewer visual artefacts than those generated by the shallow network in the second row.

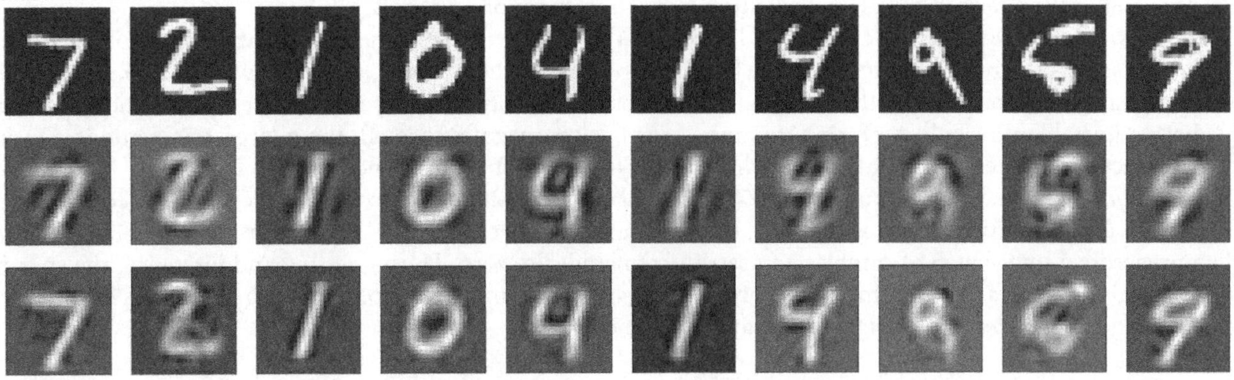

FIGURE 8.4 Ten original test images in the first row compared with the reconstructions generated by the shallow network in the second row and the deep network in the third row.

8.4 REGULARISED AND SPARSE AUTOENCODERS

As noted earlier, in an *overcomplete* autoencoder, the hidden layer can be the same size or greater in width than the input. The problem with this arrangement is that there is nothing to prevent the autoencoder from learning the identity function. Regularisation can be used to stop this from happening by encouraging sparseness in the hidden layer, ensuring that the activations of the hidden layer are mostly close to zero. To achieve this, we can add a penalty to the loss function that is a function of the activations of the hidden layer h, that is, the loss becomes

$$J(W, b) + \Omega(h). \tag{8.22}$$

Several different choices exist for the sparsity penalty:

1. The simplest choice uses L_1 regularisation as discussed in Section 4.2.2 (Aggarwal, 2018, p. 81). L_1 regularisation generates sparse solutions.
2. Another approach approximately enforces that the average activation across the training set equals some small value (Ng, 2011, pp. 14–16). Defining

$$\hat{\rho} = \frac{1}{m} \sum_{i=1}^{m} h(x^i), \tag{8.23}$$

the goal is to achieve $\hat{\rho}_j \approx \rho$ for all j, where ρ is the sparsity parameter and represents a constant close to zero, say $\rho = 0.05$. A penalty is added to the loss function to achieve this,

$$\Omega(h) = \sum_{j=1}^{s_h} KL(\rho || \hat{\rho}_j), \tag{8.24}$$

where s_h represents the number of units in the hidden layer and KL is the Kullback–Leibler divergence between a Bernoulli random variable with mean ρ and another with mean $\hat{\rho}_j$, given by

$$KL(\rho || \hat{\rho}_j) = \rho \log \frac{\rho}{\hat{\rho}_j} + (1 - \rho) \log \frac{1 - \rho}{1 - \hat{\rho}_j}. \tag{8.25}$$

This method is intended for use with sigmoid activation functions where $\hat{\rho} \leq 1$.
3. The *k-sparse autoencoder* (Makhzani and Frey, 2014) retains only the highest k activation functions in hidden layers, setting the remainder to zero. The feedforward phase occurs on the layer, followed by a selection of the k largest activation values, with remaining activations masked off (or using adaptive ReLU activation functions with adjustable thresholds). During training, error backpropagates through the k largest activations. During inference, using the top αk activations where $\alpha \geq 1$ yields better performance.
4. The *winner takes all (WTA) autoencoder* (Makhzani and Frey, 2015) enforces a lifetime sparsity constraint on hidden unit activations. During training, the WTA autoencoder keeps the $k\%$ largest activations of a hidden unit across a mini-batch of samples and sets the remainder to zero. During testing and inference, the sparsity constraint switches off. Makhzani and Frey (2015) use an asymmetric geometry with a stack of ReLU layers forming the encoder and a single linear layer for the decoder.

EXAMPLE 8.3: SPARSE AUTOENCODERS

This example trains a shallow autoencoder with a single hidden layer of the same width at the input and output layers. However, it imposes L_1 regularisation on the weights in the hidden layer (see the Jupyter Notebook `Sparse Autoencoders.ipynb`). The MNIST dataset is used again to allow comparison with the shallow and deep autoencoders in the previous example. To add L_1 regularisation in Keras, the `activity_regularizer` parameter is specified in the hidden layer, and the code to create the model is as follows.

```
class SparseAutoencoder(nn.Module):
    def __init__(self):
        super(SparseAutoencoder, self).__init__()
        self.encoder = nn.Sequential(
            nn.Linear(28*28, 28*28),
            nn.ReLU()
        )
        self.decoder = nn.Sequential(
             nn.Linear(28*28, 28*28),
             nn.Linear(28*28, 28*28)
        )
        self.l1_lambda = 10e-5

    def forward(self, x):
        x = self.encoder(x)
        x = self.decoder(x)
        return x

    def l1_regularizer(self):
        l1_loss = 0
        for param in self.encoder.parameters():
            l1_loss += torch.sum(torch.abs(param))
        return self.l1_lambda * l1_loss
```

Training of the network occurred through 200 epochs with a batch size of 256. The final network then projected the test images, with 10 examples alongside the original test images in Figure 8.5. The reconstruction visibly surpasses that of either the earlier shallow or deep networks. Extraction of the weights confirms the genuine sparsity of the hidden layer. A histogram of the absolute weight values, plotted in Figure 8.6, illustrates this sparsity. The *y*-axis of this plot uses a logarithmic scale, clearly showing that the vast majority of the 784^2 weights lie close to zero.

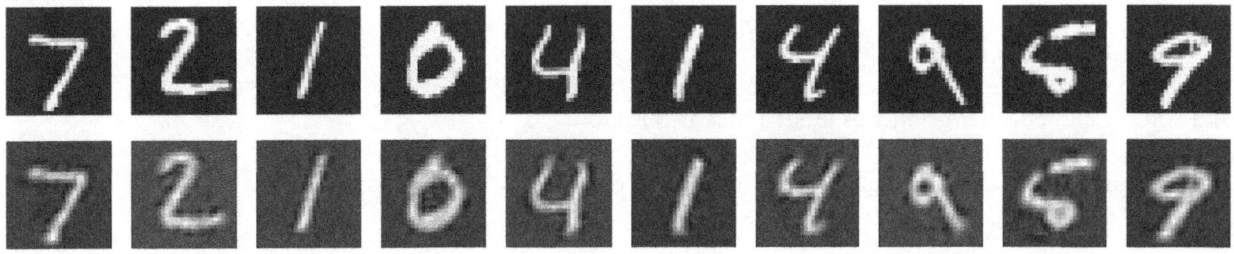

FIGURE 8.5 Ten original test images in the first row compared with the same images reconstructed by the sparse autoencoder.

(*Continued*)

(*Continued*)

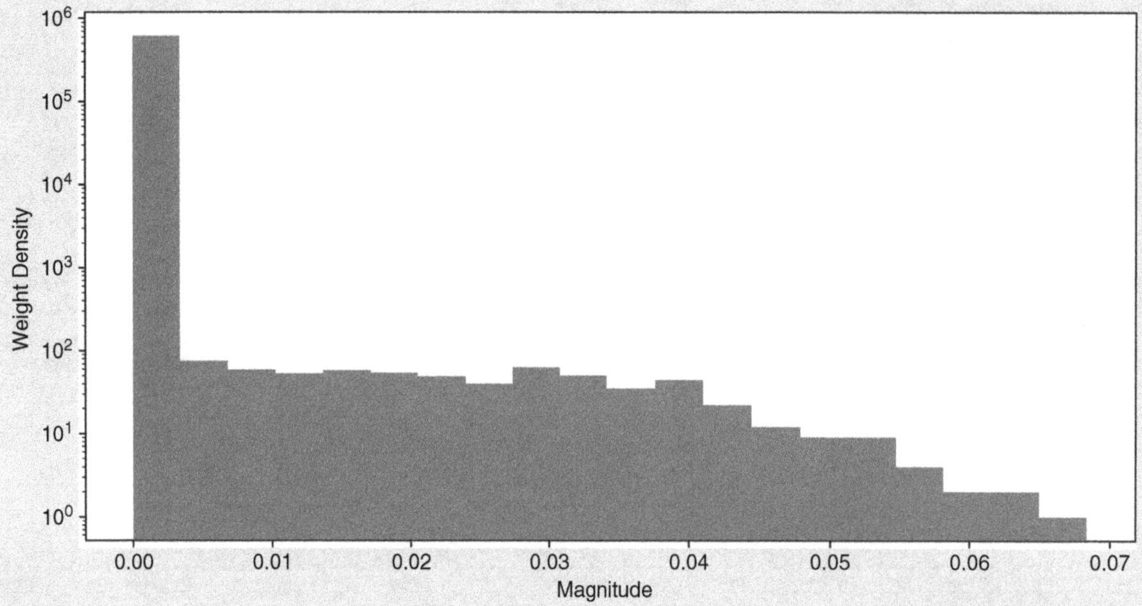

FIGURE 8.6 The distribution of the absolute value of weights in the autoencoder layer. Note the log scale on the y-axis.

8.5 DENOISING AUTOENCODERS

Denoising autoencoders (DAEs) are trained to remove noise from input images. DAEs have advantages over traditional methods because they do not produce oversmooth images (Abrahamian and Oguntayo, 2021) and are fast in operation. The network learns that the position of the noise is not important. The process to train a DAE is as follows (Goodfellow et al., 2016, p. 502):

1. Take training example $\boldsymbol{x}$.
2. Apply a corruption process to $\boldsymbol{x}$ to give $\tilde{\boldsymbol{x}}$.
3. Train the autoencoder using $\tilde{\boldsymbol{x}}$ as input and $\boldsymbol{x}$ as output.

Once trained, the DAE can remove noise from input examples.

EXAMPLE 8.4: DENOISING AUTOENCODERS

This example trains a denoising autoencoder using the MNIST dataset (see the Jupyter Notebook `Denoising Autoencoders.ipynb`). Corruption of the input training images occurs through an additive random factor, drawn from a normal distribution with a mean of 0.0 and standard deviation of 1.0, then scaled by a 'noise factor' set at 0.5 for this experiment. `random.normal` from numpy quickly generates the random samples. The `clip` function from numpy clips the final intensity values to ensure they remain in the range 0.0–1.0.

This model used convolutional layers and max pooling for downsampling and two-dimensional upsampling to mirror this in the decoder. In the output layer, the linear activation has been replaced by a sigmoid function, guaranteeing that the output remains in the range 0.0–1.0, consistent with the input. The PyTorch code to construct the model is as follows.

```
class DAE(nn.Module):
    def __init__(self):
        super(DAE, self).__init__()
        # Encoder
        self.encoder = nn.Sequential(
            nn.Conv2d(1, 32, kernel_size=3, padding=1),
            nn.ReLU(),
            nn.MaxPool2d(kernel_size=2, stride=2, padding=0),
            nn.Conv2d(32, 32, kernel_size=3, padding=1),
            nn.ReLU(),
            nn.MaxPool2d(kernel_size=2, stride=2, padding=0)
        )
        # Decoder
        self.decoder = nn.Sequential(
            nn.Conv2d(32, 32, kernel_size=3, padding=1),
            nn.ReLU(),
            nn.Upsample(scale_factor=2, mode='nearest'),
            nn.Conv2d(32, 32, kernel_size=3, padding=1),
            nn.ReLU(),
            nn.Upsample(scale_factor=2, mode='nearest'),
            nn.Conv2d(32, 1, kernel_size=3, padding=1),
            nn.Sigmoid()
        )

    def forward(self, x):
        x = self.encoder(x)
        x = self.decoder(x)
        return x
```

Figure 8.7 compares 10 original test images with the same images at the input after corruption by noise and after passing through the trained network. The reconstructed images show no trace of the noise.

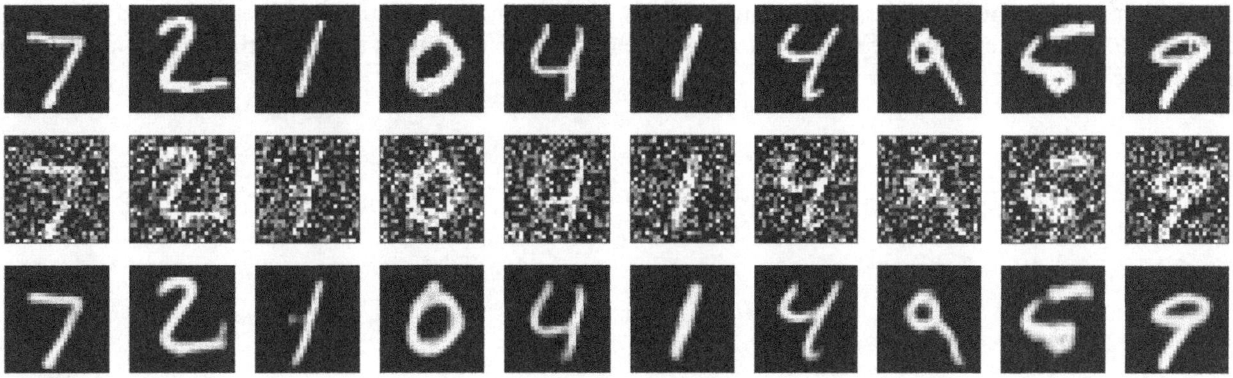

FIGURE 8.7 Ten original test images in the first row compared with the same images with added Gaussian noise in the second row and the reconstructed images in the third row.

8.6 AUTOENCODERS AND GENERATIVE MODELS

Autoencoders define a latent space at the encoder output, that is (Goodfellow et al., 2016, p. 500), the autoencoder defines two probability distributions,

$$P_{\text{encoder}}(\boldsymbol{h}|\boldsymbol{x}),$$
$$P_{\text{decoder}}(\boldsymbol{x}|\boldsymbol{h}). \tag{8.26}$$

Hence, we might imagine using the decoder generatively and sampling points in the latent space defined by $\boldsymbol{h}$ to create a new output. In practice, however, that does not work well, and Foster (2019) raises several key points:

1. The distribution of the latent space is not well defined; hence, it is not obvious how to select points to generate output.
2. The scale of the latent space is poorly understood, so it is unclear how far a point in the latent space needs to be moved to generate output with different features.
3. There is no guarantee that any given point in the latent space corresponds to meaningful output.

Solving these issues requires stepping beyond the simple autoencoder to the *variational autoencoder*, which is discussed alongside other generative models in Chapter 9.

Restricted Boltzmann machines are a generative neural network with a visible and hidden layer. As such, the geometry strongly resembles an autoencoder's encoder or decoder part. There is a close relationship between the two, and this will be further discussed in Chapter 9, which also covers RBMs.

8.7 CONCLUSION

Autoencoders have demonstrated versatility across various applications, including dimension reduction and denoising. Their ability to approximate the input through a compressed representation, or 'code', in the hidden layer has enabled significant advancements in feature extraction. Autoencoders have surpassed traditional methods like PCA and SVD in capturing complex data patterns through learned non-linear weight layers. Denoising autoencoders have demonstrated their ability to provide robust noise handling. However, the most significant development to follow from standard autoencoders is generative models, specifically the variational autoencoder and as a significant component of the current state-of-the-art image generation latent diffusion model, both of which are discussed in the next chapter.

CHAPTER 9

Generative Models

> The metal war-machines that humans called berserkers were the ultimate enemy of everything that lived. The creators of those inanimate weapons were gone, but the weapons themselves raged on across the Galaxy, endlessly repairing and replicating themselves, improving their design, and refining their killing capabilities in an eternal effort to accomplish their basic programmed task, the elimination of all life, wherever and whenever they could find it.
>
> *Berserker Throne, Fred Saberhagen (1985)*

9.1 INTRODUCTION

Generative adversarial networks (GANs) (Goodfellow et al., 2014) were introduced as a type of generative model capable of producing new images, of which StyleGAN (Karras et al., 2018, 2020b) can create photorealistic portraits of people who do not exist. GANs are just one example of a *generative model*, and in this chapter, I will present four different types of generative models that use neural networks: energy-based models (EBMs), variational autoencoders (VAEs), GANs and latent diffusion models (LDMs).

Generative models are examples of unsupervised learning, and they first appeared in the 1980s, with Boltzmann machines (Ackley et al., 1985; Hinton and Sejnowski, 1986). The central idea is as follows (Bond-Taylor et al., 2021):

- Assume the training data is drawn from a distribution $x \sim P_d$.
- Train a generative model whose samples $\tilde{x} \sim P_g$ are drawn from the same distribution.

We can also view a generative model as a distribution transformation, transforming a random variable from a source distribution that is typically either uniform $\mathcal{U}[0, 1]$ or uncorrelated normal $\mathcal{N}[0, I]$. In this way, generative models can be seen as learned equivalents of random sample generation algorithms (see, e.g., Fishman, 1996). As illustrated below, EBMs rely on *Markov chain Monte Carlo (MCMC)* techniques.

We can also compare discriminative and generative models (Zhou et al., 2020a). Given features X and classes Y, a discriminative model learns

$$P(Y|X).$$

Given classes Y and features X, a generative model learns

$$P(X|Y).$$

The generative model need not be conditioned on a class, in which case it learns

$$P(X).$$

As illustrated in Figure 9.1, generative models have numerous applications. Image generation stands out as the most well-known use of these models. Consequently, this chapter focuses primarily on image generation despite

Deep Learning in Quantitative Finance, First Edition. Andrew Green.

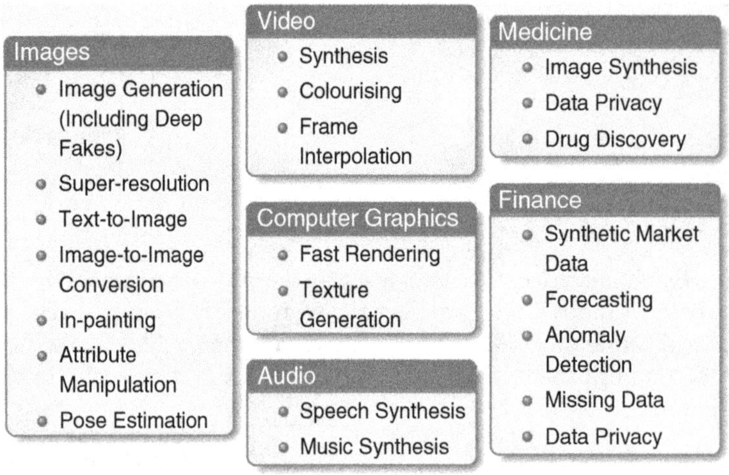

FIGURE 9.1 A range of the applications of generative models.

seeming incongruous with the book's main topic. This choice stems from the fact that generative models have been predominantly developed for image creation. Exploring generative models through image generation provides the best intuition, even though quantitative finance aims to apply these techniques to areas like synthetic market data generation. Image datasets offer accessibility and allow for the development of modestly sized models with reasonable computing resources. Chapter 18 covers financial applications of generative models, applying the techniques developed here to generate financial market data.

The major sections of this chapter discuss each of the four types of models listed earlier. Section 9.3 discusses EBMs, ranging from the various types of Boltzmann machines to the recent development of *diffusion models*. VAEs, the direct extension of autoencoders, as discussed in Chapter 8, are described in Section 9.4. GANs are the best developed of all generative models and, hence, the discussion of these models in Section 9.5 makes up a substantial part of the whole chapter. Finally, the chapter discusses LDMs, which represent the current state-of-the-art model for image generation. Before proceeding to explore the models themselves, it is essential to understand how generative models can be compared and evaluated, which is the subject of Section 9.2.

EXAMPLE 9.1: DATASETS

There are, of course, many suitable datasets available for use with generative models. In this chapter, the primary datasets used are *MNIST* and *CIFAR-10*. MNIST is monochrome with a single channel, while CIFAR-10 is colour and has three channels. These two datasets allow visual comparisons, and the comparative metrics of inception score and Fréchet inception distance are calculated for CIFAR-10. CIFAR-10 and MNIST have relatively small physical image sizes at 32 × 32 and 28 × 28, respectively. So, datasets with larger image sizes are also used in the context of higher-resolution GANs. In addition, in several cases, the galaxies dataset from Chapter 6 is used with image sizes reduced to 32 × 32, and this is a colour dataset but much more homogenous than CIFAR-10.

9.2 EVALUATING GENERATIVE MODEL PERFORMANCE

In generative modelling, we are given a dataset with samples x drawn from some real-world probability distribution $P_r(x)$. The aim is to train a model that generates samples $x \sim P_g(x)$ such that $P_g(x) \approx P_r(x)$ (Barratt and Sharma, 2018). Suppose the model admits an explicit probability density $P_g(x)$. In that case, it is possible to calculate the likelihood of a subset of the data held back from training under $P_g(x)$ as a way of assessing model performance.

However, for most models, specifically those parameterised by a neural network, $P_g(x)$ is not available directly. Techniques such as Parzen window estimates provide an approximate density function for the generative distribution, hence allowing the likelihood of a held-out set to be calculated. However, this is not the route that image generation model evaluation has taken.

Determining an image's realism relies on subjective human aesthetic judgement. However, using human judges for performance assessment proves impractical, necessitating objective metrics. Developed methods have thus applied pre-trained classifier neural networks, calculating statistics at either the output or hidden layers (Barratt and Sharma, 2018). This approach leverages the image-specific features of a trained network. Various studies have also evaluated the correlation between these metrics and human image quality assessments.

9.2.1 Inception Score

The *inception score* was introduced by Salimans et al. (2016) and uses an inception v3 network trained on the ImageNet dataset to calculate $P(y|\boldsymbol{x})$ on sample images $\boldsymbol{x}$ from the generator model. Salimans et al. (2016) aimed to create a metric that ensured that two key qualities were satisfied by the generator model:

1. Images should be clear, which implies that the inception network should be confident that there is a single object in the generated image. Hence, $P(y|\boldsymbol{x})$ should have low entropy.
2. Images should be diverse and hence $P(y)$ should have high entropy.

The inception score is defined by

$$IS(G) = \exp\left(\mathbb{E}_{x\sim P_g} D_{KL}(P(y|\boldsymbol{x})||P(y))\right), \tag{9.1}$$

where D_{KL} is the Kullback–Leibler divergence. Barratt and Sharma (2018) demonstrate that the inception score satisfies the two desired properties by relating it to mutual information I,

$$\ln(IS(G)) = I(y; \boldsymbol{x}). \tag{9.2}$$

In turn, mutual information can be related to entropy H,

$$I(y; \boldsymbol{x}) = H(y) - H(y|\boldsymbol{x}). \tag{9.3}$$

It is clear, therefore, that to obtain a high inception score, $P(y)$ needs to have high entropy and $P(y|\boldsymbol{x})$ should have low entropy.

The inception score can be calculated empirically over a batch of samples $\boldsymbol{x}^{(i)}$ from a trained generator model. $P(y|\boldsymbol{x}^{(i)})$ is obtained directly from the inception network, and then the sample marginal distribution is given by

$$\hat{P}(y) = \frac{1}{N}\sum_{i=1}^{N} P(y|\boldsymbol{x}^{(i)}), \tag{9.4}$$

which allows the inception score to be estimated.

Barratt and Sharma (2018) and others have identified several problems with the inception score in its intrinsic properties and how it has been applied. There are three critical issues with the intrinsic properties:

1. The inception score is sensitive to the particular choice of trained inception network and its weights. Multiple versions of inception are available in different model frameworks, and all have been trained using the same ImageNet dataset and show practically the same classification accuracy.
2. The original proposal from Salimans et al. (2016) was to calculate the inception score 10 times, each on a batch of 5000 images. However, given that inception was trained on ImageNet with 1000 categories, 5000 samples are insufficient to achieve accuracy. Hence, it is better to calculate the inception score over the entire generated dataset. Barratt and Sharma (2018) further propose dropping the exponentiation in the definition of the inception score.

3. To calculate the inception score, many images need to be generated and passed through the inception network. If the images differ in size from those expected by inception, that is, 299×299, then they must be rescaled, making the calculation slow and potentially memory-intensive. If it were desired to calculate the inception score during training, then the inception network would need to be loaded simultaneously as the generative and discriminator models.

Further problems with the inception score emerge from the literature. Inception was trained on ImageNet and is only valid as a measure if the generator is also trained on ImageNet when used as a classifier. The original proposal was to use the inception score in images generated from networks trained using CIFAR-10. However, this dataset's 10 categories do not align with the 1000 categories in ImageNet. Of course, the inception score would be entirely unsuited for use on a dataset like MNIST or with models trained on other popular datasets like LSUN (large-scale scene understanding). Some authors have attempted to implicitly optimise using the inception score, for example, for early stopping. Finally, Barratt and Sharma (2018) note that a high inception score can be obtained by a model that overfits and memorises the ImageNet dataset.

In practice, the inception score has now been superseded by the Fréchet inception distance.

9.2.2 Fréchet Inception Distance

The *Fréchet inception distance (FID)* was proposed by Heusel et al. (2017) as an alternative to the inception score. Recall that the key aim of generative models is to train the generator such that $P_g(x) \approx P_r(x)$, but the inception score does not compare the generator distribution with the real-world distribution as defined by the training set. The Fréchet distance is a measure of similarity between two curves that can be extended to measure the distance between probability distributions. For two multivariate normal distributions, X and Y, the Fréchet distance is given by

$$d^2\left((\boldsymbol{m}_X, \boldsymbol{\Sigma}_X), (\boldsymbol{m}_Y, \boldsymbol{\Sigma}_Y)\right) = \|\boldsymbol{m}_X - \boldsymbol{m}_Y\|_2^2 + Tr\left(\boldsymbol{\Sigma}_X + \boldsymbol{\Sigma}_Y - 2\sqrt{\boldsymbol{\Sigma}_X\boldsymbol{\Sigma}_Y}\right). \tag{9.5}$$

The FID encodes several generated and real training images into features using an inception v3 network without its classification layer, and this is a 2048-dimensional vector. The image features this vector represents are assumed to be multivariate Gaussian. The Fréchet distance is then calculated on the generated and real image vectors using Equation (9.5) to give the FID value. The closer the two distributions are, the lower the FID number.

There are still several problems with FID, although arguably less than with the inception score. The metric still uses the trained inception model, which will still not be suitable for use with very different datasets, such as MNIST (Zhou et al., 2020a). However, one could argue that the features identified by the trained inception network are, to some degree, generic and hence can be applied to different datasets other than just ImageNet. FID only considers the first two moments in its comparison, and higher-order moments are ignored. A large number of samples must be used, on the order of 50,000, along with the entire training set, and all images must be scaled and passed through the inception network, which is inevitably slow. FID is statistically biased (Chong and Forsyth, 2019) and while in general it correlates well with human perception of image quality, counterexamples have been found (Liu et al., 2018b).

9.3 ENERGY-BASED MODELS (EBMs)

All energy-based models are based on a simple equivalence between probability densities and an energy function. Any probability density function $p(x)$ for $x \in \mathbb{R}^d$ can be written (LeCun et al., 2006; Bond-Taylor et al., 2021).

$$p(x) = \frac{e^{-E(x)}}{Z}, \tag{9.6}$$

where $E(x)$ is an energy function that assigns low energy to high-probability points and

$$Z = \int e^{-E(\tilde{x})} d\tilde{x} \tag{9.7}$$

is the partition function. This representation is motivated by statistical physics and the spin-glass model in particular. The first such example of an energy-based model was the *Hopfield network*. However, the Hopfield model is deterministic and not generative. The advantages of the energy-based representation are its simplicity and stability. However, there are significant disadvantages in that it is difficult to scale to high dimensions. The most difficult and often intractable problem is the partition function calculation, which requires an integral over the state space or summation for discrete models. Fortunately, in many cases, the partition function itself is not required. One problem that cannot be ignored is the requirement to use MCMC to sample the model, which is slow. Nevertheless, the use of MCMC can be limited by clever approximations.

9.3.1 Boltzmann Machines

Boltzmann machines (Hinton and Sejnowski, 1983, 1986; Ackley et al., 1985) are fully connected networks of binary neurons in two groups, visible and hidden, as illustrated in Figure 9.2. The basic structure is identical to that of the Hopfield network. While the neurons could all be visible, Boltzmann machines with hidden units are more powerful and become universal approximators of discrete probability distributions (Le Roux and Bengio, 2008).

We define the states of the neurons as $\boldsymbol{x}$, where

$$\boldsymbol{x} = (x_1, \dots, x_q) \tag{9.8}$$

$$= (\boldsymbol{v} \wedge \boldsymbol{h}), \tag{9.9}$$

where $\boldsymbol{v} = (v_1, \dots, v_m)$ is the vector of visible nodes and $\boldsymbol{h} = (h_1, \dots, h_d)$ is the vector of hidden nodes. Like a Hopfield network, nodes are connected by a weight matrix $\boldsymbol{W}$ that is symmetric and has no self-connections so that $W_{ij} = W_{ji}$ and $W_{ii} = 0$. In a Hopfield network, each neuron is set to 0 or 1 depending deterministically on whether the energy gap between two states is positive or negative. The energy of the state $\boldsymbol{x}$ is given by

$$E(\boldsymbol{x}) = -\boldsymbol{x}^T\boldsymbol{W}\boldsymbol{x} + \boldsymbol{x}^T\boldsymbol{b}, \tag{9.10}$$

where $\boldsymbol{b}$ is a vector of bias parameters. Hence, the energy gap for a state x_i is given by

$$\begin{aligned}\Delta E_i &= E_{x_i=0} - E_{x_i=1} \\ &= \boldsymbol{W}\boldsymbol{x} + \boldsymbol{b}.\end{aligned} \tag{9.11}$$

If we divide state vector $\boldsymbol{x}$ into visible and hidden parts, the energy becomes

$$E(\boldsymbol{v} \wedge \boldsymbol{h}) = -\boldsymbol{v}^T\boldsymbol{R}\boldsymbol{v} - \boldsymbol{v}^T\bar{\boldsymbol{W}}\boldsymbol{h} - \boldsymbol{h}^T\boldsymbol{S}\boldsymbol{h} - \boldsymbol{b}^T\boldsymbol{v} - \boldsymbol{c}^T\boldsymbol{h}, \tag{9.12}$$

where there are now three weight matrices, $\boldsymbol{R}$, $\bar{\boldsymbol{W}}$ and $\boldsymbol{S}$. This representation is useful as a prelude to the introduction of *restricted* Boltzmann machines.

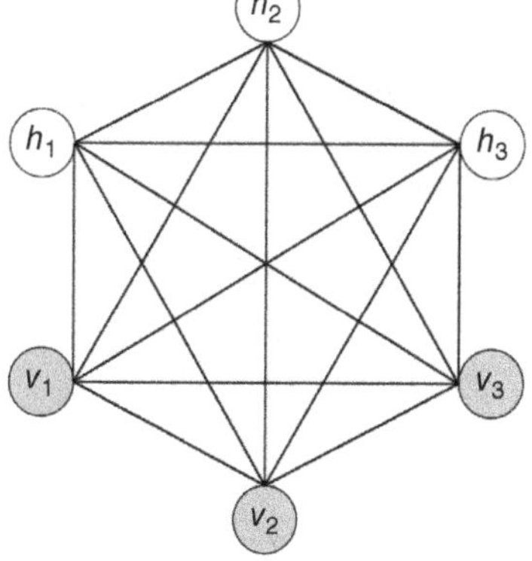

FIGURE 9.2 A Boltzmann machine with three hidden and visible units.

While the Hopfield network is deterministic, the Boltzmann machine assigns the value of state x_i probabilistically according to the Bernoulli distribution with probability (Aggarwal, 2018, p. 244)

$$\begin{aligned}P(x_i = 1|x_1, \dots x_{i-1}, x_{i+1}, \dots, x_q) \\ &= \frac{P(x_1, \dots x_{i-1}, 1, x_{i+1}, \dots, x_q)}{P(x_1, \dots x_{i-1}, 1, x_{i+1}, \dots, x_q) + P(x_1, \dots x_{i-1}, 0, x_{i+1}, \dots, x_q)} \\ &= \frac{\exp\left(-E_{x_i=1}\right)}{\exp\left(-E_{x_i=1}\right) + \exp\left(-E_{x_i=0}\right)} \\ &= \frac{1}{1+\exp\left(-\Delta E_i\right)} \\ &= \mathrm{sigmoid}(\Delta E_i).\end{aligned} \tag{9.13}$$

The probability of a state $\boldsymbol{x} = (\boldsymbol{v}, \boldsymbol{h})$ is given by

$$P(\boldsymbol{x}) = \frac{\exp\left(-E(\boldsymbol{x})\right)}{Z}, \tag{9.14}$$

and the partition function is defined by

$$Z = \sum_{\boldsymbol{x}} \exp\left(-E(\boldsymbol{x})\right) \tag{9.15}$$

$$= \sum_{\boldsymbol{v}} \sum_{\boldsymbol{h}} \exp\left(-E(\boldsymbol{v} \wedge \boldsymbol{h})\right). \tag{9.16}$$

At equilibrium, the probability distribution of the visible states $\boldsymbol{v}$ is given by

$$\begin{aligned}P(\boldsymbol{v}) &= \sum_{\boldsymbol{h}} P(\boldsymbol{v}, \boldsymbol{h}) \\ &= \frac{\sum_{\boldsymbol{h}} \exp\left(-E(\boldsymbol{v} \wedge \boldsymbol{h})\right)}{\sum_{\boldsymbol{v}} \sum_{\boldsymbol{h}} \exp\left(-E(\boldsymbol{v} \wedge \boldsymbol{h})\right)}.\end{aligned} \tag{9.17}$$

When training a Boltzmann machine, the visible units are clamped to input vectors, and the model runs until 'thermal' equilibrium is achieved. A measure of the difference between the internal state of the model at equilibrium and the model state while clamped is given by (Ackley et al., 1985, p. 154)

$$G = \sum_{\boldsymbol{v}} P_C(\boldsymbol{v}) \log \frac{P_C(\boldsymbol{v})}{P(\boldsymbol{v})}, \tag{9.18}$$

where $P_C(\boldsymbol{v})$ is the probability of the state of the visible units when clamped. This criterion should be minimised by adjusting the weight matrix and bias vector, which is done using gradient descent. An update rule requires the gradient of G with respect to the components of the weight matrix and bias vector. In Equation (9.18), only $P(\boldsymbol{v})$ is sensitive to the weight matrix and bias vector, and hence minimising G is equivalent to maximising the log-likelihood $\log P(\boldsymbol{v})$. Weight update expressions can be derived by differentiating G with respect to the weight matrix and bias vector components. To begin, differentiate the energy function[1]

$$\frac{\partial E(\boldsymbol{v} \wedge \boldsymbol{h})}{\partial W_{ij}} = x_i x_j, \tag{9.19}$$

and hence

$$\frac{\partial \exp\left(-E(\boldsymbol{v} \wedge \boldsymbol{h})\right)}{\partial W_{ij}} = x_i x_j \exp\left(-E(\boldsymbol{v} \wedge \boldsymbol{h})\right). \tag{9.20}$$

[1]A similar expression holds for the bias vector elements.

Differentiating $P(v)$ gives

$$
\begin{aligned}
\frac{\partial P(v)}{\partial W_{ij}} &= \frac{\sum_h x_i x_j \exp\left(-E(v \wedge h)\right)}{Z} - \frac{P(v)\left(\sum_{v'} \sum_{h'} \exp\left(-E(v' \wedge h')\right) x'_i x'_j\right)}{Z} \\
&= \left[\sum_h P(v \wedge h) x_i x_j - P(v) \sum_{v'} \sum_{h'} P(v' \wedge h') x'_i x'_j\right],
\end{aligned}
\tag{9.21}
$$

and hence

$$
\frac{\partial G}{\partial W_{ij}} = -\sum_v \frac{P_C(v)}{P(v)} \left[\sum_h P(v \wedge h) x_i x_j - P(v) \sum_{v'} \sum_{h'} P(v' \wedge h') x'_i x'_j\right]. \tag{9.22}
$$

By definition, the following relations must hold:

$$
P_C(v \wedge h) = P_C(h|v) P_C(v), \tag{9.23}
$$

$$
P(v \wedge h) = P(h|v) P(v). \tag{9.24}
$$

In addition, in equilibrium, the conditional distribution of hidden states must be the same whether or not the input is clamped, and so

$$
P(h|v) = P_C(h|v). \tag{9.25}
$$

Hence,

$$
P(v \wedge h) \frac{P_C(v)}{P(v)} = P_C(v \wedge h). \tag{9.26}
$$

Finally, noting that $\sum_v P(v) = 1$ gives

$$
\begin{aligned}
\frac{\partial G}{\partial W_{ij}} &= -\left[\sum_v \sum_h P_C(v \wedge h) x_i x_j - \sum_{v'} \sum_{h'} P(v \wedge h) x'_i x'_j\right] \\
&= -\left[\mathbb{E}_{\text{data}}[x_i x_j] - \mathbb{E}_{\text{model}}[x_i x_j]\right].
\end{aligned}
\tag{9.27}
$$

So, the weight and bias update equations are

$$
\Delta W_{ij} = \alpha \left[\mathbb{E}_{\text{data}}[x_i x_j] - \mathbb{E}_{\text{model}}[x_i x_j]\right], \tag{9.28}
$$

$$
\Delta b_i = \alpha \left[\mathbb{E}_{\text{data}}[x_i] - \mathbb{E}_{\text{model}}[x_i]\right]. \tag{9.29}
$$

The *data* and *model* terms require two distinct sampling types. For the data term, a randomly selected training vector clamps the input. Hidden units initialise with random values from a Bernoulli distribution where $p = 1/2$. Probabilities regenerate for each state, undergo resampling and iterate until reaching equilibrium. The final state yields the expectation under the data distribution across multiple training vectors. The model term involves unrestricted sampling with an unclamped visible vector. All states initialise randomly with $p = 1/2$, then undergo iterative sampling until equilibrium. The final states provide the model expectation. Algorithm 9.1 outlines this process.

Boltzmann machines have slow inference and training because of the large number of samples required during the time taken for the network to reach equilibrium. Because the network is fully connected, the size of the weight matrices proliferates with the number of hidden units. Hence, Boltzmann machines are no longer used in practice. A more practical alternative is the restricted Boltzmann machine, which will be discussed next.

9.3.2 Restricted Boltzmann Machines (RBMs)

RBMs were introduced under the name *harmonium* by Smolensky (1986). They are simplified versions of Boltzmann machines in which no interconnections exist between the visible and hidden units, forming two distinct layers as illustrated in Figure 9.3. Hence, the structure closely resembles the encoder of an

Algorithm 9.1: Boltzmann Machine Training

Input: Training mini-batch S
Input: Learning rate α
for $v \in S$ **do**
  $v^{(0)} \leftarrow v$;
  while *not in equilibrium* **do**
    $P(h^{(0)}|v^{(0)}) \leftarrow 0.5$ **for** $j = 1, \ldots, d$ **do**
      Sample Bernoulli random variable $h_j^{(t)} \sim P\left(h_j^{(t-1)}|v^{(t)}\right)$
$E_{\text{data}} \leftarrow \mathbb{E}[x^T x]$;
$f_{\text{data}} \leftarrow \mathbb{E}[x^T]$;
while *not in equilibrium* **do**
  $P(h^{(0)}|v^{(0)}) \leftarrow 0.5$;
  $P(v^{(0)}|h^{(0)}) \leftarrow 0.5$;
  for $j = 1, \ldots, d$ **do**
    Sample Bernoulli random variable $h_j^{(t)} \sim P\left(h_j^{(t-1)}|v^{(t)}\right)$;
  for $i = 1, \ldots, m$ **do**
    Sample Bernoulli random variable $v_i^{(t+1)} \sim P\left(v_i^{(t)}|h^{(t)}\right)$;
$E_{\text{model}} \leftarrow \mathbb{E}[x^T x]$;
$f_{\text{model}} \leftarrow \mathbb{E}[x^T]$;
$W \leftarrow W + \alpha * [E_{\text{data}} - E_{\text{model}}]$;
$b \leftarrow b + \alpha * [f_{\text{data}} - f_{\text{model}}]$;
Output: Weights W, biases b

autoencoder. Unlike an autoencoder, the activation of the units remains a random variable with a Bernoulli distribution. The energy equation, Equation (9.12), has $R = 0$ and $S = 0$, giving

$$E(v, h) = -v^T \bar{W} h - b^T v - c^T h. \tag{9.30}$$

The weight matrix $\bar{W}$ is not symmetric. The partition function Z remains intractable (Long and Servedio, 2010) and hence so does $P(v)$, however the conditional probabilities are now considerably simplified (Goodfellow et al., 2016),

$$P(h_j = 1|v) = \text{sigmoid}\left(c_j + \sum_i \bar{W}_{ij} v_i\right), \tag{9.31}$$

$$P(v_i = 1|h) = \text{sigmoid}\left(b_i + \sum_j \bar{W}_{ij} h_j\right). \tag{9.32}$$

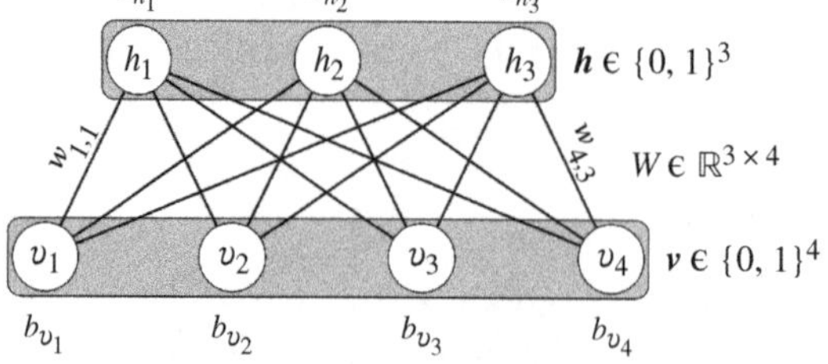

FIGURE 9.3 A restricted Boltzmann machine. *Source*: MartinThoma, Wikimedia Commons, transformed to greyscale.

In particular, if the visible state is fixed, it is possible to calculate the probabilities of the hidden states in a single step without MCMC sampling.

The approach to training an RBM follows that described above for Boltzmann machines, and the weight and bias updates are almost identical to Equations (9.28) and (9.29). Rewriting these in terms of $\bar{\boldsymbol{W}}$, $\boldsymbol{b}$ and $\boldsymbol{c}$ gives

$$\Delta \bar{W}_{ij} = \alpha[\mathbb{E}_{\text{data}}[v_i h_j] - \mathbb{E}_{\text{model}}[v_i h_j]], \tag{9.33}$$

$$\Delta b_i = \alpha\left[\mathbb{E}_{\text{data}}[v_i] - \mathbb{E}_{\text{model}}[v_i]\right], \tag{9.34}$$

$$\Delta c_i = \alpha\left[\mathbb{E}_{\text{data}}[h_i] - \mathbb{E}_{\text{model}}[h_i]\right]. \tag{9.35}$$

As with the Boltzmann machine, we need to estimate the correlation of state vectors under data and model distributions, and given the lack of connections within the two layers, this resolves the correlation of hidden and visible state vectors. It is possible to follow the same Algorithm 9.1 as described for the Boltzmann machine, except that in the first or positive phase of training to estimate the expectations under the data distribution, MCMC sampling is not needed as the conditional probability can be calculated directly using Equation (9.31). The second or negative phase of training to estimate expectations under the model distribution still requires MCMC sampling, which is slow.

The contrastive divergence algorithm presents a faster alternative (Hinton, 2000, 2010), which initialises the MCMC sampling with samples from the data distribution instead of randomly. The algorithm then performs k sampling steps, after which the expectation under the model distribution is calculated. In the early training phases, only one step of contrastive divergence is needed; later in training, the number of steps should be increased, perhaps to a maximum of 20 (Hinton, 2010; Aggarwal, 2018). Contrastive divergence introduces a bias and does not converge to the true maximum likelihood estimator. However, the bias is small (Carreira-Perpiñán and Hinton, 2005). k-Step contrastive divergence is presented in Algorithm 9.2.

Algorithm 9.2: k-Step Contrastive Divergence

Input: Training mini-batch S
Input: Learning rate α
for $\boldsymbol{v} \in S$ **do**
  $\boldsymbol{v}_{(0)} \leftarrow \boldsymbol{v}$;
  $P\left(\boldsymbol{h}_{(0)} | \boldsymbol{v}_{(0)}\right) \leftarrow sigmoid\left(c_j + \sum_i \bar{W}_{ij} v_i\right)$;
  for $t = 0, \ldots, k-1$ **do**
    $P\left(\boldsymbol{v}_{(0)} | \boldsymbol{h}_{(0)}\right) \leftarrow sigmoid\left(b_i + \sum_j \bar{W}_{ij} h_j\right)$;
    for $j = 1, \ldots, d$ **do**
      Sample Bernoulli random variable $h^j_{(t)} \sim P\left(h^j_{(t-1)} | \boldsymbol{v}_{(t)}\right)$;
    for $i = 1, \ldots, m$ **do**
      Sample Bernoulli random variable $v^i_{(t+1)} \sim P\left(v^i_{(t)} | \boldsymbol{h}_{(t)}\right)$;
$\boldsymbol{E}_{\text{data}} \leftarrow \mathbb{E}[\boldsymbol{v}^T_{(0)} \boldsymbol{h}_{(0)}]$;
$\boldsymbol{f}_{\text{data}} \leftarrow \mathbb{E}[\boldsymbol{v}^T_{(0)}]$;
$\boldsymbol{g}_{\text{data}} \leftarrow \mathbb{E}[\boldsymbol{h}^T_{(0)}]$;
$\boldsymbol{E}_{\text{model}} \leftarrow \mathbb{E}[\boldsymbol{v}^T_{(k)} \boldsymbol{h}_{(k)}]$;
$\boldsymbol{f}_{\text{model}} \leftarrow \mathbb{E}[\boldsymbol{v}^T_{(k)}]$;
$\boldsymbol{g}_{\text{model}} \leftarrow \mathbb{E}[\boldsymbol{h}^T_{(k)}]$;
$\bar{\boldsymbol{W}} \leftarrow \bar{\boldsymbol{W}} + \alpha * \left[\boldsymbol{E}_{\text{data}} - \boldsymbol{E}_{\text{model}}\right]$;
$\boldsymbol{b} \leftarrow \boldsymbol{b} + \alpha * \left[\boldsymbol{f}_{\text{data}} - \boldsymbol{f}_{\text{model}}\right]$;
$\boldsymbol{c} \leftarrow \boldsymbol{c} + \alpha * \left[\boldsymbol{g}_{\text{data}} - \boldsymbol{g}_{\text{model}}\right]$;
Output: Weights $\boldsymbol{W}$, biases $\boldsymbol{b}$ and $\boldsymbol{c}$

RBMs serve generative purposes, as demonstrated in Example 9.2 using MNIST and as a market data generator, detailed in Kondratyev and Schwarz (2020) and Chapter 18. Post-training, a random input vector with Bernoulli-distributed elements initiates the generation process. The model undergoes numerous MCMC sampling cycles to achieve 'thermal' equilibrium before reading the output vector. This process typically requires around 10^4 iterations.

Specific applications of RBMs include collaborative filtering in recommender systems (see Salakhutdinov et al., 2007; Aggarwal, 2018). RBMs also function as components in deep belief nets and deep Boltzmann machine stacks, described in Sections 9.3.3 and 9.3.4. Conventional neural networks have incorporated RBMs by transferring weights and using sigmoid activation (Aggarwal, 2018, pp. 264–268). Such stacks employed greedy pre-training of RBMs, followed by backpropagation for weight fine-tuning. This method enabled deep network construction before solving vanishing and exploding gradient problems. However, with these issues resolved, pre-trained RBM-based deep network construction has fallen out of use.

EXAMPLE 9.2: RBM TRAINED WITH MNIST

This example trains an RBM using the classic MNIST numbers dataset, and the code can be found in the Jupyter Notebook `RBM.ipynb`. First, RBM models are not included as a standard layer type in most deep learning packages, so they must be built using basic components. In this case, a Python RBM class was written using PyTorch. The weight matrix $\boldsymbol{W}$ and the two bias vectors $\boldsymbol{b}$ and $\boldsymbol{c}$ were created using PyTorch tensors. The weight matrix was initialised using samples drawn from the normal distribution with a mean of 0.0 and standard deviation of 0.01.

```
class BernoulliRBM(nn.Module):
    def __init__(self, visible_units, hidden_units, k=1, learning_rate=1e-3,
                 device=device):
        super(BernoulliRBM, self).__init__()
        self.visible_units = visible_units
        self.hidden_units = hidden_units
        self.k = k
        self.learning_rate = learning_rate
        self.device = device

        self.W = nn.Parameter(torch.randn(visible_units, hidden_units,
                              device=self.device) * 0.01, requires_grad=True)
        self.b_v = nn.Parameter(torch.zeros(visible_units,
                                device=self.device),
                                requires_grad=True)
        self.b_h = nn.Parameter(torch.zeros(hidden_units,
                                device=self.device),
                                requires_grad=True)
```

A sampling function was created to calculate the conditional probabilities $P(\boldsymbol{h}|\boldsymbol{v})$ and $P(\boldsymbol{v}|\boldsymbol{h})$.

```
def _sample(self, probs):
     return F.relu(torch.sign(probs - torch.rand_like(probs)))
```

The contrastive divergence is then implemented as follows:

```
def contrastive_divergence(self, input_data):
    v_0 = input_data.to(self.device)
    h_0_probs = torch.sigmoid(torch.matmul(v_0, self.W) + self.b_h)
```

```
    h_0 = self._sample(h_0_probs)

    for _ in range(self.k):
        v_k_probs = torch.sigmoid(torch.matmul(h_0, self.W.t()) + self.b_v)
        v_k = self._sample(v_k_probs)
        h_k_probs = torch.sigmoid(torch.matmul(v_k, self.W) + self.b_h)
        h_k = self._sample(h_k_probs)

    return v_0, h_0_probs, v_k, h_k_probs
```

The `train_step` function runs one step, calling the contrastive divergence function and then updating the weights and bias vectors.

```
def train_step(self, input_data):
    v_0, h_0_probs, v_k, h_k_probs = self.contrastive_divergence(input_data)
    positive_grad = torch.matmul(v_0.t(), h_0_probs)
    negative_grad = torch.matmul(v_k.t(), h_k_probs)

    self.W.data += self.learning_rate * \
                   (positive_grad - negative_grad) / input_data.shape[0]
    self.b_v.data += self.learning_rate * torch.mean(v_0 - v_k, dim=0)
    self.b_h.data += self.learning_rate * torch.mean(h_0_probs - h_k_probs,
                                                     dim=0)
```

Then, the training loop itself is implemented by the `train` function that implements batching with shuffling and trains the RBM through the specified number of epochs.

```
def train(self, train_tensor, batch_size=100, epochs=10):
    num_samples = train_tensor.shape[0]
    num_batches = math.ceil(num_samples / batch_size)

    tqdm_epoch = trange(epochs)
    for epoch in tqdm_epoch:
        # Shuffle the data at the beginning of each epoch
        indices = torch.randperm(num_samples)
        train_tensor_shuffled = train_tensor[indices]

        for batch_idx in range(num_batches):
            start_idx = batch_idx * batch_size
            end_idx = min(start_idx + batch_size, num_samples)
            batch = train_tensor_shuffled[start_idx:end_idx]
            self.train_step(batch)
        tqdm_epoch.set_description(f"Epoch: {epoch + 1}/{epochs}")
```

Finally, a prediction function provides the ability to reconstruct the input and generate new images. This function runs `steps` of sampling before returning the state of the visible vector.

```
def predict(self, mini_batch, steps):
    v_k = mini_batch.to(self.device)
    for k in range(steps):
```

(*Continued*)

(*Continued*)

```
        h_k_probs = torch.sigmoid(torch.matmul(v_k, self.W) + self.b_h)
        h_k = self._sample(h_k_probs)
        v_k_probs = torch.sigmoid(torch.matmul(h_k, self.W.t()) + self.b_v)
        v_k = self._sample(v_k_probs)
    return v_k.detach().cpu().numpy()
```

MNIST consists of greyscale images, while the Bernoulli RBM uses digital units. Hence, before training, the dataset was converted to a purely black (0.0) and white (1.0) representation. The input vector size was of length $28^2 = 784$, while the hidden layer contained 128 units. The model was trained through 100,000 epochs with a learning rate of 0.01 and $k = 10$. The first test was to check the reconstruction of input, and so 40 number images from the test set were input to the model. Given the input in Figure 9.4, the RBM produced the output in Figure 9.5, which is slightly noisy but reproduces the input accurately. The final step is to use the trained model to generate new images, and this is done by presenting 40 random vectors to the model in turn and allowing the model to run for 10^4 iterations to reach equilibrium before sampling the output. The generated images are shown in Figure 9.6. Some of the images are plausible as numbers, but others are noisy and contain elements of more than one numeral.

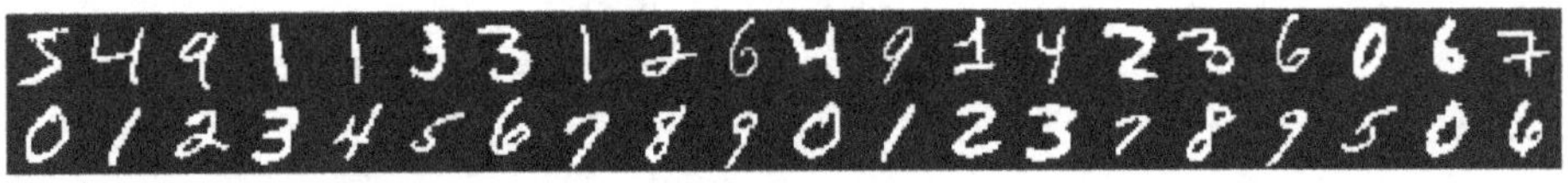

FIGURE 9.4 Forty example MNIST numbers from the test set input to the trained RBM model.

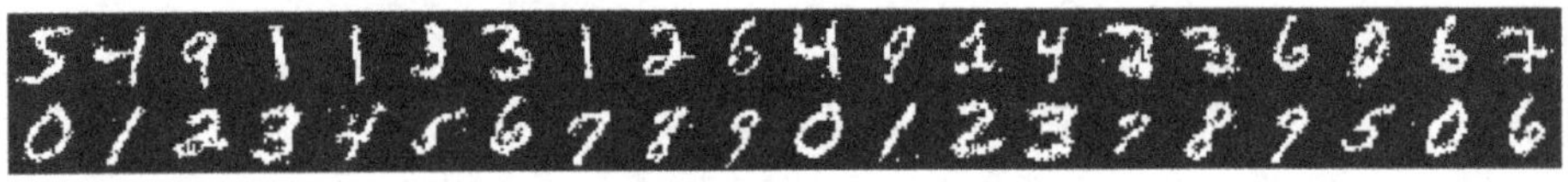

FIGURE 9.5 Forty example MNIST numbers from the test set reconstructed by the trained RBM model.

FIGURE 9.6 Forty example MNIST-style numbers generated by the trained RBM model.

9.3.3 Deep Belief Networks (DBNs)

The development of deep belief networks (DBNs) (Hinton and Salakhutdinov, 2006; Hinton, 2007b) heralded the start of the current era of *deep learning*. Before DBNs, *support vector machines* dominated the research landscape (Goodfellow et al., 2016). DBNs consist of a stack of RBMs that are trained greedily layer by layer, and, like RBMs, there are no intra-layer connections (Figure 9.7). The training process is sequential, with the top RBM trained in the standard setting using the data as input. Subsequent RBM layers are then trained using the features of the previous hidden layer as input (Hinton, 2007a). In general, no attempt is made to fine-tune the whole network after each layer is trained, but this is possible using the *wake–sleep* algorithm (see Hinton, 2007a, for details).

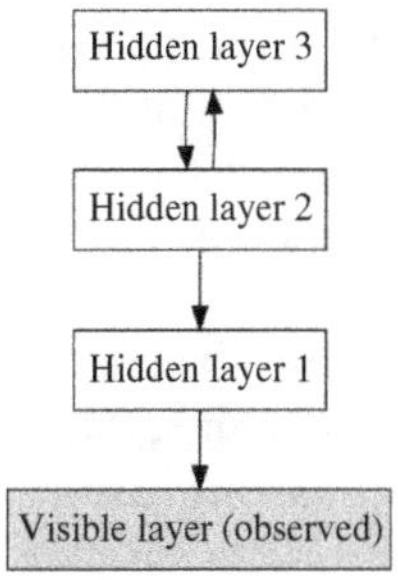

FIGURE 9.7 Deep belief network. *Source*: Qwertyus, Wikimedia Commons.

DBNs can be used as a generative model or in a supervised context. The two innermost hidden layers have undirected connections, while the others are all directed towards the input. After multiple steps of MCMC sampling in the two deepest hidden layers, a single pass through the remaining layers to the visible units produces the output (Hinton, 2007a; Goodfellow et al., 2016).

DBNs found application to a variety of problems, including a variety of classification tasks, NLP (Sarikaya et al., 2014), generating facial expressions (Susskind et al., 2008), electroencephalography (Movahedi et al., 2018) and drug discovery (Fitriawan et al., 2016). DBNs have now fallen out of favour because of the training cost and the advent of more effective alternative deep learning techniques.

9.3.4 Deep Boltzmann Machines

A *deep Boltzmann machine* (Salakhutdinov and Hinton, 2009) has the same basic structure as a DBN but has bidirectional connections between all layers. The activations are stochastic and drawn from a Bernoulli distribution, similar to the fully connected and restricted Boltzmann machines. Consider a deep Boltzmann machine with two hidden layers, $h^{(1)}$ and $h^{(2)}$. The joint probability is given by

$$p(v, h^{(1)}, h^{(2)}) = \frac{e^{-E(v,h^{(1)},h^{(2)},\theta)}}{Z(\theta)}, \tag{9.36}$$

where the energy function becomes

$$E(v, h^{(1)}, h^{(2)}, \theta) = -v^T W^{(1)} h^{(1)} - {h^{(1)}}^T W^{(2)} h^{(2)}. \tag{9.37}$$

The weights $W^{(1)}$ connect the visible layer and the first hidden layer, while $W^{(2)}$ connects the two hidden layers.[2] The deep Boltzmann machine can be rearranged into a bipartite structure with units from even layers on one side and odd on the other (Srihari, 2020a), allowing the same equations defined for the RBM to be used. The activation probabilities are given by

$$P(v_i = 1 | h) = \text{sigmoid}\left(\sum_j W_{ij}^{(1)} h_j\right), \tag{9.38}$$

$$P(h_j^{(1)} = 1 | v, h^{(2)}) = \text{sigmoid}\left(\sum_i W_{ij}^{(1)} v_i + \sum_l W_{lj}^{(2)} h_l^{(2)}\right), \tag{9.39}$$

$$P(h_j^{(2)} = 1 | h^{(2)}) = \text{sigmoid}\left(\sum_i W_{ij}^{(2)} h_i^{(2)}\right). \tag{9.40}$$

The classic approach to training a deep Boltzmann machine is to use greedy layerwise pre-training, as with the DBN, with each layer treated as an RBM and trained separately. Unlike the DBN, the layers of each RBM cannot be directly copied to the corresponding layer of the deep Boltzmann machine (Salakhutdinov and Hinton, 2009; Goodfellow et al., 2016). For the intermediate layers in the model, the weights must be halved as when training,

[2]Note that the bias terms have been included in the weight matrix for simplicity of expression.

they only have input in a single direction, while in the deep Boltzmann machine, they will input from two directions. For the top layer, the input must be doubled with tied weights used for both inputs, while to train the bottom layer, the layer is duplicated, and tied weights are used again for each half. Some joint training techniques have been developed but are not competitive with backpropagation as used with neural networks (see Goodfellow et al., 2016, pp. 662–667, for details).

For DBNs, sampling is straightforward and, as described in the previous section, only involves MCMC sampling over the top two layers. For the deep Boltzmann machine, MCMC sampling is required across all layers and is slower.

9.3.5 Deep Energy-Based Models

Recall Equation (9.6), where $E(\boldsymbol{x})$ is the energy function and

$$E_\theta(\boldsymbol{x}) : \mathbb{R}^d \rightarrow \mathbb{R}, \tag{9.41}$$

where d is the dimension of x. An energy-based model can be parameterised by any function that takes a vector input and returns a scalar. *Deep energy-based models* use a deep neural network for this purpose (Grathwohl et al., 2020; Bond-Taylor et al., 2021).

The key question is how such models should be trained. The approach is very similar to the approach used with Boltzmann machines. We want the energy function to model the data distribution $p_{\text{data}}(\boldsymbol{x})$ and hence seek the maximum likelihood solution (Du and Mordatch, 2019), and this is equivalent to minimising the negative log-likelihood of the model probability distribution,

$$\mathcal{L}(\theta) = \mathbb{E}_{\text{data}}\left[-\log p_{\text{model}}(\boldsymbol{x})\right], \tag{9.42}$$

where, from Equation (9.6),

$$-\log p_{\text{model}}(\boldsymbol{x}) = E_\theta(\boldsymbol{x}) - \log Z(\theta). \tag{9.43}$$

The gradient of $\mathcal{L}(\theta)$ in Equation (9.42) is needed to perform weight updates in the usual way, and this is given by (Ackley et al., 1985; Turner, 2005)

$$\nabla_\theta \mathcal{L}(\theta) = \mathbb{E}_{\text{data}}\left[\nabla_\theta E_\theta(\boldsymbol{x}^+)\right] - \mathbb{E}_{\text{model}}\left[\nabla_\theta E_\theta(\boldsymbol{x}^-)\right], \tag{9.44}$$

which is the equivalent of Equation (9.27). As in the Boltzmann machine case, the second term containing the negative phase expectation requires slow MCMC sampling. Recent work on deep energy-based models (Xie et al., 2016; Du and Mordatch, 2019; Nijkamp et al., 2019a,b; Grathwohl et al., 2020) has applied *stochastic gradient Langevin dynamics* to this problem and succeeded in generating image results that were competitive with GANs. GANs have now largely been superseded by diffusion models.

9.3.5.1 Stochastic Gradient Langevin Dynamics (SGLD) Stochastic gradient Langevin dynamics (SGLD) was first introduced by Welling and Teh (2011) and combined stochastic optimisation and Langevin dynamics. Given a parameter vector $\boldsymbol{\theta}$ with prior distribution $p(\boldsymbol{\theta})$, the probability of a given data item x, given parameters $\boldsymbol{\theta}$, is $p(x|\boldsymbol{\theta})$. Stochastic optimisation seeks to find the maximum a posteriori (MAP) parameters $\boldsymbol{\theta}^*$ and do so via an iterative technique with parameter updates

$$\Delta\boldsymbol{\theta}_t = \frac{\epsilon_t}{2}\left(\nabla \log p(\boldsymbol{\theta}_t) + \frac{N}{n}\sum_{i=1}^{N} \nabla \log p(x_{ti}|\boldsymbol{\theta}_t)\right), \tag{9.45}$$

where N is the total number of data items $X = \{x_i\}_i = 1^N$, n is the number of data items in a mini-batch and ϵ_t is a sequence of step sizes. The mini-batch gradient is used to approximate the gradient over the full dataset. The step sizes must be constrained to ensure convergence,

$$\sum_{t=1}^{\infty} \epsilon_t = \infty, \tag{9.46}$$

$$\sum_{t=1}^{\infty} \epsilon_t^2 < \infty, \tag{9.47}$$

and a typical choice is $\epsilon = a(b+t)^{-\gamma}$ with $\gamma \in (0.5, 1]$.

Langevin dynamics are related to the *Langevin Monte Carlo* algorithm, which can be considered as a special case of the Metropolis–Hastings algorithm with a proposal distribution (Snell, 2017)

$$Q(\boldsymbol{x}'|\boldsymbol{x}) = \mathcal{N}\left(x + \frac{1}{2}\sigma^2 \nabla \log p(x), \sigma^2 \boldsymbol{I}\right). \tag{9.48}$$

Langevin can also be considered a special case of *Hamiltonian Monte Carlo* (Neal, 2011) and Langevin dynamics are also known in quantum field theory (Kennedy, 1990). The weight update under Langevin dynamics has the form

$$\begin{aligned} \Delta\theta_t &= \frac{\epsilon}{2}\left(\nabla \log p(\theta_t) + \sum_{i=1}^{N} \nabla \log p(x_{ti}|\theta_t)\right) + \eta_t, \\ \eta_t &\sim \mathcal{N}(0, \epsilon), \end{aligned} \tag{9.49}$$

where the step size and variance of the noise term are balanced to match the variance of the posterior. The Metropolis–Hastings rejection rate and discretisation error decrease as the step size is reduced.

Welling and Teh (2011) combined the two similar updates in Equations (9.45) and (9.49) to give the SGLD algorithm with an update

$$\begin{aligned} \Delta\theta_t &= \frac{\epsilon_t}{2}\left(\nabla \log p(\theta_t) + \frac{N}{n}\sum_{i=1}^{N} \nabla \log p(x_{ti}|\theta_t)\right) + \eta_t. \\ \eta_t &\sim \mathcal{N}(0, \epsilon_t). \end{aligned} \tag{9.50}$$

The steps ϵ_t satisfy Equations (9.46) and (9.47) and hence decline to zero asymptotically. Like stochastic optimisation, the stochastic element of the gradient from using mini-batches is averaged out, and the rejection rates go to zero; hence, the acceptance–rejection step can be ignored. Welling and Teh (2011) suggest that SGLD can be used as a general-purpose algorithm that behaves like SGD in the initial phase as the noise from the stochastic gradient will dominate and then transition smoothly to approximating Langevin dynamics.

9.3.5.2 SGLD Models As noted earlier, Du and Mordatch (2019) and Nijkamp et al. (2019a,b) propose deep EBMs for image generation using the SGLD algorithm. In both cases, the SGLD update equation is given by

$$\begin{aligned} \boldsymbol{x}^{k+1} &= \boldsymbol{x}^k - \lambda \nabla_x E_\theta(\boldsymbol{x}^k) + \epsilon^{k+1}, \\ \epsilon^{k+1} &\sim \mathcal{N}(0, \sigma \boldsymbol{I}). \end{aligned} \tag{9.51}$$

As discussed above, the energy function E_θ is parameterised using a deep neural network, and gradients are obtained by backpropagation. Equation (9.51) defines a distribution $\boldsymbol{x}^K \sim q_\theta$ that in the limit $K \to \infty, \lambda \to 0$ tends to p_θ as defined by Equation (9.6).

The two models differ slightly in the algorithms used. In particular, Du and Mordatch (2019) note that there is no restriction on the choice of $\boldsymbol{x}^0$ but that the choice does make a difference to the mixing times observed. Hence, they use a *persistent contrastive divergence* approach and maintain persistent Markov chains, and this is achieved through the use of a replay buffer, B, which stores past images and is used to initialise the chains 95% of the time, with the remaining 5% initialised randomly. Nijkamp et al. (2019a,b), in contrast, always initialise the Markov chains randomly, giving them slower performance. Du and Mordatch (2019) also add spectral normalisation to all layers of the model[3] and L_2 regularisation of the energy magnitudes for both positive and negative samples. Algorithm 9.3 illustrates the approach of Du and Mordatch (2019).

[3]See Section 9.5.2.3 for a description of spectral normalisation.

Algorithm 9.3: Stochastic Gradient Langevin Dynamics

Input: Training data D, distribution $p_D(x)$, SGLD step size λ, SGLD steps K, SGLD noise σ
B $\leftarrow \emptyset$;
while *not converged* **do**
  $x_i^+ \sim p_D$;
  $x_i^0 \sim B$ (95% probability) $\mathcal{U}$ otherwise;
  Generate sample from q_θ using Langevin dynamics;
  for $k = 0$ *to* $K - 1$ **do**
    $x^{k+1} = x^k - \lambda \nabla_x E_\theta(x^k) + \epsilon^{k+1}\ \epsilon^{k+1} \sim \mathcal{N}(0, \sigma I)$;
  $x_i^- \leftarrow x^K$;
  Optimise objective $J = \alpha J_{L_2} + J_{CD}$ where $J_{L_2} = E_\theta(x_i^+)^2 + E_\theta(x_i^-)^2$;
  $J_{CD} = E_\theta(x_i^+) - E_\theta(x_i^-)$;
  $\Delta\theta \leftarrow \nabla_\theta \frac{1}{N} \sum_i \alpha \left(E_\theta(x_i^+)^2 + E_\theta(x_i^-)^2\right) + E_\theta(x_i^+) - E_\theta(x_i^-)$;
  Update θ using the Adam optimiser;
  $B \leftarrow B \cup x_i$;
Output: Parameters θ

EXAMPLE 9.3: DEEP EBM TRAINED WITH SGLD

This example illustrates an SGLD model using the MNIST, CIFAR-10 and galaxies datasets. The code is based on Lippe (2021) and illustrates the approach adopted by both Du and Mordatch (2019) and Nijkamp et al. (2019a,b). The MNIST example can be found in the Jupyter Notebook `Stochastic Gradient Langevin Dynamics with MNIST.ipynb`, with the CIFAR-10 and a galaxies example similarly named.

Two models were trained through 60 epochs, one using Du and Mordatch (2019) with 60 steps of SGLD during training and resampling from a buffer of previous images 95% of the time, and the second adopting Nijkamp et al. (2019a,b) and using 100 steps of SGLD with purely random initialisation. The training losses from both models are illustrated in Figures 9.8 and 9.9, respectively. It is clear that the approach of Du and Mordatch (2019) leads to far lower oscillations in the contrastive divergence loss than that seen with Nijkamp et al. (2019a,b).

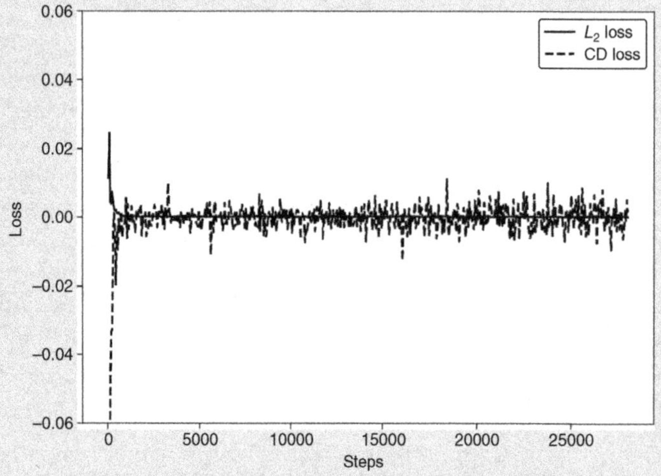

FIGURE 9.8 Du and Mordatch (2019). Model L_2 regularisation and contrastive divergence loss.

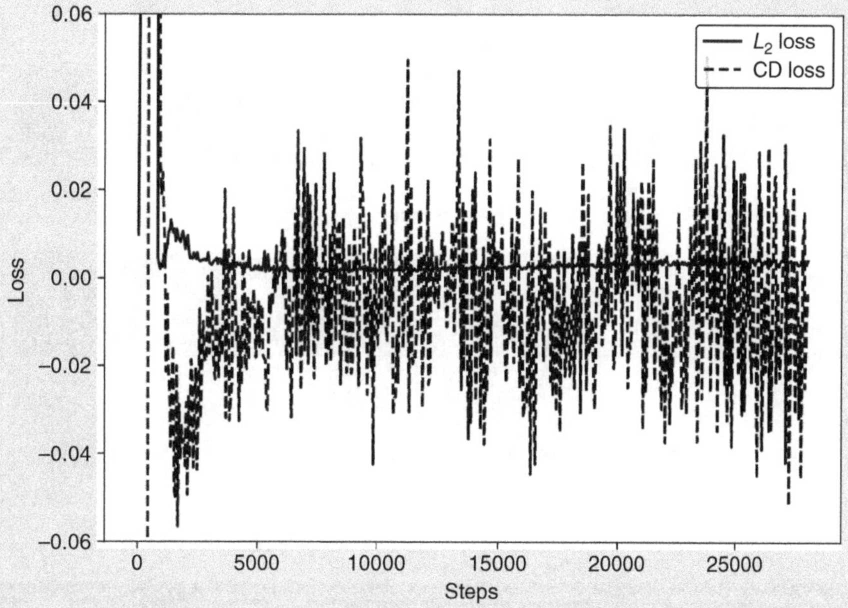

FIGURE 9.9 Nijkamp et al. (2019a,b). Model L_2 regularisation and contrastive divergence loss.

Sample images were generated from both models after training, using 256 steps of SGLD and initialised from random values. Figures 9.10 and 9.11 each show two images from Du and Mordatch (2019) and Nijkamp et al. (2019a,b), respectively, with the intermediate state shown every 32 steps. The images from Du and Mordatch (2019) perhaps settle quicker to a white number on a black background than Nijkamp et al. (2019a,b), but the second of the two images continues to show evolution to 256 steps. Nijkamp et al. (2019a,b), in contrast, has more noise after 32 steps but has settled to close the end state after 128 steps. Of course, these are only two examples from the model and may not be entirely representative. Two groups of eight final images from each model are shown in Figures 9.12 and 9.13, respectively, and here the images produced by the Nijkamp et al. (2019a,b) model appear superior to those generated by Du and Mordatch (2019).

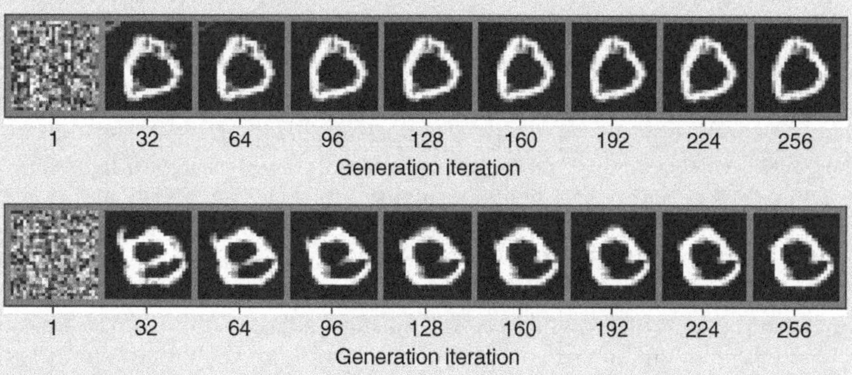

FIGURE 9.10 Two different samples drawn from the trained Du and Mordatch (2019) EBM and iterated through 256 steps of SGLD.

(Continued)

(*Continued*)

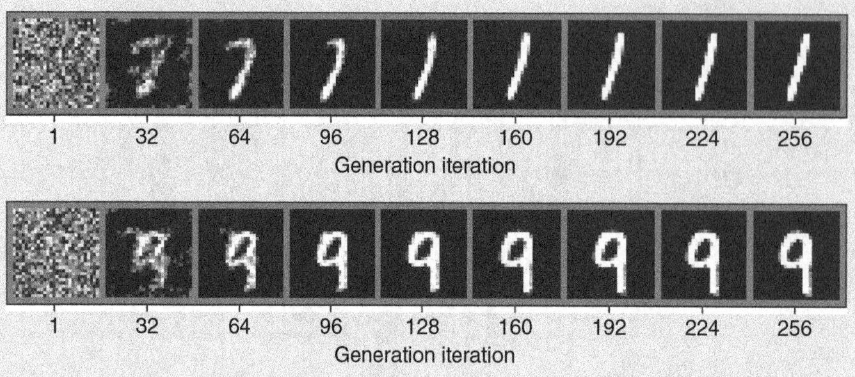

FIGURE 9.11 Two different samples drawn from the trained Nijkamp et al. (2019a,b) EBM and iterated through 256 steps of SGLD.

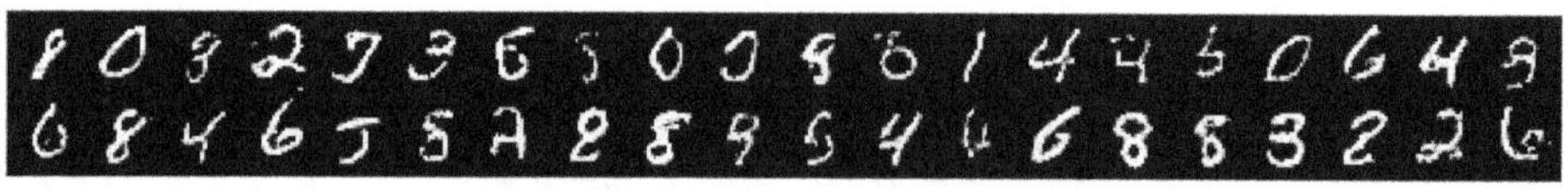

FIGURE 9.12 Forty simulated images from the Du and Mordatch (2019) model.

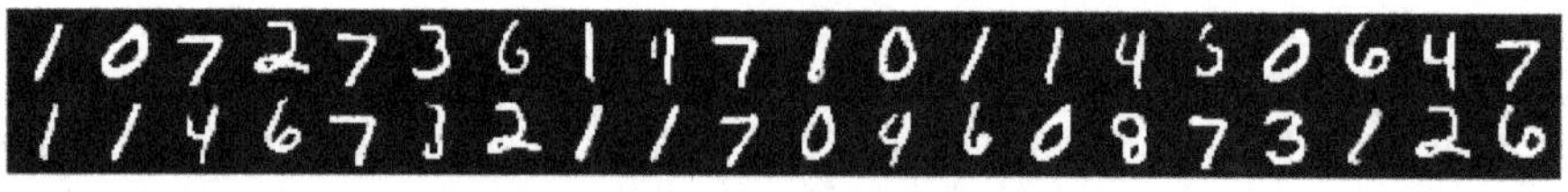

FIGURE 9.13 Forty simulated images from the Nijkamp et al. (2019a,b) model.

A more challenging example is to train a model to generate colour images using the CIFAR-10 dataset. CIFAR-10 is a challenging dataset for generative models to learn as it has 10 varied categories and only 50,000 training examples. Nevertheless, it does have small image sizes and can be tackled with moderate hardware.

The neural network model used above for MNIST does not have sufficient learning capacity to be used with CIFAR-10, and hence a larger ResNet model (see Section 6.7.5) was used with spectral normalisation (see Section 9.5.2.3) used in place of the original batch normalisation. The deep energy model was then formed of six ResNet blocks and a final linear layer. Otherwise, the code remained essentially unchanged from that used for MNIST. To evaluate the performance using inception score and Fréchet inception distance, a large batch of 32,768 images was output after every 50 epochs of training, and a second callback function was used to perform this step. Given the use of Langevin sampling during training and inference, training and sampling were prolonged. The typical execution time of an epoch was around 22 minutes on an Nvidia RTX 3060, while the generation of 32,768 sample images took around 73 minutes. Hence, the total training time was over 4 days. Only the Du and Mordatch (2019) variant was trained.

Figures 9.14 and 9.15 show final samples from the model, the first showing the generation of images as the iteration proceeds. In contrast, the second shows 64 images generated using 1024 iterations. The final images are reasonably well defined, although few are fully recognisable compared to the 64 real images from the CIFAR-10 dataset illustrated in Figure 9.16. Table 9.1 shows the inception score (IS) and Fréchet inception distance (FID) of the model as training progressed, and this was calculated using 38,086 sample images and 38,086 images drawn from CIFAR-10 in the case of FID. The inception score value is calculated by splitting the data into 10 sub-batches and averaging. IS and FID improved as training progressed, although the final scores obtained after 200 epochs are relatively modest.

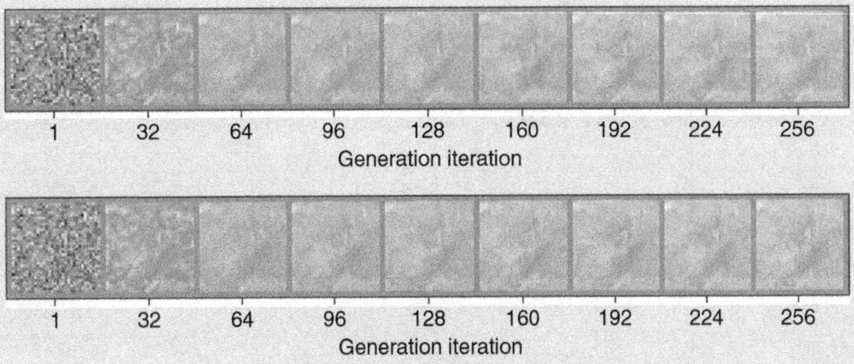

FIGURE 9.14 Two different samples drawn from the CIFAR-10 trained Du and Mordatch (2019) EBM and iterated through 256 steps of SGLD.

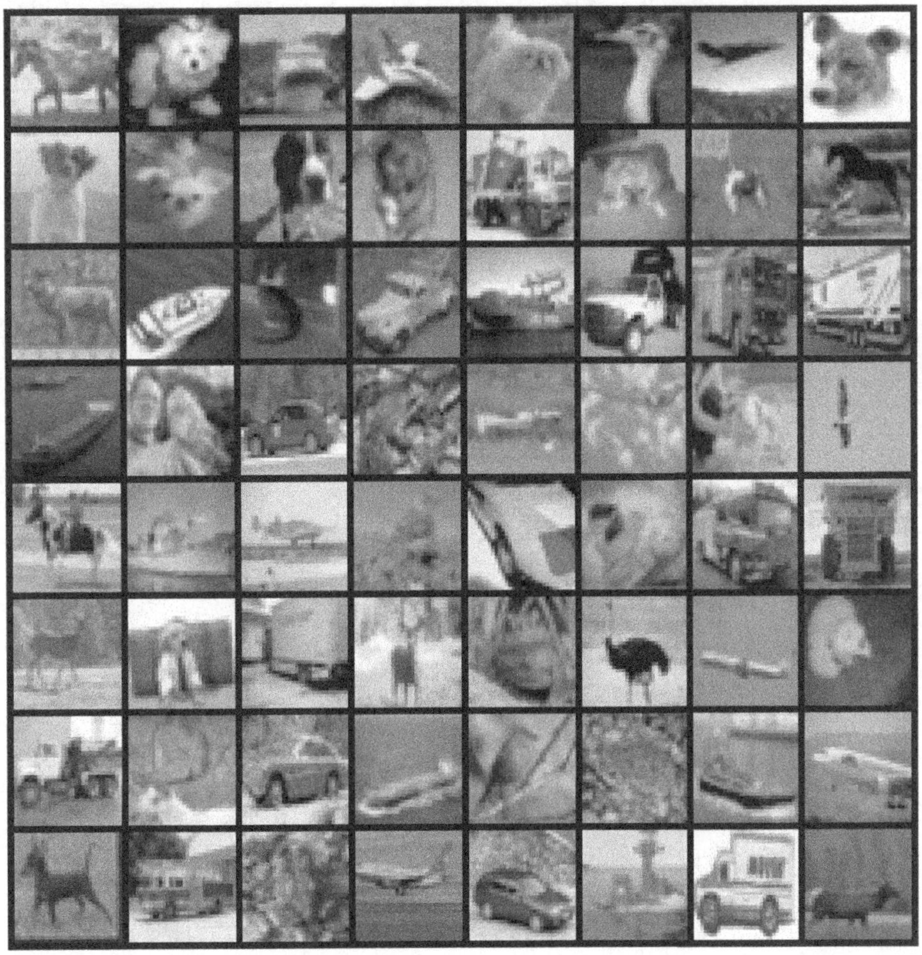

FIGURE 9.15 Sixty-four images from the CIFAR-10 dataset.

(*Continued*)

(*Continued*)

FIGURE 9.16 Sixty-four simulated images from the Du and Mordatch (2019) CIFAR-10 model with 1024 steps of iteration.

TABLE 9.1 Inception Score and Fréchet Inception Distance for the Deep Energy Model Trained Using CIFAR-10

Epoch	Inception Score	Fréchet Inception Distance
50	3.460	0.0800
100	4.104	0.0437
150	4.388	0.0221
200	4.505	0.0151

The galaxies dataset used in Chapter 6 is much more uniform than CIFAR-10 and is considerably easier to learn. The galaxies dataset was used as a third example but scaled down to the same 32 × 32 size as CIFAR-10. Another model was trained through 60 epochs with the same hyperparameters as those for the CIFAR-10 model, and the results can be found in the associated Jupyter Notebook.

9.3.6 Joint Energy-Based Model (JEM)

Recall that a classifier model learns to produce the probability of class y given input data x, $P(y|x)$, and this is done by learning a function $f_\theta(x)$ that maps the input vector to K real numbers known as *logits*, corresponding to K possible classes. These are then converted to probabilities using the softmax function,

$$P_\theta(y|x) = \frac{\exp\left(f_\theta(x)[y]\right)}{\sum_{y'} \exp\left(f_\theta(x)[y]\right)}, \tag{9.52}$$

where $f_\theta(x)[y]$ is the logit for class y.

The question posed by Grathwohl et al. (2020) is: Can a classifier model be used generatively? Implicitly, the model is learning the training set's distribution to provide classification, so is there a way to access this distribution? Grathwohl et al. (2020) provide an answer to this question by reinterpreting the logits to define $P_\theta(x, y)$,

$$P_\theta(x, y) = \frac{\exp\left(f_\theta(x)[y]\right)}{Z(\theta)} \tag{9.53}$$

$$E_\theta(x, y) = -f_\theta(x[y]), \tag{9.54}$$

where $Z(\theta)$ is the unknown normalisation factor, known as the partition function. $P_\theta(x)$ can now be obtained by marginalising out y,

$$P_\theta(x) = \sum_y P_\theta(x, y), \tag{9.55}$$

and the energy function at a data point x is given by

$$E_\theta(x) = -\log \sum_y \exp\left(f_\theta(x)[y]\right) \tag{9.56}$$

$$= -\operatorname{LogSumExp}_y\left(f_\theta(x)[y]\right). \tag{9.57}$$

There is an implicit degree of freedom present in the classifier logits as an arbitrary scalar can shift them without impact, but that is not the case here as the shift would impact $P_\theta(x)$. This extra degree of freedom allows the construction of the probability density over the input data and the joint distribution of labels and data. The conditional probability $P_\theta(y|x)$ can be recovered by dividing Equation (9.53) by Equation (9.55). This approach defines a *joint energy-based model (JEM)*.

How should a JEM be trained? Unfortunately, it is not as simple as training a classifier model and then converting it for generative use; the model must be simultaneously trained for classification and generation. Given that

$$P_\theta(x, y) = P_\theta(x)P_\theta(y|x), \tag{9.58}$$

the likelihood can be factorised,

$$\log P_\theta(x, y) = \log P_\theta(x) + \log P_\theta(y|x). \tag{9.59}$$

This likelihood factorisation is used with the two terms on the right-hand side driving optimisation to train the model. $\log P_\theta(y|x)$ is optimised using the normal cross-entropy for a classifier, while $\log P_\theta(x)$ is optimised used SGLD with gradients taken with respect to $-E_\theta(x)$ as defined in Equation (9.56). The training process is given by Algorithm 9.4.

Algorithm 9.4: Joint Energy-Based Model Training

Input: Training data D, distribution $p_D(x)$, SGLD step size λ, SGLD steps K, SGLD noise σ
B $\leftarrow \emptyset$;
while *not converged* **do**
  $x_i^+ \sim p_D$;
  $J_{XE} = \text{crossentropy}(f_\theta(x_i^+), y)$;
  $x_i^0 \sim B$ (95% probability) $\mathcal{U}$ otherwise;
  Generate sample from q_θ using Langevin dynamics;
  for $k = 0$ *to* $K - 1$ **do**
    $x^{k+1} = x^k + \lambda \nabla_x \text{LogSumExp}_y(f_\theta(x^k)[y]) + \epsilon^{k+1} \quad \epsilon^{k+1} \sim \mathcal{N}(0, \sigma I)$;
  $x_i^- \leftarrow x^K$;
  $J_{CD} = \text{LogSumExp}_{y'}(f_\theta(x^+)[y']) - \text{LogSumExp}_{y'}(f_\theta(x^-)[y'])$;
  Optimise objective $J = J_{XE} + J_{CD}$;
  Update θ using the Adam optimiser;
  $B \leftarrow B \cup x_i$;
Output: Parameters θ

EXAMPLE 9.4: JOINT ENERGY-BASED MODEL WITH MNIST

This example trains a JEM using the MNIST dataset, and it can be found in the Jupyter Notebook `Joint Energy-based Model with MNIST.ipynb`. Like the previous example, this model is adapted from Lippe (2021).

The first modification is to the neural network itself, which is now a full classification model rather than modelling only the energy function. Hence, the final layer is replaced by a dense linear layer with 10 nodes to provide the logits as output. Note that we need the logits to calculate the energy rather than a softmax function.

The `Sampler` class is almost unchanged except for the modification to handle the logits output from the CNN. To calculate the energy, the PyTorch function `logsumexp` is used on the model output, and hence the line for the energy calculation becomes

```
out_en = -torch.logsumexp(model(input_imgs), dim=1)
```

The `DeepEnergyModel` needs a few more modifications to handle the logit output of the CNN during the contrastive divergence calculation and to calculate the cross-entropy loss. Since this is also a classifier model, tracking the training and validation loss is useful. The `__init__` function adds three lines to initialise accuracy calculators for the training and validation datasets, and to initialise the cross-entropy loss class.

The training step function must be modified to reflect the new loss function. The contrastive divergence calculation remains the same, but the L_2 regularisation is removed. The call to the CNN is modified to account for the logits' return and the subsequent energy calculation for real and fake images. The cross-entropy loss is calculated using the real image logits and true label values. Finally, the training accuracy of the classifier model is calculated and logged.

The validation step is also similarly modified to calculate and log the validation accuracy. Hyperparameter values are modified from the values used with the model of Du and Mordatch (2019) and are given in Table 9.2.

TABLE 9.2 Hyperparameters Used by the Joint Energy-Based Model

Variable	Value
Initial learning rate	0.0001
Max epochs	150
SGLD steps	20
SGLD step size	1
SGLD noise	0.01

The training loss as a function of step is shown in Figure 9.17. The cross-entropy loss shows a steady decline, while the contrastive divergence loss shows the same noisy behaviour as the other models that use SGLD sampling. Eight final images are shown in Figure 9.18 and are of broadly similar quantity to those in the previous example. Of course, the underlying model is a fully fledged classifier and can be used as such. The final validation accuracy is 97.8%, which is very similar to the values obtained from the dedicated MNIST classifiers training in Chapter 6.

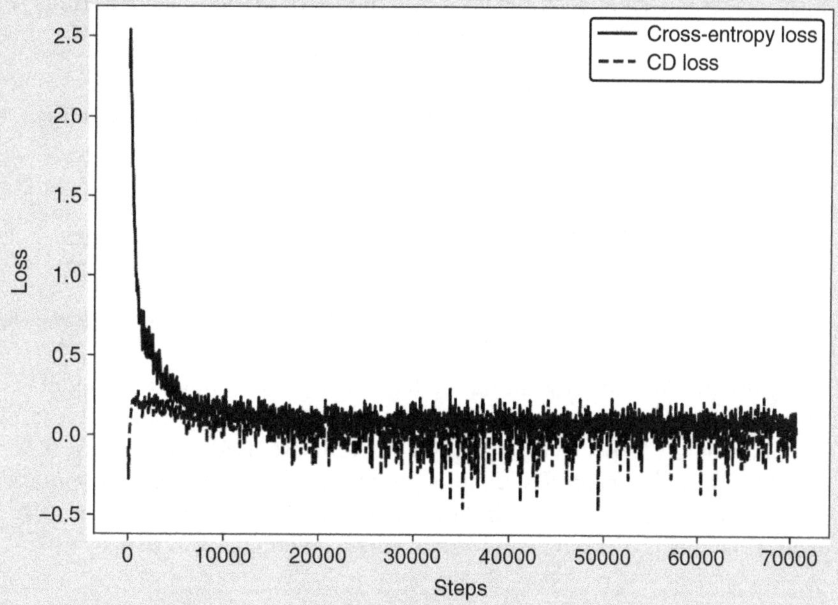

FIGURE 9.17 Grathwohl et al. (2020). Model cross-entropy and contrastive divergence losses as a function of step.

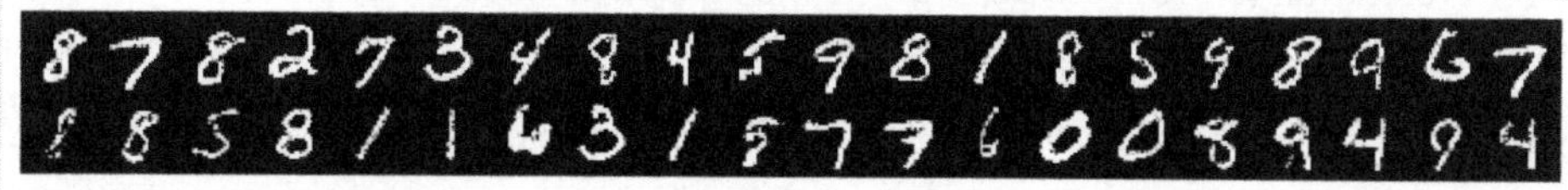

FIGURE 9.18 Forty simulated images from the Grathwohl et al. (2020) MNIST model.

9.3.7 Score-Based Models

Recall Equations (9.6) and (9.43),

$$\log p(\boldsymbol{x}) = -E(\boldsymbol{x}) - \log Z. \tag{9.60}$$

The score function is defined as the gradient of this expression,

$$s(\boldsymbol{x}) = \nabla_{\boldsymbol{x}} \log p(\boldsymbol{x}) = -\nabla_{\boldsymbol{x}} E(\boldsymbol{x}), \tag{9.61}$$

which is independent of the partition function Z as this is independent of $\boldsymbol{x}$. By eliminating the intractable partition function, the score becomes a useful base upon which to build an energy-based model (Swersky et al., 2011; Li et al., 2019).

Recall Equations (9.50) and (9.51), which define SGLD. Both expressions contain the score function, so theoretically, we could build a score-based model in the same way as the deep energy-based models but now use a deep neural network to model the score function directly rather than the energy function and then obtain the score as its gradient, and this does not offer any significant advantage over deep energy-based models and, specifically, would also suffer from the main downside of such models: slow training due to the use of MCMC in the form of Langevin sampling. If the data distribution could be used to train the score function directly, then there would be no need to use MCMC during training. Langevin sampling could generate new samples once the score function has been trained, and this is the principle behind how score-based models work.

To train a score-based model, the score function, defined as a neural network, s_{θ}, is trained using score matching, which minimises the Fisher divergence between the data and model probability distributions (Hyvärinen, 2005),

$$J(\theta) = \frac{1}{2}\mathbb{E}_{p_d(\boldsymbol{x})}\left[\|s_{\theta}(\boldsymbol{x}) - s_d(\boldsymbol{x})\|_2^2\right]. \tag{9.62}$$

Unfortunately, the score function of the data, s_d, is not usually available, so an estimate must be used. Hyvärinen (2005) applies integration by parts to Equation (9.62) to show that

$$J_{SM}(\theta) = \mathbb{E}_{p_d(\boldsymbol{x})}\left[Tr\left(\nabla_{\boldsymbol{x}} s_{\theta}(\boldsymbol{x})\right) + \frac{1}{2}\|s_{\theta}(\boldsymbol{x})\|_2^2\right] + C, \tag{9.63}$$

where C is a constant and

$$\nabla_{\boldsymbol{x}} s_{\theta}(\boldsymbol{x}) = \nabla_{\boldsymbol{x}}^2 \log p_{\theta}(\boldsymbol{x}), \tag{9.64}$$

that is, the Jacobian of s_{θ} is equal to the Hessian of the log-density function of the model. The expectation over the data distribution is straightforward and can be calculated using samples from the data. However, it remains the case that $\nabla_{\boldsymbol{x}} s_{\theta}(\boldsymbol{x})$ is computationally expensive, so approximations are used, and several different approaches are available. Shi et al. (2018) propose the *spectral Stein gradient estimator (SSGE)* as a computationally tractable way of estimating the gradient of a log-density function. Song et al. (2019) advocate the use of *sliced score matching*, which considers the projection of $\nabla_{\boldsymbol{x}} s_{\theta}(\boldsymbol{x})$ onto random vectors $\boldsymbol{v}$ giving an objective

$$J_{SSM}(\theta) = \mathbb{E}_{p_v}\mathbb{E}_{p_d(\boldsymbol{x})}\left[\boldsymbol{v}^T \nabla_{\boldsymbol{x}} s_{\theta}(\boldsymbol{x})\boldsymbol{v} + \frac{1}{2}\|s_{\theta}(\boldsymbol{x})\|_2^2\right]. \tag{9.65}$$

The term $\boldsymbol{v}^T \nabla_{\boldsymbol{x}} s_{\theta}(\boldsymbol{x})\boldsymbol{v}$ is much less computationally expensive to calculate than $tr\left(\nabla_{\boldsymbol{x}} s_{\theta}(\boldsymbol{x})\right)$ and can be calculated using algorithmic differentiation (Song et al., 2019). The most popular form of score matching used with generative models is *denoising score matching*, originally proposed by Vincent (2011). The idea here is to approximate the score using data samples that have been corrupted by noise distribution, $q_{\sigma}(\widetilde{\boldsymbol{x}}|\boldsymbol{x})$, where $q_{\sigma}(\widetilde{\boldsymbol{x}}) \equiv \int q_{\sigma}(\widetilde{\boldsymbol{x}}|\boldsymbol{x})p_d(\boldsymbol{x})d\boldsymbol{x}$. Hence, the new objective function is

$$J_{DSM}(\theta) = \frac{1}{2}\mathbb{E}_{q_{\sigma}(\widetilde{\boldsymbol{x}}|\boldsymbol{x})}\mathbb{E}_{p_d}\left[\left\|s_{\theta}(\boldsymbol{x}) - \nabla_{\theta \boldsymbol{x}} \log q_{\sigma}(\widetilde{\boldsymbol{x}}|\boldsymbol{x})\right\|_2^2\right], \tag{9.66}$$

which, if $q_{\sigma} = \mathcal{N}(\widetilde{\boldsymbol{x}}|\boldsymbol{x}, \sigma^2\boldsymbol{I})$, becomes

$$J_{DSM}(\theta) = \frac{1}{2}\mathbb{E}_{q_{\sigma}(\widetilde{\boldsymbol{x}}|\boldsymbol{x})}\mathbb{E}_{p_d}\left[\left\|s_{\theta}(\boldsymbol{x}) + \frac{\widetilde{\boldsymbol{x}} - \boldsymbol{x}}{\sigma^2}\right\|_2^2\right]. \tag{9.67}$$

Recent papers by Sohl-Dickstein et al. (2015), Li et al. (2019), Song and Ermon (2019), Song et al. (2021) and Vahdat et al. (2021) have all used denoising score matching. As an alternative to algorithmic differentiation, Pang et al. (2020) proposed the estimation of directional derivatives using finite difference approximation, leading to new objective functions for finite difference variants of sliced score matching, sliced score matching with variance reduction and denoising score matching.

DSM might be the most popular form of score matching, but it also has a problem. Models trained with a single noise level can perform the denoising task well (Saremi and Hyvärinen, 2019) but cannot generate high-quality samples (Li et al., 2019; Song and Ermon, 2019). Li et al. (2019) provide a geometric explanation of why that is the case: generally, while a data distribution is high dimensional, it typically forms a relatively low-dimensional manifold within the higher-dimensional space. Hence, the density gradient is undefined away from this manifold, making it difficult to train a valid model for the whole space. Thus, if a single noise level is used, a model that effectively removes noise from data points in the same set but does not act generatively can be constructed. Utilising multiple noise levels is essential, and there are various subtly different approaches to accomplish this, as described by Li et al. (2019) and Song and Ermon (2019).

Song et al. (2021) present a unified approach to score-based models through SDEs: instead of a finite number of noise levels, they generalise this to an infinite number through an SDE. A forward SDE is used to gradually transform a data distribution to a known prior by injecting noise, and then the associated reverse-time SDE can be used generatively. The aim is to create a diffusion process $x(t)$ such that the initial value is drawn from the data distribution $x(0) \sim p_0$ and the final value is drawn from the prior distribution $x(T) \sim p_T$. The diffusion is given by

$$dx = f(x, t)dt + g(t)dW, \tag{9.68}$$

where W is a vector Brownian motion, $f(x, t)$ is the vector-valued drift and $g(t)$ is the scalar diffusion coefficient. Anderson (1982) proves the result that a forward diffusion process generates a reverse-time representation. Given forward SDE (9.68), the reverse-time SDE is given by (Anderson, 1982; Song et al., 2021)

$$dx = \left[f(x, t) - g(t)^2 \nabla_x \log p_t(x)\right] dt + g(t)d\bar{W}, \tag{9.69}$$

where $\bar{W}$ is a Brownian motion where time flows backwards from T to 0. Given the score function $s(x) = \nabla_x \log p_t(x)$, the reverse-time SDE can be used to sample, where samples are generated from the latent distribution $x(T) \sim P_T$ and the reverse-time SDE used to obtain samples $x(0) \sim P_0$. The score is estimated using a continuous-time generalisation of DSM,

$$J_{DSM-SDE}(\theta) = \mathbb{E}_t \left\{\lambda(t)\mathbb{E}_{x(0)}\mathbb{E}_{x(t)|x(0)} \left[\left\|s_\theta(x) - \nabla_{x(t)} \log p_{0t}(x(t)|x(0))\right\|_2^2\right]\right\}, \tag{9.70}$$

where $\lambda(t)$ is a positive-weight function typically chosen so that

$$\lambda \propto \mathbb{E}\left[||\nabla_{x(t)} \log p_{0t}(x(t)|x(0))||_2^2\right], \tag{9.71}$$

t is sampled uniformly from $[0, T]$, $x(0) \sim p_0(x)$ and $x(t) \sim p_{0t}(x(t)|x(0))$.

To proceed we need to know the transition kernel $P_{0t}(x(t)|x(0))$. In the case that $f(x, t)$ is affine, the kernel is Gaussian with mean and variance often available in closed form. In the general case, the transition probability is obtained by solving the Kolmogorov forward equation.

Having trained the score function using the loss function given in Equation (9.70) with gradient descent, the reverse-time SDE can be used to sample. Any general-purpose SDE solver can solve the SDE, such as those described by Kloeden and Platen (1992). Song et al. (2021) propose *reverse diffusion sampling*, which discretises the reverse SDE in the same way as the forward SDE. Hence, given the forward SDE

$$dx = f(x, t)dt + G(t)dW, \tag{9.72}$$

and the following discretisation:

$$x_{i+1} = x_i + f_i(x_i) + G_i z_i \qquad \text{for } i = 0, \dots, N-1, \tag{9.73}$$

where $z_i \sim \mathcal{N}(0, I)$, the matching reverse-time SDE is given by

$$dx = \left[f(x.t) - G(t)G(t)^T \nabla_x \log p_t(x)\right] dt + G(t)d\bar{W}, \tag{9.74}$$

with discretisation

$$x_i = x_{i+1} - f_i(x_i) + G_{i+1}G_{i+1}^T s_{\theta^*}(x_{i+1}, i+1) + G_{i+1}z_{i+1}. \tag{9.75}$$

The model is score-based, so MCMC techniques such as Langevin sampling or Hamiltonian Monte Carlo can be used. Song et al. (2021) propose using MCMC as a *corrector* step and hence establish predictor–corrector techniques in which an SDE solver provides the prediction step and Langevin dynamics the correction step. The basic algorithm performs a double loop, with the outer loop running the discrete approximation to the SDE as a predictor and an inner loop of M steps of Langevin dynamics to refine the estimate of x_i at each time step.

Song et al. (2021) achieved record-breaking inception and FID scores using their score-based models and demonstrated high-fidelity image generation on large frames of size, 1024^2, previously only achieved using GANs.

EXAMPLE 9.5: SCORE-BASED MODEL WITH MNIST AND CIFAR-10

As an example of a score-based model, this example implements the SDE approach of Song et al. (2021) for the MNIST dataset, and it can be found in the Jupyter Notebook `Score-based Generative Modeling through SDEs.ipynb`. The model is implemented using PyTorch and is based on a Colab example by Song (2021), and a full description of the code can be found in the Colab.

The score model is a neural network with its output the same size as its input, here 28×28 with a single channel. Any autoencoder-type structure could be used, but here, a *U-Net*-type structure is chosen, derived from Ronneberger et al. (2015). The U-Net is an autoencoder-like structure with skip connections initially designed for image segmentation. It will also be used in the context of GANs later in this chapter.

The training loop was executed through 50 epochs using a batch size 32. Of course, this is a straightforward training loop using gradient descent with no sampling required, so it progresses faster than the deep energy models of earlier examples.

Once the model is trained, samples can be generated using the reverse-time SDE. For this example, a simple Euler–Maruyama discretisation of the SDE was used, although any SDE solver could replace this. The sampler generates a series of random images using a standard normal distribution and then steps these 'back' in time using the reverse SDE. A total of 512 steps are used, sufficient to generate realistic handwritten numbers. As with earlier examples, the sampler can return intermediate images.

Figure 9.19 shows two images at intervals during the 512 time steps, with good results shown at the final step with a handwritten 2 and 8 generated by the model. Figure 9.20 shows 40 image samples from the model after 512 steps.

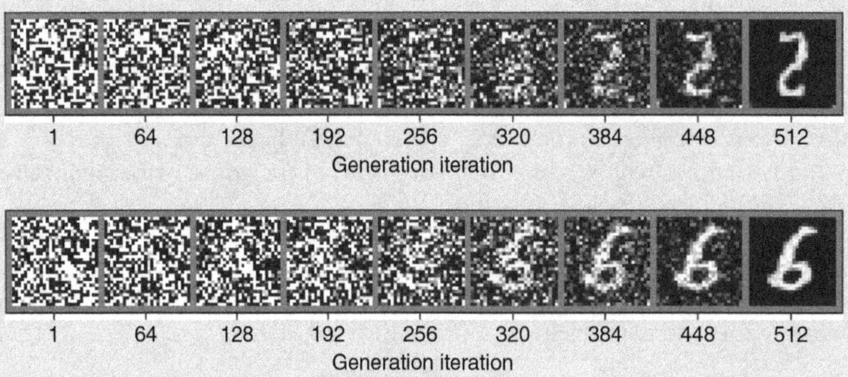

FIGURE 9.19 Two different samples drawn from the trained Song et al. (2021) score-based model and iterated through 512 sampling steps using an Euler–Maruyama SDE discretisation.

FIGURE 9.20 Forty simulated images from the score-based model (Song et al., 2021).

A second score-based model was trained using the CIFAR-10 dataset. The model used the same basic architecture for the neural network, increasing the number of channels by a factor of two for each layer, and modifying the encoder and decoder to accept three-channel colour images of size 32×32. The embedding dimension was increased to 1024. The model was trained over 3000 total epochs with a 2×10^{-4} learning rate. Figure 9.21 illustrates the final images. The results show reasonable definitions in the images, but what is represented remains unclear. Table 9.3 provides the inception scores and FID values, which show indifferent results.

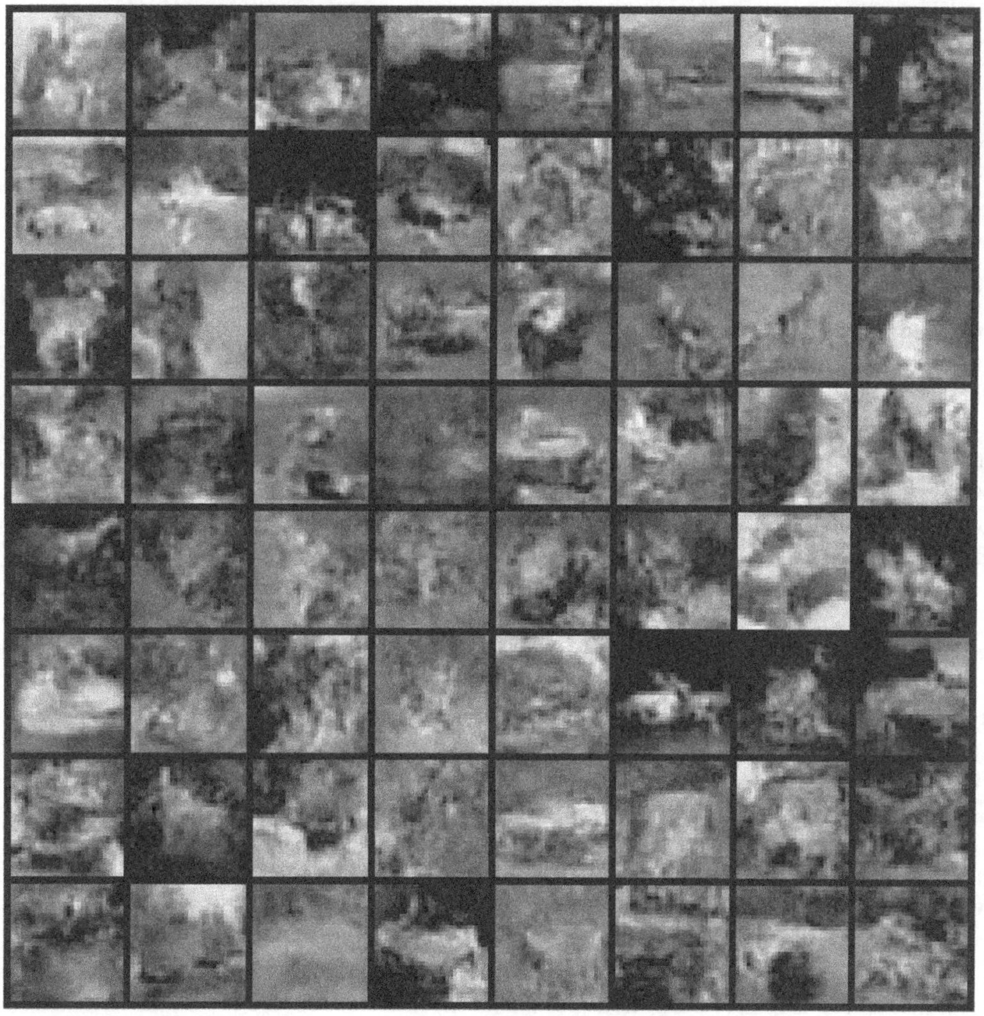

FIGURE 9.21 Sixty-four simulated images from the score-based model trained using CIFAR-10.

(Continued)

(*Continued*)

TABLE 9.3 Inception Score and Fréchet Inception Distance for the Score-Based Model Trained Using CIFAR-10

Epoch	Inception Score	Fréchet Inception Distance
600	3.371	0.0403
1200	3.725	0.0484
1800	3.509	0.0432
2400	3.641	0.0455
3000	3.705	0.0419

A third score model was trained using the galaxies dataset with the same architecture as the CIFAR-10 model. The example can be found in the Jupyter Notebook `Score-based Generative Modeling through SDEs Galaxies`. The visually excellent results demonstrate that the score-based model can work well.

9.4 VARIATIONAL AUTOENCODERS (VAEs)

9.4.1 Why *Variational*?

Chapter 8 introduced autoencoders in the context of PCA. These are seen as providing a type of non-linear PCA and dimension reduction. Autoencoders define a latent space in the middle layer; hence, theoretically, it could be used as a generative model by sampling that latent space. Section 8.6 noted three problems with such an approach:

1. The distribution of the latent space is not well defined; hence, it is not obvious how to select points to generate output.
2. The scale of the latent space is poorly understood, so it is unclear how far a point in the latent space needs to be moved to generate output with different features.
3. There is no guarantee that any given point in the latent space corresponds to meaningful output.

Before discussing *variational autoencoders*, these problems are illustrated in the context of a model trained with the MNIST dataset.

A convolutional autoencoder is used with a three-dimensional latent space. A three-dimensional latent space was explicitly used to allow visualisation, and a higher-dimensional latent space would have given better reconstruction behaviour. The encoder uses three convolutional layers, each with 32 channels, and two max pooling layers to reduce the dimension. The decoder parallels the encoder with three convolutional transpose layers, using a stride of 2 to expand the dimension back to the MNIST input of 28×28.

The model was trained through 200 epochs with a batch size of 256. Figure 9.22 illustrates a series of image reconstructions from the trained network. As can be seen, the images are a little blurred compared to the originals, reflecting the small number of dimensions in the latent space.

The first 1000 MNIST test images were encoded with the model and plotted in Figure 9.23 to understand the latent space. Some numbers have been separated spatially in the latent space, such as 0 and 7. Other numbers remain mixed and are grouped, although this is perhaps not surprising given the apparent similarity of pen strokes that form the numbers. The space is also clearly asymmetric and largely empty; hence, it is unclear how best to sample it to get effective output.

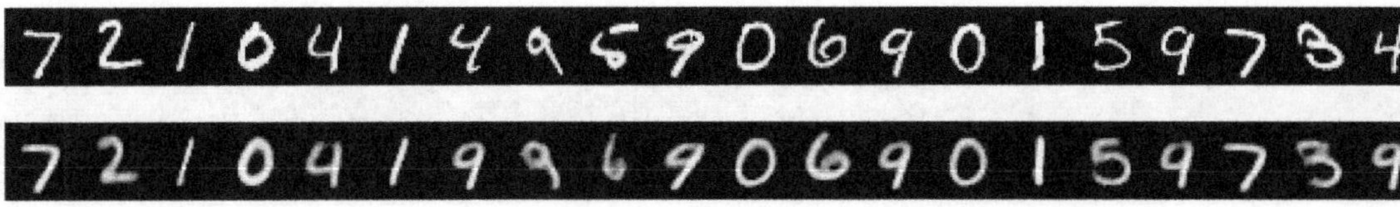

FIGURE 9.22 Twenty original test images in the first row compared with the same images reconstructed by the autoencoder.

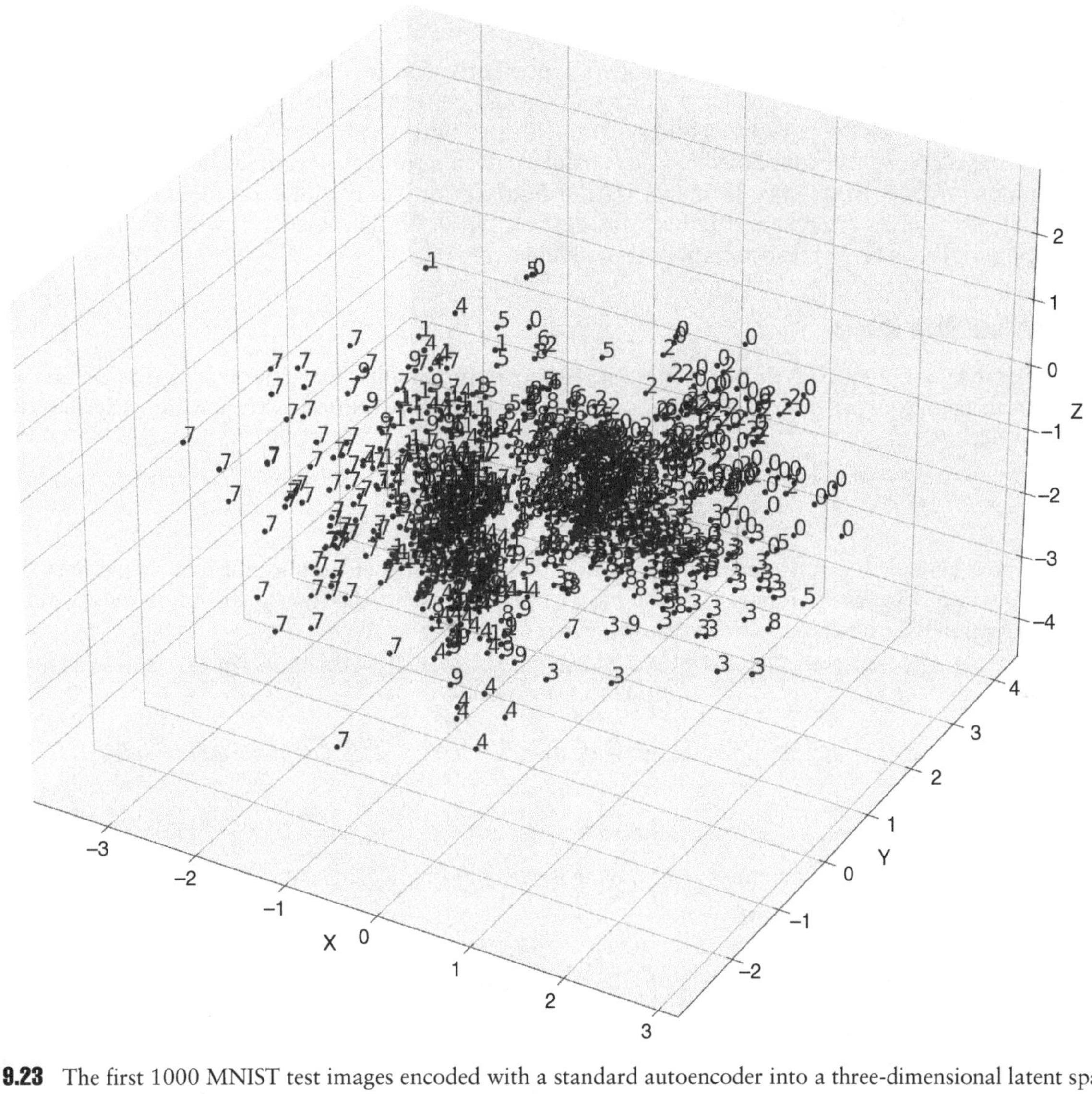

FIGURE 9.23 The first 1000 MNIST test images encoded with a standard autoencoder into a three-dimensional latent space.

Figure 9.24 shows 40 numbers sampled from the latent space. Random points were uniformly sampled in the range $(-30, 30)$ and then forward propagated through the decoder to generate the output. Some numbers look realistic and comparable to MNIST dataset examples, but others are 'smudges' with no fully formed number. The sampling is also clearly biased to specific numbers, with 2, 7 and 8 disproportionately represented. It is clear then that a standard autoencoder needs modification before it can be used generatively.

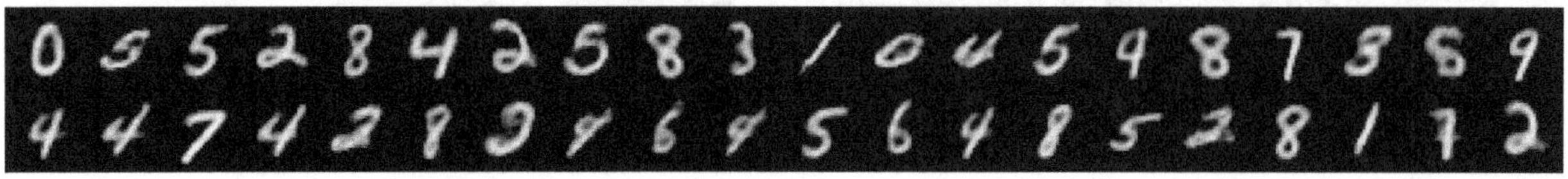

FIGURE 9.24 Forty images sampled from the latent space of a standard autoencoder.

9.4.2 Empirical View of VAEs

As described in the last section, standard autoencoders express little control over the latent space, preventing them from being used generatively. One obvious way forward would be to force the latent space to conform to some prior distribution, for which the obvious candidate would be the multivariate normal distribution $\mathcal{N}(0, I)$, and this would require the objective to be modified to add a regularisation term that penalised the difference between the latent distribution provided by the encoder model and the desired prior. The obvious choice for such a regularisation term is the Kullback–Leibler divergence (Kullback and Leibler, 1951). This, in essence, is what a variational encoder does, but a more rigorous probabilistic treatment is available.

9.4.3 Probabilistic View of VAEs

We assume that the dataset $x \in \mathcal{D}$ is drawn from some unknown probability distribution $\tilde{p}(x)$. To generate samples from the data distribution, we approximate the actual probability distribution with a parametric one (Kingma et al., 2016, p. 7),

$$x \sim p_\theta(x), \tag{9.76}$$

$$p_\theta \approx \tilde{p}(x). \tag{9.77}$$

The model is now extended to include *latent variables* z that are not observed and not part of the data (Kingma and Welling, 2019, p. 12). We then have a model $p_\theta(x, z)$ that represents the joint distribution over x and z. The marginal distribution over observed variables is then given by

$$p_\theta(x) = \int p_\theta(x, z)dz. \tag{9.78}$$

If we parameterise $p_\theta(x, z)$ with a deep neural network, then we have a *deep latent variable model (DLVM)*. This model can be factorised,

$$p_\theta(x, z) = p_\theta(z)p_\theta(x|z), \tag{9.79}$$

where we call $p_\theta(z)$ the *prior distribution* over z as it is not conditioned on data. We can also write down the *posterior distribution*,

$$p_\theta(z|x) = \frac{p_\theta(x, z)}{p_\theta(x)}. \tag{9.80}$$

The problem for DLVMs is that the marginal distribution of data, as given by Equation (9.78), is intractable and cannot be differentiated with respect to its parameters. The joint distribution $p_\theta(x, z)$ is tractable but the nature of the marginal distribution means that the posterior is also intractable and needs to be approximated.

To deal with the intractability of the true posterior, a parametric *inference model* is introduced,

$$q_\phi(z|x) \approx p_\theta(z|x), \tag{9.81}$$

where ϕ represents the *variational parameters* or an *encoder* model (Kingma and Welling, 2019, p. 15). This model is also a deep neural network, and the ϕ are the weights and biases of that network. A common choice is to use a Gaussian distribution for the posterior giving (Kingma and Welling, 2019, p. 16)

$$(\mu, \log \sigma) = \text{NeuralNet}_\phi(x), \tag{9.82}$$

$$q_\phi(z|x) = \mathcal{N}(z; \mu, \text{diag}(\sigma)). \tag{9.83}$$

The same encoder model is used for inference over the entire dataset, contrasting with traditional inference methods. This approach is a significant computational benefit, called *amortised variational inference* (Gershman and Goodman, 2014).

9.4.4 Evidence Lower Bound (ELBO)

Variational autoencoders are trained using the *evidence lower bound (ELBO)* as the optimisation objective. To see how this is obtained, consider the Kullback–Leibler divergence between the approximate and true posterior distributions (Bond-Taylor et al., 2021, p. 5),

$$\begin{aligned} D_{KL}(q_\phi(z|x)||p_\theta(z|x)) &= \mathbb{E}_{q_\phi(z|x)}\left[\ln \frac{q_\phi(z|x)}{p_\theta(z|x)}\right] \\ &= \mathbb{E}_{q_\phi(z|x)}\left[\ln q_\phi(z|x)\right] - \mathbb{E}_{q_\phi(z|x)}\left[\ln p_\theta(x, z)\right] + \ln p_\theta(x). \end{aligned} \tag{9.84}$$

Rearranging gives

$$\ln p_\theta(x) = D_{KL}(q_\phi(z|x)||p_\theta(z|x)) - \mathbb{E}_{q_\phi(z|x)}\left[\ln q_\phi(z|x)\right] + \mathbb{E}_{q_\phi(z|x)}\left[\ln p_\theta(x, z)\right]. \tag{9.85}$$

By the Gibbs inequality, $D_{KL}(Q||P) \geq 0$ and so

$$\begin{aligned} \ln p_\theta(x) &\geq -\mathbb{E}_{q_\phi(z|x)}\left[\ln q_\phi(z|x)\right] + \mathbb{E}_{q_\phi(z|x)}\left[\ln p_\theta(x, z)\right] \\ &= -\mathbb{E}_{q_\phi(z|x)}\left[\ln q_\phi(z|x)\right] + \mathbb{E}_{q_\phi(z|x)}\left[\ln p_\theta(z)\right] + \mathbb{E}_{q_\phi(z|x)}\left[\ln p_\theta(x|z)\right] \\ &= D_{KL}(q_\phi(z|x)||p_\theta(z)) + \mathbb{E}_{q_\phi(z|x)}\left[\ln p_\theta(x|z)\right] \\ &\equiv \mathcal{L}_{\theta,\phi}(x), \end{aligned} \tag{9.86}$$

where $\mathcal{L}$ defines the evidence lower bound.

9.4.5 Stochastic Gradient Descent and ELBO

To optimise parameters of the encoder, ϕ, and generative, θ, networks, unbiased gradients of the ELBO with respect to the parameters must be obtained. The gradients with respect to the generative model parameters are easy to obtain (Kingma and Welling, 2019, p. 20),

$$\begin{aligned} \nabla_\theta \mathcal{L}_{\theta,\phi}(x) &= \nabla_\theta \mathbb{E}_{q_\phi(z|x)}\left[\ln p_\theta(x, z) - \ln\ q_\phi(z|x)\right] \\ &= \mathbb{E}_{q_\phi(z|x)}\left[\nabla_\theta\left(\ln p_\theta(x, z) - \ln\ q_\phi(z|x)\right)\right] \\ &\approx \nabla_\theta\left(\ln p_\theta(x, z)\right), \end{aligned} \tag{9.87}$$

where the order of integration and differentiation have been exchanged.

The gradients with respect to the ϕ parameters are also required. Unfortunately, the order of integration and differentiation cannot be swapped as the expectation is taken with respect to the q density, which is dependent on ϕ. A change of variables, known as the *reparameterisation trick*, is used to solve this issue.

9.4.6 The Reparameterisation Trick

The reparameterisation trick expresses the random variable z in terms of another random variable ϵ that is independent of both x and ϕ,

$$z = g(\epsilon, \phi, x). \tag{9.88}$$

The gradient is then given by

$$\begin{aligned}\nabla_\phi \mathcal{L}_{\theta,\phi}(x) &= \nabla_\phi \mathbb{E}_{q_\phi(z|x)}\left[\ln p_\theta(x,z) - \ln\ q_\phi(z|x)\right]\\ &= \nabla_\phi \mathbb{E}_{p(\epsilon)}\left[\ln p_\theta(x,z) - \ln\ q_\phi(z|x)\right]\\ &\approx \nabla_\phi\left(\ln q_\phi(z|x)\right).\end{aligned} \tag{9.89}$$

A Monte Carlo estimate of the single-datapoint ELBO is formed,

$$\tilde{\mathcal{L}}_{\theta,\phi}(x) = \ln p_\theta(x,z) - \ln q_\phi(z|x), \tag{9.90}$$

the gradient of which is used in mini-batch SGD to optimise the ELBO (Kingma and Welling, 2019, p. 23). The gradient $\nabla_{\theta,\phi}\tilde{\mathcal{L}}_{\theta,\phi}(x)$ is an unbiased estimator of the exact gradient and will equal the true gradient when averaged over noise values ϵ. The remaining question is how to choose the transformation g, which should be selected to simplify the computation. Using the Gaussian described earlier, we have

$$\epsilon \sim \mathcal{N}(0, I), \tag{9.91}$$

$$z = \mu + \sigma \odot \epsilon. \tag{9.92}$$

With this specification, the loss becomes

$$\begin{aligned}\tilde{\mathcal{L}}_{\theta,\phi}(x) &= \ln p_\theta(x,z) - \ln q_\phi(z|x)\\ &= \ln p_\theta(x|z) + \ln p_\theta(z) - \ln q_\phi(z|x)\\ &= \ln p_\theta(x|z) - D_{KL}(q_\phi(z|x)||p_\theta(z))\\ &= \frac{1}{L}\sum_{l=1}^{L} \ln p_\theta(x|z^l) + \frac{1}{2}\sum_{j=1}^{J}\left(1 + \ln(\sigma_j^2) - \mu_j^2 - \sigma_j^2\right).\end{aligned} \tag{9.93}$$

The final step is to relate $\ln p_\theta(x|z)$ to the reconstruction error. We know that given z, the decoder is deterministic, and hence we have

$$\tilde{x} = f(z), \tag{9.94}$$

where f is a deterministic function. Hence we have

$$p_\theta(x|\tilde{x}) = p_\theta(x|z). \tag{9.95}$$

If we assume that this probability distribution is Gaussian, then we have

$$\ln p_\theta(x|\tilde{x}) \sim (x - \tilde{x})^2, \tag{9.96}$$

and hence the first term in the loss is seen to be the reconstruction loss. Algorithm 9.5 shows the complete training routine.

9.4.7 Marginal Likelihood

Given a trained variational autoencoder model, the probability of a datapoint can be estimated (Rezende et al., 2014; Kingma and Welling, 2019). The marginal likelihood of a data point is given by

$$\ln p_\theta(x) = \ln \mathbb{E}_{q_\phi(z|x)}\left[\frac{p_\theta(x,z)}{q_\phi(z|x)}\right]. \tag{9.97}$$

A Monte Carlo estimator of this quantity is given by

$$\ln p_\theta(x) \approx \ln\left[\frac{1}{L}\sum_{l=1}^{L}\frac{p_\theta(x,z^{(l)})}{q_\phi(z^{(l)}|x)}\right]. \tag{9.98}$$

Algorithm 9.5: Variational Autoencoder Training

Input: Training data D, learning rate α
while *not converged* **do**
  $x_i \sim p_D$ (mini-batch);
  $(\mu, \log(\sigma)) \leftarrow \text{EncoderNeuralNet}_\phi(x_i)$;
  $\epsilon \sim \mathcal{N}(0, I)$;
  $z \leftarrow \mu + \sigma \odot \epsilon$;
  $\tilde{x} \leftarrow \text{DecoderNeuralNet}_\theta(z)$;
  $J_R \leftarrow \text{crossentropy}(x, \tilde{x})$;
  $J_{KL} \leftarrow -\frac{1}{2}\sum_{j=1}^{J}(1 + \ln(\sigma_j^2) - \mu_j^2 - \sigma_j^2)$;
  Optimise objective $J = J_R + J_{KL}$;
  Update θ, ϕ using the Adam optimiser;
Output: Parameters θ, ϕ

9.4.8 Challenges with VAEs

Two critical issues are observed with variational autoencoders: blurriness or lack of fidelity of images and optimisation issues. Images generated by variational autoencoders are often reported to be blurry and lack the level of detail that rival models such as GANs are capable of producing (Dosovitskiy and Brox, 2016; Kingma and Welling, 2019; Zhou et al., 2020b). There are a variety of different explanations for this blurriness. One possible explanation is using MSE reconstruction loss (Dosovitskiy and Brox, 2016). Kingma and Welling (2019) argue that the blurriness occurs because if there is no perfect fit between $q_{D,\phi}(x, z)$ and $p_\theta(x, z)$, then the variance of the generative decoder model will end up being larger than that of the encoder model and the data. They argue that blurriness can be countered by using sufficiently general encoder and decoder models. Unfortunately, a more complex generator model increases the tendency to ignore the latent variables (Chen et al., 2017; Zhao et al., 2017). Zhao et al. (2017) argue that the problem stems from a limited ability to approximate the true prior. The Gaussian posterior is simplistic and leads to multiple data points being mapped to the same point in the latent space, giving blurriness. The way to circumvent this issue is to use more complex priors. Successful models that use complex priors are often hybrid approaches: for example, the *quantised-variational autoencoder (VQ-VAE)* embeds an autoregressive model in the latent space (Razavi et al., 2019), while *adversarial autoencoders (AAEs)* couple VAEs with adversarial training (Makhzani et al., 2015).

Bowman et al. (2016), Sønderby et al. (2016) and Kingma and Welling (2019) note that VAEs can get stuck in a stable equilibrium during training. This happens when the likelihood term $\ln p_\theta(x|z)$ is weak at the start of training, meaning $p_\theta(z) \approx q_\phi(z|x)$. To deal with this, a multiplicative weight, β, can be introduced to the Kullback–Leibler divergence term and slowly annealed from 0 to 1 during training (Bowman et al., 2016; Sønderby et al., 2016). Kingma et al. (2016) propose an alternative approach known as the method of *free bits*, which modifies the ELBO objective so that a minimum number of bits of information are encoded into each latent variable.

EXAMPLE 9.6: VARIATIONAL AUTOENCODER WITH MNIST, CIFAR-10 AND GALAXIES

In this example, a variational autoencoder is trained using the MNIST dataset and parallels the example of the standard autoencoder used generatively that was discussed in Section 9.4.1. The model retains the same structure of encoder and decoder as a regular autoencoder. The encoder needs to sample from a Gaussian distribution, so a utility layer is defined for this purpose.

```
class Sampling(nn.Module):
    def forward(self, inputs):
        mu, log_var = inputs
```

(Continued)

(*Continued*)

```
        std = torch.exp(0.5 * log_var)
        epsilon = torch.randn_like(std)
        return mu + std * epsilon
```

The encoder architecture is almost the same as a standard convolutional autoencoder, with a series of two-dimensional convolutions and max pooling layers to steadily reduce the image dimension before finally projecting the channels into a dense layer. Swish is the activation function used, and batch normalisation layers are added to help keep layer values centred and appropriately scaled. Unlike the standard autoencoder, the variational encoder does not output a point in the latent space directly; instead, it estimates the mean and variance of the distribution in the latent space. The mean and variance are then used as the parameters of the latent space distribution. The encoder model then samples from this distribution and returns the sampled point.

```
class Encoder(nn.Module):
    def __init__(self, input_dim, latent_dim):
        super(Encoder, self).__init__()
        self.conv1 = nn.Conv2d(in_channels=input_dim[0],
                               out_channels=32, kernel_size=3,
                               padding=1)
        self.bn1 = nn.BatchNorm2d(32)
        self.conv2 = nn.Conv2d(32, 32, kernel_size=3, padding=1)
        self.bn2 = nn.BatchNorm2d(32)
        self.conv3 = nn.Conv2d(32, 32, kernel_size=3, padding=1)
        self.bn3 = nn.BatchNorm2d(32)
        self.flatten = nn.Flatten()
        self.fc = nn.Linear(800, 16)
        self.mu = nn.Linear(16, latent_dim)
        self.log_var = nn.Linear(16, latent_dim)
        self.sampling = Sampling()

    def forward(self, x):
        x = F.silu(self.bn1(self.conv1(x)))
        x = F.max_pool2d(x, kernel_size=2, padding=1)
        x = F.silu(self.bn2(self.conv2(x)))
        x = F.max_pool2d(x, kernel_size=2, padding=1)
        x = F.silu(self.bn3(self.conv3(x)))
        x = F.max_pool2d(x, kernel_size=2, padding=1)
        x = self.flatten(x)
        x = F.relu(self.fc(x))
        mu = self.mu(x)
        log_var = self.log_var(x)
        z = self.sampling((mu, log_var))
        return mu, log_var, z
```

The decoder architecture is identical to a standard autoencoder, with a sequence of two-dimensional convolutional transpose layers to grow the image dimension back to 28×28. Again, swish is used as an activation function, and batch normalisation is used.

```
class Decoder(nn.Module):
    def __init__(self, latent_dim):
```

```
        super(Decoder, self).__init__()
        self.fc = nn.Linear(latent_dim, 7 * 7 * 32)
        self.deconv1 = nn.ConvTranspose2d(32, 32, kernel_size=3, stride=2,
                                          padding=1, output_padding=1)
        self.bn1 = nn.BatchNorm2d(32)
        self.deconv2 = nn.ConvTranspose2d(32, 32, kernel_size=3, stride=2,
                                          padding=1, output_padding=1)
        self.bn2 = nn.BatchNorm2d(32)
        self.deconv3 = nn.ConvTranspose2d(32, 1, kernel_size=3, padding=1)

    def forward(self, x):
        x = F.relu(self.fc(x))
        x = x.view(-1, 32, 7, 7)
        x = F.silu(self.bn1(self.deconv1(x)))
        x = F.silu(self.bn2(self.deconv2(x)))
        x = torch.sigmoid(self.deconv3(x))
        return x
```

The VAE class combined the encoder and decoder class.

```
class VAE(nn.Module):
    def __init__(self, encoder, decoder, beta=1.0):
        super(VAE, self).__init__()
        self.encoder = encoder
        self.decoder = decoder
        self.beta = beta

    def forward(self, x):
        mu, log_var, z = self.encoder(x)
        reconstruction = self.decoder(z)
        return reconstruction, mu, log_var
```

The encoder and decoder are constructed separately and then passed to the VAE model constructor. The model is then trained through 50 epochs using the Adam optimiser and a batch size of 128.

```
input_dim = (1, 28, 28)
latent_dim = 3
encoder = Encoder(input_dim=input_dim, latent_dim=latent_dim).to(device)
decoder = Decoder(latent_dim=latent_dim).to(device)
vae = VAE(encoder, decoder).to(device)
learning_rate = 0.001
optimizer = torch.optim.Adam(vae.parameters(), lr=learning_rate)
```

The VAE loss combined the reconstruction loss and the KL-divergence.

```
def vae_loss(recon_x, x, mean, log_var, beta):
    recon_loss = F.binary_cross_entropy(recon_x.view(-1, 784),
                                        x.view(-1, 784), reduction='sum')
    kld_loss = -0.5 * torch.sum(1 + log_var - mean ** 2 - log_var.exp())
    return recon_loss * beta + kld_loss, recon_loss, kld_loss
```

(Continued)

(Continued)

Once trained, the model was used to reconstruct the first 20 images from the MNIST test set, and the reconstruction is illustrated in Figure 9.25. The reconstruction images are slightly blurred compared to the original, as with the standard autoencoder. There is one significant reconstruction error in that a 5 has been reconstructed as a 0.

The first 1000 examples from the test set were encoded and plotted in the latent space in Figure 9.26. The latent space is now centred on (0,0,0) and has a range of values consistent with the Gaussian distribution.

FIGURE 9.25 Twenty original images reconstructed by the variational autoencoder. The test images are the same as in the earlier standard autoencoder case.

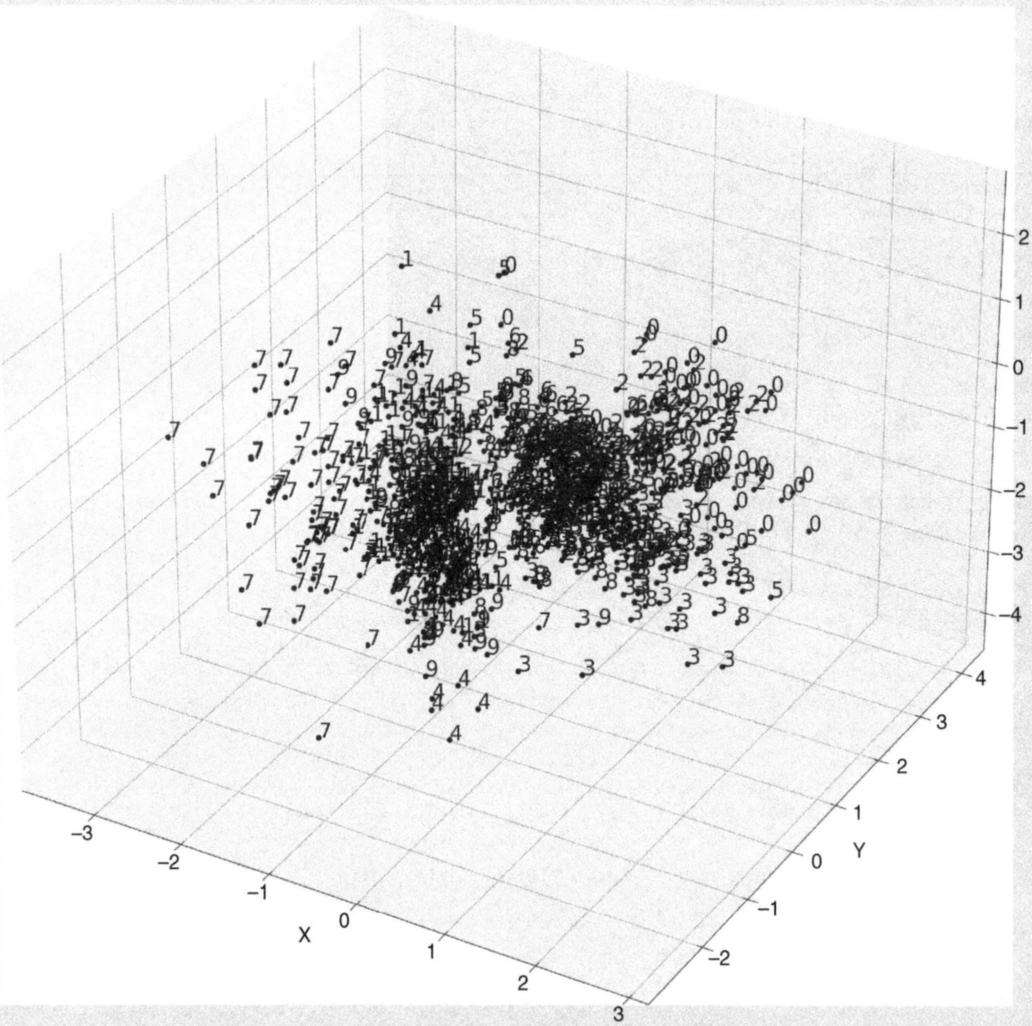

FIGURE 9.26 The first 1000 MNIST test images encoded with a variational autoencoder into a three-dimensional latent space.

Finally, 40 images were sampled from the decoder using the Gaussian distribution and are illustrated in Figure 9.27. Unlike the standard autoencoder, all of these numbers are formed. However, the images are blurred compared to the original training and test set images, and it is unclear what number some images represent.

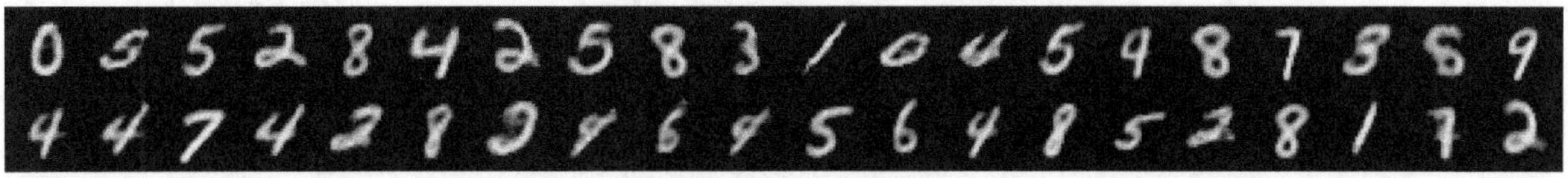

FIGURE 9.27 Forty images sampled from the latent space of a variational autoencoder.

A second VAE model was trained using CIFAR-10 through 1000 epochs. The same basic structure was used for the encoder and decoder but with increased numbers of channels, with 64, 128 and 256 used in the three convolutional layers in the encoder and 128 and 64 in the decoder transpose convolutional layers. The central dense layer was increased to 1024 and the latent dimension to 128.

As with the MNIST model, reconstruction was tested with 20 original images shown in Figure 9.28 and the corresponding reconstructions in Figure 9.29. The reconstructions are accurate but blurred compared to the original images. Figure 9.30 shows 64 images sampled from the decoder, with the resulting images blurred and indistinct. Table 9.4 shows that the inception scores FID values during training are poor, corresponding to the poor results observed in the figure.

FIGURE 9.28 Twenty test images from CIFAR-10 images.

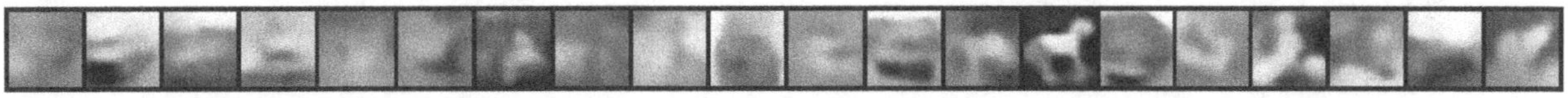

FIGURE 9.29 Twenty CIFAR-10 images reconstructed by the variational autoencoder.

A third example VAE was trained using the galaxies dataset through 200 epochs with the same architecture as that used for CIFAR-10. This example can be found in the Jupyter Notebook `VAE-Galaxies.ipynb`. The most noticeable feature of the reconstructed and sampled images is the lack of foreground stars in the original images. The VAE has 'denoised' them away, which is incorrect. The galaxy images are also clearly smoothed compared to the originals, although arguably the performance is better on this dataset than on CIFAR-10.

(*Continued*)

(*Continued*)

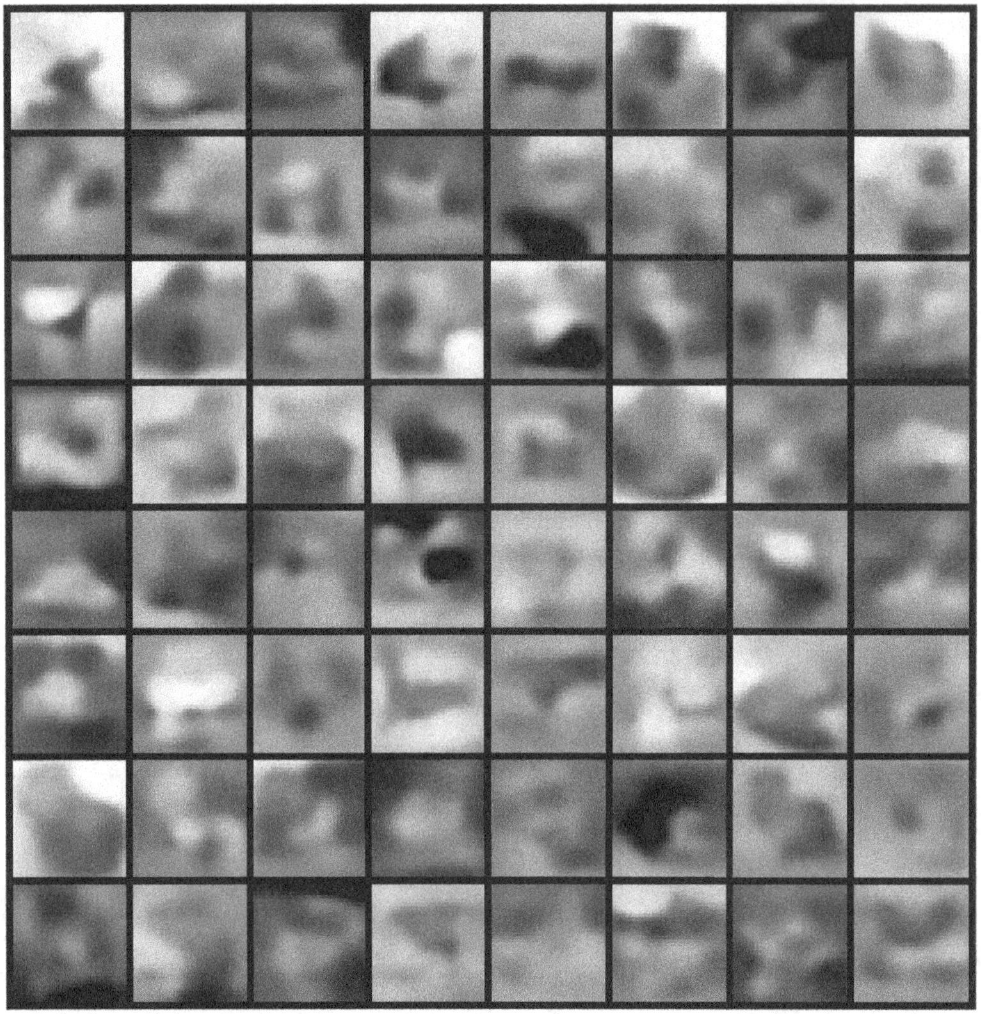

FIGURE 9.30 Sixty-four images sampled from the variational autoencoder trained on CIFAR-10.

TABLE 9.4 Inception Score and Fréchet Inception Distance for the Variational Autoencoder Trained Using CIFAR-10

Epoch	Inception Score	Fréchet Inception Distance
200	3.019	0.7241
400	3.001	0.6705
600	3.007	0.6409
800	3.117	0.6196
1000	3.102	0.6013

9.5 GENERATIVE ADVERSARIAL NETWORKS (GANs)

Generative adversarial networks (GANs) are perhaps the best-known type of deep generative model. GANs were the first generative technique to generate photorealistic images. GANs are amongst the most developed generative models and have exploded in interest since their introduction by Goodfellow et al. (2014). As discussed in Chapter 18, GANs are among the techniques used to generate synthetic market data.

This section provides a review of the critical contributions to the development of GANs, beginning with the original GAN architecture proposed by Goodfellow et al. (2014) and the first convolutional GAN, *DCGAN,* of Radford et al. (2015). Advances in GAN training methods were instrumental in their success to date, and this is discussed in Section 9.5.2, including the introduction of the Wasserstein loss function (Arjovsky et al., 2017). Controlling the generation process by conditioning an auxiliary variable or operations on the latent space has made GANs more flexible. This is discussed in Section 9.5.3. Section 9.2 discusses the evaluation of GAN performance, a complex issue in image generation. High-fidelity and high-resolution GANs have been central to their perceived success, and several such models, including *StyleGAN*, are reviewed in Section 9.5.4. GANs have also been applied to image-to-image applications such as colourising black and white photographs, and these are explored in Section 9.5.5.1. Finally, *inverse GANs* are discussed in Section 9.5.6. GANs, unlike many other generative model types, generally do not have an associated inference model that allows data to be encoded into the latent space and inverse GANs address this issue.

9.5.1 Early GANs

9.5.1.1 The First GAN Goodfellow et al. (2014) introduced generative adversarial networks. The key innovation of the approach was adversarial training, with two different models pitted against each other in a zero-sum game. In the architecture, a *generator* tries to produce images, given input random noise. In contrast, a *discriminator* classifies images it receives from both the generator and a genuine dataset as either real or fake. Both models use deep neural networks and are trained using SGD with backpropagation. Hence, GANs like VAEs do not need to use MCMC during training or sampling, which brings significant performance benefits. Training of both models proceeds in tandem as an 'arms race' in which the generator tries to generate fake images that are good enough to fool the discriminator. In contrast, the discriminator is trained in supervised fashion to recognise better which images are fake. The architecture of the GAN during training is illustrated in Figure 9.31. Once training is complete, the discriminator is discarded, and the generator model is used to create new data. The loss function applied in GANs was previously used for *noise-contrastive estimation* (Gutmann and Hyvärinen, 2012). Adversarial training had previously been applied in control theory (see, e.g., Altman, 1994) but not in the context of neural networks or generative models.

A prior is defined on the latent space as $p_z(z)$, and then the generator neural network defines a mapping from the latent space to the data space, $G(z, \theta)$. The discriminator model, $D(x, \phi)$, defines a function that returns the probability that x is drawn from the data distribution, p_d, rather than the generator distribution, p_g. The discriminator is trained to maximise the probability of correctly identifying fake and real images. In contrast, the generator is trained to minimise the probability that its samples are identified as fakes. Hence, the discriminator loss function is given by a min–max game,

$$
\begin{aligned}
J_D &= \min_G \max_D V(D, G) \\
&= \mathbb{E}_{x \sim p_d(x)}[\ln D_\phi(x)] + \mathbb{E}_{x \sim p_g}[\ln(1 - D(G(z)))].
\end{aligned} \tag{9.99}
$$

Holding the generator constant allows the objective for the discriminator to be rearranged,

$$
\begin{aligned}
\max_D V(D, G) &= \mathbb{E}_{x \sim p_d(x)}[\ln D_\phi(x)] + \mathbb{E}_{x \sim p_g}[\ln(1 - D(x))] \\
&= \mathbb{E}_{x \sim p_d}\left[\ln \frac{p_d(x)}{p_d(x) + p_g(x)}\right] + \mathbb{E}_{x \sim p_g}\left[\ln \frac{p_g(x)}{p_d(x) + p_g(x)}\right] \\
&= D_{KL}\left(p_d || \frac{1}{2}(p_d + p_g)\right) + D_{KL}\left(p_g || \frac{1}{2}(p_d + p_g)\right) + C.
\end{aligned} \tag{9.100}
$$

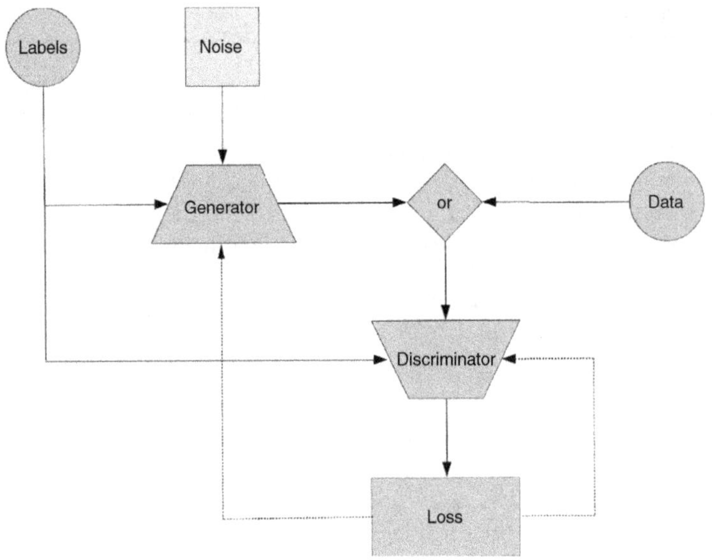

FIGURE 9.31 The architecture of a GAN with the generator and discriminator networks being trained together.

Equation (9.100) shows that the loss is equivalent to the Jenson–Shannon divergence between the generator and data distributions (Goodfellow et al., 2014; Bond-Taylor et al., 2021). Consequently, with sufficient model capacity, p_g converges to p_d. In practice, fully optimising the discriminator for each step in the generator training would be computationally expensive. Therefore, the proposed approach is to conduct k training steps on the discriminator for each step of training the generator. As long as the generator changes slowly, the discriminator will stay close to the optimal model. The full training loop is outlined in Algorithm 9.6.

Algorithm 9.6: GAN Training

Input: Training data D, learning rate α, inner loop steps k
for *no. training iterations* **do**
  for *k steps* **do**
    Sample noise $z \sim p_z$;
    $\tilde{x} \leftarrow G(\theta, z)$;
    $x \sim p_d$ (mini-batch);
    $Pred_F \leftarrow D(\phi, \tilde{x})$;
    $Pred_R \leftarrow D(\phi, x)$;
    $J_F \leftarrow \text{crossentropy}(Pred_F, \mathbf{1})$;
    $J_R \leftarrow \text{crossentropy}(Pred_R, 0)$;
    $J_D \leftarrow \frac{1}{2}(J_F + J_R)$;
    Optimise objective J_D;
    Update ϕ using SGD optimiser;
  Sample noise $z \sim p_z$;
  $\tilde{x} \leftarrow G(\theta, z)$;
  $Pred_F \leftarrow D(\phi, \tilde{x})$;
  $J_G \leftarrow \text{crossentropy}(Pred_F, \mathbf{1})$;
  Update θ using SGD optimiser;
Output: Parameters θ, ϕ

EXAMPLE 9.7: FULLY CONNECTED GAN WITH MNIST

PyTorch was used to implement the basic GAN, and the code can be found in the Jupyter Notebook `GAN.ipynb`. The MNIST dataset is loaded from torchvision, and on this occasion, the data is scaled to the range [0, 1]. A generator class represents the generator model.

```
class Generator(nn.Module):
    def __init__(self, latent_dim=10, out_dim=784, hidden_dim=128):
        super(Generator, self).__init__()
        self.gen = nn.Sequential(
            nn.Linear(latent_dim, hidden_dim),
            nn.BatchNorm1d(hidden_dim),
            nn.ReLU(inplace=True),
            nn.Linear(hidden_dim, hidden_dim * 2),
            nn.BatchNorm1d(hidden_dim * 2),
            nn.ReLU(inplace=True),
            nn.Linear(hidden_dim * 2, hidden_dim * 4),
            nn.BatchNorm1d(hidden_dim * 4),
            nn.ReLU(inplace=True),
            nn.Linear(hidden_dim * 4, hidden_dim * 8),
            nn.BatchNorm1d(hidden_dim * 8),
            nn.ReLU(inplace=True),
            nn.Linear(hidden_dim * 8, out_dim),
            nn.Sigmoid(),
        )

    def forward(self, noise):
        return self.gen(noise)
```

The generator starts with an input random vector with a default dimension of 10 and outputs a vector of length 784 to match the 28×28 size of MNIST images. The network consists of four blocks of increasing width, each with a dense layer, batch normalisation and ReLU activation. The output layer matches the scaled image range with a sigmoid activation function.

The discriminator model is a simple deep network with three dense layers of reducing dimension and leaky ReLU activation that culminates in a single sigmoid unit to act as the classifier.

```
class Discriminator(nn.Module):
    def __init__(self, in_dim=784, hidden_dim=128, neg_slope=0.2):
        super(Discriminator, self).__init__()
        self.disc = nn.Sequential(
            nn.Linear(in_dim, hidden_dim * 4),
            nn.LeakyReLU(negative_slope=neg_slope, inplace=True),
            nn.Linear(hidden_dim * 4, hidden_dim * 2),
            nn.LeakyReLU(negative_slope=neg_slope, inplace=True),
            nn.Linear(hidden_dim * 2, hidden_dim),
            nn.LeakyReLU(negative_slope=neg_slope, inplace=True),
            nn.Linear(hidden_dim, 1)
        )

    def forward(self, image):
        return self.disc(image)
```

(*Continued*)

(*Continued*)

The generator loss function calculates the binary cross-entropy between the prediction of the discriminator network for a batch of fake images and the true value, that is, 1. The aim, of course, is to update the generator network parameters in a direction that will make the images more realistic and amenable to fooling the discriminator. The loss function is given below, with the `bce_loss` an instance of the PyTorch class `BCEWithLogitsLoss` passed in as an argument.

```
def gen_loss(gen, disc, batch_size, latent_dim, bce_loss, device):
    noise = torch.randn(batch_size, latent_dim, device=device)
    fake_im = gen(noise)
    fake_pred = disc(fake_im)
    gen_loss = bce_loss(fake_pred, torch.ones_like(fake_pred))
    return gen_loss
```

The discriminator loss is the average of *fake* and *real* losses, where the fake loss is the binary cross-entropy between the prediction of the discriminator network for a batch of fake images and 0, and the real loss is the binary cross-entropy between the prediction of a batch of real images and 1. Here, the discriminator parameters should be adjusted to make the network better classify fake images from real images. The `bce_loss` argument is again an instance of the PyTorch class `BCEWithLogitsLoss`.

```
def disc_loss(gen, disc, real_im, batch_size, latent_dim, bce_loss, device):
    noise = torch.randn(batch_size, latent_dim, device=device)
    fake_im = gen(noise).detach()
    fake_pred = disc(fake_im)
    fake_loss = bce_loss(fake_pred, torch.zeros_like(fake_pred))
    real_pred = disc(real_im)
    real_loss = bce_loss(real_pred, torch.ones_like(real_pred))
    disc_loss = 0.5 * (fake_loss + real_loss)
    return disc_loss
```

The training loop is presented below, except for non-essential code blocks. The key observation is that the k parameter has been set to 1 so that the discriminator and generator network updates are directly interlaced. The Adam optimiser has been used with the learning rate set to a relatively low value of 0.0002 and the β_1 parameter set to 0.5, below the default value of 0.9.

```
gen = Generator(latent_dim).to(device)
gen_opt = Adam(gen.parameters(), lr=lr)
disc = Discriminator().to(device)
disc_opt = Adam(disc.parameters(), lr=lr)
tqdm_epoch = trange(n_epochs)
for epoch in tqdm_epoch:
    avg_gen_loss = 0.0
    avg_disc_loss = 0.0
    num_items = 0
    for real_im, _ in tqdm(train_loader):
        cur_batch_size = len(real_im)
        real_im = real_im.view(cur_batch_size, -1).to(device)
```

```
        # Update discriminator
        disc_opt.zero_grad()
        dloss = disc_loss(gen, disc, real_im, cur_batch_size,
        latent_dim, bce_loss, device)
        dloss.backward(retain_graph=True)
        disc_opt.step()

        # Update Generator
        gen_opt.zero_grad()
        gloss = gen_loss(gen, disc, cur_batch_size,
        latent_dim, bce_loss, device)
        gloss.backward(retain_graph=True)
        gen_opt.step()

        avg_gen_loss += gloss.item() * cur_batch_size
        avg_disc_loss += dloss.item() * cur_batch_size
        num_items += cur_batch_size

    ave_gen_loss = avg_gen_loss / num_items
    ave_disc_loss = avg_disc_loss / num_items
```

The GAN models were trained through 200 epochs, and the generator and discriminator training losses are presented in Figure 9.32.

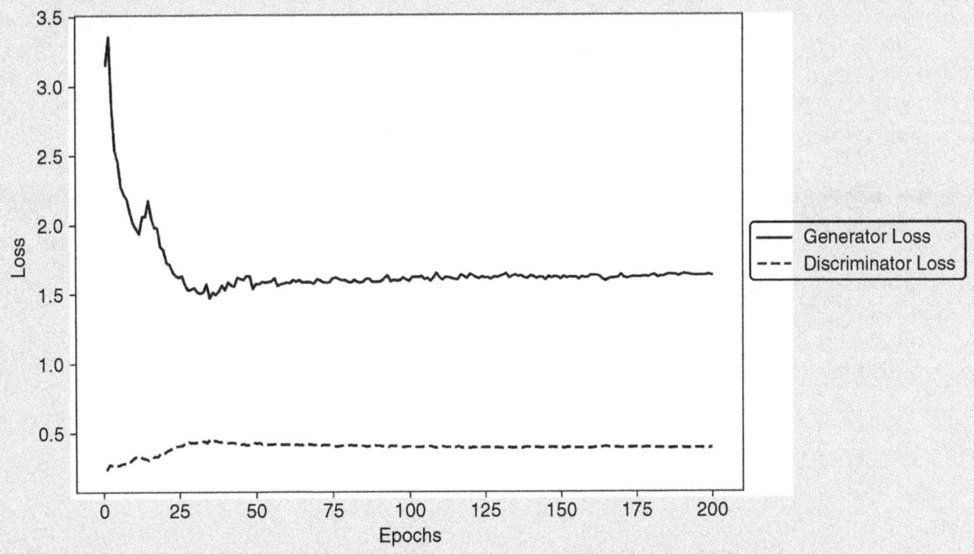

FIGURE 9.32 The generator and discriminator losses as a function of epoch for the GAN model.

A total of 40 images were generated by the final generator model and are presented in Figure 9.33.

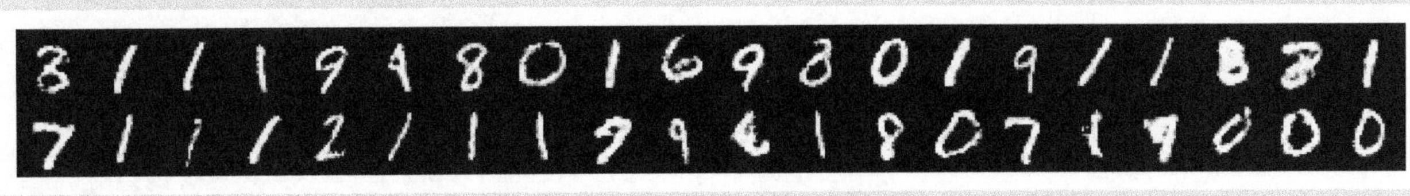

FIGURE 9.33 Forty images sampled from the latent space of a simple GAN generator model after 200 epochs.

9.5.1.2 DCGAN Radford et al. (2015) introduced DCGAN, the first GAN based on convolutions. Given the primary application to image generation, this is natural, and all subsequent image GANs also use convolutional approaches. The discriminator is a standard CNN classifier model. In DCGAN, strided convolutions were used in preference to pooling layers, allowing the model to learn its downsampling. The model also connects the convolutional layers directly to the input/output, avoiding the traditional approach of flattening the convolutional output into one or more fully connected layers before the final output. The generator model uses transpose convolutions to upsample the image, with the input random samples transformed to a four-dimensional tensor. Radford et al. (2015) also used batch normalisation to stabilise training. Example 9.8 presents a slightly modernised implementation of DCGAN.

EXAMPLE 9.8: DCGAN WITH CIFAR-10

DCGAN was trained with the CIFAR-10 dataset of colour 32 × 32 images, and the example can be found in the Jupyter Notebook `DCGAN.ipynb` The generator model takes a vector of Gaussian samples with mean 0 and variance 1 and then upsamples through four transpose convolutions to get the correct image scale. The first three layers have batch normalisation applied and use ReLU, while the output layer uses sigmoid to match the output range of [0,1].

```
class Generator(nn.Module):
    def __init__(self, latent_dim=100, out_size=32, no_channels=3):
        super(Generator, self).__init__()
        self.gen = nn.Sequential(
            nn.ConvTranspose2d(latent_dim, out_size * 4, 4, 1, 0,   4.320
                               bias=False),
            nn.BatchNorm2d(out_size * 4),
            nn.ReLU(True),
            nn.ConvTranspose2d(out_size * 4, out_size * 2, 4, 2, 1,
                               bias=False),
            nn.BatchNorm2d(out_size * 2),
            nn.ReLU(True),
            nn.ConvTranspose2d(out_size * 2, out_size, 4, 2, 1, bias=False),
            nn.BatchNorm2d(out_size),
            nn.ReLU(True),
            nn.ConvTranspose2d(out_size, no_channels, 4, 2, 1, bias=False),
            nn.Sigmoid(),
        )

    def forward(self, noise):
        return self.gen(noise)
```

The discriminator model is a straightforward sequence of convolutional layers with stride 2 ending in a sigmoid output.

```
class Discriminator(nn.Module):
    def __init__(self, in_size=32, no_channels=3, neg_slope=0.2):
        super(Discriminator, self).__init__()
        self.disc = nn.Sequential(
            nn.Conv2d(no_channels, in_size, 4, 2, 1, bias=False),
            nn.LeakyReLU(0.2, inplace=True),
            nn.Conv2d(in_size, in_size * 2, 4, 2, 1, bias=False),
            nn.BatchNorm2d(in_size * 2),
```

```
            nn.LeakyReLU(0.2, inplace=True),
            nn.Conv2d(in_size * 2, in_size * 4, 4, 2, 1, bias=False),
            nn.BatchNorm2d(in_size * 4),
            nn.LeakyReLU(0.2, inplace=True),
            nn.Conv2d(in_size * 4, 1, 4, 1, 0, bias=False),
        )

    def forward(self, image):
        return self.disc(image)
```

The loss as a function of epoch is given in Figure 9.34.

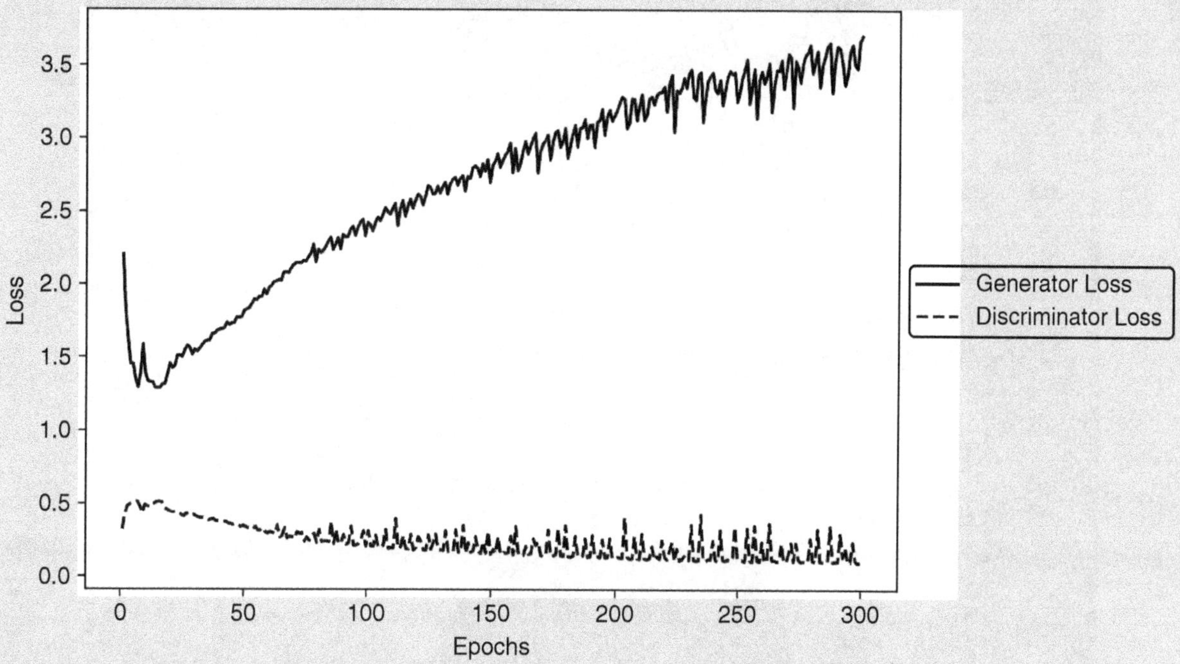

FIGURE 9.34 The generator and discriminator losses as a function of epoch for DCGAN.

A total of 64 images generated by DCGAN trained with CIFAR-10 for 300 epochs are shown in Figure 9.35. Some generated images resemble animals but lack clarity in the training set. The inception score and FID values are given in Table 9.5 and show relatively good results.

Figure 9.36 shows 40 fakes from a DCGAN trained using the MNIST dataset with an identical architecture to that used with CIFAR-10, aside from the single channel. The images were padded up to 32×32 for consistency. The performance of this GAN is clear, with a full range of digits that appear very similar to the training set. This example can be found in the Jupyter Notebook `DCGAN_MNIST.ipynb`.

(*Continued*)

(*Continued*)

FIGURE 9.35 Sixty-four images generated by a DCGAN trained using the CIFAR-10 dataset.

TABLE 9.5 Inception Score and Fréchet Inception Distance for the DCGAN Trained Using CIFAR-10

Epoch	Inception Score	Fréchet Inception Distance
50	4.985	0.0170
100	5.330	0.0097
150	5.385	0.0075
200	5.477	0.0123
250	5.428	0.0225
300	5.429	0.0318

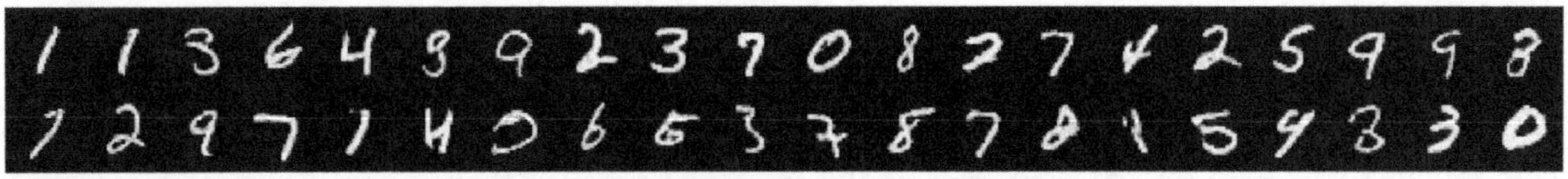

FIGURE 9.36 Forty images generated by a DCGAN trained using the MNIST dataset.

9.5.2 Stabilising GANs

GANs, for all their success, have displayed several problems either in the final images or during the training process. Section 9.5.2.1 describes the issues that can occur with GANs, while subsequent sections discuss various proposed solutions.

9.5.2.1 Problems with GANs

Artefacts. GANs, in common with other generative techniques, project from a lower-dimensional latent space to a higher-dimensional output space, typically an image. Care must be taken to avoid introducing high-frequency artefacts when performing such an operation. In the context of GANs, this phenomenon was investigated by Odena et al. (2016).

Two sources are identified for these digital artefacts: deconvolution and gradients. Upsampling through deconvolution or transposed convolution can often lead to *uneven overlap*, where the upsampling operator overlaps on some pixels more than others, and this always happens when the kernel size is not divisible by the stride. Theoretically, the model could learn weights to account for the overlap, but this tends not to happen in practice. The situation is often worse than this, even when the kernel size is divisible by the stride; models still produce chequerboard artefacts.

Odena et al. (2016) suggest that the way to avoid introducing digital artefacts is always to use a kernel size that is divisible by the stride and to change the deconvolution algorithm to one that smooths the upsampling and suggests using either *nearest-neighbour* or *bilinear* interpolation, followed by a convolutional layer. They suggest that their best results were obtained using the nearest-neighbour approach. Further, Odena et al. (2016) suggest that their results imply that the problem of chequerboard artefacts is linked to deconvolution operations rather than adversarial training and were able to give examples where they occur in other types of model. Finally, Odena et al. (2016) note that deconvolution layers also induce similar artefacts in gradients during backpropagation. They point to examples of high-frequency noise which appears in feature visualisation examples such as *DeepDream* (Mordvintsev and Tyka, 2015).

Non-Convergence. The most trying problem with GANs is getting them to converge at all. The results can be spectacular when they converge, but getting to that point is frequently challenging. Goodfellow (2016) clarifies why GANs training can be inherently unstable with gradient descent compared to most deep models. All of the models encountered up to now that have used gradient descent have a loss function that needs to be optimised, and that loss proceeds gradually 'downhill'.

GANs, in contrast, require that a Nash equilibrium be found in the two-player game formed by the generator and the discriminator. Sometimes, gradient descent successfully reaches an equilibrium, but the game oscillates between the two players in other cases. Simultaneous gradient descent is not guaranteed to converge. Goodfellow et al. (2014) show that gradient descent will converge if the updates occur in function space, but in practice, the updates are in parameter space, so there is no theorem to say whether or not GANs are guaranteed to converge.

Mode Collapse. One of the most typical types of non-convergence in GANs is *mode collapse* or the *Helvetica scenario*. In this context, a *mode* is a category of output, so with the MNIST dataset, we can say there are 10 modes. Mode collapse occurs when the generator only produces a subset of the modes in the original dataset. Complete mode collapse is rare, but partial mode collapse, where the generator only produces a subset of the possible modes in the training set, is familiar. So, for the MNIST dataset, this would translate to a GAN that only generates a few numbers, not all 10. In more general cases, mode collapse translates to a lack of variety in outputs.

Consider the objective for the generator (Srihari, 2020b),

$$\mathbb{E}_{x \sim p_g}[\ln(1 - D(G(z)))]. \tag{9.101}$$

If the generator were trained without updating the discriminator, the generated images would converge to an image x^* that is guaranteed to fool the discriminator. G would become insensitive to z. Restart the training of the discriminator, and it will then converge on detecting just this single mode. Given that G is already insensitive to the random vector, D would push the generator to find another sensitive mode. Hence, both networks become overfitted to the vulnerabilities of the other, and mode collapse has occurred.

Vanishing Gradients. If the discriminator is allowed to improve too much compared to the generator, the binary cross-entropy loss will contain flat regions (Zhou et al., 2020a). When the gradient falls to zero, the discriminator does not provide a strong enough signal to the generator, and training stops. So, for the classic GAN model, the training of the generator and discriminator must be carefully balanced so that each performance does not dominate the other. Goodfellow et al. (2014) note that early in training, the generator loss in Equation (9.101) saturates and suggests training G to maximise $\log D(G(z))$ instead.

9.5.2.2 Wasserstein GANs The training difficulties with the classic GAN model have been partly attributed to a loss function based on the Jenson–Shannon divergence. An alternative is provided by the Wasserstein-1 or *earth-mover* distance, defined by

$$W(\mathbb{P}_r, \mathbb{P}_\theta) = \inf_{\gamma \in \Pi(\mathbb{P}_r, \mathbb{P}_\theta)} \mathbb{E}_{(x,y)\sim\gamma}\left[|x - y|\right], \tag{9.102}$$

where the set of all joint distributions $\gamma(x, y)$ with marginals $\mathbb{P}_r$ and $\mathbb{P}_\theta$ is denoted by $\Pi(\mathbb{P}_r, \mathbb{P}_\theta)$. Here, γ represents how much mass must be moved from x to y and the earth-mover distance is the optimal transport policy (Arjovsky et al., 2017). The key observation from Arjovsky et al. (2017) is that $W(\mathbb{P}_r, \mathbb{P}_\theta)$ is a continuous loss function on θ and is differentiable almost everywhere, unlike the Jenson–Shannon divergence. The infinium in Equation (9.102) is intractable but the Kantorovich–Rubinstein duality (Villani, 2009; Arjovsky et al., 2017) allows it to be re-expressed as

$$W(\mathbb{P}_r, \mathbb{P}_\theta) = \sup_{\|f\|_L \leq 1} \mathbb{E}_{x\sim\mathbb{P}_r}[f(x)] - \mathbb{E}_{x\sim\mathbb{P}_\theta}[f(x)], \tag{9.103}$$

where the supremum is taken over all 1-Lipschitz functions f. A function that is K-Lipschitz continuous satisfies $\|f(x_1) - f(x_2)\| \leq K\|x_1 - x_2\|$. We can rewrite this expression once more in terms of the generator, $G(z, \boldsymbol{\theta})$, and discriminator functions, $D(x, \boldsymbol{\phi})$,

$$J_D = \mathbb{E}[D(x)] - \mathbb{E}[D(G(z))]. \tag{9.104}$$

The remaining question is how to enforce the 1-Lipschitz constraint. Arjovsky et al. (2017) propose weight clipping, something they accept is 'clearly terrible', but proceed to limit the discriminator weights to the range $[-0.01, 0.01]$. With this formulation, Algorithm 9.7 gives the training routine.

Algorithm 9.7: WGAN Training with Weight Clipping

Input: Training data D, learning rate α, inner loop steps k, clip limit c
for *no. training iterations* **do**
  for *k steps* **do**
    Sample noise $z \sim p_z$;
    $\tilde{x} \leftarrow G(\theta, z)$;
    $x \sim p_d$ (mini-batch);
    64 $Pred_F \leftarrow D(\phi, \tilde{x})$;
    $Pred_R \leftarrow D(\phi, x)$;
    $J_F \leftarrow \text{mean}(Pred_F)$;
    $J_R \leftarrow -\text{mean}(Pred_R)$;
    $J_D \leftarrow J_F + J_R$;
    Optimise objective J_D;
    Update ϕ using SGD optimiser;
    $\phi \leftarrow clip(\phi, -c, c)$;
  Sample noise $z \sim p_z$;
  $\tilde{x} \leftarrow G(\theta, 64z)$;
  $Pred_F \leftarrow D(\phi, \tilde{x})$;
  $J_G \leftarrow -\text{mean}(Pred_F)$;
  Update θ using SGD optimiser;
Output: Parameters θ, ϕ

EXAMPLE 9.9: WGAN WITH WEIGHT CLIPPING

Two models were trained using the Wasserstein loss and applying weight clipping to ensure the 1-Lipschitz constraint is satisfied, one using the CIFAR-10 dataset and the other using MNIST. The architectures were identical apart from the number of channels, and the MNIST images were padded up to 32×32. Aside from the loss functions below, much of the code was identical to the DCGAN example.

```
def gen_loss(gen, disc, batch_size, latent_dim, device):
    noise = torch.randn(batch_size, latent_dim, 1, 1, device=device)
    fake_im = gen(noise)
    fake_pred = disc(fake_im)
    gen_loss = -fake_pred.mean()
    return gen_loss

def disc_loss(gen, disc, real_im, batch_size, latent_dim, device):
    noise = torch.randn(batch_size, latent_dim, 1, 1, device=device)
    fake_im = gen(noise).detach()
    fake_pred = disc(fake_im)
    fake_loss = fake_pred.mean()
    real_pred = disc(real_im)
    real_loss = -real_pred.mean()
    disc_loss = fake_loss + real_loss
    return disc_loss
```

(*Continued*)

(*Continued*)

The name *discriminator* has been retained, although Arjovsky et al. (2017) use the term *critic* as the output is now linear. Of course, given that the logits were included in the DCGAN loss function, no change is needed to the structure of the discriminator network. The training loop needs to be modified to allow more than one step of training for the discriminator per step of generator training, and for these models, five steps were used in the inner loop for each outer-loop iteration. The discriminator weights must also be clipped and done by adding the following code inside the inner loop:

```
for p in disc.parameters():
    p.data.clamp_(-weight_cliping_limit, weight_cliping_limit)
```

The weight clipping limit was set equal to 0.01 as per Arjovsky et al. (2017). The CIFAR-10 model was trained through 300 epochs and the MNIST through 50 epochs. In both cases, the learning rate was reduced to 0.00005, and a training batch size of 256 was used. The RMSProp optimiser was used instead of Adam.

The losses in the WGAN case for CIFAR-10 are illustrated in Figure 9.37 and show that the losses for the generator and the discriminator converge on the same value. Figures 9.38 and 9.39 show 64 images from the CIFAR-10 and 40 images from MNIST models at their end state. Table 9.6 shows the inception scores and FID values during training, worse than those from the DCGAN with its original GAN loss function.

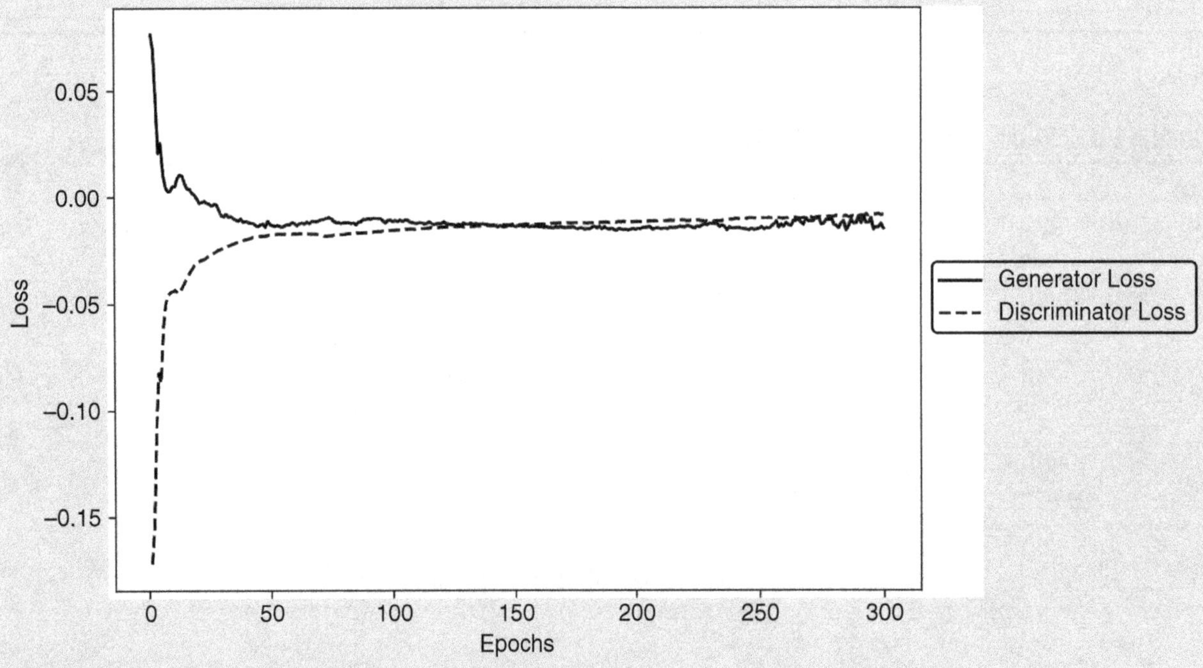

FIGURE 9.37 The generator and discriminator losses as a function of epoch for WGAN with weight clipping.

FIGURE 9.38 Sixty-four images generated by a WGAN with weight clipping trained using the CIFAR-10 dataset.

(*Continued*)

(*Continued*)

FIGURE 9.39 Forty images generated by a WGAN with weight clipping trained using the MNIST dataset.

TABLE 9.6 Inception Score and Fréchet Inception Distance for the Wasserstein GAN Trained Using CIFAR-10

Epoch	Inception Score	Fréchet Inception Distance
50	3.0917	0.0352
100	3.764	0.0258
150	4.052	0.0193
200	4.257	0.0182
250	4.198	0.0182
300	4.160	0.0182

A superior alternative to weight clipping is presented by Gulrajani et al. (2017); a penalty on the gradient norm in the form of a regularisation term. The penalty term is given by

$$\lambda \mathbb{E}_{\hat{x} \sim \mathbb{P}_{\hat{x}}} \left[\left(\left\| \nabla_{\hat{x}} D(\hat{x}) \right\|_2 - 1 \right)^2 \right], \tag{9.105}$$

where the gradient is taken on random sample points $\hat{x}$. The sample distribution $\mathbb{P}_{\hat{x}}$ is chosen to sample points uniformly on straight lines between the data distribution $\mathbb{P}_r$ and the generator distribution $\mathbb{P}_\theta$. Gulrajani et al. (2017) show that the optimal critic has straight lines between coupled points from $\mathbb{P}_r$ and $\mathbb{P}_\theta$ with gradient norm 1. A WGAN with a gradient penalty is presented in Algorithm 9.8.

Algorithm 9.8: WGAN Training with Gradient Penalty

Input: Training data D, learning rate α, inner loop steps k, penalty coefficient λ
for *no. training iterations* **do**
    for *k steps* **do**
        Sample noise $z \sim p_z$;
        $\tilde{x} \leftarrow G(\theta, z)$;
        $x \sim p_d$ (mini-batch);
        $Pred_F \leftarrow D(\phi, \tilde{x})$;
        $Pred_R \leftarrow D(\phi, x)$;
        $\epsilon \sim U[0, 1]$;
        $\hat{x} \leftarrow \epsilon x + (1 - \epsilon)\tilde{x}$;
        $J_F \leftarrow \text{mean}(Pred_F)$;
        $J_R \leftarrow -\text{mean}(Pred_R)$;
        $J_D \leftarrow J_F + J_R + \lambda \left[\left(\left\| \nabla_{\hat{x}} D(\hat{x}) \right\|_2 - 1 \right)^2 \right]$;
        Optimise objective J_D;
        Update ϕ using SGD optimiser;
    Sample noise $z \sim p_z$;
    $\tilde{x} \leftarrow G(\theta, z)$;
    $Pred_F \leftarrow D(\phi, \tilde{x})$;
    $J_G \leftarrow -\text{mean}(Pred_F)$;
    Update θ using SGD optimiser;
Output: Parameters θ, ϕ

EXAMPLE 9.10: WGAN USING GRADIENT PENALTY

Implementing the gradient penalty is relatively straightforward and just requires the discriminator loss to be modified. To calculate the gradient penalty, the model samples the uniform distribution at each point in the image space and then interpolates between a batch of real and fake images.

The gradient of the discriminator model is then calculated on the interpolated 'image', $\widehat{x}$, and the norm is calculated. Finally, the MSE criterion is used to calculate the final expression given in Equation (9.105). The remaining code is the same as for the earlier WGAN but with weight clipping removed. Sixty-four sampled images from the model trained through 300 epochs are given in Figure 9.40. Table 9.7 shows the inception scores and FID values during training. The inception score and Fréchet inception distance for the Wasserstein GAN using gradient penalty are given in Table 9.7.

FIGURE 9.40 Sixty-four images generated by a WGAN with gradient penalty trained using the CIFAR-10 dataset.

TABLE 9.7 Inception Score and Fréchet Inception Distance for the Wasserstein GAN Using Gradient Penalty Trained Using CIFAR-10

Epoch	Inception Score	Fréchet Inception Distance
50	3.643	0.0571
100	3.953	0.0439
150	4.173	0.0365
200	4.160	0.0354
250	4.026	0.0411
300	4.039	0.0507

```
def disc_loss(gen, disc, real_im, batch_size, latent_dim, device):
    noise = torch.randn(batch_size, latent_dim, 1, 1, device=device)
    fake_im = gen(noise).detach()
    fake_pred = disc(fake_im)
    fake_loss = fake_pred.mean()
    real_pred = disc(real_im)
    real_loss = -real_pred.mean()

    # Weight penalty
    epsilon = torch.rand([real_im.shape[0],1,1,1], device=device)
    epsilon = epsilon.expand(real_im.size())
    x_hat = epsilon * real_im.data  + (1 - epsilon) * fake_im.data
    x_hat = Variable(x_hat, requires_grad=True)

    Dx_hat = disc(x_hat)
    gradients = autograd.grad(outputs=Dx_hat, inputs=x_hat,
    grad_outputs=torch.ones(Dx_hat.size(), device=device),
    create_graph=True)[0].view(x_hat.size(0), -1)
    slopes = gradients.norm(2, dim=1)
    lipschitz_grad_norm = torch.ones(slopes.size(), device=device)
    gp = gp_weight * L2_criterion(slopes, lipschitz_grad_norm)

    disc_loss = fake_loss + real_loss + gp
    return disc_loss
```

9.5.2.3 Spectral Normalisation Miyato et al. (2018) introduced *spectral normalisation* as an alternative means of ensuring that the Lipschitz constraint is satisfied. The spectral norm of a matrix is the largest singular value of that matrix. A matrix W can be factorised using *singular value decomposition* (Press et al., 2007, pp. 51–63),

$$W = U\Sigma V^T, \tag{9.106}$$

where U and V are orthogonal matrices and Σ is a matrix with singular values along its diagonal. Note that Σ may be rectangular. If the singular values are ranked by size, then

$$\Sigma = \begin{pmatrix} \sigma_1 & & & \\ & \sigma_2 & & \\ & & \ddots & \\ & & & \sigma_n \end{pmatrix}, \tag{9.107}$$

and the spectral norm is defined by (Zhou et al., 2020a)

$$\sigma(\mathbf{W}) = \sigma_1. \tag{9.108}$$

Consider a neural network layer, $g(h)$. By definition, the Lipschitz norm is given by (Miyato et al., 2018, p. 3)

$$||g||_{Lip} = \sup_h \sigma(\nabla g(h)). \tag{9.109}$$

For a linear layer, $g(h) = \mathbf{W}h$, and so

$$\begin{aligned} ||g||_{Lip} &= \sup_h \sigma(\nabla \mathbf{W}h) \\ &= \sigma(\mathbf{W}). \end{aligned} \tag{9.110}$$

There is an inequality that is useful in the full network case,

$$||g_1 \circ g_2||_{Lip} \leq ||g_1||_{Lip} \cdot ||g_2||_{Lip}. \tag{9.111}$$

If the activation function a_l has Lipschitz constraint $||a_l||_{Lip} = 1$, then a bound on the Lipschitz constraint for the whole network can be found. Note that ReLU and leaky ReLU both satisfy this condition, while many others satisfy the K-Lipschitz constraint for some K (Miyato et al., 2018, p. 3, n. 1). The neural-complete neural network can be written

$$\begin{aligned} f(h_1, \theta) &= g_L(g_{L-1}(\ldots g_1(h_1))) \\ &= a_L(\mathbf{W}^L(a_{L-1}(\mathbf{W}^{L-1}(\ldots a_1(\mathbf{W}h_1))))), \end{aligned} \tag{9.112}$$

where the bias term has been ignored for clarity. Writing $g_l(h_{l-1}) = a_l(\tilde{g}_l(h_{l-1})$, $\tilde{g}_l$ is a linear layer that satisfies Equation (9.109). Then, the Lipschitz constraint for the whole network can be written as follows, where it is assumed that $||a_l||_{Lip} = 1$ for all l:

$$\begin{aligned} ||f||_{Lip} &\leq ||a_L||_{Lip} \cdot ||\tilde{g}_L||_{Lip} \cdot ||a_{L-1}||_{Lip} \cdot ||\tilde{g}_{L-1}||_{Lip} \cdots ||a_1||_{Lip} \cdot ||\tilde{g}_1||_{Lip} \\ &= \prod_{l=1}^{L} ||\tilde{g}_l||_{Lip} \\ &= \prod_{l=1}^{L} \sigma(\mathbf{W}^l). \end{aligned} \tag{9.113}$$

Hence, the Lipschitz constraint for the whole network is bounded from above by the product of the spectral norms for each layer and, if spectral normalisation is applied such that

$$\mathbf{W}^l_{SN} = \frac{\mathbf{W}^l}{\sigma(\mathbf{W}^l)}, \tag{9.114}$$

then

$$||f||_{Lip} \leq 1. \tag{9.115}$$

To perform spectral normalisation, the spectral norm needs to be calculated for each weight matrix at each step of training. Using SVD to do this would be prohibitively computationally expensive and so an alternative method must be sought. The method proposed by Miyato et al. (2018) begins with vectors $\widetilde{u}$ that are randomly generated from the uniform distribution for each weight. Then, if $\widetilde{u}$ is not orthogonal to the first left-singular vectors, which is a safe assumption if generated from the uniform distribution (Miyato et al., 2018, p. 15, n. 7), and the dominant singular values have no multiplicities,[4] then the power method can be used. The first left- and right-singular vectors are produced using the update rule

$$\widetilde{v} \leftarrow \frac{W^T \widetilde{u}}{\|W^T \widetilde{u}\|_2}, \tag{9.116}$$

$$\widetilde{u} \leftarrow \frac{W^T \widetilde{v}}{\|W^T \widetilde{v}\|_2}. \tag{9.117}$$

During updates with SGD, the weight matrix changes only slowly, and similarly, the largest singular value is small at each update. Hence, the $\widetilde{u}$ vector at each step can be used as input to iteration at the next step. Empirically, only one round of iteration was required at each step for acceptable performance. Once $\widetilde{u}$ and $\widetilde{v}$ have been obtained, the spectral norm is given by

$$\sigma(W) \approx \widetilde{u}^T W \widetilde{v}. \tag{9.118}$$

The superiority of spectral normalisation over gradient clipping is not in doubt. However, the gradient penalty method has a weakness in that it depends on the current generative distribution, which changes during training. Empirically, Miyato et al. (2018) observed that this dependence, coupled with a high learning rate, could destabilise training. Spectral normalisation is much more stable with respect to high learning rates.

EXAMPLE 9.11: SNGAN

In PyTorch there is a built-in implementation of spectral normalisation, `spectral_norm`, which can be imported from `torch.nn.utils.parametrizations`. To apply spectral normalisation to a layer, wrap it using `spectral_norm`. A model with spectral normalisation applied to the discriminator was trained through 200 epochs with the Adam optimiser using the two beta parameters of 0.5 and 0.9. The learning rate can be higher if spectral normalisation is used, and it was selected to be 0.0001. Five iterations of training of the discriminator were used for each iteration of the generator.

A total of 64 generated images from the model trained using CIFAR-10 are illustrated in Figure 9.41. These pictures are sharper than those created by any of the previous GAN models, showing the overall superiority of spectral normalisation over weight clipping and the gradient penalty. Table 9.8 shows the inception scores and FID values during training. The inception score and Fréchet inception distance for the SNGAN are given in Table 9.8.

TABLE 9.8 Inception Score and Fréchet Inception Distance for the SNGAN Trained Using CIFAR-10

Epoch	Inception Score	Fréchet Inception Distance
50	4.317	0.0563
100	5.069	0.0375
150	5.364	0.0293
200	5.599	0.0284
250	5.574	0.0281
300	5.667	0.0250

(*Continued*)

[4] A singular value is said to have multiplicity t if there are t associated linearly independent right-singular vectors and t associated linearly independent left-singular vectors (Cline and Dhillon, 2006).

(*Continued*)

FIGURE 9.41 Sixty-four images generated by an SNGAN trained using the CIFAR-10 dataset.

9.5.3 Controlling Generation

Section 9.1 noted that generative models can learn a conditional distribution $P(X|Y)$, but all the models so far discussed have learned an unconditional data distribution. In this section, GANs with controllable output are explored. Firstly, the *conditional GAN (CGAN)* uses categorical data from the input data to learn the conditional distribution, allowing users to specify a category to output when performing generation. Often, we seek finer control of the output from the generator for features in the input space for which there may or may not be categorical information available. So, for example, in the context of faces, we might seek to control eye colour or whether the output images show someone wearing a hat or glasses. Hence, Section 9.5.3.2 discusses how control can be imposed on the latent space or implied from it to provide output to a specification.

9.5.3.1 Conditional GANs Conditional GANs were first developed by Mirza and Osindero (2014). The GAN architecture must be modified to submit the labels to the generator and the discriminator to condition on them. The generator needs to know what category it should generate. In contrast, the category provides a hint to the discriminator so that if, for example, it receives an image of a bird when a cat is expected, then the discriminator knows it is a fake.

In practice, the input modifications to the generator and the discriminator are slightly different because the inputs to each network have a different form. GAN generators take a vector of latent variables, and the CGAN adds a one-hot vector containing the labels and concatenates it with the latent vector. The discriminator takes an image as input, so, as an example, in the CIFAR-10 case, it has the shape $3 \times 32 \times 32$. The labels must be passed to preserve the shape, and a channel must be added per label. The 'one-hot' representation is created with shape $categories \times height \times width$, with all the values for a given category set equal to 1 and the remaining elements 0. The image and category tensor are then concatenated together.

EXAMPLE 9.12: CGAN WITH MNIST AND CIFAR-10

Two CGAN models were trained with MNIST and CIFAR-10 and can be found in the Jupyter Notebooks `Conditional GAN with MNIST.ipynb` and `Conditional GAN with CIFAR10.ipynb`, respectively. The MNIST model was conditioned on the 10 numbers, and the CIFAR-10 model on the 10 image categories in the dataset. The SNGAN was used as the basis for both models. Only minor modifications were needed to the generator and discriminator networks. In both cases, the label dimensionality was passed as an argument to the initialisation and used to add to the size of the input to the generator and the number of input channels for the discriminator. The `forward` function was modified to take a labels tensor as an additional input, which was then concatenated with the input and passed through the network. Training labels were required. In this case, the training loop was modified to generate a one-hot representation of the labels. The basic one-hot representation is suitable for input to the generator, but it requires the number of dimensions to be expanded by two. For the discriminator, the one-hot tensor needs to be expanded to match the image dimensions so it can be concatenated along the channel axis.

The MNIST model was trained through 50 epochs, as in the SNGAN case, with all hyperparameters remaining the same. Figure 9.42 shows a grid of 10 generated images, with each column conditioned on a different digit. The results show an apparent diversity of digit styles in each row; all numbers are identifiable in each column.

For the CIFAR-10 dataset, the model was trained through 300 epochs, and the model again was almost identical to the SNGAN case. Figure 9.43 shows 10 examples of each category, each column containing a different category. The rows show considerable diversity within a category, but some categories are more easily identified than others. For example, column 2 shows some identifiable cars, while column 10 has several well-defined images of trucks. Other columns, however, are less clear. The inception score and Fréchet inception distance were also calculated every 50 epochs during training for a sample of 32,768 examples, and the results are given in Table 9.9. These results are better than those obtained by the plain SNGAN and show that the extra information in the form of the labels is benefiting image quality.

(*Continued*)

(*Continued*)

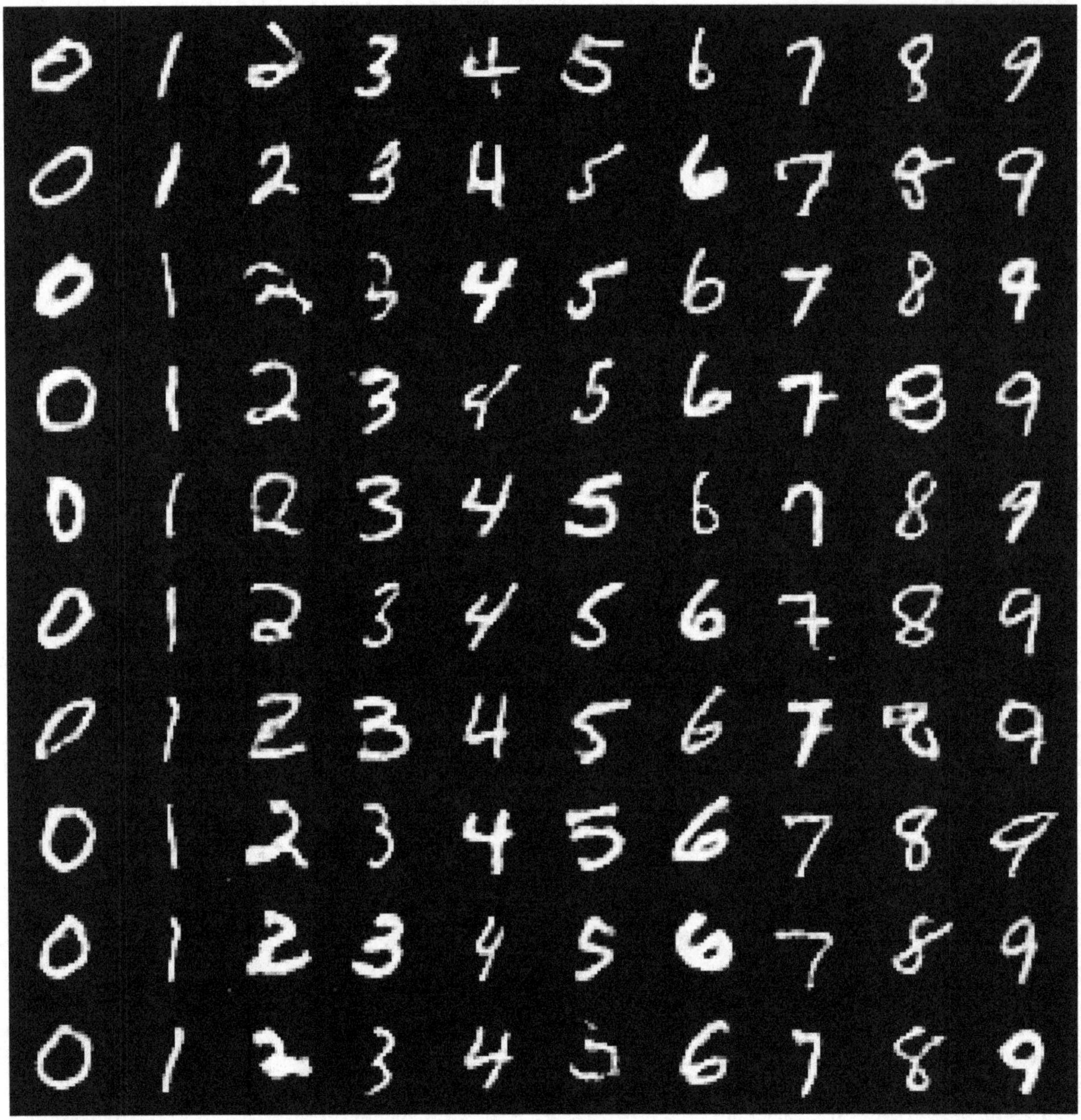

FIGURE 9.42 Hundred images generated by a CGAN trained using the MNIST dataset. The digits in the output were conditioned for each column.

FIGURE 9.43 Hundred images generated by a CGAN trained using the CIFAR-10 dataset. Each column is conditioned on one of the 10 categories in the dataset, which are in order: aeroplane, automobile, bird, cat, deer, dog, frog, horse, ship and truck.

(*Continued*)

(Continued)

TABLE 9.9 Inception Score and Fréchet Inception Distance for the CGAN Model Trained Using CIFAR-10

Epoch	Inception Score	Fréchet Inception Distance
50	4.462	0.0493
100	5.175	0.0320
150	5.564	0.0253
200	5.704	0.0218
250	5.919	0.0197
300	6.007	0.0185

9.5.3.2 InfoGAN and Unsupervised Learning The problem with the conditional GAN is that it requires supervised learning as we must supply labels to the generator and the discriminator networks. We want to be able to use unsupervised learning, given that the amount of unlabelled data dwarfs the amount of labelled data. However, we still want to be able to control generation. We know from the visualisation of features described in Section 6.6.1 that neural networks learn representations, and classification networks learn features we might wish to control. Furthermore, we know from the discussion of the variational encoder models in Section 9.4 with MNIST that regions of the latent space correspond to the different number categories; there is no reason to believe that the latent space of GANs will be any different. Hence, there is good reason to believe that smoothly changing the input vector from the latent space will vary the features of the image. Dosovitskiy et al. (2015) demonstrated that generative models can learn to model attributes of three-dimensional objects and then change properties like rotation. Radford et al. (2016) showed that GANs learn specific filters to draw objects, like classifiers learn filters to classify objects. Inspired by the application of vector arithmetic in the context of language models (Mikolov et al., 2013), they further demonstrated how simple vector arithmetic on the latent space of a GAN trained on faces could be used to add features like glasses to an image. Hence, the question becomes how to modify images effectively through the latent space.

Chen et al. (2016) proposed *InfoGAN* as an extension to GANs driven by information-theoretic considerations. The problem with GANs is that there is no a priori reason to suppose that the latent space is not highly entangled, so there is no clear relationship between the dimensions of the latent vector $\boldsymbol{z}$ and image semantics. InfoGAN is trained without label information but decomposes the latent space into semantically meaningful factors. So, for example, when training a GAN to generate numbers using the MNIST dataset, the latent input is split three ways: a vector of samples drawn from the normal distribution in common with previous models but concatenated with a one-hot representation of a 10-dimensional discrete random variable corresponding to the digit and two continuous uniform random variables designed to control the angle and thickness of the digit. The model is then trained to recover the semantics from the dataset in an unsupervised manner.

Given the latent vector $\boldsymbol{c}$ and noise vector $\boldsymbol{z}$, the generator becomes a function of both, $G(\boldsymbol{z}, \boldsymbol{c})$. The GAN can ignore the latent vector and to avoid this, Chen et al. (2016) use an information-theoretic regularisation technique. They proposed that the mutual information between latent vector $\boldsymbol{c}$ and generator distribution $G(\boldsymbol{z}, \boldsymbol{c})$, $I(\boldsymbol{c}, G(\boldsymbol{z}, \boldsymbol{c}))$, is high. Mutual information was defined in Equation (9.3) in the context of the *inception score* earlier in Section 9.2.1. Hence, Chen et al. (2016) add a regularisation term to the loss function,

$$\min_G \max_D V_I(D, G) = V(D, G) - \lambda I(\boldsymbol{c}, G(\boldsymbol{z}, \boldsymbol{c})). \tag{9.119}$$

In practice, it is not possible to maximise the mutual information directly, as it requires the posterior distribution $P(c|x)$). It is, however, possible to find a lower bound for the mutual information using *variational information maximisation* (Barber and Agakov, 2003; Chen et al., 2016),

$$I(c; G(z, c)) = H(c) - H(c \mid G(z, c)) \tag{9.120}$$
$$= \mathbb{E}_{x\sim G(z,c)}\left[\mathbb{E}_{c'\sim P(c|x)}\left[\log P\left(c' \mid x\right)\right]\right] + H(c) \tag{9.121}$$
$$= \mathbb{E}_{x\sim G(z,c)}\left[D_{\mathrm{KL}}(P(\cdot \mid x)\|Q(\cdot \mid x)) + \mathbb{E}_{c'\sim P(c|x)}\left[\log Q\left(c' \mid x\right)\right]\right] + H(c) \tag{9.122}$$
$$\geq \mathbb{E}_{x\sim G(z,c)}\left[\mathbb{E}_{c'\sim P(c|x)}\left[\log Q\left(c' \mid x\right)\right]\right] + H(c), \tag{9.123}$$

where $Q(c|x)$ approximates the true posterior $P(c|x)$. The last line inequality is obtained by recognising that the Kullback–Leibler divergence is always positive. Given $\mathbb{E}_{x\sim G(z,c)}[D_{\mathrm{KL}}(P(\cdot \mid x)\|Q(\cdot \mid x))] \to 0$ as $Q \to P$, the inequality becomes exact in the limit that the approximation approaches the posterior. Chen et al. (2016) prove the following lemma:

Lemma 9.1: *Given random variables X and Y and function $f(x, y)$, then*

$$\mathbb{E}_{x\sim X, y\sim Y|x}[f(x, y)] = \mathbb{E}_{x\sim X, y\sim Y|x, x'\sim X|y}[f(x', y)], \tag{9.124}$$

under suitable regularity conditions.

Given the lemma, a variational lower bound can be defined by

$$\begin{aligned} L_I(G, Q) &= \mathbb{E}_{c\sim P(c), x\sim G(z,c)}[\log Q(c|x)] + H(c) \\ &= \mathbb{E}_{x\sim G(z,c)}[\mathbb{E}_{c'\sim P(c|x)}[\log Q(c'|x)]] + H(c). \end{aligned} \tag{9.125}$$

Monte Carlo simulation can readily obtain this term, and $L_I(G, Q)$ can be added to the GAN loss function as a regularisation term without changing the training process. The distribution $Q(c|x)$ is parameterised as a neural network and can share most layers with the discriminator save for a final fully connected layer. Softmax is the optimal choice for output for discrete latent variables, while more choices are available for continuous variables. The loss function for categorical variables becomes the standard categorical cross-entropy between sampled input and output from the Q-network. At the same time, for continuous random variables, mean square error between input and output can be used. The weight term should be 1 for categorical variables and a lower value for continuous ones to scale them appropriately to match the other terms in the GAN loss function. $L_I(G, Q)$ converges rapidly and faster than the other GAN objectives.

EXAMPLE 9.13: InfoGAN WITH MNIST

As an example of InfoGAN, a model was trained using MNIST and can be found in the Notebook `InfoGAN with MNIST.ipynb`. The code is similar to the CGAN with a modified discriminator model and training loop. As discussed in Section 9.5.3.2 above, the input to the generator is now factored into three: an incompressible noise vector drawn from the standard normal distribution, a categorical latent variable to control the number generation represented as a 10-dimensional one-hot vector and two uniform random variables on the interval $[-1, 1]$ to control the stroke width and angle. As with CGAN, these three inputs are concatenated together before input to the generator model, although, unlike CGAN, all of these inputs are purely random. The new discriminator model now has three outputs instead of one. It now contains three neural networks: the original discriminator and the two Q-networks approximating the posterior distributions for the categorical and continuous latent variables. The new discriminator code is illustrated below, now with three linear layers for the output and the shared convolutional layers.

```
class Discriminator(nn.Module):
    def __init__(self, in_size=32, cat_dim = 10, code_dim = 2,
                 no_channels=1):
```

(Continued)

(Continued)

```
        super(Discriminator, self).__init__()
        self.disc = nn.Sequential(
            spectral_norm(nn.Conv2d(no_channels, in_size, 3, 2, 1,
                          bias=False)),
            nn.LeakyReLU(0.2, inplace=True),
            spectral_norm(nn.Conv2d(in_size, in_size * 2, 3, 2, 1,
                          bias=False)),
            nn.LeakyReLU(0.2, inplace=True),
            spectral_norm(nn.Conv2d(in_size * 2, in_size * 4, 3, 2, 1,
             content...           bias=False)),
            nn.LeakyReLU(0.2, inplace=True),
            spectral_norm(nn.Conv2d(in_size * 4, in_size * 8, 3, 2, 1,
                          bias=False)),
            nn.LeakyReLU(0.2, inplace=True)
        )
        self.adversarial = nn.Sequential(nn.Linear(in_size * 32, 1))
        self.auxiliary = nn.Sequential(
            nn.Linear(in_size * 32, cat_dim),
            nn.Softmax())
        self.code = nn.Sequential(nn.Linear(in_size * 32, code_dim))

    def forward(self, image):
        out = self.disc(image)
        out = out.view(out.shape[0], -1)
        adv_out = self.adversarial(out)
        aux_out = self.auxiliary(out)
        code_out = self.code(out)
        return adv_out, aux_out, code_out
```

The generator and discriminator are trained in the usual way, with the *Q*-outputs from the discriminator, and here, the Wasserstein loss was used. The training loop adds a new section to train the *Q* or information networks. The categorical softmax is trained using categorical cross-entropy, and the continuous variable using mean squared error.

```
info_opt.zero_grad()
sampled_labels = torch.randint(cat_dim, (cur_batch_size,), device=device)
z = torch.randn(cur_batch_size, latent_dim, device=device)
label_input = to_categorical(sampled_labels, num_columns=cat_dim,
                             device=device)
code_input = torch.rand(cur_batch_size, code_dim, device=device) * 2 - 1.0
gen_imgs = gen(z, label_input, code_input)
_, pred_label, pred_code = disc(gen_imgs)
iloss = lam_cat * cat_loss(pred_label, sampled_labels) + \
    lam_cont * cont_loss(pred_code, code_input)
iloss.backward()
info_opt.step()
```

The generator, discriminator and information networks were all trained using Adam optimisers with a learning rate of $2e^{-4}$ and beta parameters of 0.5 and 0.999. The lambda weights were 1.0 for the categorical variable and 0.1 for the continuous variables. The pure noise vector had 62 elements, and the model was trained on it for 200 epochs.

Figure 9.44 shows the loss during training for the three loss functions. As expected, the information loss has converged quickly and within a few epochs. The grid of numbers shown in Figure 9.45 is generated using the trained generator, with each column corresponding to a different category and the continuous random variables set to zero. The generator has successfully learned the 10 categories of numbers, although there is confusion between 4 and 9. Of course, the generator does not know the correct order of the integers, which is random. The numbers also all have similar stroke thickness.

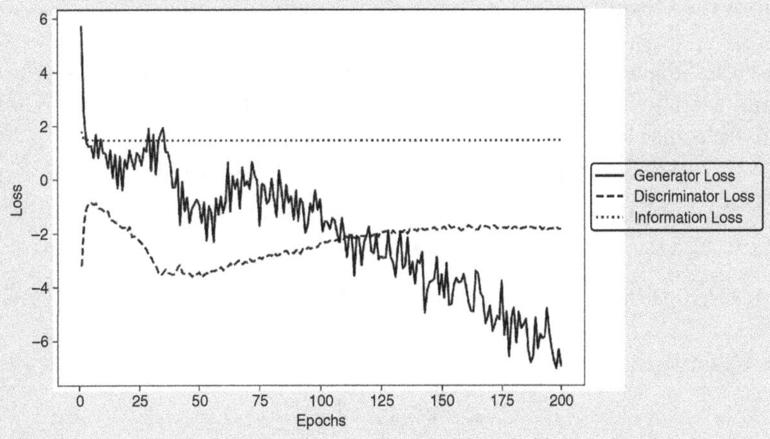

FIGURE 9.44 Loss as a function of epoch during InfoGAN training.

FIGURE 9.45 InfoGAN generated MNIST numbers where each column had a different category set, and the continuous variables were set to zero.

9.5.3.3 Interpreting the Latent Space Using existing models to control image generation or edit images rather than train a GAN specifically would be desirable, allowing state-of-the-art image-generation models such as *StyleGAN* to be used directly.

A generative model is not needed for this purpose, as demonstrated by Upchurch et al. (2017) and their *deep feature interpolation* technique, which only uses a trained convolutional network. The idea here is to change an image realistically by, for example, adjusting the subject's age or adding facial hair. A VGG-19 network trained on ImageNet is used alongside a source image x and two other sets of images: a *target* set S^t with the desired attribute and a *source* set S^s without the attribute. The following steps are then followed:

1. The target and source set images are mapped into the feature space generated by the VGG-19 network to give feature vectors ϕ^t and ϕ^s. The features were the concatenated feature values taken from the first layer of each of the last three convolutional blocks in the network.[5]
2. The average feature vectors from target and source sets are then calculated to give $\bar{\phi}^t$ and $\bar{\phi}^s$. The difference then defines the attribute vector,

$$w = \bar{\phi}^t - \bar{\phi}^s. \tag{9.126}$$

3. The image is then also mapped to the feature space, and the attribute is modified by moving along the attribute vector.
4. The final image z is reconstructed using the inverse mapping

$$z = \phi^{-1}(\phi(x) + \alpha w). \tag{9.127}$$

The inverse mapping is constructed using the approach adopted by Mahendran and Vedaldi (2015), that is, z is obtained using gradient descent with

$$z = \underset{z}{\text{argmin}} \frac{1}{2} \|(\phi(x) + \alpha w) - \phi(z)\|_2^2 + \lambda_{V^\beta} R_{V^\beta}(z), \tag{9.128}$$

where R_{V^β} is the *total variation regulariser* given by

$$R_{V^\beta}(z) = \sum_{i,j} \left((z_{i,j+1} - z_{i,j})^2 + (z_{i+1,j} - z_{i,j})^2 \right)^{\frac{\beta}{2}}, \tag{9.129}$$

and the subscripts of z are the pixel indices.

The advantages of the deep feature interpolation approach are that image reconstruction is fast and, given that only the convolutional layers of VGG are needed, it uses only around 4 GB of GPU memory (Upchurch et al., 2017, pp. 7064-7073). However, the major disadvantage lies in limiting the choice of target and source sets in which images must be aligned.

Given that vector arithmetic is effective in feature space, it is a reasonable expectation that it should also be effective when operating on the latent space of a GAN, and this is the approach adopted by Shen et al. (2020a,b) and *InterFaceGAN*. The GAN is a deterministic function, g, that maps from the latent space $\mathbb{Z} \subseteq \mathbb{R}^d$ to the image space $\mathbb{X}$. If a semantic scoring function f_S exists and maps from the image space to the semantic space $\mathbb{S}$, then it is possible to construct a mapping from latent vectors to semantic vectors,

$$s = f_S(g(z)). \tag{9.130}$$

Given two latent vectors z_1 and z_2, it has already been established by Radford et al. (2016) and others that properties change continuously when linearly interpolating between these vectors. Suppose the two vectors display two different states of a binary semantic, such as wearing and not wearing glasses. A hyperplane between the two vectors defines the separation boundary with a normal vector $\boldsymbol{n} \in \mathbb{R}^d$. A measure of separation for a latent vector and the hyperplane is defined by

$$d(\boldsymbol{n}, z) = \boldsymbol{n}^T z, \tag{9.131}$$

[5]VGG networks were discussed in Section 6.7.3.

and the change of semantic static occurs when the sign of d changes. Hence, the expectation is that the semantic space score in this one-dimensional case is linearly dependent on d,

$$f_S(g(z)) = \lambda d(\boldsymbol{n}, z). \tag{9.132}$$

It is useful to explore the multi-dimensional case. With multiple semantics, the score vector is given by

$$s \equiv f_S(g(z)) = \Lambda \boldsymbol{N}^T z, \tag{9.133}$$

where $\Lambda = \text{diag}(\lambda_1, \ldots, \lambda_m)$ and $\boldsymbol{N}$ is a matrix with columns formed by the hyperplane normal vectors $\boldsymbol{n}_i$. Given that $z \sim \mathcal{N}(0, \boldsymbol{I}_d)$,

$$s \sim \mathcal{N}(0, \boldsymbol{\Sigma}_s). \tag{9.134}$$

$$\boldsymbol{\Sigma}_s = \boldsymbol{\Lambda} \boldsymbol{N}^T \boldsymbol{N} \boldsymbol{\Lambda}. \tag{9.135}$$

So, the different semantics are only disentangled if the correlation matrix Σ_s is diagonal, which is only true if the normal vectors $\boldsymbol{n}_i$ are orthogonal.

To manipulate the latent space to generate an image with the desired properties can be achieved with a linear transformation. For a single semantic, given the hyperplane normal vector $\boldsymbol{n}$, the transformed latent vector is given by

$$\tilde{z} = z + \alpha \boldsymbol{n}. \tag{9.136}$$

For multiple semantics, unless the hyperplane normal vectors are orthogonal, varying one semantic will lead to changes in the second. Hence, Shen et al. (2020a) propose *conditional manipulation* in which orthogonal vectors are found.

The remaining question is how to identify the hyperplanes associated with different semantics. To do this, Shen et al. (2020a) use the following procedure:

1. Identify the semantics of interest and train an attribute prediction model to identify these attributes in images. Given that the work of Shen et al. (2020a) was on faces, they trained a ResNet-50 model on the CelebA dataset to simultaneously predict five attributes: smile, age, gender, eyeglasses and five-point facial landmarks.
2. Sample many images ($\sim$ 500,000) from the pre-trained GANs (PCGAN and StyleGAN in this case).
3. Predict attribute score from all images using the prediction model.
4. Use the highest and lowest 10,000 scores for each attribute and train linear SVM models to give decision boundaries.
5. The normal vectors can then be used to perform single- or multiple-attribute manipulation.

9.5.4 High-Resolution GANs

Early GANs were limited to relatively low-resolution images. A series of architectural developments beginning with *progressive growing* in 2017 saw GAN outputs scale up to 1024^2 and become photorealistic with *StyleGAN* in 2020, and this section describes the main developments. While this work is not necessarily directly relevant to quantitative finance applications, it is important to the overall development of neural networks and GANs. Only a single example of a low-resolution StyleGAN model is included here, reflecting the cost of training. Large GAN models like StyleGAN require much training, with multiple data centre GPUs.

9.5.4.1 Progressive Growing (ProGAN) The basic idea of progressive growing, as introduced by Karras et al. (2018), is to gradually increase the resolution of the GAN during training beginning at 4×4 and then steadily building up to 1024×1024. The generator and discriminator are grown in tandem, each adding an upsample and downsample block simultaneously. The new blocks are gradually 'faded-in' by adding them using a bypass route and a weight, α, that grows from an initial value of 0.0 to 1.0, as illustrated in Figure 9.46. Karras et al. (2018) used a two-stage process for each fade-in, with 800,000 real images passing through the discriminator. At the same time, α was steadily increased from 0 to 1, followed by a stabilisation period with a further 800,000 real images shown to the discriminator with α held fixed before another higher-resolution block was introduced. Real images must be shown

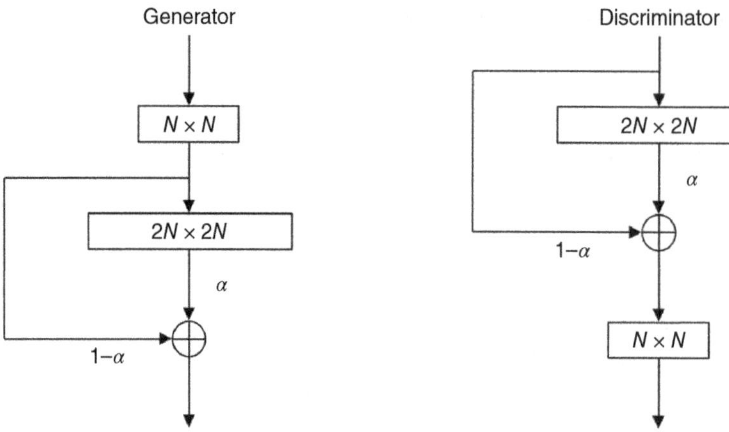

FIGURE 9.46 During the training of ProGAN, new layers are not introduced suddenly but 'faded-in' gradually. During the fade-in process, the weight of the new layer, α, is gradually increased from 0 to 1. For the discriminator, real images must be scaled appropriately to match the current image resolution, and during fade-in, images of both old and new scales are used.

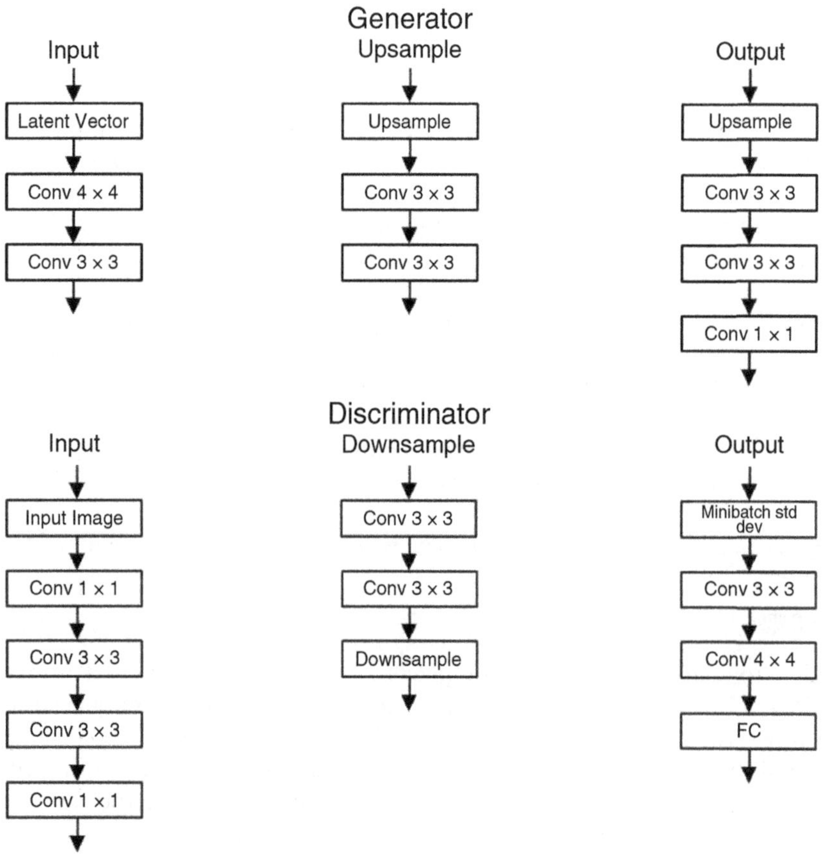

FIGURE 9.47 Generator and discriminator block definitions for ProGAN of Karras et al. (2018).

to the discriminator at reduced resolution during the growing phase. Real images of old and new resolutions are required in the fade-in period. The structure of each type of block in the generator and discriminator is shown in Figure 9.47, while the overall structure of the generator and discriminator for image output of size 1024×1024 is given in Tables 9.10 and 9.11, respectively.

Karras et al. (2018) also introduce several other innovations. As shown in Figure 9.47 and Table 9.11, the output block of the discriminator contains a mini-batch standard deviation layer. This layer calculates the standard

TABLE 9.10 The High-Level Architecture of the ProGAN Generator in Terms of Blocks as Defined in Figure 9.47

Layer	In Channels	Out Channels	Output Shape
Input	512	512	4×4
Upsample	512	512	8×8
Upsample	512	512	16×16
Upsample	512	512	32×32
Upsample	512	256	64×64
Upsample	256	128	128×128
Upsample	128	64	256×256
Upsample	64	32	512×512
Output	32	3	1024×1024

TABLE 9.11 The High-Level Architecture of the ProGAN Discriminator in Terms of Blocks as Defined in Figure 9.47. Note That the Mini-Batch Standard Deviation Injects an Additional Feature Map in the Last Layer

2018 Layer	In Channels	Out Channels	Output Shape
Input	3	32	512×512
Downsample	32	64	256×256
Downsample	64	128	128×128
Downsample	128	256	64×64
Downsample	256	512	32×32
Downsample	512	512	16×16
Downsample	512	512	8×8
Downsample	512	512	4×4
Output	513	1	1×1

deviation for each feature at each spatial location across the mini-batch and then averages over all features and locations to give a single value. This average value is then replicated across all features and locations and treated as an additional feature map fed into the remaining layers of the discriminator alongside the input from the last downsampling layer. The aim here is to encourage generated and real images to have similar summary statistics across a mini-batch, increasing diversity across generated images, and this follows from a suggestion of Salimans et al. (2016).

None of the blocks in either generator or discriminator shown in Figure 9.47 use either batch or spectral normalisation, a consistent feature of all other GAN models. Karras et al. (2018) use two techniques to normalise: equalised learning rate and pixel-wise feature vector normalisation. Rather than adopting a careful weight initialisation process, weights are initialised using the standard normal distribution and then re-weighted using a per-layer normalisation $\hat{w}_i = \frac{w_i}{c}$, where the per layer constant c is that from He et al. (2015) as described in Section 3.3.1.4. The aim is to ensure that the dynamic range of all layers and, hence, learning speed is the same. Pixel-wise feature vector normalisation is used in the generator in preference to other types of normalisation. The feature vector in each pixel is normalised to 1 after each convolutional layer using

$$b_{x,y} = \frac{a_{x,y}}{\sqrt{\frac{1}{N}\sum_{j=0}^{N-1}(a_{x,y}^{j})^2 + \epsilon}}, \tag{9.137}$$

where $\epsilon = 10e^{-8}$, N is the number of elements in the feature vector and $a_{x,y}$ is the un-normalised feature vector.

Progressive growing allowed the model to generate the first high-resolution GAN images at 1024×1024 using a new 'faces' dataset, *CelebA-HQ*. Karras et al. (2018) estimate that this approach gives a training performance gain of around 5.4 times. The approach was also tested on the much lower-resolution CIFAR-10 dataset and achieved the highest inception score at 8.80.

9.5.4.2 Self-Attention GAN (SAGAN) Recall the discussion of the receptive field of convolutional layers in Section 6.2.2 and illustrated in Figure 6.3. An individual convolutional layer has a receptive field dictated by the size of the filter. Over successive convolutional layers, the size of the receptive field grows, and theoretically, long-range effects can be captured across the image. However, Zhang et al. (2019) note that as of 2018, convolutional GANs had much more difficulty when generating images with geometric or structural patterns, such as images of dogs, when compared to those with few structural constraints, such as landscapes, and this suggested to the authors that the convolutional layers were ineffective at modelling long-range dependencies.

Taking inspiration from the success of the transformer architecture (Vaswani et al., 2017) with its use of self-attention in LLMs, Zhang et al. (2019) adapted the non-local neural networks used by Wang et al. (2018c) in the context of video to add self-attention layers to both generator and discriminator. Figure 9.48 illustrates the structure of the self-attention layers used in SAGAN. Assume that the input to the layer has C channels and N locations. The first step is to map the input feature vector $x \in \mathbb{R}^{C \times N}$ into two feature spaces via 1×1 convolutions,

$$K(x) = W_K x. \tag{9.138}$$
$$Q(x) = W_Q x. \tag{9.139}$$

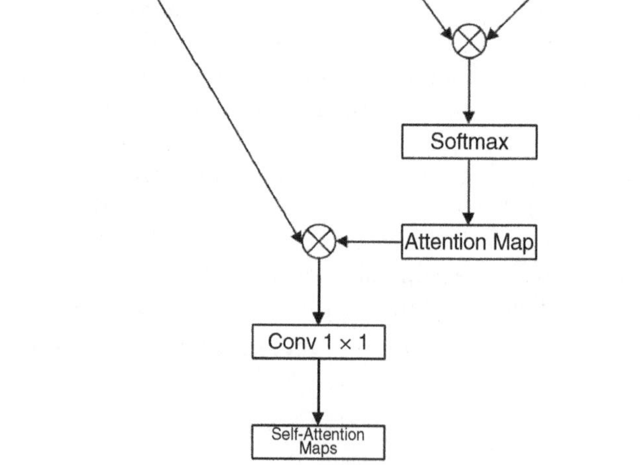

FIGURE 9.48 The structure of the self-attention layer used by SAGAN.

The attention is then calculated by applying the softmax function to the result of the matrix multiplication of Q and the transpose of K,

$$A = K(x)^T Q(x). \tag{9.140}$$

$$\beta_{ji} = \frac{\exp(A_{ij})}{\sum_i^N \exp(A_{ij})}. \tag{9.141}$$

Another convolution of the input defines a further feature space,

$$V(x) = W_V x. \tag{9.142}$$

The self-attention is given by applying a further convolution operation to the matrix product of V and the attention map β,

$$O = W_H(\beta V). \tag{9.143}$$

which is of the same dimension as the input. The final step is then to scale the self-attention with a learnable parameter γ and add it back to the input,

$$y = \gamma O + x. \tag{9.144}$$

The four weight matrices have dimension $W_K \in \mathbb{R}^{\bar{C} \times C}$, $W_Q \in \mathbb{R}^{\bar{C} \times C}$, $W_V \in \mathbb{R}^{\bar{C} \times C}$ and $W_H \in \mathbb{R}^{C \times \bar{C}}$, where $\bar{C} = \frac{C}{8}$ to reduce memory requirements at no cost in performance when tested empirically.

Zhang et al. (2019) also adopted several other innovations in SAGAN. The hinge loss was used in both the discriminator and the generator, a version of which was discussed earlier in Section 3.4.2.2,

$$\begin{aligned} J_D &= -\mathbb{E}_{(x,y)\sim p_{\text{data}}}[\min(0, -1 + D(x, y))] \\ &\quad -\mathbb{E}_{z\sim p_z, y\sim p_{\text{data}}}[\min(0, -1 - D(G(z), y))]. \\ J_G &= -\mathbb{E}_{z\sim p_z, y\sim p_{\text{data}}}[D(G(z), y))]. \end{aligned} \tag{9.145}$$

Secondly, the authors applied spectral normalisation in the generator and the discriminator to prevent parameter magnitudes from growing too large. Previous models had used spectral normalisation only in the discriminator. Finally, Zhang et al. (2019) used different learning rates for the discriminator and generator networks, allowing them to reduce the number of discriminator steps per generator stop during training, giving better overall results for the same execution time.

SAGAN only generated images of size 128 × 128, hence modestly larger than the previous generation of GANs. It is notable for its application of self-attention, which gave a significant increase in inception score and reduction in Fréchet inception distance, compared to the baseline.

9.5.4.3 BigGAN BigGAN, as developed by Brock et al. (2019), scaled up image generation to 512 × 512 without progressive growing. The model used the SAGAN architecture as a basis, including the hinge loss and several additional innovations.

The high-level generator architecture is illustrated in Figure 9.49 with three residual blocks shown, although in practice, the number of residual blocks is dictated by the final scale of the images, and so with 128, 256 and 512 scale outputs, there are five, six and seven residual blocks, respectively. The self-attention or non-local block adopted from Zhang et al. (2019) is generally placed close to the generator output immediately before the last residual block for the 128 and 256 cases and before the third-to-last in the 512 case. The detailed structure of the residual block is illustrated in Figure 9.50. As can be seen from both diagrams, each residual block receives a second input via the class-conditional batch norm (de Vries et al., 2017; Dumoulin et al., 2017). The latent vector, z, is split into sections along the channel dimension, with pieces used as input to the generator and each residual block. The class information is also passed to each residual block through a shared embedding layer. The class embedding and latent segment are concatenated and used as input to the class-conditional batch norm. This conditioning vector is then projected linearly to provide per-sample gains and biases for the two batch norms in each residual block.

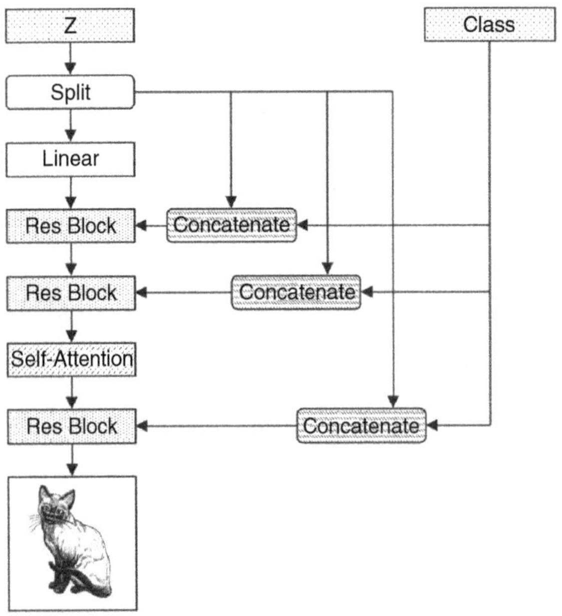

FIGURE 9.49 High-level architecture of the BigGAN generator. Note the class input and the split of the latent vector with the parts directly input to each residual block.

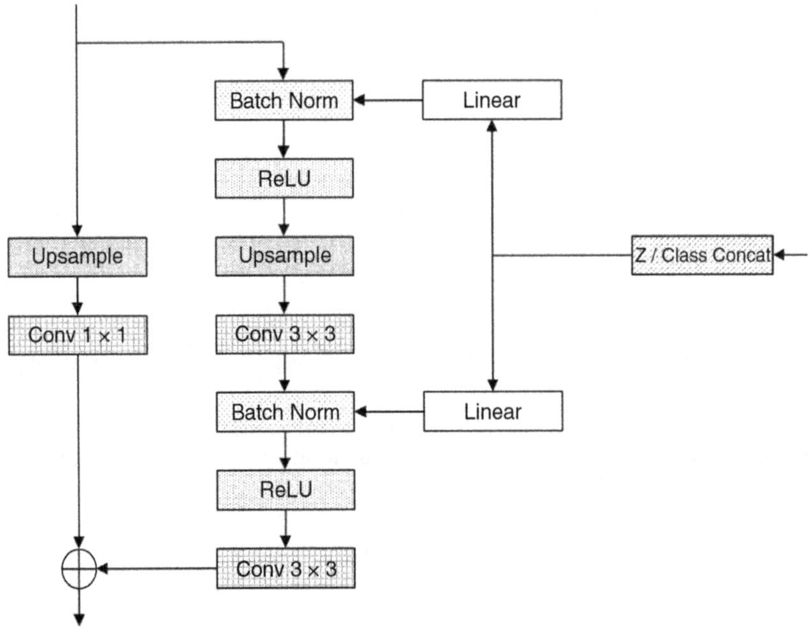

FIGURE 9.50 Detailed architecture of the generator upsampling residual block.

The BigGAN discriminator architecture is shown in Figure 9.51 and again is drawn from Zhang et al. (2019). The location of the self-attention layer is inverted with respect to the generator, lying close to the input. The downsampling residual block for the discriminator is illustrated in Figure 9.52. Class conditioning information is also passed to the discriminator through an embedding layer and added to the output.

The number of channels in both generator and discriminator is doubled in Zhang et al. (2019) and leads directly to a 21% increase in the inception score (Brock et al., 2019). The optimisation settings used are the same as Zhang et al. (2019) except that learning rates are halved. The number of discriminator steps per generator step is set at 2. Brock et al. (2019) also increased the batch sizes by a factor of 8, and this improved the inception score by 46% and

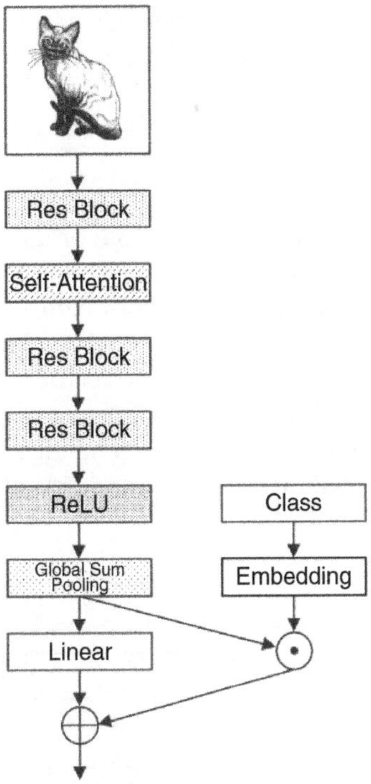

FIGURE 9.51 High-level architecture of the BigGAN discriminator. Note the class projection input through the embedding layer as additional evidence to support the discriminator.

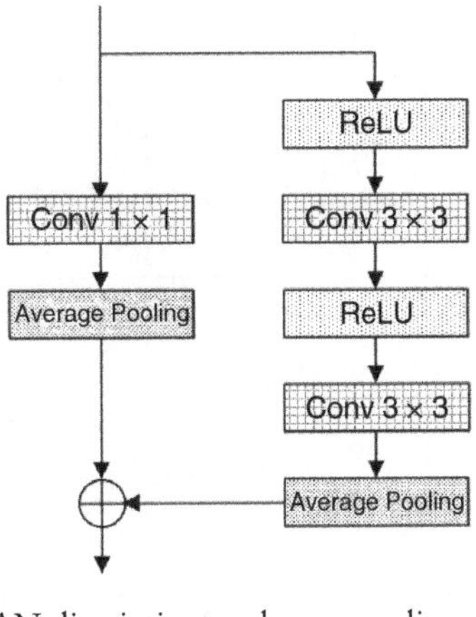

FIGURE 9.52 Detailed architecture of the BigGAN discriminator downsampling residual block.

suggested to the authors that larger batches cover more image modes and give better gradients in both generator and discriminator. However, as a consequence, models eventually become unstable and collapse.

Truncation Trick. Brock et al. (2019) introduced the *truncation trick*, which truncates the prior distribution when sampling; that is, the model is trained with the latent distribution given by $z \sim \mathcal{N}(0, I)$ but sampled using the truncated normal so that outlying samples are ignored, and this allows a trade-off to be made during sampling between variety of images and their fidelity. Some models did not perform well with truncation, giving artefacts in the output. To counteract these issues, orthogonal regularisation is used during training to enforce smoothness on the mapping from the latent space,

$$R_\beta(W) = \beta \| W^T W \cdot (\mathbf{1} - I) \|_F^2, \tag{9.146}$$

where $\mathbf{1}$ is a matrix containing all 1's and $\beta = 10^{-4}$.

9.5.4.4 StyleGAN, StyleGAN2, StyleGAN2-ADA and StyleGAN3 StyleGAN and its successors are the current leader in GAN image generation and produce photorealistic images at a resolution of 1024 × 1024. These models were developed by Tero Karras and colleagues at Nvidia Labs (Karras et al., 2019, 2020a,b, 2021). The sequence of models represents a steady evolution of the StyleGAN architecture, which is itself derived from progressive GAN (Karras et al., 2018).

StyleGAN. StyleGAN (Karras et al., 2019) derives directly from progressive GAN (Karras et al., 2018) and retains its key feature of progressive growing of the image scale during training. However, much of the architecture of the generator network is fundamentally altered, as can be seen from Figure 9.53.

The first major modification is to remove the direct input of the latent vector into the input and replace this with a learned constant tensor of size $4 \times 4 \times 512$. The latent vector $z \in \mathcal{N}(0, I)$ is still input to the network but is first passed through a *mapping network*, which consists of a neural network with eight fully connected layers to give an intermediate latent vector and latent space $w \in \mathbb{W}$. The idea is that the intermediate latent space is not bound to a fixed distribution, unlike the initial latent vector, and this allows the network to learn an appropriate

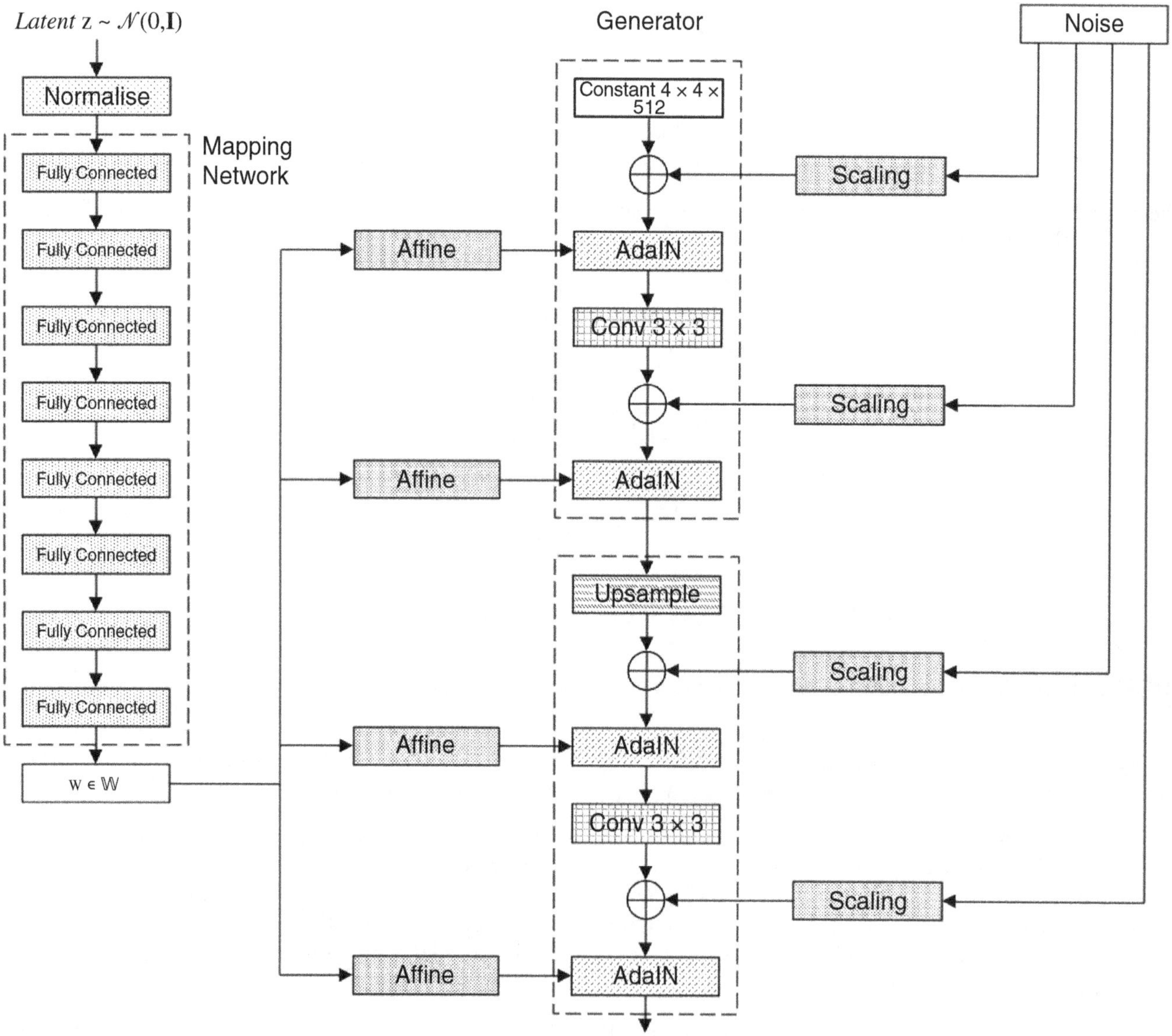

FIGURE 9.53 Architecture of the StyleGAN generator.

space to sample from as input to the generator. Karras et al. (2019) postulate that the generator is incentivised to learn a transformation that makes $\mathbb{W}$ less entangled than the input latent space and then demonstrate that this is indeed the case through analysis of the *perceptual path length* (Zhang et al., 2018). The next step is to specialise the vector w via learned affine transforms to vectors

$$y = (y_s, y_b), \tag{9.147}$$

that Karras et al. (2019) refer to as styles. These style vectors control adaptive instance normalisation (AdaIN) (Dumoulin et al., 2017; Huang and Belongie, 2017) operations after each convolution layer of the generator. The inspiration for these design elements comes from work on style transfer and image translation. AdaIN is defined by

$$AdaIN(x_i, y) = y_{s,i}\frac{x_i - \mu(x_i)}{\sigma x_i} + y_{b,i}, \tag{9.148}$$

showing that each feature map x_i is normalised separately and then scaled and shifted by the appropriate component of y.

A second noise source is provided in the form of single-channel 'images'. containing uncorrelated Gaussian samples. These are fed to each layer of the generator and broadcast to all feature maps via a learned scaling factor, distinct for each feature. The noise is added to the output of each convolution operation. The motivation for this is to provide a mechanism for the generator to add stochastic detail such as hair placement, stubble, freckles and so on in the context of portrait images.

Finally, to encourage styles to be local, that is to control only a single convolution operation, the authors employ *mixing regulation* during training. When this is used, two separate latent vectors, z_1 and z_2, are passed through the mapping network to give corresponding intermediate vectors w_1 and w_2. A crossover point is identified in the network structure, and all layers before the crossover are supplied with w_1, while those after receive w_2.

Karras et al. (2019) applied StyleGAN to several existing datasets, including CELEBA-HQ, LSUN BEDROOM, LSUN CARS and LSUN CATS. They also constructed a new high-quality dataset of human faces, Flickr Faces HQ (FFHQ). The model's lowest FID score was 5.06 on CELEBA-HQ, considerably better than the 7.3 obtained with ProGAN and 4.40 on FFHQ.

StyleGAN2. Karras et al. (2020b) introduced StyleGAN2 to address one specific defect, 'water droplets', identified in images from StyleGAN, and to improve the overall image quality. Figure 9.54 shows the revised high-level architecture.

Many images generated by StyleGAN exhibit droplet-like artifacts. Even when these droplets are not noticeable in the final image, analysis of the intermediate feature maps of the generator reveals them, beginning to appear at an image scale of 64 × 64 (Karras et al., 2020b, p. 2). Researchers isolated the problem to the AdaIN operation and found that removing it eliminated the artefacts. The authors hypothesised that the generator was finding a way

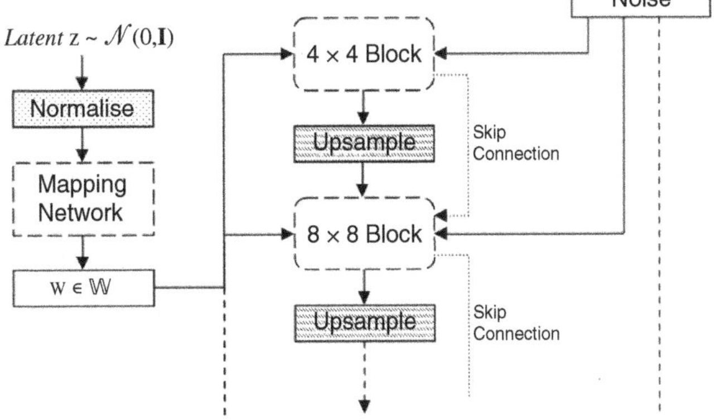

FIGURE 9.54 High-level architecture of the StyleGAN2 generator. The dashed rectangles with rounded corners are weight demodulation blocks as illustrated in Figure 9.55.

to bypass signal strength information through instance normalisation. Therefore, the next step involved finding a suitable replacement normalisation technique.

Karras et al. (2020b) proposed a series of changes to the upsampling block architecture. Firstly, the bias and noise additions were moved outside the *style block* as this gave more predictable results as they then operated on normalised data, and this also allowed the authors to drop the biasing part of AdaIN and use the standard deviation in the normalisation and modulation step. The modulation operation scales each input feature map to the convolution and hence is equivalent to scaling the convolution weights

$$w'_{ijk} = s_i w_{ijk}. \tag{9.149}$$

The normalisation step removes the scaling from the overall statistics of the convolution; hence, the weights must be divided by the standard deviation to restore a standard deviation of 1, and this is the *demodulation* operation and is given by

$$w''_{ijk} = \frac{w'_{ijk}}{\sqrt{\sum_{i,k} {w'_{ijk}}^2 + \epsilon}}, \tag{9.150}$$

where ϵ is a small number to ensure there are no problems with the division. Hence, the AdaIN operation is replaced by a modulation and demodulation step, as shown in the redesigned block in Figure 9.55.

Karras et al. (2020b) introduced four further architectural changes. Firstly, the authors removed progressive growth from the training process, although they demonstrated that the focus of training naturally shifts from lower to higher resolution during training. Secondly, the authors added skip connections to the generator, as shown in Figure 9.54. The skip connections significantly improved the perceptual path length metric, which correlated with overall image quality. Thirdly, the authors changed the discriminator to use residual blocks, as illustrated in Figure 9.56, since this was found to improve FID scores. The authors also tried residual blocks in the generator but found them detrimental and thus did not adopt them. Finally, analysis of the resolution focus during training showed that the highest resolution of 1024×1024 never gained the complete training focus, and this led the authors to double the number of feature maps in the highest-resolution layers, supposing a network capacity shortfall. The new network's high-resolution performance confirmed this supposition.

Two changes were made to the regularisation steps. The authors observed that it was unnecessary to perform regularisation for every mini-batch. It was as effective if performed at a lower frequency as calculating the main loss function, and this was termed *lazy regularisation*; regularisation terms were only calculated once every 16 batches at a considerable computational and memory saving. Finally, *path length regularisation* was introduced to give better overall performance and more consistent PPL scores. For an intermediate latent vector $w \in \mathbb{W}$, the local scaling properties of the generator $G(w)$ are given by the Jacobian,

$$J_w = \frac{\partial G(w)}{\partial w}. \tag{9.151}$$

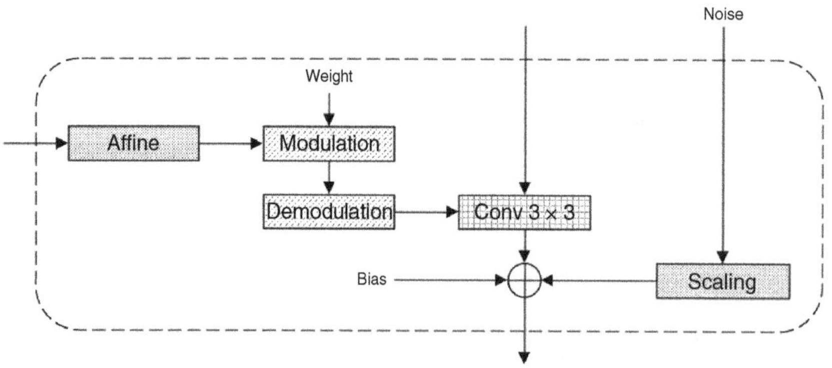

FIGURE 9.55 StyleGAN2 weight demodulation block.

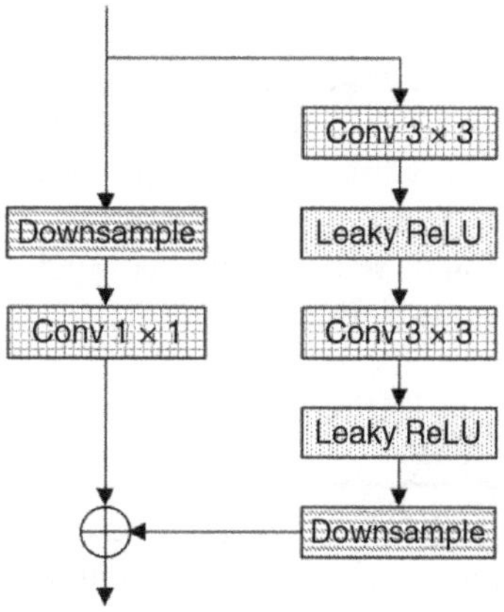

FIGURE 9.56 Detailed architecture of the StyleGAN2 discriminator downsampling residual block.

A suitable regulariser is, therefore,

$$\mathbb{E}_{w,y\sim\mathcal{N}(0,I)}(\|J_w^T y\|_2 - a)^2, \tag{9.152}$$

where y are random images with normally distributed pixel intensities. The constant a is set to be the exponential moving average of $\|J_w^T y\|_2$. Rather than calculate the Jacobian matrix directly, the following expression is used instead, as this can be calculated by backpropagation:

$$J_w^T y = \nabla_w(G(w)y). \tag{9.153}$$

StyleGAN2 removed the droplet artefact from images and significantly improved overall image quality. For example, on the FFHQ dataset, the FID score was 2.84 compared to the 4.40 obtained with StyleGAN.

StyleGAN2-ADA. Karras et al. (2020a) developed StyleGAN2-ADA as an enhanced version of StyleGAN2 designed specifically to deal with small datasets. For CNNs, data augmentation was discussed in Section 6.4 to enhance image classification models. Data augmentation would seem a likely candidate for generative models. However, there is an obvious problem in that we do not want the generator to produce augmented images with features such as rotations or random colour changes. Hence, we cannot simply augment the training set directly and naively feed these images to the discriminator as if they were all real. The way to resolve this issue is to place the augmentation step after the generator and before the discriminator for generated images so that the generator produces untransformed images. There is still a problem in that transforms can leak into the generator.

In the context of corrupted data, Bora et al. (2018) demonstrate that the GAN recovers the correct underlying data distribution as long as the corruption process is invertible. Each transformation need not be invertible, but it must be possible to discern the correct distribution. So, for example, if random rotations are chosen from 0°, 90°, 180°, 270°, then the process is only invertible if 0° has a higher probability than the other orientations (Karras et al., 2020a, p. 3). In general, many transformations can be designed to be non-leaking if they can be skipped with finite probability. Karras et al. (2020a) show that empirically, the probability of a transformation should remain under 80% to remain non-leaking. Notably, not all transformations were found to be equally beneficial, and the benefits declined with increasing dataset size. With 140,000 samples from FFHQ, augmentation became detrimental.

Rather than using a fixed augmentation probability, Karras et al. (2020a) sought to find the appropriate choice dynamically and introduced *adaptive discriminator augmentation (ADA)* for this purpose. The idea is to control the amount of augmentation based on the amount of overfitting, increase the augmentation probability as overfitting goes up and reduce it again when overfitting falls. The first step is to identify measures of overfitting, and the authors propose two:

$$r_v = \frac{\mathbb{E}[D_{\text{train}}] - \mathbb{E}[D_{\text{validation}}]}{\mathbb{E}[D_{\text{train}}] - \mathbb{E}[D_{\text{generated}}]}, \tag{9.154}$$

$$r_t = \mathbb{E}[\text{sgn}(D_{\text{train}})]. \tag{9.155}$$

Both measures range on the interval [0, 1], with $r = 0$ indicating no overfitting and $r = 1$ indicating complete overfitting. The first of the two measures requires a validation set, which may be difficult to justify given the already small training set size; hence, the second measure is more practical. The authors propose to adjust the overfitting probability up or down by a fixed amount every four mini-batches as overfitting rises and falls.

StyleGAN2-ADA was tested on CIFAR-10, among other datasets, achieving a record FID score of 2.42 in the conditional case and 2.92 in the unconditional case, and this is much lower than reported on any of the earlier models or any of the examples presented in this chapter.

EXAMPLE 9.14: StyleGAN2-ADA WITH CIFAR-10

The hardware requirements to train any of the StyleGAN variants are considerable. To train a model at 1024 × 1024 to convergence requires showing the discriminator 25 million real images. Using the StyleGAN2-ADA codebase takes 6 days and 3 hours using eight V100 GPUs (Karras and Hellsten, 2020). Even a modest model of 128 × 128 takes 4 days and 6 hours to train using 25 million real images on a single V100. Furthermore, the energy consumption is considerable; Karras et al. (2020a) report that the whole project consumed around 300 MWh of electricity, which is around 20 times the energy consumption of a UK household in a year. Hence, experiments on high-resolution GANs require significant resources beyond most research groups, let alone individuals.

It is possible to train a StyleGAN2-ADA model against the CIFAR-10 dataset in a reasonable timeframe using more modest resources, and this is best done using the official PyTorch implementation by Karras and Hellsten (2020), which can be found on GitHub at https://github.com/NVlabs/stylegan2-ada-pytorch. To install the framework, clone the repository

```
git clone https://github.com/NVlabs/stylegan2-ada-pytorch.git
```

The best way to use the framework is to build and run inside a docker container, and the following command will build the container:

```
docker build --tag sg2ada:latest
```

The CIFAR-10 dataset needs to be downloaded from https://www.cs.toronto.edu/~kriz/cifar-10-python.tar.gz and then converted to the format expected by StyleGAN2, which can be done using the command

```
python dataset_tool.py --source=~/downloads/cifar-10-python.tar.gz \
 --dest=./datasets/cifar10.zip
```

Note that a subdirectory called `datasets` will need to be set up in the root directory of the cloned repository. Once the data is in place, start a dry run using

```
./docker_run.sh python3 train.py --outdir=./training_runs \
--data=./datasets/cifar10.zip --gpus=1 --cfg=cifar --dry-run
```

Then, if everything is okay, training can be started by issuing the same command but without the `-dry-run` option. Be warned that even at 32 × 32, execution is still slow. On a current top-of-the-line gaming GPU, an RTX 4090, training through 10 million real images, took just under 15 hours. At that point, the FID measured by StyleGANs own utilities was 4.58, much better than any of the earlier models. The block of images in Figure 9.57 were generated by the trained model and are much better defined and realistic than anything generated previously.

FIGURE 9.57 Sixty-four images generated by StyleGAN2-ADA trained using CIFAR-10 after the model had been trained against 10 million real images.

StyleGAN3. When morphing from one face to another in StyleGAN2, it was noticed that fine textures such as hair were 'sticky' and did not move naturally with the rest of the image (Karras et al., 2021). While this might not sound like a significant issue, it indicates a deeper problem with how the GAN assembles the image from its features. Ideally, the GAN should have a hierarchical representation of the image so that course details control fine details. The 'texture sticking' problem shows that much of the fine detail is fixed in pixel coordinates. For GANs that produce videos, this would be a severe problem.

Karras et al. (2021) identified the cause of the problem as unintended positional references from three sources: image borders, per-pixel noise inputs and positional encodings, and aliasing. Of these, the most difficult to deal with is aliasing, which is thought to come from two sources: upsampling filters and pointwise non-linearity, such as the activation function. The network then further amplifies aliasing over multiple length scales.

As an example of aliasing, consider discretely sampling a high-frequency sinusoid with too few sampling points, as illustrated in Figure 9.58. The sample is indistinguishable from a lower-frequency signal. The high-frequency signal is lost, and an erroneous low-frequency signal is introduced. In images, aliasing can be seen in moiré patterns where a repeated pattern is imaged using too few pixels.

The solution to this problem, as proposed and implemented by Karras et al. (2021), is to eliminate from the network all sources of positional references, which reduces to making sure all operations in the generator network are equivariant with respect to translations and rotations applied to continuous input z_0,

$$G(t[z_0]; w) = t[G(z_0; w)]. \tag{9.156}$$

This necessitates redesigning many aspects of the GAN, mainly focusing on the GAN as a discrete approximation to a continuous problem rather than purely discrete operations.

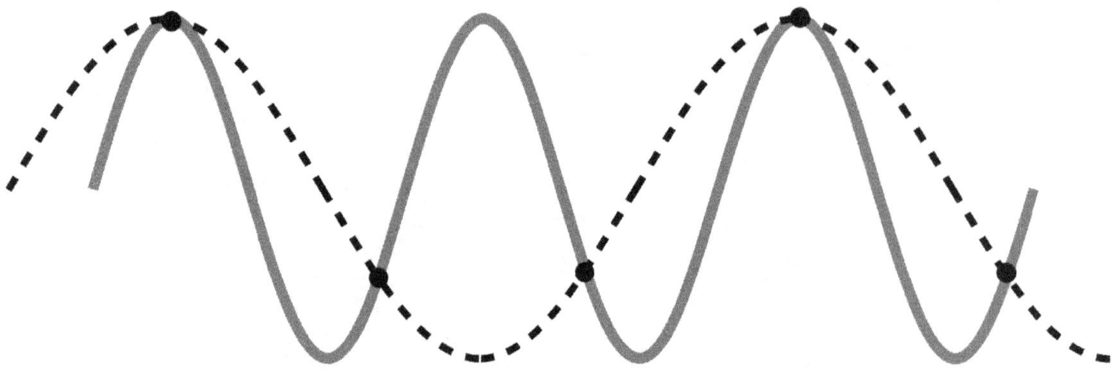

FIGURE 9.58 An example of aliasing where a high-frequency sinusoid is sampled at too low a frequency and appears indistinguishable from a lower-frequency signal.

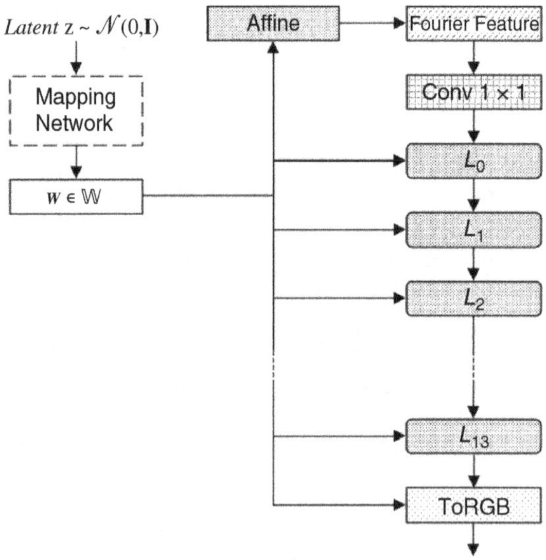

FIGURE 9.59 High-level architecture of the StyleGAN3 generator. The rounded rectangles are anti-aliasing upsampling blocks, as illustrated in Figure 9.60. The *ToRGB* block is shown in Figure 9.61.

The network design changes are listed below, with the final alias-free StyleGAN3 architecture illustrated in Figures 9.59, 9.60 and 9.61:

1. Replace the input constant layer with Fourier features (Tancik et al., 2020; Xu et al., 2021).
2. Remove the per-pixel noise input, as this is inconsistent with the desire for equivariance.
3. Reduce the mapping network depth.
4. Stop using mixing regulation and path length regulation.
5. Remove the output skip connections.
6. Add simple normalisation before each convolution by dividing the feature maps by $\sqrt{\sigma^2}$, where $\sigma^2 = \mathbb{E}[x^2]$ is the exponential moving average over all pixels and feature maps.
7. Add border padding and crop to extended size after each layer, with 10 pixels of padding sufficient.
8. Replace the bilinear 2× upsampling filter with a better low-pass filter. Use a windowed sinc function of the form (Oppenheim and Schafer, 2010) $h_K(x) = 2f_c \cdot \text{sinc}(2f_c x) \cdot w_K(x)$, where w_K is the Kaiser window function and a window of size 6 pixels was used.

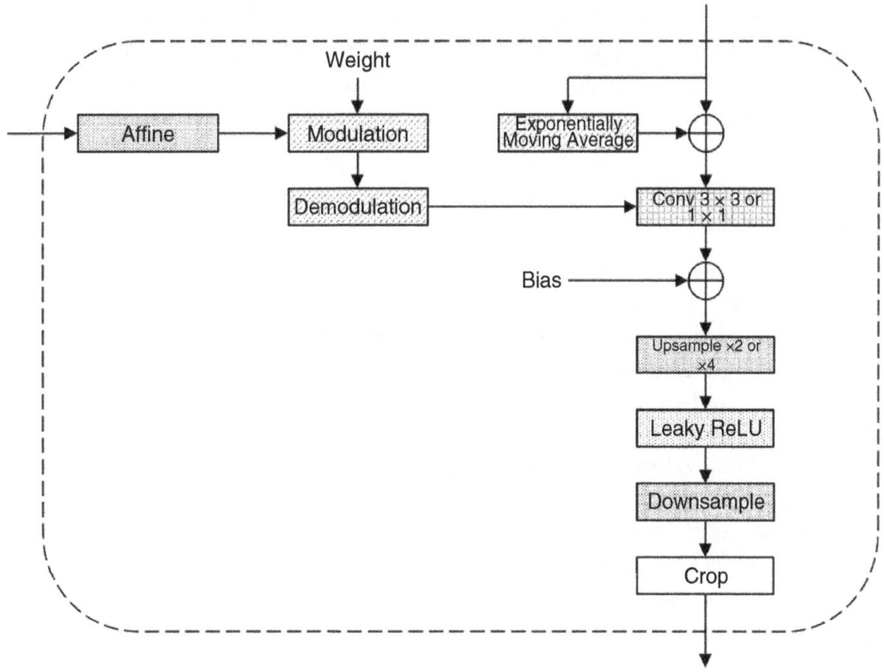

FIGURE 9.60 StyleGAN3 anti-aliasing generator upsampling block.

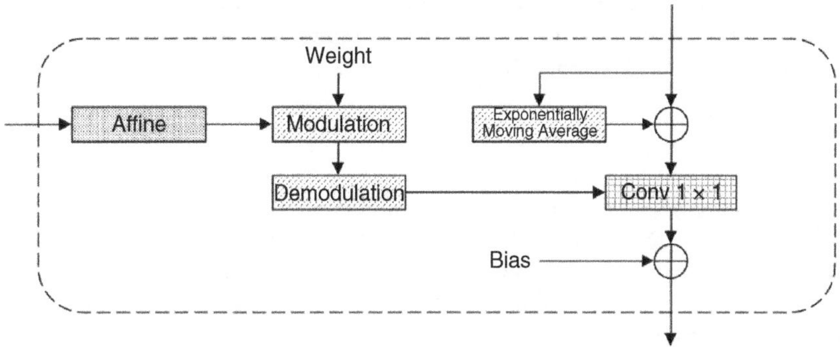

FIGURE 9.61 StyleGAN3 generator ToRGB block.

9. Filter non-linearities by sandwiching the leaky ReLU between $m \times$ *upsampling* and $m \times$ *downsampling*, with $m = 2$ found to be sufficient.
10. Lower the filter cutoff frequency to $f_c = \frac{s}{2} - f_h$ for all layers except the highest resolution to suppress aliasing.
11. Introduce a learned affine transformation that outputs global translation and rotation parameters for Fourier features.
12. Set the transition bandwidth to $f_h = \max(s/2, f_t) - f_c$ to maximise attenuation of aliasing.
13. Change the 3 × 3 convolutions on all layers to 1 × 1. The number of feature maps is doubled to compensate for the reduced capacity.
14. The sinc-based downsampling filter is replaced with a radially symmetric jinc-based one except for the last two layers.
15. Initially, blur all images the discriminator sees with a Gaussian filter and then reduce blurring from $\sigma = 10$ to 0 over the first 200,000 real images shown. This is to prevent the discriminator focusing too much on higher frequencies initially, which can cause early collapse.

This redesign process simplifies the architecture considerably while radically changing the approach to upsampling and downsampling to be equivariant. On the FFHQ, the effect of these changes is a broadly comparable FID score to StyleGAN2 but with drastically improved equivariance properties. The computational cost of training was also similar to that of StyleGAN2, although some operations required coding directly in CUDA to achieve acceptable performance.

9.5.5 Image Translation

GANs have been widely deployed for a large number of image translation tasks. Applications include:

1. In-painting, where an image has a hole that needs to be filled.
2. Blending, where two images need to be merged.
3. Removing or adding rain and snow to images.
4. Reposing portraits.
5. Style transfer such as adding zebra stripes to horses.
6. 'Cartoonifying' images, that is, translating the image to a cartoon.
7. Image segmentation, where the parts of an image are recognised and colour-coded.
8. Text-to-image translation, where an image is generated from a description.
9. Super-resolution, where an image is scaled up realistically.
10. Image-to-image translation, such as generating a map from an aerial photograph or a photorealistic image from a drawing.
11. Colourising a black and white image or video.

There are too many applications and papers to cover, so in this section *in-painting* will be discussed in detail as this directly applies to completing a set of market data with missing elements. Three landmark models will also be explored: *pix2pix* for image translation, *GauGAN* that generates photorealistic images from drawings and *CycleGAN* for style transfer.

9.5.5.1 In-Painting

Context Encoders. Denoising autoencoders were discussed in Section 8.5, and *denoising* is a similar application to *in-painting* with the difference being one of scale. In-painting usually refers to filling a large section of an image, while denoising is generally the correction of small errors in an image, such as scratches on an old photograph. The key difference between the two applications is the demand placed on the model. Denoising requires a model that can successfully examine and correct the local context of a defect. At the same time, this is insufficient for in-painting as it needs a semantic understanding of the image to fill the blank (Pathak et al., 2016). Autoencoders might seem a logical place to start building an architecture to perform in-painting, and in practice, networks use encoder–decoder structures. However, models are training adversarially with a discriminator network and hence should be seen as GAN-based.

The first GAN-based approach to in-painting was the *context encoder* developed by Pathak et al. (2016), who proposed a convolutional encoder–decoder structure. The encoder architecture is derived from the first five layers of *AlexNet*.[6] In an autoencoder, the middle layer is tightly restricted, but a small bottleneck is inappropriate, given that the image is not fully reconstructed. The middle layer needs to allow connection across the image's full size; hence, a fully connected layer would be appropriate. However, at the time Pathak et al. (2016) was writing, there was concern that a fully connected layer would lead to an explosion in the number of parameters to over 100 million, which would not have been feasible given the available GPU resources. Hence, a new type of layer was proposed, the *channel-wise fully connected layer*. This layer is only fully connected within each feature map, so if there are m feature maps of size $n \times n$, the parameters will be mn^4 compared to a fully connected layer with m^2n^4. In practice, though, a convolutional layer will span all image locations if the kernel width is big enough, and indeed, this is

[6] See Section 6.7.2.

what is used in Example 9.15. It should also be noted that, unlike a GAN, there is no random latent space as the goal is to reconstruct the missing element, not generate new images. The decoder model uses transpose convolutions to upsample the image progressively. The size of the missing area dictates the amount of upsampling, and the goal of the encoder–decoder structure is to output the missing area, given the masked input image. The discriminator model is the same as in a GAN but does not look at the entire image; instead, it compares the generated output reconstructed area with the masked area of the real input image.

The loss function for the generator consists of two terms: reconstruction loss and adversarial loss,

$$J = \lambda_{rec} J_{rec} + \lambda_{adv} J_{adv}. \tag{9.157}$$

The reconstruction loss is designed to give a pixel-wise error for the reconstruction. Given an input image $\boldsymbol{x}$ and a binary mask, $\boldsymbol{M}$, with 1 in the area to be masked and 0 otherwise, the following gives the masked part of the image:

$$\boldsymbol{M} \odot \boldsymbol{x}, \tag{9.158}$$

where $\odot$ means element-wise multiplication. The generator produces the same masked region when operating on the unmasked part of the original image, that is,

$$\boldsymbol{M} \odot G((\mathbf{1} - \boldsymbol{M}) \odot \boldsymbol{x}), \tag{9.159}$$

where $\mathbf{1}$ is a matrix of all 1s. The reconstruction loss is then either the L_2 or L_1 over the norm of the pixel-wise differences of the two, giving

$$J_{rec} = ||\boldsymbol{M} \odot (\boldsymbol{x} - G((\mathbf{1} - \boldsymbol{M}) \odot \boldsymbol{x}))||^2_{2or1}. \tag{9.160}$$

The reconstruction loss encourages the generator to correct the reconstructed image's outline. However, given that it averages over the differences in each pixel, the optimal behaviour response is to produce an average response. Hence, the reconstruction error would give a blurred image.

The adversarial loss complements the reconstruction loss and provides fine detail in the reconstructed image segment. As in a GAN, the generator participates in a two-player game with the discriminator model that is trained simultaneously, with the discriminator aiming to detect fake from real images. Here, the discriminator has to act only on the reconstructed segment rather than the whole reconstructed image, as the latter is too easily identified as fake compared to an authentic image. In Pathak et al. (2016), the original Goodfellow et al. (2014) GAN loss was applied, but the Wasserstein loss can be used instead. Example 9.15 presents a context encoder model trained using the *CelebA* dataset.

The context encoder model is designed around patching a square area of the image. The mask's area is set to a uniform value before input to the generator, and this leads to visible artefacts in the reconstructed image, within the mask area and bordering it (Liu et al., 2018a), and this led to several researchers, including, for example, Yang et al. (2017) to couple context encoder models with postprocessing techniques to improve performance. These issues can be traced to standard convolutions with the mask, and the model described in Section 9.5.5.1 is intended to correct it.

EXAMPLE 9.15: CONTEXT ENCODER WITH FLICKR FACES HQ

An example context encoder model can be found in the Jupyter Notebook `Context Encoder - FlickrFacesHQ.ipynb`. This model uses the Flickr Faces HQ dataset, which consists of 52,000 images of faces with resolution 512 × 512 (Marinez, 2020). The data was originally trawled from Flickr and hence has the biases inherent to that source, but it contains reasonable variation in age, ethnicity and image background. The images must be downloaded from the website and unzipped into a suitable directory. The example uses a subdivision with the first 49,999 images to train the model and the remaining 2000 or so used to test it.

A custom `Dataset` class is required to handle the loading and transformation of the images.

(*Continued*)

(Continued)

```
class CustomImageDataset(Dataset):
    def __init__(self, root, transforms_=None,):
        self.transform = transforms_
        self.files = sorted(glob.glob(f"{root}/*.png"))

    def __getitem__(self, index):
        img = Image.open(self.files[index % len(self.files)])
        img = self.transform(img)
        return img

    def __len__(self):
        return len(self.files)
```

For the example, the images are reduced to 128 × 128 with the set of transformations given by

```
transform = transforms.Compose([transforms.Resize((128, 128),
                                transforms.InterpolationMode.BICUBIC),
                                transforms.ToTensor()])
```

A function is used to create the masked image and to output the masked part of the image. The mask location is selected randomly, and a square mask of size 64 × 64 and applied to the mini-batch during training.

```
def apply_random_mask(img, img_size, mask_size):
    y1, x1 = np.random.randint(0, img_size - mask_size, 2)
    y2, x2 = y1 + mask_size, x1 + mask_size
    masked_part = img[:, :, y1:y2, x1:x2]
    masked_img = img.clone()
    masked_img[:, :, y1:y2, x1:x2] = 1
    return masked_img, masked_part, (x1, y1, x2, y2)
```

As described earlier, the generator model has an encoder–decoder structure with a series of downsampling blocks leading to a central convolution and then a series of upsampling blocks. The downsampling and upsampling blocks have convolution and transpose convolutions, respectively, coupled with batch normalisation and leaky ReLU activation functions. The code is given below, and it should be noted that the input is the masked image of size 128 × 128, while the output is the masked region only of size 64 × 64.

```
class Generator(nn.Module):
    def __init__(self):
        super(Generator, self).__init__()
        self.input = nn.Sequential(nn.Conv2d(3, 64, 4, 2, 1),
                                   nn.LeakyReLU(negative_slope=0.2))
        self.down1 = self.downsample_block(64, 64)
        self.down2 = self.downsample_block(64, 128)
        self.down3 = self.downsample_block(128, 256)
        self.down4 = self.downsample_block(256, 512)
        self.centre = nn.Conv2d(512, 4000, 1)
        self.up4 = self.upsample_block(4000, 512)
```

```
        self.up3 = self.upsample_block(512, 256)
        self.up2 = self.upsample_block(256, 128)
        self.up1 = self.upsample_block(128, 64)
        self.output = nn.Sequential(nn.Conv2d(64, 3, 1, 1),
                                    nn.Sigmoid())

    def downsample_block(self, in_channels, out_channels):
        block = nn.Sequential(
            nn.Conv2d(in_channels, out_channels, 4, 2, 1),
            nn.BatchNorm2d(out_channels),
            nn.LeakyReLU(negative_slope=0.2)
        )
        return block

    def upsample_block(self, in_channels, out_channels):
        block = nn.Sequential(
            nn.ConvTranspose2d(in_channels, out_channels, 4, 2, 1),
            nn.BatchNorm2d(out_channels),
            nn.LeakyReLU(negative_slope=0.2)
        )
        return block

    def forward(self, image):
        out = self.input(image)
        out = self.down1(out)
        out = self.down2(out)
        out = self.down3(out)
        out = self.down4(out)
        out = self.centre(out)
        out = self.up4(out)
        out = self.up3(out)
        out = self.up2(out)
        out = self.up1(out)
        return self.output(out)
```

The discriminator model is similar to previous examples, although instance norm layers are used in this case. The discriminator acts only on the masked part of the image with size 64×64. The training loop is almost identical to previous GAN examples, except that the loss function now consists of the weighted sum of the reconstruction or pixel loss and the adversarial loss. Here, the adversarial loss is MSE, and the pixel loss is calculated using the L_1 norm.

The model was trained through 200 epochs, giving the losses shown in Figure 9.62. Eight images from the test set were masked and passed through the final generator model. The input images are shown in Figure 9.63, while Figure 9.64 shows the same images with the mask applied. The reconstructed images are shown in Figure 9.65. The model has successfully reconstructed the shape and structure of each of the eight faces. However, the eye in the reconstructed part of the image shows a lack of diversity, with all eight appearing very similar. The reconstructed segment is still visible as a square, and the reconstruction lacks refinement compared to the original.

(*Continued*)

(*Continued*)

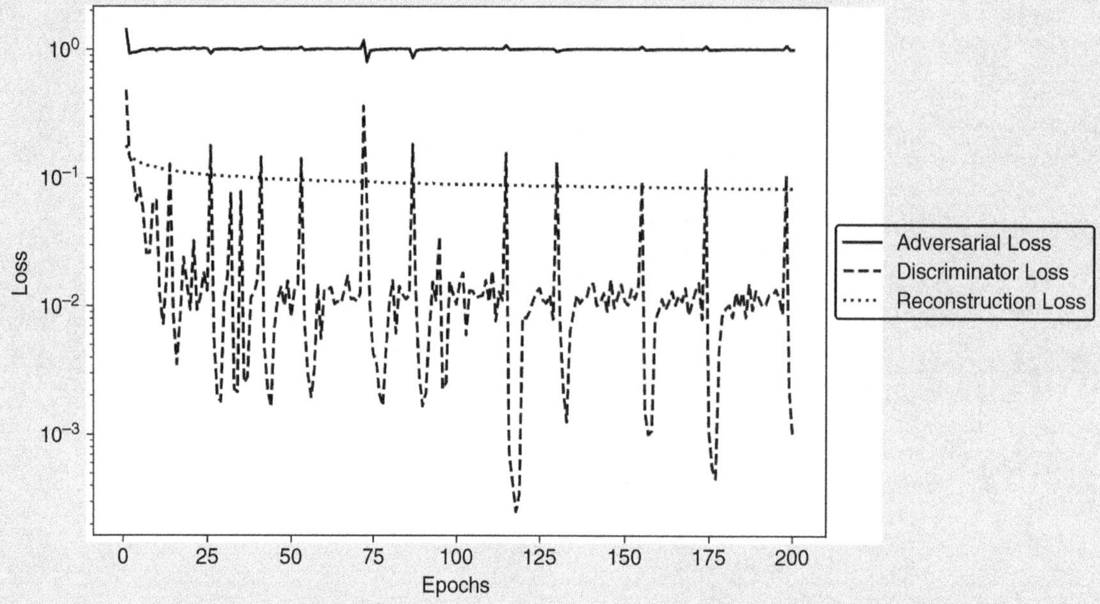

FIGURE 9.62 Losses as a function of epoch for the context encoder model trained using the Flickr Faces HQ dataset.

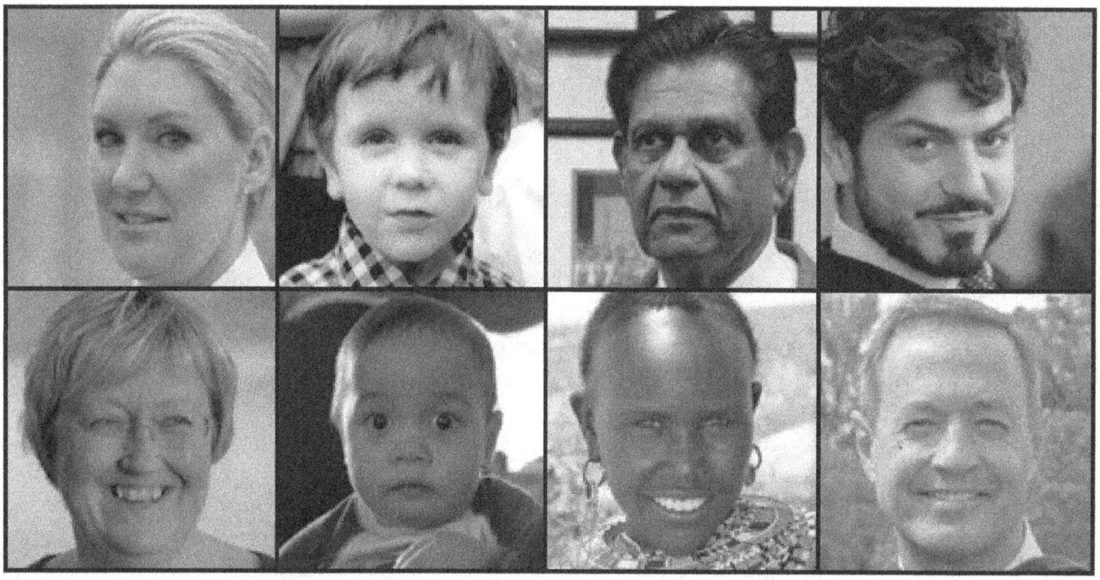

FIGURE 9.63 Eight test images from the Flickr Faces HQ dataset.

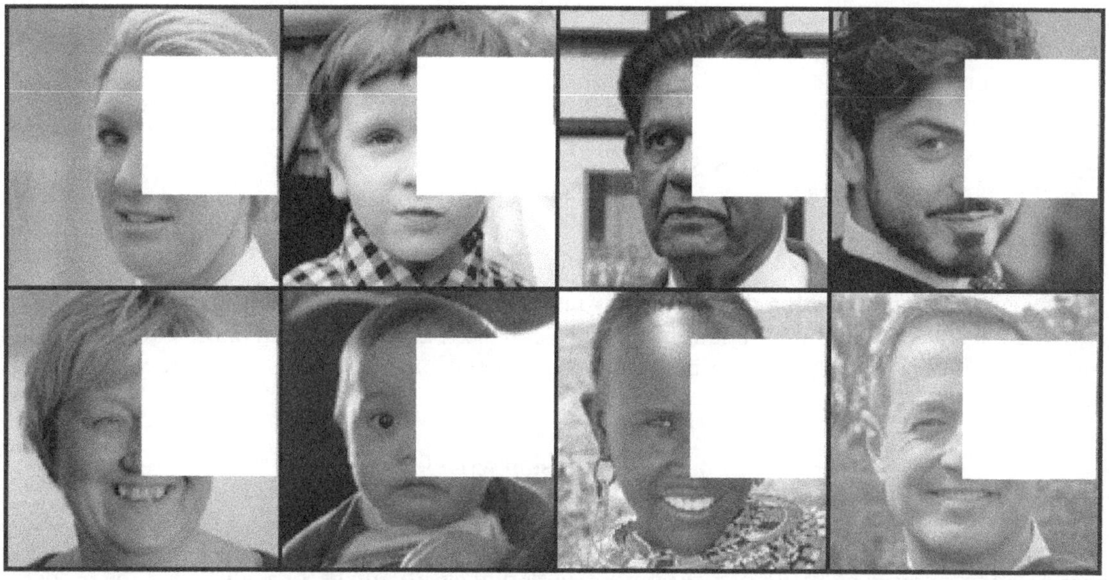

FIGURE 9.64 Eight test images from the Flickr Faces HQ dataset superimposed with a square mask.

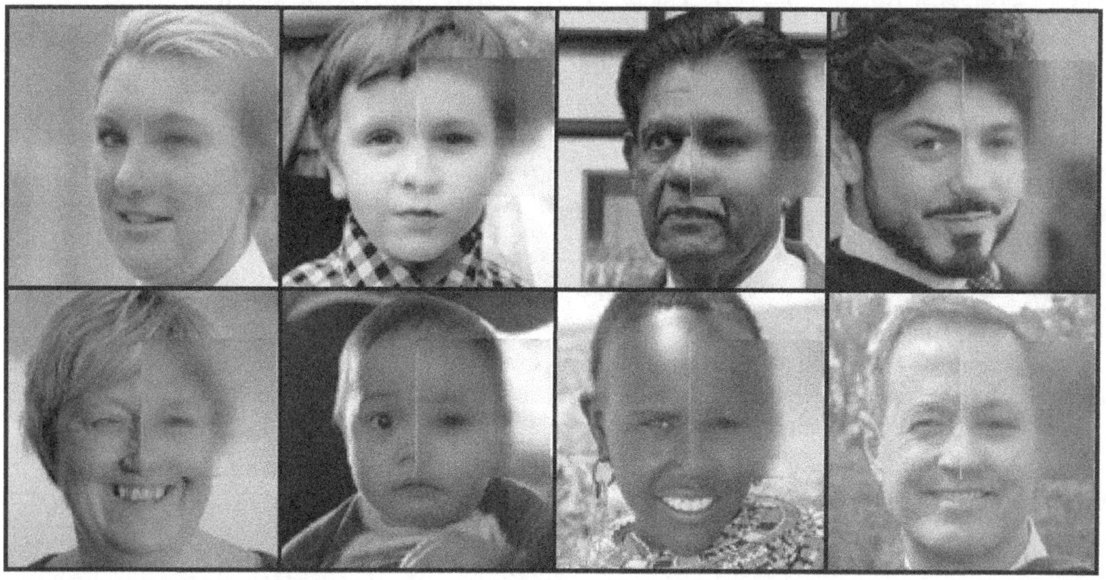

FIGURE 9.65 Eight test images from the Flickr Faces HQ dataset reconstructed using the context encoder model.

Partial Convolutions. As noted earlier, standard two-dimensional convolutions produce artefacts in masked areas, and this is because the 'mask' is normally represented by a white area with input value 1 across all channels. To address this issue, Liu et al. (2018a) propose using *partial convolutions*, coupled with a mask update step. The partial convolution is defined by

$$x' = \begin{cases} W^T(x \odot M)\dfrac{\text{sum}(\mathbf{1})}{\text{sum}(M)} + b, & \text{if sum}(M) > 0 \\ 0, & \text{otherwise} \end{cases}, \tag{9.161}$$

where $\odot$ is element-wise multiplication, M is the binary mask and matrix $\mathbf{1}$ is filled with the value 1 and has the same shape as M. The partial convolution output only depends on real values, not masked ones, and is scaled to account for the number of valid inputs. The mask is updated after a partial convolution, as elements on the boundary will now be valid,

$$m' = \begin{cases} 1, & \text{if sum}(M) > 0 \\ 0, & \text{otherwise} \end{cases}, \tag{9.162}$$

so that over successive partial convolutions, the binary mask will eventually become all 1s and the partial convolution a standard one (Li, 2020).

Liu et al. (2018a) use a U-Net-style architecture with partial convolutional layers and nearest-neighbour upsampling in the decoder. Adversarial training is not used in this case, but a series of loss functions carefully designed to elicit the desired response from the network. The first two loss terms are reconstruction errors,

$$J_{\text{hole}} = ||(\mathbf{1} - M) \odot (I_{\text{out}} - I_{gt})||_1, \tag{9.163}$$

$$J_{\text{valid}} = ||M \odot (I_{\text{out}} - I_{gt})||_1, \tag{9.164}$$

where I_{out} is the output prediction and I_{gt} is the ground truth image. The third term is the *perceptual* loss originally introduced by Gatys et al. (2015),

$$J_{\text{perceptual}} = \sum_{n=0}^{N-1} ||\psi_n(I_{\text{out}}) - \psi_n(I_{gt})||_1 + \sum_{n=0}^{N-1} ||\psi_n(I_{\text{comp}}) - \psi_n(I_{gt})||_1, \tag{9.165}$$

where I_{comp} is the output image, but with pixels from areas outside the hole regions set equal to the ground truth. The function $\psi_n()$ represents the activations from the nth selected layer of a trained VGG-16 network, and the authors used pooling layers 1 through 3. Two further similar *style* loss terms are added,

$$J_{\text{style\_out}} = \sum_{n=0}^{N-1} ||K_n(\psi_n(I_{\text{out}}))^T (\psi_n(I_{\text{out}})) - \left(\psi_n(I_{gt})\right)^T \left(\psi_n(I_{gt})\right)||_1, \tag{9.166}$$

$$J_{\text{style\_comp}} = \sum_{n=0}^{N-1} ||K_n\left(\psi_n(I_{\text{comp}})\right)^T \left(\psi_n(I_{\text{comp}})\right) - \left(\psi_n(I_{gt})\right)^T \left(\psi_n(I_{gt})\right)||_1. \tag{9.167}$$

Here, an autocorrelation calculation is performed on each feature map from the VGG-16 network, and $K_n = \frac{1}{C_n H_n W_n}$ is a normalisation factor based on the size of the feature map tensor, $\psi_n(.)$, which is $(H_n W_n) \times C_n$. The final loss term is total variation and is designed to encourage smoothness on the region of 1-pixel dilation of the hole, P,

$$J_{tv} = \sum_{(i,j)\in P,(i,j+1)\in P} ||I_{\text{comp}}^{i,j+1} - I_{\text{comp}}^{i,j}||_1 + \sum_{(i,j)\in P,(i+1,j)\in P} ||I_{\text{comp}}^{i+1,j} - I_{\text{comp}}^{i,j}||_1. \tag{9.168}$$

The weighted final loss is given by

$$J = J_{\text{valid}} + 0.6J_{\text{hole}} + 0.05J_{\text{perceptual}} + 120\left(J_{\text{style\_out}} + J_{\text{style\_comp}}\right) + 0.1J_{tv}. \tag{9.169}$$

Global and Local Discriminators, and Contextual Attention. Iizuka et al. (2017) proposed two key innovations in their approach to in-painting: the use of diluted convolutions and the use of adversarial training with two discriminator networks, one global and receiving the full image and a second local with just the region of the hole and its immediate area input. The *completion network* has an encoder–decoder form with four *dilated convolutional* layers in the centre of the network.

Figure 9.66 illustrates the dilated convolution operation. The standard convolution operation, as discussed in Section 6.2, operates a dense sliding window with width and height given by *kernel size* that is usually symmetric. The dilated convolution uses a sparse kernel where pixels are skipped; given dilation l, $l-1$ pixels are skipped. A 3×3 kernel would span 5×5 pixels and have a larger receptive field. Hence, the dilated convolution allows the network to connect features in more distant regions in the image. In the context of in-painting, the dilated convolution provides a solid mechanism to allow connections between features in different image areas, thus providing a better means of filling in the missing area. Both *Tenorflow* and *PyTorch* allow dilations to be used with their respective convolutional layers, so implementation is straightforward.

The remaining structure of the completion network is straightforward, with ReLU activation after all convolutions apart from the final one, which is normalised to the range [0, 1] with a sigmoid function. No pooling layers are used, and the image scale is reduced using strided convolutions and increased again using strided transpose convolutions. The encoder section only reduces the image resolution to one-quarter of the original. Note that Iizuka et al. (2017) do not use normalisation layers in their completion network, but many of the independent implementations of this network structure use batch normalisation.

The two context discriminator networks work in parallel. The global discriminator uses a sequence of six convolutional layers with stride 2 to reduce the input image down from the input 256×256. A final fully connected layer of length 1024 is added. The local discriminator is similar but with a smaller input size of 128×128; one less convolution is needed. The output of the two fully connected layers is concatenated and fed to a fully connected layer with a single sigmoid output representing the probability that the image is real rather than completed. Figure 9.67 illustrates the entire network structure.

Training proceeds in three separate phases. Firstly, the completion network is trained for T_C iterations using training data with the random binary mask applied to each image. The completion network is trained using an MSE loss, weighted by the mask

$$J(x, M_C) = \|M_c \odot (C(x, M_C) - x)\|_2^2. \tag{9.170}$$

In the second phase, the context discriminators are trained for T_D iterations with random binary masks using the GAN loss (Goodfellow et al., 2014),

$$\min_C \min_D \mathbb{E}[\log D(x, M_d) + \log(1 - D(C(x, M_c), M_c))]. \tag{9.171}$$

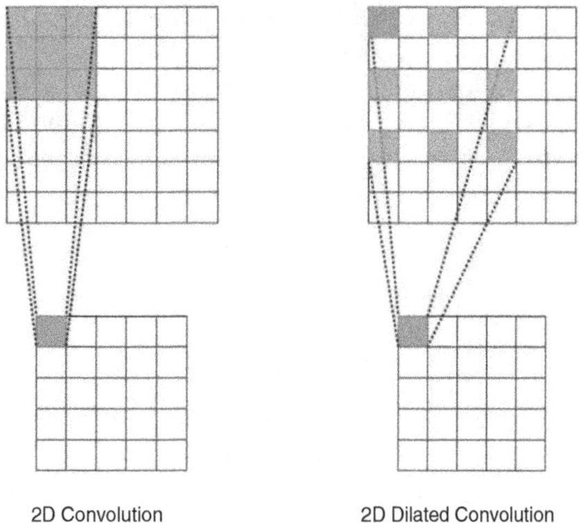

FIGURE 9.66 A normal two-dimensional convolution alongside a dilated convolution with dilation = 2.

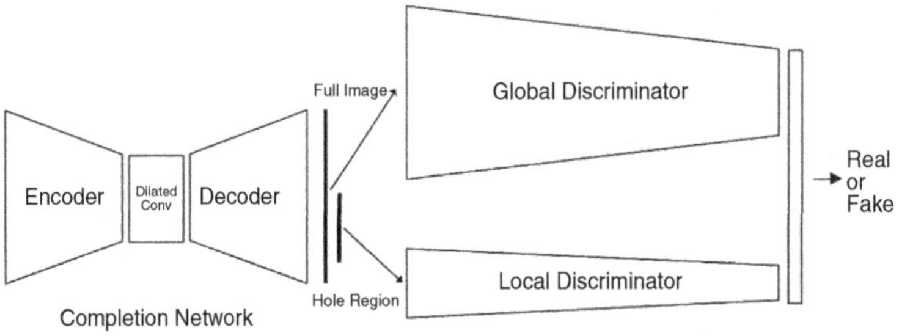

FIGURE 9.67 The full structure of the globally and locally consistent image completion networks.

Finally, the completion and discriminator networks are trained in tandem for further T_B iterations using both MSE and GAN losses, with relative weight given by hyperparameter α. Note that training is done with single holes with random aspect ratio and size; however, the trained model can complete multiple holes. Finally, Iizuka et al. (2017) note that subtle colour variation can occur in the completed regions, and hence they suggest postprocessing with blending methods.

Iizuka et al. (2017) were able to obtain what at the time were state-of-the-art results, so Yu et al. (2018) used the model as a basis for further development. The loss was changed from GAN loss to Wasserstein loss for the two discriminator networks as described in Section 9.5.2.2 with gradient penalty. Given that only the hole regions are predicted, the gradient penalty should only apply inside the hole, and hence Equation (9.105) becomes

$$\lambda \mathbb{E}_{\hat{x}\sim\mathbb{P}_{\hat{x}}}\left[\left(\|\nabla_{\hat{x}}D(\hat{x})\odot(\mathbf{1}-\mathbf{M})\|_2 - 1\right)^2\right]. \tag{9.172}$$

The pixel or reconstruction loss used the L_1 norm rather than the more often used L_2 norm. Given that the Wasserstein-1 distance in Equation (9.102) is also based on the L_1 norm, Iizuka et al. (2017) found that the combined loss was easier to train, giving greater optimisation stability. Furthermore, a *spatially discounted reconstruction loss* was introduced. Taking inspiration from reinforcement learning and recognising that pixels further from the edge of a hole region are inherently more uncertain, the weight of each hole pixel was weighted by γ^l with $\gamma = 0.99$ and l equal to the pixel distance to the nearest known pixel.

The completion network is also modified by introducing a second encoder–decoder structure operating in series with the first. The first *coarse network* gives a rough result and is strained using only the spatially discounted reconstruction loss. The second *refinement network* is trained with both reconstruction loss and WGAN-GP adversarial loss with global and local discriminators. To further enhance the ability of the refinement network to learn long relationships between features and specifically to learn when to use background patches to generate patches in hole regions, Iizuka et al. (2017) introduce a contextual attention layer. The refinement network is split into two parallel encoders, one with the contextual attention layer and one with diluted convolutions. The outputs of the encoders are then concatenated before passing into the decoder.

The aim is to match features in the 'hole regions' (foreground) with those in the surroundings (background) and apply attention. The first stage is to extract 3×3 patches from the background and reshape them as convolutional features. After this, the similarity between foreground and background patches is calculated as the inner product,

$$s_{x,y,x',y'} = \left\langle \frac{f_{x,y}}{\|f_{x,y}\|}, \frac{b_{x',y'}}{\|b_{x',y'}\|} \right\rangle. \tag{9.173}$$

The attention score for each pixel is calculated as

$$s^*_{x,y,x',y'} = \text{softmax}_{x',y'}(\lambda s_{x,y,x',y'}), \tag{9.174}$$

where λ is a constant. This can be implemented using a convolution followed by per-channel softmax. The background patches are then used as deconvolution filters to reconstruct the foreground, with overlapping pixels averaged. Finally, an *attention propagation* step is performed, and this consists of a left–right propagation with kernel size k, defined by

$$\hat{s}_{x,y,x',y'} = \sum_{i\in\{-k,\ldots,k\}} s^*_{x+i,y,x'+i,y'}, \tag{9.175}$$

and a similar top-down propagation operation. The summation can be implemented using a convolution with the identity matrix as kernel weight. This propagation step is designed to encourage coherence of attention and was found to improve in-painting results significantly.

Gated Convolution. Yu et al. (2019b) extended their earlier work (Yu et al., 2018) by introducing the *gated convolution* and making further modifications to the network architecture and training algorithm, giving *SN-PatchGAN*. The key drivers of the work are improved performance, the ability to handle arbitrarily shaped in-painting regions and the use of additional conditioning information, such as a hand-drawn sketch of a missing image region.

The gated convolution was introduced to handle the limitation of the partial convolution operation introduced by Liu et al. (2018a) and described above. Yu et al. (2019b) note that partial convolutions have four fundamental limitations. Firstly, each pixel location is marked as either valid or invalid. In contrast, pixels might have a variety of states, such as a neuron in a deeper layer with a receptive field containing both real and masked pixel locations. The second problem is that the binary state precludes additional conditional information. With stacks of partial convolutions, invalid pixels progressively disappear in deeper layers, while the gated convolution can automatically assign a 'soft mask' value. Finally, all channels share the same mask, while a gated convolution allows a more flexible weighting to be learned. The gated convolution is defined by

$$\begin{aligned} G &= W_g \cdot x, \\ F &= W_f \cdot x, \\ y &= \phi(F) \odot \sigma(G), \end{aligned} \tag{9.176}$$

where $\sigma()$ is the sigmoid function and $\phi()$ is the selected activation function; biases have been ignored for clarity. Hence, the gating matrix G defines a learned feature selection.

The authors made a few modifications to the network architecture of their previous model. They retained the completion network's original form, consisting of coarse and refinement encoder–decoder networks, including contextual attention, but replaced all convolutional layers with gated ones. Additionally, they removed the local discriminator as it was designed for use with rectangular missing image blocks rather than more general hole patterns. The global convolutional discriminator was modified to include spectral normalisation and to output a three-dimensional feature block with the same shape as the input image. Each feature corresponds to a GAN for each pixel, indicating whether it is real or fake. Training was also simplified with hinge loss, which is used for generator and discriminator networks.

Yu et al. (2019b) obtained state-of-the-art free-form mask results comparable to their previous contextual attention-based model. They were also able to illustrate the use of user-guided in-painting.

9.5.5.2 Pix2Pix Isola et al. (2017) introduced the *Pix2Pix* network, a major milestone in image-to-image translation. The applications introduced by the authors include label maps to street scenes and façades, colourisation, aerial photographs to maps, switching photographs from day to night and vice versa and sketch outlines of handbags and shoes to colour images.

The network architecture used in Pix2Pix is straightforward. The generator has a *U-Net* encoder–decoder structure of the type used earlier in Example 9.5. The U-Net has to skip connections between the corresponding downsample and upsample blocks in the encoder and decoder. These take the form of a simple concatenation of both vectors before the combined vector is passed into the next upsample block. The downsample blocks consist of a convolution followed by batch norm and leaky ReLU for all but the first block, where the batch norm is omitted. The deeper downsample and upsample blocks also use dropout layers as a source of stochasticity. Unlike standard GANs, no latent space exists; hence, dropout is the only noise source retained during inference. The upsample blocks consist of transpose convolution followed by batch norm and ReLU activation. The last layer uses convolution to map to the correct number of output channels, which is three in most applications and scales the output to $[0, 1]$ using sigmoid or $[-1, 1]$ using tahn, depending on the preference of the user.

The discriminator network is a *PatchGAN* as described in Section 9.5.5.1, meaning that the output corresponds to determining whether a patch is real or fake rather than whether or not the entire image is real or fake. Hence, the number of downsampling blocks is adjusted to reduce image size rather than a single output. The reduction factor here is 2^4, reducing from images of size 256×256 to 16×16. The discriminator downsampling blocks consist of convolution followed by batch norm and leaky ReLU, aside from the first layer, which omits the batch norm. The discriminator takes the generator input and output images as input.

The loss functions used were also standard, with GAN loss coupled with L_1 pixel loss. Training proceeds as per the standard GAN approach with iterations of generator and discriminator interleaved and the discriminator objective halved to reduce the relative speed of training the discriminator versus the generator.

Isola et al. (2017) obtained high-quality results from various applications, including when only very small datasets were used. The downside of the approach is the requirement for paired datasets for training with input and output examples. These are difficult and expensive to obtain (Hoyez et al., 2022), although fortunately, Pix2Pix does not need a large sample set for low-complexity tasks.

EXAMPLE 9.16: Pix2Pix WITH FAÇADES

An example of Pix2Pix using the façades dataset developed by Isola et al. (2017) for their model can be found in the Jupyter Notebook `Pix2Pix.ipynb`. The dataset must be downloaded first from http://efrosgans.eecs.berkeley.edu/pix2pix/datasets/ and then expanded into training, test and validation sets. The training set consists of only 400 image pairs, with around 100 each in the test and validation sets. The images are supplied as a single jpg of size 512 × 256, with the photograph on the left and the label map on the right. These need to be split into two halves when loaded. Given that the data is loaded directly from files, a custom dataset class is used and is identical to that shown in Example 9.15, apart from the difference in file format with jpg used here.

The generator structure is shown in Table 9.12, with each downsample and upsample block as described above. The instance norm variant of the batch norm was used here. The last layer in the decoder, *up1*, consists of a factor 2 `Upsample` layer, followed by `ZeroPad2d`, convolution and finally sigmoid.

TABLE 9.12 Pix2Pix Generator Architecture

Block	In Channels	Out Channels	Instance Norm	Dropout
down1	3	64		
down2	64	128	✓	
down3	128	256	✓	
down4	256	512	✓	0.5
down5	512	512	✓	0.5
down6	512	512	✓	0.5
down7	512	512	✓	0.5
down8	512	512	✓	0.5
up8	512	512	✓	0.5
up7	1024	512	✓	0.5
up6	1024	512	✓	0.5
up5	1024	512	✓	0.5
up4	1024	256	✓	
up3	512	128	✓	
up2	256	64	✓	
up1*	128	3		

The discriminator structure is shown in Table 9.13. Note that there are six input channels as the generator input and output/real output are concatenated on input to the discriminator. The output layer consists only of a `ZeroPad2d` layer followed by a convolution that returns an output of size $1 \times 16 \times 16$, and this is a PatchGAN, and so the output is an array of values rather than a single number.

TABLE 9.13 Pix2Pix Discriminator Architecture

Block	In Channels	Out Channels	Instance Norm
down1	6	64	
down2	64	128	✓
down3	128	256	✓
down4	256	512	✓
output	512	1	

The loss function is modified slightly from Isola et al. (2017) in that Wasserstein loss is used instead of GAN loss, but the pixel loss remains the L_1 norm. A weight of 100 was applied to the pixel loss. The model was trained through 1000 epochs using the Adam optimiser with a learning rate of 0.0002, $\beta_1 = 0.5$, $\beta_2 = 0.999$ and a batch size of 16. Given the small dataset, training is fast.

Figure 9.68 shows the eight test images from the dataset, while Figure 9.69 shows the corresponding label maps. The output from the trained model is given in Figure 9.70, which provides plausible reconstructions from the label maps, while not perfect.

FIGURE 9.68 Eight test images from the façades dataset.

(*Continued*)

(Continued)

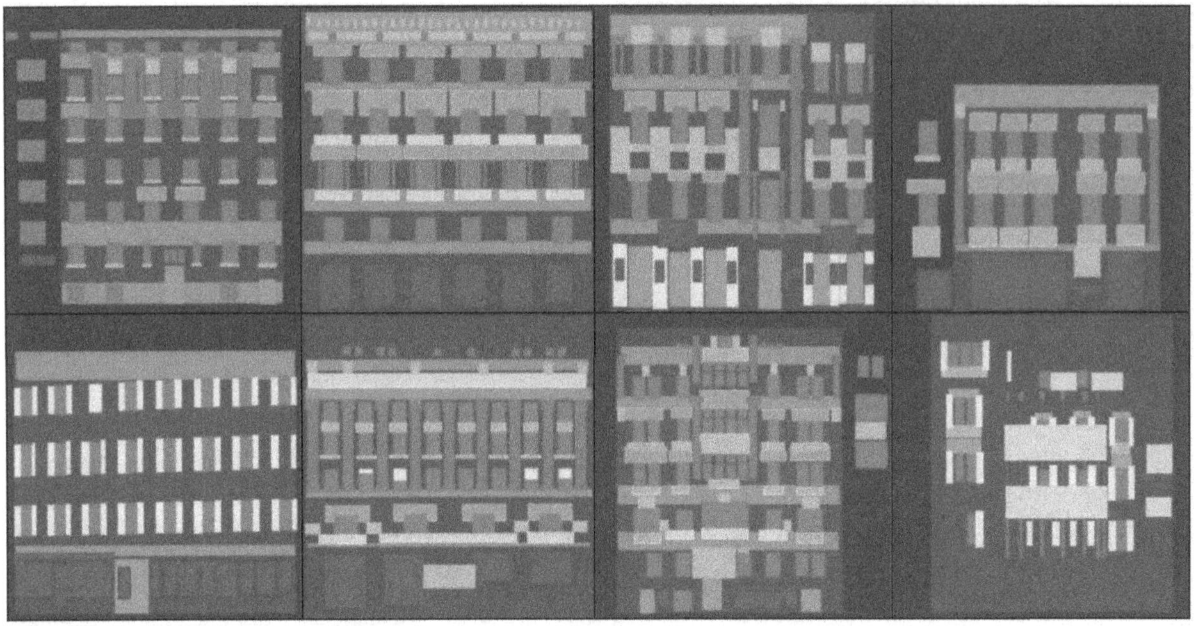

FIGURE 9.69 Eight test label maps from the façades dataset.

FIGURE 9.70 Eight sample images from the trained Pix2Pix model using the label maps as input.

9.5.5.3 GauGAN *GauGAN* and its successor, *GauGAN2,* are live interactive demonstrations of a GAN model that transforms an image segmentation map into an image. The demo can be accessed online (http://gaugan.org/gaugan2/) and was developed by Nvidia. The underlying model behind GauGAN is based on Park et al. (2019), which itself is based on *Pix2PixHD* (Wang et al., 2018a), in turn based on Johnson et al. (2016), and it is this trio of papers that is described briefly here.

The Johnson et al. (2016) Architecture. Johnson et al. (2016) designed a network architecture for style transfer and super-resolution problems. The authors proposed a two-component architecture for their work, consisting of an *image transformation* network and a *loss network*. The loss network uses a pre-trained convolutional network, VGG-16, trained on ImageNet, to measure the perceptual difference between two images. GAN-based approaches have superseded the loss network part, but the image transformation network proved influential.

The style transfer architecture from Johnson et al. (2016) is an encoder–decoder structure with a sequence of residual blocks in between. Figure 9.71 illustrates the residual block structure, and Table 9.14 gives the entire

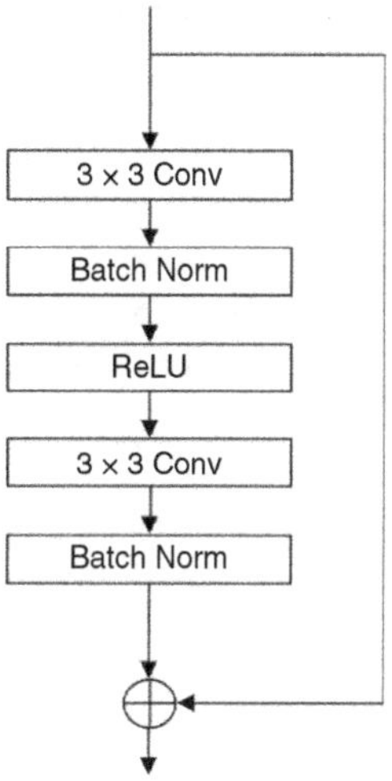

FIGURE 9.71 Design of the residual convolutional block used in Johnson et al. (2016).

TABLE 9.14 Johnson et al. (2016) Style Transfer Network

Layer	Kernel	Out Channels
Reflection padding	40 × 40	3
Conv (stride = 1)	9 × 9	32
Conv (stride = 2)	3 × 3	64
Conv (stride = 2)	3 × 3	128
Res block		128
Res block		128
Res block		128
Res block		128
Res block		128
Transpose conv (stride = 2)	3 × 3	64
Transpose conv (stride = 2)	3 × 3	32
Conv (stride = 1)	9 × 9	3

network structure. The reflection padding layer pads the outer boundary by 40 pixels and fills those pixels with the reflected values from the image. Johnson et al. (2016) were able to achieve very effective style transfer results without the use of adversarial training.

Pix2PixHD. Wang et al. (2018b) extended the previous Pix2Pix model to higher resolution, allowing the generation of 2048×1024 resolution images from a semantic label map. Pix2PixHD has three main changes from Pix2Pix: a *coarse-to-fine generator*, *multi-scale discriminators* and an *improved adversarial loss.*

The coarse-to-fine generator uses two sub-networks, with a global generator G_1 operating at a coarse scale with half the resolution in each dimension of the final image and a local enhancement network G_2 that operates at the final resolution. Hence, superficially, it has a similar approach to Iizuka et al. (2017), although the two networks are not connected serially. G_1 is based on the architecture of Johnson et al. (2016) described above, with encoder, residual blocks and decoder, and this is trained first using a reduced-resolution semantic label map. G_2 also contains the same three components. However, the output of the encoder is connected in parallel with the G_1 network, with the output of both summed together before passing into the G_2 residual blocks and then the decoder. G_2 is trained after G_1, and both networks are fine-tuned to produce the final generator.

For high-resolution images, a discriminator must have a large receptive field to discriminate between real and fake images, which can be achieved using a deep network or larger kernels. However, both choices lead to a larger model with a bigger risk of overfitting and larger memory use on GPU (Wang et al., 2018b), and this can be avoided by using multiple PatchGAN discriminators, with each one operating at a different image scale. Wang et al. (2018b) use three discriminators with a factor 2 scaling in each dimension between each pair. The architecture of all three is the same, consisting of four convolutional blocks with 4×4 convolution followed by instance norm and leaky ReLU. The four blocks have 64, 128, 256 and 512 channels. The adversarial loss becomes

$$\min_{G} \max_{D_1,D_2,D_3} \sum_{k=1,2,3} J_{GAN}(G, D_k). \tag{9.177}$$

The final change introduced into Pix2PixHD is a *feature matching loss*, which is calculated by extracting features from the layers of each discriminator model and calculating the L_1 norm between real and synthesised images. The loss is given by

$$J_{FM}(G, D_k) = \mathbb{E}_{(s,x)\sim p_{\text{data}}(s,x)} \sum_{i=1}^{T} \frac{1}{N_i} \left[\|D_k^{(i)}(s, x) - D_k^{(i)}(s, G(s))\|_1 \right], \tag{9.178}$$

where T is the total number of layers, N_i is the number of elements in each layer, s is the semantic label map and x is the associated real image. The feature matching loss is used together with the multi-discriminator GAN loss in Equation (9.177) and weighted by a factor λ.

SPADE and GauGAN. Park et al. (2019) developed the model that drives GauGAN by adapting the architecture of Pix2PixHD and adding *spatially adaptive denormalisation (SPADE).*

The problem with standard normalisation techniques, such as instance norm, argues Park et al. (2019), is that they 'wash away' information in semantic label maps. So, for example, consider two uniform segmentation maps with different values representing sky and grass. Once passed through the instance norm, both have the same and indistinguishable values. To avoid this, they introduce a different type of norm conditioned on the segmentation map that prevents information loss. Given a location with coordinates $(n, c, y, x) \in (N, C^i, H^i, W^i)$ in layer i with batch size N, channels C^i, height H^i and width W^i, the activation after normalisation is given by

$$\gamma^i_{c,y,x}(s) \frac{h^i_{n,c,y,x} - \mu^i_c}{\sigma^i_c} + \beta^i_{c,y,x}(s), \tag{9.179}$$

where $h^i_{n,c,y,x}$ is the original activation, s is the semantic label map and μ^i_c and σ^i_c are the channel-wise mean and standard deviation, defined by

$$\mu^i_c = \frac{1}{NH^iW^i}\sum_{n,y,x} h^i_{n,c,y,x}, \tag{9.180}$$

$$\sigma^i_c = \sqrt{\frac{1}{NH^iW^i}\sum_{n,y,x}\left((h^i_{n,c,y,x})^2 - (\mu^i_c)^2\right)}. \tag{9.181}$$

The SPADE block design is illustrated in Figure 9.72.

The *SPADE generator* no longer needs to have an encoder as the semantic label map is fed into the network via the SPADE normalisation blocks. Hence, the encoder structure seen in Pix2PixHD is removed entirely, and the image is initialised with a random vector as with standard GAN models. The SPADE decoder structure consists of residual blocks and upsampling layers. The SPADE residual block is shown in Figure 9.73 and is simply a residual network block with a repeated sub-block containing convolution, ReLU and SPADE block. The complete structure of the generator is given in Table 9.15, with the final output scaled either with the sigmoid or tanh functions.

The model uses the same multi-scale discriminator in Pix2PixHD, with minor modifications. A spectral norm is applied to all convolutional layers, and hinge loss is used instead of GAN loss.

An encoder can be coupled to the model to perform multi-model synthesis. In this case, a convolutional model encodes a real image to a noise vector, generating mean and variance vectors. Hence, when used in this way, the generator effectively becomes a VAE and, as might be expected, a KL divergence loss is added to the overall loss.

The GauGAN and its successors allow the generation of high-quality photorealistic images from a simple sketching tool and are helpful for visual applications and accessible to all.

9.5.5.4 CycleGAN CycleGAN (Zhu et al., 2017) is another image-to-image translation model that allows style transfer and is most memorable as the model that allowed images of horses to be converted to zebras and vice versa. The key innovation of the CycleGAN model is its use of *cycle consistency loss* and its ability to train using unpaired image sets. Pix2Pix, for example, needs a dataset with paired image and semantic label maps, which are expensive to create.

The goal of CycleGAN is to learn two mappings between datasets $\boldsymbol{X}$ and $\boldsymbol{Y}$,

$$G : X \rightarrow Y, \tag{9.182}$$

$$F : Y \rightarrow X. \tag{9.183}$$

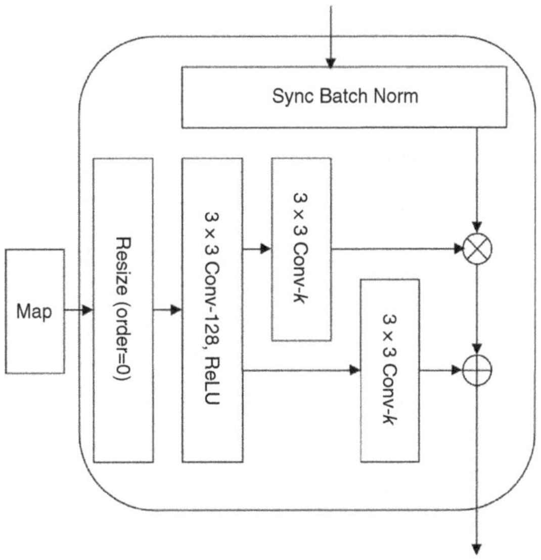

FIGURE 9.72 The SPADE normalisation block as used by Park et al. (2019).

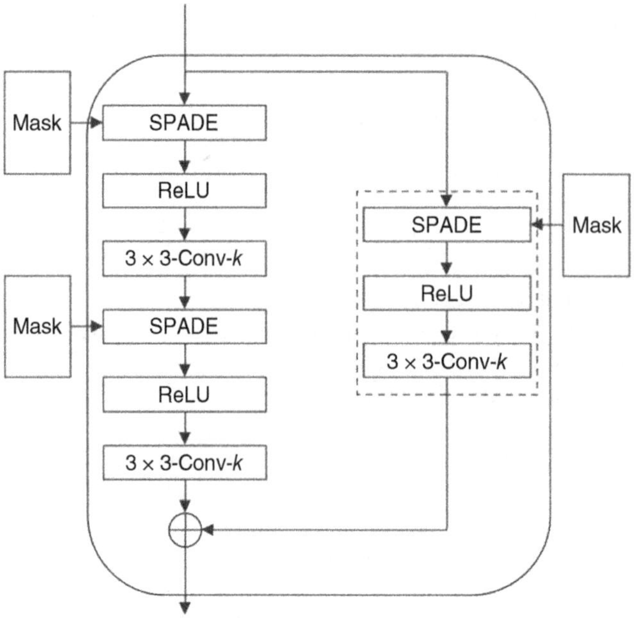

FIGURE 9.73 The SPADE residual block as used by Park et al. (2019).

TABLE 9.15 Wang et al. (2018b) SPADE Generator Structure

Layer	In Channels	Out Channels	Image Size
Linear	256	16384	
Reshape	1024	1024	4×4
SPADE ResBlk	1024	1024	4×4
Upsample	1024	1024	8×8
SPADE ResBlk	1024	1024	8×8
Upsample	1024	1024	16×16
SPADE ResBlk	1024	1024	16×16
Upsample	1024	512	32×32
SPADE ResBlk	512	512	32×32
Upsample	512	256	64×64
SPADE ResBlk	256	256	64×64
Upsample	256	128	128×128
SPADE ResBlk	128	128	128×128
Upsample	128	64	256×256
SPADE ResBlk	64	64	256×256
Upsample	64	64	512×512
3×3 Conv-3	64	3	512×512

G and F should be inverse of one another, that is,

$$F(G(x)) \approx x, \tag{9.184}$$

$$G(F(y)) \approx y. \tag{9.185}$$

To achieve this, CycleGAN trains two adversarial discriminators, D_X that distinguishes between $\{x\}$ and $\{F(y)\}$ and D_Y that distinguishes between $\{y\}$ and $\{G(x)\}$. An adversarial loss is combined with a cycle consistency loss to train the model. The adversarial loss contains two GAN loss terms for each discriminator, that is,

$$J_{GAN} = \min_G \min_{D_Y} V(D_Y, G) + \min_F \min_{D_X} V(D_X, F), \tag{9.186}$$

defined as per Equation (9.101). The cycle consistency loss is given by

$$J_{CYC} = \mathbb{E}_{x \sim p_{\text{data}}(x)} \left[||F(G(x)) - x||_1 \right] + \mathbb{E}_{y \sim p_{\text{data}}(y)} \left[||G(F(y)) - y||_1 \right]. \tag{9.187}$$

The generator architecture is based directly on that of Johnson et al. (2016) discussed above. The discriminators are 70×70 output PatchGANs, similar to those employed in Pix2Pix and Pix2PixHD.

9.5.6 GAN Inversion

GAN inversion is the process of taking an image, real or generated, and inverting it back to the latent space of a GAN. The image can then be reconstructed using the generator. Of course, the previous Section 9.5.5 discussed several models that performed precisely this inversion process using an encoder–decoder structure. However, in the cases discussed earlier, the encoder model is trained alongside the decoder to give a special-purpose model for in-painting. GAN inversion aims to project the image into the latent space of a pre-trained unconditional GAN model such as one of the StyleGANs.

Why do this? Section 9.5.3.3 shows that the latent space of a GAN can be used to manipulate the properties of an image. Hence, projecting a real image into a GAN latent space will allow that image to be manipulated or edited. Other applications include image restoration as described in Section 9.5.5.1, image interpolation, three-dimensional reconstruction from a two-dimensional image, multimodal learning and medical imaging applications (Xia et al., 2023).

Consider an unconditional GAN which maps latent vectors $z \in \mathbb{Z}$ to images $x \in \mathbb{X}$,

$$G : \mathbb{Z} \to \mathbb{X}. \tag{9.188}$$

We know that points close to each other in $\mathbb{Z}$ give images that are perceptually similar in $\mathbb{X}$. Then the GAN inversion problem is defined as (Xia et al., 2023)

$$\hat{z} = \underset{z}{\text{argmin}} l(G(z), x), \tag{9.189}$$

where l is a distance measure of visual similarity such as inception score or Fréchet inception distance (see Sections 9.2.1 and 9.2.2).

This immediately raised the question of which latent space to use. There is always a true $\mathbb{Z}$-space, the space of values sampled from the normal or uniform distribution. However, this space can be highly entangled for semantic attributes, as discussed in Section 9.5.3.3. The StyleGAN models reviewed in Section 9.5.4.4 have a second latent space $\mathbb{W}$ that is obtained using a learned transform from the original latent space $z \sim \mathcal{N}(0, \mathbf{1})$. $\mathbb{W}$ has more degrees of freedom and is less entangled than $\mathbb{Z}$ and is a better space for inversion. Other choices are possible, and Abdal et al. (2019a,b) use what they term $\mathbb{W}+$ latent space, formed from a concatenation of all the 18 different 512-dimensional w vectors used by the StyleGAN2 model. Wu et al. (2021) make a different choice, defining *StyleSpace*, the space composed of channel-wise style parameters, which are the $\mathbb{W}$ space parameters after the affine transformation step in the StyleGAN architecture. As should be clear, all of these choices are highly specific to the architecture of StyleGAN, and in general, any choice of latent space will be specific to the GAN model.

There are three basic approaches to solving Equation (9.189): learning-based, optimisation-based and a hybrid of the two. Learning-based approaches train an encoder network $E(x; \theta_E)$ that maps images x into the latent space of the GAN. The general approach is to train the encoder using the objective

$$\hat{\theta}_E = \underset{\theta_E}{\text{argmin}} \sum_n \mathcal{L}(G(E(x_n; \theta_E)), x_n), \tag{9.190}$$

for fixed G. There are several examples of this approach, including those of Perarnau et al. (2016), Zhu et al. (2016) and Bau et al. (2019a). The approaches to training the encoder model vary; Bau et al. (2019a,b), for example, adopt a layer-wise approach to GAN inversion in which each layer is progressively inverted to build the encoder. As might be expected given the prominence of StyleGAN and successors and their specialised architecture, several bespoke approaches to inversion have been proposed, including those by Alaluf et al. (2021), Richardson et al. (2021), Tov et al. (2021) and Wei et al. (2022). The main advantage of encoder-based methods is their speed, and once trained, projecting an image into the latent space is fast and involves one inference through the encoder model. The problem is that the results are often quite poor, and training the encoder well enough for accurate reconstruction is difficult.

The second way to solve Equation (9.189) is by optimisation of the latent vector. There are two approaches to optimisation here: gradient-based methods, including gradient descent optimisers like Adam, quasi-Newton methods like L-BFGS and Hamiltonian Monte Carlo; and gradient-free algorithms, including covariance matrix adaptation evolution strategy. The key issue to good performance is choosing the starting latent code well, and using a simple approach, such as choosing several starting latent codes, may be ineffective. Optimisation generally gives better results than learning-based approaches but at a considerable computational cost. Optimisation must be performed for each latent code, which is slow and requires iterative processing. Examples of this approach include Zhu et al. (2016), Abdal et al. (2019a) and Huh et al. (2020).

The final type of GAN inversion is a hybrid approach, where an encoder model is used to make the initial projection into the latent space, which is then used as the starting point for an optimiser. Hybrid approaches can be found in Zhu et al. (2016, 2020) and Bau et al. (2019a,b). One variant of this approach is Roich et al. (2021), who use *pivotal tuning inversion* with a short period of retraining to adjust the generator to reproduce the out-of-sample input image, which then allows editing to proceed with more accurate results.

EXAMPLE 9.17: INVERTING BigGAN USING OPTIMISATION

As a simple example of GAN inversion, this example, found in the Jupyter Notebook `Inverting BigGAN.ipynb`, uses a hybrid approach to invert BigGAN. The pre-trained BigGAN instance is obtained from Hugging Face (https://huggingface.co/) using the Python package `pytorch_pretrained_biggan`, which can be installed using `pip`. The model can be loaded directly from the package using

```
from pytorch_pretrained_biggan import (BigGAN, one_hot_from_names,
                                       truncated_noise_sample)
model = BigGAN.from_pretrained('biggan-deep-256').eval()
```

Note that using `eval()` as the BigGAN model is held fixed. The package is dependent on `nltk` which must also be installed and `wordnet` downloaded.

```
import nltk
nltk.download('wordnet')
```

The BigGAN model is a conditional GAN trained using ImageNet, and three example images generated are shown in Figure 9.74.

The first step is to build and train an encoder network. The model used here is a simple sequence of downsampling blocks consisting of convolution, instance norm and leaky ReLU that reduce the image dimension from 256×256 to 1×1 with 128 channels, and this is then reshaped to a one-dimensional vector as input to the BigGAN latent space. The model is trained through 50,000 iterations in which 32 images are generated from BigGAN using random vectors, and the generated images are 'round-tripped' through the encoder back into z-space. The MSE loss between the original and encoded latent vectors is used to train the encoder. The Adam optimiser was used with a learning rate of 0.002, $\beta_1 = 0.5$ and $\beta_2 = 0.999$.

FIGURE 9.74 Three images generated from BigGAN in classes dog, coffee and flower.

The purpose of the encoder is to give a good starting point for iteration using an optimiser. The optimisation process uses the encoder model to generate an initial latent vector from the given image. This latent vector is then used to generate an image using the BigGAN model, and the generated image is compared with the original image. The loss function for this has two parts, an L_1 pixel loss and *learned perceptual image patch similarity (LPIPS)* (Zhang et al., 2018). The LPIPS loss package can be installed using `pip`. The loss function is used with the Adam optimiser directly on the latent vector, with a learning rate of 0.001 and the default beta parameters. The iteration function is illustrated below. Note that a closure function is not required for the Adam optimiser but allows a broad range of optimisers to be used if desired.

```
def find_z(img, generator, img_class, truncation, device, lr=0.001,
        num_iter=5000):

    dist = torch.nn.L1Loss()
    loss_fn_vgg = lpips.LPIPS(net='vgg').to(device)
    min_loss = 10
    beta = 10

    min_z = enc(img).detach().clone().requires_grad_(True)
    optZ = torch.optim.Adam([min_z], lr=lr)

    print("Beginning Iteration.")
    tqdm_it = trange(num_iter)
    for i in tqdm_it:
        def closure():
            optZ.zero_grad()
            img_pred = generator(min_z, img_class, truncation)
            loss_d = dist(img, img_pred)
            loss_p = loss_fn_vgg(img, img_pred)
            loss = loss_d + beta * loss_p
            loss.backward()
            return loss
        optZ.step(closure)

        if (i + 1) % 100 == 0:
            img_pred = generator(min_z, img_class, truncation)
            loss_d = dist(img, img_pred)
```

(*Continued*)

(*Continued*)

```
            loss_p = loss_fn_vgg(img, img_pred)
            loss = loss_d + beta * loss_p
            print("[Iter {}] error: {}".format(i+1, loss.item()))
            comb = torch.cat((img, img_pred), 0)
            filename = 'invBigGAN_pair_' + str(i+1) + '.png'
            show_tensor_images((comb+1)/2, 2, 2, filename=filename)

    return min_z
```

As an example, the dog image from Figure 9.74 was used as the target. Figure 9.75 shows the target and the result after the encoder model and 100 iterations. The encoder model has performed reasonably well at finding a latent vector close to the original image. After 5000 iterations, the result is much closer to the target, as shown in Figure 9.76.

FIGURE 9.75 The left image is the iteration target, and the right image is the target projected through the encoder with 100 optimisation iterations.

FIGURE 9.76 The left image is the iteration target, and the right image is the target projected through the encoder with 5000 iterations of optimisation.

9.5.7 Conclusions on GANs

GANs have been the most popular generative model since their inception (Goodfellow et al., 2014), as can be seen from the vast literature on their use. Until the advent of score-based models (Song et al., 2021) and latent diffusion models (Rombach et al., 2021), GANs were largely unchallenged for realism and accuracy. The critical elements of GANs are adversarial training and discriminators rather than any particular architectural innovation. GANs will no doubt remain popular, even though diffusion models set the standard for generative AI from 2022.

9.6 LATENT DIFFUSION MODELS (LDMs)

The current state-of-the-art AI image generation is performed by *latent diffusion models (LDMs)* that derive from the work of Rombach et al. (2021). Commercial models like *Stable Diffusion* and *Midjourney* provide high-resolution text-to-image generation with modest computational demands and have become ubiquitous.

As noted above, GANs reigned supreme in image generation for the latter half of the 2010s but were not problem-free. The good results were primarily restricted to domains with limited variability. At the same time, adversarial training is difficult to stabilise and cannot easily be scaled to more complex data distributions (Rombach et al., 2021).

Diffusion models like those of Ho et al. (2020) and Song et al. (2021), discussed in Sections 9.3.5 and 9.3.7, demonstrated excellent results in several image generation domains including image synthesis (Dhariwal and Nichol, 2021; Song et al., 2021), conditional image synthesis (Ho et al., 2022) and super-resolution (Saharia et al., 2023). Diffusion models do not suffer the stability issues found with GANs. However, they are also very computationally demanding, as is evident from implementation of the score-based model in Example 9.5. So, the demand was for models with the flexibility, stability and accuracy of diffusion models but at a lower computational cost, which is what latent diffusion models provide.

LDM models operate in two stages (Rombach et al., 2021):

1. **Perceptual compression**, where the high-frequency variation is removed but limited semantic variation is learned.
2. **Semantic compression**, where the semantics of the images are learned.

LDMs explicitly separate the two processes and train a distinct model component for each one. The perceptual compression stage is performed by an autoencoder that learns a latent representation equivalent to the image space but with less computational complexity. The diffusion model then operates on the latent space, which is more suitable than the pixel space used by pure diffusion models. The high-frequency variation has been removed, and the diffusion model operates on semantic data at lower dimensionality and computational cost.

The architecture of the LDM is illustrated in Figure 9.77. The first step is the perceptual image compression, which is the left-most block in the figure, and this consists of an autoencoder that is trained using perceptual loss (Zhang et al., 2018), which is based on using the trained features of a VGG network, and a patch-based adversarial discriminator model (Isola et al., 2017), as used in *Pix2Pix* discussed in Section 9.5.5.2. The autoencoder acts to downsample the image by a factor $f = 2^m$, with factors of 4 and 8 proving to be the most effective. This latent space remains two-dimensional and distinct from more traditional autoencoder models, which flattened the latent space to one dimension, as seen in Chapter 8. Rombach et al. (2021) imposed a regularisation term to avoid high variance, testing KL and *vector quantisation* (VQ-VAE) approaches. The autoencoder is trained first before training the diffusion model.

The diffusion model itself works similarly to those described earlier. The *forward diffusion* is a Markov process that starts with a data sample and steadily adds noise over multiple steps. The denoising diffusion model learns to reverse this process and steadily reconstruct the image from the prior distribution, which is usually the standard normal. In the latent diffusion model, this process acts in the lower-dimensional latent space defined by the autoencoder model, which is computationally efficient. A time-conditioned U-Net model is the core neural network model used in the reverse process. This model predicts the noise in the latent representation at z_t and allows the iterative reconstruction of the latent space image z_0. The U-Net structure allows it to capture local features and contextual information. The denoising U-Net can also be conditioned to allow control of the synthesis process and provide a

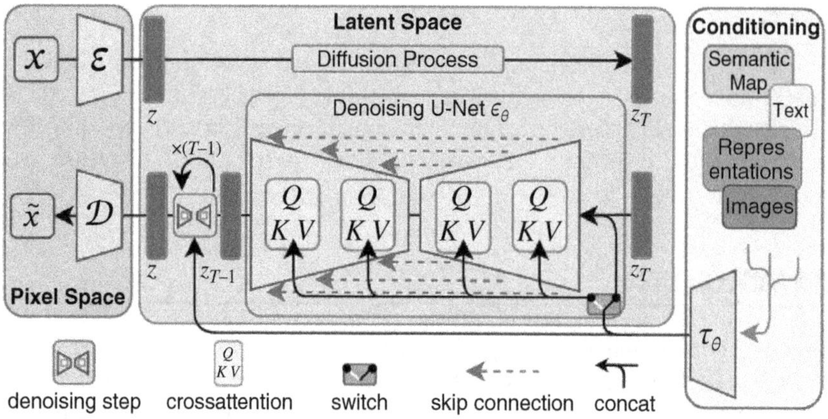

FIGURE 9.77 The structure of the LDM (Rombach et al., 2021). Image available via licence: Creative Commons Attribution 4.0 International (https://creativecommons.org/licenses/by/4.0/.) The image was scaled to 300 dpi. Print editions also converted to greyscale.

text-to-image model. Rombach et al. (2021) augment the U-Net with cross-attention to facilitate this conditioning process, as shown in Figure 9.77.

9.7 CONCLUSIONS ON GENERATIVE MODELS

This chapter has explored generative models in their native application of image generation. It has reviewed many models, from energy-based and diffusion models through variational autoencoders, GANs and the current state-of-the-art latent diffusion model. The chapter presented direct image generation and conditional models, such as in-painting and image-to-image translation. Many of these models can find applications in quantitative finance, principally by generating synthetic market data as discussed in Chapter 18.

CHAPTER 10

Deep Reinforcement Learning

I never knew what a friend was until I met Geordi. He spoke to me as though I were human. He treated me no differently from anyone else. He accepted me for what I am. And that, I have learned, is friendship. But I do not know how to say goodbye.

Lieutenant Commander Data, Star Trek: The Next Generation, 'The Next Phase' (1992)

10.1 INTRODUCTION

This chapter presents an introduction to reinforcement learning (RL). The deep learning aspect of reinforcement learning is a relatively recent innovation, and reinforcement learning has primarily developed independently of neural networks.

For a comprehensive guide to RL, the reader is referred to the seminal *Reinforcement Learning* by Sutton and Barto (2018). A more succinct introduction is provided by *Algorithms for Reinforcement Learning* by Szepesvári (2010). The Coursera specialisation *Reinforcement Learning* from the University of Alberta (White and White, 2019) is also highly recommended, as is the lecture series provided by DeepMind and UCL, beginning with the 10-lecture course from Silver (2015).

RL is *learning by doing*: machine learning where an agent learns to make decisions by performing actions in an environment to maximise cumulative reward. Unlike other machine learning paradigms, RL focuses on learning from interaction, using trial and error to discover the optimal actions to take in various situations. Notably, the RL agent's environment can change as the world changes, and indeed, the agent can change the environment in which it operates.

The theoretical treatment here largely follows Silver (2015), with input from Sutton and Barto (2018). The chapter is organised as follows: it begins with an introduction to the fundamental principles of RL in Section 10.2, where the basic ideas and terminology are established. The chapter then explores *Markov decision processes* in Section 10.3, which provides a mathematical framework for modelling decision-making in environments with stochastic outcomes. The discussion continues with *dynamic programming* in Section 10.4, and how they are used to search for optimal policies. Section 10.5 introduces Monte Carlo methods in RL that rely on sampling for policy evaluation and control. *Temporal difference learning* is discussed in Section 10.6, which combines Monte Carlo approaches with ideas drawn from dynamic programming. Section 10.7 then explores *deep reinforcement learning*, highlighting how deep learning techniques enhance the scalability and performance of traditional reinforcement learning methods, and this is followed by an examination of *policy gradient* methods in Section 10.8, which optimise policies directly by gradient ascent. Finally, the chapter concludes with *actor–critic methods* in Section 10.9, which combines the benefits of policy-based and value-based approaches, providing a comprehensive approach to solving complex reinforcement learning problems.

Deep Learning in Quantitative Finance, First Edition. Andrew Green.

10.2 KEY CONCEPTS IN REINFORCEMENT LEARNING

10.2.1 Defining RL

Definition 10.1 ***(Reinforcement Learning)*****:** *Reinforcement learning* is a machine learning paradigm in which an agent learns to make sequential decisions by interacting with an environment and receiving rewards as feedback.

Key characteristics:

- The agent learns from its actions' consequences rather than labelled examples.
- The objective is to maximise cumulative rewards over time, not just immediate outcomes.
- The learning process involves exploration (trying new actions) and exploitation (using known actions to maximise rewards).

10.2.2 Rewards

The reward function is a crucial element of reinforcement learning that quantifies the immediate feedback an agent receives after acting in a specific state.

Definition 10.2 ***(Reward Function)*****:** The reward function $R(S, A, S')$ maps the current state S, the action A and the subsequent state S' to a reward value. This reward signal $R_t \in \mathbb{R}$ provides immediate feedback to the agent about the quality or value of the action taken in the context of the current state,

$$R_t = R(S_t, A_t, S_{t+1}), \tag{10.1}$$

where R_t is the reward received at time step t, S_t is the state at time step t, A_t is the action taken at time step t and S_{t+1} is the resulting state after taking action A_t.

Key characteristics:

- **Immediate Feedback.** The reward function provides an immediate scalar value that indicates the benefit or cost of the action taken. This feedback is essential for the agent to learn which actions are favourable and which are not.
- **Guiding Behaviour.** The reward function guides the agent's behaviour towards achieving the desired objective. By maximising the cumulative reward, the agent learns to perform actions that are beneficial in the long run.
- **Task-Specific Design.** The reward function design is specific to the task and environment. Careful crafting is required to ensure alignment with the agent's goals and the problem being solved.
- **Balance Between Immediate and Future Rewards.** In many RL problems, the agent must balance the immediate reward with future rewards. This balance is typically managed through the use of discount factors in the calculation of the cumulative reward.

Examples:

- *Gaming.* In a game environment, the reward function might assign a positive reward for scoring points or achieving objectives and a negative reward for losing points or failing.
- *Robotics.* In robotic control, the reward function might reward the agent for reaching a target location and penalise it for collisions or deviations from the path.
- *Finance.* The reward function could be based on the profit or loss of trading actions.

10.2.3 Agent and Environment

Definition 10.3 ***(Agent)*****:** In reinforcement learning, the agent is the entity that makes decisions. It interacts with the environment by taking action and learns to achieve its goals through these interactions. The agent can be a software program or a physical robot. The agent executes actions A_t, obtains observations O_t and receives reward R_t.

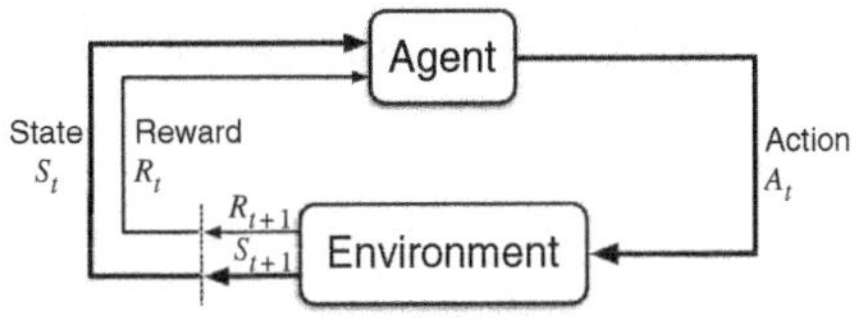

FIGURE 10.1 The relationship between agent and environment in reinforcement learning. Figure from Çetin et al. (2020), used under Creative Commons Attribution 4.0 International licence.

Definition 10.4 ***(Environment)*****:** The environment is everything the agent interacts with and is external to the agent. It provides the agent with states and rewards based on the actions taken. The environment receives action A_t, emits observations O_t and emits reward R_t.

Figure 10.1 illustrates the agent–environment interaction loop:

1. *State Perception.* At each time step t, the agent perceives the current state S_t of the environment through observation O_t.
2. *Action Selection.* Based on the current state S_t, the agent selects an action A_t according to its policy π.
3. *Environment Response.* The environment responds to the action A_t by transitioning to a new state S_{t+1} and providing a reward R_t.
4. *Learning.* The agent uses the reward R_t and the new state S_{t+1} to update its policy and value function.

Example (portfolio management):

- *State.* Current portfolio composition, asset prices, economic indicators and risk metrics.
- *Action.* Allocation of funds across different assets (e.g., stocks, bonds, commodities).
- *Reward.* Change in portfolio value, considering returns and risk.

Sequence example:

1. *State.* The agent observes the current portfolio distribution and market conditions.
2. *Action.* The agent reallocates funds by increasing bond investment and reducing stocks.
3. *Reward.* The portfolio value increases due to favourable market movements in bonds.
4. *New State.* The agent observes the new portfolio distribution and updated market conditions.

10.2.4 History and State

Definition 10.5 ***(History)*****:** The history in reinforcement learning refers to the complete sequence of observations, actions and rewards from the initial time step up to the current time step. At time step t, the history H_t can be represented as

$$H_t = (O_0, A_0, R_0, O_1, A_1, R_1, \dots, O_{t-1}, A_{t-1}, R_{t-1}, O_t). \tag{10.2}$$

The history contains all the information about the past interactions between the agent and the environment. This sequence can be used to infer the state of the environment and the agent's learning process.

Definition 10.6 ***(State)*****:** The state in reinforcement learning concisely represents the environment at a particular time step. It contains all the relevant information the agent needs to decide on the next action. At time step t, the state S_t is a function of the history H_t:

$$S_t = f(H_t), \tag{10.3}$$

where f is a function that extracts relevant information from the history to form the state. The state is a crucial component of the reinforcement learning framework. It serves as the input to the agent's decision-making process, determining which action to take next. A well-defined state space can significantly enhance the agent's ability to learn effective policies.

Example (portfolio management):

- *History*. The sequence of past portfolio allocations, asset returns and rebalancing actions.
- *State*. The current composition of the portfolio, asset prices and risk metrics (e.g., volatility, beta).

10.2.4.1 Subdivision of State The state can be subdivided into *environment*, *agent* and *information* (Silver, 2015).

Definition 10.7 ***(Environment State)*****:** The environment state, S_t^e, is the private state of the environment that is used to generate the following observation and reward. It is only sometimes visible to the agent.

Definition 10.8 ***(Agent State)*****:** The agent state S_t^a is the agent's internal state and is used to select the following action and can be any function of the history, $S_t^a = g(H_t)$.

Definition 10.9 ***(Information State)*****:** The information state contains all the useful information from the history. The state S_t is *Markov* if

$$\mathbb{P}[S_{t+1}|S_t) = \mathbb{P}(S_{t+1}|S_0, \ldots, S_t), \tag{10.4}$$

that is, the current state S_t embodies all past information, a property frequently encountered in quantitative finance.

10.2.4.2 Observability The observability of the environment can be complete or partial (Silver, 2015).

Definition 10.10 ***(Fully Observable Environment)*****:** In a fully observable environment, the agent has complete access to the current state of the environment at each time step, which means that the state S_t includes all the relevant information needed to make an optimal decision,

$$O_t = S_t^a = S_t^e. \tag{10.5}$$

Characteristics:

- *Complete Information*. The agent can observe all aspects of the environment necessary to determine the state.
- *Markov Property*. The environment typically satisfies the Markov property, where the future state depends only on the current state and action, not the history.
- *Simplified Decision-Making*. Since the agent has all the necessary information, it can make decisions based solely on the current state without inferring or estimating hidden information.

A board game like chess is an example of a fully observable environment, as the board configuration contains all the information at all times. A fully observable environment makes modelling easier, allowing simpler algorithms to be used. Unfortunately, they are rare in real-world examples as information is often unknown or hidden.

Definition 10.11 ***(Partially Observable Environment)*****:** In a partially observable environment, the agent does not have access to the complete state of the environment. Instead, it receives observations that provide incomplete or noisy information about the true state,

$$S_t^a \neq S_t^e. \tag{10.6}$$

The agent must construct its own *belief* of the environment state:

$$S_t^a = (\mathbb{P}[S_t^e = S_0], \ldots, \mathbb{P}[S_t^e = S_N]). \tag{10.7}$$

Characteristics:

- *Incomplete Information*. The observations O_t received by the agent do not fully capture the state S_t^e of the environment.
- *Hidden State*. There may be aspects of the environment's state that the agent cannot directly observe and must infer from available information.
- *History Dependence*. The agent may need to rely on a history of past observations and actions to make informed decisions, as the current observation alone may not be sufficient.

Poker is an example of a partially observable environment. The agent cannot see the opponents' cards and must make decisions based on observed actions and known cards. Partially observable environments more accurately reflect real-world scenarios, where complete information is often unavailable. However, the algorithms must handle uncertainty and may require more complex representations, such as belief states or memory mechanisms.

10.2.5 Policy, Value and State–Action Functions

The agent may include one or more of the following components (Silver, 2015):

- *Policy*. A function that determines the behaviour of the agent.
- *Value or State–Action Function*. Determines the value of a given state or a combined state–action pair.
- *Model*. The agent builds a model of the environment.

Definition 10.12 ***(Policy)*:** A policy in reinforcement learning defines the strategy used by an agent to determine its actions based on the current state. It is a mapping from states to probabilities of selecting each possible action. Two types of policy are possible:

- *Deterministic Policy* π. Maps each state to a specific action. Formally, $\pi : \mathcal{S} \to \mathcal{A}$, where $\mathcal{S}$ is the set of states and $\mathcal{A}$ is the set of actions.
- *Stochastic Policy* $\pi(a|s)$. Maps each state to a probability distribution over actions. Formally, $\pi : \mathcal{S} \to \mathbb{P}(\mathcal{A})$, where $\mathbb{P}(\mathcal{A})$ is the set of probability distributions over actions.

The agent aims to learn an optimal policy that maximises the expected cumulative reward.

Definition 10.13 ***(Value Function)*:** The value function measures the expected cumulative reward that can be obtained from a given state under a specific policy. It provides a measure of the long-term desirability of states. The state–value function $V^\pi(S)$ represents the expected cumulative reward starting from state S and following policy π.

$$V^\pi(S) = \mathbb{E}^\pi\left[\sum_{k=0}^{\infty} \gamma^k R_{t+k+1} \mid S_t = S\right], \tag{10.8}$$

where γ is the discount factor $0 \le \gamma \le 1$ and $\mathbb{E}^\pi$ denotes the expectation given that the agent follows policy π. The state–value function helps the agent evaluate the long-term benefit of being in a particular state and guides the learning process towards more rewarding states.

Definition 10.14 ***(State–Action or Q-Function)*:** The state–action function, or Q-function, measures the expected cumulative reward of taking a specific action in a given state and following a particular policy. $Q^\pi(s, a)$ represents the expected cumulative reward starting from state S, taking action A and then following policy π,

$$Q^\pi(S, A) = \mathbb{E}^\pi\left[\sum_{k=0}^{\infty} \gamma^k R_{t+k+1} \mid S_t = S, A_t = A\right]. \tag{10.9}$$

The Q-function provides a more granular evaluation than the value function, as it considers the value of specific actions in addition to the value of states. It is instrumental in action selection, allowing the agent to compare the expected returns of different actions in the same state.

10.2.6 Model

The agent may use an internal model of the environment.

Definition 10.15 *(Model)***:** In reinforcement learning, a model refers to a representation or approximation of the environment with which the agent interacts. Given the current state and action, it predicts the outcomes of the agent's actions, specifically the next state and reward. The agent can use a model to plan and make decisions about future actions without directly interacting with the real environment.

Types of model:

- *Transition Model* $P(S'|S, A)$. Represents the probability of moving from one state to another given a particular action.
- *Reward Model.* Describes the expected reward received after taking a specific action in a given state,

$$R(S, A, S') = \mathbb{E}[R|S, A, S']. \tag{10.10}$$

Using the model to simulate future actions and outcomes allows the agent to make better decisions.

EXAMPLE 10.1: MULTI-ARMED BANDIT

The multi-armed bandit problem is a classic example in reinforcement learning, where an agent must choose actions (arms) to maximise its cumulative reward over time (see, e.g., Sutton and Barto, 2018). In the bandit problem, there are multiple slot machines (arms), each with an unknown probability distribution of giving rewards. The agent can pull one arm at each time step. The agent aims to maximise its total reward over a series of pulls or time steps. The challenge arises because the agent does not know the best arm (highest average reward). Therefore, it needs to balance between *exploration*, trying out different arms to gather information about their reward distributions, and *exploitation*, leveraging the current knowledge to maximise immediate rewards.

There are several possible variations in the setup of the problem:

- Number of arms K.
- Reward distributions – each arm may have a different distribution from which rewards are generated. Common distributions include Gaussian, Bernoulli and exponential.
- Initial knowledge of rewards – whether the agent has prior knowledge about the reward distributions of the arms. In most cases, initial knowledge is assumed to be minimal or non-existent.
- Stationarity of rewards – the reward distributions of each arm remain constant over time, or they vary, requiring adaptive strategies.

This example uses 10 arms, each with rewards generated from the standard normal distribution at startup.

There are several common strategies used to solve the problem (Sutton and Barto, 2018):

- *Epsilon-Greedy.* A simple strategy where the agent chooses the arm with the highest estimated reward most of the time (exploitation) but occasionally chooses a random arm (exploration).
- *Upper Confidence Bound (UCB).* This strategy balances exploration and exploitation by choosing arms based on the upper confidence bounds of their estimated rewards. The selection of actions follows the equation

$$A_t = \underset{A}{\operatorname{argmax}} \left[Q_t(A) + c\sqrt{\frac{\ln(t+1)}{N_t(A) + \epsilon}} \right],$$

where A_t denotes the action chosen at time step t, $Q_t(A)$ represents the mean reward of action A, c is a constant controlling the balance between exploration and exploitation, $N_t(A)$ indicates the number of times action A has been chosen and ϵ prevents division by zero.

- *Thompson Sampling*. This Bayesian approach samples arms according to their posterior probability of being the best arm, combining exploration and exploitation naturally.

There are many real-world applications of bandits (Bouneffouf et al., 2020), including:

- *Online Advertising*. Choosing which advertisement to display to a user to maximise click-through rates (CTRs). Different ads represent different arms; the goal is to learn which ad performs best for different user segments.
- *Clinical Trials*. Selecting the most effective treatment from a set of potential treatments for a medical condition. Each treatment represents an arm; the reward is the patient's health outcome.
- *Recommender Systems*. To maximise user engagement or satisfaction, recommend products, movies or content to users. Each recommendation is an arm, and the reward is the user's response (click, rating, purchase).
- *Dynamic Pricing*. Adjusting prices of products in real time to maximise revenue or profit. Different price points are arms, and the reward is the revenue generated.
- *Portfolio Optimisation*. Allocating investments among different financial assets to maximise returns. Each asset represents an arm, and the reward is the financial return.

A Python class implemented the multi-arm bandit, managing the arms and the reward distribution. Member functions provide the ϵ-greedy and UCB strategies. The `step` function advances the state forward one time step.

```
class MultiArmedBandit:
    def __init__(self, num_arms):
        self.num_arms = num_arms
        self.q_true = np.random.normal(loc=0, scale=1, size=num_arms)
        self.q_estimates = np.zeros(num_arms)
        self.arm_counts = np.zeros(num_arms)
        self.total_reward = 0
        self.time_step = 0

    def reset(self):
        self.q_true = np.random.normal(loc=0, scale=1, size=self.num_arms)
        self.q_estimates = np.zeros(self.num_arms)
        self.arm_counts = np.zeros(self.num_arms)
        self.total_reward = 0
        self.time_step = 0

    def epsilon_greedy_action(self, epsilon):
        if np.random.random() < epsilon:
            # Explore: Choose a random arm
            action = np.random.randint(self.num_arms)
        else:
            # Exploit: Choose the arm with the highest estimated value
            action = np.argmax(self.q_estimates)
        return action
```

(*Continued*)

(*Continued*)

```
    def ucb_action(self, c=1):
        # Upper Confidence Bound action selection
        ucb_estimates = self.q_estimates + \
                        c * np.sqrt(np.log(self.time_step + 1) /
                        (self.arm_counts + 1e-5))
        action = np.argmax(ucb_estimates)
        return action

    def step(self, action):
        # Get reward from the chosen arm
        reward = np.random.normal(loc=self.q_true[action], scale=1)

        # Update estimates and counts
        self.arm_counts[action] += 1
        self.total_reward += reward
        self.time_step += 1
        self.q_estimates[action] += (reward - self.q_estimates[action]) / \
                                    self.arm_counts[action]

        4return reward
```

Figure 10.2 illustrates the average cumulative rewards for a 10-armed bandit with three strategies: ϵ-greedy strategy with $\epsilon = 0.1$, ϵ-greedy with $\epsilon = 0.2$ and UCB. The results were averaged over 1000 realisations. The UCB strategy produces the best results.

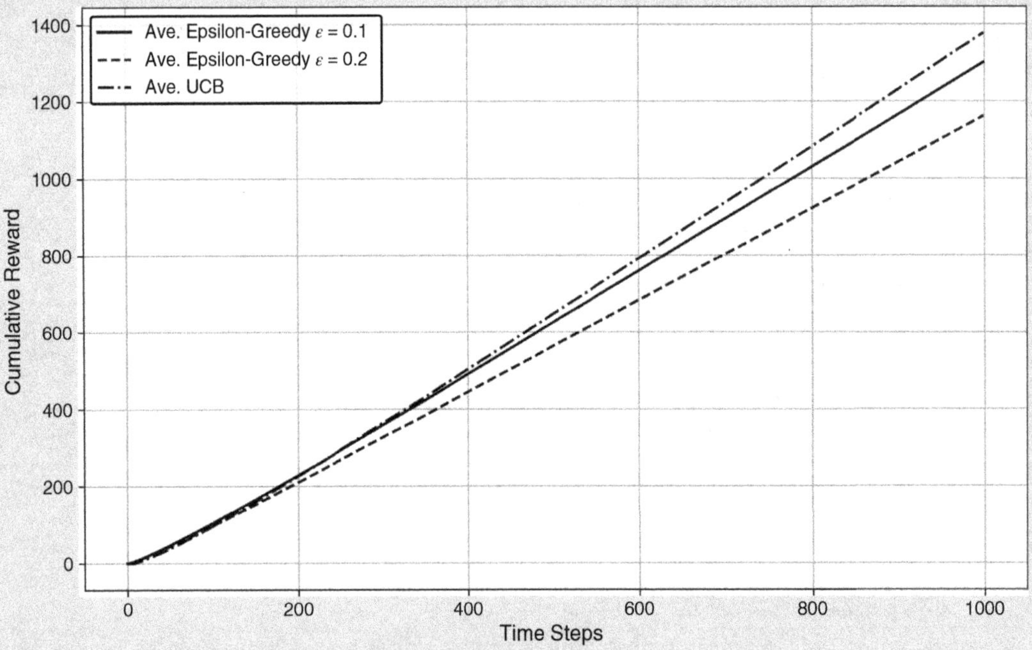

FIGURE 10.2 Average cumulative reward for a 10-armed bandit with three different strategies: ϵ-greedy strategy with $\epsilon = 0.1$, ϵ-greedy with $\epsilon = 0.2$ and UCB.

10.3 MARKOV DECISION PROCESSES (MDPs) AND THE BELLMAN EQUATIONS

The Markov decision process is a description of an environment for RL. The environment is fully observable in an MDP, and the state satisfies the Markov property (Silver, 2015). It plays a critical role as almost all RL problems are formalised as MDPs, and they are a mathematically idealised setting for RL problems (Sutton and Barto, 2018). Even problems with partial observability (*partially observable Markov decision processes (POMDPs)*) can be converted to MDPs (Silver, 2015). The *Markov reward process* is defined first, to define an MDP formally.

Definition 10.16 ***(Markov Reward Process (MRP))*:** An MRP is a stochastic process that extends the concept of a Markov chain to include rewards associated with transitions between states. Formally, an MRP is defined by a tuple $(\mathcal{S}, P, R, \gamma)$, where:

- $\mathcal{S}$ is a finite or countably infinite set of states.
- P is the state transition probability matrix, where $P_{SS'} = \mathbb{P}(S_{t+1} = S' \mid S_t = S)$.
- $R(S)$ is a reward function that maps state–action pairs to real numbers.
- γ is a discount factor that weights the importance of delayed rewards. If $\gamma \sim 0$, the evaluation is said to be *myopic*; if $\gamma \sim 1$, the evaluation is said to be *far-sighted*.

The value function defined in Equation (10.8) can be associated with an MRP. The summation can be expanded to give

$$\begin{aligned} V^{\pi}(S) &= \mathbb{E}^{\pi}\left[R_{t+1} + \gamma R_{t+2} + \gamma^2 R_{t+3} + \cdots \mid S_t = S\right] \\ &= \mathbb{E}^{\pi}\left[R_0 + \gamma\left(R_{t+1} + \gamma R_{t+2} + \cdots\right) \mid S_t = S\right]. \end{aligned} \tag{10.11}$$

Using the law of iterated expectations gives

$$\begin{aligned} V^{\pi}(S) &= \mathbb{E}^{\pi}\left[R_{t+1} + \gamma \mathbb{E}\left[R_{t+2} + \gamma R_{t+3} + \cdots\right] \mid S_t = S\right] \\ &= \mathbb{E}^{\pi}\left[R_{t+1} + \gamma V(S_{t+1}) \mid S_0 = S\right], \end{aligned} \tag{10.12}$$

and this gives the *Bellman equation* for the value function.

Definition 10.17 ***(Markov Decision Process (MDP))*:** An MDP is an extension of an MRP that includes decision-making components. It is defined by a tuple $(\mathcal{S}, \mathcal{A}, P, R, \gamma)$, where:

- $\mathcal{S}$ is a finite or countably infinite set of states.
- $\mathcal{A}$ is a finite set of actions from which the agent can choose.
- P is the state transition probability matrix, where $P_{S'|S,A} = \mathbb{P}(S_{t+1} = S' \mid S_t = S, A_t = S)$.
- $R(S, A)$ is a reward function that maps state–action pairs to real numbers.
- γ is a discount factor that weights the importance of delayed rewards.

The Q-function defined in Equation (10.9) also yields a Bellman equation, which is obtained in the same way as for the value function,

$$Q^{\pi}(S, A) = \mathbb{E}^{\pi}\left[R_{t+1} + \gamma Q^{\pi}(S_{t+1}, A_{t+1}) \mid S_t = S, A_t = A\right]. \tag{10.13}$$

The value function can be written in terms of the Q-function,

$$V^{\pi}(S) = \sum_{A \in \mathcal{A}} \pi(A|S) Q^{\pi}(S, A). \tag{10.14}$$

10.3.1 Optimal Policy

The optimal value function and state–action value function describe the maximum expected rewards achievable under the best possible strategy or policy. The optimal value function $V^*(s)$ is the maximum expected cumulative discounted reward achievable starting from state S and following the optimal policy π^*. It is defined as

$$V^*(S) = \max_{\pi} \mathbb{E}^{\pi}\left[\sum_{k=0}^{\infty} \gamma^k R_{t+k+1} \mid S_t = S\right]. \tag{10.15}$$

The optimal state–action value function $Q^*(S, A)$ is the maximum expected cumulative discounted reward achievable starting from state S, taking action A and then following the optimal policy π^* after that, defined as

$$Q^*(S, A) = \max_{\pi} \mathbb{E}^{\pi}\left[\sum_{k=0}^{\infty} \gamma^k R_{t+k+1} \mid S_t = S, A_t = A\right]. \tag{10.16}$$

A fundamental theorem and a lemma provide essential results for the optimal policy under an MDP.

Theorem 10.1 ***(Policy Improvement Theorem)***: *Let π be any policy and π' be a policy such that for all states $S \in \mathcal{S}$ (Sutton and Barto, 2018):*

$$Q^{\pi}(S, \pi'(S)) \geq V^{\pi}(S). \tag{10.17}$$

Then the policy π' must be as good as, or better than, π:

$$V^{\pi'}(S) \geq V^{\pi}(S) \quad \forall S \in \mathcal{S}. \tag{10.18}$$

Furthermore, if π' is strictly better than π for at least one state $S \in \mathcal{S}$ (i.e., $Q^{\pi}(S, \pi'(S)) > V^{\pi}(S)$), then π' is strictly better than π for all states:

$$V^{\pi'}(s) > V^{\pi}(s) \quad \forall s \in \mathcal{S}. \tag{10.19}$$

Lemma 10.1 ***(Optimal Policy Existence)***: *For an MDP there exists at least one optimal policy π^*, meaning there is a policy π^* such that $V^{\pi^*}(S) \geq V^{\pi}(S)$ for all policies π and all states $S \in \mathcal{S}$ (Bellman, 1952). All optimal policies achieve the optimal value function, $V^{\pi^*}(S) = V^*(S)$, and the optimal action–value function, $Q^{\pi^*}(S, A) = Q^*(S, A)$.*

10.4 DYNAMIC PROGRAMMING AND POLICY SEARCH

In the context of RL, dynamic programming (DP) is a collection of algorithms that can be used to search for optimal policies, given a perfect model of the environment of which MDPs are an example (Sutton, 2020). DP is a general solution method that requires two properties to be true (Silver, 2015):

- *Optimal Substructure.* The optimal solution can be decomposed into subproblems.
- *Overlapping Subproblems.* The subproblems occur often, and the solution is re-used.

MDPs satisfy both properties.[1]

The remainder of this section explores how DP can be used to find optimal policies.

[1]Dynamic programming is widely utilised in quantitative finance for solving complex optimisation problems involving sequential decision-making under uncertainty. In portfolio optimisation, dynamic programming helps determine the optimal allocation of assets over multiple periods, balancing returns and risks. Notably, it is central to models for pricing options with American and Bermudan exercises, as discussed in Section 13.3.

10.4.1 Policy Evaluation or Prediction

Policy evaluation determines the value of a given policy (Sutton and Barto, 2018). In the context of MDPs, this involves computing the state–value function, $V^{\pi}(s)$, as defined in Equation (10.8). The Bellman equation, Equation (10.14), provides a recursive formula to compute these values:

$$V^{\pi}(s) = \sum_{a} \pi(a|s) \sum_{s',r} p(s', r|s, a)[r + \gamma V^{\pi}(s')], \tag{10.20}$$

where $p(s', r|s, a)$ is the probability of transitioning to state s' and receiving reward r after taking action a in state s. Iterative methods are commonly used to solve this equation:

$$V^{k+1}(s) = \sum_{a} \pi(a|s) \sum_{s',r} p(s', r|s, a)[r + \gamma V^{k}(s')]. \tag{10.21}$$

The initial approximation V_0 can be arbitrary apart from giving terminal states value 0. Then, Equation (10.21) is used to update the policy in an algorithm called *iterative policy evaluation*. The sequence of values V^k converges to V^{π} as $k \to \infty$.

10.4.2 Policy Improvement

Policy improvement is refining a policy based on the value function obtained from policy evaluation. The goal is to find a new policy that yields a higher expected return, and this is achieved by making the policy greedy with respect to the value function.

Formally, the policy improvement step involves selecting actions that maximise the expected return for each state:

$$\begin{aligned} \pi'(s) &= \underset{a}{\text{argmax}} Q^{\pi}(s, a) \\ &= \underset{a}{\text{argmax}} \sum_{s',r} p(s', r|s, a)[r + \gamma V^{k}(s')]. \end{aligned} \tag{10.22}$$

This approach meets the policy improvement theorem's conditions; hence, any new policy π' must be least as good as the old policy π. If $\pi' = \pi$ then, from the Bellman equation,

$$\pi' = \pi = \pi^*, \tag{10.23}$$

that is, both policies are the same optimal policy.

10.4.3 Policy Iteration

Policy iteration is an algorithm used to compute the optimal policy for an MDP. It consists of two main steps: policy evaluation and policy improvement. The algorithm starts with an arbitrary policy and alternates between evaluating the current policy and improving the policy by acting greedily with respect to the current value function. The steps are repeated until the policy converges to the optimal policy, π^*:

1. ***Policy Evaluation.*** Compute V^{π} for the current policy π.
2. ***Policy Improvement.*** Update the policy by choosing actions that maximise the expected return:

$$\pi'(s) = \underset{a}{\text{argmax}} \sum_{s',r} p(s', r|s, a)[r + \gamma V^{\pi}(s')].$$

3. ***Iteration.*** Set $\pi \leftarrow \pi'$ and repeat until π converges.

10.4.4 Value Iteration

The problem with the policy iteration algorithm is that it also requires the second iterative procedure policy evaluation, which can be computationally expensive (Sutton and Barto, 2018). Value iteration, in contrast, focuses directly on finding the optimal value function, V^*. The value iteration algorithm repeatedly updates the value function using the Bellman optimality equation:

$$V^{k+1}(s) = \max_a \sum_{s',r} p(s', r|s, a)[r + \gamma V^k(s')]. \tag{10.24}$$

This process continues until the value function converges to V^*. Once V^* is found, the optimal policy π^* can be derived by choosing actions that maximise the expected return:

$$\pi^*(s) = \arg\max_a \sum_{s',r} p(s', r|s, a)[r + \gamma V^*(s')]. \tag{10.25}$$

Value iteration combines policy evaluation and improvement steps in a single update rule, making it a more straightforward yet powerful method for solving MDPs.

EXAMPLE 10.2: GRIDWORLD

The Gridworld problem is a classic example of reinforcement learning and dynamic programming. In this problem, an agent navigates a grid, moving between cells according to pre-defined actions: up, down, left, right. The objective is to reach a terminal state while maximising the cumulative reward collected. The grid contains special cells such as terminal states, where the episode ends, and holes, representing impassable obstacles. The agent starts at the top-left corner of the grid and aims to reach the bottom-right corner, navigating around any holes. Each movement incurs a small negative reward, encouraging the agent to find the shortest path to the terminal state. This environment provides a simplified yet powerful platform for exploring and understanding key reinforcement learning algorithms, such as policy iteration and value iteration, where the goal is to determine an optimal policy that guides the agent to achieve the maximum possible reward.

This example is implemented in the Jupyter Notebook `GridWorld.ipynb`. Gridworld is a Python class that maintains the different types of states, actions and rewards. The different iteration algorithms can then use this to find the optimal policy.

```
class GridworldEnv:
    def __init__(self, grid_size, holes=[]):
        self.grid_size = grid_size
        self.states = [(i, j) for i in range(grid_size)
                       for j in range(grid_size)]
        self.terminal_states = [(0, 0), (grid_size-1, grid_size-1)]
        self.actions = ['up', 'down', 'left', 'right']
        self.holes = holes
        self.rewards = {s: -1 for s in self.states}
        self.rewards[(0, 0)] = 0
        self.rewards[(grid_size-1, grid_size-1)] = 1
        self.gamma = 0.9
        for hole in holes:
            self.rewards[hole] = -np.inf  # Holes have a very negative reward

    def is_terminal(self, state):
        return state in self.terminal_states

    def is_hole(self, state):
        return state in self.holes

    def get_next_state(self, state, action):
        if self.is_terminal(state) or self.is_hole(state):
            return state
        i, j = state
```

```
        if action == 'up':
            next_state = (max(i-1, 0), j)
        elif action == 'down':
            next_state = (min(i+1, self.grid_size-1), j)
        elif action == 'left':
            next_state = (i, max(j-1, 0))
        elif action == 'right':
            next_state = (i, min(j+1, self.grid_size-1))
        if self.is_hole(next_state):
            return state
        return next_state

    def get_tprob_and_rewards(self, state, action):
        next_state = self.get_next_state(state, action)
        return [(1.0, next_state, self.rewards[next_state])]
```

In this example, a 6 × 6 grid is used, with two cells on the diagonal designated to be holes. The grid is illustrated in Figure 10.3.

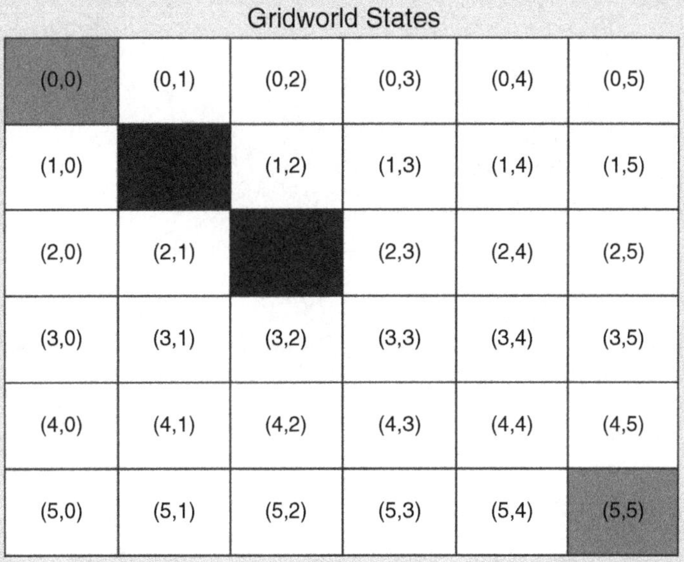

FIGURE 10.3 Gridworld states – the start state is in the top left, the terminal state in the bottom right. The black cells are holes that should be avoided.

Policy iteration was implemented to search for the optimal policy.

```
def policy_evaluation(policy, env, theta=1e-6):
    V = {s: 0 for s in env.states}
    while True:
        delta = 0
        for s in env.states:
            v = V[s]
            if not env.is_terminal(s):
                V[s] = sum([prob * (reward + env.gamma * V[next_state])
                            for prob, next_state,
                          reward in env.get_tprob_and_rewards(s, policy[s])])
```

(Continued)

(Continued)

```
            delta = max(delta, abs(v - V[s]))
        if delta < theta:
            break
    return V

def policy_improvement(V, env):
    policy = {s: np.random.choice(env.actions) for s in env.states}
    for s in env.states:
        if not env.is_terminal(s):
            action_values = []
            for a in env.actions:
                action_value = sum([prob * (reward +
                                   env.gamma * V[next_state])
                                  for prob, next_state,
                                reward in env.get_tprob_and_rewards(s, a)])
                action_values.append(action_value)
            policy[s] = env.actions[np.argmax(action_values)]
   return policy

def policy_iteration(env):
    policy = {s: np.random.choice(env.actions) for s in env.states}
    while True:
        V = policy_evaluation(policy, env)
        new_policy = policy_improvement(V, env)
        if new_policy == policy:
            break
        policy = new_policy
    return policy, V
```

The results of the policy iteration are illustrated in Figures 10.4, showing the optimal policy, and Figure 10.5, showing the value function.

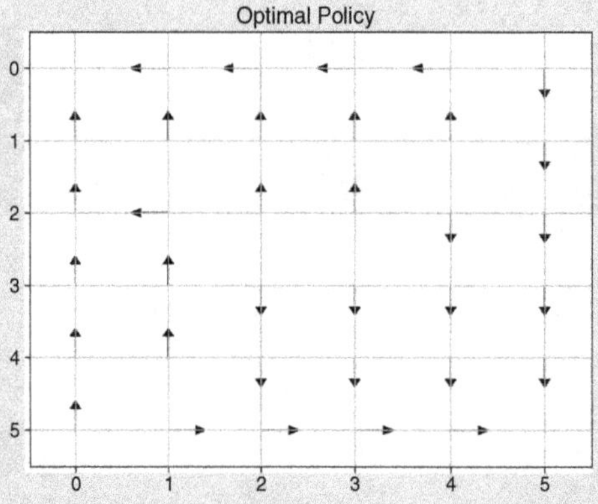

FIGURE 10.4 Optimal policy for the gridworld. The optimal choice of action in each state is shown.

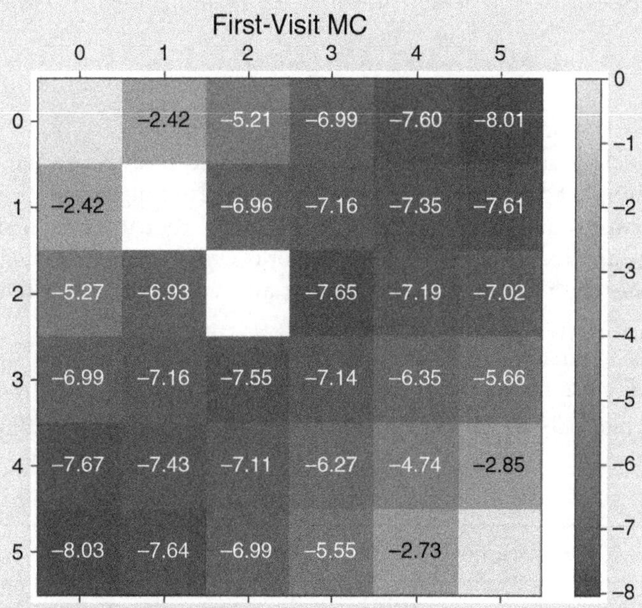

FIGURE 10.5 Optimal value function for each state in the gridworld.

Value iteration can also be used and implemented, which is much more succinct. The optimal policy is extracted from the final value function. The results are identical to those from the policy iteration, as expected.

```
def value_iteration(env, theta=1e-6):
    V = {s: 0 for s in env.states}
    while True:
        delta = 0
        for s in env.states:
            if not env.is_terminal(s):
                v = V[s]
                V[s] = max([sum([prob * (reward + env.gamma * V[next_state])
                                for prob, next_state,
                                reward in env.get_tprob_and_rewards(s, a)])
                           for a in env.actions])
                delta = max(delta, abs(v - V[s]))
        if delta < theta:
            break
     policy = policy_improvement(V, env)
     return policy, V
```

10.5 MONTE CARLO METHODS FOR RL

Monte Carlo methods in reinforcement learning are a class of algorithms that rely on random sampling to estimate the value of states and actions by averaging the returns observed from multiple episodes of interaction with the environment. Unlike other methods, Monte Carlo techniques do not require knowledge of the environment's model. They can be applied directly using sampled experiences, particularly useful in complex or unknown domains. They are especially effective for episodic tasks, where the environment naturally terminates, allowing for precise calculation of returns. However, they cannot be applied to non-episodic settings. Monte Carlo methods can use both on-policy and off-policy strategies and give flexible approaches for predicting the value of policies and discovering optimal policies.

10.5.1 Monte Carlo Prediction

Monte Carlo prediction is a technique in reinforcement learning used to estimate the value of states by averaging the returns observed from multiple episodes. This method involves running simulations to sample entire episodes of interaction with the environment and then calculating the average return for each state based on these samples. Monte Carlo prediction can be applied using either first-visit or every-visit approaches, which differ in whether they consider only the first encounter with a state in an episode or all encounters, respectively.

10.5.1.1 First-Visit MC Prediction First-visit MC prediction estimates the value of a state by averaging the returns following the first visit to that state within an episode. Each return is an i.i.d. estimate of the value of the state, and this converges to $V^{\pi}(s)$ like $\frac{1}{\sqrt{(n)}}$ by the law of large numbers (Sutton and Barto, 2018), as illustrated in Algorithm 10.1.

Algorithm 10.1: First-Visit MC Prediction

Input: Policy π, number of episodes N
Output: State–value function $V(s)$
Initialise $V(s)$ arbitrarily for all states s;
Initialise an empty list $Returns(s)$ for all states s;
for *each episode i from 1 to N* **do**
  Generate an episode $[S_1, A_1, R_2, S_2, A_2, \ldots, S_T]$ following policy π;
  Initialise an empty set $FirstVisit(s)$;
  for *each step t in the episode* **do**
    if $S_t \notin FirstVisit(S)$ **then**
      Add S_t to $FirstVisit(s)$;
      Calculate return G_t from step t to the end of the episode;
      Append G_t to $Returns(S_t)$;
      Update $V(S_t) \leftarrow \frac{1}{|Returns(S_t)|} \sum Returns(S_t)$;
    end
  end
end

10.5.1.2 Every-Visit MC Prediction Every-visit Monte Carlo estimates the value of a state by averaging the returns following every visit to that state within an episode. It can be shown to converge quadratically to $V^{\pi}(s)$ and is illustrated in Algorithm 10.2 (Singh and Sutton, 1996).

10.5.1.3 Off-Policy Prediction Using Importance Sampling Off-policy Monte Carlo methods in reinforcement learning are designed to learn the value of an optimal *target* policy while following a different *behaviour* policy, which facilitates broader exploration of the state–action space (Sutton and Barto, 2018). By employing a behaviour policy that may be more exploratory, the agent can gather diverse experiences. At the same time, *importance sampling* techniques are used to adjust the returns and correct for the differences between the behaviour policy and the target policy. This approach allows the agent to converge to an optimal policy even when the policy used to generate episodes is not optimised. Off-policy Monte Carlo methods are instrumental in scenarios where the target policy is deterministic or nearly so, but the agent must explore extensively to learn effectively.

Importance sampling under a change of probability measure is a technique for estimating expectations under one probability measure by sampling from a different measure. The change of measure is typically accomplished using a likelihood ratio, which adjusts the weights of the samples to account for the difference between the two measures.

Algorithm 10.2: Every-Visit MC Prediction

Input: Policy π, number of episodes N
Output: State–value function $V(s)$
Initialise $V(s)$ arbitrarily for all states s;
Initialise an empty list *Returns*(s) for all states s;
for *each episode i from 1 to N* **do**
  Generate an episode $[S_1, A_1, R_2, S_2, A_2, \dots, S_T]$ following policy π;
  for *each step t in the episode* **do**
    Calculate return G_t from step t to the end of the episode;
    Append G_t to *Returns*(S_t);
    Update $V(S_t) \leftarrow \frac{1}{|Returns(S_t)|} \sum Returns(S_t)$;
  end
end

Let $\mathbb{P}$ and $\mathbb{Q}$ be two probability measures on the same probability space $(\Omega, \mathcal{F})$. Suppose we want to estimate the expectation of a function $h(X)$ under the measure $\mathbb{P}$, where X is a random variable. The expectation of $h(X)$ under $\mathbb{P}$ is given by

$$\mathbb{E}_{\mathbb{P}}[h(X)] = \int_{\Omega} h(X(\omega))\, dP(\omega). \tag{10.26}$$

The Radon–Nikodym derivative $\frac{d\mathbb{P}}{d\mathbb{Q}}$ or likelihood ratio is used to adjust for the change in measure. The expectation under $\mathbb{P}$ can be rewritten as

$$\mathbb{E}_{\mathbb{P}}[h(X)] = \int_{\Omega} h(X(\omega))\, \frac{d\mathbb{P}}{d\mathbb{Q}}(\omega)\, d\mathbb{Q}(\omega). \tag{10.27}$$

The importance sampling estimator for $E_P[h(X)]$ is

$$\hat{\mathbb{E}}_{\mathbb{P}}[h(X)] = \frac{1}{n} \sum_{i=1}^{n} h(X_i)\, w(X_i), \tag{10.28}$$

where $w(X_i) = \frac{d\mathbb{P}}{d\mathbb{Q}}(X_i)$ is the likelihood ratio evaluated at the sample points.

In the context of off-policy prediction, the likelihood ratio corrects for the discrepancy between the two policies in the returns calculation. For an episode $\tau = (S_0, A_0, R_1, S_1, A_1, \dots, S_T)$, the cumulative importance sampling ratio is the product of the ratios of the target and behaviour policy probabilities for each action taken:

$$\rho(\tau) = \prod_{t=0}^{T-1} \frac{\pi(A_t|S_t)}{\mu(A_t|S_t)}. \tag{10.29}$$

The expected return under the target policy π can be estimated by weighting the return of each episode by this ratio. If G_t denotes the return following time t, the off-policy Monte Carlo estimate of the value of state S_t is

$$\begin{aligned} V^{\pi}(S_t) &= \mathbb{E}_{\mu}\left[\rho(\tau) G_t\right] = E_{\mu}\left[\left(\prod_{t=0}^{T-1} \frac{\pi(A_t|S_t)}{\mu(A_t|S_t)}\right) G_t\right] \\ &\approx \frac{1}{N} \sum_{i=1}^{N} \rho(\tau^i) G_t^i, \end{aligned} \tag{10.30}$$

where N is the number of episodes.

EXAMPLE 10.3: BLACKJACK WITH MC PREDICTION

This example uses the Blackjack environment from *Gymnasium* (Towers et al., 2023). The Blackjack environment in reinforcement learning is a simplified simulation of the classic card game, designed to provide a manageable yet challenging domain for developing and testing reinforcement learning algorithms. In this environment, the agent plays against a dealer to maximise its cumulative reward by making decisions such as hitting (drawing another card) or sticking (ending its turn). The game is played with standard Blackjack rules: the player's goal is to obtain a hand value as close as possible to 21 without exceeding it. Key aspects of this environment include the stochastic nature of card draws, the presence of hidden information (the dealer's face-down card) and the strategic trade-offs between risk and reward. The Blackjack environment is particularly valuable for studying reinforcement learning concepts such as policy evaluation, policy improvement and value function approximation in a context that balances complexity and clarity.

The environment is straightforward to instantiate:

```
import gymnasium as gym
env = gym.make('Blackjack-v1')
```

The card values in the environment are:

- Face cards (Jack, Queen, King) have a point value of 10.
- Aces can count as 11 (a 'usable ace') or 1.
- Numerical cards (2–9) have a value equal to their number.

The example will evaluate a policy where the player sticks if the score is 20 or 21 but hits otherwise, identical to an example provided by Sutton and Barto (2018).

```
def sample_policy(observation):
    score, dealer_score, usable_ace = observation
    return 0 if score >= 20 else 1  # 0: stick, 1: hit
```

Given a policy, episodes of play must be generated in which cards are dealt to the player and dealer, and this is done using the following function which interacts with the Blackjack environment:

```
def generate_episode(env, policy):
    episode = []
    observation, _ = env.reset()
    done = False
    while not done:
        action = policy(observation)
        next_observation, reward, terminated, truncated, _ = env.step(action)
        episode.append((observation, action, reward))
        observation = next_observation
        done = terminated or truncated
    return episode
```

The code for the first-visit Monte Carlo algorithm is given below, and that for the every-visit Monte Carlo is identical save for the check to see if the state–action pair has been seen already in the current episode.

```
def first_visit_mc_prediction(env, policy, num_episodes=100000):
    returns = defaultdict(list)
    value_function = defaultdict(float)

    for _ in range(num_episodes):
        episode = generate_episode(env, policy)
        state_action_pairs = set()
        for t, (state, action, reward) in enumerate(episode):
            if (state, action) not in state_action_pairs:
                state_action_pairs.add((state, action))
                G = sum(r for _, _, r in episode[t:])
                returns[(state, action)].append(G)
                value_function[(state, action)] = np.mean(returns[(state,
                                                                   action)])

    return value_function
```

A total of 100,000 episodes were run with both algorithms and the given policy. The value functions conditioned on the action and the availability of a usable ace are shown in Figures 10.6 and 10.7, respectively.

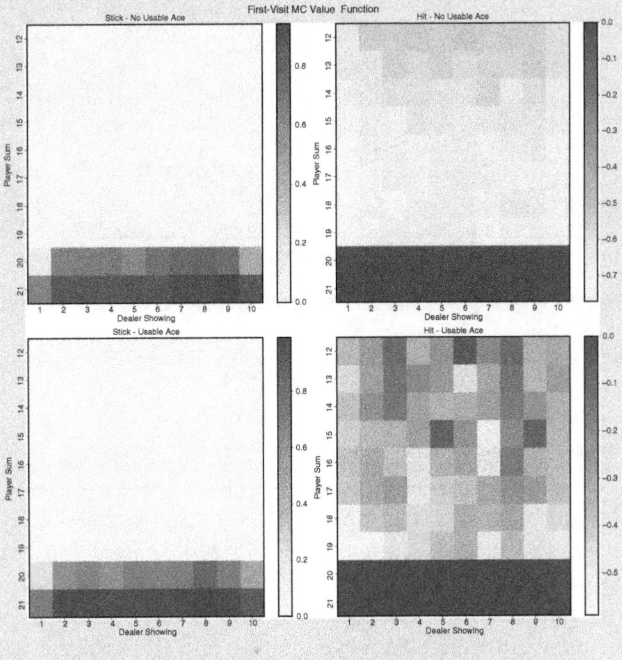

FIGURE 10.6 Value function for the first-visit Monte Carlo and the stick 20 or 21 strategy.

(Continued)

(Continued)

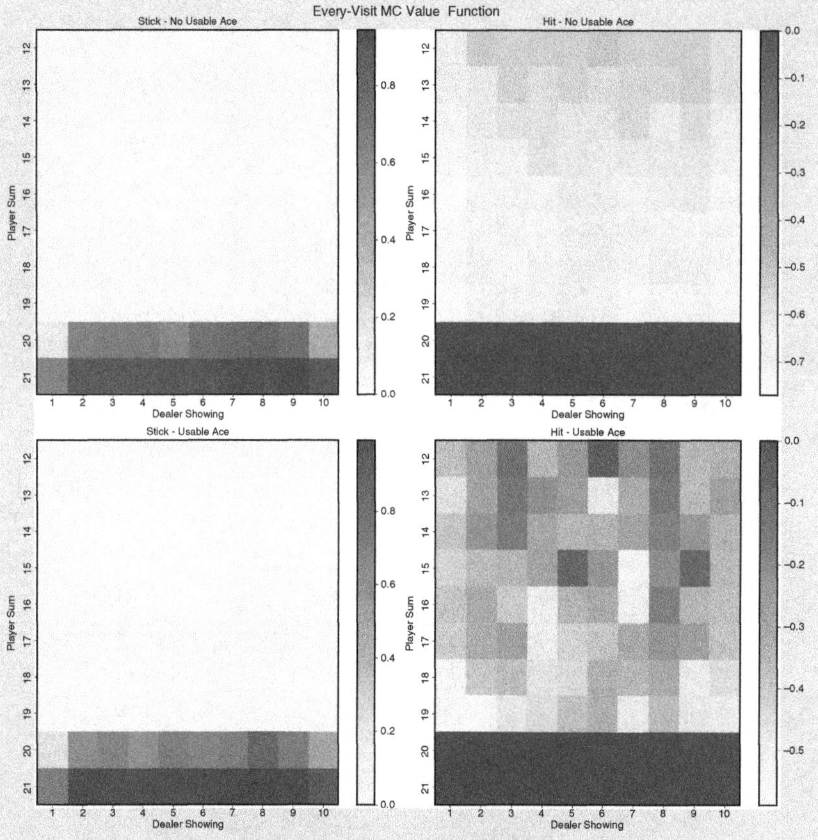

FIGURE 10.7 Value function for the every-visit Monte Carlo and the stick 20 or 21 strategy.

EXAMPLE 10.4: GRIDWORLD WITH MC PREDICTION

This example returns the earlier Gridworld (Example 10.2) and applies Monte Carlo prediction. Three algorithms are used in this case: first-visit Monte Carlo, every-visit Monte Carlo and off-policy Monte Carlo with importance sampling. The policy to be evaluated in the case of the first two algorithms is a random selection of moves: up, down, left and right. For the off-policy, this random policy is the behaviour policy, with the target policy being deterministic 'turn right' from every state, and this is not a helpful policy. However, it is one that clearly cannot be evaluated on policy.

The code to generate episodes is given below. A key element is the `max_count`, which limits the length of generated sequences of states and actions. The problem with a random policy in Gridworld is that it can wander without ever reaching the terminal state. The length of episodes is limited to 100 by default to guard against the near-infinite loop and give reasonable sampling.

```
def generate_episode(env, policy, max_count = 100):
    episode = []
    state = random.choice(env.states)
    while env.is_terminal(state):
        state = random.choice(env.states)
```

```
        count = 0
        while not env.is_terminal(state):
            if count < max_count:
                action = policy(state)
                next_state = env.get_next_state(state, action)
                reward = env.rewards[next_state]
                episode.append((state, action, reward))
                state = next_state
                count += 1
            else:
                break
    return episode
```

Implementing first-visit and every-visit Monte Carlo is essentially unchanged from the previous example. The off-policy Monte Carlo is given below, including the re-weighting. Note that the behaviour policy is assumed to be random, but it is difficult to see what other choice is realistic.

```
def off_policy_mc(env, target_policy, behavior_policy, episodes):
    V = defaultdict(float)
    C = defaultdict(float)
    for _ in trange(episodes):
        episode = generate_episode(env, behavior_policy)
        G = 0
        W = 1.0
        for t in reversed(range(len(episode))):
            state, action, reward = episode[t]
            G = env.gamma * G + reward
            C[state] += W
            V[state] += (W / C[state]) * (G - V[state])
            if action != target_policy(state):
                break
            W /= 0.25
    return V
```

After 10,000 episodes of the random policy, the value function is shown for the first-visit and every-visit Monte Carlo in Figures 10.8 and 10.9. The pattern of values is similar in both cases, as should be expected. Figure 10.10 shows the value function for the 'turn-right' policy. The only cell with a positive value is the one that can access the terminal state and its reward by turning right.

(*Continued*)

(*Continued*)

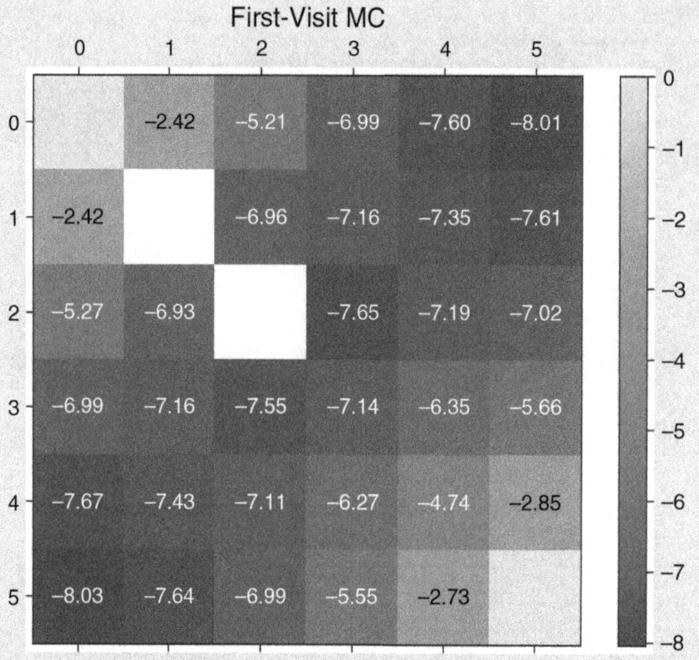

FIGURE 10.8 Value function for the first-visit Monte Carlo evaluating the random policy.

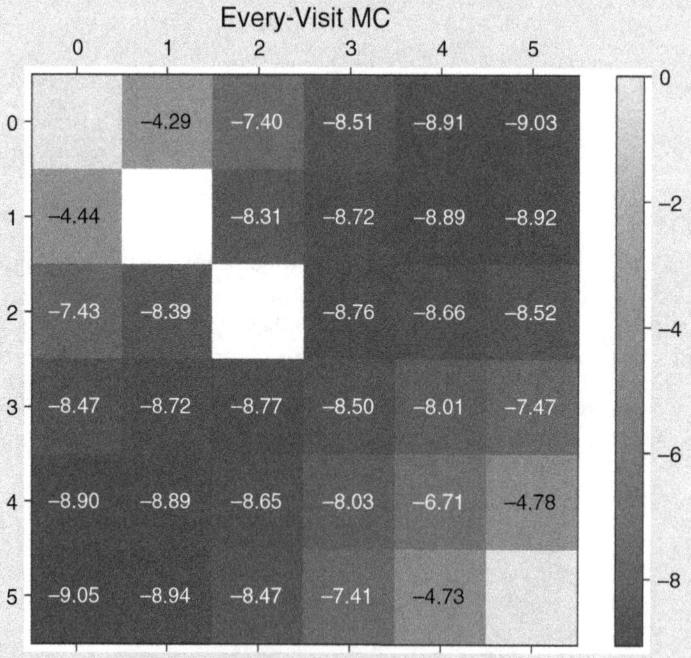

FIGURE 10.9 Value function for the every-visit Monte Carlo evaluating the random policy.

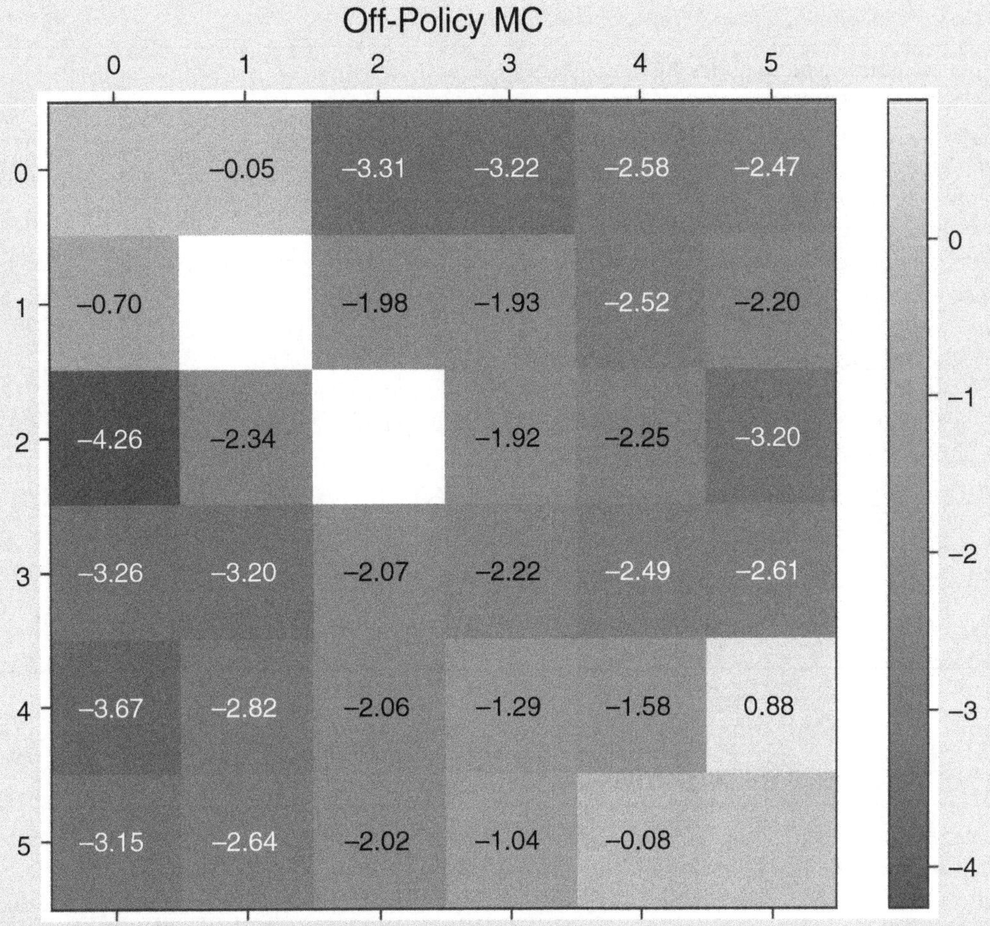

FIGURE 10.10 Value function for the off-policy Monte Carlo evaluating the 'turn right' target policy using the random behaviour policy.

10.5.2 Monte Carlo Control

Monte Carlo control aims to discover the optimal policy by learning from episodic interactions with the environment, and this is achieved through iterative processes that generate episodes using a current policy, update the action–value function based on observed returns and refine the policy to be greedy concerning the updated value estimates. The method can be applied using on-policy or off-policy strategies. Monte Carlo control, like Monte Carlo prediction, is model-free.

10.5.2.1 Exploring Starts The simplest type of Monte Carlo control is *exploring starts,* illustrated in Algorithm 10.3. This method ensures that all state–action pairs are explored by starting each episode in a randomly chosen state–action pair, and this guarantees that the learning process explores the entire state–action space, facilitating convergence to the optimal policy. The algorithm alternates between evaluation and improvement for each episode (Sutton and Barto, 2018). The convergence of the algorithm has not been proved and remains an open question, with partial solutions provided by Tsitsiklis (2003), Wang et al. (2020) and Liu (2021).

Algorithm 10.3: Exploring Starts in Monte Carlo Control

Input: Policy π, number of episodes N
Output: Action–value function $Q(s, a)$, policy π^*
Initialise $Q(s, a)$ arbitrarily for all states s and actions a;
Initialise an empty list $Returns(s, a)$ for all state–action pairs;
for *each episode i from 1 to N* **do**
  Randomly select a starting state–action pair (S_0, A_0);
  Generate an episode $[S_0, A_0, R_1, S_1, A_1, R_2, \ldots, S_T]$ following policy π;
  Initialise an empty set $Visited(s, a)$;
  for *each step t in the episode* **do**
    if $(S_t, A_t) \notin Visited(s, a)$ **then**
      Add (S_t, A_t) to $Visited(s, a)$;
      Calculate return G_t from step t to the end of the episode;
      Append G_t to $Returns(S_t, A_t)$;
      Update $Q(S_t, A_t) \leftarrow \frac{1}{|Returns(S_t,A_t)|} \sum Returns(S_t, A_t)$;
      Update $\pi(S_t) \leftarrow \text{argmax}_a\, Q(S_t, a)$;
    end
  end
end

EXAMPLE 10.5: BLACKJACK WITH MC EXPLORING STARTS

This example in the Jupyter Notebook `BlackjackMCControl.ipynb` presents the Monte Carlo exploring starts algorithm using the Blackjack environment from *Gymnasium*.

The following code block generates each episode of exploring starts. The initial state and action are generated randomly, and then the remainder of the episode, until it terminates, is generated according to the policy. If, however, the observation is not in the policy, then the following action will be generated randomly.

```
def random_policy(observation):
    return np.random.choice([0, 1])

def generate_episode_exploring_starts(env, policy):
    episode = []
    observation, _ = env.reset()
    done = False

    # Randomly select action
    action = np.random.choice([0, 1])

    while not done:
        next_observation, reward, terminated, truncated, _ = env.step(action)
        episode.append((observation, action, reward))
        observation = next_observation
        if observation in policy:
            action = policy[observation]
        else:
            action = random_policy(observation)
        done = terminated or truncated
    return episode
```

The Monte Carlo early starts code is given below. The algorithm loops over num_episodes, generating the episode using the earlier function and then updating the Q-function and the policy as per Algorithm 10.3.

```
def mc_control_es(env, num_episodes=1000000, gamma=1.0):
    Q = defaultdict(lambda: defaultdict(float))
    returns = defaultdict(lambda: defaultdict(list))
    policy = defaultdict(lambda: np.random.choice([0, 1]))

    for _ in trange(num_episodes):
        # Generate an episode using exploring starts
        episode = generate_episode_exploring_starts(env, policy)

        # Update Q-values and policy
        state_action_pairs = set()
        for t, (state, action, reward) in enumerate(episode):
        if (state, action) not in state_action_pairs:
            state_action_pairs.add((state, action))
            G =sum([gamma**i * r for i, (_, _, r) in enumerate(episode[t:])])
            returns[state][action].append(G)
            Q[state][action] = np.mean(returns[state][action])

            # Update policy (greedy with respect to Q)
            policy[state] = max(Q[state], key=Q[state].get)

    return policy, Q
```

With 10^6 episodes, the final optimal policy is shown in Figure 10.11. The policy appears almost as expected, with a tiny anomaly with the player sum at 21 and the dealer showing 5, suggesting more iterations are needed.

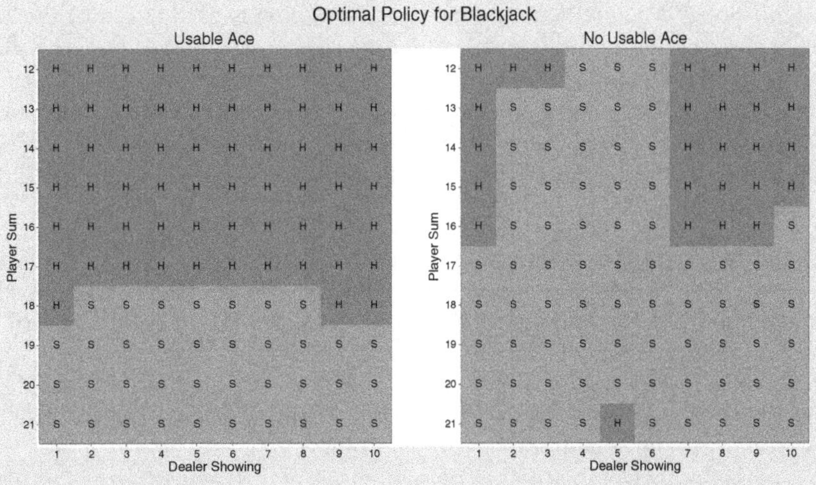

FIGURE 10.11 The optimal policy for Blackjack as a function of player score and dealer visible card after 10^6 episodes of Monte Carlo exploring starts.

10.5.2.2 On-Policy Control Exploring starts is an artificial assumption, which can be avoided by specifying a policy to generate episodes. On-policy MC uses the same policy for generating episodes and updating the policy, ensuring that the policy used to make decisions is being improved. The policy used here is ϵ-greedy, as was used in the multi-armed bandit example.

Algorithm 10.4 illustrates MC on-policy control.[2]

Algorithm 10.4: On-Policy Control with ϵ-Greedy Strategy

Input: Initial policy (ϵ-greedy) π, number of episodes N, exploration parameter ϵ
Output: Action–value function $Q(s, a)$, policy π^*
Initialise $Q(s, a)$ arbitrarily for all states s and actions a;
Initialise $Returns(s, a)$ as an empty list for all state–action pairs;
for *each episode i from 1 to N* **do**
  Generate an episode $[S_1, A_1, R_2, S_2, A_2, \dots, S_T]$ following policy π;
  for *each step t in the episode* **do**
    Calculate return G_t from step t to the end of the episode;
    Append G_t to $Returns(S_t, A_t)$;
    Update $Q(S_t, A_t) \leftarrow \frac{1}{|Returns(S_t,A_t)|} \sum Returns(S_t, A_t)$;
  end
  for *each state S_t in the episode* **do**
    Update $\pi(S_t) \leftarrow \text{argmax}_a\, Q(S_t, a)$ with probability $1 - \epsilon$, otherwise select a random action with probability ϵ;
  end
end

10.5.2.3 Off-Policy Control Off-policy MC control aims to discover the optimal policy by leveraging samples generated from a different behaviour policy. This approach allows the agent to explore the environment extensively using the behaviour policy while learning about the optimal target policy, which might be more deterministic and exploitative. As seen in off-policy MC prediction, importance sampling is used to adjust the returns from episodes generated under the behaviour policy, and this ensures that they are correctly weighted to reflect what they would have been under the target policy. Off-policy MC control is beneficial in dynamic and complex environments where direct sampling from the optimal policy is impractical, providing a robust framework for policy optimisation. Off-policy MC is presented in Algorithm 10.5. Note that the behaviour policy should be *soft,* that is, have a non-zero probability of selecting all of the actions associated with all of the states (Sutton and Barto, 2018).

EXAMPLE 10.6: GRIDWORLD WITH MC OFF-POLICY CONTROL

This example runs a search for the optimal Gridworld policy using MC off-policy control using importance sampling and can be found in the Jupyter Notebook `GridWorld-MCControl.ipynb`.

Episode generation remains identical to the previous Gridworld examples, as does the Gridworld environment itself. Here, there are two policies: the random behaviour policy, which was used in Example 10.4, and the target policy, which is greedy with respect to the Q-function.

```
def target_policy(Q, state):
    return max(env.actions, key=lambda a: Q[state][a])
```

[2] Compare with the similar on-policy first-visit Monte Carlo control algorithm in Sutton and Barto (2018).

The policy search uses the following function that implements Algorithm 10.4.

```
def off_policy_mc_control(env, num_episodes, epsilon=0.1):
    Q = defaultdict(lambda: defaultdict(float))
    C = defaultdict(lambda: defaultdict(float))

    for _ in trange(num_episodes):
        episode = generate_episode(env, behaviour_policy)
        G = 0
        W = 1.0
        for t in reversed(range(len(episode))):
            state, action, reward = episode[t]
            G = env.gamma * G + reward
            C[state][action] += W
            Q[state][action] += (W / C[state][action])*(G - Q[state][action])
            if action != target_policy(Q, state):
                break
            W /= 0.25

    # Extract the optimal policy from Q
    optimal_policy = {state: target_policy(Q, state) for state in env.states}
    return Q, optimal_policy
```

The *Q*-function and optimal policy from the off-policy MC control algorithm are shown in Figures 10.12 and 10.13. The optimal policy is very similar to the earlier policy iteration.

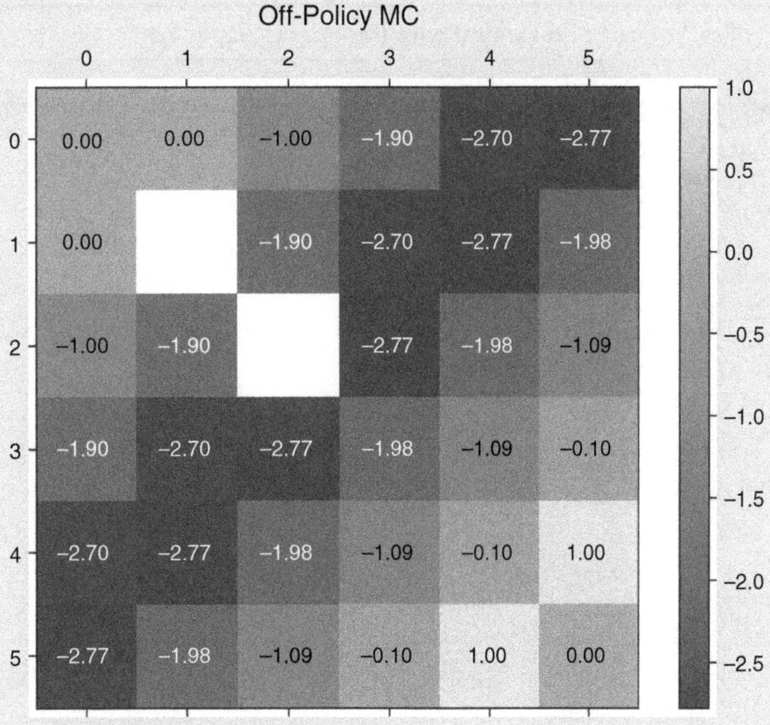

FIGURE 10.12 Optimal policy value function for Gridworld off-policy Monte Carlo control.

(Continued)

(*Continued*)

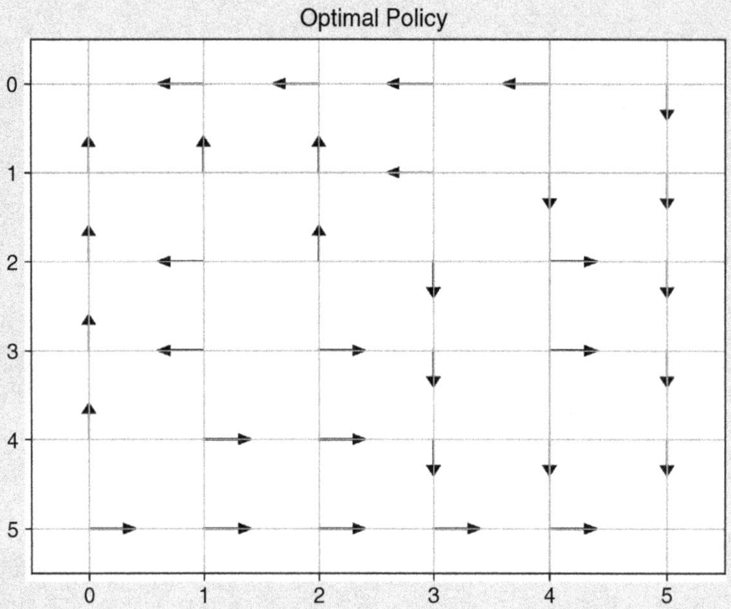

FIGURE 10.13 Optimal policy for Gridworld off-policy Monte Carlo control.

Algorithm 10.5: Off-Policy Monte Carlo Control with Importance Sampling

Input: Target policy π, behaviour policy μ, number of episodes N
Output: Action–value function $Q(s, a)$, policy π
Initialise $Q(s, a)$ arbitrarily for all states s and actions a;
Initialise $C(s, a)$ to 0 for all states s and actions a (cumulative sum of weights);
for *each episode i from 1 to N* **do**
  Generate an episode $[S_0, A_0, R_1, S_1, A_1, R_2, \ldots, S_T]$ following behaviour policy μ;
  Set $G = 0$;
  Set $W = 1$;
  for *each step t from T to 0* **do**
    $G \leftarrow \gamma G + R_{t+1}$;
    $C(S_t, A_t) \leftarrow C(S_t, A_t) + W$;
    $Q(S_t, A_t) \leftarrow Q(S_t, A_t) + \frac{W}{C(S_t, A_t)} [G - Q(S_t, A_t)]$;
    if $A_t \neq \pi(S_t)$ **then**
      break;
    end
    $W \leftarrow W \cdot \frac{1}{\mu(A_t|S_t)}$;
  end
  for *each state* S_t *in the episode* **do**
    Update $\pi(S_t) \leftarrow \arg\max_a Q(S_t, a)$;
  end
end

10.6 TD LEARNING

Temporal difference (TD) learning is a class of model-free reinforcement learning methods that combine the ideas of Monte Carlo and dynamic programming to predict and control future rewards in a given environment. Unlike Monte Carlo methods, which require complete episodes to update value estimates, TD learning updates estimates based on partially observed sequences, thus allowing for more efficient learning. The core principle of TD learning is to use the difference between successive predictions to update value functions, making it a powerful tool for learning from experience. TD learning underpinned the landmark TD-gammon application of RL to backgammon (Tesauro, 1994).

10.6.1 TD Prediction

TD prediction estimates the value of a given policy similarly to Monte Carlo (Sutton and Barto, 2018). However, unlike Monte Carlo methods, which require waiting until the end of an episode to make updates, TD prediction updates the value estimates after every step, and this allows for faster and more efficient learning, particularly in environments where episodes are long or continuous. The TD(0) update rule is a specific form of TD prediction where the value of the current state is updated based on the immediate reward and the value of the next state and is given by

$$V(s_t) \leftarrow V(s_t) + \alpha \left(r_{t+1} + \gamma V(s_{t+1}) - V(s_t)\right), \tag{10.31}$$

where α is the learning rate or step size, which can be compared with the Monte Carlo update rule for every-visit Monte Carlo,

$$V(s_t) \leftarrow V(s_t) + \alpha \left(G_t - V(s_t)\right). \tag{10.32}$$

where G_t is the actual discounted reward from the full episode as seen at time t. Hence, TD(0) estimates the discounted reward $G_t \approx r_{t+1} + \gamma V(s_{t+1})$. TD(0) in full is presented in Algorithm 10.6 (after Sutton and Barto, 2018).

Algorithm 10.6: TD(0) Prediction

Input: Policy π, learning rate α, discount factor γ, number of episodes N
Output: Value function V
Initialise $V(s)$ arbitrarily for all states s;
for *each episode* **do**
    Initialise s;
    while s *is not terminal* **do**
        Take action a according to policy π; observe reward r and next state s';
        $V(s) \leftarrow V(s) + \alpha[r + \gamma V(s') - V(s)]$;
        $s \leftarrow s'$;
    end
end

EXAMPLE 10.7: TD(0) PREDICTION IN TAXI

The 'Taxi-v3' environment in Gymnasium (Towers et al., 2023) is a classic reinforcement learning task where the agent (a taxi) must navigate a 5 × 5 grid world to pick up and drop off passengers at designated locations. The environment includes four fixed locations (labelled R, G, Y, B) and the taxi aims to efficiently transport passengers from their pickup location to their destination. The agent receives positive rewards for successfully delivering passengers and negative rewards for illegal moves, such as picking up or dropping off passengers in incorrect locations. The state space consists of the taxi's position, the passenger's location and the destination, making it a valuable benchmark for learning and evaluating reinforcement learning algorithms. The taxi environment is illustrated in Figure 10.14.

(Continued)

(Continued)

This example implements TD(0) prediction for the taxi environment in the Jupyter Notebook `TD0Prediction.ipynb`.

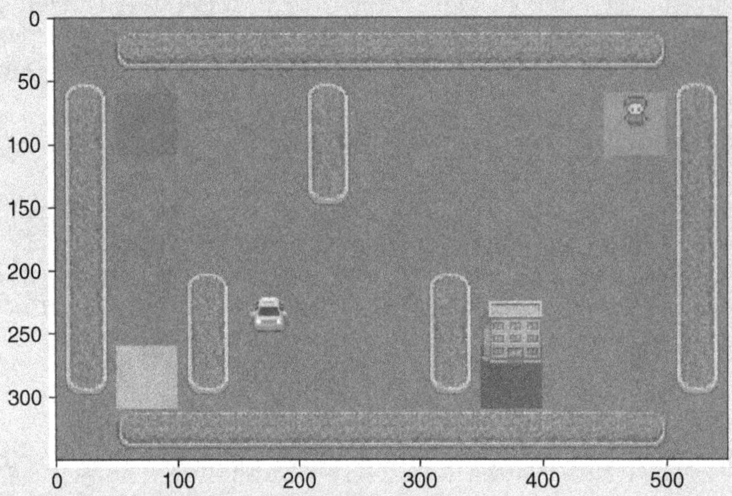

FIGURE 10.14 The taxi environment from Gymnasium.

TD(0) prediction is implemented as follows:

```
def td0_prediction(env, num_episodes):
    V = np.zeros(env.observation_space.n)

    for episode in trange(num_episodes):
        state = env.reset()[0]
        done = False

        while not done:
            action = env.action_space.sample()
            next_state, reward, done, _, _ = env.step(action)
            V[state] += alpha * (reward + gamma * V[next_state] - V[state])
            state = next_state
    return V
```

The state space of the taxi environment contains 500 points corresponding to 25 taxi locations, five passenger locations (including in the taxi) and four destinations. The reward structure is as follows:

- Penalty of 1 point per step unless another reward is triggered.
- Reward of 20 points for delivering a passenger.
- Penalty of 10 points for executing "pickup" and "drop-off" actions illegally.

The value function for the taxi locations with the passenger in the taxi and the 'red' destination after 1000 episodes is shown in Figure 10.15.

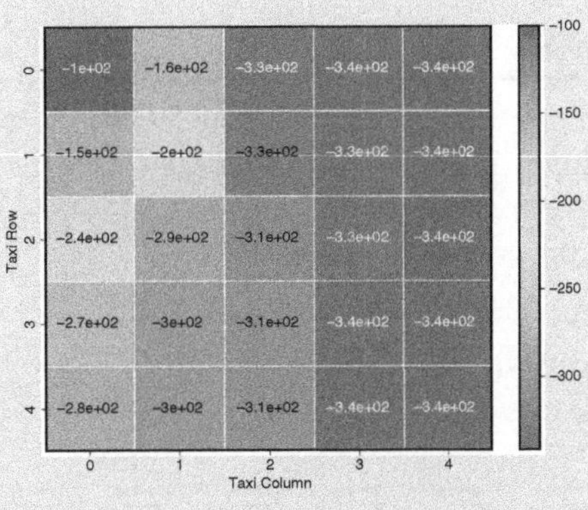

FIGURE 10.15 The taxi value function for the 25 taxi locations, with the passenger in the taxi and the 'red' destination.

10.6.2 On-Policy TD Control: SARSA

SARSA (state–action–reward–state–action) is an on-policy TD control algorithm used in reinforcement learning to learn the optimal policy that maximises the expected cumulative reward. It is 'on-policy' as the agent learns the value of its current policy. SARSA updates the action–value function $Q(s, a)$ based on the current state s, the action a taken, the reward r received, the next state s' and the following action a' chosen according to the current policy. The update rule for SARSA is given by

$$Q(s_t, a_t) \leftarrow Q(s_t, a_t) + \alpha \left(r_{t+1} + \gamma Q(s_{t+1}, a_{t+1}) - Q(s_t, a_t)\right). \tag{10.33}$$

SARSA updates the action–value function by considering the actual action taken by the agent, ensuring that the learning process is directly tied to the policy being followed, and this allows SARSA to improve the policy incrementally and converge to the optimal policy over time. SARSA is presented in Algorithm 10.7 (after Sutton and Barto, 2018).

Algorithm 10.7: SARSA: On-Policy TD Control

Input: Learning rate α, discount factor γ, number of episodes N, ϵ-greedy policy
Output: Action–value function Q
Initialise $Q(s, a)$ arbitrarily for all states s and actions a;
for *each episode* **do**
  Initialise s;
  Choose a from s using policy derived from Q (e.g., ϵ-greedy);
  while *s is not terminal* **do**
    Take action a, observe reward r and next state s';
    Choose a' from s' using policy derived from Q (e.g., ϵ-greedy);
    $Q(s, a) \leftarrow Q(s, a) + \alpha[r + \gamma Q(s', a') - Q(s, a)]$;
    $s \leftarrow s'$;
    $a \leftarrow a'$;
  end
end

EXAMPLE 10.8: GRIDWORLD WITH SARSA

This example in the Jupyter Notebook returns to the Gridworld example, using SARSA to search for the optimal policy. The SARSA algorithm is implemented using the following code block. Note that the policy is ϵ-greedy and, as a result, the episodes are truncated at a length of 100 by default.

```
def epsilon_greedy_policy(Q, state, epsilon, actions):
    if random.random() < epsilon:
        return random.choice(actions)
    else:
        return max(actions, key=lambda a: Q[state][a])

def sarsa(env, num_episodes, alpha=0.1, gamma=0.99, epsilon=0.1,
          max_count=100):
    Q = defaultdict(lambda: defaultdict(float))

    for _ in trange(num_episodes):
        state = random.choice(env.states)
        while env.is_terminal(state):
            state = random.choice(env.states)

        action = epsilon_greedy_policy(Q, state, epsilon, env.actions)
        count = 0
        while not env.is_terminal(state):
            if count < max_count:
                next_state = env.get_next_state(state, action)
                reward = env.rewards[next_state]
                next_action = epsilon_greedy_policy(Q, next_state, epsilon,
                                                    env.actions)
                td_target = reward + gamma * Q[next_state][next_action]
                td_error = td_target - Q[state][action]
                Q[state][action] += alpha * td_error
                state = next_state
                action = next_action
                count += 1
            else:
                break

    # Extract the optimal policy from Q
    optimal_policy = {state: max(env.actions, key=lambda a: Q[state][a])
                      for state in env.states}

    return Q, optimal_policy
```

The final state–value function for Gridworld after 10^6 episodes of SARSA is illustrated in Figure 10.16, which is very similar to that from the MC off-policy case.

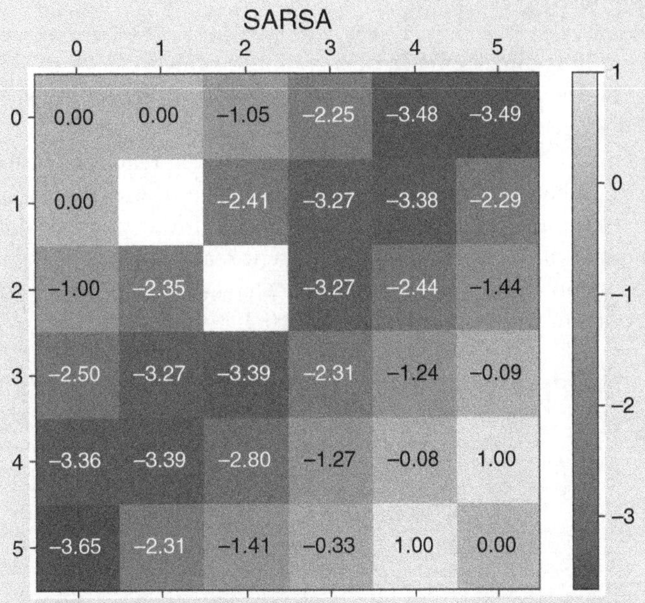

FIGURE 10.16 The state–value function for Gridworld is obtained using 10^6 episodes of SARSA.

10.6.3 Off-Policy TD Control: *Q*-Learning

Q-learning is a model-free, off-policy TD control algorithm (Watkins, 1989; Sutton and Barto, 2018). *Q*-learning updates its *Q*-values based on the maximum reward action in the next state, regardless of the agent's current policy, and this means it evaluates the optimal policy while possibly following a different policy for exploration. An ϵ-greedy policy is typically used during learning to balance exploration and exploitation. *Q*-learning is proven to converge to the optimal action–value function, given sufficient exploration and appropriate learning rate settings.

The *Q*-learning update rule is given by

$$Q(s_t, a_t) \leftarrow Q(s_t, a_t) + \alpha(r_{t+1} + \gamma \max_{a'} Q(s_{t+1}, a') - Q(s_t, a_t)), \tag{10.34}$$

and *Q*-learning is presented in Algorithm 10.8 (after Sutton and Barto, 2018).

Algorithm 10.8: *Q*-Learning: Off-Policy TD Control

Input: Learning rate α, discount factor γ, number of episodes N, ϵ-greedy policy
Output: Action–value function Q
Initialise $Q(s, a)$ arbitrarily for all states s and actions a;
for *each episode* **do**
    Initialise s;
    while *s is not terminal* **do**
        Choose a from s using policy derived from Q (e.g., ϵ-greedy);
        Take action a, observe reward r and next state s';
        $Q(s, a) \leftarrow Q(s, a) + \alpha[r + \gamma \max_{a'} Q(s', a') - Q(s, a)]$;
        $s \leftarrow s'$;
    end
end

EXAMPLE 10.9: CLIFF WALKING WITH *Q*-LEARNING

The *cliff walking* environment in Gymnasium (Towers et al., 2023) is a classic problem designed to challenge an agent's navigation skills. The environment consists of a 4×12 grid where the agent's task is to move from the starting point to the goal while avoiding a cliff.

The agent starts in the bottom-left corner of the grid and aims to reach the bottom-right corner. Between these two points lies a cliff stretching along the bottom row except for the start and goal cells. The grid contains 48 discrete states, each representing a cell. The agent can move in four possible directions: up, right, down, left. Each action incurs a penalty of -1, except when the agent reaches the goal, which gives a reward of 0. If the agent falls off the cliff by stepping into any cliff cell, it receives a heavy penalty of -100 and is reset to the starting position. The environment is illustrated in Figure 10.17.

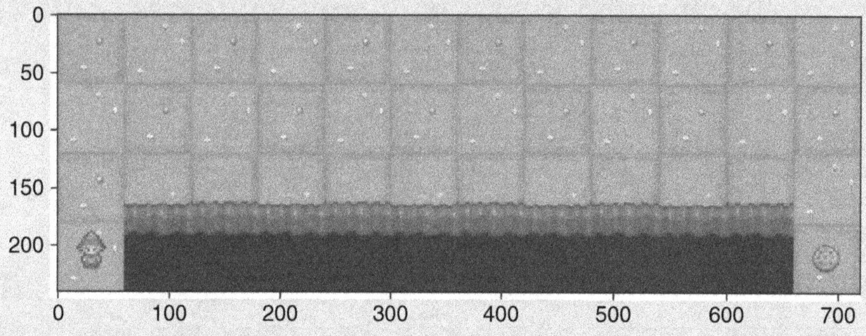

FIGURE 10.17 The cliff walking environment from Gymnasium.

The agent aims to learn a policy that maximises its cumulative reward by navigating to the goal while avoiding the cliff, and this requires balancing exploring the environment to discover safe paths and exploiting known safe paths to minimise penalties. An episode in the cliff walking environment ends when the agent either reaches the goal or falls off the cliff.

This example uses *Q*-learning to find the optimal policy when walking the cliff environment and is presented in the Jupyter Notebook `CliffWalkingQLearning.ipynb`. The *Q*-learning algorithm code is shown below, and the optimal policy is evaluated while following an ϵ-greedy behaviour policy. The function returns the state–action function, which can then be used to determine the optimal policy, shown in Figure 10.18.

```
def q_learning(env, num_episodes, epsilon=0.1):
    # Initialize the Q-table
    Q = np.zeros((env.observation_space.n, env.action_space.n))
    # Training the agent using Q-learning
    for episode in trange(num_episodes):
        state = env.reset()[0]
        done = False

        while not done:
            action = epsilon_greedy(state, Q, epsilon)
            next_state, reward, done, _, _ = env.step(action)
            next_action = np.argmax(Q[next_state])
            Q[state, action] += alpha * (reward + gamma *
                                Q[next_state, next_action] - Q[state, action])
            state = next_state
    return Q
```

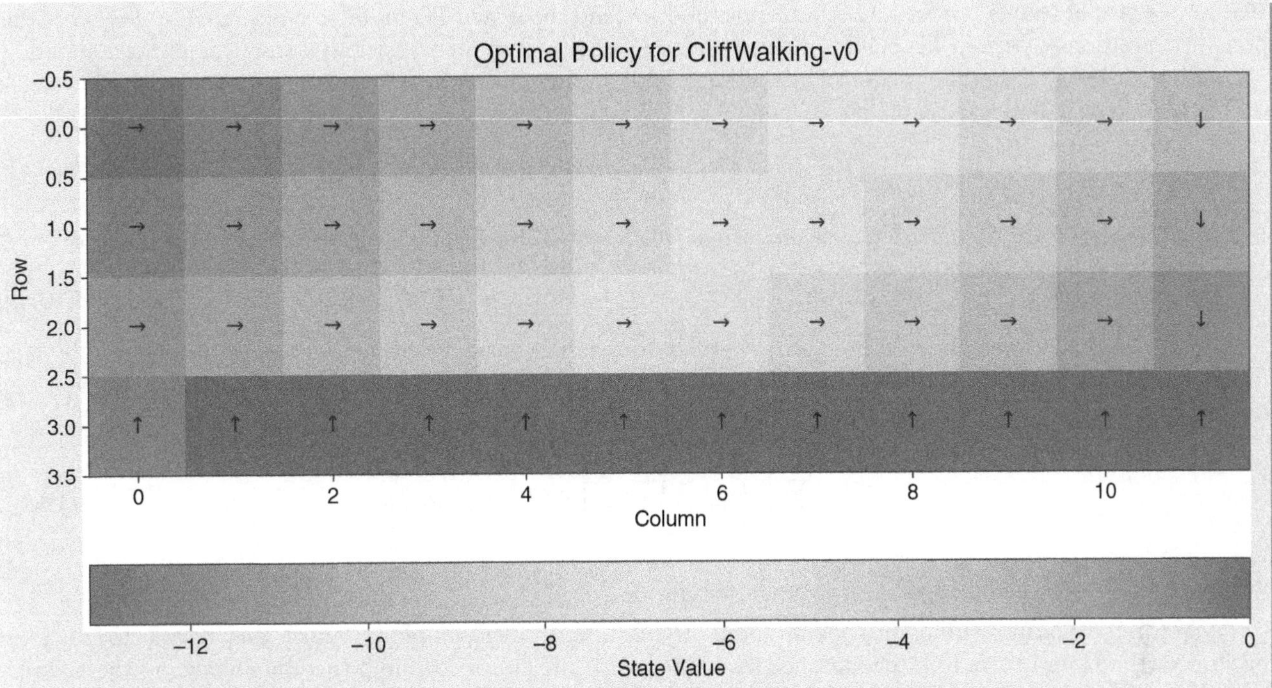

FIGURE 10.18 The cliff walking optimal policy from *Q*-learning.

10.6.4 TD and Bias–Variance Trade-Off

The TD target, defined as $r_{t+1} + \gamma V(s_{t+1})$, is a biased estimator of the true value function $V^{\pi}(s)$ (Silver, 2015). This bias arises because the TD target relies on the current estimate $V(s_{t+1})$, which may be inaccurate. However, the TD target generally has a lower variance than the return G_t, which is the total discounted reward over an entire episode. The lower variance of the TD target stems from its reliance on a single-step-ahead prediction, making updates more stable and incremental:

$$\delta_t = r_{t+1} + \gamma V(s_{t+1}) - V(s_t). \tag{10.35}$$

In contrast, the return G_t used in Monte Carlo methods includes the sum of rewards over multiple steps, resulting in higher variance due to the variability in the total episode returns.

10.6.5 *n*-Step TD

n-Step TD methods generalise the 1-step TD methods, such as TD(0) and SARSA (Sutton and Barto, 2018). In *n*-step methods, updates are based on the returns from the next *n* steps rather than just the next step or the entire episode, and this provides a balance between the high variance of Monte Carlo methods and the bias of 1-step TD methods.

10.6.5.1 *n*-Step TD Prediction *n*-Step TD prediction estimates the value function by updating the value of a state based on the cumulative rewards and value estimates over *n* future steps. The *n*-step return $G_t^{(n)}$ for a given state s_t is defined as

$$G_t^{(n)} = r_{t+1} + \gamma r_{t+2} + \gamma^2 r_{t+3} + \cdots + \gamma^{n-1} r_{t+n} + \gamma^n V(s_{t+n}). \tag{10.36}$$

The update rule for *n*-step TD prediction is then given by

$$V(s_t) \leftarrow V(s_t) + \alpha \left(G_t^{(n)} - V(s_t) \right). \tag{10.37}$$

10.6.5.2 *n*-Step TD Control n-Step TD control methods extend the n-step TD prediction approach to learn optimal policies. Variations of n-step TD control include n-step SARSA, n-step off-policy and n-step tree-backup methods.

n-Step SARSA is an on-policy control method that updates the action–value function $Q(s, a)$ based on the returns over n steps. The n-step SARSA update rule is

$$Q(s_t, a_t) \leftarrow Q(s_t, a_t) + \alpha \left(G_t^{(n)} - Q(s_t, a_t) \right), \tag{10.38}$$

where the n-step return $G_t^{(n)}$ is calculated similarly to the n-step TD prediction, but with action–value pairs:

$$G_t^{(n)} = r_{t+1} + \gamma r_{t+2} + \gamma^2 r_{t+3} + \cdots + \gamma^{n-1} r_{t+n} + \gamma^n Q(s_{t+n}, a_{t+n})'. \tag{10.39}$$

n-Step off-policy methods use a different target policy for evaluation and a behaviour policy for generating data. Importance sampling is often used to correct the discrepancy between the behaviour and target policies. The n-step off-policy return is

$$G_t^{(n)} = \sum_{k=0}^{n-1} \left(\gamma^k r_{t+k+1} \prod_{i=0}^{k-1} \rho_{t+i} \right) + \gamma^n Q(s_{t+n}, a_{t+n}), \tag{10.40}$$

where $\rho_{t+i} = \frac{\pi(a_{t+i}|s_{t+i})}{b(a_{t+i}|s_{t+i})}$ is the importance sampling ratio.

n-Step tree-backup methods provide an alternative to importance sampling (Sutton and Barto, 2018). Tree-backup methods aim to reduce the variance associated with off-policy learning, thereby enhancing the stability and efficiency of the learning process. In these methods, the value updates are computed by considering multiple future steps and the probabilities of taking various actions according to the current policy. This approach spreads the update across all possible actions, weighted by their probabilities under the policy, rather than focusing on a single sampled action. This comprehensive consideration of possible actions at each step helps mitigate the high variance from relying on a single action trajectory. The n-step tree-backup return $G_t^{(n)}$ for a given state s_t and action a_t is computed recursively as follows:

$$G_t^{(n)} = r_{t+1} + \gamma \sum_{a'} \pi(a'|s_{t+1}) \left(r_{t+2} + \gamma \sum_{a'} \pi(a'|s_{t+2}) \left(\cdots + \gamma Q(s_{t+n}, a') \right) \right). \tag{10.41}$$

10.7 DEEP Q NETWORKS (DQNs)

Deep Q Networks (DQNs) are a key advancement in deep reinforcement learning. They combine deep neural networks with Q-learning to achieve superior performance in decision-making tasks. This section explores DQNs, introducing their core principles and the motivation behind their development. It then discusses the architectural components that constitute a DQN, highlighting the role of experience replay and target networks in enhancing stability and efficiency. The loss function and optimisation techniques are then reviewed, followed by a guide to training DQNs. Lastly, this section will examine various DQN variants that have been proposed to address specific challenges and improve performance across different applications.

10.7.1 Introducing DQNs

The RL agent's performance depends on its ability to effectively estimate the value of different states and actions, guiding its policy for selecting actions. However, two challenges arise:

- **Large Discrete State and Action Spaces.** As the number of possible states and actions increases, the computational and memory requirements for storing and updating the value function or Q-function become impractically high, and this leads to the *curse of dimensionality*, where the sheer size of the state–action space makes traditional tabular methods infeasible.

- **Continuous State and Action Spaces.** When states and actions are continuous, representing the value function or Q-function for every possible state–action pair becomes impossible due to the infinite number of such pairs, and this requires methods that can generalise across similar states and actions.

To address these challenges, function approximation techniques are employed to estimate the value function or Q-function. These techniques allow the agent to generalise from limited experiences to unseen states and actions, thus making learning feasible in large or continuous spaces. Several techniques have been applied in the context of RL (Sutton and Barto, 2018), including:

- **Coarse coding** involves partitioning the state space into overlapping regions, where each region is characterised by a feature (see examples in Sutton, 1995). A state is represented by a binary vector indicating the regions with which it is associated. This method allows for generalisation across states, as states that fall into the same or overlapping regions will have similar feature representations.
  - Advantages: Simple to implement and can provide good generalisation.
  - Disadvantages: The choice of regions and their overlaps can be arbitrary and may not capture complex state dependencies.
- **Tile coding** extends coarse coding by dividing the state space into a grid of tiles and using multiple overlapping tiling (see, e.g., Stone and Sutton, 2001). Each tiling provides a different discretisation of the state space. A state is then represented by a binary vector indicating which tiles it belongs to across all tilings, creating a richer feature representation and improving generalisation.
  - Advantages: Better generalisation compared to coarse coding, especially for large state spaces.
  - Disadvantages: Requires careful tuning of the tilings and can be computationally intensive.
- **Radial basis functions** use a set of Gaussian basis functions centred at different points in the state space. A weighted sum of these basis functions approximates the value of a state. Each RBF captures local information about the state space, and the approximation is smooth due to the Gaussian functions. Other kernel-based approaches to function approximation have also been adopted.
  - Advantages: Provides smooth function approximation and can capture complex state dependencies.
  - Disadvantages: Requires selecting the centres and widths of the Gaussian functions, which can be challenging.
- **Neural networks** provide a powerful and flexible way to approximate the value function or Q-function, especially in large and continuous state and action spaces. They can automatically learn features from raw state representations and capture complex dependencies between states and actions.
  - Advantages: The ability to handle high-dimensional inputs and outputs, their capacity to generalise well from limited data and their proficiency in learning non-linear relationships within the data.
  - Disadvantages: Requirement for large amounts of data and computational resources for training, the potential for overfitting and the complexity of tuning hyperparameters to achieve optimal performance. Additionally, neural networks can be less interpretable than simpler models.

10.7.2 Architecture of DQNs

The architecture of any neural network function approximation of the Q-function depends on the form of the state and action spaces. The state space can be discrete, continuous or a hybrid of the two. Even if discrete, it can be very high dimensional: the raw Atari game frames are 210×160 pixel images with 128 colours. The action space is often discrete, representing a finite number of actions. The CartPole balance has only two actions: move left and move right. Some environments have continuous action spaces: the pendulum environment, for example, has a single continuous action over the range $[-2.0, 2.0]$ representing the torque that can be applied to the pendulum. Table 10.1 shows some example state and action spaces from environments presented by the Gymnasium package (Towers et al., 2023).

The input to a DQN can vary based on the nature of the environment and the state representation. Typically, the input includes raw pixel data from images or feature vectors derived from the state. For instance, CNNs are employed in image-based environments to process raw pixel data. A preprocessing step is often used to normalise inputs to a standard scale, reshaping them to fit the network architecture and encoding categorical variables as needed, such as one-hot encoding.

TABLE 10.1 Classic Reinforcement Learning Problems from Gymnasium Categorised by State and Action Spaces with Dimensionality

Environment	State Space	State Dimension	Action Space	Action Dimension
CartPole	Continuous	4	Discrete	2
MountainCar	Continuous	2	Discrete	3
Pendulum	Continuous	3	Continuous	1
Acrobot	Continuous	6	Discrete	3
LunarLander	Continuous	8	Discrete	4
BipedalWalker	Continuous	24	Continuous	4
Blackjack	Discrete	3	Discrete	2
FrozenLake	Discrete	16	Discrete	4
Taxi	Discrete	500	Discrete	6
CliffWalking	Discrete	48	Discrete	4
Atari games	Discrete	4,300,800	Discrete	4–18
MuJoCo environments	Continuous	Varies	Continuous	Varies

The output of the Q-function in a DQN is a vector of Q-values, with each value corresponding to the expected future rewards for taking a specific action in the current state. In environments with discrete action spaces, the output layer of the network directly provides Q-values for each possible action, forming a state–action value vector. This vector guides the agent in selecting the action with the highest Q-value, maximising expected rewards. For continuous action spaces, the output representation can be more complex, often requiring techniques like discretisation of the action space or the application of actor–critic methods, where the actor network determines the policy and the critic network estimates the Q-values. The direct output of Q-values for discrete actions simplifies decision-making, enabling efficient learning and action selection.

10.7.3 Experience Replay

Experience replay is a technique used in reinforcement learning where the agent's experiences, consisting of state, action, reward, next state and done flag, are stored in a replay buffer. Using a replay buffer is critical to DQNs but has a long history in off-policy reinforcement learning being introduced by Lin (1992). Mnih et al. (2013, 2015) used the technique to great effect in their work on Atari games.

In supervised deep learning, models are trained on large labelled datasets to learn a direct mapping from inputs to outputs, requiring substantial amounts of annotated data to achieve high performance. In contrast, reinforcement learning does not rely on labelled datasets; instead, agents learn to make decisions through interactions with an environment, using trial and error to maximise cumulative rewards. This contrast leads to significant problems when attempting to integrate deep learning with RL.

Experience replay was introduced to solve three of these problems (Mnih et al., 2013; Graesser and Keng, 2019):

1. **Breaking Temporal Correlations.** In traditional Q-learning, the agent updates the Q-values based on consecutive experiences, which can be highly correlated. Learning from such correlated samples is inefficient for deep learning models. Randomising the inputs to the neural network breaks the temporal correlations, giving more stable updates.
2. **Improved Data Efficiency.** By reusing past experiences multiple times, experience replay improves data efficiency, allowing the agent to learn more effectively from fewer environmental interactions.

3. **Averaging the Behaviour Distribution.** The randomised sampling process helps achieve better convergence by providing more diverse experiences for each training update. In on-policy learning, the agent learning experience is dictated by the states it reaches, which could lead to undesirable feedback loops. Experience replay learning is automatically off-policy.

The replay buffer is a fixed-size array where experiences are stored. During training, experiences are sampled randomly from the buffer to form mini-batches, with Mnih et al. (2013) adopting a simple uniform sampling scheme. The buffer size is thus a critical choice: a larger buffer will smooth the learning distribution but could have older and less relevant data depending on how old experiences are handled. A larger buffer will also place heavier constraints on the physical structure of the model, as data will need to be proximal to the neural network model for maximum efficiency. Given that the buffer is of fixed size, an eviction policy is needed, with Mnih et al. (2013) adopting the most straightforward first-in, first-out policy. Another important consideration in training is the *replay ratio*, which is the number of gradient updates per transition in the environment (Fedus et al., 2020). This ratio measures how frequently new experiences are gathered from the environment compared to training updates for the deep neural network.

Following the development of DQN and its use of experience replay, several enhancements have been proposed to the basic approach, including:

- **Prioritised Experience Replay (PER).** This introduces a method to sample more important experiences more frequently based on the magnitude of their temporal-difference (TD) error, which helps in learning more efficiently from critical experiences. Schaul et al. (2015) outperformed DQN with a uniform replay on 41 out of 49 Atari games. Further theoretical insight into the role played by TD error in PER is provided by Li et al. (2021), and a further enhancement to PER has been proposed by Li et al. (2024).
- Fedus et al. (2020) reveal that increasing replay capacity significantly enhances the performance of specific algorithms, particularly the Rainbow agent (see Section 10.7.5), which benefits from components like n-step returns, while the standard DQN algorithm shows minimal improvement regardless of capacity changes. The authors highlight that uncorrected n-step returns uniquely confer advantages with larger replay buffers, and they emphasise the importance of the replay ratio in contextualising performance outcomes across various deep reinforcement learning algorithms. Their findings challenge conventional wisdom about experience replay, demonstrating that the interplay between algorithmic components and data-generating mechanisms is crucial for optimising performance in deep reinforcement learning.
- **Combined Experience Replay.** Proposed by Zhang et al. (2018), the authors note that the age of experiences is critical to training performance and propose always including the latest transitions when sampling from the replay buffer.

In summary, experience replay addresses critical issues in reinforcement learning by breaking temporal correlations, improving data efficiency and averaging the behaviour distribution.

10.7.4 Training a DQN

10.7.4.1 Loss Function The Q-function estimates the expected cumulative reward for each action in a given state. The loss function measures the discrepancy between the predicted Q-values (produced by the neural network) and the target Q-values (derived from the Bellman equation). The loss function for deep Q-learning is typically defined as the mean squared error between the predicted Q-values and the target Q-values. For a given mini-batch of transitions sampled from the replay buffer, the loss function $J(\theta)$ is expressed as

$$J(\theta) = \mathbb{E}_{(s_i, a_i, r_i, s_{i+1}) \sim D}\left[\left(y_i - Q(s_i, a_i; \theta)\right)^2\right]. \tag{10.42}$$

where θ are the neural network weights, (s_i, a_i, r_i, s_{i+1}) denotes a transition in the mini-batch, $Q(s_i, a_i; \theta)$ is the predicted Q-value for taking action a_i in state s_i and y_i is the target Q-value, given by

$$y_i = \begin{cases} r_i & \text{if } s_{i+1} \text{ is a terminal state} \\ r_i + \gamma \max_{a'} Q(s_{i+1}, a'; \theta^-) & \text{otherwise} \end{cases}. \tag{10.43}$$

The gradient of the loss function $L(\theta)$ with respect to θ is given by

$$\nabla_\theta J(\theta) = \mathbb{E}_{(s_i,a_i,r_i,s_{i+1})\sim D}\left[\left(Q(s_i, a_i; \theta) - y_i\right) \nabla_\theta Q(s_i, a_i; \theta)\right] \tag{10.44}$$

and is used to update the weights of the network using SGD.

10.7.4.2 Training Algorithm

The training process for DQNs begins with the random initialisation of the action–value Q-network weights, as is standard for neural networks. The replay buffer must be sized to the required capacity.

An ϵ-greedy policy balances exploration and exploitation during training. After selecting and executing an action, the resulting transition (consisting of the current state, action, received reward and next state) is stored in the replay buffer.

Training involves repeatedly sampling mini-batches of transitions from the replay buffer. For each transition in the mini-batch, the target Q-value is computed using the Bellman equation, which incorporates the observed reward and the discounted maximum Q-value of the next state. This process helps adjust the network's weights to approximate the Q-function better.

A gradient descent step is performed on the loss between the predicted and computed target Q-values. This step updates the network weights to minimise this loss, thus refining the Q-function approximation.

This entire process is repeated across multiple episodes and time steps within each episode, gradually improving the policy that the neural network represents. Experience replay, ϵ-greedy action selection and periodic target network updates ensure that the DQN learns effectively and robustly. The process is described formally by Algorithm 10.9 (after Mnih et al., 2013).

10.7.5 DQN Variants

Since the introduction of deep Q-learning by Mnih et al. (2013), several enhancements have been proposed to the basic algorithm:

- **Double Deep Q Network (DDQN).** This variant addresses the overestimation bias inherent in DQN by decoupling the selection and evaluation of actions. DDQN achieves this by using the target network to select the best action and the online network to evaluate its value, resulting in more stable learning and improved performance (van Hasselt et al., 2015). The target network is a copy of the Q network that is periodically updated.
- **Duelling DQNs.** The duelling architecture introduces two separate estimators: one for the state–value function and one for the advantage function. The advantage function is defined by

  $$A^\pi(s, a) = Q^\pi(s, a) - V^\pi(s), \tag{10.45}$$

  and thus is the difference between the state–value function and the state–action function. In practice, the state–action function is given by

  $$Q(s, a; \theta, \alpha, \beta) = V(s; \theta, \beta) + \left(A(s, a; \theta, \alpha) - \frac{1}{|\mathcal{A}|}\sum_{a'} A\left(s, a'; \theta, \alpha\right)\right), \tag{10.46}$$

  where β and α are the weights for the V and A networks, respectively. This separation allows the network to learn which states are valuable without needing to learn the impact of each action in those states, enhancing learning efficiency and performance (Wang et al., 2016).
- **Multi-Agent DDQN (MA-DDQN).** Extending DQN to the multi-agent paradigm, MA-DDQN addresses challenges in multi-agent reward-based learning. It has been applied in tasks such as the Foraging Task and Pursuit Game, showcasing its effectiveness in collaborative and competitive multi-agent settings (Simões et al., 2017).

Algorithm 10.9: DQN Training Algorithm

Input: Number of episodes M, replay buffer capacity N, mini-batch size K, discount factor γ, learning rate α, target network update frequency C, exploration rate ϵ
Output: Trained Q-network parameters θ
Initialise replay buffer D to capacity N;
Initialise action–value function Q with random weights θ;
for *episode = 1 to M* **do**
    Initialise state s_0;
    for *t = 1 to T* **do**
        With probability ϵ, select a random action a_t;
        Otherwise, select $a_t = \arg\max_a Q(s_t, a; \theta)$;
        Execute action a_t and observe reward r_t and next state s_{t+1};
        Store transition (s_t, a_t, r_t, s_{t+1}) in D;
        if *size of D is greater than K* **then**
            Sample random mini-batch of K transitions (s_i, a_i, r_i, s_{i+1}) from D;
            for *each transition* (s_i, a_i, r_i, s_{i+1}) **do**
                Compute target y_i:

$$y_i = \begin{cases} r_i & \text{if } s_{i+1} \text{ is terminal} \\ r_i + \gamma \max_a \hat{Q}(s_{i+1}, a; \theta) & \text{otherwise} \end{cases}$$

            end
            Perform a gradient descent step on the loss:

$$L(\theta) = \frac{1}{K} \sum_{i=1}^{K} \left(y_i - Q(s_i, a_i; \theta)\right)^2$$

            with respect to the network parameters θ;
        end
    end
end

- **Rainbow DQN.** An amalgamation of several improvements to the original DQN, integrating multiple enhancements into a more powerful algorithm. The key components of Rainbow DQN are:
  - Double Q-Learning.
  - Prioritised Experience Replay.
  - Duelling DQNs.
  - Multi-Step Learning. This extends the update targets to multiple steps, which helps propagate rewards more effectively through the network (Sutton, 1988).
  - Distributional Q-Learning. This learns to approximate the distribution of returns instead of just the mean, providing a richer training signal (Bellemare et al., 2017).
  - Noisy Nets. This introduces noise into the network weights, which helps in exploration by encouraging the network to try out different actions (Fortunato et al., 2017).

  Combining these techniques results in a more robust and efficient learning algorithm that outperforms the individual components when used separately.

- **APE-X (Asynchronous Prioritised Experience Replay) DQN.** Designed to enhance scalability and efficiency in reinforcement learning by leveraging distributed computation. The key features of APE-X DQN are:
  - Distributed Training. APE-X uses multiple actors (agents) to collect experiences in parallel and a single learner to update the network, significantly increasing the speed of experience collection and training.
  - Prioritised Experience Replay.
  - Asynchronous Updates. The use of asynchronous updates allows for continuous learning and experience collection without waiting for a synchronisation point, making the training process more efficient and faster.

  APE-X DQN demonstrates that distributed approaches can scale reinforcement learning to handle more complex environments by efficiently utilising computational resources, leading to faster convergence and improved performance (Horgan et al., 2018).
- **Attention-Based DQN.** This approach integrates attention mechanisms into DQN to handle efficiency and performance issues in complex systems. By using global and local attention, the network can better focus on relevant parts of the input, improving decision-making in intricate environments (Ni et al., 2019).

EXAMPLE 10.10: DDQN AND ATARI GAMES

This example implements the DDQN model coupled with prioritised experience replay and applies it to the Atari games from the Gymnasium package. The example can be found in the Jupyter Notebook `DDQN.ipynb` and uses the Space Invaders game, but any Atari games can be used by simply changing the loaded environment.

There are two important classes in the example, `PrioritizedReplayBuffer`, which manages the replay buffer, and `QNetwork`, which is the *Q*-function approximating network. The latter is a standard CNN, which takes a batch of blocks of consecutive frames as input and outputs the action probabilities as a linear weight. The output size depends on the available actions for the specific games being played, and for Space Invaders, there are four. The PER buffer class is presented below.

```
class PrioritizedReplayBuffer:
    def __init__(self, capacity, alpha=0.6):
        self.capacity = capacity
        self.alpha = alpha
        self.buffer = []
        self.pos = 0
        self.priorities = np.zeros((capacity,), dtype=np.float32)
        self.Transition = namedtuple('Transition', ('state', 'action',
                                     'reward', 'next_state', 'done'))

    def add(self, state, action, reward, next_state, done):
        max_prio = self.priorities.max() if self.buffer else 1.0
        if len(self.buffer) < self.capacity:
            self.buffer.append(None)
        self.buffer[self.pos] = self.Transition(state, action, reward,
                                                next_state, done)
        self.priorities[self.pos] = max_prio
        self.pos = (self.pos + 1) % self.capacity

    def sample(self, batch_size, beta=0.4):
        if len(self.buffer) == self.capacity:
            prios = self.priorities
        else:
            prios = self.priorities[:self.pos]
        probs = prios ** self.alpha
        probs /= probs.sum()

        indices = np.random.choice(len(self.buffer), batch_size, p=probs)
        samples = [self.buffer[idx] for idx in indices]
```

```
        total = len(self.buffer)
        weights = (total * probs[indices]) ** (-beta)
        weights /= weights.max()
        weights = np.array(weights, dtype=np.float32)

        batch = self.Transition(*zip(*samples))
        states = np.stack(batch.state)
        actions = np.array(batch.action)
        rewards = np.array(batch.reward)
        next_states = np.stack(batch.next_state)
        dones = np.array(batch.done)

        return states, actions, rewards, next_states, dones, \\
               indices, weights

    def update_priorities(self, batch_indices, batch_priorities):
        for idx, prio in zip(batch_indices, batch_priorities):
            self.priorities[idx] = prio
```

The `PrioritizedReplayBuffer` class is designed to store transitions, which consist of a state, an action, a reward, the subsequent state and a flag indicating if the episode is done. By prioritising these transitions, the class aims to sample more significant experiences more frequently, enhancing the learning process.

When an instance of `PrioritizedReplayBuffer` is created, it initialises several key attributes. The `capacity` determines the maximum number of transitions the buffer can hold, while `alpha`, which defaults to 0.6, controls the level of prioritisation. The `buffer` is an empty list set up to store the transitions, and `pos` is an index that keeps track of where the next transition should be inserted. The `priorities` attribute is a NumPy array initialised to store the priorities of each transition, and `transition` is a named tuple that organises and stores individual transitions with elements for state, action, reward, next state and done.

Adding a transition to the buffer involves a few steps. The `add` method first determines the maximum priority currently in the buffer, defaulting to 1.0 if the buffer is empty. If the buffer has not reached capacity, a `None` value is appended to make room for the new transition. The new transition is then stored at the current `pos` index, and its priority is set to the maximum priority. The `pos` index is updated to point to the next position, wrapping around to the start of the buffer if necessary.

Sampling transitions is a process designed to reflect their importance. The `sample` method calculates the probabilities for sampling each transition by raising their priorities to the power of `alpha` and normalising them. It then randomly selects indices based on these probabilities to form the sample batch. The method also computes importance sampling weights to correct for the bias introduced by prioritisation, adjusted by a parameter `beta`. The sampled transitions are collected into arrays for states, actions, rewards, following states and done flags, along with the indices and weights.

The `update_priorities` method is used to update the priorities of transitions. It takes two lists: `batch_indices`, which are the indices of the transitions to be updated, and `batch_priorities`, which are the new priority values. The method iterates through the provided indices and updates the corresponding priorities in the `priorities` array.

The following function calculates the loss:

```
def compute_td_loss(batch_size, beta):
    s, a, r, ns, d, i, w = replay_buffer.sample(batch_size, beta)

    states = torch.FloatTensor(s).to(device)
    next_states = torch.FloatTensor(ns).to(device)
    actions = torch.LongTensor(a).to(device)
```

(*Continued*)

(Continued)

```
    rewards = torch.FloatTensor(r).to(device)
    dones = torch.FloatTensor(d).to(device)
    weights = torch.FloatTensor(w).to(device)

    q_values = q_network(states)
    next_q_values = q_network(next_states)
    next_q_state_values = target_network(next_states)

    q_value = q_values.gather(1, actions.unsqueeze(1)).squeeze(1)
    next_q_value = next_q_state_values.gather(1,
                     next_q_values.max(1)[1].unsqueeze(1)).squeeze(1)
    expected_q_value = rewards + GAMMA * next_q_value * (1 - dones)

    loss = (q_value - expected_q_value.detach()).pow(2) * weights
    prios = loss + 1e-5
    loss = loss.mean()

    optimizer.zero_grad()
    loss.backward()
    replay_buffer.update_priorities(indices, prios.data.cpu().numpy())
    optimizer.step()

    return loss
```

The function is designed to calculate the TD loss for a batch of experiences in a reinforcement learning context. This function operates by first sampling a batch of experiences from a replay buffer, using a specified batch size and a beta parameter for importance sampling.

Next, the function uses the *Q*-network to compute the *Q*-values for the current and following states. The target network is used to compute the *Q*-values for the following states, which are then used to determine the target values. The *Q*-value for the current state–action pair is extracted by gathering the *Q*-values at the indices specified by the actions. For the next *Q*-value, the maximum *Q*-value for the next state is selected and used in the calculation.

The expected *Q*-value is computed using the rewards and the discounted maximum *Q*-value of the following state, adjusted for the done flags to account for terminal states. The TD loss is then calculated as the squared difference between the current and expected *Q* values, weighted by the importance sampling weights. A small constant is added to the loss to avoid zero priorities. This loss is averaged and used to perform a gradient descent step.

Finally, the training loop is given by

```
for _ in trange(MAX_FRAMES):
    frame_idx += 1
    eps = max(EPS_END, EPS_START - frame_idx / EPS_DECAY)
    beta = min(1.0, BETA_START + frame_idx * (1.0 - BETA_START)/BETA_FRAMES)

    stacked_state = np.concatenate(state_deque, axis=0)
    action = select_action(stacked_state, eps)

    # Stochastic frame skipping
    skip = random.randint(2, 5)
    total_reward = 0
    for _ in range(skip):
```

```
            next_state, reward, done, _, _ = env.step(action)
            total_reward += reward
            if done:
                break

        next_state_processed = preprocess_frame(next_state)
        state_deque.append(next_state_processed)
        next_stacked_state = np.concatenate(state_deque, axis=0)

        replay_buffer.add(stacked_state, action, total_reward,
                          next_stacked_state, done)

        state = next_state
        episode_reward += total_reward

        if done:
            state, _ = env.reset()
            state_deque = deque([preprocess_frame(state)] * K, maxlen=K)
            all_rewards.append(episode_reward)
            episode_reward = 0

        if len(replay_buffer.buffer) > BATCH_SIZE:
            loss = compute_td_loss(BATCH_SIZE, beta)

        if frame_idx % TARGET_UPDATE == 0:
            update_target()

        if frame_idx % 1000 == 0:
            print(f'Frame: {frame_idx}, Reward: {np.mean(all_rewards[-10:])}')
```

The loop starts by incrementing the frame index and updating the ϵ value, which is used for ϵ-greedy action selection, and the β value, which is slowly annealed during training.

The current state of the environment, represented as a deque of frames, is concatenated into a single stacked state. An action is then selected based on this stacked state using an ϵ-greedy policy, where actions are chosen either randomly or based on the current policy with a probability determined by ϵ.

As discussed earlier, several frames are skipped to enhance efficiency. However, in some cases, having a fixed frequency can lead to missing significant features in the image as described by Mnih et al. (2013). Hence, a random number of frames (between two and five) are skipped. Within this skip loop, the environment executes the chosen action, returning the next state, reward and a flag indicating whether the episode is done. The total reward accumulated during these frames is summed. If the episode ends within the skip frames, the loop breaks early.

The subsequent state undergoes processing, and the deque of frames is updated with this processed state. A new stacked state is then formed by concatenating the frames within the deque, and this transition is subsequently added to the replay buffer. The state is then updated to reflect the next state, and the episode reward is incremented by the total reward accumulated during the frame skips. Upon the conclusion of an episode, the environment is reset, a new initial state is preprocessed and used to refill the deque, the episode reward is recorded and the episode reward counter is reset.

When the replay buffer exceeds the batch size, the temporal difference loss is computed using a sample of these transitions, leading to the network's training using SGD. Periodically, the target network is updated to align with the parameters of the current network.

The model uses a small buffer size of 50,000 to avoid any issues with running out of memory, which limits performance. After 10^6 frames, a full episode was captured using the trained agent, and the sequence of nine frames in Figure 10.19 illustrates the in-game action.

(*Continued*)

(*Continued*)

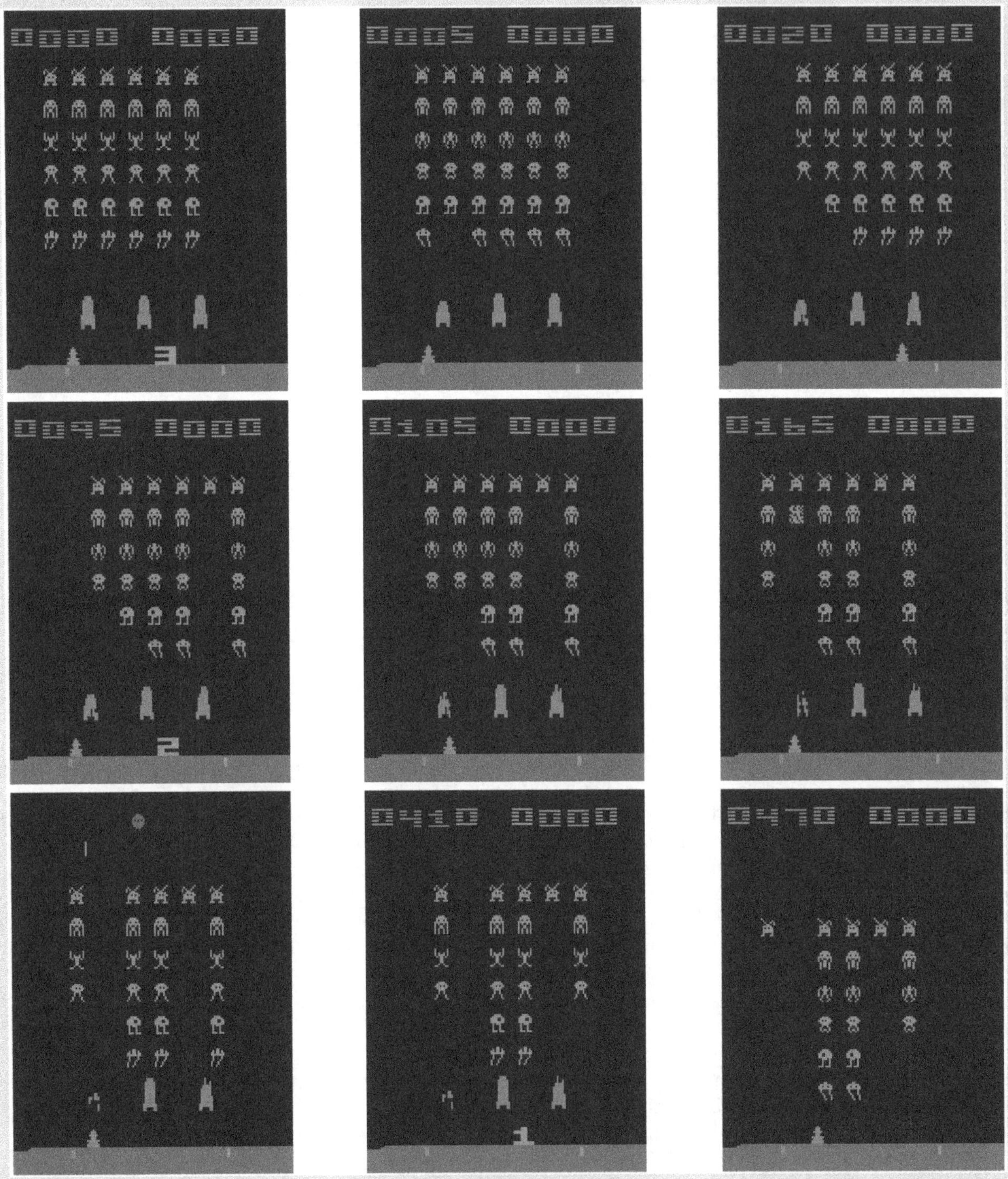

FIGURE 10.19 Nine frames from a Space Invaders game using the trained agent.

10.8 POLICY GRADIENT

10.8.1 Parameterised Policies

Earlier in this chapter, the focus was on the use of the state–value function $V(s)$ and the state–action value function $Q(s, a)$, with a policy generated from the value function, often with an ϵ-greedy approach. This section explores the alternative approach of directly defining the policy function. The policy is parametrised so that

$$\pi_\theta(a|s) = \mathbb{P}[a|s, \theta]. \tag{10.47}$$

There are a variety of approximation techniques for the policy, including linear functions and, as might be expected, neural networks (Sutton and Barto, 2018).

Different techniques are employed for discrete and continuous action spaces (Lehmann, 2024) to ensure that the policy outputs a valid probability distribution over actions. The policy can use the softmax function to convert raw action preferences (logits) into a probability distribution in discrete action spaces. Specifically, for a parameterised policy $\pi_\theta(a|s)$, the softmax function calculates the probability of each action a given state s as

$$\pi_\theta(a|s) = \frac{e^{z_a}}{\sum_b e^{z_b}}, \tag{10.48}$$

where z_a represents the preference for action a, ensuring that all probabilities are non-negative and sum to one. The policy often uses a Gaussian distribution in continuous action spaces, parameterised by a mean $\mu_\theta(s)$ and a standard deviation $\sigma_\theta(s)$. The policy $\pi_\theta(a|s)$, in this case, outputs a probability density function where actions are drawn from

$$a \sim \mathcal{N}(\mu_\theta(s), \sigma_\theta^2(s)). \tag{10.49}$$

This method allows for smooth and continuous exploration of actions, where the mean dictates the most likely action and the standard deviation controls the exploration around this mean. Both methods ensure that the policy produces valid probability distributions suitable for their respective action spaces.

Using parameterised policies enhances the agent's ability to learn and adapt to complex environments by representing the policy – the mapping from states to actions – as a function with adjustable parameters. By optimising these parameters through techniques like gradient descent, the agent can improve its decision-making process based on feedback from the environment, leading to more efficient learning and better performance in diverse and dynamic tasks.

Policy-based reinforcement learning offers several advantages, including direct optimisation of the policy, which can handle high-dimensional and continuous action spaces more effectively than value-based methods. This approach allows for stochastic policies, enhancing exploration and robustness in uncertain environments. Additionally, policy-based methods are better suited for optimising long-term strategies and handling partial observability in complex tasks. However, these methods also have disadvantages, such as higher variance in the updates, which can lead to instability and slower convergence. They often require careful tuning of hyperparameters and can be computationally intensive. Furthermore, policy-based methods may struggle with local optima and require substantial training data to achieve optimal performance (Silver, 2015).

In reinforcement learning, the policy objective function differs depending on whether the environment is episodic or continuing.

- Episodic Environments. The agent's experience is divided into episodes, each starting from an initial state and terminating at a terminal state. The policy objective function aims to maximise the expected return (total reward) over an episode. The objective function, $J(\theta)$, for a parameterised policy $\pi_\theta(a|s)$ can be defined as (Silver, 2015)

$$J(\theta) = \mathbb{E}_{\tau\sim\pi_\theta}\left[\sum_{t=0}^{T} R_t\right], \tag{10.50}$$

  where τ represents a trajectory $(s_0, a_0, s_1, a_1, \ldots, s_T)$ generated by the policy, and R_t is the reward received at time step t. The goal is to find the policy parameters θ that maximise this expected return.

- Continuing Environments. The agent's interaction with the environment is ongoing without terminal states. The policy objective function aims to maximise the expected discounted return over an infinite horizon. The objective function, $J(\theta)$, for a parameterised policy $\pi_\theta(a|s)$ can be defined as

$$J(\theta) = \mathbb{E}_{\tau\sim\pi_\theta}\left[\sum_{t=0}^{\infty} \gamma^t R_t\right], \tag{10.51}$$

where $\gamma \in [0, 1)$ is the discount factor and τ represents an infinite trajectory

$$(s_0, a_0, s_1, a_1, \ldots).$$

The objective is to optimise the policy parameters θ to maximise this expected discounted return, ensuring that the agent values immediate rewards more highly than distant future rewards.

Given the objective function, $J(\theta)$, the goal is to optimise to obtain maximum rewards. Various optimisation methods are available, but the most common is *policy gradient.*

10.8.2 Policy Gradient Theorem

The policy gradient theorem provides a foundation for the policy gradient methods in reinforcement learning. It states that the gradient of the expected return with respect to the policy parameters can be expressed as the expected value of the gradient of the log probability of the policy multiplied by the action–value function (Sutton and Barto, 2018).

Theorem 10.2 ***(Policy Gradient Theorem):*** *For a policy $\pi_\theta(a|s)$ parameterised by θ, the gradient of the expected return $J(\theta)$ with respect to θ is given by*

$$\nabla_\theta J(\theta) = \mathbb{E}_{\pi_\theta}\left[\nabla_\theta \log \pi_\theta(a|s) Q^\pi(s, a)\right]. \tag{10.52}$$

For a proof of the theorem, see, for example, Sutton and Barto (2018).

The policy gradient theorem provides the mathematical foundation for policy gradient methods by expressing the gradient in a form that can be efficiently estimated from sampled trajectories.

10.8.3 REINFORCE

The REINFORCE (REward Increment = Non-negative Factor × Offset Reinforment) algorithm was the first policy-gradient algorithm introduced by Williams (1992). The algorithm uses Monte Carlo sampling of full episodes to computer returns and estimates the policy gradient. REINFORCE is presented in full in Algorithm 10.10 (see Sutton and Barto, 2018).

Algorithm 10.10: REINFORCE Algorithm

Input: Initial policy parameters θ, learning rate α
while *not converged* **do**
  Generate an episode $\tau = (s_0, a_0, r_1, \ldots, s_{T-1}, a_{T-1}, r_T)$ using policy π_θ;
  for *each time step t in episode τ* **do**
    Compute return $G_t = \sum_{k=t+1}^{T} \gamma^{k-t-1} r_k$;
    Update policy parameters:
    $\theta \leftarrow \theta + \alpha \nabla_\theta \log \pi_\theta(a_t|s_t) G_t$
  end
end

The *REINFORCE with baseline algorithm* is an extension of the original REINFORCE algorithm, a policy gradient method in reinforcement learning. The baseline is introduced to reduce the variance of the gradient estimates without introducing bias, leading to more stable and efficient learning. To reduce the variance of this estimate, a baseline function $b(s_t)$ is introduced, typically a value function estimating the expected return from state s_t. The gradient with the baseline becomes

$$\nabla_\theta J(\theta) = \mathbb{E}_{\tau\sim\pi_\theta(\tau)}\left[\sum_{t=0}^{T} \nabla_\theta \log \pi_\theta(a_t|s_t)(R(\tau) - b(s_t))\right]. \tag{10.53}$$

The term $(R(\tau) - b(s_t))$ is called the advantage, and it measures how much better or worse the action a_t was compared to the expected return from state s_t. A common choice for the baseline $b(s_t)$ is the state–value function $V(s_t)$. REINFORCE with baseline is presented in Algorithm 10.11.

Algorithm 10.11: REINFORCE with Baseline Algorithm

Input: Initial policy parameters θ, baseline parameters ϕ, learning rates α and β
while *not converged* **do**
  Generate an episode $\tau = (s_0, a_0, r_1, \ldots, s_{T-1}, a_{T-1}, r_T)$ using policy π_θ;
  for *each time step t in episode* τ **do**
    Compute return $G_t = \sum_{k=t+1}^{T} \gamma^{k-t-1} r_k$;
    Compute baseline $b(s_t, \phi)$;
    Update baseline parameters:
    $\phi \leftarrow \phi + \beta\nabla_\phi(G_t - b(s_t, \phi))^2$;
    Update policy parameters:
    $\theta \leftarrow \theta + \alpha\nabla_\theta \log \pi_\theta(a_t|s_t)(G_t - b(s_t, \phi))$
  end
end

EXAMPLE 10.11: REINFORCE WITH LUNAR LANDER

This example is located in the Jupyter Notebook `REINFORCE.ipynb` and uses the REINFORCE algorithm to train a policy network for the lunar lander environment from Gymnasium.

The policy is parameterised by a simple two-layer neural network with 128 neurons in the first fully connected layer with ReLU activation and output with four neurons and softmax to support the four possible actions for the lunar lander. The training loop, which implements the REINFORCE algorithm, is presented below. The episode's length is truncated at 500 steps: the lander has infinite fuel and the agent can hover indefinitely. The loop samples an episode and calculates the returns from it. The neural network is trained using the gradient estimate obtained using the log probabilities output from the policy network. The first nine frames are shown in Figure 10.20.

```
def reinforce(env, policy_net, optimizer, num_episodes, device=device,
              gamma=0.99, max_steps=500):
    total_returns = list()
    for episode in trange(num_episodes):
        state, _ = env.reset()
        rewards = list()
        log_probs = list()
        done = False
```

(*Continued*)

(Continued)

```
        steps = 0
        while not done and steps < max_steps:
            action, log_prob = select_action(policy_net, state)
            next_state, reward, done, _, _ = env.step(action)
            rewards.append(reward)
            log_probs.append(log_prob)
            state = next_state
            steps += 1

        R = 0
        policy_loss = list()
        returns = list()

        for r in rewards[::-1]:
            R = r + gamma * R
            returns.insert(0, R)

        returns = torch.tensor(returns).to(device)
        returns = (returns - returns.mean()) / (returns.std() + 1e-9)

        for log_prob, R in zip(log_probs, returns):
            policy_loss.append(-log_prob * R)

        optimizer.zero_grad()
        policy_loss = torch.cat(policy_loss).sum()
        policy_loss.backward()
        optimizer.step()
        total_returns.append(R.cpu().detach().item())
        if episode % 100 == 0:
            print(f'Episode {episode}\tLast reward: {sum(rewards)}')

    return total_returns
```

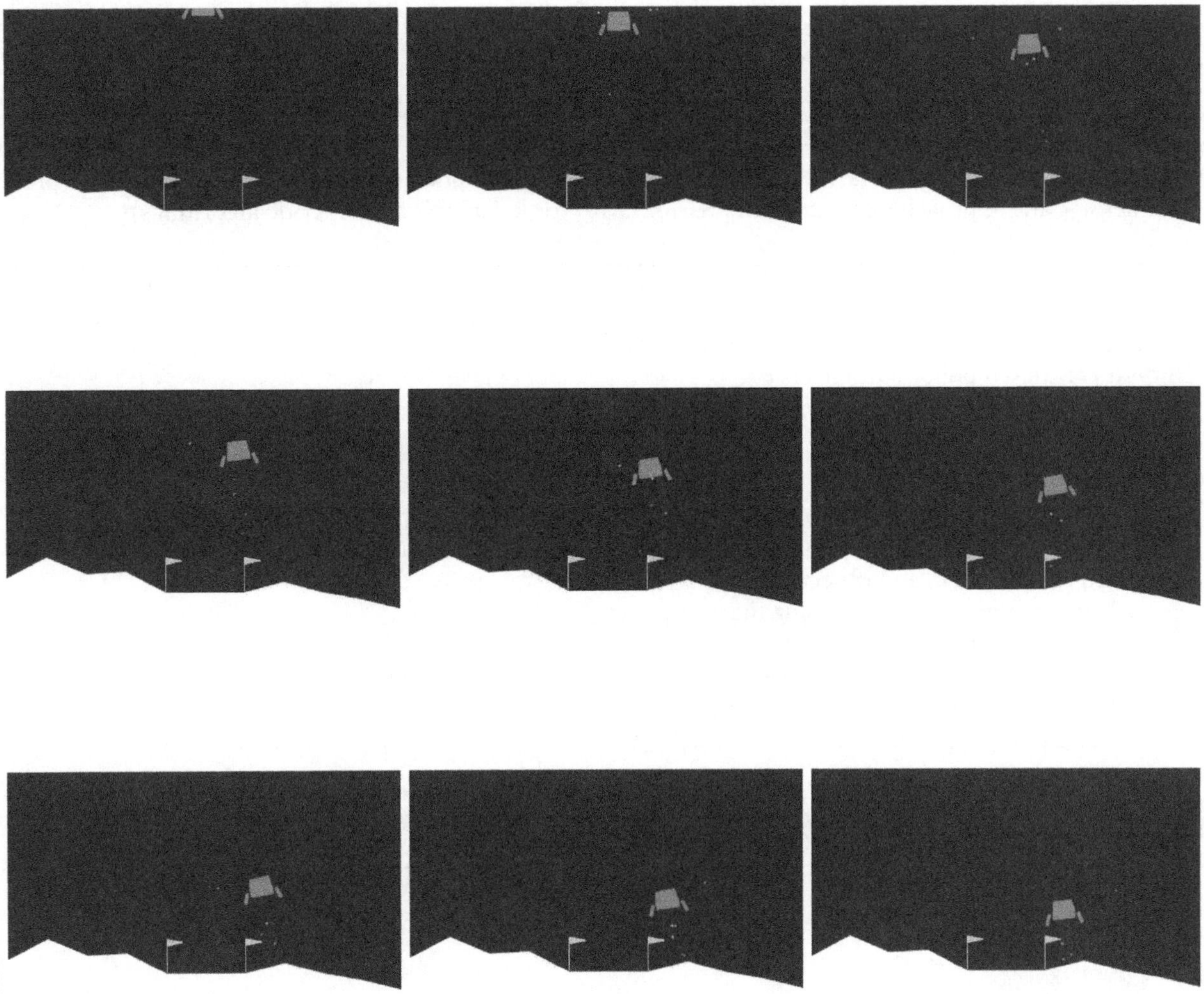

FIGURE 10.20 Nine frames from a lunar lander trained with REINFORCE.

10.9 ACTOR–CRITIC METHODS

Actor–critic methods (Konda and Tsitsiklis, 1999) are a class of reinforcement learning algorithms that combine aspects of both value-based methods and policy-based methods. These methods use two main components: the actor and the critic.

- **Actor:** The actor selects actions. It represents the policy function, which can be deterministic or stochastic. The actor adjusts the policy parameters in the direction suggested by the critic to maximise the expected reward.
- **Critic:** The critic evaluates the actions taken by the actor. It estimates the value function V or the Q-value function, which measures the expected future rewards given the current state (and action, in the case of Q-values). The critic provides feedback to the actor about how good or bad the chosen actions were, helping the actor to improve its policy.

The actor–critic methods update both the actor and the critic, leading to more efficient and stable learning. These methods are advantageous because they use the critic to reduce the variance of the gradient estimates to update the actor, leading to more stable and faster convergence than pure policy gradient methods. Algorithm 10.12 presents the basic actor–critic approach (see Sutton and Barto, 2018, for a variety of actor–critic algorithms).

Algorithm 10.12: Actor–Critic Algorithm

Input: Initial policy parameters θ, initial critic parameters w
Output: Optimised policy parameters θ

Initialise policy parameters θ and critic parameters w;
for *each episode* **do**
  Initialise state s_0;
  for *each step t in the episode* **do**
    Select action a_t according to the policy $\pi_\theta(a_t|s_t)$;
    Execute action a_t and observe reward r_{t+1} and next state s_{t+1};
    Estimate the value $V_w(s_t)$ using the critic;
    Compute TD error: $\delta_t = r_{t+1} + \gamma V_w(s_{t+1}) - V_w(s_t)$;
    Update critic parameters w: $w \leftarrow w + \alpha_c \delta_t \nabla_w V_w(s_t)$;
    Compute the policy gradient: $\nabla_\theta J(\theta) = \mathbb{E}[\delta_t \nabla_\theta \log \pi_\theta(a_t|s_t)]$;
    Update policy parameters θ: $\theta \leftarrow \theta + \alpha_a \nabla_\theta J(\theta)$;
    $s_t \leftarrow s_{t+1}$;
  end
end

10.10 CONCLUSIONS

This chapter has explored the principles behind reinforcement learning and deep reinforcement learning. It began with an overview of reinforcement learning, emphasising key components such as states, actions, rewards and the agent–environment interaction loop. It then explored the mathematical framework of Markov decision processes and the Bellman equations, which provide the foundation for RL algorithms.

Dynamic programming and Monte Carlo methods were discussed as classical approaches to solving RL problems. While effective in specific scenarios, these methods face limitations in large or continuous state and action spaces, and this led to the introduction of temporal difference learning, which combines aspects of dynamic programming and Monte Carlo methods, offering a more efficient way to learn from experience.

The chapter highlighted the evolution from traditional Q-learning to DQNs which leverage deep neural networks to approximate the Q-function. It covered the architecture, training process and various enhancements to DQNs, including experience replay, which addresses data efficiency and stability issues.

Policy gradient methods and actor–critic algorithms were introduced as powerful alternatives to value-based methods. These approaches optimise the policy, making them suitable for high-dimensional and continuous action spaces.

Deep reinforcement learning allows agents to learn complex behaviours and make intelligent decisions in dynamic environments. Integrating deep learning techniques with reinforcement learning principles has opened new possibilities and applications, from gaming to robotics. However, in quantitative finance, the application to hedging is pre-eminent, and this is explored in Chapter 19.

PART Three

Applications

CHAPTER 11

Derivative Valuation Using Neural Networks

Deckard: Replicants are like any other machine – they're either a benefit or a hazard. If they're a benefit, it's not my problem.

Blade Runner, directed by Ridley Scott (1982)

11.1 INTRODUCTION

Derivative valuation is an obvious choice for the application of deep neural networks. Early attempts to merge neural networks with derivative valuation can be attributed to works such as Malliaris and Salchenberger (1993a,b) and Hutchinson et al. (1994). These papers emerged around the second 'summer' of neural networks, indicating an early interest in applying neural networks in finance.

Research on the intersection of neural networks and derivative valuation has largely fallen into three categories:

1. Using neural networks as a non-parametric model for option valuation.
2. Employing neural networks to approximate existing parametric models for option valuation.
3. Incorporating neural networks as components within more comprehensive derivative valuation models.

This chapter will explore the first two categories in detail. Several later chapters cover the third category: high-dimensional PDE and BSDE solvers in Chapter 12; Monte Carlo models and optimal stopping in Chapter 13; static replication models in Chapter 14; volatility models in Chapter 15; and model calibration in Chapter 16. Chapter 19 covers *deep hedging* and the application of neural networks and reinforcement learning to construct hedge portfolios for derivatives.

Extensive research has been conducted on the non-parametric and parametric applications of neural networks in derivative valuation. A review by Ruf and Wang (2019) reports around 150 papers related to this theme. Unlike the general trend in neural network research, the publication frequency in this domain has remained relatively steady since the 1990s. Detailed reviews by Bennell and Sutcliffe (2004), Chen and Sutcliffe (2012) and Hahn (2013) provide a comprehensive picture of research in this area.

The chapter is organised as follows: Section 11.2 focuses on the non-parametric applications of neural networks, while Section 11.3 discusses their utility in function replication.

11.2 DERIVATIVE VALUATION USING NEURAL NETWORKS TRAINED AS NON-PARAMETRIC MODELS

The primary use case for applying neural networks to value financial derivatives is to use them as non-parametric models. These studies use historical market data to train neural networks to price options. Notably, even in research up to 2017 that used simulated data for neural network training, the main aim was to see if the network could reproduce an existing pricing model, often the Black–Scholes model. Given the many review articles on this topic, this section will concentrate on summarising the various methodologies and approaches in the literature.

Deep Learning in Quantitative Finance, First Edition. Andrew Green.

A driving factor behind using neural networks as a non-parametric alternative to traditional models such as Black–Scholes is the differences between Black–Scholes model values and market prices. Hence, the neural network model serves a role similar to empirical approaches, like the implied volatility surfaces. Implied volatility surfaces 'modify' the Black–Scholes model to reflect market patterns like skew, smile and volatility term structure. In this context, neural networks are used to determine the option price based on current market conditions, not as forecasting tools.

The following variations in approach to training ANNs as non-parametric option pricing models can be identified.

Exercise Type European and American exercise options are both used as subjects. The market data used to train the model primarily consists of exchange-traded options, where the properties of the option contract dictate the type of exercise. It is important to note that dividends matter for American options: some authors have compared the prices of American options in their trained model with those derived from a Black–Scholes benchmark. The American option price will not match the European Black–Scholes price even in theory, and the desire is that the neural network model will include the American option premium. Some authors prefer to use models such as the Barone-Adesi and Whaley model as an accurate benchmark for American option pricing (Barone-Adesi and Whaley, 1987; Lajbcygier et al., 1996).

Market Data Neural networks have been trained using options on a variety of different markets. Equity index options are the most prominent, featuring the S&P 100, S&P 500, AOSPI, IBEX 35, FTSE 100, DAX, NIKKEI 225, OMX, KOSPI 200, TAIEX, ALSI, NIFTY 50, HSI and STOXX 50 (see Table 11.1 for definitions). Besides these indices, individual stocks have also been used. Researchers have adopted different approaches to dividend treatment: some omit data periods with dividends, while others factor in the dividend yield as an input to their models. A few currency pairs have been used in the foreign exchange sector, including USD–DEM (relevant before 1999), GBP–USD and EUR–USD. Data from interest-rate instruments like the BUND and Eurodollar Futures has also been considered. Finally, one commodities asset, WTI, was used.

TABLE 11.1 Equity Index Names and Their Full Names (After Ruf and Wang, 2019)

Equity Index Name	Full Index Name
S&P 100	Standard & Poor's 100
S&P 500	Standard & Poor's 500
AOSPI	Australia All Ordinaries Share Price Index
IBEX 35	IBEX 35 Index
FTSE 100	Financial Times Stock Exchange 100
DAX	Deutscher Aktienindex (German Stock Exchange)
NIKKEI 225	Nikkei Stock Average 225
OMX	OMX Nordic Exchange
KOSPI 200	Korea Composite Stock Price Index 200
TAIEX	Taiwan Stock Exchange Capitalization Weighted Stock Index
ALSI	South Africa All Share Index
NIFTY 50	National Stock Exchange of India's benchmark index
HSI	Hang Seng Index
STOXX 50	EURO STOXX 50
WTI	West Texas Intermediate (Crude Oil)

Input Features Different authors have explored a variety of feature selections as inputs to their neural network models. These can be broadly categorised into variants of the Black–Scholes model inputs and additional features. Details of which papers apply what inputs can be found in Ruf and Wang (2019).

- **Black–Scholes Model Inputs**
  - Strike (K) and spot (S). Different representations include:
    - Directly as S and K.
    - Using the 'homogeneity hint' or moneyness: $\frac{S}{K}$.
    - Utilising $\log(S)$ in lieu of S.
    - Expressing as $\frac{(S-K)}{T}$.
  - Volatility input types:
    - Historical volatility with diverse window sizes.
    - Implied volatility.
    - Historical implied volatility.
    - At-the-money implied volatility.
    - Volatility ascertained from a Kalman filter.
    - GARCH model-derived volatility.
    - Macroeconomic variables' volatility sourced from PCA.
    - Volatility indices such as VIX.
    - Separate networks like RNNs for volatility estimation.
  - Maturity and interest rate values have been included by some authors and fixed by others.
- **Additional Features**
  - Trade volumes.
  - Open interest figures.
  - Bid and ask values for the spot.
  - Lagged spot figures.
  - Previous option values.

Network Architecture Early research papers often favoured more simplistic designs, primarily due to computational limitations before the widespread adoption of GPUs. These early models were characterised by their shallowness, often having just a single hidden layer, and their narrowness, with a typical neuron count ranging from 2 to 20. The early neural networks predominantly employed the sigmoid and tanh functions, mirroring the contemporary trends in research at the time. Some of these early models also experimented with the radial basis function as the activation function. However, as research progressed, there was a noticeable shift towards the ReLU and its variant, the leaky ReLU, again reflecting the evolving practices in ANN research.

Standard or Hybrid Model Most authors use standard neural network models that attempt to price the option directly. However, a small number of authors use a *hybrid* approach, including Andreou et al. (2002, 2006, 2010), Charalambous and Martzoukos (2005), Blynski and Faseruk (2006), Amornwattana et al. (2007), Andreou (2008) and Saxena (2008). Here, the neural network learns the difference between the market prices and a baseline model, normally the Black–Scholes model.

Train–Test Partitioning Most authors partition data into training and test sets chronologically; test data follows training data (Ruf and Wang, 2019). However, some papers adopt a different approach, such as random ordering.

Error Measures A large number of different measures of error have been applied to neural networks trained to price options, as listed in Table 11.2. In addition, the Kolmogorov–Smirnov and Diebold–Mariano statistical tests were applied in specific contexts.

Given the large number of studies, not all authors agree on the relative performance of neural networks and baseline models. However, in most cases, the neural network was able to outperform the baseline model, most often Black–Scholes, and this is not surprising given that a pure Black–Scholes model fails to capture smiles and

TABLE 11.2 Performance Metrics and Their Definitions (After Ruf and Wang (2019))

Metric (Acronym)	Equation
Mean error (ME)	$\frac{1}{n}\sum_{i=1}^{n}(y_i - \hat{y}_i)$
Mean absolute error (MAE)	$\frac{1}{n}\sum_{i=1}^{n}\lvert y_i - \hat{y}_i\rvert$
Mean absolute percentage error (MAPE)	$\frac{1}{n}\sum_{i=1}^{n}\left\lvert\frac{y_i-\hat{y}_i}{y_i}\right\rvert$
Mean squared error (MSE)	$\frac{1}{n}\sum_{i=1}^{n}(y_i - \hat{y}_i)^2$
Coefficient of determination (R^2)	$1 - \frac{\sum_{i=1}^{n}(y_i-\hat{y}_i)^2}{\sum_{i=1}^{n}(y_i-\bar{y})^2}$
Mean tracking error (MTE)	$\frac{1}{N}\sum e^{-rT_i}V(T_i)$
Mean absolute tracking error (MATE)	$\frac{1}{N}\sum e^{-rT_i}\lvert V(T_i)\rvert$
Median absolute error (MdAE)	$\sup_z\left\{\frac{1}{N}\sum \mathbf{1}_{\lvert\hat{y}_i-y_i\rvert<z} \leq 0.5\right\}$
Max error	$\max_i \lvert y_i - \hat{y}_i\rvert$
Percentage error	$\frac{y_i-\hat{y}_i}{y_i}$
Prediction error	$\sqrt{\mathrm{MTE}^2 + \frac{1}{N}\sum\left(e^{-rT_i}V(T_i) - \mathrm{MTE}\right)^2}$

skew. The result does demonstrate the potential utility of neural networks for pricing. However, it is notable that, despite many studies, neural networks have yet to be widely adopted. The market continues to use implied volatility surfaces with Black–Scholes to quote and risk-manage European options.

EXAMPLE 11.1: OPTION PRICING USING A NEURAL NETWORK TRAINED ON HISTORICAL DATA

This example leverages historical option prices to train a neural network model. Firstly, the data is obtained and prepared for use in training. The architecture of the network is determined after using a hyperparameter search with a model trained using Black–Scholes inputs, including the implied volatility. Various experiments are conducted, and their results are evaluated using the performance metrics listed in Table 11.2. The first three models are trained, replacing implied with historical volatility. The 'homogeneity hint' is also considered, using the strike/spot ratio instead of separate strike and spot inputs. Later, two models with additional inputs are explored: one incorporates open interest and the other focuses on the Greeks as inputs. Concluding the example, a model is introduced to outline the strike-dependent volatility surface.

Data Preparation

The Jupyter Notebook `DerivativePricingNonParamDataPrep.ipynb` contains the steps needed for data preparation. The culmination of this process is a structured Pandas data frame, subsequently saved as a CSV file, laying the foundation for the ensuing experiments. The steps in the process are outlined below.

1. **Data Source.** The Option Data website (https://optiondata.org/) provides complimentary option price data spanning from January to June 2013 for the US market. While this is not lengthy, the data covers many underlyings, strikes and maturities. For this example, the focus is on S&P 500 European options, and even for this period, there are some 370,000 option prices available, which is more than sufficient for this example.
2. **Data Filtering.** Given the exclusive focus on S&P 500, any extraneous data is discarded.

3. **Date Handling.** Dates in the dataset transform Pandas date–time objects from a string representation. The maturity of the options in years is deduced from the option quote and expiry dates.
4. **Interest Rate Data.** Absent interest rate data in the dataset necessitates sourcing of historical zero rates from the Federal Reserve Economic Data (FRED) database (https://fred.stlouisfed.org). Direct downloading from the FRED website yielded four distinct time series for 1, 2, 3 and 5-year zero rates:
   - https://fred.stlouisfed.org/series/THREEFY1
   - https://fred.stlouisfed.org/series/THREEFY2
   - https://fred.stlouisfed.org/series/THREEFY3
   - https://fred.stlouisfed.org/series/THREEFY5

   The data is presented in percentages and hence needs to be divided by 100 for a rate. FRED is also accessible via several Python packages, which can be used instead of downloading the data from the website in CSV form. Once the data for the four series has been obtained, the CSVs are loaded and merged into a single data frame.
5. **Interest Rate Interpolation.** The zero rate for each option is needed, and this is obtained by linearly interpolating the rates data frame for each row in the table on option maturity for the given quote date. The code appends a new column called 'rate' to the option data frame.
6. **S&P 500 Historical Data.** Though the S&P 500 closing prices are available with the option data, the role of historical volatility in subsequent experiments demands more data. The `yfinance` Python package retrieves the data from Yahoo Finance, starting 90 business days before the option data starts. This retrieval process enables the calculation of rolling historical volatility for 60, 40 and 20-day intervals using log returns. The calculated values are then added to the data frame for further analysis.
7. **Data Merging.** The SPX closing prices and historical volatility values are merged with the core option data frame.
8. **Bid and Ask Sizes.** Bid and ask size columns are not used and are NaN, so these columns are dropped.
9. **Black–Scholes Calculation.** It is worth noting that while the option implied volatility is provided for each row, the actual Black–Scholes value is not. This value is crucial for the hyperparameter optimisation step, indicating data quality issues. The standard model inputs, including the implied volatility, calculate the Black–Scholes price for each price. The `black_scholes` function, which wraps the Python version of the `QuantLib` library, is available in the `DerivModel.py` file.
10. **Price Averaging.** The bid and ask prices in the option pricing data are averaged to deduce the mid-price.
11. **Data Cleaning.** It is apparent that there are several rows where the mid-price is erroneous, and hence data cleaning is needed. So, for example, we see options with zero bid and ask prices and other rows where there is a substantial difference between the 'mid' price and the Black–Scholes value. All rows where this difference exceeded 100.0 in absolute terms were discarded; this does not entirely deal with problem data but reduces it significantly.
12. **Data Storage.** After processing and refinement, the final data frame is saved to CSV.

Model Architecture

For all the models, a single architecture was used, with the only change being the number of inputs and, hence, the size of the input layer. A small hyperparameter search was conducted in the Jupyter Notebook `DerivativePricingNonParamBS.ipynb` to obtain the optimal architecture. This notebook trained models using the standard Black–Scholes inputs: type, strike, implied volatility, maturity, rate and underlying, with Black–Scholes value as the target. Ten epochs only were used as this is sufficient to determine the best-performing model and a fixed learning rate of 0.001. A grid search was conducted to select the number of layers and their width by testing widths 64, 256, 1024 and 4096 and depths 1, 3, 5, 7 and 9. A model with

(Continued)

(Continued)

five layers and 4096 neurons in each layer, which had the lowest MSE, was selected. The feedforward model is provided as a class in the file `DerivModel.py` and allows use of a variable number of layers with variable width. The dataset was split into train, test and validation sets at a ratio of 8 : 1 : 1, with the performance evaluated using the validation set.

The intermediate layers use the 'swish' activation function described in Section 2.3.11. Note that the output layer for all the experiments was linear, which technically can give negative values for options, but this was not found to be a severe issue in practice.

Model Evaluation

To evaluate the models from the experiments, a selection of the metrics given in Table 11.2 were used: ME, MAE, MSE, R^2, MAE and max error. These were all implemented using PyTorch tensor operations and can be found in the two Python functions `compute_metrics` and `evaluate_metrics` in the supplied file `DerivMetrics.py`. The latter function also returns PyTorch tensors containing all the model results and all the targets, which facilitates the generation of scatter plots for result versus target.

Historical Volatility

What is desired here is a model that takes a series of market inputs and accurately predicts the target option 'mid' price. Five Black–Scholes inputs were used for all experiments: option type, strike price, time to maturity, risk-free interest rate and underlying asset price. Some volatility information is needed and hence, three models were trained using the 20, 40 and 60-day historical volatility, respectively, calculated using the previous n days as described above. All three models were trained through 50 epochs and evaluated, with the results shown in Table 11.3 below. The dataset was split into training and test sets in an 8 : 2 ratio. The same input data was also fed into the Black–Scholes formula to give a comparison value using the parametric model and then evaluated, with the results presented in the same table. Figure 11.1 visualises the results using scatter plots of model versus target for each point in the test set for each of the three neural network models in the left column and the corresponding Black–Scholes results in the right column. The scatter plots for each Black–Scholes model result show a wide dispersion, consistent with the lack of volatility skew and smile. All three neural network models show much less dispersion than the Black–Scholes result, with the 20-day historical case showing less than the 40 or 60-day cases.

TABLE 11.3 Performance Metrics for the Neural Network Models and the Black–Scholes Model Comparisons for Historical Volatilities

Model	ME	MAE	MSE	R^2	MAE	Max Error
20-day Hist. Vol. NN	**0.4345**	**0.7098**	**3.1176**	**0.9999**	**0.3274**	138.8226
20-day Hist. Vol. BS	-6.3077	7.5103	290.7418	0.9872	1.8303	165.7564
40-day Hist. Vol. NN	2.3106	2.5492	21.1135	0.9991	0.9316	155.7556
40-day Hist. Vol. BS	-6.5371	7.0751	266.1732	0.9890	1.5872	160.5229
60-day Hist. Vol. NN	-0.7677	1.9614	12.9560	0.9994	1.0383	153.2595
60-day Hist. Vol. BS	-6.4487	7.0440	260.7632	0.9889	1.6219	158.0498
Homogeneity hint	-0.7696	1.5402	10.2626	0.9996	0.6124	155.7917
Open interest	-2.0723	2.2785	15.6942	0.9993	1.0162	**123.7621**
Greeks	3.8669	4.1381	71.0634	0.9970	0.9596	136.9753

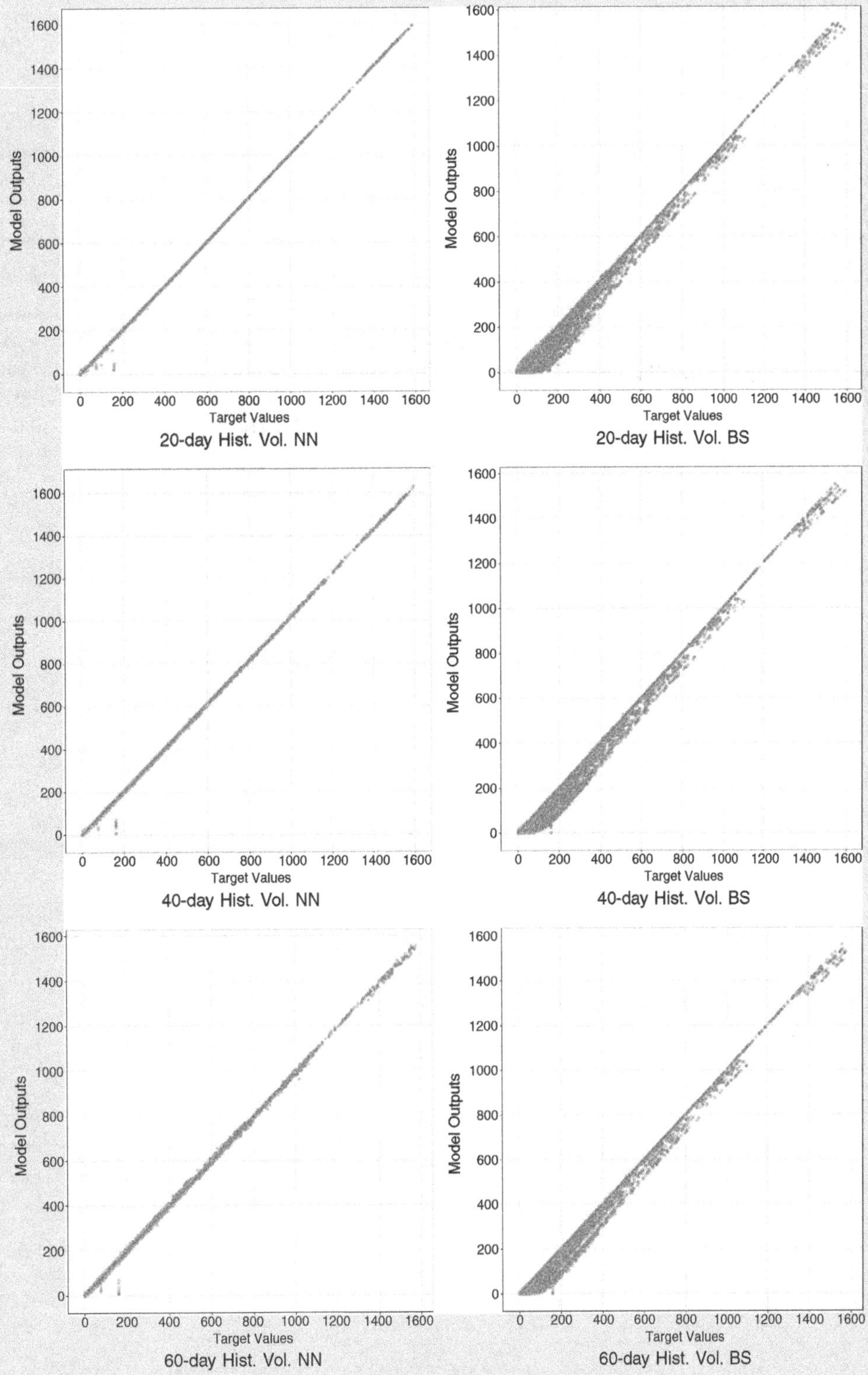

FIGURE 11.1 Scatter plots for model vs target prices with historical volatility.

(Continued)

(Continued)

Homogeneity Hint, Open Interest and Greeks

Three additional models were trained to determine if alternative inputs would be beneficial. The models included one with the homogeneity hint (`DerivativePricingNonParamHomogenity.ipynb`), another with open interest (`DerivativePricingNonParamBSHistExtraIn.ipynb`) and a third with the reported option Greeks (`DerivativePricingNonParamBSHistGreeks.ipynb`).

The homogeneity hint was first used by Hutchinson et al. (1994) and takes advantage of the fact that the Black–Scholes formula can be re-written in terms of the moneyness $\frac{S}{K}$ rather than using stock price S and K as distinct inputs. Of course, there is no guarantee that the market has the same assumption. This neural network model reduced the number of inputs to five and included moneyness instead of underlying and strike. The open interest model adds open interest as an additional input and retains separate stock price and strike inputs. The last model includes the input dataset's four supplied 'Greeks': delta, gamma, theta and vega. Hence, this model has 10 inputs in total. Figure 11.2 illustrates the scatter plots for the three models. Visually, all display more scatter than the 20-day historical volatility model.

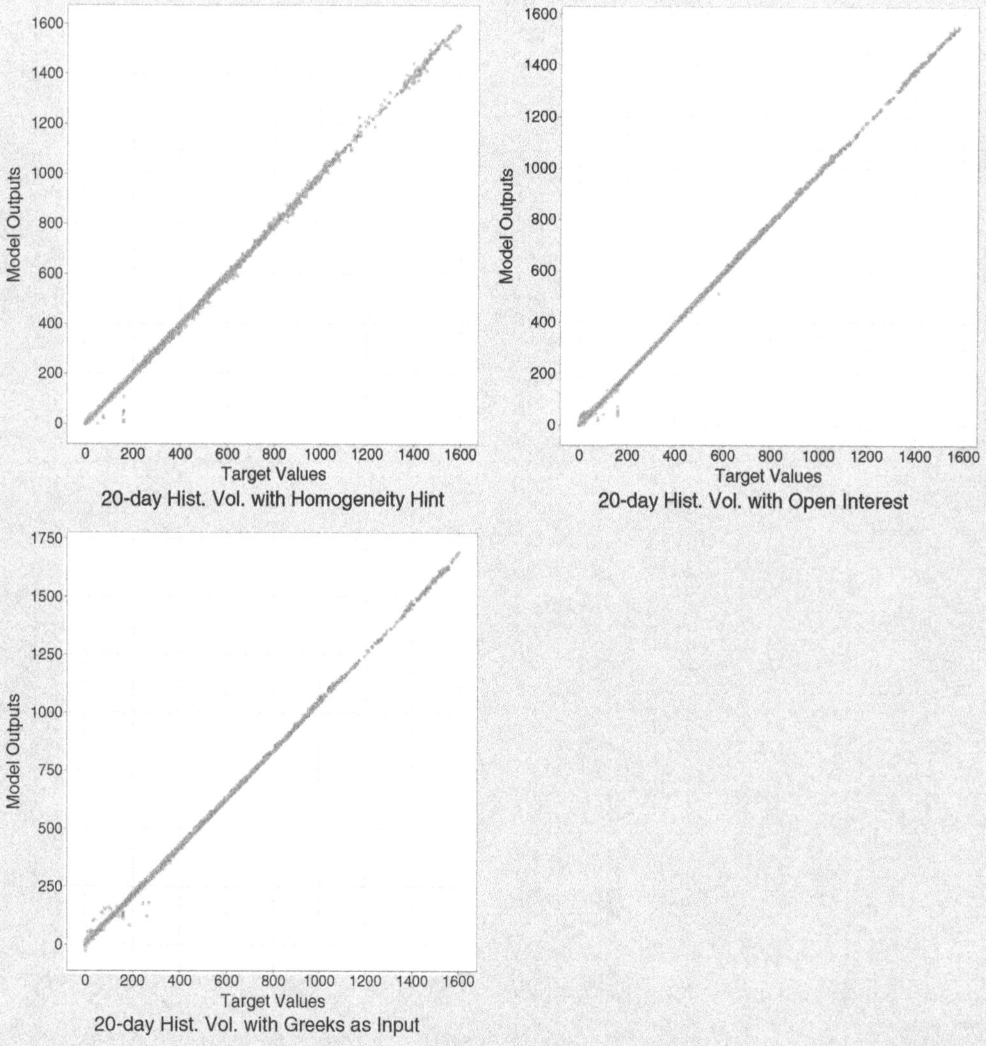

FIGURE 11.2 Scatter plots for model vs target prices for homogeneity hint, open interest as input and Greeks as inputs.

Analysis

The final results from the six neural network models are the Black–Scholes model with the three different historical volatility measures as illustrated in Table 11.3, with the best-performing model in each category shown in bold. As might be expected, the parametric Black–Scholes models all perform relatively badly. The 20-day historical volatility neural network performs best in all categories, barring max error. The homogeneity hint case is worse than using separate stock and strike inputs, which differs from many previous results. However, it remains better than the results obtained from the 40 and 60-day historical volatility models. The two models with extra inputs, the 'open interest' and 'Greeks' models, outperform the 20-day historical volatility model on max error, suggesting there is valuable information from these extra inputs even if it does not lower the dispersion in results.

Implying the Volatility Surface

As a final step, the Jupyter Notebook `DerivativePricingNonParamBSHist-ImplVol.ipynb` trains a new model with the same inputs as the 20-day historical model above. However, it is then used to infer the implied volatility surface. The neural network model price is extracted on a grid of strikes ranging from 1000 to 2000 in steps of 100 and maturities from 3 months to 3 years in steps of 3 months. This historical volatility is fixed at 10%, the rate at 10 basis points and the spot at 1500. Once the prices have been obtained, these are inverted using the Python `implied_volatility` function provided in the workbook, and this calculates the implied volatility using Newton–Raphson iteration. Figure 11.3 illustrates the resulting volatility surface.

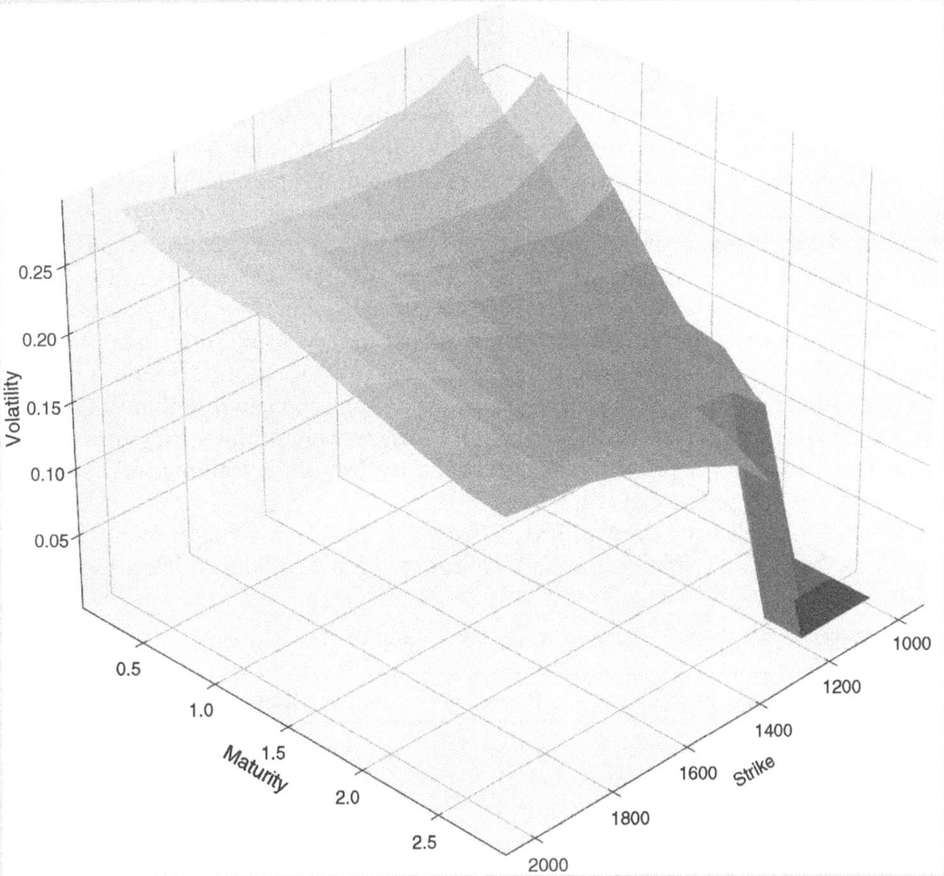

FIGURE 11.3 Volatility surface implied from the trained neural network. *Source*: MartinThoma / Wikimedia / CC BY 1.0.

11.3 DERIVATIVE VALUATION FUNCTION APPROXIMATION

The function approximation theorems detailed in Section 2.4 establish the credentials for neural network replication functions, including parametric derivative pricing models. These theorems emphasise the potential of neural networks in capturing such functions. It is no surprise to find early attempts, like the one by Hutchinson et al. (1994), to emulate the parametric Black–Scholes model using neural network structures.

The detailed review by Ruf and Wang (2019) catalogues several works centred on training neural networks with simulated data. Some of the significant papers in this context include those by Hanke (1997), Garcia and Gençay (1998), White (1998), Tsaih (1999), Galindo-Flores (2000), White (2000), le Roux and du Toit (2001), Montagna et al. (2003), Charalambous and Martzoukos (2005) and Lai (2014). A commonality in these studies is their usage of simulated data based on the Black–Scholes model, mainly to set a benchmark. The principal objective was to affirm the capability of the neural network to replicate known functions before moving on to train a model using market data directly.

However, it is worth noting that in the absence of advanced GPU computational resources, the practicality of substituting parametric functions with neural networks becomes debatable. Training efficiency diminishes in environments with limited parallelism. Parallel inference is limited or not available. Hence, the neural network's performance might be comparable to, or perhaps less efficient than, the function it seeks to mirror.

The revival of deep learning in option pricing was signalled by the work of Culkin and Das (2017), who revisited the foundational research conducted by Hutchinson et al. (1994). Culkin and Das (2017) made a persuasive argument for using deep learning by training a neural network consisting of four layers with 100 neurons each, using a dataset of 240,000 option prices. While this approach might seem modest relative to current standards, it nonetheless represented a significant improvement over 1994 capabilities. The research showcased that achieving high levels of accuracy was possible, leading to the suggestion of non-parametric models.

Following this, Ferguson and Green (2018) trained a neural network to replicate a moderately dimensional option, precisely a basket option, as discussed in Example 3.2. This study dealt with a worst-of-call option on six stocks and included 28 input features, a notable increase from the five or six features used in the Black–Scholes model. The goal was not to promote non-parametric models, often unfeasible for over-the-counter (OTC) exotic options due to limited data, but to showcase the possibility of function replication. The option was priced using a Monte Carlo simulation to achieve faster and parallel inference. Ferguson and Green (2018) highlighted the efficacy and accuracy of the model and explained the process of generating a synthetic market dataset for training, which contained millions of examples and was significantly larger than those used by other authors.

Hirsa et al. (2019) further investigated the use of deep learning to replicate various option pricing models. The study focused on European, barrier and American option pricing models using four underlying models: geometric Brownian motion; Heston; variance gamma; and variance gamma with stochastic arrival, as detailed in Table 11.4. The authors evaluated different optimisers and network configurations, concluding that the Adam optimiser and a network setup with four layers and leaky ReLU activation function were optimal for European options modelled with geometric Brownian motion. The research also assessed the effect of the training set's size and emphasised the inference's accuracy and low computational cost.

Liu et al. (2019b) advocated using deep neural networks to enable swift inference. The study explored the Black–Scholes equation, the COS (Fourier-cosine) method for the Heston model and Brent's root finder for implied

TABLE 11.4 Model Choice and Implementation in Hirsa et al. (2019)

Model	European	Barrier	American
GBM	Closed form	Closed form	Ju–Zhong approximation
VG	FFT	–	–
Heston	FFT	Monte Carlo	–
VGSA	FFT	Monte Carlo	–

volatilities (Fang and Oosterlee, 2009). A broad range of hyperparameters were examined, with the authors concluding that models capable of function approximation could be trained with accuracy, highlighting a substantial performance gain facilitated by GPUs.

Nonetheless, while neural networks have performed well within the training range, their extrapolation ability must be reviewed. Given that the range of input values can extend significantly, careful consideration of extrapolation is essential. It might not always be practical or desirable to train a neural network across a broad spectrum of input values, especially if it affects the accuracy within a more typical parameter range. To address this issue, Antonov et al. (2020) and Funahashi (2023) have introduced methods designed to manage the extrapolation behaviour of neural networks.

The remainder of this section covers two key areas. Firstly, it explores Ferguson and Green (2018), which focuses on training a neural network to replicate the pricing of a basket option. Secondly, it discusses approaches to controlling the asymptotic behaviour of deep neural networks used to replicate derivative valuation models.

11.3.1 Deeply Learning Derivatives

As noted above, Ferguson and Green (2018) was the first paper to train a neural network to replicate a multi-asset option. This section explores the example presented in Ferguson and Green (2018) in more detail.

11.3.1.1 Motivations Ferguson and Green (2018) present four key motivations stemming from several key attributes of deep neural networks (DNNs):

1. The universal approximation theorem posits that simple feedforward networks can approximate a diverse range of functions, provided certain conditions are met for the activation function (as indicated by Cybenko, 1989 and Hornik, 1991; discussed in Section 2.4).
2. DNNs are resilient against the curse of dimensionality and are scalable to valuation models with many input parameters.
3. DNNs decouple accuracy from computational cost; initial time spent in training leads to quicker and more efficient valuations later on.
4. DNNs are versatile and can replicate a diverse array of traditional models, ranging from those employing Monte Carlo simulation to finite differences and binomial trees.

11.3.1.2 Contributions Ferguson and Green (2018) make five key contributions:

1. The paper demonstrates the application of DNN models in approximating derivative valuation routines and, hence, a concrete example of a financial application.
2. The paper formulates a training methodology specific to neural network models used to approximate risk-neutral pricing models. This approach generates the training and test sets using Monte Carlo simulation and does not rely on historical market data.
3. The paper showcases the accuracy of the neural network approximation. The final neural network model exhibits lower error than the random error intrinsic to the Monte Carlo models used for training, and this suggests that the neural network can learn to filter out the random noise associated with Monte Carlo simulations.
4. The paper describes a hyperparameter search and demonstrates the effect of selecting different numbers of layers and layer width.
5. An assessment of computational performance is provided, with particular emphasis on utilising both CPU and GPU parallelism during the generation of training sets and neural network model training.

11.3.1.3 Basket Option Example Ferguson and Green (2018) use a European call option on a worst-of basket consisting of six underlying assets, which can be expressed as

$$V = \max\left(0, \min(S_1, S_2, S_3, S_4, S_5, S_6) - K\right). \tag{11.1}$$

This option type is typically valued using a Monte Carlo simulation. The choice of this example is motivated by four factors:

1. The function's dimensionality is moderate, resulting in an input space dimensionality given by $21n(n + 3) + 1$. For six underlying stocks, this yields a 28-dimensional input space.
2. Employing Monte Carlo simulation allows the exploration of deep learning in conjunction with a computationally demanding valuation procedure.
3. The problem's dimensionality can be conveniently increased by incorporating additional stocks into the basket.
4. Using a numerical technique such as Monte Carlo introduces numerical noise into the function that the model aims to approximate.

The interest rate and dividend yields are assumed to be zero, and the volatility input for each stock is assumed to be flat to simplify the example. The basket strike was fixed, and individual stock prices varied, equivalent to the 'homogeneity hint' frequently used in the single-asset case.

11.3.1.4 Training Set Generation The training set used by Ferguson and Green (2018) is generated by Monte Carlo simulation, with each input apart from the correlation matrix generated independently. The correlation matrix is generated using a variation on the Vines method, which is discussed in more detail in Section 18.4.2.1. The distributions are summarised in Table 11.5. The authors also generated three training sets with different numbers of Monte Carlo paths used in the underlying model, illustrated in Table 11.6.

Two different distributions tested the impact of the parameters in the input model distribution, A and B, as described in Table 11.7. Further, to keep the training set generation manageable in terms of computational cost, three separate training sets were generated for each distribution set, all with one million examples and using three choices of Monte Carlo path counts for the underlying QuantLib model: 1000; 10,000; and 100,000. A Jupyter Notebook, `BasketDataGeneration.ipynb`, is provided, which generates the dataset using a set of functions in the Python file `BasketDataGen.py`. A 12-core AMD threadripper with hyperthreading was used to generate the data, running 20 threads. Figure 11.4 illustrates the empirical distributions of the different inputs for datasets A and B.

TABLE 11.5 Model Input Distributions in the Training Set as Used by Ferguson and Green (2018)

Model Input	Distribution
Stock price	$100 \times \text{lognormal}(0.5, 0.25)$
Stock vols	$U(0, 1)$
Maturity (days)	x^2 where $x \sim U(1, 43)$
Correlation	$2(\beta(5, 2) - 0.5)$

TABLE 11.6 Model Input Distributions in the Training Set as Used by Ferguson and Green (2018)

Training Set	Size	Monte Carlo Paths
A	5,000,000	1,000,000
B	50,000,000	100,000
C	500,000,000	10,000

TABLE 11.7 Model Input Distributions A and B in the Training Set Used Here

Model Input	Distribution A	Distribution B
Stock price	$100 \times \text{lognormal}(0.5, 0.2)$	$100 \times \text{lognormal}(0.0, 0.4)$
Stock vols	$U(0, 1)$	$U(0, 1.5)$
Maturity (days)	x^2 where $x \sim U(1, 43)$	x^2 where $x \sim U(1, 43)$
Correlation	$2(\beta(5, 2) - 0.5)$	$2(\beta(5, 2) - 0.5)$

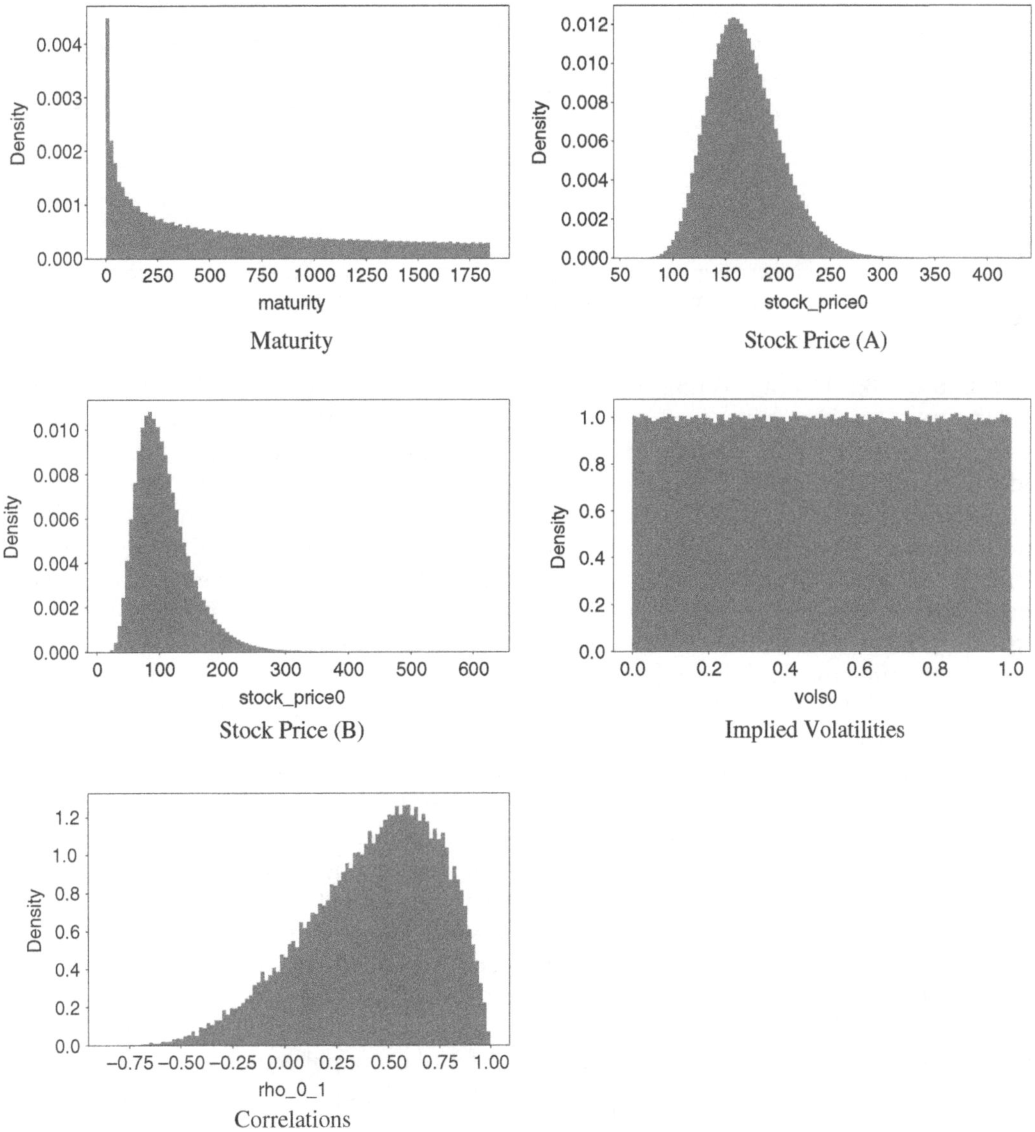

FIGURE 11.4 The empirical distributions for training sets A and B for the option maturity, stock price, implied volatility and correlations.

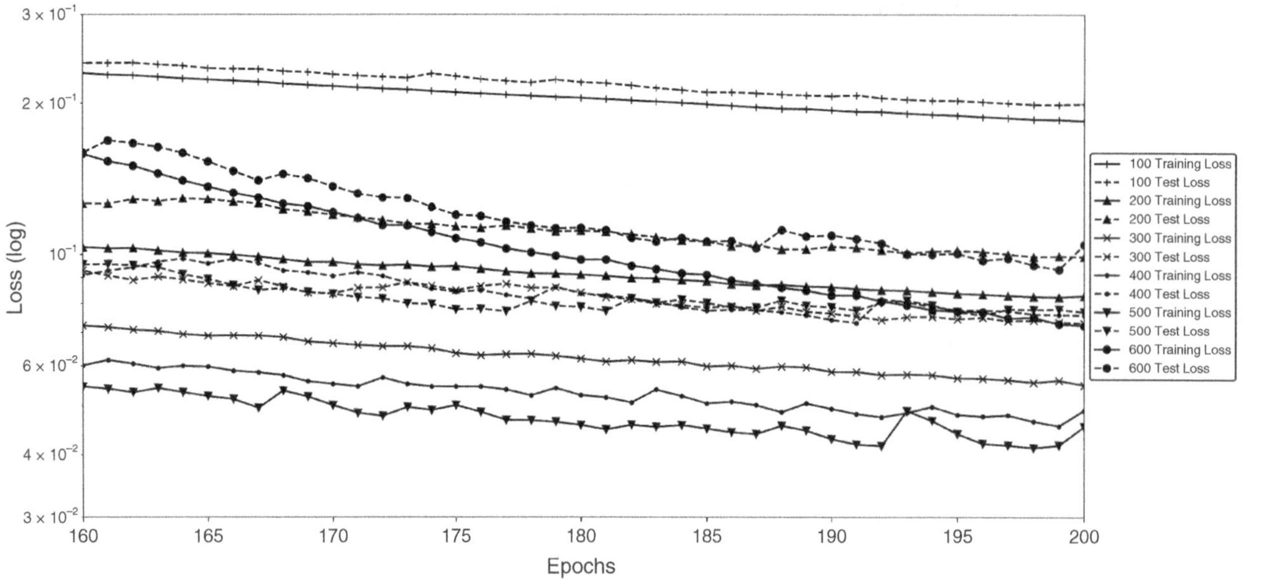

FIGURE 11.5 Width search for the basket option model – zoomed-in section for the last 40 training epochs. Note that the loss is presented on a log scale. *Source*: Qwertyus / Wikimedia / CC BY 1.0.

11.3.1.5 Hyperparameter Optimisation Ferguson and Green (2018) performed several studies to explore the best architecture. Here, two experiments are performed, first to identify the optimal width using a linear search of layer widths for a fixed network depth of six hidden layers and second to identify the optimal network depth using the previously identified width. Ferguson and Green (2018) used ReLU activation, but here, swish is used instead, with a linear output. The optimiser choice is Adam, with default parameters and a learning rate of 0.001. Dataset A was split into training and test sets, and of the one million samples, 1% were retained in the test set. The underlying option price with 100,000 Monte Carlo samples was used for training. For both experiments, the models were trained through 200 epochs.

The network width search used six widths for a fixed depth of six layers: 100, 200, 300, 400, 500 and 600. Figure 11.5 shows the smoothed training and test loss for each model evaluated as a function of epoch. The losses were smoothed for clarity. The 100-width network shows much worse test and training loss than the other models, suggesting that this model does not have sufficient representational capacity. The test loss for the network with a width of 200 also lies above the other networks aside from that with a width of 600 and again suggests a lack of network capacity. The test losses for networks with widths 300, 400 and 500 lie close together on the chart, suggesting that all these networks have saturated network capacity. The training losses of each model lie below the corresponding test loss, suggesting some degree of overtraining – the model with a width of 600 performed poorly for both test and training loss. A width of 300 was selected as the optimal choice. The network width search can be found in the Jupyter Notebook `BasketOptionWidthSearch.ipynb`.

Figure 11.6 shows the training and test losses for a depth search with 2, 4, 6, 8 and 10 hidden layers, each of 300 neurons width. The best test loss is obtained from the network with a depth of four layers, although the training loss lies below this line, suggesting there may be some overtraining. The worst-performing model had 10 layers, showing clear evidence of overtraining in this case. A four-layer architecture with 300 neurons was selected for subsequent experiments based on depth search in `BasketOptionDepthSearch.ipynb`.

11.3.1.6 Independent Test Dataset A further dataset was generated for testing purposes, and this only contains 1000 example points generated using the distributions used for dataset A. However, the Monte Carlo simulation used 10 million samples in the underlying basket option model from QuantLib. The option value is assumed to have converged fully for this example. Hence, this is used as the basis for independent evaluation of the accuracy of neural network models and evaluations of the underlying model with lower sample counts. This dataset is generated by the Jupyter Notebook `BasketDataGeneration_Accuracy.ipynb`.

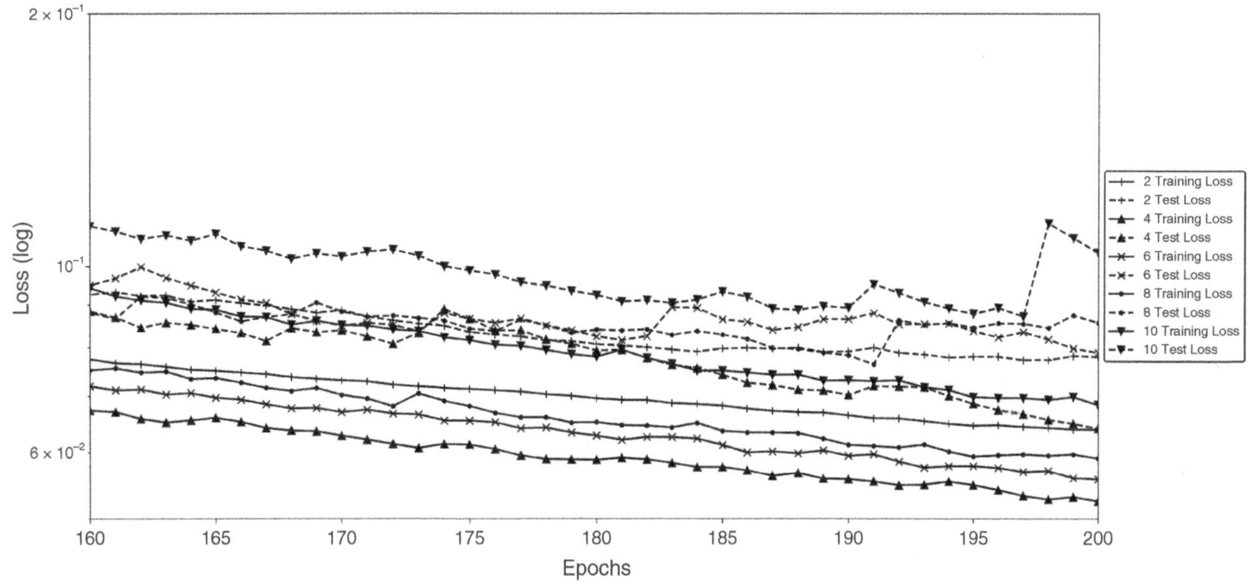

FIGURE 11.6 Network depth search for the basket option model – zoomed-in section for the last 40 training epochs. Note that the loss is presented on a log scale.

11.3.1.7 Training-Set Impact Two models were trained using the selected architecture with datasets A and B, respectively, to assess the impact of training sets on model accuracy.[1] Both models were trained using the same hyperparameters established earlier and again trained through 200 epochs. After training, the models were evaluated on the independent test dataset, and the results are given in Table 11.8. Scatter plots of the model value versus the high-quality option value for models trained on datasets A and B are illustrated in Figure 11.7. The MSE for dataset B is significantly worse than that for model A, and the scatter plot for model B shows significant dispersion away from a straight line, implying both random error and bias; this suggests that care must be taken when sampling the marginal distribution in the generation of the training set.

11.3.1.8 Monte Carlo Noise Impact A series of models were created to evaluate the effect of Monte Carlo noise on the accuracy of the trained neural network.[2] The models were trained on datasets with the same inputs but varying numbers of Monte Carlo sample paths used in the QuantLib model. The aim was to assess how the number of sample paths affects the ultimate accuracy of the network. Three different sample sizes were used – 1000, 10,000 and 100,000 paths – and all models were trained through 200 epochs as with earlier models. The accuracy of the trained neural networks and the underlying models were assessed using the independent test dataset described above.

An error analysis was conducted on each point of the independent test set to evaluate the precision of the neural networks and Monte Carlo compared to the baseline. The results of this analysis were then presented on a histogram, which is depicted in Figure 11.8. The left half of the figure shows the six outcomes of the neural networks, while the right half displays the corresponding Monte Carlo models. Visual examination of the plots shows that for the 100,000-path case, the original model errors are lower than those from the corresponding neural network.

TABLE 11.8 The MSE for Models A and B

Model	MSE
A	0.06130
B	9.33965

[1]See the Jupyter Notebook `BasketOptionTrainingSetImpact.ipynb`.

[2]See the Jupyter Notebook `BasketOptionMonteCarloNoise.ipynb`.

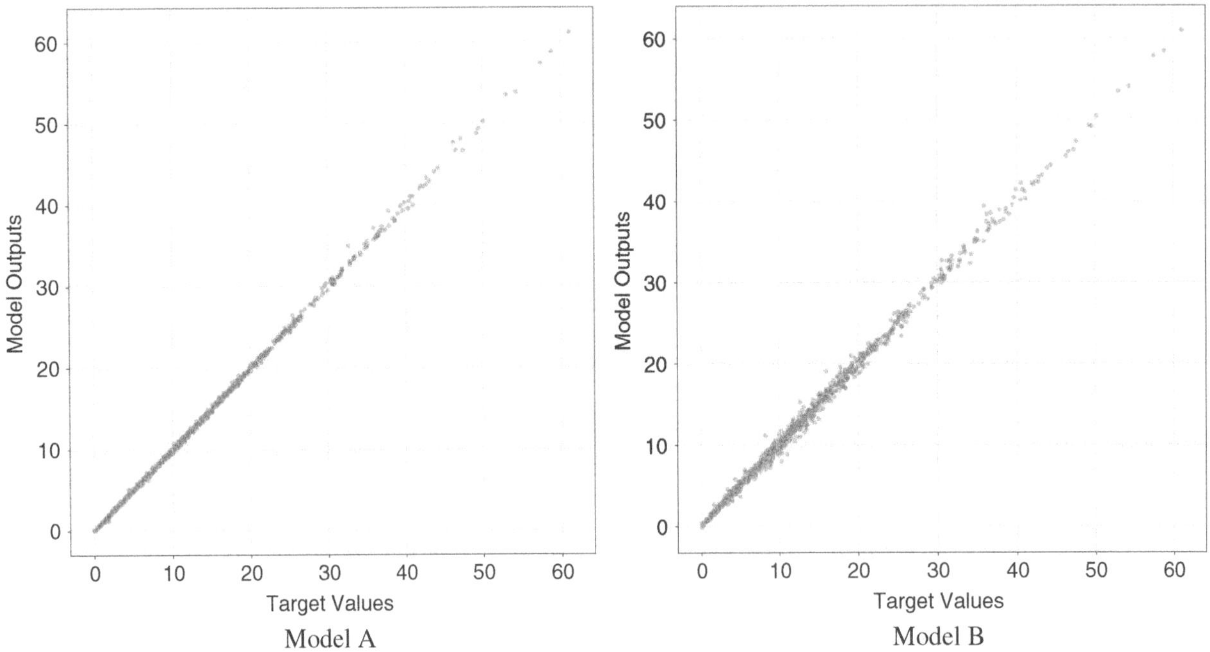

FIGURE 11.7 Scatter plot of models A and B vs the option value in the high-quality test set.

However, for the 10,000-path case, the neural network and Monte Carlo model are broadly comparable, while in the 1000-sample case, the neural network exceeds the accuracy of the underlying model. In other words, the neural network has learned to *reduce the Monte Carlo noise*.

Given that the models in Figure 11.8 were trained through 200 epochs, the impact of additional training was assessed on the 100,000 dataset. Another model was trained with the same architecture but now training through 2000 epochs. Figure 11.9 compares the accuracy obtained from this model to that of the underlying model with 100,000 samples. Compared with the 200-epoch case, it shows some improvement in accuracy, but it remains less accurate than the underlying model.

11.3.1.9 'Out-of-Sample' Model Accuracy To explore accuracy *out of sample* (i.e., outside the range where training data is either present or is of low density), the option value generated by a trained neural network was compared with that from the underlying Monte Carlo model as a function of the input parameters.[3] Given the symmetry between assets, this was performed for stock price 0, volatility 0 and correlation (0, 1). Only the specified parameter was varied, with other parameters selected to have values close to the centre of the mean of the distribution used to generate the data. Stock prices had a mean of 150 and a volatility of 50%, maturity was fixed at 1 year and all correlations were set to 40%.

Figure 11.10 shows the two model values as a function of stock price over the range 0.0 to 400.0. The model shows an excellent fit to the Monte Carlo price across the entire range, even though the training data was limited outside the range 75.0–250.0, as can be seen from Figure 11.4. Volatility was trained uniformly over the range 0% to 100%, so the accuracy was assessed over the range 0% to 300%, as illustrated in Figure 11.11. Surprisingly, the DNN and the Monte Carlo model remain reasonably closely matched across the range, despite no training data above 100% volatility. The correlation test is presented in Figure 11.12. Both DNNs and Monte Carlo show close agreement over the correlation range of –0.5 to 1.0. Below –0.5 there is poor agreement and Figure 11.4 shows a limited sampling of negative correlation points. However, the DNN shows smooth variation across the full range of correlation. At the same time, there is considerable noise in the underlying Monte Carlo model, and it is unclear how accurate it is in the range. The lack of noise suggests that the DNN has learned about Monte Carlo noise in this case, even if it is unclear from the overall error distribution.

[3]See the Jupyter Notebook `OutOfSample.ipynb`.

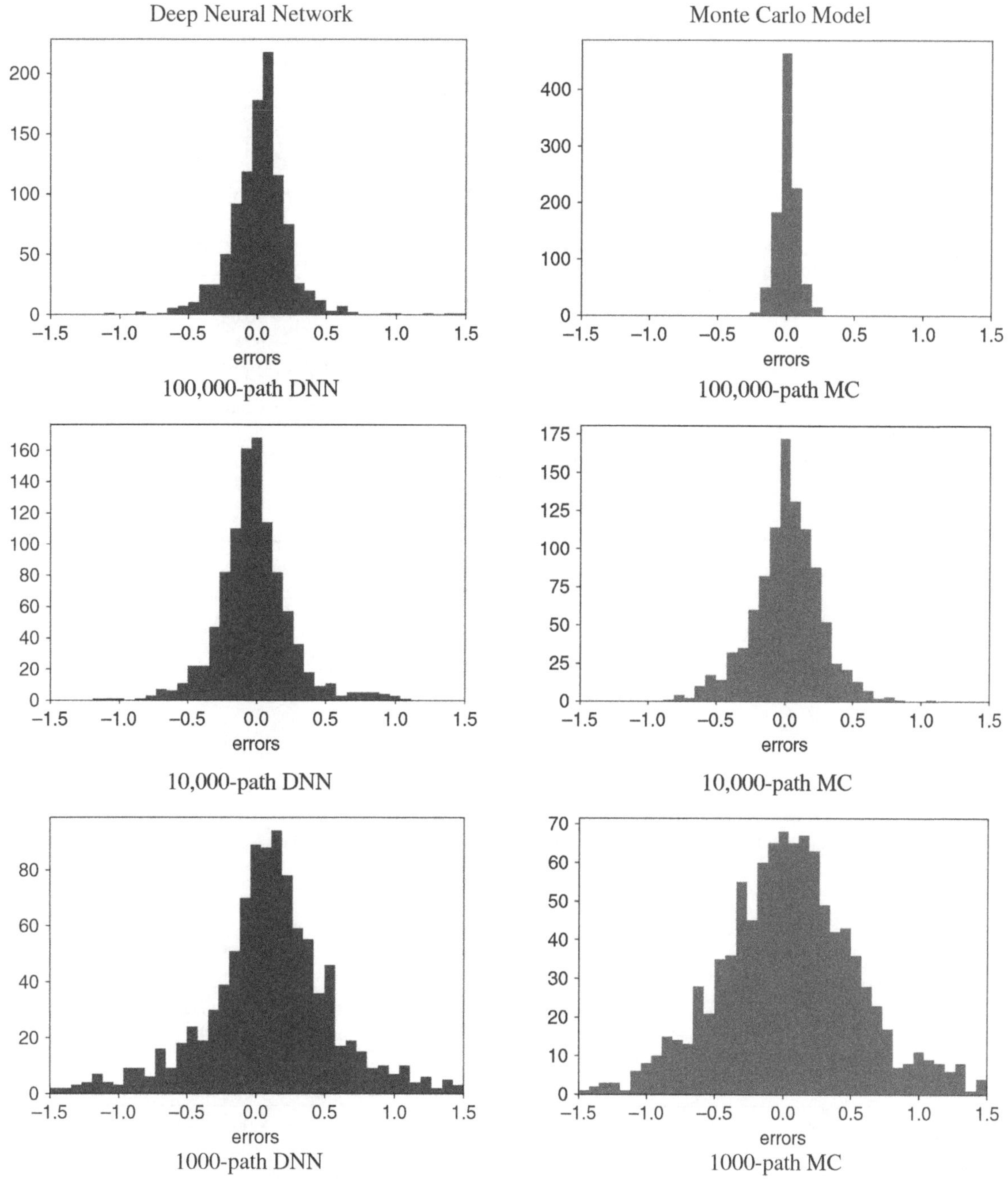

FIGURE 11.8 Error distributions for the trained deep neural networks and the underlying Monte Carlo model values used as training data. The reference value is a Monte Carlo simulation with 10 million paths.

11.3.1.10 Model Speed Table 11.9 shows the execution time for the underlying Monte Carlo model with 1000, 10,000 and 100,000 samples, and the inference time for the training DNN with a batch of 4096 examples, the equivalent inference time per example and the inference time for a batch with one example as performed on CPU (AMD 12-core threadripper) and an NVidia RTX 4090 in single precision. As expected, the Monte Carlo results show a nearly linear increase in simulation paths. Comparing the CPU and GPU results, we see that when executed as a batch, the GPU inference time is more than an order of magnitude faster than a multi-core CPU. Comparing the original model with CPU and GPU results, we see that the DNN outperforms the Monte Carlo with only 1000 paths,

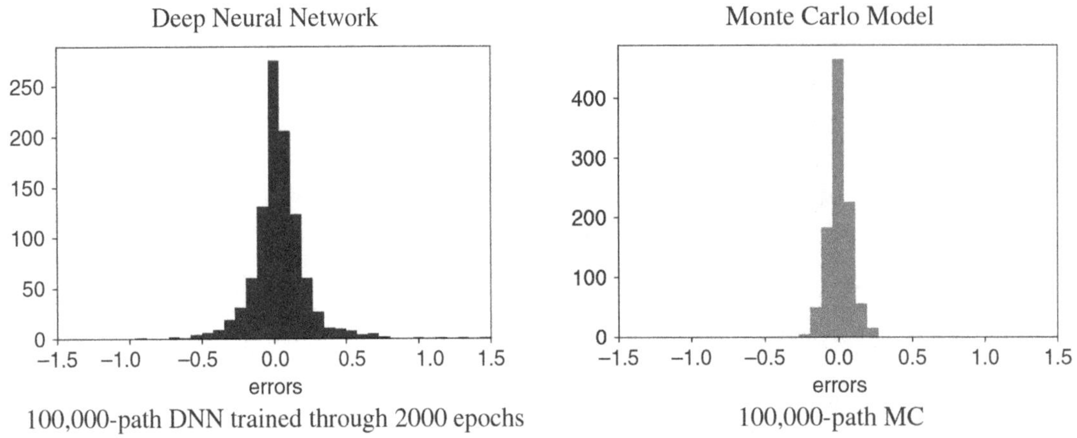

FIGURE 11.9 Error distributions for a deep neural network trained using underlying values calculated using 100,000 sample paths and trained through 2000 epochs and the underlying Monte Carlo model values used as training data. The reference value is a Monte Carlo simulation with 10 million paths.

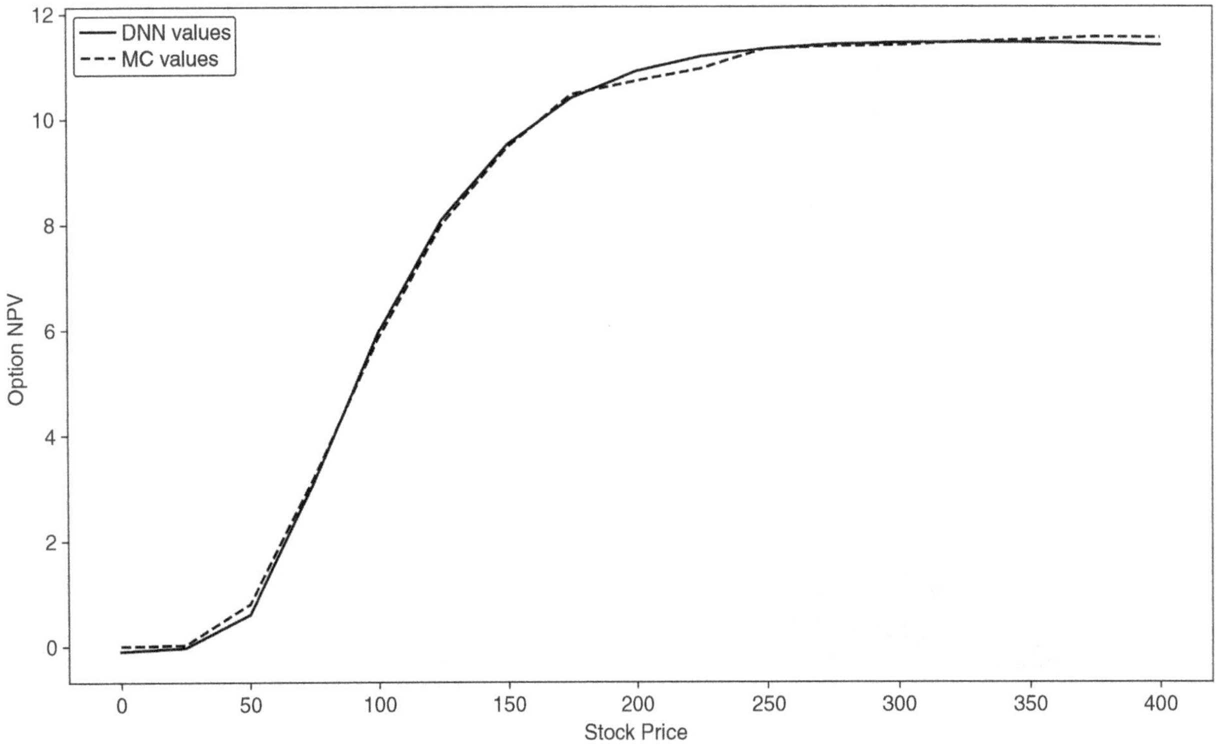

FIGURE 11.10 Deep neural network option value (100,000 dataset with 2000 epochs) vs Monte Carlo option value (100,000 samples) as a function of stock price 0.

even on a CPU with a single example. On GPU executed as a batch of 4096, the effective per-example performance is over two orders of magnitude faster than the 1000 Monte Carlo and over four orders of magnitude faster than the 100,000 Monte Carlo. In conclusion, the trained DNN model offers significant performance benefits over the underlying model, irrespective of the device used for inference. It is exceptionally performant when calculations are batched, as they would be for exposure measures or value-at-risk.

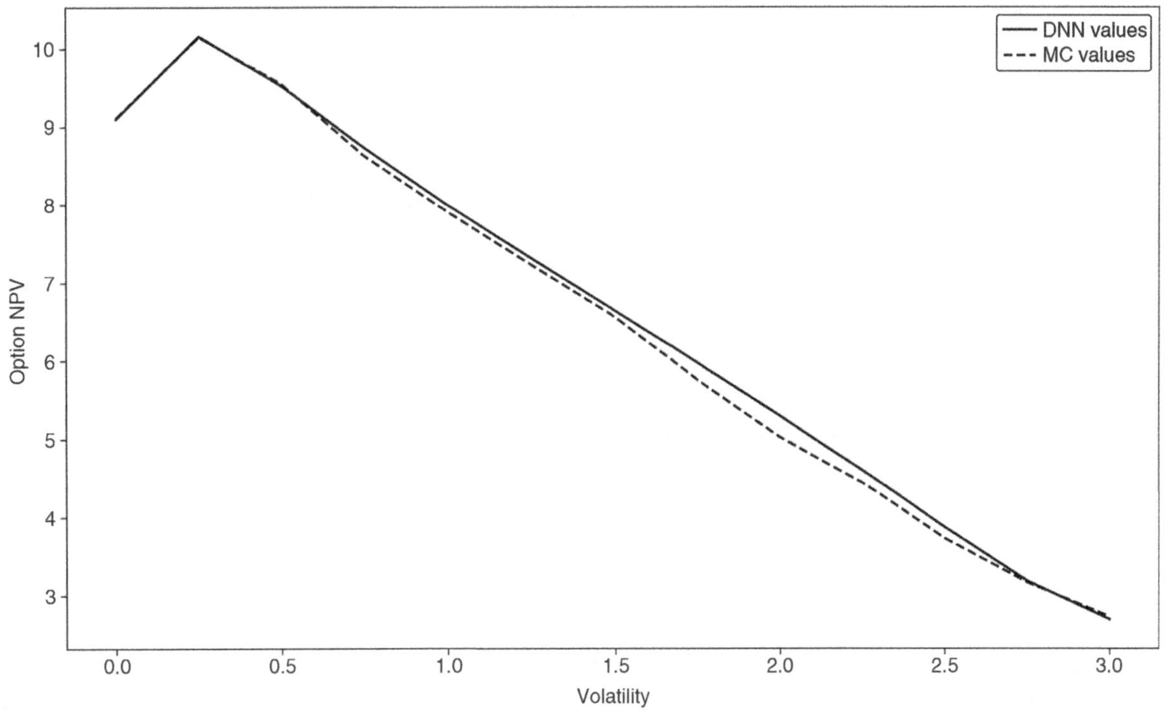

FIGURE 11.11 Deep neural network option value (100,000 dataset with 2000 epochs) vs Monte Carlo option value (100,000 samples) as a function of volatility 0.

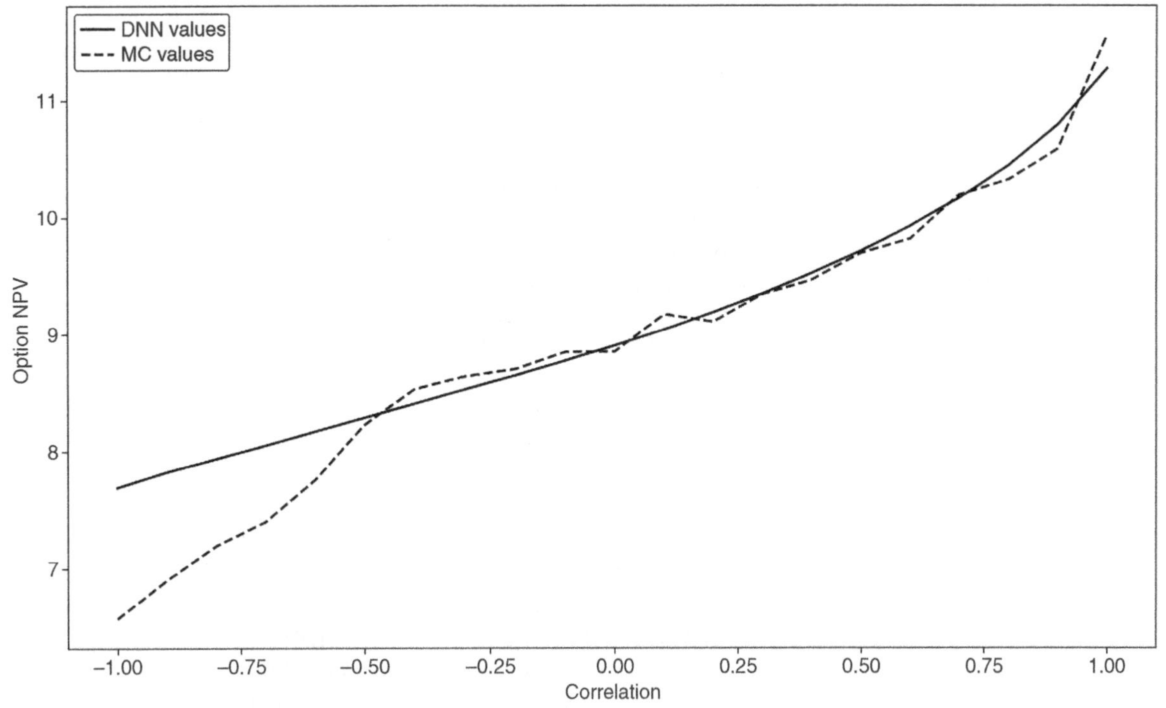

FIGURE 11.12 Deep neural network option value (100,000 dataset with 2000 epochs) vs Monte Carlo option value (100,000 samples) as a function of correlation 0.

TABLE 11.9 Evaluation Time for the Underlying Monte Carlo Model and the Trained DNN Model on CPU and GPU

Model	Time (s)
Monte Carlo 1000 samples	2.921×10^{-3}
Monte Carlo 10,000 samples	2.799×10^{-2}
Monte Carlo 100,000 samples	0.2763
DNN (CPU) batch 4096	0.5037
DNN (CPU) per example	1.230×10^{-4}
DNN (CPU) batch 1	1.247×10^{-3}
DNN (GPU) batch 4096	3.712×10^{-2}
DNN (GPU) per example	9.062×10^{-6}
DNN (GPU) batch 1	3.900×10^{-4}

11.3.2 Controlling Asymptotic Behaviour

Can the asymptotic behaviour of neural networks be controlled? As seen in Section 11.3.1.9, outside the training range, the extrapolation behaviour is not guaranteed. However, in some cases, the behaviour outside the training region is acceptable. Many derivative valuation functions have real-valued inputs, extending to positive or negative infinity. One way to approach this would be to expand the training range, potentially coupled with an appropriate functional transformation. However, this may lead to a lack of training set coverage in critical areas of the function and lead to lower accuracy overall.

Antonov et al. (2020) propose an approach to handle the asymptotic behaviour by adopting a *control variate* approach. Instead of learning the function $f(x)$ outright, a control variate function, $S(x)$, is introduced that has the same asymptotic behaviour as $f(x)$. The neural network then learns the residual function

$$R(s) = S(x) - f(x). \tag{11.2}$$

There are two critical contributions from Antonov et al. (2020): the development of a universal control variate using a multi-dimensional spline with the desired asymptotics and the design of a custom radial basis function layer to ensure that the neural network has zero asymptotic behaviour in order to blend with the control variate. Ultimately, however, this approach suffers from the curse of dimensionality. As the authors point out, splines can be slow for large numbers of nodes and dimensions, and to mitigate this issue, they use only a small number of nodes, three per dimension in four dimensions. Antonov et al. (2020) demonstrate that this works well in two and four-dimensional problems. However, it will likely remain confined to problems of modest dimension unless additional dimension reduction is used and is effective.

11.3.3 Fine-Tuning

Concerns about the accuracy of a DNN model can be addressed through fine-tuning, as the following toy example shows.[4] Returning to the basket option example, suppose the stock price data was generated using a uniform distribution over the range (0, 400.0) to address concerns about asymptotic behaviour, as this approach would put far more samples in the wings of the distribution at a cost of less in the central region.

An extensive training set of 10 million examples was generated using only 1000 Monte Carlo samples in the underlying model. Aside from the changed stock price distributions, the market data generation proceeded as described earlier. A model was trained through 200 epochs with a large but low-quality dataset. Then, as a second step, the model was fine-tuned for 50 epochs by continuing to train with the original dataset with one million examples using 100,000 Monte Carlo samples.

[4]See the Jupyter Notebook `BasketOptionAsymptotic.ipynb`.

The results are illustrated in Figure 11.13, with the left column representing the initial training phase and the right column after fine-tuning. As seen in the top row, the DNN model shows some difference in the centre of the stock price range before fine-tuning, but this disappears entirely after fine-tuning. Similarly, the scatter plots in the middle show a marked reduction in the width of the scatter after fine-tuning. Finally, the error distribution is narrowed considerably by the fine-tuning process.

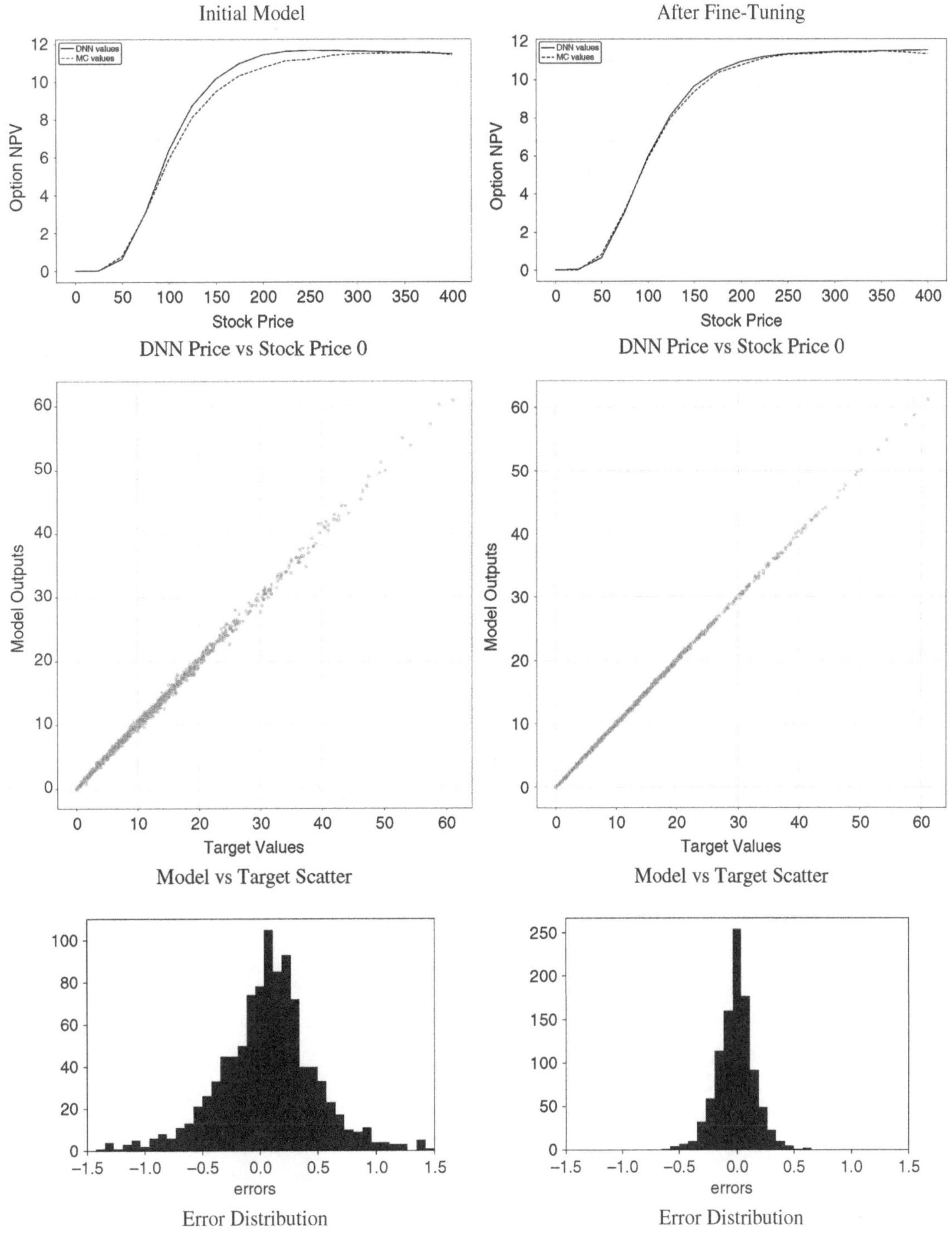

FIGURE 11.13 DNN model before and after fine-tuning.

This example shows that specific issues or regions of concern with a trained model can be addressed by additional targeted fine-tuning. Hence, concerns about overall asymptotic behaviour could be addressed using a widely dispersed training set, with fine-tuning addressing the accuracy in the centre. Similarly, if problem areas become apparent during testing, fine-tuning can be used to address them.

11.3.4 Conclusions on Derivative Valuation Function Approximation

This chapter has demonstrated the application of neural networks to approximate derivative valuation parametrically and non-parametrically. While it remains true that implied volatility coupled with the Black–Scholes model remains the approach of choice for managing vanilla options by derivative practitioners, neural networks are a valid alternative non-parametric approach. In the parametric approach, neural networks can readily be trained to replicate derivative pricing functions accurately. Hence, neural networks can provide fast inference and replace the original parametric pricing model in contexts like XVA.

CHAPTER 12

High-Dimensional PDE and BSDE Solvers

Yet across the gulf of space, minds that are to our minds as ours are to those of the beasts that perish, intellects vast and cool and unsympathetic, regarded this earth with envious eyes, and slowly and surely drew their plans against us.

H.G. Wells, The War of the Worlds (1898)

12.1 INTRODUCTION

Deep learning methods are closely identified with function approximation, but this does not mean that their only application is replicating existing functions, as illustrated in the previous chapter. As was discussed in Chapter 10, function approximation can play a role inside another algorithm; in the context of reinforcement learning, the neural networks were used to approximate the state–value function. Since 2016, several methods have been developed to solve PDEs and the closely related backward stochastic differential equations (BSDEs) utilising the function approximation of neural networks as part of the solution process, typically to approximate the solution $u(x, t)$ itself.

PDEs are found in many domains, such as physics, engineering and finance. However, why are deep PDE methods needed when suitable classical methods are available to solve PDEs numerically? The challenge is that traditional PDE solvers often use finite difference and finite element methods that use grids or meshes to discretise and solve the PDE. Unfortunately, these methods do not scale to high dimension, as was first articulated by Bellman (1961); the *curse of dimensionality*. In practice, grid-based parabolic PDE solvers cannot easily be used beyond three spatial dimensions and one of time. However, there are exceptions to this empirical rule: for example, linear parabolic PDEs can be transformed into an SDE representation via the Feynman–Kac theorem and solved by Monte Carlo methods, which do not suffer from the curse of dimensionality. However, more general non-linear PDEs cannot be transformed in this way.

Deep learning methods do not suffer from the curse of dimensionality. Following the deep learning revolution, neural networks have been used to construct various high-dimensional PDE and BSDE solvers. Amongst the most popular approaches are the *deep Galerkin method*, the d*eep BSDE* and *physics-informed neural networks*. The 'deep PDE' approach has been applied in physics, finance and elsewhere because of the scalability and flexibility presented by deep learning frameworks.

Financial applications of deep PDE and BSDE methods fall into three categories. The first is the case of high-dimensional problems such as multi-asset options. American and Bermudan options provide the second use case, and the methods are similar in many aspects to the Monte Carlo-based approaches discussed in Chapter 13. Finally, the last application applies to non-linear PDEs that arise from complex model dynamics or recursive models in XVA.

This chapter reviews deep PDE and BSDE methods as applied in finance, and foundational papers that these works rely on from 2016 to 2024. Tables 12.1–12.3 provide a summary of the works that have been included. A small number of illustrative Python examples have also been added. The chapter is organised as follows: Section 12.2 discusses the deep Galerkin method, while deep BSDEs are discussed in Section 12.3. The following Section 12.4 discusses projection and martingale solvers and Section 12.5 reviews the deep path-dependent

Deep Learning in Quantitative Finance, First Edition. Andrew Green.

PDE approach applied in rough volatility. Physics-informed neural networks are introduced in Section 12.6. Finally, deep backward dynamic programming is discussed in Section 12.7 and deep splitting in Section 12.8.

TABLE 12.1 Authors of Papers on Deep PDE and Deep BSDE Methods 2016–2018

Reference	PDE/BSDE	Method	Applications	Problem Domain
Han and Weinan (2016)			Trading costs	Finance
			Energy storage	
Han et al. (2018)	PDE	Deep BSDE	Black–Scholes with default risk	Finance
	BSDE		Hamilton–Jacobi–Bellman	Stochastic control
			Allen–Cahn equation	Physics
Sirignano and Spiliopoulos (2018)	PDE	DGM	American options	Finance
			Hamilton–Jacobi–Bellman	Stochastic control
			Burgers' equation	Fluid mechanics
Al-Aradi et al. (2018)	PDE	DGM	European call option	Finance
			American call option	
			Fokker–Plank equation	
			Stochastic optimal control	
			System risk (HJB equation)	
			Mean-field games (HJB and FP equation)	
Wang et al. (2018a)	BSDE	Deep BSDE	Bermudan swaptions	Interest rates
Vidales et al. (2018a)	PDE	Projection solver	Multi-asset Black–Scholes	Finance
		Martingale rep. solver		
		Martingale CV solver		

TABLE 12.2 Authors of Papers on Deep PDE and Deep BSDE Methods 2019–2021

Reference	PDE/BSDE	Method	Applications	Problem Domain
Fujii et al. (2019)	BSDE	Deep BSDE	American options	Finance
			FVA	XVA
Albanese et al. (2019)	BSDE	Deep BSDE	XVA	XVA
Henry-Labordère (2019b)	BSDE	Deep BSDE	CVA	XVA
			IM	

Jacquier and Oumgari (2019)	PPDE	Deep PPDE	Rough LSV	Equities
Yu et al. (2019a)	BSDE	Deep BSDE	Barrier options	Finance
Raissi et al. (2019)	PINN	PINN	Burgers' equation	Physics
			Allen–Cahn equation	
Gnoatto et al. (2020)	BSDE	Deep BSDE	XVA	XVA
Salvador et al. (2020)	PDE	PINN	European option	Finance
			European exchange option	
			American two-asset option	
Sabate-Vidales et al. (2020)	PPDE	Deep PPDE		
Beck et al. (2021)	PDE	DS	Hamilton–Jacobi–Bellman	Physics
		DGM	Non-linear Black–Scholes	Finance
			Allen–Cahn equation	
			Semi-linear heat equation	
			Sine-Gordon equation	

TABLE 12.3 Authors of Papers on Deep PDE and Deep BSDE Methods 2022–2024

Reference	PDE/BSDE	Method	Applications	Problem Domain
Geuchen et al. (2022)	PDE		'Knightian uncertainty'	Asian options
Gao et al. (2022)	BSDE	Deep BSDE	Bermudan basket	Equities
van der Meer et al. (2022)	PINN	PINN	Laplace equation	Physics
			Poisson equation	
Germain et al. (2023)	PDE	Deep BSDE	CVA	XVA
	BSDE	DGM	Portfolio allocation	Asset management
		PINN		
		DBDP		
Bichuch and Hou (2023)	BSDE	Deep BSDE	Allen–Cahn equation	Physics
			Black–Scholes with default risk	Finance
			Hamilton–Jacobi–Bellman	
			Black–Scholes	
			Burgers' equation	

(*Continued*)

TABLE 12.3 Authors of Papers on Deep PDE and Deep BSDE Methods 2022–2024 (*Continued*)

Reference	PDE/BSDE	Method	Applications	Problem Domain
Zhang et al. (2023)	PDE	MCNP	Navier–Stokes	Physics
			Diffusion equation	
			Burgers' equation	
Assabumrungrat et al. (2024)	PDE	Deep BSDE	Heston basket option	Finance
	BSDE	DBDP		
		DS		
		MDBDP		
Abbas-Turki et al. (2024)	BSDE	Deep BSDE	XVA	XVA
Peng et al. (2024)	BSDE	Deep BSDE	American options	Equities

12.2 DEEP GALERKIN METHOD (DGM)

12.2.1 Introduction

The *deep Galerkin method (DGM)* is a deep learning approach to solving high-dimensional PDEs (Sirignano and Spiliopoulos, 2018). The Galerkin method approximates the solution of a PDE using a linear combination of basis functions. The DGM derives its name from this approach, replacing the traditional basis functions with a neural network. However, it closely resembles least-squares methods such as Longstaff and Schwartz (2001).

The key innovation in DGM is its ability to scale to high dimensions, and in testing, Sirignano and Spiliopoulos (2018) successfully solved a 200-dimensional PDE. The method relies on random sampling of spatial points and, as such, is completely mesh-free, which fundamentally allows it to scale to high dimensions. It uses a DNN to approximate the solution function and can utilise all associated machinery, such as GPUs and deep learning frameworks. While it resembles least-squares methods, unlike them, it only requires a single function approximator and not a series of them used during the backward induction phase.[1]

12.2.2 Algorithm

Start with a d-dimensional parabolic PDE

$$\frac{\partial u(t,x)}{\partial t} + \mathcal{L}u(t,x) = 0, \quad (t,x) \in [0,T] \times \Omega, \tag{12.1}$$

where x is a d-dimensional vector in domain Ω. The PDE is subject to boundary conditions

$$u(0,x) = u_0(x),$$
$$u(t,x) = g(t,x), \quad x \in \partial\Omega.$$

DGM approximates the solution with a neural network

$$U_\theta(t,x) \approx u(t,x), \tag{12.2}$$

[1]See Chapter 13.

where θ are the network parameters. The derivatives in the PDE can then be calculated using automatic differentiation, and this allows the loss function by combining the equations the PDE must satisfy inside the domain Ω for the initial conditions and the boundary conditions on $\partial\Omega$. The objective function is given by

$$\begin{aligned} J(\theta) = \mathbb{E}\left[\left|\frac{\partial U_\theta}{\partial t}(t_n, x_n) + \mathcal{L}U_\theta(t_n, x_n)\right|^2\right]^2_{[0,T]\times\Omega,\nu_1(\theta)} \\ + \mathbb{E}\left[\left|U_\theta(T, w_n) - g(w_n)\right|^2\right]^2_{[0,T]\times\Omega,\nu_2(\theta)} \\ + \mathbb{E}\left[\left|U_\theta(\tau_n, z_n) - h(\tau_n, z_n)\right|^2\right]^2_{\Omega,\nu_3(\theta)}. \end{aligned} \tag{12.3}$$

Note that this involves the calculation of second derivatives, which means a third-order derivative is required when the objective gradient is taken. Sirignano and Spiliopoulos (2018) provide a Monte Carlo approximation for this second derivative, although most other authors prefer to stay with automatic differentiation throughout. SGD can then update the neural network weights. Algorithm 12.1 presents the method in full.

Algorithm 12.1: Deep Galerkin Method (DGM)

Input: PDE to solve, initial condition, boundary conditions, domain Ω, time interval $[0, T]$, neural network architecture for $U_\theta(t, x)$, training measure densities ν_1, ν_2 and ν_3, learning rate α_n, number of training iterations
Output: Trained neural network $U_{\theta^*}(t, x)$ approximating the solution of the PDE

Initialise network parameters θ
for $n = 1, 2, \ldots,$ *number of iterations* **do**
  /* Sample random points */
  Sample (t_n, x_n) from $[0, T] \times \Omega$ according to density ν_1
  Sample (τ_n, z_n) from $[0, T] \times \partial\Omega$ according to density ν_2
  Sample w_n from Ω with density ν_3;
  /* Compute loss function */
  $J(\theta) \leftarrow \mathbb{E}\left[\left|\frac{\partial U_\theta}{\partial t}(t_n, x_n) + \mathcal{L}U_\theta(t_n, x_n)\right|^2\right] + \mathbb{E}\left[\left|U_\theta(T, w_n) - g(w_n)\right|^2\right] + \mathbb{E}\left[\left|U_\theta(\tau_n, z_n) - h(\tau_n, z_n)\right|^2\right]$;
  /* Calculate gradient using automatic differentiation */
  $\nabla_\theta L(\theta) \leftarrow \frac{\partial L}{\partial \theta}$;
  /* Update network parameters using SGD */
  $\theta \leftarrow \theta - \alpha_n \nabla_\theta L(\theta)$;
end
Return θ^*;

12.2.3 Theorems

Sirignano and Spiliopoulos (2018) prove two important convergence theorems for DGM. The first theorem establishes that a multilayer feedforward network can approximate solutions of quasilinear parabolic PDEs such that there exists a $U_\theta(t, x) \approx u(t, x)$ that makes the objective function arbitrarily small, and drawing on the universal function approximation theorems to do so (Cybenko, 1989; Hornik et al., 1989, 1990; Hornik, 1991). The second theorem establishes that the neural network converges to the PDE solution as the number of layers tends to infinity. Details of the theorems and their proofs can be found in Sirignano and Spiliopoulos (2018).

12.2.4 Numerical Examples

Sirignano and Spiliopoulos (2018) explore four numerical examples as tests of DGM. The first two relate to American option pricing, which is the solution of a free boundary PDE. The authors assume the dynamics for the underlying assets,

$$dx_t^i = \mu(x_t^i)dt + \sigma(x_t^i)dW_t^i, \tag{12.4}$$

$$\rho_{ij}dt = dW_t^i dW_t^j, \tag{12.5}$$

with the American option price defined by

$$u(t,x) = \sup_{\tau \in \mathcal{T}} \mathbb{E}\left[e^{-\int_0^\tau r(u)du} h\left(x_\tau\right)\right]. \tag{12.6}$$

The option pays $h(x_t)$ at t if exercised before maturity and $h(x_T)$ at maturity if not. The option value satisfies the parabolic PDE

$$0 = \frac{\partial u}{\partial t}(t,x) + \mu(x)\cdot\frac{\partial u}{\partial x}(t,x) + \frac{1}{2}\sum_{i,j=1}^{d}\rho_{i,j}\sigma\left(x_i\right)\sigma\left(x_j\right)\frac{\partial^2 u}{\partial x_i \partial x_j}(t,x) - ru(t,x) \tag{12.7}$$
$$\forall\{(t,x) : u(t,x) > g(x)\}$$

with boundary conditions

$$u(T,x) = h_T(x),$$
$$u(t,x) \geq h_t(t,x), \quad x \in \partial\Omega,$$

where on the free boundary defined by $\{(t,x) : u(t,x) = g(x)\}$, $u(t,x)$ has a continuous first derivative. The free boundary is the exercise boundary on which optimal exercise occurs.

To handle the free boundary, Sirignano and Spiliopoulos (2018) modify the algorithm slightly to become iterative. The free boundary is determined at the start of the iteration by freezing the neural network parameters $\theta = \tilde{\theta}$ and using $\tilde{\theta}$ to generate the simulation points. The θ parameters are then updated as before using SGD. Hence, the objective function becomes

$$\begin{aligned} J(U;\theta,\tilde{\theta}) = & \left\| \frac{\partial U}{\partial t}(t,\mathbf{x};\theta) + \mu(\mathbf{x})\cdot\frac{\partial U}{\partial \mathbf{x}}(t,\mathbf{x};\theta) \right. \\ & \left. + \frac{1}{2}\sum_{i,j=1}^{d}\rho_{i,j}\sigma\left(\mathbf{x}_i\right)\sigma\left(\mathbf{x}_j\right)\frac{\partial^2 U}{\partial \mathbf{x}_i \partial \mathbf{x}_j}(t,\mathbf{x};\theta) - r\,U(t,\mathbf{x};\theta) \right\|^2_{[0,T]\times\Omega,\,\nu_1(\tilde{\theta})} \\ & + \left\|\max\left(h(\mathbf{x}) - U(t,\mathbf{x};\theta),\,0\right)\right\|^2_{[0,T]\times\Omega,\,\nu_2(\tilde{\theta})} \\ & + \left\|U(T,\mathbf{x};\theta) - h(\mathbf{x})\right\|^2_{\Omega,\,\nu_3(\tilde{\theta})}, \end{aligned} \tag{12.8}$$

where $U(t,x:\theta) \approx u(t,x)$

Sirignano and Spiliopoulos (2018) use a complex LSTM-inspired network architecture for their model, although other researchers adopt simpler feedforward networks for $U_\theta(t,x)$. The authors also use the Adam optimiser with a decreasing learning rate schedule over the training period. A total of 100,000 iterations of batches of size 1000 were performed on each of five GPUs during training, giving 500 million simulated points in total.

Sirignano and Spiliopoulos (2018) used two American option examples as test cases. The first was an American call on a geometric basket average with Black–Scholes stock dynamics, for which a semi-analytic solution exists. The error on a 200-dimensional case was only 0.22%, demonstrating that the method can be extended to high dimensionality without difficulty. The second case was an American call on the arithmetic basket average, with only a numerical solution. The authors calculated the upper and lower bounds on the option price as a benchmark in this case. In the 200-dimensional case, the error bound was 0.62%, again demonstrating the ability of DGM to scale to a high dimension.

Finally, Sirignano and Spiliopoulos (2018) considered two non-financial examples. The first was the Hamilton–Jacobi–Bellman equation for the optimal control of a stochastic heat equation. For a 21-dimensional case, the average error across the domain was only 0.1%. The second example was the Burgers' equation, which is typically encountered in areas such as fluid dynamics. Here, the authors used DGM to approximate a general solution to the PDE for different initial and boundary conditions.

A small number of other authors have explored the DGM. Al-Aradi et al. (2018) conducted a thorough review of DGM and its application to problems in quantitative finance and elsewhere. Six use cases were considered:

1. European call options (i.e., solving the Black–Scholes PDE for a simple call European call option).
2. American put options, again using Black–Scholes dynamics.
3. Fokker–Planck equation for an Ornstein–Uhlenbeck process.
4. Stochastic optimal control with two cases, the Merton problem of optimal investment with exponential utility and optimal liquidation with price impact.
5. Systemic risk using the multi-dimensional HJB equation.
6. Mean-field games for optimal liquidation, including the HJB and FP equations. Comparison was made with the solution provided by Cardaliaguet and Lehalle (2018).

Al-Aradi et al. (2018) make three observations about the DGM:

1. The choice of sampling is critical to the method's success.
2. Prior knowledge about the solution can improve accuracy and specifically allow importance sampling to be used.
3. Training time is important; sometimes, leaving the model to train longer will yield excellent results.

Two other authors have applied DGM within broader reviews of deep learning and PDE solutions: Beck et al. (2021) and Germain et al. (2023). DGM is now often considered a type of physics-informed neural network and a forerunner of this class of methods.

EXAMPLE 12.1: BLACK–SCHOLES CALL OPTION WITH DGM

The simplest example of the DGM is to apply it to the Black–Scholes PDE for a simple European call, and this is presented in the Jupyter Notebook `DGM European Option PDE.ipynb`. This implements the neural PDE solver directly using PyTorch. The PDE will be solved for the parameters in Table 12.4.

TABLE 12.4 Option Parameters

Parameter	Value	Description
r	0.05	Risk-free rate
σ	0.2	Volatility
K	100.0	Strike price
T	1.0	Maturity (years)
S_{max}	200.0	Maximum price used in domain
S_{min}	0.0	Minimum price used in domain

(*Continued*)

(*Continued*)

The first step is to define a neural network to represent the solution of the PDE, $U(t, S|\theta)$. Here, a standard feedforward network with four layers of 64 neurons is used, in contrast to the complex LSTM model proposed by Sirignano and Spiliopoulos (2018). However, the activation functions must be differentiable to the third order as the loss function contains second-order terms, which are then differentiated again for backpropagation. Hence, hyperbolic tangent was used for the hidden layers, as proposed by Sirignano and Spiliopoulos (2018), with the output layer left linear.

The boundary conditions for the PDE were defined using three simple functions for the upper at $S_{\max}$, lower at $S_{\min}$ and terminal boundary at maturity T.

```
def boundary_upper(t):
    return S_max - K * torch.exp(-r * t)

def boundary_lower(t):
    return 0.0

def terminal(S):
    return torch.max(S - K, torch.zeros_like(S))
```

The loss functions force the neural network to the solution, and as with Sirignano and Spiliopoulos (2018), there are three, corresponding to the interior solution, the S boundaries and the terminal boundary. The PDE is encoded in the residual function.

```
def pde_residual(net, t, s):
    t.requires_grad = True
    s.requires_grad = True

    V = net(t, s)

    # First derivatives
    dV_dt = torch.autograd.grad(V, t, grad_outputs=torch.ones_like(V),
                                retain_graph=True, create_graph=True)[0]
    dV_dS = torch.autograd.grad(V, s, grad_outputs=torch.ones_like(V),
                                retain_graph=True, create_graph=True)[0]

    # Second derivative
    d2V_dS2 = torch.autograd.grad(dV_dS, s,
                                  grad_outputs=torch.ones_like(dV_dS),
                                  retain_graph=True, create_graph=True)[0]

    pde = dV_dt + 0.5 * sigma**2 * s**2 * d2V_dS2 + r * s * dV_dS - r * V
    return pde
```

The boundary loss evaluates the MSE between the solution on the boundary and the boundary conditions.

```
def boundary_loss(net, t):
    # S=0 boundary
    s_zeros = torch.zeros_like(t)
    V_0 = net(t, s_zeros)
    bc_dn = boundary_lower(t)
    loss_bc_0 = torch.mean((V_0 - bc_dn)**2)

    # S=S_max boundary
    s_upper = torch.ones_like(t) * S_max
    V_up = net(t, s_upper)
    bc_up = boundary_upper(t)
    loss_bc_up = torch.mean((V_up - bc_up)**2)

    return loss_bc_0 + loss_bc_up
```

Similarly, the terminal loss evaluates the MSE between the solution and the option payoff.

```
def terminal_loss(net, s_terminal):
    tT = torch.ones_like(s_terminal) * T
    V_T = net(tT, s_terminal)
    payoff_T = terminal(s_terminal)
    return torch.mean((V_T - payoff_T)**2)
```

The training loop has several key features:

- The points on the boundaries are sampled using a *boundary batch size*, set at 2^8.
- The PDE interior is sampled using *interior batch size*, set at 2^{10}.
- The same samples are used *loops* times before resampling.
- 2000 sampling iterations are performed, giving 20,000 epochs in total.
- Optimisation uses Adam with an initial learning rate of 10^{-3}. The learning rate is then reduced by a factor of 2 if no improvement in the loss is observed over 1000 epochs (100 resamplings). In this case, the final learning rate was $7.8125e^{-6}$.
- The three loss components are equally weighted in the total loss.
- The best model parameters associated with the lowest loss are retained and used as the final solution.

The loss as a function of epoch is shown in Figure 12.1. As can be seen, training is very noisy initially, but it eventually stabilises as the learning rate decreases. The final solution is illustrated alongside the Black–Scholes solution in Figure 12.2. The neural PDE solution shows excellent agreement, apart from some slight deviation at $S_{\max}$ for some time slices.

(*Continued*)

(Continued)

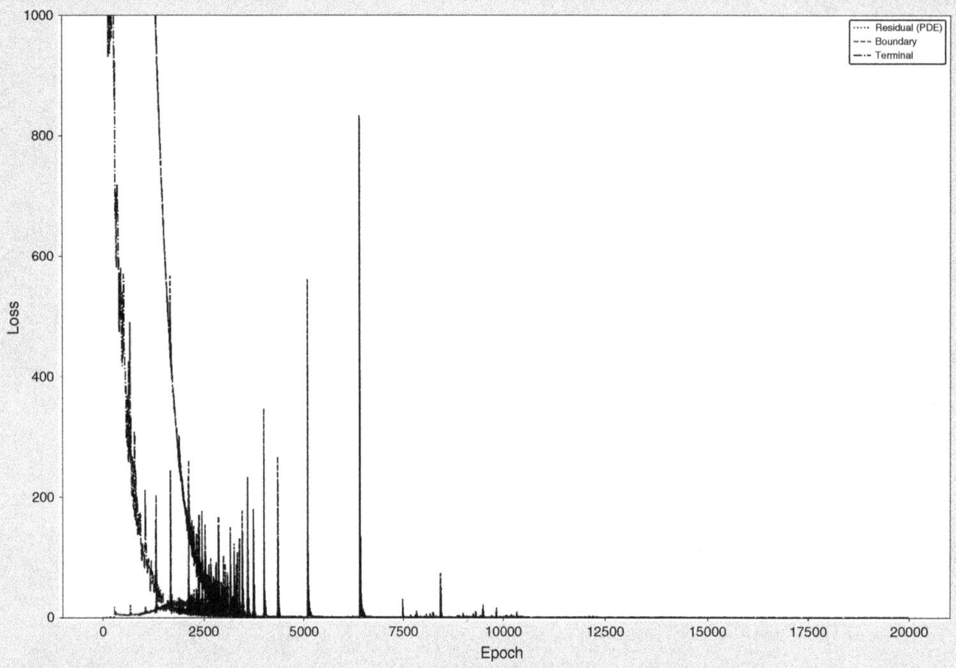

FIGURE 12.1 Loss as a function of epoch for the Black–Scholes PDE solved using DGM.

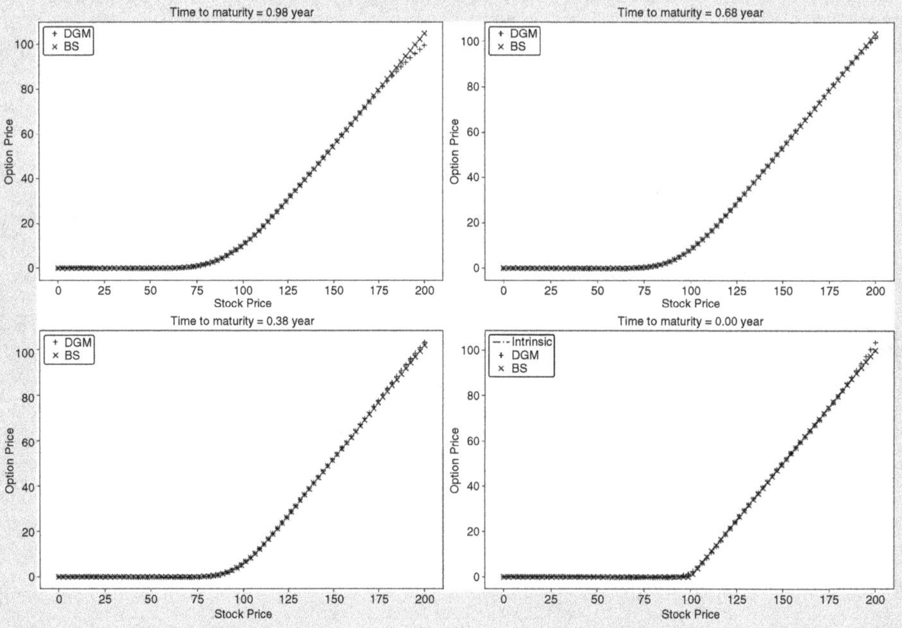

FIGURE 12.2 Comparison of the final PDE solution, $U(t, S|\theta)$, with Black–Scholes at four different time points. At final maturity, the intrinsic value is also shown.

EXAMPLE 12.2: AMERICAN BEST-OF OPTION WITH DGM

This second example of DGM prices an American 'best-of' call option and can be found in the Jupyter Notebook `DGM American Basket Option PDE.ipynb`. This is a multi-asset option with three underlying assets that are assumed to be uncorrelated to simplify the example. The volatility of all assets was 20%, the risk-free rate was 5% and the option strike was 100.

The same neural network architecture was used for this case, but the PDE and boundary conditions were changed. The terminal condition now matches the 'best-of' option.

```
def terminal(S):
    S_best = torch.max(S, dim=1, keepdim=True)[0]
    return torch.clamp(S_best - K, min=0.0)
```

The PDE is updated to reflect the multi-dimensional problem, with the zero correlation simplification, and this is coded in the PDE residual function.

```
def pde_residual(model, t, S, sigmas, r):
    t.requires_grad_(True)
    S.requires_grad_(True)

    V = model(t, S)

    # dV/dt
    dV_dt = torch.autograd.grad(
        V, t,
        grad_outputs=torch.ones_like(V),
        retain_graph=True, create_graph=True
    )[0]

    pde = dV_dt

    batch_size, n_assets = S.shape
    for i in range(n_assets):
        sigma_i = sigmas[i]
        # dV/dS_i
       dV_dSi = torch.autograd.grad(
           V, S,
           grad_outputs=torch.ones_like(V),
           retain_graph=True, create_graph=True
       )[0][:, i:i+1]

       # d2V/dS_i^2
       d2V_dSi2 = torch.autograd.grad(
           dV_dSi, S,
           grad_outputs=torch.ones_like(dV_dSi),
           retain_graph=True, create_graph=True
       )[0][:, i:i+1]

       Si = S[:, i:i+1]
       pde += r * Si * dV_dSi + 0.5 * sigma_i**2 * Si**2 * d2V_dSi2

    pde = pde - r * V
    return pde
```

(*Continued*)

(*Continued*)

The American condition is imposed by an American loss function, which replaces the boundary condition loss of the European example.

```
def american_constraint_loss(model, t, S):
    S_best = torch.max(S, dim=1, keepdim=True)[0]
    payoff =  torch.clamp(S_best - K, min=0.0)
    V = model(t, S)
    return torch.mean((torch.max(payoff, V) - V)**2)
```

The training loop remains almost the same as the previous example, with the boundary condition loss replaced by the American loss function. Training proceeded as before through 20,000 epochs with resampling every 10 epochs. The loss is illustrated in Figure 12.3.

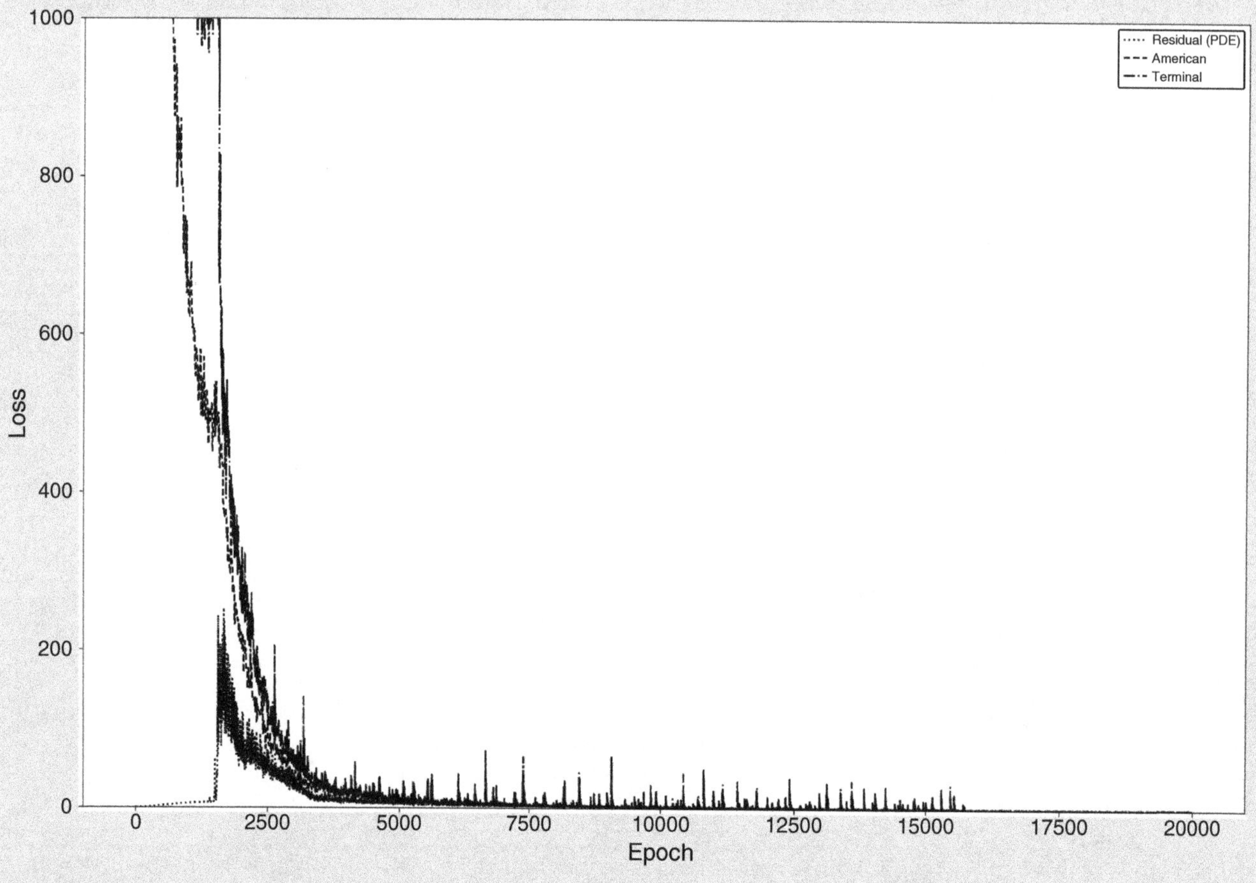

FIGURE 12.3 Loss as a function of epoch for the American best-of-basket PDE solved using DGM.

The same option was valued using the QuantLib `MCAmericanBasketEngine` to provide a comparison with the price obtained from the solution of the PDE; at $t = 0$ for spot prices of 100.0 for all three assets, the results are given in Table 12.5.

TABLE 12.5 Option Prices for the 'Best-of' American Basket Option

Model	Value
QuantLib	21.77600
DGM	23.06196

12.3 DEEP BSDE SOLVERS

Deep BSDE solvers have become a popular topic in quantitative finance and have been amongst the field's most widely implemented types of deep learning models since their introduction by Weinan et al. (2017). This section explores these solvers and their applications.

12.3.1 Introducing Backward Stochastic Differential Equations

12.3.1.1 Defining BSDEs Consider the forward SDE

$$dX_t = \mu\left(t, X_t\right) dt + \sigma\left(t, X_t\right) dW_t, \quad X_0 = x_0 \tag{12.9}$$

or in integral form,

$$X_t = x_0 + \int_0^t \mu\left(s, X_s\right) ds + \int_0^t \sigma\left(s, X_s\right) dW_s. \tag{12.10}$$

This stochastic process starts at time $t = 0$ with an initial condition x_0 and moves forward in time, and it is the standard forward equation that appears frequently in quantitative finance.

It is also possible to write down an SDE that operates backwards in time, and this is done using the pair of processes (El Karoui et al., 1997)

$$\begin{aligned} dY_t &= -f\left(Y_t, Z_t\right) dt + Z_t^* dW_t, \\ Z_T &= \xi, \end{aligned} \tag{12.11}$$

where f is a generator and ξ is the terminal condition. In integral form, this becomes

$$Y_t = \xi + \int_t^T b\left(s, Y_s, Z_s\right) ds - \int_t^T Z_s^* dW_s. \tag{12.12}$$

This expression is the BSDE and was originally introduced in the linear case by Bismut (1973) and in the general case by Pardoux and Peng (1990). Two key observations about the BSDE are that there are two processes involved, Y and Z, and not one as in the forward SDE, and that this is not simply a reversal of the forward equation: time still runs forward (Yang, 2023).[2]

The forward SDE is linked with a linear PDE via the Feynman–Kac theorem. The BSDE can similarly be linked with a semi-linear PDE (Henry-Labordère, 2019b). Consider the PDE

$$\partial_t u + \mathcal{L}u + f(u) = 0, \quad u(T, x) = g(x), \quad x \in \mathbb{R}^d, \tag{12.13}$$

[2]For a more comprehensive treatment of BSDEs and their application in quantitative finance, the reader is referred to El Karoui et al. (1997), Crépey (2013), Pardoux and Răşcanu (2014) or Zhang (2017).

where f is a non-linear function, and the operator is defined by

$$\mathcal{L} := b\nabla + \frac{1}{2}\sigma\sigma^T\nabla^2 \tag{12.14}$$

and the BSDE is linked to the PDE via

$$\begin{aligned} Y_t &= u\left(t, X_t\right), \\ Z_t &= \sigma^T\left(t, X_t\right)\nabla_x u\left(t, X_t\right). \end{aligned} \tag{12.15}$$

Solving the PDE is equivalent to solving the BSDE.

12.3.1.2 Applications of BSDEs BSDEs have been widely applied in quantitative finance, for example:

- **Pricing and Hedging in Incomplete Markets.** El Karoui et al. (1997) show how BSDEs arise when constraints are imposed on the pricing of contingent claims, such as different rates for borrowing and lending and incomplete markets.
- **Recursive Utility.** When the utility function is allowed to depend on current consumption and the expected utility of future consumption, it is said to be recursive. The recursive utility allows inter-temporal substitution preferences to be distinct from risk aversion and can better capture economic agents' preferences. The approach was introduced by Lucas (1978) (see also Robert E. Lucas, 1987) and later formalised by Epstein and Zin (1989) and the Epstein–Zin preferences. Recursive utilities are the solution of a BSDE (Duffie and Epstein, 1992; El Karoui et al., 1997).
- **Credit Risk.** BSDEs can appear in the context of defaultable contingent claims (Bielecki and Rutkowski, 2001).
- **Stochastic Control.** BSDEs are closed related to problems in stochastic control. See, for example, El Karoui et al. (1997) and Touzi (2013).
- **American Options.** Optimal stopping problems are linked to reflected backward stochastic differential equations, where the BSDE is constrained to stay above a given barrier (El Karoui et al., 1997; Esmaeeli and Imkeller, 2018). Bouchard et al. (2019) also developed BSDEs for American option pricing as an extension of the semi-linear PDE approach of Benth et al. (2003).
- **XVA.** BSDEs, as noted above, appear when the rates for borrowing and lending differ and hence automatically appear if this is the case in the context of FVA. A type of BSDE was shown to occur in the context of pricing in the presence of CCP initial margin by Agarwal et al. (2019). BSDEs also appear in some other general XVA model frameworks (Albanese et al., 2017).

12.3.2 Deep BSDE Algorithm

The deep BSDE algorithm is presented in Weinan et al. (2017) and Han et al. (2018). The authors consider semi-linear parabolic PDEs of the form

$$\begin{aligned} 0 = \frac{\partial u(t,x)}{\partial t} &+ \frac{1}{2}\mathrm{Tr}\left(\sigma\sigma^{\mathrm{T}}(t,x)\left(\mathrm{H}_x u\right)(t,x)\right) \\ &+ \nabla u(t,x)\cdot\mu(t,x) + f\left(t,x,u(t,x),\sigma^{\mathrm{T}}(t,x)\nabla u(t,x)\right), \end{aligned} \tag{12.16}$$

where Tr is the trace operator and H is the Hessian. The solution satisfies the BSDE with the form

$$\begin{aligned} u\left(t, X_t\right) = u\left(0, X_0\right) &- \int_0^t f\left(s, X_s, u\left(s, X_s\right), \sigma^{\mathrm{T}}\left(s, X_s\right)\nabla u\left(s, X_s\right)\right) ds \\ &+ \int_0^t \left[\nabla u\left(s, X_s\right)\right]^{\mathrm{T}}\sigma\left(s, X_s\right) dW_s, \end{aligned} \tag{12.17}$$

where X_t is a d-dimensional stochastic process with dynamics

$$X_t = \xi + \int_0^t \mu\left(s, X_s\right) ds + \int_0^t \sigma\left(s, X_s\right) dW_s. \tag{12.18}$$

A time partition $0 = t_0 < t_1 < \cdots < t_N = T$ is introduced and Equations (12.17) and (12.18) discretised to give

$$X_{t_{n+1}} = X_{t_n} + \mu\left(t_n, X_{t_n}\right)\Delta t_n + \sigma\left(t_n, X_{t_n}\right)\Delta W_n \tag{12.19}$$

and

$$\begin{aligned} u\left(t_{n+1}, X_{t_{n+1}}\right) \approx u\left(t_n, X_{t_n}\right) - f\left(t_n, X_{t_n}, u\left(t_n, X_{t_n}\right), \sigma^{\mathrm{T}}\left(t_n, X_{t_n}\right)\nabla u\left(t_n, X_{t_n}\right)\right)\Delta t_n \\ + \left[\nabla u\left(t_n, X_{t_n}\right)\right]^{\mathrm{T}} \sigma\left(t_n, X_{t_n}\right)\Delta W_n. \end{aligned} \tag{12.20}$$

To proceed, Han et al. (2018) approximate $z(t, X_t) = \sigma^{\mathrm{T}}(t, X_t)\nabla u(t, X_t)$ with a neural network at each t_n. The networks are then stacked based on the recursion in Equation (12.17) to form a single combined network. The loss function used to train the network is given by the MSE between the terminal condition and the neural network approximation to the solution

$$J = E\left[\left|U(t_N, X_{t_N}|\theta) - g\left(X_N\right)\right|^2\right]. \tag{12.21}$$

Training is then performed using SGD. Algorithm 12.2 gives the solution steps in full. Convergence properties of the deep BSDE algorithm are discussed in Han and Long (2020).

Algorithm 12.2: Deep BSDE Solver (see Weinan et al., 2017; Han et al., 2018; Henry-Labordère, 2019b)

Input: Number of Monte Carlo paths M, time discretisation $0 = t_0 < t_1 < \cdots < t_n = T$, payoff function g, function f
Input: Set $U(t_0, X_{t_0}) = \hat{Y}_0$ for each path m
for *each path* $m = 1, \ldots, M$ **do**
  Simulate Monte Carlo paths $(X^m_{t_1}, X^m_{t_2}, \ldots, X^m_{t_n})$.
for *each* $i = 1, \ldots, n-1$ **do**
  Parameterise the functions z_i with $n-1$ neural networks depending on weights $\theta_i = (W^i_l, b^i_l)_{1 \le l \le N_i}$.
  Set $z_i = a_{\theta_i}(X_{t_i})$.
while *not converged* **do**
  Compute the loss function:

$$J(\theta) = \frac{1}{2M}\sum_{m=1}^{M}(U(t_N, X_{t_N}) - g(X^m_{t_N}))^2.$$

  for *each path* m **do**
    for *each* $i = 0, \ldots, n-2$ **do**
      Update:

$$U^m(t_{i+1}, X^m_{t_{+i}}) = U^m(t_i, X^m_{t_i}) - f(U^m(t_i, X^m_{t_i})\Delta + a_{\theta_i}(X^m_{t_i})\sigma(t_i, X^m_{t_i})\Delta W^m_i.$$

  Update θ_i using stochastic gradient descent (SGD).

12.3.3 Deep BSDEs in Quant Finance

Since the introduction of the deep BSDE solver, many authors have sought to apply it to problems in quantitative finance. Two groups of applications can be identified: pricing of derivatives, most commonly American-style options, and XVA, including Black–Scholes with default risk. Some authors chose to tackle problems in both categories.

12.3.3.1 Pricing Fujii et al. (2019) were amongst the earliest authors to apply the deep BSDE method to quantitative finance. They extended the original methodology by introducing *asymptotic expansion* as prior knowledge. The authors then demonstrate that this approach accelerates convergence versus the original algorithm. Fujii et al. (2019) price a single-dimensional American call option as an initial test of the method and then apply the BSDE to a 50-dimensional American basket call option. The American options were priced using the reflected BSDE discussed briefly earlier. Fujii et al. (2019) also explore the Bergman (1995) model with different funding and borrow rates and a quadratic BSDE.

Bermudan swaptions priced using the Libor market model (LMM) are the subject of the paper by Wang et al. (2018a). LMM is a challenging model to use in the general case as it is non-Markovian, so the authors use a separable volatility function prescription to make the model Markovian.[3] The authors write a PDE for the European option price and then recast this as a BSDE. Following this, Wang et al. (2018a) extend the approach to Bermudan swaptions and handling the optimal stopping problem. The authors note that the original formalism for the BSDE from Weinan et al. (2017) and Han et al. (2018) is a *forward* solver; that is, it projects the option value forward in time using the SDE to the terminal time and then uses a loss function to minimise the difference between the payoff and the terminal value from the model. This forward approach is unsuited to pricing Bermudan and American-style options. For Bermudan swaptions, there is a need to handle early exercise. So Wang et al. (2018a) propose a backward solver that handles the option prices backwards from the terminal time to the initial time, handling the dynamic programming problem. The loss function is designed to minimise the variance of the initial option price. The authors consider numerical examples of both European and Bermudan swaption pricing. European forward and backward model implementations gave results comparable to a benchmark LMM implementation in QuantLib. For Bermudan swaptions, the authors considered short and long Bermudans, testing self-consistency as a function of the number of exercise opportunities rather than against a benchmark. The authors concluded that the model was performing as expected. Overall, the model performance was around 1–2 minutes for short-maturity options and 3–20 minutes for extended-maturity options, depending on the number of exercises. Testing was performed using a single V100 GPU. The implementation from Wang et al. (2018a) is not competitive with traditional approaches such as Longstaff and Schwartz (2001).

Yu et al. (2019a) apply the BSDE to the case of single barrier options on a single asset. The authors begin by writing down the PDE for the model and then recast this in probabilistic form via the Feynman–Kac theorem. This probabilistic representation allows the authors to formulate the problem as a BSDE with a terminal condition that includes the barrier condition. Once in BSDE form, Yu et al. (2019a) proceed to use the deep BSDE solver. A total of 72 test cases were used with a range of parameter values, yielding average relative errors of 1.21% against the analytic solution with 8000 iterations. Performance is slow, 4–20 seconds per 200 training iterations. However, this is a toy model rather than a practical example.

Optimal stopping is also the subject of the paper by Gao et al. (2022), who adopt the same backward version of the deep BSDE method as Wang et al. (2018a). The authors aim to provide a more rigorous foundation for the backward BSDE method by analysing its convergence properties. They can demonstrate that the error on the numerical solution is bounded by the training loss, which gives theoretical support to the approach. Gao et al. (2022) conduct numerical testing with European and Bermudan geometric put options on baskets with 1–50 underlying assets. The valuations are consistent with the analytic formula.

Assabumrungrat et al. (2024) provide an empirical study of the accuracy of deep PDE solvers, considering the deep BSDE method, deep backward dynamic programming and deep splitting. The authors identify three sources of error in deep PDE/BSDE solvers: the properties of the underlying options or assets; numerical errors from the asset simulation; and optimisation errors from DNN training. Errors from the options and assets arise, for example, from properties like the strike with deep-out-of-the-money options, which gives more significant relative pricing errors. Numerical errors from the asset simulation follow from issues like Monte Carlo discretisation. Optimisation errors from DNNs are just the previously discussed general problems inherent to training neural network models. The authors assess errors using three groups of experiments corresponding to the three types of error using a high-dimensional rainbow option with Heston model dynamics, implemented using each of the deep PDE/BSDE

[3]Technically this is only an approximate LMM model; see Andersen and Piterbarg (2010) for a more detailed discussion of this point.

solvers. Assabumrungrat et al. (2024) conclude that the deep BSDE solver is the most robust as the dynamic programming and deep splitting methods show degraded accuracy for shorter-maturity options.

A further variant of the deep BSDE solver, *deep penalty methods*, is defined by Peng et al. (2024). This method is designed to price American options and combines the penalty method (Forsyth and Vetzal, 2002; Witte and Reisinger, 2011) with the deep BSDE of Weinan et al. (2017). In the penalty method, the problem is modified to an alternate form, which can be shown to converge to the solution of the original problem. So, for example (Johnson, 2021), the PDE for an American put option

$$\begin{gathered}\frac{\partial V}{\partial t}+\frac{1}{2}\sigma^2 S^2\frac{\partial^2 V}{\partial S^2}+rS\frac{\partial V}{\partial S}-rV=0,\\ V(S,T)=\max(X-S,0),\\ V(S,t)\geq X-S\end{gathered} \tag{12.22}$$

is modified to

$$\frac{\partial V}{\partial t}+\frac{1}{2}\sigma^2 S^2\frac{\partial^2 V}{\partial S^2}+rS\frac{\partial V}{\partial S}-rV+\rho\max((X-S)-V,0)=0, \tag{12.23}$$

where solution V satisfies

$$V(S,t)\geq X-S \tag{12.24}$$

in the limit $\rho\to\infty$. Peng et al. (2024) consider the pricing of an American index put option where the index is formed of the geometric average of the underlying stocks. The authors model the stocks individually and explore a range from 10 to 100 underlying assets. They form the penalty PDE

$$\begin{aligned}&\mathcal{L}V^\lambda(t,x)-rV^\lambda(t,x)+f(t,x)+\lambda\big(p(t,x)-V^\lambda(t,x)\big)^+=0,\\ &V^\lambda(T,x)=h(x),\end{aligned} \tag{12.25}$$

where the differential operation is defined by

$$\mathcal{L}:=\frac{\partial}{\partial t}+\sum_{i=1}^{m}\sum_{j=1}^{m}a_{ij}(t,x)\frac{\partial^2}{\partial x_i\partial x_j}+\sum_{i=1}^{m}b_i(t,x)\frac{\partial}{\partial x_i}. \tag{12.26}$$

Peng et al. (2024) transform this to the following form:

$$\begin{aligned}&\mathcal{L}U(t,x)+f_1(t,x)+\lambda(-U(t,x))^+=0,\\ &U(T,x)=h_1(x),\end{aligned} \tag{12.27}$$

where

- $U(t,x):=\left(V^\lambda(t,x)-p(t,x)\right)e^{-rt}$,
- $f_1(t,x):=(f(t,x)+\mathcal{L}p(t,x)-rp(t,x))e^{-rt}$,
- $h_1(x):=(h(x)-p(T,x))e^{-rT}$,

which translates to the BSDE

$$\begin{aligned}&dY_t=\left(-f_1\left(t,X_t\right)-\lambda(-Y_t)^+\right)dt+Z_t^T dW_t,\\ &Y_T=h_1\left(X_T\right),\end{aligned} \tag{12.28}$$

to which they apply the deep BSDE method. The authors report relative errors between 0.33% and 0.56% versus the benchmark, which is the one-dimensional case to which the problem can be reduced. Runtimes were very slow; using a V100, the 10-dimensional case was executed in 6790 seconds, rising to 25,806 seconds for the 100-dimensional case.

12.3.3.2 XVA and Credit Risk Henry-Labordère (2019b) makes two key contributions to applying the deep BSDE solver to quantitative finance. Firstly, he develops a primal–dual algorithm for deep BSDE solvers. Given a semi-linear PDE and the associated BSDE, Henry-Labordère (2019b) uses stochastic control theory to find the lower bound (primal) and upper bound (dual) on the solution of the PDE.[4] Once the primal and dual have been obtained, the deep BSDE algorithm can be extended for both cases. Algorithm 12.3 gives the primal and Algorithm 12.4 gives the dual.

Algorithm 12.3: Deep BSDE Primal Algorithm from Henry-Labordère (2019b)

Input: Number of paths M, time steps $\{t_i\}_{i=1}^n$, initial condition X_0
Output: Lower bound Y_0^{Lower}
Step 1: Perform the deep BSDE solver
Obtain the (local) optimiser using the (refined) SGD:

$$Y_0^*,\ z_0^*,\ \left(z_i^* := a_{\theta_i^*}\left(X_{t_i}\right)\right)_{1\le i\le n-1}.$$

Step 2: Simulate M independent Monte Carlo paths
Generate paths $\left(X_{t_1}^m, X_{t_2}^m, \dots, X_{t_n}^m\right)$ for $1 \le m \le M$.
foreach *path* $m = 1, 2, \dots, M$ **do**

Step 3: Compute $Y_{t_i}^m$ using the Euler scheme:

$$Y_{t_{i+1}}^m - Y_{t_i}^m = -f\left(Y_{t_i}^m\right)\Delta + a_{\theta_i^*}\left(X_{t_i}^m\right)\sigma\left(t_i, X_{t_i}^m\right)\cdot \Delta W_i^m, \quad Y_0^m = Y_0^*.$$

Step 4: Simulate the processes I_t and Q_t:

$$I_{t_{i+1}}^m = I_{t_i}^m + a_{t_i}^{m,*}\Delta, \quad I_0^m := 0,$$

$$Q_{t_{i+1}}^m = Q_{t_i}^m + \exp\left(I_{t_i}^m\right) f^*\left(a_{t_i}^{m,*}\right)\Delta, \quad Q_0^m := 0,$$

where

$$a_{t_i}^{m,*} := \operatorname{argmax}\left\{aY_{t_i}^m - f^*(a)\right\}.$$

Step 5: Compute the average:

$$Y_0^{\text{Lower}} := \frac{1}{M}\sum_{m=1}^{M}\left(\exp\left(I_{t_n}^m\right) g\left(X_{t_n}^m\right) - Q_{t_n}^m\right).$$

Step 6: Lower-bound property:

$$Y_0^{\text{Lower}} \le u\left(0, X_0\right) \text{ (when } M \text{ is large)}.$$

[4]The primal–dual approach is also discussed briefly in the context of American Monte Carlo in Chapter 13.

Algorithm 12.4: Deep BSDE Dual Algorithm from Henry-Labordère (2019b)

Input: Number of paths M, time steps $\{t_i\}_{i=1}^{n}$, initial condition X_0
Output: Upper and lower bounds Y_0^{Lower} and Y_0^{Upper}
Steps 1–5: Perform the primal algorithm
From the primal algorithm, obtain Y_0^*, z_0^* and $\left(\theta_i^*\right)_{1\le i\le n-1}$.
Step 6: Minimise a functional over $\left(\theta_i\right)_{1\le i\le n-1}$ using SGD
Minimise

$$\frac{1}{M}\sum_{m=1}^{M} U_0^m,$$

where $z_{i-1} := a_{\theta_{i-1}}$ and $U_{t_{i-1}}^m$ is computed recursively as

$$U_{t_{i-1}}^m = U_{t_i}^m + f\left(U_{t_i}^m\right)\Delta - a_{\theta_{i-1}}\left(X_{t_{i-1}}^m\right)\sigma\left(t_{i-1}, X_{t_{i-1}}^m\right)\cdot \Delta W_{i-1}^m,$$

with terminal condition

$$U_{t_n}^m = g\left(X_{t_n}^m\right).$$

Remark: z_0 does not appear in the minimisation as

$$\mathbb{E}\left[z_0\sigma\left(0, X_0\right)\Delta W_0\right] = 0.$$

Gradient Computation: The gradient of U_0^m with respect to θ_i is given by

$$\frac{\partial U_0^m}{\partial \theta_i} = \prod_{k=1}^{i}\left(1 + f'\left(U_{t_k}^m\right)\Delta\right)\left(-\frac{\partial a_{\theta_i}\left(X_{t_i}^m\right)}{\partial \theta_i}\sigma\left(t_i, X_{t_i}^m\right)\cdot \Delta W_i^m\right),$$

for $i = 1, \dots, n-1$.
Step 7: Optimise and compute the upper bound
Once the optimiser converges to a (local) minimiser $\left(\theta_i^*\right)_{1\le i\le n-1}$, simulate M independent Monte Carlo paths and compute

$$Y_0^{\text{Upper}} := \frac{1}{M}\sum_{m=1}^{M} U_0^{m,*},$$

where $U_{t_{i-1}}^{m,*}$ is computed as

$$U_{t_{i-1}}^{m,*} = U_{t_i}^{m,*} + f\left(U_{t_i}^{m,*}\right)\Delta - a_{\theta_{i-1}^*}\left(X_{t_{i-1}}^m\right)\sigma\left(t_{i-1}, X_{t_{i-1}}^m\right)\cdot \Delta W_{i-1}^m,$$

with terminal condition

$$U_{t_n}^{m,*} = g\left(X_{t_n}^m\right).$$

Final Result: By construction, when M is large,

$$Y_0^{\text{Lower}} \le Y_0 \le Y_0^{\text{Upper}}.$$

The second key contribution from Henry-Labordère (2019b) is applying the deep BSDE method to CVA and initial margin. The author applies the deep primal–dual BSDE algorithm to the semi-linear 'CVA-like' PDE

$$\partial_t u^{\mathrm{CVA}} + \mathcal{L}u^{\mathrm{CVA}} + \lambda\left(\left(u^{\mathrm{CVA}}\right)^+ - u^{\mathrm{CVA}}\right) = 0,$$
$$u^{\mathrm{CVA}}(T,x) = g(x), \tag{12.29}$$

where λ is the default intensity of the counterparty. The author demonstrates tight bounds on the price in the presence of default risk for up to six underlying assets. Henry-Labordère (2019b) also considers the following 'IM-like' PDE that includes the cost of initial margin at the 99% quantile:

$$\partial_t u + \frac{1}{2}\sigma^2 \sum_{i=1}^{d} x_i^2 \partial_{x_i}^2 u + f(x, \nabla u) = 0,$$
$$f(x, \nabla u) := \beta\sqrt{\sum_{i=1}^{n}\left(x_i \partial_{x_i} u\right)^2}. \tag{12.30}$$

Again, the author demonstrates tight bounds on the price in the presence of an initial margin for up to six assets. The neural-network architecture used in both cases was a simple feedforward network with each layer having width $d + 2$, for dimensionality d. Two layers were used for the CVA example, while eight proved optimal for the IM case for $d = 2$.

Gnoatto et al. (2020) focus purely on calculating XVA using the deep BSDE algorithm. They consider two cases: XVA, which is non-recursive, and XVA, which is recursive. Standard treatments of XVA are non-recursive (Green, 2015), giving a series of integrals of the form

$$U = \mathrm{CVA} + \mathrm{DVA} + \mathrm{FCA} + \mathrm{COLVA} + \mathrm{KVA}, \tag{12.31}$$

where

$$\mathrm{CVA} = -(1 - R_C)\int_t^T \lambda_C(s) e^{-\int_t^s r(u)+\lambda_B(u)+\lambda_C(u)du}\,\mathbb{E}\left[(V(s) - C(s))^+\right] ds, \tag{12.32}$$

$$\mathrm{DVA} = -(1 - R_B)\int_t^T \lambda_B(s) e^{-\int_t^s r(u)+\lambda_B(u)+\lambda_C(u)du}\,\mathbb{E}\left[(V(s) - C(s))^-\right] ds, \tag{12.33}$$

$$\mathrm{FCA} = -(1 - R_B)\int_t^T \lambda_B(s) e^{-\int_t^s r(u)+\lambda_B(u)+\lambda_C(u)du}\,\mathbb{E}\left[(V(s) - C(s))^+\right] ds, \tag{12.34}$$

$$\mathrm{COLVA} = -\int_t^T s_X(s) e^{-\int_t^s r(u)+\lambda_B(u)+\lambda_C(u)du}\,\mathbb{E}\left[C(s)\right] ds, \tag{12.35}$$

$$\mathrm{KVA} = -\int_t^T (\gamma_K(s) - \phi r(s)) e^{-\int_t^s r(u)+\lambda_B(u)+\lambda_C(u)du}\,\mathbb{E}\left[K(s)\right] ds. \tag{12.36}$$

Here, $V(s)$ is the portfolio value, $C(s)$ is the collateral, R_B is the recovery rate for the bank, R_C is the recovery rate for the counterparty, λ_B is the bank hazard rate, λ_C is the counterparty hazard rate and r is the risk-free rate. However, some alternative treatments of XVA, such as the case previously mentioned with different borrowing and lending rates, yield a recursive model where the integrals on the right-hand side of the integrals depend on some or all of the XVA terms. One example of this is presented by Biagini et al. (2021):

$$\mathrm{CVA} = \left(1 - R^C\right) e^{-\int_t^T r(u)\,du} \mathbb{E}\left[\int_t^T \left(V(s) - C(s)\right)^+ \lambda(s)^C \, ds\right],$$

$$\mathrm{DVA} = \left(1 - R^B\right) e^{-\int_t^T r(u)\,du} \mathbb{E}\left[\int_t^T \left(V(s) - C(s)\right)^- \lambda(s)^B \, ds\right],$$

$$\begin{aligned}\mathrm{FVA} &= e^{-\int_t^T r(u)\,du} \mathbb{E}\left[\int_t^T \left(r(s)^{f,l} - r(s)\right)\left(V(s) - \mathrm{XVA}(s) - C(s)\right)^+ ds\right] \\ &\quad - e^{-\int_t^T r(u)\,du} \mathbb{E}\left[\int_t^T \left(r(s)^{f,b} - r(s)\right)\left(V(s) - \mathrm{XVA}(s) - C(s)\right)^- ds\right],\end{aligned}$$

$$\mathrm{COLVA} = e^{-\int_t^T r(u)\,du} \mathbb{E}\left[\int_t^T \left(r(s)^{c,l} - r(s)\right) C(s)^+ - \left(r(s)^{c,b} - r(s)\right) C(s)^- \, ds\right].$$

In the non-recursive case, Gnoatto et al. (2020) write down a collection of BSDEs for the value of each trade in the netting set. Solving these provides a value for each derivative on each time step and path of the driving Monte Carlo simulation. In turn, this allows the calculation of the exposure. Note, however, that the authors restrict the underlying payoffs to European style. The approach could be extended to Bermudan and American-style options, although one of the approaches to solving the American exercise discussed earlier would need to be applied. Once the BSDEs have provided the approximations for the M trade values, the XVAs are obtained using numeric integration over time and Monte Carlo paths in the usual way, with trade valuations in each Monte Carlo state provided by the deep BSDE approximation.

A second deep BSDE solver handles the recursive case; that is, Gnoatto et al. (2020) seek to solve the BSDE for XVA given by

$$\begin{cases} -\mathrm{dXVA}_t = \bar{f}(t, V_t, \mathrm{XVA}_t)\,\mathrm{d}t - \sum_{k=1}^{d} \bar{Z}_t^k \,\mathrm{d}W_t^{k,\mathbb{Q}}, \\ \mathrm{XVA}_T = 0, \end{cases}$$

where

$$\begin{aligned} \bar{f}(t, V_t, \mathrm{XVA}_t) := &- \left(1 - R^C\right)\left(V_t - C_t\right)^- \lambda_t^{C,\mathbb{Q}} \\ &+ \left(1 - R^B\right)\left(V_t - C_t\right)^+ \lambda_t^{B,\mathbb{Q}} \\ &+ \left(r_t^{f,l} - r_t\right)\left(V_t - \mathrm{XVA}_t - C_t\right)^+ - \left(r_t^{f,b} - r_t\right)\left(V_t - \mathrm{XVA}_t - C_t\right)^- \\ &+ \left(r_t^{c,l} - r_t\right) C_t^+ - \left(r_t^{c,b} - r_t\right) C_t^- - \left(r_t + \lambda_t^{C,\mathbb{Q}} + \lambda_t^{B,\mathbb{Q}}\right)\mathrm{XVA}_t. \end{aligned} \tag{12.37}$$

This BSDE is solved using another deep BSDE solver, using the portfolio value approximation generated by the first set of solvers.

The key question is how beneficial the approach described by Gnoatto et al. (2020) is, and can it be used as the basis of a practical XVA platform? If the XVA model is recursive, then there are few alternatives to the second calculation and approximation by the deep BSDE solver. However, the non-recursive case has to be competitive against traditional techniques such as standard Monte Carlo simulation with embedded trade valuation or American Monte Carlo. The trade-offs are complex; the BSDE approach naturally provides DNN approximations for trade values and expected exposures, which leads to fast inference on GPU once trained and readily available sensitivities from backpropagation. However, the training cost will be high because of the use of SGD, and that training is *online* and must be performed for every single estimation of XVA. In contrast, other techniques, such as derivative valuation approximation with neural networks as described in Chapter 11, are *offline* and, in theory, need only be performed once or at least irregularly.

Bichuch and Hou (2023) adopt a different approach to solving BSDEs to the deep BSDE method and trial their approach on several use cases, including Black–Scholes with default risk. Instead of solving the BSDE directly, they transform it to the corresponding PDE and solve for both the solution of the PDE and its gradient simultaneously. Specifying the BSDE as per Equation (12.11) and the associated semi-linear PDE by Equation (12.13), Bichuch and Hou (2023) seek to solve the coupled PDEs defined by

$$\begin{aligned} -u_t + \mathcal{L}u &= -f(t,x,u), \\ u(0,x) &= g(x), \end{aligned} \tag{12.38}$$

$$\begin{aligned} -\frac{\partial v_i}{\partial t} + \mathcal{L}v_i &= -\frac{\partial f(t,x,w)}{\partial w}\bigg|_u v_i - \frac{\partial f(t,x,u)}{\partial x_i} - \mathcal{L}_i u, \\ v_i(0,x) &= \frac{\partial g(x)}{\partial x_i}, \end{aligned} \tag{12.39}$$

where

$$\mathcal{L} = \frac{1}{2}\sum_{i,j=1}^{d} \left(\sigma\sigma^T\right)_{i,j}(x)\frac{\partial^2}{\partial x_i \partial x_j} + \sum_{i=1}^{d} b_i(x)\frac{\partial}{\partial x_i} \tag{12.40}$$

and

$$\mathcal{L}_i = \frac{1}{2}\sum_{j,k=1}^{d} \frac{\partial\left(\sigma\sigma^T\right)_{j,k}}{\partial x_i}(x)\frac{\partial^2}{\partial x_j \partial x_k} + \sum_{j=1}^{d} \frac{\partial b_j}{\partial x_i}(x)\frac{\partial}{\partial x_j}. \tag{12.41}$$

The key driver for the coupled PDE approach is that modelling the gradient directly using a neural network can ensure accurate gradient estimation, which is critical to finding a reliable control process for the BSDE. Bichuch and Hou (2023) provide several supporting converge theorems and test the approach numerically on the Allen–Cahn equation and Black–Scholes. Non-linear Black–Scholes with default risk, HJB equation and a one-dimensional Burgers-type PDE. They demonstrate that the coupled approach yields more accurate results than the deep BSDE method.

Abbas-Turki et al. (2024) consider another BSDE variant, *anticipative backward stochastic differential equations (ABSDEs)* in the context of XVA. ABSDEs were introduced by Peng and Yang (2009) and can have coefficients that depend on the conditional law of the solution beyond the current time. Hence, the equation incorporates anticipative information, which allows the model to account for situations where future expectations are relevant to current decisions. Specifically, the anticipatory BSDE is defined by

$$-dY_t = f\left(t, Y_t, Z_t, Y_{t+\delta(t)}, Z_{t+\zeta(t)}\right) dt - Z_t dW_t, \qquad t \in [0,T], \tag{12.42}$$

$$Y_t = \xi_t, \qquad t \in [T, T+K], \tag{12.43}$$

$$Z_t = \eta_t, \qquad t \in [T, T+K]. \tag{12.44}$$

As an example of this, the authors adopt the XVA framework of Albanese et al. (2021) where the XVAs are given by

$$\mathrm{CVA}_t = \mathbb{E}_t\left[\sum_c \int_t^T e^{-\int_t^s r du}\left(V_s^{(c)}\right)^+ \delta_{\tau^{(c)}}(ds)\right], \tag{12.45}$$

$$\mathrm{FVA}_t = \mathbb{E}_t\left[\int_t^T e^{-\int_t^s r du}\gamma_s^{(b)}\left(\sum_c J_s^{(c)} V_s^{(c)} - \mathrm{CVA}_s - \mathrm{FVA}_s - \max\left(\mathrm{EC}_s, \mathrm{KVA}_s\right)\right)^+ ds\right], \tag{12.46}$$

$$\mathrm{KVA}_t = \mathbb{E}_t\left[\int_t^T e^{-\int_t^s r du}\gamma_K e^{-\gamma_K(s-t)} \max\left(\mathrm{EC}_s, \mathrm{KVA}_s\right) ds\right], \tag{12.47}$$

where $V_s^{(c)}$ is the netted portfolio value for counterparty c, γ_K is the dividend rate on shareholder capital, $J_t^{(c)} = \mathbf{1}_{\{t<\tau^{(c)}\}}$ where $-dJ_t^{(c)} = \delta_{\tau^{(c)}}(dt)$ and $\delta_{\tau^{(c)}}$ is the Dirac measure at time $\tau^{(c)}$, $\gamma_s^{(b)}$ is the bank risky funding spread and r is the risk-free rate. The bank's economic capital is given by

$$\mathrm{EC}_t = \mathbb{ES}_t\left[L_{\bar{t}} - L_t\right], \tag{12.48}$$

which is the expected shortfall over the period t to later time $\bar{t}$ of the loss process given by

$$dL_t = \sum_c \left(V_t^{(c)}\right)^+ \delta_{\tau^{(c)}}(dt) + d\mathrm{CVA}_t \tag{12.49}$$

$$+\gamma_s^{(b)}\left(\sum_c J_t^{(c)} V_t^{(c)} - \mathrm{CVA}_t - \mathrm{FVA}_t - \max\left(\mathrm{EC}_t, \mathrm{KVA}_t\right)\right)^+ dt + d\mathrm{FVA}_t. \tag{12.50}$$

This XVA framework becomes an ABSDE because the economic capital is the expected shortfall of future losses. The authors define an explicit backward scheme to solve the ABSDE, where neural networks are used to approximate conditional expectations. Finally, Abbas-Turki et al. (2024) compare the 'deep ABSDE' scheme with an alternative Picard iteration algorithm, concluding that their scheme is three to four times faster.

EXAMPLE 12.3: DEEP BSDE SOLVER FOR BLACK–SCHOLES

This example implements the deep solver for the simple case of a Black–Scholes European call option and can be found in the Jupyter Notebook `BSDE Black Scholes Call.ipynb`. The deep BSDE solver uses a sequence of fully connected neural networks with two hidden layers, batch normalisation and ReLU activation, with a linear final output. The following function implements the deep BSDE solver:

```
def BSDE_BlackScholes(S0, K, sigma, r, T, M=256, N=50, hidden_dim=128,
                      max_iterations=10000, tol=1e-7, seed=42, lr=1e-2):
    start_time = time.time()
    dt = T / N
    torch.manual_seed(seed)

    # Build a network for each time step
    Z_nets = nn.ModuleList([FCNet(1, hidden_dim, 1).to(device)
                            for _ in range(N - 1)])

    # Y0 is the initial condition (to be learned) for the BSDE
    initial_guess = S0 * np.exp(r * T) \
                    + 0.5 * sigma * np.sqrt(T) * S0 - K


    Y0 = torch.tensor([initial_guess], device=device, requires_grad=True)
```

(Continued)

(Continued)

```
    # Combine all trainable parameters (Y0 and the networks' parameters)
    optimizer = optim.Adam([Y0] + list(Z_nets.parameters()), lr=lr)

    loss_lst = []
    prev_Y0 = None
    iteration = 0

    for it in tqdm(range(max_iterations)):
        iteration += 1
        # Initialize S and Y for all sample paths
        S = torch.full((M, 1), S0, device=device)
        Y = Y0.repeat(M, 1)

        # Pre-sample Brownian increments (for each time step)
        dW = torch.randn(M, N-1, device=device)*torch.sqrt(torch.tensor(dt))

        # Forward simulation along the discretized time grid
        for n in range(N - 1):
            # Compute the control process Z using
            # the nth network given the current state S
            Z = Z_nets[n](S)

            # BSDE generator: for Black-Scholes:
            f = -r * Y
            Y = Y - f * dt + Z * dW[:, n:n+1]

            # Update the underlying asset S using an exponential Euler scheme
            S = S * torch.exp((r - 0.5 * sigma ** 2) * dt \
                              + sigma * dW[:, n:n+1])

        # Compute the loss: MSE between Y and the terminal payoff
        loss = torch.mean((Y - payoff(S, K))**2)
        loss_lst.append(loss.item())

        optimizer.zero_grad()
        loss.backward()
        optimizer.step()

        # Check convergence on Y0 (the BSDE solution at time 0)
        current_Y0 = Y0.item()
        if prev_Y0 is not None:
            rel_change = abs(current_Y0 - prev_Y0) / abs(prev_Y0)
            if rel_change < tol:
                print(f"Converged at iteration {iteration}
                        with relative change in Y0: {rel_change:.2e}")
                break
            prev_Y0 = current_Y0

    end_time = time.time()
    execution_time = end_time - start_time
    return Y0.item(), loss_lst, iteration, execution_time
```

The function performs the following steps:

1. Initialise parameters and set up the time grid.
2. Create a list of feedforward networks (`FCNet`) for each time step n in $\{0, \ldots, N-2\}$.
3. Initialise the BSDE starting value Y_0.
4. Combine Y_0 and the network parameters into an Adam optimiser.
5. Iterate until convergence or maximum iterations.
   (a) Initialise the underlying asset S and BSDE solution Y with M sample paths.
   (b) Sample Brownian increments dW for each time step.
   (c) Perform forward simulation over the time grid.
      i. Compute the control process Z using the corresponding neural network.
      ii. Update Y using the BSDE equation
      $$Y_{n+1} = Y_n + rY_n dt + ZdW.$$
      iii. Update the asset price S using
      $$S_{n+1} = S_n \exp\left((r - 0.5\sigma^2)dt + \sigma dW\right).$$
   (d) Compute the loss as the mean squared error between the terminal Y and the payoff function.
   (e) Backpropagate and update the optimiser.
   (f) Check convergence of Y_0 using the relative change criterion.

A European option with a maturity of 1 year, interest rate of 5%, volatility of 20% and spot and strike price of 100 was valued. The BSDE model gave the value of 10.3297 after 108 seconds, which can be compared with the Black–Scholes model value of 10.4506. The training loss for this example is illustrated in Figure 12.4.

One-dimensional hyperparameter optimisation runs were performed to assess optimal parameter choices. Table 12.6 illustrates the results as a function of the number of time steps and shows that small time steps are needed to achieve a value close to the true Black–Scholes price. This likely partially reflects the choice of discretisation scheme for the BSDE, and other choices may yield better results. Table 12.7 shows the value as a function of the width of the hidden layers in the neural network. The impact is moderate, but a size of 128 gave the fastest convergence. The learning rate impact is shown in Table 12.8 and shows that it significantly impacts convergence speed, with the relatively large learning rate of 0.03 given the fastest time. Finally, larger batch sizes give faster convergence, as shown in Table 12.9. The overall BSDE price versus Black–Scholes price for various European calls is shown in Table 12.10.

(Continued)

(Continued)

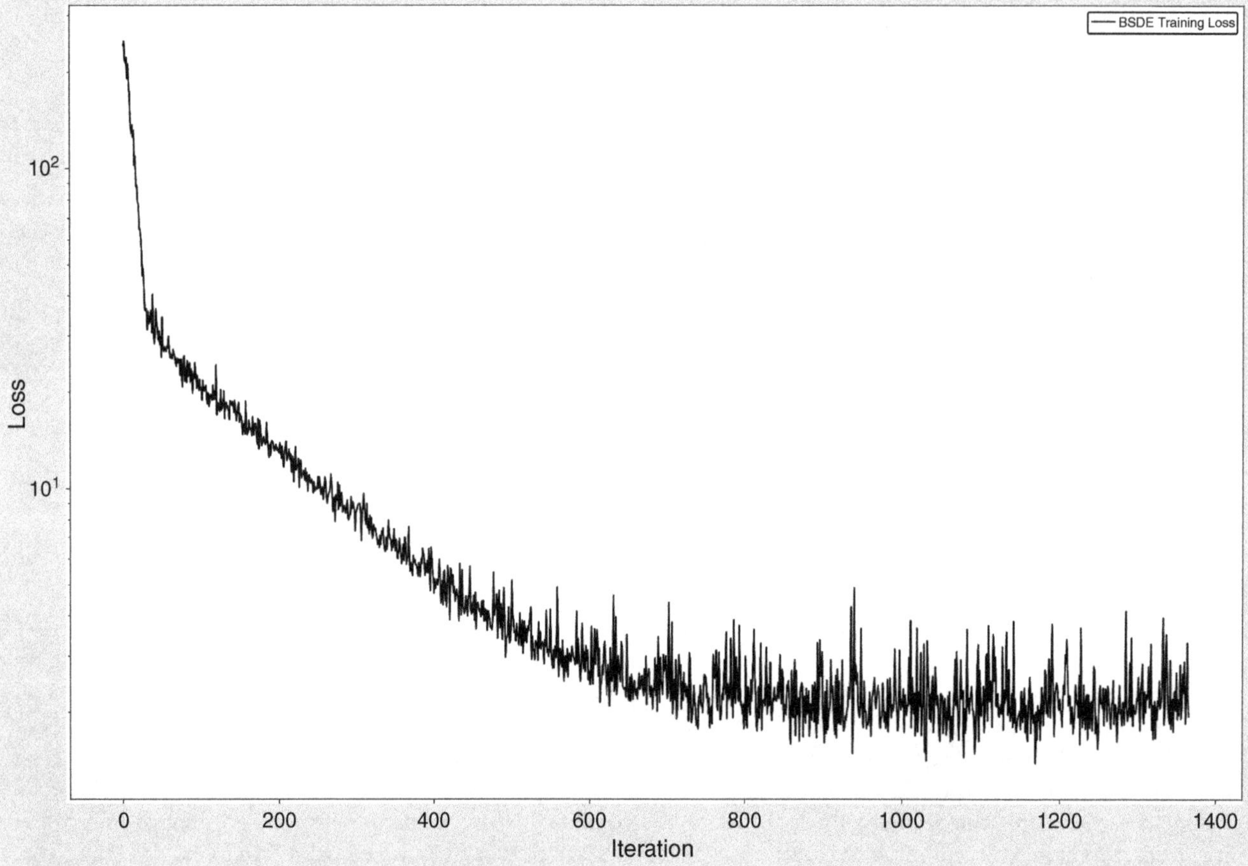

FIGURE 12.4 Loss as a function of iteration for the Black–Scholes European call option valued using the deep BSDE solver.

TABLE 12.6 BSDE Price as a Function of the Number of Time Steps

Time Steps	10	20	50	100	200
Value	9.795228	10.127690	10.329699	10.413579	10.431747
Execution time (s)	27.768716	55.436836	128.246935	149.282946	311.179115

TABLE 12.7 BSDE Price as a Function of the Network Hidden Size

Network Hidden Size	32	64	128	256	512
Value	10.319612	10.337709	10.329699	10.319538	10.338003
Execution time (s)	128.924396	168.802151	116.026306	130.714791	118.297182

TABLE 12.8 BSDE Price as a Function of the Learning Rate

Learning Rate	0.100000	0.030000	0.010000	0.003000	0.001000
Value	10.310511	10.326857	10.329699	10.330357	10.345823
Execution time (s)	899.533212	86.086900	90.009677	322.202397	715.379162

TABLE 12.9 BSDE Price as a Function of the Batch Size

Batch Size	64	256	1024
Value	10.304380	10.329699	10.328215
Execution time (s)	287.064723	133.459473	130.669918

TABLE 12.10 BSDE Price vs Black–Scholes Price for Various European Calls

Maturity (yr)	Strike	BSDE Price	Iterations	Time (s)	BS Price
0.250000	80.000000	21.015049	638	151.835967	21.021298
0.250000	90.000000	11.660649	632	151.638881	11.670087
0.250000	100.000000	4.600510	900	219.220372	4.614997
0.250000	110.000000	1.183740	3278	788.053728	1.191132
0.250000	120.000000	0.196227	2398	574.318083	0.199764
0.500000	80.000000	22.168013	766	182.970728	22.174561
0.500000	90.000000	13.482505	682	163.536399	13.498517
0.500000	100.000000	6.868236	642	154.167644	6.888729
0.500000	110.000000	2.890060	1489	356.890111	2.906471
0.500000	120.000000	1.013166	1813	435.875797	1.022615
1.000000	80.000000	24.570784	1124	269.463914	24.588835
1.000000	90.000000	16.677475	869	206.070365	16.699448
1.000000	100.000000	10.419408	837	200.025648	10.450584
1.000000	110.000000	6.013920	9698	2335.924002	6.040088
1.000000	120.000000	3.224744	1065	257.406025	3.247477

EXAMPLE 12.4: DEEP BSDE SOLVER FOR MULTI-ASSET EUROPEAN CALL WITH DEFAULT RISK

The second example is a European call option with default risk. It is identical to an example provided in Han et al. (2018), which is located in the Jupyter Notebook `BSDE Black Scholes Call with Default Risk.ipynb`. The option is worst-of call with zero strike on 100 assets that all start with the same value,

(*Continued*)

(*Continued*)

have identical volatilities of 20% and are uncorrelated. The counterparty to the option can default, and the intensity function is given by

$$Q(y) = \begin{cases} \gamma^h & y \in (-\infty, v^h) \\ \gamma^l & y \in [v^l, \infty) \\ \dfrac{\gamma^h - \gamma^l}{v^h - v^l}(y - v^h) + \gamma^h & y \in [v^h, v^l) \end{cases},$$

where y is the price of the option. This function gives three different regions for default risk, which is higher when the value of the call is low. The same parameter values were used as in Han et al. (2018): $T = 1$ (yr), recovery $\delta = 2/3$, interest rate $r = 0.02$, $\sigma = 0.2$, $v^h = 50$, $v^l = 70$, $\gamma^h = 0.2$, $\gamma^l = 0.02$.

In this case, the neural networks have an input and output dimension of 100, matching the number of assets. The training loop was modified to accommodate the 100 assets, and the default risk becomes

```
slope = (gamma_h - gamma_l) / (v_h - v_l)
Z_nets = nn.ModuleList([FCNet(d, hidden_dim, d).to(device)
                         for _ in range(N - 1)])
pbar = tqdm(range(max_iterations), desc="Training", dynamic_ncols=True)
for it in pbar:
    S = torch.full((M, d), S0, device=device)
    iteration += 1
    Y = Y0.repeat(M, 1)
    dW = torch.randn(M, N - 1, d, device=device)*torch.sqrt(torch.tensor(dt))

    # For each time step, update asset prices and the BSDE solution.
    for n in range(N - 1):
        S = S * torch.exp((r - 0.5 * sigma**2) * dt
                          + sigma * dW[:, n:n+1]).squeeze()
        Z = Z_nets[n](S)

        # BSDE drift
        piecewise_linear = F.relu(F.relu(Y - v_h) * slope \
                           + gamma_h - gamma_l) + gamma_l
        f = -((1 - delta) * piecewise_linear - r) * Y
        Y = Y - f * dt + Z * dW[:, n:n+1]

    # Terminal payoff for worst-of call.
    payoff_T = worst_of_payoff(S, K)
    loss = torch.mean((Y - payoff_T)**2)
    loss_lst.append(loss.item())

    optimizer.zero_grad()
    loss.backward()
    optimizer.step()
```

The model converged to a price of 58.5237 after 1335 seconds, comparable to the result obtained by Han et al. (2018) of 57.3 after 1607 seconds. The loss during training is illustrated in Figure 12.5.

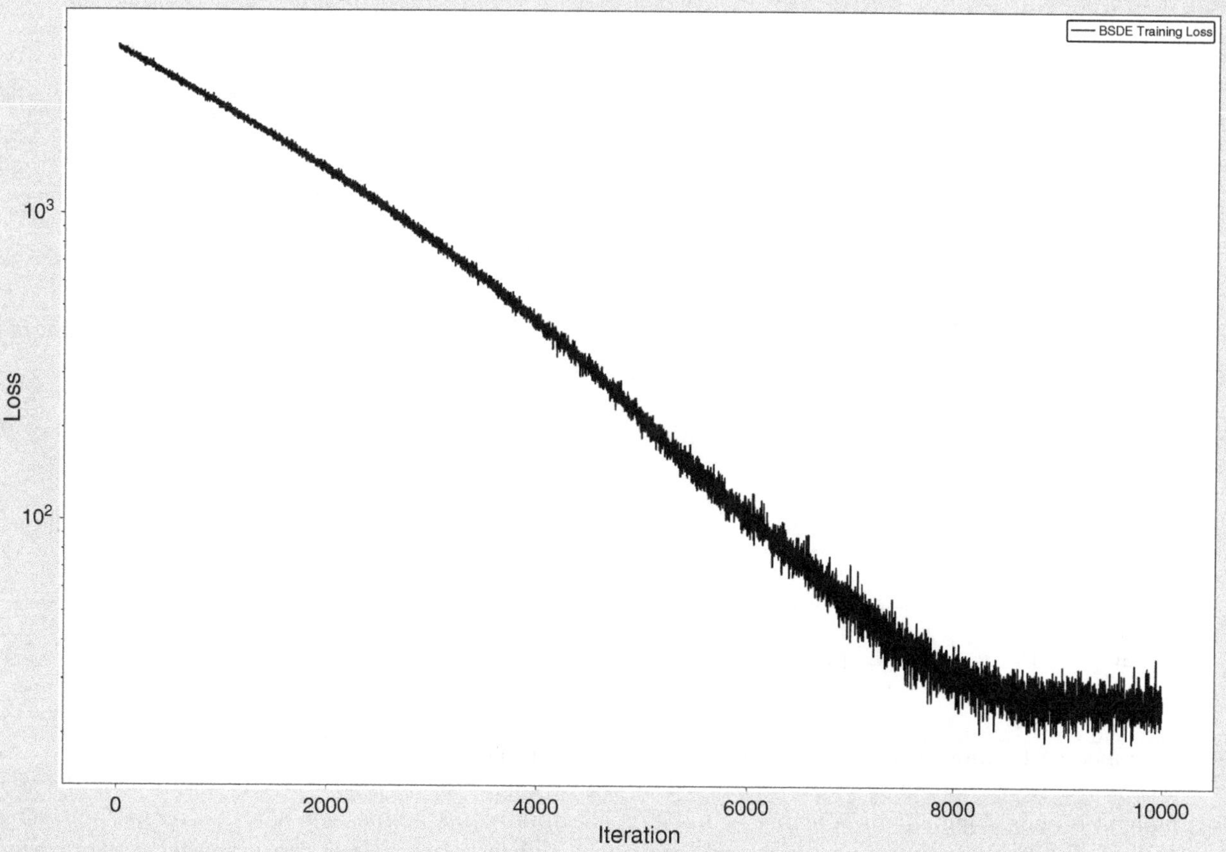

FIGURE 12.5 Loss as a function of iteration for the non-linear European basket option with default risk valued using the deep BSDE solver.

12.3.4 Conclusions on Deep BSDE Solvers

This section has reviewed BSDEs and the deep BSDE solver introduced by Weinan et al. (2017) and Han et al. (2018). BSDEs provide an alternative mathematical setting for models in quantitative finance to traditional SDEs. While SDEs are linked to linear PDEs, BSDEs are similarly linked to semi-linear PDEs by extending the Feynman–Kac theorem. Financial applications of BSDEs include pricing and hedging in incomplete markets, recursive utility models in economics, stochastic control problems, American options and XVA. The deep BSDE algorithm is an application of the function approximation capability of neural networks, used in the basic scheme to model the Z process in the BSDE. While BSDEs can solve non-linear and high-dimensional problems, they use SGD and *on-line* training, making them relatively slow compared to more traditional numerical techniques in quantitative finance.

12.4 PROJECTION AND MARTINGALE SOLVERS

Vidales et al. (2018a) introduce three types of learning algorithms for solving PDEs by deep learning. These are the *projection solver*, the *martingale representation solver* and the *martingale control variate solver*.

The projection solver is motivated by the well-known property of conditional expectations, which states that the conditional expectation of a random variable is the best approximation in the mean square sense of that variable.

Rather than work with the PDE directly, they use the probabilistic representation of it obtained using the Feynman–Kac theorem,

$$D(t,T)u\left(T,X_T^\beta;\beta\right) = v(t,x;\beta) + \int_t^T D(t,s)\partial_x u\left(s,X_s^\beta;\beta\right)\sigma\left(s,X_s^\beta;\beta\right)dW_s, \tag{12.51}$$

where $D(t,T)$ is a discount factor and β are parameters of the stochastic process for X_t. Hence

$$v(t,x;\beta) = D(t,T)g\left(X_T^\beta\right) - \int_t^T D(t,s)\partial_x u\left(s,X_s^\beta;\beta\right)\sigma\left(s,X_s^\beta;\beta\right)dW_s, \tag{12.52}$$

where $u\left(T,X_T^\beta;\beta\right) = g\left(X_T^\beta\right)$ is the option payoff. The property of conditional expectations allows the authors to write

$$\mathbb{E}\left[\left|\mathcal{X} - u\left(t,X_t^\beta;\beta\right)\right|^2\right] = \inf_{\eta\in L^2\left(\sigma\left(X_t^\beta\right)\right)} \mathbb{E}\left[|\mathcal{X}-\eta|^2\right] \tag{12.53}$$

and then seek to find $\eta = h_t\left(X_t^\beta\right)$, where h_t is parameterised by a neural network. Hence, they set up the following learning task:

$$\theta^* := \arg\min_\theta \mathbb{E}_\beta\left[\mathbb{E}_{\left(X_t^{\beta,\pi}\right)_{t\in\pi}}\left[\sum_{k=0}^{N_{\text{steps}}}\left(D\left(t_k,T\right)g\left(X_T^{\beta,\pi}\right) - h[u]_{\theta_{t_k}}\left(X_{t_k}^{\beta,\pi};\beta\right)\right)^2\right]\right], \tag{12.54}$$

where the inner expectation is calculated using Monte Carlo paths generated for $X_{t_k}^{\beta,\pi}$.

The second solver proposed by Vidales et al. (2018a) is a variant of the deep BSDE solver discussed in the previous section, as proposed initially by Weinan et al. (2017). The authors extend the deep BSDE solver to approximate the solution and gradient across all time steps and parameters. Vidales et al. (2018a) also adopt two separate neural networks for the solution and its gradient.

The last solver is a revised deep BSDE solver using a martingale control variate approach, and this is similar to the approach the same authors use in the context of learned control variates for Monte Carlo (Vidales et al., 2018b), which is discussed in detail in Section 13.2.2.

The authors test and compare the various algorithms with Monte Carlo and the DGM. First, they test on exchange options with two assets for which a solution is available through the Margrabe formula (Margrabe, 1978). They then consider the 100-asset exchange option. Narrow confidence intervals were obtained in all cases.

12.5 DEEP PATH-DEPENDENT PDEs (DPPDE)

Jacquier and Oumgari (2019) present a deep learning approach to solving path-dependent PDEs as generated by non-Markovian models such as rough local stochastic volatility. They define the model through the following equations in the physical measure:

$$\begin{aligned} S_t &= S_0 + \int_0^t \mu_r S_r\,dr + \int_0^t l\left(r,S_r,V_r\right)S_r\,dW_r, \\ V_t &= V_0 + \int_0^t K(t-r)\left(b\left(V_r\right)dr + \xi\left(V_r\right)dB_r\right), \\ d\langle W,B\rangle_t &= \rho dt, \end{aligned} \tag{12.55}$$

where W and B are two correlated Brownian motions. Given the payoff function g, the price of the derivative at time t is given by $P_t = \mathbb{E}[g(S_T)|\mathcal{F}_t]$. Then

$$P_t = P\left(t,S_t,\left(\Theta_u^t\right)_{t\le u\le T}\right), \tag{12.56}$$

where

$$\Theta_u^t := \mathbb{E}\left[V_u - \int_t^u K(u-r)b\left(r, V_r\right)dr \mid \mathcal{F}_t\right]. \tag{12.57}$$

Then, the option price satisfies a PPDE of the form

$$\left(\partial_t + \mathcal{L}_x + \mathcal{L}_{xx} + \mathcal{L}_{x\omega} + \mathcal{L}_\omega + \mathcal{L}_{\omega\omega} - r_t\right) P\left(t, S_t, \Theta^t\right) = 0, \tag{12.58}$$

where the differential operators are given by

$$\mathcal{L}_{x\omega} := \rho l(t, x, v)\xi\left(\Theta_t^t\right) x \left\langle \partial_{x,\omega}, K^t \right\rangle, \tag{12.59}$$

$$\mathcal{L}_{xx} := \frac{1}{2} l(t, x, \Theta_t^t)^2 x^2 \partial_x^2, \tag{12.60}$$

$$\mathcal{L}_x := r_t x \partial_x, \tag{12.61}$$

$$\mathcal{L}_{\omega\omega} := \frac{1}{2}\xi(\Theta_t^t)^2 \left\langle \partial_\omega^2, (K^t, K^t) \right\rangle, \tag{12.62}$$

$$\mathcal{L}_\omega := b\left(\Theta_t^t\right)\left\langle \partial_\omega, K^t \right\rangle. \tag{12.63}$$

To proceed, Jacquier and Oumgari (2019) discretise this PPDE by expressing Θ^t and K^t as sums over basis functions:

$$\widehat{\Theta}^t := \sum_{i=1}^{n} \theta_i^t \psi_n^t, \tag{12.64}$$

$$\widehat{K}^t := \sum_{i=1}^{n} \kappa_i^t \psi_n^t. \tag{12.65}$$

This allows the PPDE to be written as a high-dimensional system of PDEs

$$\partial_t \widehat{P} + \frac{1}{2}\mathrm{Tr}\left(\boldsymbol{\Sigma} \cdot \boldsymbol{\Sigma}^\top \cdot \Delta \widehat{P}\right) + \mu \cdot \nabla \widehat{P} - r_t \widehat{P} = 0, \tag{12.66}$$

where

$$\boldsymbol{\Sigma}\left(t, x, \theta^t\right) \cdot \boldsymbol{\Sigma}\left(t, x, \theta^t\right)^\top := \begin{pmatrix} \frac{1}{2} l\left(t, x, \theta^t\right)^2 & \rho l\left(t, x, \theta^t\right)\xi\left(\theta^t\right)\kappa_1^t & \cdots & \rho l\left(t, x, \theta^t\right)\xi\left(\theta^t\right)\kappa_n^t \\ \rho l\left(t, x, \theta^t\right)\xi\left(\theta^t\right)\kappa_1^t & \xi\left(\theta^t\right)^2\left(\kappa_1^t\right)^2 & \cdots & \xi\left(\theta^t\right)^2 \kappa_1^t \kappa_n^t \\ \vdots & \vdots & \ddots & \vdots \\ \rho l\left(t, x, \theta^t\right)\xi\left(\theta^t\right)\kappa_n^t & \xi\left(\theta^t\right)^2 \kappa_1^t \kappa_n^t & \cdots & \xi\left(\theta^t\right)^2 \left(\kappa_n^t\right)^2 \end{pmatrix}. \tag{12.67}$$

This expression is then transformed to a BSDE for $\widehat{P}$,

$$\widehat{P}\left(t, S_t, \theta^t\right) = \widehat{P}\left(T, S_T, \theta^T\right) + \int_t^T r_u \widehat{P}\left(u, S_u, \theta^u\right) \mathrm{d}u - \int_t^T \Sigma\left(u, S_u, \theta^u\right)^\top \cdot \nabla \widehat{P}\left(u, S_u, \theta^u\right) \mathrm{d}W_u, \tag{12.68}$$

which can be solved using the deep BSDE solver of Han et al. (2018).

The authors assessed the DPPDE approach first in the context of a simple European call option under Black–Scholes dynamics, obtaining accurate results for all tested strikes with the most significant relative errors for deep-out-of-the-money options, as might be expected. Only a minimal neural network was required, with two layers of 10 neurons each.

Jacquier and Oumgari (2019) then considered the rough stochastic local volatility model. They chose the model specification with

$$b(V) = \kappa\left(V_\infty - V\right), \tag{12.69}$$

$$\xi(V) = \nu V, \tag{12.70}$$

$$\varsigma(V) = e^V, \tag{12.71}$$

$$K(t) = \frac{t^{H-\frac{1}{2}}}{\Gamma\left(H + \frac{1}{2}\right)} \tag{12.72}$$

that gives the implied total variance (Gatheral and Jacquier, 2014)

$$w(k, T) = \frac{\vartheta_T}{2}\left\{1 + \varrho\varphi\left(\vartheta_T\right)k + \sqrt{\left(\varphi\left(\vartheta_T\right)k + \varrho\right)^2 + 1 - \varrho^2}\right\}, \tag{12.73}$$

where ϱ is a correlation parameter, θ_t is the at-the-money variance and

$$\varphi(\vartheta) = \frac{1}{\lambda\vartheta}\left(1 - \frac{1 - e^{-\lambda\vartheta}}{\lambda\vartheta}\right). \tag{12.74}$$

The deep learning approach was compared with Monte Carlo and the analytic formula for the implied variance for option maturities from 1 week to 3 years. The authors obtained good agreement for all three methods across various strikes.

12.6 PHYSICS-INFORMED NEURAL NETWORKS (PINNs)

Physics-informed neural networks (PINNs) were introduced independently by Raissi et al. (2019), although they can be considered an extension of DGM developed by Sirignano and Spiliopoulos (2018) as described earlier. In continuous time, the approach is broadly the same. Raissi et al. (2019) define a function f using

$$f(t, x) := u(t, x) + \mathfrak{N}[u], \tag{12.75}$$

where $\mathfrak{N}$ is a non-linear operator and $u(t, x) \approx u(t, x|\theta)$ is approximated by a deep neural network with parameters θ. The parameters are then learned using the MSE loss on a series of N_u points selected on the boundary of the region and N_f points in the interior,

$$J = \frac{1}{N_u}\sum_{i=1}^{N_u}\left|u\left(t_u^i, x_u^i\right) - u^i\right|^2 + \frac{1}{N_f}\sum_{i=1}^{N_f}\left|f\left(t_f^i, x_f^i\right)\right|^2. \tag{12.76}$$

The points themselves are selected using Latin hypercube sampling. The authors optimise using the L-BFGS (Zhu et al., 1997) method, although mini-batch SGD and variants can also be used.

The authors present two continuous-time examples: the one-dimensional Burgers' equation with Dirichlet boundary conditions and the Schrödinger equation with periodic boundary conditions and a complex-valued solution. For the former $N_u = 100$, $N_f = 10{,}000$, the neural network consisted of nine dense layers with 20 neurons in each and hyperbolic tangent activation functions. What is particularly notable is the ability of the neural network solution to resolve sharp features in the solution domain, such as astrophysical shock waves (Moschou et al., 2023).

Raissi et al. (2019) also consider the discrete-time case. They apply Runge–Kutta methods to obtain

$$
\begin{aligned}
u^{n+c_i} &= u^n - \Delta t \sum_{j=1}^{q} a_{ij} \mathfrak{N}\left[u^{n+c_j}\right], \quad i = 1, \dots, q, \\
u^{n+1} &= u^n - \Delta t \sum_{j=1}^{q} b_j \mathfrak{N}\left[u^{n+c_j}\right],
\end{aligned}
\tag{12.77}
$$

with $u^{n+c_j}(x) = u\left(t^n + c_j \Delta t, x\right)$ for $j = 1, \dots, q$. To solve this set of PDEs, the authors then construct a single neural network with x as input and the solution at each time step as output,

$$
\left[u_1^n(x), \dots, u_q^n(x), u_{q+1}^n(x)\right]. \tag{12.78}
$$

Van der Meer et al. (2022) further extended PINNs by firstly providing a mathematical motivation for the use of the Monte Carlo-derived loss functional given in Equation (12.76) and secondly introducing a weighting term between the two components of the loss from boundary and interior points. The authors prove two key theorems about PINNs. Noting that minimising the loss functional will lead to only an approximate solution of the PDE because minimising the Monte Carlo loss will not yield the exact minimum corresponding to the exact solution, van der Meer et al. (2022) show in their first theorem that obtaining a low loss from the Monte Carlo leads to a good approximation of the true solution. The second theorem proves that for linear PDEs, the generalised loss functional with the form

$$
J(\hat{u}) = c_1 \int_{\Omega} |\mathfrak{U}(x, \hat{u})|^p dx + c_2 \int_{\partial\Omega} |\mathfrak{F}(x, \hat{u})|^p dx_{\Gamma} \tag{12.79}
$$

is convex. Therefore, Equation (12.76) is the Monte Carlo approximation of the loss functional for $c_1 = c_2 = 1$ and $p = 2$.

Salvador et al. (2020) apply PINNs to price a series of option payoffs. The authors first consider pricing a European put with boundary and interior loss terms equally weighted, obtaining a relative error of 2.23×10^{-4} versus the analytic solution. The second case study was a European exchange option on two assets. Here, Salvador et al. (2020) explored the impact of domain size on the accuracy of the solution, finding that without modification, the relative error increased significantly as the domain size increased. To compensate, the authors introduced a combination of weight scaling and Xavier initialisation (see Section 3.3.1.3), where the initial values of the last layer of the neural network were scaled to match the maximum option value. This scaling procedure allowed the trained model to display a relative error independent of the stock price range. Single and two-asset American options were then valued using PINNs. Here, an analytic solution is unavailable for the two-asset exchange options, so the authors compared the results to the option price computed numerically using finite elements. The authors were able to obtain a relative error of $O(10^{-4})$ in the one-asset case and $O(10^{-2})$ versus FEM in the two-asset exchange options. In all cases, the neural network architecture was four layers of 20 neurons with the hyperbolic tangent activation function; like van der Meer et al. (2022), the authors used L-BFGS for optimisation, rather than SGD.

12.7 DEEP BACKWARD DYNAMIC PROGRAMMING (DBDP)

Two *deep backward dynamic programming (DBDP)* algorithms, DBDP1 and DBDP2, were introduced by Huré et al. (2020). Like Weinan et al. (2017) and Han et al. (2018), these algorithms use the BSDE representation of the PDE, but in distinction to the deep BSDE algorithm, they use a backward approach, and this allows the authors to tackle American options. The two algorithms differ in what is approximated by neural networks: in DBDP1, both the solution and its gradient are estimated using a neural network, while in DBDP2, only the solution is estimated with a neural network and the gradient is estimated by automatic differentiation. DBDP1 is shown in Algorithm 12.5 and DBDP2 in Algorithm 12.6.

Algorithm 12.5: Deep Backward Dynamic Programming 1

Input: Initialise from an estimation $U^{(1)}(t_N, X_{t_N})$ of $u(t_N, X_{T_N})$ with $\hat{U}^{(1)} = g$
for $i = N-1, \dots, 0$ **do**
Given $\hat{U}^{(1)}_{i+1}$, use a pair of deep neural networks $(U_i(.;\theta), Z_i(.;\theta)) \in \mathcal{NN}^{d,1,L,m}(\mathbb{R}^{N_m}) \times \mathcal{NN}^{d,d,L,m}(\mathbb{R}^{N_m})$ for the approximation of $(u(t_i,.), \sigma^T(t_i,.)D_x u(t_i,.))$.
Compute (by SGD) the minimiser of the expected quadratic loss function:

$$J_i^{(1)}(\theta) = \mathbb{E}\left|\hat{U}^{(1)}_{i+1}(X_{t_{i+1}}) - f(t_i, X_{t_i}, U_i(X_{t_i};\theta), Z_i(X_{t_i};\theta), \Delta t_i, \Delta W_{t_i})\right|^2, \tag{12.80}$$

$$\theta_i^* = \arg\min_{\theta\in\mathbb{R}^{N_m}} \hat{L}_i^{(1)}(\theta). \tag{12.81}$$

Update $\hat{U}^{(1)}_i = U_i(.;\theta_i^*)$ and set $\hat{Z}^{(1)}_i = Z_i(.;\theta_i^*)$.

Algorithm 12.6: Deep Backward Dynamic Programming 2

Input: Initialise with $\hat{U}^{(2)}_N = g$.
for $i = N-1, \dots, 0$ **do**
Given $\hat{U}^{(2)}_{i+1}$, use a deep neural network $U_i(.;\theta) \in \mathcal{NN}^{d,1,L,m}(\Theta_m)$.
Compute (by SGD) the minimiser of the expected quadratic loss function:

$$\begin{aligned} J_i^{(2)}(\theta) = \mathbb{E}\Big|\hat{U}^{(2)}_{i+1}(X_{t_{i+1}}) \\ - f(t_i, X_{t_i}, U_i(X_{t_i};\theta), \sigma^T(t_i, X_{t_i})\nabla_x U_i(X_{t_i};\theta), \Delta t_i, \Delta W_{t_i})\Big|^2, \end{aligned} \tag{12.82}$$

$$\theta_i^* = \arg\min_{\theta\in\Theta_m} \hat{L}_i^{(2)}(\theta). \tag{12.83}$$

Update $\hat{U}^{(2)}_i = U_i(.;\theta_i^*)$ and set $\hat{Z}^{(2)}_i = \sigma^T(t_i,.)\hat{D}_x U_i(.;\theta_i^*)$.

12.8 DEEP SPLITTING (DS)

The deep-splitting algorithm was introduced by Beck et al. (2021) to solve a class of non-linear parabolic PDEs of the form

$$\frac{\partial u(t,x)}{\partial t} = F\left(x, u(t,x), \nabla_x u(t,x)\right) + \frac{1}{2}\mathrm{Tr}\left(\sigma(x)\sigma^*(x)H_x u(t,x)\right), \tag{12.84}$$

where Tr is the trace operator and H is the Hessian. Notably, the DS algorithm can cater to fully non-linear PDEs. The differential operator is split into two parts: a linear component and a nonlinear component,

$$F\left(x, u(t,x), \nabla_x u(t,x)\right) = \langle \mu(x), \nabla_x u(t,x)\rangle_{\mathbb{R}^d} + f\left(x, u(t,x), \nabla_x u(t,x)\right), \tag{12.85}$$

with μ chosen so that f is small. The overall approach is to approximate f and then use an approximate Feynman–Kac representation to solve iteratively, and this generates recursive conditional expectation calculations that are performed using deep learning.

The authors first introduce a time partition $0 = t_0 < t_1 < \cdots < t_N$ and then the solution $u(t, x)$ is given by

$$u(t,x) = \varphi(x) + \int_0^t f(x, u(s,x), \nabla_x u(s,x))\, ds + \int_0^t \left[\frac{1}{2}\mathrm{Tr}\left(\sigma(x)\sigma^*(x)H_x u(s,x)\right) + \langle \mu(x), \nabla_x u(s,x)\rangle_{\mathbb{R}^d}\right] ds. \tag{12.86}$$

Using the discrete-time approximation and integrating the first term, coupled with simplifying assumptions that the gradient of the initial condition $\varphi(x)$ is at most growing polynomially, allows the authors to write

$$v(t,x) = v(t_n,x) + f(x, v(t_n,x), \nabla_x v(t_n,x))(t_{n+1} - t_n) + \int_{t_n}^t \left[\frac{1}{2}\mathrm{Tr}\left(\sigma(x)\sigma^*(x)H_x v(s,x)\right) + \langle \mu(x), \nabla_x v(s,x)\rangle_{\mathbb{R}^d}\right] ds, \tag{12.87}$$

where

$$v(t_n, x) \approx u(t_n, x) \quad \text{for all } n \in \{1, \ldots, N\} \tag{12.88}$$

and the approximate solution v is continuous in both arguments and has at most polynomially growing partial derivatives.

Beck et al. (2021) then proceed to form an approximate Feynman–Kac representation with the form

$$v\left(t_{n+1}, Y_{T-t_{n+1}}\right) = \mathbb{E}\Big[v\left(t_n, Y_{T-t_n}\right) + f\left(Y_{T-t_n}, v\left(t_n, Y_{T-t_n}\right), \nabla_x v\left(t_n, Y_{T-t_n}\right)\right)(t_{n+1} - t_n) \,\Big|\, Y_{T-t_{n+1}}\Big], \tag{12.89}$$

which allows the authors to formulate the problem as a recursive sequence of minimisation problems. To proceed, the approximate solution at each t_n, $v(t_n, x)$, is modelled with a neural network $V_n(t_n, x, \theta_n)$ optimised using SGD. That is, they seem to find the parameter vector θ that minimises

$$\mathbb{E}\Big[\Big\| V_n\left(\theta, Y_{T-t_n}\right) - \Big[V_{n-1}\left(\theta^{n-1}, Y_{T-t_{n-1}}\right) + f\left(Y_{T-t_{n-1}}, V_{n-1}\left(\theta^{n-1}, Y_{T-t_{n-1}}\right), \nabla_x V_{n-1}\left(\theta^{n-1}, Y_{T-t_{n-1}}\right)\right)(t_n - t_{n-1})\Big]\Big\|^2\Big]. \tag{12.90}$$

$Y + t^m$ follows an SDE, which is approximated using an Euler–Maruyama discretisation.

In common with many of the papers discussed in this chapter, Beck et al. (2021) apply their algorithm to several test cases, including the HJB equation, the non-linear Black–Scholes, Allen–Cahn-type equations, semi-linear heat equations and the sine-Gordon-type equation. For the non-linear Black–Scholes case, the authors adopt the same problem selected by Weinan et al. (2017) and Han et al. (2018) with default risk. Beck et al. (2021) applied the DS method for cases with dimensions from 10 to 10,000. The final maturity was 4 months, and 96 time steps were used. The neural network architecture was a feedforward network with a d-dimensional input layer followed by two hidden layers of size $d + 10$ with an additional 40 neurons in the cases with dimensionality in the range 0–100. The authors compared their results with the deep BSDE method (Weinan et al., 2017). Relative errors to the reference prices were in the range $O(10^{-3})$ to $O(10^{-5})$. The execution runtime on an NVidia GTX-1080 ranged from 858s for the 10-dimensional case to 23,593s for the 10,000-dimensional case. While the method is successful, the practicality of such long run times is questionable.

The DS method included the empirical study and comparison of deep PDE and BSDE solvers by Assabumrungrat et al. (2024). The test case in this study was a Heston model best-of call with 20 underlying assets. The DS exhibited significantly increased errors when the option maturity was greater than 1.25 years, which the other models under study did not exhibit.

12.9 CONCLUSIONS

This chapter has reviewed deep learning techniques applied to solve PDEs and BSDEs in quantitative finance. The two key methods of *deep BSDE solvers* and the *deep Galerkin methods*, and closely related *physics-informed neural networks*, were explored in detail with numerical examples. The chapter also explored the related techniques of *projection and martingale solvers*, *deep path-dependent PDEs*, *deep backward dynamic programming* and *deep splitting*. For the parabolic PDEs typically found in quantitative finance, some methods like DGM/PINNs can be continuous in time. However, most deep PDE approaches use time discretisation with a neural network introduced per time step. The exact use of the neural network does vary between different approaches: DGM/PINNs use the neural network to approximate the solution, while in the deep BSDE solver, the neural network is used to approximate the control process Z_t. Deep PDE and BSDE solvers can handle semi-linear through to fully non-linear PDEs and high-dimensional cases, and this makes them suitable for handling quantitative finance models that more traditional techniques either cannot be used for or are impractical. However, execution times for these solvers can be slow.

CHAPTER 13

Deep Monte Carlo and Optimal Stopping

Maybe the only significant difference between a really smart simulation and a human being was the noise they made when you punched them.

Terry Pratchett and Stephen Baxter, The Long Earth (2012)

13.1 INTRODUCTION

Monte Carlo simulation is a technique of fundamental importance for model implementation in quantitative finance (see Glasserman, 2004, for a comprehensive guide). As a solution method, it offers several key strengths:

- **Versatility.** Monte Carlo simulations can handle various problems, from option pricing and risk management to portfolio optimisation. They can be applied to virtually any model, regardless of complexity or dimensionality.
- **Flexibility.** They can incorporate complex and path-dependent features of financial instruments, which may be difficult to model analytically.
- **Non-Analytic Solutions.** Monte Carlo methods are invaluable for problems where analytical solutions are unavailable or intractable. They can approximate the distribution of potential outcomes for highly complex models.
- **Parallelisation.** The method is highly amenable to parallel computation, making it efficient to run simulations on modern computing infrastructure such as GPUs, thus speeding up the process significantly.
- **Handling High Dimensionality.** Monte Carlo simulations can manage problems in high-dimensional spaces more effectively than other numerical methods, making them suitable for multi-asset and multi-factor models.

However, Monte Carlo also displays several critical weaknesses:

- **Computationally Intensive.** Monte Carlo simulations can be very time-consuming and computationally expensive, especially for models requiring many simulations to achieve high accuracy.
- **Convergence Rate.** The convergence rate of Monte Carlo simulations is relatively slow at $\mathcal{O}\left(1/\sqrt{N}\right)$, which means that reducing the error by a factor of 10 requires 100 times more simulations.
- **American Exercise.** Standard Monte Carlo cannot price American or Bermudan-style options.

Variance reduction techniques are typically applied to address convergence and computational cost concerns. In contrast, *American* Monte Carlo methods embed ideas from dynamic programming and price options with multiple or continuous exercise.

Neural networks have been applied to Monte Carlo simulations in finance in two ways: firstly, as a form of variance reduction and secondly, as an implementation of American Monte Carlo. This chapter discusses both cases.

Deep Learning in Quantitative Finance, First Edition. Andrew Green.

Section 13.2 presents several applications of neural networks to Monte Carlo simulations. Three examples are explored; the first considers the *deep importance sampling* approach of Virrion (2020), which uses a neural network to optimise the importance sampling variance reduction technique. The second example from Vidales et al. (2018b) uses neural networks to find an optimal martingale control variate, another variance reduction technique. The final technique considered is *deep weighted Monte Carlo* from Kunsági-Máté et al. (2022), which couples a trained variational autoencoder with the weighted Monte Carlo method of Avellaneda et al. (2001).

The classic approach to pricing American and Bermudan options with Monte Carlo is the *Longstaff–Schwartz method* (Longstaff and Schwartz, 2001), which combines Monte Carlo simulations with least-squares regression. Using regression, it simulates multiple asset paths and works backwards from maturity to estimate the continuation value (the expected payoff of holding the option) at each step. This method determines the optimal exercise strategy by comparing the continuation value with the immediate exercise payoff, effectively capturing the early exercise feature through this backward induction process. This approach has also been frequently extended to applications in XVA. A large group of authors have applied deep learning to the problem of American-style options. Many of these could be considered extensions of least-squares regression, and Section 13.3 reviews these in detail.

13.2 DEEP MONTE CARLO

13.2.1 Deep Importance Sampling

Importance sampling is a variance reduction technique used in Monte Carlo simulations to improve the efficiency and accuracy of derivative pricing. The main idea behind importance sampling is to change the probability measure under which the simulation is conducted to draw more samples from the important regions of the distribution, that is, regions that contribute most to the estimated quantity.

The price of a derivative is, of course, the expected value of its payoff under the risk-neutral measure $\mathbb{Q}$:

$$\text{Price} = \mathbb{E}^{\mathbb{Q}}\left[e^{-rT}f(X_T)\right], \tag{13.1}$$

where $f(X_T)$ is the payoff function depending on the underlying asset's value X_T at maturity T, and r is the risk-free interest rate.

The Monte Carlo simulation estimates this expected value by generating N sample paths $\{X_T^{(i)}\}_{i=1}^N$ and averaging:

$$\hat{P} = \frac{1}{N}\sum_{i=1}^{N} e^{-rT} f\left(X_T^{(i)}\right). \tag{13.2}$$

However, if the payoff function $f(X_T)$ has significant contributions from rare events, then the standard Monte Carlo approach may require many samples for a precise estimate. Importance sampling addresses this issue by introducing a change of measure.

Let $g(x)$ be a probability density function that places more weight on the important regions. The original expectation under the risk-neutral measure $\mathbb{Q}$ can be rewritten using the importance sampling density $g(x)$:

$$\mathbb{E}^{\mathbb{Q}}\left[e^{-rT}f(X_T)\right] = \int e^{-rT}f(x)\frac{d\mathbb{Q}}{dg}(x)g(x)\,dx. \tag{13.3}$$

Here, $\frac{d\mathbb{Q}}{dg}(x)$ is the Radon–Nikodym derivative between $\mathbb{Q}$ and g, which represents the likelihood ratio, and this allows us to perform Monte Carlo simulations using samples drawn from $g(x)$ instead of $\mathbb{Q}$:

$$\hat{P}_{IS} = \frac{1}{N}\sum_{i=1}^{N} e^{-rT} f\left(X_T^{(i)}\right)\frac{d\mathbb{Q}}{dg}\left(X_T^{(i)}\right), \tag{13.4}$$

where $X_T^{(i)} \sim g(x)$.

Note that drift change to the Brownian motion associated with the $\mathbb{Q}$ measure to that associated with the g measure is given by

$$dW_t^{\mathbb{Q}} = dW_t + a_s\,ds, \tag{13.5}$$

with the associated Radon–Nikodym derivative given by

$$\left.\frac{d\mathbb{Q}}{dg}\right|_{\mathcal{F}_t} = \exp\left(-\int_0^t a_s\, dW_s - \frac{1}{2}\int_0^t a_s^2\, ds\right). \tag{13.6}$$

The effectiveness of importance sampling depends on the choice of $g(x)$. An optimal $g(x)$ reduces the variance of the estimator $\hat{P}_{IS}$, thus achieving more accurate results with fewer samples. The challenge lies in selecting an appropriate importance sampling density that balances computational complexity and variance reduction.

In practice, various strategies are employed to determine $g(x)$, including heuristics, optimisation methods, and leveraging knowledge about the structure of the payoff function and the underlying asset dynamics. Proper implementation of importance sampling can significantly improve the efficiency of Monte Carlo simulations for derivative pricing (Glasserman, 2004).

Virrion (2020) introduces the concept of a parameterised drift change function, $a^{\theta}(t, X_{0\le s\le t})$, which will be defined by a neural network so that

$$dW_t^{\mathbb{Q}} = dW_t^{\theta} - a^{\theta}(t, X_{0\le s\le t})\, ds, \tag{13.7}$$

and the associated Radon–Nikodym derivative is given by

$$\begin{aligned}\left.\frac{dg^{\theta}}{d\mathbb{Q}}\right|_{\mathcal{F}_t} &= \exp\left(\int_0^t a^{\theta}\left(s, X_{0\le u\le s}\right) dW_s^{\mathbb{Q}} - \frac{1}{2}\int_0^t \left(a^{\theta}\left(s, X_{0\le u\le s}\right)\right)^2 ds\right)\\ &= \exp\left(\int_0^t a^{\theta}\left(s, X_{0\le u\le s}\right) dW_s^{\theta} + \frac{1}{2}\int_0^t \left(a^{\theta}\left(s, X_{0\le u\le s}\right)\right)^2 ds\right).\end{aligned} \tag{13.8}$$

The optimal choice of measure minimises the variance of $f(X_{0\le u\le t})\frac{d\mathbb{Q}}{dg^{\theta}}$ under the sampling measure g^{θ}. So Virrion (2020) proposes the choice of neural network parameters that satisfy

$$\theta^* := \underset{\theta\in\Theta}{\operatorname{argmin}}\quad h(\theta), \tag{13.9}$$

where

$$h(\theta) := \mathbb{E}^{\mathbb{Q}^{\theta}}\left[\left(f\left(X_{0\le t\le T}^{x}\right)\frac{d\mathbb{Q}}{dg^{\theta}}\right)^2\right]. \tag{13.10}$$

To avoid changes of measure that are too dramatic, Virrion (2020) introduces a regularisation term and hence chooses the following objective function:

$$h(\theta) := \mathbb{E}^{\mathbb{Q}^{\theta}}\left[\left(f\left(X_{0\le t\le T}^{x}\right)\frac{d\mathbb{Q}}{dg^{\theta}}\right)^2\right] + \lambda \ln\left(1 + \mathbb{E}^{\mathbb{Q}^{\theta}}\left[\left(\frac{d\mathbb{Q}}{dg^{\theta}} - C\right)^{+}\right]\right), \tag{13.11}$$

for some weight λ and constant C.

EXAMPLE 13.1: DEEP IMPORTANCE SAMPLING

In this example, deep importance sampling is implemented for an arithmetic Asian option and is contained in the Jupyter Notebook `DeepImportanceSampling.ipynb`. The test option is an arithmetic Asian call option with 12 discrete observations over 1 year, with the initial stock price $S_0 = 1.0$, implied volatility $\sigma = 20\%$, interest rate $r = 5\%$ and strike $K = 1.3 \times S_0 e^{-rT}$.

(Continued)

(Continued)

The first step is to value the option using a benchmark model chosen as the PDE model in QuantLib. The basic model code to implement the pricer using Python is given below. Given that this is a PDE-based model, the execution time is relatively fast, as seen in Table 13.1. Note that this runs only on the CPU, while the Monte Carlo is written in PyTorch and runs on the GPU in this example.

TABLE 13.1 Price, Execution Time and Standard Error for the Asian Option

Model	Price	Time (s)	Std Error
PDE model	6.1386×10^{-4}	0.04619	NA
Simple MC (10^6 paths)	5.8564×10^{-4}	0.02978	8.6868×10^{-6}
Deep learning training	NA	3.578	NA
Deep IS Monte Carlo	5.7578×10^{-4}	0.0978	9.7597×10^{-7}
Simple MC (10^8 paths)	5.7664×10^{-4}	0.2083	6.2476×10^{-7}

```
def value_asian_option(S, K, r, sigma, T, option_type, n):
    calendar = ql.NullCalendar()
    day_count = ql.Actual365Fixed()

    # Set up the dates
    maturity_date = ql.Date().todaysDate() + int(T * 365)
    settlement_date = ql.Date().todaysDate()
    fixing_dates = [settlement_date + int(i * T * 365 / n)
                    for i in range(1, n + 1)]

    # Set up the option payoff and exercise type
    payoff = ql.PlainVanillaPayoff(ql.Option.Call if option_type == 'call'
                                   else ql.Option.Put, K)
    exercise = ql.EuropeanExercise(maturity_date)
    pastFixings = 0
    aRAccumulator = 0.0

    option = ql.DiscreteAveragingAsianOption(
        ql.Average.Arithmetic, aRAccumulator, pastFixings,
        fixing_dates, payoff, exercise
    )

    # Set up the Black-Scholes process
    spot_handle = ql.QuoteHandle(ql.SimpleQuote(S))
    div_ts = ql.YieldTermStructureHandle(ql.FlatForward(settlement_date,
                                                        0.0, day_count))
    flat_ts = ql.YieldTermStructureHandle(ql.FlatForward(settlement_date,
                                                         r, day_count))
    vol_ts = ql.BlackVolTermStructureHandle(ql.BlackConstantVol(
                                            settlement_date,
                                            calendar, sigma, day_count))
    bs_process = ql.BlackScholesMertonProcess(spot_handle, div_ts, flat_ts,
                                              vol_ts)

    # Set up the engine and price the option
```

```
    engine = ql.FdBlackScholesAsianEngine(bs_process, tGrid=100, xGrid=100,
                                          aGrid=50)
    option.setPricingEngine(engine)

    return option.NPV()
```

The second step is to price the same option using a Monte Carlo simulation implemented using PyTorch and numpy. Running the option price 10 times using different random number generator seeds allowed the standard error to be estimated. The code is not shown in this section but is a simplified version of the deep importance sampling version below.

The deep importance sampling model uses a neural network per time step, representing $a^{\theta}(t, X_{0\leq s\leq t})$ as defined above. The architecture is the same for all the networks apart from the input size, equal to the length of the Monte Carlo path at the particular time step. The network has two hidden layers with 64 and 32 neurons, respectively, and a ReLU activation function, followed by a single linear output.

The Monte Carlo simulation employs the neural network to adjust the drift for importance sampling, as shown in the code below. It constructs each step of the Monte Carlo path in a separate tensor, then combines them at the end to avoid in-place operations that would cause errors when computing gradients. Similarly, it constructs the weights separately for each time step, stores them in a list and later multiplies them together for the same reason. The for loop processes the time steps sequentially, generating all paths in parallel. The weights list contains the value of the Radon–Nikodym derivative for each path, re-weighting the payoff to ensure the distribution aligns with the risk-neutral measure rather than the importance sampling measure.

```
def simulate_asset_paths_nn(S0, r, sigma, T, dt, N, M, mu_models,
                            device='cpu'):
    # Initialize the tensor to store paths on the specified device
    paths = [torch.zeros((M, 1), device=device) for i in range(N+1)]
    weights_lst = list()

    # Set the initial asset price
    paths[0][:,0] = S0

    # Precompute constants
    drift = (r - 0.5 * sigma ** 2) * dt
    sqrdt = torch.sqrt(torch.tensor(dt, device=device))
    diffusion = sigma * sqrdt

    # Generate paths
    for t in range(1, N + 1):
        mu_model = mu_models[t-1]
        Z = torch.randn(M, device=device)
        concat_paths = torch.cat(paths[:t], dim=1)
        mu_shift = mu_model(concat_paths).squeeze()

        drift_IS = (r - 0.5 * sigma ** 2 - mu_shift * sigma) * dt
        weight_factor = torch.exp(-mu_shift**2 * dt / 2.0)
        paths[t][:,0] = paths[t-1][:, 0] * torch.exp(drift_IS + diffusion*Z)
        weights_lst.append(weight_factor * torch.exp(mu_shift * sqrdt * Z))

    return torch.cat(paths, dim=1), reduce(torch.mul, weights_lst)
```

The following function calculates the option average payoff, applies the max function and then discounts and re-weights the payout with the Radon–Nikodym derivative. This function is run m times to allow estimation of the standard error.

(*Continued*)

(Continued)

```
def value_asian_option_pytorch_nn(S, K, r, sigma, T, option_type, n,
                                  num_paths, seed, mu_models,
                                  device='cpu'):

    torch.manual_seed(seed)
    device = torch.device(device)

    # Time step size
    dt = T / n

    # Generate random paths with importance sampling
    paths, weights = simulate_asset_paths_nn(S, r, sigma, T, dt, n,
                                             num_paths, mu_models,
                                             device=device)

    # Calculate the average price
    average_price = paths[:, 1:].mean(dim=1)

    # Calculate payoff
    if option_type == 'call':
        payoffs = torch.maximum(average_price - K,
                                torch.tensor(0.0, device=device))
    else:
        payoffs = torch.maximum(K - average_price,
                                torch.tensor(0.0, device=device))

    # Discount payoffs
    discounted_payoffs = np.exp(-r * T) * payoffs

    # Apply importance sampling weight factor
    weighted_payoffs = discounted_payoffs * weights

    # Option price
    option_price = weighted_payoffs.mean().item()
    return option_price
```

In running the Monte Carlo simulation without training the neural networks, which acts as a test, using only the random initialisation of the neural network layers, the re-weighting ensures that the expectation aligns with the risk-neutral measure. While random initialisation may increase overall variance, it will not reduce the variance compared to sampling done in the risk-neutral measure.

The training loop is outlined below. It trains all the neural networks simultaneously using the simulation variance as the loss function. The task is completed by consolidating all network parameters into a list and passing them to a single Adam optimiser. A regularisation term to keep weights close to 1.0 is implemented, but in practice, this was not helpful, yielding better results with the `lmda` value set to 0.0. The networks were trained for 100 epochs, applying each iteration to all paths without batching.

```
def train_mu_models(S, K, r, sigma, T, option_type, n, num_paths,
    num_epochs, learning_rate, device='cpu', lmda = 0.00):
    mu_models = [MuShiftNetwork(i).to(device) for i in range(1, n + 1)]
    params = list()
```

```
    for model in mu_models:
        params += list(model.parameters())
    optimizer = optim.Adam(params, lr=learning_rate)

    for epoch in range(num_epochs):
        total_loss = 0.0
        for model in mu_models:
            model.train()
        optimizer.zero_grad()


        # Generate random paths
        paths, weights = simulate_asset_paths_nn(S, r, sigma, T, T/n, n,
                                                  num_paths, mu_models,
                                                  device=device)

        # Calculate the average price
        average_price = paths[:, 1:].mean(dim=1)

        # Calculate payoff
        if option_type == 'call':
            payoffs = torch.maximum(average_price - K,
                                    torch.tensor(0.0, device=device))
        else:
            payoffs = torch.maximum(K - average_price,
                                    torch.tensor(0.0, device=device))

        # Discount payoffs
        discounted_payoffs = np.exp(-r * T) * payoffs

        # Apply importance sampling weight factor
        weighted_payoffs = discounted_payoffs * weights


        # Calculate the variance of weighted_payoffs
        variance_loss = weighted_payoffs.var()

        # Regularization term to ensure weights remain close to 1.0
        weight_reg = ((weights - 1.0) ** 2).mean()

        # Total loss
        loss = variance_loss + lmda * weight_reg
        loss.backward()
        optimizer.step()
        total_loss += loss.item()

        print(f"Epoch {epoch+1}/{num_epochs}, Loss: {total_loss/n}")

    return mu_models
```

Table 13.1 presents the pricing for the Asian option, the execution time and standard error for the four models: benchmark PDE, simple Monte Carlo with 10^6 paths, deep importance sampling Monte Carlo and simple Monte Caro with 10^8 paths. All four models obtain comparable numerical results. The simple PDE

(*Continued*)

(*Continued*)

model is slower than the simple Monte Carlo by a factor of two, but this reflects that the Monte Carlo is GPU accelerated, while the PDE model is not. The deep importance sampling runtime is around three times that of the simple Monte Carlo, reflecting the computational cost of the re-weighting, but has a lower standard error by close to an order of magnitude. Around 100 times more paths are needed to obtain a similar variance reduction with the simple Monte Carlo, taking twice as long as the deep importance sampling model. However, this ignores the neural network training cost of 3.6 seconds. In total, this example does not provide an immediate computational benefit. However, the method does work, and variance reduction has been obtained. Higher-dimensional examples may yield a more practical use case.

13.2.2 Learning Control Variates

13.2.2.1 Control Variates Control variates are another important variance reduction technique for Monte Carlo simulation. This method leverages the correlation between the variable of interest and another variable (the control variate) with a known expected value to reduce the estimator's variance. The key idea is to use the control variate's known expectation to adjust the estimate of the target variable, thereby reducing the estimator's overall variance.

Let X be the random variable whose expected value $\mathbb{E}[X]$ we want to estimate using Monte Carlo simulation. Suppose Y is a control variate, another random variable correlated with X, with a known expected value $\mathbb{E}[Y] = \mu_Y$. The adjusted estimator using control variates is given by

$$\hat{X}_{CV} = \frac{1}{n}\sum_{i=1}^{n}(X_i - \beta(Y_i - \mu_Y)), \tag{13.12}$$

where X_i and Y_i are the ith simulated values of X and Y, and β is a coefficient that needs to be determined.

For the variance reduction to be effective, X and Y should be correlated. The closer the correlation between X and Y is to 1, the more effective the control variates method will be in reducing variance. The optimal value of β that minimises the variance of $\hat{X}_{CV}$ can be derived as follows. The variance of the adjusted estimator is given by

$$\mathrm{Var}(\hat{X}_{CV}) = \mathrm{Var}\left(\frac{1}{n}\sum_{i=1}^{n}(X_i - \beta(Y_i - \mu_Y))\right). \tag{13.13}$$

Since the terms inside the summation are i.i.d., this can be simplified to

$$\mathrm{Var}(\hat{X}_{CV}) = \frac{1}{n}\mathrm{Var}(X - \beta(Y - \mu_Y)). \tag{13.14}$$

Expanding the variance term gives

$$\mathrm{Var}(X - \beta Y) = \mathrm{Var}(X) + \beta^2\mathrm{Var}(Y) - 2\beta\mathrm{Cov}(X, Y). \tag{13.15}$$

To find the optimal β, take the derivative of the variance with respect to β and set it to zero,

$$\frac{d}{d\beta}(\mathrm{Var}(X) + \beta^2\mathrm{Var}(Y) - 2\beta\mathrm{Cov}(X, Y)) = 0, \tag{13.16}$$

which is satisfied when

$$\beta = \frac{\mathrm{Cov}(X, Y)}{\mathrm{Var}(Y)}. \tag{13.17}$$

The variance of the control variate estimator is reduced to

$$\mathrm{Var}(\hat{X}_{CV}) = \frac{1}{n}\left(\mathrm{Var}(X) - \frac{\mathrm{Cov}(X, Y)^2}{\mathrm{Var}(Y)}\right), \tag{13.18}$$

using the optimal β, which shows that the adjusted estimator's variance is always less than or equal to the variance of the original estimator, provided that Y is appropriately chosen and correlated with X.

13.2.2.2 Martingale Control Variates The martingale representation theorem (see, e.g., Shreve, 2004) provides a mechanism for identifying control variates. This approach to control variates has been adopted by several authors, including Newton (1994), Fouque and Han (2007) and Belomestny et al. (2018).

Following Vidales et al. (2018b), consider a derivative payoff given by $f((X_s)_{s\in[t,T]})$, the discounted expected value is given by

$$V_t = \mathbb{E}\left[D(t, T)f((X_s)_{s\in[t,T]})\middle|\, \mathcal{F}_t\right], \tag{13.19}$$

where $\mathcal{F}_t$ is the filtration. Given that V_T is $\mathcal{F}_T^W$ measurable and $\mathbb{E}\left[|V_T|^2\right] < \infty$, the martingale representation theorem gives

$$V_T = \mathbb{E}\left[V_T \mid \mathcal{F}_0^W\right] + \int_0^T Z_s dW_s, \tag{13.20}$$

where Z_t is a unique process adapted to $\mathcal{F}_t^W$, the filtration generated by Brownian motion W, and $\mathbb{E}\left[\int_t^T |Z_s|^2 ds\right] < \infty$. The tower property of expectations gives

$$\mathbb{E}\left[V_T \mid \mathcal{F}_t\right] = \mathbb{E}\left[V_T \mid \mathcal{F}_0^W\right] + \int_0^t Z_s dW_s. \tag{13.21}$$

Equations (13.20) and (13.21) can be combined to give

$$\mathbb{E}\left[V_T \mid \mathcal{F}_t\right] = V_T - \int_t^T Z_s dW_s. \tag{13.22}$$

Then, taking the expectation again,

$$V_t = \mathbb{E}\left[V_T \mid \mathcal{F}_t\right] = \mathbb{E}\left[\mathbb{E}\left[V_T \mid \mathcal{F}_t\right]\right] = \mathbb{E}\left[V_T - \int_t^T Z_s dW_s \mid \mathcal{F}_t\right]. \tag{13.23}$$

This gives the following Monte Carlo estimator:

$$\mathcal{V}_t^N := \frac{1}{N}\sum_{i=1}^N\left(V_T^i - \int_t^T Z_s^i dW_s^i\right), \tag{13.24}$$

which has the following properties:

$$\mathbb{E}\left[\mathcal{V}_t^N \mid \mathcal{F}_t\right] = V_t, \tag{13.25}$$

$$\mathrm{Var}\left[\mathcal{V}_t \mid \mathcal{F}_t\right] = 0. \tag{13.26}$$

So the special process Z_t generates a *martingale control variate* that reduces the variance to 0. In practice, there is no way to obtain the process Z_t. However, it is the case that any martingale can be added to the expectation without introducing bias in the result and can reduce variance if positively correlated with the payoff. For example, Fouque and Han (2007) form a martingale control variate for barrier options using the delta of a Black–Scholes option price.

13.2.2.3 Neural Martingale Control Variates Vidales et al. (2018b) seek to approximate the process Z with a neural network Z^θ, giving the Monte Carlo estimator

$$\mathcal{V}_t^{\theta,\lambda,N} := \frac{1}{N}\sum_{i=1}^{N}\left(V_T^i - \lambda \int_t^T \left(Z^\theta\right)_s^i dW_s^i\right). \tag{13.27}$$

They offer two broad approaches, one associated with a PDE solution and one not.

The PDE approach is limited to the case where the process Z can be associated with the derivative of a solution of a PDE. So, given a Markov process

$$dX_s = b\left(s, X_s\right) ds + \sigma\left(s, X_s\right) dW_s \quad t \in [t, T] \tag{13.28}$$

there is a valuation function

$$v(t,x) := \mathbb{E}\left[D(t,T)g\left(X_T\right) \mid X_t = x\right], \tag{13.29}$$

which, applying the Feynman–Kac theorem, satisfies the PDE

$$\frac{\partial v}{\partial t} + \operatorname{tr}\left(a\frac{\partial^2 v}{\partial x^2}\right) + b\frac{\partial v}{\partial x} - cv = 0. \tag{13.30}$$

Using Itô's lemma gives

$$D(t,T)v\left(T, X_T\right) = v\left(t, x_t\right) + \int_t^T D(t,s)\frac{\partial v}{\partial x}v\left(s, X_s\right)\sigma\left(s, X_s\right) dW_s. \tag{13.31}$$

Then, taking the expectation gives

$$\mathbb{E}\left[D(t,T)g\left(X_T\right) \mid \mathcal{F}_t\right] = D(t,T)g\left(X_T\right) - \int_t^T D(t,s)\frac{\partial v}{\partial x}\left(s, X_s\right)\sigma\left(s, X_s\right) dW_s. \tag{13.32}$$

Hence, the process Z_t takes the form

$$Z_t = D(t,s)\frac{\partial v}{\partial x}\left(s, X_s\right)\sigma\left(s, X_s\right). \tag{13.33}$$

The question then becomes how to approximate $\frac{\partial v}{\partial x}$ and Vidales et al. (2018b) present several options. One approach is to approximate v directly with a neural network and then use a deep PDE solver, as discussed in Chapter 12. A second alternative is to use the probabilistic representation in Equation (13.31) and treat it as a BSDE, again a method discussed in Chapter 12. A final alternative is provided through the Bismut–Elworthy–Li formula

$$\frac{\partial v(t,x)}{\partial x} = \mathbb{E}\left[\left(D(t,T)g\left(X_T\right) - g\left(X_t\right)\right)\int_t^T a(s)(\sigma(X(s)))^{-1}Y(s)dW_s \mid X_t = x\right], \tag{13.34}$$

where $a(s)$ is a continuous deterministic function such that $\int_t^T a(s)ds$ and

$$\begin{aligned} dY_s &= \partial_x b\left(s, X_s\right) Y_s ds + \sum_{j=1}^{d}\frac{\partial\sigma^{\cdot j}\left(s, X_s\right)}{\partial x}Y_s dW_s^j, \\ Y_t &= I. \end{aligned} \tag{13.35}$$

So, the Bismut–Elworthy–Li formula provides a means of approximating the process Z_t. To proceed, Vidales et al. (2018b) note that if $a\sigma^{-1}(X)Y$ is well behaved then

$$g\left(X_t\right)\mathbb{E}\left[\int_t^T a(s)(\sigma(X(s)))^{-1}Y(s)dW_s \mid X_t = x\right] = 0, \tag{13.36}$$

and hence

$$\frac{\partial v(t,x)}{\partial x} = \mathbb{E}\left[(D(t,T)g(X_T) - g(X_t))\int_t^T a(s)(\sigma(X(s)))^{-1}Y(s)dW_s \mid X_t = x\right]. \tag{13.37}$$

So a Monte Carlo estimator can be formed, with $a(s) := \frac{1}{T-t}$, giving

$$\begin{aligned}\mathcal{X} &:= (D(t,T)g(X_T) - D(t,t)g(X_t))\frac{1}{T-t}\int_t^T (\sigma(X(s)))^{-1}Y(s)dW_s \\ \frac{\partial v(t,X_t)}{\partial x} &= \mathbb{E}[\mathcal{X} \mid X_t].\end{aligned} \tag{13.38}$$

Finally, a neural network $\mathcal{R}^\theta$ can be used to approximate $\frac{\partial v(t,X_t)}{\partial x}$ and optimised:

$$\theta^* := \underset{\theta}{\operatorname{argmin}}\mathbb{E}\left[\left|\mathcal{X} - \mathcal{R}^\theta(X_t)\right|^2\right]. \tag{13.39}$$

The more general approach aims to approximate the process Z_t at discrete time steps t_k using a neural network that takes the asset path at all time steps up to the present:

$$Z_{t_k} \approx D^\pi(t,t_k)\,\mathcal{R}^{\theta_{t_k}}\left(\left(X^\pi_{t_j}\right)_{j=0}^k\right)\sigma\left(t_k,\left(X^\pi_{t_k}\right)\right). \tag{13.40}$$

The Monte Carlo estimator, as defined in Equation (13.24), is then given by

$$\mathcal{V}^{\pi,\theta,\lambda,N}_{t,T} := \frac{1}{N}\sum_{i=1}^N (D^\pi(t,T))^i g\left(\left(\left(X^\pi_{t_k}\right)_{k=0}^{N_{\text{steps}}}\right)^i\right) - \lambda M^{i,\theta}_{t_k,T}, \tag{13.41}$$

$$M^{i,\theta}_{t_k,T} := \sum_{k=1}^{M-1}(D^\pi(t,t_k))^i\left(\mathcal{R}^{\theta_{t_k}}\right)\left(\left(\left(X^\pi_{t_j}\right)_{j=0}^k\right)^i\right)\sigma\left(t_k,\left(X^\pi_{t_k}\right)^i\right)\Delta W^i_{t_{k+1}}. \tag{13.42}$$

There are two ways of choosing the neural network parameters: one to minimise the variance of the estimator and a second to optimise the correlation between the control variate and the original Monte Carlo estimator. The variance estimator is given by

$$\theta^{\star,\text{var}} := \underset{\theta}{\operatorname{argmin}}\operatorname{Var}\left[\mathcal{V}^{\pi,\theta,\lambda,N_{\text{steps}}}_{t,T}\right], \tag{13.43}$$

with $\lambda = 1$. Algorithm 13.1 presents the steps of the approach.

The alternative correlation optimisation seeks to find parameters

$$\theta^{\star,\text{cor}} := \underset{\theta}{\operatorname{argmin}}\left[1 - \left(\rho^{V_T,M^\theta_{t,T}}\right)^2\right], \tag{13.44}$$

where

$$\rho^{V_T,M^\theta_{t,T}} = \frac{\operatorname{Cov}\left(V_T, M^\theta_{t,T}\right)}{\sqrt{\operatorname{Var}[V_T]\operatorname{Var}\left[M^\theta_{t,T}\right]}}. \tag{13.45}$$

The steps in the method are given in Algorithm 13.2.

Vidales et al. (2018b) applied the deep control variates methodology to two examples: exchange options and basket options, with 2 assets and 100 assets. As with the importance sampling case described earlier, the input dimension for the neural networks was a function of the time step t_k. For a d-dimensional input layer, the two

Algorithm 13.1: Deep Control Variates Using Variance Minimisation

Input: N
Initialise θ;
for $i : 1 : N$ **do**
  Generate samples: $\left(\Delta w_{t_m}\right)_{m=1}^{M}$;
  Generate asset path: $\left(x^i_{t_m}\right)_{m=0}^{M}$;
  Compute estimator: $\mathcal{V}^{\pi,\theta,M,i}_{t,T}$;
Compute the mean: $\overline{\mathcal{V}}^{\pi,\theta,1,M}_{t,T} = \frac{1}{N}\sum_{i=1}^{N}\mathcal{V}^{\pi,\theta,1,M,i}_{t,T}$;
Optimise: $\theta^{\star,\text{var}} := \underset{\theta}{\operatorname{argmin}}\frac{1}{N}\sum_{i=1}^{N}\left(\mathcal{V}^{\pi,\theta,M,i}_{t,T} - \overline{\mathcal{V}}^{\pi,\theta,M}_{t,T}\right)$;
Output: $\theta^{\star,\text{var}}$

Algorithm 13.2: Deep Control Variates Using Correlation Maximisation

Input: N
Initialise θ;
for $i : 1 : N$ **do**
  Generate samples: $\left(\Delta w_{t_m}\right)_{m=1}^{M}$;
  Generate asset path: $\left(x^i_{t_m}\right)_{m=0}^{M}$;
  Compute: V^i_T, $M^\theta_{t,T}$;
Compute: $\overline{V_T} := \frac{1}{N}\sum_{i=1}^{N} V^i_T$;
Compute: $\overline{M^\theta_{t,T}} := \frac{1}{N}\sum_{i=1}^{N} M^{\theta,i}_{t,T}$;
Optimise: $\theta^{\star,\text{cor}} := \underset{\theta}{\operatorname{argmin}}\left[1-\left(\frac{\sum_{i=1}^{N}\left(M^{i,\theta}_{t,T}-\overline{M^\theta_{t,T}}\right)\left(\Xi^i_T-\overline{V_T}\right)}{\left(\sum_{i=1}^{N}\left(V_T-\overline{V_T}\right)^2\sum_{i=1}^{N}\left(M^{i,\theta}_{t,T}-\overline{M^\theta_{t,T}}\right)^2\right)^{1/2}}\right)^2\right]$;
Output: $\theta^{\star,\text{cor}}$

hidden layers were specified to use $20 + d$ neurons and ReLU activation functions. The output layer has a single output when approximating v and d-dimensional, approximating $\frac{\partial v}{\partial x}$. The training was performed on batches of 5000 paths with the Adam optimiser using a learning rate of 10^{-3} for the first 10,000 iterations and 10^{-4} after that.

The authors tested three learned control variate approaches: variance minimisation, correlation maximisation and the BSDE solver. Table 13.2 summarises the results obtained and the best-performing method in each case. Significant variance reduction was achieved, particularly for the high-dimensional basket option.

TABLE 13.2 Best-Performing Learned Control Variate in Vidales et al. (2018b)

Model	Method	Variance Reduction Factor
Exchange option 2	Var	132.28
Exchange option 100	BSDE	130.39
Basket option 2	Var	1228
Basket option 100	Corr	517,201

EXAMPLE 13.2: DEEP LEARNING CONTROL VARIATES

This example implements the variance-minimising control variate technique from Vidales et al. (2018b), and can be seen in the Jupyter Notebook `DeepLearningControlVariate.ipynb`. The example uses an average basket option with 10 underlying assets. For simplicity, all the initial stock prices were set at 1.0, as was the option strike. The risk-free rate was 0.05, all the dividend yields were 0.03 and the correlation matrix was the identity matrix.

A basket option pricer was constructed using QuantLib to benchmark the model. This pricer was identical to those used to generate the basket option training sets earlier, save for the payoff, which was a simple average. This model uses a Monte Carlo simulation to value the option and, as expected, it executes on the CPU.

As with the previous example, a simple Monte Carlo model was also constructed using PyTorch and GPU acceleration, which provides a performance benchmark for the deep control variate model.

The deep control variate model uses a simple feedforward network at each time step, although by default, only one time step was used for the European basket option. The network architecture was a simple feedforward network with two hidden layers. The input and output dimensions are set to be the same as the dimension of the problem, which is the number of assets; this holds for multiple time steps as well. Therefore, the neural network only considers the previous time step increment values, as specified by Equation (13.41), rather than the entire history. The output is set at the same size as the dimension and multiplied by the volatility-scaled Weiner process increments. The two hidden layers contain 64 neurons, followed by the ReLU activation function. Batch normalisation was not used and was found to be detrimental during testing.

The deep control variate model was a Python class derived from `nn.Module` containing the parameters for the Monte Carlo simulation and the generation of the martingale control variate. The first part of the class is shown here. As can be seen, this initialises the class properties, including the list of neural networks per time step, using an `nn.ModuleList`, which combines all of the network parameters; hence, all are trained simultaneously with the `DeepControlVariate` class itself.

```
def __init__(self, dim, spot_prices, volatilities, correlations, strike,
             maturity, risk_free_rate, dividend_yields,
             num_simulations=10000, num_time_steps=1, option_type='call',
             device=device):
    super(DeepControlVariate, self).__init__()
    self.dim = dim
    self.volatilities = torch.tensor(volatilities, device=device,
                                     dtype=torch.float32)
    self.strike = strike
    self.maturity = maturity
    self.risk_free_rate = risk_free_rate
    self.dividend_yields = torch.tensor(dividend_yields, device=device,
                                        dtype=torch.float32)
    self.num_simulations = num_simulations
```

(Continued)

(Continued)

```
    self.num_time_steps = num_time_steps
    self.option_type = option_type
    self.device = device
    correlations = torch.tensor(correlations, device=device,
                                dtype=torch.float32)
    self.cholesky =  torch.linalg.cholesky(correlations)
    self.df = np.exp(-self.risk_free_rate * self.maturity)
    self.network_lst = nn.ModuleList([DeepISNetwork(dim, 64) for
                                     i in range(num_time_steps)])
```

The forward method runs the Monte Carlo simulation and calculates the martingale control variate for each path, returning both tensors. During the control variate calculation, it loops over the time steps, passing the previous step increments to the corresponding neural network. The outputs are then multiplied by the volatility-scaled Wiener process increments to calculate the control variate.

```
def forward(self, S0):
    spot_prices = torch.tensor(S0, device=self.device, dtype=torch.float32)
    dt = self.maturity / self.num_time_steps
    sqrtdt = np.sqrt(dt)

    Z = torch.randn(self.num_time_steps, self.dim, self.num_simulations,
                    device=self.device)
    transformed_samples = torch.matmul(self.cholesky, Z)
    vol_sqrt_dW = self.volatilities.unsqueeze(1) * sqrtdt * \
                  transformed_samples

    # Calculate path increments and path
    dS = (self.risk_free_rate - self.dividend_yields.unsqueeze(1) - \
          0.5 * self.volatilities.unsqueeze(1)**2) * dt + \
          vol_sqrt_dW
    cum_sum = torch.cumsum(dS, dim=0)
    exp_S = torch.exp(cum_sum)
    S = spot_prices.unsqueeze(1) * exp_S

    # Calculate martingale control variate
    netZ_int_lst = list()
    for i, net in enumerate(self.network_lst):
        netZ_int_lst.append(net(dS[i].T))
    net_Z = torch.cat(netZ_int_lst)
    stoch_int = torch.matmul(net_Z, vol_sqrt_dW)
    control_variate = torch.cumsum(stoch_int, dim=0)

    return S, control_variate
```

The function train_optimise_var contains the training loop, with its core shown below. It calculates the basket option payout and the control variate adjusted payout inside the loop. The variance of the latter serves as the loss. The learning rate is adjusted by a factor of 10 every 5000 iterations, slightly slower than in Vidales et al. (2018b).

```
for it in tqdm_epoch:
    model.train()
    optimizer.zero_grad()

    lr = base_lr * 0.1**(it//5000)
    for param_group in optimizer.state_dict()['param_groups']:
        param_group['lr'] = lr

    # Forward pass
    paths, control_variate = model(spot_prices)
    basket_avg = paths[-1].mean(dim=0)

    # Calculate payoff
    if model.option_type.lower() == 'call':
        payoffs = torch.maximum(basket_avg - model.strike,
                                torch.tensor(0.0, device=device))
    else:
        payoffs = torch.maximum(model.strike - basket_avg,
                                torch.tensor(0.0, device=device))

    disc_payoffs = model.df * payoffs
    price = disc_payoffs.mean().item()
    std_error = disc_payoffs.std().item() / np.sqrt(model.num_simulations)

    MC_CV = price - model.df * control_variate
    MC_Price = MC_CV.mean()
    var_MC_CV_estimator = MC_CV.var()
    loss = var_MC_CV_estimator
    loss.backward()

    optimizer.step()
    MC_std_error = MC_CV.std().item() / np.sqrt(model.num_simulations)
```

Figures 13.1 and 13.2 show the training loss and the standard error reduction per iteration. Training is noisy, that is clear, but very significant variance reduction is achieved over the 20,000 training iterations, and the results are broadly comparable to those obtained by Vidales et al. (2018b).

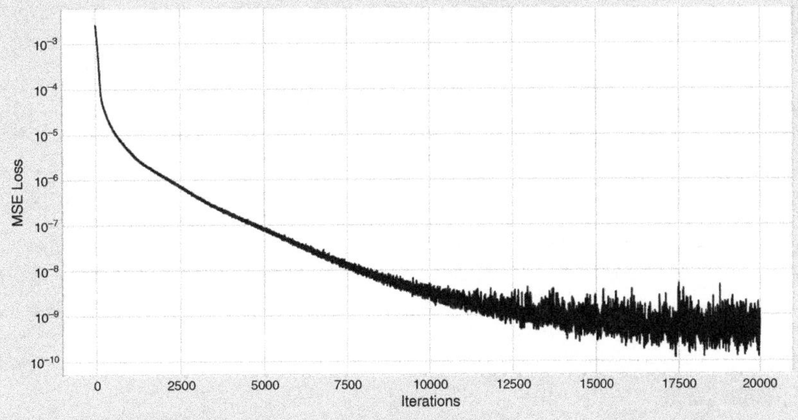

FIGURE 13.1 Loss as a function of iteration for the deep control variate Monte Carlo used to value an average basket option with 10 assets.

(Continued)

(*Continued*)

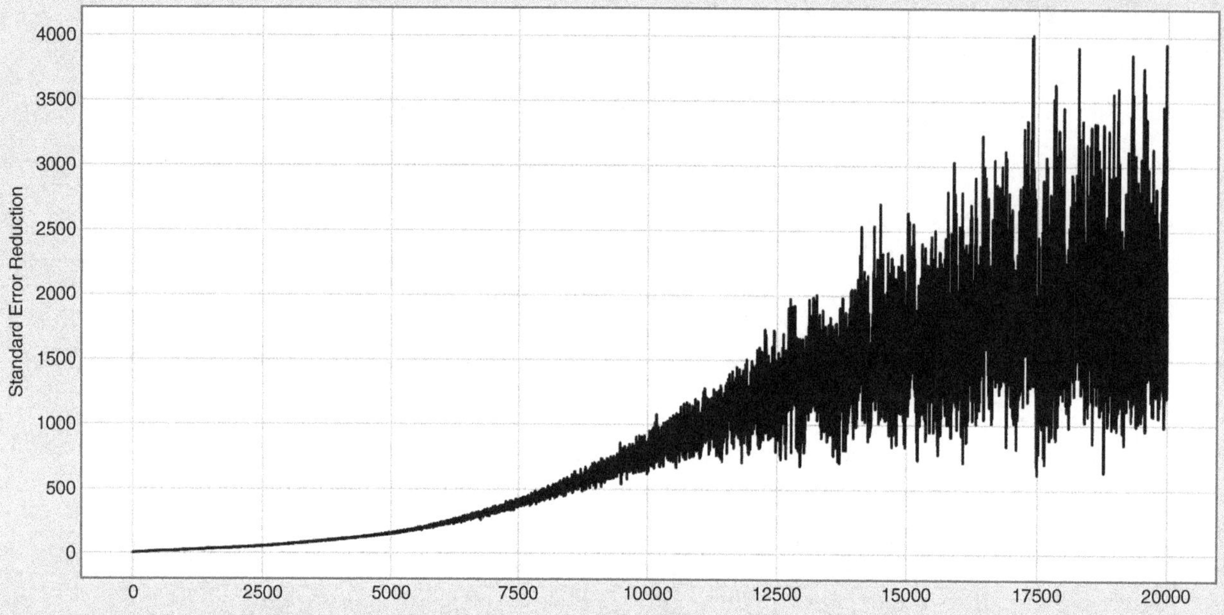

FIGURE 13.2 Variance reduction as a function of iteration for the deep control variate Monte Carlo used to value an average basket option with 10 assets.

Table 13.3 shows the price, execution time and standard error for the four different basket option models and the training time for the neural networks. The deep control variate model standard error is three orders of magnitude better than the comparable simple Monte Carlo and QuantLib models with 5000 paths. Obtaining the same standard error from the simple Monte Carlo requires a considerable increase of 10^{10} simulation paths. However, it is still not cost-effective as a large simple Monte Carlo simulation is executed in 11.3s, while 89s are required for training in the deep learning model. Given that these results are not too far apart, the method could be cost-effective with less benign payoff functions than an average basket, or the trained neural network could be used offline.

TABLE 13.3 Price, Execution Time and Standard Error for the Basket Option

Model	Price	Time (s)	Std Error
QL model (5000 paths)	0.0358	0.38	6.21×10^{-4}
Simple MC (5000 paths)	0.0359	0.002	6.23×10^{-4}
Deep learning training	NA	89	NA
Deep CV Monte Carlo	0.0354	≈ 0.004	4.1×10^{-7}
Simple MC (1×10^{10} paths)	0.0353	11.3	4.3×10^{-7}

13.2.3 Deep Weighted Monte Carlo

The *deep weighted Monte Carlo* framework from Kunsági-Máté et al. (2022) combines a generative *variational autoencoder (VAE)* with a deep learning version of the weighted Monte Carlo technique developed by Avellaneda et al. (2001). VAEs were introduced in Section 9.4 and are further discussed in the context of market data generation in Chapter 18. VAEs are trained to reconstruct volatility surfaces from their input via a Gaussian latent space in this context. Once trained, the decoder projects a volatility surface into the dimensions of the latent space, and the decoder reconstructs this surface from the latent space. As previously discussed, the decoder can be used generatively by inputting a vector of Gaussian random samples to generate a new surface. Kunsági-Máté et al. (2022) used a historical time series of GBP European swaption implied volatility surfaces for their analysis, using a strike-option maturity slice through the volatility cube with an underlying swap tenor of 2 years. They used the period from 1 September 2015 to 5 April 2019 as the training set, with the block between 9 April 2019 and 15 January 2020 as a standard test set and the early part of the COVID-19 pandemic period from 16 January 2020 to 8 October 2020 as an extreme test set. Thus, they used only a relatively small amount of training data. This approach can be applied to other types of volatility surfaces equally well, as demonstrated by Bergeron et al. (2021) and illustrated in the example below.

The VAE network used by Kunsági-Máté et al. (2022) is small with two hidden layers in both encoder and decoder, each with just 10 units and the elu activation function. The latent space used was three-dimensional, with the authors testing two- to four-dimensional ones. The Adam optimiser was used for training with the standard initial learning rate of 0.001 and a batch size equal to 32. The loss function was the standard for VAEs, $J = J_{rec} + \beta J_{KL}$ with $\beta = 5e^{-5}$.

The encoder can be used directly for encoding, or, as Kunsági-Máté et al. (2022) note, you can project a volatility surface into the latent space by optimising and searching for a point where the decoder reconstructs the given surface. Although optimisation is considerably slower than encoder inference, it can be more accurate. Therefore, the authors also trained the encoder model further using 10,000 synthetic volatility surfaces generated by the decoder. They fine-tuned the encoder with the decoder weights frozen. This fine-tuning of the encoder is optional since only the trained decoder is needed for weighted Monte Carlo simulations.

The weighted Monte Carlo technique from Avellaneda et al. (2001) is a way of adjusting a Monte Carlo simulation by re-weighting the paths in such a way as to match the prices of a set of benchmark instruments. Starting with a *prior* Monte Carlo simulation with some parameters selected to reflect an initial guess of the dynamics, the value of a discounted payoff g is given by

$$V = \frac{1}{N}\sum_{i=1}^{N} g_i, \tag{13.46}$$

where g_i is the payoff from path i and there are N Monte Carlo paths. The technique then introduces weights to update the simulated distribution to reflect the observed market,[1]

$$V = \sum_{i=1}^{N} g_i p_i, \tag{13.47}$$

where p_i is the probability weight associated with the *posterior* distribution. Given a set of M calibrating instruments with prices C_j and path payoffs $g_i j$, the weighted Monte Carlo simulation value is given by

$$C_j = \sum_{i=1}^{N} g_{ij} p_i. \tag{13.48}$$

In theory, the weights can be determined from the calibration instruments, but given that typically $N \gg M$, the system is overdetermined, and some constraints need to be introduced. Avellaneda et al. (2001) propose to minimise the *Kullback–Leibler relative entropy* between the prior and posterior distributions, given by

$$D(p \mid q) = \sum_{i=1}^{\nu} p_i \log\left(\frac{p_i}{q_i}\right), \tag{13.49}$$

which, given that $q_i = \frac{1}{N}$, becomes

$$D(p \mid q) = \log N + \sum_{i=1}^{N} p_i \log p_i. \tag{13.50}$$

[1]Implicitly, a change of probability measure is being performed.

To calibrate the model, Avellaneda et al. (2001) formulate this in terms of Lagrangian multipliers as a min–max problem

$$\underset{\lambda}{\operatorname{argmin}}\,\underset{p}{\operatorname{argmax}}\left\{-D(p\mid u)+\sum_{j=1}^{M}\lambda_j\left(\sum_{i=1}^{N}p_i g_{ij}-C_j\right)\right\}, \tag{13.51}$$

with probabilities taking the form of the Boltzmann distribution

$$p_i=\frac{1}{Z(\lambda)}\exp\left(\sum_{j=1}^{M}g_{ij}\lambda_j\right), \tag{13.52}$$

where $Z(\lambda)$ is the partition function

$$Z(\lambda)=\frac{1}{N}\sum_{i=1}^{N}\exp\left(\sum_{j=1}^{N}g_{ij}\lambda_j\right). \tag{13.53}$$

Minimising the following expression using gradient descent gives the solution:

$$\begin{aligned} W(\lambda) &= \log(Z(\lambda))-\sum_{j=1}^{M}\lambda_j C_j \\ &= \log\left\{\frac{1}{N}\sum_{i=1}^{N}\exp\left(\sum_{j=1}^{M}g_{ij}\lambda_j\right)\right\}-\sum_{j=1}^{M}\lambda_j C_j. \end{aligned} \tag{13.54}$$

Once the weights have been obtained, the Monte Carlo model can be used to value other more exotic derivatives, and Avellaneda et al. (2001) used a down-and-out barrier option as a test case.

Kunsági-Máté et al. (2022) aim to circumvent this numerical procedure using a neural network *weight decoder*,

$$p=\Phi_{WD}(z), \tag{13.55}$$

that translates from the latent space into the path weights p. Once such a model was available, it would be possible to couple this with the encoder and perform the following steps almost instantaneously:

1. Project the current volatility surface into the latent space using the enhanced encoder.
2. Generate path weights from the latent space, thus calibrating to current market prices.

The new weight decoder network proposed by the authors has two hidden layers of 20 and 49 units with an elu activation function, followed by an output with softmax applied over a layer equal to the number of Monte Carlo paths. The softmax function guarantees that the path weights sum to 1.0. The following steps are performed to train the model:

1. Generate a batch of latent space vectors by projecting the same training data into the latent space using the encoder z.
2. Generate volatility surfaces from z using the VAE decoder in evaluation mode.
3. Invert the options in the generated volatility surfaces to give call and put prices using Black–Scholes.
4. Generate path weights p from the weight decoder.
5. Use the path weights to price the same call and put options in the vol surface.
6. Measure the MSE between the reconstructed and Monte Carlo call and put prices.

Hence, the basic loss function is given by

$$J_{WD}=J_{rec-mc,call}+J_{rec-mc,put}. \tag{13.56}$$

Kunsági-Máté et al. (2022) propose adding two additional terms to the loss; one is the KL relative entropy between the prior and posterior probability weights as given by Equation (13.49) and the second through adding fictional derivatives with payoff

$$g_j = (S_{j,t_2} - S_{j,t_1}) \tag{13.57}$$

that have zero price and are designed to enforce the martingale condition. In practice, the authors found the latter term very expensive to implement and hence dropped it in favour of monitoring divergence from the martingale condition. Hence, the final loss is given by

$$J_{WD} = J_{rec-mc,call} + J_{rec-mc,put} + \delta D(p \mid q), \tag{13.58}$$

with $\delta = 1e^{-8}$. The example below implements deep weighted Monte Carlo.

EXAMPLE 13.3: DEEP WEIGHTED MONTE CARLO

This example implements the deep weighted Monte Carlo method of Kunsági-Máté et al. (2022). Two Jupyter Notebooks are provided: `Generate Implied Vol Rough Bergomi.ipynb`, which generates synthetic data, and `DeepWeightedMC-rBergomi.ipynb`, which trains a VAE and weight decoder.

Unfortunately, there is a lack of open-source volatility surface datasets. Of course, many paid data vendors can supply suitable data for models of this type. Given the need to use freely available data for these examples, synthetic volatility surfaces are generated. The data is generated by randomly sampling the parameters of a volatility surface model. *Rough Bergomi* (Christian Bayer and Gatheral, 2016) is a four-parameter model. This volatility surface is also used in Chapter 15 and is described in detail there. The Jupyter Notebook `Generate Implied Vol Rough Bergomi.ipynb` generates around 5000 sample volatility surfaces notable for their strong smiles and skews, as can be seen from the example shown in Figure 13.3.

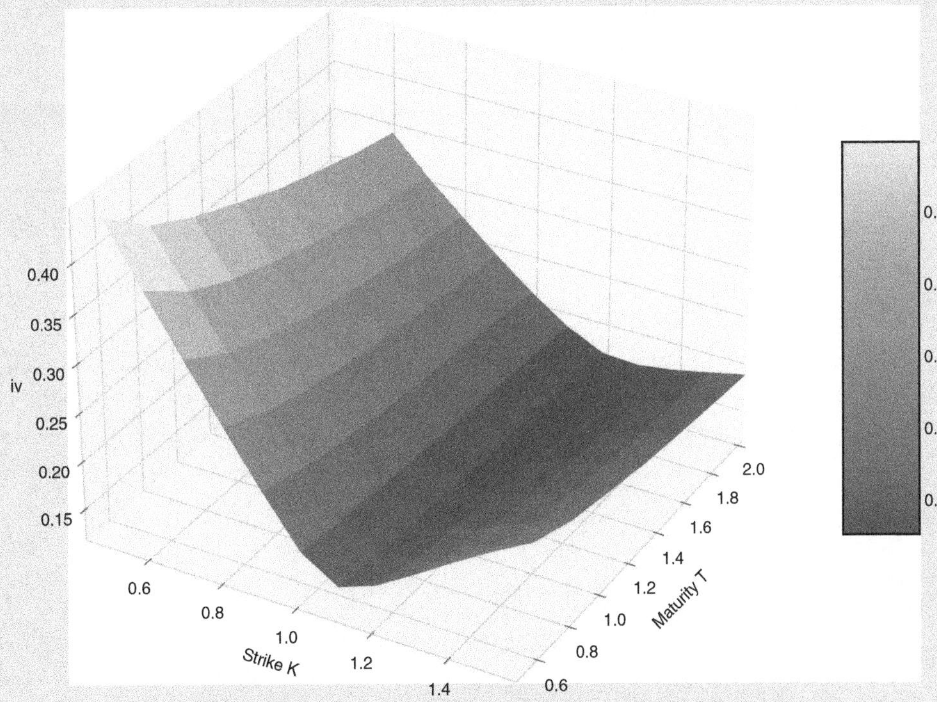

FIGURE 13.3 Example synthetic volatility surface generated from the rough Bergomi model.

(Continued)

(*Continued*)

Once the data is generated, the VAE model can be trained. The second Jupyter Notebook, `DeepWeightedMC-rBergomi.ipynb`, starts by loading the Bergomi volatility surfaces from a CSV file using Pandas. The data is then loaded into a Pandas data frame to facilitate the necessary data manipulation steps to form a PyTorch tensor.

The data is presented as a table of implied volatility points for 11 fixed strikes equally spaced between 0.5 and 1.5 and eight maturities ranging from 0.5 to 2.25 years. An index value identifies each distinct volatility surface. The implied volatility values typically range between around 15% and 50%, so it is better to scale these values to cover the range of 0–1. For this purpose, min–max scaling from scikit-learn is employed.

Next, each volatility surface is reconstructed from the flattened representation using the Pandas pivot functionality for each block of points. All the volatility surfaces are then stacked into a single three-dimensional tensor. Any surfaces with *NaN* entries are removed to ensure data cleanliness.

Since the VAE model used in this example is based on dense layers rather than convolutional layers, the last two axes of the tensor are flattened to obtain a two-dimensional tensor with a different example per row. Training and testing sets are created by splitting the first 80% of the data for training. No shuffling of the data is required as it is randomly generated.

The data is then passed to the training loop using PyTorch data loaders constructed from the training and test tensors.

The VAE model structure is shown below, with the encoder, decoder and the VAE that combines them.

```
class Encoder(nn.Module):
    def __init__(self, input_dim, hidden_dim, latent_dim):
        super(Encoder, self).__init__()
        self.fc1 = nn.Linear(input_dim, hidden_dim)
        self.fc2 = nn.Linear(hidden_dim, hidden_dim)
        self.fc_mean = nn.Linear(hidden_dim, latent_dim)
        self.fc_log_var = nn.Linear(hidden_dim, latent_dim)

    def forward(self, x):
        h = F.silu(self.fc1(x))
        h = F.silu(self.fc2(h))
        mean = self.fc_mean(h)
        log_var = self.fc_log_var(h)
        return mean, log_var
```

As can be seen, the encoder consists of two hidden layers, which were set to 16 units, with *silu* activation, which is the PyTorch name for *swish*. The output of the encoder is the mean and log variance of the latent space variables and hence consists of two linear layers of size 4.

```
class Decoder(nn.Module):
    def __init__(self, latent_dim, hidden_dim, output_dim):
        super(Decoder, self).__init__()
        self.fc1 = nn.Linear(latent_dim, hidden_dim)
        self.fc2 = nn.Linear(hidden_dim, hidden_dim)
        self.fc4 = nn.Linear(hidden_dim, output_dim)

    def forward(self, x):
        h = F.silu(self.fc1(x))
        h = F.silu(self.fc2(h))
        out = torch.sigmoid(self.fc4(h))
        return out
```

The decoder is also simple, with two hidden layers of 16 units, followed by swish activation functions and an output of size 88 and sigmoid to match the earlier min–max scaling.

```
class VAE(nn.Module):
    def __init__(self, input_dim, hidden_dim, latent_dim):
        super(VAE, self).__init__()
        self.encoder = Encoder(input_dim, hidden_dim, latent_dim)
        self.decoder = Decoder(latent_dim, hidden_dim, input_dim)

    def reparameterize(self, mean, log_var):
        std = torch.exp(0.5 * log_var)
        eps = torch.randn_like(std)
        return mean + eps * std

    def forward(self, x):
        mean, log_var = self.encoder(x)
        z = self.reparameterize(mean, log_var)
        x_recon = self.decoder(z)
        return x_recon, mean, log_var
```

The VAE model ties together the encoder and decoder models, with the `reparameterize` function providing the resampling from the latent space.

The VAE training used a training loop similar to previous examples, with the loss being the combination of the MSE reconstruction loss and KL divergence, the latter term being weighted by $\beta = 0.00005$. The model was trained through 1000 epochs, which, given the small size of the model and dataset, took just 199 seconds on an RTX 4090. The training loss as a function of epoch is shown in Figure 13.4. After training, the reconstruction loss was calculated on the training and test sets, giving 8.435×10^{-5} on the training set and 8.056×10^{-5} on the test set, the model showing good generalisation.

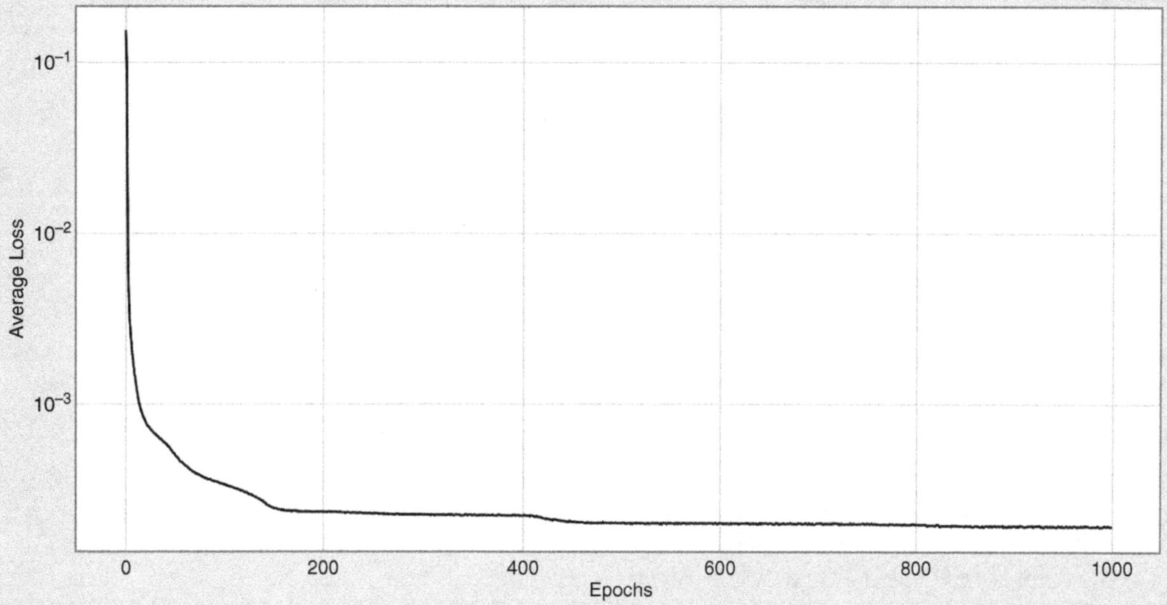

FIGURE 13.4 Deep weighted Monte Carlo VAE model training loss.

(Continued)

(*Continued*)

Kunsági-Máté et al. (2022) performed a latent space analysis, and Figure 13.5 illustrates a similar analysis performed here. Twenty plots in the figure show volatility surfaces generated from fixed points in the latent space. The centre column always shows the origin in the latent space, that is, (0, 0, 0, 0). Either side represents a single shift from that origin in the latent space, with the columns representing shifts of $-2, -1, 0, 1, 2$ and the rows representing the shifted dimension. The results are much less orthogonal than those achieved by Kunsági-Máté et al. (2022), but it seems that the third dimension of the latent space controls the degree of smile versus skew. Note that the vertical implied volatility axis remained scaled here.

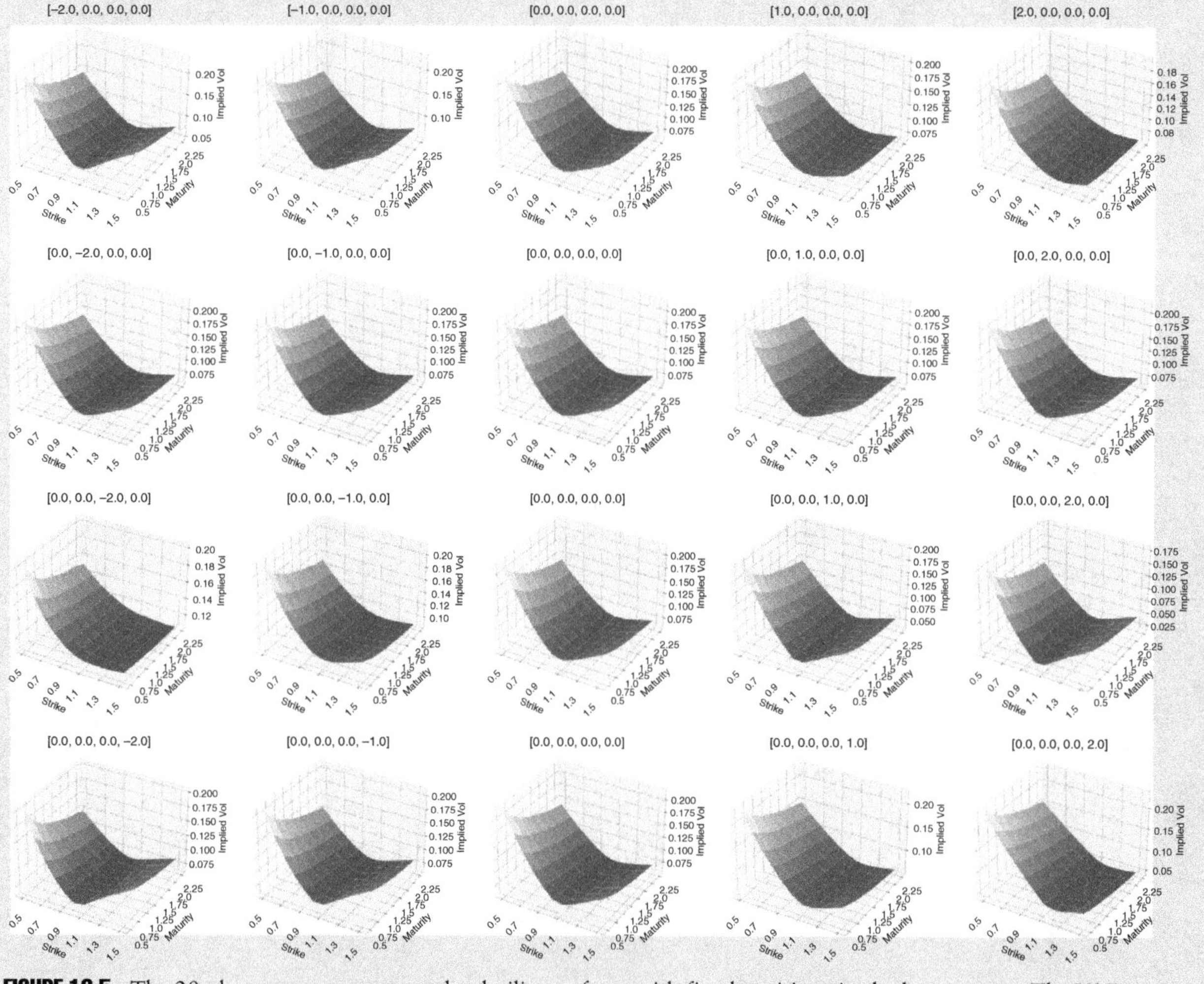

FIGURE 13.5 The 20 plots represent generated volatility surfaces with fixed positions in the latent space. The VAE was trained using around 5000 synthetic volatility surfaces generated by randomly sampling the parameters of the rough Bergomi model (see Chapter 15 for details). The latent space has four dimensions, and these were sampled using the five values (–2.0, –1.0, 0.0, 1.0, 2.0), with the four rows representing the shift in each dimension.

The deep weighted Monte Carlo decoder model is the last step. The weighted decoder network is illustrated below and uses a simple feedforward network with two hidden layers and a softmax output layer the same size as the number of Monte Carlo paths, chosen to be 4096.

```
class DeepWMCNetwork(nn.Module):
    def __init__(self, latent_size, output_size):
        super(DeepWMCNetwork, self).__init__()
        self.fc1 = nn.Linear(latent_size, 32)
        self.fc2 = nn.Linear(32, 64)
        self.fc3 = nn.Linear(64, output_size)
        self.relu = nn.ReLU()
        self.softmax = nn.Softmax()

    def forward(self, x):
        out = self.fc1(x)
        out = self.relu(out)
        out = self.fc2(out)
        out = self.relu(out)
        out = self.fc3(out)
        return self.softmax(out)
```

Another class was created to support the training of the decoder network, and this takes the parameters of the calibrating put and call options alongside those of the prior Monte Carlo simulation. The forward method takes in the latent space vector and outputs the prices of the calibrating instruments under the weighted posterior Monte Carlo simulation. Note that the prior Monte Carlo paths are generated once by the `simulate_asset_paths` function and held fixed, and this function runs a simple Monte Carlo using PyTorch and is similar to the two previous examples in this chapter.

```
class DeepWMCModel(nn.Module):
    def __init__(self, S0, r, prior_sigma, dt, num_steps, num_paths,
                 maturities, strikes, latent_size, device='cpu'):
        super(DeepWMCModel, self).__init__()
        self.S0 = S0
        self.r = r
        self.prior_sigma = prior_sigma
        self.dt = dt
        self.num_steps = num_steps
        self.num_paths = num_paths
        self.T = max(maturities)
        self.maturities = maturities
        self.strikes = strikes
        self.deepwmcnet = DeepWMCNetwork(latent_size, num_paths)
        # Generate the prior paths
        self.paths = simulate_asset_paths(S0, r, prior_sigma, maturities[-1],
                                          dt, num_steps, num_paths, device=device)

    def forward(self, z):
        weights = self.deepwmcnet(z)
        return price_calls_puts(self.paths, weights, self.strikes,
                                self.maturities, r, device)
```

The function `price_calls_puts` calculates the prices of calibrating options under the weighted Monte Carlo, operating in parallel across all paths and options for the best performance.

(*Continued*)

(*Continued*)

The training loop differs from that used by Kunsági-Máté et al. (2022) in one crucial aspect. There is no need to use actual volatility surfaces to calibrate the weighted encoder model; synthetically generated ones can be used instead, simplifying training. Hence, a block of latent space samples was generated at the start of training and then iterated using mini-batches for each epoch. The mini-batches could be shuffled for each epoch, but this was optional. A fragment of the training is shown below to illustrate the operations. In the code fragment, the `vae_decoder` is used to infer the volatility surfaces for the mini-batch. These are then rescaled back to implied volatility space. The prices of the puts and calls are calculated using the `calculate_option_prices` function, simply a parallel implementation of Black–Scholes using PyTorch to allow the generated dataset to remain on the GPU. The Kullbeck–Leibler divergence term was not included, and good results were obtained without it. For simplicity, the martingale condition has not been tested but would need to be checked using a real-world example.

```
z = torch.randn((batches, latent_size), device=device)

for it in tqdm_epoch:
    imb = 0
    loss_list = list()
    for _ in range(batches // mini_batches):
        dwc_model.train()
        optimizer.zero_grad()

        # Forward pass
        iz = z[imb:imb+mini_batches,:]
        ivs = vae_decoder(iz)
        calls, puts = dwc_model(iz)

        # unscale implied vols
        sivs = ivs * mmdiff + minscale
        rsivs = sivs.reshape((64, no_strikes, no_mats))
        vcalls = calculate_option_prices(rsivs, dwc_model.strikes,
                                         dwc_model.maturities,
                                         dwc_model.S0, dwc_model.r,
                                         device, True)
        vputs = calculate_option_prices(rsivs, dwc_model.strikes,
                                        dwc_model.maturities,
                                        dwc_model.S0, dwc_model.r,
                                        device, False)

        loss = F.mse_loss(vcalls, calls) + F.mse_loss(vputs, puts)
        loss.backward()
        optimizer.step()
        loss_list.append(loss.item())

        # Update progress bar
        tqdm_epoch.set_description(f"Iteration {it+1}/{n_iter} \
                                   - Loss: {loss:.8e}")
        imb += mini_batches

    ave_loss = sum(loss_list) / len(loss_list)
```

The weight encoder was trained through 1000 epochs with a block of 4096 samples from the latent space, with mini-batches of size 64. The Adam optimiser was used with the default learning rate of 0.001, giving the training loss shown in Figure 13.6. Training took 549 seconds to complete but could be shortened to fewer epochs. However, it would occur offline in any case.

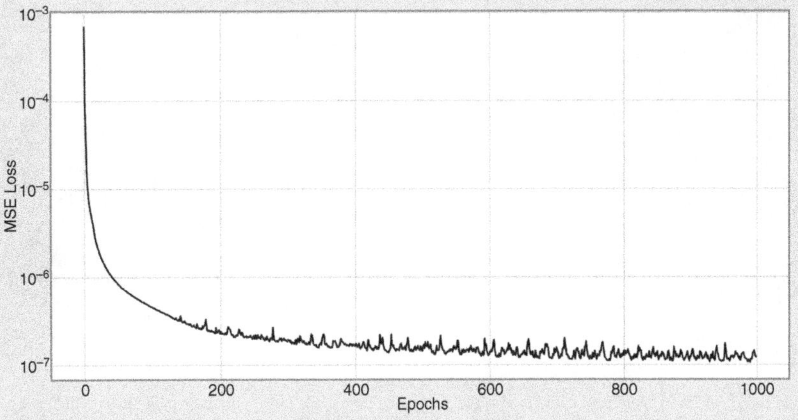

FIGURE 13.6 Deep weighted Monte Carlo weight encoder model training loss.

Finally, as an example, the trained weight encoder was used to infer the prices of calibration options for a random point in the latent space. The selected point was the vector (1.4329, −0.1552, 1.0501, 0.4988), and this gives the volatility surface illustrated in Figure 13.7 when decoded using the VAE model and rescaled. The call and put prices derived from the volatility surface are compared with those obtained from the trained weighted Monte Carlo model in Figure 13.8. At this point, the weighted Monte Carlo model is ready to price other options.

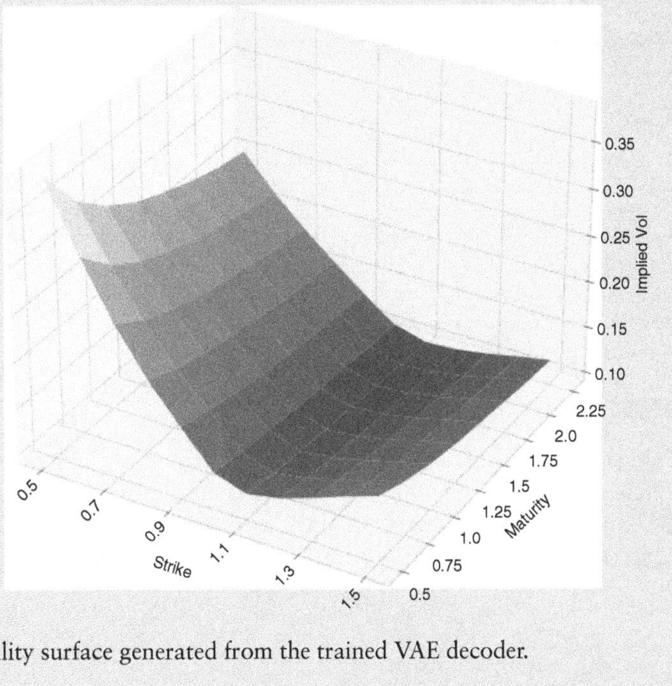

FIGURE 13.7 Example volatility surface generated from the trained VAE decoder.

(*Continued*)

(*Continued*)

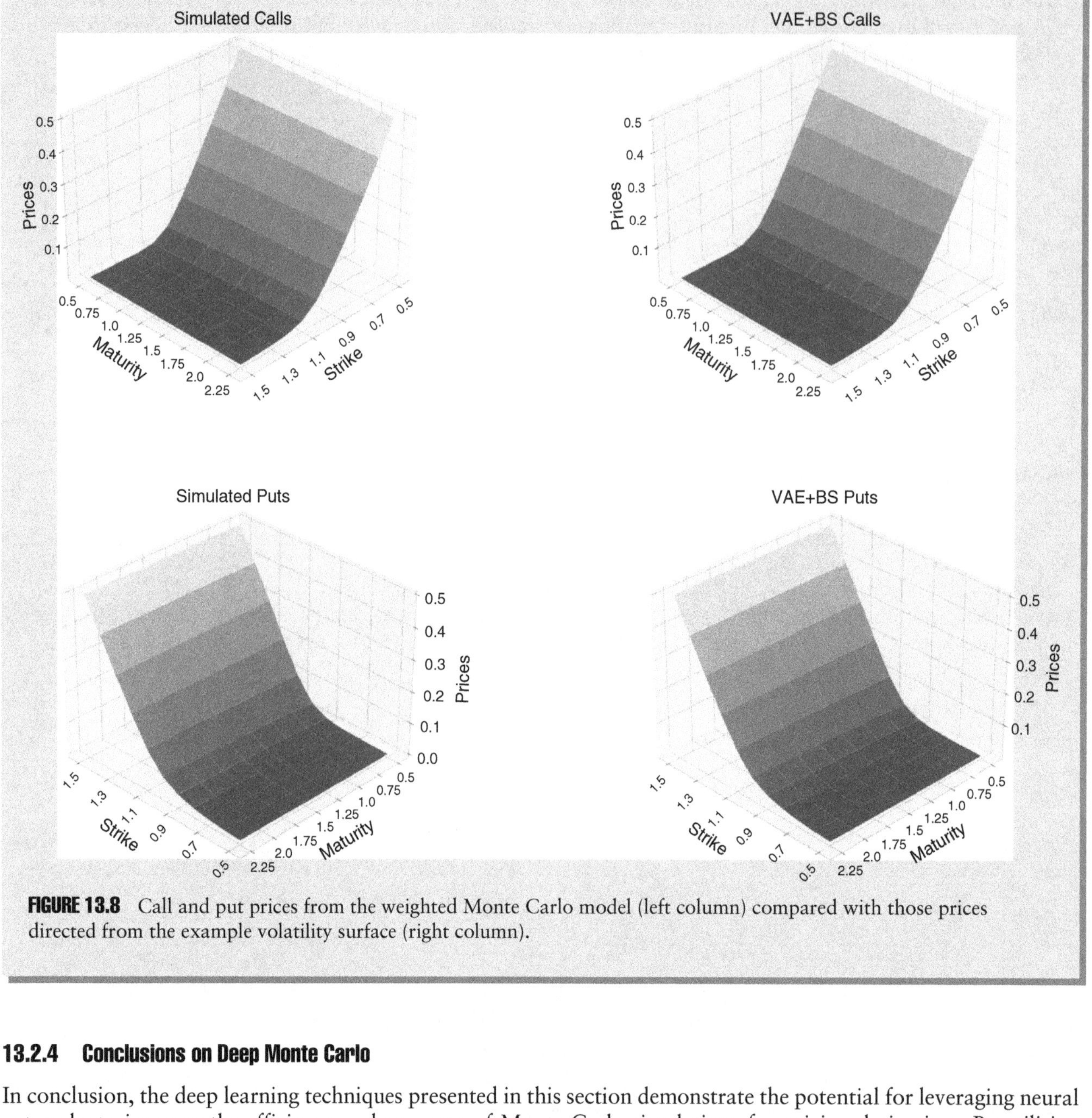

FIGURE 13.8 Call and put prices from the weighted Monte Carlo model (left column) compared with those prices directed from the example volatility surface (right column).

13.2.4 Conclusions on Deep Monte Carlo

In conclusion, the deep learning techniques presented in this section demonstrate the potential for leveraging neural networks to improve the efficiency and accuracy of Monte Carlo simulations for pricing derivatives. By utilising importance sampling, control variates and weighted Monte Carlo methods in conjunction with neural networks, these approaches aim to reduce the variance of Monte Carlo estimators, enabling more precise pricing with fewer simulation paths.

13.3 DEEP OPTIMAL STOPPING AND APPLICATIONS

13.3.1 American and Bermudan Options

American option pricing can be defined by (see, e.g., Glasserman, 2004)

$$\sup_{\tau \in \mathcal{T}} \mathbb{E}\left[e^{-\int_0^\tau r(u)du} h(\mathbf{X}_\tau)\right], \tag{13.59}$$

where τ is the stopping time in the set of possible stopping times $\mathcal{T} \in [0, T]$, r is the short rate, h is the payoff function and $\mathbf{X}_t$ is a vector-valued stochastic process. If the process $\mathbf{X}_t$ is Markovian, then the choice to exercise depends only on $\mathbf{X}_t$. A Bermudan option restricts the set of possible stopping times to a discrete set $t_1 < t_2 < \cdots < t_m$.

In the discrete exercise case with a Markovian stochastic process, the pricing problem can be formulated using dynamic programming. The value of the option at maturity t_m is given by

$$V(\mathbf{X}, t_m) = h(\mathbf{X}). \tag{13.60}$$

At a previous time step, the exercise decision relies on the decision to either exercise immediately or continue and so the value is given by

$$V(\mathbf{X}, t_{i-1}) = \max\left[h(\mathbf{X}), \mathbb{E}\left[D(t_{i-1}, t_i)V(\mathbf{X}_{t_i}) \mid \mathbf{X}_{t_{i-1}} = \mathbf{X}\right]\right], \tag{13.61}$$

where $D(t_{i-1}, t_i)$ is the discount factor between time t_{i-1} and t_i. The value of the derivative today, $V(\mathbf{X}_0, t_0)$, is given by walking backwards to t_0. This dynamic programming approach to pricing Bermudan and American options underpins the *American Monte Carlo* approaches described in this section.

13.3.1.1 Upper and Lower Bound

Given another stopping strategy $\tau^* \in \mathcal{T}$, by definition (Guo et al., 2023)

$$\sup_{\tau \in \mathcal{T}} \mathbb{E}\left[e^{-\int_0^\tau r(u)du} h(\mathbf{X}_\tau)\right] \geq \mathbb{E}\left[e^{-\int_0^{\tau^*} r(u)du} h(\mathbf{X}_{\tau^*})\right]. \tag{13.62}$$

Hence, any suboptimal strategy gives a lower bound to the value of the Bermudan callable derivative. The original pricing problem for an American option in Equation (13.59) is known as the *primal* problem,

$$V_0 = \sup_{\tau \in \mathcal{T}} \mathbb{E}\left[e^{-\int_0^\tau r(u)du} h(\mathbf{X}_\tau)\right]. \tag{13.63}$$

An upper bound can also be found using the dual formalism of Rogers (2002) and Haugh and Kogan (2004). Following Haugh and Kogan (2004), given an adapted supermartingale π_t, a dual function can be defined by

$$F(t, \pi) := e^{\int_0^t r(u)du} \mathbb{E}\left[\max_{s \in \{[t,T] \cap \mathcal{T}\}} \left(e^{-\int_0^\tau r(u)du} h(\mathbf{X}_s) - \pi_s\right)\right] + \pi_t. \tag{13.64}$$

The dual problem is to find the optimal overall supermartingales, π_t, giving a solution

$$\begin{aligned} U_0 &= \inf_\pi F(0, \pi) \\ &= \inf_\pi \mathbb{E}_0\left[\max_{t \in T} \left(e^{-\int_0^\tau r(u)du} h(\mathbf{X}_s) - \pi_s\right)\right] + \pi_0. \end{aligned} \tag{13.65}$$

Rogers (2002) and Haugh and Kogan (2004) prove that the optimal solutions of the primal and dual problems are the same, $V_0 = U_0$.

13.3.2 American Monte Carlo

The idea of augmenting Monte Carlo simulations to price American-style options was first proposed by Tilley (1993), who adopted the *stochastic bundling* approach. In Tilley's method, paths are ranked by stock price and grouped into bundles. Each bundle estimates the continuation value by taking the average value at the next step over the bundle. The continuation values can then be compared with the intrinsic value to identify the location of the early-exercise boundary.

Regression-based methods have been the mainstay of American Monte Carlo approaches, with key early contributions from Carriere (1996), Longstaff and Schwartz (2001) and Tsitsiklis and Van Roy (2001). The approach proposed by Longstaff and Schwartz (2001) has been adopted by practitioners and is presented here. Various publications provide details, including a comprehensive review by Piterbarg (2003).

To understand the algorithm's basic concept, consider valuing a Bermudan swaption, which offers multiple opportunities to enter an interest rate swap with a fixed maturity. On the last exercise date, the option resembles a European swaption, allowing entry into a swap at a fixed rate, K. Earlier exercise dates provide the option to either enter the swap or retain the option for future exercise. A standard Monte Carlo model cannot value this product as it requires decisions at each exercise date, whereas Monte Carlo paths only provide a single future state. Although Monte Carlo can value the underlying swap based on the realised yield curve, it only provides the exercise value. If Monte Carlo could also provide a continuation value at each stopping date, it would enable exercise decisions. The Longstaff–Schwartz algorithm uses polynomial regression to estimate the continuation value, providing an analytic function that approximates this value based on market state variables at each time step, effectively defining the exercise boundary.

13.3.2.1 Trade Valuation The Longstaff–Schwartz regression function determines the exercise boundary when used for trade valuation. The exercise value is used at the point on the path where the option is optimal to exercise. In simple cases, this exercise value will equal the intrinsic value, but regression functions can determine continuation and exercise values for more complex payoffs.

To estimate a regression function for derivative valuation, use the following algorithm as described in Green (2015).

1. Select *Features* (Explanatory Variables):

$$O_1(\omega, t_k), \dots, O_{n_O}(\omega, t_k). \tag{13.66}$$

These variables are features that are directly relevant to the derivative and influence exercise decisions, cash flows and valuation. For a Bermudan swaption, the typical choice is the par rate for the underlying swap and the first forward rate at each exercise date. Regression quality significantly depends on the choice of explanatory variables, necessitating careful selection and evaluation of alternatives.

2. Choose Basis Function:

$$f_1(O_i(\omega, t_k)), \dots, f_{n_f}(O_i(\omega, t_k)). \tag{13.67}$$

These functions form the basis for least-squares regression, and many choices exist. Piterbarg (2003) favours low-order polynomials for pricing to avoid sensitivity to outliers. Moreno and Navas (2003) found that the method was not strongly dependent on the choice of the polynomial,

3. Run Monte Carlo Simulation: Simulate Monte Carlo paths in the risk-neutral measure with appropriate dynamics. Include time steps on all critical trade dates, like cash flow and exercise dates.
4. Backward Induction: Start from maturity and move backwards to determine the continuation value at each step.
5. Perform Regression Algorithm:
   (a) At each observation date t_k, calculate the derivative's value as a discounted sum of future cash flows $C(\omega, t_j)$:

$$F(\omega, t_k) = \sum_{j=k+1}^{K} e^{-\int_{t_k}^{t_j} r(\omega,s)ds} C(\omega, t_j). \tag{13.68}$$

(b) Use least-squares regression of continuation values against the basis functions to calibrate coefficients α_m:

$$\min\left(\sum_{\omega}\left\|\sum_{m=1}^{n_f}\alpha_m f_m(O_i(\omega,t_k)) - F(\omega,t_k)\right\|^2, \alpha_m \in \mathcal{R}\right). \tag{13.69}$$

In Longstaff and Schwartz (2001), the regression is only run on in-the-money paths, giving higher accuracy (Giles, 2008).

6. Define Continuation Value:

$$\bar{F}(\alpha_m, O_i(\omega,t_k), t_k) = \sum_{m=1}^{n_f}\alpha_m f_m(O_i(\omega,t_k)). \tag{13.70}$$

These functions provide a valuation of the continuation value of the derivative at t_k, given state variables O_i.

7. Optimal Exercise Decision: Compare the immediate exercise value E_t with the continuation value $\bar{F}_t$:

$$V_t = \max(E_t, \bar{F}_t). \tag{13.71}$$

The option value at time t is the maximum of the immediate exercise value and the continuation value.

8. Iterate: Repeat the regression and exercise decision steps, returning to the initial valuation date.

The Longstaff–Schwartz algorithm efficiently and accurately values Bermudan-style derivatives by following this method. However, note that the Longstaff–Schwartz method has two biases: it tends to undervalue because the exercise strategy is suboptimal and overvalue because it uses the same paths to estimate the continuation value and make exercise decisions. While a second independent simulation could guarantee a lower bound, this practice is rarely implemented (Giles, 2008).

13.3.2.2 Application in XVA American Monte Carlo has been widely used in XVA calculations (Cesari et al., 2009; Green, 2015; Kenyon and Green, 2015). The estimation of future values as needed for expected exposure calculations is a very similar problem to computing the continuation value. Hence, the Longstaff–Schwartz method estimates the value of derivatives, especially Bermudan and American callable options, inside the Monte Carlo simulation used in the exposure calculation. There are some subtle differences in the XVA context:

- The regression approximation is used everywhere on a given time slice in the simulation. The accuracy of the regression function needs to extend to the wings of the value distribution. In contrast, in the valuation context, it needs to be accurate primarily around the exercise boundary, and this can mean that a different choice of features is appropriate.
- For expected exposure calculations, a different set of tenors may be used than those naturally applied to a single trade. Hence, a regression approximation may be needed on a date between exercise opportunities in XVA, while for valuation, the continuation value is only needed on the exercise dates.
- In XVA, there are typically two simulations. The first is a *calibration* Monte Carlo simulation used to estimate the regression function approximation for each time step for the particular trade. The second simulation calculates the expected exposure using the regression approximations already calibrated for the exotic trades alongside standard valuation methods for linear products.

Credit and margin valuation adjustments need to include estimation of initial margin for cleared portfolios where the counterparty is a CCP, and for bilateral margin typically using ISDA SIMM®.[2] Regression methods have been adopted as components of *dynamic initial margin (DIM)* models by, for example, Kenyon and Green (2015), Andersen et al. (2017), Anfuso et al. (2017) and Chan et al. (2018).

[2]'ISDA' and 'ISDA SIMM' are registered trademarks of the International Swaps and Derivatives Association, Inc. (ISDA).

13.3.3 Deep Optimal Stopping for Valuation and XVA

Neural networks have a relatively long history in the context of American Monte Carlo models. For example, Tsitsiklis and Van Roy (2001) suggest using a feedforward neural network as a suitable approach to approximating the value function. However, they use a linear parameterisation in the mathematical development of their model.

Haugh and Kogan (2004), in addition to developing the *dual* formalism, use a neural network with a single hidden layer to approximate the continuation value (Q-value), which they optimise using MSE loss and a Levenberg–Marquardt optimiser. The parameters from the network trained for time t were reused as the starting point for time $t-1$ during the dynamic programming phase to accelerate performance. The authors used the Q-value function to obtain lower and upper-bound estimates for Bermudan options on the maximum of 5 assets and 10 assets and a call on the geometric mean of 5 assets. Given that this paper predates the deep learning revolution and the advent of GPU computing, the execution time was an impractical 40 minutes to obtain the initial estimate of the continuation value function, 100 minutes to obtain the lower bound and a further 140 minutes to calculate the upper bound.

Kohler et al. (2010) applied neural networks in the context of the continuation function for a least-squares Monte Carlo model, replacing the polynomial regression used by Longstaff and Schwartz (2001). One key motivation for the use of neural networks was the better high-dimensional behaviour when compared to other forms of regression that suffer from the *curse of dimensionality*. They apply their model to three examples: an American put on a single stock, a strangle spread payoff on a single stock and a strangle spread payoff on a basket of five correlated stocks.

The next group of papers on American Monte Carlo using neural networks follows the popularisation of deep learning in quantitative finance. The literature identifies three approaches:

- Models that train a classifier to find the exercise boundary.
- Models that approximate the continuation value.
- A single paper that adopts a reinforcement learning approach and seeks the optimal exercise policy.

Becker et al. (2019) developed the *deep optimal stopping (DOS)* algorithm that learns the optimal stopping rule from Monte Carlo samples by decomposing the optimal stopping time into a sequence of 0–1 stopping decisions and approximating them recursively with a sequence of multilayer feedforward neural networks. This approach allows the neural network policies to approximate optimal stopping times to any degree of accuracy. They express the optimal stopping time, τ, in terms of an optimal stopping decision function, f, that is then approximated with a neural network

$$\tau_{n+1} = \sum_{m=n+1}^{N} m f^{\theta_m}\left(X_m\right) \prod_{j=n+1}^{m-1} \left(1 - f^{\theta_j}\left(X_j\right)\right). \tag{13.72}$$

The optimal stopping time satisfies

$$\mathbb{E}\left[h\left(\tau_n, X_{\tau_n}\right)\right] \geq V_n - \left(V_{n+1} - \mathbb{E}\left[h\left(\tau_{n+1}, X_{\tau_{n+1}}\right)\right]\right), \tag{13.73}$$

where $V_n = \sup_{\tau\in\mathcal{T}_n}\mathbb{E}[h\left(\tau, X_\tau\right)]$. The function f^θ provides a binary stopping decision, but the corresponding function F^θ provides the probability of stopping, with both given by the same neural network. The goal of the optimisation process is to find parameters θ such that

$$\begin{aligned}\mathbb{E}\Big[h\left(n, X_n\right) F^{\theta_n}\left(X_n\right) + h\left(\tau_{n+1}, X_{\tau_{n+1}}\right)\left(1 - F^{\theta_n}\left(X_n\right)\right)\Big] \sim \\ \sup_{\theta\in\mathbb{R}^q} \mathbb{E}\Big[h\left(n, X_n\right) F^{\theta}\left(X_n\right) + h\left(\tau_{n+1}, X_{\tau_{n+1}}\right)\left(1 - F^{\theta}\left(X_n\right)\right)\Big].\end{aligned} \tag{13.74}$$

Optimisation is performed using mini-batch gradient ascent with the Adam optimiser on the objective function given by

$$\frac{1}{K}\sum_{k=1}^{K} r_n^k(\theta), \tag{13.75}$$

where K is the number of Monte Carlo paths and

$$r_n^k(\theta) = h\left(n, x_n^k\right) F^\theta\left(x_n^k\right) + h\left(l_{n+1}^k, x_{l_{n+1}^k}^k\right)\left(1 - F^\theta\left(x_n^k\right)\right). \tag{13.76}$$

The lower and upper bounds can be computed with short runtimes and are shown to be close together in all examples tested in the paper. The paper tests the deep learning approach on three specific problems to demonstrate its accuracy and efficiency:

- Pricing of a Bermudan max-call option. This problem involves options whose payoff depends on the maximum of multiple underlying assets. The risk-neutral dynamics of the assets are assumed to follow a multidimensional Black–Scholes model.
- Pricing of a callable multi-barrier reverse convertible. In this scenario, the pricing problem becomes a $d + 1$-dimensional stopping problem, where d represents the number of assets, and one needs to track the barrier event.
- Optimal stopping of a fractional Brownian motion. This problem focuses on determining the optimal stopping time for a fractional Brownian motion process, which is not by itself Markovian. The authors transform it into a high-dimensional Markovian problem to facilitate the use of their approach.

The DOS approach was further extended and tested by Andersson and Oosterlee (2020a,b). The authors applied the DOS method to Bermudan options with both Black–Scholes and Heston dynamics and compared the performance with least-squares Monte Carlo and stochastic bundling. Andersson and Oosterlee (2020a,b) made some small optimisations to the original DOS method, such as the reuse of the parameters of the neural network at time step t as the starting point for time step $t - 1$. The authors explored the use of DOS in the context of expected exposure and PFE calculations, noting that the DOS algorithm is particularly suitable for exposure computations as it directly computes the stopping strategy rather than as a consequence of an approximate value function like most other algorithms. The DOS algorithm demonstrated strong performance compared to other methods. In Andersson and Oosterlee (2020b), consider the use of DOS for CVA calculations on portfolios of derivatives with netting. The authors adjusted the exercise strategy for the default risk of the counterparty, showing that failure to do this can lead to an overestimation of the CVA by 25%.[3]

Using a neural network to learn the continuation function is a natural approach and essentially uses deep learning as a drop-in replacement for the polynomial regression of Longstaff and Schwartz (2001). Indeed, this was precisely the approach of Kohler et al. (2010) discussed earlier. Lapeyre and Lelong (2019) follow the same technique, noting that traditional regression techniques, such as polynomial regression, may suffer from the curse of dimensionality, requiring high orders to provide accurate results, which can be computationally expensive. The authors argue that neural networks provide greater flexibility and potentially better accuracy in capturing complex relationships in the data and have been shown to scale better in high-dimensional problems than regression methods. Even relatively small neural networks with a few hundred neurons and no hidden layers have provided accurate Bermudan option pricing results. Moreover, neural networks can be trained efficiently, and in some cases, training the network only once over the data can be sufficient to fit the network at a new date, saving computational time. Lapeyre and Lelong (2019) show that neural networks provide accurate pricing results comparable to those obtained from the standard Longstaff–Schwartz algorithm.

Huge and Savine (2020) focus primarily on applying Sobolev training, as was discussed in Chapter 3. However, they include an example of using least-squares Monte Carlo with a neural network in this context. Similarly, the focus of Bayer et al. (2023) lies not with the application of neural networks to American Monte Carlo, but rather the ability of hierarchical tensor formats to alleviate the *curse of dimensionality* in pricing Bermudan options by providing efficient approximations of nominally high-dimensional functions while allowing for accurate low-rank approximations.

Guo et al. (2023) also modify the least-squares Monte Carlo approach by adopting neural networks for regression. Unlike other authors, they modify LSMC to simultaneously compute both the upper and lower bounds on the price and, in doing so, provide the upper bound at significantly reduced computational cost to other methods.

[3]Green and Kenyon (2017) noted the impact of XVA on exercise decisions.

Guo et al. (2023) also provide a variant of their approach that uses a single neural network for all time steps, which contrasts with other authors who use one neural network per time step. Finally, the approach generates a hedging strategy as a by product that can also be used as a control variate, resembling the deep control variate technique discussed above.

In contrast to the above approaches based on dynamic programming, Deschatre and Mikael (2020) adopted a method based on identifying the optimal policy. The proposed algorithm leverages reinforcement learning to address the optimal stopping time problem, formulated in terms of combinatorial optimisation. The *primal* Equation (13.59) can be written in discrete form as

$$\sup_{\tau \in \mathcal{T}_N^l} \mathbb{E}\left(\sum_{i=1}^{l} f\left(\tau_i, X_{\tau_i}\right) 1_{\tau_i \leq T}\right). \tag{13.77}$$

The key observation from Deschatre and Mikael (2020) is that the optimal stopping problem defined in the equation can be rewritten as

$$\sup_{Y} \mathbb{E}\left(\sum_{i=0}^{N} Y_i f\left(t_i, X_{t_i}\right)\right), \tag{13.78}$$

where the Y_i are a sequence of $\mathcal{F}_t$-measurable random variables taking either value 0 or 1, and subject to the following constraints:

$$\sum_{i=0}^{N} Y_i \leq l, \tag{13.79}$$

$$D_j \geq \gamma, j = 0, \ldots, N, \tag{13.80}$$

$$D_j = \gamma + t_j - \sum_{i=0}^{j-1} Y_i D_i, \tag{13.81}$$

with γ allowing for a delayed start. At each t_j, Y_j is Bernoulli distributed and depends on the state variable S_{t_j}, defined as $(X_{t_j}, \sum_{i=0}^{j-1} Y_i, D_j)$. The distribution is parameterised by a neural network with probability given by

$$\mathbb{P}\left(Y_j = 1 \mid S_{t_j}\right) = \text{sigmoid}\left(C \tanh\left(\mathbb{NN}\left(t_j, S_{t_j}, \theta\right)\right)\right) c\left(S_{t_j}\right), \tag{13.82}$$

where

$$c\left(S_{t_j}\right) = 1_{\sum_{i=0}^{j-1} Y_i < 1} 1_{D_{D_j \geq \gamma}}. \tag{13.83}$$

The neural network is trained to solve the optimal stopping problem using

$$\theta^* \in \underset{\theta \in \Theta}{\operatorname{argmax}} \ \mathbb{E}\left(\sum_{i=0}^{N} Y_i f\left(t_i, X_{t_i}\right)\right), \tag{13.84}$$

with the Y_i sampled in batches from the distribution, the remaining Monte Carlo paths of the asset fixed and SGD used to optimise the neural network parameters.

Neural networks are a natural choice for regression; hence, it is no surprise that multiple authors have applied them to American Monte Carlo models. However, neural networks will never be competitive with the raw performance provided by least-squares regression as neural networks need to be trained using SGD. In contrast, linear least-squares regression can be solved directly via simple linear algebra. The benefits of using neural networks in this context are improved accuracy, the ability to generate price bounds and the fact that neural networks do not require feature engineering. The key weakness of least-squares regression is the need to choose what state variables to use and experiment extensively to find the optimal choice; neural networks remove this requirement. The models covered in this section are summarised in Table 13.4.

TABLE 13.4 Applications of Neural Networks in American Monte Carlo Models

Authors	Application	Function Approximation	Bound
Haugh and Kogan (2004)	Bermudan option	Continuation value	Both
Kohler et al. (2010)	Bermudan option	Continuation value	Lower
Becker et al. (2019)	Bermudan option	Exercise boundary	Both
Lapeyre and Lelong (2019)	Bermudan option	Continuation value	Lower
Huge and Savine (2020)	Bermudan option	Continuation value	Lower
Andersson and Oosterlee (2020a)	Bermudan & XVA	Exercise boundary	Lower
Andersson and Oosterlee (2020b)	XVA	Exercise boundary	Lower
Deschatre and Mikael (2020)	Bermudan option	Policy gradient	Lower
Bayer et al. (2023)	Bermudan option	Continuation value	Lower
Guo et al. (2023)	Bermudan option	Continuation value	Both

EXAMPLE 13.4: DEEP AMERICAN MONTE CARLO

This example provides a simplified version of an American Monte Carlo simulation with DNNs used for regression. The classic Longstaff–Schwartz approach is provided for comparison purposes. Two versions of *deep American Monte Carlo* are included: the first is a drop-in replacement for polynomial regression using the same set of features as the Longstaff–Schwartz model, and the second uses discount bond prices for relevant dates as input. The example prices a 10-year Bermudan swaption with annual exercises and is supported by an interest rate Monte Carlo model as described below.

The example is in the Jupyter Notebook `BermudanModelRegression.ipynb`. The following four Python files contain supporting code: `lgm_ir_utility.py`, `lgm_ir_monte_carlo.py`, `ir_vanilla_swap.py` and `ir_bermudan_swaption.py`.

LGM Monte Carlo Model

Given that the option to be priced is a Bermudan swaption, a term structure interest rate model must be used to generate the Monte Carlo paths. Here, a *Hull–White* variant model, the *linear Gaussian model*, is used (Karoui et al., 1992; Hull and White, 2001) and parameterised as described in Green (2015). The dynamics are given by

$$\frac{dP_d(t,T)}{P_d(t,T)} = r_d(t)dt + \sigma_d(t,T)dW^d(t),$$

with solution

$$P_d(t,T) = \frac{P_d(0,T)}{P_d(0,t)} \exp\left\{-\frac{1}{2}\int_0^t (\sigma_d^2(s,T) - \sigma^2(s,t))ds + \int_0^t (\sigma_d(s,T) - \sigma_d(s,t))dW^d(s)\right\}.$$

The volatility is defined as follows to ensure the model is Markovian:

$$\sigma(t,T) = \phi(t)(\Psi(T) - \Psi(t)),$$
$$\Psi(t) = \textstyle\int_0^t \psi(s)ds.$$

(*Continued*)

(*Continued*)

The $\phi(t)$ and $\psi(t)$ functions are assumed to be piecewise constant. In real-world usage, the model needs to be calibrated to the prices of European swaptions, but for this example, the parameters were set to reasonable values as shown in Table 13.5.

TABLE 13.5 LGM Parameter Values

Period	ψ	ϕ
0–2Y	1.0	0.01
2–4Y	1.0	0.02
4–6Y	1.0	0.03
6–8Y	1.0	0.04
8–10Y	1.0	0.05

Two utility classes manage the model parameters. `LGMIRUtility`, defined in `lgm_ir_utility.py`, contains the model volatility parameters and calculates the required integrals numerically. `LGMIRMonteCarlo`, defined in `lgm_ir_monte_carlo.py`, runs the Monte Carlo simulation, generating a collection of yield curves for different tenors using the solution expressed in the T-forward measure. This simulation employs 2^{14} paths with all three models.

Two additional utility classes represent the underlying swap and the Bermudan swaption. `IRVanillaSwap`, defined in `ir_vanilla_swap.py`, represents the underlying swap, while `IRBermudanSwaption`, defined in `lgm_ir_monte_carlo.py`, represents the Bermudan swaption. The Bermudan swaption class includes several valuation methods to assess the represented trade.

Longstaff–Schwartz

The Longstaff–Schwartz regression model uses a polynomial regression up to fifth order in a single state variable, the par rate of the underlying swap at each exercise. The regression coefficients are obtained by multiplication with the inverse of the matrix of features. The following code block illustrates the backward induction loop.

```
def value_LS(self,
    order: int,
    lgmirutility: LGMIRUtility,
    yield_curves: dict,
    mc_params: dict,
    device: torch.device,
    dtype,
    valdate: ql.Date)-> tuple:

    mc = self._create_monte_carlo(lgmirutility, yield_curves, mc_params,
                                  device, dtype, valdate)
    numeraire_ratios = self._get_numeraire_ratios(mc)
    swap_values, par_rates = self._get_swap_values_par_rates(mc)
    option_intrinsics = self._get_option_intrinsic(swap_values,
                                                    self.ex_schedule)
```

```
    # scale by numeraire ratios
    scaled_swap_values = list()
    for inum, iswap in zip(numeraire_ratios, swap_values):
        scaled_swap_values.append(torch.mul(iswap, inum))

    scaled_option_intrinsics = list()
    for idx in range(len(option_intrinsics)):
        scaled_option_intrinsics.append(torch.mul(option_intrinsics[idx],
                                                  numeraire_ratios[idx+1]))

    # Backward induction loop
    sim_dates = mc.simulation_dates
    cont_value = scaled_option_intrinsics[-1]
    regression_data = list()
    for idate in range(len(sim_dates) - 2, 0, -1):

        # store the regression data
        ireg_data = dict()
        ireg_data["cont_value"] = cont_value.cpu().detach().numpy()
        ireg_data["par_rates"] = par_rates[idate].cpu().detach().numpy()

        # Get par rates for the relevant date
        # and generate the regression variables
        x_train_list = self._generate_polynomial_regressor(par_rates[idate],
                                                            order)
        x_ones = torch.ones_like(par_rates[idate])
        x_train_list.insert(0, x_ones)
        x_train = torch.cat(x_train_list, dim=1)
        y_train = cont_value

        # Regress
        x_train_inv = torch.pinverse(x_train)
        theta = torch.matmul(x_train_inv, y_train)
        cont_value_hat = torch.matmul(x_train, theta)
        ireg_data["inferred_value"] = cont_value_hat.cpu().detach().numpy()
        regression_data.append(ireg_data)

        # determine exercise
        cont_value = torch.max(cont_value_hat, scaled_swap_values[idate])

    return torch.mean(cont_value).cpu().detach().item(), regression_data
```

Figure 13.9 contains plots of the inferred values from the regression function versus the continuation value on the next time step. Four plots are shown: the last time step and the first three. Given the use of matrix inversion and a GPU for linear algebra, execution is swift. The final Bermudan value was \$239,330.

Neural Network LS

The first neural network model adopts the same approach as Longstaff–Schwartz, using a neural network as a simple drop-in replacement for polynomial regression. The input to the network comprises the same five powers of the par rate. The network features two hidden layers, each with 32 units combined with ReLU

(*Continued*)

(*Continued*)

activation and a linear output layer producing a single value. This neural network is consistently used and retrained to optimise performance. Training is capped at 20 epochs with a mini-batch size of 1024. Some 25% of the Monte Carlo paths are retained as an independent test set. Early stopping is implemented with a patience of 20 mini-batch steps. The code mirrors the pattern of the Longstaff–Schwartz algorithm, substituting the regression step with the neural network training loop. Due to SGD, execution is significantly slower compared to the matrix inversion in Longstaff–Schwartz.

Figure 13.10 illustrates plots of the continuation value at the next time step versus the predicted value from the neural network in the left column and the loss as a function of the training step in the right. Visual inspection of the regression shows a better fit to the continuation value than obtained using Longstaff–Schwartz, as might be expected given the non-linear regression. The final value for the Bermudan option was $229,667.

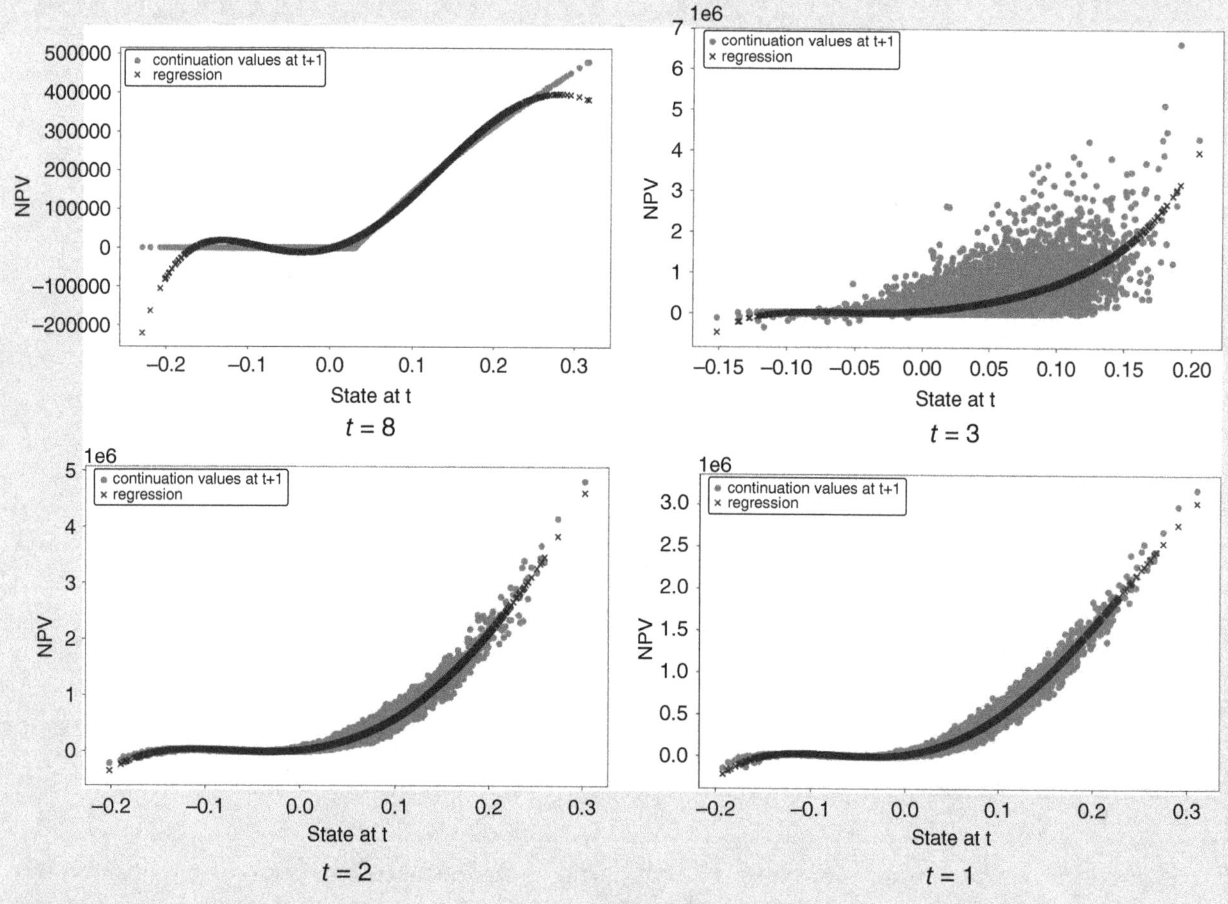

FIGURE 13.9 Continuation value at the next time step vs regression prediction for Longstaff–Schwartz.

Neural Network with ZCBs

The final model uses a neural network but with the bond prices used by the underlying swap as input rather than the par rate. Given that the underlying swap maturity decreases as a function of the time step, the input dimension differs for each step, and hence, a separate neural network was trained, and the network weights were not reused. Twenty epochs were used at each time step to train each network. The architecture of each network was otherwise the same as in the previous example.

Figure 13.11 shows the regression plots and losses for the ZCB-based model, with the regression function value showing more variety in shape than the previous example. The advantage of this approach is that the user does not have to select a particular set of features as input to the neural network. The bond prices from the simulation can be used directly and are just as effective as the par rate. The final value obtained was $258,413.

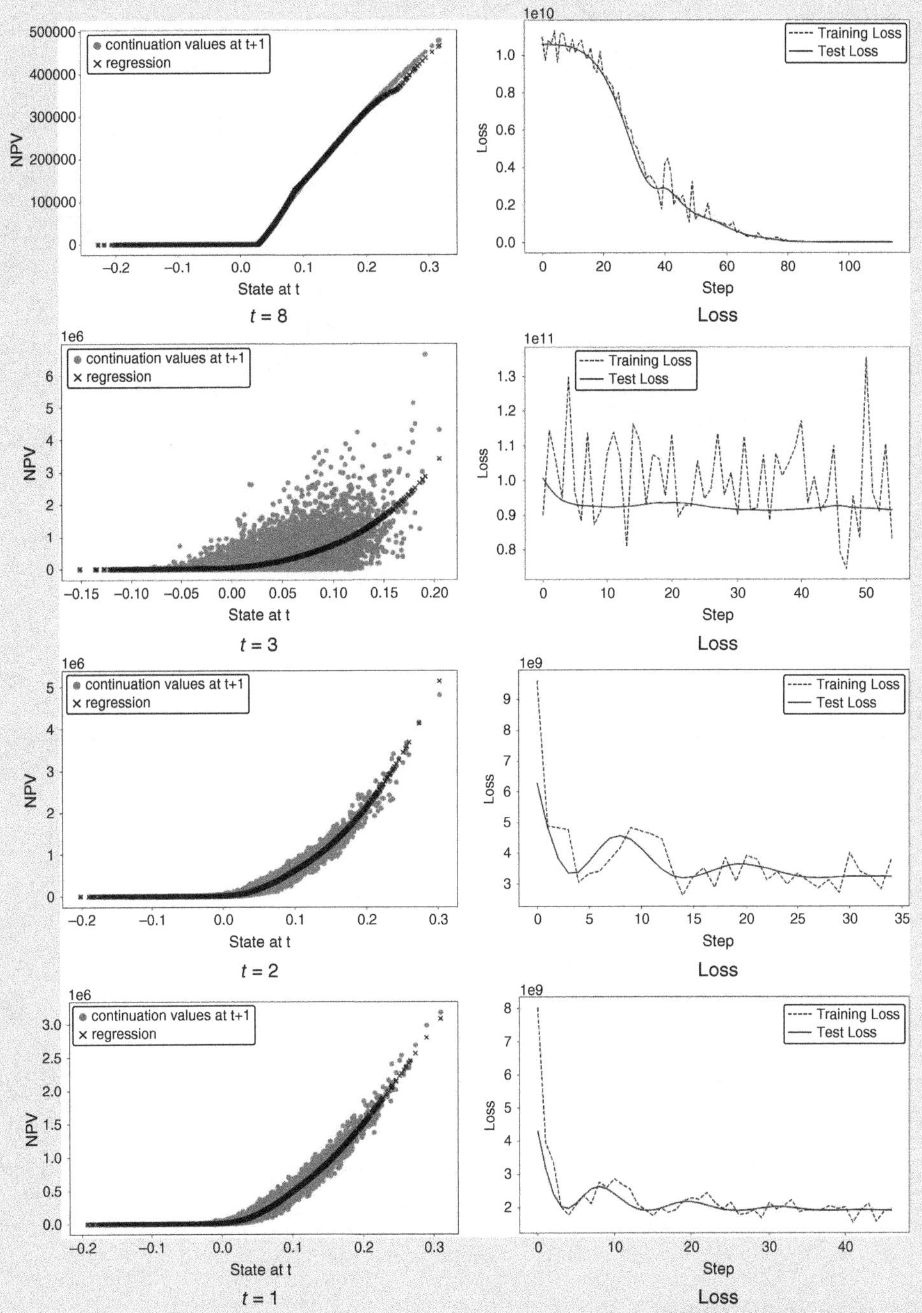

Figure 13.10 Continuation value at the next time step vs regression prediction for the DNN with polynomial input.
(*Continued*)

(Continued)

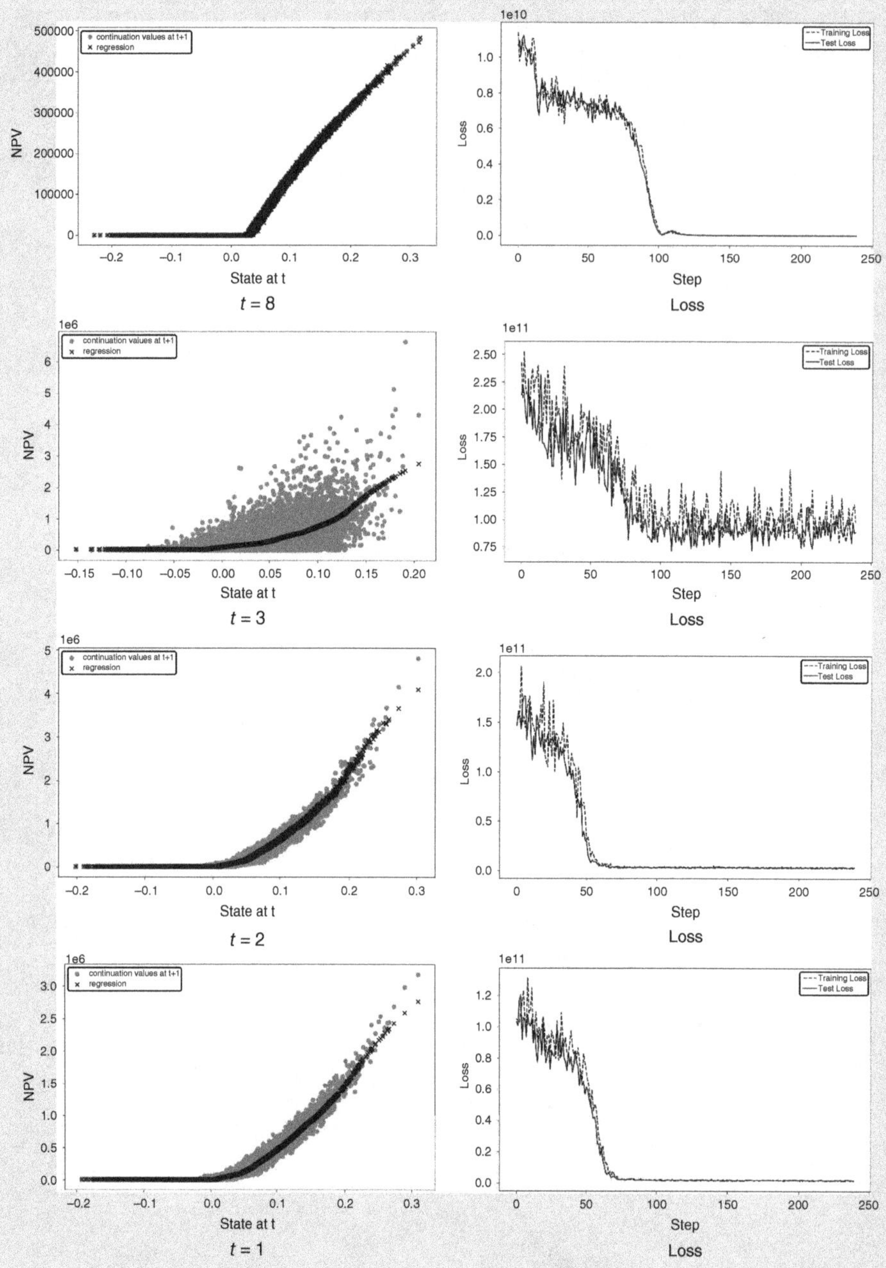

FIGURE 13.11 Continuation value at the next time step vs regression prediction for the DNN with ZCB input.

13.4 CONCLUSION: DEEP MONTE CARLO

Monte Carlo simulation and deep neural networks are not an obvious partnership. However, this chapter has demonstrated that they can be successfully paired in the context of both European and American option pricing models.

CHAPTER 14

Static Replication Using Neural Networks

Replicants are bioengineered humans designed by Tyrell Corporation for use off-world. Their enhanced strength made them ideal slave labour. After a series of violent rebellions, their manufacture became prohibited and Tyrell Corp went bankrupt. The collapse of ecosystems in the mid 2020s led to the rise of industrialist Niander Wallace, whose mastery of synthetic farming averted famine. Wallace acquired the remains of Tyrell Corp and created a new line of replicants who obey. Many older model replicants – Nexus 8s with open-ended lifespans – survived. They are hunted down and 'retired'. Those that hunt them still go by the name ... Blade Runner.

Blade Runner 2049 (directed by Denis Villeneuve, 2017)

14.1 (SEMI) STATIC REPLICATION

Dynamic hedging is a risk management strategy which involves continuously adjusting the positions of hedges to offset the risk of price movements in a portfolio of derivatives. Constructing a dynamic hedging strategy in the underlying stock and bonds is central to the development of the Black–Scholes model (Black and Scholes, 1973) and its replication argument, leading directly to the option price. The cost of a dynamic hedging strategy that is self-financing and replicates the payoff of the derivative must, by arbitrage arguments, equal the price of the option. Of course, *dynamic hedging* requires continual rebalancing of the hedge portfolio, which is impossible to achieve in practice.

A *static hedging* strategy is possible for some derivative contracts. It involves setting up a portfolio of simple derivatives, such as European puts and calls, that fully replicate the payout of the target derivative without requiring continuous rebalancing. The critical advantage of static replication is that once the portfolio is set up, it does not require the frequent adjustments typical of dynamic hedging strategies, and this not only reduces transaction costs but also simplifies the management of the portfolio. Static hedging leads to a *static replication* model that allows the development of a pricing model based on static replication of a derivative payout with portfolios of options.

A large number of authors have developed models based on static replication. Derman et al. (1995) used binomial trees as the basis of a numerical algorithm to replicate barrier options. Peter Carr and co-authors explored static replication in the context of barriers and other types of options in a series of papers: Bowie and Carr (1994), Carr and Chou (1997) and Carr et al. (1998). Further general results on static replication of barrier options were provided by Andersen et al. (2000). Several others have published further papers on different applications of static replication, often focused on barrier options, although other products, such as volatility derivatives, have also been considered.

A key result for static replication models is the relationship between the risk-neutral density, q, and the second derivative of the call price, C, provided by Breeden and Litzenberger (1978):

$$q(S, t; K, T; \Theta) = e^{r(T-t)} \frac{\partial^2 C}{\partial K^2}(S, t; K, T; \Theta), \tag{14.1}$$

Deep Learning in Quantitative Finance, First Edition. Andrew Green.

where S is the stock price, T is the maturity, K is the strike, Θ are model parameters and t is the time. A series of theoretical results for static replication were established by Carr and Wu (2013). The first key result is the spanning relationship that links the option price at time $t \leq T$ with a static position in a continuum of European options of shorter maturity $u \leq t$,

$$C(S, t; K, T; \Theta) = \int_0^\infty w(\mathcal{K})C(S, t; \mathcal{K}, u; \Theta)d\mathcal{K}, \tag{14.2}$$

where the weight is given by

$$w(\mathcal{K}) = \frac{\partial^2}{\partial \mathcal{K}^2} C(\mathcal{K}, u; K, T; \Theta). \tag{14.3}$$

The result is obtained as a consequence of the discounted expectation,

$$C(S, t; K, T; \Theta) = e^{-r(u-t)} \int_0^\infty q(S, t; \mathcal{K}, u; \Theta)C(\mathcal{K}, u; K, T; \Theta)d\mathcal{K}, \tag{14.4}$$

and Equation (14.1), with the final result obtained by integrating by parts twice and applying the boundary conditions on the option price and its first derivatives. As Carr and Wu (2013) point out, the strategy implied by Equation (14.2) is, in fact, semi-static as it implies closing the portfolio of options at some date prior to final maturity T to purchase the final option, with the portfolio providing just enough funds to do so.

It is impossible to purchase a continuum of options; hence, a finite approximation is used in practice. Carr and Wu (2013) propose approximating Equation (14.2) with a discrete approximation based on Gauss–Hermite quadrature.

Path dependence is clear in the types of trades, such as barrier and lookback options, that have often been the focus of work on static replication. Hence, Carr and Wu (2013) further extend semi-static hedging to the path-dependent case, including catering for jumps. The authors consider the case where a single payoff at maturity T depends on the price of a single asset S_{t_i} at discretely observed earlier times t_i through the use of a summary statistic H_{t_i},

$$H_{t_i} = g_i\left(H_{t_{i-1}}, S_{t_{i-1}}, S_{t_i}\right), \quad i = 1, \dots, n. \tag{14.5}$$

The model assumes one-factor Markovian dynamics and that a hedge position can be taken at time t_i in European options with a continuum of strikes at maturity at the next time step, t_{i+1}. At the final maturity, the value is assumed to be a function of the summary statistic, that is

$$V_T = \phi(H_T) \equiv f_n(S_T; H_{t_{i-1}}, S_{t_{i-1}}), \tag{14.6}$$

where the last expression follows from Equation (14.5). Following Carr and Madan (2001), any twice-differentiable function f can be spanned by options maturing at time T,

$$\begin{aligned} f_n\left(S_T; H_{t_{n-1}}, S_{t_{n-1}}\right) &= f_n\left(\kappa_n; H_{t_{n-1}}, S_{t_{n-1}}\right) \\ &+ f_n'\left(\kappa_n; H_{t_{n-1}}, S_{t_{n-1}}\right)\left[\left(S_T - \kappa_n\right)^+ - \left(\kappa_n - S_T\right)^+\right] \\ &+ \textstyle\int_0^{\kappa_n} f_n''\left(\mathcal{K}; H_{t_{n-1}}, S_{t_{n-1}}\right)\left(\mathcal{K} - S_T\right)^+ d\mathcal{K} \\ &+ \textstyle\int_{\kappa_n}^{\infty} f_n''\left(\mathcal{K}; H_{t_{n-1}}, S_{t_{n-1}}\right)\left(S_T - \mathcal{K}\right)^+ d\mathcal{K}, \end{aligned} \tag{14.7}$$

where κ_n is the expansion point, often taken as the forward price at maturity. The value of the payoff at time t_{n-1} is obtained by taking expectations of both sides of the expression, giving the result

$$\begin{aligned} V^{f_n}_{t_{n-1}} &= e^{-r(T-t_{n-1})} f_n\left(\kappa_n; H_{t_{n-1}}, S_{t_{n-1}}\right) \\ &+ f'_n\left(\kappa_n; H_{t_{n-1}}, S_{t_{n-1}}\right)\left[C_{t_{n-1}}(\kappa_n, T) - P_{t_{n-1}}(\kappa_n, T)\right] \\ &+ \int_0^{\kappa_n} f''_n\left(\mathcal{K}; H_{t_{n-1}}, S_{t_{n-1}}\right) P_{t_{n-1}}(\mathcal{K}, T) d\mathcal{K} \\ &+ \int_{\kappa_n}^{\infty} f''_n\left(\mathcal{K}; H_{t_{n-1}}, S_{t_{n-1}}\right) C_{t_{n-1}}(\mathcal{K}, T) d\mathcal{K}. \end{aligned} \tag{14.8}$$

Using the Markov property of the option price, that is

$$C_t = C(S_t, t; K, T; \Theta), \tag{14.9}$$

gives

$$\begin{aligned} V^{f_n}_{t_{n-1}} &= e^{-r(T-t_{n-1})} f_n\left(\kappa_n; H_{t_{n-1}}, S_{t_{n-1}}\right) \\ &+ f'_n\left(\kappa_n; H_{t_{n-1}}, S_{t_{n-1}}\right)\left[C\left(S_{t_{n-1}}, t_{n-1}; \kappa_n, T; \Theta\right) - P\left(S_{t_{n-1}}, t_{n-1}; \kappa_n, T; \Theta\right)\right] \\ &+ \int_0^{\kappa_n} f''_n\left(\mathcal{K}; H_{t_{n-1}}, S_{t_{n-1}}\right) P\left(S_{t_{n-1}}, t_{n-1}; \mathcal{K}, T; \Theta\right) d\mathcal{K} \\ &+ \int_{\kappa_n}^{\infty} f''_n\left(\mathcal{K}; H_{t_{n-1}}, S_{t_{n-1}}\right) C\left(S_{t_{n-1}}, t_{n-1}; \mathcal{K}, T; \Theta\right) d\mathcal{K} \\ &\equiv V\left(H_{t_{n-1}}, S_{t_{n-1}}, t_{n-1}\right), \end{aligned} \tag{14.10}$$

and hence, it is a known function of the summary statistic and stock value at the earlier time t_{n-1}. The option can be semi-statically hedged by repeating the process of obtaining the 'final' payoff to move back another step to t_{n-2}, and so on to t_0. Then, the static replication model can be used to obtain a value.

Static replication is a crucial modelling approach in quantitative finance and is an area that Peter Carr did much to develop. *Neural static replication* models, discussed in the next section, are not simply neural network versions of static replication models but are a hybrid technique. As will be seen, they are closely related to *regress later* models that apply a shallow neural network that can be interpreted in terms of static replication.

14.2 NEURAL STATIC REPLICATION

14.2.1 Regress Now or Later?

Glasserman and Yu (2004) explore the use of regression methods in Monte Carlo simulation for American option pricing. The authors identify two distinct techniques:

- **Regress Now.** This approach is the classic least-squares Monte Carlo as proposed by Carriere (1996), Longstaff and Schwartz (2001), Tsitsiklis and Van Roy (2001) and others. The neural network variant of this approach was explored in Chapter 13. At time i, these methods regress option values from time $i+1$ against basis functions at time i.
- **Regress Later.** The second technique regresses option values at time $i+1$ with basis function values also at time $i+1$. This approach is represented by the weighted Monte Carlo approach of Broadie et al. (2000). Regress later methods give less error and can provide a dual estimate of the upper bound of the option value.

14.2.2 Neural Regress Later

As was the case with least-squares Monte Carlo, several authors have developed neural network versions of regress later methods in the context of option pricing, including Souihli (2021), Hoencamp et al. (2022) and Lokeshwar et al. (2022). Hoencamp et al. (2024) also explore applying the approach to margin valuation adjustment for SIMM bilateral, initial margin.

Lokeshwar et al. (2022) define *regress later neural networks (RLNNs)* as a general algorithm for Bermudan options. The algorithm starts by generating N Monte Carlo paths through M time steps, $S_{t_0}, \dots, S_{t_M}$. The terminal option value is obtained on each path using the payoff function $V_{t_M}(S_{t_M}) = h(S_{t_M})$. A neural network $G^{\beta_{t_m}}(S_{t_m})$ is then trained to replicate the terminal option values using the MSE loss function. The algorithm then moves back a step to t_{M-1} and estimates the continuation value for each Monte Carlo path using

$$\widehat{Q}_{t_{m-1}}\left(S_{t_{m-1}}(n)\right) \approx B_{t_{m-1}} \mathbb{E}\left[\left.\frac{G^{\beta_{t_m}}\left(S_{t_m}\right)}{B_{t_m}}\right| S_{t_{m-1}}(n)\right], \tag{14.11}$$

and this is the key expression. A fast approximation of the expectation is needed, which is achieved through the interpretation of the neural network in terms of static replication. Once the continuation value is obtained, the value of the derivative at time step t_{M-1} is given by the maximum of the payout and the continuation value,

$$V_{t_{m-1}}\left(S_{t_{m-1}}(n)\right) = \max\left(h\left(S_{t_{m-1}}(n)\right), \widehat{Q}_{t_{m-1}}\left(S_{t_{m-1}}(n)\right)\right). \tag{14.12}$$

This value then forms the training set for another neural network at time step t_{M-1}, with the weights initialised from those of the neural network at the previous step. The process can be repeated to t_0 to give the final value. Algorithm 14.1 presents the method in full.

Algorithm 14.1: Regress Later Neural Network (RLNN)

Input: Payoff $h(S_{t_M})$

Generate $n = 1, \dots, N$ Monte Carlo paths at time steps $t_m = t_0, \dots t_M$;

Estimate final option value $V_{t_M} \leftarrow h(S_{t_M})$;

Initialise the neural network weights β_{t_M};

for $m = M - 1, \dots, 1$ **do**

  Train the neural network using

  $J = \operatorname{argmin}_{\beta_{t_m}}\left(\frac{1}{N}\sum_{n=1}^{N}\left(V_{t_m}\left(S_{t_m}(n)\right) - G^{\beta_{t_m}}\left(S_{t_m}(n)\right)\right)^2\right)$;

  for $n = 1, \dots, N$ **do**

    Estimate continuation value

    $\widehat{Q}_{t_{m-1}}\left(S_{t_{m-1}}(n)\right) \leftarrow B_{t_{m-1}} \mathbb{E}\left|\frac{G^{\beta_{t_m}}(S_{t_m})}{B_{t_m}}\right| S_{t_{m-1}}(n)$;

    if $h\left(S_{t_{m-1}}(n)\right) > \widehat{Q}_{t_{m-1}}\left(S_{t_{m-1}}(n)\right)$ **then**

      $V_{t_{m-1}}\left(S_{t_{m-1}}(n)\right) \leftarrow h\left(S_{t_{m-1}}(n)\right)$;

    else

      $V_{t_{m-1}}\left(S_{t_{m-1}}(n)\right) \leftarrow \widehat{Q}_{t_{m-1}}\left(S_{t_{m-1}}(n)\right)$;

  Initialise neural network weights using previous step $\beta_{t_{m-1}} \leftarrow \beta_{t_m}$;

Output: V_{t_0}

The key to the RLNN algorithm is using a shallow neural network and its interpretation in terms of static replication. Lokeshwar et al. (2022) use a network with one hidden layer using 16 neurons and a ReLU activation with a linear output layer using a single neuron. Souihli (2021) adopts a similar architecture but performs experiments using a variable hidden size up to 10^4, while Hoencamp et al. (2022) use a hidden layer with 64 neurons in the context of pricing Bermudan swaptions with one and two-factor term structure interest rate models.

Following Lokeshwar et al. (2022), the output of the hidden layer of the neural network is given by

$$o_i = \max\left(\sum_{j=1}^{d} w_{ij}x_j + b_{i1}, 0\right), \tag{14.13}$$

where the w_{ij} are the layer weights and the b_{i1} are the bias parameters. The output of the ith neuron can be interpreted as an arithmetic basket option with weights w_{ij} and strike b_{i1}. Given that there are p neurons, the hidden layer represents a collection of p basket options. The output layer has a linear activation and is given by

$$y = \left(\sum_{i=1}^{p} \omega_i o_i\right) + b_2, \tag{14.14}$$

where the ω_i are the weights of the second layer and hence represent the amount of each basket option in the portfolio and bias b_2 is the amount of risk-free bonds in the portfolio.

The conditional expectation in Equation (14.11) must be evaluated to complete the algorithm, and this is given by

$$\begin{aligned}\mathbb{E}\left[\tilde{G}^{\beta_{t_m}}\left(\mathbf{S}_{t_m}\right) \mid \mathbf{S}_t\right] &= \mathbb{E}\left[\sum_{i=1}^{p} \omega_i \max\left(\mathbf{w}_i^\top \mathbf{S}_{t_m} + b_i, 0\right) + b_2 \mid \mathbf{S}_t\right] \\ &= \sum_{i=1}^{p} \omega_i \mathbb{E}\left[\max\left(\mathbf{w}_i^\top \mathbf{S}_{t_m} + b_i, 0\right) \mid \mathbf{S}_t\right] + b_2.\end{aligned} \tag{14.15}$$

To evaluate this in the general multi-dimensional case requires a fast approximation for the valuation of an arithmetic basket option under the selected dynamics for $\boldsymbol{S}_t$.

In the single-asset case, the Bermudan continuation value becomes

$$\hat{Q}_{t_{m-1}}\left(S_{t_{m-1}}(n)\right) = \sum_{i=1}^{p} \omega_i \mathbb{E}\left[\max\left(w_i S_{t_m} + b_i, 0\right) \mid S_{t_{m-1}}\right] + b_2, \tag{14.16}$$

which is easy to interpret in terms of the prices of the forward contract and European puts and calls. There are four cases:

1. $w_i > 0, b_i > 0$. Then $w_i^\top S_{t_m} + b_i > 0$ for all S_{t_m} and so

$$\mathbb{E}\left[\max\left(w_i S_{t_m} + b_i, 0\right) \mid S_{t_{m-1}}\right] = \left(w_i^\top \mathbb{E}\left[S_{t_m} \mid S_{t_{m-1}}\right] + b_i\right),$$

which is the price of a forward contract.

2. $w_i > 0, b_i < 0$. Then

$$\mathbb{E}\left[\max\left(w_i S_{t_m} + b_i, 0\right) \mid S_{t_{m-1}}\right] = w_i = \mathbb{E}\left[\max\left(S_{t_m} + \frac{b_i}{w_i}, 0\right) \mid S_{t_{m-1}}\right].$$

which is the time t_{m-1} value of a European call option that matures at time t_m with strike $-\frac{b_i}{w_i}$.

3. $w_i < 0, b_i > 0$. Then

$$\mathbb{E}\left[\max\left(w_i S_{t_m} + b_i, 0\right) \mid S_{t_{m-1}}\right] = -w_i = \mathbb{E}\left[\max\left(-\frac{b_i}{w_i} - S_{t_m}, 0\right) \mid S_{t_{m-1}}\right],$$

which is the time t_{m-1} value of a European put option that matures at time t_m with strike $-\frac{b_i}{w_i}$.

4. $w_i < 0, b_i < 0$. Then

$$\mathbb{E}\left[\max\left(w_i S_{t_m} + b_i, 0\right) \mid S_{t_{m-1}}\right] = 0,$$

for all S_{t_m}.

In the case of geometric Brownian motion, the continuation value can be given by using the forward value, the Black–Scholes call price and the Black–Scholes put price as appropriate.

The RLNN algorithm is innovative use of shallow neural networks to perform static replication, based directly on the equivalence of a shallow network with ReLU activation and a portfolio of spanning European options. The works of Souihli (2021), Hoencamp et al. (2022) and Lokeshwar et al. (2022) have demonstrated the flexibility and effectiveness of this technique and the simplicity of its implementation.

EXAMPLE 14.1: SINGLE-ASSET BERMUDAN USING NEURAL STATIC REPLICATION

This example presents an implementation of the RLNN algorithm of Lokeshwar et al. (2022) and is featured in the Jupyter Notebook `Bermudan Static Neural Replication.ipynb`. The model will be used to price a Bermudan put option on a stock. For simplicity, the stock price is normalised to equal $S_0 = 1.0$, and the option strike $K = 1.0$, with a 1-year maturity, interest rate $r = 0.06$, volatility $\sigma = 0.2$ and 10 regularly spaced exercise opportunities.

The first step is to build a set of Monte Carlo sample paths in a PyTorch tensor, and this is coded up using standard geometric Brownian motion in the usual way, using PyTorch tensors and mathematical operations, including the standard normal random number generator, and utilising a GPU for parallelism. A total of 32,768 paths were generated directly on the GPU with a time step of 0.1 years. As a check, the European put option was priced using the discounted average of the last stock prices on the path, giving a value of 0.05193.

The model uses European options to span the Bermudan option and hence needs Black–Scholes model prices. These must be calculated directly on the GPU for performance reasons, so Black–Scholes was implemented using PyTorch. The Black–Scholes value of the European put is 0.05166.

The next step is to define the neural network and the associated training loop. The network was a simple feedforward network with one hidden layer of 64 neurons, one input, the stock price, and one output, the option value, and this was defined in the same way as previous networks using a Python class derived from `torch.nn.Module`, except that weights were initialised using the normal distribution with mean zero and standard deviation 0.01.

A training loop is needed, identical to previous examples that used early stopping (see Example 4.1). The maximum training length was 200 epochs with early stopping. In practice, the entire 200 epochs were never used at any step, with the maximum training length being 31 and the minimum just 1.

The targets for each block of neural network training are generated in the algorithm, so the data-loader objects are constructed on the fly inside the model algorithm loop. The data is split into training and validation sets, with a 70 : 30 ratio. The validation set is used to determine whether to stop training early.

The critical function in the model is estimating the continuation value, which implements Equation (14.16) and the sum over the values of the forwards, puts and calls in the static hedge portfolio. The code is illustrated below.

```
def bermudan_continuation_value(model, S_tm1, r, sigma, delta_t):
    # Extract weights and biases from the trained model
    w_i = model.fc1.weight.data
    b_i = model.fc1.bias.data
    # Assuming only one neuron in output layer
    omega_i = model.fc2.weight.data.squeeze()
    # Assuming only one bias in output layer
    b2 = model.fc2.bias.data.squeeze()
```

```
    df1 = torch.exp(r * delta_t)
    continuation_values = []

    for i in range(len(w_i)):
        if w_i[i] > 0 and b_i[i] > 0:  # Case 1
            forward_value = w_i[i] * S_tm1 * df1 + b_i[i]
            continuation_values.append(forward_value)
        elif w_i[i] > 0 and b_i[i] <= 0:  # Case 2
            strike_price = -b_i[i] / w_i[i]
            european_call_value = black_scholes(S_tm1, strike_price,
                                                delta_t, r, sigma, 'call',
                                                device=S_tm1.device)
            continuation_values.append(european_call_value * w_i[i])
        elif w_i[i] <= 0 and b_i[i] > 0:  # Case 3
            strike_price = -b_i[i] / w_i[i]
            european_put_value = black_scholes(S_tm1, strike_price,
                                               delta_t, r, sigma, 'put',
                                               device=S_tm1.device)
            continuation_values.append(european_put_value * -w_i[i])
        elif w_i[i] <= 0 and b_i[i] <= 0:  # Case 4
            continuation_values.append(torch.tensor(0.0,
                                                    device=S_tm1.device))
    return sum(omega_i[i] * continuation_values[i]
               for i in range(len(continuation_values))) + b2
```

The first step is to extract the weights and biases from the hidden and output layers of the neural network model. The function then loops over the neurons in the hidden layer, which are interpreted as the holdings of stock forward, call and put options that expire at the next step. The option prices are calculated directly on the GPU using the PyTorch function described earlier. Finally, the function sums the spanning portfolio value. Note that the function can be applied in parallel across a tensor, recognising that `S_tm1` is a vector of simulated stock prices at time t_{m-1}.

The model backward induction loop is given below.

```
paths = simulate_asset_paths(S0, r, sigma, T, dt, N, M)
strike = torch.full_like(paths[:,-1], K).to(device)

model = PricingModel(1, hidden_dim).to(device)
optimizer = Adam(model.parameters(), lr=0.001)
loss_fn = nn.MSELoss()

step_hist = dict()
values = torch.maximum(strike - paths[:,-1],
                       torch.zeros_like(strike).to(device)).detach()
for t in range(N, 0, -1):
    print('Starting timestep: {}'.format(t))

    train_loader, val_loader = create_dataloaders(paths[:, t], values)
    hist = train_model_with_early_stopping(model, train_loader, val_loader,
                                           loss_fn, optimizer, epochs)
    step_hist[t] = hist
    payoff = torch.maximum(strike - paths[:,t-1],
                           torch.zeros_like(strike).to(device)).detach()
```

(*Continued*)

(*Continued*)

```
    cont_value = bermudan_continuation_value(model, paths[:, t-1],
                                             tr.to(device),
                                             tsigma.to(device),
                                             tdt.to(device))
    values = torch.max(payoff, cont_value)

V0 = torch.mean(values).detach().cpu().item()
```

The program initialises the values array with the intrinsic value of the put at maturity and then enters the valuation loop, walking back through time steps to the start. Inside the loop, it creates data loaders using the stock prices and values for the current time t_m. The neural network model is trained using the early-stopping training loop. The model then calculates the exercise value using the stock prices from time step t_m and calculates the continuation value at the same time using the function given above. The program determines the value by taking the maximum of the exercise and continuation values before starting the next step of the loop. It obtains the final price from the value array at the last step.

A binomial tree model was used from `QuantLib` to provide a comparison, and the code to value the Bermudan put is given below.

```
import QuantLib as ql

def value_american_option(option_type, K, S, T, r, y,
                          sigma, steps=200):
    maturity = int(T * 365)
    day_count = ql.Actual365Fixed()
    evaluation_date = ql.Settings.instance().evaluationDate

    if option_type.lower() == 'call':
        payoff = ql.PlainVanillaPayoff(ql.Option.Call, K)
    elif option_type.lower() == 'put':
        payoff = ql.PlainVanillaPayoff(ql.Option.Put, K)
    else:
        raise ValueError("Invalid option type. Use 'call' or 'put'.")

    option = ql.VanillaOption(payoff, ql.AmericanExercise(evaluation_date,
                              evaluation_date+maturity))

    spot_handle = ql.QuoteHandle(ql.SimpleQuote(S))
    risk_free_curve = ql.YieldTermStructureHandle(ql.FlatForward(
                            evaluation_date,
                            ql.QuoteHandle(ql.SimpleQuote(r)), day_count))
    dividend_curve = ql.YieldTermStructureHandle(ql.FlatForward(
                            evaluation_date,
                            ql.QuoteHandle(ql.SimpleQuote(y)), day_count))
    volatility_curve = ql.BlackVolTermStructureHandle(ql.BlackConstantVol(
                            evaluation_date, ql.TARGET(),
                            ql.QuoteHandle(ql.SimpleQuote(sigma)),
                            day_count))

    process = ql.BlackScholesMertonProcess(spot_handle, dividend_curve,
                                           risk_free_curve, volatility_curve)
```

```
    binomial_engine = ql.BinomialVanillaEngine(process, 'CRR', steps)
  option.setPricingEngine(binomial_engine)

  return option.NPV()
```

The tree used 10 steps to match the 10 observations for the neural model. The value obtained from the RLNN model was 0.05635, while the binomial tree gave 0.05717. As expected, both values are slightly higher than the European put value.

The RLNN model is not competitive with the binomial tree in this context as the repeated need for neural network training is computationally intensive, even with early stopping in place. However, the binomial tree will not scale well to high dimensions and, in practice, is limited to three dimensions or less. In contrast, the RLNN model will scale to high dimensions as the Monte Carlo simulation coupled with the neural network will not suffer from the curse of dimensionality.

14.3 CONCLUSIONS ON NEURAL STATIC REPLICATION

Neural static replication models represent an innovative and practical application of neural networks as a model component. They combine traditional techniques, such as Monte Carlo simulation, regression and static replication, with neural networks. The networks here are elementary and shallow. Nevertheless, they represent a use case that leverages their utility as an effective numerical technique.

CHAPTER 15

Volatility Surfaces

Shrike is the Lord of Pain and the Angel of Final Atonement, come from a place beyond time to announce the end of the human race.

Dan Simmons, Hyperion (1989)

15.1 INTRODUCTION

Deep learning has found ready application to model calibration within quantitative finance. This chapter examines the application of deep learning to two specific areas: calibrating volatility models for constructing implied volatility surfaces and generating local volatility surfaces. The next chapter will cover model calibration in a broader context.

One of the main reasons for integrating deep learning into this area is its computational efficiency. Once adequately trained, a deep learning model can be used for direct model calibration through inference or as an efficient approximation method in parameter mapping during optimisation processes like the Levenburg–Marquardt algorithm. The speed at which a trained neural network operates can be significantly faster compared to traditional methods.

The chapter is structured as follows: in Section 15.2, stochastic volatility models that have been subjects of deep learning applications are introduced, including the Heston (1993), SABR (Hagan et al., 2002) and rough Bergomi (Christian Bayer and Gatheral, 2016) models. This section provides a foundational understanding of these models. Next, Section 15.3 reviews relevant literature and discusses the application of deep learning to these stochastic volatility models, supplemented with practical examples. Finally, Section 15.4 focuses on using deep neural networks for generating local volatility surfaces, offering an alternative to more traditional methods like the Dupire (1994) formula. This section also includes an example demonstrating the practical application of this technique.

15.2 VOLATILITY SURFACE MODELS

The Black–Scholes model has long been a cornerstone for option pricing. However, as widely understood, the model fails to explain certain market phenomena, such as the volatility smiles and skews that vary with option maturity. Despite these limitations, the Black–Scholes formula has maintained its position as a critical tool, serving as a mapping function between the implied volatility surface and option prices.

Market participants construct simple parametric implied volatility surfaces using interpolation techniques like cubic splines based on liquid option quotes available at specific strikes and maturities or on prices of risk reversals and strangles quoted at various delta levels in the FX options market. They employ these methods to interpolate and extrapolate across strikes and maturities for various purposes, such as pricing deals, valuing option portfolios and managing risk. However, these models frequently fail to capture the dynamic nature of volatility.

Deep Learning in Quantitative Finance, First Edition. Andrew Green.

Stochastic volatility model-based surfaces have been developed to overcome the limitations of existing methods. These models posit that volatility follows a stochastic process, which may correlate with the underlying asset price. Such an approach offers a more nuanced reflection of volatility dynamics, incorporating features like mean reversion, volatility clustering and leverage effects. Notably, stochastic volatility models provide a robust framework for explaining the presence of volatility smiles and skew (Gatheral, 2006).

The diffusive stochastic volatility model SABR has gained popularity in the interest rate market for managing vanilla interest rate option trading books. However, challenges arise in other markets, such as equity index options, where the extreme skews observed at short maturities are not well aligned with the assumptions of diffusive stochastic volatility models (Gatheral, 2006). This mismatch has prompted the integration of jumps into the volatility process and, ultimately, the adoption of fractional Brownian motion in models like *rough Bergomi.*

15.2.1 Definitions

Following Bayer and Stemper (2018), the market quote for an option with moneyness M and maturity T is defined as $Q(M, T)$, where $M = K/S_0$. The Black–Scholes price of an option with moneyness M and maturity T is given by $BS(M, T, \sigma)$. Then the implied volatility, $\sigma_{IV}(M, T)$, is defined by

$$Q(M, T) = BS(M, T, \sigma_{IV}(M, T)), \tag{15.1}$$

and the mapping from (M, T) to $\sigma_{IV}(M, T)$ is the *implied volatility surface*. Given a model price $P(\mu, M, T)$, which is a function of model parameters μ, the model price satisfies

$$P(\mu, M, T) = BS(M, T, \sigma_{IV}(\mu, M, T)). \tag{15.2}$$

15.2.2 Heston

The Heston (1993) model is a diffusive stochastic volatility model with dynamics given by

$$\frac{dS_t}{S_t} = [r_t - q_t]dt + \sqrt{V_t}dW_t, \tag{15.3}$$

$$dV_t = \lambda[\bar{V} - V_t]dt + \eta\sqrt{V_t}dW_t^V, \tag{15.4}$$

$$dW_t dW_t^V = \rho dt. \tag{15.5}$$

Moreover, the variance process is mean-reverting. Hence, the Heston model is a five-parameter model $(\lambda, \bar{V}, \eta, \rho, V_0)$. Several different implementations of the pricing function under Heston exist, including the original semi-analytic formula from Heston (1993), which can be numerically unstable for long maturities and high mean levels of mean reversion, a fast Fourier transform approach from Carr and Madan (1999). This improved semi-analytic approach addresses the numerical instability from Kahl and Jäckel (2005) and a version with time-dependent parameters from Benhamou et al. (2010).

15.2.3 SABR

The *stochastic alpha, beta, rho (SABR)* model (Hagan et al., 2002) is a CEV asset process with correlated lognormal stochastic volatility,

$$dF_t = \sigma_t F_t^{\beta} dW_t^F, \tag{15.6}$$

$$d\sigma_t = \nu\sigma_t dW_t^{\sigma}, \tag{15.7}$$

$$\sigma_0 = \alpha, \tag{15.8}$$

$$dW_t^F dW^{\sigma} = \rho dt. \tag{15.9}$$

It is a four-parameter model $(\alpha, \beta, \nu, \rho)$. The standard approach to determining the implied volatility, given the parameter values, is to use an approximation formula

$$\sigma_B(K, F) = \frac{\alpha}{(FK)^{(1-\beta)/2}\left\{1 + \frac{(1-\beta)^2}{24}\log^2 F/K + \frac{(1-\beta)^4}{1920}\log^4 F/K + \cdots\right\}} \times \left(\frac{z}{x(z)}\right) \times \left\{1 + \left[\frac{(1-\beta)^2}{24}\frac{\alpha^2}{(FK)^{1-\beta}} + \frac{1}{4}\frac{\rho\beta\nu\alpha}{(FK)^{(1-\beta)/2}} + \frac{2-3\rho^2}{24}\nu^2\right]T + \cdots\right., \tag{15.10}$$

where

$$z = \frac{\nu}{\alpha}(FK)^{(1-\beta)/2}\log F/K \tag{15.11}$$

and

$$x(z) = \log\left\{\frac{\sqrt{1-2\rho z + z^2} + z - \rho}{1-\rho}\right\}. \tag{15.12}$$

McGhee (2018) highlights several problems with the approximation formula:

- Displaying areas of negative implied probability within reasonable parameter ranges.
- The approximation does not match the underlying SDE.
- The formula fails to calibrate to smiles at long maturities.

In response, McGhee (2011, 2018) proposed a more accurate numerical integration scheme and a finite difference scheme, again providing better results than the original approximation formula. Several other authors have proposed improvements to the original approximation.

15.2.4 Rough Bergomi

Christian Bayer and Gatheral (2016) introduced the rough Bergomi model, which posits that financial market volatility is *rough* or irregular over time, characterised by a Hurst exponent of less than 0.5. The model employs fractional Brownian motion to describe volatility dynamics, enabling long-range dependence while being non-Markovian.[1] The model dynamics are given by

$$dS_t = S_t\sqrt{V_t}dB_t, \tag{15.13}$$

$$V_t = \xi_0(t)\exp\left(\eta W_t^H - \frac{1}{2}\eta^2 t^{2H}\right), \tag{15.14}$$

where:

- $\xi_0(t)$ is the forward variance curve, a deterministic function of time capturing the market's expectation of future variance.
- η is a volatility-of-volatility parameter, controlling the amplitude of volatility fluctuations.
- W_t^H is a fractional Brownian motion with Hurst parameter H, typically less than 0.5.
- H is the Hurst exponent, which is crucial in the rough Bergomi model, indicating the degree of roughness of the volatility path.

[1] See Chapter 18 for background on fractional Brownian motion.

The fractional Brownian motion W_t^H can be represented in terms of standard Brownian motion W_t through a process known as the Mandelbrot–Van Ness representation (Mandelbrot and Van Ness, 1968). This representation expresses W_t^H as an integral involving W_t:

$$W_t^H = \frac{1}{\Gamma\left(H+\frac{1}{2}\right)}\left(\int_{-\infty}^{0}\left[(t-s)^{H-\frac{1}{2}}-(-s)^{H-\frac{1}{2}}\right]dW_s+\int_{0}^{t}(t-s)^{H-\frac{1}{2}}dW_s\right), \tag{15.15}$$

where:

- Γ denotes the Gamma function.
- W_s is standard Brownian motion.

This expression shows how W_t^H, the fractional Brownian motion, is constructed from the integral of standard Brownian motion, W_s, weighted by a kernel that depends on the Hurst parameter H. The first integral represents the 'memory' of the fractional Brownian motion from the infinite past up to time 0, and the second integral represents the contribution from time 0 to the current time t. The Brownian motions B_t and W_t have correlation ρ in the rough Bergomi model. The model has no analytic form, and Monte Carlo simulation must be used.

15.2.5 Calibrating Volatility Models

Given a set of N market quotes of options

$$Q^i \equiv Q(M^i, T^i), \tag{15.16}$$

and associated model prices

$$P^i \equiv P(\mu, M^i, T^i), \tag{15.17}$$

model calibration is defined by

$$\mu^* = \underset{\mu}{\operatorname{argmin}} \sum_{i=1}^{N} (Q^i - P^i)^2. \tag{15.18}$$

15.3 DEEP LEARNING VOLATILITY SURFACES

Four papers, Bayer and Stemper (2018), Dimitroff et al. (2018), McGhee (2018) and Horvath et al. (2019), have explored training neural networks to either calibrate volatility surfaces directly or approximate the *pricing map*,

$$\tilde{P}(\Theta, \mu, M, T) \approx P(\mu, M, T). \tag{15.19}$$

The four papers analysed three stochastic volatility models: Heston, SABR and rough Bergomi.

Most of the papers are motivated by performance considerations and seek to obtain performant volatility surface calibrations, and this is the case for Bayer and Stemper (2018) and Horvath et al. (2019), which are primarily concerned with the rough Bergomi model. The problem, as noted earlier, is the requirement to use Monte Carlo simulation, which arises from fractional Brownian motion. A deep neural network with its fast parallel inference has significant potential to accelerate the calibration if the learned model can replace the Monte Carlo simulation. Both papers adopt the paradigm of replacing the pricing map from parameters to vanilla option prices. Horvath et al. (2019) outputs an entire grid of implied volatilities with eight maturities and 11 strikes. Surface calibration then proceeds as before, using Levenberg–Marquardt, for example. The performance gain reported by Horvath et al. (2019) was a factor of 10^4, so this aim was very clearly achieved.

Both Bayer and Stemper (2018) and Horvath et al. (2019) also use the Heston model, although this is a 'test bed' rather than any need to gain performance. The existence of a Fourier-based pricing method, which is already performant, means there is less potential gain from replacing this with a neural network. Dimitroff et al. (2018) explore the Heston model but replicate the whole calibration rather than the pricing function. Specifically, they take the input grids of implied volatilities, strikes and forwards as a function of time to maturity and output the five calibrated Heston model parameters.

McGhee (2018) considers the SABR model. As noted above, well-established analytic approximation formulas for SABR are highly performant, although with the series of problems listed earlier. Hence, McGhee (2018) seeks to use the trained neural network to replace the much more accurate but slower numerical integration and PDE schemes for SABR. The resultant neural network is 10^4 faster than the PDE approach, thus dispensing with the need to use the approximation formula at all.

Bayer and Stemper (2018), McGhee (2018) and Horvath et al. (2019) adopt fully connected network architectures. Bayer and Stemper (2018) used a four-layer network with up to 4096 units each, while McGhee (2018) only used a single layer with up to 1000 units. Horvath et al. (2019) also use a four-layer network with only 30 units per layer.

Dimitroff et al. (2018) use a completely different architecture based on the *inception* model discussed in Section 6.7.4. The model is based on treating the volatility surface as an image with the input market data consisting of grids of implied volatilities and equity forward levels for options at 11 maturities and 10 strikes expressed as a stacked tensor of dimension $11 \times 10 \times 4$ with four channels containing implied volatility, log(*strike*), forward/strike and log(*forward*). The network consists of three inception layers and six fully connected layers, including the output. Each inception layer has three convolutional kernels operating in parallel with kernels of size (1, 1), (1, 3) and (2, 1), with this choice being specifically motivated by no-arbitrage conditions on the volatility surface. The (1, 3) filters model the behaviour of the surface in the moneyness direction, while the (2, 1) filters do the same in the maturity direction.

Bayer and Stemper (2018) use a ReLU activation function, but the remaining authors opt for smooth activation functions, with Dimitroff et al. (2018) using SeLU, McGhee (2018) using softplus and Horvath et al. (2019) using ELU.

Both Bayer and Stemper (2018) and Horvath et al. (2019) use regularisation techniques, including early stopping. Bayer and Stemper (2018) also used batch normalisation, while Dimitroff et al. (2018) used L^2 regularisation but found batch norm and dropout to provide no benefit.

The training data used by Bayer and Stemper (2018), McGhee (2018) and Horvath et al. (2019) was synthetic, which is not surprising since their goal was to replicate the pricing map between model parameters and option price/Black–Scholes implied volatility. However, the approaches taken to generate the synthetic datasets were quite varied. Bayer and Stemper (2018) adopted a random sampling approach where model parameter sets were generated by sampling a suitable distribution for each parameter, with each parameter distribution independent of the others. The distributions used for parameter generation are shown in Table 15.1, where $\mathcal{N}_{trunc}[a, b, \mu, \sigma]$ is the truncated normal distribution with mean μ, variance σ and truncated to the range $[a, b]$. To sample across maturities and

TABLE 15.1 Sampling Distributions for Model Parameters as Used by Bayer and Stemper (2018) and Horvath et al. (2019)

Bayer and Stemper (2018)				Horvath et al. (2019)	
Heston	Dist	rBergomi	Dist	rBergomi	Dist
η	$\mathcal{U}[0, 5]$	η	$\mathcal{N}_{trunc}[1, 4, 2.5, 0.5]$	η	$\mathcal{U}[0.5, 4]$
ρ	$\mathcal{U}[-1, 0]$	ρ	$\mathcal{N}_{trunc}[-1, -0.5, -0.95, 0.2]$	ρ	$\mathcal{U}[-0.95, -0.1]$
λ	$\mathcal{U}[0, 10]$	H	$\mathcal{N}_{trunc}[0.01, 0.5, 0.07, 0.05]$	H	$\mathcal{U}[0.025, 0.5]$
$\bar{V}$	$\mathcal{U}[0, 1]$	V_0	$\mathcal{N}_{trunc}[0.01, 0.5, 0.07, 0.05]$	ξ_i	$\mathcal{U}[0.01, 0.16]$
V_0	$\mathcal{U}[0, 1]$				

time, Bayer and Stemper (2018) estimate a joint distribution of moneyness and time-to-maturity using weighted Gaussian kernel density estimation with market data from European call options on SPX. Horvath et al. (2019) also use a random sampling approach to generate the training set for rough Bergomi with a piecewise constant forward volatility curve,

$$\xi_0(t) = \sum_{i-1}^{n} \xi_i 1_{\{t_{i-1}<t<t_i\}}, \tag{15.20}$$

where $t_0 = 0 < t_1 < \cdots < t_n$ are option maturity dates. Horvath et al. (2019) use a grid of relative strikes (0.5, 0.6, 0.7, 0.8, 0.9, 1.0, 1.1, 1.2, 1.3, 1.4, 1.5) and maturities in years (0.1, 0.3, 0.6, 0.9, 1.2, 1.5, 1.8, 2.0). The sampling distributions are summarised in Table 15.1.

McGhee (2018) uses a sampling scheme combining a grid and random values. The author first defines the parameter ranges with fixed ranges for maturity (1 day to 2 years), initial volatility (5% to 90%) and correlation (-90% to +90%). For volatility and strike, dynamic ranges are proposed. The volatility of the volatility range is specified for maturity of 1 month at (5% to 400%) and then scaled using the formula

$$\nu_t = \nu_s \times \sqrt{\frac{T_s}{T_t}}. \tag{15.21}$$

The following expression gives the strike range:

$$K\left(\pm\eta_S, \eta_\sigma\right) = F(0,T)\exp\left(-\frac{1}{2}\frac{\alpha^2}{\nu^2}\left(e^{\nu^2 T}-1\right)\right.$$
$$\left.+\frac{\rho}{\nu}\left(\sigma\left(T,\eta_\sigma\right)-\alpha\right) \pm \eta_S\frac{\alpha}{\nu}\left(e^{\nu^2 T}-1\right)^{1/2}\right), \tag{15.22}$$

where $\eta_S = 3.5$ and $\eta_\sigma = 1.5$. Ten strikes were selected across the $\pm\eta_S$ range to represent the volatility smile. All points were input to the neural network, along with maturity T, correlation ρ, initial volatility α and volatility of volatility ν, noting that $\beta = 1$ in McGhee (2018). Models were trained separately for two time ranges $T \in [1D, 1Y]$ and $T \in [1Y, 2Y]$ within each domain split into 100 equidistant times. α, ν and ρ were split into 10 equidistant points to give a grid of input 100,000 points. A further 150,000 points were selected randomly to give the full training set.

Given the focus on replication of Heston calibration in full, Dimitroff et al. (2018) train their model using historical implied volatility surfaces. They used calibrated surfaces for 116 single stocks and three indices daily from 2012 to 2017, giving a total training set size of 183,651.

All the papers used the Adam optimiser and MSE loss as appropriate for a regression problem, except Dimitroff et al. (2018), who coupled an output sigmoid activation with cross-entropy loss.

Table 15.2 summarises the approach adopted by each of the four papers. All were able to successfully replicate either the pricing map or complete the calibration process to high levels of accuracy.

TABLE 15.2 Deep Learning and Volatility Surfaces

	Model Type			Neural Network		
Reference	Heston	SABR	Rough Bergomi	Architecture	Dataset	Approach
Bayer and Stemper (2018)	✓		✓	FC	Random sampling	Pricing map
Dimitroff et al. (2018)	✓			CNN	Historical	Calibration
McGhee (2018)		✓		FC	Grid + random sampling	Pricing map
Horvath et al. (2019)	✓		✓	FC	Grid + random sampling	Pricing map

EXAMPLE 15.1: HESTON

This example trains a neural network to replicate a Heston model implied volatility function: the Heston model price of a European call option converted to a Black–Scholes implied volatility. It then evaluates the model's performance versus the underlying Fourier transform implementation of the Heston option price.

The first step involves synthetically generating the training set in the Jupyter Notebook `Generate Heston Data.ipynb`. The Quantlib Python package provides a Heston pricing model based on the Fourier transform solution of Gatheral (2006). The following code fragment demonstrates how to price a European call option using Heston. After obtaining the price, it is necessary to calculate the corresponding Black–Scholes implied volatility using the `implied_volatility` function from the `py_vollib` Python package. The function call includes an intrinsic value check to address numerical issues and is encapsulated within a `try` ... `except` block.

```
import QuantLib as ql
from py_vollib.black_scholes.implied_volatility import implied_volatility
.
.
.

todaysDate = ql.Date(17, 2, 2024)
ql.Settings.instance().evaluationDate = todaysDate

settlementDate = todaysDate
day_count = ql.Actual365Fixed()
rfr = ql.YieldTermStructureHandle(ql.FlatForward(settlementDate, r, day_count))

div_yield = ql.YieldTermStructureHandle(ql.FlatForward(settlementDate, q, day_count))


exercise = ql.EuropeanExercise(todaysDate + maturity)
payoff = ql.PlainVanillaPayoff(ql.Option.Call, K)
european_option = ql.VanillaOption(payoff, exercise)

Spot = ql.QuoteHandle(ql.SimpleQuote(S0))
heston_process = ql.HestonProcess(rfr, div_yield, spot, V0, lamda, vbar, eta, rho)

engine = ql.AnalyticHestonEngine(ql.HestonModel(heston_process), 1e-15, int(1e6))

european_option.setPricingEngine(engine)

try:
    price = european_option.NPV()
    if price > 0 and price + K >= S0:
        iv = implied_volatility(price, S0, K, tau, r, 'c')
```

The distributions in Table 15.3, the same ones Bayer and Stemper (2018) used for the Heston parameters, guide the random sampling of model parameters, maturity and option strikes. Unlike the weighted scheme applied in earlier chapters for the basket option, the maturity sampling followed a uniform distribution, which improved the replication of Heston for longer-maturity options. The sampling of strikes also occurred uniformly, ranging between a relative strike of 0.5 and 1.5. The final training set comprised one million examples.

(*Continued*)

(*Continued*)

TABLE 15.3 Sampling Distributions for Model and Trade Parameters Used in the Heston Example.

Parameter	Distribution
η	$\mathcal{U}[0, 5]$
ρ	$\mathcal{U}[-1, 0]$
λ	$\mathcal{U}[0, 10]$
$\bar{V}$	$\mathcal{U}[0, 1]$
V_0	$\mathcal{U}[0, 1]$
Maturity	$\mathcal{U}[0.001, 5]$
K	$\mathcal{U}[0.5, 1.5]$

A standard feedforward network with four layers of 256 units each represents the neural network model architecture, incorporating batch normalisation after each layer. The network employs the swish activation function and has a linear output layer. The training process extended over 1000 epochs using the Adam optimiser with default parameters and a learning rate of 0.001, with a batch size of 1024. Figure 15.1 illustrates the test and training loss across epochs. The test loss ceases to decrease after approximately 70 epochs but shows a gradual decline after 500 epochs, indicating potential benefits from additional training. Since the training loss is lower than the test loss, the network is over-trained, which suggests the possibility of using a smaller network.

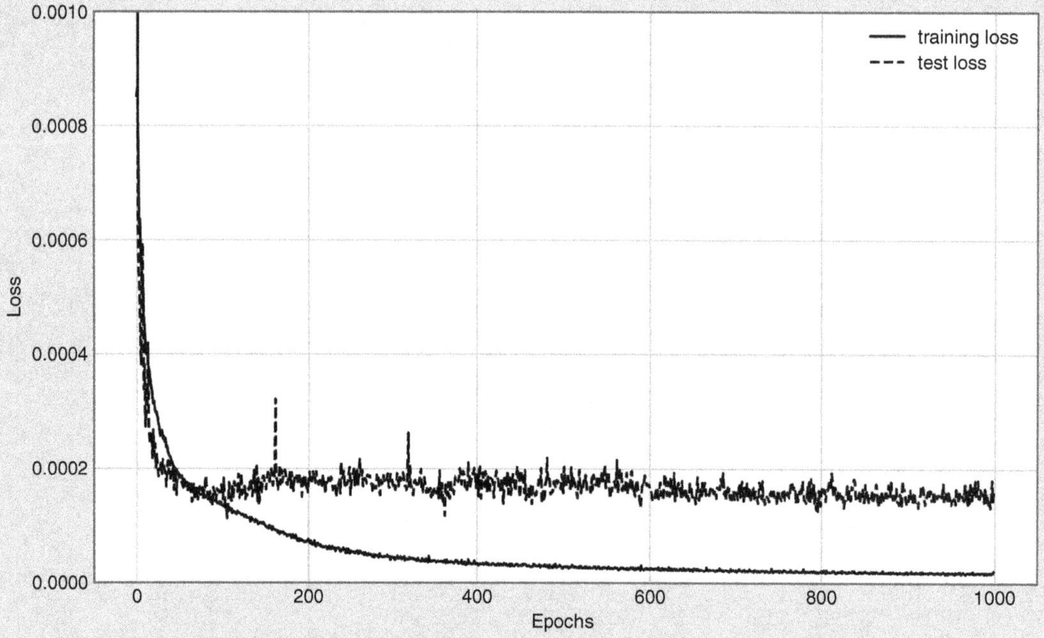

FIGURE 15.1 Training and test loss from the Heston implied volatility neural network.

Figure 15.2 compares the neural network and the Heston pricing model for parameters near the centre of the sampling distributions for eight different maturities. The two implied volatility functions are a close match across the full range of relative strikes.

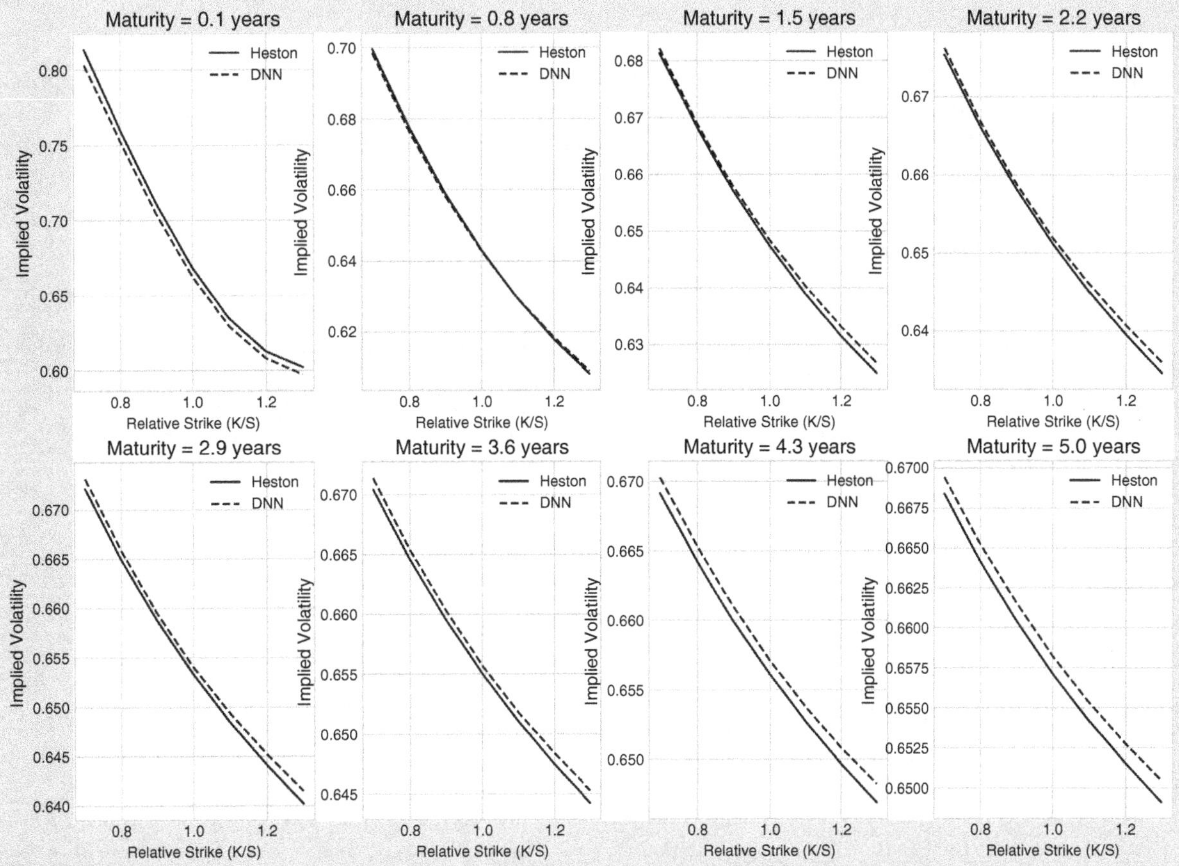

FIGURE 15.2 Smiles for different maturities from the Heston price function and the replicating neural network. The Heston model parameters were set to $\eta = 2.5, \rho = -0.5, \lambda = 5.0, \bar{v} = 0.5, V_0 = 0.5$.

EXAMPLE 15.2: ROUGH BERGOMI

This example trains a neural network to replicate the pricing map from rough Bergomi parameters to implied volatility. Unlike the case with the Heston model, rough Bergomi requires Monte Carlo simulation for option pricing, and hence, there is significant potential gain from this approach as neural network inference will be much faster than the original model, and this will be particularly beneficial in calibrating the model to a real implied volatility surface, requiring repeated option valuation of many options. As demonstrated below, the neural network can estimate all the option values in parallel, doubly saving on computational costs during calibration. The generation of training data can be found in the Jupyter Notebook `Generate Bergomi Data-Grid.ipynb` and the neural network model in `Rough Bergomi Volatility-Strike Grid.ipynb`.

The first step involves generating the training data, which, like with Heston, occurs synthetically by randomly sampling parameter values and using a rough Bergomi model implementation to generate the corresponding option price. This option price is then inverted to derive the implied volatility. The Python implementation of the rough Bergomi model is accessible in the `rbergomi` package, found at https://github.com/ryanmccrickerd/rough_bergomi. This chapter's folder contains the package's source files and the open-source licence agreement. The `rbergomi` package facilitates a rough Bergomi Monte Carlo simulation, requiring the

(*Continued*)

(*Continued*)

option pricing to be scripted in Python, as illustrated below. Notably, this function prices a series of options with varying strikes but identical maturity simultaneously, enhancing efficiency by using a single set of Monte Carlo paths for multiple options and simplifying the model's training with a fixed set of strikes instead of randomly sampled ones.

```
def simulate_rBergomi_paths(S0, Ks, T, rho, eta, H, xi_0, num_paths, num_steps):

    a = H - 0.5
    rB = rbergomi.rBergomi(n = num_steps, N = num_paths, T = T, a = a)
    dW1 = rB.dW1()
    dW2 = rB.dW2()
    Y = rB.Y(dW1)
    dB = rB.dB(dW1, dW2, rho = rho)
    V = rB.V(Y, xi = xi_0, eta = eta)
    S = rB.S(V, dB)
    ivs = dict()
    ST = S[:,-1][:,np.newaxis]
    for iK in Ks:
        call_payoff = np.maximum(ST - iK,0)
        call_price = np.mean(call_payoff, axis = 0)[:,np.newaxis].item()
        if call_price > 0 and call_price + iK > S0:
            iv = implied_volatility(call_price, S0, iK, T, 0.0, 'c')
            ivs[iK] = iv
    return ivs
```

The Monte Carlo was run with 30,000 paths and 100 time steps yearly. The remaining model and option parameters were sampled using the distributions in Table 15.4. A total of 100,000 samples were generated, with 11 strikes in each case, giving 1.1 million samples in total. Of these, around 2% were retained as the test set.

TABLE 15.4 Sampling Distributions for Model and Trade Parameters Used in the Rough Bergomi Example

Parameter	Distribution
η	$\mathcal{U}[0.5, 4.0]$
ρ	$\mathcal{U}[-0.95, -0.1]$
H	$\mathcal{U}[0.025, 0.5]$
xi_0	$\mathcal{U}[0.01, 0.16]$
Maturity	$\mathcal{U}[0.1, 2.0]$

The neural network architecture was identical to that used in the previous Heston example, save for a reduction in the size of the input to six elements, reflecting the one less model parameter of the rough Bergomi model. The model was trained through 1000 epochs, giving the learning curves shown in Figure 15.3. Adam was the optimiser, with a learning rate of 0.001 and the MSE loss function. As can be seen from the figure, both training and test loss continue to decline even after 1000 epochs, suggesting the model could have been trained further.

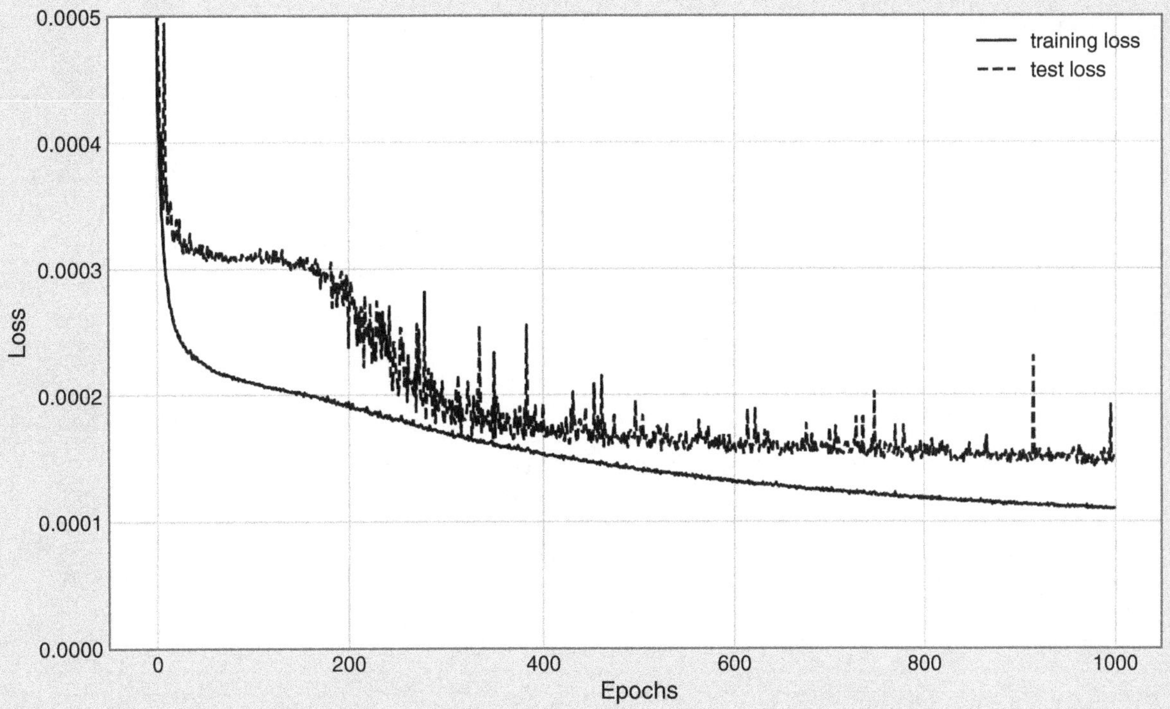

FIGURE 15.3 Training and test loss from the rough Bergomi implied volatility neural network.

After training the model, the comparison of implied volatilities from the neural network with those from the Monte Carlo simulation took place for a parameter set close to the sampling distribution's midpoints, specifically $\eta = 2.5, \rho = -0.5, H = 5.0, \xi_0 = 0.08$. The process generated volatility smiles for maturities 0.1, 0.4, 0.6, 0.9, 1.2, 1.5, 1.7 and 2.0 years with relative strikes of 0.7, 0.8, 0.9, 1.0, 1.1, 1.2 and 1.3. Due to numerical errors in the Monte Carlo simulation that sometimes resulted in non-invertible prices, the strike range was slightly compressed compared to the training set. Figure 15.4 displays the resulting smile charts, highlighting the Monte Carlo simulation's noisiness and the neural network results' smoothness. This observation aligns with the findings in Chapter 11, where the neural network effectively smoothed out the Monte Carlo noise.

The neural network model was then used to fit the rough Bergomi parameters to an actual, implied volatility surface from S&P 500 index options. The fitting test used the implied volatility surface for 27 March 2013, with the same dataset as in Chapter 11. The strike range was narrowed to $0.5 < K < 1.5$ within the neural network's training range. Maturities were confined to $0.4 < T \leq 2.0$, tighter than the training range, to exclude early maturity options with significant flat extrapolation in implied volatility across the strike range.

(*Continued*)

(*Continued*)

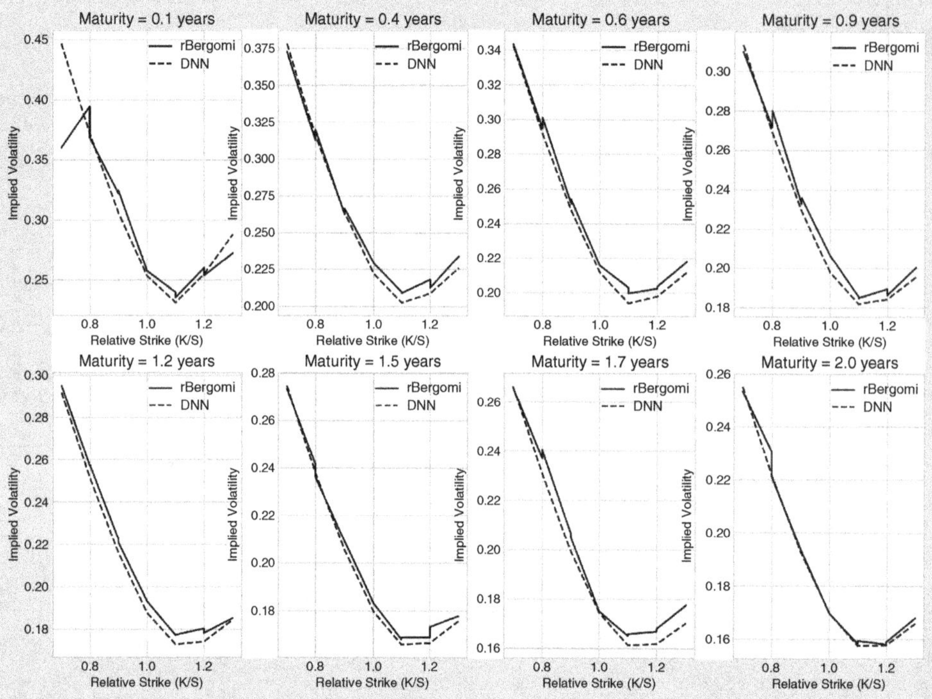

FIGURE 15.4 Smiles for different maturities from the rough Bergomi price function and the replicating neural network. The rough Bergomi model parameters were set to $\eta = 2.5, \rho = -0.5, H = 5.0, \xi_0 = 0.08$.

The fitting process utilised the `minimise` routine from `scipy.optimise`, which required an objective function. A Python class managing the neural network within the objective function handled the storage of the neural network and the scaling object. The `impliedvol` method accepts arrays of maturities and strikes for all options to be fitted. It leverages the neural network to infer implied volatilities for all options in parallel and manage the scaling of the input values.

```
class rbergomiiv:
    def __init__(self, model, sc, device):
        self.model = model
        self.sc = sc
        self.device = device

    def impliedvol(self, eta, rho, H, xi_0, mats, strikes):
        no_opt = len(mats)
        veta = np.full(no_opt, eta)
        vrho = np.full(no_opt, rho)
        vH = np.full(no_opt, H)
        vxi_0 = np.full(no_opt, xi_0)
            param_dict = {'eta': veta, 'rho': vrho,
                'H': vH, 'xi_0': vxi_0,
                'tau': mats, 'K': strikes}
        df = pd.DataFrame(param_dict)
        bergomi_X = self.sc.transform(df)
        tbergomi_X = torch.Tensor(bergomi_X).to(self.device)
        bergominn_iv = self.model(tbergomi_X)
        return bergominn_iv.squeeze().detach().cpu().numpy()
```

The objective function then takes the form

```
def objective_function(params, iv_surface, rbergomiobj):
    total_error = 0
    eta = params[0]
    rho = params[1]
    H = params[2]
    xi_0 = params[3]
    mats = iv_surface['maturity']
    strikes = iv_surface['relative_strike']
    model_iv = rbergomiobj.impliedvol(eta, rho, H, xi_0, mats, strikes)
    market_iv = iv_surface['implied_volatility'].to_numpy()
    mse = np.mean((market_iv - model_iv) ** 2)
    return mse
```

The initial parameter values were the same as those used for the sample smiles above. Bounds were set on the parameter values at the limits of the sampling ranges as shown in Table 15.4. The 'Nelder–Mead' optimisation routine was selected, and finally, the minimisation function call was made.

```
result = minimize(objective_function, initial_params,
                  args=(dfvol,bergomiivobj),
                  bounds=bounds, method=optimization_method, tol=1e-10)
```

The resulting fitted parameters were $\eta = 1.942$, $\rho = -0.149$, $H = 0.216$, $\xi_0 = 0.048$. The computation with the neural network was almost instantaneous and significantly faster than could practically be achieved with the Monte Carlo implementation, which takes around 2.35 seconds per implied volatility calculation.

Figure 15.5 shows the fitted rough Bergomi implied volatility surface against the marked data for each of the eight maturities. The chart contains the output from the trained neural network and the original Monte Carlo, although with a restricted strike range. The neural network implied volatility is consistent with the Monte Carlo model. The model-implied volatility lies above the true market volatility for the early maturities and above for the later maturities. Hence, this approach can accurately calibrate the rough Bergomi to the implied volatility option.

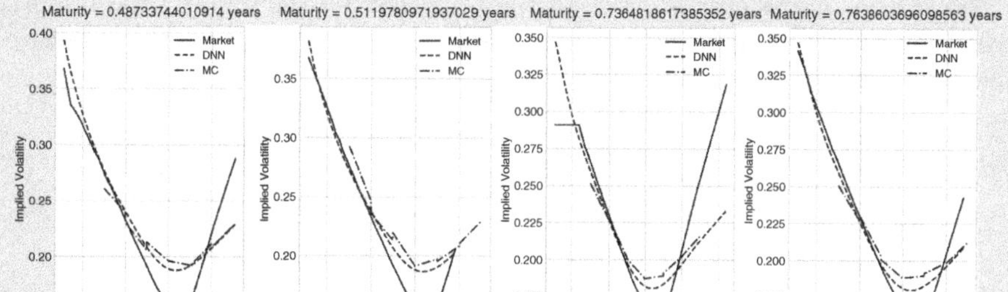

FIGURE 15.5 SPX volatility smiles for 27 March 2013 with the original market and fitted rough Bergomi model expressed using the DNN and original Monte Carlo.

15.4 DEEP LOCAL VOLATILITY

The Dupire (1994) *local volatility* model is an enduring and widely used approach to include the impact of volatility smiles and skews into option pricing. Given its fundamental importance in quantitative finance, it is unsurprising that authors have explored the use of neural networks in deriving a local volatility surface. This section begins with a summary of the local volatility model and then considers two different approaches to using neural networks. The first approach trains a neural network to match option prices, respecting the arbitrage conditions, and then automatic differentiation is used to obtain the local volatility. The second approach simultaneously fits neural networks to option prices and local volatilities in a self-consistent way.

15.4.1 The Dupire Local Volatility

The local volatility model assumes that the underlying asset follows a stochastic process under the risk-neutral measure, with SDE

$$dS_t = rS_t dt + \sigma(S_t, t)S_t dW_t, \tag{15.23}$$

where $\sigma(S_t, t)$ is the local volatility function, which depends on the asset price and time. The Dupire PDE arises from the application of Itô's lemma to a European call or put option, eliminating the stochastic term to obtain a PDE in terms of the option price, $C(S, t)$, and the underlying asset price, S. The Dupire PDE is given by

$$\frac{\partial C}{\partial t} + rS\frac{\partial C}{\partial S} + \frac{1}{2}\sigma^2(S, t)S^2\frac{\partial^2 C}{\partial S^2} - rC = 0, \tag{15.24}$$

where $C(S, t)$ is the price of the European call option. The Dupire formula is used to back out the local volatility function $\sigma(S, t)$ from market prices of European options. Rearranging the Dupire PDE and solving for $\sigma^2(S, t)$ gives

$$\sigma^2(S, t) = \frac{\frac{\partial C}{\partial t} + rS\frac{\partial C}{\partial S} + rC}{\frac{1}{2}S^2\frac{\partial^2 C}{\partial S^2}}. \tag{15.25}$$

The initial condition is set by the current price of the underlying asset, S_0, and the boundary conditions are determined by the behaviour of the option prices as they approach expiration or as the strike price approaches zero or infinity. For a European call option, the boundary conditions are

$$\begin{aligned}
T \to 0 \quad & C(S, K, T) \to \max(S - K, 0), \\
K \to 0 \quad & C(S, K, T) \to S, \\
K \to \infty \quad & C(S, K, T) \to 0.
\end{aligned}$$

Similarly, for a European put option:

$$\begin{aligned}
T \to 0 \quad & P(S, K, T) \to \max(K - S, 0), \\
K \to 0 \quad & P(S, K, T) \to 0, \\
K \to \infty \quad & P(S, K, T) \to K - S.
\end{aligned}$$

The price of European call and put options under the Dupire model must also satisfy certain upper and lower bounds for arbitrage-free conditions. For a call option:

$$S \geq C(S, K, T) \geq \max(S - Ke^{-rT}, 0).$$

Furthermore, for a put option:

$$Ke^{-rT} \geq P(S, K, T) \geq \max(Ke^{-rT} - S, 0).$$

The Dupire model imposes constraints to prevent calendar arbitrage; this is achieved when the option price is monotonically increasing,

$$\frac{\partial C(K, T)}{\partial T} \geq 0, \tag{15.26}$$

ensuring no arbitrage opportunities exist through mispricing of options with different maturities. The local volatility surface must satisfy certain convexity conditions to prevent butterfly arbitrage. Specifically, the second derivative of the call price with respect to the strike must be non-negative:

$$\frac{\partial^2 C}{\partial K^2} \geq 0. \tag{15.27}$$

15.4.2 Fitting a Local Volatility Consistent Pricing Function

Chataigner et al. (2020) approached the problem of applying neural networks to local volatility through automatic differentiation. Their approach is to fit a neural network to replicate the price of a series of discrete European calls or puts forming a volatility surface and then use the inbuilt automatic differentiation of the neural network to extract the local volatility using the Dupire formula in Equation (15.25). To avoid arbitrage, Chataigner et al. (2020) impose constraints on the neural network, and they experiment with two types, hard and soft.

The hard constraints approach imposes physical constraints on the neural network, restricts weights to be non-negative and uses convex activation functions. For hidden layers, Chataigner et al. (2020) use softplus, $\ln(1 + e^x)$, and the output uses sigmoid.

The soft constraints approach penalises arbitrage through a regularisation term in the loss function. The penalty term takes the form

$$J_{arb} = \lambda_1 \left(\frac{\partial p(T, k)}{\partial T} \right)^- + \lambda_2 \left(\frac{\partial^2 p(T, k)}{\partial k^2} \right)^- + \lambda_3 \left[\left(\zeta - \bar{a} \right)^+ + \left(\zeta - \underline{a} \right)^- \right], \tag{15.28}$$

where

- $p(T, k) = \exp\left(\int_0^T q(t)dt \right) P(T, K),$
- $k = K \exp\left(- \int_0^T (r(t) - q(t))dt \right),$
- $\zeta = \frac{\sigma^2(K,T)}{2},$
- $\bar{a}$ and $\underline{a}$ are upper and lower bounds on the local variance.

Chataigner et al. (2020) employed a two-layer neural network with 200 neurons in each hidden layer, utilising the Adam optimiser and reducing the learning rate by a factor of 10 after every 100 epochs without error improvement. The training set consisted of closing option prices with various strikes and maturities for a specific underlying. The study focused on European options on the DAX index for 7, 8 and 9 August 2001, featuring around 200 options daily. This methodology trained a separate neural network for each day, with the trained network serving as the option price function that corresponds directly to the implied volatility surface. A test set was created daily by regenerating test option prices on a regular grid from a local volatility surface, derived from the option prices using the Tikhonov calibration method cited in Crépey (2002). The model's training extended through 10,000 epochs, proceeding rapidly due to the training set's size.

The authors concluded that the hard constraint approach gave significant pricing errors and that the restrictions embedded within it restricted the expressive power of the neural network too severely. The soft constraint approach, however, successfully generated a pricing function that was free from arbitrage. The resulting local volatility was comparable to that obtained from Tikhonov regularisation, although with higher errors. Network training is slower than Tikhonov regularisation but does provide a local volatility function that can be evaluated at any point. At the same time, Tikhonov and other similar techniques require additional interpolation or calibration.

The study by Chataigner et al. (2020) on applying neural networks to local volatility extraction shows the effectiveness of soft constraints over hard constraints in generating arbitrage-free pricing functions. While hard constraints limit the network's expressive power, leading to pricing errors, soft constraints offer an accurate arbitrage-free local volatility function. Despite the longer training times and increased errors relative to methods such as Tikhonov regularisation, the soft constraint strategy offers an advantage by producing a continuous local volatility function.

15.4.3 Fitting Self-Consistent Implied and Local Volatilities

Wang et al. (2021) chose to model both the local volatility surface and option pricing function with neural networks in a self-consistent manner, training both networks with a combined loss function.

The authors adopted a change of variables as follows:

$$k = e^{-rT}\frac{K}{K_{\max}}, \tag{15.29}$$

$$t = \frac{T}{T_{\max}}, \tag{15.30}$$

and this leads to a scaled local volatility expression with the form

$$\eta(k,t) = \frac{T_{\max}}{2}\sigma^2(K,T), \tag{15.31}$$

given the Dupire equation in the form

$$f_{\text{dup}}(k,t) := \frac{\partial C}{\partial t}(k,t) - \eta(k,t)k^2\frac{\partial^2 C}{\partial k^2}(k,t) = 0. \tag{15.32}$$

The authors chose to model the local volatility directly with a neural network, that is

$$\eta_\theta(k,t) = \mathcal{N}_\eta\left(k,t;\theta_\eta\right). \tag{15.33}$$

However, for the price function, the neural network was used indirectly with the functional form

$$C_\theta(k,t) = S_0\left(1 - e^{-(1-k)\mathcal{N}_c(k,t;\theta_c)}\right), \tag{15.34}$$

$$P_\theta(k,t) = K_{\max}e^{rT_{\max}t}k\left(1 - e^{-k\mathcal{N}_p(k,t;\theta_p)}\right). \tag{15.35}$$

Wang et al. (2021) adopted a *ResNet*-style architecture with three residual blocks, each containing two sublayers with 64 neurons in each, and batch normalisation used after each layer.[2] The output activation function was softplus.

The loss function was made up of four parts,

$$J_\pi = J_{\text{fit}} + \lambda_{\text{ini}}J_{\text{ini}} + \lambda_{\text{arb}}J_{\text{arb}} + \lambda_{\text{dup}}J_{\text{dup}}. \tag{15.36}$$

[2] See Section 6.7.5.

All four components of the loss use the same weighting function,

$$w(\pi_i) := 1 + \frac{Ng(\pi_i)}{\sum_{i=1}^{N} g(\pi_i)}, \tag{15.37}$$

where

$$g(x_i) : = 0.1 \times 1_{[0,0.1)}(x_i) + x_i \times 1_{[0.1,10]}(x_i) + 10 \times 1_{[10,\infty)}(x_i), \tag{15.38}$$

$$x_i = \left(\frac{1}{N\pi_i^2} \sum_{i=1}^{N} \pi_i^2 \right), \tag{15.39}$$

where 1_A is an indicator function. Note that there is no contribution to the gradient of the loss from the weight term. The loss terms then take the following forms:

- J_{fit} is the weighted MSE on the option prices.
- J_{ini} is the weighted MSE on option prices sampled at M_1 points at $T = 0$.
- $J_{\text{arb}} = \frac{1}{M_2} \sum_{j=1}^{M_2} w\left(\frac{\partial C_\theta}{\partial t}(k_j, t_j)\right)\left(\left(-f_{\text{arb}}(k_j, t_j)\right)^+\right)^2$ is the loss associated with arbitrage conditions with $f_{\text{arb}}(k, t) := \frac{\partial C}{\partial t}(k, t) - rT_{\max}k\left(\frac{\partial C}{\partial k}(k, t)\right)^+ \geq 0.$
- $J_{\text{dup}} = \frac{1}{M_2} \sum_{j=1}^{M_2} w\left(\frac{\partial C_\theta}{\partial t}(k_j, t_j)\right)\left(f_{\text{dup}}(k_j, t_j)\right)^2$ is the Dupire loss that links the local volatility network to the price network, and is evaluated at sampled points M_2.

The training algorithm relies on a sampling of points M_1 in strike space $k \in [0, 1]$ to evaluate the initial condition constraint and M_2 points in strike and time to evaluate the arbitrage and Dupire loss terms. The two networks are trained simultaneously using the gradients of the loss with respect to the price network θ_c and to the local volatility network θ_η to update the weights in the respective models.

The authors applied their approach to a synthetic dataset and the same DAX dataset used by Chataigner et al. (2020). The synthetic dataset was constructed from an analytic local volatility model used to generate option prices via Monte Carlo to reconstruct the local volatility using the neural network.

EXAMPLE 15.3: DEEP LOCAL VOLATILITY

This example employs a synthetic local volatility surface akin to the one Wang et al. (2021) used and then generates a grid of option prices via Monte Carlo simulation. This set of option prices serves as the training data for an option price function, mirroring the approach of Chataigner et al. (2020). Estimating the local volatility function and reconstructing the original local volatility is aided by the derivatives of the price function. Two models were trained, unconstrained and constrained, the latter incorporating two constraints adopted by Chataigner et al. (2020).

Local Volatility Monte Carlo

The first step is to generate the option prices under a local volatility model, found in the Jupyter Notebook `Local Volatility Monte Carlo.ipynb`. To simplify the example, the initial stock price was 1.0, and the interest rate and dividend yield were equal to zero. The same local volatility function used by Wang et al. (2021) was adopted here; that is

$$\sigma(x, t) = 0.3 + ye^{-y},$$

(Continued)

(Continued)

where $y = (t + 0.1)\sqrt{x + 0.1}$. The resulting local volatility over the range $S \in [0.5, 1.5]$ and $T \in [0.5, 2.0]$ is illustrated as a heatmap in Figure 15.6.

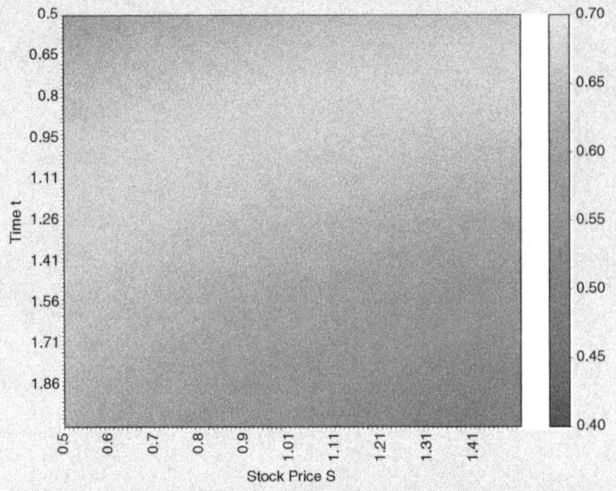

FIGURE 15.6 Local volatility surface for the analytic local volatility function.

Ten million Monte Carlo paths were constructed using the Euler approximation with a small time step, $\Delta = 0.01$, with a maximum maturity of 2 years. The paths were then used to price put options on a grid of strikes $K_i = 0.5, 0.65, \ldots, 1.5$ and maturities $T_j = 0.5, 0.65, \ldots, 2.0$ years. Once prices had been obtained for each grid point, they were saved to a CSV file for later use. The implied volatility was calculated for each option using the `implied_volatility` function from the `py_vollib` package. The resulting implied volatility surface and put price surface are shown in Figure 15.7.

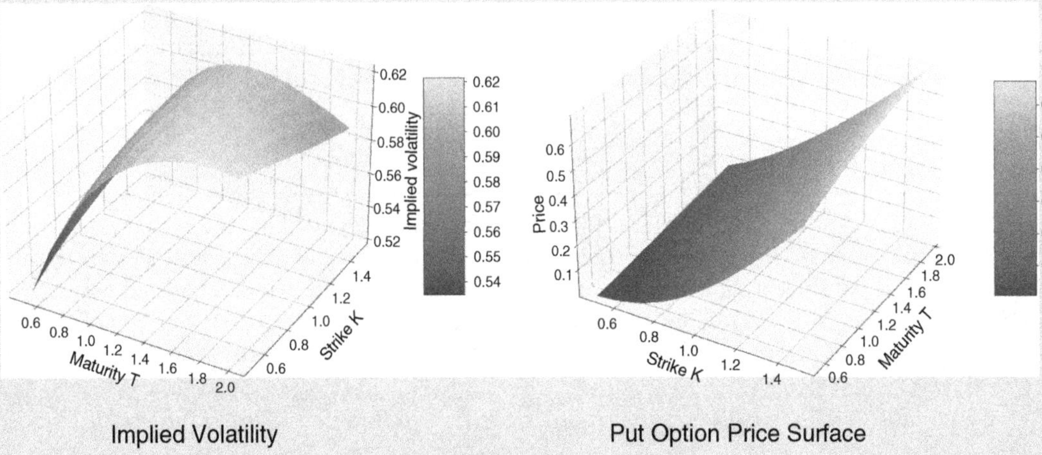

FIGURE 15.7 The resulting option implied volatility surface and put option price surface for the analytic local volatility model.

Deep Local Volatility

The next step involves training neural network models to replicate the price surface and then using the gradients of this learned function to estimate the local volatility, as demonstrated in the Jupyter Notebook `Deep Local Volatility.ipynb`. The notebook loads and prepares the option price data in the standard manner. It is crucial to recognise that the quality of the learned local volatility function will match the Monte Carlo simulation output rather than the underlying analytic function. The estimation of local volatility uses the Dupire formula applied to the option price grid, depicted as a heatmap in Figure 15.8. The numpy `gradient` function facilitates this process, as shown below, with the necessary scaling of the gradients. The figure indicates that, particularly in the central range, the Monte Carlo simulation has successfully replicated the local volatility, although edge effects are visible at low and high stock prices.

```
price_surface = df.pivot('K', 'T', 'Price')
X, Y = np.meshgrid(price_surface.columns, price_surface.index)
Z = price_surface.values
dC_dK, dC_dT = np.gradient(Z)
dC_dT /= 0.15
d2C_dK2, _ = np.gradient(dC_dK)
d2C_dK2 /= (0.05)**2
strikes = df['K'].unique()
strikes_sq = strikes**2
strikes_sq = strikes_sq.reshape(len(strikes), 1)
res = strikes_sq * d2C_dK2
local_volatility_squared = (2 * dC_dT) / (d2C_dK2 * strikes_sq)
local_volatility_squared = np.maximum(local_volatility_squared, 0.0)
local_volatility = np.sqrt(local_volatility_squared)
```

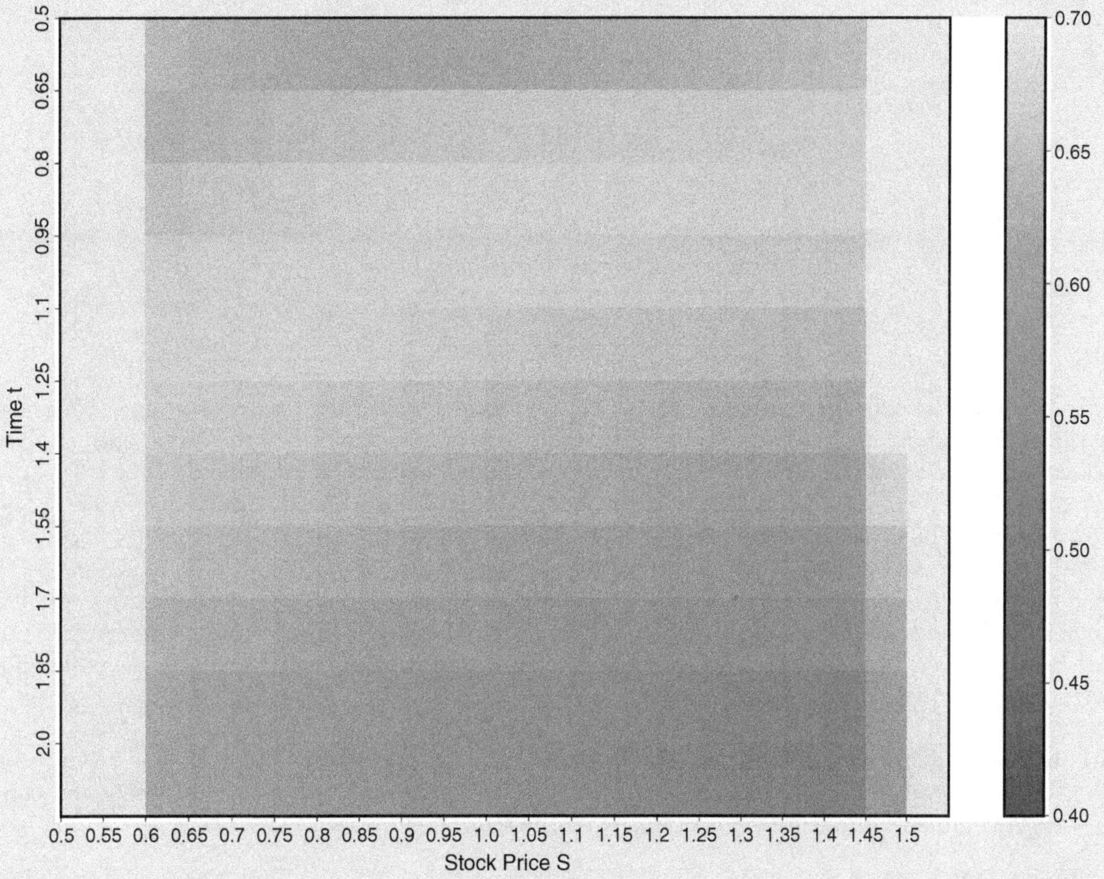

FIGURE 15.8 Local volatility surface reconstructed from the Monte Carlo put option prices.

(*Continued*)

(*Continued*)

The neural network architecture is similar to that proposed by Chataigner et al. (2020), with two layers of 256 neurons, each with the softplus activation function and followed by a batch normalisation layer. The output activation function was sigmoid.

The training loop requires the calculation of the first derivative of the price with respect to maturity and the second derivative with respect to strike, so the loss function can include the penalty if either of these is negative. The gradients were calculated using the PyTorch `grad` function. The following code fragment shows how the loss was implemented.

```
for batch_X, batch_y in train_loader:
    batch_X.requires_grad_(True)

    # Forward pass
      outputs = model(batch_X)
    loss = loss_fn(outputs.squeeze(), batch_y)

    # Calculate gradients with respect to the input
    dC_dInput = grad(outputs, batch_X, torch.ones_like(outputs),
    create_graph=True)[0]

    dC_dK, dC_dT = dC_dInput[:, 0], dC_dInput[:, 1]
    dC_dT_loss = torch.mean(torch.min(dC_dT, torch.zeros_like(dC_dT)))

    # Calculate the second derivative with respect to K (scaled)
    d2C_dK2 = grad(dC_dK, batch_X, torch.ones_like(dC_dK),
    create_graph=True)[0][:, 0]
    d2C_dK2_loss = torch.mean(torch.min(d2C_dK2,
    torch.zeros_like(d2C_dK2)))

    # Backward pass and optimisation
    optimizer.zero_grad()
    total_loss = loss - lambda1 * dC_dT_loss - lambda2 * d2C_dK2_loss
    total_loss.backward()
    optimizer.step()
```

The first model, being unconstrained, set $\lambda_1 = \lambda_2$. The model underwent training through 30,000 epochs, using the MSE loss function on the price output from the network, and employed the Adam optimiser with an initial default learning rate of 0.001. The training included a learning rate reduction when the loss plateaued, achieved via the PyTorch learning rate scheduler `ReduceLROnPlateau`. This scheduler decreases the learning rate by a specified factor if the loss does not reduce within a set number of *patience* epochs, necessitating a step with the command `scheduler.step(train_loss)` at each epoch. Here, the reduction factor was 0.3 and the patience level was 500 epochs. In the unconstrained model's case, the scheduler did not reduce the learning rate. With the training set's small size of $21 \times 11 = 231$ option prices, each epoch processed quickly, though it was expected to produce noisy learning. This expectation aligns with the observed training loss, as depicted in Figure 15.9.

Figure 15.10 shows the learned price surface generated from the trained unconstrained neural network model and the residuals versus the prices in the training set. The residuals are small, showing that the model has replicated the prices well. However, the residual surface does vary as a function of strike and maturity, suggesting the gradients of the price function may not be replicated well.

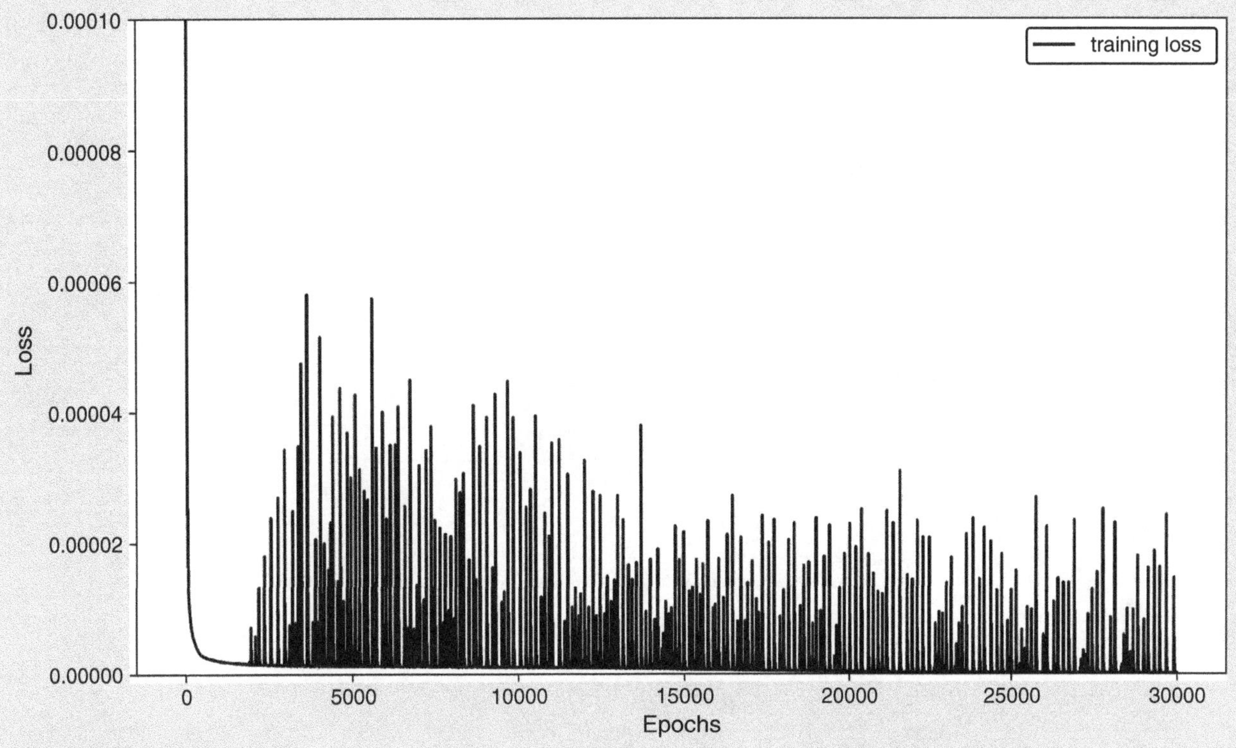

FIGURE 15.9 Training loss as a function of epoch for the unconstrained option price model.

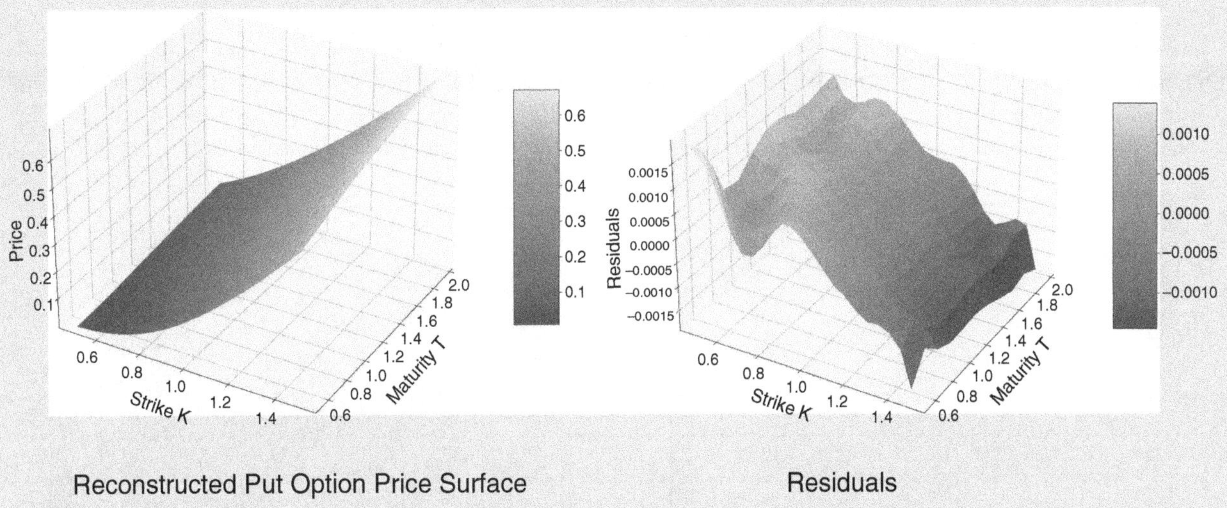

FIGURE 15.10 The price surface and residuals from the unconstrained neural network model.

The following function calculated the final local volatility from the trained model.

```
def dupire_local_volatility(model, input_tensor, r, scaler):
    model.eval()
    input_tensor.requires_grad_(True)
```

(Continued)

(*Continued*)

```
    # Predict option prices using the model
    C = model(input_tensor)

    # Calculate gradients with respect to the input
    dC_dInput = grad(C.sum(), input_tensor, create_graph=True)[0]

    dC_dK, dC_dT = dC_dInput[:, 0], dC_dInput[:, 1]

    # Calculate the second derivative with respect to K (scaled)
    d2C_dK2 = grad(dC_dK.sum(), input_tensor, create_graph=True)[0][:, 0]
    d2C_dK2 /= scaler.scale_[0]**2

# Adjust gradients for the scale of input features
    dC_dK, dC_dT = dC_dK / scaler.scale_[0], dC_dT / scaler.scale_[1]

    # Reconstructe K & T
    K, T = input_tensor[:, 0].detach()*scaler.scale_[0]+scaler.mean_[0], \
    input_tensor[:, 1].detach()*scaler.scale_[1]+scaler.mean_[1]

    # Calculate the Dupire local volatility
    lvs = (2 * dC_dT) / (d2C_dK2 * K**2)
    lv = torch.sqrt(torch.abs(lvs)).detach().cpu().numpy()

    return lv, dC_dT.detach().cpu().numpy(), \
        dC_dK.detach().cpu().numpy(), \
        d2C_dK2.detach().cpu().numpy(), K.detach().cpu().numpy(), \
        T.detach().cpu().numpy(), C.squeeze().detach().cpu().numpy()
```

The resulting heatmap for the local volatility is shown in Figure 15.11 alongside the residuals. Clear edge effects are visible on the right side of the plot at high stock price. Elsewhere, the range of local volatility is approximately correct, and the peak is in the correct location. However, there is a secondary peak on the right of the plot, and the local volatility is not well matched overall, as is clear from the residuals.

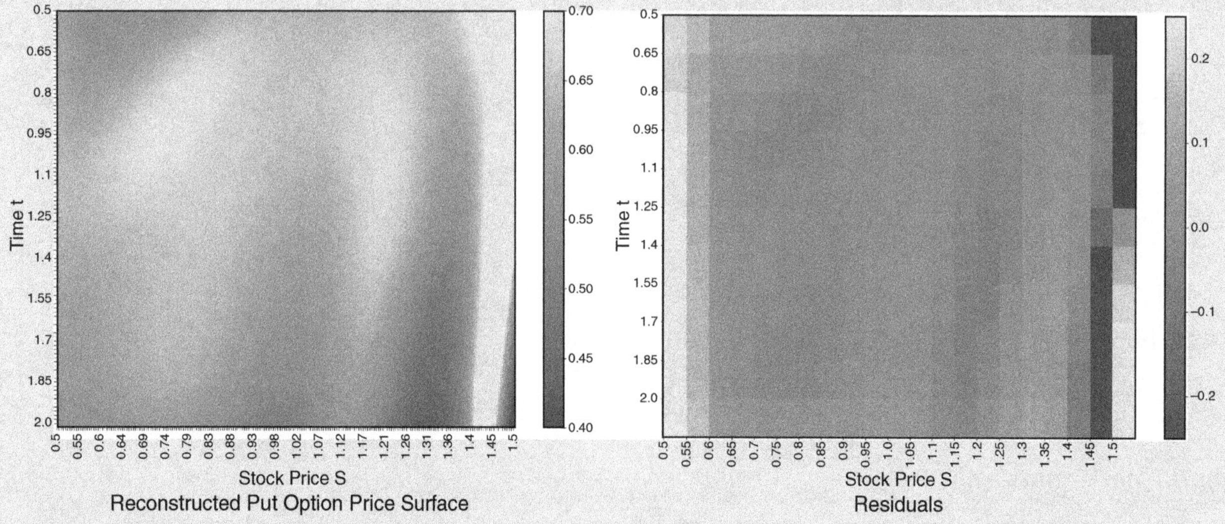

FIGURE 15.11 Local volatility surface and residuals generated by the unconstrained neural network model.

The second model included the two gradient constraints and was trained with $\lambda_1 = 0.01$ and $\lambda_2 = 100$. The Dupire constraint advocated by Chataigner et al. (2020) was not beneficial and was left out. The addition of the constraints led to the learning rate scheduler steadily reducing the learning rate from 0.001 to 5.9×10^{-9} in 10 steps. The training loss is illustrated in Figure 15.12.

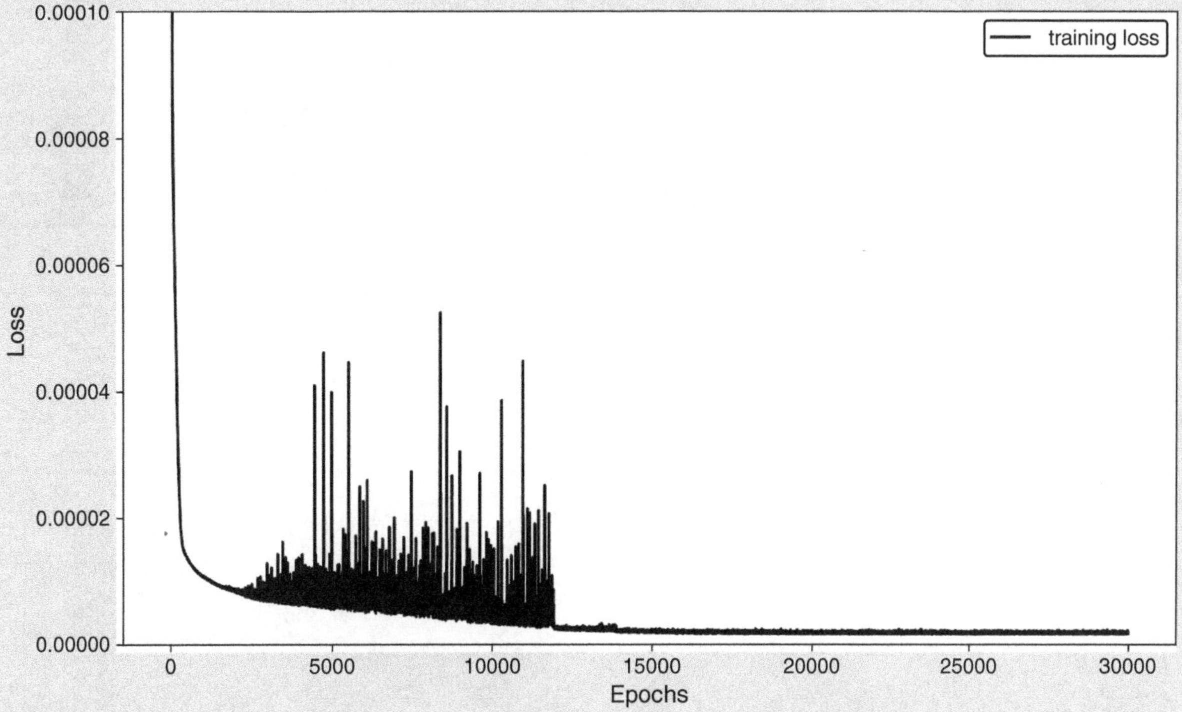

FIGURE 15.12 Training loss as a function of epoch for the constrained option price model.

The reconstructed price surface and residuals from the constrained model are shown in Figure 15.13. The residuals are broadly the same order of magnitude as those from the constrained model but flatter across the domain. Figure 15.14 shows the local volatilities and associated residuals. These show some improvement over the unconstrained case but are still some way off the original.

(*Continued*)

(Continued)

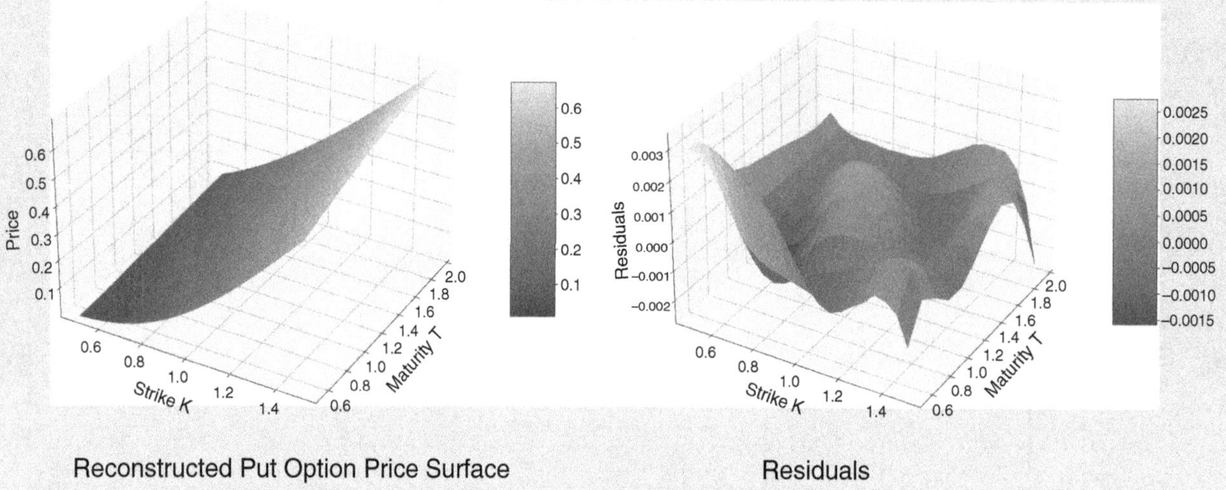

FIGURE 15.13 The price surface and residuals from the constrained neural network model.

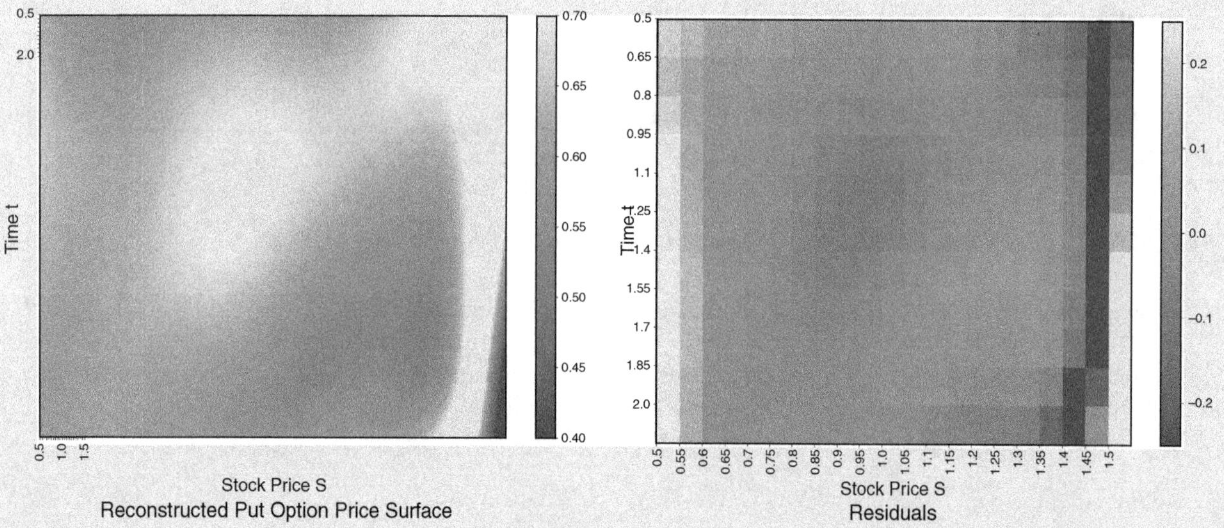

FIGURE 15.14 Local volatility surface and residuals generated by the unconstrained neural network model.

15.4.4 Conclusions on Deep Local Volatility

Using deep neural networks to approximate local volatility surfaces is an interesting idea, and this application illustrates the use of gradient-based constraints. However, the question is whether it is helpful in practice. Ultimately, this is a low-dimensional problem and might be expected to be straightforward. However, it is a challenging problem because of the tiny size of the training set. Training still takes considerable time and is far from competitive with traditional techniques. If a smooth local volatility surface is needed, then a neural network approach seems less favourable than a combination of finite differences and splines.

15.5 CONCLUSIONS

In summary, this chapter explored the application of deep learning to modelling volatility surfaces in option pricing. Several stochastic volatility models were considered, including Heston, SABR and rough Bergomi. Neural networks were successfully trained to replicate the pricing maps for these models, providing substantial computational speedups versus traditional numerical methods. Modelling the local volatility surface using neural networks while respecting no-arbitrage conditions was also demonstrated. While promising conceptually, examples show this can be challenging to implement robustly and does not offer significant advantages over more traditional techniques.

CHAPTER 16

Model Calibration

Stone Age men broke flint and found it cut things better than their own teeth did. We've created methods of transportation that work better than legs, and often do things we could only dream of, like flying. A hydraulic grip clamps on things better than a human hand. They're all tools and nobody objects to them, so why should anyone object to creating minds that are better at thinking than our own, and rulers that are better at their job than those humans who would aspire to rule?

Neal Asher, The Line of Polity (2003)

16.1 INTRODUCTION

Chapter 15 covered the calibration of volatility surface models to implied volatilities. In contrast, this chapter focuses on model calibration using neural networks. Although both chapters share similar approaches, the critical difference is that the final model in this chapter is not used for interpolation in implied volatilities. The literature shows that three categories of models have undergone *deep calibration*: the Heston model, term structure interest rate models and the large basket approximation applied to CDOs.

16.2 MODEL CALIBRATION

16.2.1 One or Two Step

As discussed in Chapter 15, there are two approaches to applying neural networks to model calibration. The most common is the *two-step* approach, in which the neural network approximates the pricing function or map as defined by Equation (15.19). The neural network is then used to provide prices of options from parameters by using the neural network in inference mode, which has the advantage that it is typically faster than the original model and vectorised, providing thousands of prices in parallel on a GPU. The pricing map is then used in place of the original function inside a standard optimisation routine as shown in Equation (15.18). The neural network is, therefore, trained using supervised learning with a series of input model parameters and option prices from the actual model as labels.

In the *one-step* approach, the neural network is trained to perform the calibration itself; that is, the input to the neural network is a collection of option prices or equivalently implied volatilities, and the output is a set of model parameters. Here, the neural network is again trained using supervised learning, but the input is now option prices, and the labels are option parameters. The one-step approach involves taking a series of option prices, calibrating the actual model using some routine and generating the calibrated model parameters to use as labels. The potential benefit of the one-step approach is significant as the neural network also replaces the calibration routine, and the model is calibrated almost instantaneously from market data.

Deep Learning in Quantitative Finance, First Edition. Andrew Green.

16.2.2 Heston

The Heston model was described in Section 15.2.2 and has proved an enduring quantitative finance model. It is popular in this context because of its simplicity and utility for testing ideas, rather than as a model to be used in real-world applications.

Liu et al. (2019a,b) consider Heston (1993) and its jump extension from Bates (1996) in the context of model calibration.[1] The authors propose a generic framework for calibrating models using a deep neural network, which they designate as a *calibration neural network (CaNN)*, illustrating the two-step approach outlined previously. In the initial step, referred to as the *forward pass*, they train an offline DNN model to emulate the pricing model, inputting model and trade parameters and generating the option implied volatility as output. Following the model's training, they proceed to the second step, in alignment with Liu et al. (2019a), termed the *backward pass*. During this stage, they solve the inverse problem by identifying the model parameters corresponding to implied volatilities. The calibration phase utilises a parallel variant of *differential evolution*, a derivative-free optimisation algorithm grounded in evolutionary computation, as described by Storn and Price (1997), and available in the `scipy` library.

Liu et al. (2019a) used the neural network geometry shown in Table 16.1 for the models trained to replicate Heston and Bates models. The sampling distributions used are shown in Table 16.2; note that Latin hypercube sampling (McKay et al., 1979) was used to generate the samples and that the training set was around one million examples in size.

The primary findings of Liu et al. (2019a,b) highlight that the use of deep learning significantly enhances the speed and reliability of calibrating model parameters for high-dimensional stochastic volatility models, effectively addressing the common challenge of getting trapped in local minima during optimisation. Numerical experiments validate CaNN's efficiency and accuracy in calibrating financial models, particularly in real-time financial applications.

Brigo et al. (2021) explore *interpretability* in the context of the Heston model, a choice motivated because it is well understood. The authors train two neural network models using Heston to facilitate the discussion on interpretability methodology for deep learning. They follow the approach of Dimitroff et al. (2018) and build models

TABLE 16.1 Properties of the Neural Networks Models Used by Liu et al. (2019a)

Property	Value
Hidden layers	4
Neurons (each layer)	200
Activation	ReLU
Dropout rate	0.0
Batch normalisation	No
Initialisation	Glorot uniform
Optimiser	Adam
Batch size	1024

[1]The Bates (1996) model has dynamics given by

$$\frac{dS_t}{S_t} = [r_t - q_t - \lambda_J \mathbb{E}[e^J - 1]]dt + \sqrt{V_t}dW_t + (e^J - 1)dX_t^P, \tag{16.1}$$

$$dV_t = \kappa[\nu - V_t]dt + \epsilon\sqrt{V_t}dW_t^V, \tag{16.2}$$

$$dW_t dW_t^V = \rho dt, \tag{16.3}$$

where X_t^P is a Poisson process of intensity λ_J with $J \sim \mathcal{N}(\mu_J, v_J^2)$.

TABLE 16.2 Sampling Range for the Heston and Bates Parameters

Model	Parameter	Value Range
Heston + Bates	Moneyness, $m = S_0/K$	$[0.6, 1.4]$
	Time to maturity, τ (year)	$[0.05, 3.0]$
	Risk-free rate, r	$[0.0\%, 5\%]$
	Correlation, ρ	$[-0.90, 0.0]$
	Reversion speed, λ	$(0, 3.0]$
	Volatility of volatility, η	$(0.01, 0.8]$
	Long average variance, $\bar{V}$	$(0.01, 0.5]$
	Initial variance, V_0	$(0.05, 0.5]$
Bates	Intensity of jumps, λ_J	$[0.0, 3.0]$
	Mean of jumps, μ_J	$[0.0, 0.4]$
	Variance of jumps, v_J^2	$[0.0, 0.3]$

to calibrate Heston parameters directly from an input matrix of implied volatilities, so the model input is an 8×11 array of volatilities corresponding to the following range of strikes and maturities:

$$\begin{aligned} K &= \{0.5, 0.6, 0.7, 0.8, 0.9, 1.0, 1.1, 1.2, 1.3, 1.4, 1.5\}, \\ T &= \{0.1, 0.3, 0.6, 0.9, 1.2, 1.5, 1.8, 2.0\}. \end{aligned} \tag{16.4}$$

The model outputs an array of the five Heston parameters. The process involved randomly sampling the five Heston parameters to generate the training set, assuming uniform distributions within the parameter ranges outlined in Table 16.3. Subsequently, the sampled parameters were utilised to compute implied volatilities for the specified grid of strikes and maturities. It is important to note that the parameter ranges employed in this study are generally narrower than those used by other researchers. Moreover, the training set comprised a relatively modest collection of 10,000 examples. Both the input and output values underwent normalisation.

Brigo et al. (2021) utilised two neural network architectures: a feedforward network (FFN) and a convolutional neural network (CNN). The FFN features an input layer with 88 units, followed by hidden layers containing 67, 49 and 25 neurons, respectively, and culminates in an output layer with five neurons. The hidden layers employ the exponential linear unit (ELU) activation function, while the output layer uses a hard sigmoid activation function. The mean squared error (MSE) is the loss function, working in conjunction with the Adam optimiser.

For the CNN, the input is a two-dimensional array sized 8×11, leading into a single two-dimensional convolutional layer with a 3×3 kernel, followed by a two-dimensional max pooling layer, and this is then connected to a dense layer with 50 neurons and, finally, a five-neuron output layer. Like the FFN, the CNN model uses ELU as the activation function in hidden layers and the hyperbolic tangent function in the output layer. The root mean squared error (RMSE) is the chosen loss function paired with the Adam optimiser.

Brigo et al. (2021) discuss two main categories of interpretability models in deep learning: local and global interpretability.

Local interpretability focuses on individual predictions, explaining the model's behaviour case by case. This approach examines how specific features influence a particular prediction, potentially revealing linear or monotonic dependencies on those features. Brigo et al. (2021) apply three different techniques: layer-wise relevance propagation (LRP) (Bach et al., 2015); local interpretable model-agnostic explanations (LIME) (Ribeiro et al., 2016); and DeepLIFT (learning important features) (Shrikumar et al., 2016, 2017). However, the authors note that local methods might be less effective in deep learning contexts due to neural networks' non-linear and non-local nature. Specifically, they note that local interpretability does not align well with financial intuition in the context of the Heston model.

Global interpretability methods provide an overarching understanding of how a model makes decisions, considering the entire model structure, including its features, weights, hyperparameters and learned components. These methods help elucidate the model's decision-making process on a broad scale, offering insights into how different features contribute to the distribution of the target outcome. The authors emphasise the utility of global interpretability tools from cooperative game theory, such as Shapley values, which have shown promise in providing meaningful insights into deep learning model behaviour. Brigo et al. (2021) implement the Shapley additive explanations (SHAP) method of Sundararajan et al. (2017) and conclude that global interpretability methods provide more reliable and consistent insights compared to local interpretability methods.

Sridi and Bilokon (2023) apply Sobolev training in the context of the Heston model, following the successful application of this technique by Huge and Savine (2020).[2] To facilitate this, the authors derive semi-analytic formulas for the partial derivatives of the Heston option price function. They then use the partial derivatives to train a DNN model to replace the original Heston function in a two-step calibration process.

The training set of 100,000 examples is generated using Latin hypercube sampling with parameters assumed uniform over the ranges given in Table 16.4, a wider range than other authors. The authors used a simple feedforward network, and the best-performing model configuration after hyperparameter tuning is given in Table 16.5. The AdamW optimiser was used with MSE loss. Overall, Sridi and Bilokon (2023) demonstrate the precision and efficacy of Sobolev training relative to standard approaches to training neural networks with values only.

Heston has proved to be a useful playground for developing *neural calibration* techniques. Researchers have successfully developed neural network architectures that can accurately replicate the Heston pricing function, enabling efficient calibration of the model parameters to market data.

TABLE 16.3 Sampling Ranges for Heston Used by Brigo et al. (2021)

Parameter	V_0	η	ρ	λ	$\bar{V}$
Range	[0.0001, 0.04]	[0.01, 1.0]	[−0.95, −0.1]	[0.0, 10.0]	[0.01, 0.2]

TABLE 16.4 Sampling Range for Heston Used by Sridi and Bilokon (2023)

Parameter	Value Range
Log moneyness, $m = \log(S_0/K)$	$[-2.0, 2.0]$
Time to maturity, τ (year)	$[0.05, 20.0]$
Risk-free rate, r	$[-0.01, 0.1]$
Correlation, ρ	$[-0.90, 0.0]$
Reversion speed, λ	$(0.005, 3.0]$
Volatility of volatility, η	$[0.1, 2.0]$
Long average variance, $\bar{V}$	$[0.0, 1.0]$
Initial variance, V_0	$[0.0, 1.0]$

[2]See Section 3.9 for a discussion of Sobolev training, known as *differential machine learning (DML)* in Huge and Savine (2020) and Sridi and Bilokon (2023).

TABLE 16.5 Configuration of the Best-Performing Model from Sridi and Bilokon (2023)

Hyperparameter	Value
Regularisation procedure	Gradient clipping
Number of hidden layers	6
Number of neurons per layer	50
Number of epochs	97
Early stopping patience	None
Gradient clipping threshold	4
Learning rate schedule	0.01

EXAMPLE 16.1: HESTON REVISITED

This example follows Dimitroff et al. (2018) and Brigo et al. (2021) and trains a CNN to calibrate the Heston model directly to an implied volatility surface. The aim is to feed into implied volatilities and directly output the Heston parameters using the trained model in inference mode.

Generating the Dataset

The dataset is generated synthetically, similar to the Heston datasets in Chapter 15, and the code can be found in the Jupyter Notebook `Generate Heston Vol Grids.ipynb`. The Heston parameters are sampled from the identical distributions in Table 15.3. However, Latin hypercube sampling is used instead of the simple independent Monte Carlo samples in previous examples. The `lhs` function from the Python package `pyDOE` was used for the purpose, and the following functions were used to generate the samples and scale them with the supplied parameter bounds.

```
def generate_lhs_samples(samples, dimensions):
    return lhs(dimensions, samples)

def scale_lhs_samples(lhs_samples, bounds):
    return np.array([sample * (bound[1] - bound[0]) +\
                     bound[0] for sample, bound in \
                     zip(lhs_samples.T, bounds)]).T
```

Once the parameters have been sampled, all the options for the relative strikes and maturities given in Equation (16.4) were priced and then inverted to implied volatility values. Of course, the inversion can fail, so only parameter sets that can be used to generate implied volatilities for all strikes and maturities successfully were included in the dataset; a total of 98,620 examples were generated. The data was then flattened and converted to a Pandas data frame, which was then saved to a CSV file.

(*Continued*)

(*Continued*)

Training and Testing the CNN

The CNN model is trained and tested in the Jupyter Notebook `Heston CNN.ipynb`. The data is first loaded and prepared from the CSV file, and then some data transformation is required to reconstruct the pairs of implied volatility surface and Heston parameters. Here, the implied volatility surface is the input, retained in two dimensions and treated as an image with a single channel, while the Heston parameter vectors form the labels. Some 4% of the dataset was retained for testing.

The CNN architecture is almost identical to that used by Brigo et al. (2021), with a single convolutional layer with a 3×3 kernel, followed by a max pooling layer with kernel size and stride 2, and two fully connected layers with 50 and 5 neurons, respectively. The swish activation is used for hidden layers, and the output is left as linear. The model was trained through 1000 epochs using the Adam optimiser with a learning rate equal to 0.001 and MSE loss. The test and training losses are shown in Figure 16.1.

After training the CNN model, its performance was compared with fitting Heston parameters using an optimisation algorithm. A specific test example was chosen from the test set and input into the CNN, which then output the calibrated Heston parameters. In parallel, Heston parameters were fitted to the same implied volatility surface using the Neader–Mead optimiser from the `scipy` library. The results from both methods were then compared with the ground truth, as detailed in Table 16.6.

It is important to note that even though the fitted Heston parameters might not match the ground truth exactly, multiple sets of Heston parameters can still produce very similar option prices and implied volatilities. The volatility smiles generated by the DNN and the fitted parameters were compared with the actual data, as shown in Figure 16.2.

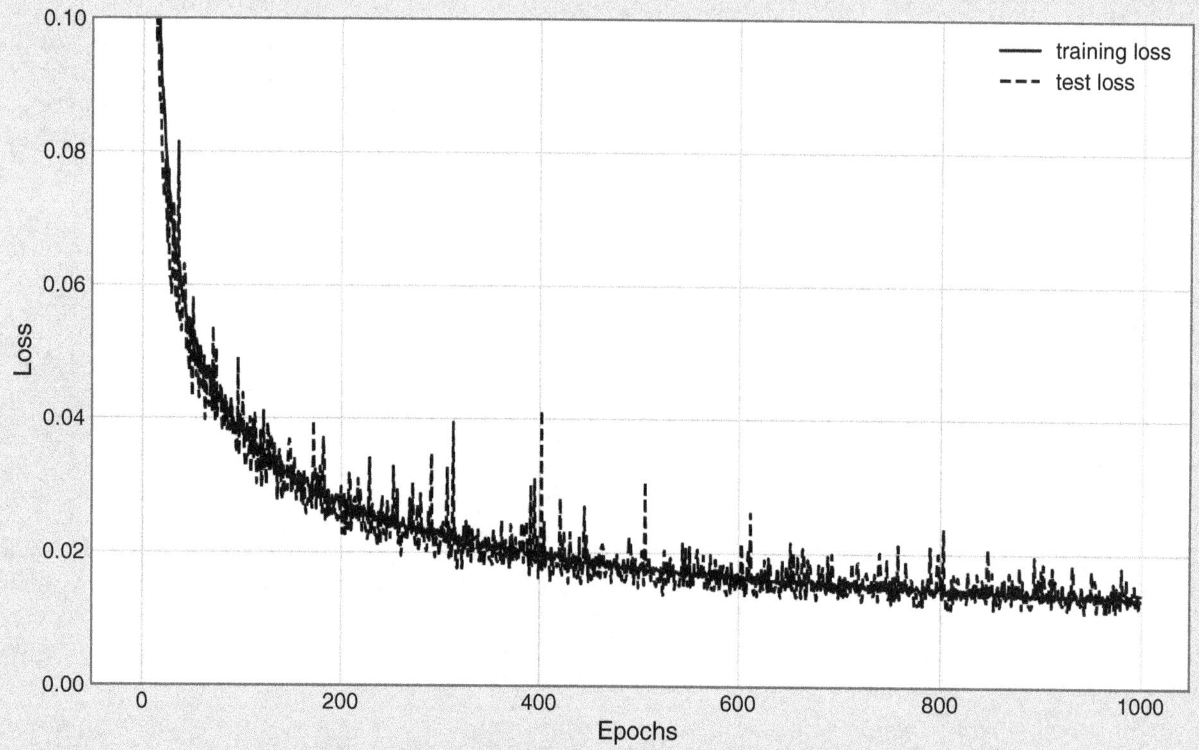

FIGURE 16.1 Training and test loss from the Heston CNN calibration neural network.

TABLE 16.6 Ground Truth Heston Parameters, the Parameters Fitted to the Volatility Surface and Those Obtained from Inference Using the CNN

Example	η	ρ	λ	$\bar{V}$	V_0
Ground truth	2.3587324	−0.72252544	7.87121519	0.88154742	0.96671401
Fitted	2.00433466	−0.72333398	6.59400624	0.91039727	0.60122428
DNN	2.389947	−0.77283645	7.9000354	0.91733974	0.9581481

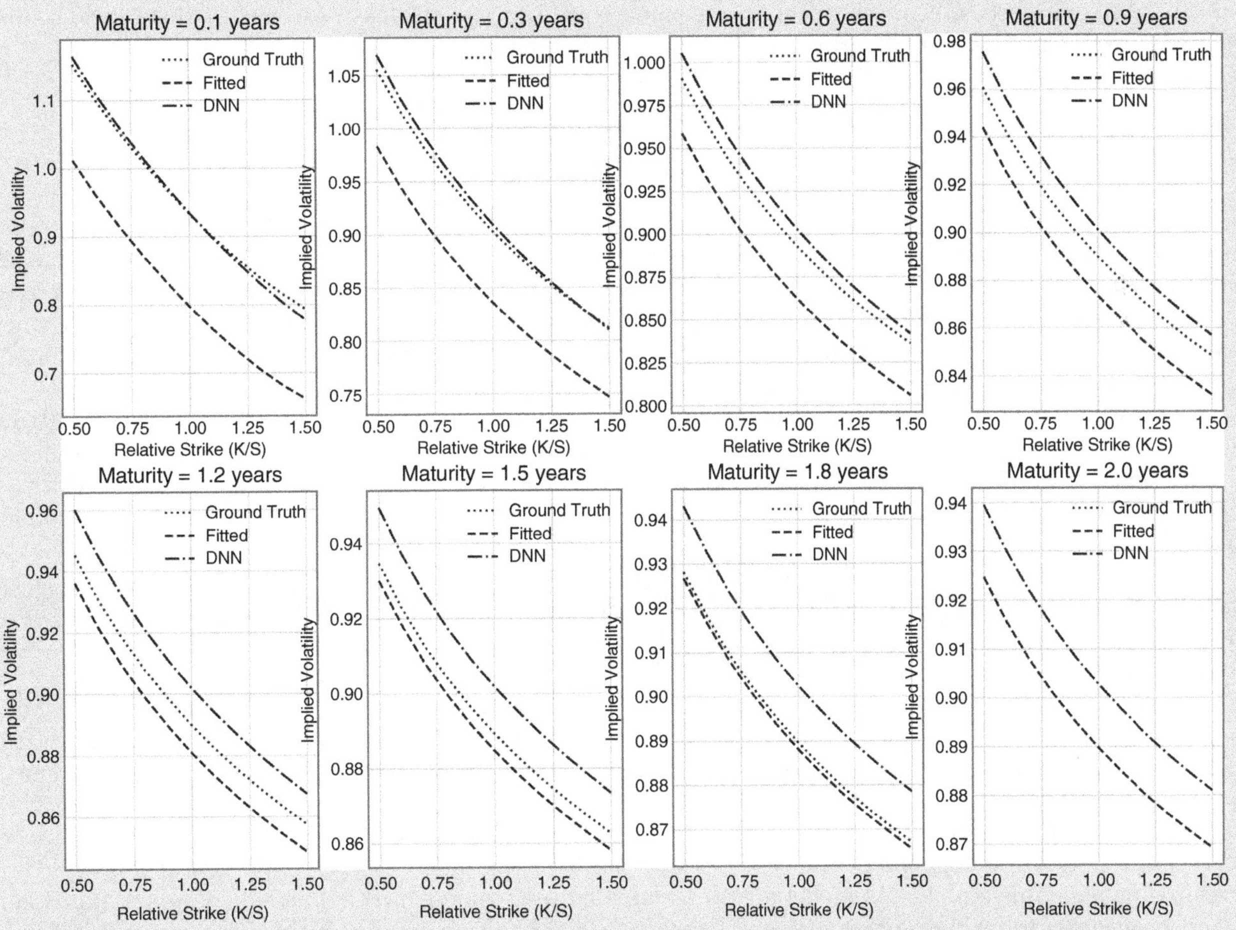

FIGURE 16.2 Smiles for different maturities compared for an example 'ground truth' implied volatility surface that was originally generated from Heston parameters set to $\eta = 2.3587324$, $\rho = -0.72333398$, $\lambda = 7.87121519$, $\bar{v} = 0.88154742$, $V_0 = 0.96671401$. The reconstructed implied volatilities are plotted for parameters fitted using the Nelder–Mead optimiser and those generated using the trained CNN.

A significant observation was the stark contrast in computational performance between the fitting routine and the DNN. The fitting process took 28,468 milliseconds, whereas the DNN completed its task in just 13 milliseconds, demonstrating that the DNN was approximately 2000 times faster. This comparison underscores the efficiency and speed advantages of using a trained DNN for parameter calibration in financial modelling.

16.2.3 Short Rate/Heath–Jarrow–Morton Models

Hernandez (2017) is one of the earliest papers in quantitative finance on using neural networks in the current revival of interest in machine learning. As such, it represents a significant milestone. The author explores the potential of neural networks to replace slow model calibration routines. As an example, Hernandez (2017) aimed to train a neural network to perform calibration for the Hull–White interest rate term structure model with the dynamics

$$dr(t) = [\theta(t) - ar(t)]dt + \sigma dW(t), \tag{16.5}$$

where $r(t)$ is the short rate at time t, $\theta(t)$ is a time-dependent function chosen to fit the initial term structure of interest rates, a is the mean reversion speed and σ is the volatility.

The training set used by Hernandez (2017) is based on historical data and the associated Hull–White model calibration. The author used GBP market data from 2 January 2013 to 1 June 2016. Swaption ATM implied volatility quotes for 156 swaptions with maturities and tenors are as follows:

$$Maturity\,(years) = 1, 2, 3, 4, 5, 6, 7, 8, 9, 10, 15, 20$$

$$Tenor\,(years) = 1, 2, 3, 4, 5, 6, 7, 8, 9, 10, 15, 20, 25$$

The 6M Libor curve, used for projection and discounting, was bootstrapped and sampled discretely at 44 points ranging from spot to 50 years with increasing intervals to serve as input for the DNN. The Hull–White model's mean reversion speed and volatility were then calibrated daily. However, this process yielded only 891 samples, deemed insufficient according to Hernandez (2017). A statistical model was developed using principal component analysis (PCA) to distil the data, aiming to retain 99.5% of the variance. This dimensionality reduction facilitated resampling, which involved creating random Gaussian vectors aligned with the data's covariance matrix.

Two distinct training sets were generated based on PCA of January 2013 to June 2014 and January 2013 to June 2015. Each new dataset, sized 150,000, was divided into training (80%) and cross-validation (20%) subsets, with the remaining real data examples allocated to the test set. The target values for the deep learning models were derived by calibrating option prices under the Hull–White model to match those obtained from the market's implied volatilities.

After hyperparameter optimisation, Hernandez (2017) selected a feedforward network with four hidden layers, each with 64 neurons and ELU activation functions. The training was run for 500 epochs using the Adam optimiser. Dropout regularisation was used with 20% probability and early stopping with patience of 50 epochs on the cross-validation set.

The key observation from the results of Hernandez (2017) was the out-of-sample performance. The model continued to perform well out of the sample for around 6 months but then required retraining. Ultimately, this reflects using a historical training set over a fixed time range that did not fully explore the potential parameter space. In practice, this is only achievable with a synthetic dataset.

Benth et al. (2020) explore the use of deep learning to calibrate a Heath–Jarrow–Morton (HJM) model applied to European options on commodity and the electricity market specifically. The primary focus of the work is to develop a fully parameterised HJM model for the forward curve in energy markets, including the specification of state-dependent volatility operators to map noise into the forward curve space. The authors derive pricing formulas for European options on swaps and forward contracts within the HJM framework. A two-step calibration approach is then used with neural networks. A feedforward neural network was trained to replicate the price function as standard with the two-step approach, which was then used to accelerate the calibration process.

The authors explore a grid-based approach where the output is a grid of option values and a pointwise approach where it is a single option price. In both cases, a small neural network with four layers, three with 30 neurons each and an output layer of size $7 \times 9 = 63$ for the grid and of size 1 for the pointwise approach, was used. The input is a vector of the seven model parameters generated using a grid of values for each parameter over a specified range. Then, a value from the grid for each parameter is randomly selected. A total of 40,000 training samples were used for the grid-based approach and 60,000 for the pointwise approach. Both training methods generate relative errors from 0% to 3%, but the grid-based method performed best overall.

TABLE 16.7 Sampling Ranges for the G2++ Model as Used by Alaya et al. (2021)

	a	b	σ	η	ρ
Min	0.02391044	0.02976928	0.03155195	0.03155851	-0.999318
Max	0.1195522	0.1488464	0.15775973	0.15779254	0.999318

The G2++ model defined by Brigo and Mercurio (2006) is the focus for Alaya et al. (2021). The G2++ model is a two-factor variant of the Hull–White model with dynamics of the form

$$dx_t = -ax_t dt + \sigma dW_t^1, \tag{16.6}$$

$$dy_t = -by_t dt + \eta dW_t^2, \tag{16.7}$$

$$r_t = x_t + y_t + \phi(t), \tag{16.8}$$

$$dW_t^1 dW_t^2 = \rho dt. \tag{16.9}$$

Here, r_t is the instantaneous short rate, x_t and y_t are the two factors following Ornstein–Uhlenbeck processes and $\phi(t)$ is a deterministic shift function.

Alaya et al. (2021) seek to use a neural network instead of a traditional calibration method applied to historical data. However, the authors use synthetic data to train the neural networks. Two approaches are explored: one using covariances or correlations for zero-coupon bonds or forward rates that were paired with a feedforward network, and a second using a block of successive zero-coupon bond curves paired with a CNN.

The first approach uses the expressions for the covariance and correlation for the G2++ model as derived by Brigo and Mercurio (2006) to generate the training data. Given the range of parameter values in Table 16.7, Alaya et al. (2021) sample these values and generate the input correlation/covariances for both zero-coupon bonds and forward rates with end dates from 1 to 12 years. Four training sets of 10,000 samples were generated, one for each combination of correlation, covariance, zero-coupon bonds and forward rates. The neural network architecture was a standard feedforward network with three hidden layers of 1000, 1500 and 1000 neurons. Hidden layers used ReLU activation with a linear output layer, and dropout was used after the last hidden layer. The model was trained through 1000 epochs with mini-batches of size 1000 using the Adam optimiser with a learning rate of 0.001, coupled with MSE loss.

The second model used a block of zero-rate curves, starting from the Euro curve on 4 November 2020; this curve was then evolved through 105 steps, each representing a week. The evolution was performed using sampled model parameters. Zero-coupon bonds with maturities at 28 tenors ranging from 1 day to 50 years were used, resulting in an input array for the model of 106×28 representing zero-coupon bond prices. Adopting a CNN architecture, the neural network commenced with a two-dimensional convolution layer using a 7×7 filter. This layer was followed by max pooling with a 7-sized kernel, leading to a dense layer with 100 neurons and a 25% dropout rate, culminating in an output layer with five nodes for the parameters.

The authors demonstrated fast calibration of the G2++ model using both approaches. Of the two types of models, the first method with zero-coupon bond covariances proved to give the most accurate results.

The three papers discussed in this section, Hernandez (2017), Benth et al. (2020) and Alaya et al. (2021), demonstrate varied approaches to the calibration of term structure models in the context of interest rates and commodities. All provide successful deep learning models that accelerate the calibration process, with Benth et al. (2020) adopting the two-step approach and the other authors the one-step approach with direct calibration of parameters.

EXAMPLE 16.2: HULL–WHITE SWAPTION CALIBRATION

This example builds a simple neural network to calibrate the parameters of the Hull–White model with constant mean reversion speed and constant volatility, as per Equation (16.5). The example is a toy model rather than a practical example but is intended to illustrate what could be achieved with a more realistic example and

(*Continued*)

(Continued)

a larger dataset. A feedforward network is trained to calibrate from a set of co-terminal European swaptions with option maturities ranging from 1 to 5 years and corresponding swap tenors from 5 to 1 year. The model takes the five option prices and the constant interest rate as input and outputs the mean reversion speed and volatility directly, so this is a one-step calibration approach. There are two Jupyter Notebooks: the dataset is generated by `Generate HW Dataset.ipynb` and the model is trained in `HW Calibration NN.ipynb`.

Generating the Training Set

The training set is generated by sampling the Hull–White parameters and interest rate and then using the model to value the co-terminal swaptions. As outlined in Table 16.8, the sampling adhered to a uniform distribution and employed the Latin hypercube strategy. Swaption pricing was executed using the Jamshidian swaption engine from QuantLib. The provided code simplifies the process using a Euribor 1-year index for projection and discounting. Although a volatility handle is a requisite for the swaption helper, the Hull–White model is the basis for the price computation. A dataset comprising one million instances was produced.

```
def price_swaptions_hw(flat_rate, hw_params, swaption_details):
    a, sigma = hw_params
    today = ql.Date.todaysDate()
    ql.Settings.instance().evaluationDate = today
    rate_handle = ql.YieldTermStructureHandle(ql.FlatForward(today,
                                              flat_rate,
                                              ql.Actual365Fixed()))
    index = ql.Euribor1Y(rate_handle)
    fixed_leg_tenor = ql.Period(1, ql.Years)
    fixed_leg_daycounter = ql.Actual360()
    floating_leg_daycounter = ql.Actual360()
    model = ql.HullWhite(rate_handle, a, sigma)
    swaption_prices = []
    for expiry, tenor in swaption_details:
        vol_handle = ql.QuoteHandle(ql.SimpleQuote(0.10))
        helper = ql.SwaptionHelper(ql.Period(expiry, ql.Years),
                                   ql.Period(tenor, ql.Years),
                                   vol_handle, index,
                                   fixed_leg_tenor,
                                   fixed_leg_daycounter,
                                   floating_leg_daycounter,
                                   rate_handle)
        engine = ql.JamshidianSwaptionEngine(model)
        helper.setPricingEngine(engine)
        swaption_prices.append(helper.modelValue())
    return swaption_prices
```

TABLE 16.8 Sampling Ranges for the Hull–White Model

Parameter	Min	Max
a	0.0	0.5
σ	0.0	0.05
Rate	0.0	0.1

Training the Model

The dataset was loaded and prepared with both input and output scaling. Input scaling used `StandardScaler` from scikit-learn, while the output scaling used `MaxMinScaler`. Some 10% of the dataset was retained for testing.

The neural network has six inputs, the five swaption prices and the interest rate, and two outputs, the Hull–White mean reversion speed a and the volatility σ. The model is a standard feedforward network with four hidden layers of 32 neurons with batch normalisation and the swish activation function. The output layer was left as a linear layer, although with max–min scaling over the range [0, 1] sigmoid is a valid alternative. The model was trained through 100 epochs using the Adam optimiser.

Figure 16.3 shows the average error magnitude for the trained model as a function of the two parameters as a heatmap. The errors are generally very low across most domains apart from close to zero mean reversion speed, and the most significant errors are for low a and high σ.

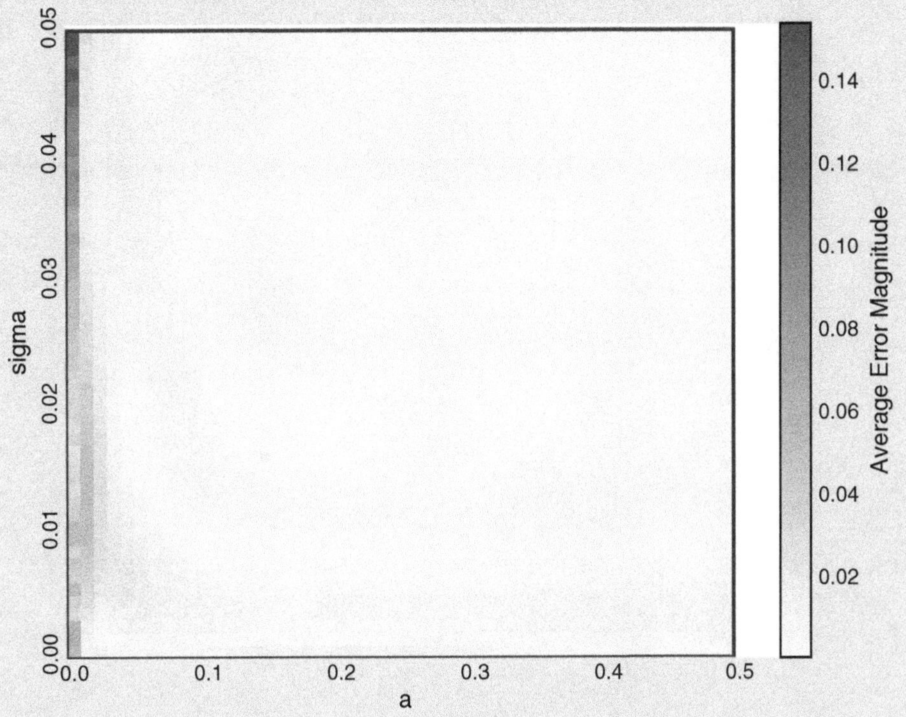

FIGURE 16.3 Errors as a function of a and σ parameters for the Hull–White calibration network.

16.2.3.1 CDOs Francesco and Kamm (2022) provide an example where deep learning is used as a component within a larger calibration routine, giving acceleration of subroutines via function approximation. The authors enhance the performance of the *large basket approximation* method developed by Bush et al. (2011); Bujok and Reisinger (2012) and Giles and Reisinger (2012) calibrate collateralised debt obligations (CDOs) to iTraxx market data. The paper introduced the use of the *Magnus expansion* to efficiently solve the large-basket stochastic partial differential equations (SPDEs) with high accuracy, providing a stable and fast numerical method for calibration.

Francesco and Kamm (2022) train two neural networks to accelerate performance. The first is an interpolation network for CDS quotes that predicts CDS quotes from Monte Carlo prices. Given parameter values, the second network is trained to find the initial distance to default. Combining both networks gives the initial distances to default for all components of the iTraxx index. The paper highlights the parallelisability of the numerical schemes involving DNNs, enabling efficient computation and scalability with GPUs.

16.3 CONCLUSION ON DEEP CALIBRATION

This chapter has demonstrated that deep calibration of models used in quant finance can be applied in practice. They can be used for markets that model spot dynamics and interest rate term structure models. While the models demonstrated here are relatively simple, the technique could be applied to more complex models. The key benefit is, of course, a significant performance gain.

CHAPTER 17

XVA

The avatar smiled silkily as it leaned closer to him, as though imparting a confidence. 'Never forget I am not this silver body, Mahrai. I am not an animal brain, I am not even some attempt to produce an AI through software running on a computer. I am a Culture Mind. We are close to gods, and on the far side'.

'We are quicker; we live faster and more completely than you do, with so many more senses, such a greater store of memories and at such a fine level of detail. We die more slowly, and we die more completely, too. Never forget I have had the chance to compare and contrast the ways of dying'.

Iain M. Banks, Look to Windward (2000)

17.1 INTRODUCTION

XVA stands for derivative valuation adjustments, which are adjustments made to the value of derivative transactions at the portfolio level rather than the individual trade level. These adjustments include credit valuation adjustment (CVA) for counterparty credit risk and funding valuation adjustment (FVA) for accounting for funding costs. Banks also use other adjustments, such as capital valuation adjustment (KVA) and margin valuation adjustment (MVA), in their derivative pricing and decision-making. FVA is now part of bank accounting policy and is included in the Basel regulatory capital framework. A more detailed explanation of XVA can be found in Green (2015) and Gregory (2020).

XVA models typically follow these computational steps:

1. Model calibration to implied market data.
2. High-dimensional Monte Carlo simulation.
3. Value the derivative portfolio inside the Monte Carlo simulation on all paths and time steps, which is a massively parallel operation.
4. Exposure calculation by taking the expectation of the relevant quantity (e.g., $\text{Max}(V - C, 0)$ for unilateral CVA).
5. Integration over the exposure profile using the relevant cost curve (e.g., survival probability curve for CVA and funding curve for FVA).

As XVA calculations are among the most computationally demanding in banking, they readily lend themselves to deep learning techniques that can accelerate the calculations. Several techniques described in earlier chapters are directly relevant:

- Chapter 16 showed how deep learning can replicate and accelerate model calibration.
- As discussed in Chapter 11, deep learning can replicate derivative valuation functions, providing models that enable parallel inference 10^5 times faster than the underlying model when using GPUs. XVA platforms can use this high-performance parallel inference to calculate expected exposures. The backpropagation algorithm can also be integrated with AAD to give fast sensitivities.

Deep Learning in Quantitative Finance, First Edition. Andrew Green.

- BSDEs are discussed in Chapter 12 and have been applied to XVA calculations. BSDEs arise naturally when XVAs become recursive in nature.
- Chapter 13 provides two deep learning methods that are directly applicable to XVA: methods to accelerate Monte Carlo simulation or to increase accuracy and the use of deep learning in place of traditional regression techniques in the Longstaff–Schwartz approach (Longstaff and Schwartz, 2001). Longstaff–Schwartz has long been used in XVA calculations, as seen from Cesari et al. (2009) and Green and Kenyon (2017). Deep learning offers significant advantages over Longstaff–Schwartz as it does not require feature engineering to identify the appropriate choice of regression variable as deep learning models learn representations. Furthermore, using Sobolev training in this context can reduce the training set size the deep learning model needs to achieve good convergence in this context (Huge and Savine, 2020).

This chapter examines two further applications of deep learning to XVA: the credit default swap (CDS) mapping problem and the direct generation of expected exposure profiles.

Banks need to calculate CVA for all counterparties for accounting and regulatory purposes. Furthermore, all CVA calculations need a survival probability curve derived from CDS quotes. However, there are only around 3000 counterparties globally for which there is a traded liquid CDS contract. Most bank counterparties will not have a liquid CDS available. In such circumstances, standard market practice is to map liquid CDS curves to counterparties using the properties of the counterparty (Green, 2015). The market practice is also enshrined in regulation, with Basel III requiring that the map be constructed based on three factors: credit rating, sector and geography. The forthcoming FRTB-CVA offers some extra flexibility on the choice of factors. Brummelhuis and Luo (2019a,b) present a machine learning approach for this problem. Here, a similar approach is explored in the context of neural networks in Section 17.2.

Given that deep learning can replicate derivative valuation functions, there is no fundamental reason why they could not be used to directly replicate an expected exposure profile of XVA, removing the need for Monte Carlo simulation. An example of this is presented by Frodé et al. (2022), which is examined in Section 17.3.

17.2 CREDIT CURVE MAPPING

When calculating CVA and assigning a credit curve to a counterparty, there are two categories: liquid, for which CDS trades, and illiquid, for which they do not trade or only trade irregularly.

Counterparties with liquid CDS contracts are relatively straightforward. When derivatives rank pari-passu with senior unsecured debt, CVA should be marked using the CDS spreads for the counterparty. Fully hedging the CVA with these CDS contracts, at least theoretically, addresses the credit spread sensitivity of CVA and the instantaneous loss on default. Complexities can arise when the counterparty has a liquid CDS, but the derivative exposure is not ranked pari-passu with senior unsecured debt. In such circumstances, the default waterfall needs to be considered.[1]

Globally, only about 3000 counterparties have quoted CDS spreads. Hence, the majority of derivatives counterparties lack quoted CDS spreads. In such cases, corporate bonds serve as an alternative source of market credit risk information, but this may not be acceptable in an accounting or regulatory context. Marking CVA for these counterparties requires using implied probability of default (PD) curves, which entails linking each counterparty to a representative CDS curve. This mapping process is under the control of each bank and is subject to oversight from bank auditors and regulators.

The mapped CDS provides a means to calculate CVA for the illiquid counterparty. It can also be the basis of hedging by an XVA management function. Such activity can help manage the P&L volatility of CVA but, unlike the situation with liquid names, does not necessarily help in the event of the actual default of the counterparty. Since the CDS is not directly linked to the counterparty, it will not provide credit protection on its default. However, as the name becomes distressed, it will likely move through credit rating categories, which could cause the mapped curve to change. Furthermore, the mapped CDS curve might react to overall market credit perceptions and widen. This behaviour may offset the lack of complete credit protection. The reverse can also happen where the name associated with the mapped CDS defaults rather than the bank counterparty, and this would yield a windfall gain for the hedging bank.

[1]This lies beyond the scope of this volume, and the reader is referred to Green (2015) for more details.

Under Basel III regulations (BCBS, 2011), the CDS mapping process for CVA capital charge, particularly for banks with internal model method (IMM) approval, must consider three factors: industry sector, rating and geography. These regulations mirror industry practice but present challenges in their implementation. The *Fundamental Review of the Credit Valuation Adjustment (CVA) Risk Framework* (FRTB-CVA) (BCBS, 2015) proposes a shift to a three-factor model with the three factors specified by the bank. However, it is unclear what additional factors could be effectively utilised. Banks could use a separate mapping process for accounting CVA, but given the regulatory capital benefits in FRTB-CVA from CDS hedging, these would unlikely differ in practice.

The availability of CDS contracts is significantly higher in the US market compared to other regions, facilitating more straightforward construction of CDS maps for US entities. Conversely, outside the United States, finding sufficient liquid CDS across all industry sectors and ratings is often challenging, making it difficult to construct an appropriate mapping. Ignoring geography could compel banks to inappropriately map many counterparties to US CDS, which may not be a suitable approach.

How should the CDS map be formulated? Classically, there are two approaches: map to the most appropriate single-name CDS and construct an artificial credit curve for each rating, sector and geography combination. In a machine learning context, these map to classification and regression problems. So, CDS map construction can be expressed as a supervised learning problem.

17.2.1 Classification Approach

Brummelhuis and Luo (2019a,b) performed a comprehensive assessment of different machine learning techniques in the context of a classifier approach to the credit curve mapping problem. The authors tested 156 classifiers from eight popular classifier families and rank-ordered their performances. The eight classifier families included:

- discriminant analysis (linear and quadratic)
- naïve Bayes
- *k*-nearest neighbours
- logistic regression
- decision trees
- support vector machines
- neural networks
- bagged decision trees

Several different variants of each model were used to give 26 tested models with six different groups of input features. Four different cases were explored for neural networks: varying the number of hidden units, Elliot sigmoid activation function,[2] purely linear activation[3] and hyperbolic tangent. In all cases, a single hidden layer was used:

The six groups of input features that were tested are given below:

$$\text{FS1}\quad \mathbf{x} = \Big(s, PD_{6m}, PD_{1y}, PD_{2y}, PD_{3y}, PD_{4y}, PD_{5y},$$
$$\sigma^{imp}_{3m}, \sigma^{imp}_{6m}, \sigma^{imp}_{12m'}, \sigma^{imp}_{18m'}, \sigma^{h}_{1m'}\sigma^{h}_{2m}, \sigma^{h}_{3m'}\sigma^{h}_{4m'}\sigma^{h}_{6m}\Big),$$
$$\text{FS2}\quad \mathbf{x} = \Big(s, PD_{5y}, \sigma^{imp}_{6m}, \sigma^{h}_{4m}\Big),$$
$$\text{FS3}\quad \mathbf{x} = \Big(s, PD_{5y}\Big),$$
$$\text{FS4}\quad \mathbf{x} = \Big(PD_{6m}, PD_{1y}, PD_{2y}, PD_{3y}, PD_{4y}, PD_{5y},$$
$$\sigma^{imp}_{3m}, \sigma^{imp}_{6m}, \sigma^{imp}_{12m'}\sigma^{imp}_{18m'}\sigma^{h}_{1m}, \sigma^{h}_{2m}, \sigma^{h}_{3m}, \sigma^{h}_{4m}, \sigma^{h}_{6m}\Big),$$
$$\text{FS5}\quad \mathbf{x} = \Big(PD_{5y}, \sigma^{imp}_{6m}, \sigma^{h}_{4m}\Big),$$
$$\text{FS6}\quad \mathbf{x} = \Big(PD_{1y}, PD_{5y}\Big),$$

---

[2]The Elliot sigmoid is a sigmoid-like function with no exponential. It is defined by Elliot$(x) = \frac{0.5(x)}{1+|x|} + 0.5$ (McCloskey, 2023).

[3]The use of a linear activation function means this case reduces simply to simple regression.

where

- s is the 5-year CDS rate. The authors selected the 5-year rate, typically the most liquid point on the CDS curve. Of course, this means the sets of features that include s, FS1–FS3, cannot be used if the CDS rate is unobservable, which is the case in most practical applications and is the driver for the CDS mapping methodology. In this case, Brummelhuis and Luo (2019a,b) say a bootstrap approach can be used where regression is run using one of the methods FS4–FS6 to predict s, which is then fed as part of FS1–FS3.
- PD_τ is the counterparty probability of default for τ equal to 6 months, 1 year, ..., 5 years.
- σ_τ^{imp} is the equity option at-the-money implied volatility for tenors τ of 3, 6, 12 and 18 months.
- σ_τ^h is the historical equity volatility calculated from log-returns for 1, 2, 3, 4 and 6 months.

Brummelhuis and Luo (2019a,b) performed extensive testing of the models, exploring intra-classifier and cross-classifier performance. For each of the eight classifier families tested, the classifier's performance was tested across several different choices of parameterisation and for all six feature selections. The authors evaluated the performance across various classifier families by individually and collectively examining the performance of eight distinct classifier families against the six feature selections, both with and without implementing PCA for feature extraction. To estimate the expected accuracy of each classifier, they implemented a 10-fold stratified cross-validation method. The classifiers were then ranked based on their expected accuracy, and their performance was compared using misclassification rates. The best-performing classifiers were the support vector machines, bagged tree and neural networks, and the k-nearest neighbour and the QDA classifiers, with naïve Bayes overall the worst performer.

17.2.2 Regression Approach

17.2.2.1 Cross-Sectional Model An alternative approach to a classifier is to use regression and to physically generate an appropriate proxy CDS spread or credit curve based on a set of input features. This approach was initially proposed by McEwen et al. (2012) and Chourdakis et al. (2013) of Nomura. The model was included in a response made in the context of industry consultation on Basel III. These factors are mathematically represented as

$$S^i_{\text{proxy}} = \prod_{j=1}^{n} m_j. \tag{17.1}$$

In this model, five primary factors are suggested: a global factor, industry sector, regional factor, rating factor and seniority factor. Notably, the three main factors – sector, region and rating – are also emphasised in Basel III regulations.

Each factor in the model is assigned a weighting factor m_j, which assumes different values based on the range of values the underlying factor can take. For instance, in the context of ratings, a Standard & Poor's-style scheme could be used, which includes 19 ratings ranging from AAA to CCC–.

To calibrate this cross-sectional model, Chourdakis et al. (2013) propose linear regression. The original equation can be reformulated in logarithmic terms as

$$y^i = \log S^i_{\text{proxy}} = \sum_{j=1}^{m} A_{ij} \log m_j. \tag{17.2}$$

Here, the summation over j encompasses all values of all factors. The matrix A_{ij} comprises indicator values. For example, if a counterparty has an AA rating, the matrix A_{ij} would have a value of 1 in the column associated with the AA rating and 0 in all other rating columns. This approach results in a *one-hot* representation of the data, as illustrated in Table 17.1.

The calibration process is completed using least-squares regression, allowing for an accurate and efficient method of determining the weightings and impact of each factor in the proxy spread. This model, therefore, offers a comprehensive and adaptable framework for analysing counterparty risks using a cross-sectional approach.

Least-squares regression is one possible model, but neural networks could also be used similarly, and the example below illustrates this.

TABLE 17.1 The 'One-Hot' Representation Used in Cross-Sectional Approach to Credit Curve Mapping (McEwen et al., 2012; Chourdakis et al., 2013)

Name	Ratings				Sectors			Regions			Seniority	
	AAA	AA+	AA	...	Financials	Telecoms	...	North America	Europe	...	Senior	Subordinated
ctpy 1	0	1	0		0	1		1	0		1	0
ctpy 2	0	0	1		1	0		0	1		1	0

EXAMPLE 17.1: USING A NEURAL NETWORK TO GENERATE PROXY CDS SPREADS

In this example, a neural network is trained to produce proxy CDS spreads based on three key factors: rating, sector and geography, as required under Basel III. One key issue here is the lack of publicly available datasets. Much of the financial data is only available on commercial subscriptions for significant data vendors. CDS spreads are one example where obtaining good-quality data outside prominent vendors is challenging. One dataset has been found at Kaggle (https://www.kaggle.com/datasets/debashish311601/credit-default-swap-cds-prices), which provides par CDS spreads for 10 annual tenor points for 661 different reference credits over the period from January 2015 to September 2021. Unfortunately, the dataset does not provide credit ratings, sectors or geographic information, which must be sourced elsewhere. The 661 names are insufficient and, as will be seen later, are reduced further because of other missing data items. The resulting minimal dataset is somewhat contrived; hence, this should be viewed as a toy model. However, the same approach illustrated here will work on larger datasets, should they be available.

Data Preparation

The data preparation for this example is complex, reflecting the need to source the CDS spreads, the sector and geographic information, and the rating information, all of which come from different sources. The Jupyter Notebook `CDS_DataPrep.ipynb` contains the data preparation steps.

The first step is to obtain the CDS data from Kaggle, and this will need a login to Kaggle, but that can be freely obtained. Once the zip file has been downloaded, it can be expanded and loaded using Pandas. The next step is to obtain a list of tickers and company names from the file, as these will be the basis of linking this data with the other sources.

```
cds_filename = 'CDS//cds.csv'
dfcds = pd.read_csv(cds_filename)
tickers = dfcds['Ticker'].unique().tolist()
companies = dfcds['Company'].unique().tolist()
```

The sector and geography information will be obtained from Yahoo Finance using the `yfinance` package. To do that, however, requires mapping the CDS file tickers or company names to the same fields for Yahoo, which do not use the same strings. Furthermore, there are multiple Yahoo tickers for a given company name. Hence, the next step is to build a map from the Yahoo name to the list of possible tickers, and this is done by accessing the information for relevant stock markets and then using them to build the map using a Python dictionary comprehension. The Yahoo ticker information is accessed using the `PyTickerSymbols` Python package.

```
from pytickersymbols import PyTickerSymbols

stock_data = PyTickerSymbols()
```

(Continued)

(Continued)

```
uk_stocks = stock_data.get_stocks_by_index('FTSE 100')
german_stocks = stock_data.get_stocks_by_index('DAX')
french_stocks = stock_data.get_stocks_by_index('CAC 40')
dj_stocks = stock_data.get_stocks_by_index('DOW JONES')
nasdaq = stock_data.get_stocks_by_index('NASDAQ 100')
sp500 = stock_data.get_stocks_by_index('S&P 500')
stk_list = list(uk_stocks) + list(german_stocks) + list(french_stocks) + \
list(dj_stocks) + list(nasdaq) + list(sp500)
name_ticker_map = {elem['name']: [tkr['yahoo'] for tkr in elem['symbols']]
for elem in stk_list}
```

Using fuzzy matching with the `fuzzywuzzy` Python library, we need to create a data frame by using the ticker and name from the CDS data and the sector and information from Yahoo to combine the sector and rating information with the CDS data. To match the ticker or the company name between the two data sources, the function `buildCompanyDataframe` first tries to match the CDS ticker with any of those in the `name_ticker_map` and then attempts to match on the company name if it fails. If no match is found, it simply skips that entry and continues.

```
import yfinance as yf
from fuzzywuzzy import process

def get_tickers(company_name, comp_dict, threshold=90):
    match, similarity = process.extractOne(company_name, comp_dict.keys())
    if similarity >= threshold:
        return comp_dict[match]
    else:
        raise Exception("Not found")

def buildCompanyDataframe(tickers, companies, name_ticker_map):
    ticker_list = list()
    name_list = list()
    country_list = list()
    sector_list = list()
    for itkr, icomp in zip(tickers, companies):
        yftkr = yf.Ticker(itkr)
        tkr_info = None
        try:
            tkr_info = yftkr.info
        except:
            try:
                tkr_lst = get_tickers(icomp, name_ticker_map, threshold=70)
                for trytkrs in tkr_lst:
                    try:
                        yftkr = yf.Ticker(trytkrs)
                        tkr_info = yftkr.info
                    except:
                        continue
            except:
                continue

       if tkr_info != None:
           try:
```

```
                country = tkr_info['country']
                sector = tkr_info['sector']
                if country != "" and sector != "":
                    ticker_list.append(itkr)
                    country_list.append(country)
                    sector_list.append(sector)
                    name_list.append(icomp)
            except:
                continue
         return ticker_list, country_list, sector_list, name_list

t_list, c_list, s_list, n_list = buildCompanyDataframe(tickers,
                                     companies, name_ticker_map)
comp_dict = {'Ticker': t_list, 'Company': n_list,
         'Sector': s_list, 'Country': c_list}
comp_df = pd.DataFrame(comp_dict)
```

The rating data has to be found in a third source. Unfortunately, it was impossible to identify a source with the appropriate corporate ratings concurrent with the credit curve time series. So, the latest publicly available rating data from S&P was used instead, and this can be accessed from http://ratingshistory.info/. Two files were used: corporate and financial. The data is in CSV format and hence can be loaded by Pandas. The rating data files contain an obligor name that must match the company name from the CDS data, and this is again performed using fuzzy matching. Multiple ratings are typically available, so the first attempt of the functions is to match 'Local Currency LT' as a preference. No rating is entered in the output dictionary if no match is found.

```
def getRating(match, df):
    dfsub = df[df['obligor_name'] == match]
    dfsubsub = dfsub[dfsub['rating_sub_type'] == 'Local Currency LT']
    if len(dfsubsub) > 0:
        return dfsubsub['rating'].iloc[0]
    elif len(dfsub) > 0:
        return dfsub['rating'].iloc[0]
    else:
        return ''

def buildRatingsDict(companies, spcorp_df, spfin_df):
    rating_dict = dict()
    spcorp_names = spcorp_df['obligor_name'].unique().tolist()
    spfin_names = spfin_df['obligor_name'].unique().tolist()
    for icomp in companies:
        match, similarity = process.extractOne(icomp, spcorp_names)
        if similarity >= 90:
            rating_dict[icomp] = getRating(match, spcorp_df)
        else:
            match, similarity = process.extractOne(icomp, spfin_names)
            if similarity >= 90:
                rating_dict[icomp] = getRating(match, spfin_df)
            else:
                continue
    return rating_dict

rating_dict = buildRatingsDict(companies, spcorp_df, spfin_df)
```

(*Continued*)

(*Continued*)

A small amount of postprocessing is needed to ensure all ratings are in the standard S&P format.

```
def remove_after_slash(input_string):
    parts = input_string.split('/', 1)
    return parts[0]

def remove_substring(original_string, substring):
    # Replace the substring with an empty string
    return original_string.replace(substring, '')

        revised_rating_dict = dict()
    for key, value in rating_dict.items():
        revised_rating_dict[key] = remove_substring(remove_after_slash(value),
                                                    'mx')
```

Now, the data can be combined in a single data frame. First, the ratings are mapped onto the sector-geography data frame using the 'Company' column as the key. Then, rows with `NaN` or blank ratings are dropped. Finally, the CDS data frame merges with the rating-sector geography data using a left join operation. Any rows with `NaN` entries are dropped, and the two copies of the 'Ticket' column are reduced to one. The final data frame can be saved down to CSV.

```
comp_df['Rating'] = comp_df['Company'].map(revised_rating_dict)
redcomp_df = comp_df.dropna()
redcomp_df = redcomp_df[redcomp_df['Rating'] != '']
combined_df = dfcds.merge(redcomp_df, on='Company', how='left')
redcomb_final = combined_df.dropna()
cds_data = redcomb_final.drop('Ticker_y', axis=1)
cds_data.rename(columns={'Ticker_x': 'Ticker'}, inplace=True)
```

Choice of Input and Output Features

The primary features included in the data are credit rating, sector and geography, which are all categorical variables. As such, they could all be one-hot encoded, concatenated together and input. However, this would only partially represent the available data, as we know there are relationships between the different data entries; they are not independent categories.

- **Credit Rating**. The rating categories are ordered from AAA down to B– in this dataset. They will be represented as ordered integers from 0 to 15, although alternatives are possible. For example, the actual relationship could be expressed using a floating-point measure of creditworthiness, such as the historical or implied default probability over some time horizon.
- **Geography**. The geography is represented as a country in this dataset, although often this will be a region such as North America or Europe. These could be encoded as categorical variables, but here, the choice is to try to represent the relationship between countries in floating-point. One option would be to use a physical measure of distance, but financial market 'distance' need not be the same as physical distance. The choice here is to use natural language embeddings from word2vec to represent the relationships between countries as vectors.

- **Sector.** The sectors also have a relationship between them, with some closer to each other. Some measures of distance could be used, such as word embeddings. Here, however, they are encoded as independent using a one-hot representation.

The most straightforward approach for the output is to generate the term structure of CDS spreads directly. However, this approach is potentially problematic as the model cannot fully respect the arbitrage relationships between CDS spreads. In other words, the resulting credit curve could imply negative hazard rates. Hence, a better approach might be to use the piecewise constant hazard rates of the standard CDS curve model as the output. The output layer could also use ReLU to ensure the desired output is positive.

Several additional steps are needed to take the raw data file generated above and prepare it for the particular choice of model input described here. The first step is to break it into data frames for each business day. Then the three fields *Date*, *Company* and *Ticker* can be dropped as they are no longer useful.

```
grouped = cds_data.groupby('Date')
dfs_by_date = [grouped.get_group(category) for category in grouped.groups]
for df in dfs_by_date:
    df.reset_index(inplace=True)
    df.drop(['Date', 'Company', 'Ticker'], axis=1, inplace=True)
```

A model is trained for the first date in the series as a first step. For this, the data is split into input features and targets.

```
target = dfs_by_date[0][['PX1', 'PX2', 'PX3', 'PX4', 'PX5',
                         'PX6', 'PX7', 'PX8', 'PX9', 'PX10']]
input_features = dfs_by_date[0][['Sector', 'Country', 'Rating']]
```

Some of the country names are not present in the word2vec embeddings, so the name needs to be replaced.

```
input_features.replace('United States', 'USA', inplace=True)
input_features.replace('United Kingdom', 'UK', inplace=True)
input_features.replace('South Korea', 'Korea', inplace=True)
```

The countries are then encoded using word2vec, and the embeddings are downloaded and managed through the `gensym` package. The embedding will give 300-dimensional vectors, which is not useful, so these are reduced to two dimensions using the t-sne algorithm from scikit-learn.

```
import gensim.downloader as api
from sklearn.manifold import TSNE

word2vec_model = api.load('word2vec-google-news-300')
embedding1 = word2vec_model[input_features['Country']]

tsne = TSNE(n_components=2, random_state=0)  # n_components can be 2 or 3
reduced_embeddings = tsne.fit_transform(embedding1)
```

(*Continued*)

(Continued)

The sectors are one-hot encoded.

```
dfsec = pd.DataFrame()
dfsec['sector_encoded'] = pd.Categorical(input_features['Sector']).codes
category_array = np.array(dfsec['sector_encoded'])
num_classes = len(np.unique(category_array))
one_hot = np.eye(num_classes)[category_array]
```

The rating strings are mapped to ordered integers and then output to a numpy array. Finally, all the input tensors are concatenated.

```
rating_map = {'AAA':0, 'AA+':1, 'AA':2, 'AA-':3, 'A+': 4, 'A': 5, 'A-': 6,
'BBB+': 7, 'BBB': 8, 'BBB-': 9, 'BB+': 10,  'BB': 11, 'BB-': 12,
'B+': 13, 'B': 14, 'B-': 15}

index_rating = input_features['Rating'].map(rating_map).to_numpy()
index_rating = index_rating.reshape(len(index_rating), 1)
input_tensor = np.concatenate([reduced_embeddings, one_hot, index_rating],
                              axis=1)
```

Training the Model

The input was scaled using standard scalar and then split into test and training datasets using `train_test_split` in the usual way, with 10% of data in the test set. A better approach would be to use balanced sampling to generate the test set and ensure all categories are represented. However, given the small size of this dataset and the fact that this is a toy example, the more straightforward approach was judged sufficient here. After splitting, PyTorch data loaders were created for training and test sets.

The model was a simple feedforward network with a single hidden layer of size 16 and swish activation. The input dimension was 14, and the output was 10, reflecting the 10 annual CDS spread points. The model was trained through 200 epochs with a batch size of 16. The Adam optimiser was used with default parameters and a learning rate equal to 0.001. Despite the small training set size, the model converged and produced results consistent with the input dataset.

Analysis

To 'test' the model, the credit curves for all ratings were generated for the combination of the United States as a country and the Consumer Credit sector, and these are presented in Table 17.2. Names from the United States dominate the training set, so there is more coverage than for other geographies. The data that is generated is plausible, with spreads rising as a function of CDS tenor and as a function of lower credit rating. Since this is a toy model, no further testing has been conducted on this example. A second example is illustrated in Table 17.3, with CDS spreads generated for all credit ratings for Japanese financials. There is only one Japanese name in the dataset for a consumer cyclical. However, the generated spreads are still realistic. More extensive analysis and testing would be required for any actual model, but the toy model here is undoubtedly encouraging.

TABLE 17.2 CDS Curves Generated by the Model for All Ratings with the United States Specified as the Country and Sector Equal to Consumer Cyclical

Rating	1 yr	2 yr	3 yr	4 yr	5 yr	6 yr	7 yr	8 yr	9 yr	10 yr
AAA	9.4	12.9	17.4	22.3	26.7	30.5	32.8	34.2	35.1	36.5
AA+	11.8	16.1	21.6	27.6	33.2	37.9	40.7	42.5	43.6	45.3
AA	14.7	20.1	26.8	34.4	41.4	47.1	50.7	52.9	54.4	56.3
AA–	18.2	24.8	33.0	42.4	51.2	58.0	62.6	65.2	67.2	69.4
A+	22.1	30.1	40.0	51.4	62.1	70.3	75.9	79.1	81.5	84.1
A	26.3	35.9	47.5	61.2	74.1	83.7	90.4	94.2	97.1	100.0
A–	30.8	41.9	55.5	71.4	86.6	97.7	105.6	110.0	113.5	116.8
BBB+	35.4	48.2	63.7	82.0	99.5	112.2	121.3	126.4	130.5	134.2
BBB	40.1	54.6	72.1	92.9	112.8	127.2	137.5	143.2	147.9	152.0
BBB–	45.0	61.3	80.8	104.2	126.5	142.5	154.2	160.5	165.8	170.4
BB+	50.0	68.1	89.7	115.8	140.6	158.3	171.3	178.3	184.4	189.3
BB	55.2	75.2	99.0	127.8	155.2	174.8	189.2	196.9	203.6	209.0
BB–	60.7	82.6	108.7	140.5	170.5	192.0	207.9	216.3	223.7	229.6
B+	66.5	90.5	118.9	153.8	186.6	210.1	227.5	236.7	245.0	251.2
B	72.5	98.7	129.7	167.8	203.6	229.2	248.2	258.2	267.2	274.0
B–	79.0	107.5	141.1	182.7	221.6	249.4	270.2	281.1	291.0	298.2

TABLE 17.3 CDS Curves Generated by the Model for All Ratings with Japan Specified as the Country and Sector Equal to Financial

Rating	0	1	2	3	4	5	6	7	8	9
AAA	6.5	8.7	12.2	15.7	19.0	21.8	23.4	24.5	25.1	26.3
AA+	9.7	13.1	17.8	23.0	27.6	31.5	34.0	35.5	36.5	37.9
AA	13.3	18.1	24.3	31.3	37.6	42.8	46.2	48.2	49.6	51.3
AA–	17.5	23.8	31.6	40.9	49.1	55.7	60.2	62.7	64.7	66.7
A+	22.2	30.2	40.0	51.7	62.1	70.4	76.0	79.2	81.8	84.1
A	27.5	37.5	49.4	63.9	76.7	86.9	93.8	97.8	101.1	103.8
A–	33.4	45.5	59.7	77.3	92.8	105.0	113.4	118.3	122.2	125.3
BBB+	39.7	54.1	70.8	91.7	110.1	124.6	134.5	140.3	145.0	148.5
BBB	46.3	63.1	82.5	106.8	128.2	145.1	156.6	163.4	168.9	172.9
BBB–	53.1	72.4	94.6	122.4	147.0	166.2	179.4	187.3	193.6	198.1
BB+	60.1	81.9	106.9	138.4	166.2	187.9	202.8	211.8	218.9	223.9

(*Continued*)

(*Continued*)

TABLE 17.3 (*Continued*)

Rating	0	1	2	3	4	5	6	7	8	9
BB	67.2	91.6	119.5	154.7	185.7	210.0	226.6	236.7	244.6	250.1
BB–	74.4	101.5	132.3	171.2	205.7	232.5	250.9	262.1	270.9	276.9
B+	81.8	111.5	145.3	188.1	226.0	255.4	275.6	288.0	297.6	304.2
B	89.2	121.7	158.5	205.1	246.5	278.5	300.6	314.0	324.6	331.7
B–	96.8	132.0	171.9	222.5	267.5	302.1	326.1	340.7	352.1	359.8

17.3 EXPOSURE CALCULATION USING NEURAL NETWORKS

Chapter 11 described how derivative deep neural networks can replicate valuation models. Is it possible to go further and use deep learning to replicate expected exposure profiles or valuation adjustments in full? There is no fundamental reason why this cannot be done; expected exposure profiles are vector quantities, and XVAs are scalars, so a neural network can be trained to replicate the models that generate these quantities, given an appropriate training set.

A clear use case would be for stand-alone XVA or exposure profile generation for individual trades. In this context, the approach can be almost identical to that adopted in the derivative value case. Generate a training set of outputs from an existing model, where market and trade data are input, then use supervised learning. However, it becomes difficult to see how this could be achieved in practice for the more general case of an exposure profile or XVA for a large netting set. The state-space size to cover this use case would be enormous, covering all possible market and trade portfolios that could be encountered in practice. However, if a training set were available or could be generated, then there is no fundamental reason why a large neural network could not be trained for this purpose.

Frodé et al. (2022) developed a neural network model to generate expected exposure profiles for interest rate swaps. They used the example of a USD 10-year payers interest rate swap, characterised by a semi-annual fixed frequency a quarterly floating frequency and a notional value of 100 million. This particular setup presented a challenge due to its 'zig-zag' exposure profile, a more complex scenario than swaps with equivalent fixed and floating frequencies.

To establish a baseline for expected exposure profiles, the researchers employed a one-factor Hull–White Monte Carlo model, executing 5000 simulation paths. The Python version of the QuantLib library was used for all the underlying financial models. It is important to note, as highlighted by Green (2015), that for interest rate swaps, an analytic solution exists so Monte Carlo is not needed for the case of a single interest rate swap.

The study's methodology involved the utilisation of 1540 historical USD yield curves spanning from 4 January 2016 to 26 January 2022. These curves were interpolated onto a monthly time grid using cubic spline interpolation. A key aspect of their approach was the implementation of data augmentation techniques to expand the number of input yield curves. Each sample underwent 5–10 augmentations, including parallel shifts, tilts, merges and multiplications between curves. The parameters for the Hull–White model, the mean-reversion speed and volatility, were selectively sampled from a set of pre-established values, as detailed in Table 17.4. The swap strike was set at the at-the-money (ATM) point for the first dataset, while the second dataset employed seven variations from the ATM, ranging between −3 and +3 basis points.

The researchers opted for a gated recurrent unit (GRU) recurrent neural network with three hidden layers to process the data. The outcome of this model was impressive: it generated highly accurate exposure profiles. These profiles aligned closely with the random error component inherent in the Monte Carlo simulations. They successfully replicated the zig-zag pattern observed in the underlying exposure profiles, demonstrating the model's efficacy.

TABLE 17.4 Hull–White Model Parameters Used in Frodé et al. (2022)

HW Parameter	Dataset 1	Dataset 2
a	$\in [0.001, 0.23]$	$\in [0.05825, 0.17275]$
σ	$\in [0.001, 0.01]$	$\in [0.00280, 0.00640]$

As Frodé et al. (2022) make clear, this is a *proof of concept model* rather than a concrete proposal to use deep learning to generate exposure profiles for interest rate swaps. It demonstrates that the approach is effective and could be applied to more complex scenarios.

EXAMPLE 17.2: NEURAL NETWORKS FOR EXPECTED EXPOSURE PROFILES

In this example, a neural network is trained to generate the expected positive exposure of a 5-year GBP interest rate swap. There are two steps: generation of the dataset and training a simple feedforward network.

Generating the Dataset

Unlike in Frodé et al. (2022), here, the analytic solution for generating the exposure profile of an interest rate swap is used (Green, 2015), which is much faster than using a Monte Carlo simulation. However, market data in the form of yield curves and implied volatilities is still required. The dataset generation example can be found in the Jupyter Notebook `Generate EE Data.ipynb`.

Yield curve generation is handled using a *generative* VAE model trained in Chapter 18 and fully described there. This model has an encoder and decoder part, but here, only the decoder that transforms points in the latent space to the space of yield curves is required. The model is loaded from the save point in the later example and used to generate yield curves. The model was trained using GBP OIS data and outputs monthly zero-rate points up to 5 years in maturity. The latent space has two dimensions, and hence, to sample, it requires two independent normally distributed samples to be input to the decoder.

```
decoder_file = 'vae_decoder.pt'
saved_model = torch.load(decoder_file)
decoder.load_state_dict(saved_model)
decoder = decoder.to(device)
```

The scaler is also needed as this is used to reverse the scaling originally used as an input to the encoder of the VAE, and this was *pickled*. Hence, *t* is loaded from the associated file.

```
scaler = load(open('scaler.pkl', 'rb'))
```

To generate 10,000 example yield curves, an array of $10{,}000 \times 2$ normal samples is generated using PyTorch and passed to the decoder, and then the output is passed through inverse scaling.

```
samples = 10000
sample_z = torch.randn((samples, 2), device=device)
s_curves = decoder(sample_z)
s_curves = scaler.inverse_transform(s_curves.detach().cpu().numpy())
```

Once the data is generated, it must be used to generate QuantLib yield curve objects. Two helper functions are defined to support this, and a series of objects must be initialised appropriately.

(*Continued*)

(*Continued*)

```
curve_matmonths = [i for i in range(1, 61)]

today = ql.Date(26, 11, 2023)
ql.Settings.instance().evaluationDate = today

calendar = ql.UnitedKingdom()
bussiness_convention = ql.Following
day_count = ql.Actual365Fixed()

settlement_days_SONIA = 0
SONIA = ql.OvernightIndex("SONIA", settlement_days_SONIA,
ql.GBPCurrency(), calendar, day_count)

def buildSONIAhelpers(tenors, ois_rates):
    OIS_helpers = []
    for i, itnr in enumerate(tenors):
        if itnr < 13:
            coupon_frequency = ql.Once
            tenor = ql.Period(intr, ql.Months)
            rate = ois_rates[i]
            OIS_helpers.append(ql.OISRateHelper(settlement_days_SONIA,
                                   tenor,
                                     ql.QuoteHandle(ql.SimpleQuote(rate/100)),
                                   SONIA))
        else:
            coupon_frequency = ql.Annual
            tenor = ql.Period(itnr, ql.Months)
            rate = ois_rates[i]
            OIS_helpers.append(ql.OISRateHelper(settlement_days_SONIA,
                                   tenor,
                                   ql.QuoteHandle(ql.SimpleQuote(rate/100)),
                                   SONIA))
    return OIS_helpers

def buildSONIACurve(tenors, ois_rates):
    sonia_ex = buildSONIAhelpers(curve_matmonths, ois_rates)
    yieldcurve = ql.PiecewiseLogCubicDiscount(today, sonia_ex, day_count)
    yieldcurve.enableExtrapolation()
    return yieldcurve
```

The function `buildSONIAhelpers` constructs a list of rate helper objects that are subsequently used by the `buildSONIACurve` to bootstrap the yield curve itself. Given that the model was trained using GBP OIS data, all conventions relate to GBP and SONIA. The implied volatility is assumed to have no term structure. It is sampled uniformly on the interval [0.0, 0.025], noting that the swaption pricing model and volatilities are normal rather than log-normal. The interest rate swaps were all payers sampled from the uniform distribution over [0%, 10%].

Given a yield curve, sampled fixed rate and implied volatility, the analytic expected positive exposure profile consists of the value of a strip of European swaptions on a regular time grid, with the option on the remaining part of the interest rate swap. A vanilla swap object must be constructed in QuantLib to price the swaption, and this requires the fixed and floating leg schedules to be constructed first, which in turn requires a series of objects to be constructed that represent the key parameters. The swap schedule is specified using a start date, an offset start tenor and then a swap maturity for the remaining trade length.

```
def buildSwap(start_date, start_tnr, swap_tenor, calendar,
              fixed_rate, curve_handle, receiver=True):
    short_conv = ql.Following
    long_conv = ql.ModifiedFollowing
    end_of_month = False
    fixed_dc = ql.Actual365Fixed()
    float_dc = ql.Actual365Fixed()
    notional = 1.0
    pay_fixed = True
    swap_start_date = start_date + start_tnr
    swap_end_date = swap_start_date + swap_tenor
    fixedLegDayCounter = ql.SimpleDayCounter()
    floatingLegDayCounter = ql.SimpleDayCounter()
    index = ql.OvernightIndex("SONIA", 0, ql.GBPCurrency(),
                              calendar, float_dc, curve_handle)

    fixedLegTenor = ql.Period(12, ql.Months)
    fixedLegAdjustment = ql.Unadjusted
    fixedLegSchedule = ql.Schedule(swap_start_date, swap_end_date,
                                   fixedLegTenor, calendar,
                                   fixedLegAdjustment,
                                   fixedLegAdjustment,
                                   ql.DateGeneration.Forward,
                                   end_of_month)

    floatingLegTenor = ql.Period(12, ql.Months)
    floatingLegAdjustment = ql.Unadjusted
    floatingLegSchedule = ql.Schedule(swap_start_date,
                                      swap_end_date,
                                      floatingLegTenor, calendar,
                                      floatingLegAdjustment,
                                      floatingLegAdjustment,
                                      ql.DateGeneration.Forward,
                                      end_of_month)

    if receiver:
        swap_pr = ql.VanillaSwap.Receiver
    else:
        swap_pr = ql.VanillaSwap.Payer
    irs = ql.VanillaSwap(swap_pr, notional, fixedLegSchedule,
                         fixed_rate, fixedLegDayCounter,
                         floatingLegSchedule,
                         index, 0, floatingLegDayCounter)
    return irs
```

Once the swap is constructed, the swaption can be created by adding an exercise and the settlement parameters at the start of the swap.

```
def buildSwaption(start_date, start_tnr, swap_tenor,
                  calendar, fixed_rate, curve_handle, receiver=True):
```

(Continued)

(*Continued*)

```
    swap = buildSwap(start_date, start_tnr, swap_tenor,
                     calendar, fixed_rate, curve_handle, receiver)
     exercise = ql.EuropeanExercise(exercise_date)
     settlementType = ql.Settlement.Physical
     settlementMethod = ql.Settlement.ParYieldCurve
     return ql.Swaption(swap, exercise, settlementType)
```

A strip of swaptions needs to be constructed with a start tenor that increases by 6 months each time and a swap tenor that reduces by a similar amount to create the expected exposure profile. The first data point on the profile has no time value, which is determined by the maximum swap value and zero. After all cash flows have occurred, the final data point on the profile should be zero.

```
def generateEPE(start_date, len_tnr, period, calendar, fixed_rate,
                curve_handle, vol, receiver):
    swap_ex = buildSwap(today, ql.Period(2, ql.Days),
                        ql.Period(len_tnr, ql.Months), calendar,
                        fixed_rate, zero_curve)
    swap_curve = ql.DiscountingSwapEngine(curve_handle)
    swap_ex.setPricingEngine(swap_curve)
    swap_npv = swap_ex.NPV()
    epe_lst = list()
    epe_lst.append(max(swap_npv, 0.0))

    cur_tnr = period
    vol_handle = ql.QuoteHandle(ql.SimpleQuote(vol))
    engine = ql.BachelierSwaptionEngine(zero_curve, vol_handle)
    while cur_tnr < len_tnr:
        swaption_ex = buildSwaption(start_date,
                                    ql.Period(cur_tnr, ql.Months),
                                    ql.Period(len_tnr - cur_tnr, ql.Months),
                                    calendar, fixed_rate, zero_curve, receiver)
    swaption_ex.setPricingEngine(engine)
    ee = swaption_ex.NPV()
    epe_lst.append(ee)
    cur_tnr = cur_tnr + period
    epe_lst.append(0.0)
    return epe_lst
```

After the EPE list is generated, it is combined with the input zero rates, volatility and fixed rate in a data frame and saved for use by the model.

Training the Model

A more straightforward approach of using a feedforward network was used, rather than the GRU-based network applied by Frodé et al. (2022), and the example can be found in the Jupyter Notebook `EPE Model.ipynb`. The dataset was loaded and split into input and target and then into training and test sets, with 1% of the one million examples used for testing. The usual feedforward network architecture was used with swish activation, an input dimension of 62, an output dimension of 11 and four hidden layers of width 400. The model was trained for 200 epochs using a batch size of 512 with the Adam optimiser and a learning rate of 0.001. Note that the input was scaled using `StandardScaler`, and the target values were scaled up to give a swap notional of one million GBP.

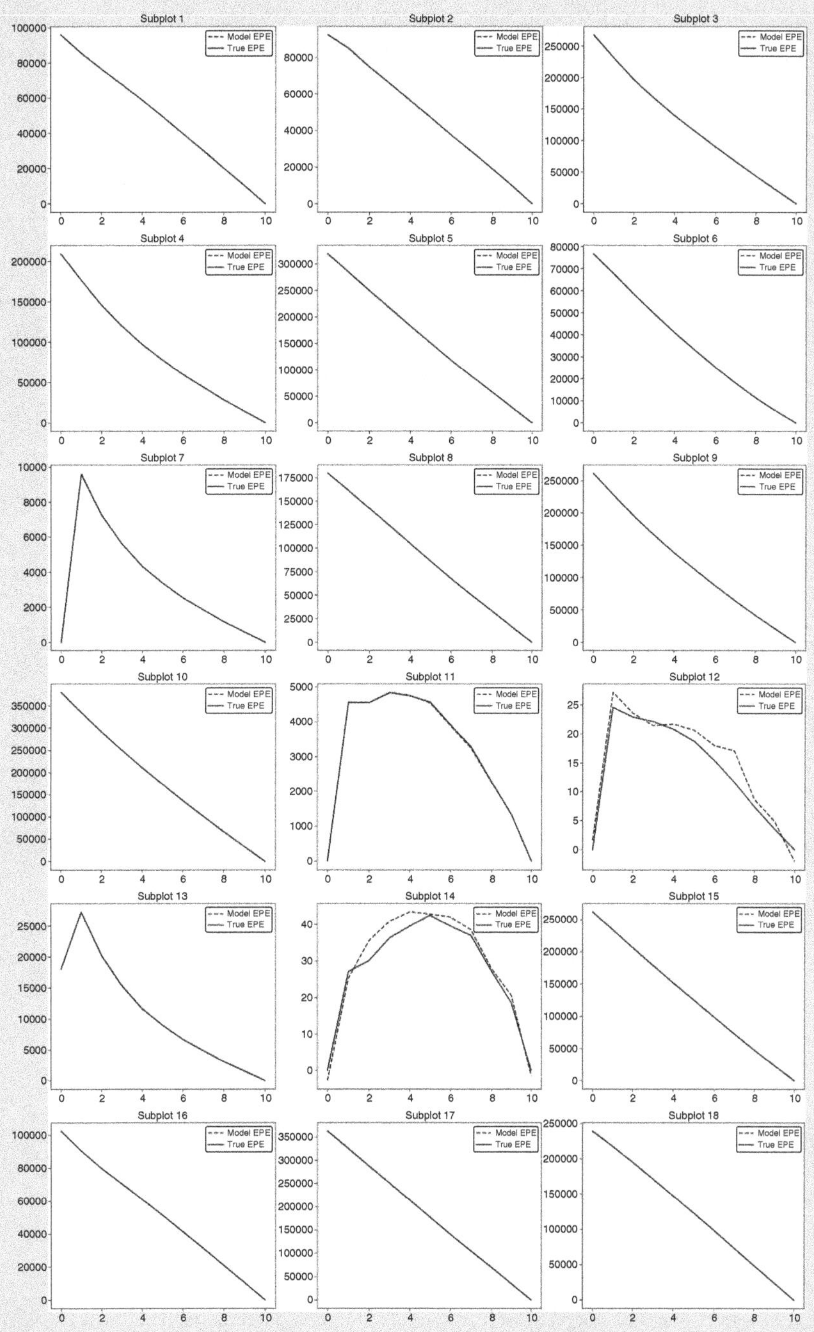

FIGURE 17.1 Eighteen exposure profiles from the test set examples compared between neural network and ground truth.

Figure 17.1 shows 18 example exposure profiles from the test set with the neural network and the ground true EPE plotted on the same chart. In all cases save for subplots 12 and 14, the two lines from the DNN and analytic solution are precisely aligned. For subplots 12 and 14, examination of the *y*-axis scale shows that the absolute exposures are tiny compared to the notional; hence, the difference here is immaterial.

17.4 CONCLUSIONS ON DEEP XVA

As is seen throughout the examples in the book, in this chapter and elsewhere, there are many potential applications of deep learning to XVA. The opportunities for deep learning in XVA range from tools to build a credit curve map, through components of XVA systems, to full XVA calculations, by replication of the provision of a full-solution capability where BSDE XVA models arise.

CHAPTER 18

Generating Realistic Market Data

Then he [The Star Child] waited, marshalling his thoughts and brooding over his still untested powers. For though he was master of the world, he was not quite sure what to do next. But he would think of something.

Arthur C. Clarke, 2001: A Space Odyssey (1968)

18.1 INTRODUCTION AND CLASSICAL METHODS

Chapter 9 reviewed generative models in their original context of image generation. However, they have also recently emerged as a powerful tool for generating synthetic data in other domains, including finance. Unlike classical methods of generating synthetic data, generative models can learn complex data distributions and generate realistic samples that are difficult to distinguish from actual data with statistical properties matching those observed in financial markets.

For years, finance has widely utilised classical methods for simulating financial time series. The simplest such model is a Gaussian random walk model where returns are assumed to follow a random walk with Gaussian increments, expressed as

$$\begin{aligned} y_t &= y_{t-1} + \epsilon_t, \\ \epsilon_t &\sim \mathcal{N}(0, \sigma), \end{aligned} \tag{18.1}$$

where y_t is the return at time t. The use of constant volatility does not match observations and limits the model. A more realistic approach would treat the volatility as stochastic, and the Heston (1993) model is a popular example. It can generate financial time series by simulating the stock price and volatility processes. The model is flexible and can capture various features of financial data, such as volatility smiles and skewness. The Heston model can be expressed mathematically as

$$\begin{aligned} dS_t &= \mu S_t dt + \sqrt{v_t} S_t dW_{1,t}, \\ dv_t &= \kappa(\theta - v_t)dt + \sigma\sqrt{v_t} dW_{2,t}, \\ dW_{1,t} dW_{2,t} &= \rho dt, \end{aligned} \tag{18.2}$$

where S_t is the stock price at time t, v_t is the instantaneous variance at time t, μ is the drift rate, κ is the speed of mean reversion, θ is the long-run average variance, σ is the volatility of the volatility and ρ is the correlation between the Brownian motions $W_{1,t}$ and $W_{2,t}$. The original introduction of the Heston model presented it as a closed-form solution for the risk-neutral pricing of options with stochastic volatility.

Deep Learning in Quantitative Finance, First Edition. Andrew Green.

A fitted econometric time series model can generate synthetic time series using resampling. The autoregressive integrated moving average (ARIMA) model is one of the most commonly used univariate models (Box and Jenkins, 1970), which can be expressed mathematically as

$$(1 - \phi_1 L - \cdots - \phi_p L^p)(1 - L)^d y_t = c + (1 + \theta_1 L + \cdots + \theta_q L^q)\epsilon_t, \tag{18.3}$$

where y_t is the time series at time t, L is the lag operator, $\phi_1, \ldots, \phi_p$ are the autoregressive coefficients, d is the degree of differencing, c is a constant, $\theta_1, \ldots, \theta_q$ are the moving average coefficients and ϵ_t is the error term.

The ARIMA model is composed of three individual components: autoregressive (AR), moving average (MA) and integrated (I).

The AR model of order p captures the dependency of the current value of the time series on its previous values (Hamilton, 1994) and is defined by

$$y_t = c + \phi_1 y_{t-1} + \phi_2 y_{t-2} + \cdots + \phi_p y_{t-p} + \epsilon_t, \tag{18.4}$$

where y_t is the time series at time t, c is a constant, $\phi_1, \ldots, \phi_p$ are the autoregressive coefficients and ϵ_t is the error term. The AR(p) model is a simple extension of the random walk, depending on p previous time-series values. The AR model is not always stationary.

The MA model of order q captures the dependency of the current value of the time series on past errors (Box and Jenkins, 1970) and is defined by

$$y_t = c + \epsilon_t + \theta_1 \epsilon_{t-1} + \theta_2 \epsilon_{t-2} + \cdots + \theta_q \epsilon_{t-q}, \tag{18.5}$$

where y_t is the time series at time t, c is a constant, $\theta_1, \ldots, \theta_q$ are the moving average coefficients and ϵ_t is the error term. The MA(q) model is a linear combination of past errors and gives a model which has autocorrelation to order q but is zero by definition for longer lags. The MA model is always stationary and can capture shock effects.

The integrated model component represents the differencing of the time series to make it stationary. The differencing operation is applied d times, denoted as $(1 - L)^d y_t$ in the ARIMA model equation. Combining the AR(p) and MA(q) models gives the ARMA(p, q) model, while adding the integrated model gives the ARIMA model.

While ARIMA models are helpful for modelling time-series data, they assume constant volatility over time. However, time-series data can exhibit conditional heteroscedasticity, where the series volatility varies over time. Engle (1982) addressed this issue by introducing the autoregressive conditional heteroscedasticity (ARCH) model. Equation (18.6) defines the ARCH model of order p,

$$\begin{aligned}
\epsilon_t &= \sigma_t z_t, \\
\sigma_t^2 &= \alpha_0 + \alpha_1 \epsilon_{t-1}^2 + \cdots + \alpha_p \epsilon_{t-p}^2, \\
z_t &\sim \mathrm{N}(0, 1),
\end{aligned} \tag{18.6}$$

where $\alpha_0, \alpha_1, \ldots, \alpha_p$ are the ARCH parameters. ARCH models fit an autoregressive model to the variance.

However, the ARCH model has some limitations, such as requiring many parameters to model long memory in volatility. The generalised autoregressive conditional heteroscedasticity (GARCH) model, proposed by Bollerslev (1986), addresses these limitations by including lagged conditional variances. The GARCH model of order (p, q) is defined as

$$\begin{aligned}
\epsilon_t &= \sigma_t z_t, \\
\sigma_t^2 &= \alpha_0 + \sum_{i=1}^{p} \alpha_i \epsilon_{t-i}^2 + \sum_{j=1}^{q} \beta_j \sigma_{t-j}^2, \\
z_t &\sim \mathrm{N}(0, 1),
\end{aligned} \tag{18.7}$$

where $\alpha_0, \alpha_1, \ldots, \alpha_p$ and $\beta_1, \ldots, \beta_q$ are the GARCH parameters.

Researchers widely use both ARCH and GARCH models for modelling and forecasting the volatility of financial time series, such as stock returns and exchange rates, as they often observe conditional heteroscedasticity

(Baillie et al., 1996; Poon and Granger, 2003). Combining these with ARIMA models enables the creation of more accurate forecasts for time-series data that exhibit autocorrelation and conditional heteroscedasticity.

In conclusion, classical methods for generating synthetic financial data have laid the foundation for understanding the complex dynamics of financial markets. These models, such as ARIMA, ARCH and GARCH, provide valuable insights into the properties of financial time series and their dependence on previous values, errors and volatility. However, despite their widespread use and flexibility, classical models still have certain limitations and may not fully capture the intricacies of real-world financial data.

In recent years, deep generative models have emerged as an increasingly powerful and promising tool for generating synthetic financial data, offering the ability to learn complex data distributions and generate realistic samples that closely resemble actual market data. The remainder of this chapter will explore various deep generative models for time-series generation, including restricted Boltzmann machines (RBMs), generative adversarial networks (GANs) and diffusion and score-based models. It will also discuss generating multivariate time series and higher-dimensional structures, such as yield curves, correlation matrices and volatility surfaces. Finally, the chapter will briefly discuss applying in-painting techniques to market data to fill in missing or incomplete data points using generative models, which can be particularly useful for dealing with real-world financial data that may have gaps or inconsistencies.

18.2 MOTIVATION AND APPLICATIONS OF SYNTHETIC FINANCIAL MARKET DATA

Why do we need synthetic market data? The need arises due to limitations in accessing high-quality and diverse financial market data, which often occur because of proprietary restrictions, data privacy concerns and the high cost of obtaining and maintaining comprehensive datasets. In such situations, synthetic financial market data emerges as a valuable alternative. It has the potential to enhance existing datasets, overcome data limitations and enable the development and evaluation of financial models and algorithms.

18.2.1 Motivation for Synthetic Financial Market Data

There are several key motivations for generating and using synthetic financial market data:

- **Data Augmentation.** By creating new data points that preserve the underlying structure and statistical properties of the original data, synthetic data can enhance existing datasets, which in turn assists in improving the performance of data-driven models by providing them with more diverse and representative training data.
- **Overcoming Data Limitations.** Synthetic data generation can overcome limitations in real-world financial data by creating additional data points, extending the period or generating data at a higher frequency, which helps to address constraints such as the limited number of data points, the period covered or the frequency of data updates in the original dataset.
- **Data Privacy and Anonymisation.** Synthetic data can help address data privacy concerns by generating data that maintains the statistical properties of the original data without revealing any sensitive or confidential information.
- **Model Development and Evaluation.** By utilising synthetic data, researchers can actively develop, test and evaluate financial models and algorithms in a controlled environment where they possess knowledge of the actual underlying dynamics. This approach facilitates a more comprehensive understanding of the models' performance, strengths and weaknesses.

18.2.2 Applications of Synthetic Financial Market Data

Synthetic financial market data has a wide range of applications across various areas of the financial industry:

- **Risk Management.** Financial institutions can use synthetic data to simulate extreme market conditions or stress scenarios that may not be present in historical data, enabling them to understand their risk exposures better and effectively manage them.

- **Portfolio Optimisation.** Synthetic data can assist in identifying optimal portfolio allocations by offering a more diverse range of market conditions and return scenarios. As a result, it leads to more robust and stable investment strategies.
- **Trading Algorithms.** Using synthetic data allows for developing, testing and refining algorithmic trading strategies. It provides a controlled environment to evaluate performance and identify potential sources of alpha.
- **Model Validation.** Financial institutions can employ synthetic data to validate and benchmark their internal models, which ensures that these models are robust, reliable and suitable for their intended purposes.
- **Machine Learning and Artificial Intelligence.** Synthetic data can be valuable for training and evaluating machine learning models and artificial intelligence algorithms. It provides a richer and more diverse set of data points and scenarios to facilitate model development.

In conclusion, synthetic financial market data offers numerous benefits and applications. It addresses data limitations and privacy concerns while providing a robust model development, evaluation and risk management tool. As data-driven methods and artificial intelligence techniques continue to gain traction in the financial industry, the importance of synthetic data is likely to grow.

18.3 TIME-SERIES GENERATION

This section will discuss various approaches for generating synthetic financial time series, covering both classical methods and advanced deep generative models. Financial time series exhibit unique properties that distinguish them from other types of time-series data, such as non-stationarity, autocorrelation and conditional heteroscedasticity. Understanding these properties is essential for developing accurate and realistic synthetic data generation models. The section will begin by exploring the properties of financial time series in Section 18.3.1 and then examine time-series generation techniques, including classical methods like ARIMA, ARCH and GARCH models, as well as modern deep generative models such as RBMs, GANs and diffusion models. This section will provide examples to illustrate the application of these techniques to financial time-series generation.

18.3.1 Empirical Properties of Financial Time Series

Financial time-series data exhibit several characteristic properties that distinguish them from other data types. These properties, also referred to as stylised facts, have been extensively documented in the literature and are crucial for understanding the behaviour of financial markets and the development of appropriate models for forecasting and risk management. Cont (2001) provides a comprehensive overview of the empirical properties of asset returns and highlights key statistical issues arising from these properties. This section discusses the most prominent empirical properties of financial time-series data.

18.3.1.1 Absence of Autocorrelation in Returns Financial asset returns exhibit little to no autocorrelation, meaning that the correlation between the returns at different time points is generally very low. Mathematically, the autocorrelation function (ACF) of returns r_t can be expressed as

$$\rho(\tau) = \frac{\mathrm{E}[(r_t - \mu)(r_{t+\tau} - \mu)]}{\sigma^2}, \tag{18.8}$$

where μ and σ^2 are the mean and variance of the returns, respectively, and τ denotes the time lag. Empirical studies show that the autocorrelation of returns is typically very close to zero for most financial assets, suggesting that past returns contain little information about future returns (Cont, 2001).

18.3.1.2 Heavy Tails The distribution of asset returns exhibits heavy tails, indicating that extreme events or large price movements occur more frequently than expected under a normal distribution. Non-Gaussian distributions like the Student's t-distribution or the stable Paretian distribution are often employed to capture these heavy tails. The heavy tails in the return distribution imply that standard risk measures, such as value-at-risk (VaR) or expected shortfall, may underestimate the actual risk exposure of a financial asset (Cont, 2001).

In the context of these heavy-tailed distributions, discussing the concept of kurtosis is important. Kurtosis is a statistical measure that describes the shape of a distribution's tails in relation to its overall shape. There are two standard definitions of kurtosis: excess kurtosis and Fisher's kurtosis. Excess kurtosis is the fourth central moment of a distribution divided by the square of the variance minus 3. This definition is often used in finance, as it directly compares a distribution's tails to a normal distribution. A distribution with excess kurtosis greater than zero is said to have heavy tails, while a distribution with excess kurtosis less than zero has light tails.

On the other hand, Fisher's kurtosis is simply the fourth central moment divided by the square of the variance. This definition is often used in fields other than finance, as it does not make a direct comparison to the normal distribution. In this chapter, the convention where the kurtosis of a normal distribution is zero is adopted, which corresponds to the definition of excess kurtosis.

18.3.1.3 Volatility Clustering Financial time-series data often exhibits volatility clustering, where periods of high volatility follow periods of high volatility, and periods of low volatility succeed periods of low volatility. The ACF of the squared returns or the absolute returns measures this behaviour:

$$\gamma(\tau) = \frac{\mathrm{E}[(|r_t| - \mu_{|r|})(|r_{t+\tau}| - \mu_{|r|})]}{\sigma^2_{|r|}}, \tag{18.9}$$

where $\mu_{|r|}$ and $\sigma^2_{|r|}$ are the mean and variance of the absolute returns, respectively. Researchers often model volatility clustering using conditional heteroscedastic models, such as the ARCH model (Engle, 1982) and the GARCH model (Bollerslev, 1986).

18.3.1.4 Leverage Effect The leverage effect indicates a negative correlation between asset returns and their volatility. It implies that when an asset experiences negative returns, its volatility tends to increase, and vice versa for positive returns. The impact of financial leverage on the riskiness of a firm's equity and the role of investor sentiment in market volatility influence this phenomenon. Volatility models, like the GARCH model, can incorporate the leverage effect by introducing an asymmetric term that captures the relationship between past returns and future volatility (Cont, 2001).

18.3.1.5 Long Memory in Volatility The volatility of financial time series often exhibits long memory, meaning that past volatility remains informative about future volatility over long time horizons. The slow decay of the squared or absolute returns ACF typically characterises long memory. To model the extended memory in volatility, researchers have developed various extensions to the GARCH model, such as the fractionally integrated GARCH (FIGARCH) model (Baillie et al., 1996) and the long-memory stochastic volatility (LMSV) model (Robinson, 2001).

18.3.1.6 Seasonality and Calendar Effects Financial time-series data can exhibit seasonality or calendar effects, such as the day-of-the-week effect, the month-of-the-year effect and the turn-of-the-month effect. These patterns can arise from various factors, such as trading activity, liquidity or investor behaviour. Time-series models can incorporate seasonality and calendar effects by introducing seasonal or deterministic components that capture the underlying periodic patterns (Cont, 2001).

18.3.1.7 Multivariate Dependencies Financial assets are often interrelated, with dependencies arising from the market, the sector or idiosyncratic factors. Different multivariate models, like the vector autoregression (VAR) model (Sims, 1980), the multivariate GARCH model (Bauwens et al., 2006) or copula-based models (Embrechts et al., 2001) can help identify and represent these dependencies. Understanding the dependencies between assets is crucial for portfolio construction, risk management and asset pricing.

18.3.2 Empirical Tests

To assess the accuracy and quality of artificial financial time series, comparing their statistical features with those observed in actual financial data is essential. This section will describe several empirical tests based on the stylised facts of financial time series, as outlined by Cont (2001). These tests aid in evaluating whether synthetic data generated by different models faithfully captures the fundamental characteristics of financial data.

18.3.2.1 Absence of Autocorrelation in Returns The first test examines the absence of autocorrelation in asset returns. Financial time series often exhibit weak or no autocorrelation in returns, as discussed by Cont (2001). The ACF of returns is computed to test for the absence of autocorrelation.

18.3.2.2 Heavy-Tailed Distribution of Returns Asset returns typically exhibit heavy-tailed distributions, which implies a higher probability of extreme events than would be expected under the Gaussian distribution. The kurtosis of the synthetic return series is compared with that of a Gaussian distribution (kurtosis equal to 3) (Cont, 2001). A kurtosis larger than 3 suggests a heavy-tailed distribution. The Jarque–Bera test (Jarque and Bera, 1980) can also be used to assess the normality of the return distribution.

18.3.2.3 Volatility Clustering In finance, it is common for time series to experience periods of volatility clustering, where episodes of low volatility concur, as do episodes of high volatility. A method recommended by Cont (2001) is used to study volatility clustering, and the ACF of squared or absolute returns is calculated. If there is significant autocorrelation in squared or absolute returns, it indicates the presence of volatility clustering.

18.3.2.4 Leverage Effect The leverage effect refers to the observed negative correlation between asset returns and changes in volatility (Cont, 2001). The cross-correlation between returns and volatility changes is calculated to test for the presence of the leverage effect. A significant negative cross-correlation suggests the leverage effect in the synthetic time series.

18.3.2.5 Long Memory in Volatility Financial time series often exhibit long memory in volatility, as noted by Cont (2001). To test for long memory, the Hurst exponent (Hurst, 1951) or the Geweke–Porter-Hudak (GPH) test (Geweke and Porter-Hudak, 1991) on the squared or absolute returns can be applied. A Hurst exponent or GPH test statistic significantly greater than 0.5 indicates long-term memory in volatility.

18.3.2.6 Discriminative and Predictive Scores The *discriminative score* is a metric used to evaluate the quality of synthetic time-series data. It trains a binary classifier, often called the *discriminator*, to distinguish between original and synthetic data points. The discriminator is usually a neural network with an input layer matching the dimensionality of the time-series data and an output layer with a single neuron activated by a sigmoid function, representing the probability that a given input is from the original dataset.

Given an original dataset O and a synthetic dataset S, the data is first split into training and test sets, typically using an 80 : 20 ratio. The training sets of O and S are combined and marked with a flag to distinguish between original and synthetic examples. The training process utilises cross-entropy loss to train the discriminator.

After training, the evaluators calculate the classification error on the test set to assess the performance of the discriminator. The classification error represents the proportion of misclassified data points in the test set, determining the discriminative score:

$$D_{\text{score}} = \frac{\text{Number of misclassified points}}{\text{Total number of points in the test set}}. \tag{18.10}$$

A lower discriminative score indicates that the synthetic data is more similar to the original data, making it more challenging for the classifier to discriminate between the two.

The *predictive score* is a metric used to evaluate the quality of synthetic time-series data. It works by training a predictive model, such as an RNN, on the synthetic data and measuring its performance on the original data. The main idea is to assess whether the synthetic data preserves the temporal dynamics of the original data, allowing the predictive model to make accurate predictions.

An RNN-based predictor with GRUs is employed to train a predictive model on the synthetic data, given an original dataset O and a synthetic dataset S. The input layer of the RNN matches the dimensionality of the time-series data, excluding the target variable. Meanwhile, the output layer consists of a single neuron activated by a sigmoid function, representing the predicted value of the target variable.

The predictive model's training process uses the L1 loss, which computes the mean absolute difference between the predicted values and the ground truth. The mean absolute error (MAE) between the predicted and actual values is used to assess model performance.

The predictive score, indicating the similarity between the synthetic and original data in terms of temporal dynamics, is determined by the MAE between the predicted and actual values of the original dataset. A lower predictive score suggests higher similarity, leading to more accurate predictions.

EXAMPLE 18.1: APPLYING EMPIRICAL TESTS TO REAL DATA

Throughout this section on time-series generation, four time series will be used consistently as an example dataset: Apple stock prices, the S&P 500 stock index, the USDJPY FX spot price and the price of gold. All four series span the 20 years from 1 January 2001 to 1 January 2021. These can be downloaded using the `yfinance` Python package, supplying the ticker as a string and the start and end dates of the desired period. The log returns are calculated from the closing prices by taking the logs and then differencing the points, which can be done using numpy.

```
import yfinance as yf
import pandas as pd
import numpy as np

def download_data(ticker, start_date, end_date):
    data = yf.download(ticker, start=start_date, end=end_date)
    return data

def log_returns(time_series):
    log_prices = np.log(time_series)
    log_returns = np.diff(log_prices)
    return log_returns
```

The four time series and the associated log returns are shown in Figures 18.1 through 18.4. Volatility clustering is immediately apparent in the returns of all four series, although present at different levels. The extreme volatility experienced in the aftermath of the collapse of Lehman Brothers on 15 September 2008 is seen in all four time series, as is the onset of the COVID-19 pandemic in March 2020.

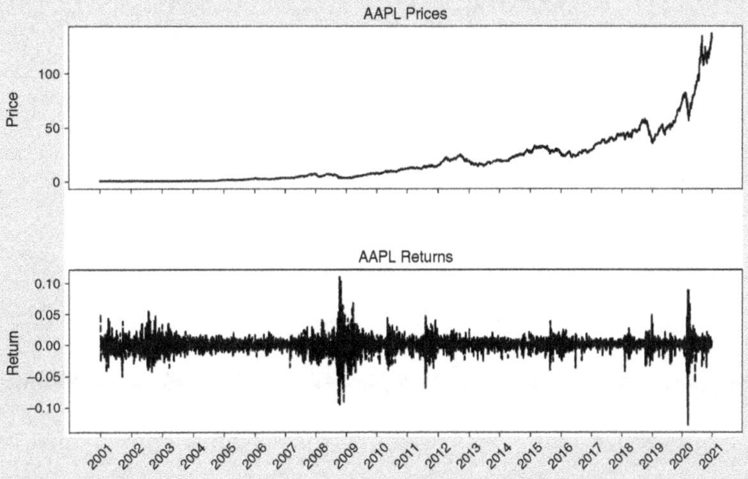

FIGURE 18.1 Apple stock price and daily log returns from 1 January 2001 to 1 January 2021.

(*Continued*)

(*Continued*)

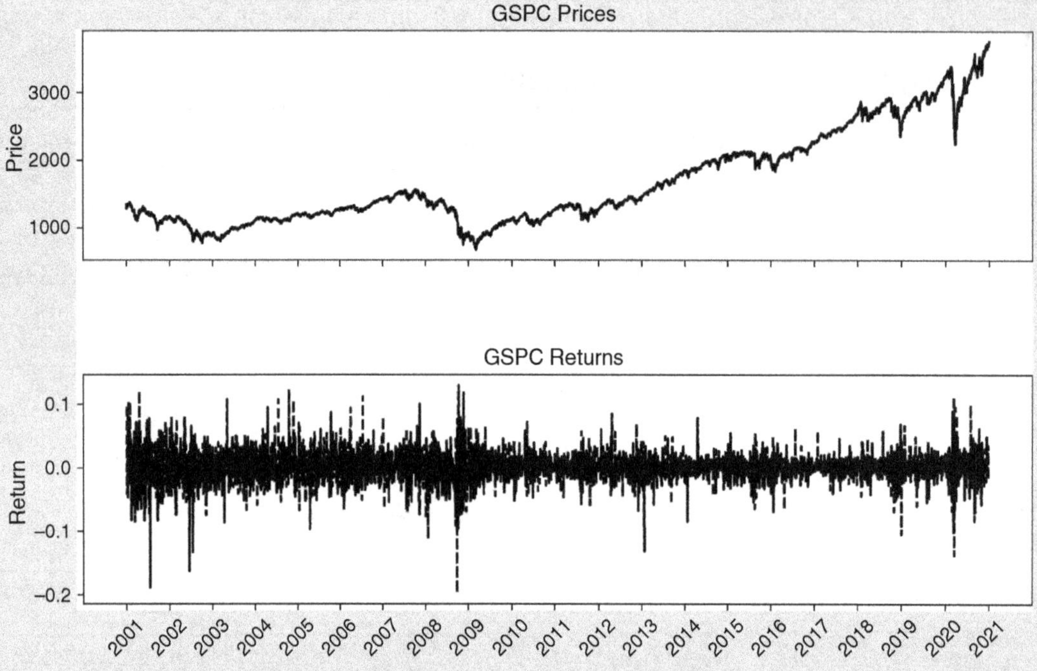

FIGURE 18.2 S&P 500 index and daily log returns from 1 January 2001 to 1 January 2021.

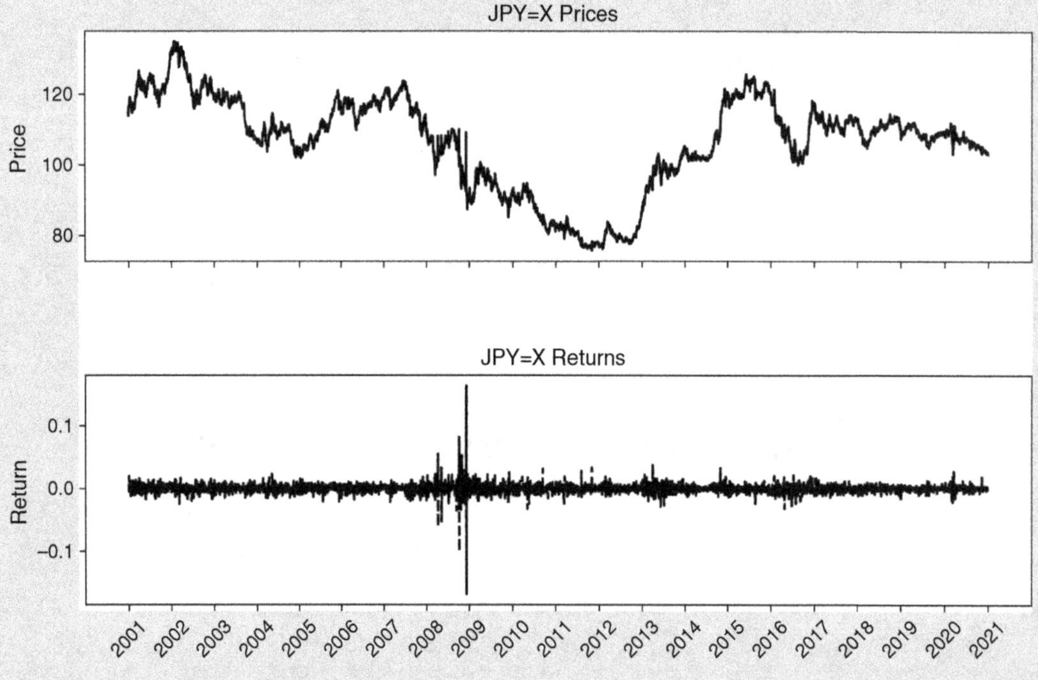

FIGURE 18.3 USDJPY and daily log returns from 1 January 2001 to 1 January 2021.

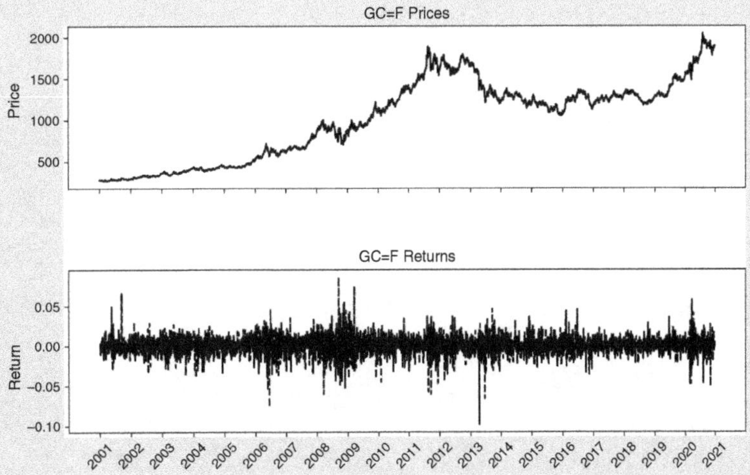

FIGURE 18.4 Gold price and daily log returns from 1 January 2001 to 1 January 2021.

Of course, pure visualisation is insufficient and hence, the tests described in Section 18.3.2 have been implemented in Python and run over the time series of returns. The tests have been implemented in Python in the file `empirical_tests.py`, using functions from the packages `scipy`, `numpy`, `statsmodels` and `hurst`. The GPH test is adapted from the R language package `LongMemoryTS` (Javier López-de-Lacalle et al., 2021).

```
import numpy as np
import pandas as pd
import matplotlib.pyplot as plt
from scipy.stats import jarque_bera, kurtosis, skew
from statsmodels.tsa.stattools import acf
from hurst import compute_Hc
from scipy.signal import periodogram

def gph(time_series, max_lag = None, min_lag=1):
    if max_lag is None:
        max_lag = len(time_series) // 2
    T = len(time_series)
    n = np.floor(T/2).astype(int)
    lambdaj = 2*np.pi/T*np.arange(1, n+1)
    _, logIj = periodogram(time_series)
    logIj = np.log(logIj[1:])
    Yj = np.log(np.abs(1 - np.exp(1j*lambdaj)))
    Ybar = np.mean(Yj[(min_lag-1):max_lag])
    d_hat = -0.5 * np.sum((Yj[(min_lag-1):max_lag] - Ybar) *
        logIj[(min_lag-1):max_lag]) /
        np.sum((Yj[(min_lag-1):max_lag] - Ybar)**2)
    return d_hat

def test_unconditional_distribution(returns):
    jb_stat, jb_pvalue = jarque_bera(returns)
    kurt = kurtosis(returns)
    skw = skew(returns)
    return jb_stat, jb_pvalue, kurt, skw
```

(*Continued*)

(*Continued*)

```
def test_volatility_clustering(returns):
    squared_returns = returns ** 2
    absolute_returns = np.abs(returns)
    acf_squared = acf(squared_returns)
    acf_absolute = acf(absolute_returns)
    return acf_squared, acf_absolute

def test_leverage_effect(returns):
    lagged_returns = returns[:-1]
    future_squared_returns = (returns[1:] ** 2)
    cross_correlation = np.correlate(lagged_returns,
                                      future_squared_returns)
    return cross_correlation[0]

def test_long_memory(returns):
    squared_returns = returns ** 2
    absolute_returns = np.abs(returns)
    gph_squared = gph(squared_returns)
    gph_absolute = gph(absolute_returns)
    H1, _, _ = compute_Hc(squared_returns)
    H2, _, _ = compute_Hc(absolute_returns)
    return H1, H2, gph_squared, gph_absolute
```

Table 18.1 presents the complete set of test statistics, providing a comprehensive overview. Additionally, in Figure 18.5, the ACF of the returns is depicted in the top panel. In contrast, the ACF of the squared returns is displayed in the bottom panel. Upon examination of the autocorrelation plots, it becomes evident that there is minimal evidence of autocorrelation in any of the series.

Furthermore, it is worth noting that all the series exhibit apparent deviations from a normal distribution, as indicated by the p-values of the Jarque–Bera test. The kurtosis values of all the series surpass the expected value of 0.0 for a normal distribution, implying heavy tails based on the Fisher definition of kurtosis.

Volatility clustering can be observed in the autocorrelation of squared returns, indicating a tendency for periods of high volatility to be followed by similarly high volatility. Additionally, all the series demonstrate a negative cross-correlation, suggesting the presence of the leverage effect.

Finally, none of the Hurst or GPH statistics exceeds the threshold of 0.5, implying that long memory in volatility is not a prominent characteristic of these time series.

TABLE 18.1 Test Statistics for the Four Real Time Series

Label	JB Stat	JB P-value	Vol	Kurt	Skew	Cross-correl	H	GPH
Apple	6.85e+03	0.0	0.37	5.71	−0.18	−5.62e−04	0.38	0.13
S&P 500	2.88e+04	0.0	0.20	11.68	−0.42	−3.51e−03	0.38	0.26
USDJPY	2.68e+06	0.0	0.12	111.37	−0.51	5.63e−03	0.48	0.45
Gold	6.41e+03	0.0	0.18	5.51	−0.28	−7.43e−04	0.39	0.12

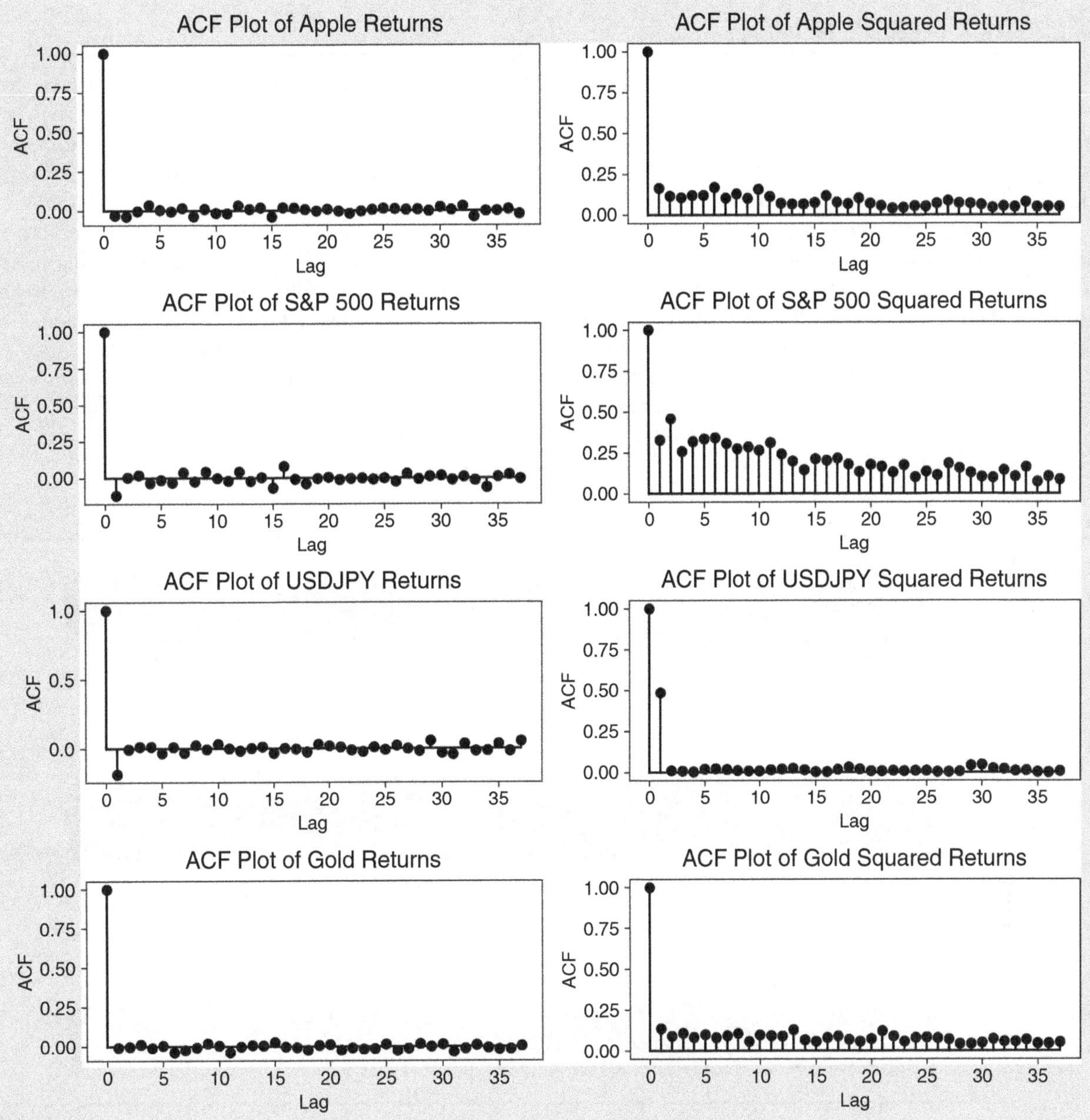

FIGURE 18.5 ACF plots for squared and absolute returns for Apple, S&P 500, USD, JPY and Gold.

18.3.3 Time-Series Generation

This section reviews the generation of univariate and multivariate time series, specifically focusing on sequences of returns for individual assets. The classical methods discussed earlier will be employed to establish a performance baseline. These methods rely on linear relationships between observations at different time lags.

Following the classical methods, more advanced deep learning approaches will be employed, including RBMs, VAEs, GANs and diffusion models.

EXAMPLE 18.2: CLASSICAL METHODS

In the introduction to this chapter, four classical time-series models – the Gaussian random walk, the Heston model, ARIMA and ARCH/GARCH models – were described. To employ these models generatively, they need to be fitted to the training sequences of returns. Subsequently, the residuals are sampled to generate synthetic time-series data. The Jupyter Notebook `Classical Models.ipynb` contains the code necessary to reproduce the results presented in this section.

Calculating the variance of returns makes it easy to fit the Gaussian random walk. Once fitted, simulating returns is just as simple. However, the simulated returns shown in Figure 18.6 bear little resemblance to historical returns because the variance remains constant, resulting in no volatility clustering. Additionally, as expected from a random walk, ACF plots for simulated returns and squared returns show no evidence of autocorrelation (Figure 18.7). Table 18.2 presents the empirical test results applied to the simulated series.

The results indicate normally distributed returns, inconsistent with the original historical data. However, the series volatility matches the historical data well. Finally, a quantile–quantile (QQ) plot in Figure 18.8 displays a marked S-shape and deviation from the straight line, indicating that the actual and simulated datasets have different distributions.

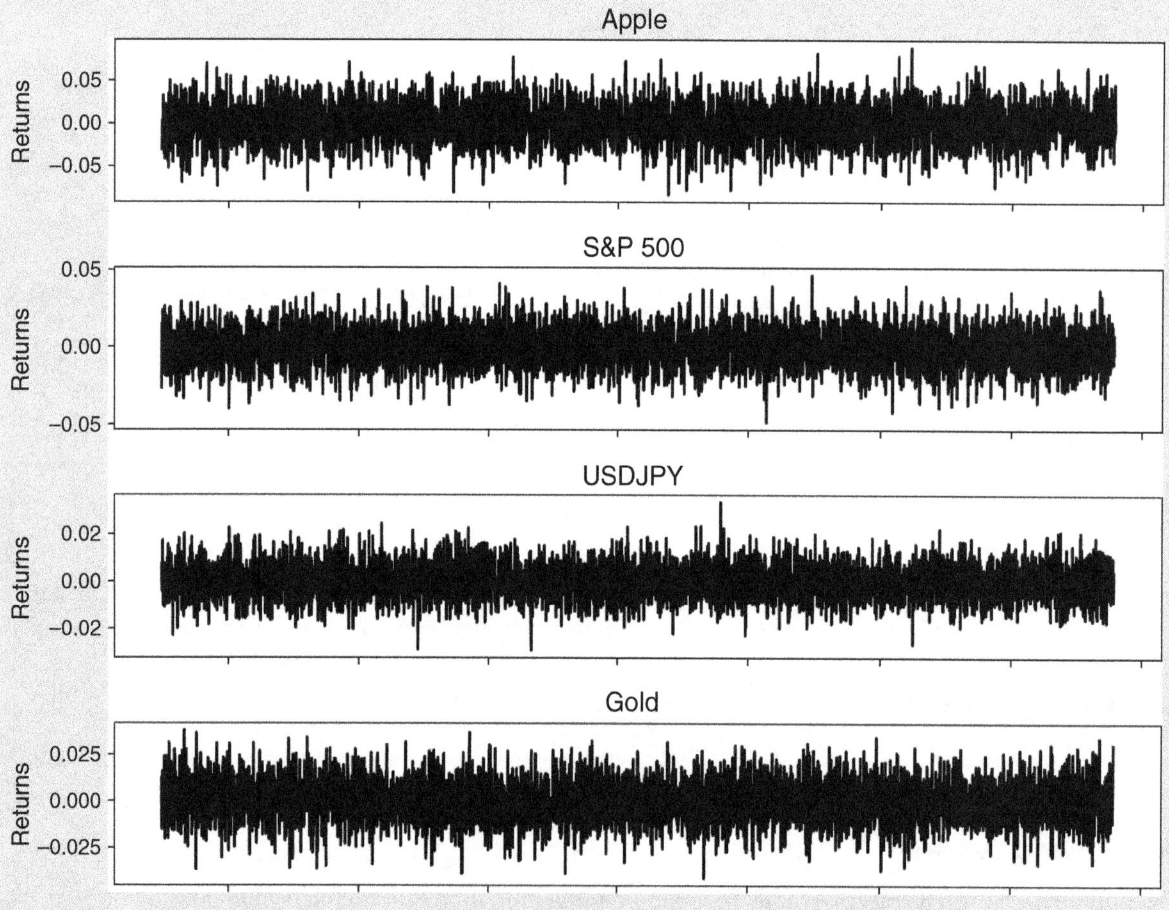

FIGURE 18.6 Simulated returns for a Gaussian random walk fitted to the four historical time series.

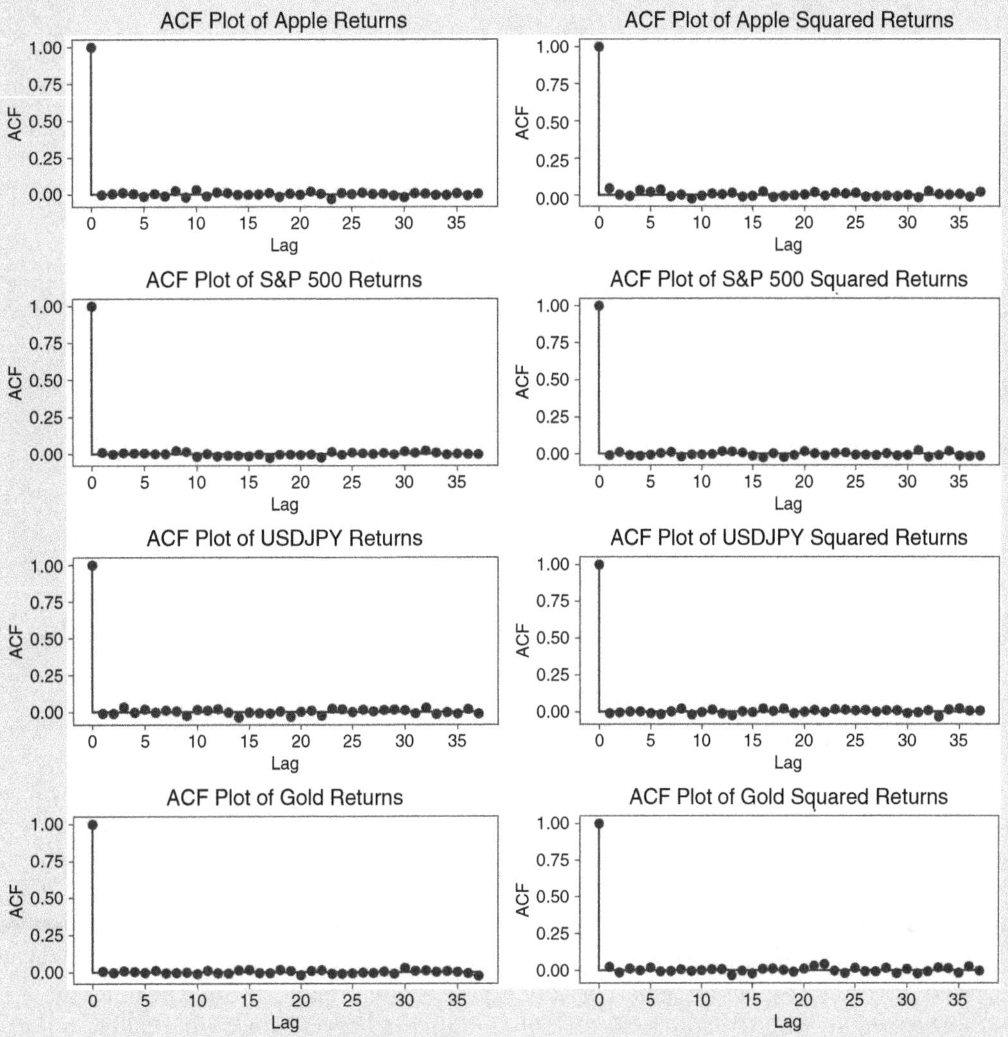

FIGURE 18.7 ACF plots for a Gaussian random walk fitted to the four historical time series.

TABLE 18.2 Test Statistics for the Four Simulated Gaussian Random Walk Time Series

Label	JB Stat	JB P-value	Vol	Kurt	Skew	Cross-correl	H	GPH
Apple	1.07	0.58	0.37	0.07	0.008	1.66e-04	0.21	-0.001
S&P 500	0.89	0.64	0.20	0.06	0.001	-2.56e-04	0.23	0.018
USDJPY	1.26	0.53	0.12	0.06	0.021	-2.14e-06	0.23	0.012
Gold	1.76	0.42	0.18	-0.04	-0.041	3.70e-04	0.21	-0.021

(Continued)

(*Continued*)

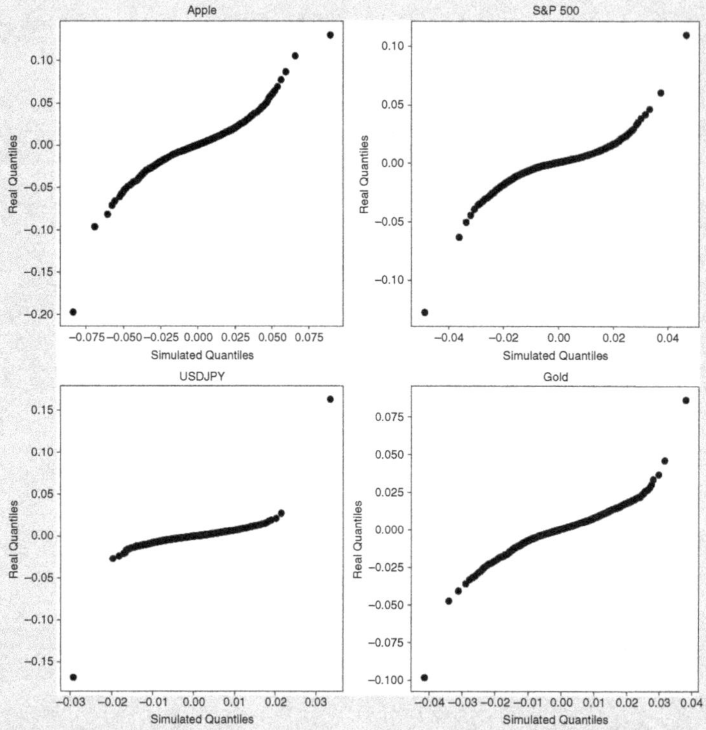

FIGURE 18.8 QQ plots for real vs simulated data for the Gaussian random walk model.

The fitting process for the Heston model is more complex, requiring the utilisation of the `svolfit` Python package. To accomplish this, the function call `svolfit.svolfit(x, dt, model='Heston', method='grid')` is employed. It is important to note that the fitting routine requires a few minutes to complete and the entire time series to be passed as input rather than just the returns. The outcome of the fitting routine is a tuple of results, with the third element containing a dictionary of the calibrated Heston parameters.

Once the parameters have been calibrated, simulated paths can be generated using the specified function.

```
def simulate_heston(heston_params, num_steps, num_paths, dt, r=0, s0=1):
    kappa, theta, sigma, rho, v0 = heston_params
    w1 = np.random.randn(num_paths, num_steps)
    w2 = rho * w1 + np.sqrt(1 - rho ** 2) * \
        np.random.randn(num_paths, num_steps)

    s = np.zeros((num_paths, num_steps + 1))
            v = np.zeros((num_paths, num_steps + 1))

    s[:, 0] = s0
    v[:, 0] = v0

    for t in range(1, num_steps + 1):
        dv = kappa * (theta - np.maximum(v[:, t - 1], 0)) * dt + sigma * \
            np.sqrt(np.maximum(v[:, t - 1], 0)) * np.sqrt(dt) * w2[:, t - 1]
        ds = r * s[:, t - 1] * dt + np.sqrt(np.maximum(v[:, t - 1], 0)) * \
            s[:, t - 1] * np.sqrt(dt) * w1[:, t - 1]
```

```
        v[:, t] = v[:, t - 1] + dv
        s[:, t] = s[:, t - 1] * np.exp(ds)

    return s, v
```

After generating the asset paths using the function, it is necessary to calculate the log returns. Figure 18.9 illustrates a plot of these simulated returns for a single path of the Heston model calibrated to the four historical time series. In contrast to the random walk, these charts depict volatility clustering. Figure 18.10 displays the ACF plots, indicating no autocorrelation in the returns. However, the squared returns exhibit autocorrelation with a gradual decay. It is worth noting that the ACF of the squared returns does not match that of the parent time series.

The empirical test results are presented in Table 18.3. The Jarque–Bera test and the kurtosis values for all four series indicate that the returns deviate from a normal distribution. While the series exhibit significant kurtosis similar to the historical data, they do not precisely match the kurtosis of the historical data. Furthermore, the volatility of the simulated returns does not closely align with that of the historical data. The Hurst and GPH statistics are consistent with those of the actual dataset, and all remain below 0.5, indicating the absence of long memory in volatility.

In Figure 18.11, the QQ plots for Apple, S&P 500 and gold demonstrate a closer alignment with the diagonal line than the Gaussian random walk. However, the simulated USDJPY series does not fit well with the original distribution.

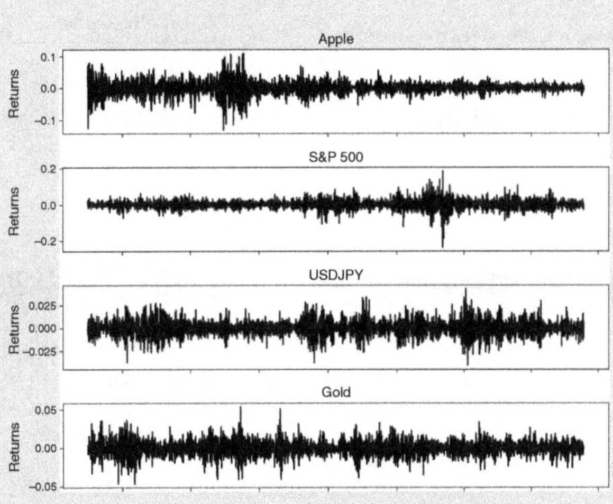

FIGURE 18.9 Simulated returns for a Heston model fitted to the four historical time series.

(Continued)

(Continued)

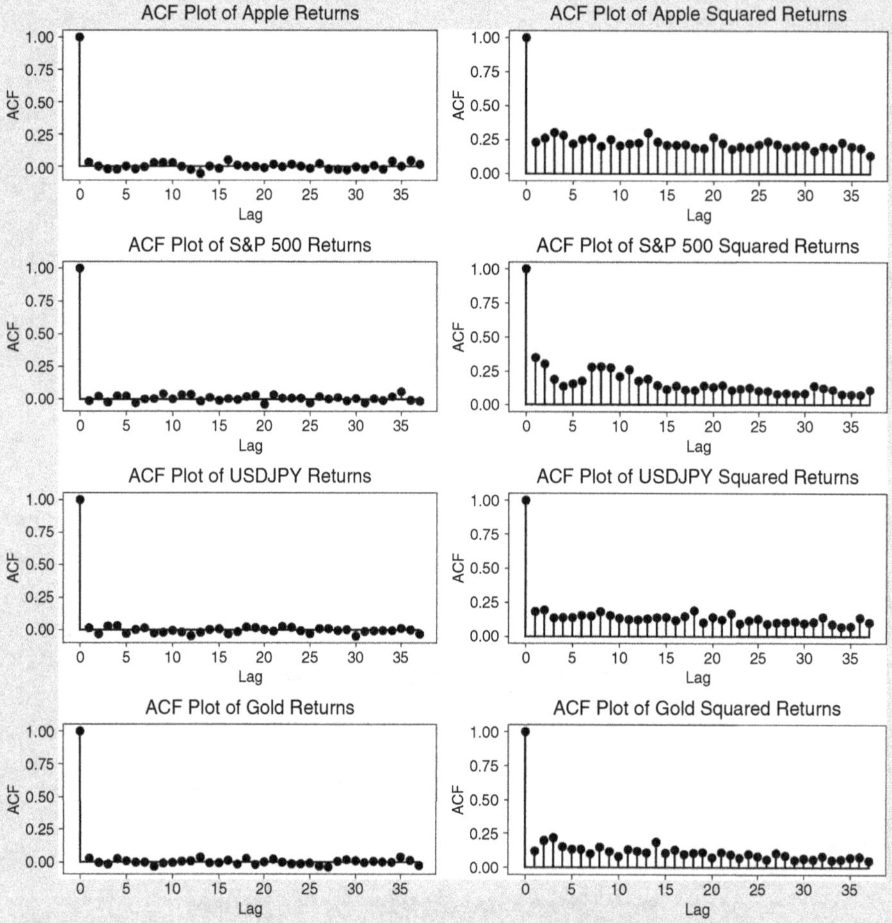

FIGURE 18.10 ACF plots for a Heston model fitted to the four historical time series.

TABLE 18.3 Test Statistics for the Four Simulated Heston Time Series

Label	JB Stat	JB P-value	Vol	Kurt	Skew	Cross-correl	H	GPH
Apple	5938.14	0.0	0.15	5.26	−0.40	−2.53e−04	0.36	0.13
S&P 500	4641.13	0.0	0.12	4.68	−0.24	−4.99e−04	0.31	0.12
USDJPY	5068.15	0.0	0.15	4.90	0.23	−7.36e−05	0.32	0.13
Gold	1010.43	0.0	0.15	2.19	0.03	1.51e−04	0.30	0.13

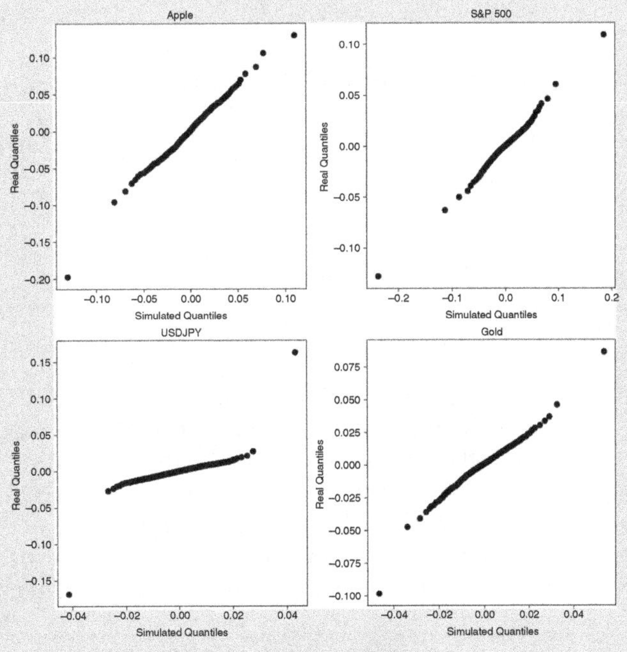

FIGURE 18.11 QQ plots for real vs simulated data for the Heston model.

The ARIMA model encompasses three integer parameters, namely p, d and q, allowing for a significant range of choices when fitting the model to each series. In this case, the ARIMA model is transformed into an ARMA model by setting $d = 0$, assuming stationarity of the mean of the log returns.

A grid search is conducted for both parameters to identify the optimal fitting model within the range of possible values for p and q. The model utilised for the grid search is sourced from the `statsmodel` package. Below is the grid search function utilised for this purpose.

```
def grid_search_arima(returns, pmax, qmax):
    best_aic = np.inf
    best_p = None
    best_q = None
    best_model = None

    for p in range(1, pmax + 1):
        for q in range(1, qmax + 1):

            try:
                model = ARIMA(returns, order=(p, 0, q)).fit()
                if model.aic < best_aic:
                    best_aic = model.aic
                    best_p = p
                    best_q = q
                    best_model = model
            except:
                continue
    return best_model, best_p, best_q
```

Table 18.4 gives the best-fitting model for each series. Once the model has been fitted, it can be simulated by calling the `simulate` function of the model-fitting results object.

(*Continued*)

(*Continued*)

TABLE 18.4 Best-Fit ARMA Parameters

Label	p	q
Apple	4	4
S&P 500	10	8
USDJPY	1	7
Gold	2	6

Figure 18.12 presents the simulated time series. It is important to note that ARIMA models cannot capture heteroscedasticity, resulting in constant volatility for the returns. The ACF plots, displayed in Figure 18.13, exhibit minimal autocorrelation in both the returns and squared returns. However, there is some evidence of short-term autocorrelation at small lags, as expected with autoregressive models.

Table 18.5 outlines the empirical test results. The volatilities align with those of the original series, but the other parameters conform to a Gaussian distribution, displaying minimal kurtosis or skewness. The QQ plots in Figure 18.14 corroborate this observation, demonstrating similarities to those of the Gaussian random walk.

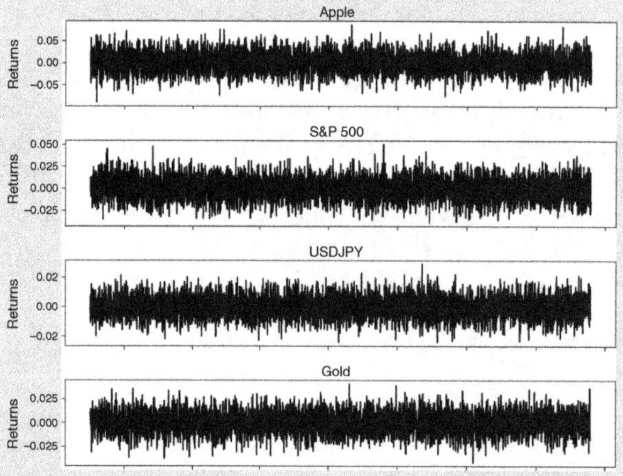

FIGURE 18.12 Simulated returns for an ARIMA model fitted to the four historical time series.

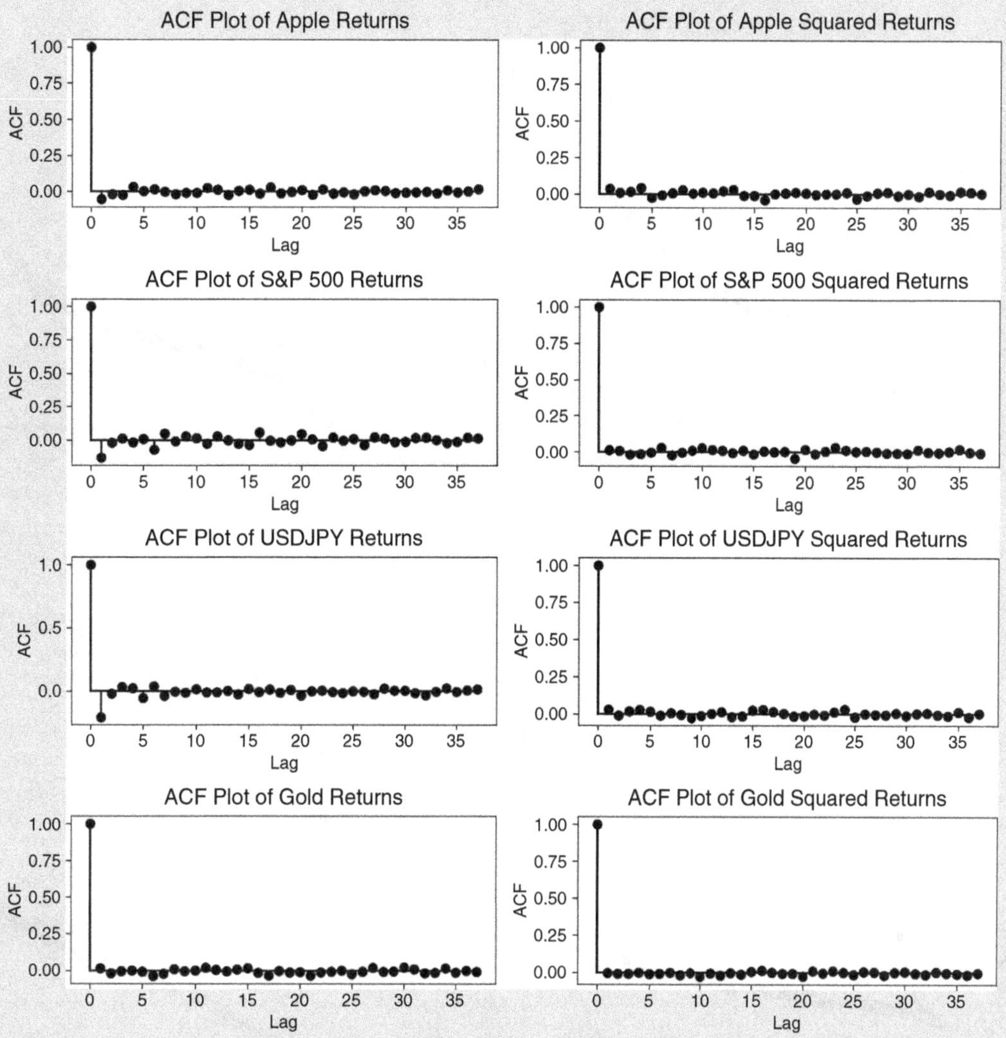

FIGURE 18.13 ACF plots for an ARIMA model fitted to the four historical time series.

TABLE 18.5 Test Statistics for the Four Simulated ARIMA Time Series

Label	JB Stat	JB P-value	Vol	Kurt	Skew	Cross-correl	H	GPH
Apple	1.15	0.56	0.37	0.05	0.03	3.33e-03	0.22	1.30e-02
S&P 500	4.36	0.11	0.20	0.14	0.02	1.51e-04	0.22	1.20e-02
USDJPY	3.42	0.18	0.12	0.09	0.05	-1.43e-05	0.18	4.12e-03
Gold	6.00	0.05	0.18	0.11	-0.06	1.51e-04	0.19	-3.42e-03

(*Continued*)

(*Continued*)

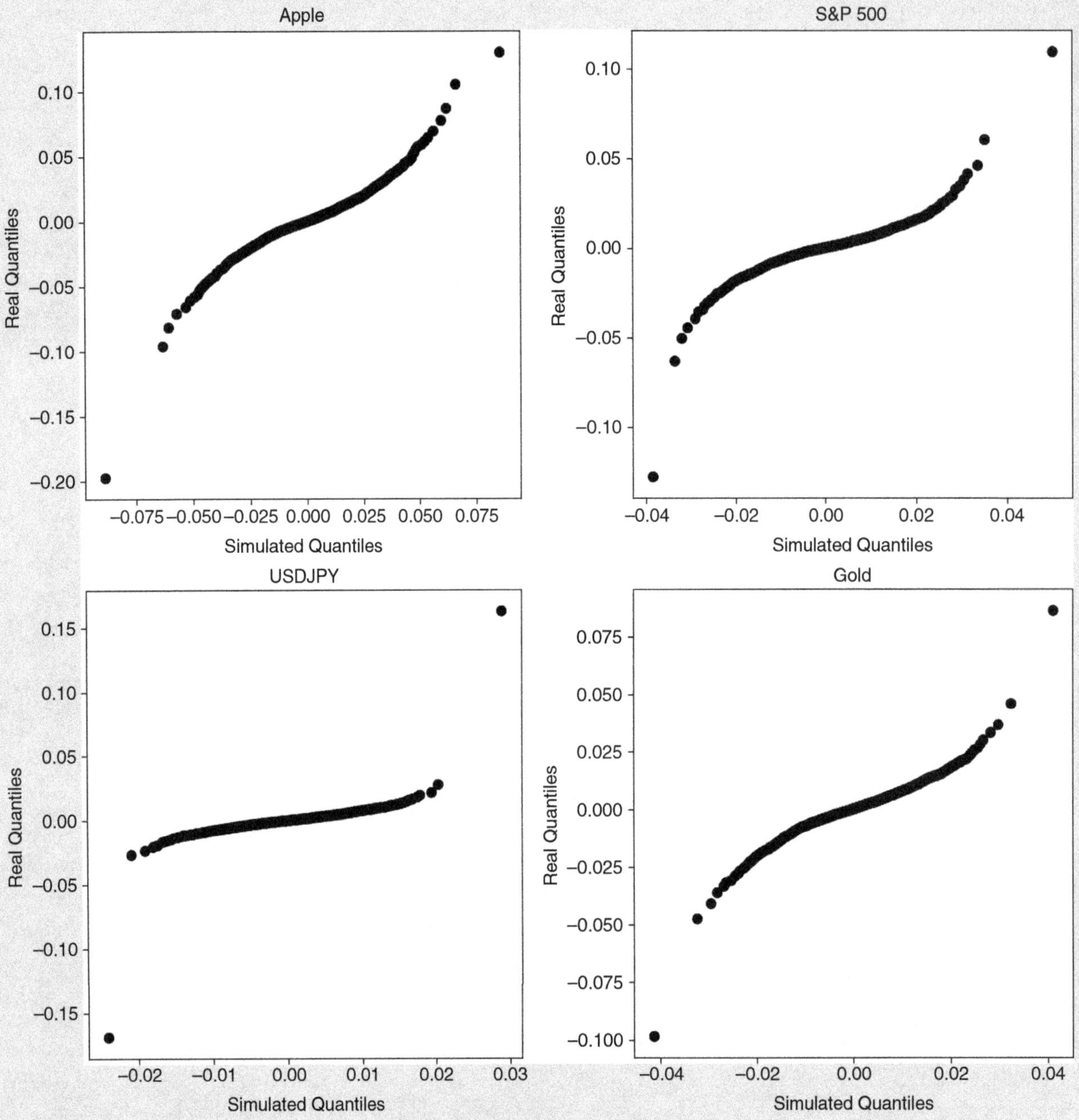

FIGURE 18.14 QQ plots for real vs simulated data for the ARIMA model.

The last classical model to be applied is GARCH, which involves two integer parameters, p and q. In this case, a grid search was conducted to identify the optimal fitting model. The `arch` package was employed to provide the GARCH model, which was fitted using the command `arch_model(returns, vol='Garch', p=p, o=0, q=q).fit()`.

Table 18.6 displays the best-fit models for each series. The simulated returns depicted in Figure 18.15 exhibit clear evidence of volatility clustering. The ACF plots for the GARCH model are shown in Figure 18.16.

There is no indication of autocorrelation in the returns; however, the squared returns display autocorrelation with a gradual decay, which aligns with the observation of volatility clustering.

Empirical test results for the simulated GARCH models are presented in Table 18.7. The Jarque–Bera test reveals that all four models significantly deviate from a Gaussian distribution. The volatility reasonably matches the historical data for all series except for the S&P 500 dataset. While all series demonstrate some level of kurtosis, they do not align with the historical series.

Finally, Figure 18.17 displays the QQ plots, illustrating nearly diagonal lines for both Apple and gold. However, like the other models examined, GARCH struggles to fit the USDJPY data effectively.

TABLE 18.6 Best-Fit GARCH Parameters

Label	p	q
Apple	1	2
S&P 500	2	2
USDJPY	2	6
Gold	1	1

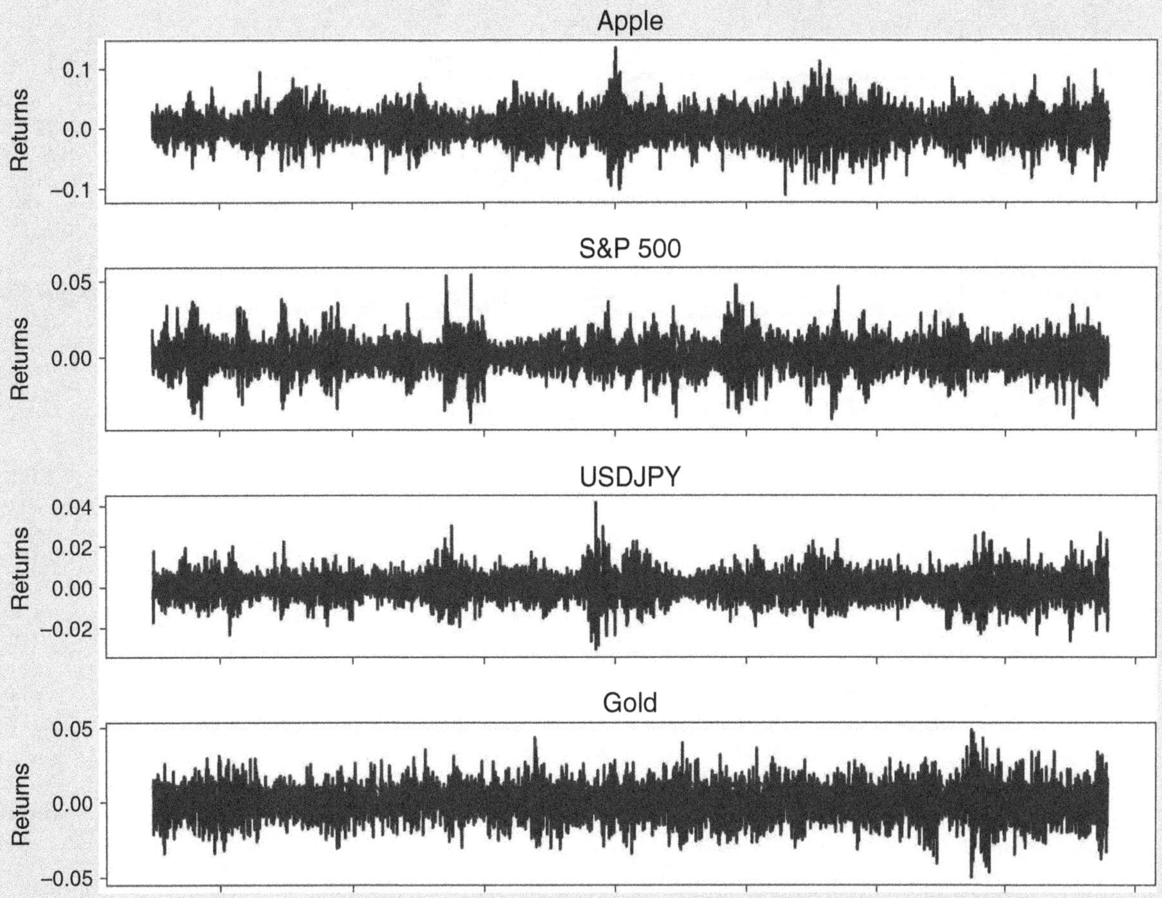

FIGURE 18.15 Simulated returns for a GARCH model fitted to the four historical time series.

(Continued)

(Continued)

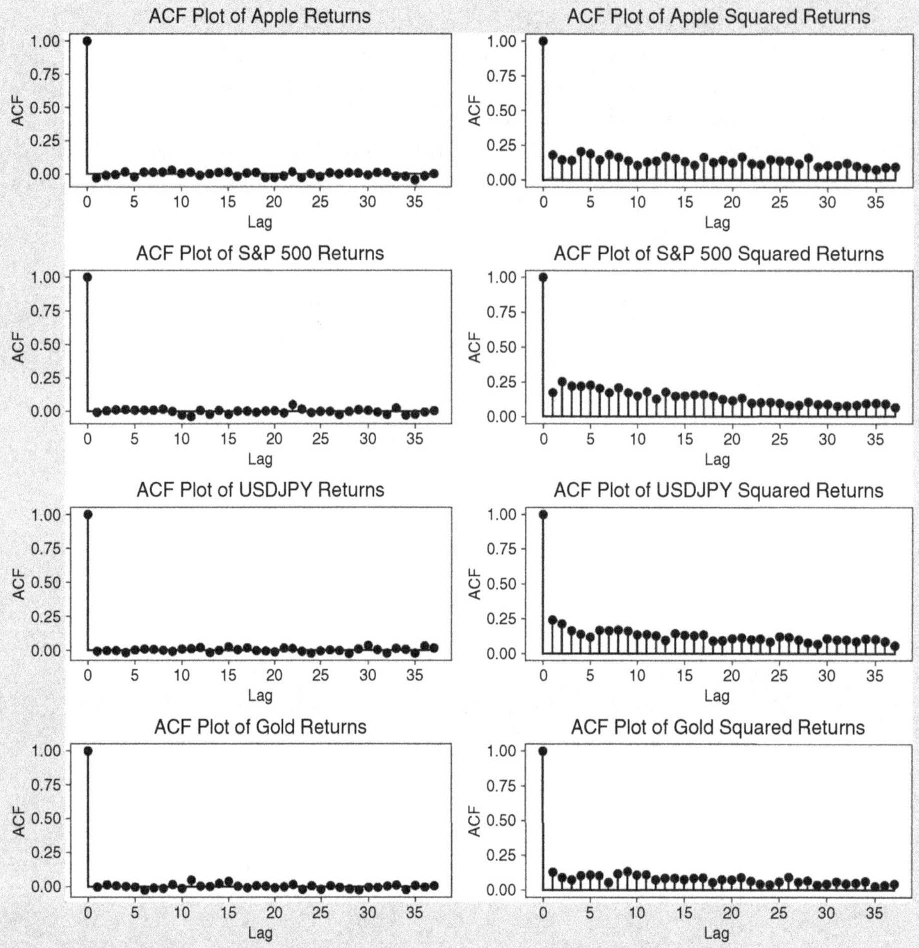

FIGURE 18.16 ACF plots for a GARCH model fitted to the four historical time series.

TABLE 18.7 Test Statistics for the Four Simulated GARCH Time Series

Label	JB Stat	JB P-value	Vol	Kurt	Skew	Cross-correl	H	GPH
Apple	595.27	0.00e+00	0.38	1.68	-0.05	5.47e-05	0.29	0.14
S&P 500	612,518.43	0.00e+00	0.42	54.06	0.05	-2.87e-02	0.41	0.20
USDJPY	1786.09	0.00e+00	0.10	2.92	-0.01	8.22e-05	0.34	0.20
Gold	19.14	6.97e-05	0.18	0.29	-0.03	4.20e-04	0.27	0.09

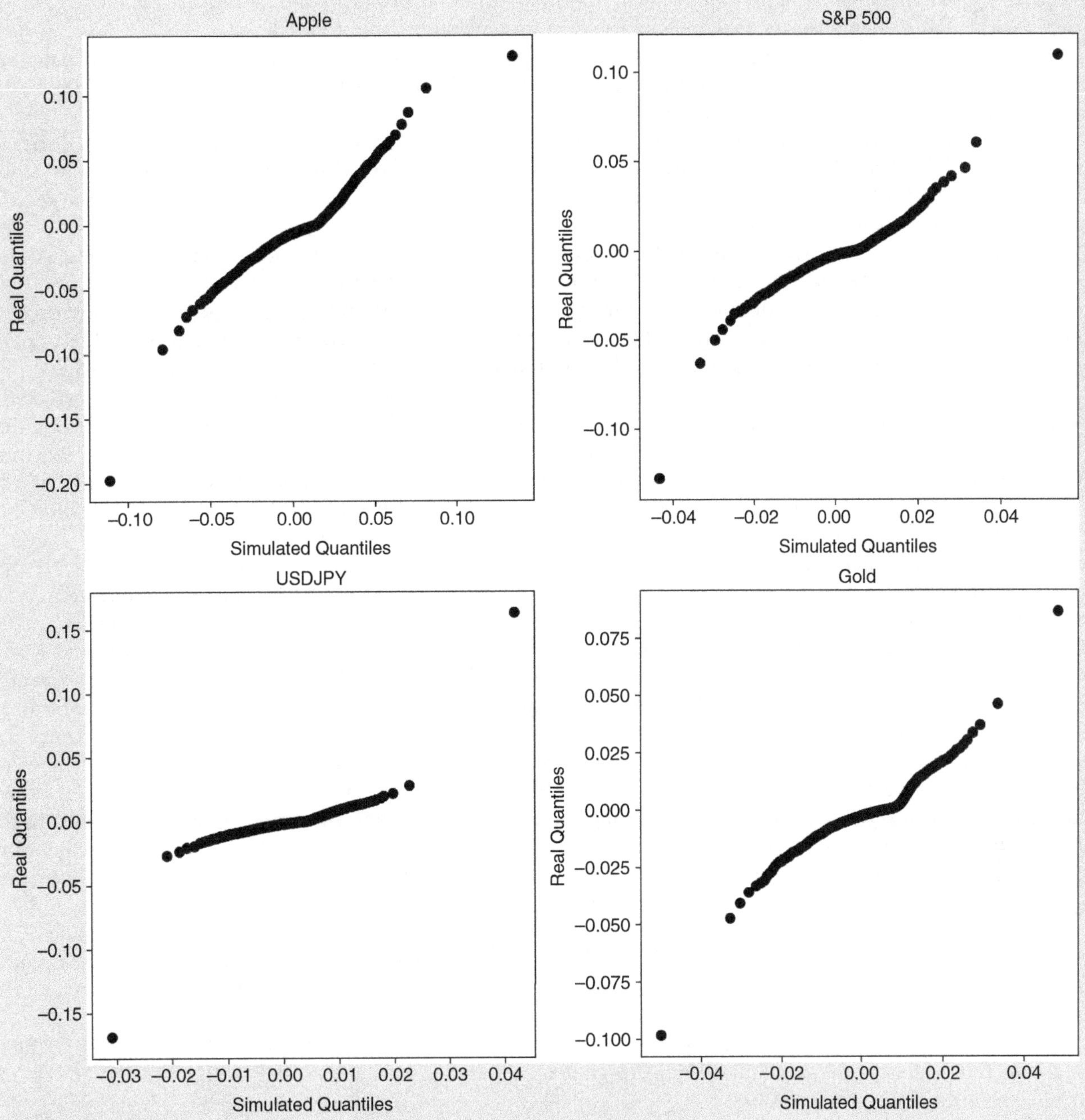

FIGURE 18.17 QQ plots for real vs simulated data for the GARCH model.

Generally, the GARCH and Heston models are the most suitable for accurately representing the original data series. On the other hand, the Gaussian random walk and ARIMA models cannot replicate specific unique characteristics of the data, such as volatility clustering. Nevertheless, none of the four models can fit the USDJPY series, and none fully match all of the statistical properties of the historical data.

18.3.3.1 RBMs Five recent papers have explored the use of RBMs to generate multivariate time-series data: Hernandez and Abad (2018), Kondratyev and Schwarz (2020), Lezmi et al. (2020), Wang (2021) and Lailler and Cohen (2022). As discussed in Section 9.3.2, RBMs and their associated training algorithms, such as contrastive divergence and Gibbs sampling, have largely fallen out of favour in the broader context of deep learning. However, in these works, RBMs demonstrate a compelling use case for generating time-series data.

Kondratyev and Schwarz (2020) employed a standard Bernoulli RBM to generate returns for multivariate time series. The returns series must first be converted into a binary representation after quantisation. Similarly, the RBM-generated samples are also binary and require the quantisation process to be inverted before use.

The authors conducted training on an RBM model using 20 years of FX spot closing prices for four currency pairs: EURUSD, GBPUSD, USDJPY and USDCAD. The RBM comprised 64 visible units, representing four 16-bit binary numbers and 30 hidden units. A small mini-batch size of 10 was utilised during training, but the specific number of training epochs was not specified.

A series of statistical tests were performed to assess the quality of the trained model. These tests demonstrated the ability of the generated samples to reconstruct rank correlation, annualised volatilities and the 1st and 99th percentiles of the training set. Additionally, Kondratyev and Schwarz (2020) illustrated good fits to the original dataset through QQ plots. Furthermore, they observed a direct relationship between the number of Gibbs sampling iterations and the observed autocorrelation, with $k = 1000$ iterations reducing the autocorrelation to 3–5.

In contrast to previous approaches, Hernandez and Abad (2018) utilise an ensemble of RBMs known as the *p-RBM*, where each RBM corresponds to a specific point in time. This modelling structure enables the representation of autocorrelation in time series, which is crucial when working with high-frequency data. The temporal structure is translated into a weight matrix and conditional probability matrices with a block structure. The p-RBM can be trained using k-step contrastive divergence. To demonstrate its effectiveness, the authors apply this model to 5-minute interval data from all 100 stocks in the NASDAQ 100 during June 2017.

On the other hand, Lezmi et al. (2020) propose the utilisation of a market generator to enhance the backtesting process of trading strategies. They explore the application of both RBMs and GANs in generating multivariate time series. Three types of RBMs are employed: a Bernoulli RBM similar to that used by Kondratyev and Schwarz (2020), a Gaussian RBM, and a conditional RBM. The Gaussian RBM has a structure identical to the Bernoulli RBM, except that the visible units are continuous with a linear output while the hidden units remain binary. Consequently, the Gaussian RBM is explicitly designed for continuous data. Both the Bernoulli and Gaussian RBMs are trained using k-step contrastive divergence.

Since the Bernoulli and Gaussian RBMs can only model static relationships between variables, Lezmi et al. (2020) propose using a conditional RBM (Taylor et al., 2007). The conditional RBM (CRBM) incorporates a third conditioning layer into the Gaussian RBM, featuring directed connections to the visible and hidden layers. In the context of time-series generation, the conditioning layer is fed d past values. Although the addition of the conditioning layer slightly modifies the energy expression, the model can still be trained using k-step contrastive divergence (see Taylor et al., 2007, for details).

To evaluate the performance of the three RBM models, Lezmi et al. (2020) test them using 5354 historical daily returns of the S&P 500 and the VIX indexes. The results demonstrate a good match in statistics between the training and simulated data for the Gaussian RBM. Moreover, the CRBM exhibits superior performance in matching the observed short-term autocorrelation.

The Master's thesis by Wang (2021) used a Bernoulli RBM alongside a conditional VAE (CVAE), a GARCH model and filtered historical simulation (FHS) to generate time series using the S&P 500 and VIX indices. He concludes that the CVAE performs best.

Finally, Lailler and Cohen (2022) conducted a benchmark study to assess the capability of RBMs in capturing the properties of multivariate distributions and preserving the dependence structure of variables. While adopting the Bernoulli RBM, the authors introduced two key innovations, namely *average sampling* and *split learning*. Despite employing $k = 1000$ steps of Gibbs sampling as used by Kondratyev and Schwarz (2020), Lailler and Cohen (2022) discovered that the distribution remained noisy. To address this, they implemented a technique where, after k steps of Gibbs sampling, an additional l steps were performed and then averaged to yield the output. In contrast to Kondratyev and Schwarz (2020), the output was defined as $\frac{1}{l}\sum_{i=1}^{l} v^{(k+i)}$ instead of $v^{(k)}$.

In other studies, such as Lezmi et al. (2020), multivariate time series were trained using a single RBM that captured the overall multivariate distribution. However, Lailler and Cohen (2022) proposed employing $N + 1$ RBMs, where N represents the number of assets. These RBMs were explicitly tasked with generating the marginal distributions of each asset and the empirical copula. The output from the copula RBM was utilised to rearrange the marginal RBM outputs, aligning them with the observed dependence structure in the training set. Additionally, the authors highlighted that split learning could be employed to parallelise the training process, significantly reducing computation time for large datasets. Notably, Lailler and Cohen (2022) concluded that combining these techniques resulted in improved results compared to Lezmi et al. (2020).

In conclusion, these five recent papers (Hernandez and Abad, 2018; Kondratyev and Schwarz, 2020; Lezmi et al., 2020; Wang, 2021; Lailler and Cohen, 2022) demonstrate the diverse and innovative applications of RBMs in generating time-series data. Despite RBMs experiencing a decline in popularity within the deep learning community, these studies establish that RBMs can still provide effective solutions for time-series generation.

EXAMPLE 18.3: BERNOULLI RBMS USED TO GENERATE UNIVARIATE TIME SERIES

To evaluate the performance of RBM models in generating time series, four RBM models were trained using the same test data as in previous examples: Apple, S&P 500, USDJPY and gold. The details of this implementation can be found in the Jupyter Notebook `RBM.ipynb`. In the case of a univariate example, the visible layer comprises 16 units, while the hidden layer consists of 30 units. Before training, the input time series is initially quantised into integer values within a range represented by a signed 16-bit integer. The code necessary for quantisation and de-quantisation is provided below.

```
def quantize(arr):
    # Get the range of the input values.
    min_val = arr.min()
    max_val = arr.max()

    # Scale the input values to the range [0, 2**16 - 1].
    arr = (arr - min_val) / (max_val - min_val) * 2**16 - 32768

    # Round the scaled values to the nearest integer.
    arr = np.round(arr)

    return arr.astype(np.int16), max_val, min_val

def dequantize(arr, max_val, min_val):
    # Scale the input values to the range [min_val, max_val].
    arr = (arr+32768) / 2**16 * (max_val - min_val) + min_val

    return arr.astype(np.float32)
```

The maximum range of floating-point values defines the range of integer values of 2^{16}. Once converted to an integer representation, the time series are converted to binary. The code to convert to and from this format is as follows:

```
def int16_to_binary_2d(int16_array):
    binary_array = np.unpackbits(int16_array.view(np.uint8)).reshape(-1, 16)
    return binary_array

def binary_2d_to_int16(binary_array):
    int16_array = np.packbits(binary_array.reshape(-1, 8)).view(np.int16)
    return int16_array
```

The models underwent training for 10,000 epochs with a mini-batch size of 100, which is time-consuming even on a modern GPU card. During inference, 1000 steps of Gibbs sampling were used, as recommended

(Continued)

(Continued)

by Kondratyev and Schwarz (2020). Generating time series is also slow because MCMC is required during inference. The series are generated in batches of 1024 until the entire length of 5031 observations is reached.

In Figure 18.18, the generated returns are displayed and visually compared to the historical returns in Figures 18.1 through 18.4. The results reveal noticeable similarities, particularly in the volatility clustering. Figure 18.19 displays the autocorrelation plots, which can be compared with Figure 18.5. As expected, the generated data shows no autocorrelation but significantly lower autocorrelations of squared returns than the original dataset. The statistical results in Table 18.8 show good agreement on volatility and kurtosis values, which are much closer to the training set than any of the classical models achieved. The skew shows reasonable agreement for gold and the S&P 500 index, but not for Apple or USDJPY. Finally, the QQ plots in Figure 18.20 show close to diagonal lines for Apple, S&P 500 and gold, and much better results for USDJPY than previously seen. Overall, the RBM achieves significantly better results than any classical model.

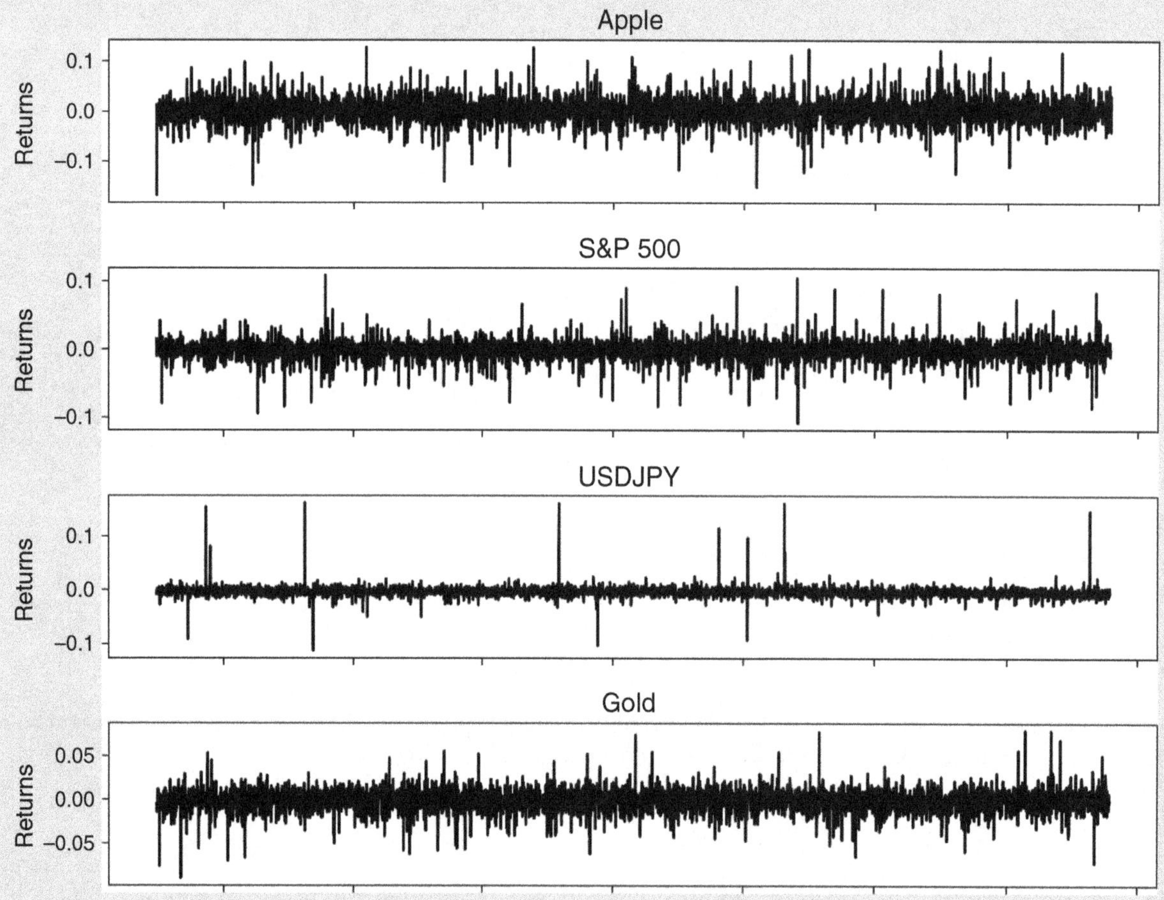

FIGURE 18.18 Simulated returns for an RBM model fitted to the four historical time series.

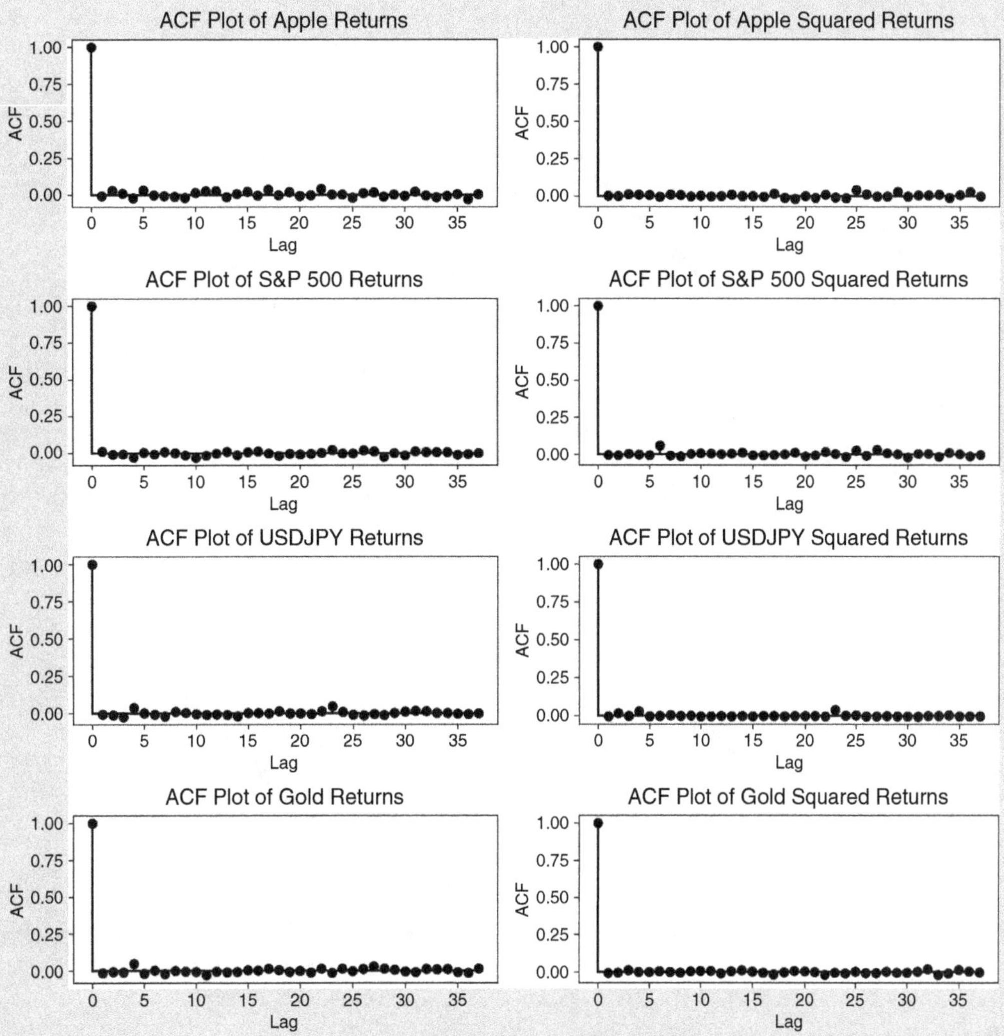

FIGURE 18.19 ACF plots for an RBM model fitted to the four historical time series.

TABLE 18.8 Test Statistics for the Four RBM-Generated Time Series

Label	JB Stat	JB P-value	Vol	Kurt	Skew	Cross-correl	H	GPH
Apple	4.61e+03	0.0	0.38	4.69	0.02	4.70e−03	0.27	0.003
S&P 500	2.93e+04	0.0	0.21	11.77	-0.54	5.79e−04	0.34	0.014
USDJPY	1.79e+06	0.0	0.12	92.23	1.92	−1.66e−03	0.46	0.007
Gold	6.99e+03	0.0	0.19	5.73	-0.34	−1.14e−03	0.29	-0.002

(*Continued*)

(Continued)

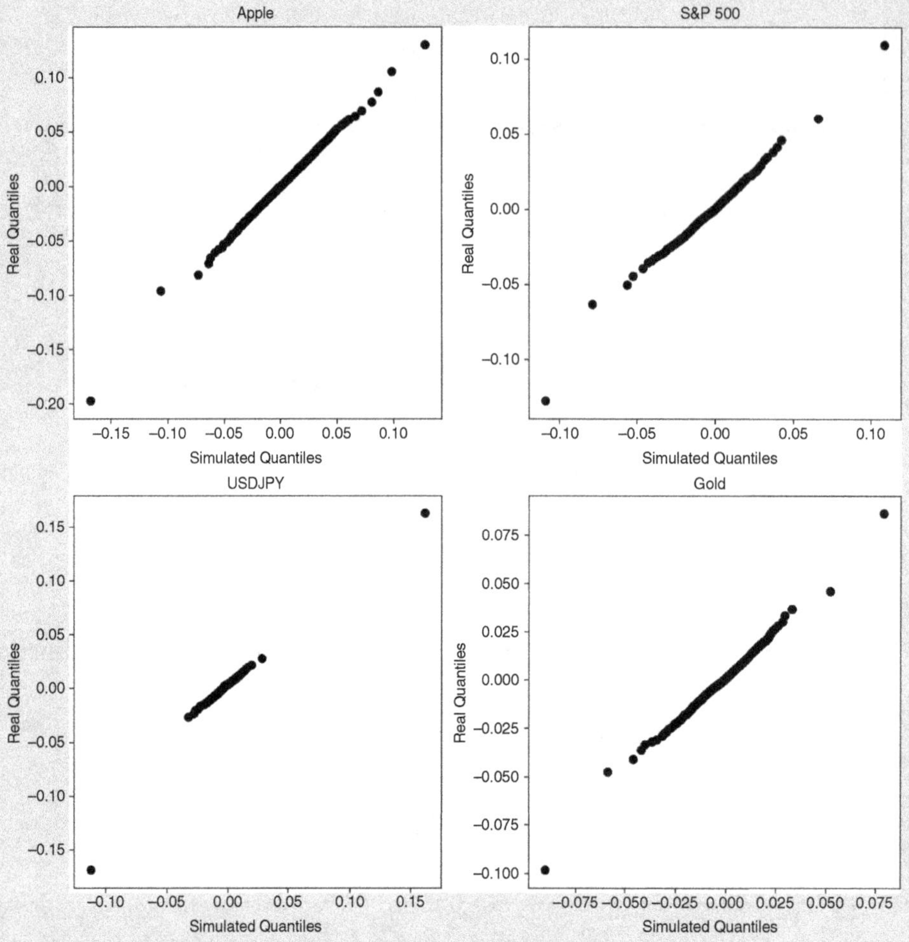

FIGURE 18.20 QQ plots for real vs simulated data for the RBM model.

18.3.3.2 VAEs Section 9.4 discussed VAEs in the context of image generation. Within that domain, two critical challenges were identified: the generation of blurry images and optimisation problems. However, these issues are not necessarily a concern for market data generation. Moreover, as noted by Bühler et al. (2020), VAEs typically require less training data than GANs with adversarial training. Consequently, VAEs have gained attention as a viable technique for generating market data. Five papers – namely Arian et al. (2020), Bühler et al. (2020), Carlsson and Lindgren (2020), Desai et al. (2021) and Wang (2021) – have adopted VAEs for this purpose.

The first consideration is determining the appropriate geometry for the input and output of the VAE. Translating the approach from the unconditional RBM to the VAE, each step in the pathway would be generated independently, resulting in a single linear input and output for a univariate time series. In contrast, the input/output dimension would match the number of time series for a multivariate generator. This approach was adopted by Wang (2021) and potentially by Arian et al. (2020), although the latter is not explicitly stated in the paper.

The simplicity of this approach implies that generating a time series of length N would require N VAE calls. However, it is essential to note that such a VAE could not model the relationship between time steps or capture any autocorrelation effects. Unlike the RBM, where some state is preserved between observations depending on the number of steps of Gibbs sampling, a VAE lacks this property. The weights remain fixed, and all stochasticity is derived from sampling the latent space.

An alternative to using a per-time-step input is to employ a fixed-size sequence as the input, which is the approach adopted by Carlsson and Lindgren (2020). They utilised an input length of 24 for Italian power demand and 120 daily log returns of stocks. Similarly, Desai et al. (2021) employed a fixed-length input in their *TimeVAE* model. Furthermore, they introduced two variant models: one utilising one-dimensional convolutional layers and another termed *interpretable*, which decomposes the time series into level, trend and seasonal components, with separate blocks for each component. While these models can learn the time dependence between steps, the input/output length remains fixed, and there is no apparent method to concatenate segments for generating longer simulated time series.

Conditioning is introduced to address this shortcoming, and the VAE input is expanded to include conditioning variables. A common choice for the conditioning variable is the value of the input immediately preceding the current one. For instance, when modelling univariate time series, Wang (2021) expanded the input from a single variable to two. Additionally, Bühler et al. (2020) utilised a CVAE within the *signatures* framework, as described below.

Rough Paths, Signatures and VAEs Rough paths and signatures are mathematical concepts utilised to study stochastic processes and irregular data. Introduced by mathematician Terry Lyons in the late 1990s, these concepts aimed to extend classical calculus to certain non-smooth, irregular functions arising in stochastic processes, such as Brownian motion (Lyons, 1998).

Rough paths generalise smooth paths (curves in an Euclidean space with continuous derivatives) to deal with irregular functions that lack well-defined derivatives, like Brownian motion. They provide a means to understand these irregular functions' structure and comprehend their properties. Rough paths can be considered enriched versions of ordinary paths with additional algebraic and analytical structures that enable meaningful integration and differentiation.

Signatures play a central role in rough path theory. They uniquely characterise the path as a sequence of iterated integrals of a given path. Essentially, the signature captures the critical information about the rough path, enabling a description of a function's behaviour controlled by the path (e.g., the solution to a differential equation driven by the path).

Rough path theory and signatures have applications in various mathematics areas, including stochastic analysis, partial differential equations and mathematical finance. In recent years, these concepts have also been applied to data analysis and machine learning, where they have been employed to develop new algorithms for analysing time-series data and learning from irregular, non-smooth datasets (Chevyrev and Kormilitzin, 2016).

Mathematically, a path's signature is defined in terms of iterated integrals. Let $X : [0, T] \to \mathbb{R}^d$ be a continuous path in a d-dimensional Euclidean space $\mathbb{R}^d$ over an interval $[0, T]$. The signature of path X is a sequence of iterated integrals, denoted as

$$\mathbb{X}_T^{<\infty} := \left(1, \mathbb{X}_t^1, \ldots, \mathbb{X}_T^n, \ldots\right), \tag{18.11}$$

where n is a non-negative integer and each $\mathbb{X}^n(X)$ is an n-fold iterated integral of path X.

The iterated integrals are defined recursively. For a single-fold iterated integral ($n = 1$), we have

$$\mathbb{X}_T^n := \int 0 < u_1 < \cdots < u_k < TdX_{u_1} \otimes \cdots \otimes dX_{u_k} \in \left(\mathbb{R}^d\right)^{\otimes n}, \tag{18.12}$$

where $dX^i(s)$ represents the differential of the ith component of path X.

It is essential to note that the signature is an infinite sequence of tensors (the iterated integrals) that grows in size as n increases. In practice, however, truncating the signature at a certain level often suffices, depending on the desired accuracy and computational constraints (Chevyrev and Kormilitzin, 2016). The truncated signature of order N is given by

$$\mathbb{X}_T^{\leq N} := \left(1, \mathbb{X}_t^1, \ldots, \mathbb{X}_T^N\right). \tag{18.13}$$

The log signature is often used and defined by

$$\log \mathbb{X}_T^{<\infty} := -\mathbb{X}_T^{<\infty} + \frac{1}{2}\left(\mathbb{X}_T^{<\infty}\right)^{\otimes 2} - \frac{1}{3}\left(\mathbb{X}_T^{<\infty}\right)^{\otimes 3} + \cdots + (-1)^n \frac{1}{n}\left(\mathbb{X}_T^{<\infty}\right)^{\otimes n} + \cdots. \tag{18.14}$$

Given that the logarithm is an invertible transformation, no information is lost when making this transformation.

Bühler et al. (2020) also apply the lead–lag or *Hoff* transformation as defined by Flint et al. (2016). This transformation can capture the volatility of a path and this led Bühler et al. (2020) to adopt it for data series at weekly and monthly frequencies. The lead–lag transformation of $\{X_{t_i}\}_{t_i \in D}$ is defined by

$$X_t^D = \left(X^{D,b}, X^{D,f}\right)$$

$$:= \begin{cases} \left(X_{t_k}, X_{t_{k+1}}\right) & t \in \left[\frac{2k}{2nT}, \frac{2k+1}{2nT}\right] \\ \left(X_{t_k}, X_{t_{k+1}} + 2(t-(2k+1))\left(X_{t_{k+2}} - X_{t_{k+1}}\right)\right) & t \in \left[\frac{2k+1}{2nT}, \frac{2k+\frac{3}{2}}{2nT}\right], \\ \left(X_{t_k} + 2\left(t - \left(2k + \frac{3}{2}\right)\right)\left(X_{t_{k+1}} - X_{t_k}\right), X_{t_{k+2}}\right) & t \in \left[\frac{2k+\frac{3}{2}}{2nT}, \frac{2k+2}{2nT}\right] \end{cases} \tag{18.15}$$

where $X^{D,b}$ is the lag component, $X^{D,f}$ is the lead component, $\{X_{t_i}\}_{t_i \in D} \subset \mathbb{R}^d$ is a d-dimensional sample and $D = \{t_i\}_{i=0}^n \subset [0, T]$ is a time partition.

Bühler et al. (2020) introduced a significant innovation by utilising the log-signature transformation as a pre- and postprocessing step in their work. Additionally, they applied the lead–lag transformation to weekly and monthly data. The model architecture employed in their study is a CVAE with a single hidden layer consisting of 50 units and a latent space of dimension 8. The authors considered conditioning on several variables, including the instantaneous volatility at the same time as the path, the level of the index at the start of the path and the log signature of the previous path. In order to assess the model's performance, signatures in the form of two-sample tests – the maximum mean discrepancy (MMD) test and the Kolmogorov–Smirnov test (Bühler, 2020) – were used.

In conclusion, rough paths and signatures are powerful mathematical tools for analysing stochastic processes and irregular data. By extending classical calculus to encompass non-smooth, irregular functions, they offer a means to comprehend the structure and properties of such functions. In this regard, Bühler et al. (2020) successfully applied these tools as a preprocessing step for a CVAE generative model for time series.

EXAMPLE 18.4: CVAE

CVAE models were trained for each of the four univariate time series mentioned earlier in this chapter: Apple, S&P 500, USDJPY and gold. The CVAE model employed a single hidden layer comprising 64 units with an eight-dimensional latent space. Furthermore, the model was conditioned on the previous training point. The following code presents the model implementation:

```
class CVAE(nn.Module):
    def __init__(self, input_size, hidden_size, latent_size,
                 condition_size):
        super(CVAE, self).__init__()
        self.encoder = nn.Sequential(
```

```
            nn.Linear(input_size + condition_size, hidden_size),
            nn.LeakyReLU(),
            nn.Linear(hidden_size, latent_size * 2)
        )
        self.decoder = nn.Sequential(
            nn.Linear(latent_size + condition_size, hidden_size),
            nn.LeakyReLU(),
            nn.Linear(hidden_size, input_size),
        )

    def reparameterize(self, mu, log_var):
        std = torch.exp(0.5 * log_var)
        eps = torch.randn_like(std)
        return mu + eps * std

    def forward(self, x, condition):
        h = torch.cat([x, condition], -1)
        latent_params = self.encoder(h)
        mu, log_var = latent_params.chunk(2, dim=-1)
        z = self.reparameterize(mu, log_var)
        z_cond = torch.cat([z, condition], -1)
        return self.decoder(z_cond), mu, log_var
```

Each model was trained for 1000 epochs using a learning rate of 0.0001. Once training was complete, time series of the same length as the training data were generated, with each simulated value conditioned on the previous one.

The simulated returns are depicted in Figure 18.21. While the returns exhibit some evidence of volatility clustering, they do not match the results obtained by the RBM model. The ACF plots for the returns are presented in Figure 18.22. We observe a small amount of autocorrelation at lag one in both the return and squared return series for Apple, S&P 500 and USDJPY, suggesting an impact from the conditioning. The statistical tests in Table 18.9 indicate a good fit for the volatility, but the present kurtosis cannot match the input data. The QQ plots in Figure 18.23 demonstrate improved results compared to the classical models, but they are not as good as those obtained from the RBM model.

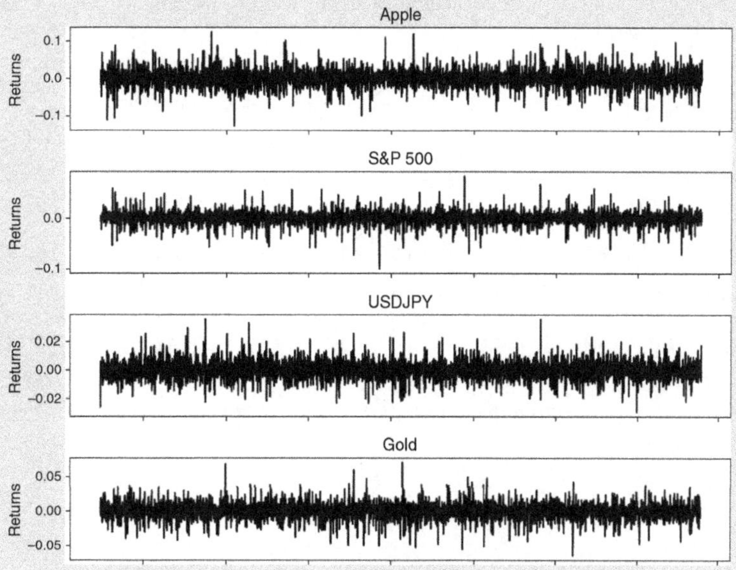

FIGURE 18.21 Simulated returns for a CVAE model fitted to the four historical time series.

(*Continued*)

(*Continued*)

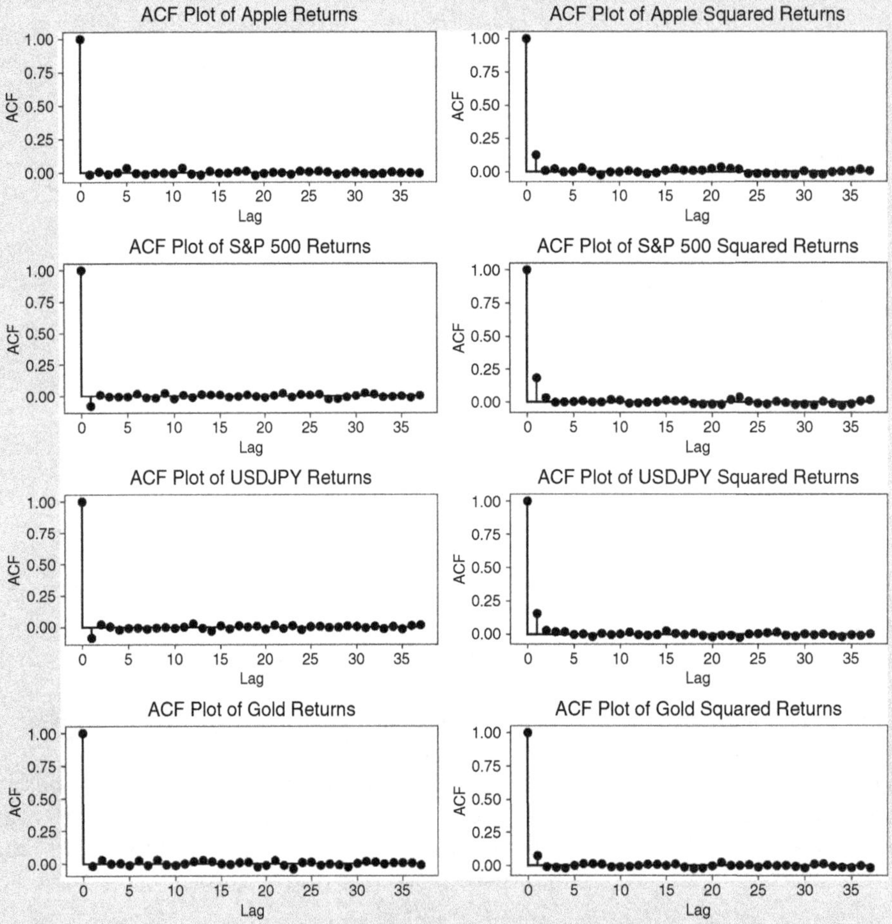

FIGURE 18.22 ACF plots for a CVAE model fitted to the four historical time series.

TABLE 18.9 Test Statistics for the Four CVAE-Generated Time Series

Label	JB Stat	JB P-value	Vol	Kurt	Skew	Cross-correl	H	GPH
Apple	2012.41	0.0	0.32	3.09	0.07	-9.85e-04	0.28	0.05
S&P 500	3633.12	0.0	0.16	4.11	-0.34	-1.13e-03	0.28	0.12
USDJPY	3730.22	0.0	0.09	4.21	0.11	-2.21e-05	0.32	0.16
Gold	1132.14	0.0	0.16	2.26	-0.27	-2.70e-04	0.27	0.02

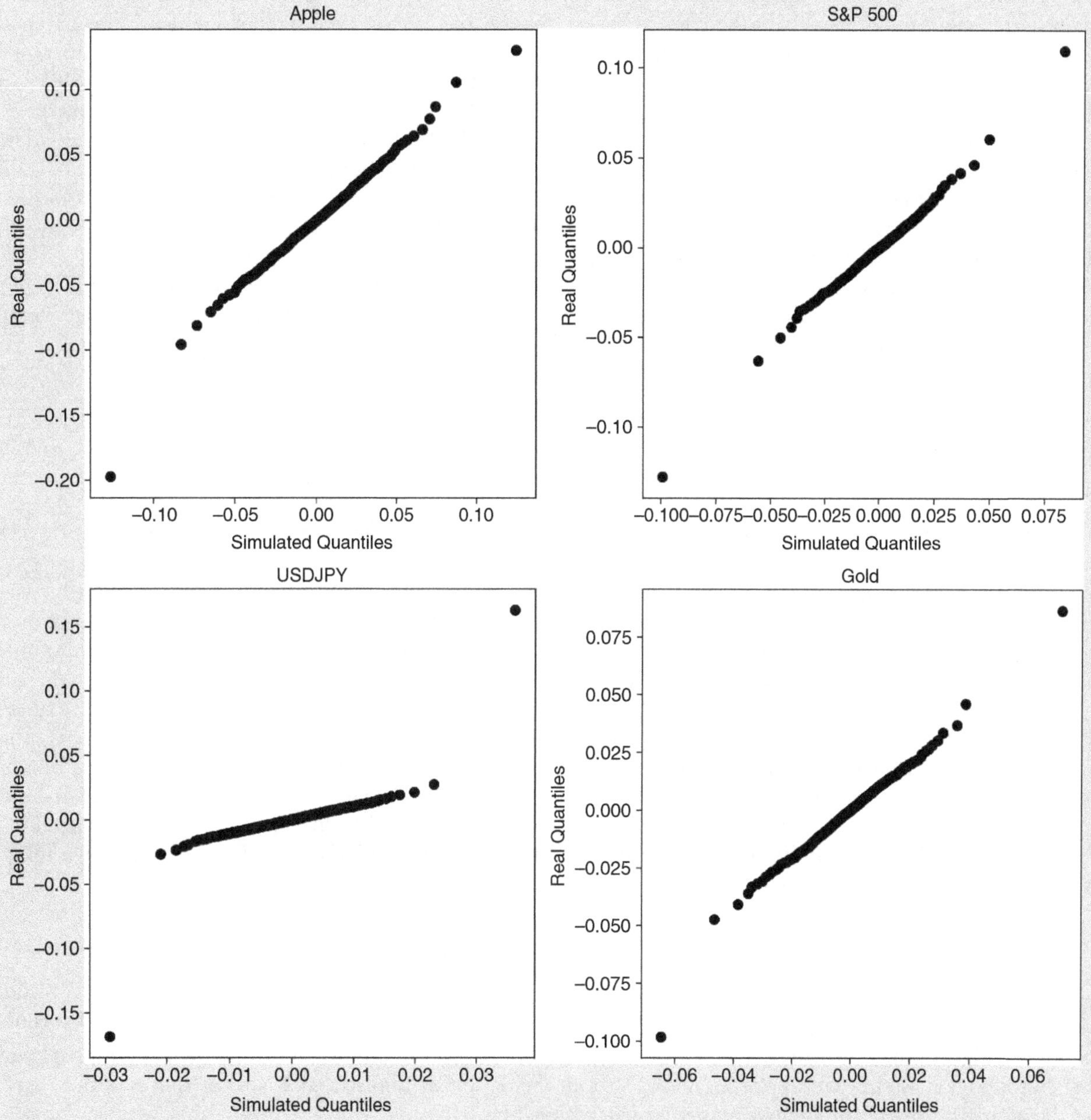

FIGURE 18.23 QQ plots for real vs simulated data for the CVAE model.

18.3.3.3 GANs Due to their impressive capacity to learn and mimic data distributions, GANs have shown promise for time-series data synthesis. This section contains a comprehensive literature review, encapsulating a broad selection of research studies that have made notable contributions to applying GANs in this domain. These include the works of Fu et al. (2019), Lin et al. (2019), Pardo (2019), Takahashi et al. (2019), Wiese et al. (2019), Yoon et al. (2019), Ni et al. (2020), Xu et al. (2020), Coletta et al. (2021), Flaig and Junike (2021), Jeha et al. (2021), Koshiyama et al. (2021), Moritz et al. (2021), Storchan et al. (2021), Cont et al. (2022), Geissler et al. (2022), Li et al. (2022) and Rusnak (2022). This thematic review centres around crucial model choices, such as loss function selection, conditioning, incorporation of convolutional layers, utilisation of autoregressive models, choice of layer normalisation, use of embedding layers, the adoption of the transformer architecture and their respective financial applications.

Loss Functions. Various loss functions have been applied to the GAN time-series models, although almost all of them derive from GAN models in the context of images. Of the 19 surveyed papers, eight use the adversarial loss equation, Equation (9.100), from Goodfellow et al. (2014). These are biased towards the earlier papers in the series from 2019, including Fu et al. (2019), Takahashi et al. (2019), Wiese et al. (2019), Yoon et al. (2019) and Koshiyama et al. (2021). Three later papers also use the original loss function: Lezmi et al. (2020), Coletta et al. (2021) and Flaig and Junike (2021). Wasserstein loss, Equation (9.102) (Arjovsky et al., 2017), is the second most popular choice of loss function, with seven papers applying it: Pardo (2019), Lin et al. (2019), Lezmi et al. (2020), Ni et al. (2020), Moritz et al. (2021), Storchan et al. (2021) and Rusnak (2022). Two groups of authors use the least-squares *LSGAN* loss, as proposed by Mao et al. (2016), while Geissler et al. (2022) apply the hinge loss, first applied in the *geometric GAN* by Lim and Ye (2017).

Pardo (2019) also applies the *relativistic average discriminator*. The relativistic average discriminator (RAD) is a variant of the original GAN discriminator that uses a relativistic average to measure the difference between real and generated samples. The loss function used in RAD is given by

$$\begin{aligned} L_{RAD} &= -\frac{1}{2}\mathbb{E}_{x\sim p_{\text{data}}}[\log(D(x) - \mathbb{E}_{z\sim p_z}[D(G(z))])] \\ &\quad -\frac{1}{2}\mathbb{E}_{z\sim p_z}[\log(D(G(z)) - \mathbb{E}_{x\sim p_{\text{data}}}[D(x)])], \end{aligned} \tag{18.16}$$

where $D(x)$ is the discriminator output for real sample x, $G(z)$ is the generator output for noise input z and $\mathbb{E}$ denotes expectation. The first term measures the probability that a real sample is classified as real, while the second term measures the probability that a generated sample is classified as real. The relativistic average in RAD involves subtracting the expected value of discriminator output on generated samples from the discriminator output on real samples, and vice versa. This approach aims to make the discriminator more robust to mode collapse and improve its ability to distinguish between real and generated samples.

Xu et al. (2020) introduce a new objective function in their COT-GAN model. The adversarial objective function employed by COT-GAN incorporates concepts from optimal transport theory. The Wasserstein distance is utilised to measure the distance between distributions, which is approximated using the Sinkhorn algorithm. The Sinkhorn algorithm, an iterative method, computes an approximation of the optimal transport plan between two distributions by iteratively scaling row and column sums until convergence. This algorithm enables efficient computation of the Wasserstein distance, which can be computationally intensive without regularisation. The final objective function for COT-GAN can be expressed as follows:

$$\hat{W}^{c,K_\phi,\epsilon}_{\text{mix},L}(\hat{x}, \hat{x}', \hat{y}_\theta, \hat{y}'_\theta) - \lambda p^\phi_M(\hat{x}), \tag{18.17}$$

where $\hat{x}$ and $\hat{x}'$ are empirical measures corresponding to two samples of the dataset, $\hat{y}_\theta$ and $\hat{y}'_\theta$ are those corresponding to two samples from ν_θ, K_ϕ is a cost function parameterised by ϕ, L is a fixed number of iterations for running the Sinkhorn algorithm, ϵ controls the strength of regularisation in the Sinkhorn algorithm, $p^\phi_M(\hat{x})$ is a penalty term that encourages consistency with prior knowledge about the data distribution and λ is a positive constant that balances these terms. The *mixed Sinkhorn divergence* is defined by

$$\widehat{\mathcal{W}}^{\text{mix}}_{c,\epsilon}\left(\hat{\mathbf{x}}, \hat{\mathbf{x}}', \hat{\mathbf{y}}_\theta, \hat{\mathbf{y}}'_\theta\right) := \mathcal{W}_{c,\epsilon}\left(\hat{\mathbf{x}}, \hat{\mathbf{y}}_\theta\right) + \mathcal{W}_{c,\epsilon}\left(\hat{\mathbf{x}}', \hat{\mathbf{y}}'_\theta\right) - \mathcal{W}_{c,\epsilon}\left(\hat{\mathbf{x}}, \hat{\mathbf{x}}'\right) - \mathcal{W}_{c,\epsilon}\left(\hat{\mathbf{y}}_\theta, \hat{\mathbf{y}}'_\theta\right). \tag{18.18}$$

Finally, in the Tail-GAN model (Cont et al., 2022), the generator G and the discriminator D are jointly trained within a bi-level optimisation framework. The objective is to minimise a specific objective function defined in the bi-level optimisation problem. Given the complexity of these constrained optimisation problems, the Lagrangian relaxation method is employed to transform the original problem into a max–min game between D and G. This transformation relies on the dual parameter λ, and it is demonstrated that, under certain conditions, this game is equivalent to the original bi-level problem. A sample-based version of the loss function is introduced in practical settings, where the actual distribution P_r is unavailable. This sample-based loss function, in comparison to the loss functions used in standard GANs and Wasserstein GANs, exhibits greater sensitivity to tail risk and provides improved approximations of α-ES (expected shortfall) and α-VaR values. The final expression of the sample-based loss function is as follows:

$$\max_{D \in \mathcal{D}} \min_{G \in \mathcal{G}} \frac{1}{Kn} \sum_{k=1}^{K} \sum_{j=1}^{n} \left[S_\alpha D(\Pi_k(q_i); i \in [n], \Pi_k(p_j)) - \lambda S_\alpha D(\Pi_k(p_i); i \in [n], \Pi_k(p_j)) \right], \tag{18.19}$$

where $p_i, p_j \sim Pr$, $q_i \sim P_G$ and S_α is the score function (Acerbi and Szekely, 2014) defined by

$$S_\alpha(v, e, x) = \frac{W_\alpha}{2} \left(1_{\{x \le v\}} - \alpha\right) \left(x^2 - v^2\right) + 1_{\{x \le v\}} e(v - x) + \alpha e \left(\frac{e}{2} - v\right),$$
$$\text{with } \frac{\text{ES}_\alpha(\mu)}{\text{VaR}_\alpha(\mu)} \ge W_\alpha \ge 1. \tag{18.20}$$

In conclusion, the reviewed studies have employed various loss functions to improve the performance of GAN-based time-series models. Adversarial loss and Wasserstein loss have emerged as the most commonly used choices. Another notable trend is the adoption of custom objective functions, as demonstrated in Tail-GAN, which focuses on addressing specific requirements of the model.

Conditioning and Autoregression. Time series represent sequential data; thus, incorporating temporal dependence is crucial for generative models. A model could not capture the observed autocorrelation in returns or squared returns without considering temporality. However, traditional GANs, initially developed for image generation, need a built-in concept of time. To address this limitation, researchers have employed one of two approaches: conditional GANs and autoregressive models integrated within the GAN architecture. These methods enable incorporating sequential characteristics into the generation process, allowing the model to capture the temporal dynamics of time-series data.

The most prevalent approach for incorporating conditioning in time-series generation is the utilisation of CGANs, as discussed in Section 9.5.3 and introduced by Mirza and Osindero (2014). A common strategy when generating a time-series segment is to employ the previous section as conditioning. For instance, Fu et al. (2019) pass the previous time-series values as conditioning. On the other hand, Koshiyama et al. (2021) utilise a more extended sequence of 252 previous observations, corresponding to 1 year of daily data, as conditioning. In the case of Pardo (2019), conditioning is performed using a sequence that matches the length of the generated sequence. Meanwhile, Lezmi et al. (2020) adopt a fixed length of 20 previous points for conditioning. Jeha et al. (2021) condition on 64 previous time-series values in their *PSA-GAN-C* model. Additionally, Geissler et al. (2022) employ 18 conditioning points in their economic scenario generation model. As discussed later, Ni et al. (2020) incorporate a signature transformation into their model and, therefore, condition on the signature of the last segment of the time series. In the work of Coletta et al. (2021), the model directly generates order data and is conditioned on N previous tuples of order data concatenated with additional features. Lastly, Rusnak (2022) utilises conditioning to incorporate prior series and macroeconomic data into the generation of synthetic financial returns, enabling the generation of data that reflects specific market conditions or economic indicators.

A few researchers have incorporated autoregressive units into GAN models. As discussed later, *TimeGAN* (Yoon et al., 2019) utilises RNNs to create an embedding from the input time series. In the case of DOPPELGANGER (Lin et al., 2019), RNNs are employed to generate time-series data iteratively, one record at a time. However, batch generation is introduced to address the RNN's challenge of capturing temporal correlations over long sequences, where the RNN generates multiple records during each iteration. Additionally, to account for important timestamps, two alternatives are employed: assuming equally spaced timestamps or using the initial timestamp of each sample along with the inter-arrival times between consecutive records as additional data. In the WGAN model proposed by Moritz et al. (2021), both the generator and discriminator utilise vanilla LSTM units. These LSTM units contain a single hidden layer and an output layer for predictions. The LSTM units, designed with a 50 timestep to align with the widely used 50-day moving average in stock trading, aim to learn from past observations to forecast future values in univariate time-series forecasting problems. Although bidirectional LSTM was considered, the authors opted for unidirectional LSTM to prevent the model from incorporating noise from future data, as their task required learning solely from past information.

In conclusion, modelling time-series data in generative models requires careful consideration of temporal dependencies.

Convolution. In the context of images and hence the original context of GANs, two-dimensional convolutional layers are standard. One-dimensional convolutions are also common in sequence applications such as natural language and audio processing and, hence, an obvious choice for time-series models. A number of authors have adopted one-dimensional convolutions in generator and discriminator architectures, including Takahashi et al. (2019), Lezmi et al. (2020), Jeha et al. (2021), Geissler et al. (2022) and Li et al. (2022).

Wiese et al. (2019) adopt the more complex temporal convolutional network (TCN) architecture designed initially by Bai et al. (2018). TCNs are convolutional architectures that have demonstrated their proficiency in various sequence-related modelling tasks, particularly for capturing long-range dependencies in sequences more effectively than recurrent architectures like LSTM or GRU. They alleviate the problem of vanishing and exploding gradients commonly encountered in RNNs. The essential component of TCNs is the dilated causal convolution. The causal convolution ensures that the output is dependent solely on past sequence elements, while dilated convolutions, often referred to as 'convolutions with holes', enhance the ability to model long-range dependencies by using increasing dilations in each layer.

The primary building block of the convolutional layer is the dilated causal convolutional operator, defined as

$$(W *^D X)_{m,t} = \sum_{i=1}^{K} \sum_{j=1}^{N_I} W_{i,j,m} \cdot X_{j,t-D(K-i)}, \tag{18.21}$$

where X is an N_I-variate sequence of length T and W is a tensor, D is the dilation factor, K is the kernel size and m ranges from 1 to N_O.

The vanilla TCN involves the composition of dilated causal convolutional layers with activation functions. Additionally, TCNs can be augmented with skip connections, enabling the incorporation of residual connections. However, TCNs have a notable limitation, as the length of the time series that can be processed is constrained by the receptive field size of the TCN. Although several extensions have been proposed to address this issue, scaling up the network to model long-range dependencies can pose computational bottlenecks and difficulties in training meaningful models.

In conclusion, TCNs have demonstrated potential in modelling time series. However, TCNs have limitations, notably the constraint on the time-series length that can be processed based on the TCN's receptive field size.

Normalisation. In computer vision applications, convolutional layers are often combined with batch normalisation. At the same time, spectral normalisation is used in conjunction with the Wasserstein loss to enforce the 1-Lipschitz condition (see Section 9.5.2.3). However, among the reviewed papers, only a few models incorporate layer normalisation. Takahashi et al. (2019) observed that batch normalisation was ineffective, resulting in highly fluctuating and strongly autocorrelated generated time series that did not resemble financial time series. Only Geissler et al. (2022) employed batch normalisation among the reviewed papers.

Spectral normalisation was utilised in three papers: Jeha et al. (2021), Geissler et al. (2022) and Rusnak (2022). Lin et al. (2019) introduced a bespoke approach called 'auto-normalisation'. This technique deviates from conventional feature normalisation in two ways. Firstly, it normalises each sample individually instead of normalising the entire dataset collectively. Secondly, it treats each time series's maximum and minimum values as random variables to be learned and generated. This approach ensures that time series have the same range during generation, effectively addressing the mode collapse problem.

Embedding. Embedding techniques have been employed in only two reviewed papers to project time-series data into a different embedding space before applying the GAN model. As mentioned, Yoon et al. (2019) introduce embedding and recovery functions within adversarial networks, enabling mappings between the feature and latent spaces. The embedding function, implemented as a recurrent network, transforms static and temporal features into latent codes. The recovery function, implemented as a feedforward network, maps these codes back to their original features. Both functions can be parameterised using any autoregressive architecture that maintains a causal ordering.

Transformers. The prevalence of transformer architectures in recent advancements in deep learning has influenced the development of GAN-based models, with four papers incorporating attention layers. In their MAS-GAN model, Storchan et al. (2021) utilise a one-dimensional self-attention layer. The PSA-GAN model proposed by Jeha et al. (2021) incorporates a central block that comprises a residual self-attention layer, leaky ReLU, spectral norm and convolution. It is noteworthy that Jeha et al. (2021) also employ the progressive, growing technique introduced in Karras et al. (2018). In an innovative approach, Li et al. (2022) adapt image-based concepts to time-series data by treating it as a tuple (C × H × W), dividing the sequence into multiple patches, applying positional encoding to each patch and employing it in a transformer GAN model. This represents the first known implementation of such an approach in the literature.

Financial Applications. Not all examined papers apply their time-series models to financial applications. Among those, the most common is modelling stock and stock index prices, primarily focusing on daily frequency and utilising the S&P 500 dataset. Several papers, such as Fu et al. (2019), Pardo (2019), Takahashi et al. (2019), Wiese et al. (2019), Yoon et al. (2019), Lezmi et al. (2020), Ni et al. (2020), Koshiyama et al. (2021) and Rusnak (2022), employ stock and stock index data. Additionally, VIX data is utilised by Pardo (2019), Lezmi et al. (2020) and Rusnak (2022). Only two papers, namely Koshiyama et al. (2021) and Rusnak (2022), focus on currency data, with the latter also incorporating bond data. Bitcoin time series is employed by Moritz et al. (2021) to train their model. Furthermore, Coletta et al. (2021) and Storchan et al. (2021) apply GANs in the context of multi-agent simulation models. Electricity prices are used by Jeha et al. (2021) and a set of non-financial time series. Economic scenarios are generated by Fu et al. (2019), Flaig and Junike (2021) and Geissler et al. (2022). Lastly, Cont et al. (2022) focus on the specialised application of generating tail risk scenarios.

Conclusions. In conclusion, time-series modelling through GANs necessitates thoughtful incorporation of temporal dependencies and sequence-specific methodologies. As evidenced by the current body of research, approaches to this challenge are varied. TCNs and transformer-based methods have demonstrated significant promise in sequence-related tasks, overcoming limitations inherent in recurrent networks, while normalisation, and embedding have seen limited use. There are a variety of financial applications, with attention given to stock data, VIX data, currency, bonds, Bitcoin and more. A summary of the models discussed in this section can be found in Table 18.10.

TABLE 18.10 A Summary of GAN Time-Series Models

Reference	Loss	Cond.	Conv.	AR	Norm.	Embed.	Trans.	Financial Applications
Fu et al. (2019)	Adver.	✓						Daily Stock, Monthly Econ.
Koshiyama et al. (2021)	Adver.	✓						Daily Stock, Currency
Yoon et al. (2019)	Adver.			✓		RNN		Daily Stock
Pardo (2019)	WGAN-GP, RaD	✓						Daily SPX, VIX
Takahashi et al. (2019)	Adver.		✓					Daily SPX
Wiese et al. (2019)	Adver.		✓					Daily SPX
Lin et al. (2019)	WGAN			✓	Auto			

(*Continued*)

TABLE 18.10 *(Continued)*

Reference	Loss	Cond.	Conv.	AR	Norm.	Embed.	Trans.	Financial Applications
Lezmi et al. (2020)	Adver., WGAN-GP	✓	✓					Daily SPX, VIX
Ni et al. (2020)	WGAN	✓				Signatures		Daily SPX, DJI
Xu et al. (2020)	COT							
Coletta et al. (2021)	Adver.	✓						Multi-Agent Sim.
Flaig and Junike (2021)	Adver.							ESG
Moritz et al. (2021)	WGAN-GP			✓				Bitcoin
Storchan et al. (2021)	WGAN-GP						✓	Multi-Agent Sim.
Jeha et al. (2021)	LSGAN	✓	✓		Spec.		✓	Electricity
Cont et al. (2022)	Score							Tail Scenarios
Geissler et al. (2022)	Hinge.	✓	✓		Spec., Batch			ESG
Rusnak (2022)	WGAN-GP	✓			Spec.		✓	Stock, Stock Idx, VIX, Currency, Bonds
Li et al. (2022)	LSGAN		✓				✓	

EXAMPLE 18.5: CGAN-MLP

As an initial example of a GAN, a model based on a multi-layer perceptron (MLP) was constructed, and the corresponding implementation can be found in the Jupyter Notebook `CGANMLP.ipynb`. The same set of four daily time-series data was used, consistent with the other examples. This model's generator and discriminator networks consist of three dense layers, with leaky ReLU activation applied to the internal layers and linear activation at the output. Both networks have hidden layers with 128 units. The training involves using a time-series window of length 32 and conditioning the model on the previous 32 data points. However, it should be noted that in this case, the conditioning information is only provided to the generator model.

The Wasserstein loss with gradient penalty (Arjovsky et al., 2017; Gulrajani et al., 2017) was employed for training. The Adam optimiser was used for the generator and discriminator, with default parameters and a learning rate of 0.0001. The training was conducted over 1000 epochs, with a batch size of 64.

The generated returns are depicted in Figure 18.24, and the corresponding ACF plots are shown in Figure 18.25. Visually, the generated returns do not exhibit the same level of variation as the original data. The ACF plots of the returns reveal a spurious spike in autocorrelation at a lag of 32, corresponding to the window size. The ACF plot for the S&P series appears noisy across all lags, whereas the other series do not exhibit this behaviour. However, the ACF plots of the squared returns approximately align with the expectation of decaying autocorrelation. As shown in Table 18.11, the statistical test results indicate poor matching of volatilities and kurtosis values by the trained model. Furthermore, all four QQ plots display an S-shape, contrary to the expectation, not solely for the 'problematic' USDJPY time series. Overall, the performance of the CGAN-MLP model falls short compared to other models examined in this study (see Figure 18.26).

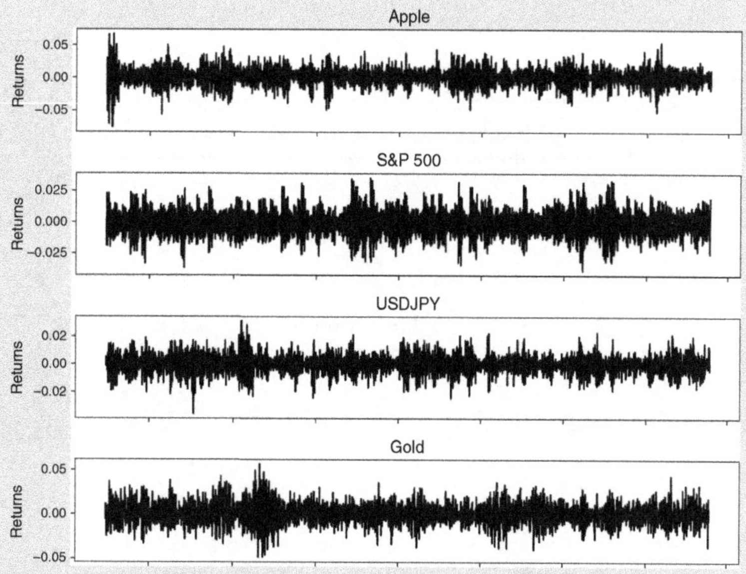

FIGURE 18.24 Simulated returns for a CGAN-MLP model fitted to the four historical time series.

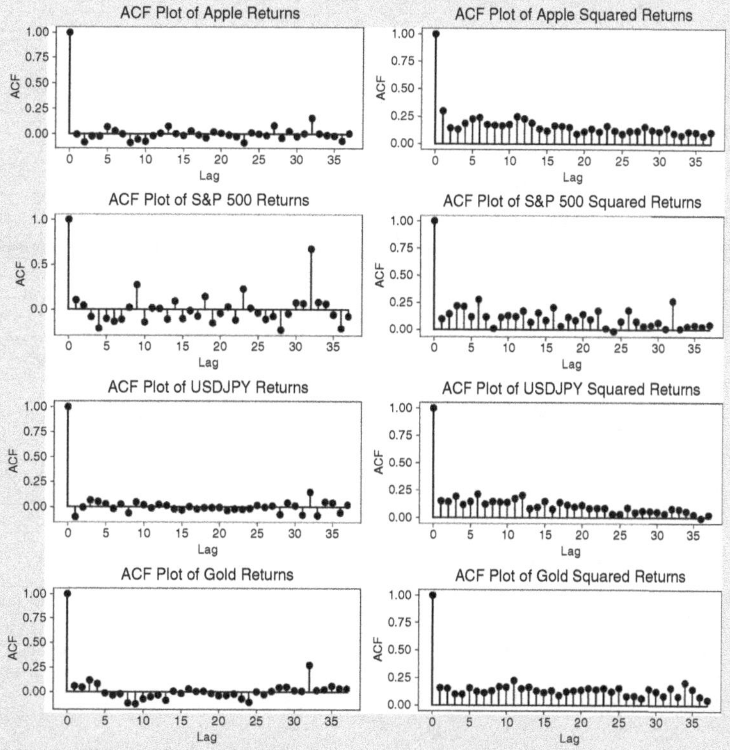

FIGURE 18.25 ACF plots for a CGAN-MLP model fitted to the four historical time series.

(Continued)

(*Continued*)

TABLE 18.11 Test Statistics for the Four CGAN-MLP-Generated Time Series

Label	JB Stat	JB P-value	Vol	Kurt	Skew	Cross-correl	H	GPH
Apple	18,900.56	0.0	0.63	9.38	0.74	6.77e–02	0.37	0.07
S&P 500	71,900.01	0.0	0.12	18.47	0.67	3.89e–04	0.42	0.29
USDJPY	10,231.32	0.0	0.21	6.98	–0.07	8.58e–04	0.37	0.09
Gold	581.75	0.0	0.09	1.66	0.07	3.87e–04	0.31	0.13

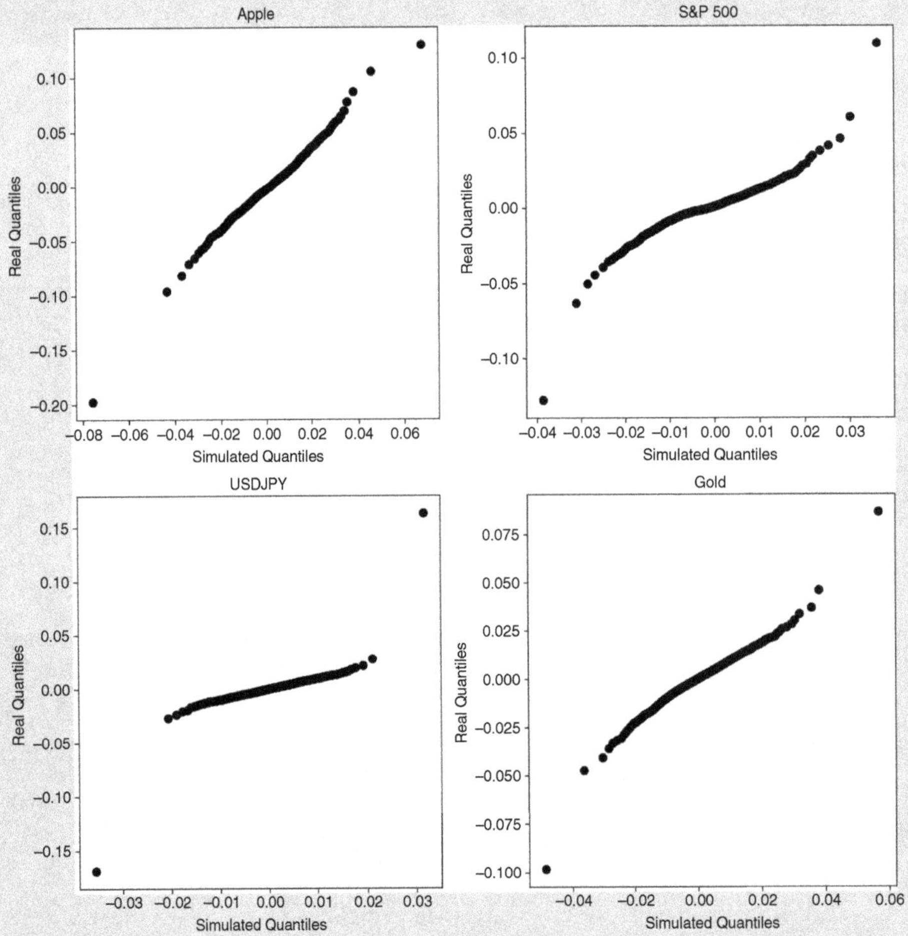

FIGURE 18.26 QQ plots for real vs simulated data for the CGAN-MLP model.

EXAMPLE 18.6: CGAN-CNN

A second GAN-based model is available in the Jupyter Notebook `CGAN-CNN.ipynb`. In this model, the dense layers of the previous example are replaced with one-dimensional convolutional layers having a kernel size of 3 and padding of 1. The generator and discriminator employ ReLU activation for the inner layers, with a linear activation for the output layer. The training process and parameters remain identical to those used in the previous *CGAN-MLP* model.

The simulated returns are depicted in Figure 18.27, and while they do exhibit periods of volatility clustering, they do not closely resemble the underlying dataset. The ACF plots in Figure 18.28 again display a spike in the returns plots at a lag of 32. However, all four plots demonstrate noise in the autocorrelation of returns. The ACF plots for squared returns exhibit a gradual decline but are noisier than the MLP model. Table 18.12 demonstrates a better fit for the variance of all four time series compared to the MLP model. The QQ plots in Figure 18.29 reveal slightly more linear results for Apple, S&P 500 and gold than the MLP model. Overall, the statistical properties demonstrate an improvement over the MLP model, but the autocorrelations exhibit spurious noise introduced by the convolutional layers.

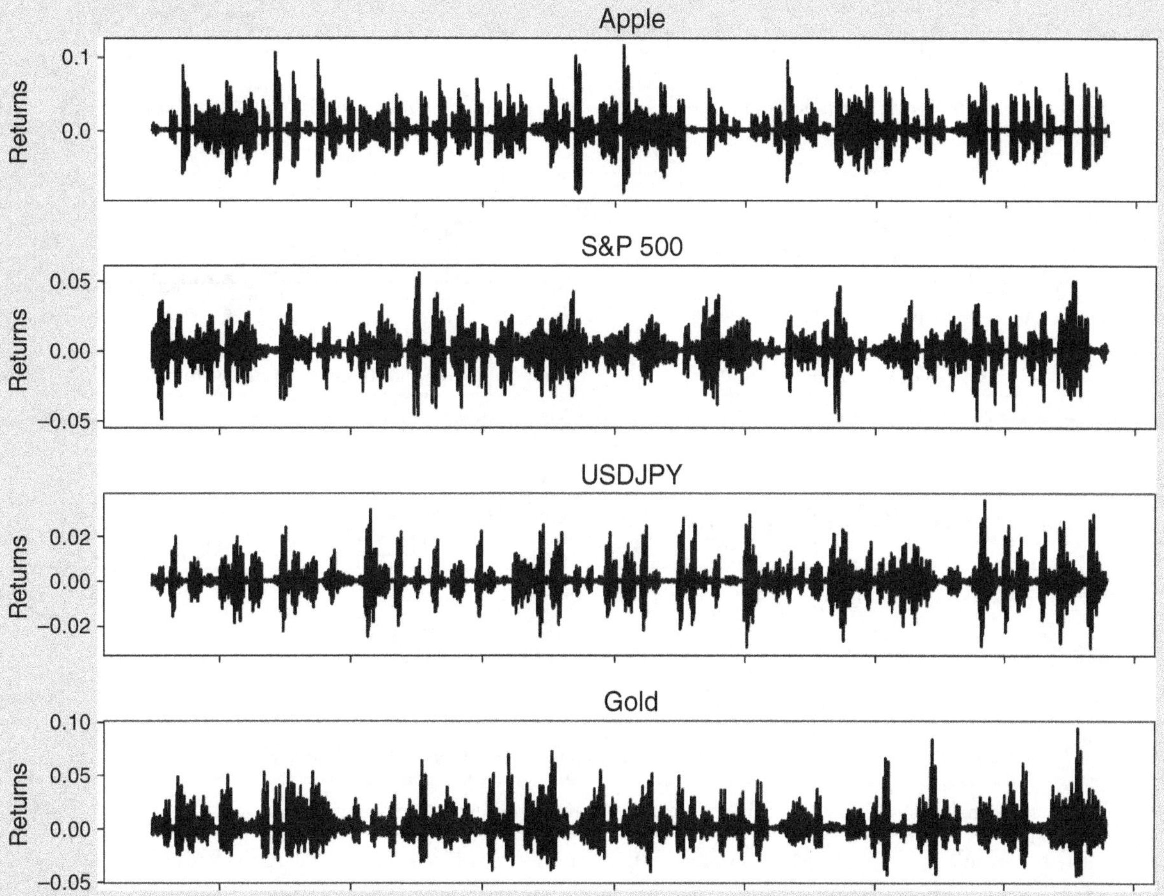

FIGURE 18.27 Simulated returns for a CGAN-CNN model fitted to the four historical time series.

(*Continued*)

(Continued)

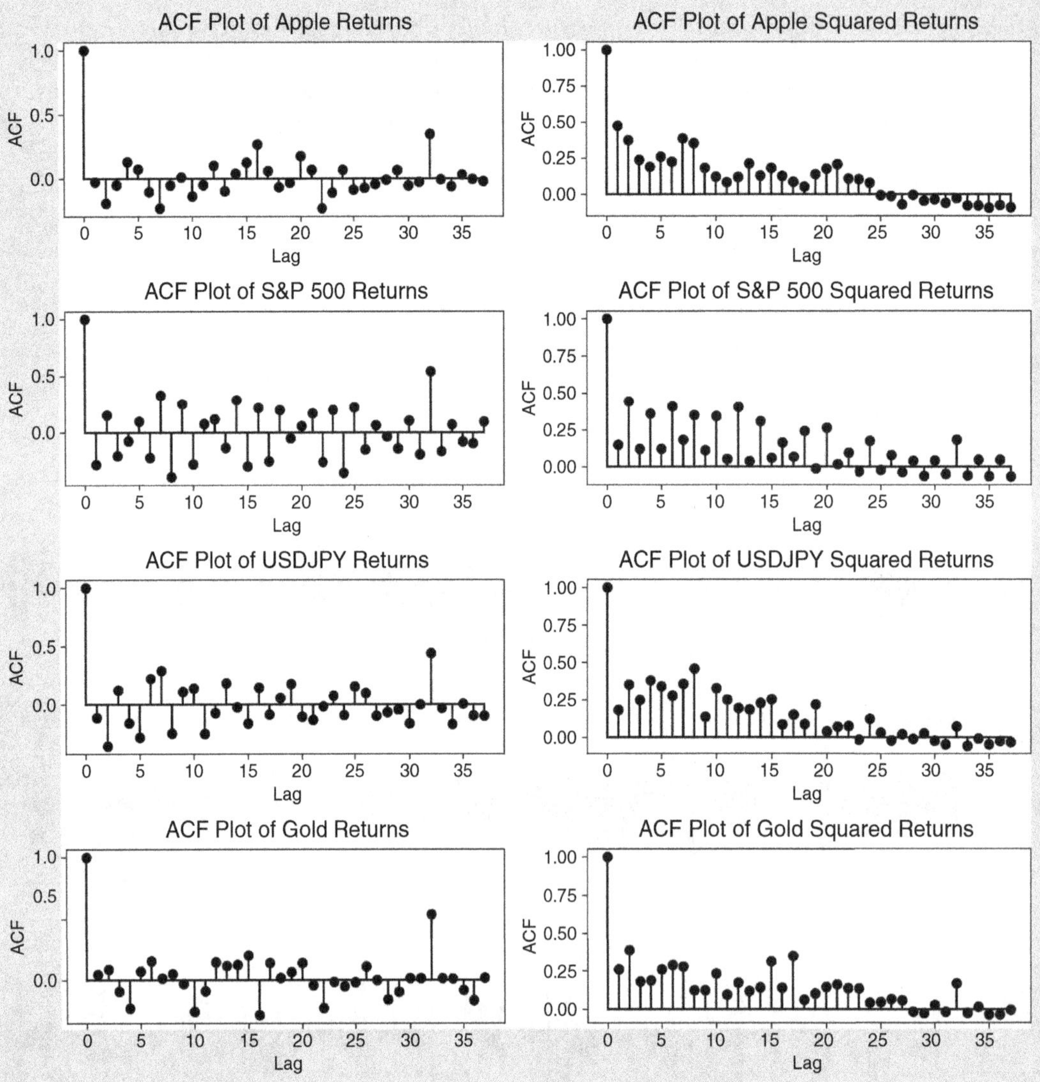

FIGURE 18.28 ACF plots for a CGAN-CNN model fitted to the four historical time series.

TABLE 18.12 Test Statistics for the Four CGAN-CNN-Generated Time Series

Label	JB Stat	JB P-value	Vol	Kurt	Skew	Cross-correl	H	GPH
Apple	3603.16	0.0	0.46	4.04	−0.48	−4.94e−02	0.25	0.26
S&P 500	1227.35	0.0	0.23	2.40	−0.17	3.38e−04	0.24	0.23
USDJPY	154.80	0.0	0.14	0.69	0.25	7.26e−04	0.24	0.22
Gold	12,431.39	0.0	0.13	7.63	−0.51	−8.04e−04	0.30	0.26

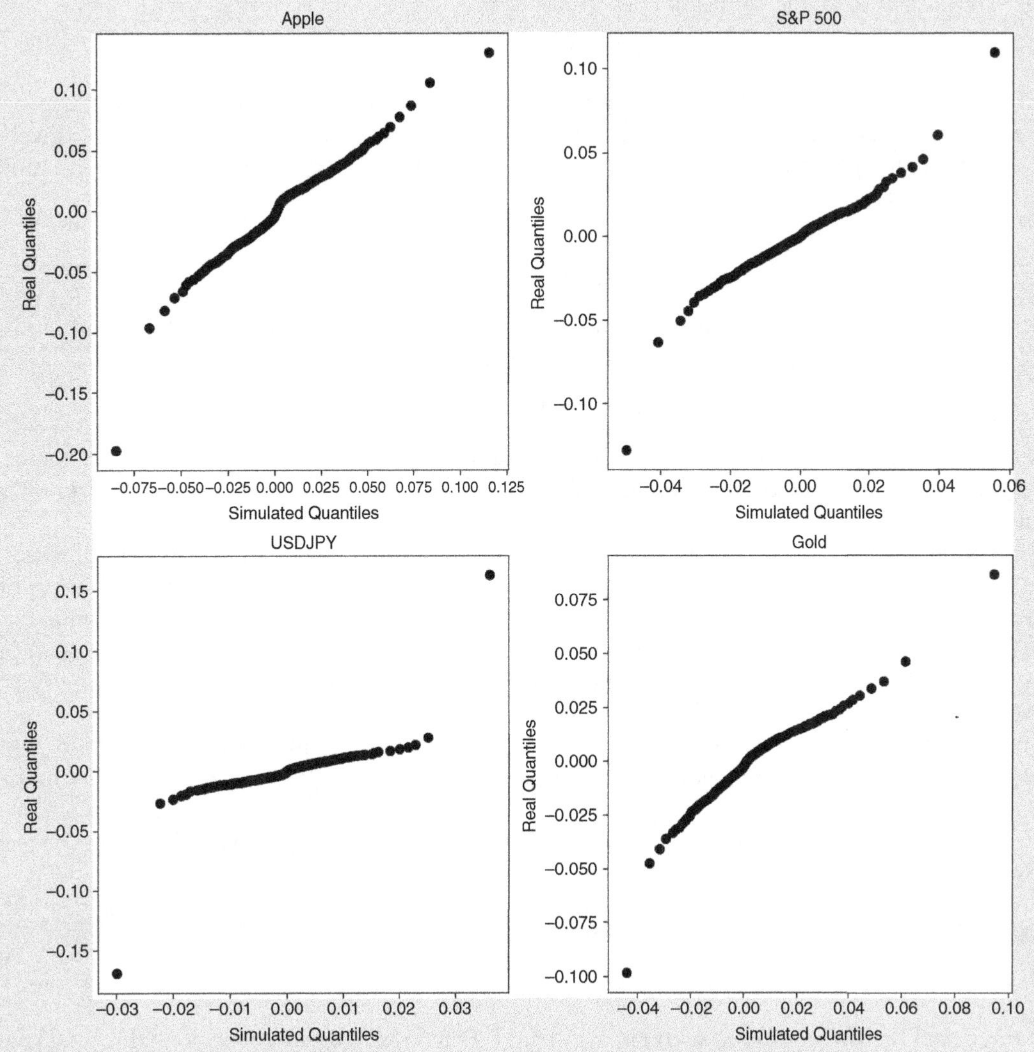

FIGURE 18.29 QQ plots for real vs simulated data for the CGAN-CNN model.

18.3.3.4 Diffusion Models This section uses diffusion models to generate synthetic time-series data. Diffusion models provide a principled framework for modelling continuous-time stochastic processes, making them well suited for generating various types of time-series data, including financial data. Two specific types of diffusion models are the focus: neural SDEs and score-based models.

Neural SDE models combine the expressive power of deep learning with the mathematical foundation of SDEs; these models leverage the flexibility of neural networks to capture the drift and diffusion coefficients of the underlying SDE, enabling the generation of realistic and diverse synthetic time series. Neural SDEs have shown promising results in various applications, including financial modelling and time-series forecasting.

Score-based models, introduced in Section 9.3.7, are a class of generative models that directly model the gradient of the data distribution. They have been extended to time-series generation, providing an alternative approach for generating synthetic data while maintaining the ability to learn complex temporal dependencies and dynamics. These models offer a different perspective on time-series generation by learning a score function that can be used to reconstruct the time series through a diffusion process.

A neural SDE has the drift and diffusion coefficients defined as neural networks,[1]

$$dX_t = b(t, X_t)dt + \sigma(t, X_t)dW_t. \tag{18.22}$$

Kidger et al. (2021) explore using SDEs as generative models for time-series data. The authors propose a new approach that combines classical SDE fitting with neural networks and Wasserstein GANs. Specifically, they use a generator–discriminator pair consisting of a neural SDE and a neural controlled differential equation (CDE) to model continuous-time generative time series.

A neural SDE of the form defines the generator:

$$dX_t = f(X_t, t; \theta)dt + g(X_t, t; \theta)dW_t, \tag{18.23}$$

where X_t is the state at time t, f and g are drift and diffusion functions parameterised by θ and W_t is Brownian motion. A neural CDE of the form defines the discriminator:

$$dY_t = h(Y_t, t; \phi)dt + \sigma(Y_t, t; \phi)dZ_t, \tag{18.24}$$

where Y_t is the state at time t, h and σ are control functions parameterised by ϕ and Z_t is another Brownian motion. The Wasserstein distance between the true data distribution and the generated distribution is used as the loss function for training.

The authors demonstrate the applicability of their approach in modelling complex temporal dynamics across various domains, including financial time-series forecasting and physical systems modelling. To exemplify its effectiveness, they apply the neural SDE model to generate time series using three datasets: a synthetic Ornstein–Uhlenbeck (OU) process, downscaled Apple/Google stock prices derived from limit orders at approximately 1-minute intervals and air quality data from Beijing. The results indicate that their approach outperforms existing methods in terms of accuracy and flexibility.

Hayashi and Nakagawa (2022) propose a novel method for generating time-series data with long-term dependencies utilising neural networks. The method is built upon fractional SDEs (fSDEs), a class of stochastic processes capable of capturing long-term dependencies in time-series data. The proposed approach, known as fSDE-Net, employs a neural network to learn the dynamics of fSDEs from input time-series data, enabling the generation of new paths by simulating the acquired dynamics.

The main contribution of this paper is the development of fSDE-Net, which generalises the neural SDE model using fractional Brownian motion with a Hurst index larger than half,

$$dX_t = f(X_t, t; \theta)dt + g(X_t, t; \theta)dB_t^H, \tag{18.25}$$

where B_t^H is fractional Brownian motion with Hirst index H. Fractional Brownian motion (fBm) is a generalisation of standard Brownian motion, characterised by its self-similarity and long-range dependence. It is defined by the continuous-time stochastic process $B_H(t)$, with Hurst parameter $H \in (0, 1)$. For $H = 0.5$, fBm becomes standard Brownian motion. The key properties of fBm are:

1. Self-similarity. For any $a > 0$, the process $B_H(at) \stackrel{d}{=} a^H B_H(t)$, where $\stackrel{d}{=}$ denotes equality in distribution.
2. Long-range dependence. The covariance function between two time points, t and s, is given by

$$E[B_H(t)B_H(s)] = \frac{1}{2}\left(|t|^{2H} + |s|^{2H} - |t - s|^{2H}\right).$$

3. Increments. The increments of fBm are not independent, unlike standard Brownian motion, but their dependence is captured by the Hurst parameter, with $H > 0.5$ indicating persistence and $H < 0.5$ indicating anti-persistence.
4. Non-Markov property. Unlike standard Brownian motion, fBm does not possess the Markov property, meaning that its future behaviour cannot be predicted solely based on its present state.

The proposed method of Hayashi and Nakagawa (2022) consists of learning and simulation. In the learning part, fSDE-Net learns the dynamics of fSDEs from input time-series data using a neural network. The training

[1]In the sense of Itô integration. Equivalently, the Stratonovich formulation can be used (Kidger et al., 2021).

algorithm is presented in Algorithm 18.1. The neural network takes as input the current state of the system and outputs the drift and diffusion coefficients of fSDEs.

Algorithm 18.1: Optimisation of fSDE-Net Generator

Input: $X_0, \ldots, X_T$ – a realised path of a stochastic process until time horizon T, sample size M, learning rate η, number of optimisation steps k
Output: $(\theta_b, \theta_\sigma)$ – the optimised parameter for fSDE-Net generator with some Hurst index H
while *not converged* **do**
  for *k steps* **do**
    Let $\hat{X}0^{(i)}, \ldots, \hat{X}T^{(i)}i = 1^M$ be the realisation of generated paths of size M and let $p\theta(t, \cdot)$ be the pdf of log-difference process, which is estimated from generated values $\hat{r}t^{(i)}i = 1^M$ where $\hat{r}t^{(i)} = \log(\frac{\hat{X}t+1^{(i)}}{\hat{X}_t^{(i)}})$.
    Compute the gradient of loss function $L(\theta) = -\frac{1}{T}\sum_{t=0}\log p_\theta(t, r_t)$.
    Descent parameters: $\theta \leftarrow \theta - \eta\nabla_\theta L(\theta)$.
  end
end

The simulation part consists of simulating new paths from learned dynamics. To simulate new paths, fSDE-Net uses an Euler–Maruyama scheme to discretise fSDEs and then applies it iteratively to generate new paths. The generated paths have the same regularity as the original path, a characteristic of fSDEs.

The authors evaluate their proposed method on both artificial and real-world datasets. They compare their method with other methods, such as RNN and SDE-Net, in terms of their ability to reproduce the distributional properties of the original paths. The results show that fSDE-Net outperforms other methods in reproducing the distributional properties of the original paths.

In their recent work, Lim et al. (2023) present an innovative approach to generative modelling of time series, termed TSGM (time-series generative model). Building upon the concept of score-based methods discussed in the context of image generation (Section 9.3.7), the proposed method utilises a conditional score network to learn the gradient of the conditional log-likelihood with respect to time. This model effectively generates realistic and accurate time-series data by incorporating the dependencies between observations. Additionally, the authors introduce a novel denoising score-matching mechanism specifically designed to account for the recurrent nature inherent in time-series generation.

TSGM is based on SDEs, which are used to model the dynamics of time-series data. The authors use two types of SDEs, namely variance preserving (VP) and sub-VP, to model different types of time-series data.

TGSM uses three neural networks, encoder and decoder networks, to map the time series to and from a latent space and a conditional score network to generate time series. RNNs are used for the encoder and decoder architectures. Let X and H denote the data and latent space, respectively. The embedding function e maps the input time-series data to the latent space, while the decoding function d maps the latent space back to the time-series data. Specifically, let $x_{1:T}$ be a time-series sample with a length of T, where x_t is a multi-dimensional observation in $x_{1:T}$ at time t. Similarly, let $h_{1:T}$ and h_t be embedded vectors. The encoder and decoder are defined recursively using RNNs as follows:

$$h_t = e(h_{t-1}, x_t), \tag{18.26}$$

$$\hat{x}_t = d(h_t). \tag{18.27}$$

At each time step t, the encoder takes as input the previous hidden state h_{t-1} and current observation x_t and outputs a new hidden state h_t. The decoder takes as input the current hidden state h_t and outputs a reconstructed observation $\hat{x}_t$. This recursive process is repeated for all time steps in the time series. This architecture efficiently encodes and decodes time-series data while capturing temporal dependencies between observations. The encoder and decoder networks are pre-trained before the conditional score network using the loss function

$$L_{ed} = \mathbb{E}_{x_{1:T}}\left[\left\|x_{1:T} - \hat{x}_{1:T}\right\|_2^2\right], \tag{18.28}$$

where $\hat{x}_{1:T} = d(e(x_{1:T}))$ is the reconstructed copy of $x_{1:T}$ by the encoder–decoder process. The training goal is to minimise this loss function, encouraging the encoder and decoder to learn a mapping between time-series data and a latent space that can accurately reconstruct input samples.

TSGM adopts a conditional score network to effectively learn the gradient of the conditional log-likelihood with respect to time. Unlike independent samples in other generation tasks, time-series observations inherently depend on previous observations. The score network in TSGM is specifically designed to learn the conditional log-likelihood based on previously generated observations. The network architecture is inspired by U-Net (Ronneberger et al., 2015) but with modifications to replace two-dimensional convolutions with one-dimensional convolutions to suit the characteristics of time-series data.

A loss function L_{score} is defined to train the network. At time step t, the model diffuses the time series $x_{s,1:t}$ using a forward SDE to the Gaussian distribution. The backward equation will then sample from and generate a new time series. Denoising score matching is used to train the model using the loss function

$$L_{\text{score}}^{\mathcal{H}} = \mathbb{E}_s \mathbb{E}_{\mathbf{h}_{1:T}} \sum_{t=1}^{T} \left[\lambda(s) l_3(t, s) \right], \tag{18.29}$$

where $l_3(t,s) = \mathbb{E}_{\mathbf{h}_t^s} \left[\left\| M_\theta \left(s, \mathbf{h}_t^s, \mathbf{h}_{t-1} \right) - \nabla_{\mathbf{h}_t^s} \log p \left(\mathbf{h}_t^s \mid \mathbf{h}_t \right) \right\|_2^2 \right]$ and $\lambda(s)$ is chosen as in Equation (9.71) (see Song et al., 2021, for more details). During the training of the conditional score-based network, the encoder and decoder can optionally be trained in an alternating fashion. Algorithm 18.2 gives the training routine in full.

Algorithm 18.2: Training SGM-Based Time-Series Synthesis Model

---

Input: Training set $x_{1:T}$, number of pre-training iterations n_{pre}, number of iterations n_{iter}, learning rate η, batch size B, use_{alt}
Output: Trained encoder and decoder networks, trained conditional score network
Initialise encoder e, decoder d and conditional score network M_θ with random weights;
for $i = 1$ *to* n_{pre} **do**
  Train e and d using L_{ed};
for $i = 1$ *to* n_{iter} **do**
  Train M_θ using $L_{\text{score}}^{\mathcal{H}}$;
  if use_{alt} **then**
    Train e and d using L_{ed}.

Comprehensive experiments with five real-world datasets and eight baselines show that the proposed method outperforms existing state-of-the-art methods regarding generation quality and diversity. The authors also visualise real and generated time-series samples on a latent space using t-SNE, which shows that their method's generation diversity is also superior to other baselines.

In conclusion, neural SDEs and diffusion models offer significant potential for generating realistic time-series data. Both approaches leverage SDEs and sit within a framework already central to quantitative finance.

EXAMPLE 18.7: SCORE-BASED MODEL

An example of a score-based model can be found in the Jupyter Notebook `Score-based TS Model.ipynb`. This model is based on the score-based model discussed in Example 9.5. The major difference between the image model and this model is that the score network is much simpler here, consisting of just two layers and a hidden layer size of 64. The code is presented below.

```
class ScoreNet(nn.Module):
    def __init__(self, input_size, hidden_size, marginal_prob_std):
```

```
        super(ScoreNet, self).__init__()
        self.fc1 = nn.Linear(input_size, hidden_size)
        self.lrelu = nn.LeakyReLU()
        self.fc2 = nn.Linear(hidden_size, input_size)
        self.marginal_prob_std = marginal_prob_std

    def forward(self, x, t):
        x = self.fc1(x)
        x = self.lrelu(x)
        x = self.fc2(x)
        x = x / self.marginal_prob_std(t)[:, None]
        return x
```

The model is unconditioned and generates new points singly. The model was trained through 1000 epochs using the Adam optimiser with standard parameters and a learning rate of 0.00001.

The simulated returns are shown in Figure 18.30 and show volatility clustering but are not well matched to the training data. The ACF plots are shown in Figure 18.31, but these show no autocorrelation in returns or squared returns as might be expected for an unconditional model. The statistics are listed in Table 18.13 and show a relatively poor fit to the statistics of the original series. The QQ plots in Figure 18.32 present linear plots for Apple, S&P 500 and gold that outperform those from the GAN models.

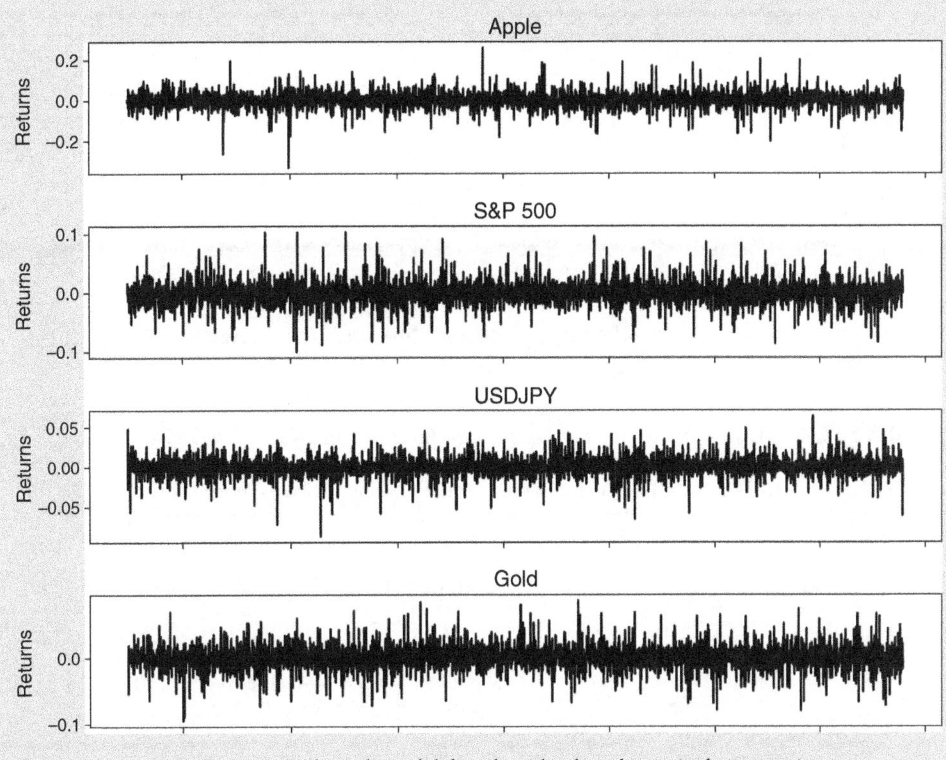

FIGURE 18.30 Simulated returns for a score-based model fitted to the four historical time series.

(*Continued*)

(*Continued*)

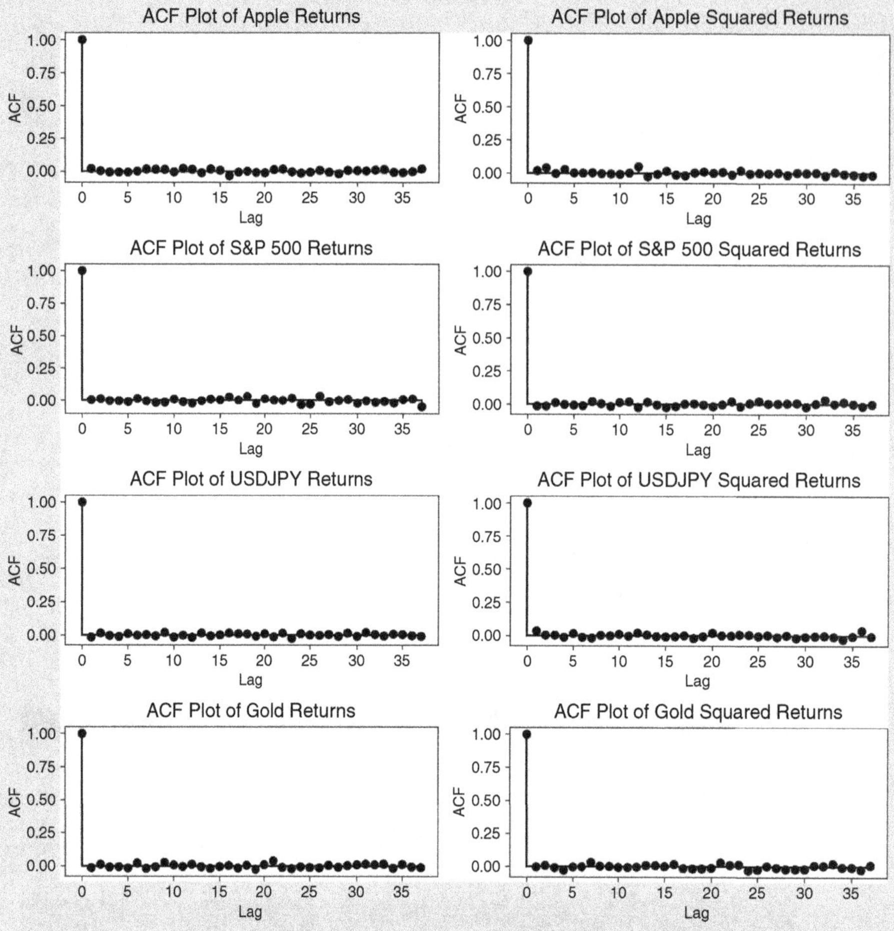

FIGURE 18.31 ACF plots for a score-based model fitted to the four historical time series.

TABLE 18.13 Test Statistics for the Four Score-Based Model-Generated Time Series

Label	JB Stat	JB P-value	Vol	Kurt	Skew	Cross-correl	H	GPH
Apple	3603.16	0.0	0.46	4.04	−0.48	−4.94e−02	0.25	0.26
S&P 500	1227.35	0.0	0.23	2.40	−0.17	3.38e−04	0.24	0.23
USDJPY	154.80	0.0	0.14	0.69	0.25	7.26e−04	0.24	0.22
Gold	12,431.39	0.0	0.13	7.63	−0.51	−8.04e−04	0.30	0.26

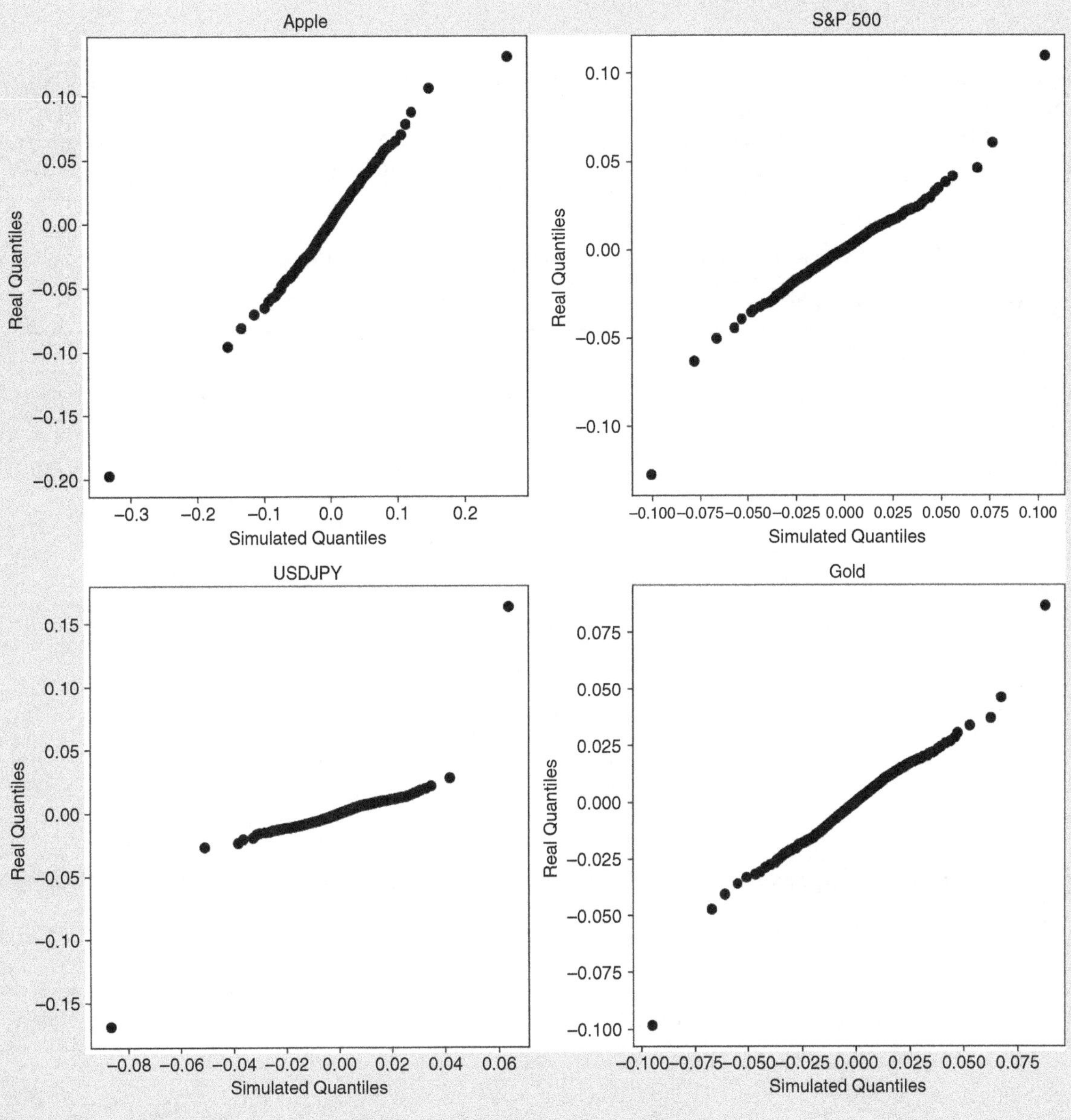

FIGURE 18.32 QQ plots for real vs simulated data for the score-based model.

18.3.4 Conclusions on Time-Series Generation

EXAMPLE 18.8: COMPARING GENERATIVE MODELS FOR TIME SERIES

Comparing all the models of the time series built in this section shows that the RBM model gives the best overall performance and is an excellent fit for the statistics of all four series. The simulated returns are visually close to the source time series and QQ plots with linear behaviour for all four, including the otherwise complex USDJPY time series. This model is not conditioned, but adding conditioning would further improve it. Table 18.14 shows the results of the predictive and discriminative scores first proposed by Yoon et al. (2019).

(*Continued*)

(Continued)

These statistics suggest that the CGAN-CNN model performs best. However, reviewing the results of all models shows that the predictive score does not have much separative power. The discriminative score shows significant differences between models but misses the clear outperformance of the RBM model. Hence, a statistical approach to testing models seems superior to building a model-based score, as has been done in the case of images.

TABLE 18.14 Predictive and Discriminative Scores for Tested Generative Models

Model	Score	Apple	S&P 500	USDJPY	Gold
Random walk	Discriminative	0.32	0.23	0.43	0.38
	Predictive	1.61e-2	8.12e-3	4.71e-3	**7.92e-3**
Heston	Discriminative	0.34	0.24	0.27	0.32
	Predictive	1.62e-2	8.07e-3	4.77e-3	7.93e-3
ARIMA	Discriminative	0.32	0.25	0.26	0.32
	Predictive	**1.61e-2**	8.10e-3	4.73e-3	8.01e-3
GARCH	Discriminative	0.42	0.42	0.44	0.40
	Predictive	1.62e-2	8.06e-3	4.73e-3	8.04e-3
RBM	Discriminative	0.38	0.30	0.03	0.35
	Predictive	1.61e-2	8.07e-3	**4.65e-3**	7.94e-3
CVAE	Discriminative	0.41	0.38	0.44	0.43
	Predictive	1.62e-2	8.07e-3	4.72e-3	7.96e-3
CGAN-MLP	Discriminative	0.19	0.04	0.42	0.31
	Predictive	1.62e-2	**8.05e-3**	4.72e-3	7.95e-3
CGAN-CNN	Discriminative	**0.02**	**0.02**	**0.004**	**0.04**
	Predictive	**1.61e-2**	**8.05e-3**	4.69e-3	8.02e-3
Score-based	Discriminative	0.26	0.22	0.19	0.26
	Predictive	1.62e-2	8.11e-3	4.73e-3	**7.92e-3**
Real data	Predictive	0.02	8.09e-3	4.69e-3	7.99e-3

Bold values are the best performing or equal best performing model for that asset and score.

18.4 GENERATING HIGHER-DIMENSIONAL MARKET DATA STRUCTURES

Expanding upon the groundwork in the previous section on time-series generation, the focus now shifts towards generating multi-dimensional market data structures, and this section reviews generating synthetic yield curves, correlation matrices and volatility surfaces.

18.4.1 Generating Yield Curves

The generation of yield curves represents a logical progression in extending generative market data models to higher dimensions beyond time series. A notable contribution in this area is presented by Sokol (2022). The author introduces a new class of models known as autoencoder market models (AEMMs), which introduce autoencoder latent variables as a substitute for the conventional state variables employed in standard model specifications.

AEMMs achieve this by employing VAE training to aggressively eliminate infeasible curve shapes, thereby ensuring that the state variables only represent valid curves. This approach circumvents the need for intricate constraints on curve dynamics, thereby preventing the generation of unrealistic curve shapes.

The paper further demonstrates that the accuracy improvement in mapping historical curve observations to model state variables, achieved through autoencoders, can be quantitatively assessed from first principles; this provides a rigorous methodology for comparing the proposed machine learning approach with its classical counterparts. The results indicate a significant and measurable enhancement in the accuracy of representing complex curve shapes when using autoencoders compared to classical methods with an equivalent number of state variables. Consequently, AEMMs outperform corresponding classical models, thereby establishing the superiority of the proposed approach.

Sokol (2022) explores three methods for transforming historical yield curve observations into autoencoder input: (a) raw market quotes such as swap rates and bond yields; (b) continuously compounded zero-coupon rates as parameterised by the Nelson–Siegel basis; and (c) piecewise constant forward rates, referred to as unsmoothed Fama–Bliss rates in economic literature. The study primarily focuses on encoding LIBOR and OIS swap curves, acknowledging the challenges of differing times-to-maturity across currencies and instruments. The limitations of the Nelson–Siegel basis are highlighted, particularly in fitting the short end of the curve, leading to the objective of developing an alternative basis for compressing swap rates with maturities from 2 to 30 years. This approach's benefits include using option (a) for curve representation, enhancing replicability by eliminating the need for curve building and avoiding interpolation. The study also emphasises the rigorous testing of the VAE, ensuring that it is genuinely 'fitting the curve' rather than 'fitting the curve builder'.

The paper explores VAEs and CVAEs, with the former used for single-currency data and the latter for multi-currency data, with the currency one-hot encoded and used for conditioning. The model is not conditioned on earlier yield curves.

Sokol (2022) emphasises the necessity for a mapping from the yield curve to the model's state variables, intended for model construction, to possess the capability of extrapolation beyond the historical data range specific to the currency under consideration; this is crucial in accommodating curve shapes that have not yet been observed in the given currency. While the CVAE independently achieves such extrapolation for each K-dimensional hyperplane, relying on data from other hyperplanes, the paper proposes an alternative approach that may offer improved effectiveness in extrapolation beyond the historical data envelope.

The proposed method involves encoding swap rates from all currencies into a shared latent space utilising a non-conditional VAE architecture and training the model using multi-currency data. The stochastic process is guided by historical data from adjacent currencies where it enters an area where no data is encoded for the modelled currency. It effectively minimises the necessity for extrapolation. Extrapolation would only be required in rare cases where the stochastic process ventures into distant regions of the latent space where no historical data for any currency is encoded. This alternative method provides a robust solution, particularly in an adequately calibrated model.

The paper comprehensively explores the application of VAEs in interest rate modelling, introducing the new model category of AEMMs. The author argues that VAEs, which have revolutionised many areas of machine learning, hold significant potential for interest rate modelling.

In conclusion, Sokol (2022) asserts that employing VAEs in interest rate modelling holds significant potential and that the newly introduced category of AEMMs can be a powerful tool for interest rate modelling.

EXAMPLE 18.9: YIELD CURVES GENERATED USING A VAE

This section showcases the training of a VAE model for yield curves, implemented in the Jupyter Notebook `Yield Curve VAE.ipynb`. Due to the limited availability of publicly accessible multi-currency data, it was not feasible to demonstrate the proposed CVAE model of Sokol (2022). Therefore, a simplified VAE model was trained using GBP OIS data provided by the Bank of England. The dataset encompasses 60 different tenors of

(*Continued*)

(*Continued*)

zero rates, ranging up to 5 years in maturity, with daily data from 2009 to the current year (2023). The data can be obtained from https://www.bankofengland.co.uk/-/media/boe/files/statistics/yield-curves/oisddata.zip, which is a compressed file comprising two spreadsheets. After unzipping, the data can be loaded into Pandas data frames and combined to form the complete dataset. The dataset is then divided into training and test sets using the `train_test_split` function and scaled using `StandardScaler` from the `sklearn` library. Subsequently, a PyTorch `DataLoader` can be constructed for the training set, reserving 10% of the dataset for testing purposes.

The VAE model shares similarities with the previously discussed CVAE for time series and the VAE model outlined in Section 9.4. However, as the data, in this case, is one-dimensional, dense layers are employed. The latent space is two-dimensional and follows a multivariate normal distribution characterised by mean μ and variance σ. The encoder model class is designed to accommodate variable depth with a block design, as depicted below. For this instance, two layers with sizes 64 and 32 were utilised.

```
class Sampling(nn.Module):
    def forward(self, inputs):
        mu, log_var = inputs
        batch = mu.shape[0]
        dim = mu.shape[1]
        epsilon = torch.randn((batch, dim), device=device)
        return mu + torch.exp(0.5 * log_var) * epsilon

class Encoder(nn.Module):
    def __init__(self, input_dim, z_dim, layer_dims, use_batch_norm,
                 use_dropout):
        super(Encoder, self).__init__()
        self.use_batch_norm = use_batch_norm
        self.use_dropout = use_dropout
        self.hidden_layers = nn.ModuleList()
        prev_dim = input_dim
        for i in layer_dims:
            self.hidden_layers.append(nn.Linear(prev_dim, i))
            if use_batch_norm:
                self.hidden_layers.append(nn.BatchNorm1d(i))
            self.hidden_layers.append(nn.LeakyReLU())
            if use_dropout:
                 self.hidden_layers.append(nn.Dropout(p = 0.25))
            prev_dim = i

        self.mu = nn.Linear(layer_dims[-1], z_dim)
        self.log_var = nn.Linear(layer_dims[-1], z_dim)
        self.sampling = Sampling()

    def forward(self, x):
        for layer in self.hidden_layers:
            x = layer(x)
        mu = self.mu(x)
        log_var = self.log_var(x)
        z = self.sampling((mu, log_var))
        return mu, log_var, z
```

The decoder model also used a block design with layer sizes 32 and 64, before the final output of 60.

```
class Decoder(nn.Module):
    def __init__(self, input_dim, z_dim, layer_dims, use_batch_norm,
                use_dropout):
        super(Decoder, self).__init__()
        self.use_batch_norm = use_batch_norm
        self.use_dropout = use_dropout
        self.hidden_layers = nn.ModuleList()
        prev_dim = z_dim
        for ilayer in layer_dims:
            self.hidden_layers.append(nn.Linear(prev_dim, ilayer))
            if use_batch_norm:
                self.hidden_layers.append(nn.BatchNorm1d(ilayer))
            self.hidden_layers.append(nn.LeakyReLU())
            if use_dropout:
                self.hidden_layers.append(nn.Dropout(p = 0.25))
            prev_dim = ilayer

        self.out = nn.Linear(layer_dims[-1], input_dim)

    def forward(self, x):
        for layer in self.hidden_layers:
            x = layer(x)
        x = self.out(x)
        return x
```

Batch normalisation and dropout were used for both encoder and decoder models. The following VAE model combined the encoder and decoder, providing the training step.

```
class VAE(nn.Module):
    def __init__(self, encoder, decoder, beta = 1.0):
        super(VAE, self).__init__()
        self.encoder = encoder
        self.decoder = decoder
        self.beta = beta

    def forward(self, x):
        mu, log_var, z = self.encoder(x)
        x_reconstructed = self.decoder(z)
        return mu, log_var, z, x_reconstructed

    def train_step(self, data, optimizer):
        optimizer.zero_grad()
        mu, log_var, z, reconstruction = self(data)
        reconstruction_loss = F.mse_loss(data, reconstruction,
                                         reduction='sum').mean()
        kl_loss = -0.5 * torch.sum(1 + log_var - mu.pow(2) -
                                   log_var.exp(), dim=1).mean()
        total_loss = reconstruction_loss + self.beta * kl_loss
        total_loss.backward()
        optimizer.step()
        return total_loss, reconstruction_loss, kl_loss
```

(Continued)

(*Continued*)

The model was trained through 1000 epochs using the Adam optimiser with default beta parameters and a learning rate of 0.001.

Figure 18.33 displays the test set projected into the latent space using the encoder, accompanied by an equal number of points randomly sampled from the same latent space. An immediate observation is the presence of outliers within the test set. Figure 18.34 explains this phenomenon by showcasing the trajectory of yield curves over time within the latent space, spanning the entire training set period. Each point on the chart corresponds to a sample taken at approximately 6-month intervals. For most of the period, the points traverse an elliptical path on the chart's left side. The outliers correspond to the period from the middle of 2022 onwards, characterised by an inflationary environment and rapidly increasing interest rates. Figure 18.35 depicts 10 sampled yield curves to further illustrate this.

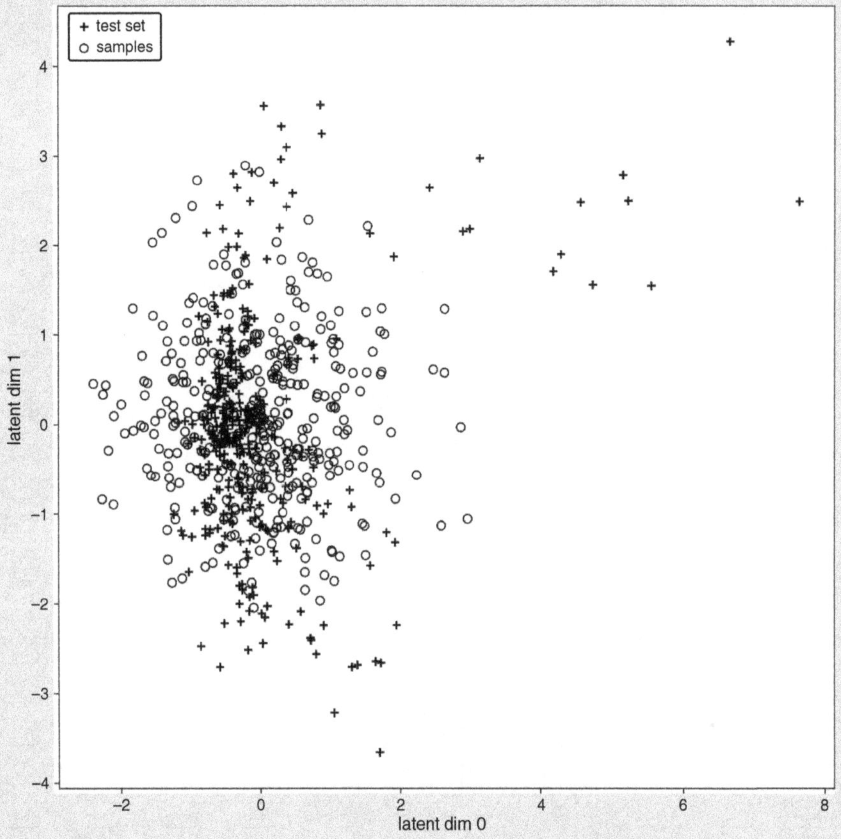

FIGURE 18.33 The GBP OIS yield curve test set encoded into the latent space of the trained VAE alongside an identical number of random samples.

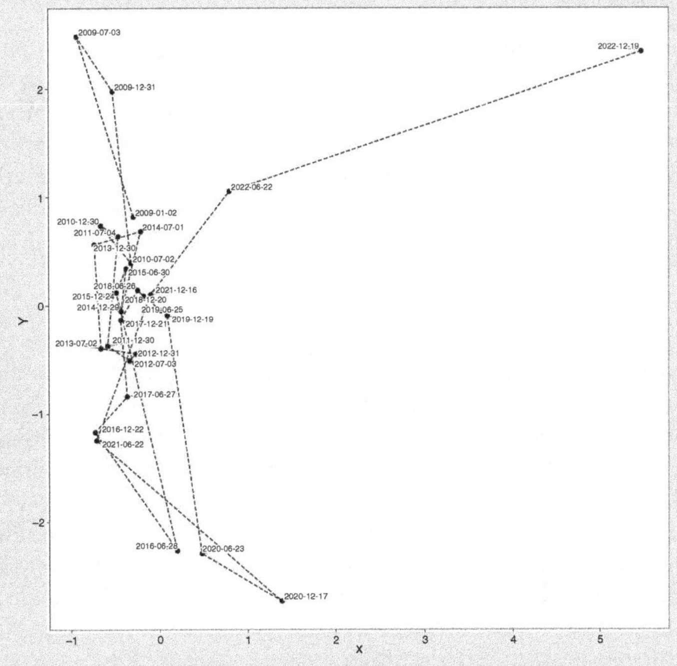

FIGURE 18.34 The path of yield curves through the latent space in the training set. Each point represents the encoded state of the GBP OIS yield curve at 6-month intervals from 2009 until 2023.

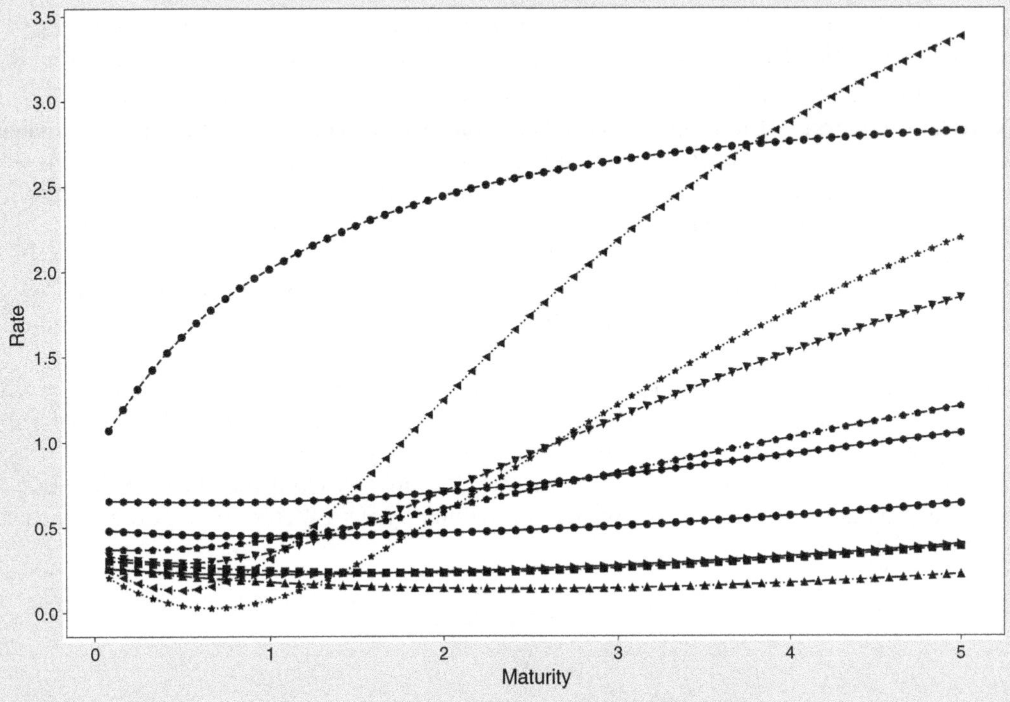

FIGURE 18.35 A set of GBP OIS yield curves sampled from the trained decoder model.

18.4.2 Generating Correlation Matrices

Given the need to generate multivariate synthetic market data, there is an apparent demand for synthetic correlation matrices. However, these correlation matrices must be valid because they have diagonal elements equal to 1, are symmetric and positive semi-definite. This section reviews the methodologies for generating correlation matrices, focusing on classical techniques and a novel approach based on GANs, known as CorrGAN. The classical methods encompass techniques such as the eigenvalue decomposition method, random gram method, sampling the Wishart distribution and the vines, onion and extended onion method. CorrGAN represents a deep learning-based approach, leveraging the power of GANs to generate realistic correlation matrices.

18.4.2.1 Classical Techniques

Eigenvalue Decomposition Method. In their paper, Davies and Higham (2000) present an algorithm for generating random correlation matrices with specified eigenvalues that are numerically stable. Their algorithm is based on the Bendel and Mickey algorithm, which uses a finite sequence of Givens rotations to introduce 1s on the diagonal of a matrix with specified eigenvalues. The authors provide new formulas for computing the Givens rotations that improve the algorithm's stability.

To generate a random correlation matrix R with specified eigenvalues $\lambda_1, \dots, \lambda_n$, the authors start by constructing a diagonal matrix D with $\lambda_1, \dots, \lambda_n$ on its diagonal. They then apply a sequence of Givens rotations to D to introduce 1s on its diagonal. The resulting matrix D' has 1s on its diagonal and non-negative eigenvalues but is not necessarily a correlation matrix.

To obtain a correlation matrix from D', the authors compute a factorisation $D' = LL^T$, where L is a lower-triangular matrix with positive diagonal entries. They then set $R = LRL^T$, where R is the desired correlation matrix. This factorisation can be computed efficiently using Cholesky decomposition. The method is implemented in the Python `scipy` library in the `stats` package as the `random_correlation` function.

Random Gram Method. The derivation of a valid correlation matrix can be achieved from any $m \times n$ matrix, $U = (u_1, \dots, u_n)$, with normalised columns, $u_j^T u_j = 1$, for $j = 1, \dots, n$. Consequently, it can be deduced that $C = U^T U$ is a positive semi-definite matrix with 1s along its diagonal. Moreover, if U has rank n, then $C = U^T U$ represents a nonsingular correlation matrix. Various methods are based on this concept, typically with $m = n$, where a random correlation matrix is obtained by generating random vectors $u_1, \dots, u_n$ on the unit sphere $S_m = \{u \in \mathbb{R}^m \mid u^T u = 1\}$. The random Gram method generates n vectors on S_n, and the resulting matrix $C = U^T U$ is a random correlation matrix (Marsaglia and Olkin, 1984; Archakov et al., 2022).

Wishart Distribution. The Wishart distribution is fundamental in multivariate statistics. It is a probability distribution over symmetric, positive-definite matrices, making it a suitable choice for generating random correlation matrices.

A random matrix W is said to have a Wishart distribution if it is an $n \times n$ matrix such that $W = XX^T$, where X is an $n \times p$ matrix whose elements are independently and normally distributed. The Wishart distribution is parameterised by the degrees of freedom ν and a scale matrix V and is denoted as $W \sim W(\nu, V)$.

To generate a random correlation matrix, we can sample a matrix from the Wishart distribution and then normalise it to have 1s on the diagonal. Given a Wishart-distributed matrix W, the corresponding correlation matrix C can be obtained as follows:

$$C_{ij} = \frac{W_{ij}}{\sqrt{W_{ii} W_{jj}}}. \tag{18.30}$$

This process ensures that C is a valid correlation matrix, as it is symmetric, positive-definite and has 1s along the diagonal.

The Wishart distribution has several important properties. The expected value of a Wishart-distributed matrix is νV, and its variance depends on ν and the elements of V. Furthermore, the eigenvalues of a Wishart-distributed matrix follow a distribution, which can be used to study the properties of the generated correlation matrices.

Vines, Onion and Extended Onion Methods. Lewandowski et al. (2009) put forth three innovative methods for the generation of random correlation matrices: the vine copula, the onion method and its extension, the extended onion method.

The vine copula method is a versatile approach that models complex dependencies between variables through a sequence of conditional correlations. This method is rooted in copulas, functions that encapsulate the dependence structure between random variables. The vine copula method constructs a vine, a tree-like structure that symbolises the conditional dependencies between variables.

The vine consists of edges that connect pairs of nodes, with each node representing a variable and each edge associated with a conditional correlation coefficient. The construction of the vine involves a two-step process. Firstly, an ordering of the variables is selected, and then trees are constructed based on this ordering. Each tree represents a collection of pairwise conditional correlations, and these trees are combined to form the final vine structure.

The onion method offers an alternative for generating random correlation matrices. This method constructs a matrix by layering correlations around an initial diagonal matrix, much like the layers of an onion. The onion method has demonstrated efficiency and precision in generating random correlation matrices.

The onion method commences with an initial diagonal matrix D with diagonal elements $d_1, d_2, \ldots, d_n$ representing the variances or standard deviations of n variables. It then constructs an upper-triangular matrix R by layering correlations around D such that R satisfies two conditions: (i) R is positive definite; (ii) R has diagonal elements equal to 1. This process can be reiterated to generate multiple random correlation matrices.

The extended onion method is a technique that constructs a correlation matrix, denoted as R, by layering correlations around an initial diagonal matrix D, similar to the onion method. However, it offers greater flexibility in selecting the joint density. Specifically, it allows for the choice of joint densities that are proportional to $\det(r)^{\eta-1}$, where $\eta > 0$ and r represents the correlation matrix. The joint density is computed using a recursive algorithm that calculates the joint density of correlations for each matrix layer. This algorithm involves a formula that incorporates the determinant of the correlation matrix and the parameter η. Moreover, the algorithm can be iterated to generate multiple random correlation matrices.

In conclusion, these three methods provide diverse approaches to generating random correlation matrices, each offering different levels of flexibility and accuracy. The selection of a specific method should be tailored to the particular requirements of the analysis and the characteristics of the data.

EXAMPLE 18.10: CLASSICAL METHODS OF GENERATING CORRELATION MATRICES

The six methods for generating random correlation matrices were implemented in Python, and the corresponding functions are presented below.

Eigenvalue Method

The eigenvalue method is implemented using the `scipy.stats` library. A numpy vector containing a set of positive eigenvalues must be provided to generate a random correlation matrix. In this implementation, the eigenvalues are generated randomly by sampling from the gamma distribution. Specifying suitable values for the shape and scale parameters of the gamma distribution is essential.

```
import numpy as np
from scipy.stats import random_correlation, wishart, beta, gamma

def generate_random_eigenvalues(N, shape, scale):
    random_values = gamma.rvs(shape, scale=scale, size=N)
    random_eigenvalues = random_values / np.sum(random_values)
    return random_eigenvalues
```

(Continued)

(Continued)

```
N = 100    # No Dimensions
shape = 1  # Shape parameter of the gamma distribution
scale = 1  # Scale parameter of the gamma distribution
eigenvalues = generate_random_eigenvalues(N, shape, scale)
eigenvalues = np.flip(np.sort(eigenvalues))*N

rng = np.random.default_rng()
ev_corr =  random_correlation.rvs(eigenvalues, random_state=rng)
```

Random Gram

The random Gram method can be implemented simply using `numpy.linalg`. First, a set of n random vectors on the unit sphere in m are generated by sampling from the standard normal distribution. Next, the correlation matrix is formed by multiplying the matrix of random vectors by its transpose.

```
def generate_random_vectors(n, m):
    vectors = np.random.normal(size=(n, m))
    vectors /= np.linalg.norm(vectors, axis=1)[:, np.newaxis]
    return vectors

def generate_gram_correlation_matrix(n, m):
    U = generate_random_vectors(n, m)
    C = np.dot(U, U.T)
    return C
```

Wishart Sampling

The Wishart distribution is also implemented in `scipy.stats`. To sample correlation matrices from the Wishart distribution, there are two steps. First, the Wishart matrix is generated by sampling with `df` degrees of freedom and the scale matrix is the identity matrix. The second step scales the matrix to be a valid correlation matrix.

```
def generate_wishart_matrix(n, df):
    scale = np.eye(n)
    W = wishart.rvs(df, scale)
    return W

def generate_wishart_correlation_matrix(W):
    std_devs = np.sqrt(np.diag(W))
    C = W / np.outer(std_devs, std_devs)
    return C

W = generate_wishart_matrix(N, N)
w_corr = generate_wishart_correlation_matrix(W)
```

Onion Method

The onion method can be implemented using numpy and the beta distribution from `scipy.stats`. The single-integer input determines the size of the output correlation matrix.

```
def generate_onion_correlation_matrix(d):
    S = np.array([[1]])
```

```
    for k in range(2, d+1):
        if k == d:
            continue
        y = beta.rvs((k-1)/2, (d-k)/2)
        r = np.sqrt(y)
        theta = np.random.randn(k-1)
        theta = theta / np.linalg.norm(theta)
        w = r * theta
        E, U = np.linalg.eig(S)
        R = U @ np.diag(np.sqrt(E)) @ U.T
        q = R @ w
        S = np.block([[S, q[:, None]], [q[None, :], 1]])
    return S
```

Extended Onion Method

The extended onion method is obtained with a small modification to the onion method function. The η parameter is described in the text above.

```
def generate_ext_onion_correlation(d, eta):
    b = eta + (d-2)/2
    u = beta.rvs(b, b)
    r12 = 2*u - 1
    S = np.array([[1, r12], [r12, 1]])
    for k in range(3, d+1):
        b = b - 1/2
        y = beta.rvs((k-1)/2, b)
        r = np.sqrt(y)
        theta = np.random.randn(k-1)
        theta = theta / np.linalg.norm(theta)
        w = r * theta
        E, U = np.linalg.eig(S)
        R = U @ np.diag(np.sqrt(E)) @ U.T
        q = R @ w
        S = np.block([[S, q[:, None]], [q[None, :], 1]])
    return S
```

Vine Copula

The vine copula method can also be implemented using numpy and the beta distribution from `scipy.stats`.

```
def generate_vine_correlation(d, eta):
    b = eta + (d-1)/2
    P = np.zeros((d, d))
    S = np.eye(d)
    for k in range(d-1):
        b = b - 1/2
        for i in range(k+1, d):
            P[k, i] = beta.rvs(b, b)
            P[k, i] = (P[k, i] - 0.5) * 2
            p = P[k, i]
            for l in range(k-1, -1, -1):
```

(*Continued*)

(Continued)

```
            p = p * np.sqrt((1 - P[l, i]**2) * (1 - P[l, k]**2)) + \
                P[l, i] * P[l, k]
        S[k, i] = p
        S[i, k] = p
return S
```

An example correlation matrix was sampled from each of the six methods. All samples were tested with Cholesky decomposition to see if there were valid correlation matrices, and all passed. The samples are illustrated in Figure 18.36. The eigenvalue method displays a clear block structure that none of the other methods display. What is immediately apparent is the lack of strong correlations in any of the matrices with the largest negative correlation values around −0.2.

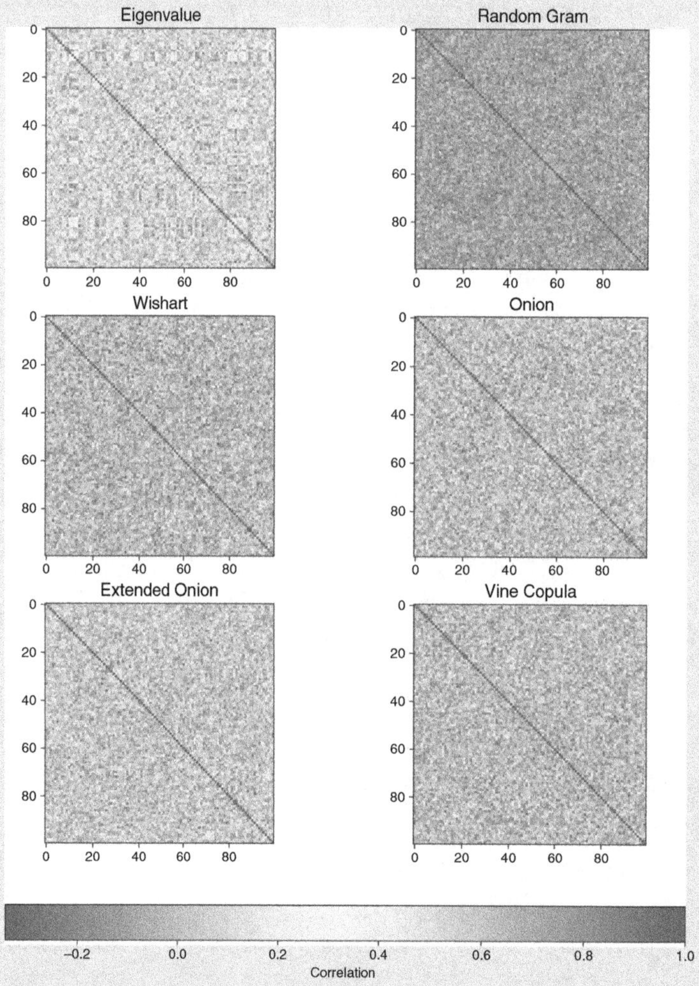

FIGURE 18.36 Correlation heatmaps for the sample matrices from the six different classical methods of generating random correlation matrices.

18.4.2.2 CorrGAN The classical methods described above are all designed to generate valid correlation matrices. However, none have much control over the sampling distribution, and none could generate correlation matrices with the strong correlations observed in financial market data.

Marti (2019) introduced a new approach to generating authentic financial correlation matrices, employing the power of GANs. The authors astutely observe the absence of an existing algorithm capable of producing suitably random financial correlation matrices that adhere to the Perron–Frobenius property.[2] This gap in empirical finance is a significant hindrance, the authors suggest. Furthermore, unlike the classical methods, the trained model will sample from the data distribution used for training.

The authors of this study have adopted a GAN architecture based on the principles of DCGAN (Radford et al., 2015), as discussed in Section 9.5.1.2. The GAN architecture utilises CNNs for the generator and discriminator components. The generator is constructed with multiple transposed convolutional layers, followed by batch normalisation and leaky ReLU activation functions. On the other hand, the discriminator consists of several convolutional layers, followed by batch normalisation and leaky ReLU activation functions. In this study, the Wasserstein GAN loss function (Arjovsky et al., 2017) is employed, incorporating gradient penalty regularisation (Gulrajani et al., 2017), as detailed in Section 9.5.2.2.

In summary, Marti (2019) presents a GAN-based approach to generating realistic financial correlation matrices. The proposed methodology exhibits promising results in recovering known stylised facts about empirical correlation matrices estimated on asset returns and holds numerous practical applications in finance. The DCGAN architecture, coupled with a modified Wasserstein GAN loss function with gradient penalty regularisation, contributes to improved training stability and prevents mode collapse.

EXAMPLE 18.11: CORRGAN ON STOCK CORRELATIONS

The implementation of CorrGAN can be found in the Jupyter Notebook `CorrGAN.ipynb`. The correlation matrix training data was prepared using a series of 32 stocks obtained through the `yfinance` package. The stock price time series used spans from 2 January 2001 to 2 January 2021, and the correlation estimation was performed using a window size of 60 observations. The Jupyter Notebook `Get Stocks Data.ipynb` contains the code for downloading the data and saving it to a CSV file. Figure 18.37 illustrates an example correlation matrix from the training set. Notably, the matrix exhibits strong correlations and displays a distinct 'blocky' structure.

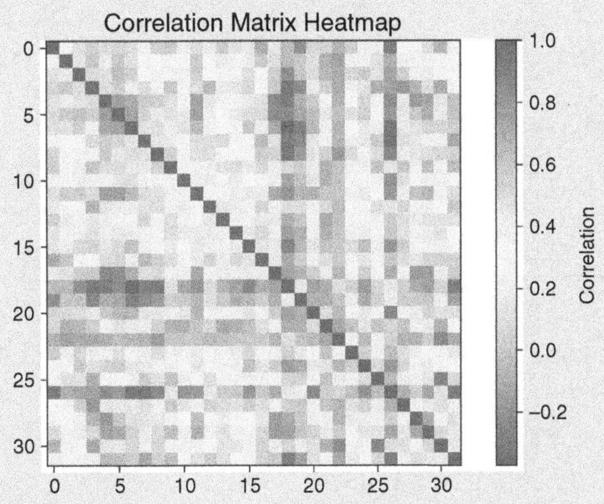

FIGURE 18.37 Correlation heatmap for a real correlation matrix for the 32 stocks calculated for 2 January 2020.

(Continued)

[2]A matrix $A \in \mathbb{R}^{n \times n}$ is said to have the Perron–Frobenius property if its dominant eigenvalue λ_1 is positive and the corresponding eigenvector $x^{(1)}$ is non-negative (Noutsos, 2006).

(*Continued*)

The generator employed in this study is identical to the one used in the DCGAN model described in Example 9.8, except for the output layer, which utilises tanh activation instead of sigmoid. The latent dimension remains at 100. On the other hand, the discriminator is similar to the one utilised in the spectral normalisation example discussed in Example 9.11, utilising leaky ReLU activation and spectral normalisation. As expected, Wasserstein loss is employed. The training follows the same procedure as DCGAN, with each iteration of generator training accompanied by five iterations of critic training. The generator and discriminator are trained using the Adam optimiser with beta parameters set to 0.5 and 0.9. The learning rate is 0.0001, and the model undergoes 50 training epochs.

An example correlation matrix generated by the trained model is presented in Figure 18.38. This matrix exhibits a wide range of correlation values similar to those observed in the training example. However, further examination of the matrix using Cholesky decomposition reveals that it does not satisfy the positive semi-definite property. Consequently, applying a *nearest correlation* algorithm as a postprocessing step will be necessary to utilise the generated matrices in real-world applications. The modified correlation matrix after this postprocessing step is depicted in Figure 18.39. A comparison between the two correlation matrices reveals that the nearest correlation algorithm has significantly altered the input matrix.

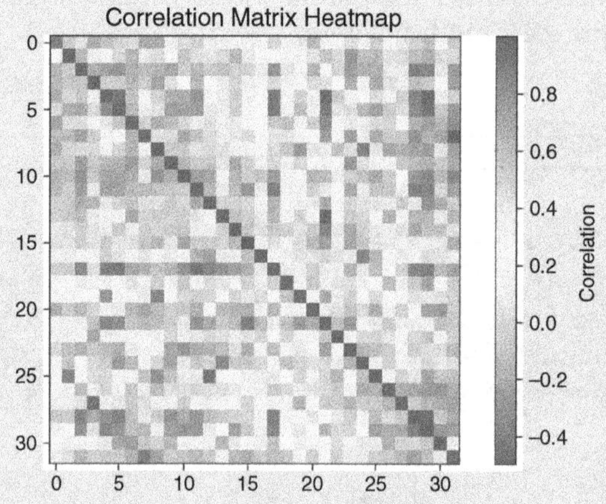

FIGURE 18.38 Correlation heatmap for a sample correlation matrix generated by CorrGAN.

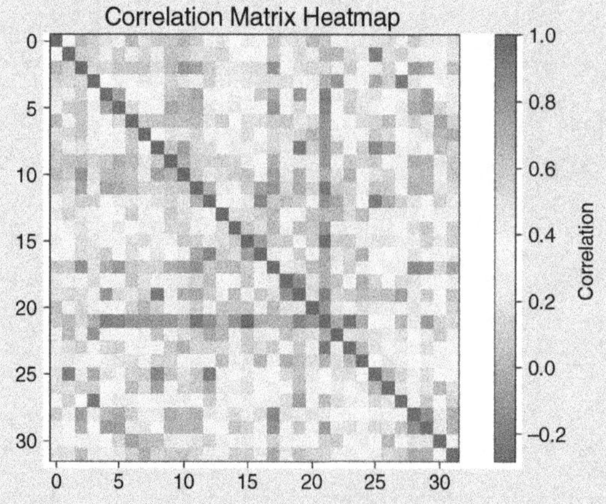

FIGURE 18.39 Correlation heatmap for a sample correlation matrix generated by CorrGAN, after postprocessing with a nearest correlation algorithm.

18.4.3 Generating Volatility Surfaces

Henry-Labordère (2019a) explores using GANs to generate synthetic SABR volatility model parameters. The author also proposes a primal–dual algorithm for computing the Wasserstein distance between two probability distributions and applies this as an enhancement over the Wasserstein loss (Arjovsky et al., 2017). The algorithm is based on a convex optimisation problem that can be solved using an iterative approach.

18.4.3.1 Primal–Dual Algorithm The primal–dual algorithm addresses the Wasserstein distance by solving two sub-problems iteratively: a primal problem and a dual problem. The primal problem focuses on finding an optimal transport plan that minimises the cost of moving mass from one distribution to another, subject to certain constraints. Conversely, the dual problem aims to determine a bounding function that provides an upper bound on the cost of the transport plan while also satisfying specific constraints. Henry-Labordère (2019a) demonstrates that repeatedly solving these two sub-problems can converge towards an optimal solution for the Wasserstein distance.

The transport plan and the bounding function are updated in each algorithm iteration using gradient descent steps. Notably, this approach does not require penalty terms or regularisation, which can introduce noise and lead to less reliable numerical outcomes. Instead, the primal–dual algorithm optimises the Wasserstein distance without introducing additional noise or bias into the computation.

The algorithm can be summarised as follows:

1. The first step is performed N_{critic} times. It involves randomly selecting N_{mini} mini-batches $(S_1^i, S_0^i)_{1\leq i\leq N_{\text{mini}}}$ from the set $(S_1^i, S_0^i)_{1\leq i\leq N}$. The weights are then updated according to the following formula:

$$\mathcal{W}_u \mapsto \mathcal{W}_u + \frac{1}{N_{\text{mini}}}\sum_{i=1}^{N_{\text{mini}}} -\nabla_{\mathcal{W}_u} u\left(T\left(S_1^i\right)\right) + \nabla_{\mathcal{W}_u} u\left(G\left(S_0^i\right)\right), \tag{18.31}$$

$$\mathcal{W}_T \mapsto \mathcal{W}_T - \frac{1}{N_{\text{mini}}}\sum_{i=1}^{N_{\text{mini}}} \left(-2\left(S_1^i - T\left(S_1^i\right)\right) - \nabla_s u\left(T\left(S_1^i\right)\right)\right) \cdot \nabla_{\mathcal{W}_T} T\left(S_1^i\right), \tag{18.32}$$

   The gradients are computed using backpropagation.

2. The second step is performed once and involves updating the weights of G as follows:

$$\mathcal{W}_G \mapsto \mathcal{W}_G - \frac{1}{N_{\text{mini}}}\sum_{i=1}^{N_{\text{mini}}} \nabla_s u\left(G\left(S_0^i\right)\right) \cdot \nabla_{\mathcal{W}_G} G\left(S_0^i\right). \tag{18.33}$$

3. The third step is to return to the first step. In practice, the optimisation is performed using the Adam algorithm with 10^6 iterations (with early stopping). For u and T (G), neural networks with linear outputs and ReLU (tanh) activation functions for the hidden layers are used.

Overall, the primal–dual algorithm proposed by the author provides a powerful tool for computing Wasserstein's distance between probability distributions. Its iterative approach allows for efficient computation without introducing additional noise or bias.

One potential limitation of this approach is that it may not be suitable for extensive datasets or high-dimensional distributions where computational complexity becomes an issue. However, this limitation could be addressed through parallelisation or other optimisation techniques.

18.4.3.2 Generating SABR Henry-Labordère (2019a) explores the calibration of SABR parameters using three GAN-based generative algorithms. The author focuses on the SABR model and its parameterisation in a six-dimensional real space, denoted as $\mathbb{R}^6$. The parameters include at-the-money volatility, skew, curvature and additional wing parameters. The author views the SABR formula as an encoder of the implied volatility smile, transforming it into a small number of parameters. This perspective aligns with machine learning methodologies, which aim to learn a compact representation of complex data.

The author compares the proposed W-primal–dual algorithm with GANs, Wasserstein GANs (W-GANs) and a normal density calibrated to the empirical distribution μ_{real}. Henry-Labordère (2019a) generates 1500 data points in $\mathbb{R}^6$ using a Gaussian transformation and evaluates the performance of the algorithms based on how closely the generated density support matches the true support of μ_{real}.

The author also considers a two-dimensional uncorrelated log-normal distribution in $\mathbb{R}^2$ with specific means and variances. He introduces 'anomalous' data modelled by the random variables $Z + 3 \times \text{sign}(Z)$, where Z follows a standard normal distribution, observing that these anomalous data points reside on the edge of the real density's support, as expected.

In the final experiment, Henry-Labordère (2019a) generates a six-dimensional density in $\mathbb{R}^6$ using a time-series model with uncorrelated normal variables. The performance of the algorithms is evaluated based on how closely the generated data, correlation, mean values and standard deviations match the actual values.

The author finds that their W-primal–dual algorithm and W-GAN perform similarly, outperforming the traditional GAN, which fails to accurately reproduce the mean and standard deviation. In conclusion, Henry-Labordère (2019a) demonstrates that GANs can be used to generate synthetic SABR parameters.

18.5 COMPLETING MARKET DATA: IMPUTING MISSING VALUES

Market data time series often require cleaning to remove erroneous values or handle missing ones. Data structures like yield curves and volatility surfaces contain multiple rates and option-implied volatilities. Such structures may miss one or more values when the data is captured, which could occur for operational reasons or because there is no market quote for the associated market instrument when the data is 'snapped'. Such missing market data elements must often be filled in before the data can be used for pricing or risk calculations. Generative deep learning models offer a potential solution to this problem. As discussed in Section 9.5.5.1, models can be trained to fill missing areas in images with realistic image data. As shown, this goes well beyond *denoising* and can deal with large missing panels and, indeed, can be used to remove undesired elements from an image altogether. Autoencoder models, often with adversarial training, are frequently used for such tasks. Bergeron et al. (2021) have tackled this problem in the context of FX option volatility surfaces, and this paper is reviewed here.

Bergeron et al. (2021) applied a VAE model to complete and synthetically generate volatility surfaces. Following Bayer et al. (2019), the authors considered two methodologies for modelling volatility surfaces using VAEs: the grid-based and pointwise approaches. The grid-based approach adheres to the traditional VAEs' architecture, using a d-dimensional latent variable to reconstruct original grid points. On the other hand, the pointwise approach leverages an alternative architecture where the option parameters (moneyness and maturity) are explicitly defined, with the decoder processing a single option's parameters along with the latent variable for the entire surface. Though Bayer et al. (2019) favoured the grid-based method, Bergeron et al. (2021) opted for the pointwise approach for its higher expressivity. This method allows the interpolation to be performed entirely by neural networks, enabling precise and efficient calculation of derivatives with respect to option parameters or 'the Greeks' using backpropagation. The performance of VAEs interpolating volatility surfaces was satisfactory even with limited data, and it was observed that additional data enhanced the results. Penalising VAEs for generating surfaces that exhibit arbitrage did not significantly improve the outcomes.

Upon training the VAE, the network parameters can be set and employed for inference tasks. The calibration procedure aims to identify the latent variables to align the decoder outputs with market data closely. Two calibration methods are proposed: using the encoder to infer the latent variables and the decoder combined with an external optimiser (like the Levenberg–Marquardt algorithm) to minimise the reconstruction loss. While the former offers computational efficiency, requiring only a single network pass, the latter becomes preferable when option data is sparse. Once calibrated, the VAE can infer unobserved option prices.

The authors evaluated their methodology by analysing OTC option data for five currency pairs: AUD/USD, USD/CAD, EUR/USD, GBP/USD and USD/MXN. The data, spanning from 2012 to 2020, was obtained from Exchange Data International. To estimate the implied volatilities, the authors utilised a grid of 40 points consisting of eight maturities and five deltas. The equations proposed by Reiswich and Wystup (2012) were employed to calculate the implied volatilities for call options, with further details available in Clark (2011).

The dataset was divided into a training set, used to train the VAE, and a validation set, which accounted for 15% of the data and covered the period from March 2020 to December 2020. During their experiments, the authors found that the choice of network architecture had minimal impact on the results. Consequently, they opted for two hidden layers in the encoder and decoder, each consisting of 32 units. The latent dimension was treated as a variable in their experiments.

To strike an optimal balance between the reconstruction loss and KL divergence, the authors conducted a random grid search to identify suitable hyperparameter choices that ensured continuity in the latent space.

Bergeron et al.'s (2021) model capability to complete volatility surfaces was assessed by randomly sampling a subset of all options observed on a given day, assuming that these represented the only known points on the volatility surface. The model was calibrated with a gradient-based optimiser, minimising the reconstruction error. All 40 option prices were then predicted using the inferred latent variables. The authors varied the number of sample points and the number of latent dimensions in the trained VAEs to evaluate the model's performance under

TABLE 18.15 Generative Deep Learning Applied to Synthetic Market Data Generation (2018–2021)

	Model Type				Application			
Reference	RBM	VAE	GAN	Diff	TS	YC	Corr	Vol
Hernandez and Abad (2018)	✓				✓			
Kondratyev and Schwarz (2020)	✓				✓			
Fu et al. (2019)			✓		✓			
Koshiyama et al. (2021)			✓		✓			
Yoon et al. (2019)			✓		✓			
Pardo (2019)			✓		✓			
Takahashi et al. (2019)			✓		✓			
Wiese et al. (2019)			✓		✓			
Henry-Labordère (2019a)			✓					✓
Lin et al. (2019)			✓		✓			
Marti (2019)			✓				✓	
Arian et al. (2020)		✓			✓			
Bühler et al. (2020)		✓			✓			
Carlsson and Lindgren (2020)		✓			✓			
Lezmi et al. (2020)	✓		✓		✓			
Ni et al. (2020)			✓		✓			
Xu et al. (2020)			✓		✓			
Bergeron et al. (2021)		✓						✓
Coletta et al. (2021)			✓		✓			
Flaig and Junike (2021)			✓		✓			
Moritz et al. (2021)			✓		✓			
Wang (2021)	✓	✓			✓			
Storchan et al. (2021)			✓		✓			
Desai et al. (2021)		✓			✓			
Jeha et al. (2021)			✓		✓			
Kidger et al. (2021)				✓	✓			
Remlinger et al. (2021)				✓	✓			

varying conditions. Initial training of VAEs on volatility surfaces from single-currency pairs was expanded to include data from multiple currencies, resulting in more robust models. Their findings suggest a similarity in the drivers of volatility surfaces across different currency pairs.

Compared to traditional volatility models like Heston, the authors' model consistently demonstrated superior performance in reconstructing volatility surfaces. The VAE offered several practical advantages, including faster price predictions that enhanced calibration efficiency. During training, the VAE also implemented regularisation techniques to promote continuity in the latent space. Moreover, the model exhibited adaptability by enabling easy retraining to handle extreme market conditions.

The authors noted that the most significant errors were observed in areas of the volatility surface corresponding to options nearing expiration. However, practitioners can adjust the weights according to their specific requirements. The approach highlighted the ease with which the VAE could be retrained using just over 10,000 surfaces to accommodate extreme market conditions.

In conclusion, Bergeron et al. (2021) demonstrated that VAEs perform well when completing volatility surfaces and require only a two-dimensional latent space to do so. The model can also generate fully synthetic surfaces by sampling the latent space of the decoder.

18.6 CONCLUSIONS: SYNTHETIC MARKET DATA

This chapter has presented a detailed examination of the process and applications of generating realistic market data. The established classical methods of time-series generation were initially revisited to provide a basis for the more advanced concepts discussed later.

In Section 18.3, the focus shifted towards the practicalities of time-series generation. The empirical properties characteristic of financial time series were explored, drawing on the seminal paper from Cont (2001), and empirical tests conducted to verify these properties. The section then reviewed several deep learning approaches to synthetic time-series generation, concluding that the RBM, a model now infrequently used, offered the best performance.

Section 18.4 tackled the creation of higher-dimensional market data structures, and this involved understanding and applying methods for generating yield curves, correlation matrices and volatility surfaces. Notably, the VAEs

TABLE 18.16 Generative Deep Learning Applied to Synthetic Market Data Generation (2022–2023)

	Model Type				Application			
Reference	RBM	VAE	GAN	Diff	TS	YC	Corr	Vol
Boursin et al. (2022)			✓		✓			
Cont et al. (2022)			✓		✓			
Geissler et al. (2022)			✓		✓			
Lailler and Cohen (2022)	✓				✓			
Richert and Buch (2022)		✓						✓
Sokol (2022)		✓				✓		
Rusnak (2022)			✓		✓			
Li et al. (2022)			✓		✓			
Hayashi and Nakagawa (2022)				✓	✓			
Choudhary et al. (2023)				✓				✓
Lim et al. (2023)				✓	✓			

used in the yield curve and volatility surface modelling also provide deeper insight into the structure and behaviour of the associated market through, via analysis of the latent space.

In the final section, a practical problem that often arises in this field was addressed: the need to fill in missing values to complete market data. Deep learning offers a mechanism to do this simply, with more realism than classical approaches.

Tables 18.15 and 18.16 present a comprehensive overview of the papers addressing the generation of synthetic market data. These tables summarise the models employed, the specific applications for which they were used and the types of market data generated.

CHAPTER 19

Deep Hedging

All reality is a game. Physics at its most fundamental, the very fabric of our universe, results directly from the interaction of certain fairly simple rules, and chance; the same description may be applied to the best, most elegant and both intellectually and aesthetically satisfying games. By being unknowable, resulting from events which, at the sub-atomic level, cannot be fully predicted, the future remains malleable, and retains the possibility of change.

The Player of Games, Iain M. Banks (1988)

19.1 INTRODUCTION

Deep hedging is an approach to risk management that leverages the power of deep learning to optimise hedging strategies in complex financial markets. Traditional approaches to risk management of asset and derivative portfolios typically combine expert knowledge provided by traders and portfolio managers coupled with portfolio sensitivities and other risk measures such as VaR, CVaR and Sharpe ratios to determine how to generate an optimal hedging strategy to achieve the institution's objective. Deep hedging offers the potential to build neural network models that can dynamically adjust positions based on a broad range of market and other financial information. Using deep neural networks enables handling non-linearities, high dimensionality and co-dependencies in real-world financial data. Most commonly, deep hedging is set implicitly or explicitly in the world of *reinforcement learning* as introduced in Chapter 10. With this approach, hedging decisions could be automated or semi-automated. However, even retaining 'humans-in-the-loop' in the process of portfolio risk management, deep hedging also offers significant insight into optimal hedging strategies in a similar way to how *Alpha Go* led human players to devise new playing strategies after observing how the reinforcement learning model played the game of Go. Derivatives can also be valued outside the traditional risk-neutral paradigm and based on the cost of the hedging strategy that allows the inclusion of market frictions.

Deep hedging emerged with the publication of a paper by the same name by Buehler et al. (2019). This paper and the large number of papers that have been published subsequently are the topic of this chapter, which presents an extended review coupled with several practical examples.

19.2 APPROACHES TO DEEP HEDGING

19.2.1 Introduction

The academic paper that led to an explosion of interest in applying deep learning to hedging and, more broadly, reinforcement learning to quantitative finance was 'Deep hedging' by Buehler et al. (2019). This paper applies deep reinforcement learning to hedge a portfolio of derivatives in the presence of market frictions, including transaction costs and liquidity limits. It does so through deep neural networks and 'standard reinforcement learning techniques'. Buehler et al. (2019) is amongst the most widely cited academic papers in quantitative finance in recent years.

Deep Learning in Quantitative Finance, First Edition. Andrew Green.

The paper makes four key contributions:

- **Deep Learning Framework.** The paper introduces a deep learning framework for generating hedging strategies, including market signals and past decisions. The approach is model-free in the RL sense in that no model of the market dynamics is assumed or learned. Indeed, an agent trained on one dataset can easily be used with a different one.
- **Handling Market Frictions.** The framework explicitly incorporates market frictions that form a significant part of real financial markets but which are excluded from most quantitative models.
- **Numerical Efficiency.** The authors demonstrate that optimal hedging strategies can be computed efficiently using small neural networks.
- **Empirical Validation.** The paper includes a series of numerical experiments that validate the proposed approach. These experiments compare the performance of the deep hedging agent against benchmarks, assess the impact of transaction costs and explore the scalability of the method.

As discussed in Chapter 10, a key element of the RL approach is the definition of the *environment* with state, action and reward functions. Buehler et al. (2019) define the state space as a discrete-time financial market with n trading dates and d hedging instruments. These instruments could include underlying assets and options, some of which may not be available for trading at $t = 0$. The portfolio being hedged, Z, consists of derivatives and underlying assets with maximum maturity T.

The action space is the amount of each hedging instrument i held at each time step t_k, δ^i_k. The trading strategy is subject to constraints such as limited liquidity or risk limits, which are included by restricting the hedging positions δ^i_k. Transaction costs for each trade are given by c^i_k and could be proportional, fixed or more complex. The final portfolio value is given by

$$\mathrm{PL}_T\left(Z, p_0, \delta\right) := -Z + p_0 + (\delta \cdot S)_T - C_T(\delta), \tag{19.1}$$

where p_0 is the initial cash position, $C_T(\delta) := \sum_{k=0}^{n} c_k\left(\delta_k - \delta_{k-1}\right)$ is the cost of the trading strategy and $(\delta \cdot S)_T := \sum_{k=0}^{n-1} \delta_k \cdot \left(S_{k+1} - S_k\right)$ is the value of the hedge portfolio.

Buehler et al. (2019) also devote considerable effort to identifying a suitable reward in the form of a risk measure and exploring the optimality of the portfolio value as given by Equation (19.1) under convex risk measures. The loss function for training the neural network is defined by

$$J(\theta) := w + \mathbb{E}\left[\ell\left(Z - \left(\delta^{\bar{\theta}} \cdot S\right)_T + C_T\left(\delta^{\bar{\theta}}\right) - w\right)\right], \tag{19.2}$$

where $w \in \mathbb{R}$ and ℓ is a convex loss function. The parameters θ are then learned using SGD.

Buehler et al. (2019) conclude by performing a series of numerical experiments to validate the approach. All the experiments use Heston market dynamics, either a single-asset process or five processes, to demonstrate scalability for the last experiment design. The initial benchmark is hedging a European option with no transaction costs with the risk measure selected to be CVaR, as given by

$$\rho(X) := \frac{1}{1-\alpha} \int_0^{1-\alpha} \mathrm{VaR}_\gamma(X)\, d\gamma. \tag{19.3}$$

In this case, deep hedging performance was similar to delta hedging using the model. The authors further explored the impact of risk preference on hedging by tuning the α parameter in Equation (19.3). Further experiments with transaction costs and a portfolio of five options on five assets were performed to show scalability to higher dimensions. The authors also explored the impact of network architectures using FFNs and RNNs.

Where does deep hedging fit in the RL pantheon? Deep hedging can be considered a form of *policy gradient*. However, the work does not adhere to the classical reinforcement learning framework and avoids the terminology commonly used in RL. Notably, more recent authors have set their work more firmly within RL, as can be seen in Buehler et al. (2022) and Murray et al. (2022).

Further early influential work on applying RL in quantitative finance are the papers of Halperin (2017, 2019), which are expanded in the book by Dixon et al. (2020). Halperin (2017) applies Q-learning to demonstrate that option pricing and hedging can be derived directly from data using the Black–Scholes model as a test environment.

While this work approximates the Q-function, it does not use a neural network, so it is beyond the scope of this chapter.

The remainder of this section explores the literature on the application of neural networks to the problem of hedging derivative portfolios. The review is approached thematically, exploring the target applications, datasets used, environment specification, RL methodology, neural network architectures and results of the studies. Tables 19.1 through 19.8 summarise the applications and environment used by each paper and the methodologies adopted, while Tables 19.9 through 19.16 later present summaries of the results of each paper.

19.2.2 Target Applications

Few authors apply deep hedging to portfolios like Bühler et al. (2020). Buehler et al. (2022) consider a portfolio again, and Lütkebohmert et al. (2021) use a butterfly option strategy, but the vast majority consider hedging a single option, most commonly a European-style option. A scattering of other option types have been used as the target: digital options were used by Buehler et al. (2021), lookback options used by Lütkebohmert et al. (2021), Hirano et al. (2023b) and Hirano (2024), Marzban et al. (2021) explored basket options and Pickard et al. (2024) targeted American-style options. In contrast, Carbonneau (2020) and Chong et al. (2021) used variable annuities.

19.2.3 Datasets

The datasets used for training and evaluation are most commonly derived from classic risk-neutral model dynamics, reflecting the ease with which large datasets can be generated by Monte Carlo simulation. Hence, almost all authors use GBM to generate a dataset, some with arbitrarily chosen parameters and others calibrated to historical returns. GBM (MJD) (Merton, 1976) is used by Carbonneau (2020), Carbonneau and Godin (2020), Carbonneau and Godin (2021) and Gong et al. (2021). Another popular choice is the SABR model (Hagan et al., 2002), which is used by Cao et al. (2021, 2022), Hientzsch (2024) and Pickard et al. (2024). Heston is also easy to simulate and is used by Buehler et al. (2019), Giurca and Borovkova (2021), Gong et al. (2021), Mikkilä and Kanniainen (2023) and Hirano (2024).

TABLE 19.1 Author Approaches to Deep Hedging: Applications

Reference	Application(s)	Duration	Frequency	Train Dataset(s)	Test Dataset(s)
Buehler et al. (2019)	Portfolios asset	30 days	D	Heston	Heston
	and derivatives			GBM	GBM
Carbonneau and Godin (2020)	Euro option	1 year	D	GARCH	GARCH
	Asian			GBM	GBM
	Lookback			MJD	MJD
Carbonneau (2020)	Variable annuities	10 years	M and Y	GBM	GBM
				MJD	MJD
Du et al. (2020)	Euro option	50 days	D	GBM	GBM
Assa et al. (2021)	Euro option	100 steps		GBM	GBM
Buehler et al. (2021)	Digital option			VAR (STOXX 50)	VAR (STOXX 50)
				GAN (STOXX 50)	GAN (STOXX 50)
Cao et al. (2021)	Euro option	1 and 3 months	D to W	GBM	GBM
				SABR	SABR

(*Continued*)

TABLE 19.1 (*Continued*)

Reference	Application(s)	Duration	Frequency	Train Dataset(s)	Test Dataset(s)
Carbonneau and Godin (2021)	Euro option	1 year	D and M	GARCH	GARCH
Chong et al. (2021)	Variable annuities			GBM	GBM
Giurca and Borovkova (2021)	Euro option	1 month to 1 year	D	GBM	GBM
				Heston	Heston
					S&P 500
Gong et al. (2021)	Euro option	30 days	D	MJD	MJD
				Heston	Heston
Hou et al. (2021)	Euro option	10 years	100 steps	GBM	GBM
Horvath et al. (2021)	Euro option	30 days	D	rBergomi (H = 0.25)	rBergomi (H! = 0.25)
Kim (2021)	Euro option	30 days	D	GBM	GBM
				GAN	GAN
Lütkebohmert et al. (2021)	Euro option	30 days	D	NGA	NGA
	Butterfly				S&P 500
	Lookback				
Marzban et al. (2021)	Euro option	1 year	M	GBM (Hist)	GBM (Hist)
	Basket option				
Vittori et al. (2021)	Euro option	61 days	305 steps	GBM	GBM
Buehler et al. (2022)	Portfolio			GBM	GBM
Cao et al. (2022)	Euro option	30 days	D	SABR	SABR
Murray et al. (2022)	Euro option	30 days	D	Heston	Heston
Cannelli et al. (2023)	Euro option	60 days	1–3 days	GBM	GBM
Fathi and Hientzsch (2023)	Euro option	30 days	D	GBM	GBM
Gao et al. (2023)	Euro option	30 days	D	Chiarella–Heston	Chiarella–Heston
				GBM	GBM
					S&P 500
Hirano et al. (2023a)	Euro option		20 steps	Heston	Heston
Hirano et al. (2023b)	Euro option		20 steps	GBM	GBM
	Lookback			Heston	Heston
					S&P 500
					BVSP

Reference	Application(s)	Duration	Frequency	Train Dataset(s)	Test Dataset(s)
Limmer and Horvath (2023)	Euro option	255 days	18 steps	GBM	GBM
					Heston
Mikkilä and Kanniainen (2023)	Euro option	5 days	60 mins	GBM	GBM
				Heston	Heston
				S&P 500	S&P 500
Szehr (2023)	Euro option	60 days		GBM	GBM
Hientzsch (2024)	Euro option	10–90 days	D	GBM	GBM
				SABR	SABR
Hirano (2024)	Euro option		20 steps	GBM	GBM
	Lookback			Heston	Heston
	Lookback			PAMS	PAMS
					S&P 500
					BVSP
Neagu et al. (2024)	Euro option	1 year	M	GBM	GBM
Pickard et al. (2024)	American option	1 year	D to W	GBM	GBM
				SABR	SABR
				Equity	Equity

TABLE 19.2 Author Approaches to Deep Hedging: Features and Methodology

Reference	Market Feature	Method	Architecture(s)	State	Action	Reward/Loss
Buehler et al. (2019)	Total costs	Deep hedging	FFN	S_k	n_{t+1}	Convex RM
	Market implied		RNN			
Carbonneau and Godin (2020)		Deep hedging	FFN	S_t	n_{t+1}	Convex RM
Carbonneau (2020)		Deep hedging	LSTM	S_t	n_{t+1}	QDH and SQDH
Du et al. (2020)	Total costs	DQN, Pop-Art, PPO	FFN	S_t, τ, n_t, K	Disc. n_{t+1}	Mean variance
Assa et al. (2021)		DDPG	FFN	S_t, τ, X_t, Y_t	n_{t+1}	Hedge error
Buehler et al. (2021)	Total costs	Deep hedging	FFN	S_t	n_{t+1}	Convex RM

(*Continued*)

TABLE 19.2 *(Continued)*

Reference	Market Feature	Method	Architecture(s)	State	Action	Reward/Loss
Cao et al. (2021)	Total costs	DDPG	FFN	S_t, τ, n_t	n_{t+1}	Mean variance
Carbonneau and Godin (2021)		Deep hedging	LSTM	S_t	n_{t+1}	Equal risk
Chong et al. (2021)		PPO	FFN	$\sum_{i=1}^{N} J_{t_k}^{(i)}, S_t, \tau$	n_{t+1}	Convex RM
Giurca and Borovkova (2021)	Total costs	DQN	FFN	$S_t, C_t, \sigma_t, \frac{\partial C_t}{\partial S_t}, n_t$	Disc. n_{t+1}	Mean variance
		DDPG				
Gong et al. (2021)	Total costs	Deep hedging	GRU	S_t	n_{t+1} if $\delta S_t > \alpha$	Convex RM
			Rand. For.			
Hou et al. (2021)	Total costs	Deep hedging	FFN	S_t	n_{t+1}	Efficient hedging
Horvath et al. (2021)	Total costs	Deep hedging	FFN	S_t	n_{t+1}	Convex RM
			RNN			
Kim (2021)	Total costs	Deep hedging	RNN	S_t	n_{t+1}	Convex RM
Lütkebohmert et al. (2021)	Total costs	Deep hedging	FFN	S_t	n_{t+1}	Convex RM
Marzban et al. (2021)		Actor–critic	FFN	S_t	n_{t+1}	DRM
Vittori et al. (2021)	Total costs	TRPO	FFN	$S_t, C_t, \frac{\partial C_t}{\partial S_t}, n_t$	n_{t+1}	TRVO
Buehler et al. (2022)	Total costs	Actor–critic	FFN	S_t	n_{t+1}	(OCE) of utility
Cao et al. (2022)	Total costs	D4PG-QR	FFN	$S_t, \Gamma_t^{\text{port}}, \nu_t^{\text{port}}, \Gamma_t^{\text{hedge}}, \nu_t^{\text{hedge}}$	n_{t+1}	(C)Var, Mean-Std.
Murray et al. (2022)	Total costs	Actor–critic	FFN	S_t	n_{t+1}	ERM
Cannelli et al. (2023)	Total costs	DQN	FFN	S_t, τ, n_t	Disc. n_{t+1}	Mean variance
		R-CMAB	FFN			
Fathi and Hientzsch (2023)	Total costs	DDPG	FFN	$S_t, C_t, \frac{\partial C_t}{\partial S_t}, n_t$	n_{t+1}	Minimum expected cost
		DTSOC				
Gao et al. (2023)	Total costs	DDPG	FFN	S_t, τ, n_t	n_{t+1}	Hedge error

Reference	Market Feature	Method	Architecture(s)	State	Action	Reward/Loss
Hirano et al. (2023a)	Total costs	Deep hedging	FFN	S_t, n_t	n_{t+1}	Hedge cost
						CVaR, ERM
Hirano et al. (2023b)	Total costs	Deep hedging	FFN	S_t, n_t	n_{t+1}	Hedge cost
						CVaR, ERM
Limmer and Horvath (2023)	Total costs	Deep hedging	GAN	S_t	n_{t+1}	ERM
Mikkilä and Kanniainen (2023)	Total costs	TD3	FFN	S_t, τ, n_t, σ_t	n_{t+1}	Mean-Std.
Szehr (2023)	Total costs	MCTS	FFN	S_t, τ, n_t	Disc. n_{t+1}	Mean variance
Hientzsch (2024)	Total costs	DDPG	FFN	S_t, τ, n_t	n_{t+1}	Minimum expected cost
		DTSOC				
Hirano (2024)	Total costs	Deep hedging	GAN	S_t, n_t	n_{t+1}	Hedge cost
						CVaR, ERM
Neagu et al. (2024)	Market implied	Policy gradi-ent	FFN	$\tau, S_t, A_t, B_t, n_t, M_t$	n_{t+1}	Semi-quadratic
Pickard et al. (2024)	Total costs	DDPG	FFN	S_t, τ, n_t	n_{t+1}	Mean variance

Horvath et al. (2021) use the *rough Bergomi* model (Christian Bayer and Gatheral, 2016) to generate their dataset, with the Hirst parameter set to 0.5 during agent training and set to a different value during testing. Hence, the dynamics are Markovian during training but non-Markovian during evaluation.

Lütkebohmert et al. (2021) adopt a *non-linear generalised affine (NGA)* process as the basis of their dataset, and this is a development of the affine process under parameter uncertainty proposed by Fadina et al. (2019). The dynamics are Markovian and take the form

$$dX_t = (b_0 + b_1 X_t)\, dt + (a_0 + a_1 X_t)^{\gamma}\, dW_t, \tag{19.4}$$

with uncertainty in the parameters b_0, b_1, a_0, a_1 and γ.

Carbonneau and Godin (2020, 2021) used a GARCH model to generate data alongside GBM and MJD.

A few researchers use historical data, most commonly for model evaluation, but some also train agents using historical time series. Giurca and Borovkova (2021), Lütkebohmert et al. (2021), Gao et al. (2023), Hirano et al. (2023b) and Hirano (2024) all use historical index data to evaluate their trained agents, most with S&P 500 data, with Hirano et al. (2023b) and Hirano (2024) adding BVSP data. Miikkulainen (2010) and Pickard et al. (2024) use historical equity and equity index data to train agents.

Two papers use agent-based models to generate the dataset: Gao et al. (2023) uses the Chiarella–Heston model that they propose as an extension of Majewski et al. (2020) and Hirano (2024) uses the PAMS multi-agent model (Hirano et al., 2023c). Buehler et al. (2021) and Kim (2021) use trained GANs to generate synthetic market data.

19.2.4 Duration and Frequency

Buehler et al. (2019) focused on hedging short-dated portfolios with a 30-day maturity, which has become the default duration for papers of this type. Almost all papers hedge a portfolio with a 1-year or less maturity. Two notable exceptions to this are Carbonneau (2020) and Hou et al. (2021), which use a maturity of 10 years.

Hedging is most commonly performed daily, with some authors considering weekly or monthly re-hedging for longer durations. Carbonneau (2020) employs annual re-hedging, reflecting the 10-year duration of the variable annuity product under consideration. Vittori et al. (2021) employ 305 re-hedging steps with a 61-day European option and examine intraday re-hedging. Mikkilä and Kanniainen (2023) utilise a short-dated option with a 5-day maturity and hourly re-hedging opportunities.

19.2.5 State and Action

The state space varies between authors but, as would be expected, always includes the current value of the underlying assets, S_t. The time to maturity of the portfolio is also a common element of the state space and is included in 10 out of 32 papers. The current hedge position, n_t, is also a frequent inclusion, with 15 papers including it. Two papers include volatility: Giurca and Borovkova (2021) use the asset volatility, while Mikkilä and Kanniainen (2023) include the Black–Scholes implied volatility. Vittori et al. (2021) hedge a European option and include both the current price of the option C_t and its delta $\frac{\partial C_t}{\partial S_t}$, as do Giurca and Borovkova (2021) and Fathi and Hientzsch (2023). Du et al. (2020) include the strike price of the option, K, in the state space. Assa et al. (2021) include the current value of the stock portfolio, X_t, and the value of the cash position, Y_t. Chong et al. (2021) use the variable annuity as the target product and hence choose to include the number of surviving policyholders $\sum_{i=1}^{N} J_{t_k}^{(i)}$, which is specific to this product. Cao et al. (2022) hedge options with options and hence include the price of the asset, the portfolio gamma Γ_t^{port}, the portfolio vega υ_t^{port}, the hedge gamma Γ_t^{hedge} and the hedge vega $\upsilon_t^{\text{hedge}}$. The study by Neagu et al. (2024) includes market impact. Hence, they include market impact persistence measures, defined by $A_t = e^{-\lambda_a}\left(A_{t-1} + (\Delta X_t)^+\right)$ and $B_t = e^{-\lambda_b}\left(B_{t-1} + (\Delta X_t)^-\right)$, in the state space alongside the asset price, hedge position and cash account value.

The action space is universally the hedge position for the next time step, n_{t+1}. Most models have a continuous action space, but a small number have discrete action spaces. Du et al. (2020) use DQN, as do Giurca and Borovkova (2021) and Cannelli et al. (2023), and hence have discrete action spaces. The Monte Carlo tree search (MCTS) algorithm used by Szehr (2023) also yields a discrete action space. Gong et al. (2021) place a constraint that re-hedging is only performed if the price move crosses a threshold α; hence, the associated action space is modified to accommodate.

19.2.6 Reward/Objective

The reward function was discussed at length in Chapter 10 and is key to providing feedback to the agent. In deep hedging, a reward function is sometimes not identified explicitly. As noted above, Buehler et al. (2019) do not use the language of RL and hence do not formally specify a reward function. However, it is clear that the specification of a convex risk measure as a function of the terminal portfolio value $\text{PL}_T(Z, p_0, \delta) := -Z + p_0 + (\delta \cdot S)_T - C_T(\delta)$ plays this role. Buehler et al. (2019) and those that adopt the deep hedging approach typically adopt CVaR as the convex risk measure,

$$u(x) = \frac{1}{1-\alpha}\int_{-\infty}^{\text{VaR}(\alpha)} x \cdot p(x)dx. \tag{19.5}$$

Carbonneau (2020) takes a different approach, using MSE and semi-MSE $x^2\mathbf{1}_{\{x>0\}}$, giving *quadratic deep hedging (QDH)* and *semi-quadratic deep hedging (SQDH)*. Neagu et al. (2024) also adopt semi-MSE. Murray et al. (2022), Hirano et al. (2023b), Limmer and Horvath (2023) and Hirano (2024) use the entropic risk measure defined by

$$u(x) = -\frac{1}{\lambda}\log \mathbb{E}[\exp(-\lambda x)]. \tag{19.6}$$

Many authors adopt a mean–variance or mean–standard deviation reward function. For example, Du and Mordatch (2019) use

$$\max_{\pi}\left(\mathbb{E}\left[w_T\right]-\frac{\kappa}{2}\mathbb{V}\left[w_T\right]\right), \tag{19.7}$$

where w_t is the agent wealth at time t. Vittori et al. (2021) use a variant of mean–variance, *TRVO*.

Assa et al. (2021) use a terminal reward only based on the hedge performance,

$$r\left(s_t, a_t\right)=\begin{cases}-\left|\left(S_T-K\right)_{+}-\left(X_T+Y_T\right)\right| & t=T \\ 0 & \text{otherwise}\end{cases}, \tag{19.8}$$

giving a negative reward for all cases where the hedge is not perfect. Hou et al. (2021) use a loss function $\mathbb{E}\left[\ell\left(\left(H-V_T\right)_{+}\right)\right]$, where

$$\ell(x)=x^p/p, p\in\mathbb{R}_{+}. \tag{19.9}$$

Here, H is the payoff function and V_T is the terminal value of the hedge portfolio.

Finally, Marzban et al. (2021) use a loss function based on the dynamic expectile risk measure, and this is defined recursively, capturing the evolution of risk over time based on the conditional distribution of future liabilities, defined by

$$\rho(X):=\bar{\rho}_0(\bar{\rho}_1(\ldots\bar{\rho}_{T-1}(X))), \tag{19.10}$$

where each $\bar{\rho}_t(\cdot)$ is an expectile risk measure that employs the conditional distribution based on the information available at time t (denoted as F_t). The τ-expectile of a random liability X is defined as

$$\bar{\rho}(X):=\arg\min_{q}\left(\tau E[(q-X)_{+}^{2}]+(1-\tau)E[(q-X)_{-}^{2}]\right). \tag{19.11}$$

19.2.7 RL Methodology

The papers reviewed here adopted a variety of RL methodologies. By far the most common is the *deep hedging* or *policy gradient* approach of Buehler et al. (2019), which, as discussed earlier, uses a deep neural network to learn the optimal policy. The approach was prevalent following the initial publication of the paper 'Deep hedging' but has declined in favour of other deep RL approaches more recently. Deep hedging has been applied by Carbonneau (2020), Carbonneau and Godin (2020), Buehler et al. (2021), Carbonneau and Godin (2021), Gong et al. (2021), Horvath et al. (2021), Hou et al. (2021), Kim (2021), Lütkebohmert et al. (2021), Hirano et al. (2023a,b), Limmer and Horvath (2023) and Hirano (2024). Neagu et al. (2024) explicitly describe their approach as *policy gradient*, while noting that it is derived from the approach of Buehler et al. (2019) and Carbonneau and Godin (2020).

As noted above, Du et al. (2020) and Giurca and Borovkova (2021) adopted deep Q-learning, introduced in Section 10.7. Du et al. (2020) also applied the *Pop-Art* variant of DQN, which is described below.

Deep deterministic policy gradient (DDPG) is another popular choice of methodology being used by Assa et al. (2021), Cao et al. (2021), Giurca and Borovkova (2021), Fathi and Hientzsch (2023), Gao et al. (2023), Hientzsch (2024) and Pickard et al. (2024). DDPG is a policy gradient method that uses an actor–critic architecture as discussed in Sections 10.8 and 10.9 and is further explored in Section 19.2.7.2.

Proximal policy optimisation (PPO) is a TD policy gradient method related to the REINFORCE algorithm described in Section 10.8.3. PPO has been adopted as one of the approaches considered by Du et al. (2020) and the sole method used by Chong et al. (2021). The closely related trust region policy optimisation (TRPO) method is used by Vittori et al. (2021). Section 19.2.7.3 discusses TRPO and PPO in detail.

Buehler et al. (2022) and Murray et al. (2022) move away from the deep hedging policy gradient algorithm to an actor–critic algorithm. As described in Section 10.9, this adds a second network to approximate the state value function. Murray et al. (2022) use a variant of the ERM function to model risk aversion. Marzban et al. (2021) also adopt a deep actor–critic approach but use a network to approximate the Q-function rather than the state value function.

Cao et al. (2022) adopt a variant of the DDPG algorithm, D4PG, as developed by Barth-Maron et al. (2018) and presented in Section 19.2.7.5. Another variant of DDPG applied in the context of deep hedging is *twin delayed deep deterministic policy gradient (TD3)*, as used by Miikkulainen (2010), described in Section 19.2.7.7. Only one paper, Cannelli et al. (2023), uses a *bandit*-based model, employing a neural risk-averse contextual multi-armed bandit as an alternative to the DQN model. DQN and neural R-CMAB models share a discrete action space, with the neural R-CMAB model detailed in Section 19.2.7.6. Finally, Szehr (2023) apply *neural Monte Carlo tree search* to deep hedging, a methodology derived from that used in AlphaGo (Silver et al., 2016), with a summary provided in Section 19.2.7.8.

19.2.7.1 DQN Pop-Art In deep Q-networks, the scale of rewards modelled in the value function can vary by several orders of magnitude, making it difficult for the model to learn and update effectively. DQN Pop-Art was introduced by van Hasselt et al. (2016) and stands for *preserving outputs precisely, while adaptively rescaling targets*, and this method dynamically normalises the target values in the Q-learning algorithm to ensure that the scale of the value function remains manageable without losing the precision of the learning signal. There are two fundamental mechanisms: normalisation of the target by maintaining a running estimate of the mean and variance and adaptive rescaling, where the algorithm adapts the network weights accordingly to preserve the outputs of the unnormalised function.

19.2.7.2 DDPG DDPG was introduced by Lillicrap et al. (2015) to target problems in RL with continuous action spaces. The key features of DDPG are as follows:

- **Actor–Critic Architecture.** Two networks representing the *actor* and the *critic*. The actor network outputs the deterministic action directly from the current state. The critic network evaluates the action by approximating the Q-value for the given state–action pair.
- **Policy Updates.** The policy (actor) is updated using the gradient of the Q-value with respect to the actions, which the critic estimates. The critic is updated by minimising the Bellman error, which is the difference between the predicted and target Q-values.
- **Exploration.** DDPG introduces noise to the deterministic policy for exploration.
- **Target Networks.** Target networks are used for both the actor and the critic to stabilise training. These target networks are copies of the actor and critic networks but are updated more slowly to provide consistent target values.
- **Experience Replay.** DDPG is an off-policy algorithm that uses a replay buffer to store past experiences.

DDPG is described by Algorithm 19.1.

19.2.7.3 TRPO and PPO TRPO, as developed by Schulman et al. (2015), is a method that ensures stable and monotonic policy improvements by constraining the size of policy updates during the training process. The key idea behind TRPO is to optimise a *surrogate* objective function while ensuring that the new policy does not deviate too much from the old one, as measured by the Kullback–Leibler divergence. This constraint, known as the trust region, helps prevent the policy from changing too abruptly, which could lead to instability and poor performance. TRPO is particularly effective for optimising extensive, non-linear policies such as those represented by neural networks. The algorithm has demonstrated robust performance across various tasks, including robotic locomotion and playing Atari games.

Schulman et al. (2017) later developed the PPO approach that builds on the ideas of TRPO but simplifies the algorithm to improve computational efficiency and ease of implementation. While TRPO requires solving a constrained optimisation problem, PPO achieves a similar effect by clipping the probability ratio between the new and old policies during updates. This clipping ensures that the updates are neither too large nor too small, maintaining stability while allowing for more flexibility than TRPO. PPO is designed to strike a balance between the advantages of TRPO and the simplicity of standard policy gradient methods. Schulman et al. (2017) demonstrated that PPO outperformed earlier methods in continuous control environments.

Algorithm 19.1: Deep Deterministic Policy Gradient (DDPG)

Initialise actor network $\mu(s|\theta^{\mu})$ and critic network $Q(s, a|\theta^{Q})$ with random weights;
Initialise target networks $\mu'(s|\theta^{\mu'})$ and $Q'(s, a|\theta^{Q'})$ with weights $\theta^{\mu'} \leftarrow \theta^{\mu}, \theta^{Q'} \leftarrow \theta^{Q}$;
Initialise replay buffer $\mathcal{R}$;
for *episode = 1 to M* **do**
  Initialise a random process $\mathcal{N}$ for action exploration;
  Receive initial state s_1;
  for $t = 1$ *to* T **do**
    Select action $a_t = \mu(s_t|\theta^{\mu}) + \mathcal{N}_t$ according to the current policy and exploration noise;
    Execute action a_t, observe reward r_t and new state s_{t+1};
    Store transition (s_t, a_t, r_t, s_{t+1}) in replay buffer $\mathcal{R}$;
    Sample a random mini-batch of N transitions (s_i, a_i, r_i, s_{i+1}) from $\mathcal{R}$;
    Set $y_i = r_i + \gamma Q'(s_{i+1}, \mu'(s_{i+1}|\theta^{\mu'})|\theta^{Q'})$;
    Update critic by minimising the loss:

$$L = \frac{1}{N}\sum_i \left(y_i - Q(s_i, a_i|\theta^{Q})\right)^2$$

    Update the actor policy using the sampled policy gradient:

$$\nabla_{\theta^{\mu}} J \approx \frac{1}{N}\sum_i \nabla_a Q(s, a|\theta^{Q})|_{s=s_i, a=\mu(s_i)} \nabla_{\theta^{\mu}} \mu(s|\theta^{\mu})|_{s_i}$$

    Soft update the target networks:

$$\theta^{Q'} \leftarrow \tau\theta^{Q} + (1-\tau)\theta^{Q'}$$

$$\theta^{\mu'} \leftarrow \tau\theta^{\mu} + (1-\tau)\theta^{\mu'}$$

  end
end

19.2.7.4 DTSOC The deep trajectory-based stochastic optimal control (DTSOC) algorithm, as applied by Fathi and Hientzsch (2023) and Hientzsch (2024), was originally proposed by Han and E (2016) and is closely related to the deep BSDE solvers by the same authors (Weinan et al., 2017; Han et al., 2018). They propose a deep learning-based framework to address high-dimensional stochastic control problems. The core idea is to approximate time-dependent controls using feedforward neural networks and utilise Monte Carlo sampling techniques to solve the problem efficiently.

The model framework is set up as follows. The hedging problem is formulated as a stochastic control problem of the form (Han and E, 2016; Fathi and Hientzsch, 2023)

$$s_{t+1} = f(s_t, a_t, \xi_t), \tag{19.12}$$

where s_t is the state, a_t is the action (control) and ξ_t is a random noise variable. The admissible actions are given by

$$a_t \in \mathcal{A}_t = \left\{ a_t(s_t) : \mathbb{R}^m \to \mathbb{R}^n \;\middle|\; \begin{array}{l} g_i(s_t, a_t) = 0 \text{ for } i = 1, \ldots, I, \forall s_t \in \mathcal{S}_t \\ h_j(s_t, a_t) \geq 0 \text{ for } j = 1, \ldots, J, \forall s_t \in \mathcal{S}_t \end{array} \right\}, \tag{19.13}$$

where $g_i(s_t, a_t)$ and $h_j(s_t, a_t)$ are constraints. The cost per step is given by $c_t = c_t(s_t, a_t, s_{t+1})$ and the terminal cost is $c_T(s_t)$. The cumulative cost is then

$$C = \sum_{t=0}^{T-1} c_t\left(s_t, a_t, s_{t+1}\right) + c_T\left(s_T\right). \tag{19.14}$$

The action is a function of the state, and a feedforward neural network approximates this,

$$a_t(s_t) \approx a_t(s_t|\theta). \tag{19.15}$$

The neural network therefore approximates the deterministic policy. The target is to minimise the expected cost,

$$\underset{a_t \in \mathcal{A}_t, t=0,\dots,T-1}{\operatorname{argmin}} \mathrm{E}[C] = \underset{a_t \in \mathcal{A}_t, t=0,\dots,T-1}{\operatorname{argmin}} \mathrm{E}\left[\sum_{t=0}^{T-1} c_t\left(s_t, a_t\left(s_t \mid \theta_t\right), s_{t+1}\right) + c_T\left(s_T\right)\right]. \tag{19.16}$$

The network architecture for the stochastic control problem consists of a stack of N feedforward neural networks, one for each time step, that are trained together. The training procedure is given in Algorithm 19.2.

Algorithm 19.2: Training Procedure for DTSOC (After Hientzsch, 2024)

Input: Network weights $\{\theta_m, m = 0, \dots, T-1\}$
Output: Optimised network weights $\{\theta_m^*, m = 0, \dots, T-1\}$
while *epoch* $\leq$ *EPOCH* **do**
  nbatch = 0;
  batchloss = 0;
  while *nbatch* $\leq$ *batch size* **do**
    $m = 0$;
    $C_{-1} = 0$;
    while $m < T$ **do**
      $a_m = \pi_{\theta_m}(s_m)$;
      $s_{m+1} = f(s_m, a_m, \xi_m)$; // `with sampled noise` ξ_m
      $C_m = C_{m-1} + c_m(s_m, a_m, s_{m+1})$;
      $m++$;
    $C_T = C_{T-1} + c_T(s_T)$;
    batchloss += $l(C_T)$;
  Calculate loss for batch: $Loss = \frac{\text{batchloss}}{\text{batch size}}$;
  Calculate gradient of *Loss* with respect to θ;
  Backpropagate updates for $\{\theta_m, m = 0, \dots, T-1\}$;
  epoch++;

19.2.7.5 D4PG The D4PG algorithm, as presented by Barth-Maron et al. (2018), is a reinforcement learning algorithm designed for continuous control tasks. It extends the DDPG algorithm by incorporating distributional perspectives, which allows for modelling the entire distribution of returns rather than just the expected return. The key components of the D4PG algorithm are as follows:

- **Distributional Reinforcement Learning.** D4PG approximates the return distribution, enhancing stability and performance.
- **N-Step Returns.** The algorithm uses (TD) N-step returns to improve the bias–variance trade-off, making the learning process more efficient.

- **Prioritised Experience Replay.** D4PG incorporates prioritised experience replay as defined in Section 10.7.3, ensuring that more significant transitions are replayed more frequently, improving learning efficiency.
- **Distributed Learning.** The algorithm is implemented within a distributed framework, enabling it to scale efficiently.

D4PG is shown in Algorithm 19.3.

Algorithm 19.3: D4PG (After Barth-Maron et al., 2018)

Input: Batch size M, trajectory length N, number of actors K, replay size R, exploration constant ϵ, initial learning rates α_0 and β_0
Output: Policy parameters θ
Initialise network weights θ, w at random;
Initialise target weights θ', $w' \leftarrow \theta$, w;
Launch K actors and replicate network weights θ, w to each actor;
for $t = 1$ **to** T **do**
  Sample M transitions $(x_{i:i+N}, a_{i:i+N-1}, r_{i:i+N-1})$ of length N from replay with priority p_i;
  Construct the target distributions
  $Y_i = \sum_{n=0}^{N-1} \gamma^n r_{i+n} + \gamma^N Z_{w'}(x_{i+N}, \pi_{\theta'}(x_{i+N}))$;
  Compute the actor and critic updates:

$$\delta_w = \frac{1}{M} \sum_i \nabla_w \left(p(Rp_i)^{-1} d_p(Y_i, Z_w(x_i, a_i)) \right)$$

$$\delta_\theta = \frac{1}{M} \sum_i \nabla_\theta \pi_\theta(x_i) \mathbb{E} \left[\nabla_a Z_w(x_i, a) \right]_{a=\pi(x_i)}$$

  Update network parameters $\theta \leftarrow \theta + \alpha_t \delta_\theta$, $w \leftarrow w + \beta_t \delta_w$;
  if t mod $t_{target} == 0$ **then**
    Update the target networks θ', $w' \leftarrow \theta$, w;
  if t mod $t_{actors} == 0$ **then**
    Replicate network weights to the actors;

Function `Actor()`:
  repeat
    Sample action $a \leftarrow \pi_\theta(x) + \epsilon N(0, 1)$;
    Execute action a, observe reward r and state x';
    Store (x, a, r, x') in replay;
  until *learner finishes*;

19.2.7.6 R-CMAB The multi-armed bandit environment was discussed in Example 10.1 in Chapter 10. Cannelli et al. (2023) employ the *risk-averse contextual multi-armed bandit (R-CMAB)* in their approach to deep hedging. Breaking this name down, *contextual* refers to the non-stationary reward distribution. The agent receives the state of the system or *context* from the environment and then needs to learn how this relates to the reward distribution. The standard MAB and CMAB agents are trained to maximise the reward only; however, as with most of the authors discussed in this chapter, the reward is modified to include risk aversion by defining it using mean variance. Given an action a, its mean variance is given by

$$MV(a) := \kappa\mu(a) - \sigma^2(a). \tag{19.17}$$

In practice, the agent only has access to the sampled results of taking action a and $X_l(a)$; hence, the sample mean and standard deviation are obtained for training purposes.

Cannelli et al. (2023) use a *neural* (R-CMAB) algorithm that leverages a neural network to predict rewards for different actions (arms) based on contextual information. Exploration is facilitated by using a Bayesian linear regression model layered on the output of the network's last layer. Random sampling predicts rewards rather than using the deterministic output from the network. The parameter vectors β_a are sampled from the posterior and combined with z_x, the output from the network's last hidden layer, giving the predicted value for the action as $v_a = \beta_a^T z_x$. As noted in the discussion of *experience replay*, the correlations in the sequence of contexts can lead to training instability, so experience relay is adopted to address this issue. The neural network weights and the posterior model are updated asynchronously to give more stable training. The Bayesian regression model layered on top of the NN is based on earlier work by Snoek et al. (2015) and Riquelme et al. (2018). The R-CMAB method is summarised in Algorithm 19.4.

Algorithm 19.4: Neural R-CMAB Algorithm (After Cannelli et al., 2023)

```
Input: Learning rate η, risk-aversion parameter λ, number of actions (arms) K, prior dist. π_0
Output: Trained agent and NN
Initialise neural network f_θ with random weights θ and replay buffer;
for each episode do
    for each time step t = 1 to T do
        Sample θ_t ~ π_t;
        Observe context x_t;
        Use NN + Bayesian to obtain best action a_t^best;
        Perform a_t and observe reward r_t;
        Store episode x_t, a_t, r_t;
        if Bayesian Update Time then
            Update posterior dist. estimate π_t using recent transitions;
        end
        if NN Training Time then
            Sample from replay buffer and train NN;
        end
    end
end
```

19.2.7.7 TD3 The TD3 algorithm, as applied by Mikkilä and Kanniainen (2023), is a DDPG development introduced by Fujimoto et al. (2018). The algorithm is designed to address two key issues: overestimation bias and variance.

Overestimation bias is a problem in RL, particularly with value-based methods that estimate the state value or state–action value functions. The actual value of an action or state is overestimated when a noisy value estimate is maximised. When function approximators like neural networks are used, the noise in estimates can lead the algorithm to assess the value of suboptimal actions being higher than they are. In turn, this leads to policy updates that are also suboptimal and the algorithm favouring actions incorrectly. Ultimately, this leads to poor performance and divergent behaviour in the learned policy.

Clipped double Q-learning is designed to address overestimation bias. Like double Q-learning, two separate Q-value estimates are maintained. However, the Q-value is also clipped for a given action by always taking the minimum of the Q-values from the two networks. In doing so, the algorithm does not take action based on biased estimates. The probability of taking a suboptimal action is reduced, leading to more reliable policy updates and improved performance.

Variance arises from error accumulation in estimating the value function. TD learning uses the estimated value of future states to update the current state, which depends on these estimates' accuracy. Hence, any inaccuracy in the estimates of states from neural networks or other function approximators can lead to errors in the TD update, which can compound over time. Noisy gradients during policy updates are the result, which can reduce the algorithm's learning speed and overall performance. Reducing variance is critical to stabilising learning and improving RL algorithms.

Two key ways of addressing variance in RL are through target networks and reducing the frequency of updates to policy networks. Section 10.7.5 included a discussion of target networks, which were used in Example 10.10. The idea of a target network is to provide stable value function estimates that are updated with a slower cadence than the main Q-network. The slower updates reduce variance in gradient estimates and help reduce oscillations induced by rapidly changing value estimates. Similarly, reducing the frequency of updates to the policy network relative to the Q-network ensures that more accurate value estimates are used to make policy adjustments. Together, both strategies increase stability and learning performance.

Target policy smoothing regularisation is another technique designed to reduce variance in RL by enforcing a smoother relationship between the value estimates of similar actions. Value functions can become sensitive to small policy changes with deterministic policies, leading to overfitting. In turn, this leads to variance in updates during training. To address this issue, 'smoothing' of the value function is used to ensure that similar actions have similar values, which is done using a SARSA-like update mechanism. Overall, policy updates become more stable, giving better convergence and performance.

TD3 combines these enhancements into the Algorithm 19.5 presented below. Fujimoto et al. (2018) evaluated the algorithm on MuJoCo continuous control tasks. They demonstrated significant performance improvements when employing TD3 compared to existing methods. In a series of evaluations across various environments, such as HalfCheetah, Hopper and Walker2d, TD3 consistently achieved higher average returns over one million time steps, showcasing its effectiveness in stabilising learning and enhancing policy performance.

Algorithm 19.5: TD3 (After Fujimoto et al., 2018)

Input: Initialise critic networks Q_{θ_1}, Q_{θ_2} and actor network π_ϕ with random parameters θ_1, θ_2, ϕ
Initialise target networks $\theta'_1 \leftarrow \theta_1, \theta'_2 \leftarrow \theta_2, \phi' \leftarrow \phi$
Initialise replay buffer B
for $t = 1$ **to** T **do**
  Select action with exploration noise $a \sim \pi(s) + \epsilon, \epsilon \sim \mathcal{N}(0, \sigma)$ and observe reward r and new state s'
  Store transition tuple (s, a, r, s') in B
  Sample mini-batch of N transitions (s, a, r, s') from B
  $\tilde{a} \leftarrow \pi_{\phi'}(s') + \epsilon, \epsilon \sim \text{clip}(\mathcal{N}(0, \tilde{\sigma}), -c, c)$
  $y \leftarrow r + \gamma \min_{i=1,2} Q_{\theta'_i}(s', \tilde{a})$
  Update critics $\theta_i \leftarrow \arg\min_{\theta_i} \frac{1}{N} \sum \left(y - Q_{\theta_i}(s, a)\right)^2$
  if t mod $d = 0$ **then**
    Update ϕ by the deterministic policy gradient:
    $\nabla_\phi J(\phi) = \frac{1}{N} \sum \nabla_a Q_{\theta_1}(s, a)|_{a=\pi_\phi(s)} \nabla_\phi \pi_\phi(s)$
    Update target networks:
    $\theta'_i \leftarrow \tau\theta_i + (1 - \tau)\theta'_i$
    $\phi' \leftarrow \tau\phi + (1 - \tau)\phi'$
  end
end

19.2.7.8 Neural MCTS Neural MCTS is the algorithm that lies behind AlphaGo (Silver et al., 2016) and its successors AlphaZero (Silver et al., 2017) and MuZero (Schrittwieser et al., 2019). MCTS has now been widely adopted in many RL applications, including chemistry, material science, electronics design, energy systems, production, combinatorial optimisation, cloud and edge computing, graph navigation, networking and communications, autonomous driving and motion planning, NLP and computer science (Kemmerling et al., 2023). This section describes the neural MCTS algorithm and its financial application by Szehr (2023).

The Game Tree. The *game tree* is a conceptual representation of all possible sequences of moves occurring in the game from the starting position. Figure 19.1 illustrates this in the context of *noughts-and-crosses*, otherwise known as *tic-tac-toe*. Each node in the tree represents a specific configuration of the game board, and each branch (or edge) represents a legal move that transitions the game from one board configuration to another.

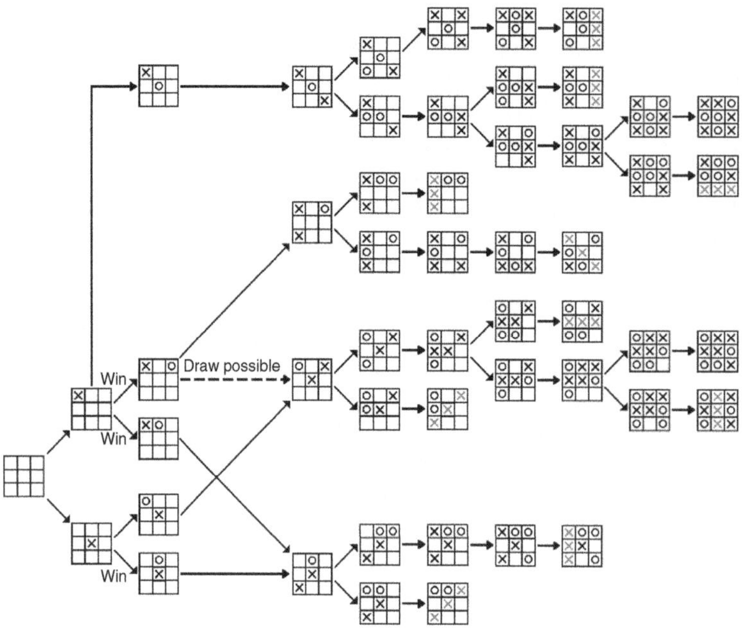

FIGURE 19.1 Game tree for *noughts-and-crosses* (*tic-tac-toe*). *Source*: Mike like0708 distributed under the Creative Commons CC0 1.0 Universal Public Domain Dedication.

Consider starting with an empty noughts-and-crosses board. The root node of the game tree represents this initial state. The first layer of children represents all possible first moves by the player who goes first (either X or O). Each of these children then has further children representing the potential responses by the second player. The tree continues to branch, with each level representing successive player moves.

The tree leaf nodes are the endpoints in the tree corresponding to a win by one layer forming a line of three, or the board becoming full, leading to a draw.

Structure of the noughts-and-crosses game tree:

1. **Root Node.** The root of the game tree represents the initial empty game board before any player makes a move.
2. **Intermediate Nodes.** These nodes represent the various configurations of the board after a sequence of moves has been made by the players. Each node has children corresponding to the possible board configurations resulting from the next player's legal moves.
3. **Branches (Edges).** A branch between two nodes represents a single move in the game. In noughts-and-crosses, the first layer has nine branches with nine empty squares, but subsequent levels have fewer branches as the board fills.
4. **Depth of the Tree.** The depth corresponds to the number of moves from the starting position. Since noughts-and-crosses is a relatively simple game, the maximum depth of the tree is nine, corresponding to a full board.
5. **Leaf Nodes.** The leaf nodes in the game tree are the endpoints for the game, as no further moves are possible or the game has been won.
   - **Win.** One player has successfully placed three of their marks (X or O) in a row, either horizontally, vertically or diagonally.
   - **Draw.** A position where all nine squares on the board are filled, but neither player has three in a row.
   - **End of Game.** If the game reaches a win or draw earlier than the ninth move, the game ends.

Tree Search. A game tree can be used to explore possible future moves and determine the best course of action. The goal is to evaluate different sequences of moves (paths in the game tree) and select the move that maximises the chances of winning or achieving a favourable outcome.

There are two forms of search, depth-first and breadth-first:

- **Depth-First Search (DFS)** explores a single path deeply before backtracking and trying other paths. DFS goes deep into the tree, which is helpful in games like chess and Go, where exploring the consequences of moves several steps ahead is critical and is an approach used by human players.
- **Breadth-First Search (BFS)** explores all possible moves at the current level before moving deeper. BFS ensures that all possible immediate responses are explored before considering longer-term strategies, which can be helpful in simpler games.

Minmax is a common tree search algorithm used in two-player games like chess (Russell and Norvig, 2021). The idea is to simulate that both players are playing optimally. The algorithm recursively explores all possible moves and counter-moves:

- **Maximising Player.** The player trying to maximise their score (typically the player whose turn it is).
- **Minimising Player.** The opponent tries to minimise the score for the maximising player.

The minmax algorithm evaluates the leaf nodes and then backpropagates these values up the tree to decide the best move. Unfortunately, minmax has high algorithmic complexity and computational cost. With a tree that is m layers deep and with b possible moves, the time complexity is $O(b^m)$, and the space complexity is $O(bm)$. The exponential time complexity makes it infeasible for complex games like chess with approximately 10^{123} states (Russell and Norvig, 2021).

The only way to make the algorithm workable for complex games is to reduce the number of game states searched by *pruning* (Russell and Norvig, 2021). Alpha–beta pruning is an optimisation of the minmax algorithm that eliminates branches in the game tree that do not need to be explored because they cannot possibly influence the final decision:

- α represents the best value the maximiser can guarantee at that level or above.
- β represents the best value the minimiser can guarantee at that level or above.

Pruning occurs when the algorithm discovers that a move will lead to a worse outcome than a previously explored path, and this allows it to skip evaluating entire subtrees, significantly reducing the number of nodes that need to be assessed. IBM's Deep Blue chess-playing computer implemented a parallel version of alpha–beta pruning using specialist hardware (Hsu et al., 1995).

MCTS. For the game of Go, the branching factor is 361, an order of magnitude greater than the 35 for chess. There are also challenges in defining an evaluation function as the game state remains uncertain until the end of the games. Hence, even *heuristic alpha–beta tree search*, one of the best deterministic search algorithms, is not sufficient and a different approach, *Monte Carlo tree search* has been adopted (Russell and Norvig, 2021).

MCTS is an RL algorithm that can be applied to games and other applications with large and complex search spaces. MCTS applies random Monte Carlo simulations to explore a large game tree in cases where a full tree search is impractical. MCTS builds a search tree by simulating random plays from a given state. The simulation results are then used to guide the search towards favourable moves. The process involves four main steps: selection, expansion, simulation and backpropagation (Russell and Norvig, 2021).

1. **Selection**
   - Objective. Traverse the tree from the root to a leaf node by selecting child nodes according to a specific strategy.
   - Process
     - Starting from the root node, recursively select child nodes that balance exploration and exploitation.
     - The most common selection strategy is UCT, which is given by the formula

$$\text{UCT} = \frac{Q(s,a)}{N(s,a)} + c \times \sqrt{\frac{\ln\ N(s)}{N(s,a)}}, \tag{19.18}$$

where $Q(s, a)$ is the state–action value function, $N(s, a)$ is the visit count of action a, $N(s)$ is the visit count of state s and c is a constant that controls the exploration–exploitation trade-off.
- The selection continues until reaching a terminal node.

2. **Expansion**
   - Objective. Expand the tree by adding one or more child nodes to the selected node.
   - Process
     - If the selected node is not a leaf node, expand it by generating one or more of its children.
     - Typically, one child node is added per iteration, corresponding to a new move in the game that has yet to be explored.
     - The expansion step ensures that the search tree grows gradually, considering possible future states as the search progresses.
3. **Simulation (Rollout)**
   - Objective. Simulate the game from the newly expanded node to the end using a simple policy to play out the rest of the game.
   - Process
     - Starting from the expanded node, simulate a complete game until a terminal state.
     - This simulation uses a default policy, which could be random or based on simple heuristics.
     - The outcome of this simulation is recorded.
4. **Backpropagation**
   - Objective. Propagate the simulation result back through the nodes in the tree, updating their statistics.
   - Process
     - After the simulation, the result is backpropagated from the expanded node to the root, updating each node's win/loss statistics along the path.
     - The node's statistics are updated by incrementing the visit count $N(s, a)$ for each node, updating the value $Q(s, a)$ to reflect the outcome.

MCTS is significantly faster than alpha–beta tree search and is linear in the depth of the tree (Russell and Norvig, 2021). Kocsis and Szepesvári (2006) demonstrated that the algorithm converges to the minmax tree search. The significant advantage of MCTS is that it does not require prior knowledge of the game mechanics and simulates according to the game rules. There are two disadvantages: the stochastic nature of the algorithm means that some moves may be missed and the algorithm does need to fully play out a game that is already a clear victory.

Neural MCTS. Silver et al. (2016) introduced two types of neural networks into the MCTS algorithm in AlphaGo, a *value network* and a *policy network*. The value network approximates the value function $v_\theta(s)$ that evaluates a given board position and predicts the likelihood of winning from that position. The value network is trained using supervised learning on state–outcome pairs (z, s), where the input is the board state and the output is the game outcome. The policy network $p_\sigma(a|s)$ approximates the policy and the probability distribution over all possible actions from the board state s. The policy network is also trained using supervised learning but from expert human moves, allowing it to learn effective human strategies. It is further refined through reinforcement learning, which optimises its move selection based on the outcomes of self-play games.

Both value and policy networks are deep CNNs with 13 layers and ReLU activation functions. The policy network has a softmax layer to output the policy, while the value network has just a single output, the state value.

Both networks are integrated into the MCTS algorithm. The policy network helps sampling actions during the search, while the value network evaluates the positions reached during the search. This combination allows AlphaGo to efficiently explore the search space and make informed decisions based on immediate move probabilities and long-term position evaluations.

There are three key advantages of neural MCTS: efficiency, scalability and learning from experience. Neural MCTS can prune large parts of the search tree that are less likely to lead to a favourable outcome. It also scales to complex games like Go and chess with vast state spaces. Finally, neural MCTS allows learning from experience, provided by expert knowledge, and then improving over time through self-play.

AlphaGo was implemented using CPU and GPU resources to optimise performance during the search and evaluation processes. The model employed a multi-threaded approach to execute simulations across CPU cores, enabling the program to run many MCTS simulations in parallel and significantly increasing the number of positions evaluated per second. The policy and value networks used GPUs for training and inference. The final model version used 48 CPUs and 8 GPUs. This configuration allowed the system to efficiently manage the large number of simulations required for effective decision-making in the game of Go.

Deep Hedging with MCTS. Szehr (2023) applies neural MCTS to deep hedging. To apply MCTS, transition probabilities $P(s'|s, a)$ are necessary, and these can be obtained in two ways. In the *pure planning problem*, the probabilities of state transitions are assumed a priori, potentially learned from real market data. In the *adversarial game problem*, the market is modelled by an independent policy that adapts dynamically, providing a more realistic representation of market behaviour. Szehr (2023) adopts the first pure planning approach.

The planning tree consists of an alternating sequence of planned decisions made by the agent and market moves. Each node in the tree represents a market state at a specific time, capturing the dynamics of the underlying asset and the derivative contract. The author used a trinomial tree model, as it allows drifts and volatilities that depend on the underlying asset. As with AlphaGo, Szehr (2023) uses neural networks for value and policy functions, with a training approach following that of the original AlphaGo model. However, the author uses a single network with two outputs rather than two distinct networks. The neutral network was a CNN but with only four layers.

Szehr (2023) applied MCTS to hedging a single European call only with a maturity of 60 days. The underlying dynamics were GBM with a volatility of 30% and no dividends. Twenty steps were used for the trinomial tree. Hedging was rewarded on the interval $[-1, 1]$, with 1 being a perfect hedge. Each training iteration consisted of 1000 episodes, with each episode consisting of 25 individual simulations. The agent operates within a discrete action space of 21 options, allowing it to buy or sell up to 10 shares or choose to make no transaction at all. The MCTS agent can learn essential hedging strategies after relatively short training periods, despite discretisation errors inherent in the state and action spaces. The introduction of transaction costs does not significantly affect the training convergence, but stochastic volatility does, requiring more training samples. Additionally, a comparison with a DQN approach shows that MCTS outperforms DQN in this context due to the challenges DQN faces with delayed rewards.

19.2.8 Network Architecture

Most authors deploy FFNs to represent value functions or policies. These networks are typically relatively shallow, with two to three hidden layers and small numbers of neurons in each layer, reflecting the simplicity of most deep hedging environments.

A small number of authors use or experiment with recurrent networks. Buehler et al. (2019) consider an RNN alongside an FFN in their original paper, as do Horvath et al. (2021) and Kim (2021). Carbonneau (2020) and Carbonneau and Godin (2021) use LSTM units in their networks, and a GRU network is used by Gong et al. (2021).

Three papers – Hirano et al. (2023b), Limmer and Horvath (2023) and Hirano (2024) – use GAN architectures. For example, Limmer and Horvath (2023) define the *robust hedging GAN*, which aims to use a model-free and algorithmic method of addressing model uncertainty by approximating optimal hedging strategies. They use three key frameworks: deep hedging, synthetic market data generation and signature methods.[1]

The robust-hedging GAN has three main components:

- **Generator.** Takes sample paths of Brownian motion and transforms them into increments of the asset price process under a specified model $\mathbb{P}$.
- **Discriminator.** Corresponds to a deep hedge instance that evaluates the generated paths. It computes the profits and losses based on a strategy defined by a neural network and assesses them using a utility functional estimator.
- **Penaliser.** The penaliser applies a penalty to the model represented by the generator, with the SigMMD metric suggested for measuring deviations from a reference model. This metric operates directly in path space and helps ensure the robustness of the generated strategies. *Signature maximum mean discrepancy (SigMMD)* is a *signature*-based metric used to measure the similarity between two probability distributions, particularly in path space.

Limmer and Horvath (2023) demonstrated improved out-of-sample performance for the hedge using their GAN model.

[1] Synthetic market data generation and signature methods were discussed in Chapter 18.

19.2.9 Results

The results of the studies discussed in this chapter are summarised in Tables 19.9 through 19.16. Not all of the studies are directly focused on developing a high-performing deep reinforcement learning agent. Nevertheless, several key themes emerge:

- **Successful Training.** Almost all the studies successfully trained an effective RL agent except for Assa et al. (2021), which required ensemble methods to obtain good performance.
- **Outperformance.** Across multiple studies, deep hedging methods outperform delta hedging, particularly in the presence of transaction costs.
- **Robustness and Adaptability.** Deep hedging is robust under parameter uncertainty, high volatility and real market data and adaptable to changing conditions.
- **Algorithmic Innovations.** There is a focus on the development and application of advanced deep RL algorithms like DDPG, PPO, actor–critic, and policy gradient methods.
- **Limitations and Challenges.** Despite the advancements, challenges remain with overfitting due to limited real-world data and the limitations of artificial market simulations. Achieving strong performance with real-world data remains the ultimate target for deep hedging.

19.2.10 Conclusions: The Deep Hedging Literature

Deep hedging has emerged as a powerful technique to optimally manage a portfolio, clearly outperforming delta hedging in the presence of transaction costs. This review has explored a large body of deep hedging research, examining target applications, datasets, environment specifications, RL methodologies and neural network architectures employed by various researchers.

Key themes that have emerged include:

1. The main focus is on hedging single options, with some extensions to portfolios and more exotic derivatives.
2. Synthetic data generated from classic risk-neutral models is commonly used, with limited historical data application, reflecting data availability.
3. The evolution from the original deep hedging framework to more sophisticated RL approaches like DDPG, PPO and neural MCTS.
4. A trend towards incorporating risk measures and market frictions into the reward/objective functions.
5. The prevalence of relatively simple feedforward neural networks, with some exploration of recurrent and GAN architectures.
6. The majority of studies can successfully train DRL agents that outperform standard benchmarks like Black–Scholes delta hedging, particularly in the presence of transaction costs.

TABLE 19.3 Author Approaches to Deep Hedging: Results

Reference	Results
Buehler et al. (2019)	The experiments assess deep hedging performance, including the impact of transaction costs and different risk preferences. The authors test in a synthetic market and analyse scalability. Results show that deep hedging outperforms traditional delta hedging.
Carbonneau and Godin (2020)	The study is focused on using deep hedging to price options using equal risk measures. ERP prices are found to be highly sensitive to asset dynamics, with time-varying volatility and regime risk further elevating residual hedging risk. ERP proves robust across various market conditions, and the approach is general and can price exotic derivatives.
Carbonneau (2020)	The study evaluates quadratic (QDH) and semi-quadratic (SQDH) deep hedging strategies, showing through Monte Carlo simulations that SQDH significantly reduces downside risk and increases expected returns compared to QDH across different market models.
Du et al. (2020)	The study finds that the DQN with Pop-Art and PPO models outperforms the standard DQN in terms of stability and efficiency in deep hedging.

Reference	Results
Assa et al. (2021)	The authors tested the DDPG model but showed that it failed to achieve convergence to the exact analytic hedging performance, regardless of training episodes or neural network architectures. To enhance performance, the authors propose using ensemble methods, specifically averaging and median approaches, which significantly improve accuracy and stability.
Buehler et al. (2021)	The paper's primary focus is to introduce a numerically efficient method for calculating risk-neutral densities for derivative paths and option prices. However, deep hedging shows that by eliminating statistical arbitrage opportunities from simulated data, the RL agent focuses on managing derivative portfolio risk, leading to more robust hedging.
Cao et al. (2021)	The authors successfully apply DDPG and show that it reduces hedging costs compared to delta hedging, especially with frequent rebalancing. The RL strategy adapts dynamically, improving cost efficiency by 31% to 42% for short-term options. It remains effective even in complex environments like stochastic volatility models.
Carbonneau and Godin (2021)	The paper examines the ERP framework for pricing and deep hedging with multiple instruments. It finds that using options in hedging reduces both equal risk prices and market incompleteness by mitigating tail risk asymmetry. ERP demonstrates its potential for flexible pricing in less liquid markets.
Chong et al. (2021)	The paper presents a two-phase deep RL approach to improve the hedging of variable annuity contracts. After additional training, the RL agent outperforms traditional delta hedging strategies in terms of profit and loss, effectively self-correcting for model miscalibration.
Giurca and Borovkova (2021)	The study compares DDPG and DQN against traditional Black–Scholes and Willmott delta strategies. RL agents outperform in markets with stochastic volatility and jumps, especially for long-maturity options, while the Willmott strategy is better for short maturities with low transaction costs. Empirical analysis shows RL agents, particularly DDPG, outperforming benchmarks on real market data.
Gong et al. (2021)	The study introduces a price change threshold in deep hedging to minimise unnecessary trading, reducing average losses while potentially increasing variance. Deep hedging outperforms traditional delta hedging, and performance in high volatility improves further when combined with a random forest classifier. GRUs are also explored.
Hou et al. (2021)	The authors demonstrate that deep partial hedging can effectively replicate modified contingent claims from efficient hedging theory for risk-neutral and risk-averse option writers without prior knowledge of the payoff profile.
Horvath et al. (2021)	The authors compared hedging methods under the rBergomi model and adapted deep hedging to a non-Markovian framework. Their deep hedge architecture outperforms the discretised perfect hedge with all tested Hurst values. The study also noted that low Hurst parameters lead to highly left-skewed profit and loss distributions with the potential for heavy losses. Increasing hedging frequency slightly reduced losses and made the profit and loss distribution less leptokurtic.
Kim (2021)	The study shows that RNN-based RL agents can learn optimal hedging strategies that minimise tail risk, particularly at high-risk aversion levels. The study also explores GAN-generated non-parametric scenarios.
Lütkebohmert et al. (2021)	The authors demonstrate that deep hedging approaches are robust under parameter uncertainty, outperforming existing hedging approaches, particularly in periods of high volatility.

(*Continued*)

TABLE 19.3 (*Continued*)

Reference	Results
Marzban et al. (2021)	The paper introduces an actor–critic RL algorithm to calculate ERP using time-consistent dynamic risk measures. The algorithm enhances risk-averse hedging strategies and ERP estimation with reasonable computational requirements by leveraging the expectile risk measure.
Vittori et al. (2021)	The authors conclude that their research shows the TRVO algorithm, a risk-averse reinforcement learning method, outperforms traditional delta hedging by balancing risk and return, adapting to different market conditions.
Buehler et al. (2022)	No numerical results.
Cao et al. (2022)	The authors show how D4PG, combined with quantile regression, can create hedging strategies aligned with the hedger's objectives, incorporating transaction costs. The RL agent effectively balances between hedging only delta and fully hedging gamma or vega alongside delta. Robustness tests confirm that these strategies are resilient to parameter estimate variations.
Murray et al. (2022)	The paper introduces an actor–critic algorithm for risk-averse stochastic control, using neural networks to approximate the policy and value function for optimal hedging. This approach adapts to various risk-aversion levels and is applied to pricing and hedging strategies in a market with stochastic volatility.
Cannelli et al. (2023)	The authors conclude that RL agents can effectively hedge derivative contracts, introducing the R-CMAB algorithm for profit and loss hedging due to its simplicity and efficiency. While RL agents perform well in simulated conditions, they risk overfitting due to limited real-world data. The R-CMAB algorithm offers a more stable and adaptive learning process than traditional methods. The authors note challenges in obtaining sufficient real-world data for hedging.
Fathi and Hientzsch (2023)	The study compared DDPG and DTSOC algorithms in stepwise mean–variance hedging, focusing on the impact of transaction costs. Both approaches effectively approximated the optimal delta hedge when transaction costs were zero and outperformed it as costs increased. While both methods performed well under varying risk aversion and market volatility, performance declined for longer maturities.
Gao et al. (2023)	The Chiarella–Heston model is introduced, outperforming traditional models in generating realistic financial data. It shows that deep hedging agents trained with this model can optimise hedging strategies across various transaction costs and perform effectively in real trading scenarios.
Hirano et al. (2023a)	The paper explores hedging a single option with multiple options. Existing learning schemes struggle with computational complexity in this nested scenario, so the authors propose a novel technique to manage it effectively. Experiments show that while classical Black–Scholes pricing can create arbitrage opportunities, their deep hedging approach eliminates them and reduces tail risks.
Hirano et al. (2023b)	Adversarial deep hedging is used to train hedging strategies without relying on a predefined price process. A generator simulates prices while the hedger and generator engage in a min-max game using adversarial learning. This approach avoids biases from explicit price modelling, and experiments show it achieves competitive hedging performance with the benchmark but not consistently exceeding it.
Limmer and Horvath (2023)	The paper shows that the robust hedging GAN effectively approximates optimal hedging strategies across various market conditions, outperforming classical methods in robustness and adaptability. The GAN successfully converges to effective strategies even when traditional methods struggle, demonstrating flexibility in handling diverse market dynamics. Using SigMMD enhances robustness against model deviations, and the GAN's hedging strategies align well with theoretical benchmarks.

Reference	Results
Mikkilä and Kanniainen (2023)	This paper uses intra-day market option data to train and test a DRL agent. It demonstrates that the DRL agent can transfer learning from simulated environments to real markets, performing well with synthetic data from a calibrated Heston model and actual market data.
Szehr (2023)	The study uses an MCTS agent for valuing and hedging derivatives, focusing on a European call option in simplified market scenarios. Trained on a trinomial tree model, the MCTS agent quickly learns effective hedging strategies and outperforms a DQN agent.
Hientzsch (2024)	The paper considers two approaches: DTSOC and an extended DDPG actor–critic method. In models without transaction costs, the RL agents matched known variance-optimal strategies: delta hedging in Black–Scholes and Bartlett's delta hedging in the SABR model. With transaction costs, the agents outperformed these strategies.
Hirano (2024)	The study evaluates the effectiveness of using artificial market simulations with the PAMS model to train deep hedging agents. Artificial market simulations can lead to more frequent tail-risk events, impacting performance, especially under risk-sensitive utility functions. The distribution of returns from artificial simulations shows longer tails than traditional models, indicating a better replication of 'market-stylised facts' (see Chapter 18). Despite these advantages, the artificial market simulation is simple and may not fully capture market dynamics. The study concludes that artificial market simulations are promising datasets for training deep hedging models.
Neagu et al. (2024)	Building on the deep hedging framework, the authors employ a policy gradient algorithm to train an FFN that maps state variables to hedging actions, with an enhanced state space accounting for liquidity issues. The study reveals that factors like portfolio value and expected return of the underlying asset significantly influence optimal hedging decisions, areas traditional delta hedging overlooks. The DRL model also adjusts rebalancing to minimise costs while protecting against risk.
Pickard et al. (2024)	The study examines the effects of hyperparameters on DRL in hedging American options, focusing on transaction cost penalties. It finds that increasing rebalancing frequency amplifies discrepancies between DRL and Black–Scholes delta due to transaction costs. Agents using quadratic transaction cost penalties consistently outperform those with linear penalties. Weekly retraining with recalibrated models further enhances performance, outperforming less frequently trained agents.

Future research directions include tackling complex multi-asset portfolios, integrating real-world data and constraints, and refining RL algorithms for financial applications. The ultimate goal is for autonomous hedging agents to be able to take over some responsibilities from human traders and risk managers.

19.3 DEEP HEDGING EXAMPLES

This section presents a series of experiments using deep hedging, or policy gradient, in the language of RL. There are four Jupyter Notebooks associated with the experiments:

- `Deep Hedging Extended Input.ipynb`
- `Deep Hedging Extended Input LSTM.ipynb`
- `Deep Hedging-MJD.ipynb`
- `Deep Hedging-MJD-LSTM.ipynb`

19.3.1 Target Application

As with most of the literature, the target for all the experiments discussed here is to hedge a single European call option. The option has a 1-year maturity and a strike at the money.

19.3.2 Datasets

The study employed two synthetic datasets: one generated by the Black–Scholes model and the second by the Merton (1976) jump-diffusion model. The Black–Scholes dataset utilised an initial stock price $S_0 = 1.0$ and volatility $\sigma = 0.2$, with interest rates set to zero for simplicity. The Merton model incorporated additional jump parameters set at $\lambda = 1.0$, $\mu_j = 0.0$ and $\sigma_j = 0.1$. Both models utilised 2^{16} paths for training and 2^{14} for evaluation.

Each time step requires option prices to provide a benchmark for the hedging strategy, the option delta. Both cases used option prices with the same input parameters as the Monte Carlo dynamics, ensuring consistent behaviour. The Black–Scholes case implemented the model and the analytic option delta directly. The Merton model call price utilised the summation closed-form formula with finite difference to calculate the delta.

19.3.3 Duration and Frequency

As noted above, the option maturity was 1 year. The model used 50 time steps for hedging, so approximately weekly re-hedging opportunities were available.

19.3.4 State and Action

The state space used for all models was the same, as was the current stock price, the current hedge position and the time to option maturity. Note that for LSTM models, a history of *window size* states is continuously supplied to the model with the window set to four. The action space was also the same for all models and continuous, being the hedge position in the underlying stock.

19.3.5 Reward/Objective

The reward function in all cases is a function of the net portfolio value at option maturity, that is

$$\text{portfolio}_T = \text{cash}_T + \text{hedge} \times S_T + \text{option}_T. \tag{19.19}$$

The cash position initialises to the negative initial value of the option, representing its sale. The process then tracks the cash position through each episode, reflecting the sale and purchase of stock to hedge the option. For models trained with transaction costs, the cash position decreases by the trade price. At each step, the cash updates according to

$$\text{cash}_t = \text{cash}_{t-1} + \text{cost}_t + \Delta_{\text{hedge}} \times S_t. \tag{19.20}$$

The study assumes proportional transaction costs, calculated as

$$\text{cost} = \text{prop} \times |\Delta_{\text{hedge}}|, \tag{19.21}$$

with the proportion set to three values for each model: 0%, 1% and 5%.

The loss is a measure of rewards obtained for a batch of simulations. The study tested four objective functions in Table 19.17. For CVaR, the testing included two percentile levels: 95% and 99%. The ERM loss utilised two lambda values: 1 and 10.

TABLE 19.4 Deep Hedging Objective Functions

Metric	Expression
MSE	$\mathbb{E}[\text{portfolio}_T^2]$
Mean variance	$-\mathbb{E}[\text{portfolio}_T] + \text{Var}[\text{portfolio}_T^2]$
CVaR(α)	$\frac{1}{1-\alpha} \int_{-\infty}^{\text{VaR}(\alpha)} x \cdot p(x)\, dx$
ERM(λ)	$-\frac{1}{\lambda} \log \mathbb{E}[\exp(-\lambda x)]$

19.3.6 Methodology

Two different neural networks, feedforward and recurrent networks, were tested for the policy network using LSTM units. The feedforward network was small, with three inputs, a single output, two hidden layers with 32 neurons and ReLU activation functions. The recurrent model was a stacked LSTM with two LSTM units, each with a hidden size of 32 units, followed by the output layer.

19.3.7 Implementation

The PyTorch implementation follows the pattern established in the other examples discussed in the book. Direct implementation of Monte Carlo paths for both Black–Scholes and Merton jump-diffusion in PyTorch allows the use of GPU for performance. Similarly, implementing option prices and deltas along each Monte Carlo path uses the PyTorch native function for performance reasons.

The training loop below demonstrates the calculation of the reward and the loss measure.

```
def train_agent(agent, optimizer, asset_paths, option_prices, option_deltas, K, r,
                sigma, T, N, transaction_cost_model, calculate_loss, batch_size=32,
                epochs=1, device=device):
    delta_T = T / N
    gamma = np.exp(-r * delta_T)  # Discount factor for reward
    agent.to(device)
    loss_lst = list()
    time_to_maturity = torch.linspace(T, 0,
                           steps=N+1, device=device).unsqueeze(0).expand(batch_size, N+1)

    for iepoch in range(epochs):
        for pathblk in trange(len(asset_paths) // batch_size,
                              desc="Training Epoch" + str(iepoch)):
            batch_start = pathblk * batch_size
            batch_end = batch_start + batch_size
            paths_batch = asset_paths[batch_start:batch_end]
            option_prices_batch = option_prices[batch_start:batch_end]
            option_deltas_batch = option_deltas[batch_start:batch_end]

            optimizer.zero_grad()

            # Initialize tensors for portfolio values and hedge positions
            portfolio_values = torch.zeros(batch_size, dtype=torch.float32).to(device)
            cash = torch.zeros(batch_size, dtype=torch.float32).to(device)
            stock_value = torch.zeros(batch_size, dtype=torch.float32).to(device)
            hedge_positions = torch.zeros(batch_size, dtype=torch.float32).to(device)


            # Iterate over each time step in parallel
            # buy the option
```

```
            cash -= option_prices_batch[:, 0]
            for t in range(N):
                # Create states in parallel
                states = torch.stack([paths_batch[:, t], hedge_positions,
                                      time_to_maturity[:,t]], dim=1).to(device)
                hedge_actions = agent(states).squeeze()

                dHedge = hedge_actions - hedge_positions
                transaction_costs = transaction_cost_model(dHedge)
                cash -= transaction_costs + dHedge * paths_batch[:, t]
                hedge_positions = hedge_actions
                stock_value = hedge_positions * paths_batch[:, t]

                portfolio_values = cash + stock_value + option_prices_batch[:, t]

            # Calculate loss and perform backpropagation
            loss = calculate_loss(portfolio_values)
            loss.backward()
            loss_lst.append(loss.item())
            optimizer.step()

    return loss_lst
```

As can be seen, each episode is run by walking down the Monte Carlo path for a mini-batch. The portfolio value, cash position, stock value and hedge position are all tracked during the episode. The cash position is initialised to the negative initial option value. Input states for the neural network combine the current stock price, the current hedge position and the option's time to maturity. The agent network outputs the policy: the new hedge position. The change in the hedge leads to the transaction cost, as calculated by the `transaction_cost_model` function and a change in the cash position to reflect the purchase or sale of the stock. The assumption that interest rates are zero means there is no need to accumulate interest costs or benefits. The stock value is updated to reflect the new stock holding and, finally, the portfolio value to reflect the current value of all the portfolio components.

The loss is calculated as a function of the portfolio value by the `calculate_loss` function given below, with the type selected using a lambda function:

```
def calculate_loss(pnl, loss_type='cvar', alpha=0.95, lmda = 1.0):
    if loss_type == 'cvar':
        sorted_pnl, _ = torch.sort(pnl)
        var_index = int((1 - alpha) * len(sorted_pnl))
        cvar = torch.mean(sorted_pnl[:var_index])
        return -cvar
    elif loss_type == 'entropic':
        return torch.log(torch.mean(torch.exp(-lmda * pnl))) / lmda
    elif loss_type == 'mean-variance':
        mean_pnl = torch.mean(pnl)
        variance_pnl = torch.var(pnl)
        return -mean_pnl + variance_pnl
    elif loss_type == 'mse':
        mse = torch.mean(pnl**2)
        return mse
    else:
        raise ValueError("Invalid loss_type.")
```

The performance of the trained agent is evaluated by the `compare_strategies` function, which repeats the portfolio tracking shown in the training loop. It uses the trained agent to generate the model hedge position and compares this with delta hedging.

19.3.8 Results

19.3.8.1 Black–Scholes with FFN and Transaction Costs The first experiment utilised the Black–Scholes dynamics described above to train a deep hedging model based on policy gradient with the feedforward network architecture. Training of the model occurred through a single epoch of 2^{16} paths with 50 time steps, using each of the six objective functions. Each choice of objective function was used to train models with three levels of proportional transaction costs, resulting in 18 models. After training, evaluation of the models used a separate set of 2^{14} Monte Carlo paths and associated option prices and deltas. Table 19.18 presents the average final profit and loss value for each case using the evaluation dataset, compared with the results of hedging using the Black–Scholes model delta. The results immediately reveal that the mean performance in all cases with non-zero transaction costs improves under the deep hedging agent compared to simple Black–Scholes hedging. Figures 19.2 and 19.3 display the distribution of final profit and loss (P&L) values using the deep hedging agent.

TABLE 19.5 Deep Hedging Agents Training Using Different Proportional Cost Values and Loss Functions

Loss Type	α	λ	Cost	Agent P&L	BS P&L
mse			0.00	−0.000011	0.000005
mse			0.01	−0.016286	−0.027681
mse			0.05	−0.040429	−0.138421
mean-variance			0.00	−0.000185	0.000005
mean-variance			0.01	−0.004413	−0.027681
mean-variance			0.05	−0.001197	−0.138421
cvar	0.95		0.00	0.000045	0.000005
cvar	0.95		0.01	−0.016379	−0.0276
cvar	0.95		0.05	−0.002650	−0.138421
cvar	0.99		0.00	−0.000475	0.000005
cvar	0.99		0.01	−0.007789	−0.027681
cvar	0.99		0.05	−0.002667	−0.138421
erm		1.0	0.00	−0.000152	0.000005
erm		1.0	0.01	−0.003308	−0.027681
erm		1.0	0.05	−0.000677	−0.138421
erm		10.0	0.00	−0.000260	0.000005
erm		10.0	0.01	−0.006751	−0.027681
erm		10.0	0.05	−0.014108	−0.138421
mse			0.00	−0.000228	0.000005
mse			0.01	−0.014703	−0.027681
mse			0.05	−0.036212	−0.138421

(Continued)

TABLE 19.5 (*Continued*)

Loss Type	α	λ	Cost	Agent P&L	BS P&L
mean-variance			0.00	-0.000377	0.000005
mean-variance			0.01	-0.004661	-0.027681
mean-variance			0.05	-0.001746	-0.138421
cvar	0.95		0.00	-0.000353	0.000005
cvar	0.95		0.01	-0.000852	-0.027681
cvar	0.95		0.05	-0.001363	-0.138421
cvar	0.99		0.00	-0.000556	0.000005
cvar	0.99		0.01	-0.000777	-0.027681
cvar	0.99		0.05	-0.000845	-0.138421
erm		1.0	0.00	-0.000302	0.000005
erm		1.0	0.01	-0.003584	-0.027681
erm		1.0	0.05	-0.000671	-0.138421
erm		10.0	0.00	-0.000212	0.000005
erm		10.0	0.01	-0.009891	-0.027681
erm		10.0	0.05	-0.011898	-0.138421

Here, the input features were the stock price, the option's time to maturity and the current hedge position. A feedforward network was used with two hidden layers of 32 neurons each. The results show the average final P&L compared to that obtained using Black–Scholes delta hedging. All models were trained and evaluated using simulated GBM dynamics with $S_0 = 1.0, r = 0.0, \sigma = 0.2, T = 1.0$, time steps = 50.
Here, the input features were the stock price, the option's time to maturity and the current hedge position. An LSTM cell was used with two hidden layers of 32 neurons each. The results show the average final P&L compared to that obtained using Black–Scholes delta hedging. All models were trained and evaluated using simulated GBM dynamics with $S_0 = 1.0, r = 0.0, \sigma = 0.2, T = 1.0$, time steps = 50.

Comparing the distributions for deep hedging and Black–Scholes hedging under MSE is instructive. For zero transaction costs, the two distributions are superimposed on top of one another, demonstrating that in this case, the deep hedging agent has learned to replicate Black–Scholes hedging, which is the optimal choice if intending to minimise hedging errors – the behaviour driven by the MSE loss. As the transaction costs increase, delta hedging will lead to losses, as each rebalancing will cost additional funds. In these two cases, the deep hedging agent performs better with the distribution offset on the positive side of the delta hedging mean.

The behaviour of hedging under the remaining five objective functions differs from Black–Scholes hedging behaviour because there is implicit or explicit risk aversion. The distribution of outcomes for these models is generally asymmetric, with a long tail to the positive and a concentration on the negative side but curtailing the loss level. The CVaR 95% shows less extreme behaviour than the 99% case. Still, both ERM models are similar, even with different lambda values, as the transaction cost increases the performance differential compared to Black–Scholes hedging as the model adapts to the cost of trading.

19.3.8.2 MJD with FFN and Transaction Costs The experiment was repeated using MJD dynamics. In this case, the option price was obtained using the Merton summation formula, and the delta hedging was performed using the MJD option delta. The results can be found in Table 19.19 and Figures 19.4 and 19.5.

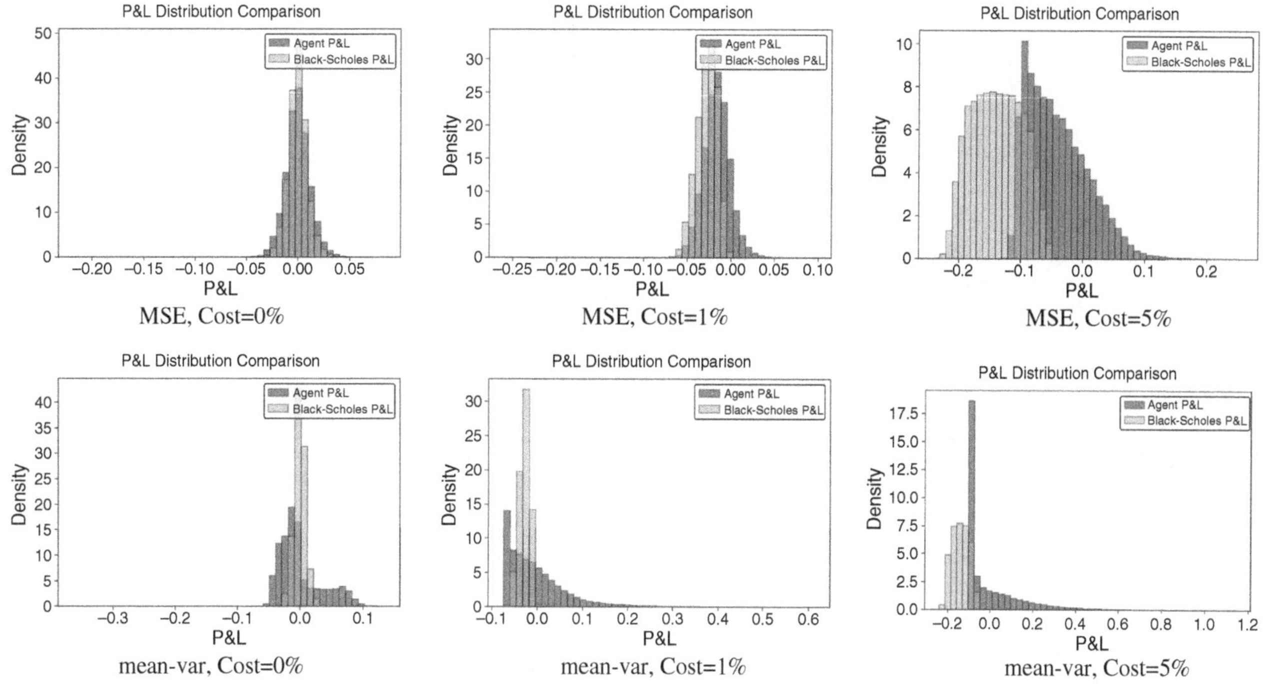

FIGURE 19.2 Deep hedging agents underwent training using different proportional cost values (columns) and different loss functions (rows). The input features comprised the stock price, the option's time to maturity and the current hedge position. The model employed a feedforward network with two hidden layers of 32 neurons each. The plots display the distribution of results compared to Black–Scholes delta hedging using an independent evaluation dataset. Training and evaluation of all models used simulated GBM dynamics with parameters $S_0 = 1.0$, $r = 0.0$, $\sigma = 0.2$, $T = 1.0$, time steps = 50.

Reviewing the mean performance on the evaluation set in Table 19.19 shows that, again, the deep hedging agent outperforms the delta hedging example in all cases, although the differential is smaller than in the Black–Scholes case. Outperformance increases as a result of transaction costs. The mean model performance is similar for all choices of objective function.

The P&L distribution charts show a broadly similar pattern to those from the Black–Scholes case, although the width of the distribution is narrower than that observed from simple delta hedging.

19.3.8.3 LSTM Versions The Black–Scholes and MJD experiments were repeated with the LSTM-based architecture. The Black–Scholes results can be found in Table 19.20 and Figures 19.6 and 19.7, with the MJD results in Table 19.21 and Figures 19.8 and 19.9.

Comparing the mean values for each test case with Black–Scholes hedging shows the same pattern as the feedforward network, outperforming Black–Scholes hedging with non-zero transaction costs in all instances. However, the distribution results are different, with a wider dispersion than shown with the FFN model. At least part of this dispersion will relate to the delay imposed because of the window size. Unlike delta hedging activity, the recurrent model requires a stack of states to be input, which means the deep hedging agent does not start hedging immediately. However, the LSTM model underperforms the simple feedforward network.

In contrast, the MJD LSTM models show broadly similar performance for both mean and dispersion compared to those obtained with the FFN.

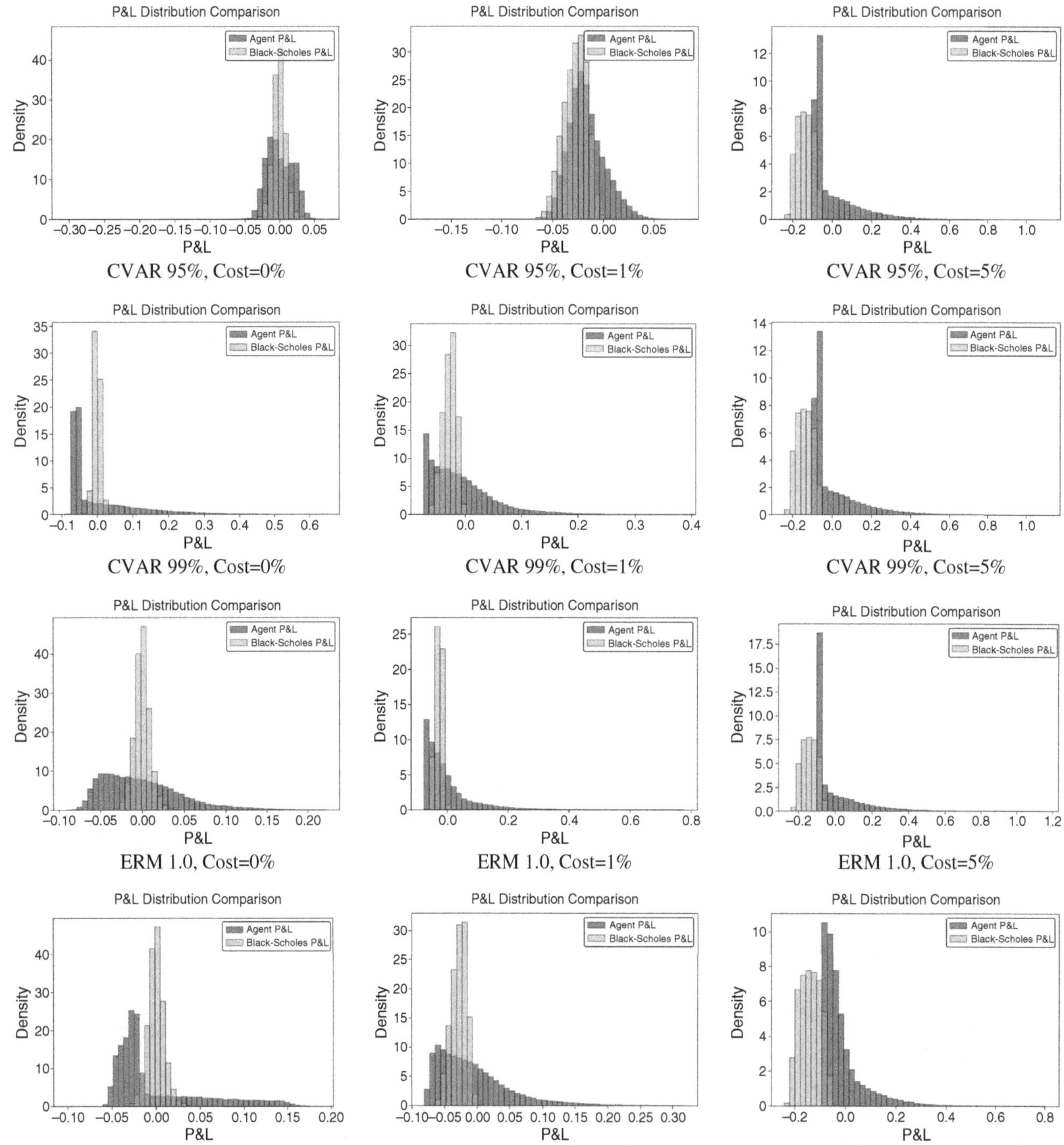

FIGURE 19.3 Deep hedging agents underwent training using different proportional cost values (columns) and different loss functions (rows). The input features comprised the stock price, the option's time to maturity and the current hedge position. The model employed a feedforward network with two hidden layers of 32 neurons each. The plots display the distribution of results compared to Black–Scholes delta hedging using an independent evaluation dataset. Training and evaluation of all models used simulated GBM dynamics with parameters $S_0 = 1.0$, $r = 0.0$, $\sigma = 0.2$, $T = 1.0$, time steps = 50.

TABLE 19.6 Deep Hedging Agents Training Using Different Proportional Cost Values and Loss Functions

Loss Type	α	λ	Cost	Agent P&L	MJD P&L
mse			0.00	−0.151721	−0.152634
mse			0.01	−0.162270	−0.205300
mse			0.05	−0.188236	−0.415966
mean-variance			0.00	−0.151103	−0.152634
mean-variance			0.01	−0.155112	−0.205300
mean-variance			0.05	−0.153085	−0.415966
cvar	0.95		0.00	−0.151519	−0.152634
cvar	0.95		0.01	−0.166465	−0.205300
cvar	0.95		0.05	−0.152037	−0.415966
cvar	0.99		0.00	−0.150845	−0.152634
cvar	0.99		0.01	−0.151500	−0.205300
cvar	0.99		0.05	−0.152032	−0.415966
erm		1.0	0.00	−0.150785	−0.152634
erm		1.0	0.01	−0.153415	−0.205300
erm		1.0	0.05	−0.149657	−0.415966
erm		10.0	0.00	−0.151664	−0.152634
erm		10.0	0.01	−0.162483	−0.205300
erm		10.0	0.05	−0.165587	−0.415966
mse			0.00	−0.151794	−0.152634
mse			0.01	−0.161846	−0.205300
mse			0.05	−0.172994	−0.415966
mean-variance			0.00	−0.151596	−0.152634
mean-variance			0.01	−0.155239	−0.205300
mean-variance			0.05	−0.151448	−0.415966
cvar	0.95		0.00	−0.150560	−0.152634
cvar	0.95		0.01	−0.152464	−0.205300
cvar	0.95		0.05	−0.150124	−0.415966
cvar	0.99		0.00	−0.149617	−0.152634
cvar	0.99		0.01	−0.149726	−0.205300
cvar	0.99		0.05	−0.150108	−0.415966
erm		1.0	0.00	−0.151072	−0.152634
erm		1.0	0.01	−0.153367	−0.205300

(*Continued*)

TABLE 19.6 *(Continued)*

Loss Type	α	λ	Cost	Agent P&L	MJD P&L
erm		1.0	0.05	-0.150033	-0.415966
erm		10.0	0.00	-0.151573	-0.152634
erm		10.0	0.01	-0.161866	-0.205300
erm		10.0	0.05	-0.162932	-0.415966

Here, the input features were the stock price, the option's time to maturity and the current hedge position. A feedforward network was used with two hidden layers of 32 neurons each. The results show the average final P&L compared to that obtained using MJD delta hedging. All models were trained and evaluated using simulated MJD dynamics with $S_0 = 1.0, r = 0.0, \sigma = 0.2, T = 1.0, \mu_j = 0.0, \sigma_j = 0.1, \lambda_j = 1.0$, time steps = 50.

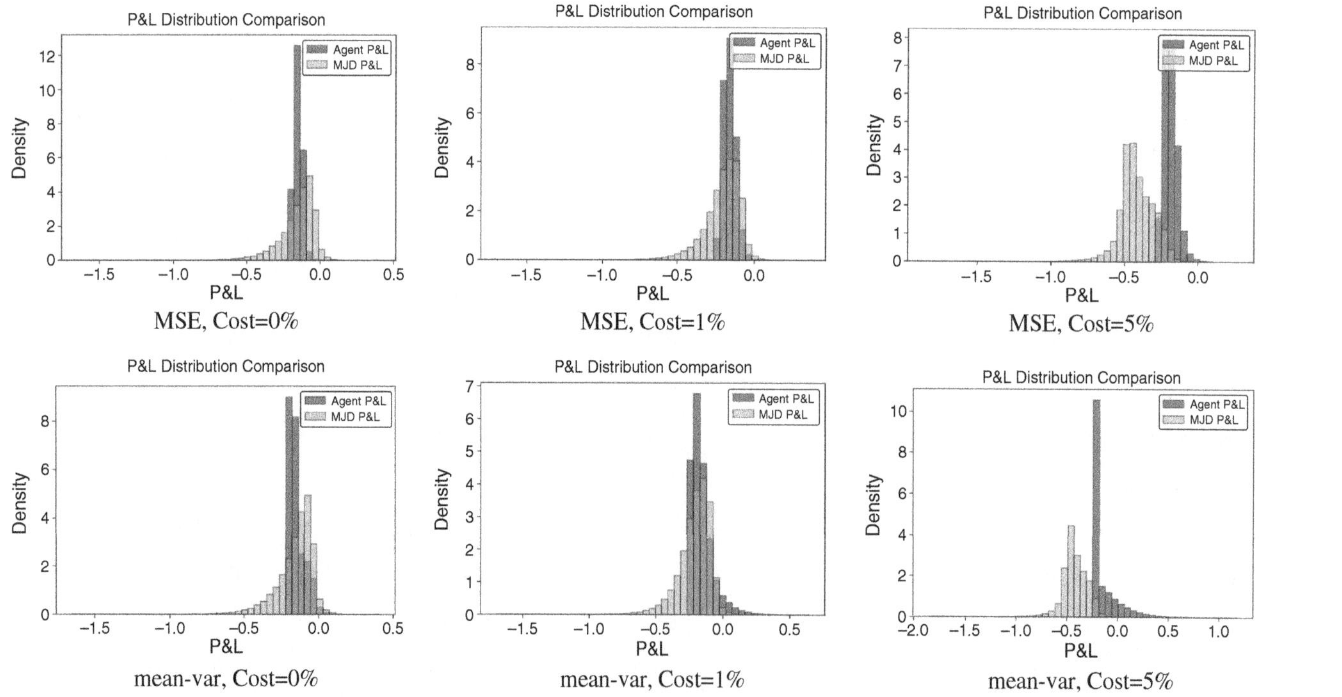

FIGURE 19.4 Deep hedging agents training using different proportional cost values (columns) and different loss functions (rows). Here, the input features were the stock price, the option's time to maturity and the current hedge position. A feedforward network was used with two hidden layers of 32 neurons each. The plots show the distribution of results compared to MJD delta hedging using an independent evaluation dataset. All models were trained and evaluated using simulated Merton jump-diffusion dynamics with $S_0 = 1.0, r = 0.0, \sigma = 0.2, T = 1.0, \mu_j = 0.0, \sigma_j = 0.1, \lambda_j = 1.0$, time steps = 50.

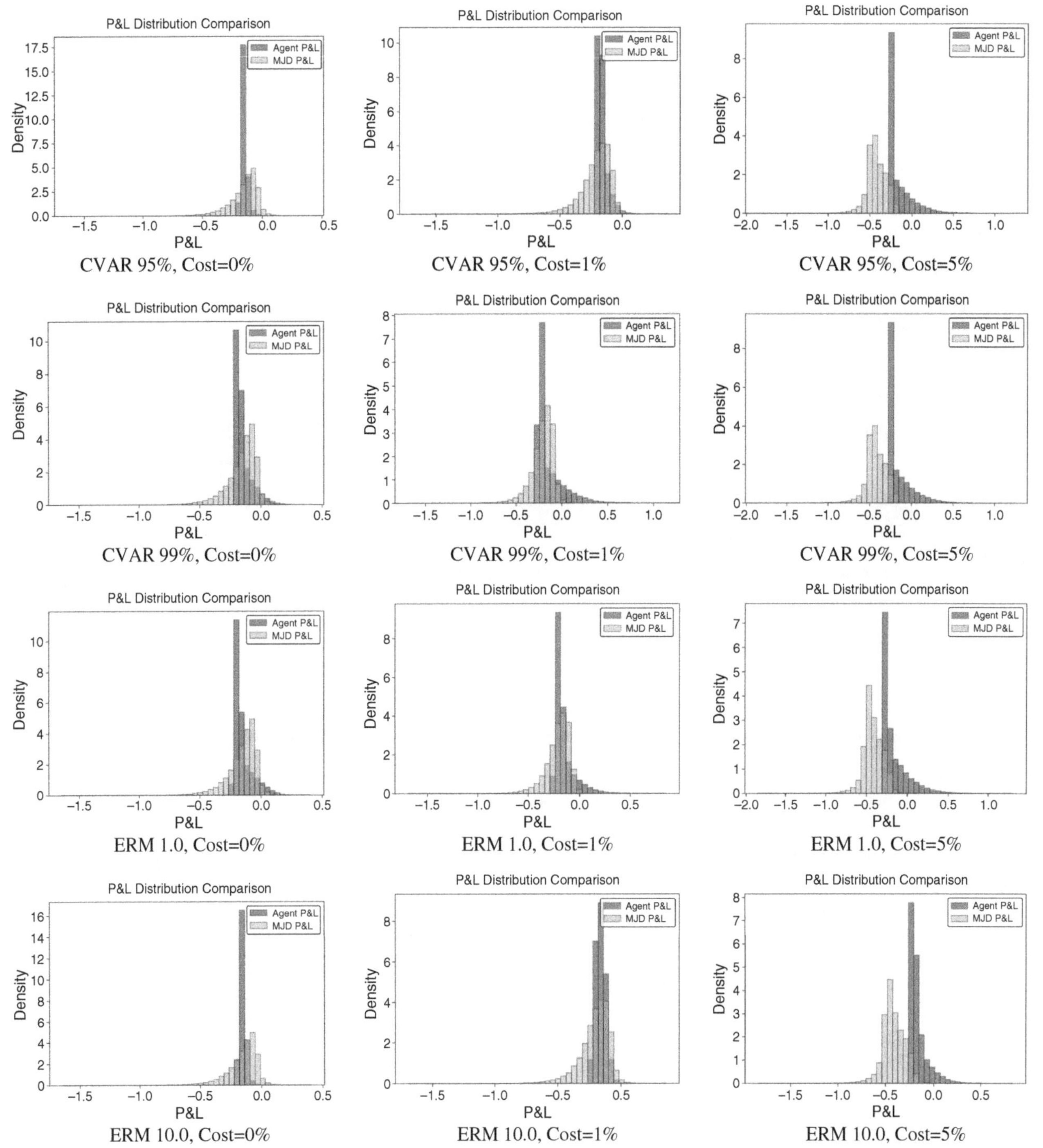

FIGURE 19.5 Deep hedging agents training using different proportional cost values (columns) and different loss functions (rows). Here, the input features were the stock price, the option's time to maturity and the current hedge position. A feedforward network was used with two hidden layers of 32 neurons each. The plots show the distribution of results compared to MJD delta hedging using an independent evaluation dataset. All models were trained and evaluated using simulated Merton jump-diffusion dynamics with $S_0 = 1.0$, $r = 0.0$, $\sigma = 0.2$, $T = 1.0$, $\mu_j = 0.0$, $\sigma_j = 0.1$, $\lambda_j = 1.0$, time steps = 50.

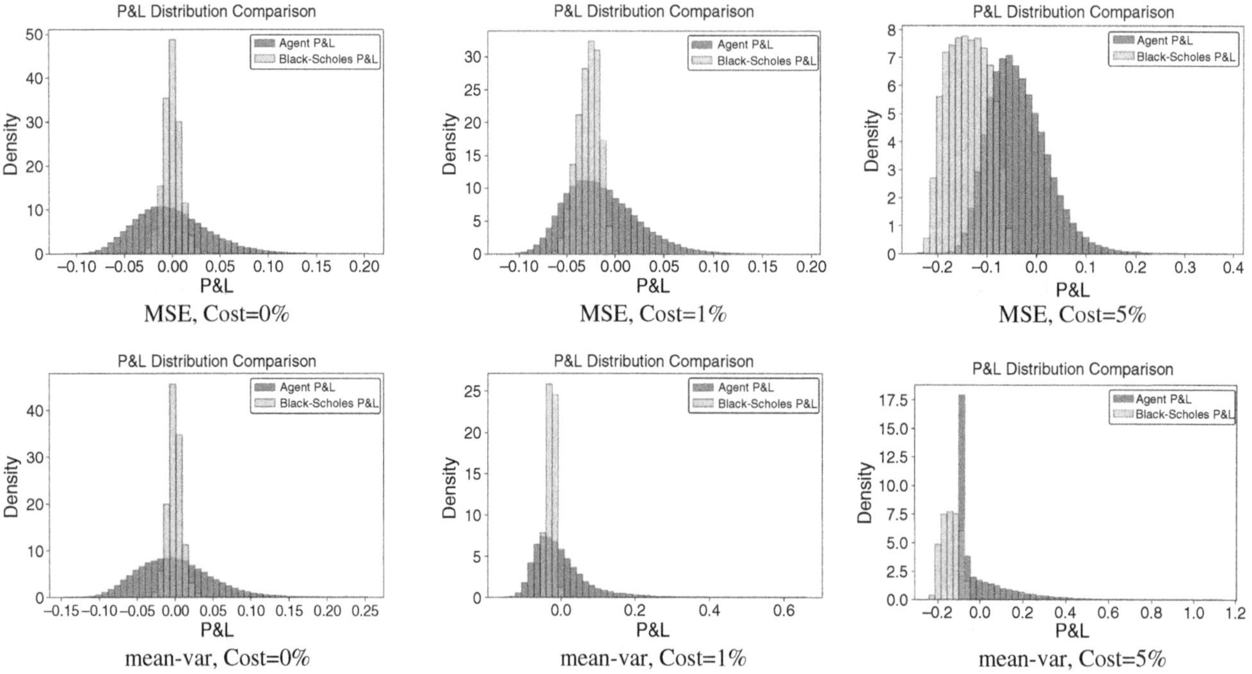

FIGURE 19.6 Deep hedging agents training using different proportional cost values (columns) and different loss functions (rows). Here, the input features were the stock price, the option's time to maturity and the current hedge position. An LSTM cell was used with two hidden layers of 32 neurons each. The plots show the distribution of results compared to Black–Scholes delta hedging using an independent evaluation dataset. All models were trained and evaluated using simulated GBM dynamics with $S_0 = 1.0$, $r = 0.0$, $\sigma = 0.2$, $T = 1.0$, time steps = 50.

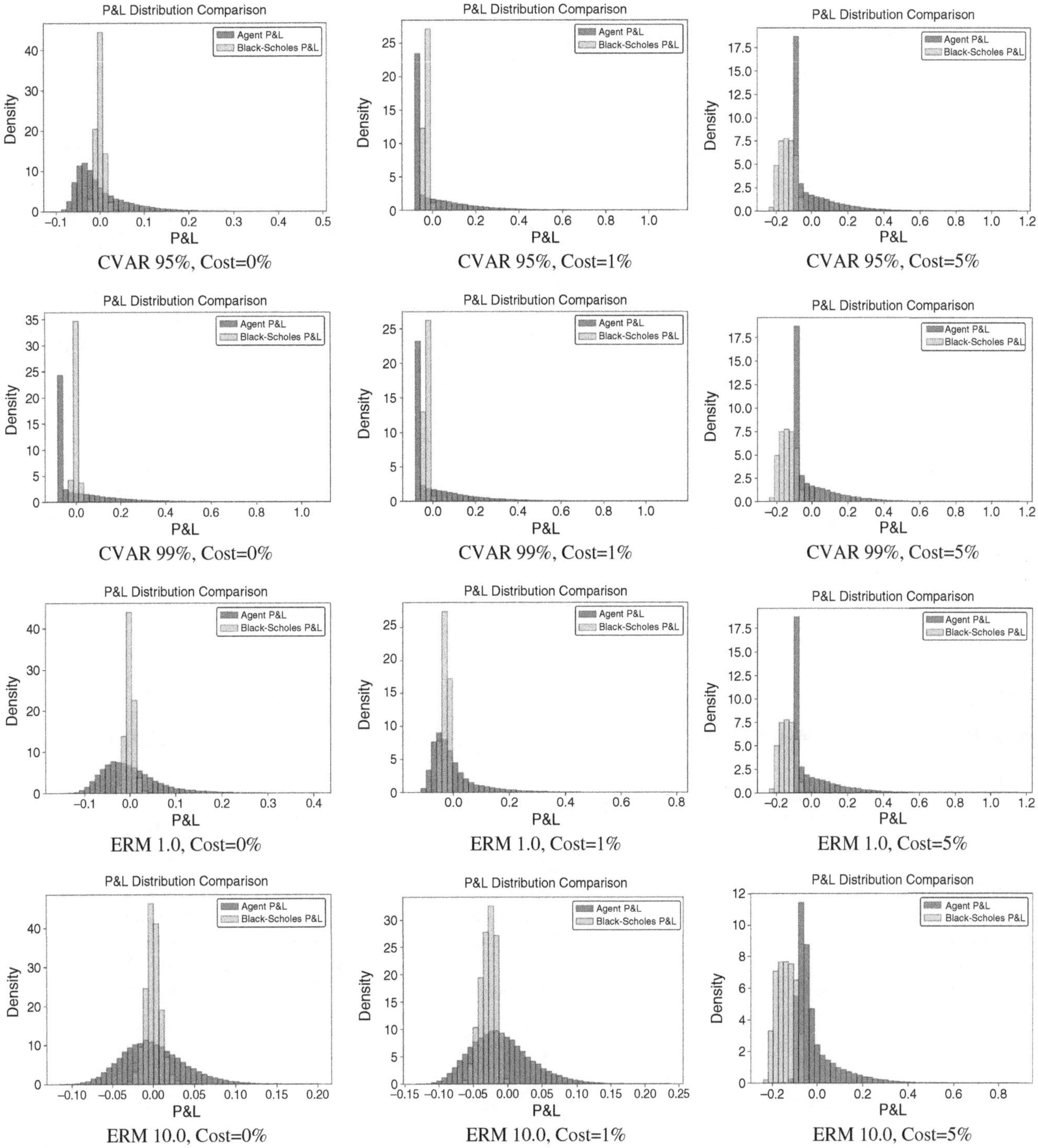

FIGURE 19.7 Deep hedging agents training using different proportional cost values (columns) and different loss functions (rows). Here, the input features were the stock price, the option's time to maturity and the current hedge position. An LSTM cell was used with two hidden layers of 32 neurons each. The plots show the distribution of results compared to Black–Scholes delta hedging using an independent evaluation dataset. All models were trained and evaluated using simulated GBM dynamics with $S_0 = 1.0$, $r = 0.0$, $\sigma = 0.2$, $T = 1.0$, time steps = 50. Note that both Black–Scholes and LSTM start hedging after 10 steps, reflecting the window size for the LSTM unit.

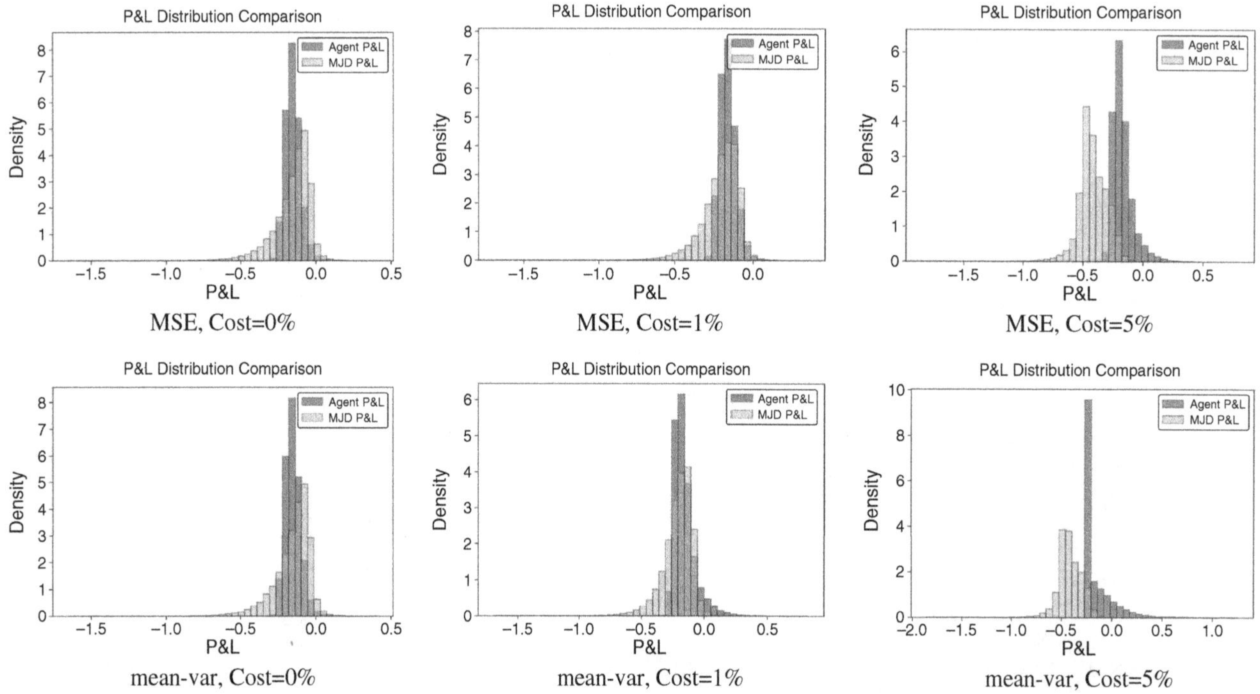

FIGURE 19.8 Deep hedging agents training using different proportional cost values (columns) and different loss functions (rows). Here, the input features were the stock price, the option's time to maturity and the current hedge position. An LSTM cell was used with two hidden layers of 32 neurons each. The plots show the distribution of results compared to Black–Scholes delta hedging using an independent evaluation dataset. All models were trained and evaluated using simulated Merton jump-diffusion dynamics with $S_0 = 1.0$, $r = 0.0$, $\sigma = 0.2$, $T = 1.0$, $\mu_j = 0.0$, $\sigma_j = 0.1$, $\lambda_j = 1.0$, time steps = 50.

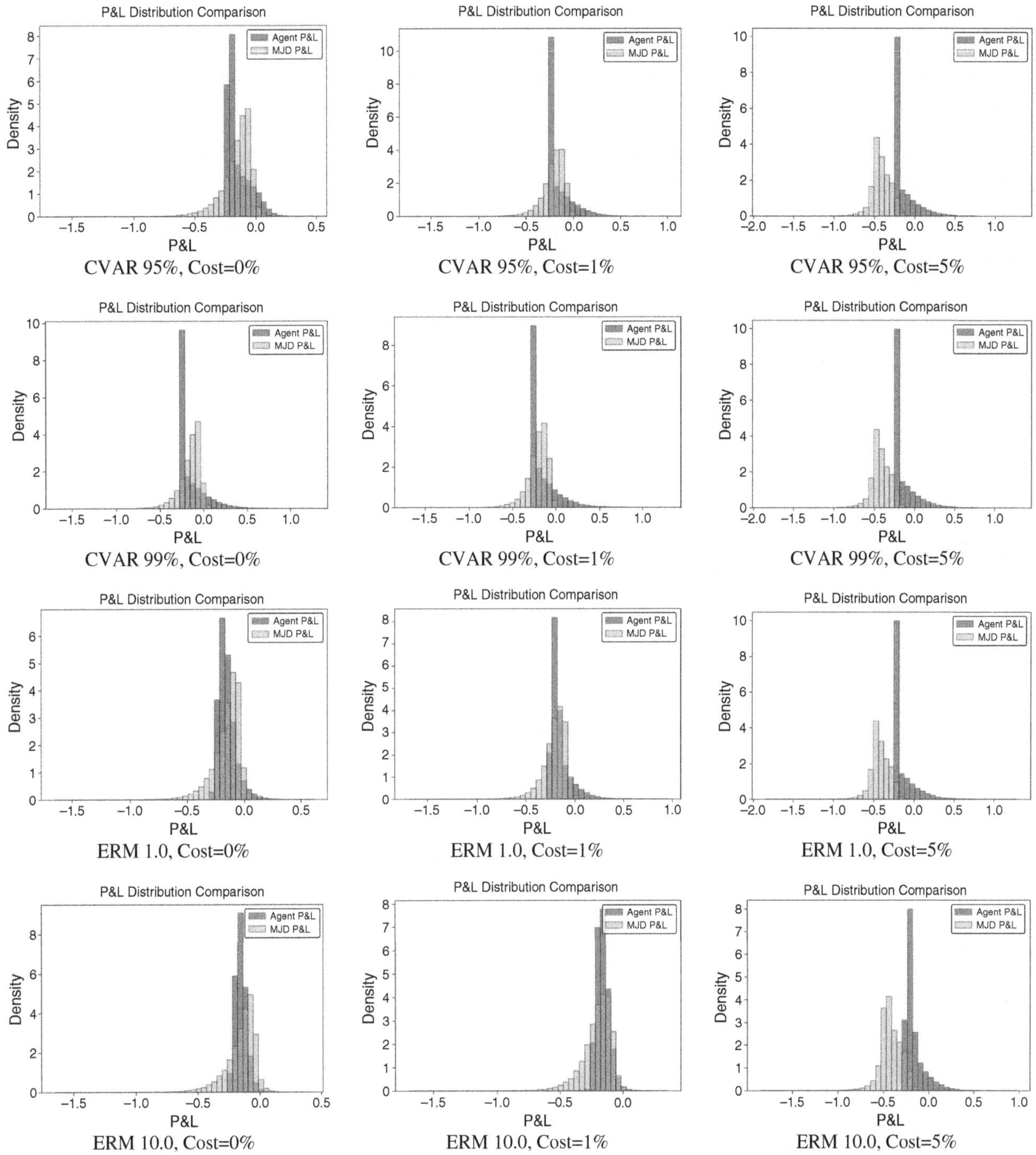

FIGURE 19.9 Deep hedging agents training using different proportional cost values (columns) and different loss functions (rows). Here, the input features were the stock price, the option's time to maturity and the current hedge position. An LSTM cell was used with two hidden layers of 32 neurons each. The plots show the distribution of results compared to MJD delta hedging using an independent evaluation dataset. All models were trained and evaluated using simulated Merton jump-diffusion dynamics with $S_0 = 1.0, r = 0.0, \sigma = 0.2, T = 1.0, \mu_j = 0.0, \sigma_j = 0.1, \lambda_j = 1.0$, time steps = 50.

19.4 CONCLUSION

The exploration of deep hedging, as presented through various models and methodologies in this chapter, underscores its significant potential in revolutionising risk management in financial markets. By leveraging deep reinforcement learning techniques, deep hedging enables the creation of strategies that dynamically adjust to market conditions, outperforming traditional hedging methods, particularly in complex scenarios involving transaction costs and market frictions. The experiments performed here and by other authors demonstrate the robustness of these models in synthetic and real-world environments. However, not all models perform equally well, indicating that model selection and architecture tuning are crucial for achieving optimal performance. As deep hedging evolves, future research should focus on enhancing these models' adaptability and scalability to handle realistic derivative portfolios and real-world data, aiming towards fully autonomous hedging solutions that could significantly reduce reliance on human intervention in risk management.

PART Four

The Future

CHAPTER 20

The Future Quant

An Outside Context Problem was the sort of thing most civilisations encountered just once, which they tended to encounter rather in the same way a sentence encountered a full stop.

Iain M. Banks, Excession (1996)

20.1 CONCLUSION ON DEEP LEARNING

This book has provided a guide to deep learning and its application to problems in traditional quantitative finance. The text in Part II provided the essential foundations of deep learning methodology in their original context. The book covered the main architectures of deep learning models, beginning with feedforward networks, before discussing convolutional layers and recurrent neural networks. The now ubiquitous transformer architecture built on the various attention mechanisms was introduced as part of sequence models but can now be found in many different types of network architecture. Training methodology for neural networks was reviewed: gradient-based training for weights and biases and optimisation approaches for hyperparameters that cannot be trained using SGD. The final chapters of Part II introduced more advanced topics. Autoencoders were briefly introduced in their simplest form before moving on to generative models, where encoder–decoder structures play a critical role. Finally, deep reinforcement learning was explored, a topic worthy of a book-length treatment.

Part III provided a tour of a wide range of deep learning applications in traditional quantitative finance areas. The most straightforward application, replicating derivative pricing functions, was shown to be both achievable and yield significant performance benefits at inference time. Chapters explored how deep learning can benefit standard numerical techniques like PDE solvers and Monte Carlo simulations. PDEs and BSDEs can be solved with a variety of deep learning algorithms. While these techniques are unlikely to ever be competitive with standard numerical methods in simpler use cases, they can tackle high-dimensional problems that standard techniques cannot solve. In several innovative ways, Monte Carlo can be accelerated by deep neural networks and by providing new approaches to optimal stopping problems that do not suffer from the limitations of approaches like Longstaff and Schwartz (2001). Static replication models have been used in quant finance to provide models in specific contexts, and they are equivalent to neural networks. Volatility surfaces and model calibration are closely related problems; volatility surfaces are calibrated to the prices of vanilla options, while model calibration is a more general problem of calibrating model parameters to the prices of hedging instruments. Function approximation by neural networks allows these problems to be accelerated; in particular, volatility surface models like rough Bergomi that rely on slow Monte Carlo for calibration can be rapidly calibrated using a trained neural network. XVA can benefit from deep learning models in several areas, notably making use of fast derivative pricing for neural networks and enhanced ways of handling optimal stopping. In addition, Chapter 17 demonstrated how neural networks could be applied to the credit curve mapping problem and replicate expected exposure profiles directly.

Deep Learning in Quantitative Finance, First Edition. Andrew Green.

Chapter 18 presented one of the most innovative applications of generative deep learning, generating synthetic market data. There are many potential benefits from synthetic data, from testing to model risk management. *Deep hedging* is perhaps the deep learning topic that has generated the most interest in quantitative finance and was discussed in Chapter 19. Deep hedging offers the prospect of at least semi-automating derivative hedging operations.

Several topics were omitted from Part III for reasons of space and available time. Even in quantitative finance, the applications of deep neural networks are many and varied. Notable amongst the omissions are *neural SDEs*, where the drift and diffusion coefficients of SDEs become neural networks, applications of deep learning to problems in asset management, including strategy selection and risk management, and order book management. Quantum neural networks were also excluded as, while quantum computers are clearly on the horizon, the current noisy intermediate-scale machines do not offer significant benefits. Also omitted is any discussion on ethics and AI; however, given that this book focuses on numerical methods, this is a lower concern in this context than it is in others.

Deep learning models are not a panacea. Many of the examples provided work well, but some do not. Some models are impractically slow to use or at least not competitive with existing numerical approaches. Deep learning models are frequently opaque, which sometimes extends to training and inference. Deep learning is data intensive, although techniques like data augmentation and Sobolev training provide some respite from this.

Notwithstanding the challenges, I hope the book shows that deep learning is a valuable adjunct to existing quantitative finance techniques.

20.2 THE FUTURE OF QUANTITATIVE ANALYTICS

Is AI an 'outside context problem' for quantitative finance? Will AI replace quant analysts and developers in banks, funds and software vendors? At the time of writing, there are several news stories that big tech is considering replacing software engineers with AI (Marks, 2025; Oekmwa, 2025). Will quants suffer the same fate?

Firstly, it is essential to clarify what is proposed here: replacing coders with large language models (LLMs). Coding is a central part of the role of quant analysts and developers, but it is not the only part. The other two key quant skills are business analysis, the ability to relate the needs of finance professionals like traders to mathematics and code, and mathematics itself. It is important to remember that an LLM is a statistical model of language, that is all. LLMs have not been featured heavily in this text as they are not pertinent to the applications that have been included. LLMs are certainly not going to replace business analysis any time soon. While research into AI models that can do mathematics is ongoing, the LLMs in mainstream use cannot operate at anything near the level required of quants (Ahn et al., 2024). The coding aspect of quantitative finance can be supported by LLM use in the form of copilots. These will certainly boost productivity (Kalliamvakou, 2024) and will automate the more routine tasks, leaving quants to focus on the more challenging and interesting aspects of the job. Can LLMs help write the type of code featured in this book: yes, and LLMs were used to accelerate code development for this book. LLMs can, in many cases, 'type' code faster than the author. So, will LLMs replace quants in the near future? No. However, quants who use LLMs effectively may replace those that cannot.

20.3 THE FUTURE QUANT

What do the skills of future quants look like? They look very much like those of present quants:

- Mathematics, of which *stochastic calculus* will remain critical.
- Business knowledge and analysis: where the quant will work with business staff like traders, structurers and sales to understand business problems and translate them into mathematical models and code implementation.
- Numerical methods: familiarity with traditional numerical techniques like PDE solvers and Monte Carlo.
- Coding in C++, Python and other languages.

However, I think two new skills will also be needed:

- Familiarity with deep learning models as another numerical method.
- Ability to leverage AI productivity tools.

The best quants will be able to leverage all the available tools and generate business benefits, but that has not changed and will not change.

20.4 A FINAL WORD

This book explored how deep learning can be applied in quantitative finance. It has been an enjoyable, if lengthy, project. I hope you have enjoyed reading the book and found it helpful.

Bibliography

Lokman Abbas-Turki, Stéphane Crépey, Botao Li and Bouazza Saadeddine. An Explicit Scheme for Pathwise XVA Computations. *ArXiv*, 2024.

Rameen Abdal, Yipeng Qin and Peter Wonka. Image2StyleGAN: How to Embed Images Into the StyleGAN Latent Space? *ArXiv*, 2019a.

Rameen Abdal, Yipeng Qin and Peter Wonka. Image2StyleGAN++: How to Edit the Embedded Images? *ArXiv*, 2019b.

Melania Abrahamian and Sijuade Oguntayo. Denoising Images: How to Use Autoencoders to Produce Clearer Images [Tutorial]. *Omdena*, April 2021.

Carlo Acerbi and Balazs Szekely. Back-testing expected shortfall. *Risk*, 27(11):76–81, 2014.

David H. Ackley, Geoffrey E. Hinton and Terrence J. Sejnowski. A learning algorithm for Boltzmann machines. *Cognitive Science*, 9(1):147–169, 1985.

A. Agarwal, S. De Marco, E. Gobet, J. G. López-Salas, F. Noubiagain and A. Zhou. Numerical approximations of McKean anticipative backward stochastic differential equations arising in initial margin requirements. *ESAIM: ProcS*, 65:1–26, 2019.

Charu Aggarwal. *Neural Networks and Deep Learning: A Textbook*. Springer, Cham, 2018.

Sabeen Ahmed, Ian E. Nielsen, Aakash Tripathi, Shamoon Siddiqui, Ravi P. Ramachandran and Ghulam Rasool. Transformers in time-series analysis: A tutorial. *Circuits, Systems, and Signal Processing*, 42(12):7433–7466, 2023.

Janice Ahn, Rishu Verma, Renze Lou, Di Liu, Rui Zhang and Wenpeng Yin. Large language models for mathematical reasoning: Progresses and challenges. In Neele Falk, Sara Papi and Mike Zhang (Eds), *Proceedings of the 18th Conference of the European Chapter of the Association for Computational Linguistics: Student Research Workshop*, pp. 225–237, St. Julian's, Malta, March 2024. Association for Computational Linguistics.

Takuya Akiba, Shotaro Sano, Toshihiko Yanase, Takeru Ohta and Masanori Koyama. Optuna: A next-generation hyperparameter optimization framework. In *Proceedings of the 25th ACM SIGKDD International Conference on Knowledge Discovery and Data Mining*, 2019.

Ali Al-Aradi, Adolfo Correia, Danilo Naiff, Gabriel Jardim and Yuri Saporito. Solving Nonlinear and High-Dimensional Partial Differential Equations via Deep Learning. *ArXiv*, 2018.

Yuval Alaluf, Or Patashnik and Daniel Cohen-Or. ReStyle: A residual-based styleGAN encoder via iterative refinement. In *Proceedings of the IEEE/CVF International Conference on Computer Vision (ICCV)*, pp. 6711–6720, October 2021.

Mohamed Ben Alaya, Ahmed Kebaier and Djibril Sarr. Deep Calibration of Interest Rates Model. *ArXiv*, 2021.

Claudio Albanese, Simone Caenazzo and Stéphane Crépey. Credit, funding, margin and capital valuation adjustments for bilateral portfolios. *Probability, Uncertainty and Quantitative Risk*, 2(1):7, 2017.

Claudio Albanese, Stéphane Crépey, Rodney Hoskinson and Bouazza Saadeddine. XVA Analysis from the Balance Sheet. *ArXiv*, 2019.

Claudio Albanese, Stéphane Crépey, Rodney Hoskinson and Bouazza Saadeddine. XVA analysis from the balance sheet. *Quantitative Finance*, 21(1):99–123, January 2021.

E. Altman. Flow control using the theory of zero sum Markov games. *IEEE Transactions on Automatic Control*, 39(4): 814–818, 1994.

S. Amornwattana, D. Enke and C. H. Dagli. A hybrid option pricing model using a neural network for estimating volatility. *International Journal of General Systems*, 36(5):558–573, 2007.

Leif Andersen, Michael Pykhtin and Alexander Sokol. Does initial margin eliminate counterparty risk? *Risk*, 30(5):74–79, 2017.

Leif B. G. Andersen, Jesper Andreasen and David A. Eliezer. Static replication of barrier options: Some general results, 2000. Available at SSRN: https://ssrn.com/abstract=220010.

Leif B. G. Andersen and Vladimir V. Piterbarg. *Interest Rate Modeling. Volume 2: Term Structure Models*. Atlantic Financial Press, New York, 2010.

Brian D. O. Anderson. Reverse-time diffusion equation models. *Stochastic Processes and their Applications*, 12(3): 313–326, 1982.

Kristoffer Andersson and Cornelis Oosterlee. A Deep Learning Approach for Computations of Exposure Profiles for High-dimensional Bermudan Options. *ArXiv*, 2020a.

Deep Learning in Quantitative Finance, First Edition. Andrew Green.

Kristoffer Andersson and Cornelis W. Oosterlee. Deep Learning for CVA Computations of Large Portfolios of Financial Derivatives. *ArXiv*, 2020b.

P. C. Andreou. Parametric and nonparametric functional estimation for options pricing with applications in hedging and trading. PhD thesis, University of Cyprus, 2008.

P. C. Andreou, C. Charalambous and S. H. Martzoukos. Critical assessment of option pricing methods using artificial neural networks. In *International Conference on Artificial Neural Networks*, pp. 1131–1136, 2002.

P. C. Andreou, C. Charalambous and S. H. Martzoukos. Robust artificial neural networks for pricing of European options. *Computational Economics*, 27(2–3):329–351, 2006.

P. C. Andreou, C. Charalambous and S. H. Martzoukos. Generalized parameter functions for option pricing. *Journal of Banking & Finance*, 34(3):633–646, 2010.

Fabrizio Anfuso, Daniel Aziz, Klearchos Loukopoulos and Paul Giltinan. A sound modelling and backtesting framework for forecasting initial margin requirements. *Risk*, May: 86–91, 2017.

Alexandre Antonov, Michael Konikov and Vladimir V. Piterbarg. Neural networks with asymptotics control, 2020. Available at SSRN: https://ssrn.com/abstract=3544698.

Walter Appel. *Mathematics for Physics and Physicists*. Princeton University Press, Princeton, NJ, 2007.

Ilya Archakov, Peter Reinhard Hansen and Yiyao Luo. A New Method for Generating Random Correlation Matrices. *ArXiv*, 2022.

Hamidreza Arian, Mehrdad Moghimi, Ehsan Tabatabaei and Shiva Zamani. Encoded Value-at-Risk: A Predictive Machine for Financial Risk Management. *ArXiv*, 2020.

Martin Arjovsky, Soumith Chintala and Léon Bottou. Wasserstein GAN. *ArXiv*, 2017.

Hirbod Assa, Chris Kenyon and Haodong Zhang. Assessing reinforcement delta hedging, 2021. Available at SSRN: https://ssrn.com/abstract=3918375.

Rawin Assabumrungrat, Kentaro Minami and Masanori Hirano. Error analysis of option pricing via deep PDE solvers: Empirical study. In *16th IIAI International Congress on Advanced Applied Informatics (IIAI-AAI)*, pp. 329–336, Los Alamitos, CA, USA, July 2024. IEEE Computer Society.

Marco Avellaneda, Robert Buff, Craig Friedman, Nicolas Grandechamp, Lukasz Kruk and Joshua Newman. Weighted Monte Carlo: A new technique for calibrating asset-pricing models. *International Journal of Theoretical and Applied Finance*, 4(1):91–119, 2001.

V. I. Avrutskiy. Enhancing approximation abilities of neural networks by training derivatives. *IEEE Transactions on Neural Networks and Learning Systems*, 32(2):916–924, 2021.

Reza Azad, Amirhossein Kazerouni, Moein Heidari, Ehsan Khodapanah Aghdam, Amirali Molaei, Yiwei Jia, Abin Jose, Rijo Roy and Dorit Merhof. Advances in medical image analysis with vision transformers: A comprehensive review. *Medical Image Analysis*, 91:103000, 2024.

Sebastian Bach, Alexander Binder, Grégoire Montavon, Frederick Klauschen, Klaus-Robert Müller and Wojciech Samek. On pixel-wise explanations for non-linear classifier decisions by layer-wise relevance propagation. *PloS One*, 10(7):e0130140, 2015.

Dzmitry Bahdanau, Kyunghyun Cho and Yoshua Bengio. Neural machine translation by jointly learning to align and translate. In Yoshua Bengio and Yann LeCun (Eds), *3rd International Conference on Learning Representations, ICLR 2015*, San Diego, CA, USA, May 7–9, 2015, Conference Track Proceedings.

Shaojie Bai, J. Zico Kolter and Vladlen Koltun. An Empirical Evaluation of Generic Convolutional and Recurrent Networks for Sequence Modeling. *ArXiv*, 2018.

Richard T. Baillie, Tim Bollerslev and Hans Ole Mikkelsen. Fractionally integrated GARCH: A study of high frequency UK inflation. *Journal of Applied Econometrics*, 11(3):225–242, 1996.

David Barber and Felix Agakov. Information maximization in noisy channels: A variational approach. In S. Thrun, L. Saul and B. Schölkopf (Eds), *Advances in Neural Information Processing Systems*, volume 16. MIT Press, Cambridge, MA, 2003.

Giovanni Barone-Adesi and Robert E. Whaley. Efficient analytic approximation of American option values. *The Journal of Finance*, 42(2):301–320, 1987.

Shane Barratt and Rishi Sharma. A Note on the Inception Score. *ArXiv*, 2018.

A. R. Barron. Universal approximation bounds for superpositions of a sigmoidal function. *IEEE Transactions on Information Theory*, 39(3):930–945, 1993.

Gabriel Barth-Maron, Matthew W. Hoffman, David Budden, Will Dabney, Dan Horgan, Dhruva TB, Alistair Muldal, Nicolas Heess and Timothy Lillicrap. Distributed Distributional Deterministic Policy Gradients. *ArXiv*, 2018.

David S. Bates. Jumps and stochastic volatility: Exchange rate processes implicit in Deutsche mark options. *The Review of Financial Studies*, 9(1):69–107, 1996.

David Bau, Jun-Yan Zhu, Jonas Wulff, William Peebles, Hendrik Strobelt, Bolei Zhou and Antonio Torralba. Inverting layers of a large generator. In *ICLR Debugging Machine Learning Models Workshop*, 2019a.

David Bau, Jun-Yan Zhu, Jonas Wulff, William Peebles, Hendrik Strobelt, Bolei Zhou and Antonio Torralba. Seeing what a GAN cannot generate. In *Proceedings of the International Conference Computer Vision (ICCV)*, 2019b.

Luc Bauwens, Sebastien Laurent and Jeroen V. K. Rombouts. Multivariate GARCH models: A survey. *Journal of Applied Econometrics*, 21(1):79–109, 2006.

Jonathan Baxter. Learning internal representations. In *Proceedings of the Eighth Annual Conference on Computational Learning Theory*, COLT '95, pp. 311–320, New York, NY, USA, 1995. Association for Computing Machinery.

Christian Bayer and Benjamin Stemper. Deep Calibration of Rough Stochastic Volatility Models. *ArXiv*, 2018.

Christian Bayer, Blanka Horvath, Aitor Muguruza, Benjamin Stemper and Mehdi Tomas. On Deep Calibration of (Rough) Stochastic Volatility Models. *ArXiv*, 2019.

Christian Bayer, Martin Eigel, Leon Sallandt and Philipp Trunschke. Pricing high-dimensional Bermudan options with hierarchical tensor formats. *SIAM Journal on Financial Mathematics*, 14(2):383–406, 2023.

BCBS. *Basel III: A Global Regulatory Framework for More Resilient Banks and Banking Systems*. Bank for International Settlements, Basel, 2011.

BCBS. *Fundamental Review of the Credit Valuation Adjustment (CVA) Risk Framework – Consultative Document*. Bank for International Settlements, Basel, 2015.

Christian Beck, Sebastian Becker, Patrick Cheridito, Arnulf Jentzen and Ariel Neufeld. Deep splitting method for parabolic PDEs. *SIAM Journal on Scientific Computing*, 43(5):A3135–A3154, 2021.

Sebastien Becker, Patrick Cheridito and Arnulf Jentzen. Deep optimal stopping. *Journal of Machine Learning Research*, 20:1–25, 2019.

Marc G. Bellemare, Will Dabney and Rémi Munos. A distributional perspective on reinforcement learning. In *Proceedings of the 34th International Conference on Machine Learning – Volume 70*, ICML'17, pp. 449–458. JMLR.org, 2017.

Richard Bellman. On the theory of dynamic programming. *Proceedings of the National Academy of Sciences of the United States of America*, 38(8):716–719, 1952.

Richard E. Bellman. *Adaptive Control Processes*. Princeton University Press, Princeton, NJ, 1961.

Denis Belomestny, Stefan Häfner, Tigran Nagapetyan and Mikhail Urusov. Variance reduction for discretised diffusions via regression. *Journal of Mathematical Analysis and Applications*, 458(1):393–418, 2018.

Y. Bengio, P. Simard and P. Frasconi. Learning long-term dependencies with gradient descent is difficult. *IEEE Transactions on Neural Networks*, 5(2):157–166, March 1994.

Yoshua Bengio, Réjean Ducharme, Pascal Vincent and Christian Janvin. A neural probabilistic language model. *Journal of Machine Learning Research*, 3:1137–1155, 2003.

Yoshua Bengio, Aaron Courville and Pascal Vincent. Representation learning: A review and new perspectives. *IEEE Transactions on Pattern Analysis and Machine Intelligence*, 35(8):1798–1828, 2013.

E. Benhamou, E. Gobet and M. Miri. Time dependent Heston model. *SIAM Journal on Financial Mathematics*, 1(1):289–325, 2010.

Julia Bennell and Charles Sutcliffe. Black–Scholes versus artificial neural networks in pricing FTSE 100 options. *Intelligent Systems in Accounting, Finance and Management*, 12(4):243–260, 2004.

Fred E. Benth, Kenneth H. Karlsen and Kristin Reikvam. A semilinear Black and Scholes partial differential equation for valuing American options. *Finance and Stochastics*, 7(3):277–298, 2003.

Fred Espen Benth, Nils Detering and Silvia Lavagnini. Accuracy of Deep Learning in Calibrating HJM Forward Curves. *ArXiv*, 2020.

Maxime Bergeron, Nicholas Fung, John Hull and Zissis Poulos. Variational Autoencoders: A Hands-Off Approach to Volatility. *ArXiv*, 2021.

Yaacov Z. Bergman. Option pricing with differential interest rates. *The Review of Financial Studies*, 8(2):475–500, 1995.

James Bergstra and Yoshua Bengio. Random search for hyper-parameter optimization. *Journal of Machine Learning Research*, 13:281–305, 2012.

James Bergstra, Rémi Bardenet, Yoshua Bengio and Balázs Kégl. Algorithms for hyper-parameter optimization. In *Proceedings of the 24th International Conference on Neural Information Processing Systems*, NIPS'11, pp. 2546–2554, Red Hook, NY, USA, 2011. Curran Associates Inc.

Francesca Biagini, Alessandro Gnoatto and Immacolata Oliva. A unified approach to xVA with CSA discounting and initial margin. *SIAM Journal on Financial Mathematics*, 12(3):1013–1053, 2021.

Maxim Bichuch and Jiahao Hou. Deep PDE solution to BSDE. *Digital Finance*, 6(4):727–758, 2023.

Tomasz R. Bielecki and Marek Rutkowski. *Credit Risk: Modeling, Valuation and Hedging*. Springer, Berlin, 1st edition, 2001.

Christopher M. Bishop. *Pattern Recognition and Machine Learning*.2006Springer, Berlin,

Jean-Michel Bismut. Conjugate convex functions in optimal stochastic control. *Journal of Mathematical Analysis and Applications*, 44(2):384–404, 1973.

Fischer Black. The pricing of commodity contracts. *Journal of Financial Economics*, 3:167–179, 1976.

Fischer Black and Myron Scholes. The pricing of options and corporate liabilities. *Journal of Political Economy*, 81(3):637–654, 1973.

Hendrik Blockeel. *Hypothesis Space*. Springer, Boston, MA, 2010.

L. Blynski and A. Faseruk. Comparison of the effectiveness of option price forecasting: Black–Scholes vs. simple and hybrid neural networks. *Journal of Financial Management & Analysis*, 19(2):46–58, 2006.

Tim Bollerslev. Generalized autoregressive conditional heteroskedasticity. *Journal of Econometrics*, 31(3):307–327, 1986.

Sam Bond-Taylor, Adam Leach, Yang Long and Chris G. Willcocks. Deep Generative Modelling: A Comparative Review of VAEs, GANs, Normalizing Flows, Energy-Based and Autoregressive Models. *ArXiv*, 2021.

Ashish Bora, Eric Price and Alexandros G. Dimakis. AmbientGAN: Generative models from lossy measurements. In *International Conference on Learning Representations*, 2018.

Bruno Bouchard, Ki Wai Chau, Arij Manai and Ahmed Sid-Ali. Monte-Carlo methods for the pricing of American options: A semilinear BSDE point of view. *ESAIM: ProcS*, 65:294–308x, 2019.

Djallel Bouneffouf, Irina Rish and Charu Aggarwal. Survey on applications of multi-armed and contextual bandits. In *2020 IEEE Congress on Evolutionary Computation (CEC)*, pp. 1–8. IEEE Press, New York, 2020.

H. Bourlard and Y. Kamp. Auto-association by multilayer perceptrons and singular value decomposition. *Biological Cybernetics*, 59:291–294, 1988.

Nicolas Boursin, Carl Remlinger, Joseph Mikael and Carol Anne Hargreaves. Deep Generators on Commodity Markets; Application to Deep Hedging. *ArXiv*, 2022.

Jonathan Bowie and Peter Carr. Static simplicity. *Risk*, 7(8):45–49, 1994.

Samuel R. Bowman, Luke Vilnis, Oriol Vinyals, Andrew Dai, Rafal Jozefowicz and Samy Bengio. Generating sentences from a continuous space. In *Proceedings of The 20th SIGNLL Conference on Computational Natural Language Learning*, pp. 10–21, Berlin, Germany, August 2016. Association for Computational Linguistics.

George E. P. Box and Gwilym M. Jenkins. *Time Series Analysis: Forecasting and Control*. Holden-Day, San Francisco, 1970.

Achi Brandt. Multi-level adaptive solutions to boundary-value problems. *Mathematics of Computation*, 31:333–390, 1977.

Douglas T. Breeden and Robert H. Litzenberger. Prices of state-contingent claims implicit in option prices. *The Journal of Business*, 51(4):621–651, 1978.

Damiano Brigo and Fabio Mercurio. *Interest Rate Models – Theory and Practice*. Springer, New York, 2nd edition, 2006.

Damiano Brigo, Xiaoshan Huang, Andrea Pallavicini and Haitz Sáez de Ocáriz Borde. Interpretability in deep learning for finance: A case study for the Heston model, 2021. Available at SSRN: https://ssrn.com/abstract=3829947.

Mark Broadie, Paul Glasserman and Zachary Ha. Pricing American options by simulation using a stochastic mesh with optimized weights. In S. P. Uryasev (Ed.), *Probabilistic Constrained Optimization. Nonconvex Optimization and Its Applications*, volume 49, pp. 26–44. Springer, Boston, MA, 2000.

Andrew Brock, Jeff Donahue and Karen Simonyan. Large Scale GAN Training for High Fidelity Natural Image Synthesis. *ArXiv*, 2019.

Tom B. Brown, Benjamin Mann, Nick Ryder, Melanie Subbiah, Jared Kaplan, Prafulla Dhariwal, Arvind Neelakantan, Pranav Shyam, Girish Sastry, Amanda Askell, Sandhini Agarwal, Ariel Herbert-Voss, Gretchen Krueger, Tom Henighan, Rewon Child, Aditya Ramesh, Daniel M. Ziegler, Jeffrey Wu, Clemens Winter, Christopher Hesse, Mark Chen, Eric Sigler, Mateusz Litwin, Scott Gray, Benjamin Chess, Jack Clark, Christopher Berner, Sam McCandlish, Alec Radford, Ilya Sutskever and Dario Amodei. Language Models are Few-Shot Learners. *ArXiv*, 2020.

Jason Brownlee. How to use data scaling improve deep learning model stability and performance, 2019a. https://machinelearningmastery.com/how-to-improve-neural-network-stability-and-modeling-performance-with-data-scaling/.

Jason Brownlee. How to visualize filters and feature maps in convolutional neural networks, 2019b. https://machinelearningmastery.com/how-to-visualize-filters-and-feature-maps-in-convolutional-neural-networks/.

Raymond Brummelhuis and Zhongmin Luo. CDS proxy construction via machine learning techniques—Part I: Methodology and results. *The Journal of Financial Data Science*, 1(2):111–127, 2019a.

Raymond Brummelhuis and Zhongmin Luo. CDS proxy construction via machine learning techniques—Part II: Parametrization, correlation, benchmarking. *The Journal of Financial Data Science*, 1(2):128–151, 2019b.

Hans Buehler, Lukas Gonon, Josef Teichmann, Ben Wood, Baranidharan Mohan and Jonathan Kochems. Deep hedging. *Quantitative Finance*, 19(8):1271–1291, 2019.

Hans Buehler, Phillip Murray, Mikko S. Pakkanen and Ben Wood. Deep Hedging: Learning to Remove the Drift under Trading Frictions with Minimal Equivalent Near-Martingale Measures. *ArXiv*, 2021.

Hans Buehler, Phillip Murray and Ben Wood. Deep Bellman Hedging. *ArXiv*, 2022.

K. Bujok and C. Reisinger. Numerical valuation of basket credit derivatives in structural jump-diffusion models. *Journal of Computational Finance*, 15(4):115–158, 2012.

N. Bush, B. M. Hambly, H. Haworth, L. Jin and C. Reisinger. Stochastic evolution equations in portfolio credit modelling. *SIAM Journal on Financial Mathematics*, 2(1):627–664, 2011.

Hans Bühler, Blanka Horvath, Terry Lyons, Imanol Perez Arribas and Ben Wood. A Data-Driven Market Simulator for Small Data Environments. *ArXiv*, 2020.

Loris Cannelli, Giuseppe Nuti, Marzio Sala and Oleg Szehr. Hedging using reinforcement learning: Contextual k-armed bandit versus Q-learning. *The Journal of Finance and Data Science*, 9:100101, 2023.

Jay Cao, Jacky Chen, John Hull and Zissis Poulos. Deep hedging of derivatives using reinforcement learning. *The Journal of Financial Data Science*, 3(1):10–27, 2021.

Jay Cao, Jacky Chen, Soroush Farghadani, John Hull, Zissis Poulos, Zeyu Wang and Jun Yuan. Gamma and Vega Hedging Using Deep Distributional Reinforcement Learning. *ArXiv*, 2022.

Alexandre Carbonneau. Deep Hedging of Long-Term Financial Derivatives. *ArXiv*, 2020.

Alexandre Carbonneau and Frédéric Godin. Equal Risk Pricing of Derivatives with Deep Hedging. *ArXiv*, 2020.

Alexandre Carbonneau and Frédéric Godin. Deep Equal Risk Pricing of Financial Derivatives with Multiple Hedging Instruments. *ArXiv*, 2021.

Pierre Cardaliaguet and Charles-Albert Lehalle. Mean field game of controls and an application to trade crowding. *Mathematics and Financial Economics*, 12:335–363, 2018.

Filip Carlsson and Philip Lindgren. Deep Scenario Generation of Financial Markets, 2020. https://www.diva-portal.org/smash/get/diva2:1432666/FULLTEXT02.pdf.

P. Carr and D. Madan. Optimal positioning in derivative securities. *Quantitative Finance*, 1(1):19–37, 2001.

Peter Carr and Andrew Chou. Hedging complex barrier options, 1997.

Peter Carr and Dilip Madan. Option valuation using the fast fourier transform. *Journal of Computational Finance*, 2(4): 61–73, 1999.

Peter Carr and Liuren Wu. Static hedging of standard options. *Journal of Financial Econometrics*, 12(1):3–46, 2013.

Peter Carr, Katrina Ellis and Vishal Gupta. Static hedging of exotic options. *The Journal of Finance*, 53(3):1165–1190, 1998.

Miguel Á. Carreira-Perpiñán and Geoffrey Hinton. On contrastive divergence learning. In Robert G. Cowell and Zoubin Ghahramani (Eds), *Proceedings of the Tenth International Workshop on Artificial Intelligence and Statistics*, volume R5 of *Proceedings of Machine Learning Research*, pp. 33–40. PMLR, 6–8 January 2005.

Jacques F. Carriere. Valuation of the early-exercise price for options using simulations and nonparametric regression. *Insurance: Mathematics and Economics*, 19(1):19–30, 1996.

Rich Caruana. Multitask learning. *Machine Learning*, 28(1):41–75, 1997.

A.-L. Cauchy. Méthode générale pour la résolution des systèmes d'équations simultanées. *Comptes rendus de l'Académie des Sciences Paris*, 25:536–538, 1847.

Giovanni Cesari, John Aquilina, Niels Charpillon, Zltako Filipovic, Gordon Lee and Ion Manda. *Modelling, Pricing and Hedging Counterparty Credit Exposure*. Springer, New York, 2009.

Ender Çetin, Cristina Barrado and Enric Pastor. Counter a drone in a complex neighborhood area by deep reinforcement learning. *Sensors*, 20:2320, April 2020.

Justin Chan, Shengyao Zhu and Boris Tourtzevitch. Modelling forward initial margin requirements for bilateral trading. In Leif Andersen and Michael Pykhtin (Eds), *Margin in Derivatives Trading*. 2018. Risk.net

C. Charalambous and S. H. Martzoukos. Hybrid artificial neural networks for efficient valuation of real options and financial derivatives. *Computational Management Science*, 2(2):155–161, 2005.

Marc Chataigner, Stéphane Crépey and Matthew Dixon. Deep Local Volatility. *ArXiv*, 2020.

Fei Chen and Charles Sutcliffe. Pricing and hedging short sterling options using neural networks. *Intelligent Systems in Accounting, Finance and Management*, 19(2):128–149, 2012.

Xi Chen, Yan Duan, Rein Houthooft, John Schulman, Ilya Sutskever and Pieter Abbeel. InfoGAN: Interpretable Representation Learning by Information Maximizing Generative Adversarial Nets. *ArXiv*, 2016.

Xi Chen, Diederik P. Kingma, Tim Salimans, Yan Duan, Prafulla Dhariwal, John Schulman, Ilya Sutskever and Pieter Abbeel. Variational lossy autoencoder. In *5th International Conference on Learning Representations, ICLR 2017*, Toulon, France, April 24–26, 2017, Conference Track Proceedings.

Ilya Chevyrev and Andrey Kormilitzin. A Primer on the Signature Method in Machine Learning. *ArXiv*, 2016.

Kyunghyun Cho, Bart van Merriënboer, Caglar Gulcehre, Dzmitry Bahdanau, Fethi Bougares, Holger Schwenk and Yoshua Bengio. Learning phrase representations using RNN encoder–decoder for statistical machine translation. In Alessandro Moschitti, Bo Pang and Walter Daelemans (Eds), *Proceedings of the 2014 Conference on Empirical Methods in Natural Language Processing (EMNLP)*, pp. 1724–1734, Doha, Qatar, October 2014. Association for Computational Linguistics.

François Chollet. *Deep Learning with Python*. Manning Publications, New York, 2018.

François Chollet et al. Keras [Blog], 2015. https://blog.keras.io/author/francois-chollet.html.

Min Jin Chong and David Forsyth. Effectively Unbiased FID and Inception Score and Where to Find Them. *ArXiv*, 2019.

Wing Fung Chong, Haoen Cui and Yuxuan Li. Pseudo-Model-Free Hedging for Variable Annuities via Deep Reinforcement Learning. *ArXiv*, 2021.

Vedant Choudhary, Sebastian Jaimungal and Maxime Bergeron. FuNVol: A Multi-Asset Implied Volatility Market Simulator Using Functional Principal Components and Neural SDEs. *ArXiv*, 2023.

Yoni Choukroun and Lior Wolf. Geometric transformer for end-to-end molecule properties prediction. In Lud De Raedt (Ed.), *Proceedings of the Thirty-First International Joint Conference on Artificial Intelligence, IJCAI-22*, pp. 2895–2901. International Joint Conferences on Artificial Intelligence Organization, July 2022.

Kyriakos Chourdakis, Eduardo Epperlein, Marc Jeannin and James McEwen. A cross-section across CVA. 2013. https://www.nomura.com/resources/europe/pdfs/cva-cross-section.pdf.

Peter Friz, Christian Bayer and Jim Gatheral. Pricing under rough volatility. *Quantitative Finance*, 16(6):887–904, 2016.

Iain J. Clark. *Foreign Exchange Option Pricing: A Practitioners Guide*. Wiley, Chichester, 2011.

Djork-Arné Clevert, Thomas Unterthiner and Sepp Hochreiter. Fast and Accurate Deep Network Learning by Exponential Linear Units (ELUs). *ArXiv*, 2016.

A. K. Cline and I. S. Dhillon. Computation of the singular value decomposition. In L. Hogben (Ed.), *Handbook of Linear Algebra*, pp. 45-1–45-13. CRC Press, Boca Raton, FL, 2006.

Andrea Coletta, Matteo Prata, Michele Conti, Emanuele Mercanti, Novella Bartolini, Aymeric Moulin, Svitlana Vyetrenko and Tucker Balch. Towards Realistic Market Simulations: A Generative Adversarial Networks Approach. *ArXiv*, 2021.

R. Cont. Empirical properties of asset returns: Stylized facts and statistical issues. *Quantitative Finance*, 1(2):223–236, 2001.

Rama Cont, Mihai Cucuringu, Renyuan Xu and Chao Zhang. Tail-GAN: Nonparametric Scenario Generation for Tail Risk Estimation. *ArXiv*, 2022.

S. Crépey. Calibration of the local volatility in a trinomial tree using Tikhonov regularization. *Inverse Problems*, 19(1):91, 2002.

Stéphane Crépey. *Financial Modeling: A Backward Stochastic Differential Equations Perspective*. Springer, Berlin, 1st edition, 2013.

R. Culkin and S. R. Das. Machine learning in finance: The case of deep learning for option pricing. *Journal of Investment Management*, 15(4):92–100, 2017.

G. Cybenko. Approximation by superpositions of a sigmoidal function. *Mathematics of Control, Signals and Systems*, 2(4):303–314, 1989.

Wojciech Marian Czarnecki, Simon Osindero, Max Jaderberg, Grzegorz Świrszcz and Razvan Pascanu. Sobolev Training for Neural Networks. *ArXiv*, 2017.

Yann N. Dauphin, Razvan Pascanu, Caglar Gulcehre, Kyunghyun Cho, Surya Ganguli and Yoshua Bengio. Identifying and attacking the saddle point problem in high-dimensional non-convex optimization. In *Proceedings of the 27th International Conference on Neural Information Processing Systems – Volume 2*, NIPS'14, pp. 2933–2941, Cambridge, MA, USA, 2014. MIT Press.

Philip I. Davies and Nicholas J. Higham. Numerically stable generation of correlation matrices and their factors. *BIT Numerical Mathematics*, 40(4):640–651, 2000.

Harm de Vries, Florian Strub, Jeremie Mary, Hugo Larochelle, Olivier Pietquin and Aaron C. Courville. Modulating early visual processing by language. In I. Guyon, U. Von Luxburg, S. Bengio, H. Wallach, R. Fergus, S. Vishwanathan and R. Garnett (Eds), *Advances in Neural Information Processing Systems*, volume 30. Curran Associates, New York, 2017.

Moto Dei. 6 More Evaluation Metrics Data Scientists Should Be Familiar with — Lessons from A High-Rank Kagglers' New Book. https://medium.com/data-science/6-more-evaluation-metrics-data-scientists-should-be-familiar-with-lessons-from-a-high-rank-d7756611efc4.

Emanuel Derman, Deniz Ergener and Iraj Kani. Static options replication. *Journal of Derivatives*, 2(4):78–95, 1995.

Abhyuday Desai, Cynthia Freeman, Zuhui Wang and Ian Beaver. Timevae: A Variational Auto-Encoder for Multivariate Time Series Generation. *ArXiv*, 2021.

Thomas Deschatre and Joseph Mikael. Deep Combinatorial Optimisation for Optimal Stopping Time Problems: Application to Swing Options Pricing. *ArXiv*, 2020.

Jacob Devlin, Ming-Wei Chang, Kenton Lee and Kristina Toutanova. Bert: Pre-Training of Deep Bidirectional Transformers for Language Understanding. *ArXiv*, 2018.

Y. Geeta Dharani, Nimisha Nair, Pallavi Satpathy and Jabez Christopher. Covariate Shift: A Review and Analysis on Classifiers. In *2019 Global Conference for Advancement in Technology (GCAT)*, pp. 1–6, October 2019.

Prafulla Dhariwal and Alex Nichol. Diffusion Models Beat GANs on Image Synthesis. *ArXiv*, 2021.

Georgi Dimitroff, Dirk Röder and Christian P. Fries. Volatility model calibration with convolutional neural networks, 2018. Available at SSRN: https://ssrn.com/abstract=3252432.

Matthew F. Dixon, Igor Halperin and Paul Bilokon. *Machine Learning in Finance: From Theory to Practice*. Springer, Berlin, 2020.

Alexey Dosovitskiy and Thomas Brox. Generating images with perceptual similarity metrics based on deep networks. In D. Lee, M. Sugiyama, U. Luxburg, I. Guyon and R. Garnett (Eds), *Advances in Neural Information Processing Systems*, volume 29. Curran Associates, New York, 2016.

Alexey Dosovitskiy, Jost Tobias Springenberg and Thomas Brox. Learning to generate chairs with convolutional neural networks. In *2015 IEEE Conference on Computer Vision and Pattern Recognition (CVPR)*, pp. 1538–1546, 2015.

Alexey Dosovitskiy, Lucas Beyer, Alexander Kolesnikov, Dirk Weissenborn, Xiaohua Zhai, Thomas Unterthiner, Mostafa Dehghani, Matthias Minderer, Georg Heigold, Sylvain Gelly, Jakob Uszkoreit and Neil Houlsby. An Image Is Worth 16×16 Words: Transformers for Image Recognition at Scale. In *International Conference on Learning Representations (ICLR)*, 2021.

Iddo Drori. *The Science of Deep Learning*. Cambridge University Press, Cambridge, 2022.

H. Drucker and Y. Le Cun. Improving generalization performance using double backpropagation. *IEEE Transactions on Neural Networks*, 3(6):991–997, 1992.

Jiayi Du, Muyang Jin, Petter N. Kolm, Gordon Ritter, Yixuan Wang and Bofei Zhang. Deep reinforcement learning for option replication and hedging. *Journal of Financial Data Science*, 2(2):44–57, 2020.

Yilun Du and Igor Mordatch. Implicit generation and modeling with energy based models. In H. Wallach, H. Larochelle, A. Beygelzimer, F. d'Alché-Buc, E. Fox and R. Garnett (Eds), *Advances in Neural Information Processing Systems*, volume 32. Curran Associates, New York, 2019.

John Duchi, Elad Hazan and Yoram Singer. Adaptive subgradient methods for online learning and stochastic optimization. *Journal of Machine Learning Research*, 12:2121–2159, 2011.

Darrell Duffie and Larry G. Epstein. Stochastic differential utility. *Econometrica*, 60(2):353–394, 1992.

Vincent Dumoulin, Jonathon Shlens and Manjunath Kudlur. A learned representation for artistic style. In *5th International Conference on Learning Representations, ICLR 2017,* Toulon, France, April 24–26, 2017, Conference Track Proceedings.

Bruno Dupire. Pricing with a smile. *Risk*, 7(1):18–20, 1994.

Nadir Durrani, Barry Haddow, Philipp Koehn and Kenneth Heafield. Edinburgh's phrase-based machine translation systems for WMT-14. In Ondřej Bojar, Christian Buck, Christian Federmann, Barry Haddow, Philipp Koehn, Christof Monz, Matt Post and Lucia Specia (Eds), *Proceedings of the Ninth Workshop on Statistical Machine Translation*, pp. 97–104, Baltimore, MD, USA, June 2014. Association for Computational Linguistics.

Carl Eckart and Gale Young. The approximation of one matrix by another of lower rank. *Psychometrika*, 1(3):211–218, 1936.

J. Eisenstein. *Introduction to Natural Language Processing*. Adaptive Computation and Machine Learning Series. MIT Press, Cambridge, MA, 2019.

N. El Karoui, S. Peng and M. C. Quenez. Backward stochastic differential equations in finance. *Mathematical Finance*, 7(1):1–71, 1997.

Paul Embrechts, Alexander J. McNeil and Daniel Straumann. Correlation and dependence in risk management: Properties and pitfalls. In M. A. H. Dempster (Ed.), *Risk Management: Value at Risk and Beyond,* pp. 176–223. Cambridge University Press, Cambridge, 2001.

Robert F. Engle. Autoregressive conditional heteroskedasticity with estimates of the variance of United Kingdom inflation. *Econometrica*, 50(4):987–1007, 1982.

Larry G. Epstein and Stanley E. Zin. Substitution, risk aversion, and the temporal behavior of consumption and asset returns: A theoretical framework. *Econometrica*, 57(4):937–969, 1989.

N. E. D. A. Esmaeeli and P. E. T. E. R. Imkeller. American options with asymmetric information and reflected BSDE. *Bernoulli*, 24(2):1394–1426, 2018.

Tolulope Fadina, Ariel Neufeld and Thorsten Schmidt. Affine processes under parameter uncertainty. *Probability, Uncertainty and Quantitative Risk*, 4(1):5, 2019.

Stefan Falkner, Aaron Klein and Frank Hutter. BOHB: Robust and efficient hyperparameter optimization at scale. In Jennifer Dy and Andreas Krause (Eds), *Proceedings of the 35th International Conference on Machine Learning*, volume 80 of *Proceedings of Machine Learning Research*, pp. 1437–1446, Stockholmsmässan, Stockholm, Sweden, 10–15 July 2018. PMLR.

F. Fang and C. W. Oosterlee. A novel pricing method for European options based on Fourier-cosine series expansions. *SIAM Journal on Scientific Computing*, 31(2):826–848, 2009.

Ali Fathi and Bernhard Hientzsch. A Comparison of Reinforcement Learning and Deep Trajectory Based Stochastic Control Agents for Stepwise Mean-Variance Hedging. *ArXiv*, 2023.

Tom Fawcett. An introduction to ROC analysis. *Pattern Recognition Letters*, 27:861–874, 2006.

William Fedus, Prajit Ramachandran, Rishabh Agarwal, Yoshua Bengio, Hugo Larochelle, Mark Rowland and Will Dabney. Revisiting Fundamentals of Experience Replay. *ArXiv*, 2020.

Ryan Ferguson and Andrew Green. Deeply Learning Derivatives. *ArXiv*, 2018.

Matthias Feurer and Frank Hutter. *Hyperparameter Optimization*. Springer International, Cham, 2019.

George S. Fishman. *Monte Carlo: Concepts, Algorithms and Applications*. Springer, New York, 1996.

Aries Fitriawan, Ito Wasito, Arida Ferti Syafiandini, Mukhlis Amien and Arry Yanuar. Multi-label classification using deep belief networks for virtual screening of multi-target drug. In *2016 International Conference on Computer, Control, Informatics and its Applications (IC3INA)*, pp. 102–107, 2016.

Solveig Flaig and Gero Junike. Scenario Generation for Market Risk Models Using Generative Neural Networks. *ArXiv*, 2021.

Harriet Flint, Ben Hambly and Terry Lyons. Discretely sampled signals and the rough Hoff process. *Stochastic Processes and their Applications*, 126(9):2593–2614, 2016.

P. A. Forsyth and K. R. Vetzal. Quadratic convergence for valuing American options using a penalty method. *SIAM Journal on Scientific Computing*, 23(6):2095–2122, 2002.

Meire Fortunato, Mohammad Gheshlaghi Azar, Bilal Piot, Jacob Menick, Ian Osband, Alex Graves, Vlad Mnih, Remi Munos, Demis Hassabis, Olivier Pietquin, Charles Blundell and Shane Legg. Noisy Networks for Exploration. *ArXiv*, 2017.

David Foster. *Generative Deep Learning*. O'Reilly, Sebastopol, CA, 2019.

Jean-Pierre Fouque and Chuan-Hsiang Han. A martingale control variate method for option pricing with stochastic volatility. *ESAIM: Probability and Statistics*, 11:40–54, 2007.

Marco Di Francesco and Kevin Kamm. CDO Calibration via Magnus Expansion and Deep Learning. *ArXiv*, 2022.

Isabelle Frodé, Viktor Sambergs and Shengyao Zhu. Neural networks for credit risk and xVA in a front office pricing environment, 2022. Available at SSRN: https://ssrn.com/abstract=4136123.

Rao Fu, Jie Chen, Shutian Zeng, Yiping Zhuang and Agus Sudjianto. Time Series Simulation by Conditional Generative Adversarial Net. *ArXiv*, 2019.

Masaaki Fujii, Akihiko Takahashi and Masayuki Takahashi. Asymptotic expansion as prior knowledge in deep learning method for high dimensional BSDEs. *Asia-Pacific Financial Markets*, 26(3):391–408, 2019.

Scott Fujimoto, Herke Hoof and David Meger. Addressing function approximation error in actor–critic methods. In *International Conference on Machine Learning*, pp. 1587–1596. PMLR, 2018.

Hideharu Funahashi. Deep learning for derivatives pricing: A comparative study of asymptotic and quasi-process corrections, 2023. Available at SSRN: https://ssrn.com/abstract=4553139.

J. Galindo-Flores. A framework for comparative analysis of statistical and machine learning methods: An application to the Black–Scholes option pricing model. In Yaser S. Abu-Mostafa, Blake LeBaron, Andrew W. Lo and Andreas S. Weigend (Eds), *Computational Finance 1999*, pp. 635–660. MIT Press, Cambridge, MA, 2000.

Chengfan Gao, Siping Gao, Ruimeng Hu and Zimu Zhu. Convergence of the Backward Deep BSDE Method with Applications to Optimal Stopping Problems. *ArXiv*, 2022.

Kang Gao, Stephen Weston, Perukrishnen Vytelingum, Namid R. Stillman, Wayne Luk and Ce Guo. Deeper Hedging: A New Agent-Based Model for Effective Deep Hedging. *ArXiv*, 2023.

R. Garcia and R. Gençay. Option pricing with neural networks and a homogeneity hint. In Apostolos-Paul N. Refenes, Andrew N. Burgess and John E. Moody (Eds), *Decision Technologies for Computational Finance: Proceedings of the Fifth International Conference on Computational Finance*, pp. 195–205. Springer, Dordrecht, 1998.

Jim Gatheral. *The Volatility Surface: A Practitioner's Guide*. Wiley Finance Series. Wiley, Hoboken, NJ, 2006.

Jim Gatheral and Antoine Jacquier. Arbitrage-free SVI volatility surfaces. *Quantitative Finance*, 14(1):59–71, 2014.

Leon A. Gatys, Alexander S. Ecker and Matthias Bethge. A Neural Algorithm of Artistic Style. *ArXiv*, 2015.

Christophe Geissler, Nicolas Morizet, Matteo Rizzato and Julien Wallart. Generative Adversarial Networks Applied to Synthetic Financial Scenarios Generation. *ArXiv*, 2022.

Maximilien Germain, Huyên Pham and Xavier Warin. Neural networks-based algorithms for stochastic control and PDEs in finance. In Agostino Capponi and Charles-Albert Lehalle (Eds), *Machine Learning and Data Sciences for Financial Markets: A Guide to Contemporary Practices*. Cambridge University Press, Cambridge, 2023.

F. A. Gers and J. Schmidhuber. Recurrent nets that time and count. In *Proceedings of the IEEE-INNS-ENNS International Joint Conference on Neural Networks. IJCNN 2000. Neural Computing: New Challenges and Perspectives for the New Millennium*, volume 3, pp. 189–194, 2000.

Samuel Gershman and Noah Goodman. Amortized inference in probabilistic reasoning. *Proceedings of the Annual Meeting of the Cognitive Science Society*, volume 36, pp. 517–522, 2014.

Benedikt Geuchen, Katharina Oberpriller and Thorsten Schmidt. Classical and Deep Pricing for Path-Dependent Options in Non-Linear Generalized Affine Models. *ArXiv*, 2022.

John Geweke and Susan Porter-Hudak. Estimating the persistence of deviations from purchasing power parity. *Journal of International Economics*, 31(3–4):311–329, 1991.

Michael B. Giles and Christoph Reisinger. Stochastic finite differences and multilevel Monte Carlo for a class of SPDEs in finance. *SIAM Journal on Financial Mathematics*, 3(1):572–592, 2012.

Mike Giles. Advanced Monte Carlo methods: American options. 2008. https://www2.maths.ox.ac.uk/~gilesm/mc/module_6/american.pdf.

Mike Giles and Paul Glasserman. Smoking adjoints: Fast Monte Carlo Greeks. *Risk*, 19:92–96, 2006.

Igor Gitman and Boris Ginsburg. Comparison of Batch Normalization and Weight Normalization Algorithms for the Large-Scale Image Classification. *ArXiv*, 2017.

Alexandru Giurca and Svetlana Borovkova. Delta hedging of derivatives using deep reinforcement learning, 2021. Available at SSRN: https://ssrn.com/abstract=3847272.

Paul Glasserman. *Monte Carlo Methods in Financial Engineering*. Springer, Berlin, 2004.

Paul Glasserman and Bin Yu. Simulation for American options: Regression now or regression later? In *Monte Carlo and Quasi-Monte Carlo Methods 2002: Proceedings of a Conference held at the National University of Singapore, Republic of Singapore, November 25–28, 2002*, pp. 213–226. Springer, Berlin, 2004.

Xavier Glorot and Yoshua Bengio. Understanding the difficulty of training deep feedforward neural networks. In Yee Whye Teh and Mike Titterington (Eds), *Proceedings of Machine Learning Research*, volume 9 of *Proceedings of Machine Learning Research*, pp. 249–256, Chia Laguna Resort, Sardinia, Italy, 13–15 May 2010. JMLR Workshop and Conference Proceedings.

Xavier Glorot, Antoine Bordes and Yoshua Bengio. Deep sparse rectifier neural networks. In Geoffrey Gordon, David Dunson and Miroslav Dudík (Eds), *Proceedings of Machine Learning Research*, volume 15 of *Proceedings of Machine Learning Research*, pp. 315–323, Fort Lauderdale, FL, USA, 11–13 April 2011. JMLR Workshop and Conference Proceedings.

Alessandro Gnoatto, Athena Picarelli and Christoph Reisinger. Deep xVA Solver – A Neural Network Based Counterparty Credit Risk Management Framework. *ArXiv*, 2020.

Zheng Gong, Carmine Ventre and John O'Hara. The Efficient Hedging Frontier with Deep Neural Networks. *ArXiv*, 2021.

Ian Goodfellow. NIPS 2016 Tutorial: Generative Adversarial Networks. *ArXiv*, 2016.

Ian Goodfellow, Yoshua Bengio and Aaron Courville. *Deep Learning*. MIT Press, Cambridge, MA, 2016.

Ian J. Goodfellow, Jean Pouget-Abadie, Mehdi Mirza, Bing Xu, David Warde-Farley, Sherjil Ozair, Aaron Courville and Yoshua Bengio. Generative adversarial nets. In *Proceedings of the 27th International Conference on Neural Information Processing Systems – Volume 2*, NIPS'14, pp. 2672–2680, Cambridge, MA, USA, 2014. MIT Press.

Laura Graesser and Wah Loon Keng. *Foundations of Deep Reinforcement Learning: Theory and Practice in Python*. Addison-Wesley, Boston, MA, 1st edition, 2019.

Margherita Grandini, Enrico Bagli and Giorgio Visani. Metrics for Multi-Class Classification: An Overview. *ArXiv*, 2020.

Will Grathwohl, Kuan-Chieh Wang, Jörn-Henrik Jacobsen, David Duvenaud, Mohammad Norouzi and Kevin Swersky. Your Classifier Is Secretly an Energy Based Model and You Should Treat It Like One. *ArXiv*, 2020.

Andrew Green. *XVA: Credit, Funding and Capital Valuation Adjustments*. Wiley, Chichester, 2015.

Andrew Green and Chris Kenyon. XVA at the Exercise Boundary. *Risk*, 3 February 2017. https://www.risk.net/cutting-edge/banking/3847981/xva-at-the-exercise-boundary.

Andrew David Green. Cosmological applications of multi-grid methods. PhD thesis, University of Oxford, 2000.

Jon Gregory. *The xVA Challenge: Counterparty Risk, Funding, Collateral, Capital and Initial Margin*. Wiley, Chichester, 2020.

Katarína Grešová, Vlastimil Martinek, David Čechák, Petr Šimeček and Panagiotis Alexiou. Genomic benchmarks: A collection of datasets for genomic sequence classification. *BMC Genomic Data*, 24(1):25, 2023.

Andreas Griewank and Andrea Walther. *Evaluating Derivatives: Principles and Techniques of Algorithmic Differentiation*. SIAM, Philadelphia, PA, 2nd edition, 2008.

Roger Grosse. Bayesian hyperparameter optimization, 2017. https://www.cs.toronto.edu/~rgrosse/courses/csc321_2017/slides/lec21.pdf.

Prince Grover. 5 Regression Loss Functions All Machine Learners Should Know, June 2018. https://www.comet.com/site/blog/5-regression-loss-functions-all-machine-learners-should-know/.

Ken Gu and Akshay Budhkar. A package for learning on tabular and text data with transformers. In Amir Zadeh, Louis-Philippe Morency, Paul Pu Liang, Candace Ross, Ruslan Salakhutdinov, Soujanya Poria, Erik Cambria and Kelly Shi (Eds), *Proceedings of the Third Workshop on Multimodal Artificial Intelligence*, pp. 69–73, Mexico City, Mexico, June 2021. Association for Computational Linguistics.

Ishaan Gulrajani, Faruk Ahmed, Martin Arjovsky, Vincent Dumoulin and Aaron Courville. Improved Training of Wasserstein GANs. *ArXiv*, 2017.

Ivan Guo, Nicolas Langrené and Jiahao Wu. Simultaneous Upper and Lower Bounds of American Option Prices with Hedging via Neural Networks. *ArXiv*, 2023.

Michael U. Gutmann and Aapo Hyvärinen. Noise-contrastive estimation of unnormalized statistical models, with applications to natural image statistics. *Journal of Machine Learning Research*, 13(11):307–361, 2012.

Road Gylberth. Cross-Entropy and Maximum Likelihood Estimation, February 2019. https://medium.com/konvergen/cross-entropy-and-maximum-likelihood-estimation-58942b52517a.

P. S. Hagan, D. Kumar, A. S. Lesniewski and D. E. Woodward. Managing smile risk. *Wilmott Magazine*, 1:84–108, July 2002.

J. T. Hahn. Option pricing using artificial neural networks: The Australian perspective. PhD thesis, Bond University, Queensland, 2013.

Richard H. R. Hahnloser, Rahul Sarpeshkar, Misha A. Mahowald, Rodney J. Douglas and H. Sebastian Seung. Digital selection and analogue amplification coexist in a cortex-inspired silicon circuit. *Nature*, 405:947–951, June 2000.

Igor Halperin. QLBS: Q-Learner in the Black-Scholes(-Merton) Worlds. *ArXiv*, 2017.

Igor Halperin. The QLBS Q-learner goes nuqlear: Fitted Q iteration, inverse RL, and option portfolios. *Quantitative Finance*, 19(9):1543–1553, 2019.

James D. Hamilton. *Time Series Analysis*. Princeton University Press, Princeton, NJ, 1994.

Jiequn Han and Weinan E. Deep Learning Approximation for Stochastic Control Problems. *ArXiv*, 2016.

Jiequn Han and Jihao Long. Convergence of the deep BSDE method for coupled FBSDEs. *Probability, Uncertainty and Quantitative Risk*, 5(1):5, 2020.

Jiequn Han, Arnulf Jentzen and Weinan E. Solving high-dimensional partial differential equations using deep learning. *Proceedings of the National Academy of Sciences*, 115(34):8505–8510, 2018.

David J. Hand and Robert J. Till. A simple generalisation of the area under the roc curve for multiple class classification problems. *Machine Learning*, 45(2):171–186, 2001.

Boris Hanin. Universal function approximation by deep neural nets with bounded width and ReLU activations. *Mathematics*, 7(10):10.3390/math7100992, 2019.

M. Hanke. Neural network approximation of option pricing formulas for analytically intractable option pricing models. *Journal of Computational Intelligence in Finance*, 5(5):20–27, 1997.

Thomas Hartmann, Matthias Kissel and Klaus Diepold. Sobolev Training with Higher Order Derivatives, 2019. file:///E:/Downloads/fp_hartmann.pdf.

M. B. Haugh and L. Kogan. Pricing American options: A duality approach. *Operations Research*, 52:258–270, 2004.

Kohei Hayashi and Kei Nakagawa. Fractional SDE-Net: Generation of Time Series Data with Long-Term Memory. *ArXiv*, 2022.

K. He, X. Zhang, S. Ren and J. Sun. Delving deep into rectifiers: Surpassing human-level performance on ImageNet classification. In *2015 IEEE International Conference on Computer Vision (ICCV)*, pp. 1026–1034, December 2015.

K. He, X. Zhang, S. Ren and J. Sun. Deep residual learning for image recognition. In *2016 IEEE Conference on Computer Vision and Pattern Recognition (CVPR)*, pp. 770–778, June 2016.

Jeff Heaton. The number of hidden layers, 2017. https://www.heatonresearch.com/2017/06/01/hidden-layers.html.

Dan Hendrycks and Kevin Gimpel. Gaussian Error Linear Units (GELUs). *ArXiv*, 2016.

Pierre Henry-Labordère. Generative models for financial data, 2019a. Available at SSRN: https://ssrn.com/abstract=3408007.

Pierre Henry-Labordère. CVA and IM: Welcome to the machine. *Risk*, March 2019b.

Andres Hernandez. Model calibration with neural networks. *Risk*, June 2017.

Jefferson Hernandez and Andres G. Abad. Learning from Multivariate Discrete Sequential Data Using a Restricted Boltzmann Machine Model. *ArXiv*, 2018.

Steven L. Heston. A closed-form solution for options with stochastic volatility with applications to bond and currency options. *Review of Financial Studies*, 6(2):327–343, 1993.

Martin Heusel, Hubert Ramsauer, Thomas Unterthiner, Bernhard Nessler and Sepp Hochreiter. GANs trained by a two time-scale update rule converge to a local Nash equilibrium. In *Proceedings of the 31st International Conference on Neural Information Processing Systems*, NIPS'17, pp. 6629–6640, Red Hook, NY, USA, 2017. Curran Associates Inc.

Bernhard Hientzsch. Reinforcement Learning and Deep Stochastic Optimal Control for Final Quadratic Hedging. *ArXiv*, 2024.

G. E. Hinton and R. R. Salakhutdinov. Reducing the dimensionality of data with neural networks. *Science*, 313(5786): 504–507, 2006.

G. E. Hinton and T. J. Sejnowski. Learning and relearning in Boltzmann machines. In David E. Rumelhart, James L. McClelland and CORPORATE PDP Research Group (Eds), *Parallel Distributed Processing: Explorations in the Microstructure of Cognition*, volume 1, pp. 282–317. MIT Press, Cambridge, MA, 1986.

Geoffrey Hinton. 2007 NIPS Tutorial on: Deep Belief Nets, 2007a. https://www.cs.toronto.edu/~hinton/nipstutorial/nipstut3.pdf.

Geoffrey Hinton. A Practical Guide to Training Restricted Boltzmann Machines. Technical Report UTML TR 2010–003, Department of Computer Science, University of Toronto, August 2010.

Geoffrey Hinton, Nitish Srivastava and Kevin Swersky. Lecture 6e rmsprop: Divide the gradient by a running average of its recent magnitude, 2014. https://www.cs.toronto.edu/~tijmen/csc321/slides/lecture_slides_lec6.pdf.

Geoffrey E. Hinton. Learning translation invariant recognition in a massively parallel networks. In J. W. de Bakker, A. J. Nijman and P. C. Treleaven (Eds), *PARLE Parallel Architectures and Languages Europe*, pp. 1–13. Springer, Berlin, 1987.

Geoffrey E. Hinton. Training Products of Experts by Minimizing Contrastive Divergence. Technical Report GCNU TR 2000-004, Gatsby Computational Neuroscience Unit, University College London, 2000.

Geoffrey E. Hinton. Learning multiple layers of representation. *Trends in Cognitive Sciences*, 11:428–434, 2007b.

Geoffrey E. Hinton and Terrence J. Sejnowski. Optimal perceptual inference. In *Proceedings of the IEEE Conference on Computer Vision and Pattern Recognition*, pp. 448–453, Washington, D.C., 1983.

Geoffrey E. Hinton, Nitish Srivastava, Alex Krizhevsky, Ilya Sutskever and Ruslan R. Salakhutdinov. Improving Neural Networks by Preventing Co-Adaptation of Feature Detectors. *ArXiv*, 2012.

Masanori Hirano. Experimental Analysis of Deep Hedging Using Artificial Market Simulations for Underlying Asset Simulators. *ArXiv*, 2024.

Masanori Hirano, Kentaro Imajo, Kentaro Minami and Takuya Shimada. Efficient Learning of Nested Deep Hedging Using Multiple Options. *ArXiv*, 2023a.

Masanori Hirano, Kentaro Minami and Kentaro Imajo. Adversarial Deep Hedging: Learning to Hedge Without Price Process Modeling. *ArXiv*, 2023b.

Masanori Hirano, Ryosuke Takata and Kiyoshi Izumi. PAMS: Platform for Artificial Market Simulations. *ArXiv*, 2023c.

Ali Hirsa, Tugce Karatas and Amir Oskoui. Supervised Deep Neural Networks (DNNs) for Pricing/Calibration of Vanilla/Exotic Options Under Various Different Processes. *ArXiv*, 2019.

Jonathan Ho, Ajay Jain and Pieter Abbeel. Denoising Diffusion Probabilistic Models. *ArXiv*, 2020.

Jonathan Ho, Chitwan Saharia, William Chan, David J. Fleet, Mohammad Norouzi and Tim Salimans. Cascaded diffusion models for high fidelity image generation. *Journal of Machine Learning Research,* 23(1):1–33, 2022.

Sepp Hochreiter and Jürgen Schmidhuber. Long short-term memory. *Neural Computation*, 9(8):1735–1780, 1997.

J. H. Hoencamp, S. Jain and B. D. Kandhai. A static replication approach for callable interest rate derivatives: Mathematical foundations and efficient estimation of SIMM-MVA. *Quantitative Finance*, 24(3–4):409–432, 2024.

Jori Hoencamp, Shashi Jain and Drona Kandhai. A Semi-Static Replication Approach to Efficient Hedging and Pricing of Callable IR Derivatives. *ArXiv*, 2022.

Dan Horgan, John Quan, David Budden, Gabriel Barth-Maron, Matteo Hessel, Hado van Hasselt and David Silver. Distributed Prioritized Experience Replay. *ArXiv*, 2018.

Kurt Hornik. Approximation capabilities of multilayer feedforward networks. *Neural Networks*, 4(2):251–257, 1991.

Kurt Hornik, Maxwell Stinchcombe and Halbert White. Multilayer feedforward networks are universal approximators. *Neural Networks*, 2(5):359–366, 1989.

Kurt Hornik, Maxwell Stinchcombe and Halbert White. Universal approximation of an unknown mapping and its derivatives using multilayer feedforward networks. *Neural Networks*, 3(5):551–560, 1990.

Blanka Horvath, Aitor Muguruza and Mehdi Tomas. Deep Learning Volatility. *ArXiv*, 2019.

Blanka Horvath, Josef Teichmann and Zan Zuric. Deep Hedging Under Rough Volatility. *ArXiv*, 2021.

Songyan Hou, Thomas Krabichler and Marcus Wunsch. Deep Partial Hedging. *ArXiv*, 2021.

Henri Hoyez, Cédric Schockaert, Jason Rambach, Bruno Mirbach and Didier Stricker. Unsupervised image-to-image translation: A review. *Sensors (Basel, Switzerland)*, 22:8540, November 2022.

Feng-hsiung Hsu, Murray S. Campbell and A. Joseph Hoane. Deep Blue system overview. In *Proceedings of the 9th International Conference on Supercomputing*, ICS '95, pp. 240–244, New York, NY, USA, 1995. Association for Computing Machinery.

Xun Huang and Serge Belongie. Arbitrary style transfer in real-time with adaptive instance normalization. In *Proceedings of the IEEE International Conference on Computer Vision (ICCV)*, October 2017.

Brian Huge and Antoine Savine. Differential machine learning: The shape of things to come. *Risk*, 33, September 2020.

Minyoung Huh, Richard Zhang, Jun-Yan Zhu, Sylvain Paris and Aaron Hertzmann. Transforming and projecting images to class-conditional generative networks, 2020. https://www.ecva.net/papers/eccv_2020/papers_ECCV/papers/123470018.pdf.

John C. Hull and Alan White. One factor term structure models and SuperCalibration. *Financial Analysts Journal*, 57(6): 34–43, 2001.

Harold E. Hurst. Long-term storage capacity of reservoirs. *Transactions of the American Society of Civil Engineers*, 116(1):770–799, 1951.

C. Huré, H. Pham and X. Warin. Deep backward schemes for high-dimensional nonlinear PDEs. *Mathematics of Computation*, 89:1547–1579, 2020.

J. M Hutchinson, A. W. Lo and T. Poggio. A nonparametric approach to pricing and hedging derivative securities via learning networks. *The Journal of Finance*, 49(3):851–889, 1994.

Frank Hutter, Lars Kotthoff and Joaquin Vanschoren (Eds), *Automated Machine Learning: Methods, Systems, Challenges.* Springer Nature, Cham, 2019.

Aapo Hyvärinen. Estimation of non-normalized statistical models by score matching. *Journal of Machine Learning Research*, 6:695–709, December 2005.

Satoshi Iizuka, Edgar Simo-Serra and Hiroshi Ishikawa. Globally and locally consistent image completion. *ACM Transactions on Graphics*, 36(4):1–14, 2017.

Sergey Ioffe and Christian Szegedy. Batch normalization: Accelerating deep network training by reducing internal covariate shift. In *Proceedings of the 32nd International Conference on Machine Learning – Volume 37*, ICML'15, pp. 448–456. JMLR.org, 2015.

Phillip Isola, Jun-Yan Zhu, Tinghui Zhou and Alexei A. Efros. Image-to-image translation with conditional adversarial networks. In *2017 IEEE Conference on Computer Vision and Pattern Recognition (CVPR)*, pp. 5967–5976, 2017.

Paul Jaccard. *Nouvelles Recherches sur la Distribution Florale.* Rouge, Lausanne, 1908.

Antoine Jacquier and Mugad Oumgari. Deep PPDEs for rough local stochastic volatility, 2019. https://www.ma.imperial.ac.uk/~ajacquie/index_files/JO%20-%20RoughVolPPDE_Final.pdf.

Max Jaderberg, Valentin Dalibard, Simon Osindero, Wojciech M. Czarnecki, Jeff Donahue, Ali Razavi, Oriol Vinyals, Tim Green, Iain Dunning, Karen Simonyan, Chrisantha Fernando and Koray Kavukcuoglu. Population Based Training of Neural Networks. *ArXiv*, 2017.

Kevin Jamieson and Ameet Talwalkar. Non-stochastic best arm identification and hyperparameter optimization. In Arthur Gretton and Christian C. Robert (Eds), *Proceedings of the 19th International Conference on Artificial Intelligence and Statistics*, volume 51 of *Proceedings of Machine Learning Research*, pp. 240–248, Cadiz, Spain, 9–11 May 2016. PMLR.

Carlos M. Jarque and Anil K. Bera. An efficient test for normality, homoscedasticity and serial independence of regression residuals. *Economics Letters*, 6(3):255–259, 1980.

Javier López-de-Lacalle, Artur Lemonte and Igor Rychlik. LongMemoryTS: Long Memory Time Series, 2021. https://search.r-project.org/CRAN/refmans/LongMemoryTS/html/LongMemoryTS.html.

Paul Jeha, Michael Bohlke-Schneider, Pedro Mercado, Shubham Kapoor, Nirwan Rajbir Singh, Valentin Flunkert, Jan Gasthau and Tim Januschowski. PSA-GAN: Progressive Self Attention GANs for Synthetic Time Series. *ArXiv*, 2021.

F. Jelinek, R. L. Mercer, L. R. Bahl and J. K. Baker. Perplexity—a measure of the difficulty of speech recognition tasks. *The Journal of the Acoustical Society of America*, 62(S1):S63–S63, 8 2005.

Justin Johnson, Alexandre Alahi and Li Fei-Fei. Perceptual losses for real-time style transfer and super-resolution. In Bastian Leibe, Jiri Matas, Nicu Sebe and Max Welling (Eds), *Computer Vision – ECCV 2016*, pp. 694–711, Cham, 2016. Springer International Publishing.

Paul V. Johnson. American options, 2021. https://personalpages.manchester.ac.uk/staff/paul.johnson-2/resources/math60082/lab-math60082-8.pdf.

I. T. Jolliffe. *Principle Component Analysis*. Springer, Berlin, 2002.

Dan Jurafsky and James H. Martin. *Speech and Language Processing* (3rd edition draft). Stanford University, Stanford, CA, 2023.

Christian Kahl and Peter Jäckel. Not-so-complex logarithms in the Heston model. *Wilmott Magazine*, 19(9):94–103, 2005.

Eirini Kalliamvakou. Research: quantifying GitHub Copilot's impact on developer productivity and happiness, 2024. https://github.blog/news-insights/research/research-quantifying-github-copilots-impact-on-developer-productivity-and-happiness/.

N. El Karoui, R. Myneni and R. Viswanathan. Arbitrage Pricing and Hedging of Interest Rate Claims with State Variables I. Working Paper Paris VI and Stanford University, 1992.

Tero Karras and Janne Hellsten. StyleGAN2-ADA – Official PyTorch implementation, 2020.

Tero Karras, Samuli Laine and Timo Aila. A Style-Based Generator Architecture for Generative Adversarial Networks. *ArXiv*, 2018.

Tero Karras, Samuli Laine and Timo Aila. A style-based generator architecture for generative adversarial networks. In *Proceedings of the IEEE/CVF Conference on Computer Vision and Pattern Recognition (CVPR)*, June 2019.

Tero Karras, Miika Aittala, Janne Hellsten, Samuli Laine, Jaakko Lehtinen and Timo Aila. Training generative adversarial networks with limited data. In H. Larochelle, M. Ranzato, R. Hadsell, M. F. Balcan and H. Lin (Eds), *Advances in Neural Information Processing Systems*, volume 33, pp. 12104–12114. Curran Associates, Inc., 2020a.

Tero Karras, Samuli Laine, Miika Aittala, Janne Hellsten, Jaakko Lehtinen and Timo Aila. Analyzing and improving the image quality of StyleGAN. In *2020 IEEE/CVF Conference on Computer Vision and Pattern Recognition (CVPR)*, pp. 8107–8116, Seattle, WA, USA, 2020b.

Tero Karras, Miika Aittala, Samuli Laine, Erik Härkönen, Janne Hellsten, Jaakko Lehtinen and Timo Aila. Alias-free generative adversarial networks. In M. Ranzato, A. Beygelzimer, Y. Dauphin, P. S. Liang and J. Wortman Vaughan (Eds), *Advances in Neural Information Processing Systems*, volume 34, pp. 852–863. Curran Associates, Inc., 2021.

Marco Kemmerling, Daniel Lütticke and Robert H. Schmitt. Beyond Games: A Systematic Review of Neural Monte Carlo Tree Search Applications. *ArXiv*, 2023.

A. D. Kennedy. *The Theory of Hybrid Stochastic Algorithms*. Springer, Boston, MA, 1990.

Chris Kenyon and Andrew Green. Efficient XVA management: Pricing, hedging, and allocation. *Risk*, 28(8), 2015.

Mitesh M. Khapra. CS7015 (Deep Learning): Lecture 8, 2019.

Patrick Kidger and Terry Lyons. Universal approximation with deep narrow networks. In Jacob Abernethy and Shivani Agarwal (Eds), *ArXiv*, volume 125 of *Proceedings of Machine Learning Research*, pp. 2306–2327. PMLR, 9–12 July 2020.

Patrick Kidger, James Foster, Xuechen Li, Harald Oberhauser and Terry Lyons. Neural SDEs as Infinite-Dimensional GANs. *ArXiv*, 2021.

Hyunsu Kim. Deep Hedging, Generative Adversarial Networks, and Beyond. *ArXiv*, 2021.

Diederik P. Kingma and Jimmy Ba. Adam: A method for stochastic optimization. In Yoshua Bengio and Yann LeCun (Eds), *3rd International Conference on Learning Representations, ICLR 2015,* San Diego, CA, USA, 7–9 May 2015, Conference Track Proceedings 2015.

Diederik P. Kingma and Max Welling. An introduction to variational autoencoders. *Foundations and Trends® in Machine Learning*, 12(4):307–392, 2019.

Diederik P. Kingma, Tim Salimans, Rafal Jozefowicz, Xi Chen, Ilya Sutskever and Max Welling. Improved variational inference with inverse autoregressive flow. In *Proceedings of the 30th International Conference on Neural Information Processing Systems*, NIPS'16, pp. 4743–4751, Red Hook, NY, USA, 2016. Curran Associates, Inc.

Matthias Kissel and Klaus Diepold. Sobolev training with approximated derivatives for black-box function regression with neural networks. In Ulf Brefeld, Elisa Fromont, Andreas Hotho, Arno Knobbe, Marloes Maathuis and Céline Robardet (Eds), *Machine Learning and Knowledge Discovery in Databases*, pp. 399–414, Cham, 2020. Springer International Publishing.

Günter Klambauer, Thomas Unterthiner, Andreas Mayr and Sepp Hochreiter. Self-normalizing neural networks. In *31st Conference on Neural Information Processing Systems (NIPS 2017)*, Long Beach, CA, USA, 2017.

Peter A. Kloeden and Ekhardt Platen. *Numerical Solution of Stochastic Differential Equations*. Springer, Berlin, 1992.

Levente Kocsis and Csaba Szepesvári. Bandit based Monte-Carlo planning. In Johannes Fürnkranz, Tobias Scheffer and Myra Spiliopoulou (Eds), *Machine Learning: ECML 2006*, pp. 282–293. Springer, Berlin, 2006.

Michael Kohler, Adam Krzyżak and Nebojsa Todorovic. Pricing of high-dimensional American options by neural networks. *Mathematical Finance*, 20(3):383–410, 2010.

Vijay Konda and John Tsitsiklis. Actor–critic algorithms. In S. Solla, T. Leen and K. Müller (Eds), *Advances in Neural Information Processing Systems*, volume 12. MIT Press, Cambridge, MA, 1999.

Alexei Kondratyev and Christian Schwarz. The market generator. *Risk*, 5 February 2020.

Adriano Koshiyama, Nick Firoozye and Philip Treleaven. Generative adversarial networks for financial trading strategies fine-tuning and combination. *Quantitative Finance*, 21(5):797–813, 2021.

Mark A. Kramer. Nonlinear principal component analysis using autoassociative neural networks. *AIChE Journal*, 37(2):233–243, 1991.

Alex Krizhevsky. Learning Multiple Layers of Features from Tiny Images. Technical Report, University of Toronto, 2009.

Alex Krizhevsky, Ilya Sutskever and Geoffrey E. Hinton. Imagenet classification with deep convolutional neural networks. In *Proceedings of the 25th International Conference on Neural Information Processing Systems – Volume 1*, NIPS'12, pp. 1097–1105, Red Hook, NY, USA, 2012. Curran Associates, Inc.

Anders Krogh and John A. Hertz. A simple weight decay can improve generalization. In J. E. Moody, S. J. Hanson and R. P. Lippmann (Eds), *Advances in Neural Information Processing Systems 4*, pp. 950–957. Morgan-Kaufmann, Burlington, MA,1992.

Jan Kukačka, Vladimir Golkov and Daniel Cremers. Regularization for Deep Learning: A Taxonomy. *ArXiv*, 2017.

S. Kullback and R. A. Leibler. On information and sufficiency. *The Annals of Mathematical Statistics*, 22(1):79–86, 1951.

Sándor Kunsági-Máté, Gábor Fáth, István Csabai and Gábor Molnár-Sáska. Deep Weighted Monte Carlo: A Hybrid Option Pricing Framework Using Neural Networks. *ArXiv*, 2022.

Jean Lahoud, Jiale Cao, Fahad Shahbaz Khan, Hisham Cholakkal, Rao Muhammad Anwer, Salman Khan and Ming-Hsuan Yang. 3D Vision with Transformers: A Survey. *ArXiv*, 2022.

W.-N. Lai. Comparison of methods to estimate option implied risk-neutral densities. *Quantitative Finance*, 14(10): 1839–1855, 2014.

Alexandre Lailler and Samson Cohen. Improving market data generation with restricted Boltzmann machines, 2022. Available at SSRN: https://ssrn.com/abstract=4020037.

P. Lajbcygier, C. Boek, A. Flitman and M. Palaniswami. Comparing conventional and artificial neural network models for the pricing of options on futures. *NeuroVe$T Journal*, 4(5):16–24, 1996.

Bernard Lapeyre and Jérôme Lelong. Neural Network Regression for Bermudan Option Pricing. *ArXiv*, 2019.

L. J. le Roux and G. S. du Toit. Emulating the Black & Scholes model with a neural network. *Southern African Business Review*, 5(1):54–57, 2001.

Nicolas Le Roux and Yoshua Bengio. Representational power of restricted Boltzmann machines and deep belief networks. *Neural Computation*, 20:1631–49, June 2008.

Y. LeCun. Modeles connexionnistes de l'apprentissage (connectionist learning models). PhD thesis, Université P. et M. Curie (Paris 6), June 1987.

Y. LeCun, B. Boser, J. S. Denker, D. Henderson, R. E. Howard, W. Hubbard and L. D. Jackel. Backpropagation applied to handwritten zip code recognition. *Neural Computation*, 1(4):541–551, 1989.

Y. LeCun, L. Bottou, Y. Bengio and P. Haffner. Gradient-based learning applied to document recognition. *Proceedings of the IEEE*, 86(11):2278–2324, 1998a.

Yann LeCun, Léon Bottou, Genevieve B. Orr and Klaus-Robert Müller. Efficient backprop. In *Neural Networks: Tricks of the Trade, This Book Is an Outgrowth of a 1996 NIPS Workshop*, pp. 9–50, Springer, Berlin, 1998b.

Yann LeCun, Sumit Chopra, Raia Hadsell, Marc'Aurelio Ranzato and Fu Jie Huang. A tutorial on energy-based learning. In G. BakIr, T. Hofmann, B. Schölkopf, A. J. Smola, B. Taskar and S. V. N. Vishwanathan (Eds), *Predicting Structured Data*. MIT Press, Cambridge, MA, 2006.

Yann LeCun, Corinna Cortes and Christopher J. C. Burges. MNIST Database of Handwritten Digits, 2012. https://archive.ics.uci.edu/dataset/683/mnist+database+of+handwritten+digits.

J. Lee and J. Oh. Hybrid learning of mapping and its Jacobian in multilayer neural networks. *Neural Computation*, 9(5):937–958, 1997.

Matthias Lehmann. The Definitive Guide to Policy Gradients in Deep Reinforcement Learning: Theory, Algorithms and Implementations. *ArXiv*, 2024.

Moshe Leshno, Vladimir Ya. Lin, Allan Pinkus and Shimon Schocken. Multilayer feedforward networks with a nonpolynomial activation function can approximate any function. *Neural Networks*, 6(6):861–867, 1993.

Henry Leung and Jo Bovy. Galaxy10 decals dataset, 2017. https://archive.ics.uci.edu/datasets?search=Henry+Leung+and+Jo+Bovy.+Galaxy10+decals+dataset.

Vladimir I. Levenshtein. Binary codes capable of correcting deletions, insertions, and reversals. *Doklady Akademii Nauk SSSR*, 163(4):845–848, 1965.

Daniel Lewandowski, Dorota Kurowicka and Harry Joe. Generating random correlation matrices based on vines and extended onion method. *Journal of Multivariate Analysis*, 100(9):1989–2001, 2009.

Mike Lewis, Yinhan Liu, Naman Goyal, Marjan Ghazvininejad, Abdelrahman Mohamed, Omer Levy, Veselin Stoyanov and Luke Zettlemoyer. BART: Denoising sequence-to-sequence pre-training for natural language generation, translation, and comprehension. In Dan Jurafsky, Joyce Chai, Natalie Schluter and Joel Tetreault (Eds), *Proceedings of the 58th Annual Meeting of the Association for Computational Linguistics*, pp. 7871–7880, July 2020. Association for Computational Linguistics.

Edmond Lezmi, Jules Roche, Thierry Roncalli and Jiali Xu. Improving the robustness of trading strategy backtesting with Boltzmann machines and generative adversarial networks, 2020. Available at SSRN: https://ssrn.com/abstract=3645473.

Ang A. Li, Zongqing Lu and Chenglin Miao. Revisiting Prioritized Experience Replay: A Value Perspective. *ArXiv*, 2021.

Chu-Tak Li. Pushing the limits of deep image inpainting using partial convolutions, 2020. https://towardsdatascience.com/pushing-the-limits-of-deep-image-inpainting-using-partial-convolutions-ed5520775ab4/.

Fei-Fei Li, Ranjay Krishna and Danfei Xu. CS231n: Convolutional Neural Networks for Visual Recognition, 2020. Stanford University, Stanford, CA.

Hu Li, Xuezhong Qian and Wei Song. Prioritized experience replay based on dynamics priority. *Scientific Reports*, 14(1):6014, 2024.

Liam Li, Kevin Jamieson, Afshin Rostamizadeh, Ekaterina Gonina, Moritz Hardt, Benjamin Recht and Ameet Talwalkar. A System for Massively Parallel Hyperparameter Tuning. *ArXiv*, 2018a.

Lisha Li, Kevin Jamieson, Giulia DeSalvo, Afshin Rostamizadeh and Ameet Talwalkar. Hyperband: A novel bandit-based approach to hyperparameter optimization. *Journal of Machine Learning Research*, 18(185):1–52, 2018b.

Xiaomin Li, Vangelis Metsis, Huangyingrui Wang and Anne Hee Hiong Ngu. TTS-GAN: A Transformer-Based Time-Series Generative Adversarial Network. *ArXiv*, 2022.

Zengyi Li, Yubei Chen and Friedrich T. Sommer. Learning Energy-Based Models in High-Dimensional Spaces with Multi-Scale Denoising Score Matching. *ArXiv*, 2019.

Timothy P. Lillicrap, Jonathan J. Hunt, Alexander Pritzel, Nicolas Heess, Tom Erez, Yuval Tassa, David Silver and Daan Wierstra. Continuous Control with Deep Reinforcement Learning. *ArXiv*, 2015.

Haksoo Lim, Minjung Kim, Sewon Park and Noseong Park. Regular Time-Series Generation Using SGM. *ArXiv*, 2023.

Jae Hyun Lim and Jong Chul Ye. Geometric GAN. *ArXiv*, 2017.

Yannick Limmer and Blanka Horvath. Robust Hedging GANs. *ArXiv*, 2023.

Chin-Yew Lin. ROUGE: A package for automatic evaluation of summaries. In *Text Summarization Branches Out*, pp. 74–81, Barcelona, Spain, July 2004. Association for Computational Linguistics.

Chin-Yew Lin and Eduard Hovy. Automatic evaluation of summaries using N-gram co-occurrence statistics. In *Proceedings of the 2003 Human Language Technology Conference of the North American Chapter of the Association for Computational Linguistics*, pp. 150–157, 2003.

Chin-Yew Lin and Franz Josef Och. Automatic evaluation of machine translation quality using longest common subsequence and skip-bigram statistics. In *Proceedings of the 42nd Annual Meeting of the Association for Computational Linguistics (ACL-04)*, pp. 605–612, Barcelona, Spain, July 2004.

Haoning Lin, Zhenwei Shi and Zhengxia Zou. Maritime semantic labeling of optical remote sensing images with multi-scale fully convolutional network. *Remote Sensing*, 9:480, May 2017.

Long-Ji Lin. Self-improving reactive agents based on reinforcement learning, planning and teaching. *Machine Learning*, 8(3):293–321, 1992.

Min Lin, Qiang Chen and Shuicheng Yan. Network in Network. *ArXiv*, 2013.

Zinan Lin, Alankar Jain, Chen Wang, Giulia Fanti and Vyas Sekar. Using GANs for Sharing Networked Time Series Data: Challenges, Initial Promise, and Open Questions. *ArXiv*, 2019.

Chris J. Lintott, Kevin Schawinski, Anže Slosar, Kate Land, Steven Bamford, Daniel Thomas, M. Jordan Raddick, Robert C. Nichol, Alex Szalay, Dan Andreescu, Phil Murray and Jan Vandenberg. Galaxy Zoo: Morphologies derived from visual inspection of galaxies from the Sloan Digital Sky Survey. *Monthly Notices of the Royal Astronomical Society*, 389(3): 1179–1189, 2008.

Philip Lippe. Tutorial 8: Deep Energy-Based Generative Models, 2021. https://uvadlc-notebooks.readthedocs.io/en/latest/tutorial_notebooks/tutorial8/Deep_Energy_Models.html.

Guilin Liu, Fitsum A. Reda, Kevin J. Shih, Ting-Chun Wang, Andrew Tao and Bryan Catanzaro. Image inpainting for irregular holes using partial convolutions. In Vittorio Ferrari, Martial Hebert, Cristian Sminchisescu and Yair Weiss (Eds), *Computer Vision – ECCV 2018*, pp. 89–105, Cham, 2018a. Springer International Publishing.

Jun Liu. On the convergence of reinforcement learning with Monte Carlo exploring starts. *Automatica*, 129:109693, 2021.

Shaohui Liu, Yi Wei, Jiwen Lu and Jie Zhou. An Improved Evaluation Framework for Generative Adversarial Networks. *ArXiv*, 2018b.

Shuaiqiang Liu, Anastasia Borovykh, Lech A. Grzelak and Cornelis W. Oosterlee. A Neural Network-Based Framework for Financial Model Calibration. *ArXiv*, 2019a.

Shuaiqiang Liu, Cornelis W. Oosterlee and Sander M. Bohte. Pricing Options and Computing Implied Volatilities Using Neural Networks. *ArXiv*, 2019b.

Yinhan Liu, Myle Ott, Naman Goyal, Jingfei Du, Mandar Joshi, Danqi Chen, Omer Levy, Mike Lewis, Luke Zettlemoyer and Veselin Stoyanov. RoBERTa: A Robustly Optimized BERT Pretraining Approach. *ArXiv*, 2019c.

Vikranth Lokeshwar, Vikram Bharadwaj and Shashi Jain. Explainable neural network for pricing and universal static hedging of contingent claims. *Applied Mathematics and Computation*, 417:126775, March 2022.

Philip M. Long and Rocco A. Servedio. Restricted Boltzmann machines are hard to approximately evaluate or simulate. In *Proceedings of the 27th International Conference on Machine Learning*, ICML'10, pp. 703–710, Madison, WI, USA, 2010. Omnipress.

Francis Longstaff and Eduardo Schwartz. Valuing American options by simulation: A simple least-squares approach. *The Review of Financial Studies*, 14(1):113–147, 2001.

Zhou Lu, Hongming Pu, Feicheng Wang, Zhiqiang Hu and Liwei Wang. The expressive power of neural networks: A view from the width. In I. Guyon, U. V. Luxburg, S. Bengio, H. Wallach, R. Fergus, S. Vishwanathan and R. Garnett (Eds), *Advances in Neural Information Processing Systems 30*, pp. 6231–6239, 2017. Curran Associates, Inc.

Robert E. Lucas. Asset prices in an exchange economy. *Econometrica*, 46(6):1429–1445, 1978.

Ping Luo, Xinjiang Wang, Wenqi Shao and Zhanglin Peng. Towards Understanding Regularization in Batch Normalization. *ArXiv*, 2018.

Thang Luong, Hieu Pham and Christopher D. Manning. Effective approaches to attention-based neural machine translation. In *Proceedings of the 2015 Conference on Empirical Methods in Natural Language Processing*, pp. 1412–1421, Lisbon, Portugal, September 2015. Association for Computational Linguistics.

Terry Lyons. Differential equations driven by rough signals. *Revista Matemática Iberoamericana*, 14(2):215–310, 1998.

Eva Lütkebohmert, Thorsten Schmidt and Julian Sester. Robust Deep Hedging. *ArXiv*, 2021.

A. L. Maas, Y. A. Hannun and A. Y. Ng. Rectifier nonlinearities improve neural network acoustic models. In *ICML Workshop on Deep Learning for Audio, Speech, and Language Processing*, 2013.

Aravindh Mahendran and Andrea Vedaldi. Understanding deep image representations by inverting them. In *IEEE Conference on Computer Vision and Pattern Recognition*, 2015.

Adam A. Majewski, Stefano Ciliberti and Jean-Philippe Bouchaud. Co-existence of trend and value in financial markets: Estimating an extended Chiarella model. *Journal of Economic Dynamics and Control*, 112:103791, March 2020.

Alireza Makhzani and Brendan Frey. k-Sparse Autoencoders. *ArXiv*, 2014.

Alireza Makhzani and Brendan Frey. Winner-take-all autoencoders. In *Proceedings of the 28th International Conference on Neural Information Processing Systems – Volume 2*, NIPS'15, pp. 2791–2799, Cambridge, MA, USA, 2015. MIT Press.

Alireza Makhzani, Jonathon Shlens, Navdeep Jaitly, Ian Goodfellow and Brendan Frey. Adversarial Autoencoders. *ArXiv*, 2015.

Anthony Malakian. Scotiabank turns to cloud GPUs for risk calculations. *Waterstechnology*, July 2019. https://www.waterstechnology.com/data-management/4465306/scotiabank-turns-to-cloud-gpus-for-risk-calculations.

M. Malliaris and L. Salchenberger. Beating the best: A neural network challenges the Black–Scholes formula. In *Proceedings of 9th IEEE Conference on Artificial Intelligence for Applications*, pp. 445–449, 1993a.

Mary Malliaris and Linda Salchenberger. A neural network model for estimating option prices. *Applied Intelligence*, 3(3):193–206, 1993b.

Benoit B. Mandelbrot and John W. Van Ness. Fractional Brownian motions, fractional noises and applications. *SIAM Review*, 10(4):422–437, 1968.

Christopher D. Manning, Prabhakar Raghavan and Hinrich Schütze. *Introduction to Information Retrieval*. Cambridge University Press, Cambridge, 2008.

Xudong Mao, Qing Li, Haoran Xie, Raymond Y. K. Lau, Zhen Wang and Stephen Paul Smolley. Least Squares Generative Adversarial Networks. *ArXiv*, 2016.

William Margrabe. The value of an option to exchange one asset for another. *The Journal of Finance*, 33(1):177–186, 1978.

Hector Marinez. Flickr-Faces-HQ Dataset (FFHQ), 2020. https://www.kaggle.com/datasets/arnaud58/flickrfaceshq-dataset-ffhq.

Gene Marks. Business tech news: Zuckerberg says AI will replace mid-level engineers soon. *Forbes*, 26 January 2025.

George Marsaglia and Ingram Olkin. Generating correlation matrices. *SIAM Journal on Scientific and Statistical Computing*, 5(2):470–475, 1984.

James Martens. Deep learning via hessian-free optimization. In *Proceedings of the 27th International Conference on Machine Learning*, ICML'10, pp. 735–742, Madison, WI, USA, 2010. Omnipress.

Gautier Marti. CorrGAN: Sampling Realistic Financial Correlation Matrices Using Generative Adversarial Networks. *ArXiv*, 2019.

Saeed Marzban, Erick Delage and Jonathan Yumeng Li. Deep Reinforcement Learning for Equal Risk Pricing and Hedging Under Dynamic Expectile Risk Measures. *ArXiv*, 2021.

R. Masuoka. Noise robustness of EBNN learning. In *Proceedings of 1993 International Conference on Neural Networks (IJCNN-93)*, Nagoya, Japan, volume 2, pp. 1665–1668, October 1993.

Benjamin McCloskey. Elliot activation function: What is it and is it effective? 2023. https://towardsdatascience.com/elliot-activation-function-what-is-it-and-is-it-effective-59b63ec1fd8a/.

Warren S. McCulloch and Walter Pitts. A logical calculus of the ideas immanent in nervous activity. *Bulletin of Mathematical Biophysics*, 5:115–133, 1943.

J. McEwen, C. Kyriakos and M. Jeannin. Cross-section methodology for proxy spreads and recovery rates. *Nomura*, 2012.

William A. McGhee. An artificial neural network representation of the SABR stochastic volatility model, 2018. Available at SSRN: https://ssrn.com/abstract=3288882.

William Alexander McGhee. An efficient implementation of stochastic volatility by the method of conditional integration. In *ICBI Global Derivatives and Risk Management*, 2011.

M. D. McKay, R. J. Beckman and W. J. Conover. A comparison of three methods for selecting values of input variables in the analysis of output from a computer code. *Technometrics*, 21(2):239–245, 1979.

Robert C. Merton. Option pricing when underlying stock returns are discontinuous. *Journal of Financial Economics*, 3:125–144, 1976.

Cade Metz. Meet GPT-3. It has learned to code (and blog and argue). *The New York Times*, 24 November 2020.

Risto Miikkulainen. *Topology of a Neural Network*, pp. 988–989. Springer, Boston, MA, 2010.

Oskari Mikkilä and Juho Kanniainen. Empirical deep hedging. *Quantitative Finance*, 23(1):111–122, 2023.

Tomas Mikolov, Martin Karafiát, Lukas Burget, Jan Cernocký and Sanjeev Khudanpur. Recurrent neural network based language model, 2010. https://www.isca-archive.org/interspeech_2010/mikolov10_interspeech.html.

Tomas Mikolov, Ilya Sutskever, Kai Chen, Greg S. Corrado and Jeff Dean. Distributed representations of words and phrases and their compositionality. In C. J. Burges, L. Bottou, M. Welling, Z. Ghahramani and K. Q. Weinberger (Eds), *Advances in Neural Information Processing Systems*, volume 26. Curran Associates, New York, 2013.

Tomáš Mikolov. Statistical language models based on neural networks. PhD thesis, Brno University of Technology, 2012.

Mehdi Mirza and Simon Osindero. Conditional Generative Adversarial Nets. *ArXiv*, 2014.

Divyanshu Mishra. Translation Invariance vs Translation Equivariance, 2020. https://medium.com/data-science/translational-invariance-vs-translational-equivariance-f9fbc8fca63a.

Tom Michael Mitchell and S. Thrun. Explanation-based neural network learning for robot control. In *Advances in Neural Information Processing Systems 5 (NIPS 1992)*, 1992.

Takeru Miyato, Toshiki Kataoka, Masanori Koyama and Yuichi Yoshida. Spectral Normalization for Generative Adversarial Networks. *ArXiv*, 2018.

Volodymyr Mnih, Koray Kavukcuoglu, David Silver, Alex Graves, Ioannis Antonoglou, Daan Wierstra and Martin A. Riedmiller. Playing Atari with Deep Reinforcement Learning, 2013. https://www.cs.toronto.edu/~vmnih/docs/dqn.pdf.

Volodymyr Mnih, Koray Kavukcuoglu, David Silver, Andrei A. Rusu, Joel Veness, Marc G. Bellemare, Alex Graves, Martin Riedmiller, Andreas K. Fidjeland, Georg Ostrovski, Stig Petersen, Charles Beattie, Amir Sadik, Ioannis Antonoglou, Helen King, Dharshan Kumaran, Daan Wierstra, Shane Legg and Demis Hassabis. Human-level control through deep reinforcement learning. *Nature*, 518(7540):529–533, 2015.

G. Montagna, M. Morelli, O. Nicrosini, P. Amato and M. Farina. Pricing derivatives by path integral and neural networks. *Physica A: Statistical Mechanics and its Applications*, 324(1–2):189–195, 2003.

Guido F. Montufar, Razvan Pascanu, Kyunghyun Cho and Yoshua Bengio. On the number of linear regions of deep neural networks. In Z. Ghahramani, M. Welling, C. Cortes, N. D. Lawrence and K. Q. Weinberger (Eds), *Advances in Neural Information Processing Systems 27*, pp. 2924–2932. Curran Associates, New York, 2014.

John E. Moody. The effective number of parameters: An analysis of generalization and regularization in nonlinear learning systems. In J. E. Moody, S. J. Hanson and R. P. Lippmann (Eds), *Advances in Neural Information Processing Systems 4*, pp. 847–854. Morgan-Kaufmann, Burlington, MA, 1992.

Alexander Mordvintsev, Christopher Olahand and Mike Tyka. Inceptionism: Going Deeper into Neural Networks, 2015. https://research.google/blog/inceptionism-going-deeper-into-neural-networks/.

Manuel Moreno and Javier F. Navas. On the robustness of least-squares Monte Carlo (LSM) for pricing American derivatives. *Review of Derivatives Research*, 6(2):107–128, 2003.

Pfenninger Moritz, Daniel Nico Bigler, Samuel Rikli and Joerg Osterrieder. Wasserstein GAN: Deep Generation Applied on Financial Time Series. *ArXiv*, 2021.

S. P. Moschou, E. Hicks, R. Y. Parekh, D. Mathew, S. Majumdar and N. Vlahakis. Physics-informed neural networks for modeling astrophysical shocks. *Machine Learning: Science and Technology*, 4(3):035032, 2023.

Younes Bensouda Mourri, Lukasz Kaiser and Eddy Shyu. Natural language processing with sequence models, 2021. https://www.coursera.org/learn/sequence-models-in-nlp.

Faezeh Movahedi, James L. Coyle and Ervin Sejdic. Deep belief networks for electroencephalography: A review of recent contributions and future outlooks. *IEEE Journal of Biomedical and Health Informatics*, 22:642–652, May 2018.

David Murphy. The doom loop in sovereign exposures. *Financial Times*, 12 April 2012.

Phillip Murray, Ben Wood, Hans Buehler, Magnus Wiese and Mikko S. Pakkanen. Deep Hedging: Continuous Reinforcement Learning for Hedging of General Portfolios Across Multiple Risk Aversions. *ArXiv*, 2022.

Vinod Nair and Geoffrey E. Hinton. Rectified linear units improve restricted Boltzmann machines. In *Proceedings of the 27th International Conference on Machine Learning*, ICML'10, pp. 807–814, Madison, WI, USA, 2010. Omnipress.

Uwe Naumann. *The Art of Differentiating Computer Programs: An Introduction to Algorithmic Differentiation (Software, Environments and Tools)*. SIAM, Philadelphia, PA, 2012.

Andrei Neagu, Frédéric Godin, Clarence Simard and Leila Kosseim. Deep Hedging with Market Impact. *ArXiv*, 2024.

Radford M. Neal. MCMC Using Hamiltonian dynamics. In Steve Brooks, Andrew Gelman, Galin L. Jones and Xiao-Li Meng (Eds), *Handbook of Markov Chain Monte Carlo*, chapter 5. CRC Press, Boca Raton, FL, May 2011.

Y. Nesterov. A method for unconstrained convex minimization problem with the rate of convergence $O(1/k^2)$. *Soviet Mathematics Doklady*, 27:372–376, 1983.

Nigel J. Newton. Variance reduction for simulated diffusions. *SIAM Journal on Applied Mathematics*, 54(6):1780–1805, 1994.

Andrew Ng. Sparse autoencoder, 2011. https://web.stanford.edu/class/cs294a/sparseAutoencoder_2011new.pdf.

Andrew Ng. Neural networks and deep learning, 2018a. https://www.coursera.org/learn/neural-networks-deep-learning.

Andrew Ng. Improving deep neural networks, 2018b. https://www.coursera.org/learn/deep-neural-network.

Andrew Ng. Improving deep neural networks: Hyperparameter tuning, regularization and optimization, 2018c. https://www.coursera.org/learn/deep-neural-network.

Andrew Ng. Sequence models, 2018d. https://www.coursera.org/learn/nlp-sequence-models.

Andrew Ng. Machine learning specialization, 2018e, https://www.coursera.org/specializations/machine-learning-introduction.

Hao Ni, Lukasz Szpruch, Magnus Wiese, Shujian Liao and Baoren Xiao. Conditional Sig-Wasserstein GANs for Time Series Generation. *ArXiv*, 2020.

Kun Ni, Danning Yu and Yunlong Liu. Attention-based deep Q-network in complex systems. In *Neural Information Processing*, pp. 323–332, Cham, 2019. Springer International Publishing.

Erik Nijkamp, Mitch Hill, Tian Han, Song-Chun Zhu and Ying Nian Wu. On the Anatomy of MCMC-Based Maximum Likelihood Learning of Energy-Based Models. *ArXiv*, 2019a.

Erik Nijkamp, Mitch Hill, Song-Chun Zhu and Ying Nian Wu. *Learning Non-Convergent Non-Persistent Short-Run MCMC Toward Energy-Based Model*. Curran Associates, New York, 2019b.

Dimitrios Noutsos. On Perron–Frobenius property of matrices having some negative entries. *Linear Algebra and its Applications*, 412(2):132–153, 2006.

NVIDIA Corporation. *NVIDIA CUDA Programming Guide. Version 1.0*, June 2007.

Augustus Odena, Vincent Dumoulin and Chris Olah. Deconvolution and checkerboard artifacts, 2016. https://distill.pub/2016/deconv-checkerboard/.

Kavin Oekmwa. OpenAI's Sam Altman claims AI will 'gradually' replace software engineers — creating an urgent need to master 'AI tools'. https://www.windowscentral.com/software-apps/openai-sam-altman-ai-will-gradually-replace-software-engineers.

OpenAI. Gpt-4 Technical Report. *ArXiv*, 2023.

Alan V. Oppenheim and Ronald W. Schafer. *Discrete-Time Signal Processing*. Prentice-Hall, Englewood Cliffs, NJ, 3rd edition, 2010.

Swarnima Pandey. How to choose the size of the convolution filter or kernel size for CNN? *Medium*, 2020. https://medium.com/analytics-vidhya/how-to-choose-the-size-of-the-convolution-filter-or-kernel-size-for-cnn-86a55a1e2d15.

Tianyu Pang, Kun Xu, Chongxuan Li, Yang Song, Stefano Ermon and Jun Zhu. Efficient learning of generative models via finite-difference score matching. In H. Larochelle, M. Ranzato, R. Hadsell, M. F. Balcan and H. Lin (Eds), *Advances in Neural Information Processing Systems*, volume 33, pp. 19175–19188. Curran Associates, New York, 2020.

Kishore Papineni, Salim Roukos, Todd Ward and Wei-Jing Zhu. Bleu: A method for automatic evaluation of machine translation. In Pierre Isabelle, Eugene Charniak and Dekang Lin (Eds), *Proceedings of the 40th Annual Meeting of the Association for Computational Linguistics*, pp. 311–318, Philadelphia, PA, USA, July 2002. Association for Computational Linguistics.

Fernando De Meer Pardo. Enriching financial datasets with generative adversarial networks. Master's thesis, Deflt University of Technology, 2019.

E. Pardoux and S. G. Peng. Adapted solution of a backward stochastic differential equation. *Systems & Control Letters*, 14(1):55–61, 1990.

Etienne Pardoux and Aurel Răşcanu. *Stochastic Differential Equations, Backward SDEs, Partial Differential Equations*. Springer, Cham, 1st edition, 2014.

Taesung Park, Ming-Yu Liu, Ting-Chun Wang and Jun-Yan Zhu. Semantic image synthesis with spatially-adaptive normalization. In *2019 IEEE/CVF Conference on Computer Vision and Pattern Recognition (CVPR)*, 2019.

Razvan Pascanu, Tomas Mikolov and Yoshua Bengio. On the Difficulty of Training Recurrent Neural Networks. *ArXiv*, 2012.

D. Pathak, P. Krahenbuhl, J. Donahue, T. Darrell and A. A. Efros. Context encoders: Feature learning by inpainting. In *2016 IEEE Conference on Computer Vision and Pattern Recognition (CVPR)*, pp. 2536–2544, Los Alamitos, CA, USA, June 2016. IEEE Computer Society.

F. Pedregosa, G. Varoquaux, A. Gramfort, V. Michel, B. Thirion, O. Grisel, M. Blondel, P. Prettenhofer, R. Weiss, V. Dubourg, J. Vanderplas, A. Passos, D. Cournapeau, M. Brucher, M. Perrot and E. Duchesnay. Scikit-learn: Machine learning in Python. *Journal of Machine Learning Research*, 12:2825–2830, 2011.

Shige Peng and Zhe Yang. Anticipated backward stochastic differential equations. *The Annals of Probability*, 37(3): 877–902, 2009.

Yunfei Peng, Pengyu Wei and Wei Wei. Deep Penalty Methods: A Class of Deep Learning Algorithms for Solving High Dimensional Optimal Stopping Problems. *ArXiv*, 2024.

Guim Perarnau, Joost van de Weijer, Bogdan Raducanu and Jose M. Álvarez. Invertible Conditional GANs for Image Editing. *ArXiv*, 2016.

David L. Phillips. A technique for the numerical solution of certain integral equations of the first kind. *Journal of the ACM*, 9(1):84–97, 1962.

Reilly Pickard, F. Wredenhagen and Y. Lawryshyn. Optimizing Deep Reinforcement Learning for American Put Option Hedging. *ArXiv*, 2024.

Vladimir Piterbarg. A practitioner's guide to pricing and hedging callable Libor exotics in forward Libor models. Available at SSRN: https://ssrn.com/abstract=427084.

Boris Polyak. Some methods of speeding up the convergence of iteration methods. *USSR Computational Mathematics and Mathematical Physics*, 4:1–17, December 1964.

Ser-Huang Poon and Clive W. J. Granger. *Forecasting Volatility in Financial Markets: A Review*, volume 41. American Economic Association, Nashville, TN, 2003.

William H. Press, Saul A. Teukolsky, William T. Vetterling and Brian P. Flannery. *Numerical Recipes: The Art of Scientific Computing*. Cambridge University Press, Cambridge, 3rd edition, 2007.

Foster Provost and Peter Domingos. Well-trained PETs: Improving probability estimation trees. *CDERE Working Paper #00-04-IS*, Stern School of Business, NYU, NY, 2000.

A. Pukrittayakamee, M. Malshe, M. Hagan, L. M. Raff, R. Narulkar, S. Bukkapatnum and R. Komanduri. Simultaneous fitting of a potential-energy surface and its corresponding force fields using feedforward neural networks. *The Journal of Chemical Physics*, 130(13):134101, 2009.

Alec Radford, Luke Metz and Soumith Chintala. Unsupervised Representation Learning with Deep Convolutional Generative Adversarial Networks. *ArXiv, 2015.*

Alec Radford, Luke Metz and Soumith Chintala. Unsupervised Representation Learning with Deep Convolutional Generative Adversarial Networks [revised]. *ArXiv,* 2016.

Alec Radford, Karthik Narasimhan, Tim Salimans and Ilya Sutskever. Improving Language Understanding by Generative Pre-training. Technical Report, Open AI, 2018.

Alec Radford, Jeff Wu, Rewon Child, David Luan, Dario Amodei and Ilya Sutskever. Language Models Are Unsupervised Multitask Learners. Technical Report, Open AI, 2019.

Colin Raffel, Noam M. Shazeer, Adam Roberts, Katherine Lee, Sharan Narang, Michael Matena, Yanqi Zhou, Wei Li and Peter J. Liu. Exploring the limits of transfer learning with a unified text-to-text transformer. *Journal of Machine Learning Research*, 21:140:1–140:67, 2019.

M. Raissi, P. Perdikaris and G.E. Karniadakis. Physics-informed neural networks: A deep learning framework for solving forward and inverse problems involving nonlinear partial differential equations. *Journal of Computational Physics*, 378:686–707, 2019.

Prajit Ramachandran, Barret Zoph and Quoc V. Le. Searching for Activation Functions. *ArXiv*, 2017.

Carl Edward Rasmussen and Christopher K. I. Williams. *Gaussian Processes for Machine Learning*. MIT Press, Cambridge, MA, 2006.

Ali Razavi, Aäron van den Oord and Oriol Vinyals. *Generating Diverse High-Fidelity Images with VQ-VAE-2*. Curran Associates, New York, 2019.

Dimitri Reiswich and Uwe Wystup. FX volatility smile construction. *Wilmott*, 2012(60):58–69, 2012.

Carl Remlinger, Joseph Mikael and Romuald Elie. Conditional Loss and Deep Euler Scheme for Time Series Generation. *ArXiv*, 2021.

Jason D. M. Rennie. Loss functions for preference levels: Regression with discrete ordered labels. In *Proceedings of the IJCAI Multidisciplinary Workshop on Advances in Preference Handling*, pp. 180–186, 2005.

Danilo Jimenez Rezende, Shakir Mohamed and Daan Wierstra. Stochastic backpropagation and approximate inference in deep generative models. In Eric P. Xing and Tony Jebara (Eds), *Proceedings of the 31st International Conference on Machine Learning*, volume 32 of *Proceedings of Machine Learning Research*, pp. 1278–1286, Beijing, China, 22–24 June 2014. PMLR.

Marco Tulio Ribeiro, Sameer Singh and Carlos Guestrin. 'Why should I trust you?': Explaining the predictions of any classifier. In *Proceedings of the 22nd ACM SIGKDD International Conference on Knowledge Discovery and Data Mining*, KDD '16, pp. 1135–1144, New York, NY, USA, 2016. Association for Computing Machinery.

Elad Richardson, Yuval Alaluf, Or Patashnik, Yotam Nitzan, Yaniv Azar, Stav Shapiro and Daniel Cohen-Or. Encoding in style: A StyleGAN encoder for image-to-image translation. In *2021 IEEE/CVF Conference on Computer Vision and Pattern Recognition (CVPR)*, pp. 2287–2296, 2021.

Ivo Richert and Robert Buch. Interpolation of Missing Swaption Volatility Data Using Gibbs Sampling on Variational Autoencoders. *ArXiv*, 2022.

Salah Rifai, Pascal Vincent, Xavier Muller, Xavier Glorot and Yoshua Bengio. Contractive auto-encoders: Explicit invariance during feature extraction. In *Proceedings of the 28th International Conference on Machine Learning*, ICML'11, pp. 833–840, Madison, WI, USA, 2011. Omnipress.

Carlos Riquelme, George Tucker and Jasper Snoek. Deep Bayesian Bandits Showdown: An Empirical Comparison of Bayesian Deep Networks for Thompson Sampling. *ArXiv*, 2018.

Robert E. Lucas, Jr. *Models of Business Cycles*. Yrjö Jahnsson Lectures. Blackwell, Oxford, 1987.

Peter M. Robinson. The memory of stochastic volatility models. *Journal of Econometrics*, 101(2):195–218, 2001.

L. C. G. Rogers. Monte Carlo valuation of American options. *Mathematical Finance*, 12(3):271–286, 2002.

Daniel Roich, Ron Mokady, Amit H Bermano and Daniel Cohen-Or. Pivotal tuning for latent-based editing of real images. *ACM Transactions on Graphics*, 42(1):1–13, 2021.

Robin Rombach, Andreas Blattmann, Dominik Lorenz, Patrick Esser and Björn Ommer. High-Resolution Image Synthesis with Latent Diffusion Models. *ArXiv*, 2021.

Olaf Ronneberger, Philipp Fischer and Thomas Brox. U-Net: Convolutional Networks for Biomedical Image Segmentation. *ArXiv*, 2015.

Framk Rosenblatt. The Perceptron: A Perceiving and Recognizing Automaton. Technical Report, Cornell Aeronautics Laboratory, 1957.

Sebastian Ruder. An Overview of Gradient Descent Optimization Algorithms. *ArXiv*, 2016.

Johannes Ruf and Weiguan Wang. Neural Networks for Option Pricing and Hedging: A Literature Review. *ArXiv*, 2019.

David E. Rumelhart, Geoffrey E. Hinton and Ronald J. Williams. Learning representations by back-propagating errors. *Nature*, 323(6088):533–536, 1986.

Alexander Rusnak. Conditional synthetic financial time series with generative adversarial networks. Master's thesis, Digital Humanities Institute, College of Humanities and Social Sciences, EPFL, 2022.

Olga Russakovsky, Jia Deng, Hao Su, Jonathan Krause, Sanjeev Satheesh, Sean Ma, Zhiheng Huang, Andrej Karpathy, Aditya Khosla, Michael Bernstein, Alexander C. Berg and Li Fei-Fei. ImageNet large scale visual recognition challenge. *International Journal of Computer Vision (IJCV)*, 115(3):211–252, 2015.

Stuart Russell and Peter Norvig. *Artificial Intelligence, Global Edition A Modern Approach*. Pearson, Berlin, 2021.

Marc Sabate-Vidales, David Šiška and Lukasz Szpruch. Solving Path Dependent PDEs with LSTM Networks and Path Signatures. *ArXiv*, 2020.

Chitwan Saharia, Jonathan Ho, William Chan, Tim Salimans, David J. Fleet and Mohammad Norouzi. Image super-resolution via iterative refinement. *IEEE Transactions on Pattern Analysis and Machine Intelligence*, 45(4):4713–4726, 2023.

Ruslan Salakhutdinov and Geoffrey Hinton. Deep Boltzmann machines. In David van Dyk and Max Welling (Eds), *Proceedings of the Twelfth International Conference on Artificial Intelligence and Statistics*, volume 5 of *Proceedings of Machine Learning Research*, pp. 448–455, Hilton Clearwater Beach Resort, Clearwater Beach, FL, USA, 16–18 April 2009. PMLR.

Ruslan Salakhutdinov, Andriy Mnih and Geoffrey Hinton. Restricted Boltzmann machines for collaborative filtering. In *Proceedings of the 24th International Conference on Machine Learning*, ICML'07, pp. 791–798, New York, NY, USA, 2007. Association for Computing Machinery.

Tim Salimans, Ian Goodfellow, Wojciech Zaremba, Vicki Cheung, Alec Radford and Xi Chen. Improved techniques for training GANs. In *Proceedings of the 30th International Conference on Neural Information Processing Systems*, NIPS'16, pp. 2234–2242, Red Hook, NY, USA, 2016. Curran Associates Inc.

Beatriz Salvador, Cornelis W. Oosterlee and Remco van der Meer. Financial Option Valuation by Unsupervised Learning with Artificial Neural Networks. *ArXiv*, 2020.

Fadil Santosa and William W. Symes. Linear inversion of band-limited reflection seismograms. *SIAM Journal on Scientific and Statistical Computing*, 7(4):1307–1330, 1986.

Saeed Saremi and Aapo Hyvärinen. Neural empirical Bayes. *Journal of Machine Learning Research*, 20(181):1–23, 2019.

Ruhi Sarikaya, Geoffrey E. Hinton and Anoop Deoras. Application of deep belief networks for natural language understanding. *IEEE/ACM Transactions on Audio, Speech, and Language Processing*, 22(4):778–784, 2014.

Antoine Savine. *Modern Computational Finance: AAD and Parallel Simulations with Professional Implementation in C++*. Wiley, Hoboken, NJ, 2019.

Andrew M. Saxe, James L. McClelland and Surya Ganguli. Learning hierarchical categories in deep neural networks. In Markus Knauff, Michael Pauen, Natalie Sebanz and Ipke Wachsmuth (Eds), *Proceedings of the 35th Annual Meeting of the Cognitive Science Society, CogSci 2013*, Berlin, Germany, July 31–August 3, 2013. cognitivesciencesociety.org.

A. Saxena. Valuation of S&P CNX Nifty options: Comparison of Black–Scholes and hybrid ANN model. In *Proceedings SAS Global Forum*, 2008.

Tom Schaul, John Quan, Ioannis Antonoglou and David Silver. Prioritized Experience Replay. *ArXiv*, 2015.

Julian Schrittwieser, Ioannis Antonoglou, Thomas Hubert, Karen Simonyan, Laurent Sifre, Simon Schmitt, Arthur Guez, Edward Lockhart, Demis Hassabis, Thore Graepel, Timothy Lillicrap and David Silver. Mastering Atari, Go, Chess and Shogi by Planning with a Learned Model. *ArXiv*, 2019.

John Schulman, Sergey Levine, Pieter Abbeel, Michael Jordan and Philipp Moritz. Trust region policy optimization. In Francis Bach and David Blei (Eds), *Proceedings of the 32nd International Conference on Machine Learning*, volume 37 of *Proceedings of Machine Learning Research*, pp. 1889–1897, Lille, France, 7–9 July 2015. PMLR.

John Schulman, Filip Wolski, Prafulla Dhariwal, Alec Radford and Oleg Klimov. Proximal Policy Optimization Algorithms. *ArXiv*, 2017.

Ramprasaath R. Selvaraju, Michael Cogswell, Abhishek Das, Ramakrishna Vedantam, Devi Parikh and Dhruv Batra. Grad-CAM: Visual explanations from deep networks via gradient-based localization. In *Proceedings of the IEEE International Conference on Computer Vision (ICCV)*, October 2017.

C. E. Shannon. Prediction and entropy of printed english. *Bell System Technical Journal*, 30(1):50–64, 1951.

Yujun Shen, Jinjin Gu, Xiaoou Tang and Bolei Zhou. Interpreting the latent space of GANs for semantic face editing. In *Conference on Computer Vision and Pattern Recognition (CVPR)*, 2020a.

Yujun Shen, Ceyuan Yang, Xiaoou Tang and Bolei Zhou. InterFaceGAN: Interpreting the disentangled face representation learned by GANs. *IEEE Transactions on Pattern Analysis and Machine Intelligence (TPAMI)*, 2020b.

Jiaxin Shi, Shengyang Sun and Jun Zhu. A Spectral Approach to Gradient Estimation for Implicit Distributions. *ArXiv*, 2018.

Steven E. Shreve. *Stochastic Calculus for Finance II: Continuous-Time Models*. Springer, New York, 2004.

Avanti Shrikumar, Peyton Greenside, Anna Shcherbina and Anshul Kundaje. Not Just a Black Box: Learning Important Features Through Propagating Activation Differences. *ArXiv*, 2016.

Avanti Shrikumar, Peyton Greenside and Anshul Kundaje. Learning important features through propagating activation differences. In *International Conference on Machine Learning*, pp. 3145–3153. PMLR, 2017.

David Silver. UCL Lecture Course on Reinforcement Learning [YouTube], 2015.

David Silver, Aja Huang, Chris J. Maddison, Arthur Guez, Laurent Sifre, George van den Driessche, Julian Schrittwieser, Ioannis Antonoglou, Veda Panneershelvam, Marc Lanctot, Sander Dieleman, Dominik Grewe, John Nham, Nal Kalchbrenner, Ilya Sutskever, Timothy Lillicrap, Madeleine Leach, Koray Kavukcuoglu, Thore Graepel and Demis Hassabis. Mastering the game of Go with deep neural networks and tree search. *Nature*, 529(7587):484–489, 2016.

David Silver, Julian Schrittwieser, Karen Simonyan, Ioannis Antonoglou, Aja Huang, Arthur Guez, Thomas Hubert, Lucas Baker, Matthew Lai, Adrian Bolton, Yutian Chen, Timothy Lillicrap, Fan Hui, Laurent Sifre, George van den Driessche, Thore Graepel and Demis Hassabis. Mastering the game of Go without human knowledge. *Nature*, 550(7676):354–359, 2017.

Karen Simonyan and Andrew Zisserman. Very deep convolutional networks for large-scale image recognition. In *International Conference on Learning Representations*, 2015.

Christopher A. Sims. Macroeconomics and reality. *Econometrica*, 48(1):1–48, 1980.

David Simões, Nuno Lau and Luís Paulo Reis. Multi-agent double deep Q-networks. In *Progress in Artificial Intelligence*, pp. 123–134, Cham, 2017. Springer International.

Satinder P. Singh and Richard S. Sutton. Reinforcement learning with replacing eligibility traces. *Machine Learning*, 22(1):123–158, 1996.

Justin Sirignano and Konstantinos Spiliopoulos. DGM: A deep learning algorithm for solving partial differential equations. *Journal of Computational Physics*, 375:1339–1364, 2018.

V. A. Skvortsov. Borel function, 2012. http://encyclopediaofmath.org/index.php?title=Borel_function&oldid=29100.

P. Smolensky. *Information Processing in Dynamical Systems: Foundations of Harmony Theory*. MIT Press, Cambridge, MA, 1986.

Jake Snell. Gradient-based MCMC, March 2017. https://www.cs.toronto.edu/~jessebett/CSC412/content/week8/grad_mcmc.pdf.

Jasper Snoek, Hugo Larochelle and Ryan P. Adams. Practical Bayesian optimization of machine learning algorithms. In F. Pereira, C. J. C. Burges, L. Bottou and K. Q. Weinberger (Eds), *Advances in Neural Information Processing Systems*, volume 25, pp. 2951–2959. Curran Associates, New York, 2012.

Jasper Snoek, Oren Rippel, Kevin Swersky, Ryan Kiros, Nadathur Satish, Narayanan Sundaram, Md. Mostofa Ali Patwary, Prabhat Prabhat and Ryan P. Adams. Scalable Bayesian optimization using deep neural networks. In *Proceedings of the 32nd International Conference on Machine Learning – Volume 37*, ICML'15, pp. 2171–2180, 2015.

I. M. Sobol. On the distribution of points in a cube and the approximate evaluation of integrals. *USSR Computational Mathematics and Mathematical Physics*, 7(4):86–112, 1967.

Jascha Sohl-Dickstein, Eric Weiss, Niru Maheswaranathan and Surya Ganguli. Deep unsupervised learning using nonequilibrium thermodynamics. In Francis Bach and David Blei (Eds), *Proceedings of the 32nd International Conference on Machine Learning*, volume 37 of *Proceedings of Machine Learning Research*, pp. 2256–2265, Lille, France, 7–9 July 2015. PMLR.

Alexander Sokol. Autoencoder market models for interest rates. Available at SSRN: https://ssrn.com/abstract=4300756.

Casper Kaae Sønderby, Tapani Raiko, Lars Maaløe, Søren Kaae Sønderby and Ole Winther. Ladder variational autoencoders. In *Proceedings of the 30th International Conference on Neural Information Processing Systems*, NIPS'16, pp. 3745–3753, Red Hook, NY, USA, 2016. Curran Associates Inc.

Yang Song. Tutorial on Score-Based Generative Modeling (PyTorch).ipynb [YouTube], 2021.

Yang Song and Stefano Ermon. Generative Modeling by Estimating Gradients of the Data Distribution. *ArXiv*, 2019.

Yang Song, Sahaj Garg, Jiaxin Shi and Stefano Ermon. Sliced Score Matching: A Scalable Approach to Density and Score Estimation. *ArXiv*, 2019.

Yang Song, Jascha Sohl-Dickstein, Diederik P. Kingma, Abhishek Kumar, Stefano Ermon and Ben Poole. Score-based generative modeling through stochastic differential equations. In *International Conference on Learning Representations*, 2021.

Oussama Souihli. Neural static replication. Available at SSRN: https://ssrn.com/abstract=4050520.

Jost Tobias Springenberg, Alexey Dosovitskiy, Thomas Brox and Martin Riedmiller. Striving for Simplicity: The All Convolutional Net. *ArXiv*, 2014.

Abir Sridi and Paul Bilokon. Applying Deep Learning to Calibrate Stochastic Volatility Models. *ArXiv*, 2023.

Sargur N. Srihari. Deep Boltzmann Machines, 2020a. https://cedar.buffalo.edu/~srihari/CSE676/20.4-DeepBoltzmann.pdf.

Sargur N. Srihari. GAN: Mode Collapse, 2020b. https://cedar.buffalo.edu/~srihari/CSE676/22.3-GAN%20Mode%20Collapse.pdf.

Nitish Srivastava, Geoffrey Hinton, Alex Krizhevsky, Ilya Sutskever and Ruslan Salakhutdinov. Dropout: A simple way to prevent neural networks from overfitting. *Journal of Machine Learning Research*, 15(1):1929–1958, 2014.

Rupesh Kumar Srivastava, Klaus Greff and Jürgen Schmidhuber. Highway Networks. *ArXiv*, 2015a.

Rupesh Kumar Srivastava, Klaus Greff and Jürgen Schmidhuber. Training Very Deep Networks. *ArXiv*, 2015b.

Peter Stone and Richard S. Sutton. Scaling reinforcement learning toward RoboCup soccer. In *Proceedings of the Eighteenth International Conference on Machine Learning*, ICML'01, pp. 537–544, San Francisco, CA, USA, 2001. Morgan Kaufmann Publishers Inc.

Victor Storchan, Svitlana Vyetrenko and Tucker Balch. Learning Who Is in the Market from Time Series: Market Participant Discovery Through Adversarial Calibration of Multi-agent Simulators. *ArXiv*, 2021.

Rainer Storn and Kenneth Price. Differential evolution – a simple and efficient heuristic for global optimization over continuous spaces. *Journal of Global Optimization*, 11(4):341–359, 1997.

Mukund Sundararajan, Ankur Taly and Qiqi Yan. Axiomatic attribution for deep networks. In *Proceedings of the 34th International Conference on Machine Learning – Volume 70*, ICML'17, pp. 3319–3328. JMLR.org, 2017.

David Sussillo and L. F. Abbott. Random Walk Initialization for Training Very Deep Feedforward Networks. *ArXiv*, 2014.

Joshua M. Susskind, Geoffrey E. Hinton, Javier R. Movellan and Adam K. Anderson. Generating facial expressions with deep belief nets. In Jimmy Or (Ed.), *Affective Computing*, chapter 23, pp. 421–440. IntechOpen, May 2008.

Ilya Sutskever, James Martens, George Dahl and Geoffrey Hinton. On the importance of initialization and momentum in deep learning. In Sanjoy Dasgupta and David McAllester (Eds), *Proceedings of the 30th International Conference on Machine Learning*, volume 28 of *Proceedings of Machine Learning Research*, pp. 1139–1147, Atlanta, GA, USA, 17–19 June 2013. PMLR.

Ilya Sutskever, Oriol Vinyals and Quoc V. Le. Sequence to sequence learning with neural networks. In *NIPS'14: Proceedings of the 28th International Conference on Neural Information Processing Systems*, volume 2, pp. 3104–3112, 2014.

Richard S. Sutton. Two problems with backpropagation and other steepest-descent learning procedures for networks. In *Proceedings of the Eighth Annual Conference of the Cognitive Science Society*, 1986.

Richard S. Sutton. Learning to predict by the methods of temporal differences. *Machine Learning*, 3(1):9–44, 1988.

Richard S. Sutton. Generalization in reinforcement learning: Successful examples using sparse coarse coding. In D. Touretzky, M. C. Mozer and M. Hasselmo (Eds), *Advances in Neural Information Processing Systems*, volume 8. MIT Press, Cambridge, MA, 1995.

Richard S. Sutton. John McCarthy's definition of intelligence. *Journal of Artificial General Intelligence*, 11(2):66–67, 2020.

Richard S. Sutton and Andrew G. Barto. *Reinforcement Learning: An Introduction*. MIT Press, Cambridge, MA, 2nd edition, 2018.

Kevin Swersky, Marc'Aurelio Ranzato, David Buchman, Benjamin M. Marlin and Nandode Freitas. On autoencoders and score matching for energy based models. In *Proceedings of the 28th International Conference on Machine Learning*, ICML'11, pp. 1201–1208, Madison, WI, USA, 2011. Omnipress.

C. Szegedy, V. Vanhoucke, S. Ioffe, J. Shlens and Z. Wojna. Rethinking the inception architecture for computer vision. In *2016 IEEE Conference on Computer Vision and Pattern Recognition (CVPR)*, pp. 2818–2826, June 2016.

Christian Szegedy, Wojciech Zaremba, Ilya Sutskever, Joan Bruna, Dumitru Erhan, Ian Goodfellow and Rob Fergus. Intriguing Properties of Neural Networks. *ArXiv*, 2013.

Christian Szegedy, Wei Liu, Yangqing Jia, Pierre Sermanet, Scott Reed, Dragomir Anguelov, Dumitru Erhan, Vincent Vanhoucke and Andrew Rabinovich. Going Deeper with Convolutions. *ArXiv*, 2014.

Oleg Szehr. Hedging of financial derivative contracts via Monte Carlo tree search. *Journal of Computational Finance*, 27(2):47–80, 2023.

C. Szepesvári. Algorithms for reinforcement learning. *Synthesis Lectures on Artificial Intelligence and Machine Learning*, 4:1–103, 2010.

Shuntaro Takahashi, Yu Chen and Kumiko Tanaka-Ishii. Modeling financial time-series with generative adversarial networks. *Physica A: Statistical Mechanics and its Applications*, 527:121261, 2019.

Hong Hui Tan and King Hann Lim. Review of second-order optimization techniques in artificial neural networks backpropagation. *IOP Conference Series: Materials Science and Engineering*, 495:012003, June 2019.

Matthew Tancik, Pratul Srinivasan, Ben Mildenhall, Sara Fridovich-Keil, Nithin Raghavan, Utkarsh Singhal, Ravi Ramamoorthi, Jonathan Barron and Ren Ng. Fourier features let networks learn high frequency functions in low dimensional domains. In H. Larochelle, M. Ranzato, R. Hadsell, M. F. Balcan and H. Lin (Eds), *Advances in Neural Information Processing Systems*, volume 33, pp. 7537–7547. Curran Associates, Inc., 2020.

Graham W. Taylor, Geoffrey E. Hinton and Sam T. Roweis. Two distributed-state models for generating high-dimensional time series. In *2007 IEEE International Conference on Acoustics, Speech and Signal Processing – ICASSP'07*, volume 4, pp. IV–65. IEEE, 2007.

Gerald Tesauro. Td-gammon, a self-teaching backgammon program, achieves master-level play. *Neural Computation*, 6(2):215–219, 1994.

Robert Tibshirani. Regression shrinkage and selection via the lasso. *Journal of the Royal Statistical Society: Series B (Methodological)*, 58(1):267–288, 1996.

A. N. Tikhonov. On the stability of inverse problems. *Proceedings of the USSR Academy of Sciences*, 39:195–198, 1943.

J. Tilley. Valuing American options in a path simulation model. *Transactions of the Society of Actuaries*, 45:83–104, 1993.

Nizar Touzi. *Optimal Stochastic Control, Stochastic Target Problems, and Backward SDE*. Fields Institute Monographs. Springer, New York, 1st edition, 2013.

Omer Tov, Yuval Alaluf, Yotam Nitzan, Or Patashnik and Daniel Cohen-Or. Designing an encoder for StyleGAN image manipulation. *ACM Transactions on Graphics*, 40(4):1–14, July 2021.

Mark Towers, Jordan K. Terry, Ariel Kwiatkowski, John U. Balis, Gianluca de Cola, Tristan Deleu, Manuel Goulão, Andreas Kallinteris, Arjun KG, Markus Krimmel, Rodrigo Perez-Vicente, Andrea Pierré, Sander Schulhoff, Jun Jet Tai, Andrew Tan Jin Shen and Omar G. Younis. Gymnasium: A standard interface for reinforcement learning environments. *Zenodo*, March 2023.

Shubhendu Trivedi and Risi Kondor. Lecture 7 Convolutional Neural Networks, April 2017. https://shubhendutrivedi.org/files/CMSC-DLcourse/Lecture7_pauses.pdf.

U. Trottenberg, C. W. Oosterlee and A. Schüller. *Multigrid*. Academic Press, New York, 2001.

R. Tsaih. Sensitivity analysis, neural networks, and finance. In *IJCNN'99. International Joint Conference on Neural Networks. Proceedings*, volume 6, pp. 3830–3835. IEEE, New York, 1999.

J. N. Tsitsiklis and B. Van Roy. Regression methods for pricing complex American-style options. *IEEE Transactions on Neural Networks*, 12(4):694–703, 2001.

John N. Tsitsiklis. On the convergence of optimistic policy iteration. *Journal of Machine Learning Research*, 3:59–72, 2003.

Richard Turner. CD notes [personal communication], 2005.

Paul Upchurch, Jacob Gardner, Geoff Pleiss, Robert Pless, Noah Snavely, Kavita Bala and Kilian Weinberger. Deep feature interpolation for image content changes. In *Computer Vision and Pattern Recognition (CVPR)*, 2017.

Arash Vahdat, Karsten Kreis and Jan Kautz. Score-Based Generative Modeling in Latent Space. *ArXiv*, 2021.

Remco van der Meer, Cornelis W. Oosterlee and Anastasia Borovykh. Optimally weighted loss functions for solving PDEs with neural networks. *Journal of Computational and Applied Mathematics*, 405:113887, 2022.

Hado van Hasselt, Arthur Guez and David Silver. Deep Reinforcement Learning with Double Q-learning. *ArXiv*, 2015.

Hado van Hasselt, Arthur Guez, Matteo Hessel, Volodymyr Mnih and David Silver. Learning values across many orders of magnitude. In *Proceedings of the 30th International Conference on Neural Information Processing Systems*, NIPS'16, pp. 4294–4302, Red Hook, NY, USA, 2016. Curran Associates Inc.

Ashish Vaswani, Noam Shazeer, Niki Parmar, Jakob Uszkoreit, Llion Jones, Aidan N. Gomez, Łukasz Kaiser and Illia Polosukhin. Attention is all you need. In *Proceedings of the 31st International Conference on Neural Information Processing Systems*, NIPS'17, pp. 6000–6010, Red Hook, NY, USA, 2017. Curran Associates Inc.

Marc Sabate Vidales, David Siska and Lukasz Szpruch. Unbiased Deep Solvers for Parametric PDEs. *ArXiv*, 2018a.

Marc Sabate Vidales, David Siska and Lukasz Szpruch. Martingale Functional Control Variates via Deep Learning. *ArXiv*, 2018b.

Cédric Villani. *Optimal Transport: Old and New*. Springer, Berlin, 2009.

Pascal Vincent. A connection between score matching and denoising autoencoders. *Neural Computation*, 23(7):1661–1674, 2011.

Benjamin Virrion. Deep Importance Sampling. *ArXiv*, 2020.

Edoardo Vittori, Michele Trapletti and Marcello Restelli. Option hedging with risk averse reinforcement learning. In *Proceedings of the First ACM International Conference on AI in Finance*, ICAIF'20, New York, NY, USA, 2021. Association for Computing Machinery.

Che Wang, Shuhan Yuan, Kai Shao and Keith Ross. On the Convergence of the Monte Carlo Exploring Starts Algorithm for Reinforcement Learning. *ArXiv*, 2020.

Haojie Wang, Han Chen, Agus Sudjianto, Richard Liu and Qi Shen. Deep Learning-Based BSDE Solver for Libor Market Model with Application to Bermudan Swaption Pricing and Hedging. *ArXiv*, 2018a.

Rui Wang. Discriminating Modelling Approaches for Point in Time Economic Scenario Generation. *ArXiv*, 2021.

Ting-Chun Wang, Ming-Yu Liu, Jun-Yan Zhu, Andrew Tao, Jan Kautz and Bryan Catanzaro. High-resolution image synthesis and semantic manipulation with conditional GANs. In *2018 IEEE/CVF Conference on Computer Vision and Pattern Recognition*, pp. 8798–8807, 2018b.

Xiaolong Wang, Ross Girshick, Abhinav Gupta and Kaiming He. Non-local neural networks. In *Proceedings of the IEEE Conference on Computer Vision and Pattern Recognition (CVPR)*, June 2018c.

Zhe Wang, Nicolas Privault and Claude Guet. Deep Self-Consistent Learning of Local Volatility. *ArXiv*, 2021.

Ziyu Wang, Tom Schaul, Matteo Hessel, Hado Van Hasselt, Marc Lanctot and Nando De Freitas. Dueling network architectures for deep reinforcement learning. In *Proceedings of the 33rd International Conference on International Conference on Machine Learning – Volume 48*, ICML'16, pp. 1995–2003. JMLR.org, 2016.

C. J. C. H. Watkins. Learning from delayed rewards. PhD thesis, University of Cambridge, Cambridge, 1989.

Tianyi Wei, Dongdong Chen, Wenbo Zhou, Jing Liao, Weiming Zhang, Lu Yuan, Gang Hua and Nenghai Yu. E2Style: Improve the efficiency and effectiveness of StyleGAN inversion. *IEEE Transactions on Image Processing*, 2022.

E. Weinan, Jiequn Han and Arnulf Jentzen. Deep learning-based numerical methods for high-dimensional parabolic partial differential equations and backward stochastic differential equations. *Communications in Mathematics and Statistics*, 5(4):349–380, 2017.

B. L. Welch. The generalization of 'Student's' problem when several different population variances are involved. *Biometrika*, 34(1–2):28–35, 1947.

Max Welling and Yee Whye Teh. Bayesian learning via stochastic gradient Langevin dynamics. In *Proceedings of the 28th International Conference on Machine Learning*, ICML'11, pp. 681–688, Madison, WI, USA, 2011. Omnipress.

A. White. *Pricing Options with Futures-Style Margining: a Genetic Adaptive Neural Network Approach*. Garland Publishing, New York, 2000.

A. J. White. A genetic adaptive neural network approach to pricing options: A simulation analysis. *Journal of Computational Intelligence in Finance*, 6(2):13–23, 1998.

Martha White and Adam White. Fundamentals of reinforcement learning, 2019. https://www.coursera.org/learn/fundamentals-of-reinforcement-learning.

B. Widrow and M. E. Huff. Adaptive Switching Circuits. Technical Report 1553-1, Solid-State Electronics Laboratory, Stanford Electronics Laboratories, June 1960.

Magnus Wiese, Robert Knobloch, Ralf Korn and Peter Kretschmer. Quant GANs: Deep Generation of Financial Time Series. *ArXiv*, 2019.

Ronald J. Williams. Simple statistical gradient-following algorithms for connectionist reinforcement learning. *Machine Learning*, 8(3):229–256, 1992.

D. Randall Wilson and Tony R. Martinez. The general inefficiency of batch training for gradient descent learning. *Neural Networks*, 16:1429–1451, 2003.

Essam Wisam. Language modeling with LSTMs in PyTorch, 2022. https://medium.com/data-science/language-modeling-with-lstms-in-pytorch-381a26badcbf.

James B. Witkoskie and Douglas J. Doren. Neural network models of potential energy surfaces: Prototypical examples. *Journal of Chemical Theory and Computation*, 1:14–23, January 2005.

J. H. Witte and C. Reisinger. A penalty method for the numerical solution of Hamilton–Jacobi–Bellman (HJB) equations in finance. *SIAM Journal on Numerical Analysis*, 49(1):213–231, 2011.

Zongze Wu, Dani Lischinski and Eli Shechtman. StyleSpace analysis: Disentangled controls for StyleGAN image generation. In *Proceedings of the IEEE/CVF Conference on Computer Vision and Pattern Recognition (CVPR)*, pp. 12863–12872, June 2021.

Weihao Xia, Yulun Zhang, Yujiu Yang, Jing-Hao Xue, Bolei Zhou and Ming-Hsuan Yang. GAN inversion: A survey. *IEEE Transactions on Pattern Analysis and Machine Intelligence*, 45(3):3121–3138, 2023.

Han Xiao, Kashif Rasul and Roland Vollgraf. Fashion-MNIST: A Novel Image Dataset for Benchmarking Machine Learning Algorithms. *ArXiv*, 2017.

Jianwen Xie, Yang Lu, Song-Chun Zhu and Ying Nian Wu. A theory of generative ConvNet. In *Proceedings of the 33rd International Conference on Machine Learning – Volume 48*, ICML'16, pp. 2635–2644. JMLR.org, 2016.

Rui Xu, Xintao Wang, Kai Chen, Bolei Zhou and Chen Change Loy. Positional encoding as spatial inductive bias in GANs. In *Proceedings of the IEEE/CVF Conference on Computer Vision and Pattern Recognition (CVPR)*, pp. 13569–13578, June 2021.

Tianlin Xu, Li Wenliang, Michael Munn and Beatrice Acciaio. COT-GAN: Generating sequential data via causal optimal transport. In *Proceedings of the 34th International Conference on Neural Information Processing Systems*, NIPS'20, Red Hook, NY, USA, 2020. Curran Associates Inc.

Chao Yang, Xin Lu, Zhe Lin, Eli Shechtman, Oliver Wang and Hao Li. High-resolution image inpainting using multi-scale neural patch synthesis. In *2017 IEEE Conference on Computer Vision and Pattern Recognition (CVPR)*, pp. 4076–4084, 2017.

Weiye Yang. Backward Stochastic Differential Equations in Financial Mathematics. *ArXiv*, 2023.

Zhilin Yang, Zihang Dai, Yiming Yang, Jaime Carbonell, Ruslan Salakhutdinov and Quoc V. Le. *XLNet: Generalized Autoregressive Pretraining for Language Understanding*. Curran Associates, New York, 2019.

I-Cheng Yeh and Che-hui Lien. The comparisons of data mining techniques for the predictive accuracy of probability of default of credit card clients. *Expert Systems Applications*, 36(2):2473–2480, 2009.

Jinsung Yoon, Daniel Jarrett and Mihaela van der Schaar. Time-series generative adversarial networks. In H. Wallach, H. Larochelle, A. Beygelzimer, F. d'Alché-Buc, E. Fox and R. Garnett (Eds), *Advances in Neural Information Processing Systems*, volume 32. Curran Associates, New York, 2019.

Bing Yu, Xiaojing Xing and Agus Sudjianto. Deep-Learning Based Numerical BSDE Method for Barrier Options. *ArXiv*, 2019a.

Jiahui Yu, Zhe Lin, Jimei Yang, Xiaohui Shen, Xin Lu and Thomas S. Huang. Generative Image Inpainting with Contextual Attention. *ArXiv*, 2018.

Jiahui Yu, Zhe Lin, Jimei Yang, Xiaohui Shen, Xin Lu and Thomas Huang. Free-form image inpainting with gated convolution. In *2019 IEEE/CVF International Conference on Computer Vision (ICCV)*, pp. 4470–4479, 2019b.

Tong Yu and Hong Zhu. Hyper-Parameter Optimization: A Review of Algorithms and Applications. *ArXiv*, 2020.

Matthew D. Zeiler. ADADELTA: An Adaptive Learning Rate Method. *ArXiv*, 2012.

Matthew D. Zeiler and Rob Fergus. Visualizing and Understanding Convolutional Networks. *ArXiv*, 2013.

Chiyuan Zhang, Samy Bengio, Moritz Hardt, Benjamin Recht and Oriol Vinyals. Understanding Deep Learning Requires Rethinking Generalization. *ArXiv*, 2016.

G. Zhang and H. Li. Effectiveness of Scaled Exponentially-Regularized Linear Units (SERLUs). *ArXiv*, 2018.

Han Zhang, Ian Goodfellow, Dimitris Metaxas and Augustus Odena. Self-attention generative adversarial networks. In Kamalika Chaudhuri and Ruslan Salakhutdinov (Eds), *Proceedings of the 36th International Conference on Machine Learning*, volume 97 of *Proceedings of Machine Learning Research*, pp. 7354–7363. PMLR, 9–15 June 2019.

Jianfeng Zhang. *Backward Stochastic Differential Equations: From Linear to Fully Nonlinear Theory*. Probability Theory and Stochastic Modelling. Springer, New York, 1st edition, 2017.

Richard Zhang, Phillip Isola, Alexei A. Efros, Eli Shechtman and Oliver Wang. The Unreasonable Effectiveness of Deep Features as a Perceptual Metric. *ArXiv*, 2018.

Rui Zhang, Qi Meng, Rongchan Zhu, Yue Wang, Wenlei Shi, Shihua Zhang, Zhi-Ming Ma and Tie-Yan Liu. Monte Carlo Neural Operator for Learning PDEs via Probabilistic Representation. *ArXiv*, 2023.

Tong Zhang. Solving large scale linear prediction problems using stochastic gradient descent algorithms. In *Proceedings of the Twenty-First International Conference on Machine Learning*, ICML'04, p. 116, New York, NY, USA, 2004. Association for Computing Machinery.

Shengjia Zhao, Jiaming Song and Stefano Ermon. Towards Deeper Understanding of Variational Autoencoding Models. *ArXiv*, 2017.

Sharon Zhou, Eda Zhou and Eric Zelikman. Build basic generative adversarial networks (GANs), 2020a. https://www.coursera.org/learn/build-basic-generative-adversarial-networks-gans.

Sharon Zhou, Eda Zhou and Eric Zelikman. Build better generative adversarial networks (GANs), 2020b. https://www.coursera.org/learn/build-better-generative-adversarial-networks-gans.

C. Zhu, R. H. Byrd, P. Lu and J. Nocedal. Algorithm 778: l-bfgs-b. *ACM Transactions on Mathematical Software*, 23: 550–560, 1997.

Jiapeng Zhu, Yujun Shen, Deli Zhao and Bolei Zhou. In-domain GAN inversion for real image editing. In *Proceedings of European Conference on Computer Vision (ECCV)*, 2020.

Jun-Yan Zhu, Philipp Krähenbühl, Eli Shechtman and Alexei A. Efros. Generative visual manipulation on the natural image manifold. In Bastian Leibe, Jiri Matas, Nicu Sebe and Max Welling (Eds), *Computer Vision – ECCV 2016*, pp. 597–613, Cham, 2016. Springer International.

Jun-Yan Zhu, Taesung Park, Phillip Isola and Alexei A. Efros. Unpaired Image-to-Image Translation Using Cycle-Consistent Adversarial Networks. *ArXiv*, 2017.

Index

Note: Page numbers in *italics* and **bold** refers to figures and tables respectively.

Deep Learning in Quantitative Finance, First Edition. Andrew Green.

E

S

W

X

Y

Z